Data Center Fundamentals

Mauricio Arregoces, CCIE No. 3285
Maurizio Portolani

Cisco Press

Cisco Press
800 East 96th Street
Indianapolis, IN 46240 USA

Data Center Fundamentals

Mauricio Arregoces

Maurizio Portolani

Published by:
Cisco Press
800 East 96th Street
Indianapolis, IN 46240 USA

ISBN: 1-58705-023-4

Library of Congress Cataloging-in-Publication Number: 2001086631

Printed in the United States of America 8 9 0

Eighth Printing June 2012

Trademark Acknowledgments

All terms mentioned in this book that are known to be trademarks or service marks have been appropriately capitalized. Cisco Press or Cisco Systems, Inc., cannot attest to the accuracy of this information. Use of a term in this book should not be regarded as affecting the validity of any trademark or service mark.

Warning and Disclaimer

This book is designed to provide information about Data Center technologies. Every effort has been made to make this book as complete and as accurate as possible, but no warranty or fitness is implied.

The information is provided on an "as is" basis. The authors, Cisco Press, and Cisco Systems, Inc., shall have neither liability nor responsibility to any person or entity with respect to any loss or damages arising from the information contained in this book or from the use of the discs or programs that may accompany it.

The opinions expressed in this book belong to the author and are not necessarily those of Cisco Systems, Inc.

Feedback Information

At Cisco Press, our goal is to create in-depth technical books of the highest quality and value. Each book is crafted with care and precision, undergoing rigorous development that involves the unique expertise of members from the professional technical community.

Readers' feedback is a natural continuation of this process. If you have any comments regarding how we could improve the quality of this book or otherwise alter it to better suit your needs, you can contact us through e-mail at feedback@ciscopress.com. Please make sure to include the book title and ISBN in your message.

We greatly appreciate your assistance.

Corporate and Government Sales

Cisco Press offers excellent discounts on this book when ordered in quantity for bulk purchases or special sales. For more information, please contact:

U.S. Corporate and Government Sales 1-800-382-3419 corpsales@pearsontechgroup.com

For sales outside of the U.S. please contact: **International Sales** 1-317-581-3793 international@pearsontechgroup.com

Publisher	John Wait
Editor-In-Chief	John Kane
Cisco Representative	Anthony Wolfenden
Cisco Press Program Manager	Nannette M. Noble
Production Manager	Patrick Kanouse
Development Editors	Christopher Cleveland Betsey Henkels
Senior Project Editor	Sheri Cain
Copy Editors	Krista Hansing, Kris Simmons
Technical Editors	Mario Baldi, Robert Batz, Mark Gallo, Ron Hromoko, Fabio Maino, Scott Van de Houten, Stefano Testa, Brian Walck
Team Coordinator	Tammi Barnett
Cover Designer	Louisa Adair
Composition	Octal Publishing, Inc.
Indexers	Tim Wright, Eric Schroeder
Proofreader	Angela Rosio

Corporate Headquarters
Cisco Systems, Inc.
170 West Tasman Drive
San Jose, CA 95134-1706
USA
www.cisco.com
Tel: 408 526-4000
800 553-NETS (6387)
Fax: 408 526-4100

European Headquarters
Cisco Systems International BV
Haarlerbergpark
Haarlerbergweg 13-19
1101 CH Amsterdam
The Netherlands
www-europe.cisco.com
Tel: 31 0 20 357 1000
Fax: 31 0 20 357 1100

Americas Headquarters
Cisco Systems, Inc.
170 West Tasman Drive
San Jose, CA 95134-1706
USA
www.cisco.com
Tel: 408 526-7660
Fax: 408 527-0883

Asia Pacific Headquarters
Cisco Systems, Inc.
Capital Tower
168 Robinson Road
#22-01 to #29-01
Singapore 068912
www.cisco.com
Tel: +65 6317 7777
Fax: +65 6317 7799

Printed in the USA

About the Authors

Mauricio Arregoces, CCIE No. 3285, is the manager of the Cisco Enterprise Solutions Engineering team on Data Center designs. He has been in the networking industry for 17 years and has been involved in designing, implementing, and maintaining large-scale enterprise networks. Mauricio holds a B.S. degree in computer science from the Colombian School of Engineering and a M.S. degree in computer science from California State University at Northridge.

Maurizio Portolani is a network design consultant at Cisco Systems Inc., involved in architecting and validating large-scale Data Center designs.

Maurizio has filed patents on advanced spanning-tree and load-balancing features, and is the author of several Cisco Data Center solution architectures that cover the Layer 2 and Layer 3 design, load balancing, security, DNS, SSL offloading, and integration with application environments.

Maurizio also works closely with various technology teams at Cisco to define and validate new features that enhance Cisco product support for customer system level solutions. Maurizio has designed product features in areas such as spanning-tree, SSL, and HTTP persistence mainly for the Catalyst 6500 family.

About the Contributor

Martin Pueblas, CCIE No. 2133, CISSP No. 40844, technical marketing engineer, Central Marketing Organization, Cisco Systems, Inc.

Martin contributed to the content in the security-related chapters in this book (Chapters 5, 15, and 21).

Martin is a network security expert with more than ten years of experience in the networking industry who obtained his CCIE certification in 1996 and recently achieved his CISSP. Martin joined Cisco in 1998 and since then has held a variety of technical positions.

In 2000, Martin joined the Advanced Engineering Services team as a network design consultant, where he provided design and security consulting services to large corporations and service providers. During this period, Martin wrote a variety of technical documents, including design guides and white papers that define the Cisco best practices for security and virtual private networks (VPNs).

In late 2001, Martin began his current position as a technical marketing engineer for security and VPN technologies. As part of his current responsibilities, Martin is leading the development of a security architecture for service providers. Before joining Cisco Systems, Martin worked for a Cisco Gold partner in South America, where he provided support, consulting, and training services to numerous customers and partners in Latin America.

About the Technical Reviewers

Mario Baldi is associate professor on the tenure track at the Computer Engineering Department of Torino Polytechnic, Torino, Italy, and vice president for Protocol Architecture at Synchrodyne Networks, Inc., New York.

He received his M.S. degree *summa cum laude* in electrical engineering in 1993 and his Ph.D. in computer and system engineering in 1998, both from Torino Polytechnic. He was assistant professor on the tenure track at Torino Polytechnic from 1997 to 2002. He joined Synchrodyne Networks, Inc., in November 1999.

Mario has been a visiting researcher at the IBM T.J. Watson Research Center, Yorktown Heights, New York; at Columbia University, New York; and at the International Computer Science Institute (ICSI), Berkeley, California.

As part of his extensive research activity at Torino Polytechnic, Mario has been leading various networking research projects involving universities and industrial partners, funded by the European Union, local government, and various companies, including telecommunications carriers, such as Infostrada and Telecom Italia, and research institutions, such as Telecom Italia Labs.

Mario provides on a regular basis consultancy and training services, both directly to companies and through various training and network consultancy centers.

Mario has co-authored more than 50 papers on various networking related topics and two books, one on internetworking and one on switched LANs.

Robert (Bob) Batz is a technical leader in the Cisco Mobile Wireless group. Bob develops software for content networking services, primarily addressing the mobile wireless space. He has also developed and sustained load-balancer products, frequently working closely with the TAC support teams in Cisco to resolve customer issues and to assist with network designs. Bob has been at Cisco for eight years and has been working in the content networking area for four years.

Mark Gallo is a technical manager with America Online, where he leads a group of engineers responsible for the design and deployment of the domestic corporate intranet. His network certifications include CCNP and CCDP. He has led several engineering groups responsible for designing and implementing enterprise LANs and international IP networks. He has a B.S. in electrical engineering from the University of Pittsburgh. Mark resides in northern Virginia with his wife, Betsy, and son, Paul.

Fabio Maino is a senior security architect at the San Jose–based Andiamo Systems, recently acquired by Cisco Systems. Fabio is one of the major contributors of the INCITS T11 Fibre Channel Security Protocols (FC-SP) working group, which is designing the security layer of the next-generation Fibre Channel architecture. Fabio is also an active contributor to the activities of the Internet Engineering Task Force (IETF) Simple Network Management Protocol version 3 (SNMPv3) working group, where he recently proposed an Advanced Encryption System (AES) extension for the USM security model.

Fabio received an M.Sc. degree in electronic engineering and a Ph.D. in computer and system engineering from Torino Polytechnic, Torino, Italy, in 1994 and 1999, respectively. During his Ph.D. studies, he was a guest researcher at Hewlett-Packard, working on VerSecure; then, he researched public-key infrastructure in Torino and finally moved to San Jose. After joining Cisco Systems at the beginning of 2000, he moved to Andiamo Systems with the original group of engineers that founded the company.

Scott Van de Houten, CCIE No. 1640, is a distinguished systems engineer for the Technical Operations group. He is currently a technical lead for the Enterprise Routing and Switching Technology leadership program. His responsibilities include developing customer requirements for the product teams and customer technical consulting. Scott has been with Cisco for 11 years and has worked as a network engineer for 17 years.

Stefano Testa joined Cisco Systems, Inc., in 1998, as part of the Catalyst 6500 software development team. He moved to technical marketing in 2000, initially focusing on content switching and geographic load balancing. Then, Stefano expanded his role to cover security products, such as SSL and firewall modules. Stefano works closely with Cisco field teams to help large customers design fully redundant, high-performance integrated Data Centers and content-aware solutions. He also works on a daily basis with multiple Cisco engineering teams on future software releases, network management, and platforms for L4-7 services.

Cisco Press gratefully acknowledges the efforts of technical reviewers **Ron Hromoko** and **Brian Walck**; their contributions helped ensure the quality and accuracy of the text.

Dedications

Mauricio Arregoces:

To my wife Frances, whose support, patience, and encouragement got me through the writing of this book.

To my daughter, Gabrielle, who lets me see the wonders of the world through her eyes.

To my son, Julian, who constantly reminds me of the right priorities in life through his candid self.

To my family, who gave me time and understanding during the many days, nights, and weekends I spent away from them working on this project.

Maurizio Portolani:

I dedicate this book to Rosangela and Stefano for their continued support and understanding and to Margherita, Alda, and Leonardo for their example of hard work and strength that helped me during the long nights of work. I want to thank Giovanni, whose religious love for books always inspired me. A special thanks to all my friends who bore with my schedule during the last two years of hard work.

Acknowledgments

Mauricio Arregoces and Maurizio Portolani:

To John Kane, our executive editor, for his constant encouragement and support through the evolution of the book and for his understanding and willingness to look past our many schedule slips.

To Chris Cleveland, our development editor, for his keen eye, great work, and always helpful attitude, without whom the book would certainly not be what it is.

To Bob Batz, Brian Walck, Ron Hromoko, Scott Van deHouten, Stefano Testa, Mario Baldi, and Fabio Maino, whose feedback contributed to the quality of the book.

Very special thanks to Fabio Maino for helping us on security topics. Fabio, your strength and optimism are beyond words.

To Martin Pueblas, who contributed substance and knowledge on matters of cryptography and overall security.

To Patrick Folstrom, who helped us understand the world of Domain Name System (DNS) and for his accurate review of the DNS-related topics.

And to the Cisco Press team behind the scenes for supporting this project for making this book a reality.

Mauricio Arregoces:

To Maurizio, for his dedication, appetite for knowledge, and search for perfection. You kept me honest and focused; may you find the perfect mountain.

Maurizio Portolani:

I want to especially thank Mauricio for his vision, which made it possible to develop a book on such an interesting topic. Thank you for involving me in this project for the past two years, for the help and encouragement, and for the focus on quality.

Contents at a Glance

Table of Contents

Icons Used in This Book

Cisco uses the following standard icons to represent different networking devices. You will encounter several of these icons within this book.

Router

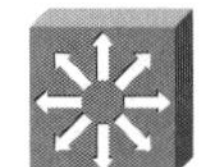
Multilayer Switch

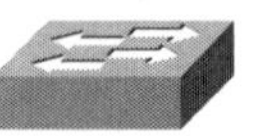
Switch

Firewalls

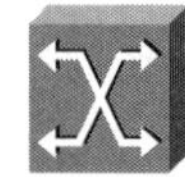
ATM Switch

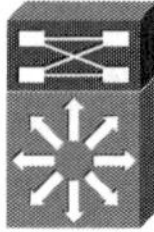
Route/Switch Processor

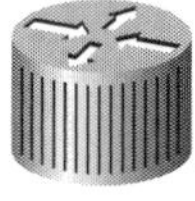
Cisco 7500 Series Router

ISDN/Frame Relay switch

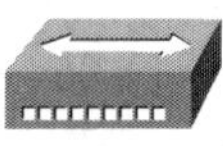
Hub

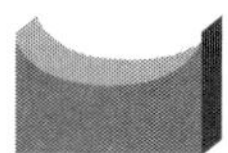
Bridge

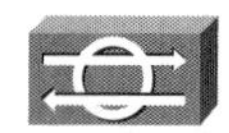
Intrusion Detection System

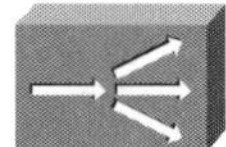
Load Balancer

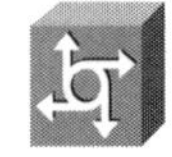
Access Server

CiscoSecure Scanner

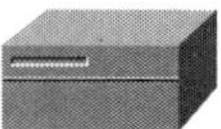
IP/TV Broadcast Server

Cisco CallManager

Cisco Directory Server

PC

Laptop

Cisco Works Workstation

Web Browser

Web Server

Network Cloud

Concentrator

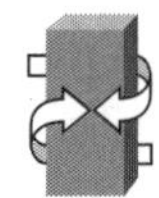
Gateway

Fax

File Server

Printer

VPN Concentrator

Phone

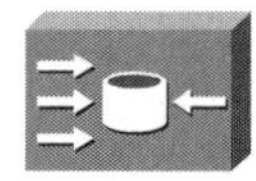
Cache or Content Engine

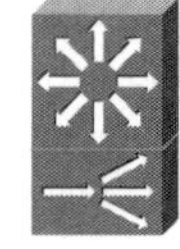
Multilayer Switch with Load Balancer

SSL Offloader

Tape Subsystem

Fibre Channel Switch

DWDM-CWDM

Storage Subsystem

Command Syntax Conventions

The conventions used to present command syntax in this book are the same conventions used in the Cisco IOS Command Reference. The Command Reference describes these conventions as follows:

- Vertical bars (|) separate alternative, mutually exclusive elements.
- Square brackets [ ] indicate optional elements.
- Braces { } indicate a required choice.
- Braces within brackets [{ }] indicate a required choice within an optional element.
- **Boldface** indicates commands and keywords that are entered literally as shown. In actual configuration examples and output (not general command syntax), boldface indicates commands that the user manually enters (such as a **show** command).
- *Italics* indicate arguments for which you supply actual values.

Introduction

Data Centers are complex systems encompassing a wide variety of technologies that are constantly evolving. Designing and maintaining a Data Center network requires skills and knowledge that range from routing and switching to load balancing and security, including the essential knowledge of servers and applications.

This books addresses both fundamental information such as the protocols used by switches and routers; the protocols used in application environments; the network technology used to build the Data Center infrastructure and secure, scale, and manage the application environments; and design best practices. We hope this book becomes your Data Center reference on protocols, technology, and design.

Motivation for Writing This Book

While speaking to networkers abroad on the topic of server load balancing, we realized that we could only convey the benefits of the technology by explaining application layer information and describing the larger design issues common in application environments.

Often through discussions with customers, the subjects related to load balancing take a back seat as issues of integration with the entire Data Center take the forefront. This book attempts to cover the breadth and depth of the Data Center IP network. The storage network and distributed Data Center topics will be the subjects of other books.

Having designed campus and Data Center networks, and having developed and supported technologies that are often referred to as *content networking* (load balancing, Secure Socket Layer [SSL] offloading, and DNS routing), we felt the need for a book that described these topics in a single place and focused on what is relevant to the Data Center. This area is what this book is about: it is an all-encompassing view of Data Centers from routing and switching technologies to application-aware technologies.

Who Should Read This Book

This book is intended for any person or organization seeking to understand Data Center networks: the fundamental protocols used by the applications and the network, the typical network technologies, and their design aspects. The book is meant to be both a reference on protocols and technology and a design and implementation guide for personnel responsible for planning, designing, implementing, and operating Data Center networks.

Chapter Organization

This book has six parts. This book is designed to be read in order from the overview of the Data Center environment, through the server farms and infrastructure protocols, to security and load-balancing concepts, before you reach the Data Center design chapters. This organization also allows you to go directly to the desired chapter if you already know the information in the previous chapters.

Part I, "An Introduction to Server Farms," includes chapters that contain an overview of the architecture of Data Centers, servers, and applications. This part also introduces the security and load-balancing technology:

- Chapter 1, "Overview of Data Centers," presents Data Center environments, the Data Center architecture, and services that are used as a guide to the rest of the book.
- Chapter 2, "Server Architecture Overview," explores the architecture of servers. This chapter covers topics such as how servers process TCP and User Datagram Protocol (UDP) traffic, how processes and threads are used, and server health.

- Chapter 3, "Application Architectures Overview," explores the application environments and how applications are architected. This chapter includes discussions on the relation between the application architectures and the design of the Data Center, the n-tier model, HTML and XML, user-agent technologies, web server technologies, and clustering technologies. This chapter introduces application concepts that are developed in Chapter 18 and Chapter 19.
- Chapter 4, "Data Center Design Overview," discusses the types of server farms on Data Centers, generic and alternative Layer 2 and Layer 3 designs, multitier designs, high availability, Data Center services, and trends that might affect Data Center designs.
- Chapter 5, "Data Center Security Overview," discusses threats, vulnerabilities and common attacks, network security devices such as firewalls and intrusion detection systems (IDSs), and other fundamental security concepts such as cryptography; VPNs; and authentication, authorization and accounting (AAA).
- Chapter 6, "Server Load-Balancing Overview," discusses reasons for load balancing, fundamental load-balancing concepts, high-availability considerations, and generic load-balancing architectures. The fundamental load-balancing concepts include Layer 4 and Layer 5 load balancing, session tracking, session persistence, and server health.

Part II, "Server Farm Protocols," explores the fundamental protocols used in server farms:

- Chapter 7, "IP, TCP, and UDP," explores the protocol headers details and their relevance to network design issues.
- Chapter 8, "HTTP and Related Concepts," discusses key concepts such as Uniform Resource Identifiers (URIs) and URLs, Multipurpose Internet Mail Extension (MIME) and its relation to HTTP entities, and HTTP header details. Chapter 8 provides additional information on the operation of HTTP, the different versions and their performance characteristics.
- Chapter 9, "SSL and TLS," discusses SSL operations with specific focus on SSL session establishment, ciphersuites, and SSL performance considerations. Chapter 15 provides additional information on the public-key infrastructure (PKI), certificates, and more security-related aspects of SSL.
- Chapter 10, "DNS Essentials and Site-Selection Considerations," explores how the DNS namespace is organized, the DNS components in the Internet, how the DNS resolution process works, DNS configuration options, DNS server placement in the network, and how to use DNS to distribute application requests to multiple Data Centers.
- Chapter 11, "Streaming Protocols Overview," discusses HTTP and real streaming, the use of TCP and UDP in streaming, analog and digital video, coders-decoders (codecs), packetization, the streaming transport formats, unicast, multicast and stream splitting, and encoding mechanisms.

Part III, "Infrastructure Protocols," explores the fundamental Layer 2 and Layer 3 protocols as well as IBM Data Center technologies:

- Chapter 12, "Layer 2 Protocol Essentials," discusses Ethernet frame types; the difference between unicast, multicast, and broadcast frames; physical layer characteristics of Ethernet technologies; jumbo frames; trunks and channels; and a variety of spanning-tree concepts. Chapter 20 provides the design best practices applied to the concepts described in this chapter.
- Chapter 13, "Layer 3 Protocol Essentials," discusses the Address Resolution Protocol (ARP); gateway redundancy protocols such as Hot Standby Router Protocol (HSRP), VRRP and GLBP; and routing-protocol essentials for Open Shortest Path First (OSPF) and Enhanced Interior Gateway Routing Protocol (EIGRP). Chapter 20 provides the design best practices applied to the concepts described in this chapter.

- Chapter 14, "IBM Data Center Technology," discusses mainframe attachment options, IBM networking, Systems Network Architecture (SNA) switching, Sysplex, TN3270, and current IBM Data Center designs.

Part IV, "Security and Server Load Balancing," explores the security protocols and technology, load-balancing operations, server health management, session tracking and cookies, and persistence mechanisms on load balancers:

- Chapter 15, "Security Protocols and Technologies," discusses cryptography, U.S. government–related topics about cryptography, PKI, transport security protocols (SSL and IP Security [IPSec]), authentication protocols and technologies, and network management security. This chapter also complements Chapter 9 with regards to the security design aspects of SSL and introduces the concept of SSL VPNs.
- Chapter 16, "Load-Balancing Modes and Predictors," discusses the load-balancing modes of operation, server load-balancing algorithms, and cache farm load-balancing algorithms.
- Chapter 17, "Server Health Management," discusses server health management through load balancers, SNMP, server failure detection and checking, in-band and out-of-band probes, and case studies on server checking for web hosting and e-commerce applications.
- Chapter 18, "Session Tracking and Cookies," explores the concept of user sessions from an application point of view. This chapter explains nonpersistent cookies, cookies in general, how servers track user sessions, session persistence on clusters of servers, and the challenges of dealing with HTTP and HTTPS. Chapter 19 further expands the topic of session persistence in load-balancing deployments.
- Chapter 19, "Persistence Mechanisms on Load Balancers," explains session persistence in relation to load balancing; discusses key persistence mechanisms, including source-IP sticky, cookie-URL sticky, HTTP redirection sticky, and SSL sticky; and presents a case study using an e-commerce application. Chapter 19 is based on the applications introduced in Chapter 3 and Chapter 18.

Part V, "Data Center Design," explores the details behind designing the Data Center infrastructure, the integration of security into the infrastructure design, and the performance of Data Center devices:

- Chapter 20, "Designing the Data Center Infrastructure," discusses router switching paths, essential Data Center design concepts, and the design best practices of the infrastructure by explaining the configuration of Layer 2 and Layer 3 features and protocols that are described in Chapter 12 and 13.
- Chapter 21, "Integrating Security into the Infrastructure," discusses the concept of security zones and how to design application security at the Internet Edge and at intranet server farms. This chapter explains alternative designs and how to implement secure management.
- Chapter 22, "Performance Metrics of Data Center Devices," discusses the Data Center traffic patterns and performance metrics of various Data Center devices, including proposed metrics for devices for which there are none and no standard methodology exists (such as load balancers and SSL offloaders).

Part VI, "Appendixes," is the final part of this book:

- Appendix A, "Character Sets," covers multiple character sets, including ASCII, the extended ASCII sets, and the ISO-8859-1 set.
- Appendix B, "HTTP Header Fields," explains the details of HTTP header fields that were not described in Chapter 8.
- Appendix C, "Video Encoding Mechanisms," explains the removal of special and temporal redundancy in codecs with special focus on MPEG.
- Appendix D, "Loopback Interface Configuration Procedures," provides an explanation about configuring a machine with multiple IP addresses used as loopbacks for certain load-balancing modes of operation.

- Appendix E, "Configuring Servers to Insert Cookies," examines several alternatives for configuring cookie insertion on web servers.
- Appendix F, "Client-Side and Server-Side Programming," provides excerpts of client-side programs to help you understand the differences and similarities between JavaScripts, Java applets, and ActiveX controls. The section on server-side programming explains the differences between CGI, servlets, and Active Server Pages (ASP) in terms of operating-system implications (threads versus processes). This appendix explains the adoption of certain technologies in today's enterprise applications and the performance and availability implications.

PART I

An Introduction to Server Farms

This chapter covers the following topics:

- Overview of the role of a Data Center in the enterprise
- Overview of the evolution of application environments
- The blueprint of the Data Center architecture
- The services provided by the Data Center network

CHAPTER 1

Overview of Data Centers

This chapter presents an overview of enterprise Data Center environments, current application environment trends, the Data Center network architecture, and the services provided by the architecture. The approach to develop the architecture of the Data Center network is typically an internal process based on the requirement of the enterprise. This chapter provides the design criteria used by the authors to define the Data Center design best practices presented throughout the book.

Data Centers Defined

Data Centers house critical computing resources in controlled environments and under centralized management, which enable enterprises to operate around the clock or according to their business needs. These computing resources include mainframes; web and application servers; file and print servers; messaging servers; application software and the operating systems that run them; storage subsystems; and the network infrastructure, whether IP or storage-area network (SAN). Applications range from internal financial and human resources to external e-commerce and business-to-business applications. Additionally, a number of servers support network operations and network-based applications. Network operation applications include Network Time Protocol (NTP); TN3270; FTP; Domain Name System (DNS); Dynamic Host Configuration Protocol (DHCP); Simple Network Management Protocol (SNMP); TFTP; Network File System (NFS); and network-based applications, including IP telephony, video streaming over IP, IP video conferencing, and so on.

According to a report from the Renewable Energy Policy Project on Energy Smart Data Centers, Data Centers are

> . . . an essential component of the infrastructure supporting the Internet and the digital commerce and electronic communication sector. Continued growth of these sectors requires a reliable infrastructure because . . . interruptions in digital services can have significant economic consequences.

Virtually, every enterprise has one or more Data Centers. Some have evolved rapidly to accommodate various enterprise application environments using distinct operating systems and hardware platforms. The evolution has resulted in complex and disparate environments that are expensive to manage and maintain. In addition to the application environment, the supporting network infrastructure might not have changed fast enough to be flexible in accommodating ongoing redundancy, scalability, security, and management requirements.

A Data Center network design lacking in any of these areas risks not being able to sustain the expected service level agreements (SLAs). Data Center downtime, service degradation, or the inability to roll new services implies that SLAs are not met, which leads to a loss of access to critical resources and a quantifiable impact on normal business operation. The impact could be as simple as increased response time or as severe as loss of data.

Data Center Goals

The benefits provided by a Data Center include traditional business-oriented goals such as the support for business operations around the clock (resiliency), lowering the total cost of operation and the maintenance needed to sustain the business functions (total cost of ownership), and the rapid deployment of applications and consolidation of computing resources (flexibility).

These business goals generate a number of information technology (IT) initiatives, including the following:

- Business continuance
- Increased security in the Data Center
- Application, server, and Data Center consolidation
- Integration of applications whether client/server and multitier (n-tier), or web services-related applications
- Storage consolidation

These IT initiatives are a combination of the need to address short-term problems and establishing a long-term strategic direction, all of which require an architectural approach to avoid unnecessary instability if the Data Center network is not flexible enough to accommodate future changes. The design criteria are

- Availability
- Scalability
- Security
- Performance
- Manageability

These design criteria are applied to these distinct functional areas of a Data Center network:

- **Infrastructure services**—Routing, switching, and server-farm architecture
- **Application services**—Load balancing, Secure Socket Layer (SSL) offloading, and caching

- **Security services**—Packet filtering and inspection, intrusion detection, and intrusion prevention
- **Storage services**—SAN architecture, Fibre Channel switching, backup, and archival
- **Business continuance**—SAN extension, site selection, and Data Center interconnectivity

The details of these services are discussed later in this chapter.

Data Center Facilities

Because Data Centers house critical computing resources, enterprises must make special arrangements with respect to both the facilities that house the equipment and the personnel required for a 24-by-7 operation. These facilities are likely to support a high concentration of server resources and network infrastructure. The demands posed by these resources, coupled with the business criticality of the applications, create the need to address the following areas:

- Power capacity
- Cooling capacity
- Cabling
- Temperature and humidity controls
- Fire and smoke systems
- Physical security: restricted access and surveillance systems
- Rack space and raised floors

Discussing the facilities where the Data Center resides and the related planning functions is outside the scope of this book.

The sections that follow introduce the role of the Data Center in the enterprise network.

Roles of Data Centers in the Enterprise

Figure 1-1 presents the different building blocks used in the typical enterprise network and illustrates the location of the Data Center within that architecture.

The building blocks of this typical enterprise network include

- Campus network
- Private WAN
- Remote access
- Internet server farm
- Extranet server farm
- Intranet server farm

Figure 1-1 *Data Centers in the Enterprise*

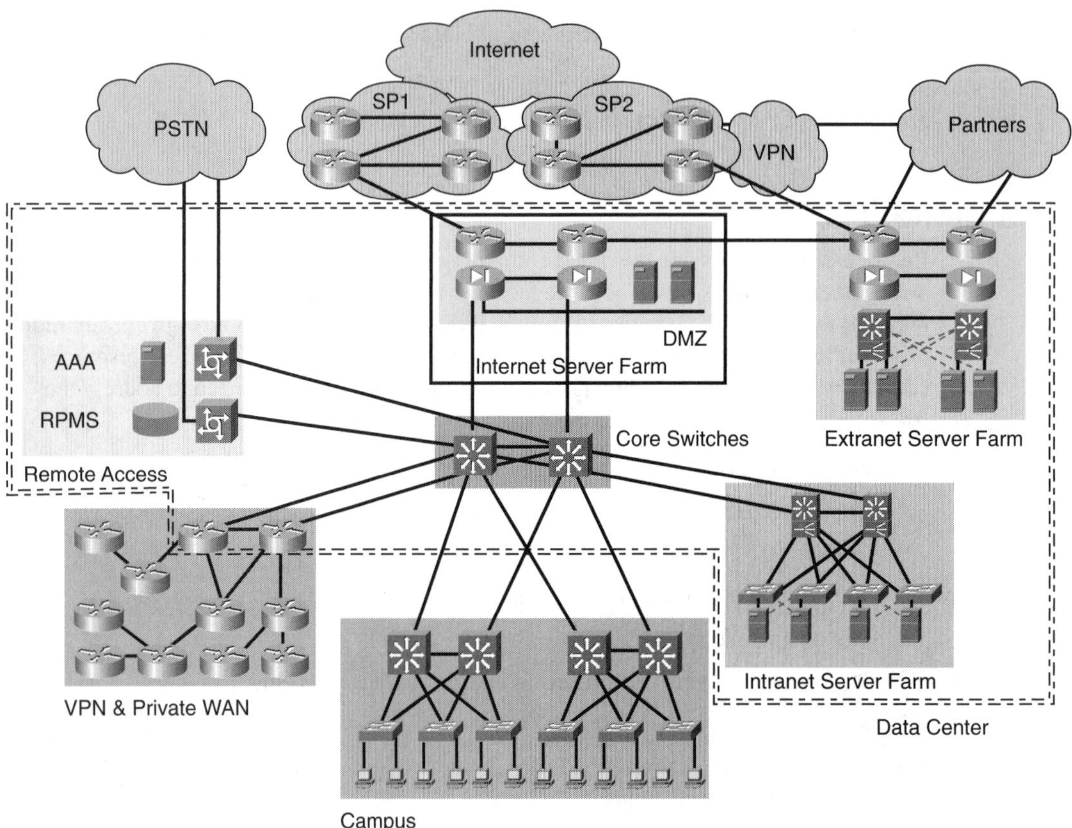

Data Centers typically house many components that support the infrastructure building blocks, such as the core switches of the campus network or the edge routers of the private WAN. Data Center designs can include any or all of the building blocks in Figure 1-1, including any or all server farm types. Each type of server farm can be a separate physical entity, depending on the business requirements of the enterprise. For example, a company might build a single Data Center and share all resources, such as servers, firewalls, routers, switches, and so on. Another company might require that the three server farms be physically separated with no shared equipment. This book focuses on the details of architecting server farms in the context of a highly available and scalable Data Center. These server farms support a wide number of enterprise applications.

Enterprise applications typically focus on one of the following major business areas:

- Customer relationship management (CRM)
- Enterprise resource planning (ERP)

- Supply chain management (SCM)
- Sales force automation (SFA)
- Order processing
- E-commerce

Roles of Data Centers in the Service Provider Environment

Data Centers in service provider (SP) environments, known as Internet Data Centers (IDCs), unlike in enterprise environments, are the source of revenue that supports collocated server farms for enterprise customers. The SP Data Center is a service-oriented environment built to house, or *host*, an enterprise customer's application environment under tightly controlled SLAs for uptime and availability. Enterprises also build IDCs when the sole reason for the Data Center is to support Internet-facing applications.

The IDCs are separated from the SP internal Data Centers that support the internal business applications environments.

Whether built for internal facing or collocated applications, application environments follow specific application architectural models such as the classic client/server or the n-tier model.

Application Architecture Models

Application architectures are constantly evolving, adapting to new requirements, and using new technologies. The most pervasive models are the client/server and n-tier models that refer to how applications use the functional elements of communication exchange. The client/server model, in fact, has evolved to the n-tier model, which most enterprise software application vendors currently use in application architectures. This section introduces both models and the evolutionary steps from client/server to the n-tier model.

The Client/Server Model and Its Evolution

The classic client/server model describes the communication between an application and a user through the use of a server and a client. The classic client/server model consists of the following:

- A thick client that provides a graphical user interface (GUI) on top of an application or business logic where some processing occurs
- A server where the remaining business logic resides

Thick client is an expression referring to the complexity of the business logic (software) required on the client side and the necessary hardware to support it. A thick client is then a portion of the application code running at the client's computer that has the responsibility of retrieving data from the server and presenting it to the client. The thick client code requires a fair amount of processing capacity and resources to run in addition to the management overhead caused by loading and maintaining it on the client base.

The server side is a single server running the presentation, application, and database code that uses multiple internal processes to communicate information across these distinct functions. The exchange of information between client and server is mostly data because the thick client performs local presentation functions so that the end user can interact with the application using a local user interface.

Client/server applications are still widely used, yet the client and server use proprietary interfaces and message formats that different applications cannot easily share. Part **a** of Figure 1-2 shows the client/server model.

Figure 1-2 *Client/Server and n-Tier Application Interaction*

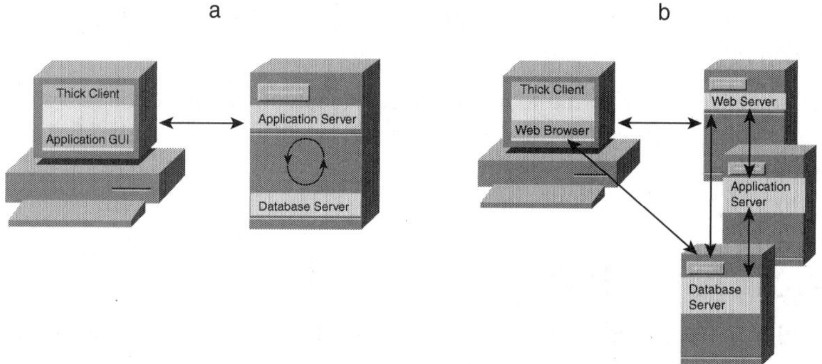

The most fundamental changes to the thick client and single-server model started when web-based applications first appeared. Web-based applications rely on more standard interfaces and message formats where applications are easier to share. HTML and HTTP provide a standard framework that allows generic clients such as web browsers to communicate with generic applications as long as they use web servers for the presentation function. HTML describes how the client should render the data; HTTP is the transport protocol used to carry HTML data. Netscape Communicator and Microsoft Internet Explorer are examples of clients (web browsers); Apache, Netscape Enterprise Server, and Microsoft Internet Information Server (IIS) are examples of web servers.

The migration from the classic client/server to a web-based architecture implies the use of thin clients (web browsers), web servers, application servers, and database servers. The web browser interacts with web servers and application servers, and the web servers interact with application servers and database servers. These distinct functions supported by the servers are referred to as *tiers*, which, in addition to the client tier, refer to the *n-tier model*.

The n-Tier Model

Part **b** of Figure 1-2 shows the n-tier model. Figure 1-2 presents the evolution from the classic client/server model to the n-tier model. The client/server model uses the thick client with its own business logic and GUI to interact with a server that provides the counterpart business logic and database functions on the same physical device. The n-tier model uses a thin client and a web browser to access the data in many different ways. The server side of the n-tier model is divided into distinct functional areas that include the web, application, and database servers.

The n-tier model relies on a standard web architecture where the web browser formats and presents the information received from the web server. The server side in the web architecture consists of multiple and distinct servers that are functionally separate. The n-tier model can be the client and a web server; or the client, the web server, and an application server; or the client, web, application, and database servers. This model is more scalable and manageable, and even though it is more complex than the classic client/server model, it enables application environments to evolve toward distributed computing environments.

The n-tier model marks a significant step in the evolution of distributed computing from the classic client/server model. The n-tier model provides a mechanism to increase performance and maintainability of client/server applications while the control and management of application code is simplified.

Figure 1-3 introduces the n-tier model and maps each tier to a partial list of currently available technologies at each tier.

Figure 1-3 *n-Tier Model*

Notice that the client-facing servers provide the interface to access the business logic at the application tier. Although some applications provide a non-web–based front end, current trends indicate the process of "web-transforming" business applications is well underway.

This process implies that the front end relies on a web-based interface to face the users which interacts with a middle layer of applications that obtain data from the back-end systems.

These middle tier applications and the back-end database systems are distinct pieces of logic that perform specific functions. The logical separation of front-end application and back-end functions has enabled their physical separation. The implications are that the web and application servers, as well as application and database servers, no longer have to coexist in the same physical server. This separation increases the scalability of the services and eases the management of large-scale server farms. From a network perspective, these groups of servers performing distinct functions could also be physically separated into different network segments for security and manageability reasons.

Chapter 3, "Application Architectures Overview," discusses the details on applications that follow the n-tier model and the implications on the design of the Data Center.

Multitier Architecture Application Environment

Multitier architectures refer to the Data Center server farms supporting applications that provide a logical and physical separation between various application functions, such as web, application, and database (n-tier model). The network architecture is then dictated by the requirements of applications in use and their specific availability, scalability, and security and management goals. For each server-side tier, there is a one-to-one mapping to a network segment that supports the specific application function and its requirements. Because the resulting network segments are closely aligned with the tiered applications, they are described in reference to the different application tiers.

Figure 1-4 presents the mapping from the n-tier model to the supporting network segments used in a multitier design.

Figure 1-4 *Multitier Network Segments*

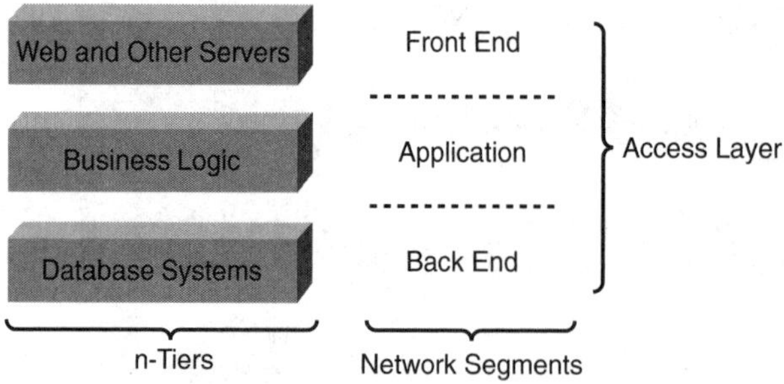

The web server tier is mapped to the *front-end segment*, the business logic to the *application segment*, and the database tier to the *back-end segment*. Notice that all the segments supporting the server farm connect to access layer switches, which in a multitier architecture are different access switches supporting the various server functions.

The evolution of application architectures and departing from multitier application environments still requires a network to support the interaction between the communicating entities. For example, a web service (defined as "A web service is a software system designed to support interoperable machine-to-machine interaction over a network" by the W3C web services architecture document) still refers to the network element. In this case, the network would be used for networked resources that support such interaction realiably. This layer of abstraction does not necesarily translate on to a layered network design as much as the capability of the network to support networked applications, resources, and their interaction.

The following section presents a high-level overview of the distinct network layers of the Data Center architecture.

Data Center Architecture

The enterprise Data Center architecture is inclusive of many functional areas, as presented earlier in Figure 1-1. The focus of this section is the architecture of a generic enterprise Data Center connected to the Internet and supporting an intranet server farm. Other types of server farms, explained in Chapter 4, "Data Center Design Overview," follow the same architecture used for intranet server farms yet with different scalability, security, and management requirements. Figure 1-5 introduces the topology of the Data Center architecture.

Figure 1-5 *Topology of an Enterprise Data Center Architecture*

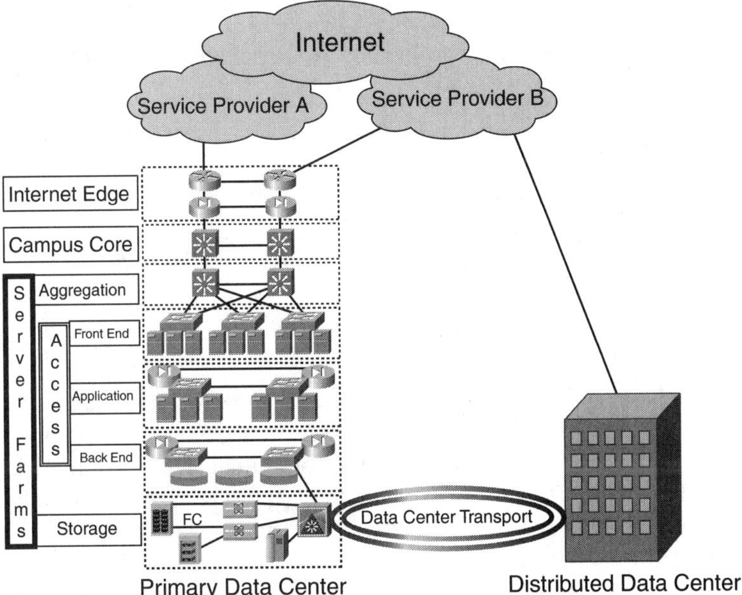

Figure 1-5 shows a fully redundant enterprise Data Center supporting the following areas:

- No single point of failure—redundant components
- Redundant Data Centers

Although the focus of this book is the architecture of an IP network that supports server farms, we include explanations pertaining to how the server farms are connected to the rest of the enterprise network for the sake of clarity and thoroughness. The core connectivity functions supported by Data Centers are Internet Edge connectivity, campus connectivity, and server-farm connectivity, as presented in Figure 1-5.

The Internet Edge provides the connectivity from the enterprise to the Internet and its associated redundancy and security functions, such as the following:

- Redundant connections to different service providers
- External and internal routing through exterior border gateway protocol (EBGP) and interior border gateway protocol (IBGP)
- Edge security to control access from the Internet
- Control for access to the Internet from the enterprise clients

The campus core switches provide connectivity between the Internet Edge, the intranet server farms, the campus network, and the private WAN. The core switches physically connect to the devices that provide access to other major network areas, such as the private WAN edge routers, the server-farm aggregation switches, and campus distribution switches.

As depicted in Figure 1-6, the following are the network layers of the server farm:

- Aggregation layer
- Access layer
  - Front-end segment
  - Application segment
  - Back-end segment
- Storage layer
- Data Center transport layer

Some of these layers depend on the specific implementation of the n-tier model or the requirements for Data Center-to-Data-Center connectivity, which implies that they might not exist in every Data Center implementation. Although some of these layers might be optional in the Data Center architecture, they represent the trend in continuing to build highly available and scalable enterprise Data Centers. This trend specifically applies to the storage and Data Center transport layers supporting storage consolidation, backup and archival consolidation, high-speed mirroring or clustering between remote server farms, and so on.

The sections that follow present the specific details of each layer.

Aggregation Layer

The aggregation layer is the aggregation point for devices that provide services to all server farms. These devices are multilayer switches, firewalls, load balancers, and other devices that typically support services across all servers. The multilayer switches are referred to as aggregation switches because of the aggregation function they perform. Service devices are shared by all server farms. Specific server farms are likely to span multiple access switches for redundancy, thus making the aggregation switches the logical connection point for service devices, instead of the access switches.

If connected to the front-end Layer 2 switches, these service devices might not offer optimal services by creating less than optimal traffic paths between them and servers connected to different front-end switches. Additionally, if the service devices are off of the aggregation switches, the traffic paths are deterministic and predictable and simpler to manage and maintain. Figure 1-6 shows the typical devices at the aggregation layer.

Figure 1-6 *Aggregation and Access Layers*

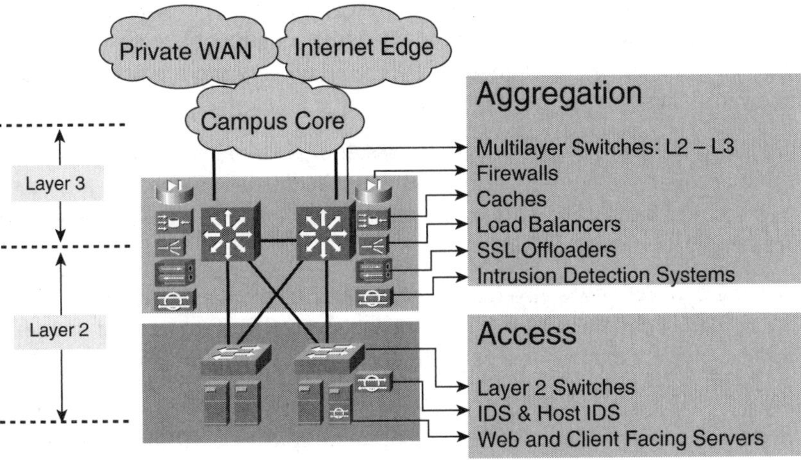

As depicted in Figure 1-6, the aggregation switches provide basic infrastructure services and connectivity for other service devices. The aggregation layer is analogous to the traditional distribution layer in the campus network in its Layer 3 and Layer 2 functionality.

The aggregation switches support the traditional switching of packets at Layer 3 and Layer 2 in addition to the protocols and features to support Layer 3 and Layer 2 connectivity. A more in-depth explanation on the specific services provided by the aggregation layer appears in the section, "Data Center Services."

Access Layer

The access layer provides Layer 2 connectivity and Layer 2 features to the server farm. Because in a multitier server farm, each server function could be located on different access switches on different segments, the following section explains the details of each segment.

Front-End Segment

The front-end segment consists of Layer 2 switches, security devices or features, and the front-end server farms. See the section, "Data Center Services" for a detailed description of the features provided by the devices at this layer. The front-end segment is analogous to the traditional access layer of the hierarchical campus network design and provides the same functionality. The access switches are connected to the aggregation switches in the manner depicted in Figure 1-6. The front-end server farms typically include FTP, Telnet, TN3270 (mainframe terminals), Simple Mail Transfer Protocol (SMTP), web servers, DNS servers, and other business application servers, in addition to network-based application servers such as IP television (IPTV) broadcast servers and IP telephony call managers that are not placed at the aggregation layer because of port density or other design requirements.

The specific network features required in the front-end segment depend on the servers and their functions. For example, if a network supports video streaming over IP, it might require multicast, or if it supports Voice over IP (VoIP), quality of service (QoS) must be enabled. Layer 2 connectivity through VLANs is required between servers and load balancers or firewalls that segregate server farms.

The need for Layer 2 adjacency is the result of Network Address Translation (NAT) and other header rewrite functions performed by load balancers or firewalls on traffic destined to the server farm. The return traffic must be processed by the same device that performed the header rewrite operations.

Layer 2 connectivity is also required between servers that use clustering for high availability or require communicating on the same subnet. This requirement implies that multiple access switches supporting front-end servers can support the same set of VLANs to provide layer adjacency between them.

Security features include Address Resolution Protocol (ARP) inspection, broadcast suppression, private VLANs, and others that are enabled to counteract Layer 2 attacks. Security devices include network-based intrusion detection systems (IDSs) and host-based IDSs to monitor and detect intruders and prevent vulnerabilities from being exploited. In general, the infrastructure components such as the Layer 2 switches provide intelligent network services that enable front-end servers to provide their functions.

Note that the front-end servers are typically taxed in their I/O and CPU capabilities. For I/O, this strain is a direct result of serving content to the end users; for CPU, it is the connection rate and the number of concurrent connections needed to be processed.

Scaling mechanisms for front-end servers typically include adding more servers with identical content and then equally distributing the load they receive using load balancers. Load balancers distribute the load (or load balance) based on Layer 4 or Layer 5 information. Layer 4 is widely used for front-end servers to sustain a high connection rate without necessarily overwhelming the servers. See Chapter 22, "Performance Metrics of Data Center Devices," to understand the performance of servers and load balancers under load.

Scaling mechanisms for web servers also include the use of SSL offloaders and Reverse Proxy Caching (RPC). Refer to Chapter 9, "SSL and TLS," for more information about the use of SSL and its performance implications.

Application Segment

The application segment has the same network infrastructure components as the front-end segment and the application servers. The features required by the application segment are almost identical to those needed in the front-end segment, albeit with additional security. This segment relies strictly on Layer 2 connectivity, yet the additional security is a direct requirement of how much protection the application servers need because they have direct access to the database systems. Depending on the security policies, this segment uses firewalls between web and application servers, IDSs, and host IDSs. Like the front-end segment, the application segment infrastructure must support intelligent network services as a direct result of the functions provided by the application services.

Application servers run a portion of the software used by business applications and provide the communication logic between the front end and the back end, which is typically referred to as the *middleware* or *business logic*. Application servers translate user requests to commands that the back-end database systems understand. Increasing the security at this segment focuses on controlling the protocols used between the front-end servers and the application servers to avoid trust exploitation and attacks that exploit known application vulnerabilities. Figure 1-7 introduces the front-end, application, and back-end segments in a logical topology.

Note that the application servers are typically CPU-stressed because they need to support the business logic. Scaling mechanisms for application servers also include load balancers. Load balancers can select the right application server based on Layer 5 information.

Deep packet inspection on load balancers allows the partitioning of application server farms by content. Some server farms could be dedicated to selecting a server farm based on the scripting language (.cgi, .jsp, and so on). This arrangement allows application administrators to control and manage the server behavior more efficiently.

Figure 1-7 *Access Layer Segments*

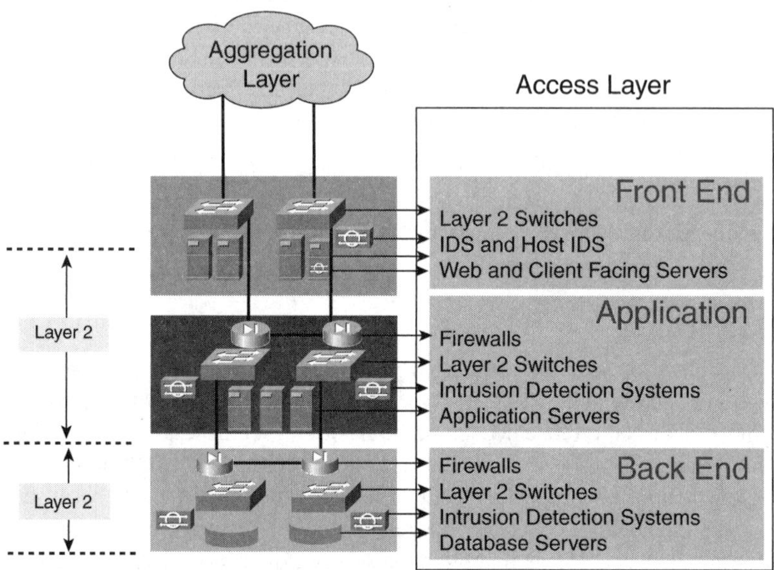

Back-End Segment

The back-end segment is the same as the previous two segments except that it supports the connectivity to database servers. The back-end segment features are almost identical to those at the application segment, yet the security considerations are more stringent and aim at protecting the data, critical or not.

The hardware supporting the database systems ranges from medium-sized servers to high-end servers, some with direct locally attached storage and others using disk arrays attached to a SAN. When the storage is separated, the database server is connected to both the Ethernet switch and the SAN. The connection to the SAN is through a Fibre Channel interface. Figure 1-8 presents the back-end segment in reference to the storage layer. Notice the connections from the database server to the back-end segment and storage layer.

Note that in other connectivity alternatives, the security requirements do not call for physical separation between the different server tiers. These alternatives are discussed in Chapter 4.

Storage Layer

The storage layer consists of the storage infrastructure such as Fibre Channel switches and routers that support small computer system interface (SCSI) over IP (iSCSI) or Fibre Channel over IP (FCIP). Storage network devices provide the connectivity to servers, storage devices such as disk subsystems, and tape subsystems.

NOTE SAN environments in Data Centers commonly use Fibre Channel to connect servers to the storage device and to transmit SCSI commands between them. Storage networks allow the transport of SCSI commands over the network. This transport is possible over the Fibre Channel infrastructure or over IP using FCIP and iSCSI.

FCIP and iSCSI are the emerging Internet Engineering Task Force (IETF) standards that enable SCSI access and connectivity over IP.

The network used by these storage devices is referred to as a SAN. The Data Center is the location where the consolidation of applications, servers, and storage occurs and where the highest concentration of servers is likely, thus where SANs are located. The current trends in server and storage consolidation are the result of the need for increased efficiency in the application environments and for lower costs of operation.

Data Center environments are expected to support high-speed communication between servers and storage and between storage devices. These high-speed environments require block-level access to the information supported by SAN technology. There are also requirements to support file-level access specifically for applications that use Network Attached Storage (NAS) technology. Figure 1-8 introduces the storage layer and the typical elements of single and distributed Data Center environments.

Figure 1-8 shows a number of database servers as well as tape and disk arrays connected to the Fibre Channel switches. Servers connected to the Fibre Channel switches are typically critical servers and always dual-homed. Other common alternatives to increase availability include mirroring, replication, and clustering between database systems or storage devices. These alternatives typically require the data to be housed in multiple facilities, thus lowering the likelihood of a site failure preventing normal systems operation. Site failures are recovered by replicas of the data at different sites, thus creating the need for distributed Data Centers and distributed server farms and the obvious transport technologies to enable communication between them. The following section discusses Data Center transport alternatives.

Figure 1-8 *Storage and Transport Layers*

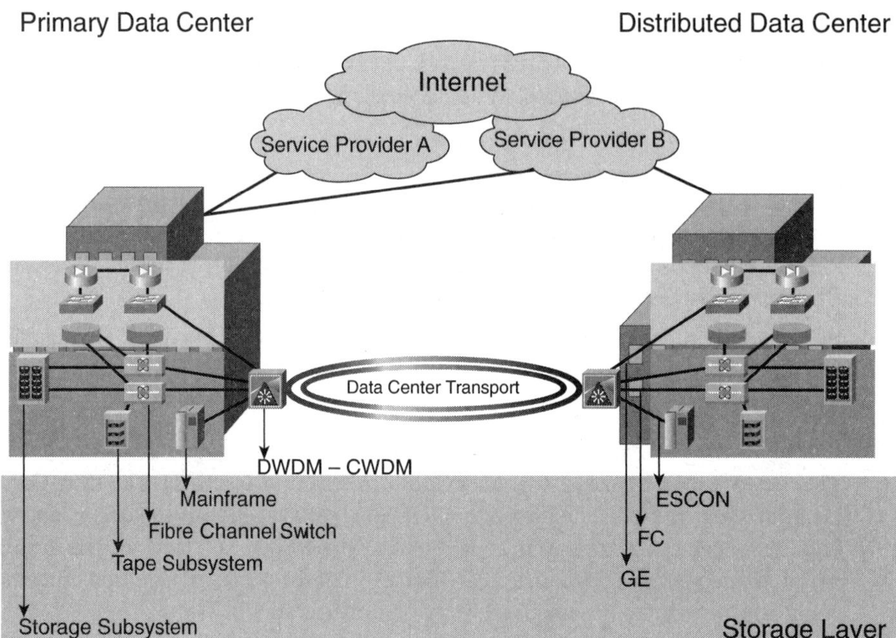

Data Center Transport Layer

The Data Center transport layer includes the transport technologies required for the following purposes:

- Communication between distributed Data Centers for rerouting client-to-server traffic
- Communication between distributed server farms located in distributed Data Centers for the purposes of remote mirroring, replication, or clustering

Transport technologies must support a wide range of requirements for bandwidth and latency depending on the traffic profiles, which imply a number of media types ranging from Ethernet to Fibre Channel.

For user-to-server communication, the possible technologies include Frame Relay, ATM, DS channels in the form of T1/E1 circuits, Metro Ethernet, and SONET.

For server-to-server and storage-to-storage communication, the technologies required are dictated by server media types and the transport technology that supports them transparently. For example, as depicted in Figure 1-8, storage devices use Fibre Channel and Enterprise

Systems Connectivity (ESCON), which should be supported by the metro optical transport infrastructure between the distributed server farms.

If ATM and Gigabit Ethernet (GE) are used between distributed server farms, the metro optical transport could consolidate the use of fiber more efficiently. For example, instead of having dedicated fiber for ESCON, GE, and ATM, the metro optical technology could transport them concurrently.

The likely transport technologies are dark fiber, coarse wavelength division multiplexing (CWDM), and dense wavelength division multiplexing (DWDM), which offer transparent connectivity (Layer 1 transport) between distributed Data Centers for media types such as GE, Fibre Channel, ESCON, and fiber connectivity (FICON).

Note that distributed Data Centers often exist to increase availability and redundancy in application environments. The most common driving factors are disaster recovery and business continuance, which rely on the specific application environments and the capabilities offered by the transport technologies.

- Blade servers
- Grid computing
- Web services
- Service-oriented Data Centers

All these trends influence the Data Center in one way or another. Some short-term trends force design changes, while some long-term trends force a more strategic view of the architecture.

For example, the need to lower operational costs and achieve better computing capacity at a relatively low price leads to the use of blade servers. Blade servers require a different topology when using Ethernet switches inside the blade chassis, which requires planning on port density, slot density, oversubscription, redundancy, connectivity, rack space, power consumption, heat dissipation, weight, and cabling. Blade servers can also support compute grids. Compute grids might be geographically distributed, which requires a clear understanding of the protocols used by the grid middleware for provisioning and load distribution, as well as the potential interaction between a compute grid and a data grid.

Blade servers can also be used to replace 1RU servers on web-based applications because of scalability reasons or the deployment or tiered applications. This physical separation of tiers and the ever-increased need for security leads to application layer firewalls.

An example of this is the explicit definition for application layer security is (included in the Web Services Architecture [WSA] document). Security on Web Services is in reference to a secure environment for online processes from a security and privacy perspective. The development of the WSA focuses on the identification of threats to security and privacy and the architect features that are needed to respond to those threats. The infrastructure to support such security is expected to be consistently supported by applications that are expected to be distributed on the network. Past experiences suggest that some computationally repeatable tasks would, over time, be offloaded to network devices, and that the additional network intelligence provides a more robust infrastructure to complement Web Services security (consistency- and performance-wise).

Finally, a services-oriented Data Center implies a radical change on how Data Centers are viewed by their users, which invariably requires a radical change in the integration of the likely services. In this case, interoperability and manageability of the service devices become a priority for the Data Center designers. Current trends speak to the Utility Data Center from HP and On Demand (computing) form IBM, in which both closer integration of available services and the manner in which they are managed and provisioned is adaptable to the organization. This adaptability comes from the use of standard interfaces between the integrated services, but go beyond to support virtualization and self-healing capabilities. Whatever these terms end up bringing to the Data Center, the conclusion is obvious: The Data Center is the location where users, applications, data, and the network infrastructure converge. The result of current trends will change the ways in which the Data Center is architected and managed.

Chapter 4 discusses some of these trends in more detail. The following section discusses the different services a Data Center is expected to support.

Data Center Services

This section presents an overview of the services supported by the Data Center architecture. Related technology and features make up each service. Each service enhances the manner in which the network operates in each of the functional service areas defined earlier in the chapter. The following sections introduce each service area and its associated features. Figure 1-9 introduces the Data Center services.

Figure 1-9 *Data Center Services*

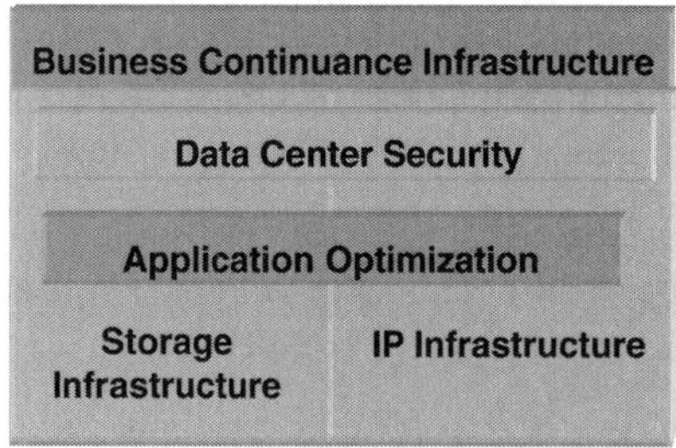

As depicted in Figure 1-9, services in the Data Center are not only related to one another but are also, in certain cases, dependent on each other. The IP and storage infrastructure services are the pillars of all other services because they provide the fundamental building blocks of any network and thus of any service. After the infrastructure is in place, you can build server farms to support the application environments. These environments could be optimized utilizing network technology, hence the name *application services*. Security is a service expected to leverage security features on the networking devices that support all other services in addition to using specific security technology. Finally, the business continuance infrastructure, as a service aimed at achieving the highest possible redundancy level. The highest redundancy level is possible by using both the services of the primary Data Center and their best practices on building a distributed Data Center environment.

IP Infrastructure Services

Infrastructure services include all core features needed for the Data Center IP infrastructure to function and serve as the foundation, along with the storage infrastructure, of all other Data Center services. The IP infrastructure features are organized as follows:

- Layer 2
- Layer 3
- Intelligent Network Services

Layer 2 features support the Layer 2 adjacency between the server farms and the service devices (VLAN's); enable media access; and support a fast convergence, loop-free, predictable, and scalable Layer 2 domain. Layer 2 domain features ensure the Spanning Tree Protocol (STP) convergence time for deterministic topologies is in single-digit seconds and that the failover and failback scenarios are predictable.

STP is available on Cisco network devices in three versions: Per VLAN Spanning Tree Plus (PVST+), Rapid PVST+ (which combines PVST+ and IEEE 802.1w), and Multiple Spanning Tree (IEEE 801.1s combined with IEEE 802.1w). VLANs and trunking (IEEE 802.1Q) are features that make it possible to virtualize the physical infrastructure and, as a consequence, consolidate server-farm segments. Additional features and protocols increase the availability of the Layer 2 network, such as Loopguard, Unidirectional Link Detection (UDLD), PortFast, and the Link Aggregation Control Protocol (LACP or IEEE 802.3ad).

Layer 3 features enable a fast-convergence routed network, including redundancy for basic Layer 3 services such as default gateway support. The purpose is to maintain a highly available Layer 3 environment in the Data Center where the network operation is predictable under normal and failure conditions. The list of available features includes the support for static routing, Border Gateway Protocol (BGP) and Interior Gateway Protocols (IGPs) such as Open Shortest Path First (OSPF), Enhanced Interior Gateway Routing Protocol (EIGRP), Intermediate System-to-Intermediate System (IS-IS), gateway redundancy protocols such as the Hot Standby Routing Protocol (HSRP), Multigroup HSRP (MHSRP), and Virtual Router Redundancy Protocol (VRRP) for default gateway support.

Intelligent network services encompass a number of features that enable application services network-wide. The most common features are QoS and multicast. Yet there are other important intelligent network services such as private VLANs (PVLANs) and policy-based routing

(PBR). These features enable applications, such as live or on-demand video streaming and IP telephony, in addition to the classic set of enterprise applications.

QoS in the Data Center is important for two reasons—marking at the source of application traffic and the port-based rate-limiting capabilities that enforce proper QoS service class as traffic leaves the server farms. For marked packets, it is expected that the rest of the enterprise network enforces the same QoS policies for an end-to-end QoS service over the entire network.

Multicast in the Data Center enables the capabilities needed to reach multiple users concurrently. Because the Data Center is the source of the application traffic, such as live video streaming over IP, multicast must be supported at the server-farm level (VLANs, where the source of the multicast stream is generated). As with QoS, the rest of the enterprise network must either be multicast-enabled or use tunnels to get the multicast stream to the intended destinations.

Application Services

Application services include a number of features that enhance the network awareness of applications and use network intelligence to optimize application environments. These features are equally available to scale server-farm performance, to perform packet inspection at Layer 4 or Layer 5, and to improve server response time. The server-farm features are organized by the devices that support them. The following is a list of those features:

- Load balancing
- Caching
- SSL termination

Load balancers perform two core functions:

- Scale and distribute the load to server farms
- Track server health to ensure high availability

To perform these functions, load balancers virtualize the services offered by the server farms by front-ending and controlling the incoming requests to those services. The load balancers distribute requests across multiple servers based on Layer 4 or Layer 5 information. The mechanisms for tracking server health include both in-band monitoring and out-of-band probing with the intent of not forwarding traffic to servers that are not operational. You also can add new servers, thus scaling the capacity of a server farm, without any disruption to existing services.

Layer 5 capabilities on a load balancer allow you to segment server farms by the content they serve. For example, you can separate a group of servers dedicated to serve streaming video (running multiple video servers) from other groups of servers running scripts and application code. The load balancer can determine that a request for an .mpg file (a video file using MPEG) goes to the first group and that a request for a .cgi file (a script file) goes to the second group.

Server farms benefit from caching features, specifically working in RPC mode. Caches operating in RPC mode are placed near the server farm to intercept requests sent to the server farm, thus offloading the serving of static content from the servers. The cache keeps a copy of the content, which is available to any subsequent request for the same content, so that the server farm does not have to process the requests. The process of offloading occurs transparently for both the user and the server farm.

SSL offloading features use an SSL device to offload the processing of SSL sessions from server farms. The key advantage to this approach is that the SSL termination device offloads SSL key negotiation and the encryption/decryption process away from the server farm. An additional advantage is the capability to process packets based on information in the payload that would otherwise be encrypted. Being able to see the payload allows the load balancer to distribute the load based on Layer 4 or Layer 5 information before re-encrypting the packets and sending them off to the proper server.

Security Services

Security services include the features and technologies used to secure the Data Center infrastructure and application environments. Given the variety of likely targets in the Data Center, it is important to use a systems approach to securing the Data Center. This comprehensive approach considers the use of all possible security tools in addition to hardening every network device and using a secure management infrastructure. The security tools and features are as follows:

- Access control lists (ACLs)
- Firewalls
- IDSs and host IDSs
- Secure management
- Layer 2 and Layer 3 security features

ACLs filter packets. Packet filtering through ACLs can prevent unwanted access to network infrastructure devices and, to a lesser extent, protect server-farm application services. ACLs are applied on routers (RACLs) to filter routed packets and to VLANs (VACLs) to filter intra-VLAN traffic. Other features that use ACLs are QoS and security, which are enabled for specific ACLs.

An important feature of ACLs is the capability to perform packet inspection and classification without causing performance bottlenecks. You can perform this lookup process in hardware, in which case the ACLs operate at the speed of the media (wire speed).

The placement of firewalls marks a clear delineation between highly secured and loosely secured network perimeters. Although the typical location for firewalls remains the Internet

Edge and the edge of the Data Center, they are also used in multitier server-farm environments to increase security between the different tiers.

IDSs proactively address security issues. Intruder detection and the subsequent notification are fundamental steps for highly secure Data Centers where the goal is to protect the data. Host IDSs enable real-time analysis and reaction to hacking attempts on database, application, and Web servers. The host IDS can identify the attack and prevent access to server resources before any unauthorized transactions occur.

Secure management include the use of SNMP version 3; Secure Shell (SSH); authentication, authorization, and accounting (AAA) services; and an isolated LAN housing the management systems. SNMPv3 and SSH support secure monitoring and access to manage network devices. AAA provides one more layer of security by preventing users access unless they are authorized and by ensuring controlled user access to the network and network devices with a predefined profile. The transactions of all authorized and authenticated users are logged for accounting purposes, for billing, or for postmortem analysis.

Storage Services

Storage services include the capability of consolidating direct attached disks by using disk arrays that are connected to the network. This setup provides a more effective disk utilization mechanism and allows the centralization of storage management. Two additional services are the capability of consolidating multiple isolated SANs on to the same larger SAN and the virtualization of storage so that multiple servers concurrently use the same set of disk arrays.

Consolidating isolated SANs on to one SAN requires the use of virtual SAN (VSAN) technology available on the SAN switches. VSANs are equivalent to VLANs yet are supported by SAN switches instead of Ethernet switches. The concurrent use of disk arrays by multiple servers is possible through various network-based mechanisms supported by the SAN switch to build logical paths from servers to storage arrays.

Other storage services include the support for FCIP and iSCSI on the same storage network infrastructure. FCIP connects SANs that are geographically distributed, and iSCSI is a lower-cost alternative to Fibre Channel. These services are used both in local SANs and SANs that might be extended beyond a single Data Center. The SAN extension subject is discussed in the next section.

Business Continuance Infrastructure Services

Business continuance infrastructure services support the highest levels of application availability through the use of networking technology in the three major areas described next.

- Site selection
- SAN extension
- Data Center interconnectivity

Site selection refers to the features that allow the automatic detection of the failure of a Data Center on the application level and the subsequent reroute of all requests to an available site and server farm. You can use the technology for site selection over the Internet or the intranet. The mechanisms for site selection vary from the use of DNS to the host routes and the routed network.

SAN extension refers to the process of stretching an existing SAN to a secondary location, which could be located in the same Data Center or on a different geographical location. You make this extension to allow the replication of the data from the primary to the secondary SAN. Depending on the distance, the application transaction rate, and the latency between the distributed Data Centers, the replication is synchronous or asynchronous. For more information on replication technologies consult Chapter 3.

Data Center interconnectivity services are connectivity alternatives provided by various technologies. These connectivity alternatives support the communication requirements for site selection and SAN extension. The section, "Data Center Transport Layer" earlier in this chapter discussed the available technologies.

Summary

Data Centers are strategic components of an enterprise that house the critical assets of the business: applications, data, and the computing infrastructure. The Data Center network is vital to sustaining the normal operations of the business. The Data Center network architecture is driven by business requirements.

The criteria that guide the design of a Data Center are availability, scalability, security, performance, and manageability. The Data Center designs described in this book are based on these principles.

The distinct services likely offered by the Data Center network include IP infrastructure connectivity, SAN infrastructure connectivity, application optimizations, security, and business continuance.

The IP infrastructure connectivity function refers to routing and switching. The SAN function refers to the Fibre Channel fabric switching. The application optimization functions include load balancing, caching, and SSL offloading. The security function refers to the use of ACLs, firewalls, IDSs, and secure management. The business continuance function refers to the use of site selection (IP based or DNS based), SAN extension, and Data Center Interconnectivity.

The design process consists of choosing among the available options for each function (IP connectivity, application optimization, security, and business continuance), based on how it meets the high availability, scalability, security, performance, and manageability requirements.

Additionally, the design process must take into account the current trends in application environments you have or are likely to deploy—such as the n-tier model, the adoption of blade servers, or the use of grid computing—and the Data Center network layers to support the aforementioned services. Once the application requirements are clear, the Data Center architecture needs to be qualified to ensure it meets its objectives and satisfies such requirements.

This book primarily focuses on IP-related functions, including the infrastructure design, application optimization, and security.

This chapter covers the following topics:

- Network interface card basics
- Server processing of network traffic from the Ethernet driver to the socket layer
- TCP and UDP algorithms and timeouts applied to simple applications
- The workings of multiprocess and multithreaded servers, and the implications on server availability
- The behavior of the client TCP/IP stack in the presence of server failure
- An example of a web server configuration
- The Window Scale option and its support for higher throughput on high-speed networks
- Jumbo frames and their optimization of servers' performance
- Reverse proxy caches and their improvement of application performance
- The importance of load balancers in Data Centers to monitor the health of servers and to avoid server overload

CHAPTER 2

Server Architecture Overview

Data Centers provide a centralized location to host applications. The architecture of applications has changed significantly from the master-slave model, which was predominant in the 1970s and '80s, to the client/server model, which is predominant today. The client/server model is characterized by distributed architectures: The server functions are performed by a number of computers or processes specialized in particular operations. Chapter 1, "Overview of Data Centers," presents an example of an interaction between client and server, and Chapter 3, "Application Architectures Overview," presents more detail about the architecture of today's applications.

This chapter focuses on the networking aspects of client/server architectures and, more specifically, on the server hardware and software components that relate to the processing of network traffic, such as the network interface card (NIC), the Ethernet driver, and the TCP/IP stack.

Understanding these topics is essential for comprehending network design choices such as the use of reverse proxy caching, the use of load balancers for server health monitoring, the need for jumbo frames, and the need for NIC features such as interrupt coalescing.

The traffic profile of two simple but different applications, such as Telnet and HTTP, introduces the key algorithms and settings of TCP. Knowing these TCP algorithms and settings is key to troubleshooting network problems and to correctly design highly available Data Centers. Throughout this book, you find information about several other applications and servers, such as DNS servers, servlet engines, and streaming servers.

The last part of this chapter provides an example of the configuration of a server—specifically, a web server. A web server was chosen because HTTP is the most commonly used protocol for accessing applications.

This section is also crucial to understanding Chapter 3 because it provides background information on how applications function from operating system and network perspectives. It is assumed that you are already familiar with basic concepts such as the TCP connection establishment, sequence numbers, and acknowledgments (ACKs). If not, read the beginning of Chapter 7, "IP, TCP, and UDP."

Network Attachment

Servers and clients attach to the network via network interface cards (NIC). This section covers relevant aspects of using NICs when designing a Data Center network.

Servers can also be attached to a storage-area network by means of host bus adapters (HBAs) for Fibre Channel connectivity. For a high-level overview of the role storage networks play in Data Centers, see Chapter 1. No further detail is provided in this book on storage networks.

Mainframes offer a variety of attachment options. For more information, see Chapter 14, "IBM Data Center Technology."

Network Interface Cards

Network interface cards (NICs), also known as network adapters or adapters for short, provide connectivity between hosts (client and servers) and LANs. NICs translate the computer data into signals to be transmitted on the network, and vice versa.

Most NICs in use today are Fast Ethernet, but Gigabit Ethernet cards are becoming popular, and 10-Gigabit Ethernet adapters are already available. NICs negotiate the speed of the transmission and the duplex settings with the switch to which they connect.

Chapter 12, "Layer 2 Protocol Essentials," gives more details of how the IEEE 802 specifications map to the NIC functionalities. Chapter 20, "Designing the Data Center Infrastructure," describes how to properly configure the switch ports used by hosts (servers or clients), including the speed and duplex settings.

NOTE In networking terminology, the ports on a switch that connect to a server or a client are typically called access ports.

Adapters have buffers whose size varies according to the model and the vendor; Gigabit adapters typically have 64-KB onboard buffers. Incoming traffic from the network is stored in the buffer and eventually passed to the memory. When the data is ready to be transferred, the adapter triggers a hardware interrupt to invoke the server's CPU. NICs typically offer several options to reduce the number of interrupts to the system processors and the involvement of the CPU in moving the data.

Most server adapters offer the following features:

- **Direct Memory Access (DMA)**—This facilitates the transfer of data from the NIC to the computer memory without involving the system processor.
- **Interrupt coalescing**—This reduces the number of interrupts sent by the NIC to the CPU by delaying the notification of a newly arrived packet. This feature is especially useful with Gigabit Ethernet NICs because the number of interrupts per second at wire rate can take 50 percent or more of the server CPU.
- **Jumbo frames support**—This supports the use of bigger Ethernet frames (typically 9-KB frames). Using jumbo frames also alleviates the interrupts to the CPU and allows higher throughput (see the section, "Jumbo Frames," later in this chapter).
- **IEEE 802.1Q support**—This supports the connection of a server to several VLANs (see Chapter 12 for more information about IEEE 802.1Q).
- **TCP/IP offloading**—Some NICs can offload part of the TCP processing from the OS TCP stack. NICs supporting TCP offloading typically offer TCP checksum calculation and segmentation functions that can significantly reduce the CPU utilization.
- **Fault tolerance and load balancing**—These features facilitate attaching a server to the network with multiple ports, to increase availability and performance (see the next section in this chapter).
- **IEEE 802.3ad support**—802.3ad is a protocol that allows negotiation between ports of separate devices to form a channel (see Chapter 12 for more information).

Server Multihoming

It is possible and likely for a single server to use multiple NICs for both redundancy and performance. The connectivity between the server and the network device (switch) can be composed of several ports out of a single NIC or of several ports, one per NIC. For the purpose of this discussion, the difference is irrelevant. The key point is that a single server connects to one or multiple switches with multiple ports.

Most NIC vendors offer configurations that allow multiple ports to work together (some vendors call this a "teaming" configuration), as depicted in Figure 2-1.

Figure 2-1 *Server Attachment with Multiple Ports: (a) Fault Tolerance, (b) Load Balancing, and (c) Link Aggregation*

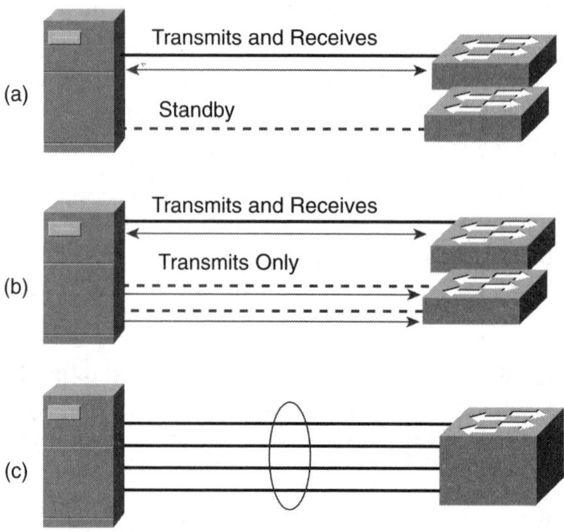

The list that follows details the three options—a, b, and c—shown in Figure 2-1:

- **Fault tolerance**—One port (or NIC) is active (receives and transmits traffic) while the other ports are in standby (these ports don't forward or receive traffic). When the active port fails, one of the ports that was previously in standby takes over with the same MAC address. This option is depicted as option **a** in Figure 2-1.
- **Load balancing**—Only one port receives traffic; all the ports transmit traffic. If the receive port fails, a new port is elected for the receive function. In Figure 2-1, this is option **b**.
- **Link aggregation**—A number of ports (NICs) form a bundle that logically looks like a single link with a bandwidth equivalent to the sum of the bandwidth of each single link. Cisco calls this configuration an EtherChannel. In Figure 2-1, this is option **c**.

Chapter 20 provides more details on how to connect servers to the network infrastructure with multiple NICs.

PCI and PCI-X Buses

NICs provide the interface between the host's CPU and the network, and translate parallel data from the bus into a serial transmission on the wire. The bus allows the communication between the CPU/memory and the NIC.

The predominant bus architecture today is Peripheral Component Interface (PCI), which Intel originally developed. PCI is typically deployed as a 32-bit bus at 33 MHz, which allows a maximum theoretical bandwidth of 133 MBps (1.064 Gbps). Using a gigabit NIC in conjunction with a 32-bit PCI bus could overwhelm the bus by saturating the available bandwidth.

This explains the availability of 64-bit PCI buses with 66 MHz, which provides for a peak bandwidth of 533 MBps (4.25 Gbps). This bandwidth can still be a bottleneck when deploying multiple NICs for server multihoming because 4-Gbps NICs could again saturate the bus.

The solution consists of using the PCI-X technology, which is an extension to the PCI bus standard. PCI-X was developed by Compaq, Hewlett Packard, and IBM. PCI-X is a 64-bit bus that operates at 133 MHz, allowing a peak bandwidth of 1.066 GBps (about 8 Gbps).

High-performance NICs for servers typically use the PCI-X or 64-bit PCI technologies.

Client and Server Packet Processing

This section describes how operating systems (OSs) handle the processing of IP packets on a host (either a client or a server) and how data flows from the network to the application, and vice versa.

A high-level discussion of user mode and kernel provides a foundation for understanding the functional and performance implications of how the driver, TCP/IP stack, and applications are invoked in an operating system.

The remainder of the section describes how the kernel deals with the network functions.

User Mode and Kernel Mode

The kernel of an OS provides the core services, including the management of threads and processes, interrupt handling, and the management of input/output (I/O) operations. UNIX-based operating systems have a kernel that handles all possible services, from process management to network operations. Other OSs provide a microkernel that handles operations such as thread scheduling, memory management, and interrupt handling. When using OS with microkernels, support for I/O operations or process management is offered by separate services.

The system services (I/O handling, memory management, thread scheduling, and so on) execute in kernel mode. Applications execute in user mode. Code executing in kernel mode has access to the system memory and direct access to the hardware.

Applications that need to perform I/O operations use specific interfaces (in UNIX, these are called system calls) that eventually cause the process to change and run in kernel mode.

Figure 2-2 shows how applications interface with the kernel to perform network operations. The socket layer provides an abstraction for the underlying protocols.

Figure 2-2 *User Mode and Kernel Mode for I/O Processing*

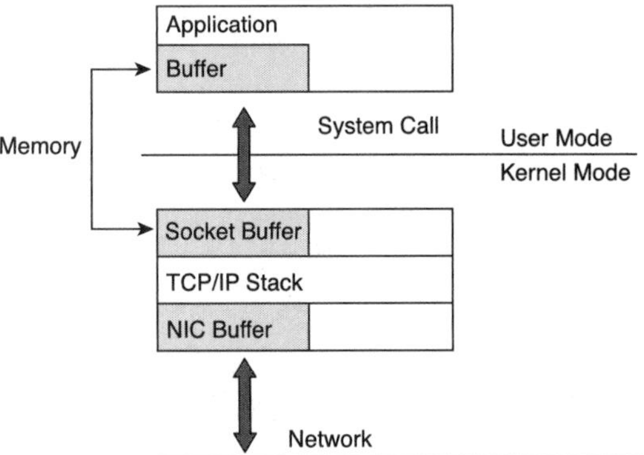

When an application must send traffic on the network, it invokes a system call from the process where it runs, which causes the invocation of procedures from the socket layer. This also causes the change of execution mode in the process from user mode to kernel mode. The process data is copied into the memory buffers used by the kernel. Figure 2-2 shows the switch from user to kernel mode; notice that data is copied between memory buffers.

Input processing occurs when a new packet is received by the NIC and the interrupt invokes the Ethernet driver (kernel mode). Eventually, the kernel wakes up the process waiting for incoming traffic. The data is copied from the socket buffer to the process.

As just described, changing between user mode and kernel mode requires copying between the application buffer and the socket buffer for the data structures holding the data for transmission on the network or the data received from the network.

Ethernet Driver

NICs typically provide Layer 2 functionalities (sometimes they also provide some TCP offloading, as previously described in this chapter). A NIC picks up three main traffic types:

- **Broadcasts**—These are frames with a destination MAC address of ffff.ffff.ffff. Every station on the LAN segment inspects broadcast traffic.
- **Unicast**—These are frames whose destination MAC address matches the NIC MAC address. Normally, on a given LAN segment, only one station is configured to pick up the traffic destined for a given MAC.

- **Multicast**—On a given LAN segment, several stations accept the traffic destined for a multicast MAC. If the host is not configured to accept specific multicast MAC, the NIC does not pass it to the TCP/IP stack.

The NIC receiving the frame generates a hardware interrupt to the CPU that triggers the driver for the interface to handle the frame. Assuming that the NIC is Ethernet, the driver performs a number of actions, which include examining the Type/Length field to distinguish Ethernet v2 from 802.3 frames and eventually queuing the frame into either the IP queue or the Address Resolution Protocol (ARP) queue. At this point, the driver generates a software interrupt to invoke the IP processing.

Server TCP/IP Processing

A server application based on TCP waits for incoming connections on specific Layer 4 ports (see "bind()" in the "Sockets" section, which follows this section). A client requesting an application sends a TCP SYN to one of these ports and performs a TCP handshake with the server (see Chapter 7 for details about the TCP handshake). Example 2-1 shows which ports the server is listening to by using the command **netstat –a**. The previous command also displays information about the send and receive queue.

Example 2-1 shows, among others, the following servers: an Apache HTTP server configured for SSL (see the line :https), a DNS server (see the line :domain), a Telnet server, and an FTP server.

Example 2-1 *Determining the Ports a Server Is Listening To*

```
[root@localhost admin]# netstat -a
Active Internet connections (servers and established)
Proto Recv-Q Send-Q Local Address          Foreign Address        State
tcp        0      0 10.20.5.14:telnet      10.21.4.5:1073         ESTABLISHED
tcp        0      0 10.20.5.14:domain      *:*                    LISTEN
tcp        0      0 mp5:domain             *:*                    LISTEN
tcp        0      0 *:www                  *:*                    LISTEN
tcp        0      0 *:https                *:*                    LISTEN
tcp        0      0 *:587                  *:*                    LISTEN
tcp        0      0 *:smtp                 *:*                    LISTEN
tcp        0      0 *:printer              *:*                    LISTEN
tcp        0      0 *:ssh                  *:*                    LISTEN
tcp        0      0 *:login                *:*                    LISTEN
tcp        0      0 *:shell                *:*                    LISTEN
tcp        0      0 *:telnet               *:*                    LISTEN
tcp        0      0 *:ftp                  *:*                    LISTEN
tcp        0      0 *:finger               *:*                    LISTEN
tcp        0      0 *:auth                 *:*                    LISTEN
tcp        0      0 *:1024                 *:*                    LISTEN
tcp        0      0 *:sunrpc               *:*                    LISTEN
udp        0      0 *:2154                 *:*
udp        0      0 10.20.5.14:domain      *:*
```

The typical connection status that you can observe is either LISTEN (before the connection is established), TIME_WAIT (right after the connection has been closed), or ESTABLISHED if the connection is active. In Example 2-1, you can see a Telnet connection to this server from the client 10.20.5.15.

The server can take a number of possible states, including LISTEN, TIME_WAIT, and ESTABLISHED. Figure 2-3 shows the TCP state machine for reference.

Figure 2-3 *TCP State Machine with Highlighted Sequence of States Taken by a Server*

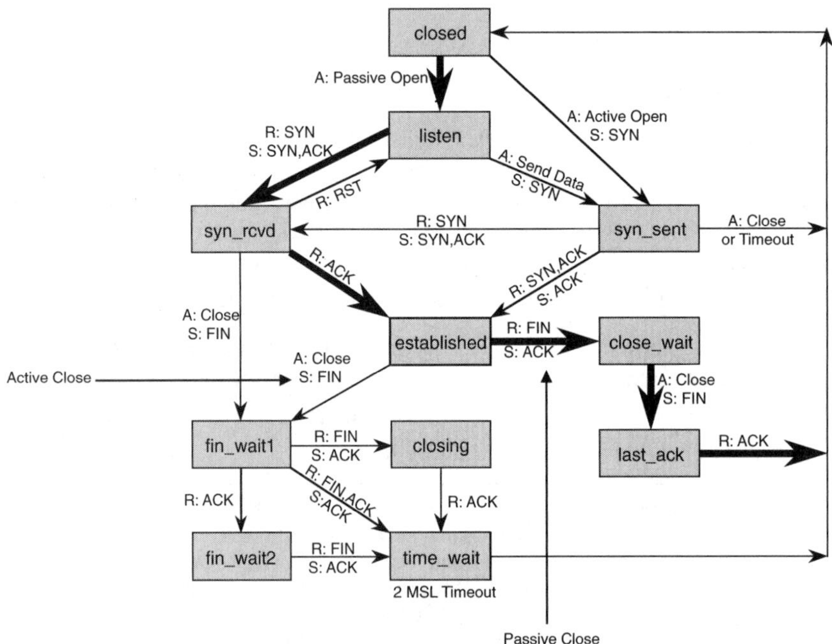

The bold arrows show the typical states taken by a connection on a server: At the reception of a SYN, a server responds with a SYN ACK, which brings the state to SYN-RCVD (passive open). After receiving one ACK, the connection is in the ESTABLISHED state. From the ESTABLISHED state, the typical server connection closure is initiated by the client (passive close).

Connections often can be stuck in a state, as described in the following list, and this is the symptom of a problem:

- **SYN-RCVD**—The server has received a SYN (passive open), and it has sent a SYN ACK but has not received an ACK back from the client. Among the possible causes is an asymmetric traffic path. The traffic from the client hits a device that performs NAT on the destination IP to the real server IP address. The traffic from the server instead could bypass the device that translates the IP address. As a result, the client does not recognize the source of the SYN ACK.

- **SYN-SENT**—The server has sent a SYN (active open) but has not received a SYN ACK from the client. Among the possible causes, the routing could be misconfigured.
- **FIN-WAIT1**—The server has sent a FIN but has not received an ACK or a FIN ACK. Among the possible causes for this problem, the client could be down as the result of either an administrative action (power cycling) or a failure.

The previous list shows that analyzing the output of the **netstat –a** command can help you detect problems that relate either to a network misconfiguration (routing issues) or to an anomaly on the client. For more details about the other possible states of a connection, refer to the book *TCP/IP Illustrated*, by Richard Stevens (Addison-Wesley, 1994).

The closure of the TCP connection can take the form of a FIN handshake or a TCP RST (see Chapter 7). When either side of a connection sends a TCP FIN, the other entity can finish sending the content of its send buffer and eventually close the connection.

When either the client or the server sends a TCP RST, it means that the connection is closing, and the data left in the send buffer of either entity is discarded. Under normal conditions, either side of an application should close connections with the TCP FIN sequence, but there are exceptions; for example, some browsers use TCP RSTs.

For some applications, receiving a TCP RST is the symptom of a failure on the client side. As a result, these applications can throw an exception when they see this type of closure. This is sometimes the case for servlet engines (see the Chapter 3 for more information on servlet engines).

Sockets

Sockets provide application processes with a protocol-independent interface to the network communication. In UNIX, the communication between the process and the OS (kernel) uses system calls.

The following list shows the sequence of system calls used by a server that uses TCP as the transport protocol:

1. **Socket()**—Creates a socket for streams (TCP). The socket descriptor created on the server defines the capability of the server to accept connections of a specific type, for the IP address defined by the Bind() call.
2. **Bind()**—Associates the socket with a local IP address and Layer 4 port number.
3. **Listen()**—Defines the length of the receive queue for incoming connection requests.

4 **Accept()**—Used by the server to wait for incoming connection requests. This call puts the process in a waiting state for incoming connections. When a new connection request is received, the accept call returns a new socket descriptor. This descriptor references a specific client connection to the server.

5 **Read()/Write()**—Exchange data between the server and the client.

Client applications based on TCP use the socket() and connect() calls to establish the connection to the server, and write() and read() calls to exchange data.

Server applications based on UDP use different system calls than those listed because UDP does not establish connections between the client and the server. As a result, there is no need to use the Listen() and Accept() system calls on a UDP server. The following list shows the sequence of system calls used by a server using UDP as the transport protocol:

1 **Socket()**—This call creates a socket descriptor of the datagram type.

2 **Bind()**—This call binds the socket descriptor to an IP address and a port.

3 **Recvfrom()**—A process calling recvfrom() waits for incoming connections. When UDP datagrams arrive, recvfrom() returns the IP address of the client together with the datagram.

4 **Sendto()**—This call sends datagrams to the IP address specified in the parameters to this call.

Sockets allow options to be defined to control the TCP and UDP functions in the kernel, such as these:

- **SO_KEEPALIVE**—This option controls the capability of TCP to verify whether an idle connection is still alive by sending a keepalive probe after a configurable amount of time (the default is 2 hours). If no ACK is received, the socket is closed. For more information, see the section, "TCP Timeout."
- **SO_RCVBUF**—TCP or UDP receives buffer size. This buffer size is used as the receive window by the TCP protocol during the handshake.
- **SO_SNDBUF**—TCP or UDP send buffer size.

Server applications that enable the SO_KEEPALIVE option should configure an appropriate TCP KEEPALIVE. Under normal conditions, for many applications a TCP connection is never idle for 2 hours. The implication of using the default setting is the possibility of keeping servers' resources allocated for clients that did not close connections.

The receive buffer size has a direct implication on the performance of TCP transfers. Suppose that the two communicating entities are host A and host B, and suppose that the receive buffer configured on host B is 64 KB. Assuming that the maximum segment size (MSS) is 1460 bytes, host A can send 44 segments (64 KB/1460 bytes, rounded to an even number of MSS) without receiving any acknowledgements from host B. When you compare this with a transfer in which host A can send only one segment after receiving an ACK from host B, the benefit in terms of throughput is evident.

Typical TCP window sizes can range from 8 to 64 KB, or more if the OS supports the Window Scale option (defined in RFC 1323). For more information about the Window Scale option, see Chapter 7. This chapter provides additional information about the use of the Window Scale option in the section, "High-Speed Networks and the Window Scale Option."

TCP and Server Applications

Applications based on TCP take advantage of the features offered by TCP, such as reliability, flow control, and congestion avoidance. The purpose of this section is to provide examples of TCP applications and to identify some of its reliability, flow control, and congestion-avoidance features. Chapter 7 provides more details for each one of these algorithms.

This chapter analyzes two traffic profiles:

- **Interactive traffic**—With Telnet. Telnet is an interactive application that generates a limited amount of traffic on a network. This means that, most of the time, the transmit buffer is empty or filled with small segments.
- **Bulk transfer**—With a Hypertext Transfer Protocol (HTTP) transfer of a big object. In this case, the transmit buffer is continuously filled, and most of the segments sent over the network are as big as the maximum segment size (typically 1460 bytes).

Segments, Datagrams, and Frames

TCP data is a stream of bytes. The application data goes into the TCP send buffer; in the case of Telnet, the application data could be a sequence of keystrokes. TCP is unaware of keystrokes; for TCP, the send buffer contains a sequence of bytes.

For the duration of the TCP connection, the TCP stack takes data from the send buffer and slices the stream of bytes into chunks (called segments) to send on the network.

Figure 2-4 can help you understand how application data is turned into frames to transmit on the network. At the top of the figure, you can see the application generating records of different sizes.

Figure 2-4 *TCP Processing of Application Data*

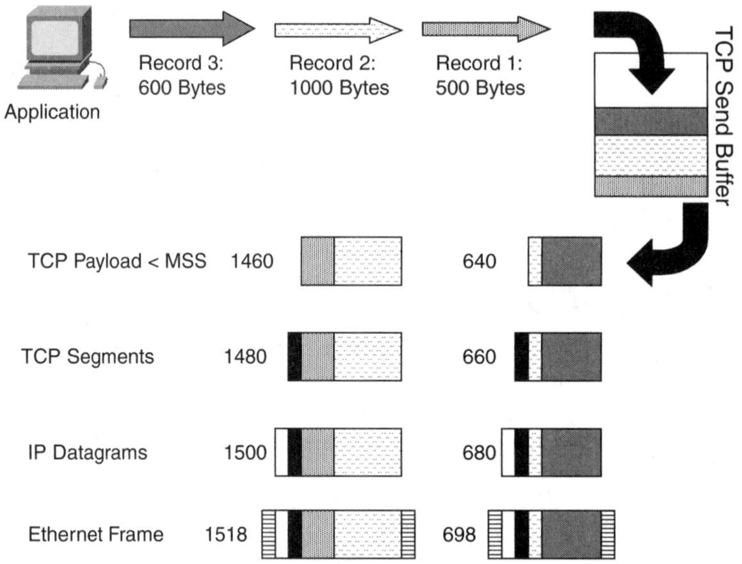

These records end in the TCP send buffer. From the TCP point of view, all these records together are a stream of bytes to be sent on the network. TCP takes this data out of the send buffer to form segments. A TCP header with a TCP payload is called a segment.

When forming segments, TCP tries to fill the maximum segment size (MSS) which, on an Ethernet LAN, is typically 1460 bytes. The MSS specifies how big the payload of a TCP segment can be for it to be compatible with the maximum transmission unit (MTU) of the physical network between the sender and the receiver.

In Figure 2-4, you can see that the application writes three records in the TCP send buffer. TCP forms the first segment with two records—the first record and a portion of the second. The second segment is formed by the remaining portion of the second record and by the third record.

The size of the first segment is 1480, which equals the MSS (1460 bytes) plus the TCP header (20 bytes). This segment plus the IP header form a datagram. As a result, its size grows to 1500 bytes because the IP header is 20 bytes.

The IP datagram plus the Ethernet header and the trailer become an Ethernet frame; its size is 1518 bytes (the MTU size).

TCP Interactive Traffic Profile

The Telnet application mainly transmits keystrokes from a client computer to the server and sends back to the client the characters to be displayed.

The traces in this section were captured using tcpdump. Notice that, with the exception of the connection-establishment segments, tcpdump shows the sequence number as the offset from the initial values instead of their absolute value. Also notice that:

The notation is *first:last(nbytes)*, which means "sequence numbers first up to but not including last," which is *nbytes* bytes of user data.

Connection Setup

Example 2-2 shows the trace of the beginning of a Telnet session. The client 10.21.4.5 opens a TCP connection to port 23 on 10.20.5.14 from a random source port (1159). The TCP handshake is the sequence of SYN (see the S in the trace) followed by a SYN ACK (the second frame in the example) and by the ACK.

Each segment carries a sequence number that tells the receiver how to compose the byte stream with all the received segments. For example, the first byte of the TCP payload in the last segment is 13 bytes away from the first byte of the data stream (13:28). The sequence number between two consecutive segments is increased by the amount of data—compare Frame 4 with the last frame. Frame 4 carried a TCP segment with a payload of 12 bytes, and it was the first segment carrying data; as a result, the next segment's sequence number is the sequence number in Frame 4 augmented by 12.

In Example 2-2, you do not see the sequence number, but you see the "offset" from the initial value; for example, in the last frame, the sequence number really is (730524282 + 13).

Example 2-2 *TCP Connection Setup and First Few Frames of a Telnet Session*

```
1  09.1064 10.21.4.5.1159 > 10.20.5.14.telnet: S 4196118748:4196118748(0)
     win 32120 <mss 1460
2  09.1068 10.20.5.14.telnet > 10.21.4.5.1159: S 730524282:730524282(0)
     ack 4196118749 win 32120 <mss 1460
3  09.1068 10.21.4.5.1159 > 10.20.5.14.telnet: . ack 1 win 32120
4  09.1143 10.20.5.14.telnet > 10.21.4.5.1159: P 1:13(12) ack 1 win 32120
5  09.1144 10.21.4.5.1159 > 10.20.5.14.telnet: . ack 13 win 32120
6  09.1312 10.21.4.5.1159 > 10.20.5.14.telnet: P 1:25(24) ack 13 win 32120
7  09.1315 10.20.5.14.telnet > 10.21.4.5.1159: . ack 25 win 32120
8  09.1315 10.21.4.5.1159 > 10.20.5.14.telnet: P 25:28(3) ack 13 win 32120
9  09.1315 10.20.5.14.telnet > 10.21.4.5.1159: P 13:28(15) ack 25 win 32120
```

The sequence number's initial value can be seen in the SYN, SYN ACK sequence. Chapter 7 provides insight on how these initial numbers are generated.

It is assumed that the reader is already familiar with the meaning of the ACK flag. In Frame 5 for example, 10.21.4.5 "ack 13" acknowledges having received the 12th byte from 10.20.5.14 and communicates that it expects to receive the 13th byte.

Among the TCP fields shown in Example 2-2, notice the presence of the MSS field. In the first frame, the client 10.21.4.5 reports to the server that the maximum TCP payload that it can receive is 1460 bytes. As a result, the server makes sure to packetize the byte stream in chunks no bigger than 1460 bytes. The second frame has the same meaning but for the opposite direction—the server notifies the client about its MSS.

Maximum Segment Size

The maximum transmission unit (MTU) is the maximum frame payload size available along the path between the client and the server. The maximum segment size (MSS) in TCP is 1460 bytes, which is equivalent to an MTU of 1500 bytes, which, in turn, is equivalent to the maximum Ethernet frame size of 1518 bytes.

According to RFC 879, a "host should not send datagrams larger than 576 octets unless they have specific knowledge that the destination host is prepared to accept larger datagrams." A maximum datagram size of 576 bytes translates to a TCP segment size of 536 bytes. The MSS is the maximum amount of data that TCP should send per segment to avoid fragmentation of the IP packets. The MSS is communicated by the client to the server, and vice versa, at the connection setup. Each entity calculates its MSS based on the network it connects to. For example, a host connected to an Ethernet network should communicate an MSS of 1460. Client machines typically set the MSS to 536 bytes when connected via modems.

TCP Retransmission

As previously stated, a TCP packet with the ACK bit set notifies the sender which byte the receiver is expecting. In Example 2-2, the segment sent by the client at 15.187 sec tells the server that the client is expecting the 13th byte.

The ACK also communicates to the server that all the bytes previously sent have been received. If the server does not receive an acknowledgment for the segments sent previously, it would have to retransmit them. How long does the server wait before retransmitting?

Example 2-3 shows an established Telnet session between 10.21.4.5 and 10.20.5.14, a session in which the server sends a segment and no ACK comes back from the client. After 200 ms (calculated from the timestamps, 20.964 sec to 30.764 sec) the server performs a retransmission, and still no ACK comes back.

The server then retransmits again, this time after 400 ms. No ACK comes back, and the server retransmits after 800 ms. The length of the timeout for these retransmissions depends on the operating system settings. Typically, you can configure this parameter either for the total timeout (which could be 2 minutes, for example) or for the number of retries performed (for example, 15 times).

Example 2-3 *TCP Retransmission*

```
20.764487 eth0 > 10.20.5.14.telnet > 10.21.4.5.1159: P 94:95(1)
20.964405 eth0 > 10.20.5.14.telnet > 10.21.4.5.1159: P 94:95(1)
21.364403 eth0 > 10.20.5.14.telnet > 10.21.4.5.1159: P 94:95(1)
22.164406 eth0 > 10.20.5.14.telnet > 10.21.4.5.1159: P 94:95(1)
[...]
```

Delayed ACK

Example 2-4 shows the continuation of the Telnet session of Example 2-2. In Example 2-4, the user on the client types three characters. In the first frame, the client sends the keystroke to the server. Notice the size of the payload—1 byte. The server sends back 1 byte of data and also ACKs the reception of the 94th byte.

The interesting portion of the trace is the fact that the client does not ACK the server's segment immediately. At 37.051 sec, the client sends an ACK with 0 bytes to ACK the segment received at 37.031 sec, which is 20 ms later. Why is the ACK from the client delayed by 20 ms?

The reason for this is that TCP delays sending the ACK when the send buffer is empty because it tries to piggyback the ACK on a data packet. In this example, the TCP send buffer on 10.21.5.4 is empty at 37.03 sec; as a result, TCP waits and eventually sends a TCP segment with 0 bytes of data, just to acknowledge the server's segment.

Example 2-4 *TCP Delayed ACKs in a Telnet Session*

```
1  37.031228 10.21.4.5.1159 > 10.20.5.14.telnet: P 94:95(1) ack 215 win 32120
2  37.031658 10.20.5.14.telnet > 10.21.4.5.1159: P 215:216(1) ack 95 win 32120
3  37.051145 10.21.4.5.1159 > 10.20.5.14.telnet: . ack 216 win 32120

4  42.391209 10.21.4.5.1159 > 10.20.5.14.telnet: P 95:96(1) ack 216 win 32120
5  42.391623 10.20.5.14.telnet > 10.21.4.5.1159: P 216:217(1) ack 96 win 32120
6  42.411145 10.21.4.5.1159 > 10.20.5.14.telnet: . ack 217 win 32120
```

To avoid causing retransmissions on the sender host, the timeout for the ACK delay should not be too long. Considering the behavior of the host machine in Example 2-3, in this setup, the delayed ACK timer must be less than 200 ms.

Nagle Algorithm

If you do cut and paste a string to the client's Telnet session, you likely will observe the sequence of packets that you see in Example 2-5. In this example, the send buffer on the client receives from the application a sequence of 81 noncontiguous bytes. The client application sends those bytes in records of 16 bytes, 40 bytes, 22 bytes, and so forth.

TCP does not send these segments one after the other; instead, it sends one segment, waits for the ACK, sends another segment, waits again for the ACK, and so forth.

This is because the Nagle algorithm mandates that a host cannot have more than one unacknowledged small segment on the network. A small segment is defined as a segment that is smaller than the maximum segment size.

In Example 2-5, you see that the client sends 16 bytes at 12.021 seconds, waits for an ACK, then sends 40 bytes at 12.03 seconds, waits for an ACK, and so forth.

Example 2-5 *Nagle Algorithm*

```
12.021223 10.21.4.5.1159 > 10.20.5.14.telnet: P 97:113(16) ack 218 win 32120
12.021686 10.20.5.14.telnet > 10.21.4.5.1159: P 218:219(1) ack 113 win 32120
12.031181 10.21.4.5.1159 > 10.20.5.14.telnet: P 113:153(40) ack 219 win 32120
12.031458 10.20.5.14.telnet > 10.21.4.5.1159: P 219:234(15) ack 153 win 32120
12.041176 10.21.4.5.1159 > 10.20.5.14.telnet: P 153:175(22) ack 234 win 32120
12.041447 10.20.5.14.telnet > 10.21.4.5.1159: P 234:274(40) ack 175 win 32120
12.061143 10.21.4.5.1159 > 10.20.5.14.telnet: . ack 274 win 32120
12.061405 10.20.5.14.telnet > 10.21.4.5.1159: P 274:298(24) ack 175 win 32120
```

Connection Closure

Example 2-6 shows how Telnet closes the connection between the client and the server:

1. The client sends a FIN at 18.7512 sec.
2. The server responds with an ACK at 18.7515 sec.
3. The server then sends a FIN at 18.7519 sec.
4. The client ACKs at 18.7519 sec.

Example 2-6 *TCP Connection Closure*

```
18.751245 10.21.4.5.1159 > 10.20.5.14.telnet: F 178:178(0) ack 301 win 32120
18.751526 10.20.5.14.telnet > 10.21.4.5.1159: . ack 179 win 32120
18.751936 10.20.5.14.telnet > 10.21.4.5.1159: F 301:301(0) ack 179 win 32120
18.751959 10.21.4.5.1159 > 10.20.5.14.telnet: . ack 302 win 32120
```

TCP Bulk Transfer Traffic Profile

Example 2-7 shows the use of the Hypertext Transfer Protocol (HTTP) to download a 100-MB object from a web page.

Among the characteristics that you should observe in traces of TCP bulk transfers are the use of the TCP receive window and the fact that most segments carry a payload of MSS (1460) bytes.

Full-size TCP segments are used because the application keeps the TCP send buffer full, just as it does on the server in Example 2-7.

The client, in turn, has a TCP receive buffer filling in while the client application empties it. The client uses the TCP receive window for flow-control purposes by notifying the server of the size of the receive buffer. You can see this in Example 2-7 by looking at Frame 7.

Example 2-7 *HTTP Bulk Transfer and Segment Size*

```
1  30.316225 < 10.21.4.5.1122 > 10.20.5.14.www: S 2777311705:2777311705(0) win 32120
   <mss 1460>
2  30.316241 > 10.20.5.14.www > 10.21.4.5.1122: S 3157467248:3157467248(0) ack
  2777311706 win 32120mss 146060>
3  30.316383 < 10.21.4.5.1122 > 10.20.5.14.www: P 1:317(316) ack 1 win 32120
4  30.316415 > 10.20.5.14.www > 10.21.4.5.1122: . 1:1(0) ack 317 win 31804
5  30.317416 > 10.20.5.14.www > 10.21.4.5.1122: P 1:1461(1460) ack 317 win 32120
6  30.317434 > 10.20.5.14.www > 10.21.4.5.1122: P 1461:2921(1460) ack 317 win 32120
7  30.318150 < 10.21.4.5.1122 > 10.20.5.14.www: . 317:317(0) ack 1461 win 30660
[...]
```

TCP Windows

Receive buffers on host machines influence the TCP receive window advertised by the receiver to the sender.

In TCP, two windows decide how many segments the sender can transmit without receiving an ACK from the receiver:

- **Receive window**—This is the amount of space available in the receiver TCP buffer.
- **Congestion window**—The sender uses this window to avoid causing congestion in the network.

The size of the congestion window is determined by the slow start algorithm and the congestion-avoidance algorithm. The sender needs to ensure that it does not cause congestion in the network and does not overwhelm the receiver. As a result, the sender sends a number of segments whose total size in bytes is less than the minimum of each window.

The windowing mechanism limits the number of segments that the sender can send when the transmit buffer is continuously filled. This is typically the case for bulk transfers such as FTP or even HTTP.

In Example 2-8, the client sends ACKs with no data, and the TCP receive window progressively reduces as follows:

- 32,120 bytes at 30.3163 sec
- 30,660 bytes at 30.3181 sec
- 29,200 at 30.3188 sec

This means that the application on the client side is slow at retrieving data from the TCP receive buffer; as a result, the space available in the buffer reduces.

The receive window on the server side does not really change because the client is not sending any data to the server.

Example 2-8 *Client Receive Window*

```
30.316225 < 10.21.4.5.1122 > 10.20.5.14.www: S 2777311705:2777311705(0)
  win 32120 <mss 1460>
30.316241 > 10.20.5.14.www > 10.21.4.5.1122: S 3157467248:3157467248(0)
  ack 2777311706 win 32120 <mss 1460>
30.316383 < 10.21.4.5.1122 > 10.20.5.14.www: P 1:317(316) ack 1 win 32120
30.316415 > 10.20.5.14.www > 10.21.4.5.1122: . 1:1(0) ack 317 win 31804
30.317416 > 10.20.5.14.www > 10.21.4.5.1122: P 1:1461(1460) ack 317 win 32120
30.317434 > 10.20.5.14.www > 10.21.4.5.1122: P 1461:2921(1460) ack 317 win 32120
30.318150 < 10.21.4.5.1122 > 10.20.5.14.www: . 317:317(0) ack 1461 win 30660
30.318217 > 10.20.5.14.www > 10.21.4.5.1122: P 2921:4381(1460) ack 317 win 32120
30.318227 > 10.20.5.14.www > 10.21.4.5.1122: P 4381:5841(1460) ack 317 win 32120
30.318846 < 10.21.4.5.1122 > 10.20.5.14.www: . 317:317(0) ack 4381 win 29200
30.318880 > 10.20.5.14.www > 10.21.4.5.1122: P 5841:7301(1460) ack 317 win 32120
30.318888 > 10.20.5.14.www > 10.21.4.5.1122: P 7301:8761(1460) ack 317 win 32120
30.318898 > 10.20.5.14.www > 10.21.4.5.1122: P 8761:10221(1460) ack 317 win 32120
```

ACK Scheme

RFC 1122, "Requirements for Internet Hosts," calls for one ACK every two full-size segments. The OS used on the client in Example 2-9 ACKs follows the standard:

- At 30.3181 sec, the client ACKs the reception of data up to byte 1460 (which is the frame received at 30.3174 sec).
- The next ACK at 30.3188 sec ACKs the reception of bytes up to 4380 (which is the frame received at 30.3182 sec).

Example 2-9 *ACKing Every Other Segment*

```
30.316225 < 10.21.4.5.1122 > 10.20.5.14.www: S 2777311705:2777311705(0)
  win 32120 <mss 1460>
30.316241 > 10.20.5.14.www > 10.21.4.5.1122: S 3157467248:3157467248(0)
  ack 2777311706 win 32120 <mss 1460>
30.316383 < 10.21.4.5.1122 > 10.20.5.14.www: P 1:317(316) ack 1 win 32120
30.316415 > 10.20.5.14.www > 10.21.4.5.1122: . 1:1(0) ack 317 win 31804
30.317416 > 10.20.5.14.www > 10.21.4.5.1122: P 1:1461(1460) ack 317 win 32120
30.317434 > 10.20.5.14.www > 10.21.4.5.1122: P 1461:2921(1460) ack 317 win 32120
30.318150 < 10.21.4.5.1122 > 10.20.5.14.www: . 317:317(0) ack 1461 win 30660
30.318217 > 10.20.5.14.www > 10.21.4.5.1122: P 2921:4381(1460) ack 317 win 32120
30.318227 > 10.20.5.14.www > 10.21.4.5.1122: P 4381:5841(1460) ack 317 win 32120
30.318846 < 10.21.4.5.1122 > 10.20.5.14.www: . 317:317(0) ack 4381 win 29200
30.318880 > 10.20.5.14.www > 10.21.4.5.1122: P 5841:7301(1460) ack 317 win 32120
30.318888 > 10.20.5.14.www > 10.21.4.5.1122: P 7301:8761(1460) ack 317 win 32120

30.318898 > 10.20.5.14.www > 10.21.4.5.1122: P 8761:10221(1460) ack 317 win 32120
```

Other rules that govern how the client or the server ACK include the need for immediate ACKs at the reception of an out-of-order packet and the need to communicate an update of the receive window.

For more information about these mechanisms, see Chapter 7.

High-Speed Networks and the Window Scale Option

By analyzing the behavior of TCP, you understand that the sender uses the minimum of two windows (receive or offered window and congestion window) to determine the size of a single burst. After sending the burst, the host waits for ACKs before sending new segments. The round-trip time measures how long a host waits to receive ACKs from the receiver. A typical round-trip time for a campus network is 10 ms; across a WAN, this number can increase to 100 ms.

Assuming that there is no congestion on the network, the maximum theoretical burst that a host can send is determined by the offered window of the receiver. The maximum offered window that TCP can advertise is 64 KB.

Assuming that a server uses a Gigabit Ethernet NIC, a possible scenario that you could observe is a server sending the full buffer of 64 KB, then waiting for 10 ms for the first ACK to come back, and then bursting again. The throughput of such a transfer would be equal to 64 KB * 8 (bits/byte) / RTT = 51 Mbps, which is far below the gigabit rate. For the servers to achieve a wire-rate gigabit transfer, they would need to be on the same local segment with a RTT of less then 1 ms.

The conclusion is that, when dealing with high-speed networks such as Gigabit Ethernet, the maximum window size allowed by TCP (64 KB) is not enough to achieve wire-rate gigabit between two hosts. This phenomenon is more apparent on a WAN than it is on a LAN segment because the longer distances that signals have to travel on the WAN cause longer delays.

The parameter used to measure the window size that allows maximizing the throughput is called Bandwidth Delay Product (BDP). The BDP equals the smaller bandwidth in the path between two hosts, multiplied by the round-trip time. In the case of a gigabit campus network with 10 ms of RTT between two servers and the servers being gigabit attached, the BDP equals this:

$$(1 \text{ Gbps} * 10 \text{ ms})/8 = 1.25 \text{ MB}$$

Considering that TCP allows hosts to advertise a maximum of 64 KB, to achieve a gigabit wire rate, you need to configure the servers to advertise larger windows. This requires the use of the Window Scale option. Chapter 7 explains how the Window Scale option works.

UDP and Server Applications

UDP is a connectionless protocol and does not have any error-correction or flow-control capabilities. When using UDP, these functions can be provided by the application.

UDP is often preferred over TCP for delay-sensitive applications such as video or audio streaming because TCP algorithms and timeouts could introduce delays in case of packet loss or congestion. By using UDP, applications that are not sensitive to the drop of packets can continue without having to wait for retransmissions. Chapter 11, "Streaming Protocols Overview," provides more details about streaming applications.

UDP applications listen to Layer 4 ports that you can see by using **netstat –a** on UNIX OSs, as in Example 2-10. This example shows the output for a Trivial File Transfer Protocol (TFTP) server (UDP port 69).

Example 2-10 *Layer 4 Ports for UDP-Based Applications on a Server*

```
admin@server-4 ids]# netstat -a
Active Internet connections (servers and established)
Proto Recv-Q Send-Q Local Address           Foreign Address         State
udp        0      0 *:tftp                  *:*
```

Example 2-11 shows the trace for a TFTP transfer between 10.21.4.5 (the client) and 10.20.5.14 (the server). The server sends data messages to the client, and the client application acknowledges each packet sent by the server.

Example 2-11 *TFTP Transfer*

```
13:05:30.433033 eth0 < 10.21.4.5.1026 > 10.20.5.14.tftp: 17 RRQ "IDS2.img"
13:05:30.481342 eth0 > 10.20.5.14.1274 > 10.21.4.5.1026: udp 516
13:05:30.481892 eth0 < 10.21.4.5.1026 > 10.20.5.14.1274: udp 4
13:05:30.481933 eth0 > 10.20.5.14.1274 > 10.21.4.5.1026: udp 516
13:05:30.482316 eth0 < 10.21.4.5.1026 > 10.20.5.14.1274: udp 4
13:05:30.482335 eth0 > 10.20.5.14.1274 > 10.21.4.5.1026: udp 516
13:05:30.482711 eth0 < 10.21.4.5.1026 > 10.20.5.14.1274: udp 4
13:05:30.482729 eth0 > 10.20.5.14.1274 > 10.21.4.5.1026: udp 516
```

All the packets from the server to the client have the same size—516 bytes composed of 512 bytes of data, 2 bytes of block number, and 2 bytes of opcode. UDP applications normally limit the size of datagrams to 512 bytes, with the notable exception of the Network File System, which creates datagrams as big as 8192 bytes. Using datagrams of 512 bytes avoids the need for fragmentation because this number is smaller than typical MTUs.

Server Availability

High availability is one of the key design considerations of a Data Center. Chapter 20 describes how to design a highly available infrastructure; Chapter 17, "Server Health Management," describes how a load-balancing device can monitor the availability of applications and servers.

This section provides the necessary background on the operating systems aspects of an application and the implications on the availability of the application. No matter how robust the application is, failures are always possible. This section explains how the TCP stack of the client behaves in the presence of a server failure.

The section, "Increasing Server Availability with Load Balancing," introduces the use of hardware load-balancing devices to work around server failures.

Processes and Threads

Server applications are basically processes listening on certain Layer 4 ports. Examples of applications/servers are web servers, common gateway interface (CGI) applications, Active Server Pages (ASP) servers, servlet engines, and so on.

Server implementations differ depending on how incoming connections are handled. A process can be spawned on a per-connection basis by another process listening on multiple ports (such as inetd in UNIX), or it can be a *standalone* server forking when new connections arrive.

Additionally, servers can be categorized as *forking* servers if they rely on creating different processes to serve new connections, or *threaded* servers if they rely on threads instead. Example 2-12 shows the processes in a Linux system running an HTTP forking server. When launching the web server, you have the root process and one child (process 31785).

Example 2-12 *Processes on a Standalone HTTP Server Before Receiving Clients' Requests*

```
[admin@localhost conf]# ps -ef | grep httpd
root         31784     1  0 21:44 ?        00:00:00 /usr/sbin/httpd
httpserver   31785 31784  0 21:44 ?        00:00:00 /usr/sbin/httpd
```

In Example 2-12, you see a standalone implementation. The main process is like a supervisor to the activities of the other server processes and typically does not perform I/O operations.

NOTE Example 2-12 does not reflect the default settings of the HTTP server. Parameters have been changed to show the creation of new processes for new incoming connections. A regular web server configuration would create many more processes.

When one client sends a connection request, a new process is created, as you can see in Example 2-13. If the same client continues to open connections without closing them, new child processes are created to handle the new connections.

Example 2-13 *HTTP Server Spawns a New Process to Serve a Client's Request*

```
[admin@localhost conf]# ps -ef | grep httpd
root      31784     1  0 21:44 ?        00:00:00 /usr/sbin/httpd -D HAVE_PERL
httpserver   31785 31784  0 21:44 ?        00:00:00 /usr/sbin/httpd -D HAVE_PERL
httpserver   31833 31784  0 21:46 ?        00:00:00 /usr/sbin/httpd -D HAVE_PERL
```

Threads are similar to processes, in that they allow concurrent operation, but they execute inside the same process and have less overhead than processes. Processes have separate memory space and file descriptors; threads are separate execution instances that share the same memory space. At a very high level, you can think of threads as separate program counters inside the same process.

If you executed the same tests as those in Examples 2-12 and 2-13 but used a threaded server, you would see a single process handling multiple connections.

FastCGI is an example of a multiprocess application server. Servlet engines (which are basically Java Virtual Machines) are examples of threaded servers.

The main differences between forking servers and threaded servers are as follows:

- **Performance**—Context switching between threads is much lighter than between processes, so the impact of an increasing number of connections on the CPU utilization is less with threaded servers than with forking servers. Because of this, threaded servers are more efficient than forking servers.
- **Robustness**—When you run an application inside a single process, the failure of one thread can affect the entire process and the other connections with it. A forking server is more robust because a main process does not deal with I/O operations. Additionally, this process periodically kills the child processes, which prevents memory leaks from crashing the server. If one child fails, other connections still succeed. As a result, forking servers are more robust than threaded servers.
- **Shared state information**—When dealing with a client that sends requests to the same application over a period of time, you typically want to save the session (state) information about this client. Processes do not share memory, which means that dispatching client's connections to different processes forces the application developer to use temporary files or databases to save state information. Threads running in a single process share the memory space, which makes it possible to save the state information across multiple connections of the same application.

Today's servers can be forking, threaded, and hybrid. Hybrid servers keep a number of active processes for the same application and allow each process to serve a number of connections by using the threaded approach. You can make implementations of threaded servers more robust by launching several instances of them.

Multiprocess servers provide a solution to the need of sharing state information by writing this information on temporary files shared across servers or by using mechanisms such as session affinity.

FastCGI is an example of a multiprocess application server with session affinity. CGI initially had limitations related to the creation of a separate process for each connection request with performance and session state limitations. FastCGI solves the problem by providing the option of running as a multithreaded server or implementing session affinity. (For more information about CGI, see Chapter 3.)

A robust application can be built by using multiprocess server and building multitier server farms. As an example, the business logic of the application can execute as a script in a different process than the web server. If the script has an infinite loop, the web server is unaffected. For more information about multitier architectures, see Chapter 3.

TCP and UDP Connections to a Failed Server

No matter how robust the design of the application is, server failures are still possible for the following reasons:

- Power failure
- Hard disk failures
- NIC failures
- Cable failures
- Software bugs
- Memory leaks
- Disk data corruption
- Configuration errors

Depending on the server failure, the client detects the failure for an established connection as follows:

- **Server process fails**—The server sends a TCP FIN to the client, or the client sends a TCP segment and receives a TCP RST. In case of UDP, the server sends an ICMP port unreachable message.
- **Server machine fails or loses network connectivity**—The TCP connection times out on the client, unless the application has other mechanisms to detect the failure and close the connection.

When a client sends a request to an application for a new connection, there are two possible results, depending on which failure affects the server:

- **Server process failed**—The client sends a TCP SYN, and the server sends a TCP FIN. In case of UDP, the server sends an ICMP port unreachable message.
- **Server machine failed or lost network connectivity**—The client sends TCP SYNs for a number of times (these SYN packets are called TCP SYN retransmissions), depending on the operating system implementation of the TCP stack.

TCP Timeout

When a server is disconnected from the network or powered down, no data flows back to the client, and the connection can stay idle for hours. The TCP stack can keep a connection idle for a configurable amount of time. Because the default is typically two or three hours, however, it is up to the application to age out connections.

As an example, in the case of FTP on Linux, if you use **proftpd** in the configuration file proftpd.conf, you can set the parameter **TimeoutIdle** *TimeoutIdle* seconds (in which the default is 600 seconds) to age out connections that have been idle for the configured timeout.

If the application keeps the TCP connection idle for more than 2 hours, the TCP stack sends a *TCP keepalive* to verify that the peer entity (client or server) is still alive. The sender not receiving a response sends a number of keepalives (a typical number is 9) at an interval of approximately every 1 minute and eventually closes the TCP connection.

Although the recommendation is to not change the TCP keepalive defaults, on most OSs, you can change the value of the TCP keepalive. On UNIX-based OSs, this variable can take the name of tcp_keepalive_interval, tcp_keepidle, and tcp_keepalive_time. In Windows, this variable is called KeepAliveTime. The socket interface also allows the application to decide whether TCP should implement the keepalive mechanism.

SYN Retransmission

When a client tries to open a connection to a failed server, the TCP stack reacts by retransmitting the SYN for a number of times, depending on the OS. Windows 2000 and XP perform two retransmissions; other OSs perform more. The timeout depends on the number of retransmissions and the interval between them.

The following list shows the behavior of three OSs:

- **Windows**—Uses TcpMaxConnectRetransmissions, which is 3 SYNs in Windows NT and 2 SYNs in Windows 2000. This translates into a timeout of 22 seconds in Windows 2000 (with the first retransmission happening in 3 sec) and 45 seconds in Windows NT.
- **Solaris**—Uses tcp_ip_abort_cinterval, which is the timeout when TCP performs an active open and, by default, is four minutes. The total number of retransmissions depends on other parameters, such as the retransmission interval.
- **Linux**—Uses tcp_syn_retries with a default of 10.

TIP Understanding the SYN retransmission mechanism is key to using the in-band health-monitoring feature of load-balancing devices. For more details, see Chapter 17.

Status of HTTP Applications

The previous section dealt with the impact of a failed server on TCP and UDP traffic. Another scenario could be an application whose process is alive and capable of accepting new connections, yet is not functioning properly. This section analyzes the behavior of a web server and how the server informs the client about possible errors.

From a black box point of view, a web server is a device that receives HTTP requests from a client and returns three types of answers:

- **Static web page or web page information**—A static web page is the simplest type of output from a web server. Such a page consists of HTML code that seldom changes, together with GIFs and similar objects.
- **Dynamic web page**—A page is dynamically generated by input from the client (such as a search page), a change in objects that are displayed (such as a playlist on an Internet radio), and information randomly generated (such as stock quotes of commercial banners).
- **Error message or status code**—All HTTP responses include a status code. The typical status message when everything is fine is "200 Ok." If some failure occurs, a web server returns error messages (for example, "404 Not found").

Status codes in the 400 range refer to client-side issues; the 500 range is for status code on server-side issues. Chapter 8, "HTTP and Related Concepts," describes the status codes in more detail.

Examples of the 400 status codes are as follows:

- **Bad request 400**—A syntax error exists in the URL.
- **Unauthorized 401**—The user identified by the user-agent field is not authorized to get the content requested.
- **Forbidden 403**—The client does not have privileges for the page.
- **Not found 404**—The requested URL is not available. The URL either is no longer active or is temporarily disabled.

Examples of the 500 error code are as follows:

- **Internal error 500**—The server has an internal software error that prevents it from sending the HTML document to you.
- **Service unavailable 503**—The server is processing too many requests.
- **Gateway timeout 504**—The connection is timing out.
- **HTTP version not supported 505**—The client is requesting a version that the server does not support.

As emerges from this description, a server can be alive, can accept TCP connections, and can report error codes to the client. In the case of HTTP, the 500 error codes relate mainly to server-side issues. For more information about HTTP error codes, see Chapter 8.

Configuring a Web Server

This section describes the configuration of a web server to illustrate the concepts discussed thus far that relate to both OS and TCP aspects of applications. An HTTP server is used for the example because it is typically the front end of most server farms.

This section covers the configuration of an Apache web server (httpd.conf file).

Configuring TCP and HTTP Parameters

Each of the multiple processes spawned by Apache listens for incoming connections on a number of ports and IP addresses. The Listen directive lets you specify these parameters.

All processes listen to the same IP addresses and ports. If you want the HTTP server to listen on multiple IP addresses, you must first configure the TCP stack to accept traffic destined to multiple IP addresses. This technique is called *aliasing*. On a Linux machine, it can be achieved as in Example 2-14.

Example 2-14 *Configuring IP Address Aliasing*

```
ifconfig eth0:1 10.10.10.11 netmask 255.255.255.0
ifconfig eth0:2 10.10.10.12 netmask 255.255.255.0
```

The Listen directive in Apache (see Example 2-15) tells the server which IP addresses and port to use.

Example 2-15 *Configuring IP Addresses and Ports on the HTTP Server*

```
Listen 10.10.10.11:80
Listen 10.10.10.11:8080
```

This server listens to TCP connections on ports 80 and 8080 for the IP address 10.10.10.11.

You can also configure the following parameters, mainly for performance reasons:

- **Maximum number of concurrent connections**—The MaxClient directive controls the maximum number of connections the server accepts.
- **HTTP 1.1 persistence**—Usually, you control the use of HTTP1.1 persistent connections by using Keepalive On/Off. You control how long Apache waits for a subsequent HTTP persistent request with the command **KeepaliveTimeout**. You can also limit the number of requests sent on the same persistent connection with **MaxKeepaliveRequests**.

For more information about HTTP 1.1, see Chapter 8.

Server Processes

Servers can be activated and deactivated. Activating a server means creating a collection of processes that are waiting for incoming connections.

You have control over how many unused (spare) servers (meaning processes) you can have at any given time by using the commands **MinSpareServers** and **MaxSpareServers**.

You can also define how many servers start when Apache is launched with the command **StartServers**.

In theory, you could run multiple instances of servers (each instance composed of several processes) to separate the document space.

Directories

A web server has to serve pages, which are stored on the disk according to some directory structure. The root for this directory structure is defined by the DocumentRoot directive. The directive ScriptAlias tells where the scripts (executables) are stored.

For the Secure Socket Layer (SSL), a web server can listen to port 443. SSL requests are assigned to a different directory than the clear-text content. Notice that no separate process is spawned for the SSL. All the active processes for the web server are ready to take connections for port 443, as with any other port.

As pointed out in the previous section, to avoid sharing the same document space between HTTP and HTTPS, it is possible to start multiple servers independently of each other, in which case you would start a separate server for SSL.

Virtual Hosting

As a general rule, there is no need to launch multiple HTTP servers on the same machine because of a feature called *virtual hosting.*

Virtual hosting is a popular technique used on HTTP servers to host multiple domains on a single-server machine. For example, one single server could be hosting www1.example.com and www2.example.com.

Each domain uses the following:

- Different directory trees
- Different log files

Virtual hosting can be achieved in four different ways:

- By running several instances of the same server (which is not virtual hosting, by definition)
- By using multiple IP addresses on the same server machine
- By using multiple Layer 4 ports on the same server machine
- By using the HTTP Host tag header

This section explains how to configure virtual hosting on an Apache web server. If you need more information, refer to http://httpd.apache.org/docs/vhosts/.

Running Multiple Servers on the Same Machine

This technique is an alternative to virtual hosting and involves launching a separate HTTP server on a single machine for each hosted web site. Each server, in turn, is made of several processes.

Each server can process specific connections based either on the IP address or on the Layer 4 port. For example, you could have two HTTP servers on the same machine, listening to the IP addresses 192.168.1.1 and 192.168.1.2, respectively. www1.example.com maps to the IP address 192.168.1.1, and www2.example.com maps to the IP address 192.168.1.2.

The configurations for the two HTTP servers would contain the lines in Example 2-16 for the server hosting www1.example.com and the lines in Example 2-17 for the server hosting www2.example.com.

Example 2-16 *Configuration of the HTTP Server for www1.example.com*

```
BindAddress 192.168.1.1
Port 80
```

Example 2-17 *Configuration of the HTTP Server for www2.example.com*

```
BindAddress 192.168.1.2
Port 80
```

Of course, having the server listen to multiple IP addresses requires configuring multiple IP addresses on the same NIC. Notice the use of the BindAddress directive (as opposed to the Listen directive), which forces the server to listen to one single IP address, and the Port directive, which forces the server to listen to a single Layer 4 port.

Using Multiple IP Addresses on the Same Machine

With this approach, also called IP-based virtual web hosting, a single instance of a web server can listen on multiple IP addresses for incoming TCP connections, as long as these IP addresses are configured in both the server and the interface configuration. The server is capable of multiplexing incoming requests for different IP addresses to different web pages.

When using a single server instance, you configure multiple Listen statements instead of Bind. The children processes of the main HTTP daemon all listen on multiple sockets; when a new connection arrives, only one child gets the connection.

An example of a configuration file for an Apache web server hosting www1.example.com and www2.example.com is shown in Example 2-18.

Example 2-18 *IP-Based Virtual Hosting Configuration*

```
Listen 192.168.1.1:80
Listen 192.168.1.2:80
[...]
<VirtualHost 192.168.1.1>
Servername www1.example.com
Documentroot /home/httpd/html/foo1
</VirtualHost>
<VirtualHost 192.168.1.2>
Servername www2.example.com
Documentroot /home/httpd/html/foo2
</VirtualHost>
```

Using Multiple Layer 4 Ports on the Same Machine

With this method, also called port-based virtual hosting, a single IP is required for both www1.example.com and www2.example.com. Each website domain name maps to the same IP address. For example, www1.example.com maps to 192.168.1.1, and www2.example.com maps 192.168.1.1 as well.

The Layer 4 ports that the server is listening to are different; for example, www1.example.com receives traffic on port 8081, and www2.example.com receives traffic on port 8082. A single instance of a web server can listen on multiple Layer 4 ports incoming to TCP connections to the same IP address.

In the case of Apache, you use multiple Listen statements to force the server to listen on multiple ports. The children processes of the main HTTP daemon all listen on multiple sockets; when a new connection arrives, only one child gets the connection.

Example 2-19 shows an example configuration file for an Apache web server hosting www1.example.com and www2.example.com.

Example 2-19 *Port-Based Virtual Hosting Configuration*

```
Listen 192.168.1.1:8081
Listen 192.168.1.1:8082
[...]
<VirtualHost 192.168.1.1:8081>
Servername www1.example.com
Documentroot /home/httpd/html/foo1
</VirtualHost>
<VirtualHost 192.168.1.1:8082>
Servername www2.example.com
Documentroot /home/httpd/html/foo2
</VirtualHost>
```

Using the HTTP Host Tag Header

With this method, also called name-based virtual hosting, a server decides which HTML page to deliver by looking at the Host tag of the HTTP request.

Starting with HTTP/1.1, all the HTTP requests must carry the domain name in the Host header. Example 2-20 shows the content of an HTTP GET request for www1.example.com and www2.example.com.

Example 2-20 *Host TAG in the HTTP Requests for www1.example.com and www2.example.com*

```
HTTP GET /index.html HTTP/1.1
Host: www1.example.com

HTTP GET /index.html HTTP/1.1
Host: www2.example.com
```

www1.example.com and www2.example.com can map to the same IP address, and the server is capable of pulling the content from the right directory by matching the Host tag.

Apache supports the Host tag virtual hosting configuration by means of the directive <VirtualHost>. Example 2-21 shows the configuration.

Example 2-21 *Name-Based Virtual Hosting Configuration*

```
NameVirtualHost 192.168.1.1
[...]
<VirtualHost 192.168.1.1>
UseCanonicalName DNS
Servername www1.example.com
Documentroot /home/httpd/html/foo1
</VirtualHost>
<VirtualHost 192.168.1.1>
UseCanonicalName DNS
Servername www2.example.com
Documentroot /home/httpd/html/foo2
</VirtualHost>
```

Network Architecture Design Options

This section describes some network design options that you can consider when building a Data Center to optimize server performance and increase application availability.

Increasing Server Performance

Now that you understand the OS aspects of server applications and how the TCP stack works, you can take advantage of network products and features to optimize the use of the servers in a Data Center. Optimizing the server performance involves a combination of many factors:

- Use of faster bus architectures. This topic was covered in the section, "PCI and PCI-X Buses."
- Use of the Window Scale option. This topic was described in the section, "High-Speed Networks and the Window Scale Option."
- Bundling multiple NICs in EtherChannels. This topic was described in the section, "Server Multihoming." More information about using multiple NICs from a single server and the network design aspects of this technique can be found in Chapter 20.
- Alleviating the CPU load by using interrupt coalescing.
- Alleviating the CPU load by using TCP offloading.
- Alleviating the CPU load by using jumbo frames.
- Using reverse proxy caching to deliver static content.

This section provides additional details about jumbo frames and reverse proxy caching.

Jumbo Frames

After reading the section, "Client and Server Packet Processing," you should be aware of the amount of processing involved in the reception of an interrupt from a NIC in relation to the arrival of a packet.

The overhead associated with the processing of each interrupt can be a limiting factor in the achievable throughput because the CPU could be busy processing hardware interrupts without performing any other operation on the incoming traffic.

With the adoption of Gigabit Ethernet NICs, the number of interrupts per second that arrive at the CPU can range from about 81,000 (with 1518-byte frames) to about 1,488,000 (with 64-byte frames).

NOTE In Gigabit Ethernet, the interpacket gap is equivalent to 20 bytes. As a result, the number of packets per second for 64-byte frames can be calculated as follows:

1 Gbps ÷ 84 * 8 = 1.488 million packets per second

Similarly, the number of packets per second for 1518 frames equals:

1 Gbps ÷ 1538 bytes * 8, which is 81,274 packets per second

The consequence is that wire-rate Gigabit Ethernet traffic could take up to the full CPU utilization, even with gigahertz processors. This is the result of interrupt processing and excessive context switching.

Two main solutions to this problem exist:

- **Interrupt coalescing**—This mechanism consists of delaying the interrupt generation from the NIC to the CPU. When invoked, the CPU must process a number of packets instead of just one.
- **Jumbo frames**—This mechanism uses frames larger than the 1500 MTU.

Interrupt coalescing is a feature available on NICs that does not require any extra network configuration. Jumbo frames allow throughput improvements and require configuration on the NICs as well as the network.

Jumbo frames are bigger than 1518 bytes. As a result, throughput increases, the CPU utilization decreases, and sending more data per frame achieves higher efficiency because of the per-packet ratio of data to control information.

How can an Ethernet frame be bigger than the maximum transmission unit? Ethernet specifications mandate a maximum frame size of 1518 bytes (1500 MTU), but, in reality, frames can exceed the 1518-byte size as long as the algorithm for the cyclic redundancy check (CRC) does not deteriorate (this happens with frames bigger than 12,000 bytes).

The typical size for jumbo frames is approximately 9000 bytes, which is well below the limits of the CRC and big enough to carry UDP Network File System (NFS).

In terms of network configuration, support for jumbo frames needs to be enabled on a per-port basis on switches and routers in the path between servers exchanging this type of traffic.

If jumbo packets go out to an interface of an intermediate network device with a smaller MTU, they are fragmented. The network device that needs to fragment performs this operation in software with an obvious performance impact.

Reverse Proxy Caching

Having a kernel mode and a user mode increases the reliability of servers regarding the operations performed by the applications. The drawback of separating the two modes is performance, which degrades depending on the number of times that the data is copied within the server when there is a transition from user mode to kernel mode, and vice versa (see the section, "User Mode and Kernel Mode").

A solution to this problem involves deploying kernel caches in the form of either separate appliances or servers. Deployment of caches in Data Center environments typically goes by the name of reverse proxy caching.

Typically, a proxy cache is just a server, but it runs in kernel mode because it does not need to host a number of different applications. As a result, with the hardware being equivalent, a proxy cache is faster than a server in delivering static objects because of the reduced overhead on data processing. Figure 2-5 shows the architecture of a typical Data Center and highlights the placement of cache engines in relation to the aggregation switches.

Figure 2-5 *Cache Attachment in a Data Center*

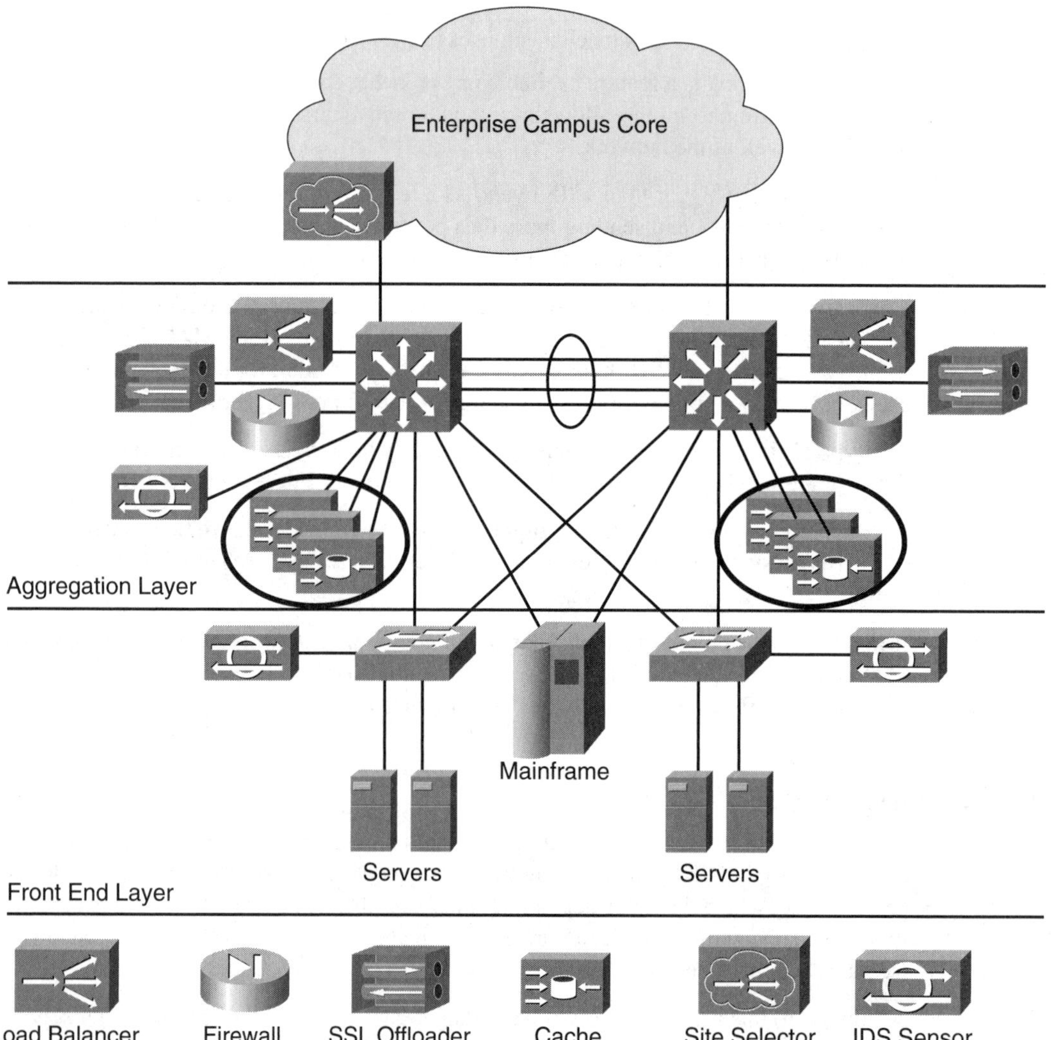

Another benefit of deploying caches is outlined in Chapter 3. Using caches can simplify the design of multitier server farms.

Increasing Server Availability with Load Balancing

Clustering of application servers increases the availability of the server farm impacted by server failures. Clustering consists of using multiple-server computers to provide a single application that is virtually running on a single server. The application runs effectively on multiple servers, but the end user thinks he is accessing a single server.

Clustering provides both load distribution and high availability. Clustering can be used to scale a server farm. Instead of adding processors to a single computer, you can use a farm of computers of the same power; the end result is a virtual server of higher processing power than a single device.

Clustering typically refers to the combination of load-balancing traffic to a number of servers and the capability of these servers to share resources such as a storage disk subsystem or a tape drive. This section focuses on how load balancers can increase server availability.

Figure 2-6 shows the placement of a load-balancing device in a Data Center. A load-balancer is placed in the path between clients and servers. There, it can provide a number of server farm services besides pure load distribution, including limiting the number of connections to a server and assigning connection requests to healthy servers.

Preventing Server Overload

When a server becomes overloaded with connections, it can experience severe performance degradation. The large number of connections results in the spawning of a large number of processes and threads, which causes degradation because of the following factors:

- **Too much context switching**—This happens because the more connections there are, the more processes/threads are present on the server.
- **Too much memory swapping**—The more processes and threads are active on a server, the more memory you need. The OS starts swapping to disk, which, in turn, increases the CPU utilization.

A load-balancer protects the server from receiving more than a configured number of connections. For example, on the Cisco Content Switching Module, you can set maxconns under the "real" server configuration. The load-balancer then waits until the connections are closed and, when they go below a configure threshold (minconns), starts assigning new connections to the server.

Figure 2-6 *Load Balancers in a Data Center*

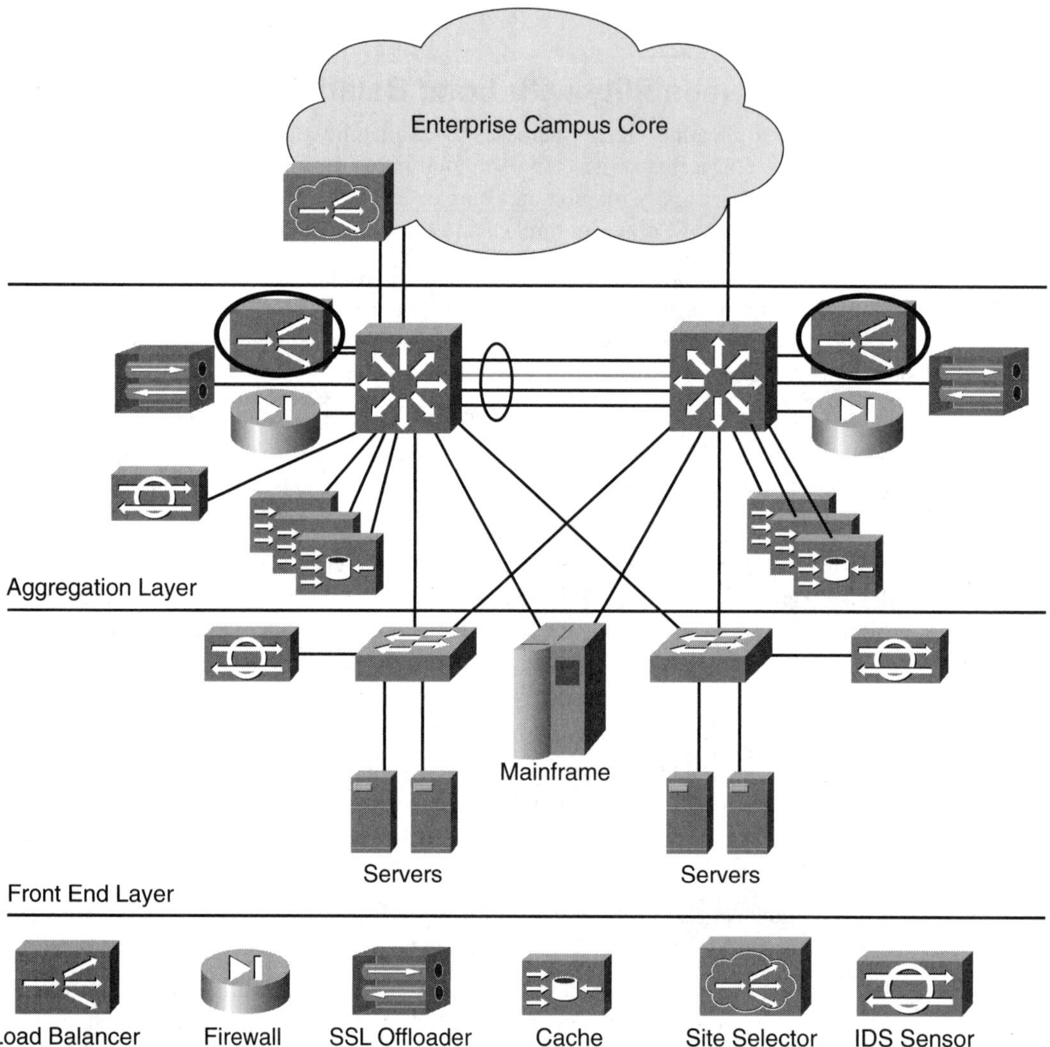

TIP

Processes and threads require a certain amount of memory. On a forking server, the maximum number of connections is bound to the maximum number of processes that can be spawned.

On a multiprocess-threaded server, the number of connections equals the number of threads per child times the number of processes.

If you can find out how much memory is required by each process and thread, and consequently how many processes * threads you can have running at the same time, you can decide how many connections the server can tolerate.

Even if you managed to estimate how many connections the server should be capable of accepting, an overload is possible. When available, one possible method of protecting your servers is to periodically monitor CPU and memory utilization from an external device.

Monitoring TCP Connections

An incoming request for a TCP-based application to a server port that is not open usually causes the server to send a TCP reset (RST) as a response to the client. As a result, the client application displays an error message and no connection is established.

Some server platforms behave differently. An actual TCP handshake to a port is possible even if the associated application is not running.

Using a load-balancing device to front-end a pool of servers provides monitoring of the server health status and can address both server behaviors through the following methods:

- By monitoring the TCP connection setup between a client and a server, and taking proper action if the server does not answer client SYN packets or if it sends RST packets. This mechanism is called in-band health monitoring.
- By monitoring the load on the servers and adjusting the weight of the servers when CPU and memory rise above certain thresholds.
- By monitoring the error messages returned by an HTTP server by sending HTTP requests from the load-balancer with "probes," or by monitoring the HTTP error messages returned by the server to a client (this mechanism is called return error code checks).

Each method has pros and cons. In-band health verification can detect that the SYN sent by a client went unanswered and can reassign a retransmitted SYN to a healthy server. The advantage of in-band health verification is that this type of monitoring is nonintrusive, meaning that the load-balancer does not generate additional traffic to the server. The disadvantage is that the client experiences a delay of a few seconds because of the TCP retransmission timer.

Monitoring servers by periodically sending probes makes it possible for a load-balancer to identify a faulty server independently of clients' connections, possibly before connections are assigned to it. The limitations of probes relate to the fact that they are an intrusive method of monitoring a server. For example, a probe might use a TCP RST to close a connection, and some servers might react to a TCP RST by throwing an exception (servlet engines sometimes do).

For more information about these topics, see Chapter 17.

Summary

Today's Data Centers are based on client/server architectures that rely on TCP/IP for the network communication. Servers receive the traffic from network interface cards and pass the data to the application via sockets. NICs implement Layer 2 functions such as speed negotiation, collision detection, serialization, and deserialization. NICs can be and should be connected to the infrastructure with teaming for increased availability. Chapter 20 provides more information about the design of a highly available infrastructure in the presence of dual-attached NICs.

Data that arrives on a NIC is initially processed by the Ethernet driver, then is passed up to the TCP stack, and eventually is copied to the socket buffer. Understanding the basics of packet processing in current OSs helps troubleshooting network problems and making design decisions on issues such as the need for reverse proxy caching, jumbo frames, interrupt coalescing, and the receive window size.

Network traces of an interactive TCP application and of a bulk transfer show how the TCP stack operates while client and server communicate. The traces show how TCP optimizes the use of the network and implements flow control during a session. Knowing TCP algorithms and timeouts also helps when troubleshooting problems of performance and making the right choice on which socket options to use when writing an application. Chapter 7 provides more details about the TCP protocol. In Chapter 11, you can see TCP and UDP applied to streaming applications.

A server application can be thought of as one or more Layer 4 ports waiting for incoming connections and one or more processes. Servers can be made of multiple processes for robustness and can use threads as well for optimized performance and sharing of session information. Even multiprocess servers can fail. In this case, the client receives a TCP FIN or a TCP RST, or, when setting up a new connection, the client does not receive any SYN ACK. Understanding the failure scenarios and how TCP behaves in such conditions is important when designing network services for a highly available application.

Network devices provide the infrastructure for TCP/IP applications and can also optimize server performance and increase server availability. Jumbo frames, for example, can optimize the achievable throughput of a server by using frames larger than the regular 1518 bytes. Reverse proxy caching also helps optimize server performance by delivering objects from a kernel-level cache. Load balancing can prevent server overload and can monitor connections between clients and servers to identify malfunctioning servers. Chapter 17 provides detailed information on how to provide application availability with load-balancing devices.

This chapter also provides a section that shows how the concepts explained in this chapter apply to a simple configuration of a web server. For more information about the HTTP-related options, see Chapter 8.

For Further Reading

Stevens, Richard. *TCP/IP Illustrated*, Volume I: *The Protocols.* Boston: Addison-Wesley, 1994.

———. *TCP/IP Illustrated*, Volume II: *The Implementation*. Boston: Addison-Wesley, 1995.

This chapter covers the following topics:

- The relationship between application architectures and network design relative to Enterprise Application Integration (EAI) efforts
- The use of web services and remote procedure call (RPC) technologies in web-based multitier serverfarms
- The use of HTML and Extensible Markup Language (XML) in the Data Center and how it relates to web services
- User-agent technologies: browsers and client-side programming technologies such as JavaScript, applets, and ActiveX controls
- Web-server and application-server essentials, and server-side programming technologies such as Common Gateway Interface (CGI), Java servlets, and Active Server Pages (ASP)
- Database and middleware essential concepts
- Clustering essentials and how clusters interoperate with storage-area networks (SANs), and how to stretch a server or storage cluster geographically
- A case study: how to design a Data Center network that provides high availability and security with multitier applications and with explanations on where to perform hardware load balancing, where to perform clustering, how to create different security zones in a Data Center by means of firewalls, and which Intrusion Detection System (IDS) signatures to enable in a Data Center environment

CHAPTER 3

Application Architectures Overview

The purpose of Data Centers is to host application environments and the servers that support them. Enterprise applications range from Internet portals to e-commerce, customer relationship management (CRM), collaboration, enterprise resource planning (ERP), and more.

Enterprises either develop these applications internally and run them on application servers such as IBM WebSphere, BEA Weblogic, or Oracle 9i, or they use commercial applications made by vendors such as SAP, Oracle, and Siebel. Each application is unique in its purpose, architecture, and associated traffic patterns, yet there are common elements to both homegrown and commercial applications.

For example, a significant number of today's applications use a web-based front end, which implies the following:

- The client is a web browser such as Microsoft Internet Explorer or Netscape Communicator.
- The client and the server use HTTP as the protocol for communicating.
- The data transferred by HTTP is in HTML format.
- The server has a process that understands HTTP and can exchange data with the application and with the client.

Because the design of a Data Center results from understanding the application characteristics, this chapter provides a high-level overview of today's applications.

The following list highlights key reasons why it is important to understand application architectures for a successful Data Center design:

- Upgrades to new versions of a given application might require a different network design. For example, an application that once ran the presentation logic (web front end) and the business logic (application middleware) on the same server might migrate to a tiered model where the presentation logic and the business logic run on separate servers.

- The need to integrate applications (a process that is referred to as EAI) might require the creation of new traffic paths between servers that were previously isolated. For example, you can address the need to web-enable legacy applications running on mainframes with middleware software running on application servers. This solution requires a new communication path between application servers and mainframes in addition to or in replacement of the direct connectivity between terminal clients and mainframes.
- The security design of a Data Center requires understanding the application environment to create security zones and to deploy IDS signatures in a meaningful way.
- The need to scale the performance of application servers might require hardware load balancing and SSL offloading. Taking full advantage of hardware load balancing requires also understanding how web and application servers are deployed.
- The need to deploy clustered applications for disaster recovery requires data replication, which in turns requires understanding how applications store data.
- The need to exchange information with business partners on extranet environments requires the right network design and security considerations to connect the two networks and to allow a secure communication exchange between them.

This chapter describes the way enterprise applications use HTTP and the Secure Socket Layer (SSL). HTTP is explained in Chapter 8, "HTTP and Related Concepts," and SSL is explained in Chapter 9, "SSL and TLS" and in Chapter 15, "Security Protocols and Technologies."

This chapter is also the foundation to understanding Chapter 18, "Session Tracking and Cookies"; Chapter 19, "Persistence Mechanisms on Load Balancers"; Chapter 21, "Integrating Security into the Infrastructure."

Taxonomy of Applications and Hosted Servers

As previously mentioned, the main goal of Data Centers is to host applications that the end user invokes remotely to retrieve data or perform some task, such as placing orders, making reservations, communicating with a remote party, or retrieving documentation. The many categories of enterprise applications include portals, e-commerce applications, ERP, CRM, supply-chain management, and collaboration tools.

The purpose of *portal* applications is to operate as the gateway to various information sources and tools tailored to a specific community of users. Portals are web pages hosted on web servers: they provide information in the form of HTML pages transmitted on top of HTTP. HTML pages in turn support a number of other objects, such as Word or PDF documents, other web pages, and multimedia content via *anchors*. (Read the section "HTML.")

E-commerce and business-to-business applications make it possible to browse catalogs and place orders securely. The user interface for these applications is still built in HTML format and carried on HTTP. Transactions are secured with SSL.

Collaborative applications integrate the communication between remote parties by using e-mails, document sharing, online messaging, and conferencing.

From an architectural point of view, applications execute on a number of servers, which provide the user interface (web servers), the application logic (application servers), and a system to save and retrieve data (database servers); for more information, read the section, "Multitier Applications."

Besides these servers, several other services support applications and network management: they include file servers, Domain Name System (DNS) servers, directory servers, RADIUS servers, and Certificate Authority (CA) servers.

This list summarizes the servers that you can typically find in a Data Center:

- **Web servers**—These servers provide the presentation function for most applications. The simplest use of a web server is as a portal for a company on the Internet. For more information, read the section, "Web Servers." Apache, Netscape Enterprise Server, and Microsoft Internet Information Server (IIS) are examples.
- **Application servers**—These servers execute the business logic function of a multitier application. For more information, read the section, "Server-Side Programming." Examples are BEA Weblogic, IBM WebSphere, Oracle 9i, Apache Tomcat, and Sun ONE application servers.
- **Database servers**—These servers store and manage records of data. One of the key functions of a database server is maintaining structured tables and returning the content in the order and format that is requested by the client application. For more information about database servers, read the section, "Database Access." Examples of database servers include Oracle 9i, IBM databases (DB2, Informix, IMS, and U2), and Sybase.
- **E-mail servers**—Electronic mail is probably the most popular collaboration application on the Internet, together with HTTP applications. The architecture of e-mail applications usually consists of three components—the user agent on the client's desktop, a mailbox that stores e-mails and interacts with the user agent, and a mail server. The protocols used by these components are the Post Office Protocol (POP3, RFC 1939), the Internet Message Access Protocol (IMAP, RFC 3501), and the Simple Mail Transfer Protocol (SMTP, RFC 2821). Examples of e-mail servers are Sendmail Inc., Microsoft Exchange, Lotus Notes and Domino, Oracle Collaboration Suite, and Sun ONE messaging servers.
- **File servers**—These servers provide shared remote storage for other servers in the Data Center and users on the network. The protocols used to access files on file servers are either the Network File System (NFS, RFC 3530) protocol (for UNIX-based operating systems) or the Common Internet File System (CIFS) protocol (for Microsoft Windows applications). Examples of file servers include Network Appliance Filers, EMC Celerra, IBM TotalStorage, and Microsoft Windows Storage Server 2003.

- **Directory servers**—These servers provide a database in a predefined format (a subset of International Organization for Standardization [ISO] X.500) that stores enterprise information about users, printers, servers, and digital certificates. The Lightweight Directory Access Protocol (LDAP, RFC 3494) is used by client applications (such as servers executing middleware software or authentication servers) to consult directory servers. Examples of directory servers include the Microsoft Active Directory, Novell eDirectory, Sun ONE directory server, Oracle Internet Directory, and IBM directory server.
- **DNS servers**—DNS servers, among other services, provide the translation of domain names into their associated IP addresses. Chapter 10, "DNS Essentials and Site Selection Considerations," describes the DNS protocol and its uses. Examples of DNS servers include BIND, Novell DNS server, Microsoft DNS server, and Cisco Network Registrar.
- **DHCP servers**—Dynamic Host Configuration Protocol (DHCP, RFC 2131) servers assign IP addresses dynamically to requesting clients. Typical clients are desktop machines in an enterprise network. Examples of DHCP servers include the Internet Software Consortium (ISC) DHCP server, Novell DHCP server, Microsoft DHCP server, IBM DHCP server, and Cisco Network Registrar.
- **RADIUS servers**—Remote Access Dial-In User Service (RADIUS, RFC 2865) servers—and in general, authentication, authorization, and accounting (AAA) servers—authenticate network administrators, dial-up users, virtual private network (VPN) clients, Internet users (with HTTP cut-through proxy or authentication proxy), and desktop users (with IEEE 802.1x). Examples of authentication servers include CiscoSecure Access Control Server (CSACS) and Microsoft Windows 2000 Internet Authentication Server (IAS). For more information about AAA, read Chapter 15, "Security Protocols and Technology."
- **CA servers**—CA servers are required to build the public-key infrastructure (PKI) for the distribution of public keys when deploying SSL or IP Security (IPSec) applications. E-commerce applications (i.e. applications using HTTP on SSL), IPSec VPNs, SSL VPNs, TN3270 on SSL, and identity-based network access (802.1x authenticated desktops) are examples of applications that require a CA server. CA servers can be hosted in-house or outsourced. Examples of CA servers that you can use to build an in-house PKI are Entrust servers, Sun ONE certificate servers, and Microsoft Windows CA servers. Chapter 9 describes the SSL protocol. Chapter 15 provides details about the PKI technology.
- **Streaming servers**—Streaming servers allow the distribution of Video on Demand or live events to desktops in the enterprise network or to Internet clients. Streaming servers include Cisco IPTV, Apple QuickTime Streaming, Microsoft Windows Media, and Progressive Real servers. Chapter 11, "Streaming Protocols Overview," provides more information about streaming protocols and products.

- **TN3270 servers**—TN3270 servers provide client access to mainframes' Systems Network Architecture (SNA) applications via Telnet. A TN3270 server is a computer that implements both a TCP/IP stack and an SNA stack. The software running on the TN3270 server translates the characters from the format used on terminals to the ASCII format and vice-versa. It converts clients' characters in SNA data streams. Several standards, such as RFC 1576 and RFC 2355, describe how the TN3270 implementations work. For more information about TN3270, read Chapter 14, "IBM Data Center Technology."

Integration of Applications

Data Centers typically host servers running several different operating systems and applications based on diverse software architectures.

The diversity of hardware and software platforms in a single Data Center is the result of many factors, which include the rapid evolution of application technologies, the consolidation of server farms from companies that have been merged, and simply the parallel and independent implementation of software without a plan to share data across multiple systems.

This diversity of applications comes with a management burden and the need to share the same data. These challenges are the reason for the current trend of simplification and integration. This section explains what the Enterprise Application Integration (EAI) is, which software technologies have emerged to make the integration possible, and what is the likely impact on the network traffic patterns.

Enterprise Application Integration

Enterprise business-critical applications such as databases, reservation systems, and parts-ordering tools have existed long before the Internet, and they were originally developed to execute on systems such as IBM mainframes.

In recent years, enterprises have decided to let remote internal users, business partners, and online customers access their applications. Rewriting applications to make them fully web-based poses a risk to stability, complexity, and availability, which have long been solved in the existing software.

The solution is to web-enable existing applications. This task is not just about placing a web server in front of a mainframe but providing an easy-to-use interface and consolidating and automating business processes. This operation can be complex because a business process requires several different applications, which might not be designed to interoperate with each other. The integration process is typically referred to as *Enterprise Application Integration (EAI)*.

The software design model that simplifies the integration and development of applications is called the *n-tier model*, and the software that glues these servers and applications together is called *middleware*.

Middleware can translate HTTP requests into the specific protocols of legacy applications. An example of this approach comes from the technologies that enable the integration of IBM Customer Information Control System (CICS) applications. IBM's redbook *Revealed! Architecting Web Access to CICS* (http://www.redbooks.ibm.com/) provides an excellent reference.

A higher integration between applications requires the use of distributed object technologies, such as Enterprise Java Beans (EJB), Distributed Component Object Model (DCOM), Common Object Request Broker Architecture (CORBA), or Web Services. This topic is described in the section, "Middleware."

Network Design Implications of EAI

EAI has an important implication for the network design. The immediate consequence is that servers which were previously isolated need to communicate. This step requires creating new communication paths and security zones, which translates into Layer 2, Layer 3, and security considerations.

The network design that matches the software n-tier model segregates server farms of different types to provide isolation from possible attacks. You can design this segregation with VLANs and access control lists (ACLs) on routers or enforce it with firewalls.

The network designer needs to assess the impact of server-to-server protocols and database access protocols. Remote Procedure Calls (RPC), Java Remote Method Invocation (RMI), Object RPC (ORPC), Internet Inter ORB (Object Request Broker) Protocol (IIOP), Simple Object Access Protocol (SOAP), and various SQL transport protocols might open dynamically negotiated ports. Addressing this risk is often a challenge in designing ACLs, or it can be as easy as enabling the appropriate fixup on a firewall. (Read Chapter 5, "Data Center Security Overview," for more information.)

The other implication of application integration is the increased use of web servers for the presentation of the user interface. User interfaces are built as HTML pages carried in the HTTP payload.

The use of web-based applications increases the number of HTTP requests, and the use of web-associated technologies increases the number of DNS requests. Client machines sending HTTP requests to servers initially send DNS requests by indicating the server name in order to determine its IP address. This step is necessary for a user requesting a web page from a browser as well as a Java application calling a remote method. The higher number of DNS and HTTP requests (HTTP uses TCP, thus increasing the number of TCP connection requests) drives the need for scalability and load distribution between a pool of servers.

(Read Chapter 6, "Server Load-Balancing Overview," and Chapter 16, "Load-Balancing Modes and Predictors," for more information.)

Permitting access to internal applications from business partners also requires careful design in the extranet. In this environment, network address translation (NAT) is fundamental to avoiding conflicting private IP addresses. (Both companies might use the same private address range.) NAT is a Layer 3 function that needs to be application-aware. Chapter 13, "Layer 3 Protocol Essentials," provides information about NAT, its capabilities, and the devices that support this feature.

Another, less apparent, implication of EAI is the need to provide *application* functions from network devices. Consider the various operating systems and server platforms in a Data Center and the need to provide similar services to these applications, such as load distribution, server health monitoring, encryption, and remote access. By providing these application services on network devices, it is possible to ease the integration and the consolidation of multiple server platforms. For example, a network SSL device can decrypt traffic for UNIX-based servers as well as Microsoft Windows servers. The SSL configuration is unique across multiple servers. The same concept applies to the use of load balancers or VPN concentrators.

The following section discusses a model to build open application environments that can easily accommodate the need to integrate various hardware and software platforms, besides being scalable and resilient to failures.

Multitier Applications

Most enterprise applications today are developed according to the *multitier* or *n-tier* model. Applications developed to follow the n-tier model are refered to as multitier applications as the various application functions are provided by different server tiers. According to this model, the application functions are divided into the following software tiers:

- **The client tier**—The client software (usually called the *user agent*) allows the interaction between the user and the application. With web-based applications, the client tier (usually a browser) renders the user interface (which is generated by the presentation tier) by interpreting the HTML, Java applets, and ActiveX controls.
- **The presentation tier**—This software provides the visualization functions for the application. The presentation tier comprises static objects such as images, form fields to receive the client's input, and dynamically generated objects to display the results of the computation of the application tier. On web-based applications, the presentation tier is implemented by web servers.
- **The application tier**—This software provides the business logic. The application tier receives procedure invocations from the presentation tier, to which it returns the result of the computation. The application tier also communicates with the database tier to store and retrieve data. You implement the application tier either with scripting

languages on web servers or on application servers. The typical technologies are CGI; ASP; Java Server Pages (JSP); Java servlets; or, for more complex applications, object-oriented middleware such as EJB, DCOM, and CORBA.

- **The database tier**—This software stores application data, such as catalogs and user information. The software that implements the business logic connects to database servers to retrieve and save data.

Some of these functions are provided either on a single server machine or on multiple machines that communicate over the network. How the functions are separated and whether they execute on multiple machines depends on how the vendor architected the application (if the tiers are modular enough to be placed on different servers) and the scalability and resiliency requirements of the application. Figure 3-1 shows some possible multitier Data Center designs.

Figure 3-1 *The n-Tier Model*

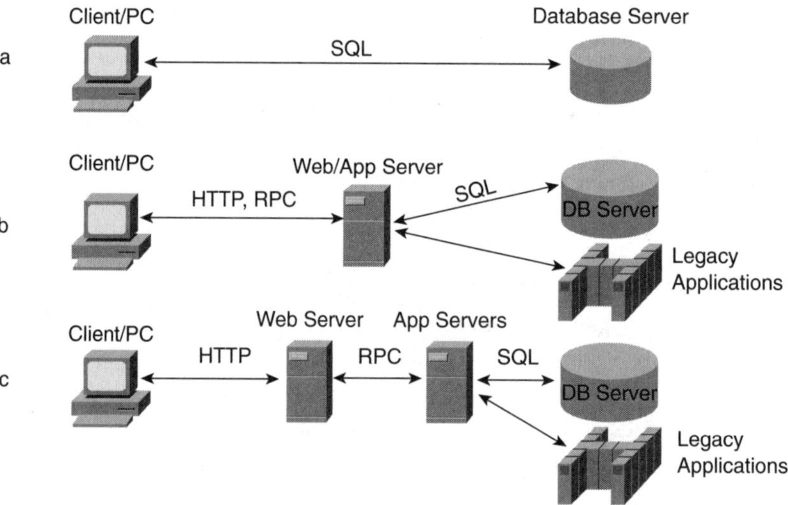

Part **a** of Figure 3-1 shows a two-tier model. The PC is the client and implements most of the processing logic, which is why the client software is called a *thick client*. The PC connects to a remote database server to retrieve data.

Part **b** of Figure 3-1 shows a three-tier architecture. The client mainly implements the presentation logic; the application processing happens on the application server, which in turn retrieves data from a database server. The software on the PC is considered a *thin client*, which means that it does not perform much processing besides rendering the information returned by the server. Part **b** of Figure 3-1 also shows that the application server can provide the gateway function with legacy applications.

Part **c** of Figure 3-1 shows a four-tier architecture. The client has not changed, but the functions of the application servers are separated in a presentation function, typically implemented by web servers, and an application logic function, implemented on application servers. The application servers retrieve data from database servers. The application servers also provide access to legacy applications from web-based applications.

This chapter explains each tier of the architecture, the client-side technologies, web servers, server-side programming, and connectivity to the database tier. A section on middleware explains how you can distribute the business logic on multiple application servers by using the component technologies.

Markup Languages: HTML and XML

The web browser is the ubiquitous client software in use today. Browsers send HTTP requests (typically HTTP GET and POST requests) to web servers.

Clients might request static content by sending HTTP GET requests for such objects as /index.html and /image.gif, or they might send variables to the remote application by appending variable names and values to HTTP POST or GET requests.

Web and application servers return HTTP responses with HTML data. HTML describes how a browser should display data, which is why HTML is suitable for formatting the user interface of an application.

NOTE For more information about HTTP, see Chapter 8.

One challenge with using HTML to render documents is that users might retrieve information by using clients other than web browsers. These include wireless phones, handheld devices, and IP phones. Formatting documents for these clients is different from formatting for desktop computers because of the differences in the screen size and the capabilities of the software that displays the text.

XML is a markup language that is used by web-based applications to describe data without formatting information. An XML document can be formatted differently according to the client that is requesting it.

Besides providing the functions just described, XML is becoming a key component in building business-to-business and e-commerce applications because it provides a standard way to describe data. In fact, you can use XML in conjunction with SOAP to enable the communication between remote servers of different operating systems on top of HTTP.

Load balancing, SSL offloading, caching, and content-transformation devices are designed to integrate with web-based applications. For example, you can design the HTML data and the forwarding decisions of a load balancer (such as the Cisco Content Switching Module) to interoperate: the *anchors* in the HTML code can be matched by the load balancer, which is useful for *session persistence* (see Chapter 19). As another example, a load balancer can be dynamically configured by an application by means of XML messages. (This topic is described in Chapter 17, "Server Health Management.")

Knowing basic concepts about HTML and XML is necessary to understand the functionalities of network products that are HTTP and SSL aware, and as a consequence, it helps you take advantage of their functions and integrate these products in a Data Center environment.

HTML

HTML describes how a browser should display text on a screen. Servers use HTML to build the user interface to applications in the Data Center.

HTML provides the following functionalities:

- Text and paragraph formatting
- Inclusion and formatting of images
- Linking to other documents or web pages
- Creation of tables
- Creation of forms
- Creation of image maps

For more information about HTML, refer to http://www.w3c.org/MarkUp/.

NOTE The World Wide Web Consortium (W3C) is an organization that develops standard web technologies. W3C standards are called *recommendations*. HTML and XML are described in W3C recommendations.

Suppose that the user enters the URL http://www.example.com/ in a browser. The browser resolves the DNS name www.example.com to the IP address, such as 192.0.2.80, and it sends an HTTP request to 192.0.2.80. The web server returns the content of the local file index.html. The HTTP response includes the HTML document. (The HTTP headers indicate Content-Type: text/html.)

Example 3-1 shows a simple HTML document. The <html> and </html> tags delimit the document. The <title> and </title> tags surround the document title.

Example 3-1 *Example of HTML Code from index.html*

```
<html>
<head>
<title>Personal Page</title>
</head>
<body>
<h2><img src="images/bullet.gif"> Data Center Design </h2>
<p> Click on the following links to download the documents </p>
<p><a href="http://www.example.com/document1.zip"> Design Best Practices </a></p>
<p><a href="http://www.example.com/document2.zip"> Load balancing overview </a></p>
</body>
</html>
```

The main portion of the document constitutes the body, which is enclosed in the <body> and </body> tags. Within the body, the <p> and </p> tags delimit the paragraphs. An example of a paragraph from Example 3-1 is "<p> Click on the following links to download the documents </p>". The browser simply displays the sentence as a separate paragraph. Figure 3-2 shows how the browser renders the HTML code of Example 3-1.

Notice the bullet image at the left of the heading "Data Center Design." You insert images by using the <img> element, which specifies the source for the picture. When the browser reads the tag, it sends an HTTP request for the image. The web server sends an HTTP response with Content-type: image/gif and the image data. The browser displays the image according to what the HTML code specifies.

Figure 3-2 *Rendering of a Simple Web Page on a Browser*

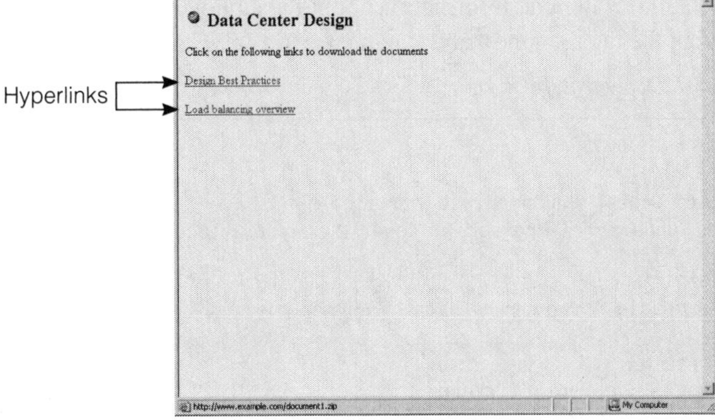

Special text visible in Figure 3-2 appears in bold and underlined format. The user can click on this text, and depending on the content, the browser either displays a new page or downloads the content referenced by this text.

In Example 3-1, it is possible to read the URL associated with the text visible in Figure 3-2. The text displayed by the browser, "Design Best Practices," is associated with the URL http://www.example.com/document1.zip. You make this association by using the <a href> tag, also called an *anchor*. When the user clicks the "Design Best Practices" text, the browser resolves www.example.com to its IP address, sends an HTTP GET to the IP address, and retrieves the file document1.zip using HTTP.

XML

XML is a data-description language. Whereas HTML describes how some text should appear on a computer screen, XML describes the type of data present in the text. Think of a simple analogy with the records of a database. The fields in the record have a name that describes the field type (such as the name, address, and phone number of a customer).

An XML document includes the field descriptions (such as <name>, <address>, and <phone number>) and their values. The application that uploads the XML file can exchange this information with another application, or it can format the text for a client. This flexibility makes XML suitable for server-to-server communication, where the presentation function is not required, and for user interfaces that need to be displayed on multiple client types: PCs, wireless devices, and handhelds. This section explains how.

Example 3-2 shows a simple XML document. This document includes the information about a book. The tags <title> and </title> include the title of the book, and the tags <author> and </author> include information about the authors, which in this case is the names included in the tags <name> and </name>.

Example 3-2 *Example of an XML Document, book.xml*

```
<?xml version = "1.0"?>
<book>
   <title> Data Center Fundamentals </title>
   <subtitle> Fundamental Protocols, Layer 2, Layer 3, Security and Load Balancing
   </subtitle>
   <author id="1">
     <name> Mauricio Arregoces </name>
   </author>
   <author id="2">
     <name>Maurizio Portolani </name>
   </author>
   <editor>Cisco Press</editor>
</book>
```

As it emerges from Example 3-2 in XML, the tags describe the type of data included in the tags. For the purpose of this book, this description of XML is sufficient; for more information, refer to the URL http://www.w3c.org/XML/. What is really important to understand in this section is the use of XML in a Data Center.

An XML document can be rendered differently based on the user agent that is requesting it. An application server can generate data in XML format. An XML parser on the server loads the XML document into memory; transcoder software provides the formatting for the XML document based on the user agent that is requesting it. If the user agent is a web browser, the document is formatted in HTML; if it is a handheld device, the document is formatted with compact HTML (cHTML); and if it is a wireless phone, the document is formatted with the Wireless Markup Language (WML).

NOTE For more information about cHTML, refer to the W3C note "Compact HTML for Small Information Appliances."

For more information about WML, refer to http://www.wapforum.com.

Another important application of XML is facilitating the exchange of data between servers. SOAP makes it possible to invoke remote calls and to exchange messages between servers of different operating systems. SOAP relies on XML for the description of data. SOAP traffic is carried on HTTP.

NOTE The concept of SOAP is similar to that of RPC, Java RMI, CORBA, IIOP, and ORPC.

For more information about SOAP, refer to http://www.w3.org/TR/SOAP/ or http://msdn.microsoft.com/library/en-us/dnsoapspec/html/soapspecindex.asp.

User Agents

The client side of an application is software that runs on a personal computer, a workstation, a personal digital assistant (PDA) device, or a web-enabled phone and uses the network to send requests to a server in a Data Center. Client applications, also called user agents, are categorized as follows:

- **Thick clients**—Clients that perform significant amounts of processing and access servers mainly to retrieve data.
- **Thin clients**—Client applications that mainly display the results of processing done on servers. A thin client deals with the presentation layer of the application. A web browser is an example of a thin client.

Web browsers, e-mail clients, and streaming players are examples of client software. Web browsers implement presentation functions based on the HTML code sent by the server and basic functions such as data validation and confirmations based on code sent by the server and executed locally on the client. Among the key technologies used to implement these functions, you should be familiar with the following: helpers, plug-ins, JavaScript, applets, and ActiveX controls. Most vendors' applications rely on one or more of these technologies for functions implemented on the client side.

Browsers

Web browsers are the most popular Internet client. A web browser is a client application that communicates with a web server, and its main purpose is to render HTML files on a computer screen. The user interacts with the browser either by entering URLs into the Address bar of the browser or by clicking the hyperlinks of HTML documents.

In addition to HTML, a browser renders several multimedia types. When a specific media type is not supported natively in the browser, helper programs and plug-ins help with this task. (See the section "Helpers and Plug-Ins.")

The browser features that interest the network designer the most are

- The support for HTTP 1.1 (read Chapter 8 for more information)
- How browsers handle the resolution of domain names (read Chapter 10)
- The support for SSL (read Chapter 9)
- The use of cookies for HTTP session-state management (read Chapter 18)
- The use of proxy servers for Internet access (read Chapter 19)

The most popular browsers at the time of this writing are Microsoft Internet Explorer and Netscape Communicator.

Helpers and Plug-Ins

The browser launches a helper application when it receives a content type that it cannot natively display. For example, a browser that requests a video and audio stream launches a player, which in turn contacts the streaming server.

Figure 3-3 shows the helper applications for Netscape. For each Multipurpose Internet Mail Extensions (MIME) type, there is a handler, which is the helper application. For example, Figure 3-3 shows that the Content-type video/x-ms-wmx is handled by Microsoft Windows Media Player.

NOTE For more information about MIME types, see Chapter 8.

Figure 3-3 *Helper Applications*

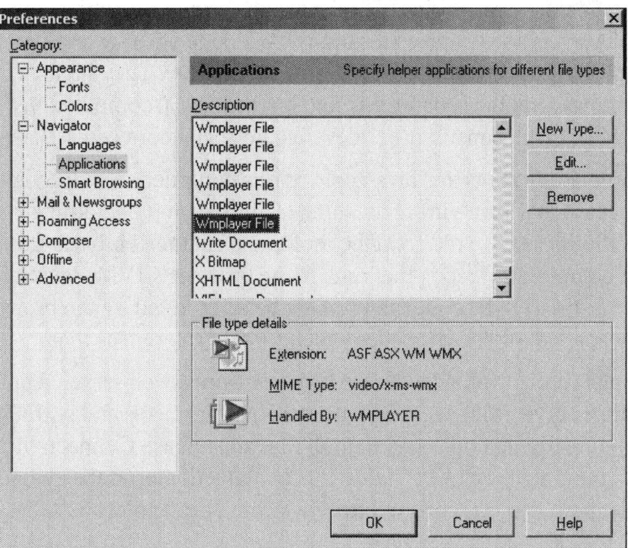

Plug-ins provide a more integrated solution than helpers do. For example, a browser that requests a streaming content can load the player plug-in into its memory instead of launching it as an external application. Plug-ins applications run from the browser memory, and consequently, the content usually appears within the window of the browser.

With Netscape, the plug-in files are usually located in the directory C:\Program Files\Netscape\Communicator\Program\Plugins. These files are mainly dynamic link libraries (DLLs) and are linked dynamically when the browser is launched.

Client-Side Programming

As previously mentioned, a browser is a thin client: it mainly implements the presentation function. Sometimes, an application needs to provide functions dynamically, such as executing simple procedures like data validations. You provide these functions with client-side scripting. Compiled code such as Java applets and ActiveX controls can execute more complex operations.

The main technologies for client-side programming are the following:

- **JavaScript**—JavaScript is a client-side scripting language that is interpreted by the browser. JavaScript provides the HTML code with several functionalities that can be implemented on the client side (in the browser). They include control of the browser windows, graphic capabilities, and mathematical computations. For more information on JavaScript, consult http://devedge.netscape.com/central/javascript/.
- **Applets**—Applets are Java applications compiled in bytecode format that can be executed in a Java virtual machine (JVM) on any operating system. Java applets and JavaScript are two different technologies, but they both use Java syntax. A Java applet is a compiled bytecode that runs in the browser's JVM; JavaScript is the source-code part of the HTML code, and it must be interpreted by the browser. Applets are independent of HTML code, which merely references them.

  Applets are downloaded by the browser from a web server. Applets can connect to the remote server with sockets, with the RMI protocol, and with IIOP. Applets can connect directly to a database with the Java Database Connectivity (JDBC) application program interface (API). (JDBC is explained later in the chapter.) For more information about applets, consult http://java.sun.com/applets/.
- **ActiveX**—ActiveX means many things, but for the purpose of our discussion, we are interested in ActiveX controls, which are developed by Microsoft and similar to applets. ActiveX controls are binary code downloaded to the client machine by a browser. They execute on the client machine just as applets do. An ActiveX control can open connections to a remote server, just as an applet does. The protocol that is used to invoke remote methods is DCOM. For more information about ActiveX controls, refer to http://www.microsoft.com/windows/ie/press/whitepaper/iwhite/white003.htm.

For more information about these client-side technologies, see Appendix F, "Client-Side and Server-Side Programming."

NOTE A JVM is an abstraction of a processor with its own registers and instruction set. Java applications are compiled in a bytecode format that runs in a JVM. The JVM is what makes the compiled Java code portable across operating systems and hardware platforms because it provides virtualization of the underlying hardware.

Web Servers

The first tier of servers for web-based applications consists of web servers. Web servers process HTTP requests and return HTTP responses.

Chapter 2, "Server Architecture Overview," already illustrates how to configure an HTTP server and the strategies used to process requests from multiple users simultaneously with multiprocessing and multithreading.

The most basic HTTP server is a device that accepts HTTP requests from browsers; looks up files on the local disk; and returns text, images, documents. A web server also needs to be able to terminate SSL: it needs to decrypt secure HTTP (HTTPS) requests, retrieve the requested object, encrypt the HTTP response, and send it back to the browser.

HTTP servers can return a wide variety of Content-types. Examples are text/html, image/gif, image/jpeg, and video/quicktime. HTTP uses MIME-like messages to describe the content of HTTP responses so that the browser can correctly visualize it. (You can find more information about MIME in Chapter 8.)

The section "Markup Languages: HTML and XML" provides an example of static HTML content (refer to Example 3-1). A server machine hosting a web server can also provide dynamic processing by executing applications, connecting to the database servers, and delivering the results to the client in HTML format.

The application technologies include CGI, JSP, and ASP. The section, "Server-Side Programming" provides more detail about these technologies.

Server-Side Programming

Web servers can provide static content, business logic, and database access. The main capability offered by web servers is delivering static content. The business-logic intelligence and the capability to access databases is provided by additional modules, to which the web server hands off specific fields of a URL, or by application servers, to which the web server delegates the processing of the business logic. The case study at the end of the section provides an example of how clients interact with web-based applications by means of HTTP and dynamically generated HTML.

NOTE All the server-side programming technologies described in this section provide mechanisms to manage the state of user sessions with web-based applications. These mechanisms include cookies, rewritten URLs, and form hidden fields.

Chapter 18 provides more information about how these mechanisms relate to the HTTP protocol, and provides examples of Java servlet code for session tracking with HTTP.

Chapter 19 describes how to integrate application servers implementing servlets with load balancers.

Web Programming Technologies Overview

One of the easiest ways to run business logic on a web server is to execute programs on the web server itself. With server-side programming, the client (the browser, basically) receives HTML code that is the result of executing the program on the server. With server-side scripting, the client cannot see the source code that generates the HTML page (which is different from client-side scripting).

Server-side programming technologies can be categorized as follows:

- **Scripting**—Scripting consists of embedding lines of code in HTML files that are named with the extension of a scripting language, which is interpreted at runtime by the server. Examples of scripting languages are PHP: Hypertext Processor (PHP) and JavaScript.
- **Server-specific APIs**—These APIs are the interface to procedures provided by the web-server software. These APIs are invoked from the HTML code. Examples of this technology are Internet Server API (ISAPI) and Netscape Server API (NSAPI).
- **Precompiled code**—This methodology consists of compiling the software and invoking the compiled code from the web server. Examples of this technology are Java servlets and server-side ActiveX components.

The following list includes the main server-side programming technologies:

- **ISAPI**—These APIs are specific to the Microsoft IIS web server and can be invoked from within the HTML code.
- **NSAPI**—These APIs are specific to the Netscape web server and can be invoked from within the HTML code.
- **PHP**—This scripting language can be embedded into the HTML code and is interpreted at runtime; the web server has a built-in interpreter for PHP. The <?php and ?> delimiters enclose the scripting code. The files containing PHP code have the .php extension.
- **Server-side JavaScript**—Server-side JavaScript is equivalent to client-side JavaScript, except that the server-side script is delimited by the tag <server> instead of <script>.
- **CGI scripts**—CGI is a protocol that allows communication between users and the application via a web server. The Practical Extraction and Report Language (Perl) is the most popular language used to build CGI applications.
- **Servlets and JSPs**—These Java classes are executed by a JVM, which is embedded into a web server.
- **ASPs**—ASP is Microsoft server-side scripting technology. It is similar in concept to JSP but differs in the programming language and the portability.

- **Server-side ActiveX components**—When developing ASP pages, it is possible to include ActiveX server components written in a programming language that can differ from the language used for scripting. The compiled code can be called from the ASP page.

Server-side programs can run from the memory space of the web server—with the risk that incorrect programming can affect the web server itself—or they can run as a separate process. Comparing CGI and Java servlets helps you understand the implication of either architecture.

CGI is one of the first technologies to be adopted for server-side programming of web-based applications. CGI programs spawn separate processes for each request. The life of the program is kept short, which minimizes the impact of code that could be buggy on further requests.

This behavior provides robustness for CGI applications but is also subject to the following limitations:

- **Performance**—CGI creates processes for each client request even when multiple requests come from the same client.
- **Complex data persistence**—Creating separate processes for requests that belong to the same client session requires CGI to continuously save on the disk temporary data that must be shared.
- **Complex handling of database server connectivity**—Multiple requests from the same client that require access to the database imply closing and opening of new database connections because processes are created and killed for each connection.

NOTE Most of the listed limitations that originally affected CGI have been addressed by FastCGI. FastCGI provides easier session affinity (or data persistence) than CGI because a single client can be assigned to the same application process for the duration of a session, making it possible to cache previous selections in the process memory.

The preceding list highlights some of the reasons that brought about Java servlets. Unlike CGI, servlets use multiple threads instead of processes to handle multiple clients requesting the same servlet. Because of the threaded architecture, data persistence for a returning client is typically easier to manage than in CGI.

Java servlets and JSP execute in a JVM, which is always running. JSP and servlet code is only compiled the very first time that it is requested.

Each approach has pros and cons: running scripts in the web-server memory space makes the application faster, but executing scripts in a separate process makes the application more robust. For more information about these technologies, see Appendix F, "Client-Side and Server-Side Programming."

Case Study: Web-Client Interaction with Java Servlets

One of the reasons why you should be interested in understanding server-side programming is to realize how you can integrate hardware load balancing with specific application environments. This case study provides the foundation to understanding the examples in Chapter 18 and 19. Chapter 18 provides information about the use of servlets to keep state information about a user's session; Chapter 19 explains how to use a Cisco Content Switching Module to provide session persistence without changing the servlet application.

The servlet technology is similar to applets, but the difference is that servlets run on servers instead of clients. A servlet is a Java class (which is bytecode) that executes on a server.

Servlets run in a special environment that is referred to as a "container" or a "servlet engine." A container handles the creation of servlet instances, their initialization, and the distribution of incoming requests; in brief, the servlet container manages the life cycle of the servlet. Like applets, servlets are loaded and executed in a JVM.

Servlet engines can run inside application servers or inside web servers. Examples of web and application servers that support servlets include BEA Weblogic and IBM WebSphere.

Servlet engines and the web server can run on the same physical machine or on separate machines. In the first case, the web server uses interprocess communication to pass HTTP requests to the servlet engine. In the second case, HTTP requests that require application processing are exchanged on the network using a format that depends on the application server vendor.

Clients send HTTP requests to the web server with a Uniform Resource Identifier (URI) that specifies the servlet application. For example, a browser sends an HTTP request to www.example.com with the URI /examples/servlet/SessionTracking?musicpreference=rock. The /examples/servlet/SessionTracking identifies the application, and musicpreference=rock is the input to the servlet.

The server returns the result of the computation in the data portion of the HTTP response in HTML format. Example 3-3 shows a possible output from the application SessionTracking in HTML format.

Example 3-3 shows that the application expects some input from the user: the hyperlinks are built to provide input about the user choices ?musicpreference=classical and ?musicpreference=rock. Notice that because the hyperlinks do not specify the domain name, it is assumed that the HTTP requests are to be sent to the same domain name as the main document.

NOTE The URIs in the hyperlinks of Example 3-3 are called relative URIs because they are relative to the URI of the main document. If the main URI is http://www.example.com/index.html, the hyperlink <a href=SessionTracking?musicpreference=classical"> is translated by the browser into <a href=http://www.example.com/SessionTracking?musicpreference=classical">.

For more information about URLs and URIs, see Chapter 8.

The same application also includes *Form fields*, which is another mechanism provided by HTML for the application to receive input from the user.

Example 3-3 *Example of HTML Code Dynamically Generated by a Servlet*

```
<html>
<head><title> Simple example of HTML code </title></head>
<body>
<p> Your choice is Rock </p>
<p><a href="SessionTracking?musicpreference=classical" > Click here to select the
  classic collection </a></p>
<p><a href="SessionTracking?musicpreference=rock" > Click here to select the rock
  collection </a></p>

<form action="SessionTracking" method = GET>
<p> Fill in with your music preference </p>
<input type=text name=musicpreference>
<input type=submit value="click here to submit">
</form>

</body>
</html>
```

Middleware

As previously explained, multitier web-based applications require the integration between multiple server tiers, some of which could come from legacy systems. *Middleware* is the technology that allows this integration because it lets application software running on diverse operating systems communicate.

Middleware functions are often categorized as follows:

- **Object middleware**—This category allows the creation of distributed object-oriented applications. CORBA-based brokers, RMI, ActiveX/DCOM, and SOAP belong to this category.

- **Transaction middleware**—This middleware updates several databases and resources with Atomic, Consistent, Isolation, Durable (ACID) transactions; that is, if the transaction does not succeed, a rollback procedure is performed. Transaction Processing (TP) monitors such as IBM CICS provide these functions.
- **Messaging middleware**—Messaging is typically used for asynchronous communication. Integrating applications across a WAN is one example of using messaging middleware. IBM WebSphere MQ and BEA MessageQ are examples of messaging products.
- **Database middleware**—JDBC and Open Database Connectivity (ODBC) interfaces and database management systems (DBMSs) are examples of this middleware type. DBMS solutions typically provide a number of services such as support for load distribution, redundancy, and security.

Each category of middleware can exist as a software product or is part of a software product that implements multiple functions.

The most widely used middleware software environments today are

- **Java 2 Enterprise Edition (J2EE)**—Sun Microsystems's architecture for multitier applications is based on Java. Among its assets is the portability of the architecture across multiple operating systems because it is based on Java and because it is compatible with most web servers.
- **Microsoft .NET**—Previously called Distributed internetwork Application Architecture (DNA), Microsoft .NET is Microsoft's architecture for multitier applications. .NET executes on Windows operating systems (such as Windows 2000 Server and Windows XP). Among the advantages of this architecture is the number of different languages supported.
- **CORBA**—Middleware that is compliant with CORBA lets you develop applications in a number of different languages and permits communication between computers running different operating systems.

Today's applications, whether commercial or home-grown, typically rely on the J2EE technology, Microsoft .NET, or CORBA.

J2EE-based software is characterized by the use of applets for client-side programming, servlets, and JSP for server-side programming and uses JDBC as the interface for database access. The J2EE technology for distributed object-oriented computing is based on EJB.

Microsoft .NET software relies on ActiveX controls for client-side programming, ASP for server-side programming, and ODBC and ActiveX Data Objects (ADO) as the interface for database access. The .NET technology for distributed object-oriented computing is based on DCOM objects.

CORBA is an open architecture that provides transport for the communications between objects in the network and also provides services such as life cycle for the objects, persistence, naming for remote objects, transaction services, and security. You can write the applications in several languages, including Java and C++. Notice that CORBA is not a product but a specification maintained by an organization called the Object Management Group (OMG).

Table 3-1 maps the client and server functions previously examined in this chapter to the J2EE and .NET architectures.

Table 3-1 *Main Software Architectures for Web-Based Applications and Associated Technologies*

	Client Application	Scripting Language	Database Interface	Components	Transport Protocol
J2EE	Browser, Java applet	JSPs and servlets	JDBC	EJB	RMI
.NET	Browser, ActiveX control	ASPs	ODBC	DCOM objects	ORPC

Components: EJBs and DCOM

Among the key software characteristics of the J2EE and .NET technology is that they allow the development of object-oriented distributed applications, which are based on components. *Components* are small binary applications that can be used by several other applications. Java Beans and Component Object Model (COM) objects follow this paradigm.

COM and Java Beans are locally available components. The logical evolution of this paradigm is to make the components available across the network. Remotely accessible Java Beans are called EJB, and remotely accessible COM objects are called DCOM objects.

In multitier environments, remote objects typically implement the business logic and run on a separate server from the one that provides the presentation logic.

In a J2EE-based application, Java servlets can provide the presentation functions and EJBs can provide the business logic and interface with the database server. The servlet container communicates with the EJB container with the RMI protocol.

A .NET application can use ASP for presentation purposes and execute the business logic on a DCOM component. The communication between the IIS server and the remote component uses the ORPC protocol.

Network Traffic Patterns: RPC, RMI, ORPC, IIOP

RPCs do not qualify as remote-object technology, yet they provide a simple reference to understanding the network characteristics of such technologies as RMI, ORPC, and IIOP.

An RPC is a procedure invoked from one computer and executed on a different computer. The client computer calls a procedure on the remote computer, on which the procedure waits for requests; once it receives one, it executes the call and returns the results to the client.

The sequence assumes that the client already knows which server can execute the RPC and which protocol and port it is listening to. A mechanism called *binding* takes care of finding this information.

When the client needs to execute a remote call, it sends a query to a well-known port used by RPC, TCP port 111 (the software service listening on this port is called the *portmapper*). The server receives the query with the ID of the procedure that the client needs to invoke. The client also specifies the transport protocol, either TCP or User Datagram Protocol (UDP). The server responds with the port number to which the client should connect.

The presence of a dynamically negotiated port can be a challenge when RPC goes through a firewall unless the firewall explicitly supports the RPC protocol. The reason is that when the client and servers try to connect on the dynamically negotiated port, the firewall, not being configured to allow that port, drops the connection. An RPC-aware firewall instead can spoof the negotiation and open the port that was negotiated. Cisco IOS Context Based Access Control (CBAC), Cisco PIX Firewalls, and the Firewall Services Modules (FWSM) have support for RPC.

RMI is a set of APIs that allow applets or servlets to call remote methods. In RMI, the client-side machine sends a request to TCP port 1099 (the software service listening on this port is called the *registry*). After contacting the server, the client receives the information about the remote object, which includes the hostname and port number of the computer to which it must connect.

Example 3-4 shows the packet that the server sends to the client, when the server IP address is 10.20.20.10 and the port communicated to the client is 0x08ae, which is 2222 in decimal notation. The use of dynamically negotiated ports is typically a problem with firewalls as described for RPC, unless the firewall is RMI aware.

Example 3-4 also highlights the presence of an embedded IP address. This embedded address can be a problem if the server IP address is subject to NAT. A firewall between the client-side machine and the server might not have the capability to translate embedded IP addresses for this specific protocol.

Example 3-4 *An RMI Packet*

```
Java RMI
    Input Stream Message: ReturnData
    Serialization Data
Java Serialization
    Magic: 0xaced
    Version: 5
[...]
00a0  2e 72 6d 69 2e 73 65 72 76 65 72 2e 52 65 6d 6f   .rmi.server.Remo
00b0  74 65 4f 62 6a 65 63 74 d3 61 b4 91 0c 61 33 1e   teObject.a...a3.
00c0  03 00 00 70 78 70 77 34 00 0a 55 6e 69 63 61 73   ...pxpw4..Unicas
00d0  74 52 65 66 00 0b 31 30 2e 32 30 2e 32 30 2e 31   tRef..10.20.20.1
00e0  30 00 00 08 ae 00 00 00 00 00 00 00 00 00 19 29   0..............)
```

NOTE For more information about RMI, refer to http://java.sun.com/products/jdk/rmi/.

For more information on how to pass RMI through firewalls, refer to http://java.sun.com/products/jdk/1.2/docs/guide/rmi/spec/rmi-arch.doc5.html.

DCOM is a library that allows communication among components in the network. With DCOM, a client computer can invoke methods on a remote object. DCOM uses ORPC as the wire format.

In DCOM, a client contacts the server on the TCP or UDP port 153 and obtains the reference to a dynamic port for invoking the method for the remote object.

Just like RPC and RMI, using DCOM through a firewall can be difficult because of dynamically negotiated ports. The section, "Using RMI and DCOM Through a Firewall" provides additional details on how to pass these protocols through a firewall.

NOTE For more information on how to pass DCOM (i.e., ORPC) through firewalls, refer to http://www.microsoft.com/com/wpaper/dcomfw.asp.

CORBA can locate remote objects by means of the ORB, which is software that resides in each server and client in the network. The transport protocol used in the context of CORBA is IIOP. With IIOP, a client uses TCP port 683 to connect to the *naming* service (the equivalent of the registry in RMI) on the server. The server provides the client with the port number where the object is listening for incoming requests. This process can present a problem with firewalls unless the firewall can understand IIOP. Like RPC, RMI, and DCOM, IIOP might not work through a firewall in presence of NAT.

NOTE For more information about IIOP, refer to http://www.omg.org/library/iiop4.html.

Database Access

Databases provide an organized collection of data. Application servers provide processing and storing of data from and into database systems.

The database servers are typically separated from the application servers, or from the PCs that have direct access, by firewalls. This separation requires configuring the firewall to allow Layer 4 protocols and ports that are specific to the installed database system. This section explains where to find the information about the traffic characteristics of databases.

SQL enables you to manage access to the database system by giving you the ability to retrieve specific information or save new information. SQL is an American National Standards Institute (ANSI) and Open Systems Interconnection (OSI) standard in database querying, and it is used by commercial DBMSs, such as Microsoft SQL Server, Oracle, and Sybase, as well as open source DBMSs, such as mSQL or MySQL.

Each DBMS product has different access procedures. A driver installed on the application server provides access to the database. For example, if the application server uses servlets, you would install a JDBC driver provided by the DBMS vendor.

Each programming language accesses databases through a database interface. Good database interfaces make it possible to write applications almost independently of the DBMS they interface to.

Commonly used interfaces are

- JDBC—The interface for Java
- DBI—The interface for Perl
- dbx—The PHP interface
- ODBC—A Microsoft library for applications written in C that is based on SQL
- ActiveX Data Objects (ADO)—Another Microsoft interface to access databases with object-oriented software

Example 3-5 shows what the JDBC interface looks like. For more information about JDBC, refer to http://java.sun.com/products/jdbc/.

Example 3-5 *Database Access with Java*

```
DriverManager.getConnection("jdbc:mysql://10.10.20.14:3306/ski", "username",
  "password");
```

It is important to notice that the traffic pattern between the application server and the database system depends on the database vendor. A Java application using JDBC to connect to MySQL generates a different traffic pattern from the same Java application using JDBC to connect to an Oracle database server.

To find out which ports need to be open on a firewall, you consult the documentation of the database vendor.

The Layer 4 port can also be configurable in the application code, as Example 3-5 shows. (In the example, the TCP port is set to the default for MySQL, which is 3306.)

NOTE Different DBMSs use different ports: MySQL uses 3306, mSQL uses 4333, Microsoft SQL Server uses 1433, Microsoft SQL Monitor uses 1434, and Oracle uses port 1521.

Network Architecture Considerations

Application architectures dictate several aspects of the network design. The section, "Integration of Applications" already outlined some of the design implications of integrating applications and how network devices can help. This section provides additional network design considerations that are driven by application requirements. The two main areas of interest are high availability and security.

High availability is provided by *clustering*, which means executing the same application on multiple servers while providing a single view of the system to the user. How you implement clustering depends on the application. In some cases, you implement clustering by performing server *load balancing* either in hardware or in software; in this chapter, we call this approach simply load balancing. Clustering also refers to the combination of load balancing traffic to a number of servers and the capability of these servers to share resources like a storage disk subsystem; in this section, we call this approach *clustering*.

Security refers to the need to segregate server farms by using firewalls and at the same time to open ports on the firewalls to let the legitimate server-to-server traffic pass. You provide this security by enabling application-specific *fixups* or by configuring ACLs (read Chapter 5).

Load Balancing

The concept of load balancing was introduced in Chapter 2. Chapter 6 describes the load-balancing concepts that are mentioned in this section.

Server load balancing is balancing traffic load across a group of servers. The load balancer is in charge of distributing the load and ensuring the recipients of the load are available.

Load balancing can be performed by software running on the servers or by hardware devices that are in the path between the client and the server farm.

It is out of the scope of this book to describe in detail how software load balancing works, but it is important to understand that software load balancing is subject to scalability limitations.

TIP Software *load balancing* typically requires that all the servers see the clients' requests even if each request is answered by only one server.

This mechanism causes *flooding* of each client request in the Data Center LAN. (Read Chapter 12, "Layer 2 Protocol Essentials," for more information.) *Flooding* means that a single client request which arrives to the server farm is forwarded to all ports on the LAN.

The mechanism that forwards incoming requests to all the servers in the server farm uses multicast MAC addresses or *dummy* unicasts in the Data Center LAN.

A *dummy* unicast MAC address is a MAC that is never used by the servers as a source MAC address when forwarding traffic, so it is never learned by the Ethernet switches. The router device that forwards traffic on the server LAN uses either the multicast MAC address or the dummy unicast as the destination MAC address to reach the servers. Both MAC addresses cause flooding of this traffic on the server LAN.

This flooding is undesirable because it consumes bandwidth. Additionally, all the servers see the client's traffic even if only one server is responding to the client's request. For these reasons, software load balancing is subject to scalability limitations.

Hardware load balancing is a more efficient mechanism for load distribution and high availability because it forwards each client request to only one server in the server farm, thus preserving the LAN bandwidth and optimizing the server-farm performance.

Load balancing is typically applied to these server categories: web servers, application servers, e-mail servers, DNS servers, RADIUS servers, streaming servers, and TN3270 servers.

You can configure load balancers to load-balance almost every protocol used by the applications, but they also have additional intelligence for certain protocols. HTTP is the protocol that load balancers understand better. In addition to HTTP, Cisco load balancers provide special support for SSL, DNS, FTP, POP2, POP3, SMTP, IMAP, streaming protocols, RADIUS, and the Wireless Session Protocol (WSP).

In addition to these protocols, a load balancer can operate on an unlimited number of protocols. You can configure load balancing for a given application if you know the following:

- **The Layer 4 protocols and ports used by the application**—(Often referred to as the *port mappings*.) If the port mappings are well known, you can configure a load balancer to intercept only the protocol/port pairs of interest.
- **Whether or not the application negotiates dynamic ports**—If the application negotiates Layer 4 ports dynamically, these ports cannot be specifically configured on the load balancer. The solution to this problem is to use a *wildcard* Layer 4 port.

- **Whether or not the application uses embedded IP addresses**—Load balancers perform NAT, which means that they hide the real address of the servers (which could be a private IP address) by translating it to a different IP address (which could be a public IP address). This mode of operation is referred to as *directed mode*. If the protocol used by the application carries IP addresses embedded in the payload of TCP or UDP, the load balancer might not be capable of translating these *embedded IP addresses*. The solution is to use the load balancer in *dispatch mode*. Protocols such as FTP or the streaming protocols often do not require dispatch mode because they are automatically translated by the load balancer.

All the protocol/port mappings (including mappings with wildcards) of a given application need to be grouped for the purpose of *session persistence*.

TIP The concepts described in this section apply to the virtual server configuration of a load balancer. Read Chapter 6 to know what a virtual server is, the load-balancing modes of operation (directed mode and dispatch mode), and the basics of session persistence.

Read Chapter 19 for more information about session persistence.

Clustering

Clustering indicates the use of multiple servers that operate as a single device. Clustering provides high availability and load distribution. Business-critical applications are always deployed on clustered servers.

For some applications, such as database servers, e-mail servers, and file servers, clustering requires sharing the storage system so that when one element in the cluster fails, the remaining servers have access to the data that was previously processed by the failed device.

Figure 3-4 shows the topology of a cluster of two servers.

Figure 3-4 *A Two-Node Cluster*

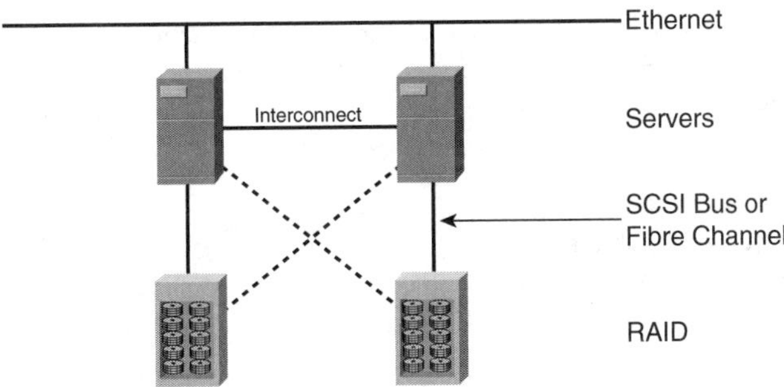

The connectivity between the servers and the storage systems is provided by the I/O channel, which can be a Small Computer System Interface (SCSI) bus, Fibre Channel, Enterprise System Connection (ESCON), or Fibre Connectivity (FICON).

NOTE For more information about ESCON and FICON, see Chapter 14.

As shown in Figure 3-4, clustered topologies are characterized by the following:

- A connection to the Ethernet network on a LAN where the servers receive client requests.
- An *interconnect cable* (or network) that connects the servers directly. The servers use this connection to monitor each other and sometimes to transfer data as well. In most cases, the interconnect can be an Ethernet crossover cable or an Ethernet switch.
- A storage system such as a Redundant Array of Independent Disks (RAID) connected to the servers in the cluster via a SCSI bus or a Fibre Channel network.

Cluster Models

If you want to configure servers to form a cluster, the server needs to run software that implements the clustering functions. Examples are Veritas Cluster Server, HP TruCluster Server, Microsoft Windows NT/2000 Cluster Service (MSCS), Solaris Sun Cluster, HP OpenVMS, and IBM Parallel Sysplex.

NOTE For more information about the IBM Parallel Sysplex, read Chapter 14.

The clustering software can support these clustering options:

- **Active/standby two-node cluster**—This cluster consists of two servers attached to a RAID. One server is active and processes the clients' requests. Data is continuously mirrored from the disks assigned to the primary server to the disks assigned to the backup server. When the primary server fails, the backup server takes over with the same IP address and provides access to the same data that was available on the primary server.
- **Active/active shared nothing**—This architecture consists of a pair of servers, both attached to RAID systems of disks. Even if the disks are physically connected to both servers, each array is owned by one server. Figure 3-4 shows this type of topology.

If a server fails, the other server takes over the operations of the failed server and uses the extra storage connection to mount the volumes previously controlled by the failed server.

- **Active/active shared everything**—This architecture consists of servers connected to the same storage system where the servers can access the same files. A locking system provided by the cluster software prevents concurrent access to a given file. Active/active shared everything clusters are typically used to build clusters with multiple servers. Figure 3-5 shows a cluster of servers connected with Fibre Channel to a shared storage system.

Figure 3-5 *Fibre Channel Storage Cluster*

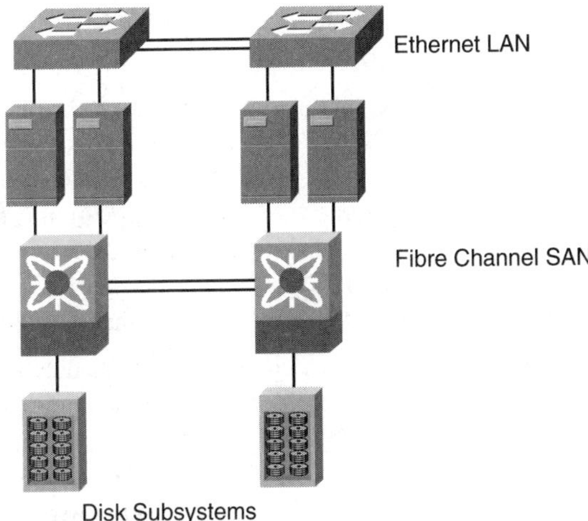

Key network considerations for integrating clusters into the Data Center are the following:

- The traffic exchanged among the servers in the cluster for monitoring purposes can be multicast or unicast. Unicast is preferable because it preserves the LAN bandwidth.
- Active/active shared everything topologies need to replace the interconnect cable with one or more switches in general with a LAN segment.
- Active/active shared everything topologies call for the use of a SAN to connect servers to storage devices, as shown in Figure 3-5.

Geographical Clustering

Geographical clustering consists of clustering servers that are located at different geographical facilities.

TIP By extending clusters geographically, it is possible to make the same application data available at multiple Data Centers, which is the prerequisite to deploying geographical load distribution such as DNS-based site selection. For more information on site selection, see Chapter 10.

The number-one requirement of geographical clustering is that the data available in one Data Center must be replicated at the remote Data Center. The second requirement is that the network must be capable of forwarding client requests to the servers in either Data Center location.

The data replication for cluster environments can take advantage of technologies such as *disk replication* or *host-based replication*:

- **Disk replication**—This technique replicates data at the block level. When the servers of the cluster in the main Data Center write to the disk array, the disk-replication software generates the I/O write to a disk array in the remote Data Center. With this mechanism, the servers are unaware that the replication is taking place because the operation is performed by the disk-management software. Examples of this type of software are EMC Symmetrix Data Remote Facility (SRDF), IBM Peer-to-Peer Remote Copy (PPRC), HP Data Replication Manager (DRM), and Hitachi Truecopy.
- **Host-based replication**—This technique replicates data at the file-system level. Between the file system and the disk driver is the volume manager, which is software that manages the disks and creates a logical view of the physical devices for the use of the file system. With host replication, the volume manager on the server duplicates the writes to the storage system. Examples of this software are Microsoft Windows Local Disk Manager (LDM) and Veritas Volume Manager.

Designing a cluster solution requires validating which type of technology is supported by the clustering software and whether the replication technology is *synchronous* or *asynchronous*.

Synchronous replication means that the server which is performing the write to disk waits for an acknowledgment of the success of the write. Asynchronous replication means that the server does not have to wait for an acknowledgment.

Synchronous technologies are suitable for low-latency networks such as a LAN or when Data Centers are no more than 100 kilometers (km) away. In all other cases, it is preferable to use asynchronous replication. The software typically provides the option to choose either mechanism.

The network design for data replication needs to consider the use of a SAN for the connectivity of the servers to the storage system and the need to connect Data Centers either via the WAN or with metro-optical technologies such as dense wave division multiplexing

(DWDM) and coarse wave division multiplexing (CWDM). You can extend the SAN geographically with the following technologies:

- **iSCSI**—Internet SCSI consists of sending SCSI commands on IP. If you install an iSCSI driver on the server, the volume manager can send SCSI commands to the Ethernet network interface card (NIC). You can use iSCSI for host-based replication to send write commands to a remote storage system through the WAN.
- **Fibre Channel over IP (FCIP)**—This technique consists of tunneling Fibre Channel through the IP network by using routers with a Fibre Channel Port Adapter or a Fibre Channel switch/director with Gigabit Ethernet ports and FCIP capability (such as the Cisco MDS9000 family).
- **SAN extension via CWDM or DWDM**—This technique consists in using CWDM or DWDM to provide Layer 1 connectivity for the SAN between two Data Centers. With DWDM, it is possible to carry Fibre Channel, ESCON, FICON, and Gigabit Ethernet between Data Centers on the same fiber. Figure 3-6 depicts the use of DWDM equipment to multiplex the storage transport protocols into one fiber and demultiplex them at the remote Data Center.

Figure 3-6 *Using DWDM to Connect Distributed Data Centers*

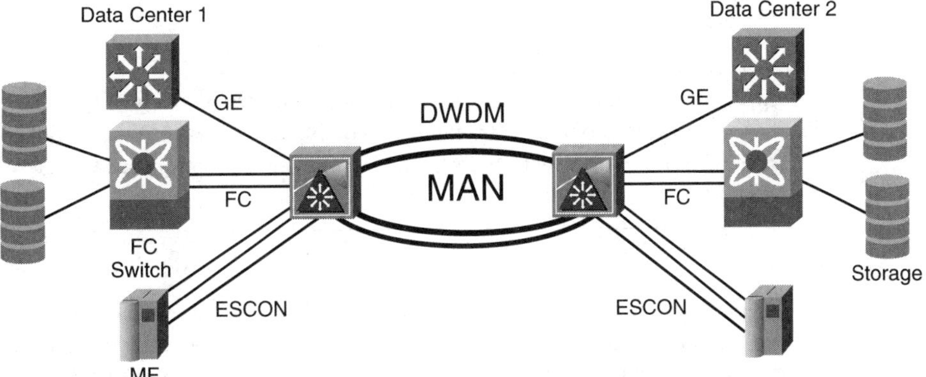

You need to combine the data-replication technologies with a clustering technology that provides a single image of the system of servers. Depending on the clustering software, it might be a requirement that the servers of either Data Center location be on the same LAN. Servers that belong to the same cluster should be able to exchange traffic at Layer 2 between Data Centers. You can use metro-optical technologies such as CWDM or DWDM to extend the LAN by carrying Gigabit Ethernet to the remote Data Center, as depicted in Figure 3-6.

When you choose the transport technology that connects the Data Centers, you should consider the data-replication requirements as well as the possible need to extend the local subnet. Pay careful consideration to stretching a local subnet over the WAN because WANs are built using a hierarchical approach to the IP addressing scheme and the interior gateway protocols (IGPs).

It is out of the scope of this book to describe each transport technology, but as a reference, this list describes the typical options:

- **WAN connectivity**—A typical option for Data Center connectivity over the WAN is to use FCIP over a service provider or enterprise synchronous optical network/synchronous digital hierarchy (SONET/SDH) transport. Replication using an FCIP transport can be synchronous over shorter metropolitan distances with low-latency links but is typically asynchronous over longer distances to avoid impacting application performance from the increased latency.
- **Dark Fiber**—Enterprises can connect Data Centers via dark fiber-enabling transport of Gigabit Ethernet or Fibre Channel or further aggregation through deployment of CWDM, DWDM, Dynamic Packet Transport/Resilient Packet Ring (DPT/RPR), or SONET/SDH.
- **Wavelength services**—In some areas, enterprises can connect Data Centers by leasing wavelength services from a service provider. From a technology standpoint, this choice equates to using a channel from a DWDM network. It enables Gigabit Ethernet, RPR, Fibre Channel, or SONET/SDH connectivity between Data Centers.

NOTE To optimize the use of the WAN bandwidth in high round-trip time (RTT), FCIP-capable devices—such as the Cisco MDS9000 family—you typically use the Window Scale Option (RFC 1323). (For more information about the Window Scale Option, see Chapter 7, "IP, TCP, and UDP").

When designing the Data Center connectivity for high availability, one of the key considerations is the distance between the Data Centers. When you choose the distance, consider whether both Data Centers are within the threat radius of a potential disaster.

The achievable distance depends on the Layer 2 transport technology itself, and Chapter 12 provides the information that applies to Gigabit Ethernet. It also depends on the latency that can be tolerated by the applications that perform the data replication and the applications that perform the disk writes.

Security

Chapter 15 describes the security technologies that are typically used in a Data Center. The deployment of these technologies varies based on whether they are applied at the Internet Edge or in the intranet server farm.

This list summarizes the aspects of the security design that relate to the architecture of the application environment of the Data Center:

- **Security zones**—Server farms are assigned to different virtual LANs (VLANs), and firewalls separate these VLANs and server farms. Servers with similar security requirements are connected on the same LAN and are kept separated from servers that have different requirements. For example, in a multitier application architecture, web servers and database servers are on separate VLANs, and they communicate through a firewall.
- **Port mappings**—Knowing which applications are used in the Data Center lets you decide which protocol/port pairs to open on a firewall. For those applications that open dynamic ports, the best option is to enable fixups on the firewall. A *fixup* is a feature tailored to a specific application, which can listen to the negotiation of dynamic ports between a client and a server and open these ports for the specific flow. This arrangement limits the exposure of the servers to attacks that can take advantage of services which are not in use but have not been disabled on the servers.
- **Signatures**—IDS sensors can detect attacks of many different types. IDS sensors deployed at the Internet Edge should be configured differently from IDS sensors deployed in front of the server farm. For the Internet Edge, it is appropriate to identify possible attacks to the client software carried with client-side programming technologies. IDS sensors placed in front of the server farm should use signatures that capture attacks specific to the server and applications in use.

A common challenge when using firewalls in a multitier server farm is protocols that use dynamically negotiated ports and embedded IP addresses. It is easy to use firewalls with these protocols if they are supported as fixups.

Typical fixups available on Cisco firewalls include HTTP, SMTP, Real Time Streaming Protocol (RTSP), FTP, LDAP, Sun RPC, SQL*NET, H.323, Trivial File Transfer Protocol (TFTP), UNIX rlogin, rexec, rsh, and Internet Control Message Protocol (ICMP).

NOTE For updated information about the supported protocols, refer to the Cisco documentation available on http://www.cisco.com.

Dynamically negotiated ports and embedded IP addresses are typical of the protocols that are used between web/application servers and distributed components and between web/application servers and database servers. Some workarounds are necessary to pass these protocols through the firewalls if the firewall does not support them.

Using RMI and DCOM Through a Firewall

When using RMI for remote communication through firewalls, if you open only port 1099 for the connection to the registry, the communication will not work. After contacting the registry for the reference to the object, the actual call is executed on another port. Another possible problem is performing NAT on the firewall because the firewall does not translate the embedded IP address communicated by the registry to the client.

The trace in Example 3-6 shows a client machine 10.20.20.23 contacting a server machine on port 1099 (packet 1). Packet 10 shows the same client machine contacting the server on port 1067 with another TCP connection. 1099 is, of course, the registry port, and 1067 is the port assigned to the specific object being called. This port is dynamically negotiated, and there is no way for the firewall to know that it needs to open port 1067.

Example 3-6 *RMI Trace*

```
Source                Destination           Protocol Info
1  10.20.20.23           10.20.20.10           TCP      2375 > 1099 [SYN]
2  10.20.20.10           10.20.20.23           TCP      1099 > 2375 [SYN, ACK]
3  10.20.20.23           10.20.20.10           TCP      2375 > 1099 [ACK]
4  10.20.20.23           10.20.20.10           RMI      JRMI, Version: 2,
  StreamProtocol
5  10.20.20.10           10.20.20.23           RMI      JRMI, ProtocolAck
6  10.20.20.23           10.20.20.10           RMI      Continuation
7  10.20.20.23           10.20.20.10           RMI      JRMI, Call
8  10.20.20.10           10.20.20.23           TCP      1099 > 2375 [ACK]
9  10.20.20.10           10.20.20.23           RMI      JRMI, ReturnData
10 10.20.20.23           10.20.20.10           TCP      2376 > 1067 [SYN]
11 10.20.20.10           10.20.20.23           TCP      1067 > 2376 [SYN, ACK]
12 10.20.20.23           10.20.20.10           TCP      2376 > 1067 [ACK]
13 10.20.20.23           10.20.20.10           RMI      JRMI, Version: 2,
  StreamProtocol
14 10.20.20.10           10.20.20.23           RMI      JRMI, ProtocolAck
15 10.20.20.23           10.20.20.10           RMI      Continuation
16 10.20.20.23           10.20.20.10           RMI      JRMI, Call
```

There are several workarounds to make RMI work through the firewalls, and they are described at http://java.sun.com/products/jdk/1.2/docs/guide/rmi/spec/rmi-arch.doc11.html and http://java.sun.com/j2se/1.4.1/docs/guide/rmi/faq.html.

Having a firewall in the path between a DCOM client and a DCOM server can be challenging. DCOM uses the well-known port 135, but the method calls are carried on the top of a dynamically negotiated port. Typically firewalls do not understand DCOM, which means that you need to open a range of ports for DCOM communication.

Another problem is the presence of the server IP address embedded in the response to the client: if the firewall is configured for NAT, this IP is not translated because the firewall does not typically read into the DCOM packets.

The solution to the first problem consists of modifying the configuration on the server machine by using the tool DCOMCFG or by changing the registry file to use a specific range of ports. The registry key is at HKEY_LOCAL_MACHINE\Software\Microsoft\Rpc\Internet.

By doing this step and by configuring the same range of ports on the firewall, you gain better control on the traffic allowed through the firewall.

For more information, refer to the following article at http://msdn.microsoft.com/library/en-us/dndcom/html/msdn_dcomfirewall.asp and the Microsoft documentation.

IDS Signatures

Chapter 5 and Chapter 21 describe the placement of IDS sensors in the Data Center. Network IDS sensors make it possible for the network administrator to monitor the server-farm subnets for traffic that is trying to exploit server vulnerabilities.

The IDS sensors closer to the servers should capture attacks directed to the servers' operating systems, and you should enable only the signatures that apply to the specific application environment. For example, if the business logic is built with CGI, it makes sense to enable signatures like the following:

- WWW count-cgi overflow
- WWW TEST-CGI attack
- WWW CGI valid shell access
- WWW imagemap.cgi attack
- WWW IRIX infosrch.cgi attack

If the application servers in use are based on servlets, you should enable signatures like the following:

- WWW Sun Java Server access
- *.jsp/*.jhtml Java execution
- Java Web Server command exec

If the web servers are Microsoft IIS servers, you should enable the following signatures:

- WWW IIS view source attack
- IIS MDAC RDS buffer overflow
- IIS 5 Translate: f source disclosure
- IIS executable file command exec

The preceding signatures detect attacks against servers. Other signatures detect attacks against clients. The right place to detect these attacks is at the Internet Edge because the enterprise clients connect to the Internet through the firewalls at the Internet Edge. The signatures that you should turn on detect attacks based on client-side programming technologies such as Java applets, ActiveX controls, and JavaScript. Examples of these signatures are

- ActiveX: Active Setup control file upload bug
- Java hostile applet
- Internet Explorer file access bug

The preceding list just provides examples of signatures to enable; there are several more signatures available on Cisco IDS sensors. You can find information about the signatures supported on Cisco IDS devices on the Cisco Secure Encyclopedia at http://www.cisco.com/pcgi-bin/front.x/csec/csecHome.pl.

Multitier Design Case Study

This section illustrates typical multitier architectures and which network design considerations are driven by the application architecture.

The components of web-based multi-tier applications can be placed in a Data Center in many fashions, some of which are pictured in Figure 3-7.

Clients from the Internet or an intranet communicate with web servers. The business logic runs in the application servers, and the database behind the application servers provides storage for data.

You can split the application servers into two separate tiers, one running servlets and JSP, for example, and another providing storage for the components. Part **a** of Figure 3-7 shows the split design, in which the web servers communicate with the servlet engines and the servlet engines access the components available on EJB containers.

In part **a** of Figure 3-7, the web server acts as a proxy for the client request that necessitates dynamically generated web pages: the web server is configured with plug-in software that delivers the client's HTTP request to the servlet engine. As a result, the operations of the first and second tier of servers in part a of Figure 3-7 are as follows:

- **Web servers**—Provide static content, terminate SSL, and wrap requests for other applications into protocols such as AJP and hand them off to the application servers
- **Application servers**—Provide mainly JSP, servlets in servlet engines, and EJB capabilities in EJB containers

A different design uses servlet engines as the first tier of servers because application servers are also HTTP servers. This simplified design is visible in part **b** of Figure 3-7.

Figure 3-7 *Components of Multitier Applications*

a

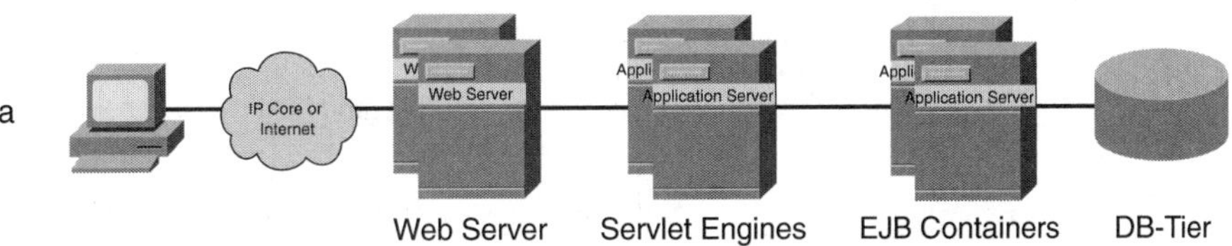

b

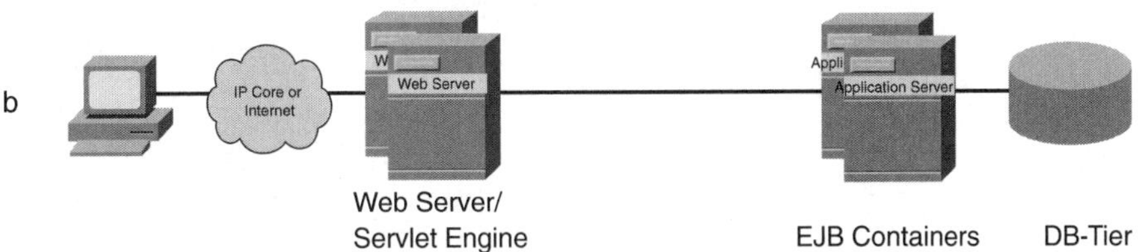

The design of part **a** of Figure 3-7 is more secure because the web servers do not provide any business logic, so for an attack to compromise the application servers, it first needs to compromise the web servers.

Part **b** of Figure 3-7 is a simpler design and more efficient in handling client requests. This section focuses on the design of part **b** of Figure 3-7.

High Availability

Figure 3-8 shows a sample architecture for high availability of a Data Center hosting web applications.

NOTE Notice that Figure 3-8 represents a logical topology and focuses on the functions provided by the network components, not on the number of devices. In an actual network, you would have to deploy redundant load balancers, multiple caches, and multiple SSL offloaders.

Chapter 4, "Data Center Design Overview," describes the design of a fully redundant network.

Figure 3-8 *High Availability for Multitier Applications*

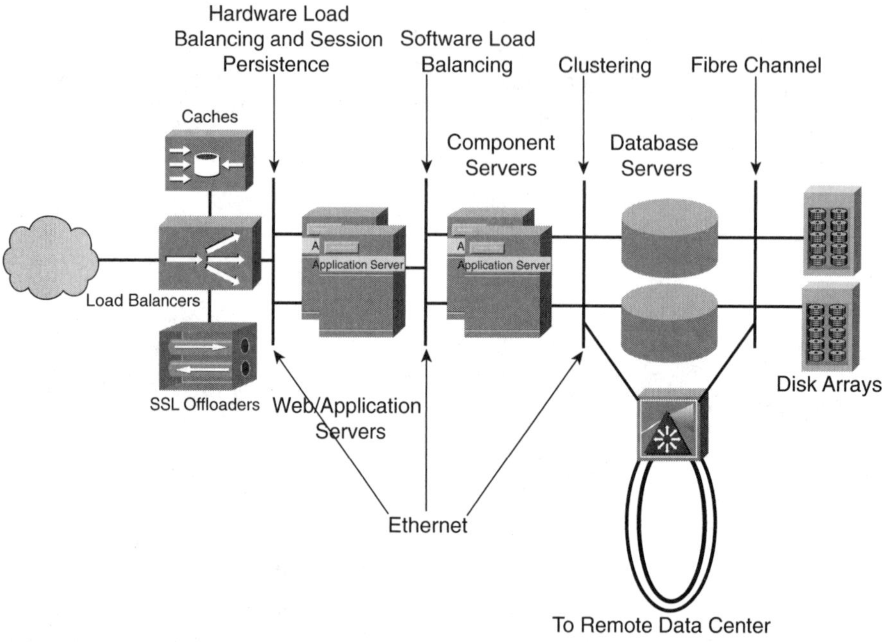

The network devices provide the following services:

- Ethernet switches (not displayed in the picture) provide server attachment to the LAN. Fibre Channel switches (not displayed in the picture) provide server attachment to the SAN.
- The load balancer intercepts HTTP requests. If the request is for a specific application, the load balancer sends the request to the application servers; otherwise, the load balancer sends the request to the cache engines. If the request is encrypted, it is sent to the SSL offloading devices.
- Cache engines store static content and client-side scripts, thus optimizing the application servers for business-logic processing.
- SSL offloaders decrypt traffic carried on SSL, thus offloading the web and application servers from decrypting HTTPS traffic.

Figure 3-8 shows the redundancy mechanisms adopted at each tier of servers.

One key design consideration is that the transient state information of the user session is kept local in the memory of the web/application server. Every time the server receives a new HTTP request from a client, it retrieves this information. Using a database to store and retrieve the session information would be extremely inefficient. The persistent information about a user, such as the orders placed by the user or the account information, should be stored on the database.

The web and application servers rely on hardware load balancing as the high-availability mechanism. You can configure hardware load balancing for session persistence to ensure that a client is consistently assigned to a given web/application server during a user session. The transient state information about the user session is available on the server that the client is assigned to. You can find more information about session persistence by reading Chapters 18 and 19.

TIP Session persistence for web applications is a performance optimization. A design that does not require session persistence consists of sharing the transient state information among web and application servers by saving this information in a shared folder or writing to a database.

Client requests could then be assigned to any server, but for each request, the server would have to retrieve the information from a database, which does not scale well.

High availability between the web/application server and the server that hosts the object components (such as the EJB container) is provided by software-based load balancing.

High availability for the database servers is based on clustering. The database servers are attached to the Ethernet network and to the Fibre Channel network. A DWDM device allows the extension of the cluster across Data Centers.

Security

In multitier application environments, each tier of servers should communicate to another tier of servers via a firewall. The purpose is to isolate compromised servers to prevent the propagation of an attack.

Figure 3-9 shows the logical topology of a multitier server farm with firewalls between each tier. Figure 3-9 also shows the presence of IDS sensors with signatures appropriately tuned for each tier.

The physical topology for the application environment described in Figure 3-9 would consist of a fully redundant topology (such as the one described in Chapter 4), where server farms are segregated by VLANs. (For more information on VLANs, read Chapter 12.) Figure 3-10 clarifies by presenting a physical topology.

Figure 3-9 *Security for Multitier Applications*

Web Server
Application Server
Application Server
Web-Tier
Servlet Engines
EJB Containers
DB-Tier

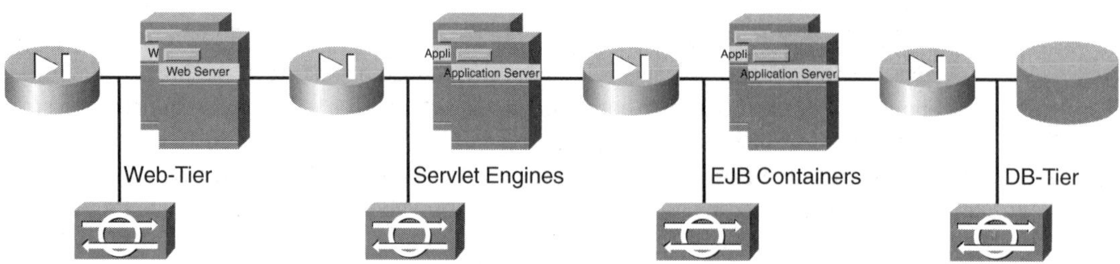

Figure 3-10 *Physical Topology for the Attachment of Security Devices*

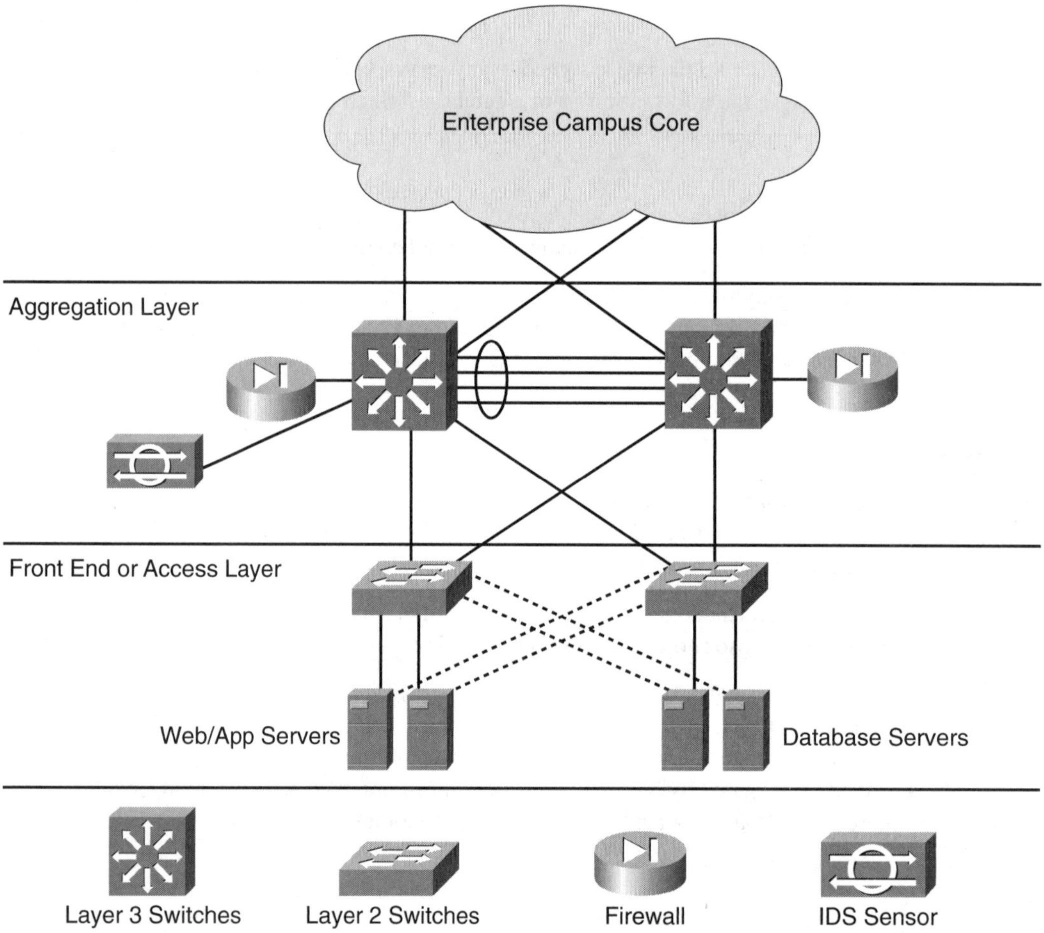

Enterprise Campus Core
Aggregation Layer
Front End or Access Layer
Web/App Servers
Database Servers
Layer 3 Switches
Layer 2 Switches
Firewall
IDS Sensor

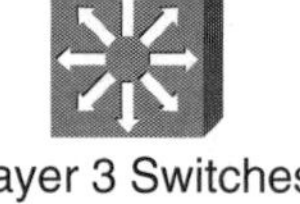

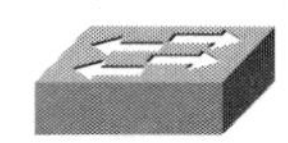

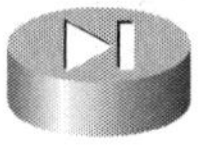

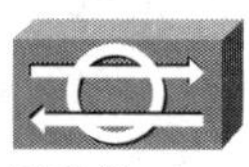

All the servers—web and application servers, component servers, database servers—are attached to the same LAN infrastructure and segregated by VLANs.

Instead of having separate physical firewalls between each server farm, the physical topology uses a single pair of firewalls that route between VLANs. Similarly, you would not have one IDS sensor per server-farm segment on a single device configured to monitor all the server-farm VLANs. You would be using multiple IDS devices if the amount of traffic to monitor exceeds the capacity of a single IDS device.

Summary

The network design of a Data Center is driven by the architecture of the application that needs to be supported. Understanding the application environments used today makes it easier to design the network to provide application high availability and security.

The two main software architectures used today are Sun J2EE and Microsoft .NET. Their respective client-side technologies include JavaScript, applets, and ActiveX components. Their respective server-side technologies include Java servlets and ASP.

Today's applications, whether developed in-house or commercially, are typically based either on the J2EE or the .NET architecture. These architectures let you build multitier applications. Multitier architectures require specific choices in terms of high availability: some server tiers rely on hardware load balancing, and other server tiers use clustering.

You can apply hardware load balancing to a multitude of servers. It is typically necessary to perform hardware load balancing for web and application servers, DNS servers, RADIUS servers, and streaming servers. Session persistence is necessary to optimize the servers' performance.

You use clustering to achieve high availability in the deployment of SANs. If the cluster is extended geographically, you need to evaluate the requirements of the applications that write the data as well as the software that performs data replication. These requirements are typically expressed in terms of latency and throughput. The requirements decide the transport technology and the distance between redundant Data Centers.

The security design of the Data Center consists of placing firewalls between server tiers and of opening ports based on the applications present in the Data Center. RMI, DCOM, and IIOP are typical protocols used within a Data Center. Sometimes, it is difficult to make these protocols work through a firewall; this chapter references documents that explain how to integrate the applications which use these protocols with the firewalls.

Another aspect of the security design consists of enabling IDS signatures in the Data Center and at the Internet Edge. The IDS sensors closer to the servers should capture attacks related to the specific operating systems and application architecture of the server farm. If the server farm is based on the .NET architecture, you should enabled signatures for IIS vulnerabilities; if the server farm is based on J2EE software, you should enable signatures for attacks that exploit servlets, JSP, and Java-based technologies in general.

For Further Reading

Britton, Chris. *IT Architectures and Middleware: Strategies for Building Large, Integrated Systems*. Addison Wesley, 2000.

Deitel, Harvey, Paul Deitel, and Tem Nieto. *Internet & World Wide Web: How to Program*. Prentice Hall, 2001.

This chapter covers the following topics:

- Types of server farms and Data Centers
- Data Center topologies
- Fully redundant Layer 2 and Layer 3 designs
- Fully redundant Layer 2 and Layer 3 designs with services

CHAPTER 4

Data Center Design Overview

This chapter focuses on three main properties of Data Center architectures: scalability, flexibility, and high availability. Data Centers are rapidly evolving to accommodate higher expectations for growth, consolidation, and security. Although the traditional Layer 2 and Layer 3 designs have not changed drastically over the last few years, stringent demands for uptime and service availability, coupled with new technology and protocols, make the design efforts more challenging and demanding.

Demands for scalability, flexibility, and high availability can be summarized as follows:

- **Scalability**—The Data Center must support fast and seamless growth without major disruptions.
- **Flexibility**—The Data Center must support new services without a major overhaul of its infrastructure.
- **High availability**—The Data Center must have no single point of failure and should offer predictable uptime (related to hard failures).

NOTE A hard failure is a failure in which the component must be replaced to return to an operational steady state.

Scalability translates into the capability to sustain rapid growth in performance, the number of devices hosted in the Data Center, and the amount and quality of the services offered. Higher performance implies tolerance to very short-term changes in traffic patterns without packet loss and longer-term plans mapping growth trends to the capacity of the Data Center.

Scalability on the number of hosted devices refers to being capable of seamlessly adding more ports for servers, routers, switches, and any other service devices, such as server load balancers, firewalls, IDSs, and SSL offloaders. Higher density also includes slot density because the number of slots ultimately determines the potential growth of the system.

Flexibility translates into designs that accommodate new service offerings without requiring the complete redesign of the architecture or drastic changes outside the normal periods scheduled for maintenance. The approach to flexibility is a modular design in which the characteristics of the modules are known, and the steps to add more modules are simple.

High availability translates into a fully redundant architecture in which all possible hard failures are predictable and deterministic. This implies that each possible component's failure has a predetermined failover and fallback time, and that the worst-case scenario for a failure condition is still within the acceptable failover limits and is within the requirements as measured from an application availability viewpoint. This means that although the time of failure and recovery of a network component should be predictable and known, the more important time involves the user's perception of the time to recover application service.

NOTE After a failure, the recovery time could be measured from the perspective of the Layer 2 environment (the spanning tree) or from a Layer 3 perspective (the routed network), yet the application availability ultimately matters to the user. If the failure is such that the user connection times out, then, regardless of the convergence time, the network convergence does not satisfy the application requirements. In a Data Center design, it is important to measure recovery time from the perspectives of both the network and the application to ensure a predictable network recovery time for the user (application service).

Figure 4-1 presents an overview of the Data Center, which, as a facility, includes a number of the building blocks and components of the larger enterprise network architecture.

This books deals primarily with the engineering of application environments and their integration to the remaining enterprise network. Different types of server farms support the application environments, yet this book focuses on understanding, designing, deploying, and maintaining the server farms supporting intranet application environments. The actual engineering of the different server farm types—Internet, extranet, and intranet server farms—does not vary much from type to type; however, their integration with the rest of the architecture is different. The design choices that differ for each type of server farm are the result of their main functional purpose. This leads to a specific location for their placement, security considerations, redundancy, scalability, and performance. In addition to the server farm concepts, a brief discussion on the types of server farms further clarifies these points.

NOTE The figures in this chapter contain a wide variety of Cisco icons. Refer to the section, "Icons Used in This Book" (just before the "Introduction") for a list of icons and their descriptions.

Figure 4-1 *Overview of Data Center Topology*

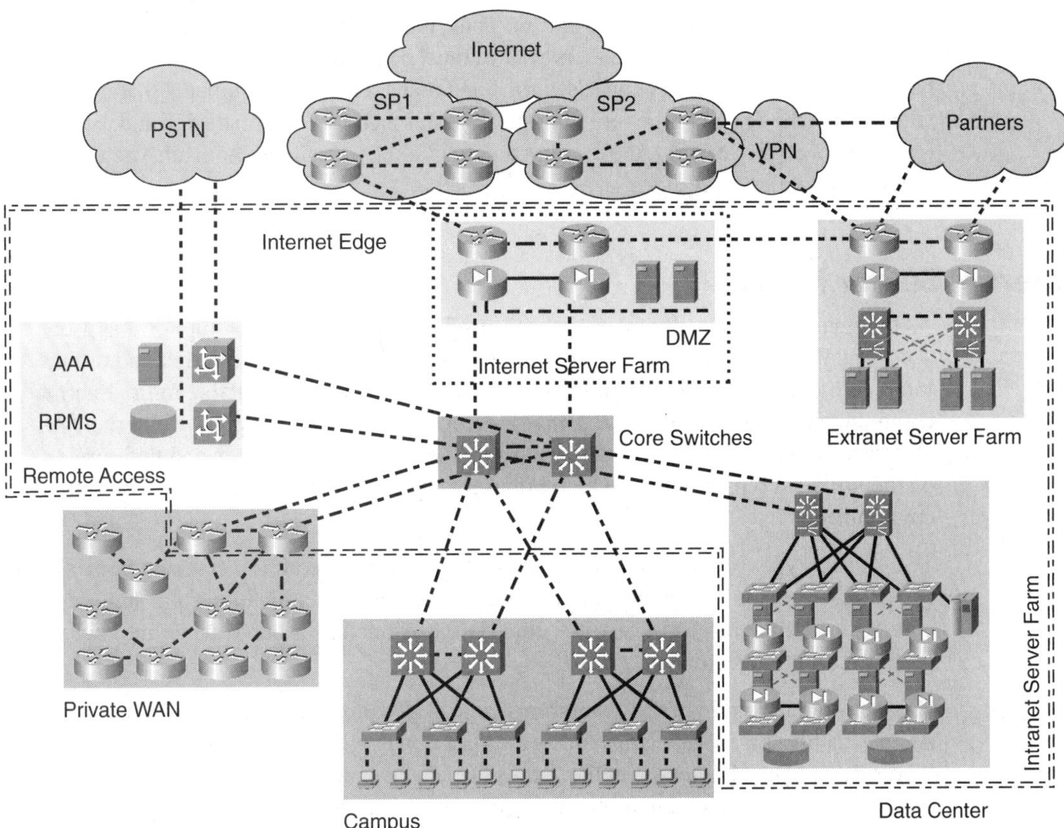

Types of Server Farms and Data Centers

As depicted in Figure 4-1, three distinct types of server farms exist:

- Internet
- Extranet
- Intranet

All three types reside in a Data Center and often in the same Data Center facility, which generally is referred to as the *corporate Data Center* or *enterprise Data Center*. If the sole purpose of the Data Center is to support Internet-facing applications and server farms, the Data Center is referred to as an *Internet Data Center*.

Server farms are at the heart of the Data Center. In fact, Data Centers are built to support at least one type of server farm. Although different types of server farms share many architectural requirements, their objectives differ. Thus, the particular set of Data Center requirements depends on which type of server farm must be supported. Each type of server farm has a distinct set of infrastructure, security, and management requirements that must be addressed in the design of the server farm. Although each server farm design and its specific topology might be different, the design guidelines apply equally to them all. The following sections introduce server farms.

Internet Server Farms

As their name indicates, Internet server farms face the Internet. This implies that users accessing the server farms primarily are located somewhere on the Internet and use the Internet to reach the server farm. Internet server farms are then available to the Internet community at large and support business-to-consumer services. Typically, internal users also have access to the Internet server farms. The server farm services and their users rely on the use of web interfaces and web browsers, which makes them pervasive on Internet environments.

Two distinct types of Internet server farms exist. The dedicated Internet server farm, shown in Figure 4-2, is built to support large-scale Internet-facing applications that support the core business function. Typically, the core business function is based on an Internet presence or Internet commerce.

In general, dedicated Internet server farms exist to sustain the enterprise's e-business goals. Architecturally, these server farms follow the Data Center architecture introduced in Chapter 1, "Overview of Data Centers," yet the details of each layer and the necessary layers are determined by the application environment requirements. Security and scalability are a major concern in this type of server farm. On one hand, most users accessing the server farm are located on the Internet, thereby introducing higher security risks; on the other hand, the number of likely users is very high, which could easily cause scalability problems.

The Data Center that supports this type of server farm is often referred to as an Internet Data Center (IDC). IDCs are built both by enterprises to support their own e-business infrastructure and by service providers selling hosting services, thus allowing enterprises to collocate the e-business infrastructure in the provider's network.

The next type of Internet server farm, shown in Figure 4-3, is built to support Internet-based applications in addition to Internet access from the enterprise. This means that the infrastructure supporting the server farms also is used to support Internet access from enterprise users. These server farms typically are located in the demilitarized zone (DMZ) because they are part of the enterprise network yet are accessible from the Internet. These server farms are referred to as DMZ server farms, to differentiate them from the dedicated Internet server farms.

Figure 4-2 *Dedicated Internet Server Farms*

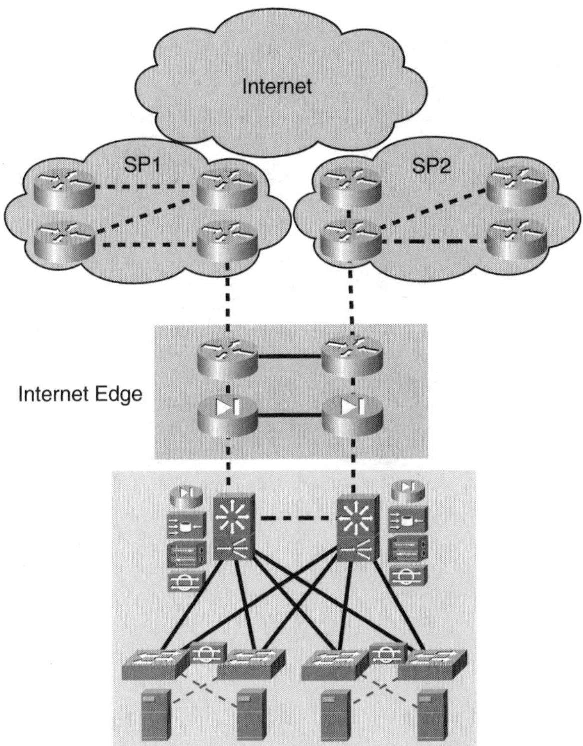

These server farms support services such as e-commerce and are the access door to portals for more generic applications used by both Internet and intranet users. The scalability considerations depend on how large the expected user base is. Security requirements are also very stringent because the security policies are aimed at protecting the server farms from external users while keeping the enterprise's network safe. Note that, under this model, the enterprise network supports the campus, the private WAN, and the intranet server farm.

NOTE Notice that Figure 4-3 depicts a small number of servers located on a segment off the firewalls. Depending on the requirements, the small number of servers could become hundreds or thousands, which would change the topology to include a set of Layer 3 switches and as many Layers 2 switches for server connectivity as needed.

Figure 4-3 *DMZ Server Farms*

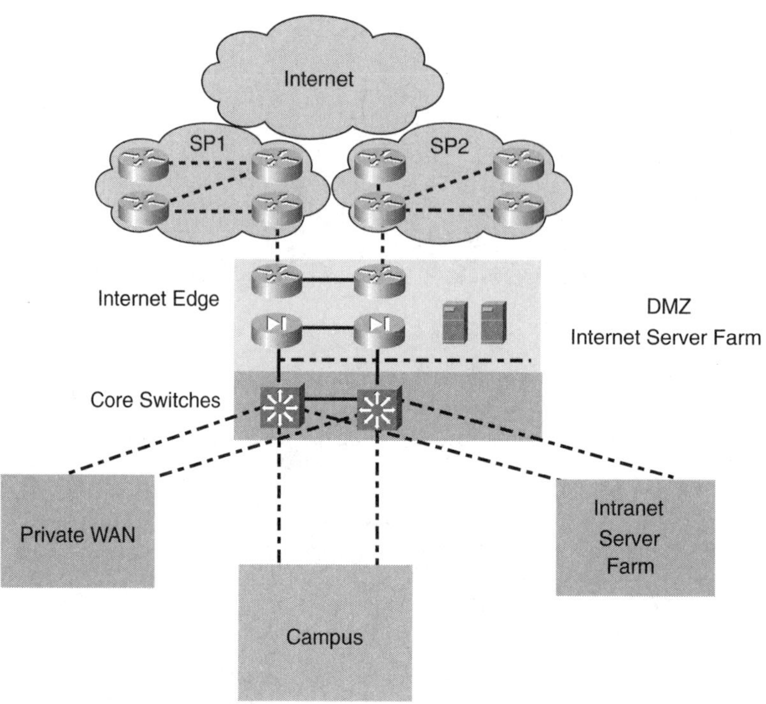

Intranet Server Farms

The evolution of the client/server model and the wide adoption of web-based applications on the Internet was the foundation for building intranets. Intranet server farms resemble the Internet server farms in their ease of access, yet they are available only to the enterprise's internal users. As described earlier in this chapter, intranet server farms include most of the enterprise-critical computing resources that support business processes and internal applications. This list of critical resources includes midrange and mainframe systems that support a wide variety of applications. Figure 4-4 illustrates the intranet server farm.

Notice that the intranet server farm module is connected to the core switches that form a portion of the enterprise backbone and provide connectivity between the private WAN and Internet Edge modules. The users accessing the intranet server farm are located in the campus and private WAN. Internet users typically are not permitted access to the intranet; however, internal users using the Internet as transport have access to the intranet using virtual private network (VPN) technology.

Figure 4-4 *Intranet Server Farms*

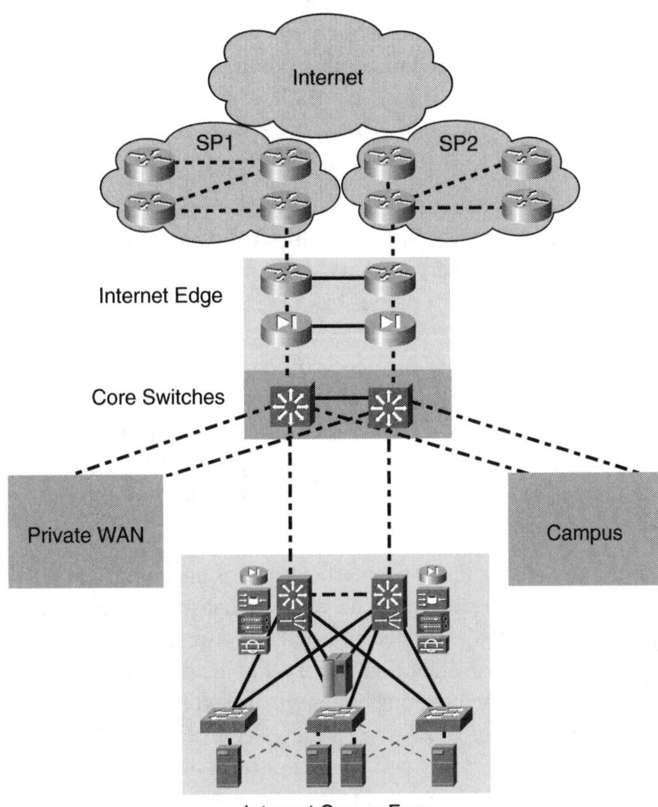

The Internet Edge module supports several functions that include the following:

- Securing the enterprise network
- Controlling Internet access from the intranet
- Controlling access to the Internet server farms

The Data Center provides additional security to further protect the data in the intranet server farm. This is accomplished by applying the security policies to the edge of the Data Center as well as to the applicable application tiers when attempting to harden communication between servers on different tiers. The security design applied to each tier depends on the architecture of the applications and the desired security level.

The access requirements of enterprise users dictate the size and architecture of the server farms. The growing number of users, as well as the higher load imposed by rich applications, increases the demand placed on the server farm. This demand forces scalability to become a critical design criterion, along with high availability, security, and management.

Extranet Server Farms

From a functional perspective, extranet server farms sit between Internet and intranet server farms. Extranet server farms continue the trend of using web-based applications, but, unlike Internet- or intranet-based server farms, they are accessed only by a selected group of users that are neither Internet- nor intranet-based. Extranet server farms are mainly available to business partners that are considered external yet trusted users. The main purpose for extranets is to improve business-to-business communication by allowing faster exchange of information in a user-friendly and secure environment. This reduces time to market and the cost of conducting business. The communication between the enterprise and its business partners, traditionally supported by dedicated links, rapidly is being migrated to a VPN infrastructure because of the ease of the setup, lower costs, and the support for concurrent voice, video, and data traffic over an IP network.

As explained previously, the concept of extranet is analogous to the IDC, in that the server farm is at the edge of the enterprise network. Because the purpose of the extranet is to provide server farm services to trusted external end users, there are special security considerations. These security considerations imply that the business partners have access to a subset of the business applications but are restricted from accessing the rest of the enterprise network. Figure 4-5 shows the extranet server farm. Notice that the extranet server farm is accessible to internal users, yet access from the extranet to the intranet is prevented or highly secured. Typically, access from the extranet to the intranet is restricted through the use of firewalls.

Many factors must be considered in the design of the extranet topology, including scalability, availability, and security. Dedicated firewalls and routers in the extranet are the result of a highly secure and scalable network infrastructure for partner connectivity, yet if there are only a small number of partners to deal with, you can leverage the existing Internet Edge infrastructure. Some partners require direct connectivity or dedicated private links, and others expect secure connections through VPN links. The architecture of the server farm does not change whether you are designing Internet or intranet server farms. The design guidelines apply equally to all types of server farms, yet the specifics of the design are dictated by the application environment requirements.

Figure 4-5 *Extranet Server Farms*

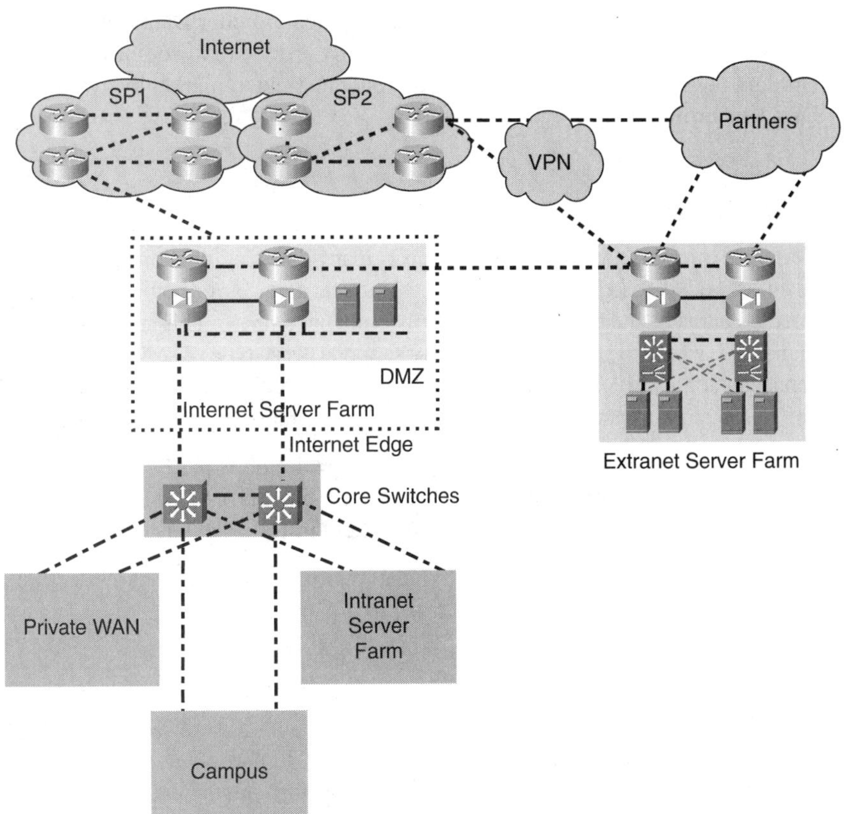

The following section discusses the types of Data Centers briefly mentioned in this section.

Internet Data Center

Internet Data Centers (IDCs) traditionally are built and operated by service providers, yet enterprises whose business model is based on Internet commerce also build and operate IDCs. The architecture of enterprise IDCs is very similar to that of the service provider IDCs, but the requirements for scalability are typically lower because the user base tends to be smaller and there are fewer services compared with those of SP IDCs hosting multiple customers.

In fact, the architecture of the IDC is the same as that presented in Figure 4-2. An interesting consideration of enterprise IDCs is that if the business model calls for it, the facilities used by the Data Center could be collocated in a service provider Data Center, but it remains under the control of the enterprise. This typically is done to lower the costs associated with building the server farm and reducing a product's time to market by avoiding building a Data Center internally from the ground up.

Corporate Data Center

Corporate or enterprise Data Centers support many different functions that enable various business models based on Internet services, intranet services, or both. As a result, support for Internet, intranet, and extranet server farms is not uncommon. This concept was depicted in Figure 4-1, where the Data Center facility supports every type of server farm and also is connected to the rest of the enterprise network—private WAN, campus, Internet Edge, and so on. The support of intranet server farms is still the primary target of corporate Data Centers.

Enterprise Data Centers are evolving, and this evolution is partly a result of new trends in application environments, such as the n-tier, web services, and grid computing, but it results mainly because of the criticality of the data held in Data Centers.

The following section discusses the typical topologies used in the architecture of the Data Center.

Data Center Topologies

This section discusses Data Center topologies and, in particular, the server farm topology. Initially, the discussion focuses on the traffic flow through the network infrastructure (on a generic topology) from a logical viewpoint and then from a physical viewpoint.

Generic Layer 3/Layer 2 Designs

The generic Layer 3/Layer 2 designs are based on the most common ways of deploying server farms. Figure 4-6 depicts a generic server farm topology that supports a number of servers.

NOTE Notice that the distribution layer now is referred to as the aggregation layer resulting from becoming the aggregation point for most, if not all, services beyond the traditional Layer 2 and Layer 3.

Figure 4-6 *Generic Server Farm Design*

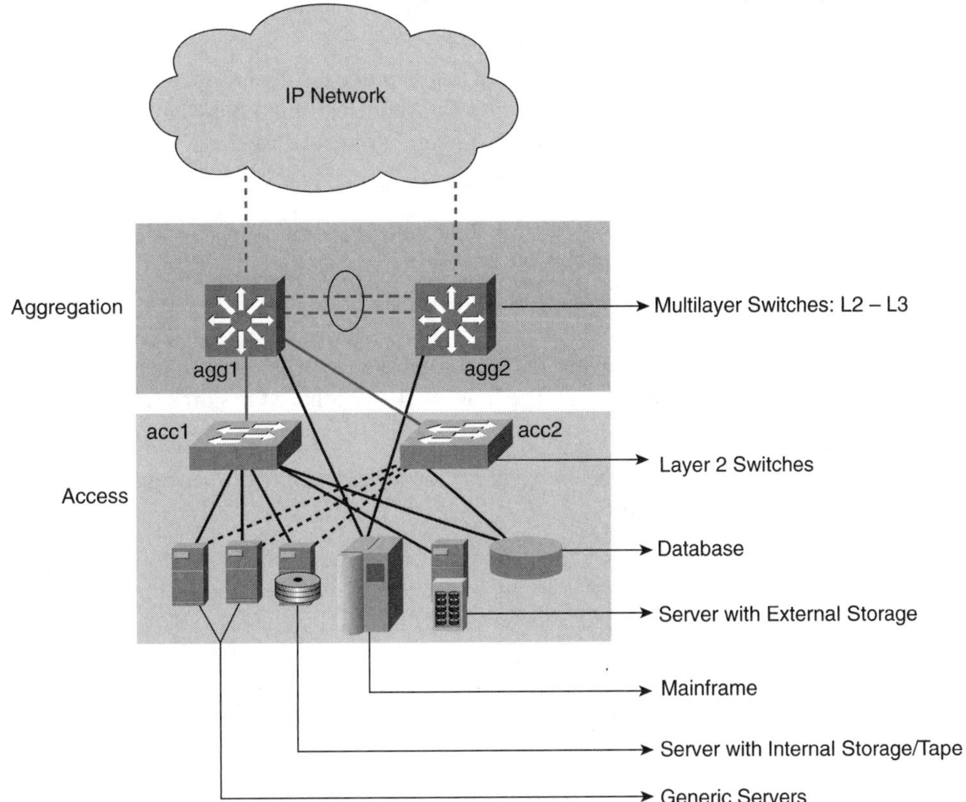

The highlights of the topology are the aggregation-layer switches that perform key Layer 3 and Layer 2 functions, the access-layer switches that provide connectivity to the servers in the server farm, and the connectivity between the aggregation and access layer switches.

The key Layer 3 functions performed by the aggregation switches are as follows:

- Forwarding packets based on Layer 3 information between the server farm and the rest of the network
- Maintaining a "view" of the routed network that is expected to change dynamically as network changes take place
- Supporting default gateways for the server farms

The key Layer 2 functions performed by the aggregation switches are as follows:

- Spanning Tree Protocol (STP) 802.1d between aggregation and access switches to build a loop-free forwarding topology.
- STP enhancements beyond 802.1d that improve the default spanning-tree behavior, such as 802.1s, 802.1w, Uplinkfast, Backbonefast, and Loopguard. For more information, refer to Chapter 12, "Layer 2 Protocol Essentials."
- VLANs for logical separation of server farms.
- Other services, such as multicast and ACLs for services such as QoS, security, rate limiting, broadcast suppression, and so on.

The access-layer switches provide direct connectivity to the server farm. The types of servers in the server farm include generic servers such as DNS, DHCP, FTP, and Telnet; mainframes using SNA over IP or IP; and database servers. Notice that some servers have both internal disks (storage) and tape units, and others have the storage externally connected (typically SCSI).

The connectivity between the two aggregation switches and between aggregation and access switches is as follows:

- EtherChannel between aggregation switches. The channel is in trunk mode, which allows the physical links to support as many VLANs as needed (limited to 4096 VLANs resulting from the 12-bit VLAN ID).
- Single or multiple links (EtherChannel, depending on how much oversubscription is expected in the links) from each access switch to each aggregation switch (uplinks). These links are also trunks, thus allowing multiple VLANs through a single physical path.
- Servers dual-homed to different access switches for redundancy. The NIC used by the server is presumed to have two ports in an active-standby configuration. When the primary port fails, the standby takes over, utilizing the same MAC and IP addresses that the active port was using. For more information about dual-homed servers, refer to Chapter 2, "Server Architecture Overview."

The typical configuration for the server farm environment just described is presented in Figure 4-7.

Figure 4-7 shows the location for the critical services required by the server farm. These services are explicitly configured as follows:

- agg1 is explicitly configured as the STP root.
- agg2 is explicitly configured as the secondary root.
- agg1 is explicitly configured as the primary default gateway.
- agg2 is explicitly configured as the standby or secondary default gateway.

Figure 4-7 *Common Server Farm Environment*

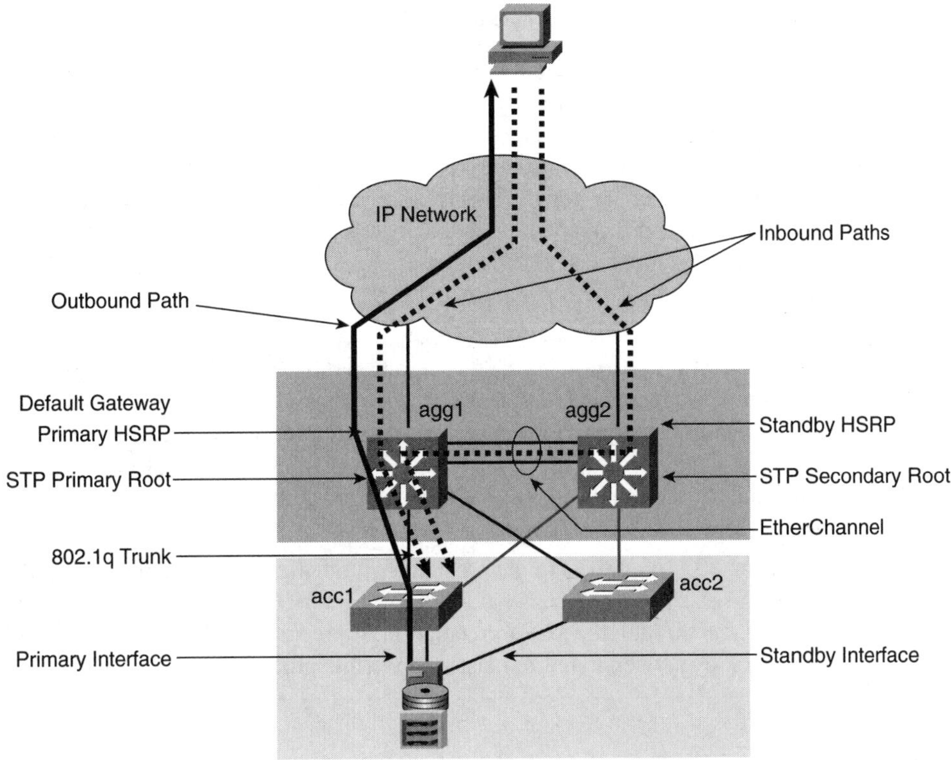

NOTE The explicit definition of these critical functions sets the primary and alternate paths to and from the server farm. Notice that there is no single point of failure in the architecture, and the paths are now deterministic.

Other STP services or protocols, such as UplinkFast, are also explicitly defined between the aggregation and access layers. These services/protocols are used to lower convergence time during failover conditions from the 802.d standard of roughly 50 seconds to 1 to 3 seconds.

In this topology, the servers are configured to use the agg1 switch as the primary default gateway, which means that outbound traffic from the servers follows the direct path to the agg1 switch. Inbound traffic can arrive at either aggregation switch, yet the traffic can reach the server farm only through agg1 because the links from agg2 to the access switches are not forwarding (blocking). The inbound paths are represented by the dotted arrows, and the outbound path is represented by the solid arrow.

The next step is to have predictable failover and fallback behavior, which is much simpler when you have deterministic primary and alternate paths. This is achieved by failing every component in the primary path and recording and tuning the failover time to the backup component until the requirements are satisfied. The same process must be done for falling back to the original primary device. This is because the failover and fallback processes are not the same. In certain instances, the fallback can be done manually instead of automatically, to prevent certain undesirable conditions.

NOTE When using 802.1d. if the primary STP root fails and the secondary takes over, when it comes back up, it automatically takes over because it has a lower priority. In an active server farm environment, you might not want to have the STP topology change automatically, particularly when the convergence time is in the range of 50 seconds. However, this behavior is not applicable when using 802.1w, in which the fallback process takes only a few seconds.

Whether using 802.1d or 802.1w, the process is automatic, unlike when using HSRP, in which the user can control the behavior of the primary HSRP peer when it becomes operational again through the use of preemption. If preemption is not used, the user has manual control over when to return mastership to the initial master HSRP peer.

The use of STP is the result of a Layer 2 topology, which might have loops that require an automatic mechanism to be detected and avoided. An important question is whether there is a need for Layer 2 in a server farm environment. This topic is discussed in the following section.

For more information about the details of the Layer 2 design, see Chapter 20, "Designing the Data Center Infrastructure."

The Need for Layer 2 at the Access Layer

Access switches traditionally have been Layer 2 switches. This holds true also for the campus network wiring closet. This discussion is focused strictly on the Data Center because it has distinct and specific requirements, some similar to and some different than those for the wiring closets.

The reason access switches in the Data Center traditionally have been Layer 2 is the result of the following requirements:

- When they share specific properties, servers typically are grouped on the same VLAN. These properties could be as simple as ownership by the same department or performance of the same function (file and print services, FTP, and so on). Some servers that perform the same function might need to communicate with one another, whether as a result of a clustering protocol or simply as part of the application function. This communication exchange should be on the same subnet and sometimes is possible only on the same subnet if the clustering protocol heartbeats or the server-to-server application packets are not routable.
- Servers are typically dual-homed so that each leg connects to a different access switch for redundancy. If the adapter in use has a standby interface that uses the same MAC and IP addresses after a failure, the active and standby interfaces must be on the same VLAN (same default gateway).
- Server farm growth occurs horizontally, which means that new servers are added to the same VLANs or IP subnets where other servers that perform the same functions are located. If the Layer 2 switches hosting the servers run out of ports, the same VLANs or subnets must be supported on a new set of Layer 2 switches. This allows flexibility in growth and prevents having to connect two access switches.
- When using stateful devices that provide services to the server farms, such as load balancers and firewalls, these stateful devices expect to see both the inbound and outbound traffic use the same path. They also need to constantly exchange connection and session state information, which requires Layer 2 adjacency. More details on these requirements are discussed in the section, "Access Layer," which is under the section, "Multiple Tier Designs."

Using just Layer 3 at the access layer would prevent dual-homing, Layer 2 adjacency between servers on different access switches, and Layer 2 adjacency between service devices. Yet if these requirements are not common on your server farm, you could consider a Layer 3 environment in the access layer. Before you decide what is best, it is important that you read the section titled "Fully Redundant Layer 2 and Layer 3 Designs with Services," later in the chapter. New service trends impose a new set of requirements in the architecture that must be considered before deciding which strategy works best for your Data Center.

The reasons for migrating away from a Layer 2 access switch design are motivated by the need to drift away from spanning tree because of the slow convergence time and the operation challenges of running a controlled loopless topology and troubleshooting loops when they occur. Although this is true when using 802.1d, environments that take advantage of 802.1w combined with Loopguard have the following characteristics: They do not suffer from the same problems, they are as stable as Layer 3 environments, and they support low convergence times.

NOTE The STP standard 802.1d has limitations in addressing certain conditions in addition to its convergence time, yet a fair amount of spanning tree–related problems are the result of misconfiguration or rogue STP devices that appear on the network and "bridge" between Layer 2 domains. More information on this topic is presented in Chapter 12.

The next section discusses an alternate solution for a topology with spanning tree that does not present the STP problems or limitations.

Alternate Layer 3/Layer 2 Designs

Figure 4-8 presents an alternate Layer 3/Layer 2 design resulting from the need to address STP limitations.

Figure 4-8 *Loopless Topology*

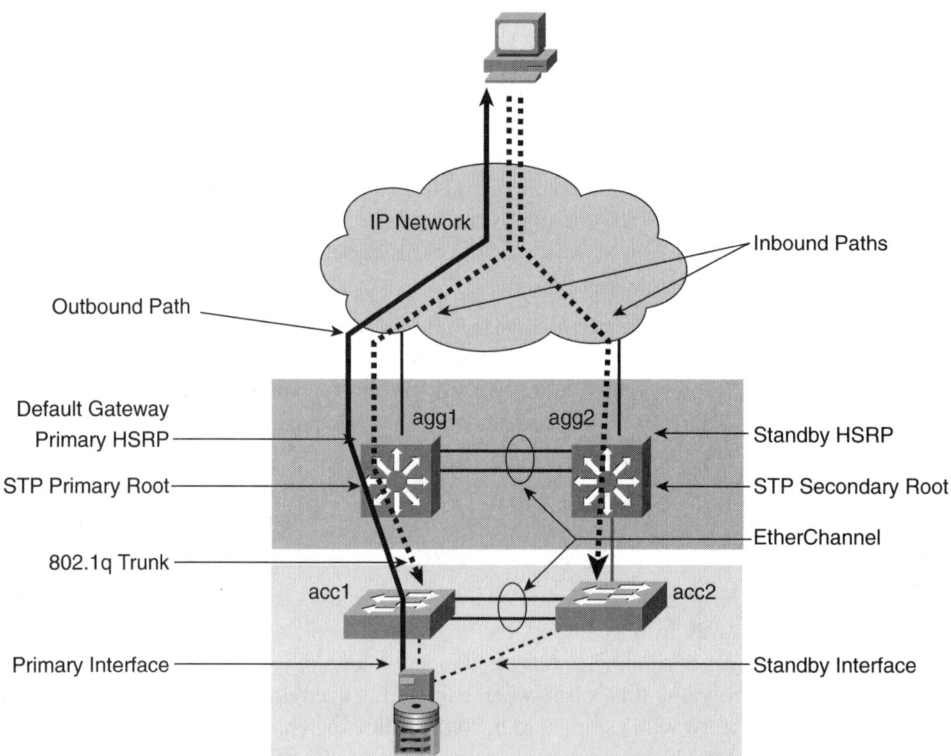

Figure 4-8 presents a topology in which the network purposely is designed not to have loops. Although STP is running, its limitations do not present a problem. This loopless topology is accomplished by removing or not allowing the VLAN(s), used at the access-layer switches, through the trunk between the two aggregation switches. This basically prevents a loop in the topology while it supports the requirements behind the need for Layer 2.

In this topology, the servers are configured to use the agg1 switch as the primary default gateway. This means that outbound traffic from the servers connected to acc2 traverses the link between the two access switches. Inbound traffic can use either aggregation switch because both have active (nonblocking) paths to the access switches. The inbound paths are represented by the dotted arrows, and the outbound path is represented by the solid arrows.

This topology is not without its own challenges. These challenges are discussed later in the chapter after other information related to the deployment of services becomes available.

Multiple-Tier Designs

Most applications conform to either the client/server model or the n-tier model, which implies most networks, and server farms support these application environments. The tiers supported by the Data Center infrastructure are driven by the specific applications and could be any combination in the spectrum of applications from the client/server to the client/web server/application server/database server. When you identify the communication requirements between tiers, you can determine the needed specific network services. The communication requirements between tiers are typically higher scalability, performance, and security. These could translate to load balancing between tiers for scalability and performance, or SSL between tiers for encrypted transactions, or simply firewalling and intrusion detection between the web and application tier for more security.

Figure 4-9 introduces a topology that helps illustrate the previous discussion.

Notice that Figure 4-9 is a logical diagram that depicts layer-to-layer connectivity through the network infrastructure. This implies that the actual physical topology might be different. The separation between layers simply shows that the different server functions could be physically separated. The physical separation could be a design preference or the result of specific requirements that address communication between tiers.

For example, when dealing with web servers, the most common problem is scaling the web tier to serve many concurrent users. This translates into deploying more web servers that have similar characteristics and the same content so that user requests can be equally fulfilled by any of them. This, in turn, requires the use of a load balancer in front of the server farm that hides the number of servers and virtualizes their services. To the users, the specific service is still supported on a single server, yet the load balancer dynamically picks a server to fulfill the request.

Figure 4-9 *Multiple-Tier Application Environments*

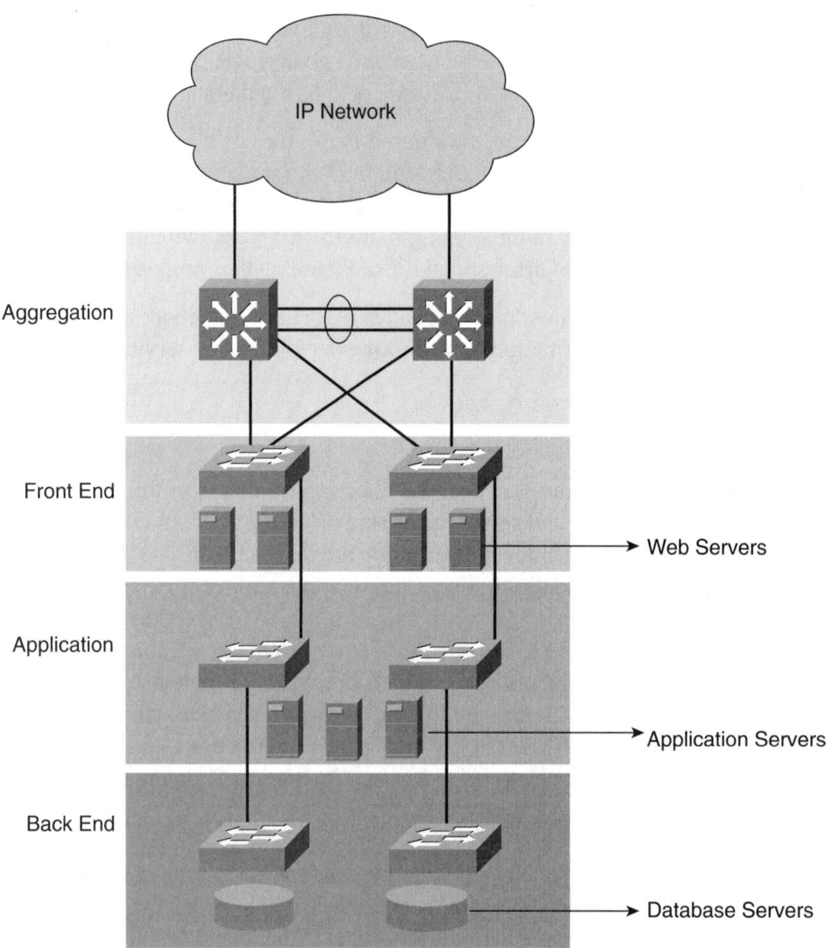

Suppose that you have multiple types of web servers supporting different applications, and some of these applications follow the n-tier model. The server farm could be partitioned along the lines of applications or functions. All web servers, regardless of the application(s) they support, could be part of the same server farm on the same subnet, and the application servers could be part of a separate server farm on a different subnet and different VLAN.

Following the same logic used to scale the web tier, a load balancer logically could be placed between the web tier and the application tier to scale the application tier from the web tier perspective. A single web server now has multiple application servers to access.

The same set of arguments holds true for the need for security at the web tier and a separate set of security considerations at the application tier. This implies that firewall and intrusion-detection capabilities are distinct at each layer and, therefore, are customized for the requirements of the application and the database tiers. SSL offloading is another example of a function that the server farm infrastructure might support and can be deployed at the web tier, the application tier, and the database tier. However, its use depends upon the application environment using SSL to encrypt client-to-server and server-to-server traffic.

Expanded Multitier Design

The previous discussion leads to the concept of deploying multiple network-based services in the architecture. These services are introduced in Figure 4-10 through the use of icons that depict the function or service performed by the network device.

NOTE Figure 4-10 introduces the icons used through this chapter to depict the services provided by network devices in the Data Center.

The different icons are placed in front of the servers for which they perform the functions. At the aggregation layer, you find the load balancer, firewall, SSL offloader, intrusion-detection system, and cache. These services are available through service modules (line cards that could be inserted into the aggregation switch) or appliances. An important point to consider when dealing with service devices is that they provide scalability and high availability beyond the capacity of the server farm, and that to maintain the basic premise of "no single point of failure," at least two must be deployed. If you have more than one (and considering you are dealing with redundancy of application environments), the failover and fallback processes require special mechanisms to recover the connection context, in addition to the Layer 2 and Layer 3 paths. This simple concept of redundancy at the application layer has profound implications in the network design.

Figure 4-10 *Network Service Icons*

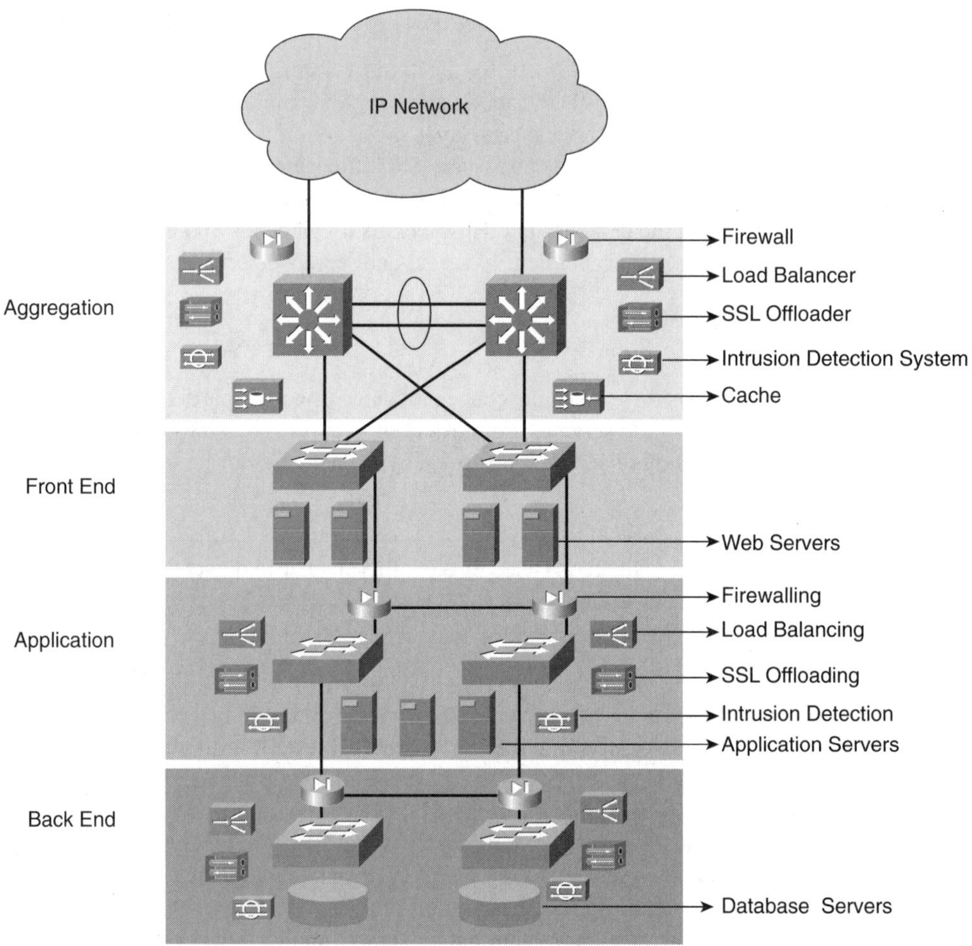

A number of these network service devices are replicated in front of the application layer to provide services to the application servers. Notice in Figure 4-10 that there is physical separation between the tiers of servers. This separation is one alternative to the server farm design. Physical separation is used to achieve greater control over the deployment and scalability of services. The expanded design is more costly because it uses more devices, yet it allows for more control and better scalability because the devices in the path handle only a portion of the traffic. For example, placing a firewall between tiers is regarded as a more secure approach because of the physical separation between the Layer 2 switches.

This argument is correct, yet it is likely to be much more related to an existing security policy than a real threat. Having logical instead of physical separation simply requires a consistent application of security policies to ensure that the expanded security zone is as secure logically as it is physically.

This brings the discussion to another alternative of designing the multitier server farm, an alternative in which there is no physical separation, but rather a logical separation between tiers, as presented in the next section.

Collapsed Multitier Design

A collapsed multitier design is one in which all the server farms are directly connected at the access layer to the aggregation switches, and there is no physical separation between the Layer 2 switches that support the different tiers. Figure 4-11 presents the collapsed design.

Figure 4-11 *Collapsed Multiple-Tier Design*

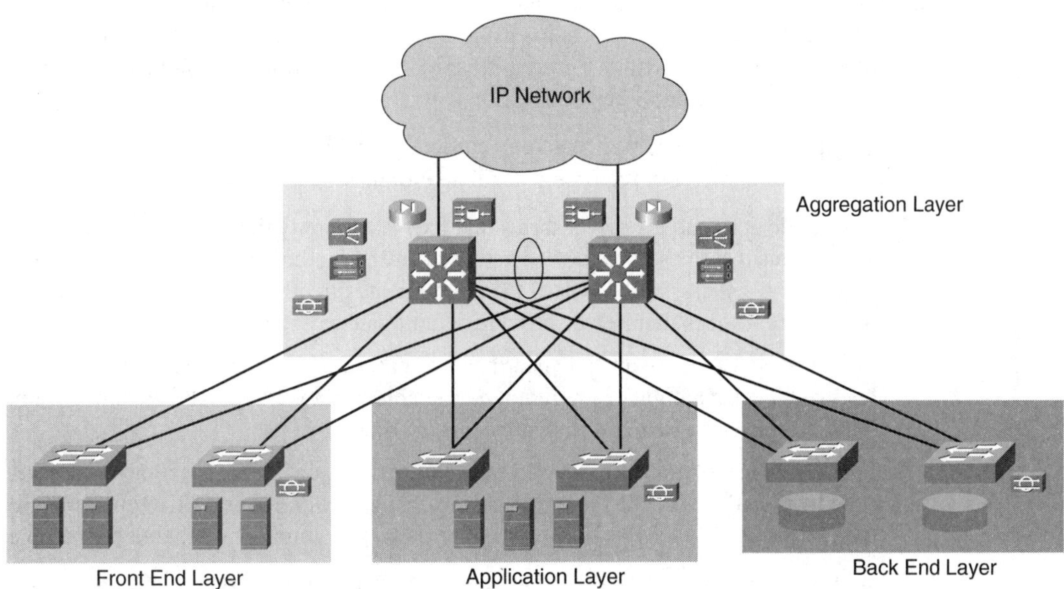

Notice that in this design, the services again are concentrated at the aggregation layer, and the service devices now are used by the front-end tier and between tiers. Using a collapsed model, there is no need to have a set of load balancers or SSL offloaders dedicated to a particular tier. This reduces cost, yet the management of devices is more challenging and the performance demands are higher. The service devices, such as the firewalls, protect all server tiers from outside the Data Center, but also from each other. The load balancer also can be used concurrently to load-balance traffic from client to web servers, and traffic from web servers to application servers.

Notice that the design in Figure 4-11 shows each type of server farm on a different set of switches. Other collapsed designs might combine the same physical Layer 2 switches to house web applications and database servers concurrently. This implies merely that the servers logically are located on different IP subnets and VLANs, yet the service devices still are used concurrently for the front end and between tiers. Notice that the service devices are always in pairs. Pairing avoids the single point of failure throughout the architecture. However, both service devices in the pair communicate with each other, which falls into the discussion of whether you need Layer 2 or Layer 3 at the access layer.

The Need for Layer 2 at the Access Layer

Each pair of service devices must maintain state information about the connections the pair is handling. This requires a mechanism to determine the active device (master) and another mechanism to exchange connection state information on a regular basis. The goal of the dual–service device configuration is to ensure that, upon failure, the redundant device not only can continue service without interruption, but also seamlessly can failover without disrupting the current established connections.

In addition to the requirements brought up earlier about the need for Layer 2, this section discusses in depth the set of requirements related to the service devices:

- Service devices and the server farms that they serve are typically Layer 2–adjacent. This means that the service device has a leg sitting on the same subnet and VLAN used by the servers, which is used to communicate directly with them. Often, in fact, the service devices themselves provide default gateway support for the server farm.
- Service devices must exchange heartbeats as part of their redundancy protocol. The heartbeat packets might or might not be routable; if they are routable, you might not want the exchange to go through unnecessary Layer 3 hops.
- Service devices operating in stateful failover need to exchange connection and session state information. For the most part, this exchange is done over a VLAN common to the two devices. Much like the heartbeat packets, they might or might not be routable.
- If the service devices provide default gateway support for the server farm, they must be adjacent to the servers.

After considering all the requirements for Layer 2 at the access layer, it is important to note that although it is possible to have topologies such as the one presented in Figure 4-8, which supports Layer 2 in the access layer, the topology depicted in Figure 4-7 is preferred. Topologies with loops are also supportable if they take advantages of protocols such as 802.1w and features such as Loopguard.

NOTE To date, most common implementations use Layer 2 at the access layer and rely on the Spanning Tree Protocols and Cisco enhancements to lower convergence times and achieve stability, as depicted in Figure 4-7. Few use the loopless topology. The main reasons relate to whether it is possible to have a loopless topology, given the restrictions imposed by the requirements, and, if possible, whether the setup is simple enough for support, maintenance, and management reasons. Dual-homing requires Layer 2 adjacency between access switches to carry the same VLANs, and redundant stateful service devices need Layer 2 adjacency to work properly. Therefore, it is important to carefully consider the requirements when designing the server farm network infrastructure.

The following section discusses topics related to the topology of the server farms.

Fully Redundant Layer 2 and Layer 3 Designs

Up to this point, all the topologies that have been presented are fully redundant. This section explains the various aspects of a redundant and scalable Data Center design by presenting multiple possible design alternatives, highlighting sound practices, and pointing out practices to be avoided.

The Need for Redundancy

Figure 4-12 explains the steps in building a redundant topology.

Figure 4-12 depicts the logical steps in designing the server farm infrastructure. The process starts with a Layer 3 switch that provides ports for direct server connectivity and routing to the core. A Layer 2 switch could be used, but the Layer 3 switch limits the broadcasts and flooding to and from the server farms. This is option **a** in Figure 4-12. The main problem with the design labeled **a** is that there are multiple single point of failure problems: There is a single NIC and a single switch, and if the NIC or switch fails, the server and applications become unavailable.

The solution is twofold:

- Make the components of the single switch redundant, such as dual power supplies and dual supervisors.
- Add a second switch.

Redundant components make the single switch more tolerant, yet if the switch fails, the server farm is unavailable. Option **b** shows the next step, in which a redundant Layer 3 switch is added.

Figure 4-12 *Multilayer Redundant Design*

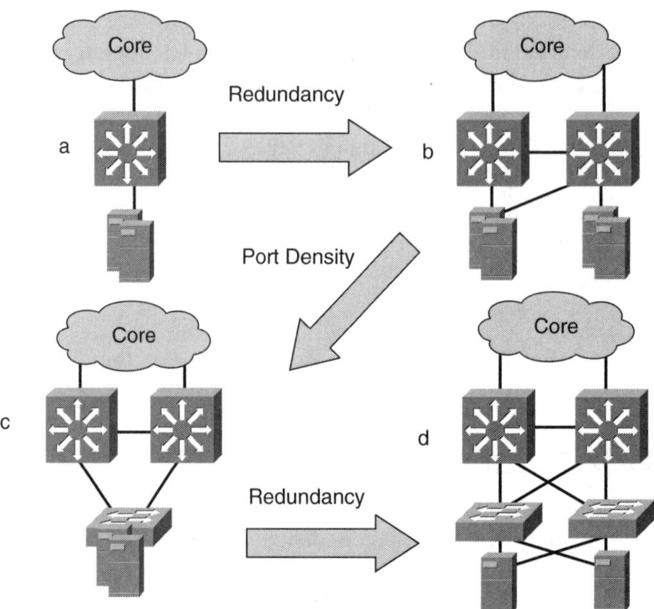

By having two Layer 3 switches and spreading servers on both of them, you achieve a higher level of redundancy in which the failure of one Layer 3 switch does not completely compromise the application environment. The environment is not completely compromised when the servers are dual-homed, so if one of the Layer 3 switches fails, the servers still can recover by using the connection to the second switch.

In options **a** and **b**, the port density is limited to the capacity of the two switches. As the demands for more ports increase for the server and other service devices, and when the maximum capacity has been reached, adding new ports becomes cumbersome, particularly when trying to maintain Layer 2 adjacency between servers.

The mechanism used to grow the server farm is presented in option **c**. You add Layer 2 access switches to the topology to provide direct server connectivity. Figure 4-12 depicts the Layer 2 switches connected to both Layer 3 aggregation switches. The two uplinks, one to each aggregation switch, provide redundancy from the access to the aggregation switches, giving the server farm an alternate path to reach the Layer 3 switches.

The design described in option **c** still has a problem. If the Layer 2 switch fails, the servers lose their only means of communication. The solution is to dual-home servers to two different Layer 2 switches, as depicted in option **d** of Figure 4-12.

NOTE Throughout this book, the terms *access layer* and *access switches* refer to the switches used to provide port density. The terms *aggregation layer* and *aggregation switches* refer to the switches used both to aggregate the traffic to and from the access switches and to connect service devices (load balancers, SSL offloaders, firewalls, caches, and so on).

The *aggregation switches* are Layer 3 switches, which means that they have a built-in router that can forward traffic at wire speed.

The *access switches* are predominantly Layer 2 switches, yet they could be Layer 3 switches merely operating in Layer 2 mode for the server farms.

Layer 2 and Layer 3 in Access Layer

Option **d** in Figure 4-12 is detailed in option **a** of Figure 4-13.

Figure 4-13 *Layer 3 and Layer 2 in the Data Center*

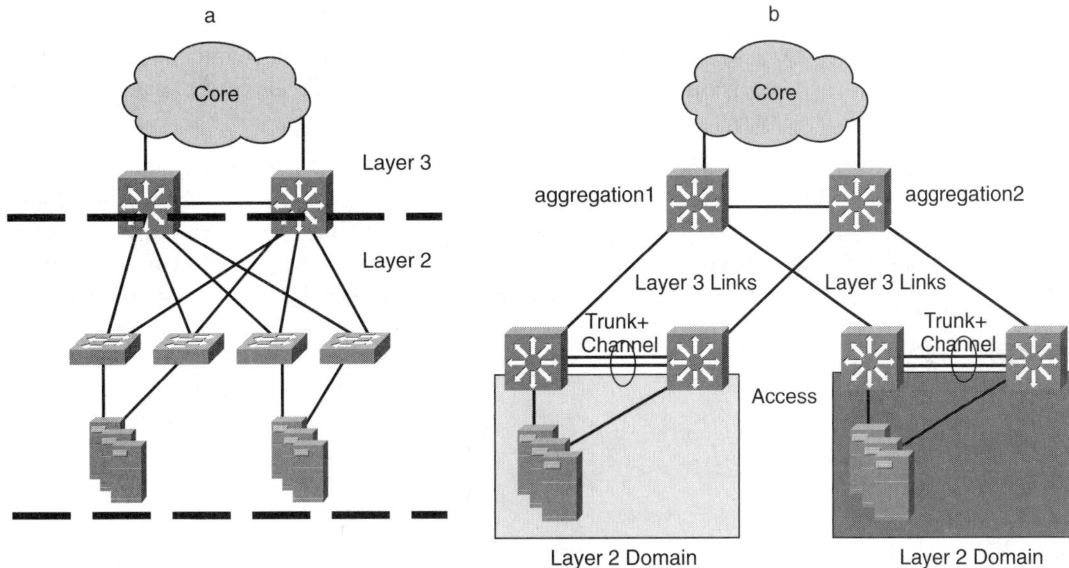

Figure 4-13 presents the scope of the Layer 2 domain(s) from the servers to the aggregation switches. Redundancy in the Layer 2 domain is achieved mainly by using spanning tree, whereas in Layer 3, redundancy is achieved through the use of routing protocols.

Historically, routing protocols have proven more stable than spanning tree, which makes one question the wisdom of using Layer 2 instead of Layer 3 at the access layer. This topic was discussed previously in the "Need for Layer 2 at the Access Layer" section. As shown in option **b** in Figure 4-13, using Layer 2 at the access layer does not prevent the building of pure Layer 3 designs because of the routing between the access and distribution layer or the supporting Layer 2 between access switches.

The design depicted in option **a** of Figure 4-13 is the most generic design that provides redundancy, scalability, and flexibility. Flexibility relates to the fact that the design makes it easy to add service appliances at the aggregation layer with minimal changes to the rest of the design. A simpler design such as that depicted in option **b** of Figure 4-13 might better suit the requirements of a small server farm.

Layer 2, Loops, and Spanning Tree

The Layer 2 domains should make you think immediately of loops. Every network designer has experienced Layer 2 loops in the network. When Layer 2 loops occur, packets are replicated an infinite number of times, bringing down the network. Under normal conditions, the Spanning Tree Protocol keeps the logical topology free of loops. Unfortunately, physical failures such as unidirectional links, incorrect wiring, rogue bridging devices, or bugs can cause loops to occur.

Fortunately, the introduction of 802.1w has addressed many of the limitations of the original spanning tree algorithm, and features such as Loopguard fix the issue of malfunctioning transceivers or bugs.

Still, the experience of deploying legacy spanning tree drives network designers to try to design the Layer 2 topology free of loops. In the Data Center, this is sometimes possible. An example of this type of design is depicted in Figure 4-14. As you can see, the Layer 2 domain (VLAN) that hosts the subnet 10.0.0.*x* is not trunked between the two aggregation switches, and neither is 10.0.1.*x*. Notice that GigE3/1 and GigE3/2 are not bridged together.

Figure 4-14 *Loop-Free Layer 2 Design*

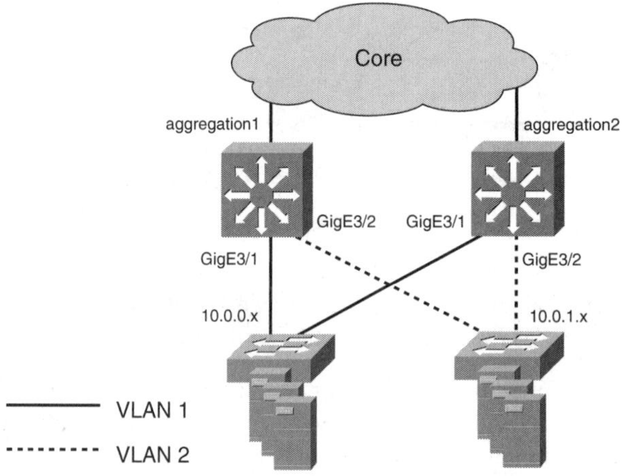

TIP It is possible to build a loop-free access layer if you manage to keep subnets specific to a single access switch. If subnets must span multiple access switches, you should have a "looped" topology. This is the case when you have dual-attached servers because NIC cards configured for "teaming" typically use a floating IP and MAC address, which means that both interfaces belong to the same subnet.

Keep in mind that a "loop-free" topology is not necessarily better. Specific requirements such as those mandated by content switches actually might require the additional path provided by a "looped" topology.

Also notice that a "looped" topology simply means that any Layer 2 device can reach any other Layer 2 device from at least two different physical paths. This does not mean that you have a "forwarding loop," in which packets are replicated infinite times: Spanning tree prevents this from happening.

In a "looped" topology, malfunctioning switches can cause Layer 2 loops. In a loop-free topology, there is no chance for a Layer 2 loop because there are no redundant Layer 2 paths.

If the number of ports must increase for any reason (dual-attached servers, more servers, and so forth), you could follow the approach of daisy-chaining Layer 2 switches, as shown in Figure 4-15.

Figure 4-15 *Alternate Loop-Free Layer 2 Design*

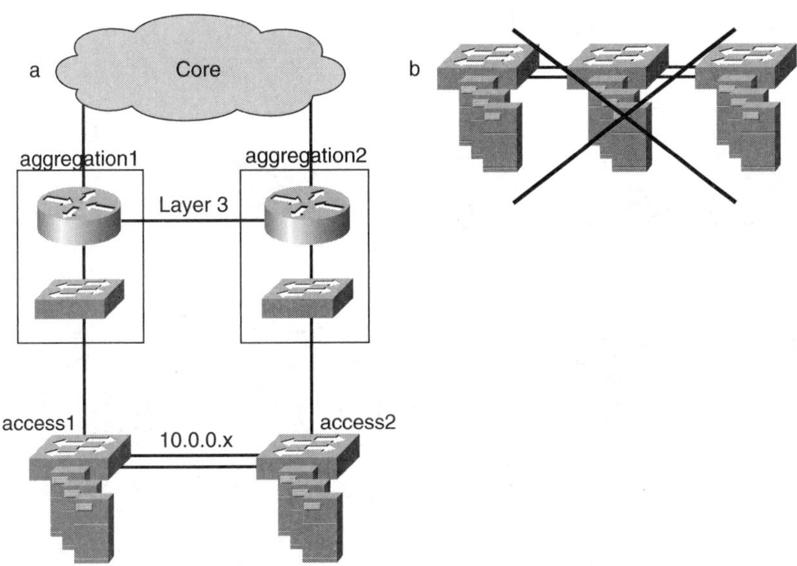

To help you visualize a Layer 2 loop-free topology, Figure 4-15 shows each aggregation switch broken up as a router and a Layer 2 switch.

The problem with topology **a** is that breaking the links between the two access switches would create a discontinuous subnet—this problem can be fixed with an EtherChannel between the access switches.

The other problem occurs when there are not enough ports for servers. If a number of servers need to be inserted into the same subnet 10.0.0.*x*, you cannot add a switch between the two existing servers, as presented in option **b** of Figure 4-15. This is because there is no workaround to the failure of the middle switch, which would create a split subnet. This design is not intrinsically wrong, but it is not optimal.

Both the topologies depicted in Figures 4-14 and 4-15 should migrate to a looped topology as soon as you have any of the following requirements:

- An increase in the number of servers on a given subnet
- Dual-attached NIC cards
- The spread of existing servers for a given subnet on a number of different access switches
- The insertion of stateful network service devices (such as load balancers) that operate in active/standby mode

Options **a** and **b** in Figure 4-16 show how introducing additional access switches on the existing subnet creates "looped topologies." In both **a** and **b**, GigE3/1 and GigE3/2 are bridged together.

Figure 4-16 *Redundant Topologies with Physical Layer 2 Loops*

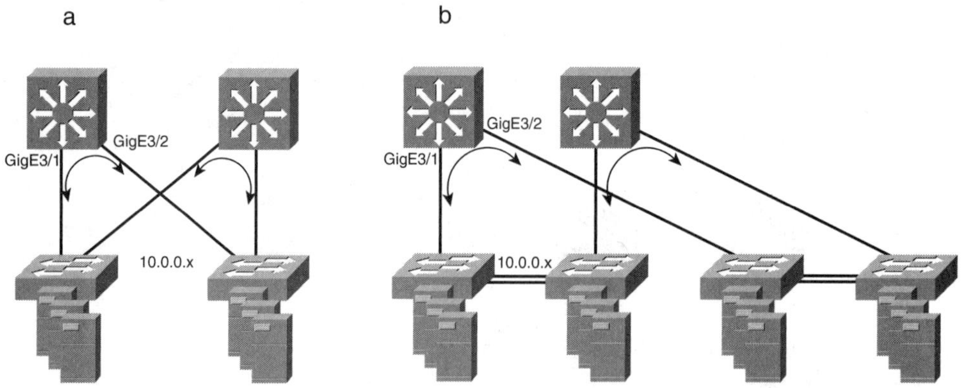

If the requirement is to implement a topology that brings Layer 3 to the access layer, the topology that addresses the requirements of dual-attached servers is pictured in Figure 4-17.

Figure 4-17 *Redundant Topology with Layer 3 to the Access Switches*

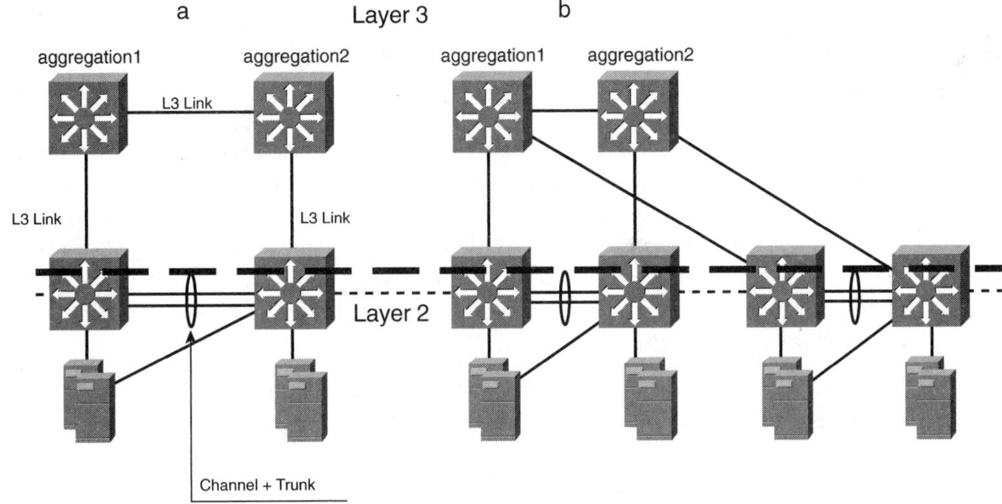

Notice in option **a** of Figure 4-17, almost all the links are Layer 3 links, whereas the access switches have a trunk (on a channel) to provide the same subnet on two different switches. This trunk also carries a Layer 3 VLAN, which basically is used merely to make the two switches neighbors from a routing point of view. The dashed line in Figure 4-17 shows the scope of the Layer 2 domain.

Option **b** in Figure 4-17 shows how to grow the size of the server farm with this type of design. Notice that when deploying pairs of access switches, each pair has a set of subnets disjointed from the subnets of any other pair. For example, one pair of access switches hosts subnets 10.0.1.*x* and 10.0.2.*x*; the other pair cannot host the same subnets simply because it connects to the aggregation layer with Layer 3 links.

NOTE If you compare the design in Figure 4-17 with option **b** in Figure 4-12, the natural questions are these: Why is there an aggregation layer, and are the access switches not directly connected to the core? These are valid points, and the answer actually depends on the size of the Data Center. Remember that the access layer is added for reasons of port density, whereas the aggregation layer is used mainly to attach appliances, such as load-balancing devices, firewalls, caches, and so on.

So far, the discussions have centered on redundant Layer 2 and Layer 3 designs. The Layer 3 switch provides the default gateway for the server farms in all the topologies introduced thus far. Default gateway support, however, could also be provided by other service devices, such as load balancers and firewalls. The next section explores the alternatives.

Fully Redundant Layer 2 and Layer 3 Designs with Services

After discussing the build-out of a fully redundant Layer 2 and Layer 3 topology and considering the foundation of the Data Center, the focus becomes the design issues related to other Data Center services. These services are aimed at improving security and scaling the performance of application services by offloading processing away from the server farm to the network. These services include security, load balancing, SSL offloading, and caching; they are supported by a number of networking devices that must be integrated into the infrastructure following the design requirements.

Additionally, this section discusses application environment trends brought about by technology advancements in either applications, the application infrastructure, or the network infrastructure.

Additional Services

At the aggregation layer, in addition to Layer 2 and Layer 3, the Data Center might need to support the following devices:

- Firewalls
- Intrusion Detection Systems (IDSs)
- Load balancers
- SSL offloaders
- Caches

It is important to discuss design issues when supporting some of these devices.

Service devices bring their own requirements that could change certain aspects of the design—for instance, the exchange state or status information, the NAT function that they perform on the source or destination IP addresses that forces them to be in the inbound and outbound path, and so on.

Service devices can be deployed using service modules integrated in the aggregation switches or as appliances connected to the aggregation switches. Both deployments require network connectivity and forethought about the actual traffic path.

Firewalls and load balancers may support the default gateway function on behalf of the server farms. Default gateway support traditionally has been provided by the router, so with two additional alternatives, you need to decide which is the default gateway and in which order traffic is processed through the multiple devices. Firewalls and load balancers are capable of providing stateful failover, which is supported by specific redundancy protocols. The protocols, which are specific to the firewalls or load balancers, must be supported by the design. SSL offloaders are typically used with load balancers and require the same considerations, with one exception: They do not support default gateway services.

IDSs are transparent to the design, which means that they integrate well with any existing design. The main consideration with regard to IDSs is their placement, which depends on selecting the location to analyze traffic and the traffic types to be monitored.

Caches, on the other hand, are deployed in reverse proxy cache mode. The placement of the caches and the mechanism for directing traffic to them impact the Data Center design. The options for traffic redirection are the Web Cache Communication Protocol (WCCP) on the Layer 2 or Layer 3 switches, and load balancers to distribute the load among the cache cluster. In either case, the cache or cache cluster changes the basic traffic path to the server farm when in use.

The following section presents the multiple deployment options.

Service Deployment Options

Two options exist when deploying Data Center services: using service modules integrated into the aggregation switch and using appliances connected to the aggregation switch. Figure 4-18 shows the two options.

Figure 4-18 *Service Deployment Options*

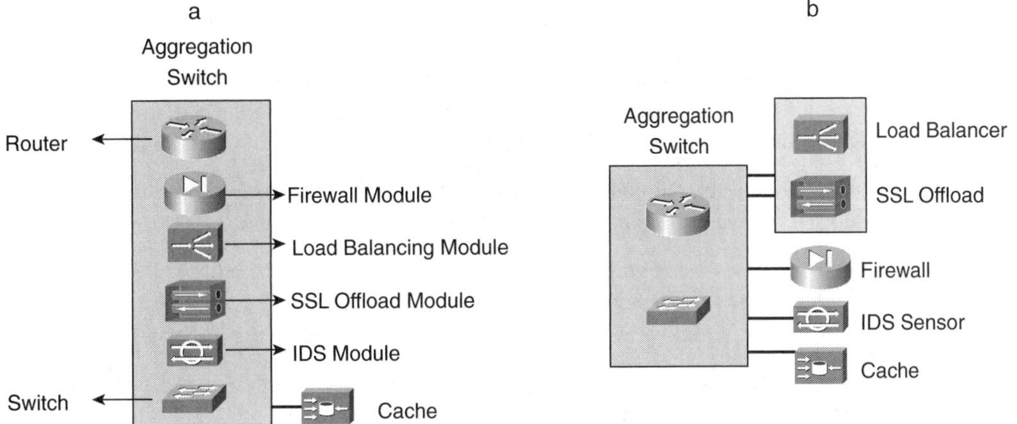

Option **a** shows the integrated design. The aggregation switch is represented by a router (Layer 3) and a switch (Layer 2) as the key components of the foundation (shown to the left) and by a firewall, load balancer, SSL module, and IDS module (shown to the right as add-on services). The service modules communicate with the routing and switching components in the chassis through the backplane.

Option **b** shows the appliance-based design. The aggregation switch provides the routing and switching functions. Other services are provided by appliances that are connected directly to the aggregation switches.

NOTE Designs that use both modules and appliances are also possible. The most common case is when using caches, which are appliances, in both design options. Current trends on Data Center services lean toward integrated services. Evidence of this integration trend is the proliferation of services modules in the Catalyst 6500 family and the use of blade servers and blade chassis to collapse multiple services in one device.

A thoughtful approach to the design issues in selecting the traffic flow across different devices is required whether you are considering option **a**, option **b**, or any combination of the options in Figure 4-18. This means that you should explicitly select the default gateway and the order in which the packets from the client to the server are processed. The designs that use appliances require more care because you must be concerned with physical connectivity issues, interoperability, and the compatibility of protocols.

Design Considerations with Service Devices

Up to this point, several issues related to integrating service devices in the Data Center design have been mentioned. They are related to whether you run Layer 2 or Layer 3 at the access layer, whether you use appliance or modules, whether they are stateful or stateless, and whether they require you to change the default gateway location away from the router. Changing the default gateway location forces you to determine the order in which the packet needs to be processed through the aggregation switch and service devices.

Figure 4-19 presents the possible alternatives for default gateway support using service modules. The design implications of each alternative are discussed next.

Figure 4-19 shows the aggregation switch, a Catalyst 6500 using a firewall service module, and a content-switching module, in addition to the routing and switching functions provided by the Multilayer Switch Feature Card (MSFC) and the Supervisor Module.

The one constant factor in the design is the location of the switch providing server connectivity; it is adjacent to the server farm.

Figure 4-19 *Service Module Interoperability Alternatives*

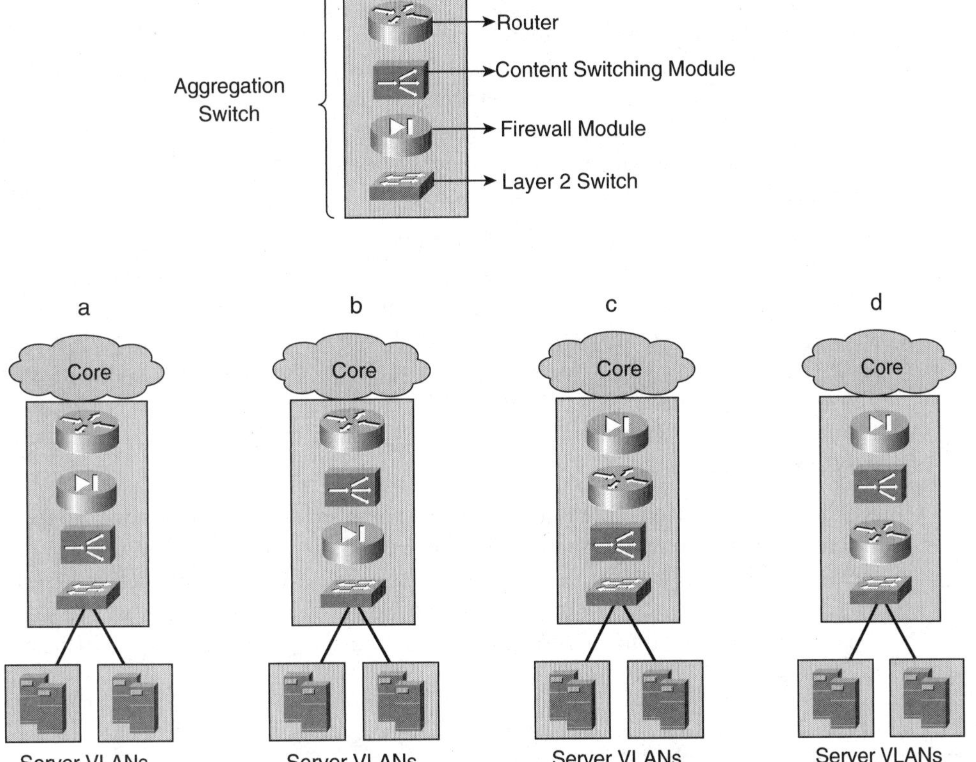

Option **a** presents the router facing the core IP network, the content-switching module facing the server farm, and the firewall module between them firewalling all server farms. If the content switch operates as a router (route mode), it becomes the default gateway for the server farm. However, if it operates as a bridge (bridge mode), the default gateway would be the firewall. This configuration facilitates the creation of multiple instances of the firewall and content switch combination for the segregation and load balancing of each server farm independently.

Option **b** has the firewall facing the server farm and the content switch between the router and the firewall. Whether operating in router mode or bridge mode, the firewall configuration must enable server health-management (health probes) traffic from the content-switching module to the server farm; this adds management and configuration tasks to the design. Note that, in this design, the firewall provides the default gateway support for the server farm.

Option **c** shows the firewall facing the core IP network, the content switch facing the server farm, and the firewall module between the router and the content-switching module. Placing a firewall at the edge of the intranet server farms requires the firewall to have "router-like" routing capabilities, to ease the integration with the routed network while segregating all the server farms concurrently. This makes the capability to secure each server farm independently more difficult because the content switch and the router could route packets between the server farm without going through the firewall. Depending on whether the content-switching module operates in router or bridge mode, the default gateway could be the content switch or the router, respectively.

Option **d** displays the firewall module facing the core IP network, the router facing the server farm, and the content-switching module in between. This option presents some of the same challenges as option **c** in terms of the firewall supporting IGPs and the inability to segregate each server farm independently. The design, however, has one key advantage: The router is the default gateway for the server farm. Using the router as the default gateway allows the server farms to take advantage of some key protocols, such as HSRP, and features, such as HSRP tracking, QoS, the DHCP relay function, and so on, that are only available on routers.

All the previous design options are possible—some are more flexible, some are more secure, and some are more complex. The choice should be based on knowing the requirements as well as the advantages and restrictions of each. The different design issues associated with the viable options are discussed in the different chapters in Part V. Chapter 21, "Integrating Security into the Infrastructure," addresses the network design in the context of firewalls.

Application Environment Trends

Undoubtedly, the most critical trends are those related to how applications are being developed and are expected to work on the network. These trends can be classified arbitrarily into two major areas:

- Application architectures
- Network infrastructure

Application Architecture Trends

Application architecture trends include the evolution of the classic client/server model to the more specialized n-tier model, web services, specific application architectures, the server and client software (operating systems), application clients, the server and client hardware, and middleware used to integrate distributed applications in heterogeneous environments.

The more visible trends of application architectures are the wide adoption of web technology in conjunction with the use of the n-tier model to functionally segment distinct server types. Currently, web, application, and database servers are the basic types, yet they are combined in many ways (depending on the vendor of the application and how the buyer wants to implement it).

This functional partitioning demands that the network be smarter about securing and scaling the tiers independently. For instance, the n-tier model's web tier layer created the need for smaller and faster servers used to scale up the front-end function. This resulted in 1RU (rack unit) servers, which offer adequate performance for web servers at a low cost and minimal infrastructure requirements (power and rack space).

Web services are bringing a service-oriented approach to the use of different and distinct distributed applications that are accessible using standard messages over Internet protocols. Web services rely initially on the transport functions of the network and eventually on using the network as an extension to provide computing capacity to the distributed application environments by offloading tasks to network hardware.

NOTE The World Wide Web consortium (W3C) defines a web service as "a software application identified by a URI, whose interfaces and binding are capable of being defined, described, and discovered by XML artifacts and supports direct interactions with other software applications using XML-based messages via Internet-based protocols." For more information on web services and its architecture, consult the W3C at www.w3.org.

Grid computing is another trend that actually brings the applications and the network closer together by treating the servers as a network of CPUs in which the applications use the most available CPU on the network. Other trends related to grid computing include blade servers as an alternative to 1RU servers, to provide higher CPU density per RU, lower power consumption per server, and an additional benefit of lower cabling requirements. Blade servers are servers on blades (or modules) that are inserted into a chassis, much like network modules or line cards are inserted on a switch chassis. Using blade servers in blade chassis enables you to centralize the server-management functions (one chassis instead of however many servers are in the chassis), requires less cables (one set per chassis instead of one set per server), and provides higher computing and memory capacity per rack unit.

However, the blade server technology is still young, which explains the variety of flavors, architectures, connectivity options, and features.

An instance of middleware is the software used in the management and control of distributed CPUs in a grid of computers that can be 1RU or blade servers. This specific middleware virtualizes the use of CPUs so that the applications are given a CPU cycle from CPUs on the network instead of through the traditional manner.

Network Infrastructure Trends

The network infrastructure is growing smarter and more application-aware, and it thereby supports application environments both by offloading some computationally intense tasks to the network (typically hardware-based) and by replacing some functions performed by servers that could be better handled by networking devices.

Load balancing is a good example of a function performed by the network that replaces clustering protocols used by servers for high availability. Clustering protocols tend to be software-based, hard to manage, and not very scalable in providing a function that the network performs well using hardware.

Trends such as blade servers bring new design considerations. Most blade server chassis (blade chassis, for short) in the market support both an option to provide redundant Ethernet switches inside the chassis and as an option to connect the blade servers to the network using pass-through links, with the chassis simply providing at least twice as many uplinks as servers in the chassis, to allow dual-homing.

Figure 4-20 presents both connectivity alternatives for a blade chassis.

Figure 4-20 *Blade Server Chassis Server Connectivity*

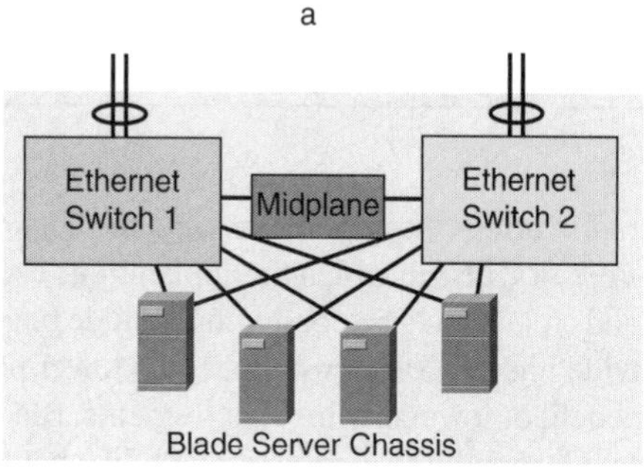

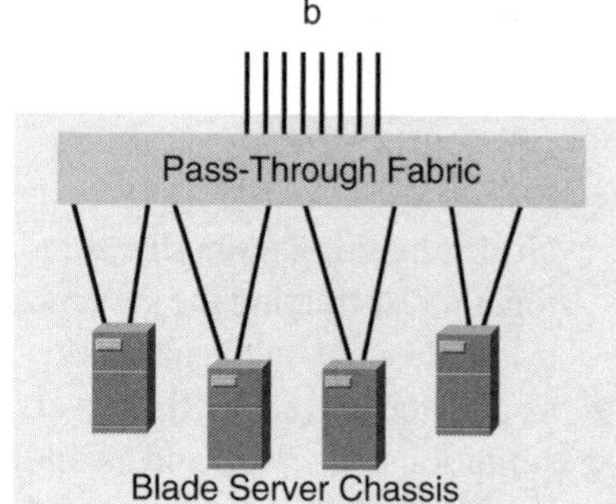

Option **a** in Figure 4-20 shows a blade server chassis in which each blade server is connected to each of the blade chassis's redundant Layer 2 Ethernet switches. Each blade chassis's Ethernet switch provides a number of uplinks that can be channeled to the IP network. The number of uplinks is typically smaller than the combined number of links per server, which requires planning for oversubscription, particularly if the servers are Gigabit Ethernet–attached. The midplane is the fabric used for management tasks, that is, control plane traffic such as switch status.

Option **b** in Figure 4-20 presents the pass-through option in which the servers are dual-homed and preconnected to a pass-through fabric that provides the connectivity to the IP network. This option does not use Ethernet switches inside the chassis. The pass-through fabric is as simple as a patch panel that conserves the properties of the server NICs, but it also could become a more intelligent fabric, adding new features and allowing blade server vendors to differentiate their products. Either approach you take to connect blade servers to your network requires careful consideration on short- and long-term design implications.

For instance, if the choice is to utilize the redundant Ethernet switches in the blade chassis, you have the following design alternatives to consider:

- How to use the redundant Ethernet switches' uplinks for connectivity
- Whether to connect the blade chassis to the access or aggregation switches
- What level of oversubscription is tolerable

Figure 4-21 displays two connectivity choices utilizing the uplinks on the redundant Ethernet switches. For redundancy, two switches are used to connect the uplinks from the blade chassis. Switches A and B, the small clouds in the IP network cloud, provide a redundant network fabric to the blade chassis to avoid single point of failure issues.

Figure 4-21 *Blade Chassis Uplink Connectivity*

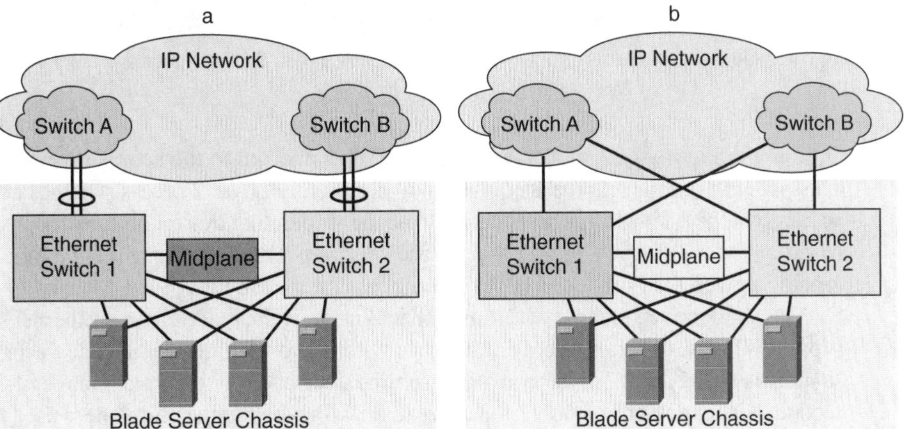

Option **a** in Figure 4-21 shows all the uplinks from both blade chassis' Ethernet switches connected to a single switch in the IP network. This allows the uplinks to be channeled. In contrast, option **b** in Figure 4-21 shows each blade chassis Ethernet switch connected to each IP network switch, also avoiding a single point of failure. This presents the advantage of having a direct link to either switch A or switch B, thus avoiding unnecessary hops. Additionally, if each blade chassis Ethernet switch supports more than two uplinks, they can also be channeled to switches A and B for greater redundancy and higher bandwidth.

The next step is to determine whether to connect the blade chassis to the access-layer switches, as is traditionally done with servers, or to the aggregation layer switches. Figure 4-22 displays the connectivity options for the next-hop switches from the blade chassis.

Figure 4-22 *Blade Chassis Next-Hop Switch*

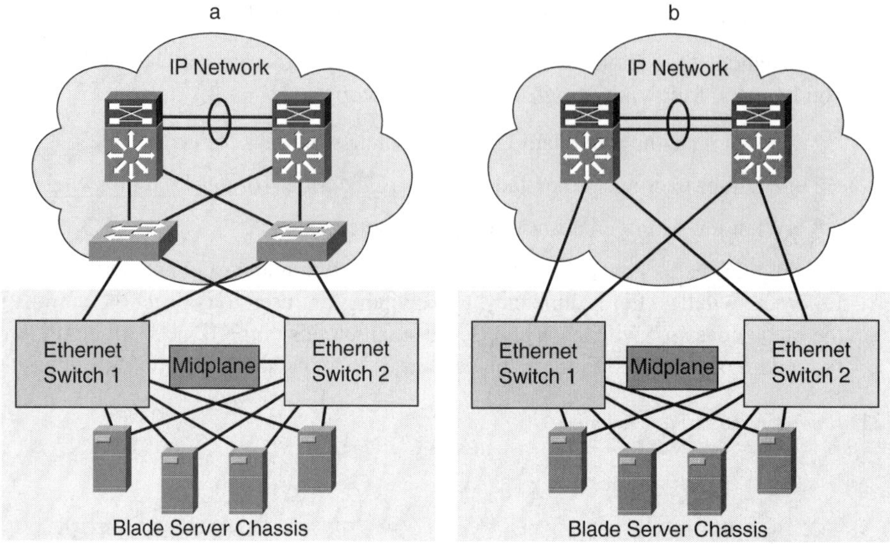

Option **a** in Figure 4-22 shows the blade chassis connected to the access-layer switches. This particular design choice is equivalent to connecting Layer 2 access switches to Layer 2 access switches. The design must take into account spanning tree recommendations, which, based on the topology of option **a** in Figure 4-22, are aimed at determining a loop-free topology given the number of Layer 2 switches and the amount of available paths to the STP root and the secondary root from each leaf node. If the blade chassis Ethernet switches support 802.1w, the convergence time stays within two to three seconds; however, if the support is strictly 802.1d, the convergence time goes back to the typical range of 30 to 50 seconds. Other design considerations have to do with whether the midplane is used for more than management and switch-to-switch control traffic communication functions. If for some reason the midplane also is used to bridge VLANs (forward Bridge Protocol Data Units, or BPDUs) the STP topology needs to be considered carefully. The design goals remain making the topology predictable and deterministic. This implies that you need to explicitly set up root and bridge priorities and analyze the possible failure scenarios to make sure they support the requirements of the applications.

Option **b** in Figure 4-22 shows the blade chassis Ethernet switches directly connected to the aggregation switches. This is the preferred alternative because it lends itself to being more deterministic and supporting lower convergence times. Much like in the previous option, if the blade chassis Ethernet switches do not support 802.1w or some of the STP enhancements such as Uplinkfast and Loopguard, the convergence time would be in the range of 30 to 50 seconds. The topology still needs to be made deterministic and predictable by explicitly setting up root and bridge priorities and testing the failures scenarios.

How to scale the blade server farm is another consideration. Scalability on server environments is done simply by adding pairs of access switches for redundancy and connecting them to the aggregation switches, as shown in option **a** in Figure 4-23.

Figure 4-23 *Server Farm Scalability*

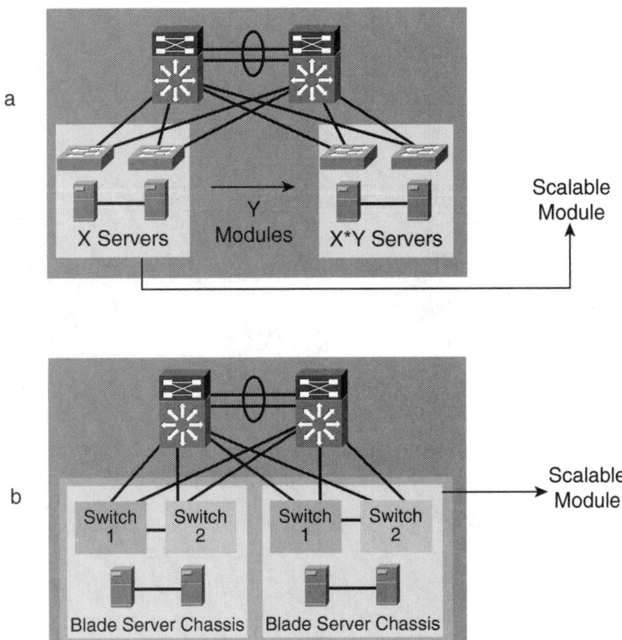

If a single scalable server module supports X servers (limited by port density), higher scalability is achieved by replicating the scalable module Y times (limited by slot density in the aggregation switch). The total number of servers could be X * Y. Depending on the access switch port density and the aggregation switch slot density, this could grow to thousands of servers. Scaling the number of blade servers might require a slightly different strategy. Because blade chassis with Ethernet switches are the access layer, the amount of blade server is limited to the number of slots and ports per slot at the aggregation switches. Option **b** in Figure 4-23 shows this alternative.

Notice that the scalable module is now the aggregation switch along with a set number of blade chassis. This is because the aggregation switch has a limit to the number of slots that can be used for blade chassis. In addition, line cards used to support blade server uplinks now receive aggregate server traffic, thus requiring less oversubscription. This leads to fewer ports used per line card. So, the total number of blade servers is limited somewhat by the slot and port density. Even though this design alternative is likely to support hundreds of blade servers and satisfy the requirements for a fast-growing server farm environment, you must have a plan for what to do if you need to increase your server farm beyond what the current design supports. Figure 4-24 shows this alternative.

Figure 4-24 *Core Layer Within the Data Center*

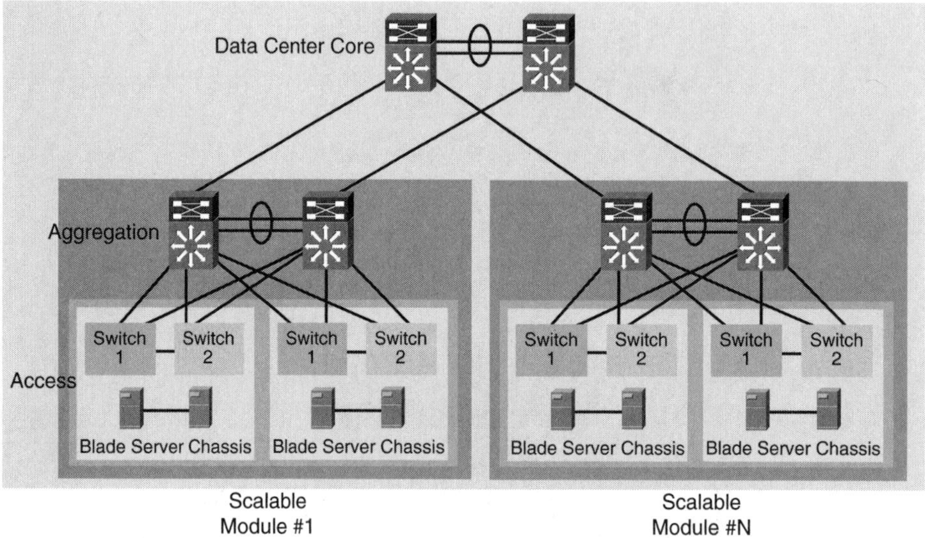

Figure 4-24 introduces a new layer in the Data Center: the core layer. The core layer is used to aggregate as many server blade modules as needed, but the number is limited to the port and slot capacity to the aggregation switches. The pass-through option might not require as much planning because the blade chassis do not have redundant Ethernet switches. The uplinks are connected to the access layer, which is equivalent to current designs in which servers are dual-homed to a redundant set of access switches.

Setting aside the connectivity, port density, slot density, and scalability considerations, other areas, such as oversubscription, uplink capacity, and service deployment options, might require design and testing before the Data Center architecture is established.

Additional trends include the dual-homing of servers, the migration from Fast Ethernet to Gigabit Ethernet, application firewalls, and the use of transparent network service devices. Application firewalls are firewalls that are more in tune with application behavior than ordinary firewalls, thus making the firewalling process more granular to application information in addition to just network or transport layer information. For instance, an application firewall might be capable of identifying not only that a packet is TCP and that the information in the TCP payload is HTTP, but also that the request comes from a specific high-priority user and is a SQL request for sensitive payroll information, which requires a higher security service level.

Transparent network services include firewalling, load balancing, SSL offloading, and so on. These services are provided by network devices with minimal interoperability issues that leave the existing designs unchanged. These transparent services could apply to traditional network services such as load balancing and firewalling, yet they are implemented to minimize disruption and changes in the application environment. This approach might include using physical devices as if they were distinct logical entities providing services to different server farms concurrently. This implies that the administration of those services, such as configuration changes or troubleshooting efforts, is isolated to the specific logical service. Think of it as a single physical firewall that is deployed to support many server farms concurrently where access to the CLI and configuration commands is available only to users who have been granted access to the specific server farm firewall service. This would appear to the user as a completely separate firewall.

Some of these trends are ongoing, and some are barely starting. Some will require special design and architectural considerations, and some will be adopted seamlessly. Others will not exist long enough for concern.

Summary

Data Centers are very dynamic environments hosting multiple types of server farms that all support key business applications. The design of the Data Center involves a variety of aspects related to how applications are architected, how they are deployed, and their network infrastructure.

A sound approach to design involves using a combination of architectural principles, such as scalability, flexibility, and high availability, as well as applying those principles to the requirements of the application environment. The result should be an architecture that meets the current needs but that is flexible enough to evolve to meet the needs of short- and long-term trends.

A solid foundation for Data Center design is based on a redundant, scalable, and flexible Layer 2 and Layer 3 infrastructure in which the behavior is both predictable and deterministic. The infrastructure also should accommodate service devices that perform key functions aimed at scaling or securing application environments. The deployment of service devices such as firewalls, load balancers, SSL offloaders, and caches requires careful planning.

The planning efforts must ensure that the desired behavior is achieved in the following areas: redundancy protocols between service devices, the exchange of connection and session information between stateful devices, the location of default gateway services, and the traffic path through the Data Center infrastructure from device to device.

Additional considerations require an architectural approach to deal with the application environment trends and the requirements that are imposed on the network infrastructure. Subsequent chapters in the book dig deeper into the specifics of Data Center and server farm designs.

This chapter covers the following topics:

- The need for a secure Data Center
- Security vulnerabilities and common attacks
- The Data Center network security infrastructure
- Fundamental security concepts
- A framework for applying security in the Data Center

CHAPTER 5

Data Center Security Overview

This chapter provides an overview of the typical security issues that affect Data Centers and presents the general guidelines to secure a Data Center in a systematic manner that helps maintain an adequate security level as the Data Center evolves. This chapter also discusses the importance of security policies, secure management, incident response, and attack mitigation.

The Need for a Secure Data Center

Data Centers are key components of enterprise networks. The Data Center houses the enterprise applications and data, hence the need for proper security. Losing data and applications can impact the organization's ability to conduct business.

The large volume of information and the criticality of the services housed in Data Centers make them likely targets; in fact, the number of reported attacks, including those that affect Data Centers, continues to grow year by year ([CERT/CC] Statistics 1988-2002, Computer Security Institute/Federal Bureau of Investigation [CSI/FBI] 2001). Denial of service (DoS), theft of confidential information, data alteration, and data loss are some of the common security problems afflicting Data Center environments.

New forms of attacks are continuously developed; both attacks and attack tools are becoming more sophisticated and attack frequency is increasing. The section, "Common Attacks" presents a classification of these and explains the security challenges they pose to the enterprise.

Understanding the issues associated with network attacks on Data Centers requires awareness of the factors that contribute to their proliferation. On one hand, the expansion of the Internet and the growing complexity of protocols and applications used in Data Centers result in an increasing number of exploitable vulnerabilities. For example, as applications become more complex, there are more chances for inconsistent installations. On the other hand, hackers use the openness of the Internet to communicate and develop automated tools that facilitate the identification and exploitation of those vulnerabilities. Many attack tools are widely available on the Internet and are designed to execute highly sophisticated attacks using simple user interfaces, which makes them accessible to anyone.

Attacks are also initiated by internal trusted personnel, according to the 2001 CSI/FBI report "Computer Crime and Security Survey." In fact, studies show that internal attacks tend to be more damaging because of the variety and amount of information available inside organizations. The term *hackers*, which has traditionally been associated with people external to an organization, now includes people internal to the organization.

NOTE The Computer Crime and Security survey is conducted by the CSI with the participation of the FBI Computer Intrusion Squad in San Francisco. The survey has been published every year for the past eight years.

Network attacks are real, and they do pose a serious threat to an organization. Risk reduction to acceptable levels should account for measures against internal as well as external threats.

Vulnerabilities and Common Attacks

The following terms often used in security discussions are important to define in the context of security in Data Centers:

- **Threat**—An event that poses some harm to the Data Center or its resources
- **Vulnerability**—A deficiency on a system or resource whose exploitation leads to the materialization of the threat
- **Attack**—The actual exploitation of a vulnerability to make a threat reality

Applied to a web application, for example, a threat could be the loss of the application server's capability to process requests from legitimate users. The vulnerability could be that the server is running a software version known to be susceptible to buffer-overflow attacks. The attack would be the event of a hacker actually exploiting the vulnerability via a buffer overflow that brings down the server.

Threats

Data Centers are vulnerable to threats that affect the rest of the enterprise network and to threats that are specific to the Data Center.

The following are some of the most common threats to Data Centers:

- DoS
- Breach of confidential information
- Data theft or alteration

- Unauthorized use of compute resources
- Identity theft

All these common threats are somewhat obvious and self-explanatory; therefore, the rest of this section covers some generic vulnerabilities and some of the most common attacks.

Vulnerabilities

Most of the vulnerabilities found today originated in at least one of the following areas:

- **Implementation**—Software and protocols flaws, incorrect or faulty software design, incomplete testing, etc.
- **Configuration**—Elements not properly configured, use of defaults, and so on.
- **Design**—Ineffective or inadequate security design, lack of or inappropriate implementation of redundancy mechanisms, etc.

The following section discusses the details of the most common vulnerabilities and their relation to source problems.

Exploitation of Out-of-Date Software

Running out-of-date software and using insecure default configurations are the top two causes of security incidents. Most attacks to Data Centers today exploit well-known vulnerabilities that are usually discovered and announced months before the first attack takes place.

The worms CodeRed, Nimda, and SQL Slammer are good examples of exploited known vulnerabilities that could have been avoided.

Recently, CodeRed and Nimda severely impacted the Internet worldwide by exploiting a series of vulnerabilities in Windows Internet Information Server (IIS) systems, which were discovered before the first incident was reported.

In late January 2003, the SQL Slammer worm infected more than 250,000 hosts in less than two hours, severely affecting communications over the Internet and additionally impacting bank ATM networks. SQL Slammer exploited a well-known flaw in Microsoft SQL Server 2000, which was officially reported by Microsoft on July 2002, approximately six months prior to the first attack.

This clearly indicates that systems are not kept updated. You can avoid a significant number of exploits on the Internet by using the latest releases of software.

Exploitation of Software Defaults

The second most common cause behind exploits is the use of default configuration values. Many systems are shipped with default accounts and passwords, which are exploited for unauthorized access and theft of information, among other threats.

TIP As a rule of thumb, you should never put a system in production unless you change its default usernames and passwords. Furthermore, once it is in production, you should maintain the system with the latest security patches, with the adequate configuration to mitigate the latest security vulnerabilities, and with a mechanism to select and change passwords regularly.

Common Attacks

After talking about threats and vulnerabilities, the following sections discuss how they are exploited by the most frequent attacks.

Scanning or Probing

Rather than an attack, this activity precedes an attack to gain access by discovering information about a system or network. This reconnaissance activity usually preludes a more severe security incident. The term *probe* refers to an individual attempt, whereas a *scan* consists of a large number of probes by an automated tool.

A port scan is an example of scanning whose purpose is to identify the services that a host is running. During a port scan, the offender basically tries to open a TCP connection to each of the well-known ports, such FTP, Telnet, HTTP, Simple Mail Transfer Protocol (SMTP), and so on. Then, the offender can direct more precise attacks to those ports the host is listening on.

In many cases, the volume of information generated by the probes can consume existing bandwidth and other resources, resulting in Denial of Service (DoS).

DoS

The goal of a *DoS* attack is to degrade service to the point that legitimate users are unable to conduct their regular activities. DoS attacks can take many different forms, but the most common case consists of generating large volumes of data to deliberately consume limited resources such as bandwidth, CPU cycles, and memory blocks.

A *SYN flood* is a good example in which the attacker generates large amounts of TCP connection requests that are not intended to be established. Because a system must maintain these connections, referred to as *embryonic* connections, the system eventually runs out of resources and fails to respond to new legitimate connections.

A *smurf* is another classic example of a DoS attack where the attacker sends a large volume of Internet Control Message Protocol (ICMP) echo requests to broadcast IP addresses, using the IP address of a victim system as the source. Then, the victim system receives the replies from every single host that received the ICMP request.

Figure 5-1 illustrates a smurf attack in which the attacker forges a packet with the source IP address of a victim and the packet is sent to a known broadcast address. Because the packet is directed to a broadcast address, the directly connected router sends a copy of the packet to each device behind that broadcast address. Then, each device replies with a separate packet, which results in an overwhelming volume of responses directed to the victim.

Figure 5-1 *Smurf, a DoS Attack Example*

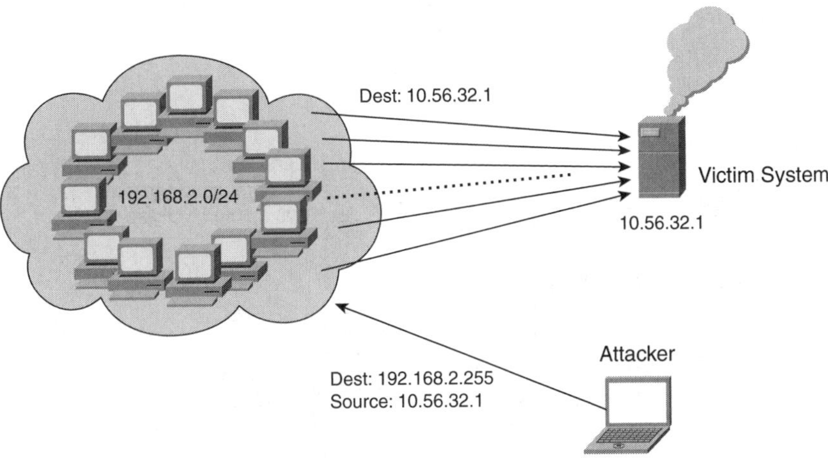

A DoS attack can also consist of generating a single malformed packet that exploits a flaw in an application or protocol stack. Ping of death (PoD) is a good example. PoD sends an ICMP echo packet that violates the maximum size of the packet. Some old TCP/IP stacks did not verify the packet size and ended up allocating more memory than needed, which eventually causes a system crash.

In Data Centers, most DoS attacks target server farms primarily by sending the servers large volumes of traffic. A large volume of traffic over the network could lead to network congestion, which is an indirect result of the DoS attack.

Distributed Denial of Service

Distributed denial-of-service (DDoS) attacks are a particular case of DoS attacks where a large number of systems are compromised and used as the source of traffic on a synchronized attack. DDoS attacks work in a hierarchical model typically consisting of clients, handlers, and agents.

The client is the system used by the attacker to control all the handlers and instruct the attack. The handlers are compromised systems that run a special program that gives the attacker the ability to control multiple agents concurrently.

The agents are the end systems that, once compromised, are used to generate an attack against a specific target (a system or network). Figure 5-2 presents the hierarchical structure of a DDoS attack.

Figure 5-2 *DDoS Attack*

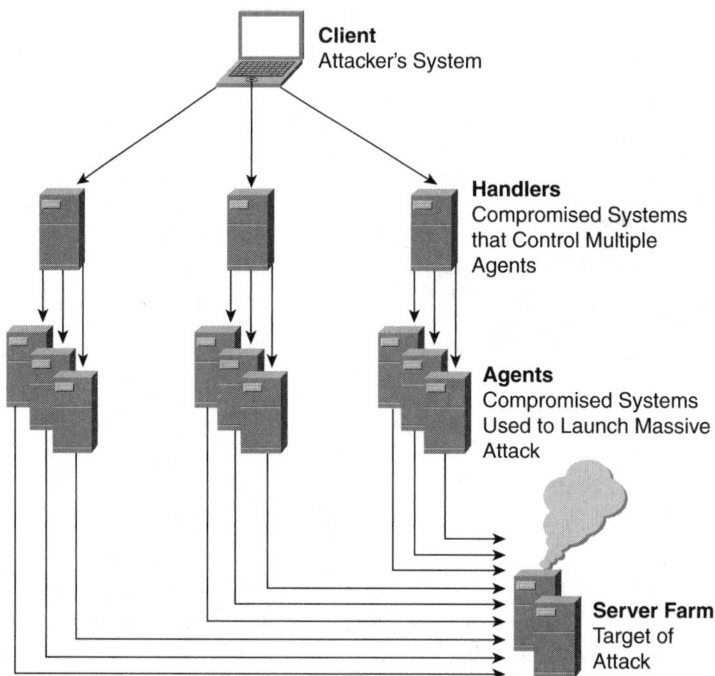

With this hierarchical approach, hackers can easily compromise and manage thousands of devices with devastating effectiveness. Trinoo, Tribe Flood Network (TFN), and Stacheldraht are examples of tools used for DDoS attacks.

Similarly to DoS attacks in Data Centers, DDoS attacks target servers rather than the network infrastructure. However, because of the potential volume of traffic generated during DDoS attacks, the network could be congested and networking devices might also be affected.

Unauthorized Access

Unauthorized access consists of gaining access to restricted resources by using a valid account or a backdoor. An account compromise is a type of unauthorized access where someone other than the account owner uses the privileges associated with the compromised account.

A backdoor is a purposely planted vulnerability, which can affect systems that leave unrestricted guest accounts or programs that allow unauthorized users to gain access. An account compromise is a serious security incident that might lead to loss of data, data alteration, and even theft of services. In the context of Data Centers, unauthorized access attacks frequently happen on web servers with poor authentication controls.

A special case of unauthorized access is *network intrusion*. Network intrusion defines the attack where an external intruder gains access to internal network resources. Backdoors and IP spoofing attacks are typical cases that lead to network intrusions.

Eavesdropping

Eavesdropping is the unauthorized interception of information that travels on the network. This information might contain confidential data such as usernames and passwords. Packet capturing is a typical case of eavesdropping where an attacker uses packet-capturing software to monitor packets so that he or she can see the data that crosses a network segment. The most common cases of eavesdropping in Data Centers include intercepting typical and critical user transactions such as logon sessions.

Viruses and Worms

Viruses and *worms* are both cases of malicious code that, when executed, produces undesired results on the infected system. The malicious code usually remains hidden in the system until the damage is discovered. The difference between viruses and worms is the way they auto-replicate. Worms are self-replicating programs that propagate without any human intervention. Viruses are also self-replicating programs, but they need some kind of action on part of the user to infect the system, such as executing an infected file in an e-mail attachment.

CodeRed, Nimda, and SQL Slammer are examples of worms that affect servers in Data Centers.

Internet Infrastructure Attacks

Internet infrastructure attacks target the critical components of the Internet infrastructure rather than individual systems or networks. These attacks are becoming more frequent and mostly affect service providers. Domain Name System (DNS) servers, edge routers, cache clusters, and access servers are some of the devices targeted by these attacks.

An example of an infrastructure attack is the massive DDoS attack conducted in October 2002, which severely affected 9 of the 13 root DNS servers. In this instance, the attacker overwhelmed the root servers with a ping flood, which generated 10 times the normal traffic volume the servers typically handle.

Trust Exploitation

These attacks exploit the trust relationships that computer systems have to communicate. Communications in networked environments are always based on trust. For example, when a web server communicates with a back-end database, a trust relationship exists between the two systems. If an attacker can forge his identity, appearing to be coming from the web server, he or she can gain unauthorized access to the database. Figure 5-3 displays a trust-exploitation situation.

Figure 5-3 *Trust Exploitation*

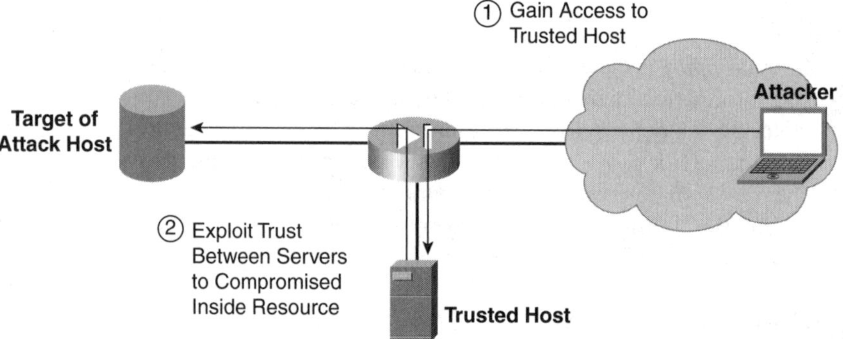

In Figure 5-3, the attacker gains access to a host that is trusted by the target host. Once access is granted to the attacker, the target host is unable to determine the malicious interaction with the trusted host, which might lead to loss, corruption, or stolen data.

Session Hijacking

Session hijacking consists of stealing a legitimate session established between a target and a trusted host. The attacker intercepts the session and makes the target believe it is communicating with the trusted host.

Multiple mechanisms are typically used in session hijacking. *IP spoofing* is one of them. IP spoofing consists of using the source IP address of the trusted system. This method is extremely easy because in many cases, identity is solely based on IP addresses. The fact that most of the routing and forwarding happens on destination IP addresses only makes the attack easier.

TCP initial sequence number (ISN) guessing is another common mechanism in which the hacker intercepts the initial segment exchange (TCP SYN) and predicts the following ISN in the response (TCP SYN/ACK).

NOTE Consult Chapter 7, "IP, TCP, and UDP," for more information on TCP's ISN selection and SYN cookies.

Connectionless protocols such as User Datagram Protocol (UDP) are by nature easier to spoof because there are no sequence numbers and states to predict.

Buffer Overflow Attacks

A *buffer overflow* occurs when a program allocates memory buffer space beyond what it had reserved; it results in memory corruption affecting the data stored in the memory areas that were overflowed.

Buffer overflows are programming errors that many times pass undetected during testing efforts. After they discover the error, attackers can exploit buffer overflows to crash the victim's system and even gain unauthorized access and potentially execute arbitrary commands on the compromised system. A buffer overflow is a problem that can potentially affect any system running software, from servers to network devices; however, in reality, these attacks are mainly conducted against the operating systems of application servers.

Layer 2 Attacks

Layer 2 attacks exploit the vulnerabilities of data link layer protocols and their implementations on Layer 2 switching platforms. One of the characteristics of Layer 2 attacks is that the attacker must be connected to the same LAN as the victims.

Address Resolution Protocol (ARP) spoofing and MAC flooding are examples of attacks that fall into this category:

- **ARP spoofing**—An attack in which the attacker forges the identity of a trusted system by spoofing the system's IP address. ARP spoofing attacks take advantage of the fact that ARP does not provide any control that proves that a particular MAC address truly corresponds to a given IP address. The attacker exploits that vulnerability by sending to the LAN segment an unsolicited, forged ARP reply for the IP address of the gateway that contains its own MAC address, as illustrated in Figure 5-4. When victims update their ARP caches, they unwittingly start sending packets to the attacker instead of the intended gateway.

Figure 5-4 *ARP Spoofing, a Layer 2 Attack*

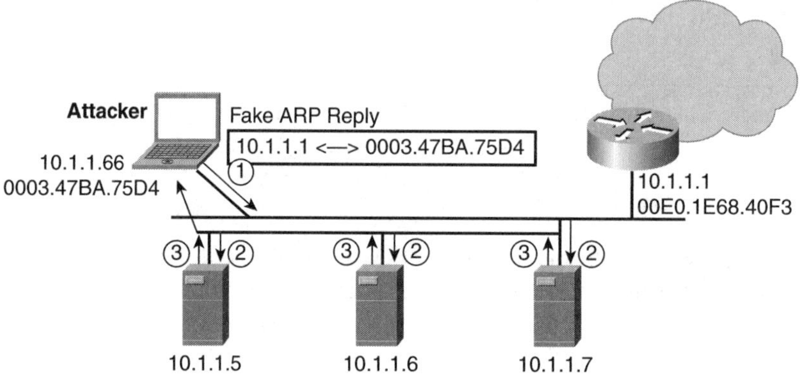

In Figure 5-4, Step 1 is the attacker sending an unsolicited ARP reply with its MAC address and the IP address of the default gateway. The hosts on the segment see the ARP reply and update their ARP cache in Step 2. When the hosts need to talk to the default gateway, Step 3, the destination MAC and IP addresses correspond to the attacker's system, therefore forcing all traffic to it. The attacker can then monitor all traffic destined to the default gateway.

- **MAC flooding**—Another type of attack that exploits the fact that switches start flooding packets when their MAC address tables get full and they receive a packet destined to a MAC address that is not in the table. In this attack, the offender starts flooding the switch with packets containing bogus source MAC addresses. When the number of MAC addresses reaches the maximum capacity of the Layer 2 forwarding table, all the traffic for that specific VLAN is flooded to all the ports. The attack is meant to flood the VLAN with traffic, and secondarily, this attack makes it possible for a malicious host to capture all the traffic sent on a specific VLAN.

NOTE Chapter 12, "Layer 2 Protocol Essentials," explains the use of the MAC address table for Ethernet switching. Chapter 13, "Layer 3 Protocol Essentials," explains the use of the ARP in the Data Center.

For more information about Layer 2 attacks and their mitigation, you can refer to the results of the study conducted by Cisco Systems and @stake at http://www.cisco.com/warp/public/cc/pd/si/casi/ca6000/tech/stake_wp.pdf.

- **VLAN hopping**—A malicious host on VLAN A sends traffic tagged with an 802.1Q tag of VLAN B (different from the one it belongs to). If the access port where the packet is received is also the native VLAN of the trunks, the packet eventually is forwarded to VLAN B, without being routed. This mechanism would allow the host to bypass access control lists (ACLs) set on routers.

NOTE Proper configuration of Cisco Layer 2 switches makes these attacks ineffective. Consult Chapter 21, "Integrating Security into the Infrstructure," for more information.

Network Security Infrastructure

The network security infrastructure includes the security tools used in the Data Center to enforce security policies. The tools include packet-filtering technologies such as ACLs and firewalls and intrusion detection systems (IDSs) both network-based and host-based. The following sections discuss these security tools.

ACLs

ACLs are filtering mechanisms explicitly defined based on packet header information to permit or deny traffic on specific interfaces. An ACL is typically set up as a list that is applied sequentially on the packets until a match is found. Once the match is found, the associated permit or deny operation is applied.

ACLs have an implicit "deny all," which is the last item at the end of the ACL when they are created. ACLs are used to perform basic packet filtering by devices that are not expected to understand the connection context of those packets.

ACLs are used in multiple locations within the Data Center such as the Internet Edge and the intranet server farm. These ACLs are applied to control access to network devices and to specific applications. ACLs are available on Cisco routers as well as firewalls. The following sections describe the types of access lists available.

Standard and Extended Access Lists

The following describes standard and extended access lists:

- **Standard ACLs**—A standard ACL is the simplest type of ACL; it filters traffic solely based on source IP addresses. Standard ACLs are typically deployed to control access to network devices for network management or remote access. For example, you can configure a standard ACL in a router to specify which systems are allowed to Telnet to it. Because of their lack of granularity, standard ACLs are not the recommended option for traffic filtering. In Cisco routers, standard ACLs are configured with a number between 1 and 99.

- **Extended ACLs**—Extended ACL filtering decisions can be based on source and destination IP addresses, Layer 4 protocol, Layer 4 ports, ICMP message type and code, type of service, and precedence. In Cisco routers, you can define extended ACLs by name or by a number in the 100 to 199 range.

Example 5-1 shows the use of a standard ACL for management purposes. You can configure Cisco routers via HTTP. The ACL in Example 5-1 shows how you control access to a router's HTTP server: Only clients from the 10.1.1.x subnet can configure the router via HTTP.

Example 5-1 *Standard Access Lists*

```
ip http access-class securemanagement
ip access-list standard securemanagement
permit 10.1.1.0 0.0.0.255
! (Note: all other access implicitly denied)
```

Example 5-2 shows the use of extended ACLs to restrict the access to interface Ethernet 0 only for the traffic directed to a mail server (TCP/25) and an HTTP (TCP/80) server. All the other traffic is denied.

Example 5-2 *Extended Access Lists*

```
access-list 101 permit tcp any 170.34.54.2 eq 25
access-list 101 permit tcp any 170.34.54.5 eq 80

interface ethernet 0
 ip access-group 101 in
```

Router ACLs and VLAN ACLs

Router ACLs (RACLs) are a typical feature of Cisco routers: they apply to traffic destined to a router interface, either in the form of a physical port or in the form of a VLAN interface. Traffic traverses an interface through the ACL and, only if permitted, is forwarded according to the routing table.

Example 5-2 shows how you normally assign an IOS ACL to an interface. Example 5-3 shows how you assign the access list from Example 5-2 to a VLAN interface, VLAN 10. Notice the presence of the **in** keyword, which means that traffic leaving interface VLAN 10 is allowed. Only inbound traffic on the interface VLAN 10 is filtered.

Example 5-3 *IOS Access Lists*

```
Interface VLAN10
 ip access-group 101 in
```

NOTE *Inbound* and *outbound* refer to the router interface, whether it is a physical interface or a VLAN interface. Traffic with a destination MAC address of the router interface is considered inbound. Traffic sourced from the router interface is considered outbound.

VLAN ACLs (VACLs) are ACLs applied to traffic switched at Layer 2. VLAN ACLs do not have a concept of direction. IOS ACLs are either applied as "in" or "out"; VACLs are applied to all the traffic traversing a VLAN.

Example 5-4 shows a VACL in which the access map matches the ACL 101 (from Example 5-2), and if a match occurs, the traffic is forwarded. Otherwise, the implicit deny takes place. The **vlan filter** command assigns the VACL to VLAN 10.

Example 5-4 *VACL*

```
Aggregation(config)#vlan access-map vaclwebserver
Aggregation(config-access-map)#match ip address 101
Aggregation(config-access-map)#action forward
Aggregation(config)#vlan filter vaclwebserver vlan-list 10
```

Notice that there is no concept of direction. As a result, access list 101 allows traffic to the e-mail and web servers, but the return traffic from the servers is denied. To fix this problem, you have to modify access list 101 with additional entries to permit traffic from 170.34.54.2 and .5 to any destination.

Dynamic ACLs (Lock and Key)

Dynamic ACLs and *lock* and *key* are both names for an advanced type of ACL that allows an authenticated user to pass traffic that otherwise would be denied. When lock and key is configured, the user first needs to authenticate to the router by opening a Telnet session. As soon as the user is authenticated, a dynamic ACL entry is appended to the interface ACL, which opens the user's temporary access through the router. The dynamic entry is built based on template, and it automatically includes the source IP address of the authenticated user.

Lock and key is a useful feature in cases where temporary access should be granted to users, and it can be combined with strong authentication mechanisms such as TACACS+. One of the limitations of lock and key is that you can use only one template at a time. All users share the same access criteria, which is not suitable with multiple groups of users who have different access needs. A solution to that problem is the use of downloadable per-user ACLs with TACACS+.

Example 5-5 illustrates a configuration of lock and key.

Example 5-5 *Lock and Key Access List*

```
username mary password mysecret
interface ethernet1
 ip address 172.16.19.3 255.255.255.0
 ip access-group 111 in
access-list 111 permit tcp any host 172.16.19.3 eq telnet
access-list 111 dynamic controllist timeout 120 permit ip any any
line vty 0
login local
autocommand access-enable timeout 5
```

In this example, once the user Mary is successfully authenticated, a new dynamic entry is appended to the end of ACL 111. This entry includes the source IP address of the host used by Mary, which gives her full access to the network.

Reflexive ACLs

Reflexive ACLs are an advanced type of ACL that lets you filter IP packets based on upper-layer session information. These ACLs typically increase the functionality of routers configured as packet-filtering firewalls. Reflexive ACLs restrict sessions to those initiated from a secured segment and deny any attempts coming from an unsecured interface.

Reflexive ACLs are temporary entries that are nested to an existing extended named ACL. They are never applied to an interface by themselves. The temporary entries are created as soon as a new IP connection (TCP or UDP) is created, and they are removed as it ends.

Example 5-6 shows a reflexive ACL applied to the external interface of a router, the interface connecting to the Internet service provider (ISP).

Example 5-6 *Reflexive ACLs*

```
interface Serial 1
 description Access to the Internet via this interface
 ip access-group outinboundfilters in
 ip access-group inoutboundfilters out
!
ip reflexive-list timeout 120
!
ip access-list extended inoutboundfilters
 permit tcp any any reflect tcptraffic
!
ip access-list extended outinboundfilters
 permit bgp any any
 evaluate tcptraffic
!
```

This ACL allows TCP traffic from the internal network to reach the Internet using the filters defined in **outboundfilters**. The **reflect tcptraffic** statement builds access-list entries to append to the ACL **inboundfilters** based on outbound TCP connections (leaving the interface).

Traffic from the Internet to the internal network is blocked by **inboundfilters** unless the traffic is Border Gateway Protocol (BGP) or it belongs to a TCP connection originating from the network. The **evaluate tcptraffic** statement permits the traffic belonging to TCP connections originating from the internal network.

Firewalls

A *firewall* is a sophisticated filtering device that separates LAN segments, giving each segment a different security level and establishing a security perimeter that controls the traffic flow between segments. Firewalls are typically deployed in strategic locations and commonly work as the only pass-through point to sensitive resources. For example, firewalls are most commonly deployed at the Internet Edge where they act as boundary to the internal networks.

Firewalls are expected to perform critical functions in recognizing specific applications to better secure the application resources, and they are expected to perform these functions in the primary traffic paths by creating a boundary between the secure and unsecured areas. The considerations are as follows:

- **Performance**—Firewalls are typically deployed to separate the secured and unsecured areas of a network. This separation forces the firewall to be in the primary traffic path, potentially exposed to large volumes of data. Performance becomes a natural design factor to ensure that the firewall meets the particular requirements. Some typical parameters used to measure a firewall's capacity are packets per second (throughput), connections per second, and concurrent connections. These metrics are explained in detail in Chapter 22, "Performance Metrics of Data Center Devices."
- **Application support**—Another important aspect is the capability of a firewall to control and protect a particular application or protocol, such as Telnet, FTP, and HTTP. The firewall is expected to understand application-level packet exchanges to determine whether packets do follow the application behavior and, if they do not, to deny the traffic.

There are different types of firewalls based on their packet-processing capabilities and their awareness of application-level information:

- Packet-filtering firewalls
- Proxy firewalls
- Stateful firewalls
- Hybrid firewalls

Packet-Filtering Firewalls

Packet-filtering firewalls, often referred to as screening routers, are network devices that filter packets based on header information. A router configured with ACLs is an example of this type of firewall. The capability to identify different protocols and applications depends on the granularity of the filters. For example, you can use extended ACLs to specify which TCP/UDP ports are permitted or blocked.

Packet-filtering firewalls are the most basic class of firewalls and have the following characteristics:

- Access rules are static and cannot handle protocols that dynamically negotiate the port used in the communication flows. For example, streaming video session use multiple concurrent connections. A control connection tracks the streaming session, synchronizes the client and server, and feeds the streaming video. The ports and the transport protocols are dynamically negotiated when the session is established, forcing a static firewall configuration to support the likely protocols and ports. Having all the likely ports open is unnecessary and could lead to exploitation by an attacker.
- The firewalls cannot determine whether inbound packets belong to established connections. This type of firewall does not track the state of the connections, so it is unable to block packets that might belong to an existing connection. In addition, because of their stateless nature, packet-filtering firewalls cannot identify the sequence of packet exchange and whether a protocol is being violated, and consequently can permit harmful packets that do not correspond to legitimate connections.
- The firewalls cannot inspect the payload of packets to perform the adequate changes or read the appropriate information. Many protocols insert IP address information inside the payload portion of packets. This type of firewall cannot modify the embedded IP addresses, consequently breaking the communication if the routers use address translation.

NOTE Some packet-filtering firewalls support a special feature that, by using the **established** keyword, identifies and processes packets that belong to an existing connection according to the particular ACL.

Proxy Firewalls

Proxy firewalls, also known as application-level proxies, are application-specific firewalls that are frequently implemented in software. These firewalls are specially designed to protect applications associated with well-known ports and are typically limited to SMTP, HTTP, Telnet, and FTP. The protection comes from the capability to identify the application protocol exchange and determine whether the packets comply with the exchange. The proxy firewalls proxy outbound connections for specific protocols, thus implicitly denying incoming traffic that does not belong to outbound initiated connections. Microsoft Proxy Server is an example of a proxy firewall.

The proxy firewall acts as an intermediary for all the connections initiated by clients. Every time a client needs to establish a session, the request is first sent to the firewall, which initiates a request to the desired location or service on behalf of the client. This process typically requires the client to be configured to use the proxy. Another typical characteristic of proxy firewalls is that all connections are established using the public IP address of the firewall, hiding the real (and private) IP addresses of the clients. Proxy firewalls implemented in a transparent manner are an exception to this rule, and they do maintain the client IP addresses. The transparent implementation is one in which the firewalls are inserted in the traffic path without requiring changes to the addressing schemes or client configuration.

One of the advantages of proxy firewalls is the level of intelligence they provide for the supported applications and protocols. The proxy firewalls keep track of connections and their packets. The application intelligence allows them to identify when flows are dynamically negotiated and modify the access rules to permit the corresponding traffic. In addition, they can inspect the payload of packets and change the interior address information to make network address translation (NAT) possible. Proxy firewalls also provide advanced services such as authentication, content filtering, caching, and accounting for the supported protocols.

Some disadvantages of proxy firewalls follow:

- Proxy-firewall processing is resource-intensive; therefore, performance and scalability tend to be lower than with other types of firewalls.
- Client configuration, if required, increases the deployment, maintenance, and administration tasks.
- Outside a handful of applications, the proxy firewall has limited support for additional applications.

Stateful Firewalls

Stateful firewalls keep track of connection state and only permit packets that match legitimate connections. IOS Firewall, PIX Firewall, and the Catalyst 6500 Firewall Services Module are examples of stateful firewalls.

The state of the connections is generally maintained in connection tables that are dynamically updated as data flows are established and ended. These connection tables are not reserved for connection-oriented protocols such as TCP; they also maintain the state of data flows for connectionless protocols such as UDP. There are no standards for defining the information that should be maintained by a stateful firewall, but typically connection entries at least include the following:

- Protocol
- Source and destination IP addresses
- Source and destination UDP/TCP ports
- TCP sequence numbers
- TCP flags
- Connection duration

In addition to knowing which packets correspond to existing connections, thereby reducing the chances of spoofing attacks, stateful firewalls also perform application-level inspection for certain applications. This task allows them to check and change payload information such as embedded IP addresses or to identify malformed packets, providing an additional level of security.

Stateful firewalls are also capable of providing protection against common DoS attacks such as TCP SYN floods. DoS protection keeps track of embryonic connections (connections that are in the process of being established). Firewalls then can limit the total number of embryonic connections per server, and once a predefined threshold is reached, they simply ignore new requests until the number of pending connections returns to an acceptable value. In more sophisticated implementations, when the threshold is reached, the firewall can use TCP SYN cookies to avoid the effects of DoS attacks.

NOTE For more information on TCP SYN cookies, see Chapter 7, "IP, TCP, and UDP."

Stateful firewalls in general perform better and offer greater capacity than proxy servers because they do not need to proxy client connections and use hardware to offload some of the more intense computational tasks. Multiple mechanisms are commonly used to accelerate the processing of packets. A common method consists in checking every incoming packet against the connection table, which you can implement using hardware. Then, only packets matching a connection entry are inspected at the application level as needed.

Hybrid Firewalls

Hybrid firewalls combine the behavior of the previous types of firewalls, including key features that make the firewalls more flexible and intelligent in dealing with application traffic. The comprehensive feature set is the basis for the most common types of firewalls. Hybrid firewalls can be proxy, stateful, or packet-filtering firewalls in addition to application-level inspection firewalls with advanced services such as authentication, content filtering, and accounting. The PIX Firewall and Catalyst 6500 Firewall Services Module are examples of hybrid firewalls.

When the PIX Firewall is configured in cut-through proxy mode, a user first needs to authenticate to the firewall. If the authentication succeeds, the connection is proxied and a new entry is added to the connection state table. When packets that belong to the same connection arrive, they are sent directly to the stateful engine for processing, dramatically reducing the processing cycles. You can also configure the PIX Firewall to work in conjunction with filtering engines such as Websense and N2H2, which control the user activity on the Internet while keeping detailed records of the usage of the network resources.

NOTE Websense and N2H2 are host-based systems that provide application-layer intelligence used to filter traffic based on specific application-layer information. A common example is to filter based on either the URL in an HTTP request or the object type (.mov, .jpg, .mpg, etc.).

For more information on Websense or N2H2, consult http://www.websense.com/ and http://www.n2h2.com/.

Figure 5-5 presents a cut-through proxy mode environment and the steps in processing traffic through the firewall.

Figure 5-5 *PIX Cut-Through Proxy*

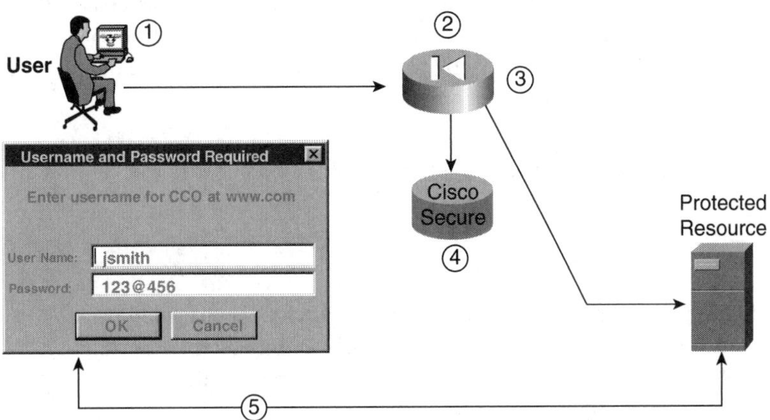

The process in Figure 5-5 follows:

1 The user makes a request to a protected resource.
2 The firewall receives the request and knows it is configured to proxy the request and challenge the user.

3. The firewall challenges the user for a username and password, authenticates the user, and checks the security policy on a RADIUS or TACACS+ server.
4. The firewall now can initiate a request on behalf of the user.
5. The connection is established, and the user can interact with the server holding the object associated with the request.

Common Firewall Limitations

Firewalls are useful tools for network security, but as with every tool, they have limitations worth understanding. Once you understand these limitations, your design choices and security-policy implementations have a greater chance of meeting the desired service levels.

The following list shows some challenges of firewalls:

- Firewalls cannot establish any correlation between different events, so they cannot block some attacks that are performed in multiple stages. For example, CodeRed propagates via HTTP and exploits a well-known vulnerability on Microsoft's IIS servers versions 4 and 5 via a buffer-overflow attack. The propagation process does not violate any of the protocol rules of HTTP, and once vulnerable servers are compromised, the worm uses them to scan for new vulnerable systems. Firewalls typically do not have the intelligence to detect the relation between these types of events. In this case, firewalls treat the propagation and the scan as completely independent events.
- Firewalls cannot actively respond against attacks. Firewalls basically block or permit packets based on the access rules configured and according to the context of connections, but typically by themselves, they do not have the mechanisms to dynamically block an ongoing attack.

These common limitations are typically addressed by devices that are specifically designed for those tasks. These devices are IDSs.

IDSs

IDSs are real-time systems that can detect intruders and suspicious activities and report them to a monitoring system. They are configured to block or mitigate intrusions in progress and eventually immunize the systems from future attacks.

IDSs have two fundamental components:

- **Sensors**—Appliances and software agents that analyze the traffic on the network or the resource usage on end systems to identify intrusions and suspicious activities. Sensors can be network-based or host-based.
- **IDS management**—Single- or multi-device system used to configure and administer sensors and to additionally collect all the alarm information generated by the sensors.

The sensors are equivalent to surveillance tools, and IDS management is the control center watching the information produced by the surveillance tools. Figure 5-6 shows the components of an IDS environment.

Figure 5-6 *IDS Environment*

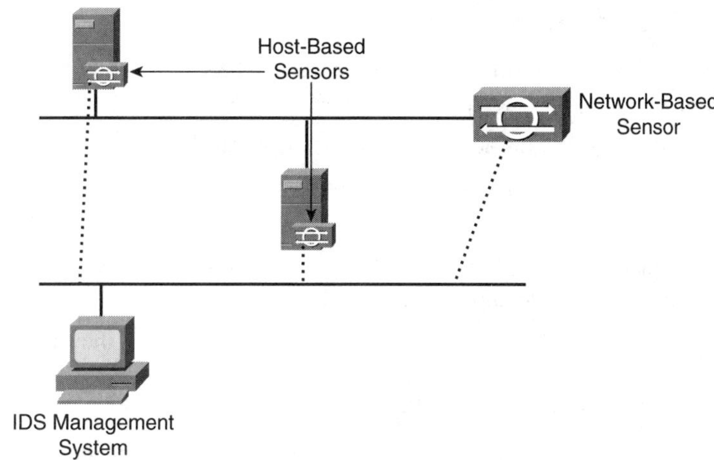

In Figure 5-6, IDSs are placed on the network, network-based IDSs (NIDSs), and on hosts, host-based IDS (HIDSs), monitoring traffic and sending their information to the IDS management system.

Network-Based IDSs

Network-based sensors are systems that connect to network segments and inspect traffic to detect intrusions and suspicious activities. These sensors are available as software on routers (IOS IDS) and firewalls (PIX IDS), standalone appliances, or hardware modules such as the Cisco IDS-4250 appliance and the IDS Module for Catalyst 6500. Standalone appliances and modules provide a more comprehensive level of support than the IDS solutions based on integrated software.

Network-based sensors usually use two network interfaces, one that connects to the network being monitored and another one to a secure segment that provides access to a management system. The monitoring interface does not have a MAC address, so it is unable to send traffic. The switch port where the IDS is connected sees all the traffic mirrored by the switch. The management interface does have a MAC address and an IP address to communicate with the IDS management.

Although you can configure some sensors to use a single interface for both functions, it is recommended to use separate interfaces to isolate the management infrastructure from the segments where traffic is monitored.

Which segments need monitoring by an IDS is a question better answered by the critically of the systems and the type of traffic expected. The recommendation is to start deploying network-based sensors on those network segments where attacks are more likely to come through (that is, at the Internet Edge) and on the segments housing mission-critical servers.

Host-Based IDSs

Host-based sensors are software agents that run on the systems to be protected. These types of agents provide protection at different levels:

- Identify and prevent malicious behavior beforehand
- Shield some specific applications by blocking suspicious packets before they reach the application
- Automatically maintain the server operating-system update with the appropriate patches to mitigate known vulnerabilities

One of the principle characteristics of host-based sensors is that they are operating-system–specific and aware of certain applications. There are different agents for Unix or Windows systems as well as for Apache or IIS servers.

Host-based IDSs are recommended in systems that receive connections from untrusted parties, systems that house mission-critical applications, and systems that receive traffic that cannot be protected by other means (i.e. encrypted traffic that gets decrypted on the system).

Network-Based Versus Host-Based IDSs

Network-based and host-based IDSs both have their own advantages and limitations, yet they are complementary technologies.

Network-based systems protect all the devices that are accessible through the segment where they are connected and can easily identify activities such as scans, but network-based sensors do not have any end-system visibility and cannot determine whether an attack on a system was successful. Network-based sensors are also unable to monitor and analyze encrypted traffic.

Host-based sensors do have visibility for what is occurring on the end system and can proactively block attacks to the operating system. The HIDS agents are centrally managed and are expected to consume some server resources. The effect on server performance depends on the configuration yet is reasonable enough that it does not impact the server.

IDSs could be further classified by how they perform the monitoring functions. The following section discusses the two types.

Anomaly-Based Versus Signature-Based IDS

There are two approaches IDS systems use to detect intrusions and suspicious activities: anomalies and signatures.

Anomaly-based systems define normal activities in terms of network traffic and system-resource usage so that any deviation from the defined baseline is consider an attack. Anomaly-based systems are typically rolled out with the learning period in which all relevant parameters are analyzed.

For example, an anomaly-based system determines what is the normal distribution of the traffic per protocol type, how many connections per second a particular server receives, etc., after which it generate alarms any time there is a significant deviation from the statistical values.

Signature-based systems work in a different way. They explicitly define which activity should be considered malicious, which is identified by a particular signature, and compare the traffic and resource utilization with the signature. A match in the comparison would indicate the presence of a malicious event. In the comparison process, each and every packet is compared against the signature. It is important to note that signature patterns can be dispersed in multiple packets, so the network-based system must reassemble the session and eventually perform the protocol analysis.

Signatures

Signatures are templates used by IDSs to determine unusual behaviors on the network that could be considered security violations. An IDS compares these templates against traffic patterns or specific traffic conversations, looking for a match. A match implies that an anomaly has been detected and an action is required. The action could be just sending an alarm or sending an alarm and applying a measure designed to stop the anomaly.

Signatures are grouped according to the types of attacks they attempt to match:

- **Embedded signatures**—Specific, known attack signatures that come with the IDS. The user cannot change these signatures.
- **Connection signatures**—Protocol-specific signatures configurable by the user. The protocol definition (TCP/UDP) could include the port number.
- **String-matching signatures**—Attack signatures based on portions of the payload in packets. The signatures use a regular expression to perform the string-matching function on the packet. These signatures are user-configurable.
- **ACL signatures**—Policy-violation signatures logged by network devices. These signatures require the network devices to log ACL violations and to communicate with the IDS via syslog before alarms are generated. These signatures are user-configurable.

Typical IDS Response Actions

Most IDSs are capable of responding to identified security incidents using specific mechanisms:

- **IP session login**—This response is the least aggressive response and consists of logging the entire IP session that corresponds to a detected intrusion. The logs are commonly used for forensic analysis to determine the details of the event and identify where the security gap was and how to correct it. This information can also be use as evidence if law enforcement is required.
- **TCP resets**—You can configure the IDS to generate TCP resets on behalf of a victim system. This setting is helpful in case the attack is launched using a TCP connection. The IDS sends a TCP reset generated using the source IP address of the victim and a random MAC address to avoid conflicts with Layer 2 switches and the MAC address of the victim.
- **Shunning or blocking**—The IDS can instruct a network device such as a router, switch, or firewall to dynamically apply an ACL to block the traffic coming from an attacker. This response is the most aggressive response and can result in a self-induced DoS problem when it accidentally blocks valid traffic. In this type of scenario, the IDS can communicate with the shunning devices using various protocols such as Telnet and Secure Shell (SSH). Figure 5-7 illustrates a shunning example.

Figure 5-7 *Shunning Example*

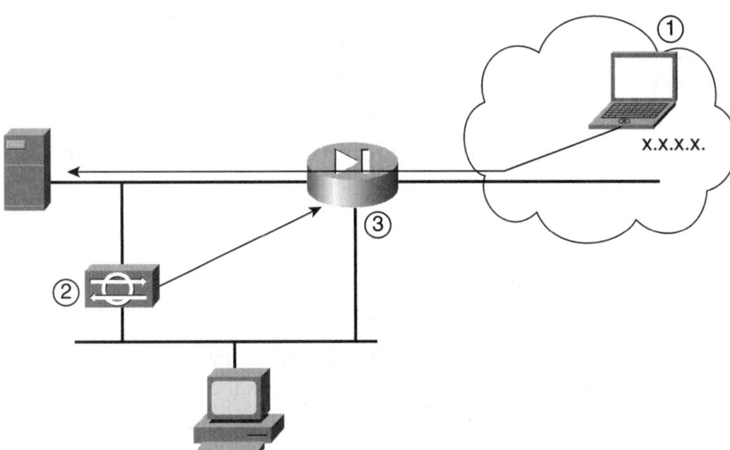

The transactions depicted in Figure 5-7 follow:

1. The attacker launches an attack that passes through the firewalls.
2. The IDS detects the attack.
3. The IDS downloads an ACL on the firewall to block the attack. All packets from *x.x.x.x* are denied.

IDSs should use response actions when there is a clear understanding of the protocols and applications involved. You should selectively deploy the actions, starting with only a few signatures, and expand gradually as you gain more understanding about the application environment.

Layer 2 Security

Cisco Layer 2 switches provide tools to prevent the common Layer 2 attacks introduced in the section, "Common Attacks," earlier in the chapter. More details on where to use them is provided in Chapter 21.

Port Security

Port security is a feature that permits you to configure a switch port to only accept packets coming with a trusted source MAC address. You can manually configure the trusted MAC addresses, or the switch can learn them dynamically. When a packet arrives with a nontrusted MAC address, the switch can either shut down the port or selectively drop the offending packets.

TIP In most cases, it is more convenient to configure a port to selectively drop the offending packets rather than shut down the port. For example, if port security shuts down the port, a MAC flooding attack would result in a DoS to legitimate application traffic because the port would be brought down.

Example 5-7 shows the configuration of a switch for port security. With this configuration, only the host with MAC address 00-90-2b-03-34-08 can send traffic to this port.

Example 5-7 *Port Security Configuration for a Single MAC Address*

```
Access(config)#interface FastEthernet2/1
Access(config-if)#switchport mode access
Access(config-if)#switchport port-security
Access(config-if)#switchport port-security mac-address 00-90-2b-03-34-08
```

A more flexible configuration consists of specifying the maximum number of MAC addresses allowed on a specific port, as shown in Example 5-8. With this configuration, the switch learns five MAC addresses from the port. After it learns these MAC addresses, traffic with a source MAC different from any of those five is dropped.

Example 5-8 *Port Security Configuration to Allow 5 MAC Addresses*

```
Access(config)#interface FastEthernet2/1
Access(config-if)#switchport mode access
Access(config-if)#switchport port-security
Access(config-if)#switchport port-security maximum 5
```

ARP Inspection

ARP inspection is a feature that lets you specify the mapping between the default gateway IP address and its MAC address. If the switch sees a gratuitous ARP carrying an invalid mapping, the switch drops the packet. This process prevents ARP spoofing attacks known as *man-in-the-middle* attacks.

ARP inspection requires the use of VACLs because the gratuitous ARP is not destined to the router but to the local subnet.

NOTE The ARP inspection feature is currently available in the Catalyst 6500 for CatOS 7.5 and higher. Private VLANs and port security can protect from ARP spoofing as well.

There are two commands for ARP inspection. One enables the ARP inspection feature using the following command:

```
set security acl ip arp-inspection
```

The second one configures the switch to drop packets based on the MAC address in the Ethernet header not matching the MAC in the ARP header:

```
set security acl arp-inspection match-mac enable
```

It can also drop packets based on illegal MAC or IP addresses:

```
set security acl arp-inspection address-validation enable
```

Illegal MAC addresses include 00-00-00-00-00-00, FF-FF-FF-FF-FF-FF, and multicast MAC addresses, and illegal IP addresses include 0.0.0.0, 255.255.255.222, and multicast IP addresses.

An additional command aimed at limiting the number of ARP on a per-port basis is

```
set port arp-inspection mod/port drop-threshold rate shutdown-threshold rate
```

Private VLANs

Private VLANs permit the isolation of ports from one another within the same VLAN. You use three types of ports to achieve this isolation:

- **Promiscuous ports**—Can communicate with all other ports
- **Isolated ports**—Can only communicate with promiscuous ports
- **Community ports**—Can only communicate with promiscuous ports and other ports within the same community

These ports are associated with three types of VLANs:

- **Primary VLAN**—Carries traffic from promiscuous ports to isolated, community, and other promiscuous ports. Traffic from the primary VLAN can be forwarded to either isolated or community VLANs.
- **Isolated VLAN**—Carries traffic from isolated ports to promiscuous ports. Server ports attached to the same isolated VLANs cannot talk to each other; the server traffic can only go to the router.
- **Community VLAN**—Carries traffic between community ports and to promiscuous ports. You can configure multiple community VLANs in a private VLAN.

Figure 5-8 illustrates the concept of a private VLAN. The ports on the same community VLAN (the dashed line) can communicate with each other and to the promiscuous port (which is on the primary VLAN). The ports on the isolated VLANs (the continuous line and the dotted line) cannot talk to the community VLANs, to other isolated VLANs, or even to other ports assigned to the same isolated VLAN.

Figure 5-8 *Private VLANs*

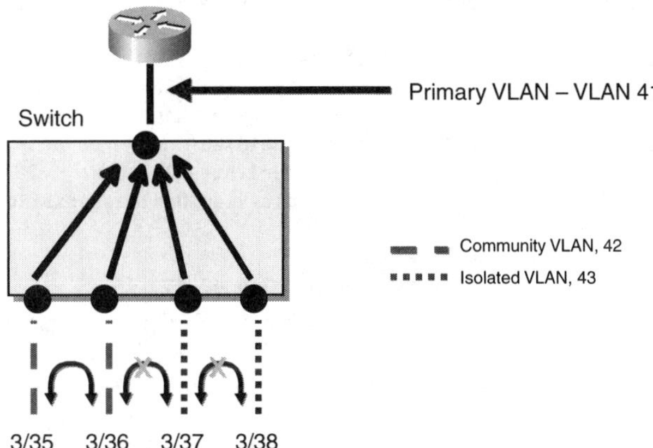

All the ports can send traffic to the promiscuous ports and receive traffic from the promiscuous port. The key point to keep in mind is that private VLANs are designed to segregate traffic that belongs to the same subnet/primary VLAN. Normally, this process would require allocating more subnets in such a way that you can filter subnet-to-subnet traffic.

With private VLANs, you can use a single subnet and force all the server-generated traffic to go to a promiscuous port, which typically is a router port (or a VLAN interface). By doing so, you protect servers from Layer 2 attacks such as ARP spoofing.

Example 5-8 shows the configuration for the setup in Figure 5-9. VLAN 41 is defined as a primary VLAN, VLAN 42 is set as a community VLAN, and VLAN 43 is an isolated VLAN. The example also shows the necessary mappings to define ports 3/35 and 3/36 as community and ports 3/37 and 3/38 as isolated. You configure the router interface VLAN 10 as a promiscuous port by defining the private VLAN mapping.

Example 5-9 *Private VLAN Configuration*

```
Aggregation(config)#vlan 41
Aggregation(config-vlan)#private-vlan primary
Aggregation(config)#vlan 42
Aggregation(config-vlan)#private-vlan community
Aggregation(config)#vlan 43
Aggregation(config-vlan)#private-vlan isolated
Aggregation(config)#vlan 41
Aggregation(config-vlan)#private-vlan association 42,43

Aggregation(config)#interface FastEthernet3/35
Aggregation(config-if)#switchport mode private-vlan host
Aggregation(config-if)#switchport private-vlan host-association 41 42
Aggregation(config)#interface FastEthernet3/36
Aggregation(config-if)#switchport mode private-vlan host
Aggregation(config-if)#switchport private-vlan host-association 41 42

Aggregation(config)#interface FastEthernet3/37
Aggregation(config-if)#switchport mode private-vlan host
Aggregation(config-if)#switchport private-vlan host-association 41 43
Aggregation(config)#interface FastEthernet3/38
Aggregation(config-if)#switchport mode private-vlan host
Aggregation(config-if)#switchport private-vlan host-association 41 43

Aggregation(config)#interface VLAN 41
Aggregation(config-if)#private-vlan mapping 42,43
```

NOTE Private VLANs are available in different Catalyst switches, and even though the functionality is equivalent, command syntax and specifics change from one platform to the other.

802.1Q Tag All

The problem of VLAN hopping derives from the fact that 802.1Q carries untagged traffic that belongs to the same VLAN as the native VLAN of the trunk port. If a host sends traffic with a VLAN tag (VLAN 20, for example) on an access port whose VLAN is the same as the native VLAN of a trunk (VLAN 10 for example), the host's traffic goes on the trunk (by virtue of transparent bridging).

The switch at the other end of the trunk interprets the VLAN tag 20 correctly as the VLAN that the traffic needs to be put on. What happens is that a host configured on VLAN 10 manages to forward traffic to VLAN 20, just because VLAN 10 is also the native VLAN of an 802.1Q trunk.

If all the VLANs on the 802.1Q trunk were tagged, this problem would not occur. The solution consists of enabling VLAN tagging on all switches. Using **vlan dot1q tag native** basically tells the switch to also tag the packets corresponding to the native VLAN.

Private VLANs and Firewalls

You can use private VLANs in the Data Center in conjunction with firewalls. Firewalls are typically configured with multiple demilitarized zones (DMZs) to filter server-to-server traffic passing from one subnet to another subnet. The firewall performs the routing function, the firewall being the default gateway for the servers, and in addition to routing traffic, it also applies stateful inspection and access lists.

In Figure 5-9, you can see a firewall connected to a Layer 2 switch either with separate ports or with a trunk. The continuous line is the VLAN for the web servers, for example, and the dashed line is the VLAN for the application servers.

The default gateway for the servers is the firewall. Traffic from the web servers to the application servers is routed by the firewall, which also applies ACLs and performs stateful inspection.

Traffic local to the web server subnet does not go through the firewall. Using private VLANs, the traffic can be further segmented and kept local to a subset of the server farm.

At the bottom of Figure 5-9, you can see that the web servers cannot communicate directly with each other because they are assigned to isolated VLANs. The same is true for the application servers.

Figure 5-9 *Private VLANs and Firewalls*

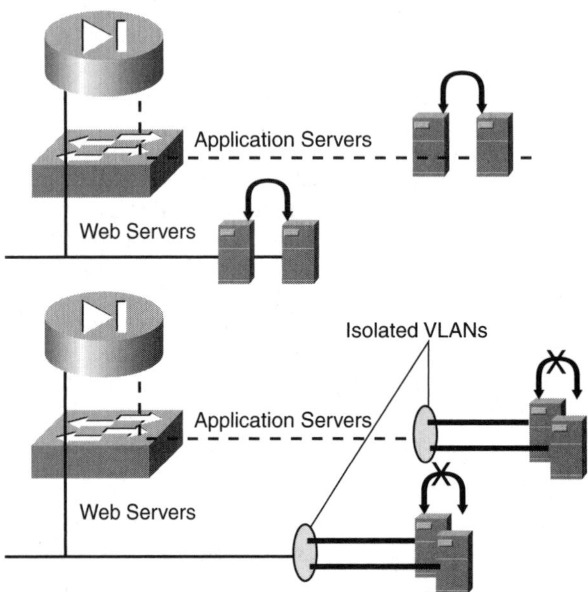

Security Fundamentals

This section discusses fundamental security concepts such as encryption; encryption algorithms (referred to as ciphers); authentication, authorization, and accounting (AAA); and virtual private networks (VPNs). Chapter 15, "Security Protocols and Technology," provides additional details on these technologies.

Cryptography

Cryptography is simply the science of encrypting and decrypting information. Cryptography has multiple uses in a Data Center: the encryption of transactions from client to server, encryption of communication between a user and a managed device, encryption of the communication channel between two sites, and so on.

Encryption is the process of transforming data into a format that cannot be read by anyone except the intended receiver. Encryption uses algorithms called *ciphers*, which are based on mathematical transformations applied to the original information. In this process, the original information (*plaintext*) is processed along with an encrypting key to produce a *ciphertext*, or the resulting scrambled data.

Decryption is the reverse process in which the receiver obtains the original plaintext from the ciphertext, which is possible with the right set of credentials or decryption keys. A key is a randomly generated string used to encrypt and decrypt information. Figure 5-10 illustrates the processes of encryption and decryption.

Figure 5-10 *Encryption and Decryption Example*

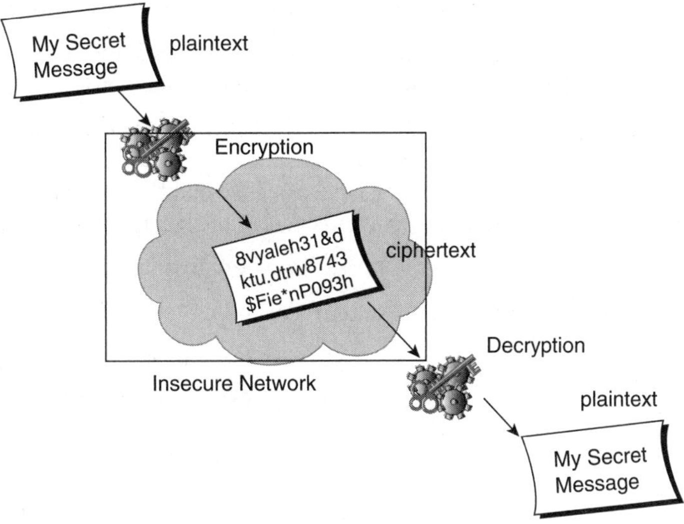

In Figure 5-10, the message that needs to be encrypted is considered plaintext. The plaintext is encrypted using the encryption algorithm and the encryption key, producing an encrypted message called ciphertext. The ciphertext is then sent over the network; it remains confidential because the data cannot be seen without decrypting it and decryption cannot occur without the proper keys. Once the ciphertext arrives at its intended destination, it is decrypted and presented in plaintext to the application.

Cryptography is typically associated with confidentiality but also provides for integrity, nonrepudiation, authentication, and antireplay protection:

- **Confidentiality**—Ensures that the information cannot be read by anybody but the intended receiver. The information is encrypted in a format that cannot be understood by anyone but the entity holding the appropriate key to decrypt it.
- **Integrity**—Ensures that the information is consistent and that no unauthorized modification can happen without being detected. The encryption software signs each packet with a secret key. When the intended destination receives the packet, the signature is checked to make sure the packet has not been changed in transit and that it was signed with the right key.

- **Nonrepudiation**—Means a sender cannot deny it was the source of the signed information sent. Public-key cryptography provides nonrepudiation when the sender uses a private key that is only known and controlled by the sender, and only the corresponding public key can decrypt what was encrypted with the private key. Because the owner of the key is unique, you know the message was sent by that owner.

  The sender cannot deny the origin of the information once it is successfully decrypted with a public key that indicates that the right private key was used for encryption.
- **Authentication**—Allows the sender and receiver to confirm each other's identity to make sure they are communicating with the intended party.
- **Antireplay protection**—Used at the IP packet level to ensure that packets are not intercepted, modified, and inserted back in the communication stream between client and server. The software checks the sequence number of the packets arriving to the destination. The sequence number is part of the header of the encryption protocol.

Data Center security uses encryption with two primary purposes:

- To protect the confidentiality of user's data
- To secure the communications over the management infrastructure

IP Security (IPSec), SSH, Secure Socket Layer (SSL), and Transport LAN Service (TLS) are examples of widely deployed protocols that you can use to secure the communication in Data Centers.

As explained at the beginning of this section, encryption and decryption algorithms are typically based on complex mathematical transformations and on the use of keys. Some algorithms use the same key for encryption and decryption, but others use a pair of keys.

Symmetric Encryption

In *symmetric* encryption algorithms, encryption and decryption happen using a unique key. In symmetric encryption, both sender and receiver share the same key, which must be maintained in secrecy. For that reason, symmetric encryption algorithms are also known as *secret-key* algorithms. Figure 5-11 illustrates the concept of symmetric encryption.

Figure 5-11 *Symmetric Encryption*

In Figure 5-11, the sender and receiver share the same key, which implies on one hand that the key is used for the encryption/decryption process and on the other that the exchange of the key is critical to maintain the confidentiality of the data.

In general, symmetric algorithms are faster when encrypting/decrypting than asymmetric algorithms. Symmetric algorithms are commonly deployed to provide payload encryption only. Encryption through symmetric algorithms provides confidentiality; however, it does not provide authentication and nonrepudiation.

One of the evident challenges of this type of algorithms is the secure distribution of the secret key shared by sender and receiver. Another problem is that each pair of users needs a secret key, which poses a challenge when symmetric encryption is deployed on a large scale because of key management.

Data Encryption Standard (DES), Triple DES (3DES), Rivest Cipher 4 (RC4), International Data Encryptions Algorithm (IDEA), and Advanced Encryption Standard (AES) are examples of symmetric encryption algorithms.

Asymmetric Encryption

Asymmetric encryption, also referred to as *public-key cryptography*, uses two separate keys for *encryption* and decryption. One of the keys is called the *private key*, and it is maintained in secrecy by the sender. The other key is known as *public key*, and it is known to everyone who needs to communicate with the owner of the key. The *public key* is calculated from the private key but uses mathematical functions such that the reverse operation is practically unfeasible. Obtaining a private key from a public key should be computationally not viable.

Asymmetric encryption provides authentication, integrity, and confidentially services. Authentication and integrity are together the most common use for asymmetric algorithms. In general, asymmetric algorithms are slower than symmetric algorithms when encrypting; for that reason, they are typically used to encrypt only light-volume data such as key distribution, whereas symmetric algorithms are the preferred option for bulk encryption.

On the other hand, asymmetric algorithms simplify the problem of key distribution and scale better than symmetric encryption, which makes them a more attractive option for authentication services.

One of the characteristics of asymmetric encryption is that the key pairs are such that any of the keys can decrypt what was encrypted with the other key. In this way, the public key can decrypt what was encrypted with the private key, which is done for authentication. Likewise, the private key can decrypt what was encrypted using the public key, which is used for confidentiality.

Figure 5-12 depicts how an asymmetric encryption algorithm uses a pair of keys to provide confidentiality.

Figure 5-12 *Asymmetric Encryption for Confidentiality*

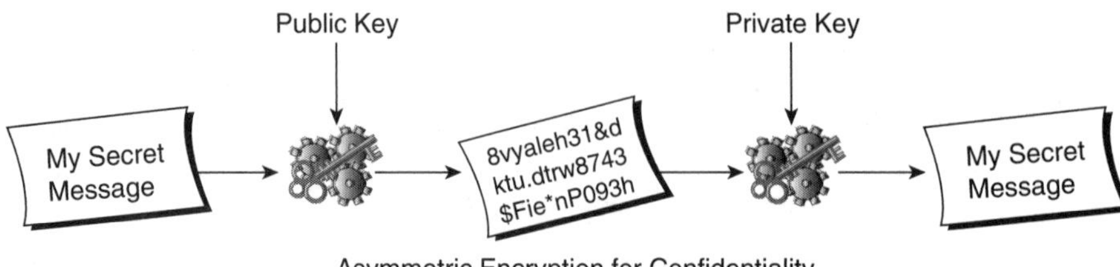

In this example, the sender encrypts the data using the receiver's public key, and the receiver decrypts the ciphertext using its secret key, which is only known to the receiver.

Figure 5-13 shows how you can use asymmetric encryption for origin authentication and nonrepudiation. In this example, the sender encrypts the data using the private key. Then, the receiver decrypts the ciphertext using the sender's public key. The ciphertext can be successfully decrypted only if it has been encrypted with the right secret key. Because the sender is the only one in possession of the secret key, if a message is successfully decrypted, that indicates that it actually came from the sender. This procedure is typically used for digital signatures.

Figure 5-13 *Asymmetric Encryption for Authentication*

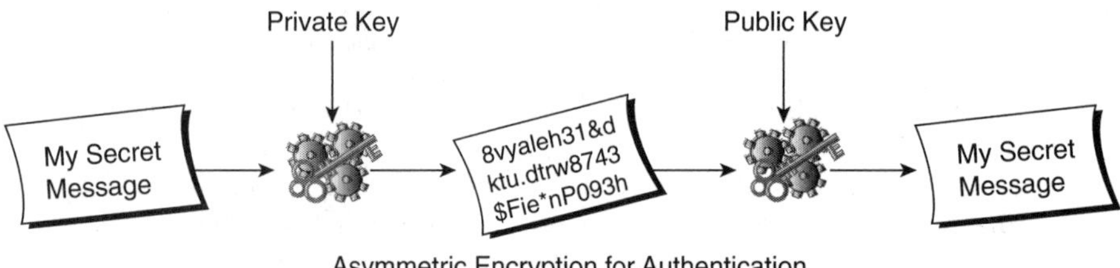

Rivest, Shamir, and Adleman (RSA), Digital Signature Algorithm (DSA), and Elliptic Curve Cryptosystem (ECC) are examples of asymmetric algorithms.

Symmetric algorithms are further divided into two categories, depending on whether encryption\decryption is done on blocks or over streams of data:

- **Block ciphers**—Refer to a symmetric algorithm in which the plaintext is divided into fixed-length blocks that are then transformed into cipher blocks of the same length, typically 64 bits.
- **Stream ciphers**—Process the plaintext on bits rather than blocks by using a simpler yet faster algorithm. With stream ciphers, the plaintext is typically processed with a random sequence of bits called the *keystream*, commonly using a simple XOR operation.

In practice, stream ciphers are faster, but because of the difficulty of generating truly random keystreams, they are not as secure as block ciphers. RC4 is an example of widely used stream cipher. The Rijndael algorithm, DES in Electronic Code Book (ECB) and Cipher Block Chaining (CBC) modes, and RC6 are examples of block ciphers.

In addition to encryption/decryption algorithms, mechanisms should ensure that data has not been changed while in transit.

Cryptographic Hashing Algorithms

A *cryptographic hash algorithm* is a one-way function that takes a variable-length input and produces a fixed-size output called a digest, hash, or fingerprint. This fingerprint is appended to the packet and used by the receiver to determine the authenticity of the data.

The resulting fingerprint is expected to be cryptographically strong. Being cryptographically strong implies that you cannot easily find the fingerprint by computing the original data (re-image resistance) and it is difficult to find different data that produces the same fingerprint (collision resistance).

Figure 5-14 illustrates the concept behind hash algorithms.

Figure 5-14 *Cryptographic Hash Algorithm*

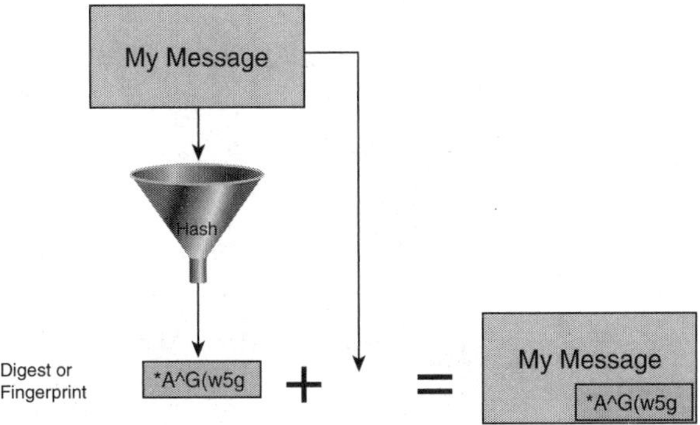

In Figure 5-14, the hash algorithm derives the fingerprint that is added to the message. The receiver verifies the fingerprint and concludes that the message is authentic.

Hash algorithms are typically used for data integrity, where the original message is transmitted with its corresponding fingerprint. When the message is received, the receiver calculates the digest from the message, and the resulting digest is compared to the fingerprint. A match means that the message has not been altered in transit.

This type of implementation is useful for data integrity but does not provide any security for the data in transit. In fact, these algorithms are susceptible to man-in-the-middle attacks, where an attacker intercepts the message, changes it, and appends a new fingerprint without being detected.

Hashing algorithms are also called message digest algorithms. Message Digest 5 (MD5) and Secure Hash Algorithm 1 (SHA-1) are widely deployed cryptographic hashing algorithms. SHA-1 is considered more secure than MD5 because it produces a longer fingerprint (160 versus 128 bits), but the computation of a longer digest makes it slower. To solve this problem of man-in-the-middle attacks, you use cryptographic hash message authentication codes (HMACs).

Cryptographic HMACs

HMACs are hash algorithms that, in addition to data integrity, provide authentication with a secret key, which is only known to the sender and receiver. HMACs provide protection from man-in-the-middle attacks. Keyed MD5 and Key SHA-1 are examples of HMACs.

Figure 5-15 illustrates HMACs.

Figure 5-15 *Hash Message Authentication Code*

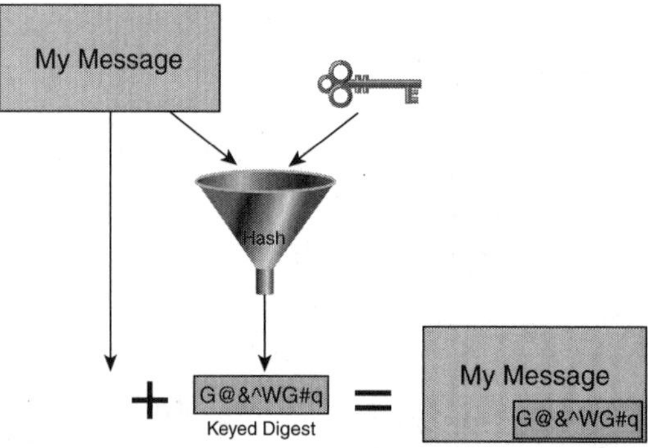

In Figure 5-15, the sender uses a secret key, only known between the sender and receiver, to execute the hash function and create the digest. This digest, called the *authenticity tag*, is based on both the shared secret key and the information being transmitted. The receiver calculates the authentication tag and compares it to the received one. If the authenticity tags match, the message is considered authentic. This keyed mechanism provides an additional layer of protection over cryptographic hash algorithms in dealing with man-in-the-middle attacks.

TIP You can use HMACs for routing update authentication. You can configure two neighboring routers with the same secret key, which is used to calculate the HMAC on the routing updates. As an example, you can configure Open Shortest Path First (OSPF) for routing authentication with the following commands:

```
router(config-router)#area area-id authentication message-digest
router(config-if)#ip ospf message-digest-key 1 md5 key
```

Digital Signatures

A *digital signature* is an electronic mechanism used to prove the authenticity and integrity of a piece of information by applying public-key cryptography to the hashed message.

When using HMACs, both sender and receiver share the same secret key, and because both know the same key, any of the parties can deny being the source of a message.

Digital signatures overcome this problem by using public-key cryptography, which provides nonrepudiation. Figure 5-16 illustrates the concept of digital signatures.

Figure 5-16 *Digital Signature*

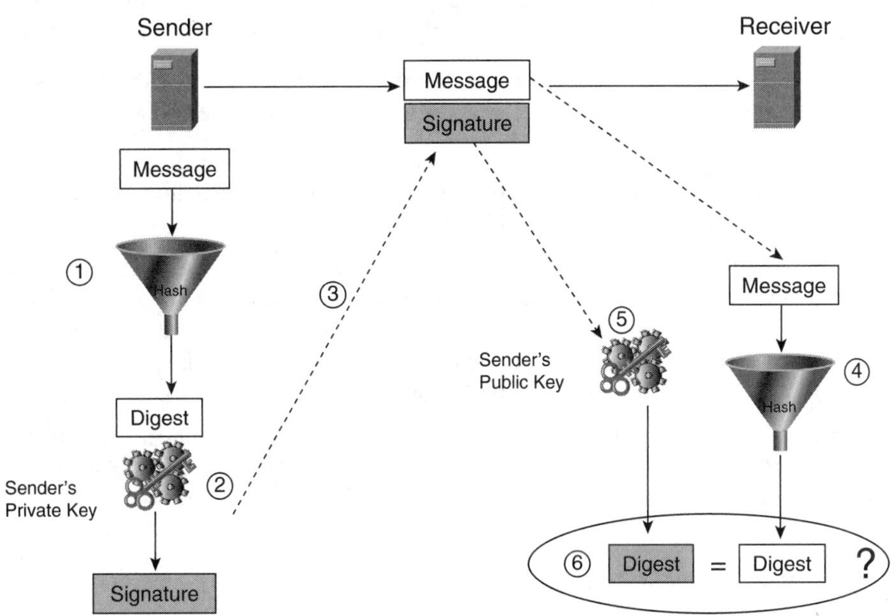

The following are the steps an entity using digital signatures takes when sending a message, as depicted in Figure 5-16:

1 The message is first processed with a hash function such as SHA-1 or MD5.

2 Then, the resulting fingerprint is encrypted using the sender's private key. This encrypted fingerprint is considered the *signature*.

3 The signature is appended to the message and the message is sent.

4 The receiving party takes the message and processes it with the same hash function, which results in a message fingerprint.

5 The receiver decrypts the "signature" sent along with the message using the sender's public key.

6 Finally, the receiver compares the unencrypted signature to the message fingerprint. If they match, the message was not changed while in transit, and the sender is the originator the receiver expected to hear from.

Virtual Private Networks

A VPN in its most generic definition can be described as a virtual link between two entities that allows them to communicate securely over a public network like the Internet.

VPNs use tunneling technologies combined with encryption and authentication services, which are provided through protocols such as IPSec. There are two main applications for VPNs:

- **Site-to-site**—A VPN that typically provides the communication between two distinct locations using routers or VPN concentrators.
- **Remote access**—A VPN that allows remote users to access a central location via a secure communication channel between end users and a VPN router or VPN concentrator. In this scenario, a VPN device is deployed at the central side, which terminates all the VPN connections. At the remote-user end is VPN client software or hardware that enables the communication to the VPN device.

Remote-access VPNs have multiple uses in Data Center environments: giving access to the applications hosted in the Data Center, updating secure content, and managing Data Centers.

Site-to-site VPNs are mainly used in extranets to connect business partners and provide access to business-to-business applications.

SSL and IPSec are technologies typically used to implement VPNs. Chapter 15 provides additional details about these technologies. Chapter 21 provides information about the use of these technologies in the Data Center.

AAA

AAA is a framework that defines the control of access to network resources such as those in Data Centers (routers, switches, firewalls, servers, and so on). The framework controls access, enforces policies, and provides audit trails, all key areas for security and network management. Essentially, by implementing AAA, an organization can determine and enforce which users can access what resources and for what kind of purposes and provide a record of what the user does once access is granted.

AAA provides three basic services:

- **Authentication**—Proves that a user is who she or he claims to be. Multiple mechanisms prove a user's identity, from usernames and passwords to biometrics. A *biometric* is a unique characteristic of a human that is used by the authentication process to verify identity. Biometrics include the retina, fingerprints, voice, and so on.
- **Authorization**—Defines what a user is allowed to do. Authorization is typically used to restrict what systems a user is allowed to access and which commands the user can execute on them.
- **Accounting**—Consists of keeping records of user activity. Accounting is commonly used for billing and change-control tracking purposes.

Many protocols provide access control under the AAA framework, but the two most common are TACACS+ and RADIUS. For more information on TACACS and RADIUS, see Chapter 15.

Data Center Security Framework

The process of securing a Data Center requires both a comprehensive system-analysis approach and an ongoing process that improves the security levels as the Data Center evolves. The Data Center is constantly evolving as new applications or services become available. Attacks are becoming more sophisticated and more frequent. These trends require a steady evaluation of security readiness.

A key component of the security-readiness evaluation is the policies that govern the application of security in the network including the Data Center. The application includes both the design best practices and the implementation details.

This section explains the key components of a sound security framework from a system-planning perspective. Because the details of applying these components to the network are driven by the particular business needs of an organization, discussing them is outside the scope of this chapter.

Security Policies

The *security policy* defines what activities are considered acceptable or unacceptable by the organization. Security policies are only effective when supported by the entire enterprise organization and when deployed with the corresponding procedures, standards, and guidelines that define the details on how security is ultimately implemented.

The security policy, in conjunction with the accompanying procedures, defines the security strategy of the organization. The security policy and procedures also help delimit and determine responsibilities: who is responsible for what and what to do in case an incident takes place. This kind of up-front planning helps organizations control the effects and impact of security incidents, which translates to a lesser economic impact and a more resilient business.

The evaluation of security readiness, referred to as the security life cycle, is anchored in the security policies. The security life cycle has multiple phases to ensure that the security readiness is known and quantifiable.

Security Life Cycle

The *security life cycle* is the constant evaluation cycle that refines the state of security readiness and adapts the security policy to the network architecture. There are many versions of security cycles, with varying numbers of steps and names, yet their goals all aim at constantly and consistently refining security readiness. The following security life cycle, presented in Figure 5-17, is often quoted and well understood in the security industry:

- Assess
- Design
- Deploy
- Maintain

Notice that the life cycle is applied to a system; whether it's the network or the Data Center, the cycle processes are the same. The system in this case is the Data Center network, yet the security life cycle must reflect a network-wide effort to be effective.

Figure 5-17 *Security Life Cycle*

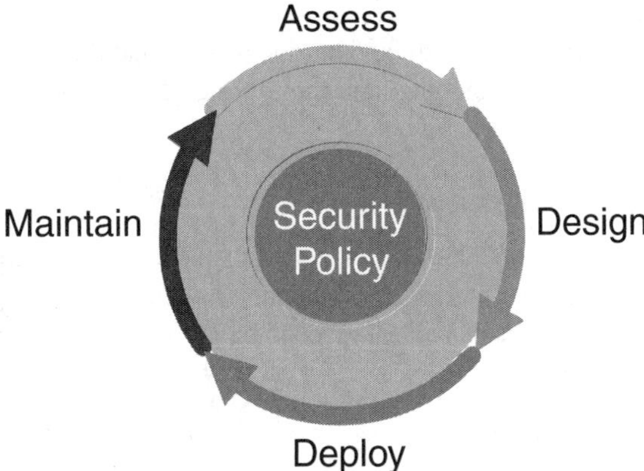

The security life cycle is an ongoing process that you document both at its initial state and after every cycle. This documentation ensures that the results are measurable and comparable to determine noticeable improvements. The following are the details of the security cycle:

- **Assessment**—The process of auditing, testing, and verifying the system vulnerabilities through risk analysis. The output of the assessment process is a list of the critical components of the system; the current level of risk to known vulnerabilities; and a list, if any, of the requirements that will be fed to the design process. In the Data Center, the critical components are mission-critical servers and the infrastructure devices that support them, such as routers, switches, and firewalls. The vulnerabilities are those that could affect the critical components. Often, the assessment process includes testing various elements and the system.
- **Design**—The process of applying the security policy and the requirements resulting from the assessment process to the security design. A recommendation in this phase is to group devices with similar security requirements in security zones where the consistency of applying policies is easier to maintain. Chapter 21 discusses design aspects of integrating security into the existing architecture.
- **Deployment**—The process of implementing the specific security design recommendations into the network architecture. In this careful integration step, security policies and the overarching network architecture are consistent with one another.

- **Maintenance**—The process of keeping the application of security policies consistent throughout the network by monitoring that the best practices and recommendations, are in effect. In addition to a clear set of maintenance procedures, this phase includes the infrastructure (software and hardware tools and their usage policies) that sustains the provisioning, managing, and monitoring of the system.

Secure Management Framework

Because a compromise on the management infrastructure can lead to disastrous consequences, the network design must include mechanisms to secure the management infrastructure. This section presents various alternatives to help you achieve a secure management infrastructure.

Isolating the Management Infrastructure

Isolating the management infrastructure from the Data Center infrastructure prevents access to the Data Center from the management segments, which are typically considered secure and trusted. Isolation comes from a separate physical infrastructure or logical segregation through VLANs. Figure 5-18 illustrates the concept.

Figure 5-18 *Physical and Logical Segregation*

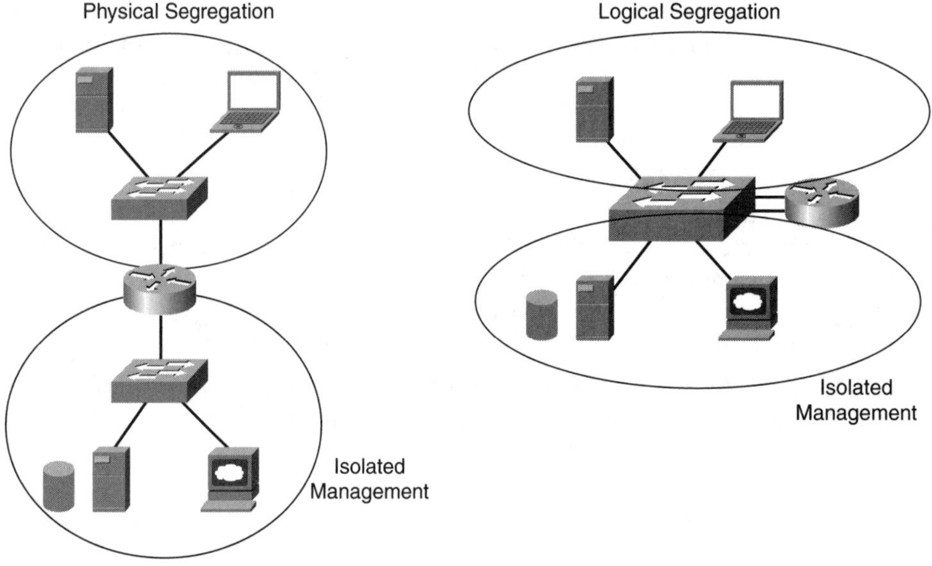

You create physical isolation by deploying separate hardware devices; for example, use two LAN switches—one to connect all management workstations and managed devices and another to connect user servers and workstations. Physical segregation is considered the most secure way to achieve isolation, yet logical separation is just as secure if the security policies, design, and implementation are consistent. Logical segregation could be as simple as configuring VLANs for managing traffic and normal user data. Chapter 21 explains some common segregation mechanisms for an effective implementation.

Encryption of Control Data

Using encryption for the communication between the managed and management devices provides authenticity for the sessions and confidentiality for accounts and passwords. Telnet, SNMPv1, and many other protocols commonly used for device-management functions exchange data in cleartext. SNMP v3, however, provides a robust set of user-based security mechanisms not available in SNMP v1.

The use of encryption between managed and management devices provides a mechanism to guarantee authenticity and privacy in the communication exchange. The protocols for this purpose might be provided with the application, such as SSH for secure Telnet. Additional protocols might be those used for transport on the network, such as IPSec, or for the application, such as SSL for Secure HTTP (HTTPS).

NOTE Chapter 9, "SSL and TLS," explains the details of SSL, and Chapter 15 explains common technologies available for encryption, such as IPSec.

Strong Authentication for Access Control

Using strong authentication mechanisms allows you to effectively control the access to both the management and managed devices. Chapter 15 discusses the concept of AAA, which is the pillar for an effective access-control environment.

Strong authentication uses multiple advanced authentication schemes such as dynamic passwords and digital certificates. *Dynamic passwords* are dynamic tokens generated by software or hardware based on specific keys. The device generating the token is exclusively assigned to the user, and it is also password-protected. The token is used for authentication when the user requests access to a system, thus offering multiple authentication steps before a successful attempt is possible.

Digital certificates are also unique pieces of information assigned to a client based on his or her identity. The certificate is issued by an organization that certifies the authenticity of the client. The owner of the certificate uses it to gain access to systems that can verify the authenticity of the certificate with the organization that issued it.

Incident Response and Attack Mitigation

Incident response and attack mitigation are two of the most important aspects of the strategic planning for the maintenance of a Data Center. *Incident response* consists of the definition of the procedures and mechanisms in place to react when a security incident takes place.

Before incident response is initiated, log analysis must take place. This step calls for a robust mechanism to capture and analyze logs that could be used to determine the details of the attack so that the response to the incident focuses on the right problem. Incident response defines such things as who to contact and what to do when something wrong happens. *Attack mitigation* relates directly to incident response and consists of establishing the necessary security mechanisms to reduce or remove the effects of a security incident, such as a DDoS attack.

Incident response and attack mitigation also implement technologies such as intrusion detection. In practice, without an appropriate plan, these technologies are little help.

Summary

This chapter discussed many basic concepts related to security. The design of security in the Data Center requires understanding the security threats, the attacks, and the technology to counter them.

You can use such tools as ACLs, firewalls, IDSs, and security features on switches and routers to mitigate the effects of attacks against servers and network devices.

Designing the Data Center requires configuring the appropriate ciphers on SSL and IPSec devices, generating and installing certificates, and enabling HMAC on routers—all of which require an understanding of the key concepts of cryptography, AAA, and VPNs. This chapter provided an overview of these concepts, which are further analyzed in Chapter 15.

Creating security policies, secure management, and incident response and attack mitigation are as important as understanding the technology. The last part of this chapter described the key considerations for creating a Data Center security framework.

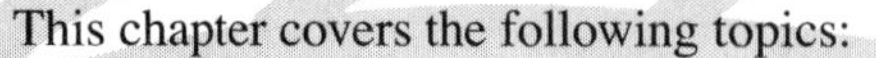

This chapter covers the following topics:

- Definition of load balancing
- Key concepts of load balancing
- Planning for high availability
- Generic load-balancer architecture

CHAPTER 6

Server Load-Balancing Overview

This chapter discusses concepts related to server load balancing. The term *content switching* is analogous to server load balancing. The capabilities of a content switch are considered to be a superset of the capabilities of a server load balancer. The main difference is the capability of a content switch to perform load balancing based on information beyond Layer 3 or Layer 4, such as an HTTP URL or an HTTP cookie. In this book, the term *load balancer* covers devices known as content switches and as server load balancers because the authors believe that there is no fundamental difference between them.

NOTE In this book, mention of Layer 3, Layer 4, and Layer 5 is made in reference to the TCP/IP protocol suite. The treatment of the layers is consistent with the TCP/IP protocol suite throughout this book unless otherwise noted.

This chapter introduces fundamental concepts and features that are key to understanding load balancers, and it serves as the foundation for other basic and more advanced concepts that are introduced in Parts III and IV.

Before describing the basic operational details of load balancers, it is important to describe how bridges and routers forward packets, and the differences between their operations and those of load balancers. Load balancers perform similar functions and, in certain cases, are flexible enough to perform both bridging and routing functions.

Load Balancing Defined

Load balancing is simply the capability to balance traffic load across a group of devices. This implies that the load balancer is placed in the traffic path of those devices being load-balanced. The load balancer's role is to distribute the load and ensure that the recipients of the load are available. Load balancing has various uses, including server load balancing and cache load balancing.

Load Balancing Functions

The most fundamental requirement behind load balancing is scalability. Traditional scaling methods, as presented in Figure 6-1, include vertical scaling and horizontal scaling.

Figure 6-1 *Scaling Methods*

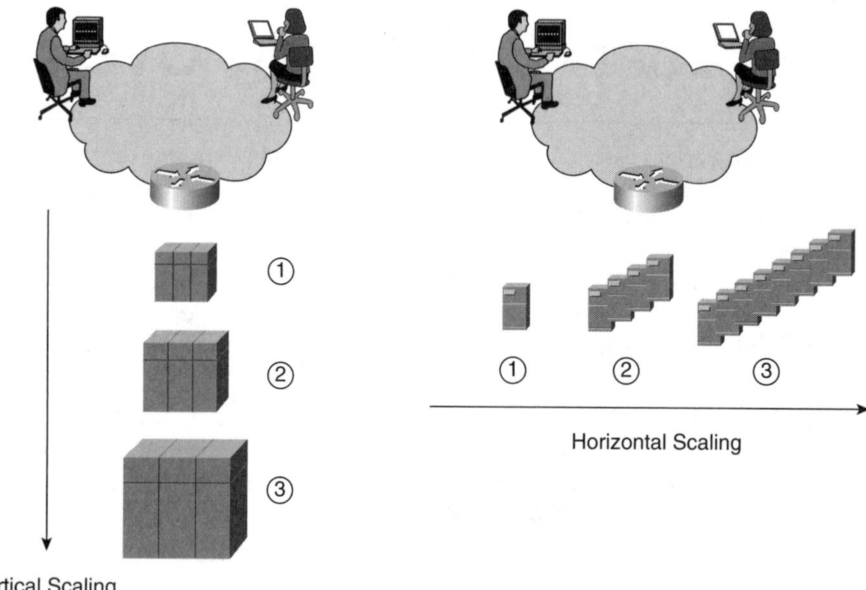

Vertical scaling implies adding more CPU capacity to the service device by increasing the number of processors or adding faster processors, more memory, newer and faster components, and so on. Every step shown in Figure 6-1 provides additional performance at an incremental price, which could be significant if the base system is upgraded completely. Horizontal scaling implies that more devices of similar or better capacity are added. Again, at every stage, you add more processing capacity; however, the existing equipment is not upgraded and the incremental cost is the result of the new systems that are added. This upgrade path is typically more cost-effective than the path for vertical scaling. Overall, the scaling methods increase the transaction rates offered by the system. Using vertical scaling, the service identified by a particular IP address, protocol, and port number is under the control of the single device. In horizontal scaling, the service belongs to many service devices, which requires a mechanism to distribute the load.

Before load balancers were available, the mechanism that was used to distribute the traffic load between servers was DNS round-robin. The DNS server, also known as the name server that was responsible for the domain used by servers supporting a specific service, would reply with a specific IP address. This IP address was one of a few in the available address records that matched the service name (host name) that the name server used in round-robin for each response. The round-robin process distributed the load to the different servers in the address records. The following section explains the details of using DNS round-robin to load-balance.

NOTE For more information about the domain name system, see Chapter 10, "DNS Essentials and Site Selection Considerations."

DNS Round-Robin

DNS round-robin was a popular technique used before load balancers were available to distribute traffic load. DNS round-robin is still used today, but load balancers have gained greater popularity because of the additional benefits they offer.

The following is a typical DNS round-robin configuration:

1. The name server holds a zone file that contains multiple address (A) records for the same subdomain pointing to different servers:

   www.example.com IN A 192.0.2.80

   www.example.com IN A 192.0.2.50

2. The name server sends all the A records for a single request, and the order of the records is determined by the options configured.
3. The name server can be configured to return the records in a round-robin fashion. This is done by using the directive rrset-order in the /etc/named.conf file, as shown in Example 6-1.
4. Subsequent DNS resolution requests from DNS proxies receive the IP addresses for the same service in a different order, thus initiating connections with the different servers.

Example 6-1 *DNS Round-Robin Configuration*

```
options {
        directory "/var/named";
        rrset-order {
           class IN type A name "www.example.com" order cyclic;
        };
};
```

DNS round-robin, however, presents many challenges, including the following:

- Uneven load distribution
- Undetermined server health
- Undetermined server load

Figure 6-2 shows the challenges in dealing with a DNS round-robin as a mechanism to scale environments that have several devices offering the same services.

Figure 6-2 *DNS Round-Robin Challenges*

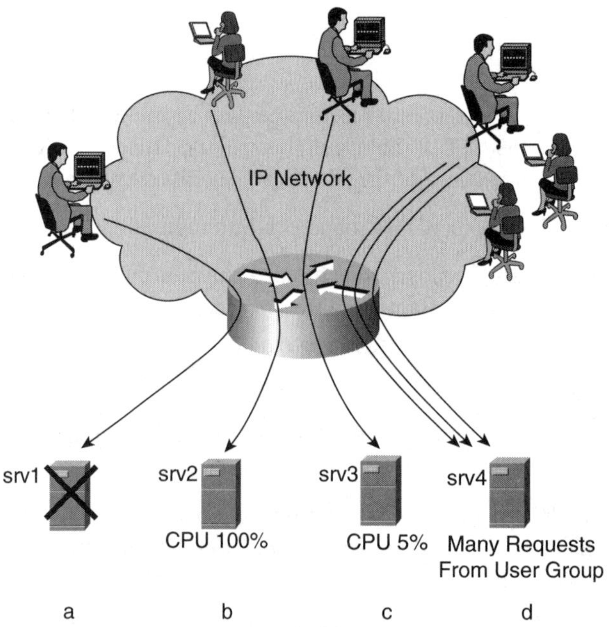

Because the load distribution is simply based on client requests, the likely load that each server receives is not even. Option **a** in Figure 6-2 shows a request sent to a server that is no longer available. The name server is not aware of the status of the server associated with the A record, so it could still include it in a DNS response. Options **b** and **c** in Figure 6-2 show a server with a 100 percent CPU load still receiving requests from clients, and a server with 5 percent CPU receiving the same number of requests. The name server is also unaware of the server load and thus cannot remove the server's A record from a DNS response or indicate that more requests are to be sent to srv3. Option **d** in Figure 6-2 shows a server receiving many requests from a user group that could be using a DNS proxy that responded with the IP address of srv4. The name server cannot control the number of requests that a single server receives.

Load balancers can address all the problems associated with DNS round-robin, yet they also are used for more advanced functions. These advanced functions include increased service scalability, server and application health monitoring, load monitoring, and load distribution based on application server address (IP address or subnet), service information (protocol and port number), and application information. Load balancers can scale the performance of a service and offer a number of algorithms for load distribution, server health monitoring, and server load monitoring. The following sections describe some of the most common applications that use load balancers.

Server Load Balancing

As its name indicates, server load balancing is load balancing of traffic among servers. Figure 6-3 presents the basic idea behind server load balancing.

Figure 6-3 *Server Load Balancing*

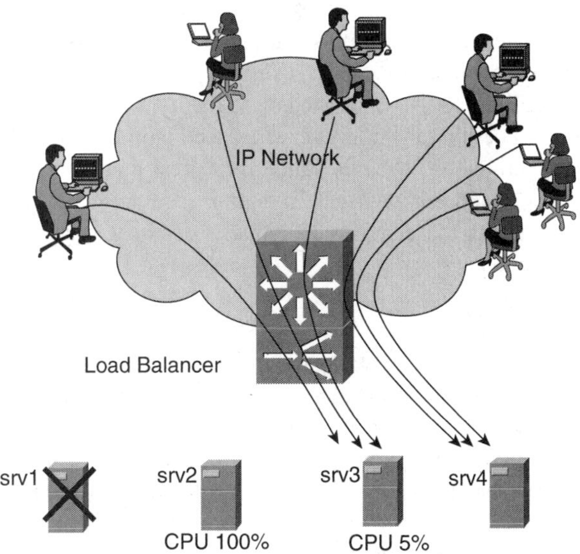

In Figure 6-3, the server load balancer is capable of determining that srv1 and srv2 should not receive any new connections because the servers are offline and beyond the maximum allowed capacity respectively. The connections then are load-balanced using a simple round-robin algorithm so that each server receives an even load (or close to even load) of the incoming requests.

The application that is being load-balanced may also require special treatment. For example, in an e-commerce environment, the requirements might include the following:

- All TCP connections to port 80 from the same user should be sent to the same server.
- All subsequent connections to TCP port 443 from the same user should be sent to the same server used for the previous port 80 connections.

This simply means that the user might be conducting an online transaction, such as buying a book. The transaction requires that the contents of the shopping cart be available at all times during the connection and also as a new encrypted connection is opened for the checkout process. Other requirements that could be the result of security policies or service-level agreements might include all users from certain source IP addresses being sent only to a subset of servers in the server farm.

An implication of load balancing is the virtualization of the service being advertised. The load balancer must take over the service so that it can determine what to do with the traffic load. In doing so, the load balancer assumes the IP address used by the service and hides the IP addresses of the servers supporting the actual service. This makes the load balancer a virtual server using a virtual address hiding the real addresses of the real servers. The load balancer does not replace the server; it simply pretends to be the server so that the clients think they are talking to the server, when, in reality, they are interacting with the load balancer. Remember that the many servers used behind the load balancer are all hidden from the users through the use of a single IP address that is sent back to the clients in DNS responses. This IP address is virtual, in that no specific server is associated with it, but rather a load balancer that receives all requests destined to it.

Cache Load Balancing

Cache load balancing is the distribution of load across a group of available caches. Cache load balancing, like server load balancing, distributes the load among the caches. However, unlike server load balancing, cache load balancing attempts to maximize the cache hit ratio. Cache hit ratio refers to the ratio of requests for content sent to the cache for which there is a copy of the requested content in the cache that could be used in the response. Notice that the request for content is a hit when the cache does not need to retrieve the requested content from a server. The load-balancing algorithm needs to ensure that the load is load-balanced while also considering the likelihood that the selected cache has a copy of the requested content.

If the selected cached does not have the requested content, before a response is sent back to the client, the cache must retrieve the content from the origin server. If a traditional round-robin load-balancing algorithm is used on a cache farm, sequential requests for the same content would be sent to different caches, defeating the purpose of the cache farm. The purpose of the cache farm is to offload CPU capacity from the server farm by processing and responding to requests for static content. The members of the cache farm store frequently accessed content to reduce the number of requests for content to the server farm, thus relieving the load.

NOTE The caching mechanism used to offload servers in the Data Center is called the Reverse Proxy Cache, or RPC. Load balancers and other network devices, such as routers and switches, support the RPC. Load balancers use specific algorithms to redirect the request to the cache farm, whereas routers and switches use the Web Cache Communication Protocol (WCCP).

Other Load-Balancing Applications

Other requirements resulting in the need for load balancing include devices that support VPN termination and firewall services. As with servers and caches, the goal is to scale the VPN and firewall services by placing a load balancer in front of the service devices (VPN concentrators and firewalls) to distribute the traffic load.

VPN/IPSec Load Balancing

VPN/IPSec load balancing involves scaling VPN/IPSec termination points by increasing the number of VPN/IPSec tunnels that could be established at the VPN aggregation point. Figure 6-4 shows a VPN aggregation point, which is behind a load balancer that distributes the IPSec traffic to the appropriate VPN concentrator.

Figure 6-4 *VPN/IPSec Load Balancing*

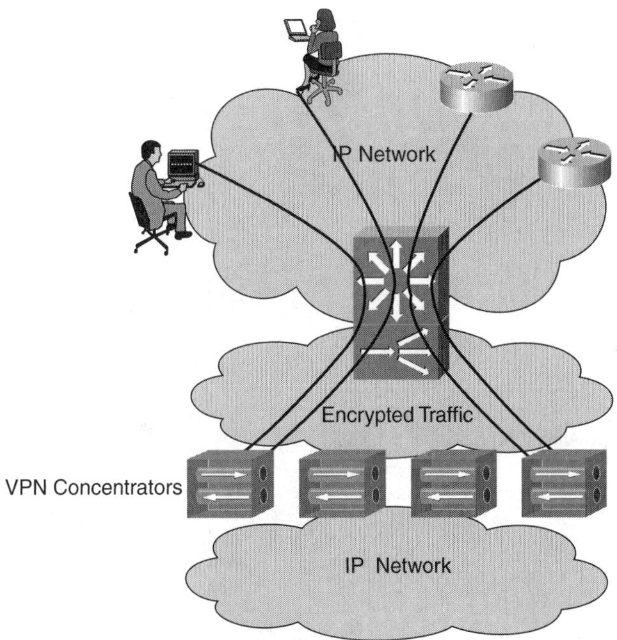

Note that IPSec load balancing requires the load balancer to understand some aspects of the protocols it is trying to load-balance. IPSec uses IP protocol values 50 and 51, so the load balancer must be capable of at least identifying the protocols and the packet format to extract the information used for load balancing.

NOTE For more information on how IPSec operates, see Chapter 15, "Security Protocols and Technology."

Firewall Load Balancing

Firewall load balancing typically scales firewall services at the edge of the enterprise network to the Internet. In a firewall load-balancing setup, the firewalls are placed between two layers of load balancers. However, unlike with VPN/IPSec load balancing, firewall load balancing deals with whichever protocols the firewalls deal with; depending on the network location, they can be exposed to a wide range of protocols in the TCP/IP protocol suite. This might require the load balancers to understand more than just the most commonly used protocols or to develop a mechanism to ensure the proper selection of the firewall for both inbound and outbound traffic. Figure 6-5 presents a high-level view of a firewall load-balancing topology.

Figure 6-5 *Firewall Load Balancing*

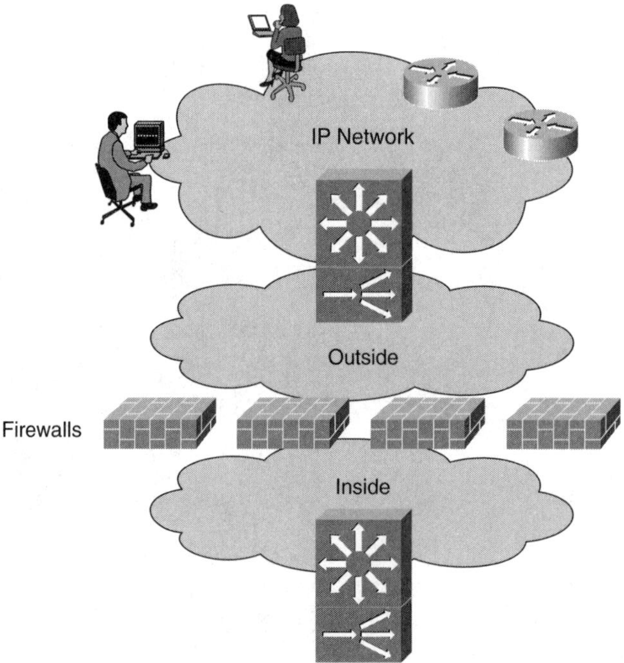

Firewalls can operate in Layer 3 mode or Layer 2 mode. In Layer 3 mode, firewalls route packets between subnets. In Layer 2 mode, firewalls bridge packets, which implies that they are transparent to the network operation. To function properly, load balancers used for firewall load balancing are required to understand both firewall operation modes. Additionally, firewalls can exchange connection information between themselves, which requires that the load balancer avoid impacting their exchange.

Based on experience, the benefits of firewall load balancing are marginal and often offset by the complexity introduced by the design. This does not mean that firewall load balancing is not useful, but it does mean that the requirements and benefits must be clearly understood before you decide to implement and support a firewall load-balancing environment. Follow these simple guidelines to make sure that you reap the benefits of firewall load balancing:

- Firewall load balancing is a viable option if you cannot achieve the desired performance with faster firewalls. It is much simpler to deploy a faster and more capable firewall to fix a firewall-scaling problem than to deploy a complex firewall load-balancing solution.
- Make sure that the load balancer is capable of achieving the performance required by the aggregate number of firewalls, and allow some room for growth.
- Make sure that the load balancer is capable of dealing with the mode of operation of the firewalls and that it does not diminish the high-availability behavior of the firewalls.
- If the installation is so complex that only you understand it, there is most likely a simpler installation possible.

So far, this chapter has covered the need for load balancing as a basis for discussing some fundamental concepts behind load balancing.

Key Concepts of Load Balancing

This section introduces some basic yet fundamental concepts related to load balancing. Refer to Figure 6-6 throughout this section for the discussion about the different load-balancing concepts.

Figure 6-6 *A Server Load-Balancing Setup*

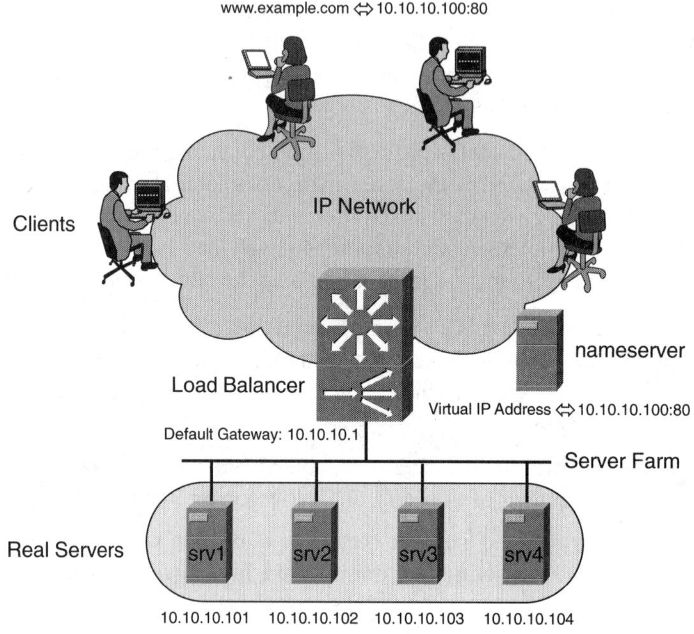

Figure 6-6 demonstrates the following key concepts:

- **Clients**—The originators of requests.
- **www.example.com**—The advertised service identified by the IP address 10.10.10.100 and supported by the server farm.
- **Virtual IP address (VIP)**—The IP address that identifies the service supported by the load balancer. It is called virtual because no server is associated with it, and it exists only in the load balancer.

NOTE An exception to the rule of the VIP address not supported by the servers exists. Servers are configured to support the VIP address when the load balancer is operating either in dispatch or direct server return modes. Dispatch and direct server return are described in Chapter 16, "Load-Balancing Modes and Predictors."

The load balancer may advertise the virtual IP address by participating directly in a routing process or injecting a host static route. In certain cases, the load balancer does not participate in the routing process or inject a host route, which implies the closest router must be used to advertise the IP address or subnet associated with the service.

- **Real servers**—The actual servers that support the services in the server farm.
- **Server farm**—A group of servers that can be associated by supporting the same application. In IOS, the term *server farm* has a specific meaning: It is a group of servers that support a load-balanced service.
- **Default gateway**—The IP address of the default gateway used by the server farm.

The load-balancing process is described in the following section.

Load-Balancing Process

The client sends a DNS request to determine the IP address of www.example.com. The name server responds to the request with the IP address 10.10.10.100, which is the virtual IP address configured on the load balancer. The request to the VIP is routed until it is received by the load balancer. The load-balancing process is initiated when a connection request destined to the VIP arrives at the load balancer. The load balancer receives the request and parses enough information (such as the IP address, protocol, and port number) to determine what to do with the packet.

Because this is a new connection request, no pre-existing information about the connection is associated with the request. The load balancer applies the appropriate content policies, which might require a Layer 4 or Layer 5 lookup before selecting a real server.

NOTE Layer 4 refers to the transport layer (TCP, UDP, and so on), and the lookup is expected on the transport header information. Layer 5 refers to the application layer (HTTP, SMTP, and so on), and the lookup is expected in the application layer header information. More details on Layer 4 and Layer 5 processing are discussed in forthcoming sections.

The layers are in reference to the TCP/IP protocol stack, the details of which are explained in Chapter 7, "IP, TCP, and UDP."

The connection request eventually is forwarded to the selected real server. After a connection is accepted by the server, an entry is added to a table that keeps track of connection activity—the connection table.

Before the load balancer sends the packet, it calculates the checksum, if needed, and rewrites the appropriate header information (IP addresses, port numbers, and acknowledgments (ACK) and sequence (SEQ) numbers, if dealing with TCP). On the response from the server, the load balancer updates the packet and forwards it back to the client. The connection table entry is then updated with the full connection information, which is used on fast lookups for packets that belong to an existing connection. The load balancer performs a number of tasks, which are applied consistently to every connection:

- Layer 4 load balancing
- Layer 5 load balancing
- Connection tracking
- Connection persistence
- Session persistence
- Server health

The following sections describe these tasks in greater detail.

Layer 4 Load Balancing

Layer 4 load balancing refers to the process in which the load balancer uses Layer 4 information to apply content policies on which to make the load-balancing decision. Layer 4 information includes the protocol and source and destination port numbers. Figure 6-7 presents an example of a Layer 4 connection through a load balancer.

Notice in Figure 6-7 that the load balancer is capable of applying policies and performing server selection as the SYN or connection request is received. This is because all the information required for server selection, protocol, and port number is present in the first packet.

Layer 5 Load Balancing

Layer 5, or application layer, load balancing refers to the process in which the load balancer uses Layer 5 information to apply content policies and make the load-balancing decisions. Layer 5 information typically refers to the Layer 5 protocol, such as HTTP, SMTP, and FTP, that is found in the payload of a packet. The content policies could be applied to information such as an HTTP URL, an HTTP cookie, or the HTTP header field user agent. Depending on the Layer 5 protocols, the information used by the content policy could be anywhere in the payload, and it could range in size from a small number of bytes to a few thousand that span multiple packets.

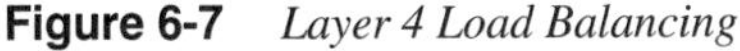

Figure 6-7 *Layer 4 Load Balancing*

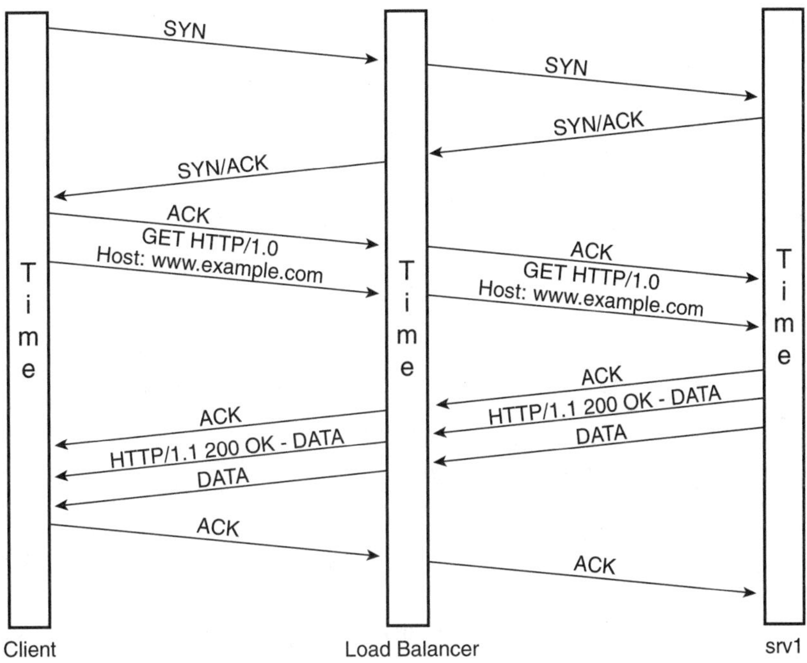

The parsing for Layer 5 information has some major implications. Figure 6-8 shows a typical TCP connection through a load balancer configured to load-balance based on an HTTP URL.

As shown in Figure 6-8, the processing of a connection that requires lookup beyond Layer 4 demands the load balancer to fully complete the connection setup before it can apply a content policy and make the load-balancing decision. The load balancer is spoofing the TCP connection to parse Layer 5 information before selecting a real server. After the content policy has been applied and the server has been selected, the load balancer must not only rewrite the Layer 4 header information, but also adjust the sequence (SEQ) and acknowledgment (ACK) numbers because it is initiating a connection to the selected real server.

NOTE For more information on TCP, see Chapter 7. For the details of connection spoofing, see Chapter 16.

Figure 6-8 *Layer 5 Load Balancing*

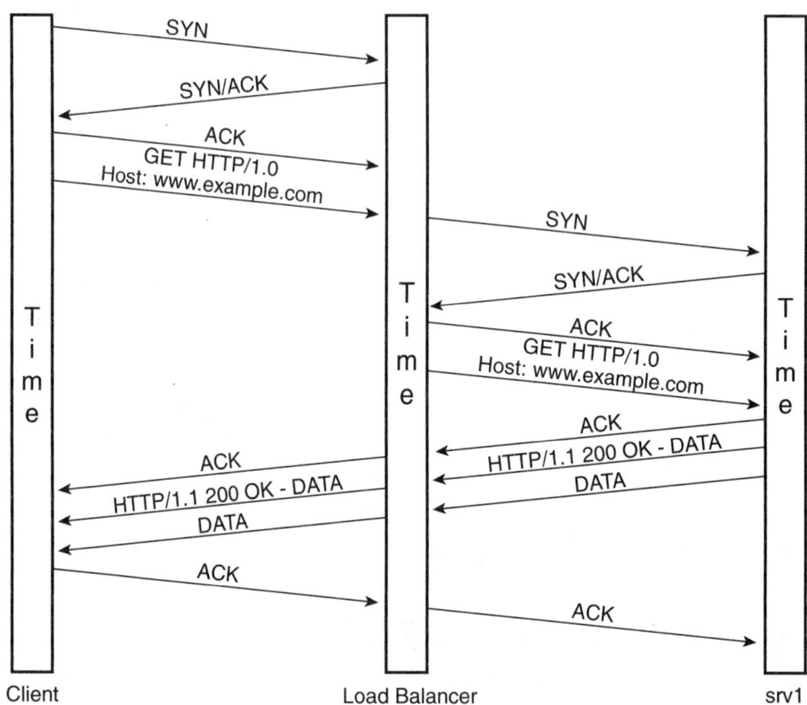

Realize that after the connection is established with the server, the load balancer is required to adjust the SEQ and ACK for every packet destined to the server or the client. These tasks are added to the normal tasks that TCP performs on a connection, such as flow control and error correction.

Connection Tracking

Connection tracking refers to the mechanism used by the load balancer to maintain state information related to the active connections between clients and servers. Two distinct uses exist for the connection information collected by the load balancer.

The primary purpose of the connection information is to simplify the tasks associated with packet flow lookup and rewrite by recording information such as the inbound and outbound interfaces, source and destination IP address, protocol, and source and destination port numbers. This information is recorded and typically stored in fast accessible memory, otherwise know as shortcut tables.

The other purpose of tracking connection information is to replicate that information to a backup device, which can use the information for recovery of connection state in case of a failure in the primary load balancer.

This information includes some of the previous information in addition to Layer 4 and Layer 5 protocol-specific details that would be required to recover from a failure. For example, for TCP, the SEQ and ACK numbers are needed in addition to the source and destination IP addresses, protocol, and port numbers.

Connection tracking is also important as the means of determining the availability and health of the server farm. This topic is discussed later in this chapter.

Connection Persistence

The concept of connection persistence is no different from the HTTP persistent connection discussed in Chapter 8, "HTTP and Related Concepts." In this chapter, however, the discussion focuses on how the concept of connection persistence applies to a load balancer and its capability to support persistence. This feature is particularly important when using the load balancer for Layer 5 tasks and when the client and server are using HTTP/1.1. The support for connection persistence is twofold:

- The basic mechanisms ensure that the TCP connection remains open for subsequent HTTP requests.
- The load balancer is capable of selecting a different real server for every HTTP request that it receives.

A load balancer must be transparent to HTTP persistent connections because it is required to support TCP and HTTP standard behavior. Handling the HTTP requests independently, however, is an enhancement in which the load balancer can send each HTTP request to a different real server based on Layer 5 information such as the URL. The load balancer must maintain an open connection with the client to be capable of continuing to receive HTTP requests. This implies that the load balancer should be capable of dealing with the mechanisms used on persistent connections. This concept is explained in detail in Chapter 16 in the "Connection Remapping" section.

Session Persistence

Session persistence refers to the capability of the load balancer to logically group multiple connections from the same client transaction to the virtual service. The virtual service is one or more VIPs that support an application. Session persistence is also known as *stickiness* or *sticky connections* because the goal is to stick two or more connections together as part of a single session.

This grouping is done to ensure the connections are handled and forwarded to the groups of servers that are aware of and expect to see the remaining connections. This ensures that the client has a successful interaction with the application. Load balancers typically keep a table for session persistence of sticky connections. This table is used to match incoming requests to existing connections so that they can be grouped together.

The classical and best example of session persistence is an e-commerce transaction in which the client buys some items online. Figure 6-9 represents this transaction.

Figure 6-9 *Session Persistence*

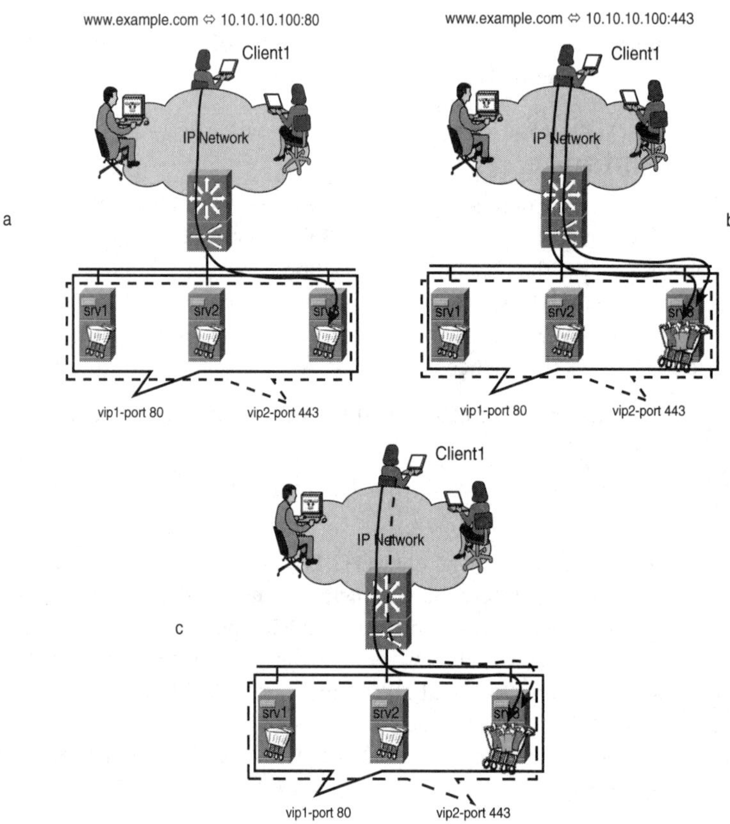

Figure 6-9 presents just three steps of the online shopping session. In option **a** of Figure 6-9, Client1 connects to the VIP related to www.example.com. When the connection is established, Client1 selects the items to buy. This step is depicted by two connections to the same server used to select the items to buy. These items are placed in the shopping cart displayed in option **b** of Figure 6-9. So far, the connection has been with VIP1, and the associated packets have been directed to srv1 on port 80.

In option **c** of Figure 6-9, Client1 selects the last item that is placed in the shopping cart of srv3 and is now ready to finish the transaction by paying online. At this point, Client1 is directed to www.example.com:443 to ensure that any sensitive information, such as the credit card number, phone number, or address, is encrypted and kept confidential. This causes Client1 to initiate a new connection to vip2 (TCP port 443), which uses secure HTTP (HTTPS or HTTP over SSL), thereby encrypting all the data between client and server. For the sake of the example, assume that the servers supporting www.example.com:80 and www.example.com:443 (srv1, srv2 and srv3) do not exchange the shopping cart content with one another.

The load balancer must then be capable of detecting that the new TCP connection should be sent to srv3, where the contents of the shopping cart are kept. This logical grouping of the connections to vip1 and vip2 from the same client to the same server is session persistence. If the load balancer cannot provide that functionality, the transaction might not complete and the online retailer might have lost a customer. The following section discusses the challenges of dealing with session persistence and the solutions to those challenges.

Session-Persistence Problems and Solutions

The most common session-persistence problems are related to client identification by the load balancer so that the load balancer can send the user connections to the right server. The load balancer keeps a table to track connections related to sessions. This table is referred to as the *sticky table*.

NOTE This chapter introduces the topic of session persistence by explaining what it is, what its main problems and challenges are, and what solutions are possible. Chapter 18, "Session Tracking and Cookies" and Chapter 19, "Persistence Mechanisms on Load Balancers" discuss the technical details in depth.

For session-persistence purposes, the simplest mechanism of identifying the user is through the source IP address. Regardless of the destination VIP or port numbers, the multiple connections could be sent to the same server. This method, which is referred to as *source IP sticky,* works well if the source IP remains constant across multiple connections. This is possible on an intranet where address translation typically is not used and you have control over how the network is implemented. Unfortunately, this is not as simple when dealing with Internet-facing applications in which there is no control over how the client software is configured. A common problem that breaks session persistence based on source IP address is related to the use of proxy servers. Using proxy server farms to support Internet access is common and can cause a user to change the IP address when new connections are generated; therefore, the load balancer no longer is capable of identifying and sticking the connections together.

The solution to this problem seems logical: Use some kind of information that uniquely identifies the user, whether using a single or multiple IP addresses. One mechanism, probably the most widely used in the Internet today, is the use of cookies. The load balancer is configured to look for a cookie value that could be matched to a specific user. This mechanism is known as *cookie sticky.*

NOTE Cookies are placed by the servers on the clients and are used consistently by the clients because they are set when communicating with the server. For more information on cookies, see Chapter 18.

Two types of cookie sticky mechanisms exist:

- **Cookie insert**—The load balancer places the cookie in the client that uses it for stickiness.
- **Cookie passive**—The server places the cookie that is used by the load balancer for stickiness.

The load balancer parses the selected cookie value. When it finds a match in the sticky table, it forwards the packets to the server associated with the specific entry. However, note that cookie sticky mechanisms work only if the load balancer can access the unencrypted cookie. Cookies are encrypted along with the rest of the HTTP payload using HTTPS. HTTPS typically is used to secure sensitive data, such as personal credit card information, during the checkout process of an online purchase. Using encrypted cookies breaks cookie sticky as the preferred sticky mechanism when dealing with encrypted transactions.

The load balancer can solve this problem in one of two ways:

- The load balancer tracks some unique SSL client information.
- The load balancer decrypts the connection to parse the cookie value.

As explained in Chapter 9, "SSL and TLS," the SSL ID uniquely identifies a user. The load balancer is then configured to use the SSL ID for stickiness. The SSL ID used for stickiness has mixed success, for the following reasons:

- The SSL ID is clear text on SSL version 3 and TLS version 1, yet it is encrypted on SSL v2.
- The SSL ID can be renegotiated (rehandshake) by the server or the client after the SSL connection has been established.

If SSL versions before v3 are used, the load balancer fails to stick the different connections for the same session because it cannot identify the SSL ID. When using SSL v3 or TLS, the load balancer identifies the SSL ID. However, if the SSL ID changes during an established SSL connection, the load balancer might not be capable of determining the new SSL ID, which prevents the unencrypted and encrypted connections from being logically grouped.

NOTE Remember that SSL sticky is applicable to SSL-only transactions, such as online banking, in which the initial connection is made using HTTPS. This means that the online shopping cart problem cannot be resolved by SSL sticky if there are connections other than HTTPS.

The other approach is for the load balancer to decrypt the connection, which implies that the SSL connection is established with the load balancer instead of the server. This practice is increasing noticeably as load balancers integrate SSL into their architectures. When the load balancer is capable of looking into what normally would be encrypted, the doors are opened for a number of alternatives, including cookie sticky.

Yet another mechanism for session persistence is HTTP redirection. Figure 6-10 represents HTTP redirection used as a persistence mechanism.

In option **a** of Figure 6-10, the client sends a connection request to the VIP (192.0.2.100) associated with the specific service (www.example.com). The load balancer spoofs the TCP connection until it can determine the URL in the request. The load balancer applies the content policies and sends an HTTP redirection (response code 302) indication in the response pointing to a different URL (srv3.example.com). This new URL is associated with a different IP address (192.0.2.113), which is associated with a VIP that maps to a single real server (10.10.10.103). This mapping to a single real server is the key to HTTP redirection sticky. The real server, srv3, is configured to have all the URLs related to local content be relative to its host and domain names. The basic goal is to ensure that all subsequent TCP connections, regardless of the port number, that are the result of the interaction between Client1 and srv3 are sent to srv3. In essence, the load balancer is not ensuring persistence in any particular way, other than directing connections to srv3 that are associated with its VIP. This mechanism is not affected by changes to the source IP address, the cookie encryption, or the fact that the SSL ID is not in clear text or changes during the connection. The caveats associated with this mechanism are as follows:

- The URL sent back to the client is different than the original one.
- For every real server, there must be a single VIP.
- Every VIP must resolve to a distinct host name.

Chapter 18 explores the topic of session persistence in more detail.

Figure 6-10 *HTTP Redirection Sticky*

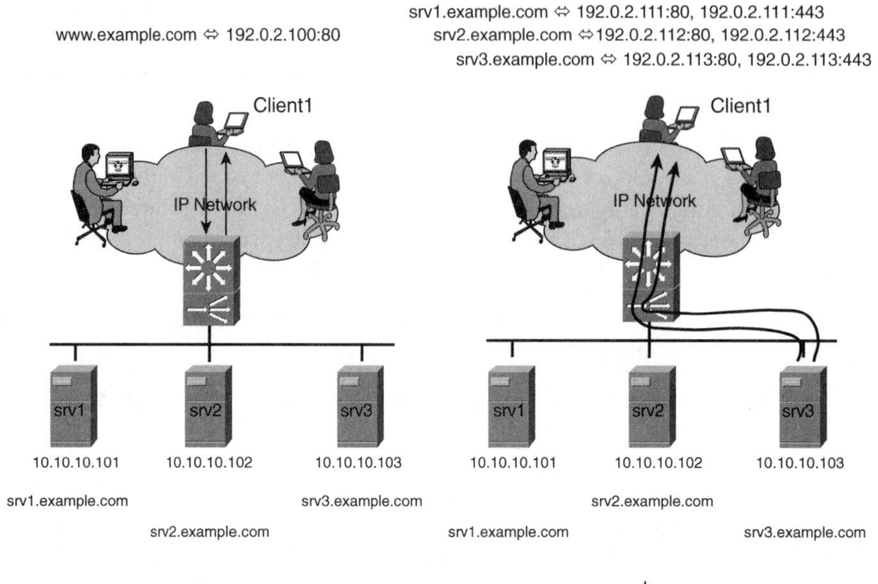

Server Health

Server health refers to the status of the servers in the server farm and the mechanisms used by the load balancer to track such status. The server health can be tracked in-band or out-of-band.

In-Band Server Health Tracking

In-band server health tracking refers to the load balancer monitoring packet activity related to active connections, which indicates whether the server is active. In its most basic form, the load balancer passively monitors packet activity to and from the server, which proves that the server is active, yet it does not guarantee that the application is behaving properly. This mechanism is inexpensive in terms of its processing requirements from the load balancer and should be the preferred choice for overall server health tracking. In-band mechanisms do not lend themselves well to application health tracking because the load balancer is required to understand the details of the application interaction to determine whether the application appears to be working as expected. Out-of-band tracking methods are better suited for this task.

Out-of-Band Server Health Tracking

Out-of-band server health tracking refers to the load balancer actively probing servers for specific application-related information to determine their health. Several mechanisms are available for out-of-band probing. The mechanisms vary depending on the type of health information required from the server. The following are the most common categories:

- Server availability
- Application availability
- Application consistency

Server availability requires the simplest of all probing mechanisms. A ping determines whether the server is available. The assumption is that if a server does not respond to an ICMP echo request, the server is offline and the load balancer should take the appropriate action. The appropriate action is to logically remove the real server from the server farm so that no new connections are sent to it.

Application availability requires a bit more work. The load balancer must generate a probe that can test both that the application is responding and thus listening on the expected port, and that it is responding in the expected manner. This implies, for example, that when initiating an HTTP connection request to port 80 for a particular URL, the connection is established properly (handshake is completed) and the HTTP connection request is responded to. If an HTTP GET was sent in the request, the response must include the contents associated with the URL in the GET request.

In addition to ensuring that the server is available, application consistency monitors the data provided by the application that issues the response. This consistency is monitored by comparing the content returned by the servers with a copy of the expected content and determining whether there is a match. This comparison is done between the checksum of the content returned in the response with a previous checksum value of the same content. If there is a match, the content is considered consistent. Typically, the checksum value is calculated the first time the probe is used. The load balancer stores the value to use in subsequent probing activities. For more information on this topic, see Chapter 17, "Server Health Management."

High Availability Considerations

Because of the importance of the tasks performed by load balancers and their location in the network, load balancers are required to provide very high levels of redundancy, availability, and predictability. These attributes require careful planning and understanding of the Data Center design. Redundancy simply implies the need for a backup device that is capable of taking over the critical functions performed by the load balancer with minimal or no disruption. High availability is related to the expected uptime provided by the system as a whole, including the rest of the infrastructure. Predictability refers to having an environment that offers predictable failover and convergence times, and a predictable traffic path during steady state and failure conditions. The following sections discuss the details related to highly available environments.

Because redundant designs offer no single point of failure, multiple load balancers are required for the same server farm. Figure 6-11 introduces a redundant design.

Figure 6-11 *Redundant Load-Balancing Design*

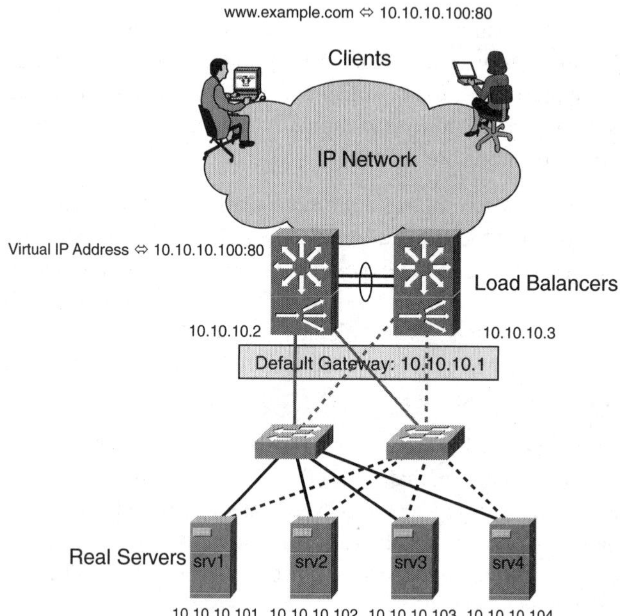

Notice the following details:

- Each load balancer requires two IP addresses: one used as the floating IP address for the default gateway, and a second for IP connectivity. Only the active load balancer uses the floating IP address.
- The load balancers run a redundancy protocol that determines the mastership and ownership of the default gateway address.
- Two load balancers are in place, with one acting as the default gateway and the other on standby.

Each server is configured to point to the default gateway address, regardless of which load balancer is currently active. The overall goal is to allow servers to continue to operate if the primary load balancer fails, and to ensure that the failover process can prevent active connections and sessions from being affected. This requires the two load balancers to exchange information about their status, as well as existing connections and session state information. The protocol used to track the status of the load balancer and the mechanism to determine which load balancer should be active generically is called redundancy protocol. The mechanism used to communicate connection and session state information generically is called stateful failover.

Redundancy Protocol

The redundancy protocol used between the load balancers monitors the status of the load balancer and initiates the actions leading to the failover from active to standby, or from the fallback mechanism back to the original active load balancer. It should be noted that the redundancy protocol is specific to the load balancers and sometimes is not based on any standard protocols. The fact that the redundancy protocols are proprietary should not be considered as bad. Typically, these redundancy protocols are transparent to the operation of the server farm, so they do not need to be interoperable with other devices.

The monitoring process relies on active probing or passive monitoring of heartbeats from the peer. Because the load balancers might be providing default gateway services, it is expected that the protocol used for default gateway redundancy (HSRP, VRRP, and so on) is used by the redundancy protocol. Figure 6-12 shows a redundant environment in which slb1 is the primary load balancer and default gateway.

Figure 6-12 *Redundant Topology Details*

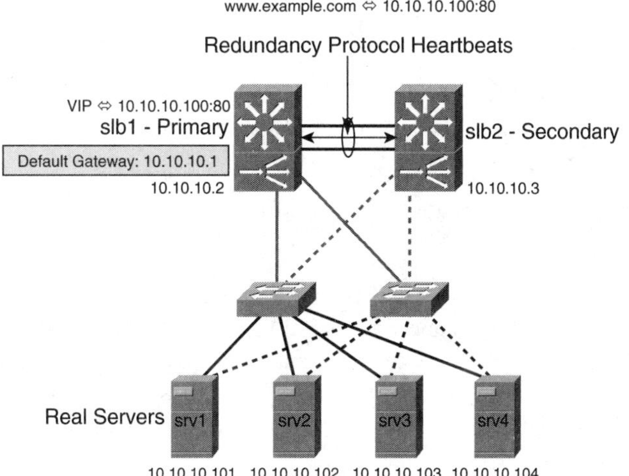

The configuration in Figure 6-12 implies that when a VIP fails on the primary load balancer and the secondary takes over the VIP, it also assumes the responsibility for default gateway support.

NOTE It is recommended that the active load balancer, whether an appliance or a module, be directly connected to the Spanning Tree Protocol (STP) root.

The heartbeats are exchanged over a dedicated link between the two load balancers. Most redundancy protocols are tunable, enabling you to match the default gateway protocol behavior and giving you control over the timing of the failover process. When deploying two load balancers, you could consider using them in an active-standby or active-active configuration.

Active-Standby Load-Balancing Configuration

Active-standby environments have a pair of load balancers, yet only one of them is active at all times. This configuration is shown in Figure 6-12. In Figure 6-12, slb1 is the primary load balancer and the default gateway. Being the primary load balancer implies that it owns and receives all traffic destined to the VIP. These configurations are predictable and simpler to troubleshoot than active-active configurations. The connection or session-state information is unidirectional from active to standby, there is a single active service location, and there typically is a single forwarding path to the access-layer switches. This makes management and troubleshooting simpler than in the active-active alternative.

Active-Active Load-Balancing Configuration

Active-active environments have a pair of load balancers that are both active at all times. This permits two possibilities:

- Both load balancers are active for different VIPs.
- Both load balancers are active for the same VIP.

When both load balancers are active for different VIPs, the configuration is set up explicitly by assigning each load balancer a specific VIP. The other load balancer is in standby mode for that VIP. If the servers for the different VIPs are on the same subnet and the load balancers are providing default gateway services, it is recommended that the servers point to the load balancer that supports the VIP associated with their service. This configuration is displayed in Figure 6-13.

Figure 6-13 *Active-Active Load-Balancing Configuration for Different VIPs*

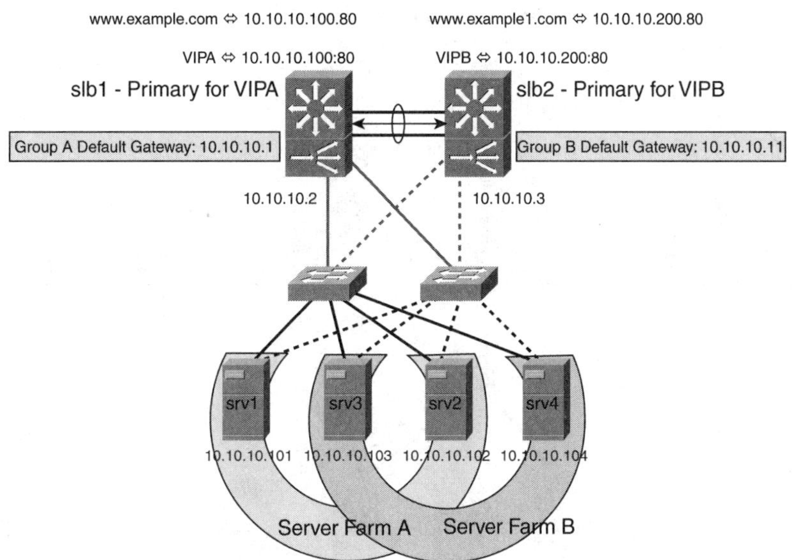

VIPA, supported by server farm A, is active on slb1. Therefore, srv1 and srv2 should point to slb1 as the default gateway on IP address 10.10.10.1. VIPB, supported by server farm B, is active on slb2. Therefore, srv3 and srv4 should point to slb2 as the default gateway on IP address 10.10.10.11. This configuration is equivalent to having multiple HSRP groups for default gateway redundancy. Notice that in Figure 6-13, the servers that belong to the same server farm are staggered across the multiple access switches. Upon failure, not all the servers that support the same service are disrupted, achieving yet another level of control in the failover process.

The next alternative is to have the same VIP active on both load balancers concurrently. This configuration presents a number of challenges, some of which might offset the perceived benefit of such a configuration. Figure 6-14 displays an active-active load-balancing environment for the same VIP.

The main challenge with an active-active setup for the same VIP is the result of having the same MAC and IP addresses active in two different places concurrently. The problem arises from the requirement that the load balancers receive all packets for the same connection, and all connections from the same session. The devices that are upstream from the load balancers, which are routers or Layer 3 switches, are typically not aware of connections or sessions. These devices select the best path for sending the traffic. Depending on the cost of each of the paths and the internal switching mechanisms of the devices, the traffic might be switched on a per-packet basis, on source/destination IP addresses, and so on.

Figure 6-14 *Active-Active Load-Balancing Configuration for the Same VIP*

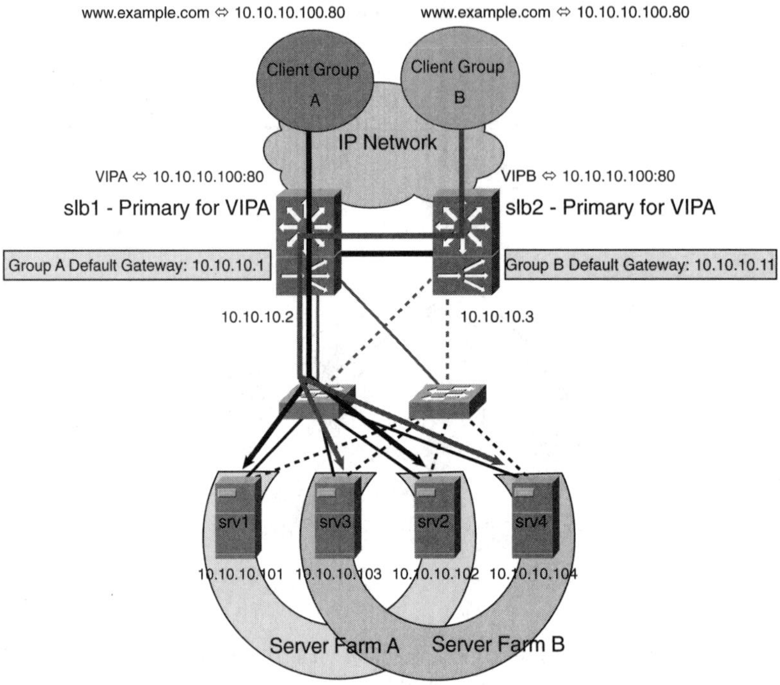

To make this work, the upstream devices need to ensure that the same load balancer sees all packets for a single connection, and all connections for the same session. This is possible by using policy-based routing (PBR) to direct traffic that matches certain parameters through specific traffic paths. The parameters are the source addresses used by the clients. This address space is divided in two, giving each half access to a VIP instance consistently. Figure 6-14 shows the paths that traffic takes when the source address space is divided.

NOTE An important consideration on an active-active environment is the fact that any one of the load balancers in the redundant configuration must be capable of handling the combined load if the other redundant load balancer fails.

The additional configuration efforts and added complexity to support active-active load-balancing environments, particularly when the same VIP is active on the two load balancers, are significant. The perceived benefits of active-active load-balancing environments typically are related to higher performance achieved because the two load balancers work simultaneously.

Connection and Session State Failover

The requirements for the exchange of connection state information between the pair of load balancers are dictated by the needs of the applications. The application environments can vary from basic web browsing that is characterized by short-lived sessions, to long-lived sessions such as VPN. Although the load balancers are expected to support the exchange of connection and session information for this wide range of applications, not all of them require or benefit from stateful failover.

Connections that last anywhere from less than a second to a few seconds are called short-lived connections and do not benefit from having state information in the secondary load balancer because the failure of the primary load balancer is unlikely to break such a connection. If multiple short-lived connections are part of a session that lasts more than a few seconds, the state information in the secondary load balancer is useful upon the failure of the primary load balancer. The secondary load balancer would have enough information to recover the session so that any new connections could be sent to the same server.

Connections that last longer than a few seconds or minutes, even hours and days, are referred to as long-lived connections and do benefit from the secondary load balancer having state information. This information is used to recover the actual connection and to guarantee that new connections of an existing session are sent to the same real server. The following sections cover the state failover options.

Stateless Failover

Stateless failover offers only failover from primary to secondary load balancer, without the recovery of connection or session information. After the primary has failed and the secondary has detected the failure, the secondary takes over the functions and handles all new requests. This option is well suited for environments that have short-lived connections.

Sticky Failover

As its name implies, sticky failover offers replication of the sticky tables needed to ensure that existing or new connections are sent to the correct server. This kind of failover is well suited for short-lived connections that require stickiness or sessions that are composed primarily of short-lived connections.

Stateful Failover

The stateful failover option replicates connection and session state information between the pair of load balancers. Stateful failover requires the load balancers to exchange state information at a predetermined and constant rate, which ensures that the failover of the primary load balancer is recoverable and that the active connections are not affected. This option is well suited for long-lived connections or sessions.

Generic Load Balancer Architecture

The load-balancing overview cannot be complete without the description of the architecture of a load balancer. This is an important topic because load balancers provide a new set of application services that require some special software and hardware features to make the processing possible at reasonable rates. Not all load balancers are created equal, yet there are a fair amount of commonalities among them. This section introduces a generic architecture that is not specific to a product yet that describes the main possible components found on a load balancer.

Generic Architecture Components

The following lists components described in the generic architecture that support fundamental processing functions in the load balancer. Some of these components can be combined on specific hardware architectures, yet the functions remain constant. Figure 6-15 presents a generic architecture used on a load balancer.

Figure 6-15 *Generic Architecture of a Load Balancer*

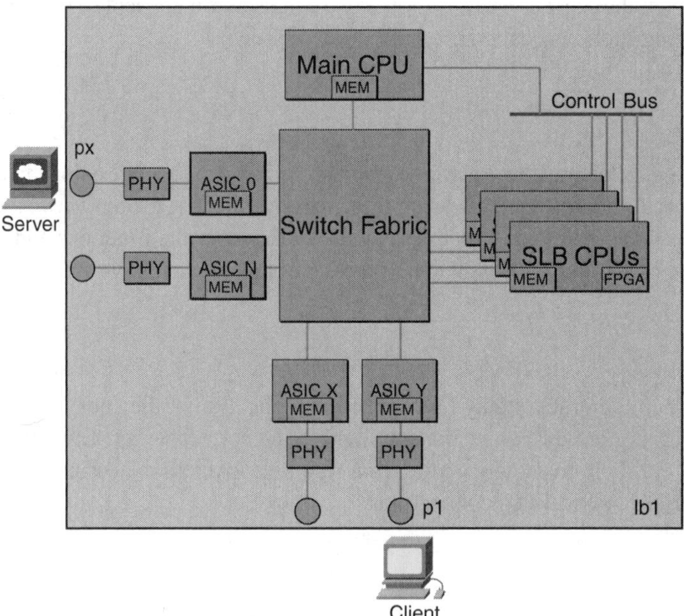

The main components of the architecture are as follows:

- Switch fabric
- Main processor or CPU

- LB processors
- Control bus
- Interface ASICs
- Memory components

The switch fabric provides the connectivity between the interfaces, the LB processors, and the main CPU. The main processor performs the control functions, such as configuration and management of the components and processing of control traffic. It uses the control bus to transmit and receive control information to and from the LB processors. The LB processors perform the different intelligent operations on the packets, such as pattern matching, TCP spoofing, and so on. When you have multiple processors, each is specialized for a certain task, yet they all complement each other. The ASICs automate the packet rewrite functions, which offload the other processors from the burden. Memory is used throughout for different purposes. The main CPU uses memory for connection and session tables, the LB processors for specific connection information, and the ASICs at the interface level for connection information associated with the particular interface.

An example of the operation of this architecture is as follows:

1. The client sends a new connection request to VIPA that is supported by lb1 (load balancer 1) in Figure 6-15.
2. lb1 receives the packet on a specific port p1.
3. A lookup process using the 5-tuple (source/destination IP, source/destination port, and protocol number) takes place to determine whether the packet is part of an existing connection or a new connection. In the latter case, the packet is a connection request (SYN), so the lookup process comes back empty.
4. The packet is forwarded to the main CPU for processing. The main CPU processing steps are as follows:
   a. Selection of the content policies that should be applied to the packet
   b. Application by the lb processors of the appropriate policies to the packet
   c. Selection of the real server by the main CPU
   d. Creation of a new entry in the connection table (MEM) and other potential memory locations (interface MEM) for the specific connection
5. After a server is selected, the header re-write operations take place (interface ASIC), and the packet is forwarded to the selected real server.
6. The interface memory is updated with the header re-write information to be used in subsequent packets.

When a packet that belongs to an existing connection arrives, policies are applied to it. The packet then is forwarded to the appropriate interface based on the connection table, and the interface ASIC performs the header rewrite tasks before forwarding the packet.

Depending on the hardware architecture, there are variations to where the processing takes place. In certain cases, ASICs at the port level help the processing by keeping track of connection information so that they can rewrite header information before the packet is forwarded, thereby offloading the main CPU from processing.

A common approach to offloading the main CPU is to add more processors that share the connection-processing load. The load sharing is done either by assigning connections to processors or by assigning different tasks to each processor. The tasks per processor then are executed sequentially on each packet as the packet moves through the processors. Because the processors are organized in pipeline fashion, they also execute their precise tasks concurrently, yet on the different packets moving through the pipeline.

The forwarding operation can take advantage of a switch fabric if it is present, or it can just happen on a bus in older architectures. If a fabric is present, the logic to perform the rewrite most likely is located on the ports. The alternative is to have central logic that rewrites the Layer 2 information to Layer 4 information.

In the architecture of a load balancer, certain components could become bottlenecks in a load balancer when processing high amounts of traffic. The most critical components that could affect the overall performance of the load balancer are described in greater detail in the next section.

Critical Components of a Load Balancer

Based on previous discussions, you could conclude that three critical areas are related to the performance of a load balancer, each with its own set of critical components: CPU processing capacity, memory, and switching capacity. These areas depend, in turn, on the critical components that support them.

CPU processing capacity is used for control functions, which include but are not limited to connection creation and teardown, deep packet inspection, Layer 2 functions such as Spanning Tree Protocol (STP), and Internal Gateway Protocols (IGPs).

Memory holds packet and connection information for transit traffic. Transit traffic applied to load balancers when connection state information must be maintained increases the overall demand for memory utilization.

Switch fabric allows transit traffic and other control messages to be communicated among multiple ports concurrently. In addition to each port capacity, the switch fabric capacity determines the overall raw bandwidth available.

Each critical area is then bound to one or multiple components that are coupled tightly to the previously described connection types.

The critical components are presented in Table 6-1.

Table 6-1 *Critical Components for Load Balancing*

Performance Impact Areas	Critical Components
Processing capacity	Main or central CPU, port ASICs, dedicated processors
Memory	DRAM, port memory, CAM
Switching capacity	Shared bus, switch fabric, port capacity

Table 6-1 reflects the main areas in question and the critical components per area. The components listed are deemed critical because they determine the performance capacity of the load balancer. The performance capacity is quantified by performance metrics, and the performance metrics are related to the critical components.

The processing of both short-lived and long-lived connections is tightly coupled with the critical components. Before explaining this relationship, it is important to state the following:

- The critical components are finite resources.
- A real traffic mix is composed of a combination of short-lived and long-lived connections that are changing constantly.

The one assumption that can be made is that the traffic patterns for any one network include a combination of short-lived and long-lived connections that can exceed the capacity of a load balancer. The processing capacity limits are related to the critical components, which are the components of a load balancer that are worth monitoring. The topic of measuring performance metrics of load balancers is discussed in detail in Chapter 22, "Performance Metrics of Data Center Devices."

Summary

This chapter described various fundamental concepts of load balancing that aid in understanding how load balancers work, what they do, and how to design networks that use them.

Load balancers are used in a variety of configurations to solve distinct problems that typically are related to scalability. They are deployed in front of farms of devices to increase the overall capacity of the farms while offering high availability and extended application-aware features.

Load balancers operate at multiple layers and perform critical functions on behalf of the server farm. The section, "Key Concepts of Load Balancing," introduced the details of how load balancers perform processing tasks at various stages and varying depth. The depth ranges from Layer 2 (MAC) through Layer 5 (applications such as HTTP), yet load balancing could operate at Layer 3 (IP) and Layer 4 (TCP/UDP) as well.

High availability is a major design consideration when deploying load balancers. The different options are driven by the application requirements. This means that careful consideration of design details leads to a better implementation.

Finally, this chapter explained the processing details and architectural issues in a generic architecture for a load balancer. Understanding the components and their functions enables you to determine which of the critical components is likely to be affected first by the traffic load and also enables you to determine track and understand the implications of the traffic types on the load balancer, and vice versa.

PART II

Server Farm Protocols

Chapter 7 IP, TCP, and UDP

Chapter 8 HTTP and Related Concepts

Chapter 9 SSL and TLS

Chapter 10 DNS Essentials and Site-Selection Considerations

Chapter 11 Streaming Protocols Overview

This chapter covers the following topics:

- Layers and protocols
- IP
- TCP
- UDP

CHAPTER 7

IP, TCP, and UDP

This chapter introduces the fundamental protocols used in intranets and, in particular, the server farms supporting web-based services. A number of other networking devices, such as firewalls, load balancers, and Secure Socket Layer (SSL) offloading devices, are also exposed to the operation of these fundamental protocols. These protocols include Transport Control Protocol (TCP) and User Datagram Protocol (UDP) at Layer 4 and Hypertext Transfer Protocol (HTTP) at Layer 5, which combined make a substantial percentage of traffic destined to the server farms in the Data Center.

The information in this chapter is not meant to be a tutorial on the protocols or a comprehensive explanation of their operation, but rather a focused view of their most relevant aspects. These aspects are viewed in relation to the operation of the server farm and the networking devices used to optimize the application services supported by the server farm. Because the operation of server stateful firewall's load balancers, SSL offloaders, and content engines depends on these protocols, it is important to understand their behavior before examining the interaction with the network devices. These interactions are transparent to clients and servers alike, which means that the expected behavior of the load balancers or SSL offloaders is the same as that of a server or a client. The flow of packets that belong to a single connection, or multiple logically related connections (a session), is monitored and to a certain extent controlled by these networking devices. For this reason, it is important to delve into the protocol details.

Layers and Protocols

Before discussing the fundamental protocols, it is important to introduce the relationship between the protocols and the layers they represent. Server load balancers, for example, operate at different layers, which are often named differently according to their operation. These labels include Layer 4, Layer 7, or Layers 5 through 7, referring to the layers of the packets in which the server load balancing is performed.

The classical model used to describe the layered approach to protocols is the Open System Interconnection (OSI) reference model, which is depicted in Figure 7-1.

Figure 7-1 *Layers in the OSI Model*

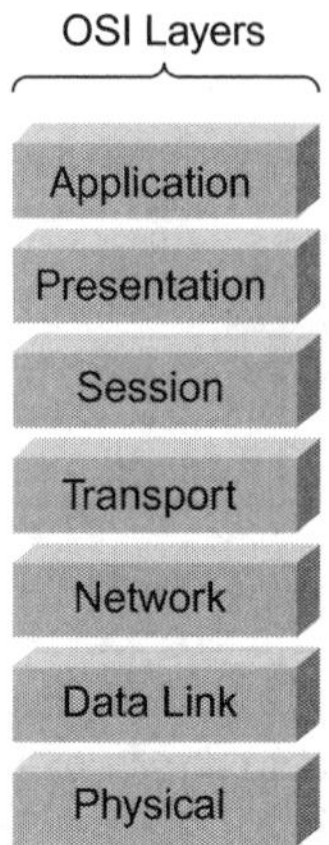

The layers in Figure 7-1 represent the typical layers required in a protocol stack to efficiently partition functional tasks in each layer while permitting layer-to-layer communication through clearly identified interfaces. When referring to Layer 5 or Layer 7, the general assumption is that the layers are those defined in the OSI model. Unfortunately, the OSI model does not completely map to existing protocol stacks such as TCP/IP. TCP/IP in fact does not use seven layers; thus, the concept of Layers 5 through 7 does not apply. Figure 7-2 presents the mapping from the OSI model to the TCP/IP protocol stack.

Figure 7-2 *OSI to TCP/IP Layer Mappings*

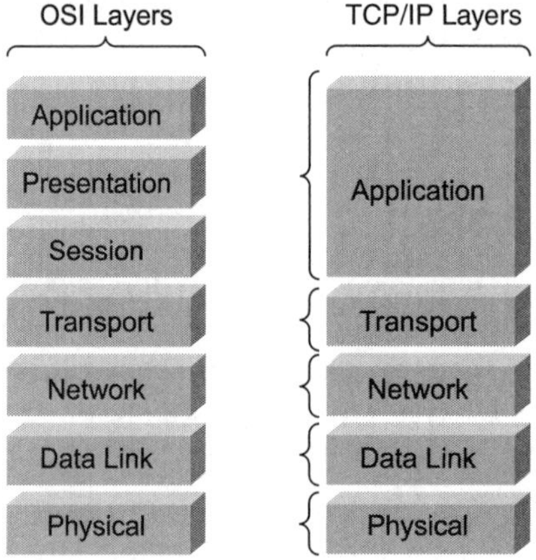

As shown in Figure 7-2, the TCP/IP stack does not have Layer 6 or Layer 7. The application layer of the TCP/IP stack, Layer 5, corresponds to the session, presentation, and application layers of the OSI model. Applications that run on top of a TCP/IP stack must perform the tasks and functions that the OSI Layers 5 through 7 support, all in the same layer. When referring to Layers 5 through 7 and applications that run on TCP/IP, the implication is that the session, presentation, and application functions are distinct, although they are supported by the application layer. For example, a SQL request that uses TCP as the transport protocol could potentially have information from a user making the request. This information (user ID, such as a name or account number) is different from requests originated by a different user. From the perspective of the TCP/IP protocol stack, these different requests are simply considered part of the TCP payload, but the information they contain might be important to the application. The user ID is then considered a Layer 7 piece of information.

For the purposes of this book, Layer 5 refers to the Layer 5 of the TCP/IP stack and is meant to group all relevant pieces of information that appear in the TCP/IP payload. We do so for consistency in the book and to accurately refer to the TCP/IP protocol stack. Referring to URL switching as Layer 7 switching simply implies Layer 7 of the OSI model instead of the TCP/IP protocol stack.

Figure 7-3 describes how the protocols in the TCP/IP stack map to the various layers of the TCP/IP stack.

Figure 7-3 *TCP/IP Protocols*

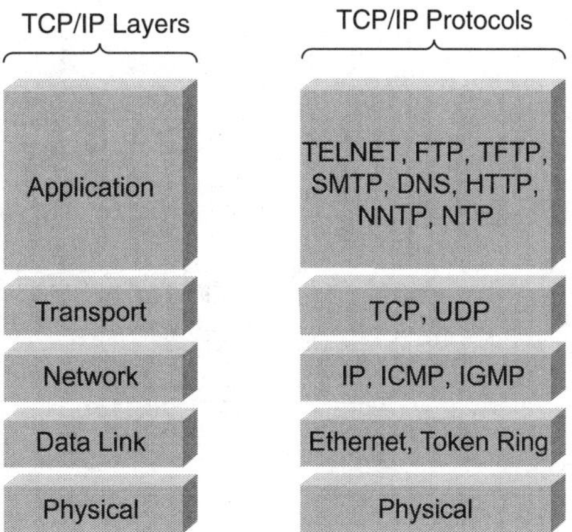

The TCP/IP protocol suite includes many protocols organized in layers. Each layer is responsible for a different function of the communication exchange.

NOTE The physical layer is not considered a layer of the TCP/IP suite yet is included here for completeness.

This book focuses on the protocols at the transport and application layers that are commonly found in server farm environments and, in particular, those that make up the majority of any given traffic mix. These protocols include TCP and UDP at the transport layer and HTTP, FTP, DNS, RTP, FTP, and many others at the application layer.

Notice that the application layer protocols use the transport protocols TCP and UDP, which implies that the application layer protocols rely on the flow control and error correction and detection characteristics of the transport layer protocols if available. For example, HTTP uses TCP and relies on the connection-oriented nature of TCP. It implies that HTTP does not need to support flow control and error correction because TCP provides these capabilities.

Before delving into the details of transport protocols, it is important to understand some aspects of the IP protocol, how it encapsulates TCP and UDP, and the header details. Figure 7-4 introduces the encapsulation steps as data is sent from the application down the protocol stack.

Figure 7-4 *Encapsulation*

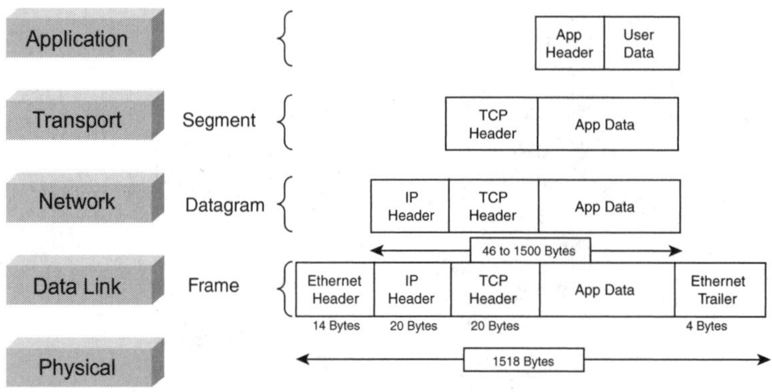

As application data comes down the protocol stack, it is encapsulated into the transport protocol payload (TCP or UDP), which in turn is encapsulated onto the network protocol (IP), which is placed into an Ethernet frame.

As the application data is made available to the TCP/IP stack, the stream of bytes uses a specific name that denotes the protocol stack layer handling the stream. A TCP or UDP chunk of data is referred to as a *segment*, an IP chunk of data is a *datagram*, and an Ethernet chunk of data is a *frame*. *Packet* describes a chunk of data going from the IP layer to the network interface (data link layer); however, it is not exactly the same as a datagram. As defined in Stevens,[1] "A packet can be either an IP datagram or a fragment of an IP datagram."

This book uses the terms *packet*, *datagram*, *segment*, and *frame* as defined in this section.

NOTE Ethernet was first proposed as a standard protocol by Xerox, DEC, and Intel, and it became the basis for the 802.3, the IEEE standard for Ethernet and Ethernet II. The 802.3 and Ethernet II (also known as Ethernet v2) formats are slightly different. 802.3 uses the length field instead of the type field used by Ethernet v2. For more information on the frame formats and their differences, see Chapter 12, "Layer 2 Protocol Essentials."

In this book, the references to Ethernet are specific to the Ethernet v2 standard unless noted otherwise. Traffic captures throughout the book show Ethernet II, referring to the Ethernet v2 standard and therefore using the Ethernet v2 header format.

IP

The original specification of IP is available in RFC 0791. Like many other protocols in the TCP/IP suite, IP has been evolving. The latest IP specification, IP version 6 (IPv6), also known as IP Next Generation (IPng), is available in RFC 2460, which is part of a long list of specifications related to IPV6. This list, controlled by the IETF IPv6 working group, appears at http://www.ietf.org/html.charters/ipv6-charter.html.

NOTE This book addresses applications and the infrastructure that rely mainly on IPv4.

As previously shown in Figure 7-3, IP operates at the network layer, and it is a connectionless protocol. Being connectionless implies that IP is not aware of the concept of a connection between two entities, and therefore it does not maintain state information between the parties communicating. IP is used by the transport protocols TCP and UDP. The header and payload of the transport protocols are encapsulated, as shown in Figure 7-5.

Figure 7-5 *Protocol Encapsulation*

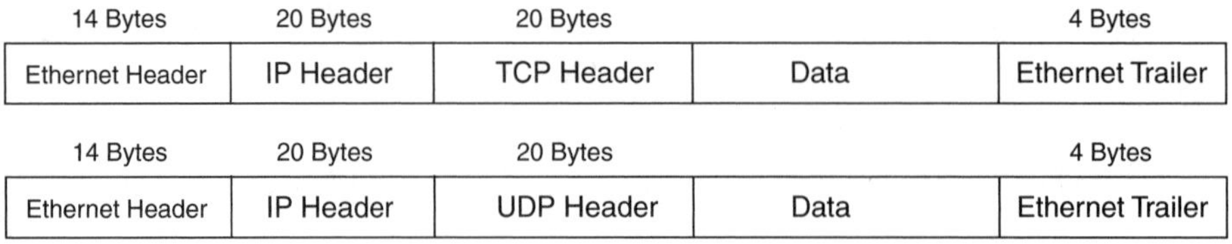

14 Bytes	20 Bytes	20 Bytes		4 Bytes
Ethernet Header	IP Header	TCP Header	Data	Ethernet Trailer

14 Bytes	20 Bytes	20 Bytes		4 Bytes
Ethernet Header	IP Header	UDP Header	Data	Ethernet Trailer

IP Header

Figure 7-6 illustrates the IP header.

Figure 7-6 *IP Header*

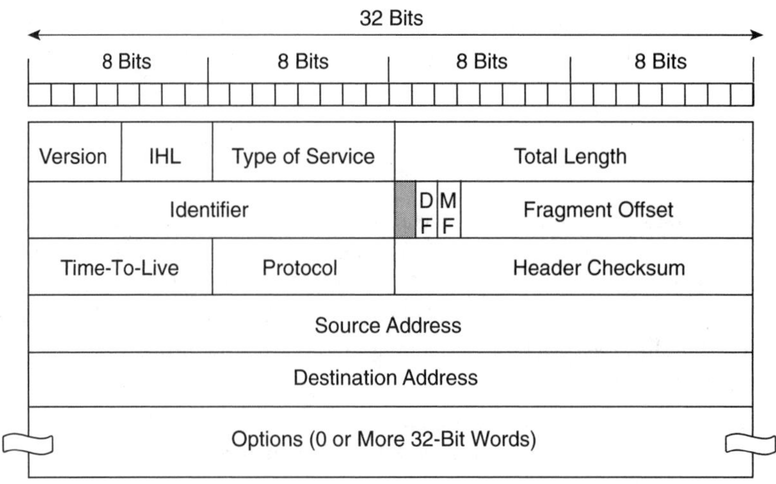

The fields in the IP header control the communication exchange between the two parties. Each field carries specific information explained in the sections that follow.

Version Field

Version is a 4-bit field that specifies the version of IP in use by the server and receiver. Table 7-1 describes the current IP version numbers.

Table 7-1 *IP Version Field*

Binary	Decimal	Version	RFC
0000	0	Reserved	—
0001, 0010, 0011	1-3	Unassigned	—
0100	4	IPv4 (standard IP)	791
0101	5	Stream IP Datagram Mode (experimental)	1190
0110	6	IPv6, also known as IPng	1883
0111	7	TP/IX: The Next Internet	1475
1000	8	The "P" Internet Protocol (PIP)	1621
1001	9	TCP and UDP over Bigger Addresses (TUBA)	1347
1010–1110	10–14	Unassigned	—
1111	15	Reserved	—

The Internet Assigned Numbers Authority (IANA) in RFC 2780 provides the guidelines for the allocation of "Values in the Internet Protocol and Related Headers." The IANA addresses fields for the following protocol headers:

- IPv4
- IPv6
- Internet Control Message Protocol (ICMP)
- UDP
- TCP

Some of the IANA guidelines affect how the IPv4 fields are used. These effects are discussed in sections that are relevant to each field. For instance, RFC 2780 specifies how the high-order bit of the version field is used for TCP/IP (RFC 1144) header compression and how the three high-order bits are used for IP (RFC 2507) header compression.

NOTE You typically use TCP/IP header compression on low-speed serial lines on which bandwidth is scarce. When header compression is in use, the IP version field is ignored. The header information on a compressed packet is different from that of a noncompressed packet. For more information, see the three sections about header compression later in this chapter.

Header Length Field

Header length is a 4-bit field specifying the number of 4-byte words in the IP header, which yields a maximum value of 60 bytes:

60 Bytes = 15 (maximum field value) * 4-byte words

The typical value of this field is 5 (20 bytes) in the absence of options.

Type of Service Field

Type of service is an 8-bit field known as the TOS field, which originally consisted of a 3-bit precedence field, 4 TOS bits, and an unused bit (bit 0). The 8-bit field, referred to as the differentiated services (DS) field, which superseded the TOS definition, is divided in a 6-bit differentiated services code point (DSCP) and a 2-bit field currently unused. The use of the DS field, defined in RFC 2474, is further explained in RFC 2475, "An Architecture for Differentiated Services." RFC 2481, a Proposal to add Explicit Congestion Notification (ECN) to IP, presents an experimental use of the currently unused bits and in section 19 describes a brief historical definition for the TOS bit.

RFC 3168 obsoletes RFC 2481 and updates RFC 2474 by defining an ECN field in the IP header.

Under this previous definition, depicted in part A of Figure 7-7, the TOS bits were divided into a 3-bit precedence field, a 4-bit TOS field, and the unused 0 bit.

Figure 7-7 *TOS Definition*

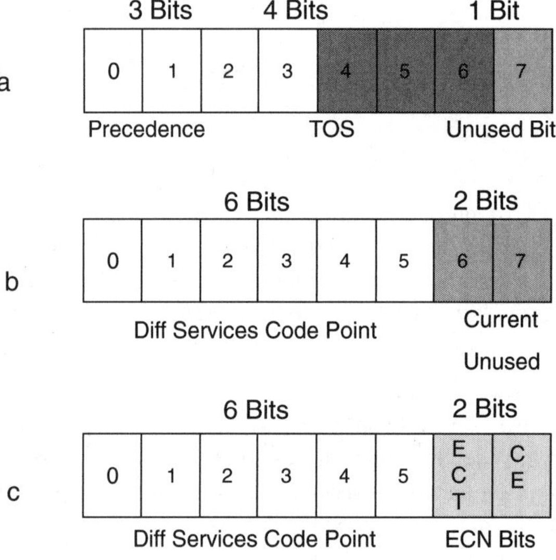

Table 7-2 shows how the precedence bits (bits 0, 1, and 2, starting from the high-order bit) are mapped (as specified in RFC 1349).

Table 7-2 *Precedence Bits*

Precedence Bits	Priority
000	Routine
001	Priority
010	Immediate
011	Flash
100	Flash override
101	Critic/ECP
110	Internetwork control
111	Network control

Table 7-3 shows how the TOS field bits are mapped (as specified in RFC 791 and RFC 1349).

Table 7-3 *Type of Service Bits*

TOS Bits	Semantics
0000	Normal service (default value)
Bit 6: 0001	0: Normal monetary cost 1: Low monetary cost
Bit 5: 0010	0: Normal reliability 1: High reliability
Bit 4: 0100	0: Normal throughput 1: High throughput
Bit 3: 1000	0: Normal delay 1: Low delay

Although the DS approach is adopted and its support is pervasive on networking equipment, the previous specification of the TOS field is still applicable. This point is important especially when it comes to applying quality of service (QoS) to IP network traffic.

Part B of Figure 7-7 depicts the interim step before the ECN bit was explicitly added to the TCP header. (ECN is no longer experimental.) The TOS field now consists of 6 bits allocated for the DSCP and 2 unused bits. Part C of Figure 7-7 presents the new definition for the previously unused bits. The new definition, in RFC 3168, specifies the 2-bit field as the ECN codepoint with four possible values (the possible combination of their binary values). The ECN capable transport (ECT) codepoints 10 and 01, or ETC(0) and ETC(1), indicate that the endpoints of the transport protocol are ECN capable. The other codepoints, 00 and 11, indicate that the codepoints are not ECN capable and that there is congestion in the endpoints, respectively. Congestion experienced is also known as CE. Table 7-4 displays the bit in reference to other ECN values.

Table 7-4 *ECN Field Values*

ECT	CE	Semantics
0	0	No ECT endpoints
0	1	ECT(1)
1	0	ECT(0)
1	1	Congestion experienced

Refer to RFC 3168 for more details regarding the ECN field.

Total Length Field

Total length is a 16-bit field that carries the total length of the IP datagram, including the header in chunks of 8 bytes (octets). A 16-bit field yields a maximum value of 65,535 bytes in an IP datagram.

TIP Subtracting the header length from the total length yields the IP datagram payload size.

Identifier Field

The identifier is a 16-bit field that identifies the fragments of a fragmented IP datagram. The identifier is incremented by the source when it transmits a new IP datagram. The identifier field with the flags and fragmented offset fields are used to reassemble fragmented datagrams.

IP datagrams are fragmented when they exceed the maximum transmission unit (MTU) of a particular segment they traverse. This process implies that either the source host or an intermediate router placing the datagram in the segment performs the fragmentation. The host or router fragments the datagram in pieces that do not exceed the MTU and places the same number in the identifier field. The destination host uses the ID to reassemble the datagram.

NOTE The MTU size depends on the encapsulation used by the data link layer protocol, which is typically 1500 (1492 bytes with the Logical Link Control [LLC] and Subnetwork Access Protocol [SNAP] headers) for Ethernet v2 and 802.3.

Path MTU refers to the smallest MTU found in the path the packets traverse between source and destination hosts. The path is assumed to have more than one data link segment.

The fragmentation is performed based on the MTU, which implies it is done potentially at the source hosts or intermediate routers.

Flags Field

The flags field is a 3-bit field that contains information about IP datagram fragmentation. The first bit is unused. The second bit is the Don't Fragment (DF) bit, which when set to 0, indicates the packet is not to be fragmented. A packet that cannot be fragmented is discarded by the router, which sends an ICMP "Fragmentation Needed and Don't Fragment Flag Set" message back to the source host. The third bit is the More Fragments (MF) bit that signals whether there are more fragments expected. The router sets this bit to 1 in all fragments and 0 in the last fragment. The destination host expects to receive fragments until the MF bit equals 0.

Fragment Offset Field

The fragment offset field is a 13-bit field that carries the offset of the fragment from the header of the original datagram in chunks of 8 bytes. Because fragments could arrive out of order to the destination hosts, the offset value allows the host to reassemble them in the correct order.

NOTE If a fragment from an IP datagram is lost, all fragments from the IP datagram must be discarded. Hence, the entire IP datagram must be retransmitted, which again requires fragmentation. Because fragment loss increases packet retransmission, congestion might be exacerbated if the loss is due to link load conditions.

Time-To-Live Field

The Time-To-Live field (TTL) is an 8-bit field that specifies how long the packet should live, which is counted in terms of the number of routers traversed by the datagram (hop count). The initial TTL value is selected by the source host, and it is recommended to use 64. Often, other values are used to limit the time, in hops, that the packet should live. This TTL keeps packets from lingering on the network unnecessarily.

The TTL is decremented by 1 by every router it traverses. After the TTL has been decremented to 0, the packet is discarded, and an ICMP **time-to-live equals 0 during transit** message is sent to the source host.

NOTE The **traceroute** program uses the TTL to determine the "route" or path from the source host to the destination host. The **traceroute** program sends a datagram with a TTL of 1 to the destination host. The intermediate router decrements the TTL to 0, discards the packet, and sends the ICMP "time exceeded" message back, which permits the source host to identify the first router in the path. The source host sends the datagram, this time with a TTL value of 2, which reaches the second intermediate router. This process is repeated until the final destination is reached and the path is recorded to the source host.

A router that receives a datagram in which the TTL field is 0 must discard it and send back an ICMP "time exceeded" message to the source host.

This detail is important to note: When the datagram finally reaches the destination host with TTL 1, the host returns an ICMP "port unreachable" message instead of a "time exceeded" message, which makes it possible for the source host to determine that it has reached the destination host. The "port unreachable" message results from the destination port being in an unlikely range supported by the destination host (greater than 30,000).

Protocol Field

The protocol field is an 8-bit field that identifies the protocol in use. Most protocols in the TCP/IP suite rely on IP, which requires some kind of identification for the specific protocol using the IP layer.

Table 7-5 lists the most common protocols.

Table 7-5 *Protocol Number Table*

Decimal	Keyword	Protocol	References
0	HOPOPT	IPv6 Hop-by-Hop Option	RFC 1883
1	ICMP	Internet Control Message Protocol	RFC 792
2	IGMP	Internet Group Management Protocol	RFC 1112
3	GGP	Gateway-to-Gateway Protocol	RFC 823
4	IP	IP in IP (encapsulation)	RFC 2003
5	ST	Stream	RFC 1190, RFC 1819

Table 7-5 *Protocol Number Table (Continued)*

Decimal	Keyword	Protocol	References
6	TCP	Transmission Control Protocol	RFC 793
8	EGP	Exterior Gateway Protocol	RFC 888, DLM 1
9	IGP	Any private interior gateway (used by Cisco for its IGRP)	IANA
16	CHAOS	Chaos	NC 3
17	UDP	User Datagram	RFC 768, JBP
29	ISO-TP4	ISO Transport Protocol Class 4	RFC 905, RC 77
30	NETBLT	Bulk Data Transfer	RFC 969, DDC 1
35	IDPR	Inter-Domain Policy Routing	MXS1
41	IPv6	IP Version 6	Deering
43	IPv6-Route	Routing Header for IPv6	Deering
44	IPv6-Frag	Fragment Header for IPv6	Deering
45	IDRP	Inter-Domain Routing Protocol	Sue Hares
46	RSVP	Resource Reservation Protocol	Bob Braden
47	GRE	General Routing Encapsulation	Tony Li
48	MHRP	Mobile Host Routing Protocol	David Johnson
50	ESP	Encapsulating Security Payload for IPv6	RFC 1827
51	AH	Authentication Header for IPv6	RFC 1826
55	MOBILE	IP Mobility	Perkins
56	TLSP	Transport Layer Security Protocol using Kryptonet key management	Oberg
58	IPv6-ICMP	ICMP for IPv6	RFC 1883
59	IPv6-NoNxt	No Next Header for IPv6	RFC 1883
60	IPv6-Opts	Destination Options for IPv6	RFC 1883
80	ISO-IP	International Organization for Standardization IP	MTR
83	VINES	VINES	BXH
85	NSFNET-IGP	National Science Foundation Network IGP	HWB

continues

Table 7-5 *Protocol Number Table (Continued)*

Decimal	Keyword	Protocol	References
88	EIGRP	Enhanced Interior Gateway Routing Protocol	Cisco, GXS
89	OSPFIGP	Open Shortest Path First Interior Gateway Protocol	RFC 1583, JTM 4
94	IPIP	IP-within-IP Encapsulation	JI6
95	MICP	Mobile Internetworking Control Protocol	JI6
97	ETHERIP	Ethernet-within-IP Encapsulation	RFC 3378
98	ENCAP	Encapsulation Header	RFC 1241, RXB3
102	PNNI	Private Network-Network Interface over IP	Callon
103	PIM	Protocol Independent Multicast	Farinacci
108	IPComp	IP Payload Compression	RFC 2393
111	IPX-in-IP	Internetwork Packet Exchange in IP	Lee
112	VRRP	Virtual Router Redundancy Protocol	Hinden
113	PGM	Pragmatic General Multicast Reliable Transport Protocol	Speakman
114		Any 0-hop protocol	IANA
115	L2TP	Layer 2 Tunneling Protocol	Aboba
121	SMP	Simple Message Protocol	Ekblad
132	SCTP	Stream Control Transmission Protocol	Stewart
133	FC	Fibre Channel	Rajagopal
135-254		Unassigned	IANA
255		Reserved	IANA

You can find the complete list of protocols at http://www.iana.org/assignments/protocol-numbers.

Header Checksum Field

The header checksum field is a 16-bit field that contains the checksum of the IP header only. The checksum is calculated by using the 16-bit 1s complement sum of the header. On arrival, the receiver of the datagram performs its own checksum calculation on the header and determines whether the datagram needs to be discarded.

The next layer protocols are in many cases responsible for their own checksum calculations, which in TCP and UDP include fields from the IP header as well.

Source Address and Destination Address Fields

Both the source address and destination address are 32-bit fields that carry the source and destination IP addresses.

Options Field

The options field is a variable-length field in which the actual chunks come in 32-bit size portions that carry optional information used by the datagram. This field is optional and might not be present on every IP packet. The following are the currently defined options:

- **Source Routing**—Source routing is the ability to route packets based on information contained in the source route fields. The information in the source route fields is placed by the source host. Intermediate routers must obey the source routes. There are two types of source routing: loose source route (LSR) and strict source route (SSR).

  LSR permits a router to pick the next hop router used to forward the datagram based on the route indicated in the source route field. The IP header carries only a number of IP addresses to use to route but not all of them. SSR forces intermediate routers to follow the routes specified in the source route field.

- **Record Route**—The record route (RR) option makes each router record its own IP address. The ping program uses this option to issue an RR in the datagram, which includes an ICMP echo request message. Each router the datagram traverses adds its IP address to the options field. When the destination host receives the datagram, it sends back an ICMP echo reply with all the recorded IP addresses. All routers in the return path add their own addresses to the datagram, which implies that the source host has the IP addresses of the routers in the forward and reverse paths.
- **Timestamp**—The timestamp is similar to the RR option, except that it adds the time when the packet touched each router. In addition to the 3 bytes used for the IP option, length and pointer, there are two more fields in use: the overflow (4 bits) and the flags (4 bits) fields. The overflow field is incremented by the routers when there is no room left in the header. The flags field is used to signal whether the routers should record the timestamp only (0 value), timestamp with IP address (1 value), or a timestamp when the router's IP address matches the next IP address in the pre-initialized list of IP addresses. When IP addresses and timestamps are used, there could be up to four pairs (IP address and timestamp) in the options part of the IP header. Each timestamp requires 4 bytes.
- **Security and Handling Restrictions**—RFC 1108 describes in detail the use of the options for security and handling restrictions.

TIP The length of the IP header is limited by the size of the IP header length field of 4 bits. This limit implies that the maximum length of the IP header is 60 bytes, minus the fixed 20 bytes from the header, leaving 40 bytes for options. There are 3 bytes used: 1 byte for the IP option, 1 byte for the length of the RR option, and 1 byte for the pointer field to signal the start of the current IP addresses list (typically the fourth byte). It leaves room for nine IP addresses, which across a large network might not be enough to record all hops. After the ninth IP address is recorded, the pointer field points to byte 40, indicating that the list is full.

The following section discusses specific details of TCP that are relevant to Data Centers and server farm environments. This information is relevant when describing the interaction of application-aware network devices such as server load balancers and caches with application traffic.

IP Header Compression

For more information on IP header compression, see the sections, "TCP Header Compression" and "UDP Header Compression."

TCP

TCP, originally defined in RFC 793, provides a reliable host-to-host communication service (also referred to as client-to-server). From the discussion in the previous section, you understand that IP does not offer a reliable connection. The extent of IP's reliability is the ability to determine whether the IP header has been changed through the checksum field. TCP was designed to address the following areas, some of which are defined in RFC 793:

- Basic data transfer (byte-stream service)
- Reliability
- Flow control
- Multiplexing
- Connections

Basic data transfer refers to the capability for a continuous data transfer, which is bidirectional sender-to-receiver and receiver-to-sender. The implication is a mechanism that allows the upper layers of the stack to tell the TCP process to send data immediately. This process is possible because of the *push* flag, which is discussed in detail in the section, "TCP Control Flags." An important aspect of the basic data transfer is TCP's capability for continuous data transfer, which is better described as a byte-stream service. TCP is not based on the concept of application data boundaries such as records or block.

TCP simply receives data from the application layer of the stack, stuffs the data into a segment, and sends it down to the stack. The applications are expected to control the contextual boundaries of the data because TCP just sends streams from one end to the other. In some cases, the TCP protocol stack might wait for more data from the application to send a larger segment, thus increasing efficiency. Because the stream is just a number of bytes, the state information about the connection requires knowledge of the transmitted and received bytes. It uses two key pieces of information:

- Sequence number (SEQ)
- Acknowledgement number (ACK)

Both sequence and acknowledgement numbers use bytes or rather, the byte numbers of the data being sent or received, to keep track of the state, which is easier to control as it maps directly to the byte stream.

Reliability refers to the capability of TCP to recover from any kind of error condition that could prevent the successful communication between sender and receiver. TCP expects the datagrams to be acknowledged (ACK) within a timeout interval, after which it attempts retransmissions for a period of time before ceasing any attempts. Sequence numbers related to each segment are used to order the segments because they could have arrived out of order. Finally, a checksum over the entire segment ensures that there is no damage to the payload or header. If there is damage, the segment is discarded.

Flow control refers to the capability of the receiver to control the amount of data the sender is sending. The receiver sends the window size (advertised window) along with every ACK that tells the sender how many bytes can be sent after a specific segment SEQ. This process allows the receiver to throttle back the amount of data being received.

Multiplexing refer to the capability of TCP to maintain many simultaneous processes in a single host. It uses port numbers, which identify distinct application processes. The application process and the network address form a socket. Different connections can use a single socket, yet a connection between two hosts is uniquely identified by the pair of sockets (source and destination addresses and source and destination port numbers).

Connection refers to the concept of a communication stream between two devices for which state is maintained. The state is maintained to ensure the communication process is successful for as long as it is active. Additionally, the aforementioned control mechanisms of SEQ and window size help maintain reliability and flow control. TCP ensures reliability by using flow-control mechanisms to control the conversation, and error correction and detection to handle communication problems when they appear.

TCP is also known for its connection-oriented service in which a connection between server and receiver is established before they start the data exchange. This initial connection uses what is referred to as a three-way handshake, which is explained in detail in the "TCP Connection Overview" section of this chapter.

The reliability offered by TCP results from handling the host-to-host communication in the following manner:

- Selecting the preferred size of portion of data to send.
- Maintaining a timer when a segment is sent. An acknowledgement of the segment is expected, and if it is not received, the portion of data is retransmitted.
- Tagging each segment being sent with a SEQ so that the receiver is able to order the data.
- Using a mechanism to throttle the traffic flow between sender and receiver by means of a window that increases as packets are successfully received or decreases as packets are dropped.

As with the previous section on IP, this section is not meant to be a tutorial on TCP but rather a focused explanation of the topics that are critical for Data Center design, planning, support, and engineering staff to understand.

TCP Header

This section on TCP presents a summary of the TCP header fields and introduces concepts that are critical in the understanding of TCP as it relates to devices that interact with the TCP connection, purposely or transparently, when processing server farm traffic.

TCP as IP has changed over the years. RFC 3168 has updated RFC 793. Some of the new changes in RFC 3168 affect the use of two TOS bits for ECN in the IP header and some include changes to the TCP header. We introduce these changes as we explain the different fields in the TCP header.

Figure 7-8 introduces the TCP header, as defined in RFC 793.

Figure 7-8 *TCP Header*

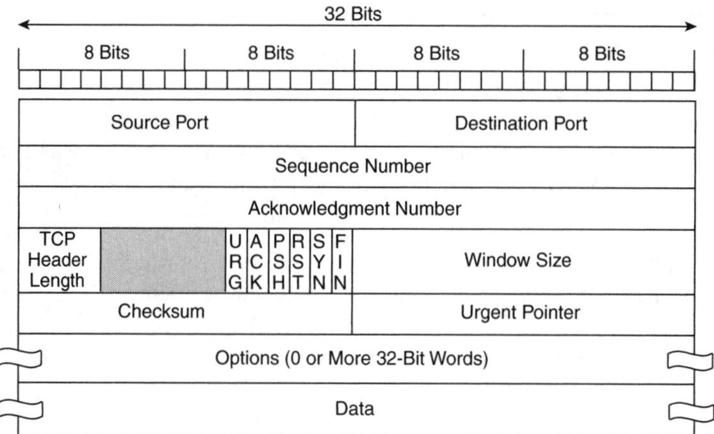

The sections that follow introduce the details of each field in the TCP header.

Source Port and Destination Port Fields

The source and destination port number fields are each 16 bits. (Values range from 1 to 65,535.) Port numbers uniquely identify an application process at the source and destination hosts. An application process running on a host uses a unique port number that could be multiplexed.

Figure 7-9 presents an example of multiplexing in which Client1 and Client2 have established connections with Server1. Client1 and Client2 are connected to Server1 using the same destination port (port 80), yet their source ports are unique. Each combination of source/destination port number identifies a unique connection.

Figure 7-9 *TCP Connections*

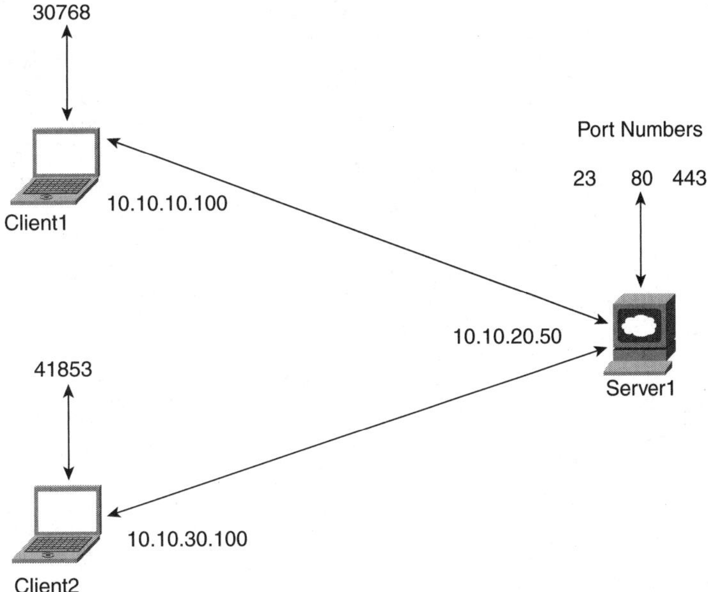

The application process listens on a specific port for all incoming traffic, in this case from Client1 and Client2. The host, Server1, must provide a mechanism to handle multiple connections on the same port concurrently. The combination of source and destination port numbers and IP addresses identifies a single and unique connection between sender and receiver.

TIP The port numbers were traditionally documented in the "assigned numbers" RFCs, which have become obsolete regularly since RFC 739. (RFC 739 obsoleted both RFC 604, "Assigned Link Numbers," and RFC 503, "Socket Number List.") RFC 3232 obsoleted, which was the 1994 snapshot of the assigned list and indicates, officially, that the assigned number list is an online database accessible through the web at http://www.iana.org. The list of port numbers appears at http://www.iana.org/assignments/port-numbers.

Table 7-6 lists well-known port numbers and their associated protocols.

Table 7-6 *Well-Known Port Numbers and Associated Protocols*

Keyword	Decimal	Description
ftp-data	20/tcp	FTP (default data)
ftp-data	20/udp	FTP (default data)
ftp	21/tcp	FTP (control)
ftp	21/udp	FTP (control)
ssh	22/tcp	Secure Shell (SSH) remote login protocol
ssh	22/udp	SSH remote login protocol
telnet	23/tcp	Telnet
telnet	23/udp	Telnet
smtp	25/tcp	Simple Mail Transfer Protocol (SMTP)
smtp	25/udp	SMTP
domain	53/tcp	Domain Name System (DNS)
domain	53/udp	DNS
tacacs-ds	65/tcp	TACACS (database service)
tacacs-ds	65/udp	TACACS (database service)
tftp	69/tcp	Trivial File Transfer Protocol (TFTP)
tftp	69/udp	TFTP
finger	79/tcp	Finger
finger	79/udp	Finger
http	80/tcp	HTTP
http	80/udp	HTTP
www	80/tcp	HTTP
www	80/udp	HTTP

Table 7-6 *Well-Known Port Numbers and Associated Protocols (Continued)*

Keyword	Decimal	Description
www-http	80/tcp	HTTP
www-http	80/udp	HTTP
kerberos	88/tcp	Kerberos
kerberos	88/udp	Kerberos
pop2	109/tcp	Post Office Protocol (POP) Version 2
pop2	109/udp	POP Version 2
pop3	110/tcp	POP Version 3
pop3	110/udp	POP Version 3
nntp	119/tcp	Network News Transfer Protocol (NNTP)
nntp	119/udp	NNTP
ntp	123/tcp	Network Time Protocol (NTP)
ntp	123/udp	NTP
snmp	161/tcp	Simple Network Management Protocol (SNMP)
snmp	161/udp	SNMP
snmptrap	162/tcp	SNMPTRAP
snmptrap	162/udp	SNMPTRAP
bgp	179/tcp	Border Gateway Protocol (BGP)
bgp	179/udp	BGP
rsvp_tunnel	363/tcp	Resource Reservation Protocol (RSVP) Tunnel
rsvp_tunnel	363/udp	RSVP Tunnel
https	443/tcp	HTTP over Transport Layer Security/Secure Socket Layer (TLS/SSL)
https	443/udp	HTTP over TLS/SSL

The list of port numbers is organized as follows:

- Well-known ports: 0–1023
- Registered Ports: 1024–49,151
- Dynamic or private ports: 49,152–65,535

Registered ports are ports that have been explicitly reserved for specific applications by request yet they "can be used by ordinary user processes or programs executed by ordinary users," as defined by RFC 1340. A good example of registered ports is the Hot Standby Router Protocol (HSRP):

```
hsrp        1985/tcp   HSRP
hsrp        1985/udp   HSRP
```

NOTE The list shows both TCP and UDP used as transport, which indicates the protocol port number has been reserved instead of it supported using UDP and TCP.

The dynamic or private port range is used by hosts to obtain a randomly generated port number when there is no port associated with the application.

Sequence Number Field

The sequence number field is a 32-bit field that identifies the first byte of data in the specific segment. TCP labels each byte in the communication stream with a sequence number and the sequence number of the first byte in the data that is sent. When a new connection is being established (the SYN flag is set), the sequence number field contains the initial sequence number (ISN) selected by the host for the connection. The ISN must be selected using the host clock to ensure the randomness of the actual number. Because TCP poses no restriction on a connection used repeatedly, it is important that TCP is capable of identifying potential duplicate segments for different instances of the same connection. TCP avoids this problem by preventing duplicate sequence numbers on the network for different instances of the same connection. The ISN selection is based on the clock incrementing every so often so that the ISN values are able to cycle less frequently than the maximum lifetime of a segment. This process prevents the same sequence number from being used simultaneously. RFC 793 specified the maximum segment lifetime (MSL) to be 2 minutes yet flexible to more practical values applicable in operational networks.

TIP The selection of the ISN depends on the implementation of the TCP/IP stack on each host. Current implementations might not be compliant with the RFC 973 specification. The implications of a nonrandom selection of the ISN could imply a repeatable pattern that could be predicted, which opens the door for potential connection hijacks or prevents the successful completion of a connection handshake.

Certain TCP protocol stack implementations support *SYN cookies*. SYN cookies provide a choice in the values of the ISN, which are used to prevent SYN flood attacks. SYN flood attacks are designed to keep the SYN queue on the server full. The SYN cookie mechanism protects the SYN queue by selecting an ISN (the cookie value) based on a Message Digest 5 (MD5) of the source and destination IP addresses and port numbers. When the queue is full, it still sends a SYN/ACK but keeps no connection state information. If the final ACK for the three-way handshake is received, the server recalculates the original information that had come with the initial SYN. The original information is encoded into the sequence number of the reply to the SYN packet. The acknowledgement number in the last packet of the three-way handshake will be the sequence number that was sent plus 1. When the acknowledgement arrives, 1 is subtracted and the number decoded. Using this mechanism, the server does not have to remember any connection information.

SYN cookies are supported in Linux and FreeBSD, but they are not enabled by default. The following command enables them:

```
> /proc/sys/net/ipv4/tcp_syncookies
```

There are some restrictions in using SYN cookies: the server must reject TCP options such as large windows and selective acknowledgement. The large window restriction is because the ISN is a 32-bit field.

There is research underway to resolve the current side effects of SYN cookies. For more information on SYN cookies, consult http://cr.yp.to/syncookies.html.

Acknowledgement Number Field

The acknowledgement number field is a 32-bit field that identifies the sequence number the sender of the acknowledgment is expecting to receive next. The sender of the acknowledgement uses the sequence number of the last segment plus 1, which corresponds to the next byte the sender expects plus 1 byte. This field is used only when the ACK flag is set, which is after the connection is established. After the connection is established the field is always set and the ACK flag is always on (set to 1).

NOTE A TCP connection between sender and receiver is full duplex, which implies that it supports concurrent information exchanges from sender to receiver and from receiver to sender. Each side of the connection is controlled independently by its own sequence and acknowledgement numbers, which ensures that flow control is accomplished on either direction independently. The section, "TCP Connection Overview" provides more information about this topic.

According to the delayed ACK algorithm, TCP can delay an ACK for as long as two full-sized (one ACK for every second full-size segment) segments but no more than 500 milliseconds. TCP specifies the last byte that was successfully received. If it receives a new segment that does not correspond to the next chunk of contiguous bytes, TCP has to send an acknowledgment to indicate the expected byte, even if the segment just received was successful. TCP has no mechanism to provide negative acknowledgment or to acknowledge that a chunk of data was successfully received.

Selective Acknowledgment (SACK) is a mechanism that could be used by the receiver to acknowledge all the segments that might have been succesfully received so that the sender only retransmitts the segments that have been lost. More information on Delayed ACK and SACK is introduced later in this chapter.

TCP Header Length Field

The TCP header length field is a 4-bit header that carries the total length of the TCP header in 32-bit words (4-byte chunks). The maximum header length is 60 bytes (16 * 4), which leaves room for 40 bytes of options because the set fields are 20 bytes.

The next 4 bits are reserved.

NOTE In RFC 793, the 6 bits following the header length field were reserved. RFC 3168 updates RFC 793 and takes 2 reserved bits for new control flags, leaving 4 reserved bits. The next section, "TCP Control Flags," explains the new flags.

TCP Control Flags

Figure 7-10 illustrates the eight control flags, per RFC 793 and RFC 3168.

Figure 7-10 *TCP Control Flags*

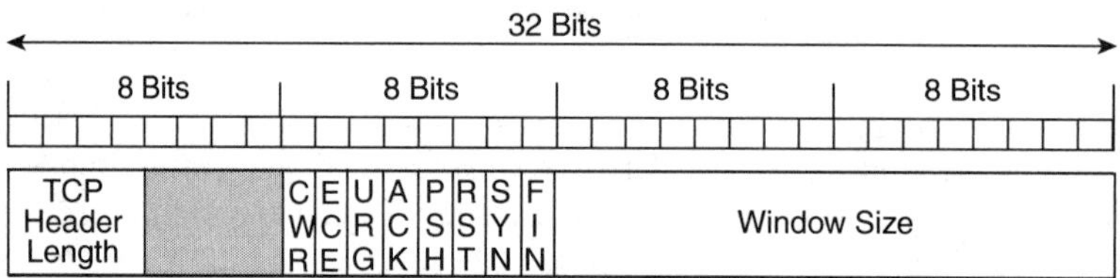

- **CWR and ECE**—ECN uses the ECT and CE flags in the IP header, introduced in the "Type of Service" section, for signaling between routers and endpoints. ECN uses CWR and ECE for TCP endpoint-to-TCP endpoint signaling. Refer to RFC 3168 section 6.1 for more details on how these flags are used.
- **URG**—The sender uses this Urgent Pointer flag, when set, to indicate to the receiver that the receiver should accept urgent data. The receiver uses it to indicate to the sender when the user has received the last byte of urgent data. When set, this flag indicates that the urgent pointer field value should be used.

- **ACK**—The Acknowledgment flag, when set, indicates that the segment is used to acknowledge the successful reception up to the byte indicated by the acknowledgement value.
- **PSH**—The Push flag indicates to the receiver that it should pass the received data to the application as soon as possible.

NOTE An example of the use of the PSH flag is a Telnet session in which each character is sent as it is typed. The traffic trace in Figure 7-11 highlights a specific packet when the user enters the character "q" as the final sequence to finish a Telnet connection (by typing quit on a Cisco console server).

The effect of the PSH flag is to immediately send the packet even though the payload only contains the character "q."

Figure 7-11 *Telnet Session with PSH Flag*

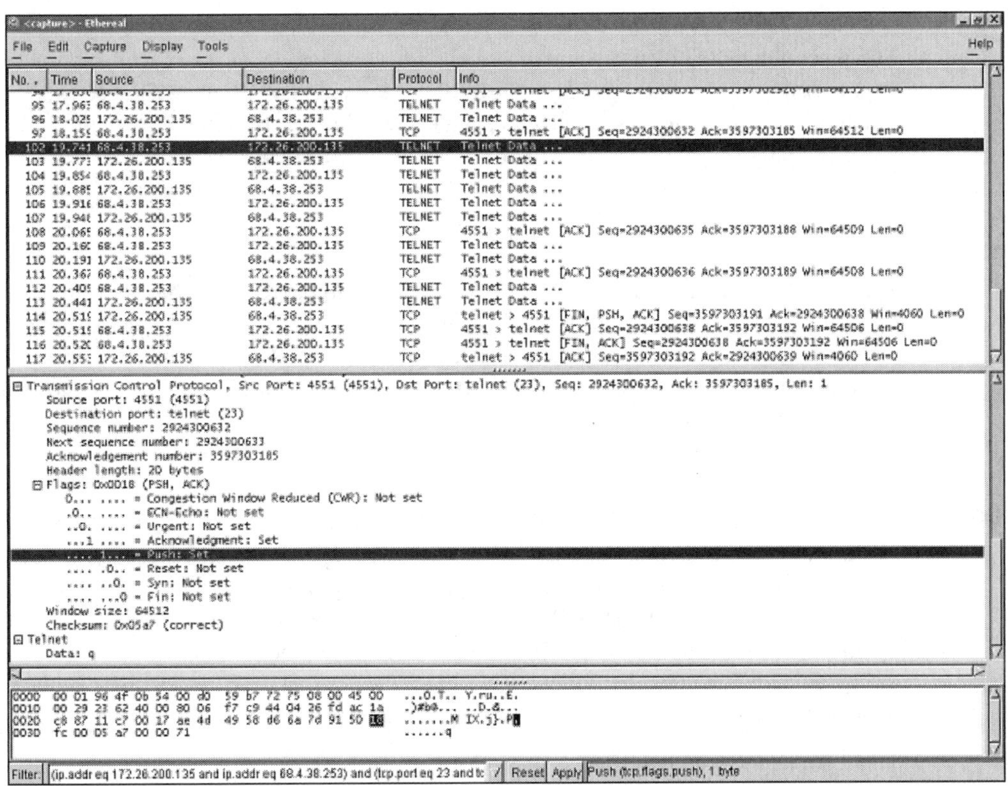

- **RST**—The Reset flag notifies the receiver to reset the connection.
- **SYN**—The Synchronize sequence number flag indicates to the receiver that the sequence numbers should be synchronized. The SYN flag, when set, indicates a connection request from the sender to the receiver.
- **FIN**—The Finished control flag indicates that the sender has finished sending data. The receiver then proceeds to close that half of the connection.

Window Size Field

The window size field is a 16-bit field used for flow control between the sender and receiver. The sender and receiver each advertise their own window size. The size indicates the number of bytes, starting with the byte indicated by the acknowledgment field, that the sender of the segment is willing to receive. The maximum size of the window is 65,535 bytes (without the use of the Window Scale option).

Checksum Field

The checksum field is a 16-bit field that carries the value which must be calculated for every segment and which must cover both the TCP header and the TCP data. The receiver calculates and compares the checksum against the value received in the segment, and if it is different, the segment is discarded and not acknowledged.

Urgent Pointer Field

The urgent pointer field is a 16-bit field that indicates to the receiver that the value is an offset that must be added to the sequence number field to produce the sequence number of the last byte or urgent data. This field is used only when the URG flag is set. The receiver is notified of the urgent data (by the URG flag and urgent pointer value) in the data stream, and the receiver decides what to do when the notification is received.

Options Field

The options field is a variable-length field ranging from 0 to 40 bytes that carries TCP options. A few of the most common TCP options are the MSS, the window scale (windows larger than 65,535 bytes), the TCP selective acknowledgement (SACK), and the timestamp option (round-trip time measurement for data segments). Some of these options are discussed in the sections that follow. RFC 793 indicates that a TCP stack must support all options, and it indicates the defined options (at the time of the writing).

There are two alternatives for the option format:

- A single byte for the option kind
- A byte for the option kind, a byte for the length, and the option-data bytes

Kind refers to the type of option and *length* to its value in bytes. Table 7-7 lists the kind options defined in RFC 793.

Table 7-7 *3-Byte Option Format*

Kind	Length	Meaning
0	—	End of option list
1	—	No operation
2	4	MSS

Other options have other values and might have variable length, such as the SACK option. See the section, "TCP SACK Option" for more information on its type and length.

TCP Connection Overview

This section explains how a TCP connection is established and terminated. As introduced earlier, the connection-oriented nature of TCP requires the protocol to keep state information on the connection and perform certain functions, such as flow control and error correction, to ensure a successful connection. Before data is transmitted between sender and receiver, a TCP connection must be established. Figure 7-12 provides a quick overview of a TCP connection.

Figure 7-12 *TCP Connection Overview*

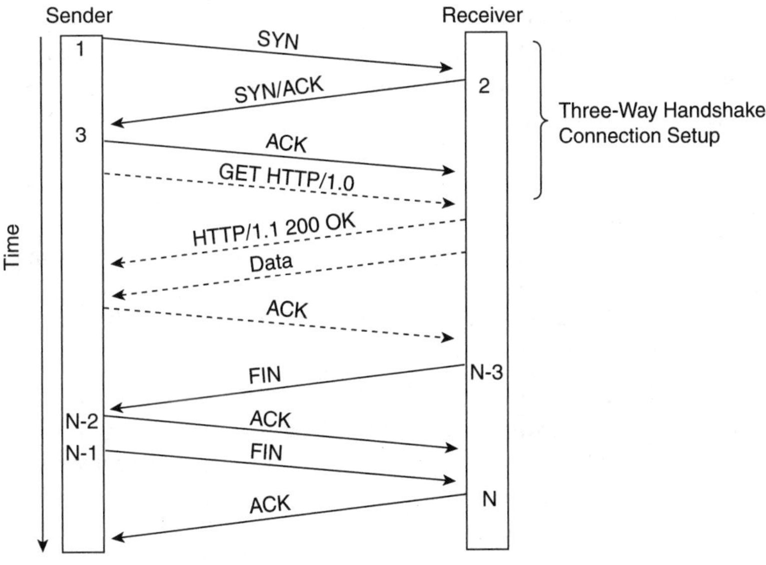

The initiator of the connection is referred to as the *sender* and the destination of that connection as the *receiver*. The following sequence describes the connection establishment process, also known as three-way handshake:

1 **SYN segment**—The sender sends a TCP segment with the SYN flag set, the port number it expects to use in the receiver's end, and its ISN. This segment is considered a connection request.

2 **SYN/ACK segment**—The receiver responds to the connection request with its own segment that contains a SYN, the source port from the received segment as the destination port, the original destination port as the source port, its own ISN, and an ACK (ACK flag set) that acknowledges the sender's connection request. Note that the ACK is the sender's SEQ plus 1. The receiver has agreed to establish a connection and has initiated its side of the connection.

3 **ACK segment**—The sender acknowledges the receiver's SYN (setting the ACK flag) using the receiver's SEQ plus 1 as the ACK.

Once Step 3 is finished, the TCP connection has been established.

After the connection is established, the sender and receiver start exchanging information. Note that in Figure 7-12, the application layer protocol is HTTP. The information exchange for a different application layer protocol would be different.

After the data exchange, one of the two parties initiates the connection termination exchange (step N-3 in Figure 7-12). It does so by sending a segment with the FIN flag set. The sender acknowledges the reception of the FIN as soon as possible to avoid further delays from the interaction with the application layer (step N-2 in Figure 7-12) and then replies with a FIN/ACK (step N-1 in Figure 7-12). The receiver then acknowledges the FIN/ACK with an ACK (step N in Figure 7-12) and the connection is terminated. Keep in mind that this process is the normal but not the only connection-termination process. The section, "Connection Termination" introduces alternatives.

Connection Establishment

This section provides an in-depth description of the connection-establishment process. To better illustrate the process, we use a real connection. The connection is between a host on the Internet, the client, and the server supporting the Apache Software Foundation site, http://www.apache.org, which we refer to simply as the server.

The client runs Microsoft Windows, the browser is Netscape Communicator 4.76, and the server runs the Apache web server on a UNIX-based OS. The client is set to "never cache," which is inefficient from the client's perspective but ensures the content is always retrieved from the network and not the local cache.

NOTE The traffic analyzer is a shareware tool named Ethereal. You can find more information at http://www.ethereal.com.

Figure 7-13 presents the full content (text format) of the first frame sent by the host. (Segment 1 was frame 11 on the captured trace.)

Figure 7-13 *TCP Connection Establishment: Segment 1*

```
Frame 11 (62 bytes on wire, 62 bytes captured)
    Arrival Time: Nov 17, 2002 11:20:17.972332000
    Time delta from previous packet: 0.000000000 seconds
    Time relative to first packet: 3.883534000 seconds
    Frame Number: 11
    Packet Length: 62 bytes
    Capture Length: 62 bytes
Ethernet II, Src: 00:d0:59:b7:72:75, Dst: 00:10:67:00:b7:eb
    Destination: 00:10:67:00:b7:eb (Redback_00:b7:eb)
    Source: 00:d0:59:b7:72:75 (AMBIT_b7:72:75)
    Type: IP (0x0800)
Internet Protocol, Src Addr: 64.174.163.54 (64.174.163.54), Dst Addr: 63.251.56.142 (63.251.56.142)
    Version: 4
    Header length: 20 bytes
    Differentiated Services Field: 0x00 (DSCP 0x00: Default; ECN: 0x00)
        0000 00.. = Differentiated Services Codepoint: Default (0x00)
        .... ..0. = ECN-Capable Transport (ECT): 0
        .... ...0 = ECN-CE: 0
    Total Length: 48
    Identification: 0x3716
    Flags: 0x04
        .1.. = Don't fragment: Set
        ..0. = More fragments: Not set
    Fragment offset: 0
    Time to live: 128
    Protocol: TCP (0x06)
    Header checksum: 0x6744 (correct)
    Source: 64.174.163.54 (64.174.163.54)
    Destination: 63.251.56.142 (63.251.56.142)
Transmission Control Protocol, Src Port: 1351 (1351), Dst Port: http (80), Seq: 857121131, Ack: 0, Len: 0
    Source port: 1351 (1351)
    Destination port: http (80)
    Sequence number: 857121131
    Header length: 28 bytes
    Flags: 0x0002 (SYN)
        0... .... = Congestion Window Reduced (CWR): Not set
        .0.. .... = ECN-Echo: Not set
        ..0. .... = Urgent: Not set
        ...0 .... = Acknowledgment: Not set
        .... 0... = Push: Not set
        .... .0.. = Reset: Not set
        .... ..1. = Syn: Set
        .... ...0 = Fin: Not set
    Window size: 64512
    Checksum: 0x50fc (correct)
    Options: (8 bytes)
        Maximum segment size: 1360 bytes
        NOP
        NOP
        SACK permitted
```

The total frame size of 62 bytes consists of the source and destination MAC addresses (12 bytes), 2 bytes for the protocol type, 20 bytes for the IP header, and 28 bytes for the TCP header (including options). There is no TCP payload because this is the first datagram of a new connection.

At the IP layer, the segment has the DF bit set and a TTL of 128. Although the DF bit is set, it is highly unlikely that this TCP segment would be fragmented due to the small size of the

TCP SYN segment. This point is also true for the SYN-ACK and ACK that make up the rest of the TCP handshake because they are small, which implies that the DF bit would be set. At the TCP layer, the client is using port 80 as the destination and 1351 as the source port (randomly generated). The ISN is 857121131, and because this request is a connection request, the SYN bit is set. Notice the header size is 28 bytes, which includes the 20 bytes for the fixed part of the header and 8 bytes for options. The window size is specified as 64,512 bytes, the MSS is 1360 bytes, and SACKs are permitted.

NOTE The window size is 64,512 bytes instead of the default 16K typical of the Windows 2000 TCP/IP stack. This windows size value is controlled by **TCPWindowSize**. This option appears with all other TCP/IP parameters in the Registry under the following Registry key:

```
HKEY_LOCAL_MACHINE
    \SYSTEM
        \CurrentControlSet
            \Services:
                \Tcpip
                    \Parameters
```

TIP The MTU size of the client was manually set up as 1400 bytes to keep the virtual private network (VPN) client software from exceeding the maximum size of 1518 bytes of an Ethernet frame when the IPSec header is added.

The server responds to the connection request. Figure 7-14 shows the full frame with the server response.

Frame 12 corresponds to Segment 2, the response from server to client. At the TCP layer, the server is using 80 as the source port and 1351 as the destination, ensuring it is communicating with the right client (destination IP address) and the right application process. Note that the SEQ 3560831726 that is generated by the server is used for the server-to-client connection, and the ACK 857121132 indicates to the client the next byte it expects to see, which is the ISN + 1. The flags SYN and ACK indicate to the client the connection request from the server and the acknowledgement from the client's connection request. Note also that the window size indicated by the server is 57,344 (the number of bytes the server will accept), and the MSS is 1460. The MSS option adds 4 bytes to the TCP header for 24 bytes.

Figure 7-14 *TCP Connection Establishment: Segment 2*

```
Frame 12 (60 bytes on wire, 60 bytes captured)
    Arrival Time: Nov 17, 2002 11:20:17.994692000
    Time delta from previous packet: 0.022360000 seconds
    Time relative to first packet: 3.905894000 seconds
    Frame Number: 12
    Packet Length: 60 bytes
    Capture Length: 60 bytes
Ethernet II, Src: 00:10:67:00:b7:eb, Dst: 00:d0:59:b7:72:75
    Destination: 00:d0:59:b7:72:75 (AMBIT_b7:72:75)
    Source: 00:10:67:00:b7:eb (Redback_00:b7:eb)
    Type: IP (0x0800)
    Trailer: 0000
Internet Protocol, Src Addr: 63.251.56.142 (63.251.56.142), Dst Addr: 64.174.163.54 (64.174.163.54)
    Version: 4
    Header length: 20 bytes
    Differentiated Services Field: 0x00 (DSCP 0x00: Default; ECN: 0x00)
        0000 00.. = Differentiated Services Codepoint: Default (0x00)
        .... ..0. = ECN-Capable Transport (ECT): 0
        .... ...0 = ECN-CE: 0
    Total Length: 44
    Identification: 0xcaa9
    Flags: 0x04
        .1.. = Don't fragment: Set
        ..0. = More fragments: Not set
    Fragment offset: 0
    Time to live: 56
    Protocol: TCP (0x06)
    Header checksum: 0x1bb5 (correct)
    Source: 63.251.56.142 (63.251.56.142)
    Destination: 64.174.163.54 (64.174.163.54)
Transmission Control Protocol, Src Port: http (80), Dst Port: 1351 (1351), Seq: 3560831726, Ack: 857121132, Len: 0
    Source port: http (80)
    Destination port: 1351 (1351)
    Sequence number: 3560831726
    Acknowledgement number: 857121132
    Header length: 24 bytes
    Flags: 0x0012 (SYN, ACK)
        0... .... = Congestion Window Reduced (CWR): Not set
        .0.. .... = ECN-Echo: Not set
        ..0. .... = Urgent: Not set
        ...1 .... = Acknowledgment: Set
        .... 0... = Push: Not set
        .... .0.. = Reset: Not set
        .... ..1. = Syn: Set
        .... ...0 = Fin: Not set
    Window size: 57344
    Checksum: 0xb261 (correct)
    Options: (4 bytes)
        Maximum segment size: 1460 bytes
```

The next segment is the response from the client back to the server, Segment 3 (frame 13). This segment, presented in Figure 7-15, is the acknowledgement of the server's SYN; it is the final segment of the TCP handshake. The ACK 3560831727 is the server side ISN + 1, and the SEQ 857121132 is the previous client SEQ + 1, because no data has been sent yet.

The next segment is the actual HTTP request from the client to the server, which is possible now that the TCP connection between them is established. Note that the window size from the client's perspective remains the same, 64,512, and there is no MSS information in the TCP header, so the header size is 20 bytes (no options).

Once the web page is downloaded, which implies the client has received and acknowledged the content of the page to the server, the connection-termination process starts.

Figure 7-15 *TCP Connection Establishment: Segment 3*

```
full http connection to apache.org + FIN frame 3.txt - Notepad
File Edit Format Help
Frame 13 (54 bytes on wire, 54 bytes captured)
    Arrival Time: Nov 17, 2002 11:20:17.994713000
    Time delta from previous packet: 0.000021000 seconds
    Time relative to first packet: 3.905915000 seconds
    Frame Number: 13
    Packet Length: 54 bytes
    Capture Length: 54 bytes
Ethernet II, Src: 00:d0:59:b7:72:75, Dst: 00:10:67:00:b7:eb
    Destination: 00:10:67:00:b7:eb (Redback_00:b7:eb)
    Source: 00:d0:59:b7:72:75 (AMBIT_b7:72:75)
    Type: IP (0x0800)
Internet Protocol, Src Addr: 64.174.163.54 (64.174.163.54), Dst Addr: 63.251.56.142 (63.251.56.142)
    Version: 4
    Header length: 20 bytes
    Differentiated Services Field: 0x00 (DSCP 0x00: Default; ECN: 0x00)
        0000 00.. = Differentiated Services Codepoint: Default (0x00)
        .... ..0. = ECN-Capable Transport (ECT): 0
        .... ...0 = ECN-CE: 0
    Total Length: 40
    Identification: 0x3717
    Flags: 0x04
        .1.. = Don't fragment: Set
        ..0. = More fragments: Not set
    Fragment offset: 0
    Time to live: 128
    Protocol: TCP (0x06)
    Header checksum: 0x674b (correct)
    Source: 64.174.163.54 (64.174.163.54)
    Destination: 63.251.56.142 (63.251.56.142)
Transmission Control Protocol, Src Port: 1351 (1351), Dst Port: http (80), Seq: 857121132, Ack: 3560831727, Len: 0
    Source port: 1351 (1351)
    Destination port: http (80)
    Sequence number: 857121132
    Acknowledgement number: 3560831727
    Header length: 20 bytes
    Flags: 0x0010 (ACK)
        0... .... = Congestion Window Reduced (CWR): Not set
        .0.. .... = ECN-Echo: Not set
        ..0. .... = Urgent: Not set
        ...1 .... = Acknowledgment: Set
        .... 0... = Push: Not set
        .... .0.. = Reset: Not set
        .... ..0. = Syn: Not set
        .... ...0 = Fin: Not set
    Window size: 64512
    Checksum: 0xae1e (correct)
```

Connection Termination

This section provides an in-depth description of the connection-termination process. Before continuing with the connection introduced in the "Connection Establishment" section, it is important to introduce some basic concepts behind the connection-termination process.

The connection-termination process is similar to the connection-establishment process in which the sender and receiver agree to terminate the connection and exchange a few segments to do so. The termination process, however, requires one more segment than the establishment process—because of the half-close concept explained later in this chapter.

As depicted in Figure 7-12, the FIN sent by the receiver indicates that the sending of data is finished. The sender's ACK acknowledges the reception of the FIN and notifies the application process. The sender may continue to send data, and after it is finished, it sends a FIN, which is acknowledged by the receiver, at which point the connection is closed. Note in Figure 7-12 that the connection-termination process was initiated by the server (receiver), which is common in an HTTP transaction.

Continuing with the trace and after skipping the data transfer, the connection-termination process starts. Figure 7-16 shows the FIN sent by the server initiating the connection termination.

Figure 7-16 *TCP Connection Termination: Segment N-3*

```
full http connection to apache.org + FIN frame 27.txt - Notepad
File  Edit  Format  Help
Frame 27 (60 bytes on wire, 60 bytes captured)
    Arrival Time: Nov 17, 2002 11:20:23.055815000
    Time delta from previous packet: 4.926198000 seconds
    Time relative to first packet: 8.967017000 seconds
    Frame Number: 27
    Packet Length: 60 bytes
    Capture Length: 60 bytes
Ethernet II, Src: 00:10:67:00:b7:eb, Dst: 00:d0:59:b7:72:75
    Destination: 00:d0:59:b7:72:75 (AMBIT_b7:72:75)
    Source: 00:10:67:00:b7:eb (Redback_00:b7:eb)
    Type: IP (0x0800)
    Trailer: 000000000000
Internet Protocol, Src Addr: 63.251.56.142 (63.251.56.142), Dst Addr: 64.174.163.54 (64.174.163.54)
    Version: 4
    Header length: 20 bytes
    Differentiated Services Field: 0x00 (DSCP 0x00: Default; ECN: 0x00)
        0000 00.. = Differentiated Services Codepoint: Default (0x00)
        .... ..0. = ECN-Capable Transport (ECT): 0
        .... ...0 = ECN-CE: 0
    Total Length: 40
    Identification: 0xd8d5
    Flags: 0x04
        .1.. = Don't fragment: Set
        ..0. = More fragments: Not set
    Fragment offset: 0
    Time to live: 56
    Protocol: TCP (0x06)
    Header checksum: 0x0d8d (correct)
    Source: 63.251.56.142 (63.251.56.142)
    Destination: 64.174.163.54 (64.174.163.54)
Transmission Control Protocol, Src Port: http (80), Dst Port: 1351 (1351), Seq: 3560839781, Ack: 857121415, Len: 0
    Source port: http (80)
    Destination port: 1351 (1351)
    Sequence number: 3560839781
    Acknowledgement number: 857121415
    Header length: 20 bytes
    Flags: 0x0011 (FIN, ACK)
        0... .... = Congestion Window Reduced (CWR): Not set
        .0.. .... = ECN-Echo: Not set
        ..0. .... = Urgent: Not set
        ...1 .... = Acknowledgment: Set
        .... 0... = Push: Not set
        .... .0.. = Reset: Not set
        .... ..0. = Syn: Not set
        .... ...1 = Fin: Set
    Window size: 58480
    Checksum: 0xa51c (correct)
```

Frame 27 corresponds to the FIN from the server to the client. The segment also acknowledges the previously received data, which explains the set ACK flag. The ACK is 857121415 and the SEQ 3560839781, resulting from the data exchange that took place.

The response from the client side acknowledges the FIN (the ACK flag is set) using ACK 3560839782 and SEQ 857121415. The detail of this segment appears in Figure 7-17, which corresponds to frame 28.

The FIN from the client is sent almost 4 seconds (sec) later and corresponds to frame 79 in the trace, which appears in Figure 7-18. The ACK is 3560839782 and the SEQ 857121415, which are, as expected, the same as the previous frame from the client to the server because there has not been any activity between them.

Figure 7-17 *TCP Connection Termination: Segment N-2*

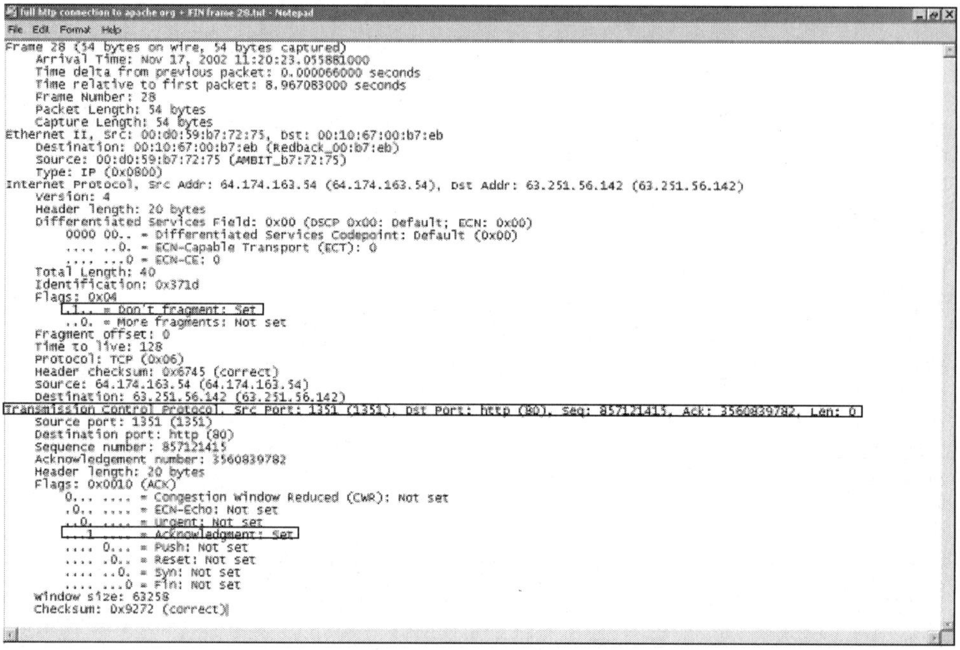

```
full http connection to apache.org - FIN frame 28.txt - Notepad
File Edit Format Help
Frame 28 (54 bytes on wire, 54 bytes captured)
    Arrival Time: Nov 17, 2002 11:20:23.055881000
    Time delta from previous packet: 0.000066000 seconds
    Time relative to first packet: 8.967083000 seconds
    Frame Number: 28
    Packet Length: 54 bytes
    Capture Length: 54 bytes
Ethernet II, Src: 00:d0:59:b7:72:75, Dst: 00:10:67:00:b7:eb
    Destination: 00:10:67:00:b7:eb (Redback_00:b7:eb)
    Source: 00:d0:59:b7:72:75 (AMBIT_b7:72:75)
    Type: IP (0x0800)
Internet Protocol, Src Addr: 64.174.163.54 (64.174.163.54), Dst Addr: 63.251.56.142 (63.251.56.142)
    Version: 4
    Header length: 20 bytes
    Differentiated Services Field: 0x00 (DSCP 0x00: Default; ECN: 0x00)
        0000 00.. = Differentiated Services Codepoint: Default (0x00)
        .... ..0. = ECN-Capable Transport (ECT): 0
        .... ...0 = ECN-CE: 0
    Total Length: 40
    Identification: 0x371d
    Flags: 0x04
        .1.. = Don't fragment: Set
        ..0. = More fragments: Not set
    Fragment offset: 0
    Time to live: 128
    Protocol: TCP (0x06)
    Header checksum: 0x6745 (correct)
    Source: 64.174.163.54 (64.174.163.54)
    Destination: 63.251.56.142 (63.251.56.142)
Transmission Control Protocol, Src Port: 1351 (1351), Dst Port: http (80), Seq: 857121415, Ack: 3560839782, Len: 0
    Source port: 1351 (1351)
    Destination port: http (80)
    Sequence number: 857121415
    Acknowledgement number: 3560839782
    Header length: 20 bytes
    Flags: 0x0010 (ACK)
        0... .... = Congestion Window Reduced (CWR): Not set
        .0.. .... = ECN-Echo: Not set
        ..0. .... = Urgent: Not set
        ...1 .... = Acknowledgment: Set
        .... 0... = Push: Not set
        .... .0.. = Reset: Not set
        .... ..0. = Syn: Not set
        .... ...0 = Fin: Not set
    Window size: 63258
    Checksum: 0x9272 (correct)
```

Figure 7-18 *TCP Connection Termination: Segment N-1*

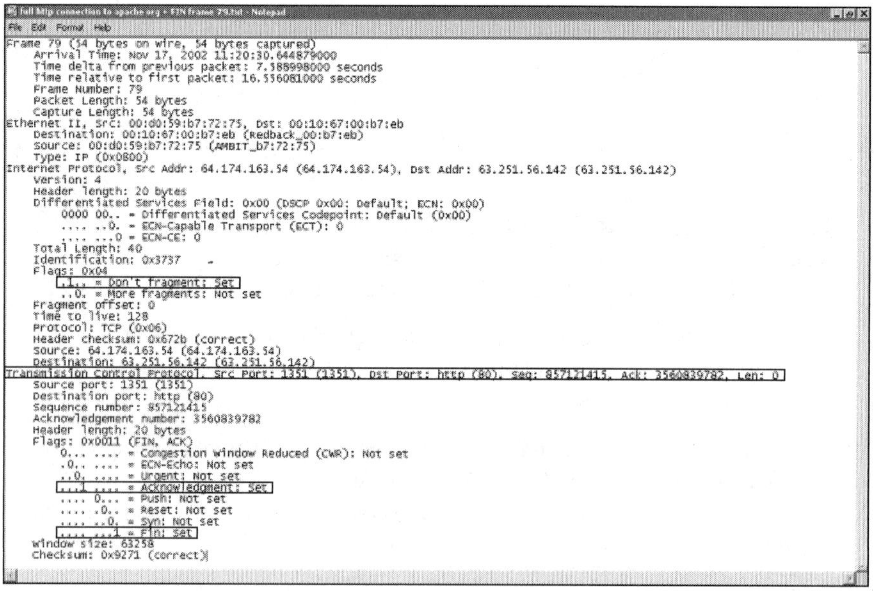

```
full http connection to apache.org - FIN frame 79.txt - Notepad
File Edit Format Help
Frame 79 (54 bytes on wire, 54 bytes captured)
    Arrival Time: Nov 17, 2002 11:20:30.644879000
    Time delta from previous packet: 7.588998000 seconds
    Time relative to first packet: 16.556081000 seconds
    Frame Number: 79
    Packet Length: 54 bytes
    Capture Length: 54 bytes
Ethernet II, Src: 00:d0:59:b7:72:75, Dst: 00:10:67:00:b7:eb
    Destination: 00:10:67:00:b7:eb (Redback_00:b7:eb)
    Source: 00:d0:59:b7:72:75 (AMBIT_b7:72:75)
    Type: IP (0x0800)
Internet Protocol, Src Addr: 64.174.163.54 (64.174.163.54), Dst Addr: 63.251.56.142 (63.251.56.142)
    Version: 4
    Header length: 20 bytes
    Differentiated Services Field: 0x00 (DSCP 0x00: Default; ECN: 0x00)
        0000 00.. = Differentiated Services Codepoint: Default (0x00)
        .... ..0. = ECN-Capable Transport (ECT): 0
        .... ...0 = ECN-CE: 0
    Total Length: 40
    Identification: 0x3737
    Flags: 0x04
        .1.. = Don't fragment: Set
        ..0. = More fragments: Not set
    Fragment offset: 0
    Time to live: 128
    Protocol: TCP (0x06)
    Header checksum: 0x672b (correct)
    Source: 64.174.163.54 (64.174.163.54)
    Destination: 63.251.56.142 (63.251.56.142)
Transmission Control Protocol, Src Port: 1351 (1351), Dst Port: http (80), Seq: 857121415, Ack: 3560839782, Len: 0
    Source port: 1351 (1351)
    Destination port: http (80)
    Sequence number: 857121415
    Acknowledgement number: 3560839782
    Header length: 20 bytes
    Flags: 0x0011 (FIN, ACK)
        0... .... = Congestion Window Reduced (CWR): Not set
        .0.. .... = ECN-Echo: Not set
        ..0. .... = Urgent: Not set
        ...1 .... = Acknowledgment: Set
        .... 0... = Push: Not set
        .... .0.. = Reset: Not set
        .... ..0. = Syn: Not set
        .... ...1 = Fin: Set
    Window size: 63258
    Checksum: 0x9271 (correct)
```

Figure 7-19 shows that the final segment (frame 81) is the acknowledgement from the server to the client's FIN. The ACK is 857121416 (client's SEQ + 1) and the SEQ 3560839782, which corresponds to the client's ACK number.

Figure 7-19 *TCP Connection Termination: Segment N*

```
Frame 81 (60 bytes on wire, 60 bytes captured)
    Arrival Time: Nov 17, 2002 11:20:30.697438000
    Time delta from previous packet: 0.052559000 seconds
    Time relative to first packet: 16.608640000 seconds
    Frame Number: 81
    Packet Length: 60 bytes
    Capture Length: 60 bytes
Ethernet II, Src: 00:10:67:00:b7:eb, Dst: 00:d0:59:b7:72:75
    Destination: 00:d0:59:b7:72:75 (AMBIT_b7:72:75)
    Source: 00:10:67:00:b7:eb (Redback_00:b7:eb)
    Type: IP (0x0800)
    Trailer: 000000000000
Internet Protocol, Src Addr: 63.251.56.142 (63.251.56.142), Dst Addr: 64.174.163.54 (64.174.163.54)
    Version: 4
    Header length: 20 bytes
    Differentiated Services Field: 0x00 (DSCP 0x00: Default; ECN: 0x00)
        0000 00.. = Differentiated Services Codepoint: Default (0x00)
        .... ..0. = ECN-Capable Transport (ECT): 0
        .... ...0 = ECN-CE: 0
    Total Length: 40
    Identification: 0xf0da
    Flags: 0x04
        .1.. = Don't fragment: Set
        ..0. = More fragments: Not set
    Fragment offset: 0
    Time to live: 56
    Protocol: TCP (0x06)
    Header checksum: 0xf587 (correct)
    Source: 63.251.56.142 (63.251.56.142)
    Destination: 64.174.163.54 (64.174.163.54)
Transmission Control Protocol, Src Port: http (80), Dst Port: 1351 (1351), Seq: 3560839782, Ack: 857121416, Len: 0
    Source port: http (80)
    Destination port: 1351 (1351)
    Sequence number: 3560839782
    Acknowledgement number: 857121416
    Header length: 20 bytes
    Flags: 0x0010 (ACK)
        0... .... = Congestion Window Reduced (CWR): Not set
        .0.. .... = ECN-Echo: Not set
        ..0. .... = Urgent: Not set
        ...1 .... = Acknowledgment: Set
        .... 0... = Push: Not set
        .... .0.. = Reset: Not set
        .... ..0. = Syn: Not set
        .... ...0 = Fin: Not set
    Window size: 58480
    Checksum: 0xa51b (correct)
```

There are other potential connection-termination alternatives such as the client sending a reset (RST flag set) to the server, which terminates the connection without further segment exchanges. Closing the client's browser, for example, causes the client to issue RST for every active connection.

TIP When you close the browser, Netscape Communicator 4.76 and Internet Explorer 5.5 behave similarly. On all active connections, an RST is sent from the client to the server. Other traces show the Internet Explorer browser sending an RST after some period of inactivity.

TCP Flow Control

Flow control, one of the main properties of TCP, is supported by a collection of features. In general, flow control means being able to control the communication flow between sender and receiver. Part of the flow-control mechanism is the use of ACKs and SEQs that, as indicated in previous sections, provide the structure to establish and terminate a connection, signal received packets, and retransmit if necessary. However, other areas are equally important, such as the sliding window mechanism and congestion control. The following sections discuss these topics.

Timeout and Retransmission

TCP uses retransmission to ensure that segments are delivered in the absence of feedback from the receiver. A timer controls the retransmission timing when ACKs are outstanding, a process referred to as retransmission timeout (RTO). As stated in RFC 1122, "Requirements for Internet Hosts: Communication Layers":

"the algorithm suggested in RFC 793 for calculating the retransmission timeout is now known to be inadequate . . ."

There were two known problems with the RTO calculations specified in RFC 793:

- The accurate measurement of round-trip times (RTTs) is difficult when there are retransmissions.
- The algorithm to compute the smoothed RTT is inadequate because it incorrectly assumed that the variance in RTT values would be small and constant.

These problems were solved by Karn's and Jacobson's algorithms, respectively:

- Karn's algorithm for selecting RTT measurements ensures that ambiguous RTTs will not corrupt the calculation of the smoothed RTT.
- Jacobson's algorithm for computing the smoothed RTT incorporates a simple measure of the variance.

RFC 1122 specifies that both Karn's and Jacobson's algorithms must be supported by a host TCP/IP stack, and it recommends that for a new connection that the RTT and RTO values should be initialized as 0 and 3 sec, respectively.

RFC 2988, "Computing TCP's Retransmission Timer," codifies the algorithm for setting the RTO, expands on the discussion of RTO calculation (section 4.2.3.1) of RFC 1122, and upgrades the requirement of supporting the algorithm from a *should* to a *must*.

Sliding Windows

The sliding window is one of TCP's flow control mechanisms that defines the maximum amount of data (segments) the sender is able to send before receiving an ACK. The amount of data sent is determined by the number of segments that the receiver's advertised window size is able to accept.

Each side of the connection advertises the number of bytes (receive window size) it is willing to receive from the other peer (starting with the ACK). The window advertised by the receiver is the *receive window* (also called the offered window). The window size reflects how much buffer space the receiving side has available for new data coming in, which implies it changes during the connection. The sender must not exceed the receiver window size, so it adjusts the size and number of segments sent.

The following list specifically defines some of the terms related to congestion control out of RFC 2581:

- **Sender maximum segment size (SMSS)**—The size of the largest segment that the sender can transmit. This value can be based on the MTU of the network, the path MTU discovery algorithm, the RMSS (see next item), or other factors.
- **Receiver maximum segment size (RMSS)**—The size of the largest segment the receiver will accept. This value is specified in the MSS option sent by the receiver during connection startup.
- **Receiver window (rwnd)**—The most recently advertised receiver window.
- **Congestion window (cwnd)**—A TCP state variable that limits the amount of data TCP can send. At any given time, a TCP must not send data with a SEQ higher than the sum of the highest acknowledged SEQ and the minimum of cwnd and rwnd.
- **Initial window (IW)**—The size of the sender's congestion window after the three-way handshake is completed.
- **Loss window (LW)**—The size of the congestion window after a TCP sender detects loss using its retransmission timer.
- **Restart window (RW)**—The size of the congestion window after a TCP restarts transmission after an idle period.
- **Flight size**—The amount of data that has been sent but not yet acknowledged.

The size of the initial window, which is the initial value of the cwnd, is defined as less or equal to 2 * SMSS bytes and must not be more than two segments.

The sender window "slides" as datagrams are acknowledged. The process is better described using an example. As presented in Figure 7-20, the receiver has advertised a window size of 4.

The sender has sent segments 1 and 2, which have been acknowledged, and segments 3, 4, and 5, which have not been acknowledged. Because the receiver window size is 4 and there are three unacknowledged segments, it can send one more immediately. It cannot send segments 6, 7, and 8 until the window slides to the right, which occurs only after the reception of an ACK for the sent but unacknowledged segments (3, 4, and 5 in this case).

Retransmission occurs for packets that have been unacknowledged and for which the timeout has expired.

Figure 7-20 *Sliding Window*

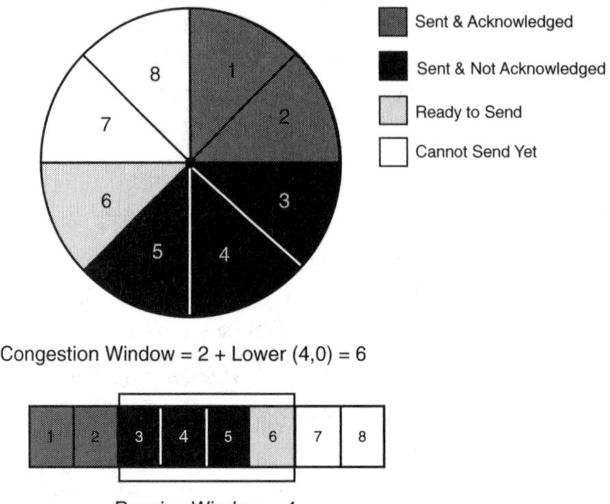

Sometimes using the sliding window protocol yields poor TCP performance even when the sender and receiver have adequate buffers and available buffer space. This problem is described as the Silly Window Syndrome (SWS), and it is explained in the section, "Nagle Algorithm" later in this chapter.

Congestion Control

Congestion control mechanisms are used when there is excessive load in the system. RFC 2581 defines four new protocols for TCP that deal with congestion control in addition to the timeout and retransmission algorithms:

- Slow start
- Congestion avoidance
- Fast retransmit
- Fast recovery

Slow Start and Congestion Avoidance

Slow start and congestion avoidance are both sender-side TCP flow-control measures. They control the amount of data being injected into the network.

Slow start addresses a situation in which the sender injects multiple segments into the network at the beginning of a transmission or after a packet drop has occurred (retransmission). The number of bytes injected depends on the window size of the receiver. In case of a packet drop, the receiver is not able to acknowledge more segments until the lost segment arrives. At some point, the sender would have sent bytes up to its window size, and it is forced to wait until the retransmission occurs. Sending to the entire window size could lead to congestion because the network might not be able to absorb all of it. A less aggressive sending behavior is more appropriate. Slow start observes the rate at which acknowledgements are returned and injects packets accordingly.

Congestion avoidance simply addresses packet loss as a result of congestion somewhere on the network between the endpoints (sender and receiver). The congestion avoidance kicks in when timeouts or duplicate ACKs are detected, and it reduces the rate of packets injected into the network.

Two state variables are added to TCP: slow start threshold (ssthresh) and cwnd.

The ssthresh controls whether TCP uses the slow start or congestion avoidance algorithm to control packets entering the network. The cwnd limits the amount of traffic the sender puts on the network. The need for transmission control comes from the unknown network conditions that make TCP slowly probe the network's available capacity to avoid congestion.

Although the two algorithms are independent, cwnd is used in conjunction with slow start, and the minimum value between them determines the data transmission, as defined in RFC 2581.

The following are the steps followed by the combined algorithm (as documented in RFC 2001 and RFC 2581):

1. TCP initializes the cwnd to 1 or 2 segments and the ssthresh to 65,535 bytes.
2. TCP uses the minimum value between cwnd and the receiver's advertised window as the amount to send.
3. When congestion is detected (timeout or duplicate ACKs), the ssthresh is updated with the value of half the current window size. If the congestion is caused by a timeout, the cwnd is set to 1 segment.

When data is acknowledged by the other end, the cwnd increases depending on whether slow start or congestion avoidance is active.

In general if the cwnd is less than the ssthresh, TCP is in slow start; if the cwnd is greater than the ssthresh, TCP is in congestion avoidance; and if the cwnd is equal to the ssthresh, either algorithm could be used. RFC 2581 indicates that TCP must implement both slow start and congestion avoidance.

Fast Retransmission and Fast Recovery

Fast retransmission and fast recovery enhance the congestion-avoidance process. Fast retransmission avoids having to wait for a retransmission timeout (expired timer) to retransmit. This behavior is triggered by receiving three duplicate ACKs (4 ACKs) without any segments between them as an indication that a segment has been lost.

Fast recovery kicks in afterwards by controlling the transmission of data until no more duplicate ACKs are received. Fast recovery does not leverage slow start to control the transmission of new data until a nonduplicate ACK arrives because the sender knows a duplicate segment was received. The receipt implies that a copy of the segment is in the receiver's buffer, indicating that there is data flowing, the segment itself is no longer consuming network resources, and the sender can continue to transmit new segments. The flow of data would be reduced suddenly if TCP went into slow start.

Fast retransmission and fast recovery are typically implemented together, yet RFC 2581 indicates they *should* be implemented, which makes them optional. For details on their support, consult the specific OS manuals.

Delayed ACK and Immediate ACK

Delayed acknowledgments are ACKs that are intentionally delayed by TCP, hoping to have data to send in the same direction so that it can piggyback the ACK. This process is often referred to as *ACK piggyback*. The treatment of delayed ACKs is specified in RFC 1122, and it has the following considerations:

- Both the network and the hosts experience increased efficiency because fewer segments are sent.
- An ACK should not be excessively delayed (less than 0.5 sec).

As indicated earlier in the chapter, in a stream of full-sized segments, the ACK is sent every two segments, which increases the efficiency of TCP.

The Windows 2000 TCP/IP implementation specifies the following:

"As data is received by TCP on a connection, it only sends an acknowledgment back if one of the following conditions is met:

- No ACK was sent for the previous segment received.
- A segment is received, but no other segment arrives within 200 milliseconds for that connection.

In summary, normally an ACK is sent for every other TCP segment received on a connection, unless the delayed ACK timer (200 milliseconds) expires. The delayed ACK timer can be adjusted through the **TcpDelAckTicks** registry parameter, which is new in Windows 2000."

Immediate ACK is a slightly different subject dealing with fast retransmits and fast recovery. As specified in RFC 2581, "TCP Congestion Control," immediate ACKs are generated by TCP on the receiving end as a result of the following reasons:

- An out-of-order segment arrives
- An incoming segment fills in all or part of a sequence space gap

For out-of-order segments, the immediate ACKs notify the sender that a segment was received out-of-order, and indicate the expected SEQ. In the sequence space-gap case, the immediate ACK enables the sender to recover faster from a loss through a retransmission timeout or fast retransmit.

Nagle Algorithm

The Nagle algorithm is used to lower the number of small segments sent by TCP. RFC 896, "Congestion Control in IP/TCP Internetworks," defines the Nagle algorithm and describes congestion problems resulting from the interaction between the network and the transport layers. In RFC 896, Nagle refers to two main problems, the small packet problem and the source-quench problem.

The small packet problem occurs when a heavily loaded network has many small packets (little data). This situation leads to congestion, lost segments, retransmissions, and large end-to-end delay. The solution to the small packet problem is to reduce the number of small segments by delaying the transmission of small packets for a short time by waiting for the acknowledgement to the last segment sent, thus enabling the possibility that more data becomes available to send in a segment.

Full-sized segments are transmitted immediately.

The short time is defined as 200 milliseconds (ms) to 500 ms with only one segment to be outstanding without an acknowledgement. When more small segments are generated while waiting for the ACK for the first segment, the segments are merged into a larger segment. You see the advantages of the algorithm predominantly in interactive applications such as Telnet.

The Nagle algorithm is typically enabled on hosts, but you can disable it using the TCP socket option **TCP_NODELAY,** which is available in Microsoft Windows and Linux (Red Hat).

NOTE For more information on the Nagle algorithm and Microsoft Winsock, see the knowledge base article http://support.microsoft.com/default.aspx?scid=kb;en-us;214397, which discusses design issues when sending small data segments over TCP with Winsock. For more information on the Nagle algorithm and Linux, visit http://www.europe.redhat.com /documentation/man-pages/man7/tcp.7.php3.

The Nagle algorithm also provides a solution to the SWS problem. According to RFC 1122, the SWS problem is defined as a stable pattern of small incremental window movements resulting in extremely poor TCP performance.

SWS is the result of the receiver advancing the right window edge as buffer space becomes available to receive data and the sender using an incremental window, without regard to how small the additional data to be sent should be. The consequence is a stable pattern of very small datagrams sent even though the sender and receiver have a larger usable buffer space for the connection. The solution to SWS is based on algorithms applied to both sender and receiver.

On the sender side, the Nagle algorithm prevents sending small chunks of data at a time. On the receiver side, an algorithm referred to as the SWS avoidance algorithm determines when the right window edge can be advanced to avoid advertising small window increments.

Table 7-8 lists several OSs and their support for some of the aforementioned RFCs and algorithms.

Table 7-8 *Operating Systems Algorithm Support*

Operating System	RFC 1191 Path MTU Discovery	RFC 1323	Default Maximum Socket Size	Default TCP Socket Buffer Size	Default UDP Socket Buffer Size	RFC 2018 SACKs
FreeBDS 2.1.5	Yes	Yes	256 KB	16 KB	40 KB	Available in some versions
Linux 2.4 or later	Yes	Yes	64 KB	32 KB	32 KB	Yes
Solaris 7	Yes	Yes	1 MB TCP 256 KB UDP	8 KB	8 KB	Yes
Windows 2000, Windows XP	Yes	Yes	1 GB	8 KB		Yes
HPUX 11	Yes	Yes	>31 MB	32 KB	64 KB	
IAX 4.1	No	Yes	64 KB	16 KB	41,600 receive; 9216 send	

NOTE Table 7-8 displays a subset of the information available at http://www.psc.edu/networking/tcp_friendly.html under the performance tuning section.

For more information about algorithm support, consult the manual for your specific OS.

TCP Half Close

As introduced earlier, TCP allows for full-duplex communication in which both the sender and receiver have the capability of transmitting simultaneously. This communication is supported by having two logical unidirectional relationships, one from client to server and the other one from server to client. Each relationship has its own flow-control mechanism, which manifests itself by using independent SEQ and ACK for each.

TCP allows one of the nodes in the communication to end its relation and stop its output while still receiving data from the other end. As presented in Figure 7-21, the server acknowledges the sender's FIN sending back an ACK, and it continues to send data to the sender.

Figure 7-21 *TCP Half-Close Overview*

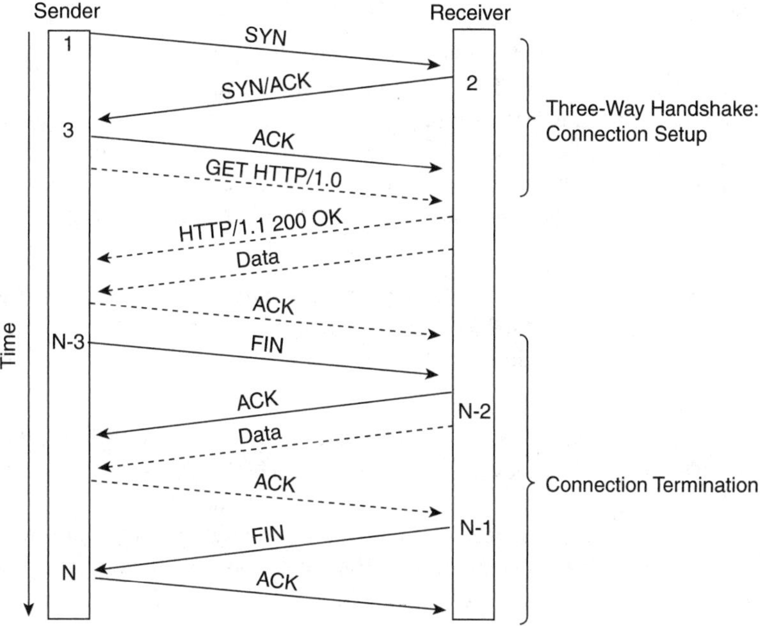

The result of the half close is an extra segment required to completely close the TCP connection.

MSS Option

The MSS is the maximum size of the TCP data portion that the sender sends to the receiver. The MSS is determined by subtracting the IP and TCP headers (usually 20 bytes from the TCP segment and 20 from the IP header), which is the maximum TCP segment size minus 40 bytes. The two most common MSS values are 536 and 1460 for hosts behind a modem or an Ethernet segment, respectively, as described in Chapter 2, "Server Architecture Overview."

MSS is one of the options of TCP that can be announced only when a connection is established, and it indicates the number of bytes the sender of the segment is able to receive. The MSS is a 2-byte option defined in RFC 879, which specifies the following:

"Hosts must not send datagrams larger than 576 octets unless they have specific knowledge that the destination host is prepared to accept larger datagrams."

This rule implies the sender and receiver have a mechanism to tell the other what its MSS value is. They do so by using the options field in the TCP header.

According to RFC 879, the default IP maximum datagram size (MTU) is 576, and the default TCP MSS is 536. The MSS is not negotiated, just announced between the two peers during the connection establishment. Note that in Figure 7-13 (SYN), the MSS from the client is announced as 1360 in the connection request (SYN), which is the MTU size defined with the VPN client tool minus the IP and TCP header. The response from the server, Figure 7-14 (SYN/ACK), communicates the server's MSS as 1460, which implies the MTU is 1500 bytes.

The server chooses the MSS to send as the minimum value between the MTU minus the IP and TCP headers and the MSS of the client. If IP or TCP options are included in the datagram, the MSS should still conform, which implies that the data portion of the segment must be adjusted.

MSS is the means by which the sender and receiver inform each other of the maximum size of the TCP data chunk they are able to receive. The MSS, however, does not address the larger issue of intermediate devices between the end nodes supporting their MSS values. This concept is important because intermediate nodes might not be able to handle the MSS of the end nodes, which would lead to fragmentation and all its related problems. The relationship between the MTU size, the MSS, and the path MTU is explained in the next section.

Path MTU Discovery Option

Path MTU discovery (PMTUD) is the mechanism used to determine the maximum size of the MTU in the path, or path MTU (PMTU), between the end nodes. Discovering the PMTU is primarily useful to avoid fragmentation in the path. PMTUD dynamically figures out the PMTU, which is effectively the lowest MTU of any one link in the path between the end nodes.

PMTUD was first defined in RFC 1063, which was later obsoleted by RFC 1191, "Path MTU Discovery." The technique used by the PMTUD is rather simple: A host sends an initial datagram with the size of the MTU for that interface with the DF bit set. (The DF bit is a flag in the IP header that indicates Don't Fragment when set.) Any router in the path with a lower MTU discards the datagram and returns an ICMP message (ICMP type 4) equivalent to "fragmentation needed and DF set" back to the source. This message is also referred to as a "datagram too big" message. The sender estimates a new size for the datagram, and the process takes place until the PMTU is found or the datagram DF bit is unset, which permits fragmentation.

RFC 1191 specifies that intermediate devices such as routers report their MTUs in the unused version of the IP header, which is the only proposed change. The RFC also specifies that hosts supporting PMTUD must decrease their MTUs as soon as they detect the exceeding of a particular MTU along the path. Detecting an increase in the PMTU is also possible, yet it requires active probing. RFC 1191 recommends the following timers:

- Sending a datagram bigger than the current MTU no less than 10 minutes (min) before the latest "datagram too big" message was received
- Sending a datagram bigger than the current MTU no less than 1 min after a successful MTU increase

Figure 7-22 presents the ICMP message header, including the proposed change on RFC 1191.

Figure 7-22 *PMTUD ICMP Header Details*

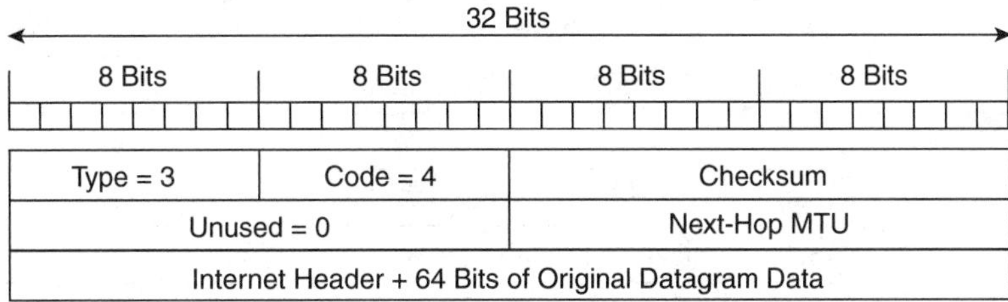

The lower 16 bits of the unused field in the ICMP header are used to carry the MTU of the next hop. The field contains the size in bytes of the largest datagram that could be forwarded by the device. Type 3 ICMP messages include the following code numbers:

- 0 = net unreachable
- 1 = host unreachable
- 2 = protocol unreachable
- 3 = port unreachable
- 4 = fragmentation needed and DF set
- 5 = source route failed

The format defined in RFC 1191 applies to code 4, fragmentation needed and DF set. RFC 1191 also offers a limited number of MTU values to try, to minimize the attempts to control the "search" for the appropriate PMTU. Table 7-9 documents these MTU values. (The plateau column established the maximum value to try.)

Table 7-9 *Recommended MTU Values*

Plateau	MTU	Comments	Reference
	65,535	Official maximum MTU	RFC 791
	65,535	Hyperchannel	RFC 1044
65,535			
32,000		Just in case	
	17,914	16 MB IBM Token Ring	ref. [6]
17,914			
	8166	IEEE 802.4	RFC 1042
8166			
	4464	IEEE 802.5 (4 MB max)	RFC 1042
	4352	Fiber Distributed Data Interface (FDDI) (revised)	RFC 1188
4352 (1%)			
	2048	Wideband Network	RFC 907
	2002	IEEE 802.5 (4 MB recommended)	RFC 1042
2002 (2%)			
	1536	Exp. Ethernet Nets	RFC 895
	1500	Ethernet Networks	RFC 894
	1500	Point-to-Point (default)	RFC 1134
	1492	IEEE 802.3	RFC 1042
1492 (3%)			
	1006	Serial Line Internet Protocol (SLIP)	RFC 1055
	1006	ARPANET	BBN 1822
1006			
	576	X.25 Networks	RFC 877
	544	DEC IP Portal	ref. [10]
	512	NETBIOS	RFC 1088
	508	IEEE 802/Source-Rt Bridge	RFC 1042
	508	ARCNET	RFC 1051

Table 7-9 *Recommended MTU Values (Continued)*

Plateau	MTU	Comments	Reference
508 (13%)			
	296	Point-to-Point (low delay)	RFC 1144
296			
68		Official minimum MTU	RFC 791

traceroute is also an option to determine the PMTU. It is similar to the ICMP method proposed in RFC 1191 in that datagrams are sent with the DF bit set until the PMTU is found. If the intermediate device is able to send the PMTU, the process is shortened; otherwise, the program is likely to step through the RFC 1191–proposed MTU values.

NOTE Note that MSS is applicable to TCP only. UDP does not have such an option. PMTUD and **traceroute** are options available to UDP as well. These alternatives are discussed in the UDP section.

In practice, both the approach proposed by RFC 1191 and **traceroute** as mechanisms to discover the PMTU are challenged. Several of the issues are described in the next section.

Issues with PMTUD

PMTUD issues are well documented in RFC 2923, "TCP Problems with Path MTU Discovery." This section presents one of the most common problems known as the *black-hole problem*. Other problems related to Path MTU discovery and TCP are documented in detail in RFC 2923, and general problems with TCP implementations are documented in RFC 2525, "Known TCP Implementation Problems."

The black-hole problem is described as malformed ICMP messages or filters on routers or firewalls that drop ICMP messages or ICMP messages that have to traverse IP Security (IPSec), IP-in-IP, or generic routing encapsulation (GRE) tunnels along the path from source to destination. The problem is that ICMP messages associated with PMTUD or **traceroute** do not arrive to the source, which is unable to determine whether the MTU size is appropriate or it needs to retry with a lower MTU.

The implications, as pointed out in RFC 2923, are that the problem is difficult to debug as regular ICMP packets work, but bulk data transfers do not work as soon as they exceed the MTU. The practical recommendations, related to Cisco routers, include the following:

- When dealing with GRE tunnels, routers "act like hosts" and perform PMTUD when configured with the **tunnel path-mtu-discovery** command so that the DF bit is copied from the inner IP header to the outer (GRE + IP) header.
- When initiating TCP connections on routers, you use the **ip tcp path-mtu-discovery** command to enable TCP MTU path discovery.
- When filtering ICMP, block specifically the ICMP traffic that needs to be denied, thus avoiding dropping the ICMP responses unnecessarily. An example of such an access list follows:

  ```
  access-list 199 permit icmp any any packet-too-big
  access-list 199 deny icmp any any
  access-list permit ip any any
  ```

  The first statement corresponds to an ICMP error "fragmentation needed and DF set," which is permitted; then, all other ICMP packets are denied; and finally, all other IP traffic is permitted.
- When dealing with IPSec tunnels, some configuration commands permit modifying PMTUD processing by allowing changes to the DF bit to clear it, set it, or copy it from the original IP header to the IPSec IP header. This feature is referred to as "DF bit override functionality."

NOTE To obtain more information go to http://www.cisco.com and search on "DF bit override."

TCP recovers from the black-hole problem naturally by timing out. Because the behavior can be erratic (default-sized ICMP echoes and basic MTU or smaller packets would work, but bulk data transfers do not), you need a simple troubleshooting procedure.

From a Cisco router adjacent to the end source or destination device, send an ICMP packet using the default size and the IP address of the source or destination (whichever is adjacent) to the other peer. (You can specify the source IP address using the extended option from the Cisco IOS Software command line.) If this test works, which proves the two hosts can communicate (note that by default the DF bit is not set), try the same process with a packet using the MTU size and with the DF bit set and see whether it works. If it works, but you have experienced a failure before, it is very possible that the current path differs from that used during the failure. If it does not work, try it with the DF bit not set, which leads to fragmentation. If this test works, you are now able to diagnose the problem. If it still does not work, try lowering the packet MTU size until you are able to get through. After you determine that a device "causes" the black-hole problem, you could capture the traffic, and determine its IP address and potentially its domain name so you can find a contact responsible for its configuration.

Other information you might find useful includes how to control enabling and disabling PMTUD on hosts given the various OSs available. The following sections cover some of the more common OSs.

Windows 2000 and Windows NT

The following information was extracted from the "TCP/IP and NBT Configuration Parameters for Windows 2000 or Windows NT" knowledge base article 120642 (http://support.microsoft.com/default.aspx?scid=kb;en-us;120642).

NOTE More information on Microsoft's TCP/IP stack implementation details appears at http://www.microsoft.com/windows2000/docs/tcpip2000.doc.

All the following TCP/IP parameters are Registry values that are located under one of two different subkeys of HKEY_LOCAL_MACHINE\SYSTEM\CurrentControlSet\Services\Tcpip\Parameters*Adapter Name*\Parameters\Tcpip:

- EnablePMTUBHDetect
  - Key: Tcpip\Parameters
  - Value Type: REG_DWORD - Boolean
  - Valid Range: 0,1 (False, True)
  - Default: 0 (False)
  - Description: Setting this parameter to 1 (True) causes TCP to try to detect "black-hole" routers while doing PMTUD. A black-hole router does not return ICMP destination unreachable messages when it needs to fragment an IP datagram with the DF bit set. TCP depends on receiving these messages to perform PMTUD. With this feature enabled, TCP tries to send segments without the DF bit set if several retransmissions of a segment go unacknowledged. If the segment is acknowledged as a result, the MSS is decreased and the DF bit is set in future packets on the connection. Enabling black-hole detection increases the maximum number of retransmissions performed for a given segment.

- EnablePMTUDiscovery
  - Key: Tcpip\Parameters
  - Value Type: REG_DWORD - Boolean
  - Valid Range: 0,1 (False, True)
  - Default: 1 (True)
  - Description: Setting this parameter to 1 (True) causes TCP to attempt to discover the MTU or largest packet size over the path to a remote host. By discovering the PMTU and limiting TCP segments to this size, TCP can eliminate fragmentation at routers along the path that connect networks with different MTUs. Fragmentation adversely affects TCP throughput and network congestion. Setting this parameter to 0 causes an MTU of 576 bytes to be used for all connections that are not to machines on the local subnet.

From a Windows command prompt, you can use the following command to manually determine potential black-hole issues:

```
ping -f -n number of pings -l size destination ip address
```

NOTE Cisco routers comply with RFC 1191 in the treatment of PMTUD. A router returns an ICMP message indicating "fragmentation needed and DF bit set," including the MTU of the next-hop network in the ICMP header field, as shown in Figure 7-22.

Windows 95 and Windows 98

The following information was extracted from the "Windows TCP/IP Registry Entries" knowledge base article 158474 (http://support.microsoft.com/default.aspx?scid=KB;en-us;q158474).

The following value entries, which are described in this article, do not normally exist in the Windows Registry; you must add them to the following Registry key:

```
HKEY_LOCAL_MACHINE\System\CurrentControlSet\Services\VxD\MSTCP
```

- PMTUBlackHoleDetect = 0 or 1
  - Data Type: DWORD
  - For Windows 98, the data type is a string value.
  - Specifies whether the stack attempts to detect MTU routers that do not send back ICMP fragmentation-needed messages. Setting this parameter when it is not needed can cause performance degradation. The default is 0.

- PMTUDiscovery = 0 or 1
  - Data Type: DWORD
  - For Windows 98, the data type is a string value.
  - Specifies whether Microsoft TCP/IP attempts to perform PMTU discovery as specified in RFC 1191. The default is 1.

Solaris 2

The following information was extracted from *TCP/IP Illustrated,* Volume I.

Using the configuration program **ndd**, which permits reconfiguring the kernel without having to rebuild it, you can disable or enable PMTUD and set the MSS. The following are the commands:

- Disable PMTUD:

```
ndd -set /dev/ip ip_path_mtu_discovery 0
```

- Set MSS to 1460:

```
$ ndd -set /dev/tcp tcp_mss_max 1460
```

Linux (Red Hat)

The following information was extracted from a Linux programmer's manual at http://www.europe.redhat.com/documentation/man-pages/man7/ip.7.php3:

IP_PMTU_DISCOVER sets or receives the PMTUD setting for a socket. When it is enabled, Linux performs PMTUD as defined in RFC 1191 on this socket. The DF flag is set on all outgoing datagrams. The system-wide default is controlled by the **ip_no_pmtu_disc sysctl** for **SOCK_STREAM** sockets and disabled on all others. The user can retrieve the PMTU using the **IP_MTU** or the **IP_RECVERR** options:

PMTUD Flags	Meaning
IP_PMTUDISC_WANT	Use per-route settings
IP_PMTUDISC_DONT	Never do PMTUD
IP_PMTUDISC_DO	Always do PMTUD

When PMTUD is enabled, the kernel automatically keeps track of the PMTU per destination host. Packets sent from datagram (including raw) sockets that are larger than the MTU are rejected with **EMSGSIZE**. When it is connected to a specific peer, the currently known PMTU can be retrieved conveniently using the **IP_MTU** socket option (after a **EMSGSIZE** error occurs). It can change over time. For connectionless sockets with many destinations, you can access the new MTU using the error queue (see **IP_RECVERR**). While

PMTUD is in progress, initial packets from datagram sockets might be dropped. Applications using UDP should be aware of this point and not take it into account for their packet retransmit strategy.

To bootstrap the PMTUD process on unconnected sockets, it is possible to start with a big datagram size (up to 64KB-headers bytes long) and let it shrink by updates of the PMTU.

To get an initial estimate of the PMTU, connect a datagram socket to the destination address and retrieve the MTU by calling with the **IP_MTU** option.

As mentioned earlier, in general PMTUD support is mainly found on TCP implementations, not UDP, so as you troubleshoot, this point is important to keep in mind.

TCP SACK Option

TCP SACK was first defined in RFC 1072, "TCP Extensions for Long-Delay Paths," which was made obsolete by RFC 2018. The primary purpose of SACK is the ability to acknowledge several successfully received segments so that the sender only retransmits the lost segments. TCP performance is typically impacted when multiple packets are lost on the same window of data. The loss of a packet is known to the sender after, at least, an RTT.

SACK uses two options:

- SACK-permitted indicates that the SACK option can be used once the connection is established. SACK-permitted is sent in SYN packets.
- SACK is used over an established connection after obtaining permission through the SACK-permitted option. The SACK option is sent by the host receiving the data to the host that is sending the data on a simplex data flow. The other simplex data flow, in the opposite direction, is treated independently.

The SACK-permitted option, kind or type 4, is a 2-byte option, as depicted in part A of Figure 7-23, sent only in a SYN packet. An example of a SACK-permitted option is documented in Figure 7-11 under the options field. SACK-permitted is the last option, and it corresponds to the connection request (SYN) from the client to server.

The SACK option, kind or type 5, is a variable-length option, depicted in part B of Figure 7-23, used only after permission is obtained with SACK-permitted.

The receiver informs the sender that a noncontiguous block of data has been received. The receiver expects to receive the missing block in the sequence space. When missing segments are received, the data receiver increases the ACK (advancing the left window). The SACK option data field contains blocks of contiguous sequence space corresponding to received data. Each contiguous block of data received is identified by two 4-byte numbers that map to the left-edge and right-edge blocks, respectively.

Figure 7-23 *SACK-Permitted and SACK Options*

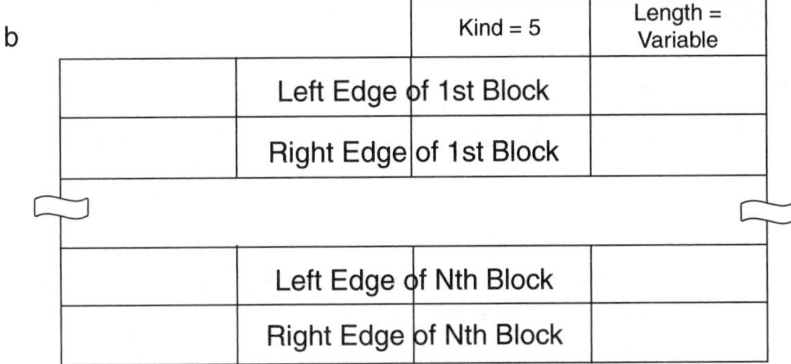

The left-edge block is the first SEQ of the block, and the right edge is the SEQ that follows the last SEQ of the block. This setup implies that between blocks (to the right of block x and the left of block x+1), there are segments that have not been received.

Given that the option field is up to 40 bytes, a SACK option is able to carry up to 4 blocks (4 blocks * 8 bytes each + 2 bytes for the kind and length). The timestamp option is typically used concurrently with SACK, and it reduces the overall number of blocks to 3. The next section explains the details.

NOTE Microsoft knowledge base article 224829 provides a description of Microsoft Windows 2000 TCP features that include SACK as well as timestamp and window scale (http://support.microsoft.com/default.aspx?scid=kb;en-us;224829). This article contains explanations of the operation of the option and the mechanisms to change the values through the Registry.

In Linux, TCP SACK is enabled by the **tcp_sack** sysctls, which can be accessed by the **/proc/sys/net/ipv4/*** files or with the interface. (See http://www.europe.redhat.com/documentation/man-pages/man7/tcp.7.php3.)

Timestamp Option

The TCP timestamp, a 10-byte option, was also introduced in RFC 1072 (along with SACK) to allow a sender to place a timestamp on every segment. It also allows the receiver to return the timestamp in an acknowledgement so that the receiver can accurately measure the RTT. Figure 7-24 introduces the timestamp option fields.

Figure 7-24 *Timestamp Option Fields*

1 Byte	1 Byte	4 Bytes	4 Bytes
Kind=8	Length=10	Timestamp Value TSval	Timestamp Echo Reply TSecr

Using timestamps lets you avoid a number of issues resulting from changing traffic conditions. The most obvious problem concerns the average RTT being used in the calculation for retransmission: if the actual RTT increases, the number of retransmissions increases. TCP would have to continuously calculate an accurate average RTT, which, as referenced in the RFC, would be computationally heavy and under certain error conditions, impossible to calculate. RFC 1323 made RFC 1072 obsolete, clarified some issues, and corrected some ambiguity. (Refer to Appendix C, "Video Encoding Mechanisms" for more details on RFC 1323.) Two important changes are

- Timestamp values could be shared by both Round Trip Time Measurement (RTTM) and Protection Against Wrapped Sequence Numbers (PAWS).
- Timestamps can be placed on ACKs as well as data segments.

As pointed out in RFC 1323, "TCP implements reliable data delivery by retransmitting segments that are not acknowledged within some retransmission timeout (RTO) interval . . . RTO is determined by estimating the mean and variance of the measured round-trip time (RTT)"—thus the importance of an accurate RTT.

Because timestamps can occur in either simplex flow (sender to receiver or receiver to sender), they should be supported for each flow, which is why the timestamp value and timestamp reply are present in a single timestamp option. The timestamp value field contains the current value of the TCP clock of the sender. The timestamp reply field contains the timestamp value sent by the peer in the TCP connection (its timestamp value field,) and it is valid if the ACK bit is set.

In Linux, timestamps are enabled by the **tcp_timestamps** sysctls, which can be accessed by the **/proc/sys/net/ipv4/*** files or with the interface. (See http://www.europe.redhat.com/documentation/man-pages/man7/tcp.7.php3.)

Window Scale Option

The window scale is a 3-byte option that allows TCP to expand the window size limited by the TCP header. The TCP header allocates 16 bits for the window size, which limits the maximum window size to 65 KB (2^{16}). The TCP window scale option permits window sizes beyond 65 KB, expanding the window size to 32 bits and using a scale factor to carry the 32-bits value in the 16-bits window size field (TCP header). The window scale option field carries the scale factor.

This option is only sent on SYN segments, which means the window scale is fixed in either simplex flow until the end of the connection. When the window scale option is used, both the sender and receiver indicate they are ready to use window scaling and communicate the scale factor to use on each receiving window.

Figure 7-25 presents the window scale option fields.

Figure 7-25 *Window Scale Option Fields*

1 Byte	1 Byte	1 Byte
Kind = 3	Length = 3	Shift cnt

The kind or type field value is 3 and the length is 3. The last field of 1 byte is used to carry the shift count. The sender uses the shift count to right-shift its receive window values the number of bits indicated in the shift.cnt field.

For more information on the window scale operation, consult RFC 1323.

In Linux, TCP SACK is enabled by the **tcp_windows_scaling** sysctls, which can be accessed by the **/proc/sys/net/ipv4/*** files or with the interface. (See http://www.europe.redhat.com/documentation/man-pages/man7/tcp.7.php3.)

PAWS

PAWS lets TCP avoid having the same SEQ used concurrently on a different connection on the same host. In networks that support speeds such as 1 Gigabit per second (Gbps), the SEQ can be wrapped in approximately 34 sec, so at some point there could be two packets with the same SEQ. To avoid this potential confusion, the TCP timestamp is used to timestamp every segment. The timestamp value is sent back to the sender, compared to a duplicate segment, and discarded if the timestamp is less than other timestamps recently received on the connection.

For more details on PAWS, consult section 3 of RFC 1323.

TCP Header Compression

Some of the early work on header compression was done by Van Jacobson in early 1990. This work is documented in RFC 1144, "Compressing TCP/IP Headers for Low-Speed Serial Links," and proves that TCP/IP headers can be compressed to an average in the 3 bytes range. The benefits of header compression mainly focus on improving efficiency and reducing response time on interactive sessions such as Telnet and rlogin, in which the ratio of header bytes to data is high. Bulk data transfers are more efficient, so the benefit of header compression is not significant.

More recent work for IP header compression, including TCP and UDP, is documented in RFC 2507, which is on the standards track. Header compression can be applied to IPv4, IPv6, TCP, and UDP.

The following are the advantages described by RFC 2507, which are mainly applicable to low- and medium-speed links:

- Improve interactive response time
- Allow use of small packets for bulk data with good line efficiency
- Allow use of small packets for delay-sensitive, low data-rate traffic
- Decrease header overhead
- Reduce packet loss rate over lossy links

The principle behind header compression is to avoid sending the header fields that are likely to remain constant through the life of the connection. Figure 7-26 highlights the fields that do not change during the connection (the shaded fields), as stated in RFC 1144.

The headers shown are the minimum size headers (no options in use), which equal 40 bytes, 20 for the IP header and 20 for the TCP header. The number of unchanged bytes is equivalent to 50 percent of the original header size. The context used by the headers can be occasionally communicated, through a full packet header, so that the subsequent compressed headers can be received in reference to the pre-established context.

The compression process occurs only after a connection is established and on packets that belong to an active connection. Figure 7-27 presents the compressed header.

Note that Figure 7-27 displays the compressed packet formats defined in RFC 1144 (part a in Figure 7-27) and later in RFC 2507 (part b in Figure 7-27). Byte 0 in part a in Figure 7-27, which corresponds to byte 1 in part b, is referred to as the *change mask* that determines how the remaining fields are interpreted. The change mask determines which of the fields that are expected to change has changed. A value of 1 in the specific change-mask bit implies the related field has changed.

The connection number (byte 1 in part a of Figure 7-27), which was flagged by the C bit, has been eliminated in part b because the connection identifier (CID) is always present (byte 0 in part b).

Figure 7-26 *IP and TCP Header Fields*

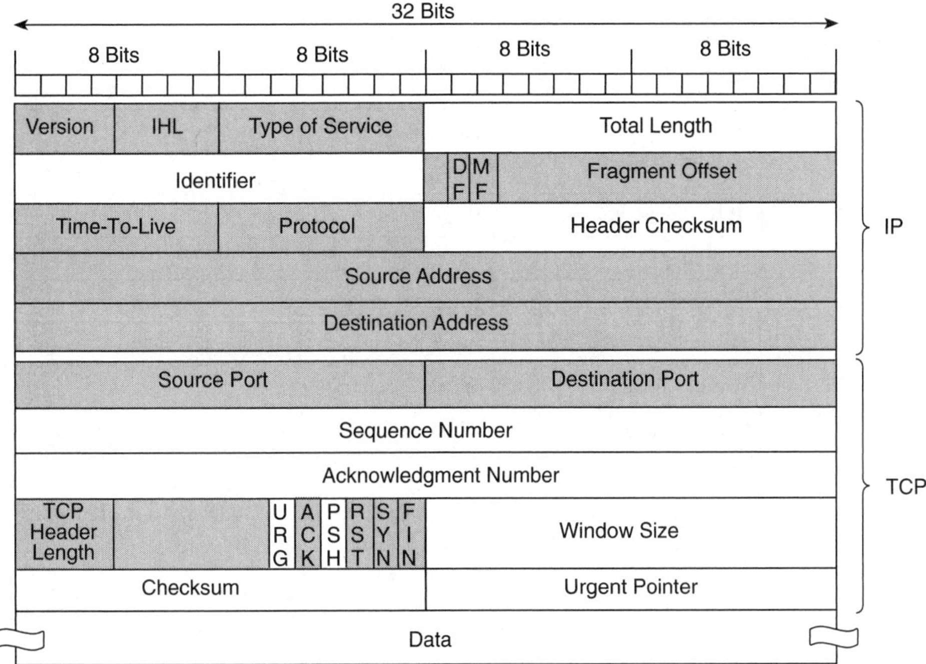

Figure 7-27 *Compressed Packet Format*

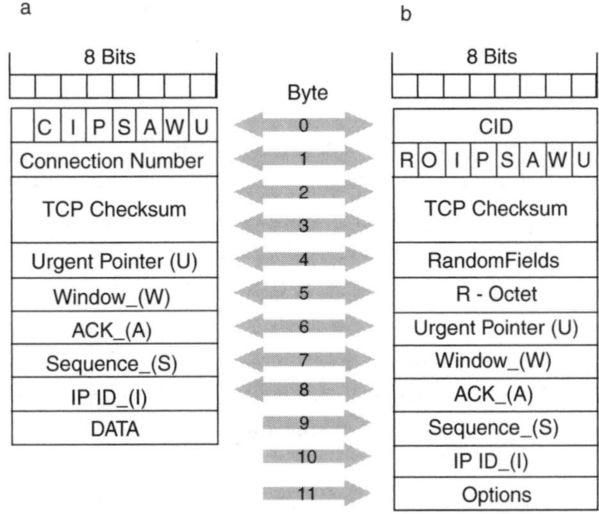

All the other bits correspond to the fields in Table 7-9.

Table 7-10 *New Mapping of Header Compression Fields*

Bit	RFC 1144	RFC 2507
C	Connection ID	N/A
R	N/A	R-Octet
O	N/A	Options
I	IP ID delta	IP ID delta
P	Push flag	Push flag
S	Sequence delta	Sequence delta
A	Acknowledgment delta	Acknowledgment delta
W	Window delta	Window delta
U	Urgent pointer	Urgent pointer

The CID is used to send the context, which keeps track of the IP version (IPv4 or IPv6) and the random fields that might be present.

The "delta" (Δ shown in the diagrams) is the difference in value between the field in this header and the field on the previous header. The delta value is expected to be small, which makes it cheaper to send than the complete new value.

The I bit signals whether it is an IPv4 header (set to 1) immediately before the TCP header. The R bit is used for random fields to be included "as is" in a compressed header because they are expected to change unpredictably. The header-compression work is applicable mainly to point-to-point links one hop at a time.

For more information on header compression, refer to RFC 1144 and RFC 2507.

NOTE Microsoft's TCP/IP stack implementation supports RFC 1144. See http://www.microsoft.com/windows2000/docs/tcpip2000.doc for more details.

To disable IP header compression on a Microsoft TCP/IP stack, refer to the knowledge base article at http://support.microsoft.com/default.aspx?scid=kb;en-us;161986.

You enable IP header compression on Cisco routers by using the command **ip tcp header-compression**. Header compression is supported on serial lines using Frame Relay, high-level data link control (HDLC), or Point-to-Point Protocol (PPP) encapsulation.

UDP

UDP, originally defined in RFC 768, provides a datagram host-to-host (also referred to as client-to-server) communication service with minimum protocol overhead. The protocol, as defined in RFC 768, is "transaction oriented, and delivery and duplicate protection are not guaranteed." Unlike TCP, UDP does not have the concept of a connection between two peers. UDP is in fact referred to as a connectionless protocol and does not have the structure required for a connection-state tracking mechanism.

In UDP, datagrams are sent without expectations of acknowledgments, timeouts, or retransmissions. Some applications built on UDP, such as TFTP, actually provide some means of reliability by retransmitting if packet acknowledgements are not received. The following sections discuss the UDP header format, UDP transaction, and header compression.

UDP Header

Figure 7-28 introduces the UDP header format.

Figure 7-28 *UDP Header Format*

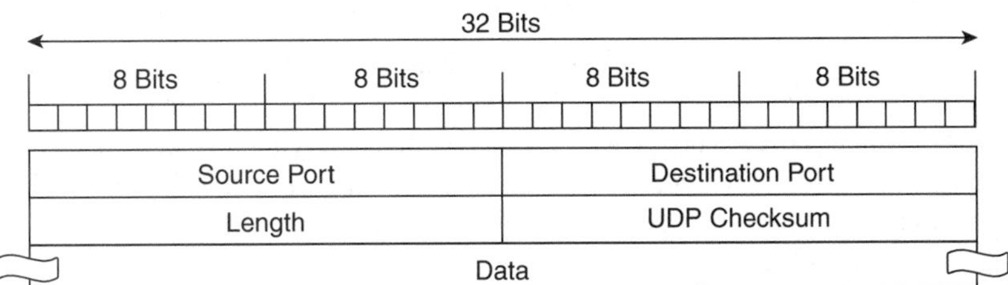

As is visible in the UDP header format, the number of fields in a UDP header is less than that for TCP and amounts to 8 bytes instead of 20. The following sections introduce the header fields.

Source Port Field

The source port field is a 16-bit field that indicates the process port number of the sender that the receiver can use to communicate back if required. The source port is not always used, and it has the value 0 when not in use.

Destination Port Field

The destination port field is also a 16-bit field used to identify the process in the receiving host.

Length Field

The length field is a 16-bit field that indicates the length of the entire datagram, including the header and the data. The minimum header length is 8 bytes.

Checksum Field

The checksum field is a 16-bit field that indicates whether there is any corruption in the datagram. The checksum calculation, as described in RFC 768, is "the 16-bit one's complement of the one's complement sum of a pseudo header of information from the IP header, the UDP header, and the data, padded with zero octets at the end (if necessary) to make a multiple of two octets." This process basically means using the content of the pseudo header (which also includes a portion of the IP header) to come up with a padded value (the value may be padded if it is not multiple of 2 bytes) to which the 1s complement operation is applied. Except for the pseudo header, the checksum calculation is the same as that with TCP, but unlike TCP, the inclusion of the checksum is optional.

The pseudo header, as shown in Figure 7-29, contains the source and destination IP addresses, the protocol, and the UDP length fields. The header provides this information in case the datagrams are not properly routed so the receiving host can check that the received datagram arrived at the correct destination. The RFC specifies that in the IP stack, there should be a mechanism that allows UDP to determine the source and destination IP address and the protocol field from the IP header.

Figure 7-29 *UDP Pseudo Header Format*

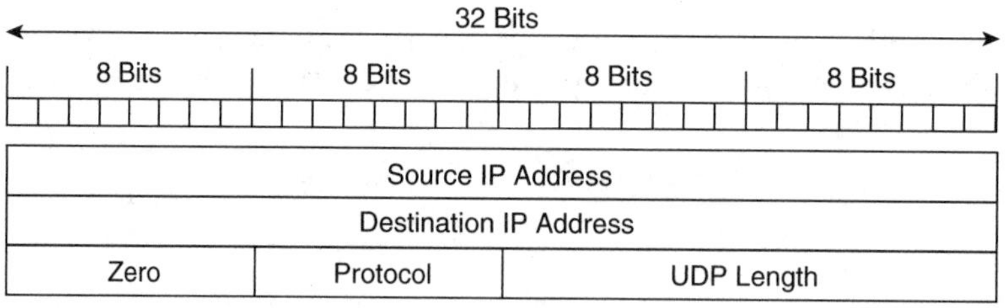

Using the same procedure as in TCP, the receiver uses the checksum field to calculate and compare against the checksum value it received in the segment, and if they are different, the segment is discarded.

UDP Transaction Overview

A UDP transaction is a datagram-oriented exchange in which a single datagram is the result of a process's output operation (transaction oriented). Even though the protocol itself does not have flow control and error correction built in, there are mechanisms used by applications to provide some basic error control. The best example is TFTP.

The first TFTP specification is documented in RFC 0783. RFC 0783 has been made obsolete by RFC 1350, which has been updated by the following RFCs: RFC 1782, RFC 1783, RFC 1784, RFC 1785, RFC 2347, RFC 2348, and RFC 2349. According to the specification, each packet is acknowledged independently, which implies that the TFTP protocol has its own mechanism to guarantee data transfer.

You need a few more pieces of information regarding TFTP to understand a UDP transaction. During a TFTP transaction, every datagram is expected to be acknowledged in order. If a datagram goes unacknowledged, the sender retransmits after a timeout. An acknowledgment contains the number of the block of data being acknowledged. A data block has a fixed size of 512 bytes.

Table 7-11 defines the TFTP opcode values.

Table 7-11 *TFTP Opcode Values*

Opcode	Operation
1	Read request (RRQ)
2	Write request (WRQ)
3	Data (DATA)
4	Acknowledgment (ACK)
5	Error (ERROR)

Figure 7-30 presents the first frame (frame number 60 in the trace) of a TFTP transaction in which the sender (Catalyst 7603) requested the file c6slb-apc.3-1-1a.bin (the content-switching module 3.1 software release from a Windows 2000 laptop running the Cisco TFTP server software).

Figure 7-30 *Frame 1 of TFTP Transfer*

```
60 6.895874 64.174.163.52 64.174.163.51 TFTP Read Request, File: c6slb-apc.3-1-1a.bin, Transfer type: octet
⊟ Frame 60 (71 bytes on wire, 71 bytes captured)
    Arrival Time: Dec 30, 2002 11:23:36.112595000
    Time delta from previous packet: 0.000069000 seconds
    Time relative to first packet: 6.895874000 seconds
    Frame Number: 60
    Packet Length: 71 bytes
    Capture Length: 71 bytes
⊟ Ethernet II, Src: 00:08:a3:7f:d2:8a, Dst: 00:03:47:0f:14:7a
    Destination: 00:03:47:0f:14:7a (Intel_0f:14:7a)
    Source: 00:08:a3:7f:d2:8a (Cisco_7f:d2:8a)
    Type: IP (0x0800)
⊟ Internet Protocol, Src Addr: 64.174.163.52 (64.174.163.52), Dst Addr: 64.174.163.51 (64.174.163.51)
    Version: 4
    Header length: 20 bytes
  ⊟ Differentiated Services Field: 0x00 (DSCP 0x00: Default; ECN: 0x00)
      0000 00.. = Differentiated Services Codepoint: Default (0x00)
      .... ..0. = ECN-Capable Transport (ECT): 0
      .... ...0 = ECN-CE: 0
    Total Length: 57
    Identification: 0x0000
  ⊟ Flags: 0x00
      .0.. = Don't fragment: Not set
      ..0. = More fragments: Not set
    Fragment offset: 0
    Time to live: 255
    Protocol: UDP (0x11)
    Header checksum: 0xf3ef (correct)
    Source: 64.174.163.52 (64.174.163.52)
    Destination: 64.174.163.51 (64.174.163.51)
⊟ User Datagram Protocol, Src Port: 55244 (55244), Dst Port: tftp (69)
    Source port: 55244 (55244)
    Destination port: tftp (69)
    Length: 37
    Checksum: 0x6b7a (correct)
⊟ Trivial File Transfer Protocol
    Opcode: Read Request (1)
    Source File: c6slb-apc.3-1-1a.bin
    Type: octet

0000  00 03 47 0f 14 7a 00 08  a3 7f d2 8a 08 00 45 00   ..G..z.. ......E.
0010  00 39 00 00 00 00 ff 11  f3 ef 40 ae a3 34 40 ae   .9...... ..@..4@.
0020  a3 33 d7 cc 00 45 00 25  6b 7a 00 01 63 36 73 6c   .3...E.% kz..c6sl
0030  62 2d 61 70 63 2e 33 2d  31 2d 31 61 2e 62 69 6e   b-apc.3- 1-1a.bin
0040  00 6f 63 74 65 74 00                               .octet.
```

The highlighted areas of the frame show the IP is UDP (0x11), and under the UP section, it shows the source port (a random source port 55244) and the well-known TFTP destination port (UDP port 69). Under the TFTP section, the frame displays the type of operation (opcode for a GET), the file to be transferred (source file c6slb-apc.3-1-1a.bin), and the type of transfer. (An octet implies a binary transfer.)

Figure 7-31 illustrates the return from the TFTP server.

Because a formal connection request is not present, an acknowledgment is not expected, so the response from the server already includes a portion of the requested file. The GET is equivalent to a "read." If the TFTP operation were a PUT, equivalent to a "write," the request must be acknowledged first before any data is sent. The important areas to focus on in frame 61 are that the source port is not the well-known UDP port 69 but rather one randomly selected (port 1878); the destination port does match the original sender's source port (port 55244). Additionally, the opcode is 3 for data, and the block of data being transferred is the first block. (The first block is always number 1.) The total size of the frame is 558 bytes, made of 18 bytes of Ethernet II header, 20 bytes of IP header, 8 bytes of UDP header, and 512 bytes of the UDP payload (fixed size).

Figure 7-31 *Frame 2 of TFTP Transfer*

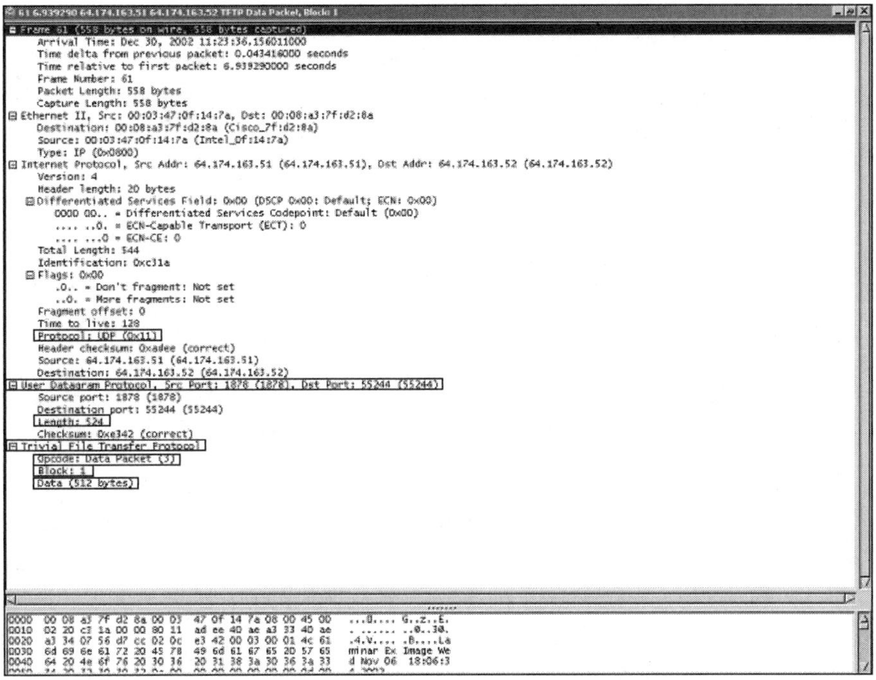

```
61 6.939290 64.174.163.51 64.174.163.52 TFTP Data Packet, Block: 1
⊟ Frame 61 (558 bytes on wire, 558 bytes captured)
    Arrival Time: Dec 30, 2002 11:23:36.156011000
    Time delta from previous packet: 0.043416000 seconds
    Time relative to first packet: 6.939290000 seconds
    Frame Number: 61
    Packet Length: 558 bytes
    Capture Length: 558 bytes
⊟ Ethernet II, Src: 00:03:47:0f:14:7a, Dst: 00:08:a3:7f:d2:8a
    Destination: 00:08:a3:7f:d2:8a (Cisco_7f:d2:8a)
    Source: 00:03:47:0f:14:7a (Intel_0f:14:7a)
    Type: IP (0x0800)
⊟ Internet Protocol, Src Addr: 64.174.163.51 (64.174.163.51), Dst Addr: 64.174.163.52 (64.174.163.52)
    Version: 4
    Header length: 20 bytes
  ⊟ Differentiated Services Field: 0x00 (DSCP 0x00: Default; ECN: 0x00)
      0000 00.. = Differentiated Services Codepoint: Default (0x00)
      .... ..0. = ECN-Capable Transport (ECT): 0
      .... ...0 = ECN-CE: 0
    Total Length: 544
    Identification: 0xc31a
  ⊟ Flags: 0x00
      .0.. = Don't fragment: Not set
      ..0. = More fragments: Not set
    Fragment offset: 0
    Time to live: 128
    Protocol: UDP (0x11)
    Header checksum: 0xadee (correct)
    Source: 64.174.163.51 (64.174.163.51)
    Destination: 64.174.163.52 (64.174.163.52)
⊟ User Datagram Protocol, Src Port: 1878 (1878), Dst Port: 55244 (55244)
    Source port: 1878 (1878)
    Destination port: 55244 (55244)
    Length: 524
    Checksum: 0xe342 (correct)
⊟ Trivial File Transfer Protocol
    Opcode: Data Packet (3)
    Block: 1
    Data (512 bytes)

0000  00 08 a3 7f d2 8a 00 03  47 0f 14 7a 08 00 45 00   ........ G..z..E.
0010  02 20 c3 1a 00 00 80 11  ad ee 40 ae a3 33 40 ae   . ...... ..@..3@.
0020  a3 34 07 56 d7 cc 02 0c  e3 42 00 03 00 01 4c 61   .4.V.... .B....La
0030  6d 69 6e 61 72 20 45 78  49 6d 61 67 65 20 57 65   minar Ex Image We
0040  64 20 4e 6f 76 20 30 36  20 31 38 3a 30 36 3a 33   d Nov 06  18:06:3
```

The next frame contains the acknowledgment to the first data block. The frame details appear in Figure 7-32.

The important details to note are that the entire header details remain the same (source and destination ports) and that this frame acknowledges the first data block sent.

The next frames of the transaction are data blocks sent sequentially and an acknowledgment for each block sent in return. The end of the transaction is implicitly signaled when a data block less than 512 bytes is sent. This last data block for the transaction in the example appears in Figure 7-33.

Figure 7-32 *Frame 3 of TFTP Transfer*

```
62 6.939884 64.174.163.52 64.174.163.51 TFTP Acknowledgement, Block: 1
Frame 62 (60 bytes on wire, 60 bytes captured)
    Arrival Time: Dec 30, 2002 11:23:36.156605000
    Time delta from previous packet: 0.000594000 seconds
    Time relative to first packet: 6.939884000 seconds
    Frame Number: 62
    Packet Length: 60 bytes
    Capture Length: 60 bytes
Ethernet II, Src: 00:08:a3:7f:d2:8a, Dst: 00:03:47:0f:14:7a
    Destination: 00:03:47:0f:14:7a (Intel_0f:14:7a)
    Source: 00:08:a3:7f:d2:8a (Cisco_7f:d2:8a)
    Type: IP (0x0800)
    Trailer: 0000000000000000000000000000
Internet Protocol, Src Addr: 64.174.163.52 (64.174.163.52), Dst Addr: 64.174.163.51 (64.174.163.51)
    Version: 4
    Header length: 20 bytes
  Differentiated Services Field: 0x00 (DSCP 0x00: Default; ECN: 0x00)
      0000 00.. = Differentiated Services Codepoint: Default (0x00)
      .... ..0. = ECN-Capable Transport (ECT): 0
      .... ...0 = ECN-CE: 0
    Total Length: 32
    Identification: 0x0001
  Flags: 0x00
      .0.. = Don't fragment: Not set
      ..0. = More fragments: Not set
    Fragment offset: 0
    Time to live: 255
    Protocol: UDP (0x11)
    Header checksum: 0xf407 (correct)
    Source: 64.174.163.52 (64.174.163.52)
    Destination: 64.174.163.51 (64.174.163.51)
User Datagram Protocol, Src Port: 55244 (55244), Dst Port: 1878 (1878)
    Source port: 55244 (55244)
    Destination port: 1878 (1878)
    Length: 12
    Checksum: 0x58ea (correct)
Trivial File Transfer Protocol
    Opcode: Acknowledgement (4)
    Block: 1

0000  00 03 47 0f 14 7a 00 08  a3 7f d2 8a 08 00 45 00   ..G..z.. .......E.
0010  00 20 00 01 00 00 ff 11  f4 07 40 ae a3 34 40 ae   . ...... ..@..4@.
0020  a3 33 d7 cc 07 56 00 0c  58 ea 00 04 00 01 00 00   .3...V.. X.......
0030  00 00 00 00 00 00 00 00  00 00 00 00               ........ ....
```

Figure 7-33 *Frame n-1 of TFTP Transfer*

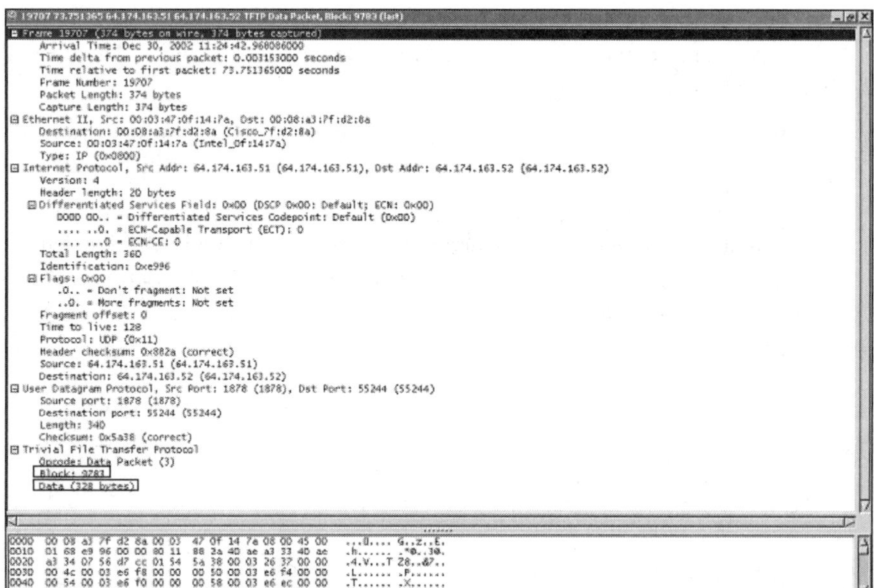

The highlighted areas of frame 19707 (n-1 with n being the last frame) show that the block sent is 9783 and the size of the data portion is 328 bytes, which is lower than 512 bytes, thus signaling the last block. The next frame (19708 or n) shows the acknowledgment of the last received block, block 9783. This frame, shown in Figure 7-34, is the last frame of the TFTP transaction.

Figure 7-34 *Frame n of TFTP Transfer*

```
19708 73.751776 64.174.163.52 64.174.163.51 TFTP Acknowledgement, Block: 9783
⊟ Frame 19708 (60 bytes on wire, 60 bytes captured)
    Arrival Time: Dec 30, 2002 11:24:42.968497000
    Time delta from previous packet: 0.000411000 seconds
    Time relative to first packet: 73.751776000 seconds
    Frame Number: 19708
    Packet Length: 60 bytes
    Capture Length: 60 bytes
⊟ Ethernet II, Src: 00:08:a3:7f:d2:8a, Dst: 00:03:47:0f:14:7a
    Destination: 00:03:47:0f:14:7a (Intel_0f:14:7a)
    Source: 00:08:a3:7f:d2:8a (Cisco_7f:d2:8a)
    Type: IP (0x0800)
    Trailer: 000000000000000000000000000
⊟ Internet Protocol, Src Addr: 64.174.163.52 (64.174.163.52), Dst Addr: 64.174.163.51 (64.174.163.51)
    Version: 4
    Header length: 20 bytes
  ⊟ Differentiated Services Field: 0x00 (DSCP 0x00: Default; ECN: 0x00)
      0000 00.. = Differentiated Services Codepoint: Default (0x00)
      .... ..0. = ECN-Capable Transport (ECT): 0
      .... ...0 = ECN-CE: 0
    Total Length: 32
    Identification: 0x2637
  ⊟ Flags: 0x00
      .0.. = Don't fragment: Not set
      ..0. = More fragments: Not set
    Fragment offset: 0
    Time to live: 255
    Protocol: UDP (0x11)
    Header checksum: 0xcdd1 (correct)
    Source: 64.174.163.52 (64.174.163.52)
    Destination: 64.174.163.51 (64.174.163.51)
⊟ User Datagram Protocol, Src Port: 55244 (55244), Dst Port: 1878 (1878)
    Source port: 55244 (55244)
    Destination port: 1878 (1878)
    Length: 12
    Checksum: 0x32b4 (correct)
⊟ Trivial File Transfer Protocol
    Opcode: Acknowledgement (4)
    Block: 9783

0000  00 03 47 0f 14 7a 00 08  a3 7f d2 8a 08 00 45 00   ..G..z.. ......E.
0010  00 20 26 37 00 00 ff 11  cd d1 40 ae a3 34 40 ae   . &7.... ..@..4@.
0020  a3 33 d7 cc 07 56 00 0c  32 b4 00 04 26 37 00 00   .3...V.. 2...&7..
0030  00 00 00 00 00 00 00 00  00 00 00 00               ........ ....
```

The TFTP example shows that even though UDP does not offer any sophisticated mechanisms for flow control and error detection or correction, it is still possible to maintain certain levels of reliability by building it into the application. UDP still provides a lower overhead alternative to TCP.

UDP Header Compression

UDP header compression, also discussed in RFC 2507, follows the same principles of compression applied to TCP and has the same overall benefits. The UDP header can be compressed down to 2 bytes. Both the source and destination source ports remain the same during the life of the connection, and the length must match the length of previous headers, which leaves the checksum (2 bytes) as the field that changes regularly.

Figure 7-35 presents two compressed non-TCP header formats.

Figure 7-35 *Compressed Non-TCP Header Formats*

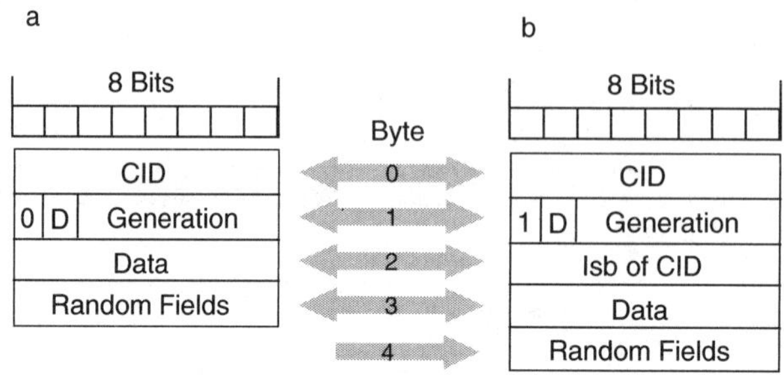

The context ID (CID) can be either 8 or 16 bits, and it is determined by the first bit of the second byte. If the bit equals 1, the next byte holds the least significant bits of the CID. The D bit on the second byte determines whether there is data (if bit = 1). A simple explanation for *generation* is a version related to a particular context identified by a CID.

For more information on the specific meaning of the generation field and the need behind 8- or 16-bit CIDs, refer to RFC 2507.

More recent work on IP/UDP compression is available through several RFCs. For example, RFC 2508 deals with the compression of IP, UDP, and Real Time Protocol (RTP) headers. RFC 3095 deals with Robust Header Compression (ROHC) for IP/UDP/RTP, IP/UDP, and IP/ESP and a number of other RFCs related with ROHC. RFC 2508 describes compression mechanisms specific to IP/UDP/RTP on low-speed serial links, whereas RFC 3095 describes compression mechanisms useful for links with significant error rates and long RTTs. Both RFCs are on the standards track.

Summary

IP is simply the most prevalent network layer protocol on the Internet and intranets to date.

The TCP/IP protocols suite supports two transport protocols: TCP and UDP.

TCP, a connection-oriented protocol, provides reliability and flow control. It guarantees error detection and correction and packet delivery for applications needing such features. TCP continues to evolve by improving its operation and functions to better utilize network resources.

UDP, a connectionless protocol, provides no reliability or flow control, yet it offers low overhead, which makes it the choice for applications in which low overhead is important and reliability is not critical.

Understanding each of these protocols and their behavioral implications is fundamental to the Data Center, where they come together as the source or destination of traffic. The Data Center is an environment where application awareness makes the knowledge about the protocol's operation relevant and key to architectural and design considerations.

TCP offers a number of services better suited for applications that require certain service guarantess and can tolerate the header overhead and flow control issues and need error correction and detection. UDP, on the other hand, offers less overhead and fewer services, yet it is useful for application where packet loss is less sensitive but time delays are more problematic.

The use of devices such as firewalls and load balancers requires you understand how the protocols in the TCP/IP suite work to ensure the operational behavior is the expected one.

A good understanding of the working details of IP, TCP and UDP help you design and operate a better network.

References

[1]Stevens, Richard W. *The Protocols (TCP/IP Illustrated,* Volume I*).* Addison-Wesley, 1994.

This chapter covers the following topics:

- The concepts of URI, URL, URN, and MIME
- An overview of HTTP, including its operation, message format, and versions
- A discussion on the differences between HTTP/1.0 and HTTP/1.1 and their performance implications
- A discussion on HTTP header types: General, Request, Reponse, and Entity Headers

CHAPTER 8

HTTP and Related Concepts

HTTP is the most widely used protocol for web applications, both on the Internet and on intranets. HTTP, which relies on TCP as the transport protocol, is used to carry many types of objects or content such as text, images, and video, yet it also allows file transfers and video streaming. Chapter 3, "Application Architectures Overview," discusses applications that use HTTP, and Chapter 11, "Streaming Protocols Overview," describes HTTP streaming.

This chapter describes the functional and operational aspects of HTTP and presents examples of its use based on traffic captured when real transactions are conducted. This chapter also presents concepts related to HTTP that are fundamental to the full understanding of how HTTP works. These include the treatment of resources as the object of a request or response, and the messages used by the peers in the HTTP transaction (request/response interaction).

Resources and Messages

The HTTP specification provides a set of commands, referred to as *methods*, that indicate the purpose of the communication exchange (request or response) in addition to some basic functionality used to retrieve, update, and search information. This "information" is typically referred to as a resource or resources, and they must be clearly defined so that they are handled in a nonambiguous manner. This definition includes an identification, location, and name that are universally recognized and accepted so the resources can be used in a variety of applications by a number of protocols, including HTTP. For example, if a user is trying to perform a search on the web for a particular web page, the identification, location, and name must be unique to ensure a successful result (whether the object of the search exists or not).

Another equally important aspect is the format of the pieces of information used in the communication exchange between peers when dealing with resources. These pieces of information are call messages, and like resources, they too must be clearly defined. The HTTP specification relies on how resources are identified (URI), located (URL), and named (URN) to execute the proper operation. Messages, the information unit between HTTP peers, are based on the Multipurpose Internet Mail Extensions (MIME) definitions. The following sections discuss these concepts.

URIs

RFC 1630, "Uniform Resource Identifiers in WWW," introduced the concept of Uniform Resource Identifiers (URIs) to "encode the name and addresses of objects on the Internet." The goal of encoding the name and address of an object is to create a universal set that abstracts the idea of a generic object yet uniquely identifies each object. For example, the object book.txt could exist in many places, so to uniquely identify one in a particular location, you use a URI.

The URI for http://www.example.com/book.txt ensures that book.txt is uniquely identified and different from http://www.example/books/book.txt.

NOTE You can find all RFCs online at http://www.ietf.org/in-notes/rfc*xxxx*.txt, where *xxxx* is the number of the RFC. If you do not know the number of the RFC, you can try searching by topic at http://www.rfc-editor.org/cgi-bin/rfcsearch.pl.

A URI is a member of the universal namespace, which consists of all registered names and addresses that correspond to registered protocols. A Uniform Record Locator (URL), informally discussed in RFC 1630, is a form of URI that maps an address to the access network protocol. Paraphrasing the World Wide Web Consortium (W3C), a "URL is an informal term associated with popular URI schemes: FTP, HTTP, mailto:." Universal Resource Name (URN) is also a URI that is intended to be location independent. Figure 8-1 shows a graphical representation of URLs, URNs, and their relation to URIs.

Figure 8-1 *URIs*

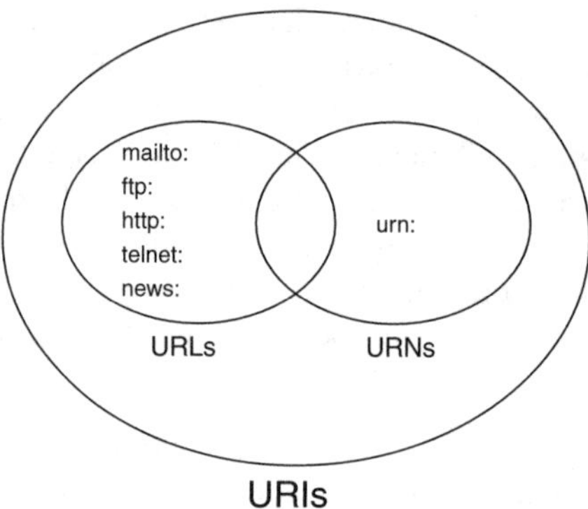

Notice that both URLs and URNs are subsets of URIs.

The syntax of a URI contains a naming scheme, followed by a string that follows the format of the function specified by the naming scheme. As presented in Figure 8-2, the scheme is HTTP, and the path, which is a function of the HTTP naming scheme, is http://www.cisco.com/go/srnd.

Figure 8-2 *URI Syntax*

The scheme and the path are separated by a colon, which is also a part of the syntax of URLs and URNs.

URIs can be relative or absolute. The following section presents the details. The generic syntax of URIs is further defined in RFC 2396, which merges the URLs in RFC 1737 and relative URLs in RFC 1808 into a generic URI syntax.

The URI definition, from RFC 2396, is based on the following tenets:

- *Uniform* refers to
  - Being able to have multiple access mechanisms (FTP, HTTP, and so on) for the same URIs
  - Preventing the erroneous interpretation of these URIs by using a standard rule set, regardless of the access method, which also allows the addition of new types of URIs
- *Resource* refers to
  - Any piece of content (an object such as a text file, video clip, image, and so on) that has an identity which remains unchanged as it is used as part of a superset of objects (entities) that change over time
- *Identifier* refers to
  - An object that can be used to reference resources, such as the characters and syntax of a URI

Relative or Partial URIs

Partial or *relative* URIs are an abbreviated form used to describe an object that is related to other objects, with which it shares certain parts of the URI. Related objects can refer to each other, and if they are moved, relative URIs prevent the references to those objects from changing. In general, partial URLs do not use colons before any slash, and any reference made to the objects is understood to be relative to the common information.

Figure 8-3 presents an example of relative URIs.

Figure 8-3 *Partial or Relative URI*

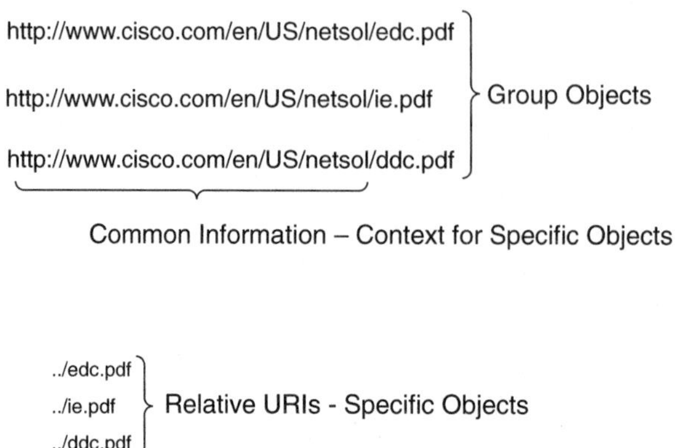

The common information shared by all objects is http://www.cisco.com/en/US/netsol, which is a combination of the scheme and a portion of the path. In this case, all URLs are relative to the common information. This common information could be described as the *context* URI, which all other URIs are related to and relative from. Example 8-1 shows relative URIs on a web page (HTML code) that references objects (highlighted) relative to the site.

Example 8-1 *Relative URI*

```
<p><a href="../Terms"><img border="0" alt="WYY" src="../Icons/WWW/example_home"></a>
<a href="../Architecture/"><img src="../Icons/arch" width="212" height="48"
alt="Architecture Domain" border="0"></a></p>
```

Notice under the **href** attribute, used as a hyperlink, the string **../** preceding the relative URI. If the site changes, the objects referenced by the web page could remain the same because they would be relative to the new site.

Absolute or Full URIs

Absolute or *full* URI refers to the complete form when describing an object. It makes the references to objects change as the objects move. Absolute URIs conserve their full names and the reference to them is based on those full names. Figure 8-4 presents the same object referenced in Figure 8-3 but using absolute URIs, which implies that the notation on the web page where they are referenced uses the absolute URI.

Figure 8-4 *Absolute or Full URIs*

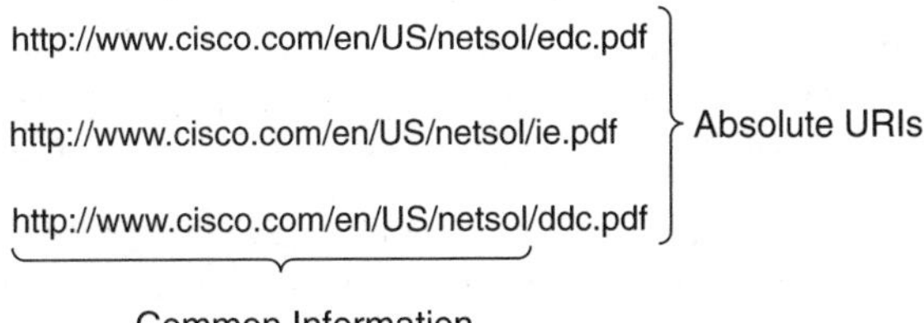

In general, absolute URIs use colons before any slash. This slash is one of the main differentiators between relative and absolute URIs. An absolute URL would contain the scheme and path, with the object part of the path, as in http://www.cisco.com/en/US/netsol/ddc.pdf.

Example 8-2 presents an example of the notation that would appear on a web page.

Example 8-2 *Absolute URI*

```
<a href="http://www.example.com/files"><img src="/images/asf_logo_wide.gif"
alt="The Example Web Page" align="left" border="0"/></a>
```

Notice that the shaded area includes **http://**, which makes the reference absolute, yet the image **img src** has a relative reference to the href attribute. This reference means that the object asf_logo_wide.gif is retrieved from www.example.com/files/images/asf_logo_wide.gif using HTTP.

Absolute URIs are quite common when referencing objects that exist on other pages, but if the objects are all in the same location, a relative URI seems more appropriate. From the perspective of the client, nothing should change, and regardless of the location, the object should be available. The server's perspective is slightly different because changing URIs requires maintenance. The use of relative URIs allows the web administrator to be more flexible in the treatment of URIs.

TIP A good discussion on whether the URIs need to change and the use of URIs appears at http://www.w3.org/Provider/Style/URI.html.

Rules for Naming Relative and Absolute URIs

There are specific rules in the use of relative URIs, which rely on syntax properties of URIs and such characters as / and other path elements (.. or .). Some of these characters have a meaning reserved for the representation of the hierarchical space that is recognized by clients and servers. The rules (according to RFC 1630) are as follows:

- If the scheme parts are different, you must give the whole absolute URI. Otherwise, you can omit the scheme. For example, if a single resource object uses both FTP and HTTP as the access mechanisms, you must use the absolute form. This rule helps you avoid applying the wrong access mechanism to an object because it is not supported by either the object or the server (such as trying to FTP a video file on a streaming-only server).
- If the relative URI starts with at least two consecutive slashes, everything from the context URI up to (but not including) the first occurrence of exactly the same number of consecutive slashes (which has no greater number of consecutive slashes anywhere to the right of it) is taken to be the same and so prepended to the partial URL to form the full URL. From the URIs http://www.example.com/files/book.txt and http://www.example.com/files/book1.txt, the context URI is http://www.example.com/files/ and the relative URIs are /book.txt and /book1.txt.
- Otherwise, the last part of the path of the context URI (anything following the rightmost slash) is removed, and the partial URI is appended in its place.
- Within the result, all occurrences of *xxx/../* or */.* are recursively removed, where *xxx*, .., and . are complete path elements.

These concepts are best explained with an example.

Table 8-1 shows the partial URIs for the objects on the table and uses magic://a/b/c//d/e/ as the context URI.

Table 8-1 *Relative URIs Example*

Object	Absolute URI
G	magic://a/b/c//d/e/g
/g	magic://a/g
//g	magic://g
../g	magic://a/b/c//d/g
g:h	g:h

Table 8-2 shows a more concrete example related to the context URL http://www.cisco.com/en/US/netsol/.

Table 8-2 *Mapping from Relative to Absolute URI*

Relative URI	Absolute URI
edc.pdf	http://www.cisco.com/en/US/netsol/edc.pdf
../edc.pdf	http://www.cisco.com/en/US/edc.pdf
./edc.pdf	http://www.cisco.com/en/US/netsol/edc.pdf

Table 8-3 lists some of the defined schemes currently available.

Table 8-3 *Defined URI Schemes*

Scheme	Scheme Details
http	Hypertext Transfer Protocol
ftp	File Transfer Protocol
gopher	Gopher protocol
mailto	Electronic mail address
news	Usenet news
telnet, rlogin, and tn3270	Reference to interactive sessions
wais	Wide Area Information Servers
File	Local file access

The generic syntax for URIs and URL is discussed in RFC 1630 under the sections "BNF of Generic URI Syntax" and "BNF of Generic URL Syntax."

URLs

RFC 1738 documents the URL specification. RFC 1738 discusses the syntax and semantics of URLs, and their specification is designed to meet the requirements documented in "Functional Requirements for Internet Resource Locators" in RFC 1736.

NOTE The L in URL stands for *locators*, which implies that URL means more than one locator, as specified in RFC 1738. In the same RFC, URLs is mentioned to imply *Universal Resource Locators*. For consistency and simplicity, references to *URL* indicate the generic *Universal Resource Locator*, and references to *URLs indicate Universal Record Locators* or more than one URL.

URLs, as defined in RFC 1738, locate resources by providing identification to the resource location. Once the resource is located, a number of operations can be performed on the resource. These operations are methods that are specified for each URL scheme. The following is the syntax of a URL:

<scheme>:<scheme-specific-part>

The scheme part could be one of the values in Table 8.3, and the *scheme-specific-part* depends on the scheme. The section "URL Encoding" provides more information about URL syntax.

NOTE RFC 1738 Section 5 explains the BNF form of the URL syntax in more detail. BNF stands for Backus Naur Form, and it refers to a formal notation initially used to describe the syntax of a given language that has since been extended to other types of languages.

Relative and Absolute URLs

The concept of a relative URL is similar yet not identical to that of the relative URI. URLs are, in some cases, used to locate resources that contain pointers to other resources. These pointers are links where the location to the other resource is represented by an expression that references the same place as the first URL, except with a specified path. This arrangement implies that there is a hierarchical structure in how the URLs are specified to support relative links. The hierarchy, like the one used in file systems, uses / to separate components.

RFC 1808, "Relative Uniform Resource Locators," defines the syntax and semantics of relative URLs. Relative URLs are used in situations where the URL references a resource without specifying its context because it is well-defined and inherited. You do not have to specify the context in every instance or change it when the location of the file system changes. The base document containing the reference carries the context used by the relative URL. The length of a relative URL is shortened from the absolute version, and the use of . and .. is common to interpret the relative path.

Absolute URLs make no reference to portions of the URL or specify a relative path. They include the entire scheme, and they are not used in reference to any other URL. The schemes supported are the same supported by URIs.

URL Encoding

The need to encode the URL comes from the mechanism used to interpret characters in a nonambiguous way. For example, imagine a hyperlink on a web page to the following document.

The "Data Center Architecture and Design Guide" is a hyperlink on a web page that points to the file www.cisco.com/en/US/netsol/Data Center Arch Design Guide v1.txt, which is kept in a file system that allows spaces in the filename. The hyperlink that the web page uses, which you can likely see by placing the cursor over the link, must encode the spaces because they would otherwise be interpreted by the browser, thus breaking the link to the actual file. If the filename contains more special characters that you do not want the browser to interpret, what can you do? The answer is to encode those special characters in a way that the browser can see and determine the real meaning of the character. Encoding those characters requires both a mechanism to signal that they are encoded and rules to encode and decode such characters.

URLs are strings of characters that follow the basic <scheme>:<scheme-specific-part> syntax. These characters are letters, digits, and special characters that can be represented in a number of ways. Most URL schemes use the US-ASCII character set to represent the sequence of characters in the URL, with 1 byte per character.

Other representations might use the hexadecimal value of the ASCII character, which implies the character must be encoded. The % sign signals that the next character in the sequence is encoded. Using a hexadecimal representation, the next two characters (hexadecimal digits) following the % represent the value of a single ASCII character.

The general guidelines for encoding characters are explained in detail in RFC 1738.

The following is the general guideline related to URL encoding:

"Bytes must be encoded if they have no corresponding graphic character within the US-ASCII coded character set, if the use of the corresponding character is unsafe, or if the corresponding character is reserved for some other interpretation within the particular URL scheme."

These guidelines apply to one of three possible issues:

- Characters are not available in the US-ASCII character set.
- Characters are unsafe to use.
- Characters are reserved.

For characters that are not available in the US-ASCII character set, the following guidelines apply:

- URLs are written only with the graphic printable characters of the US-ASCII coded character set.
- The bytes 80 to FF hexadecimal (128 to 255 decimal) are not used in US-ASCII.
- The bytes 00 to 1F (0 to 31 decimal, which are nonprintable characters) and 7F hexadecimal (127 decimal, a nonprintable character corresponding to the delete operation) represent control characters and must be encoded.

NOTE For more information on the ASCII character set, consult Appendix A, “Character Sets.”

For unsafe characters, the general rule is that all unsafe characters must be encoded. The following is a list of unsafe characters, as described in RFC 1738:

- **The space character (ASCII decimal value 20)**—It is unsafe because significant spaces might disappear and insignificant spaces might be introduced when a URL is transcribed, typeset, or put through a word-processing program.
- **The characters < and >**—They are unsafe because they are used as the delimiters around a URL.
- **The quote mark (“)**—It is unsafe because it is used to delimit URLs in some systems.
- **The character #**—It is unsafe because it is used on the web and in other systems to delimit a URL from a fragment/anchor identifier that might follow it.
- **The character %**—It is unsafe because it is used for encoding other characters.
- **The characters {, }, |, \, ^, ~, [,], and `**—These characters are unsafe because gateways and other transport agents are known to sometimes modify them.

For reserved characters, the guidelines specify that those characters which carry a special meaning must be encoded to preserve the semantics given in the context of the URL. The following is a list of common reserved characters:

- The characters ;, /, ?, :, @, =, and & are reserved.
- No other characters may be reserved within a scheme.

For reserved characters, the interpretation of a URL might not be the same when the character is encoded as when the character is unencoded. You can use only the following characters unencoded within a URL:

- Alphanumeric characters
- The special characters $, -, _, ., +, !, *, ‘, (,), and “
- Reserved characters used for their reserved purposes

This list does not imply that you cannot encode characters which are not required to be encoded. These characters, if not used for a reserved purpose, can be encoded within the scheme-specific part or a URL. The following section presents the specific syntax of some of the most common schemes currently available.

URL Syntax for Specific Schemes

This section presents the syntax of the URLs for the FTP, HTTP, Mailto, and Telnet schemes. An important bit of information to notice is that URLs are related not just to HTTP but also to all the other schemes mentioned in RFC 1630 and RFC 1738.

The generic URL syntax, often referred to as common Internet scheme syntax, follows:

//<user>:<password>@<host>:<port>/<url-path>

Note that the scheme-specific part varies depending on the specific protocol in use, yet the common scheme syntax is used for the scheme-specific data.

The URL for FTP is as follows:

ftp://<host>:<port>/<cwd1>/<cwd2>/.../<cwdN>/<name>;type=<typecode>

The URL for HTTP is as follows:

http://<host>:<port>/<path>?<searchpart>

This address would be equivalent to an anonymous FTP transfer, yet you should still be able to use username and password by following the common Internet scheme syntax. The example is as follows: You are trying to download a file using FTP from your browser from the rfc-editor.org site. Following the Internet scheme syntax, you would type

A: ftp://anonymous:anonymous@example.com@ftp.rfc-editor.org/in-notes/rfc2616.tx

You can also type

B: ftp://ftp.rfc-editor.org/in-notes/rfc2616.txt

Part A uses the FTP USER and PASS commands to pass on the username and password, and part B follows the **anonymous** convention in which the username is anonymous and the password is the e-mail address of the user. You can try this example on real sites, but be aware that the password is cleartext. Using the Internet scheme on a page is even more dangerous because you code the name and password in the page, and anyone who has access to the page can see the name and password.

The URL for Mailto is as follows:

mailto:<RFC 822-addr-spec>

The URL for Telnet is as follows:

telnet://<user>:<password>@<host>:<port>/

URNs

The concept of a URN, although not new, is fairly esoteric to many people because its adoption and use is not widespread. Although it seems it remains an experimental concept, it brings a number of advantages to the use of resources:

- Resources could be identified by their names instead of their locations, which allows a permanent relation between the name and the resource.
- The access mechanism is decoupled from the resource, which allows organizations to choose the most convenient access mechanism.

An example is the best way to explain these advantages.

Suppose you are trying to find more information on a book for which you know the title and ISBN but not the publisher. You have to search first for the publisher's website, and if there is one and you can find it, you then search the site, hoping to find the specific book. You certainly need to spend time researching the product, but it might not lead to finding the product-specific details. Publishers do have fairly robust online infrastructures, which means search engines could yield results fairly quickly, but that will not happen if are looking for products that are not mainstream and the search results give you hundreds of places to try finding more information.

If URNs were used and there was a namespace for the barcode, you could just use the barcode to access the resource information directly. Applying it to the resource type where the specific resource is permanently identified by a unique name makes the process of finding information about it simple and closer to how humans conduct business.

URNs exist to uniquely identify resources independent from their locations. RFC 1737, "Requirements for Uniform Resource Names," states that

". . .the purpose or function of a URN is to provide a globally unique, persistent identifier used for recognition, for access to characteristics of the resource or for access to the resource itself."

URNs support two kinds of requirements:

- The functional capabilities of URNs
- URN encoding in data streams and written communications

The functional capabilities requirements address primarily the global scope of an object so that

- It is uniquely identified regardless of the location.
- There is a permanent relation between the name and the object being named.
- The translation from URN to URL is possible and seamless.

The requirements for URN encoding focus on encoding the string of characters so that it meets some basic criteria. These criteria include consistency in the encoding whether it is text, e-mail, or another type so that humans can transcribe them regardless of the protocols used to transport them and so that computers can also parse URNs.

The URN syntax is used to encode characters so that protocols can transport them. The URN syntax is defined in RFC 2141 as follows:

<URN> ::= "urn:" <NID> ":" <NSS>

NID is the namespace identifier, and NSS is the namespace-specific string.

NOTE The leading urn: sequence is case-insensitive.

URN Namespace

The namespace definition for URNs, specified in RFC 3403, refers to a template to define the namespace and the mechanism for associating an identifier or NID.

NOTE The NIDs are registered with the Internet Assigned Number Authority (IANA). Consult http://www.iana.org/assignments/urn-namespaces.

Namespaces are divided into three categories:

- Experimental
- Informal
- Formal

The experimental namespaces are intended for internal or experimental uses and are not explicitly registered with the IANA.

The informal namespaces can be registered with the IANA and are required to maintain a well-managed URN space, as defined in RFC 3406. The difference between informal and formal namespaces is the handling of the NID. Informal namespaces are assigned an alphanumeric NID. Table 8-4 presents the most current list of registered informal namespaces.

Table 8-4 *Registered Informal Namespaces*

URN Namespaces	Value	Reference
urn-1	1	[urn-1]
urn-2	2	[urn-2]
urn-3	3	[urn-3]
urn-4	4	[urn-4]
urn-5	5	[urn-5]

You use formal namespaces when the publication of the NID and the namespace are beneficial to a subset of Internet users. Formal namespaces must be globally functional and available outside internal networks (not connected to the Internet). Table 8-5 presents the most current list of registered formal namespaces.

Table 8-5 *Registered Formal Namespaces*

URN Namespaces	Value	Reference
IETF	1	RFC 2648
PIN	2	RFC 3043
ISSN	3	RFC 3044
OID	4	RFC 3061
NEWSML	5	RFC 3085
OASIS	6	RFC 3121
XMLORG	7	RFC 3120
Publicid	8	RFC 3151
ISBN	9	RFC 3187
NBN	10	RFC 3188

URIs, URLs, and URNs

The terms URI and URL are often misunderstood, interchanged, and used out of context, but the term URN is not necessarily recognized. RFC 2396 discusses the different concepts in Section 1.2. As previously mentioned, URIs refer to resource identifiers that include both locators and names. URLs are a subset of URIs that identify resources through the network location, and URNs uniquely identify resources through names. Both URLs and URNs are subsets of URIs, and the key difference between them is the persistent nature of URNs (global and permanent name identification).

Section 2.3 of RFC 3305 also discusses the confusion around URIs, URLs, and URNs and references two distinct views and time spans during which the bulk of RFCs covering URIs were introduced. These two views, called *classical* and *contemporary*, are not consistent in the partitioning of URI space.

In the classical view, a resource identifier specifies either the location (URL) or the name (URN), which is independent from the location. A URI was either a URL or URN.

In the contemporary view, the distinction between the different types of resource identifications, URL or URN, is not as important. *Identification schemes* are generally URI schemes where each scheme can define a namespace. A namespace is not a URL scheme or a URI scheme. A URL does not refer to a subset of the URI space, yet it informally identifies a resource via the representation of its primary access mechanism.

A good example is "http." http is a URI scheme, and an http URI is a URL. The expression *URL scheme* is not frequently used, but it refers to subclasses of URI schemes that do not include URNs. Furthermore, a URN scheme "urn:" is just another URI scheme. Each URI scheme has a defined subspace called a namespace. A set of URNs in urn:isbn:<isbn number> forms a namespace.

Figure 8-5 presents a contemporary view, in contrast to Figure 8-1, which presents the classical view.

Figure 8-5 *URIs: Contemporary View*

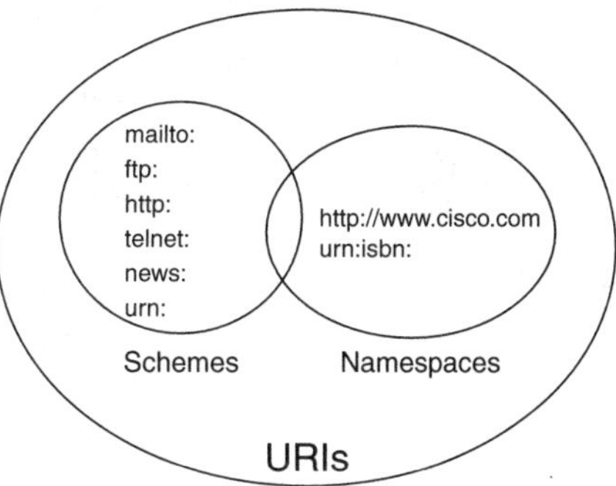

For more details, refer to RFC 3305.

MIME

MIME is the format for encoding and decoding nontext (non-ASCII) messages between peers over the Internet and on intranets. The applications that use MIME messages include e-mail, and it is similar to the format used between web browsers and web servers to exchange messages. The MIME format is quite flexible, thus allowing messages to contain text, images, audio, video, and specific application data while providing protection against the potential corruption of messages. Without a common format, peers exchanging information or messages might not understand each other, but most importantly, if the message contains more than text (images, video, and audio), a text-only format would not work. An e-mail, for example, might contain text and attachments. If the attachment is a document created with a specific application such as text editor, the receiving end must be able to understand and separate the text portion from the attachment before presenting it to the user.

The most current MIME specification contains five parts:

- RFC 2045 is part 1 and specifies the various headers used to describe the structure of MIME messages.
- RFC 2046 is part 2 and defines the general structure of the MIME media typing system and defines an initial set of media types.

- RFC 2047 is part 3 and describes extensions to RFC 822 to allow non–US-ASCII text data in Internet mail header fields.
- RFC 2048 is part 4 and specifies various IANA registration procedures for MIME-related facilities.
- RFC 2049 is part 5 and describes MIME conformance criteria as well as providing some illustrative examples of MIME message formats, acknowledgments, and the bibliography.

NOTE MIME was first described in RFC 1341, "Mechanisms for Specifying and Describing the Format of Internet Message Bodies," and RFC 1342, "Representation of Non-ASCII Text in Internet Message Headers." RFC 1521 and RFC 1522 obsoleted RFC 1341 and RFC 1342, respectively. RFC 1521 and RFC 1522 are part 1 and part 2 of the MIME specification. The MIME specification is continually being revised, and the latest revision obsoletes RFC 1521 and RFC 1522.

The MIME information presented in this section is a complement to the various topics that the chapter discusses, and its relevance comes from the fact that HTTP uses MIME-like messages and MIME specifications for object or entity definitions, such as the character sets and the media types. An *entity* is simply a finite piece of content (an object) and its characteristics. These characteristics that describe pieces of content are transferred through entity headers.

RFC 822 defined the format of Internet text messages, and its format has been adopted beyond the Internet and beyond mail messages. RFC 822 does not include formats for messages that include video, audio, images, or other languages. The MIME specification is intended to address the issues not covered by RFC 822 and some that are beyond RFC 822. The MIME specification tries to keep compatibility with RFC 822 messages, and it defines the following MIME-specific mechanisms:

- A MIME version header field, which allows the identification of MIME messages versus messages from previous specifications.
- A Content-Type header field used to specify the media type and subtype of the content in the message.
- A Content-Transfer-Encoding header field used to specify the encoding applied to the content in the message.
- Two new header fields, Content-ID and Content-Description, used to provide more description of the message content.
- Example 8-3 displays an e-mail transaction.

Example 8-3 *MIME Headers*

```
220 server.cisco.com ESMTP Sendmail 8.8.6 (PHNE_14041)/CISCO.SERVER.1.2 ready at
Tue, 24 Jun 2003 15:22:07 -0700 (PDT)
EHLO mylaptop.cisco.com
250-server.cisco.com Hello san-jose.cisco.com [10.21.97.194], pleased to meet you
250-EXPN
250-VERB
250-8BITMIME
250-SIZE 50000000
250-DSN
250-ONEX
250-ETRN
250-XUSR
250 HELP
RSET
250 Reset state
MAIL FROM:<source-user>
250 <source-user>... Sender ok
RCPT TO:<destination-user@cisco.com>
250 <destination-user@cisco.com>... Recipient ok
DATA
354 Enter mail, end with "." on a line by itself
Message-Id: <4.3.2.7.2.20030624152034.00b5ddd0@server.cisco.com>
X-Sender: source-user@server.cisco.com
X-Mailer: EMAIL APPLICATION Version x.x.x
Date: Tue, 24 Jun 2003 15:21:23 -0700
To: destination-user@cisco.com
From: My name <source-user>
Subject: Capturing a MIME encoded message...
Mime-Version: 1.0
Content-Type: text/plain; charset="us-ascii"; format=flowed

This is the body of the email...

Thanks,

mo

.
250 PAA20707 Message accepted for delivery
QUIT
221 server.cisco.com closing connection
```

Notice that the shaded lines display the MIME version and Content-Type headers followed by additional header information: Character-Set and Format. The protocol used for the transport of e-mail host-to-host is Simple Mail Transfer Protocol (SMTP).

MIME and HTTP Entities

HTTP since HTTP/1.0 uses MIME-like messages. Section 19.4 of RFC 2616, "Differences Between HTTP Entities and RFC 1045 Entities," provides details of the relationship between HTTP and MIME messages.

The differences in the entities between MIME and HTTP messages are the result of the difference in the features between HTTP and RFC 2045.

The HTTP features were selected for performance reasons, to provide greater flexibility in the use of new media types, to make comparisons easier, and to provide compatibility with earlier HTTP servers and clients. The following is a summary of the differences between HTTP and MIME messages:

- **MIME-Version**—HTTP is not considered a MIME-compliant protocol; however, HTTP/1.1 messages can contain a single MIME-Version field to indicate the version of MIME used in the message.
- **Conversion to canonical form**—RFC 1045 requires Internet mail to be converted to canonical form before being transferred. HTTP allows a few more forms for message transmission.
- **Conversion of date formats**—HTTP uses a restricted set to simplify date comparisons.
- **Content-Encoding**—MIME does not include a Content-Encoding like field.
- **Content-Transfer-Encoding**—It is not used by HTTP.
- **Transfer-Encoding**—It is used by HTTP but not used by MIME.
- **MHTML and line-length limitations**—MHTML has line-length limitations that HTTP does not have.

The following sections discuss the characters sets and media types that HTTP uses but are referenced from the MIME specifications.

Character Sets

Character sets are a series of tables used to convert a sequence of bytes into a sequence of characters. The definition of character sets allows various types of character encodings to be used as character sets. These character sets can be mapped from simple sets to more complex ones, and the MIME definition must include the mapping procedure. This procedure ensures compatibility and consistency when mapping between different sets, which could be required, for example, when translating to a different language.

Simple character sets where there is a one-to-one mapping between a byte and a character include the ISO-10646, US-ASCII, and ISO-8859-1 character sets.

NOTE HTTP uses but is not limited to ISO-8859-1. SMTP uses US-ASCII.

Character sets are also referred to as *coded character sets*. For more information on the semantics of character sets, consult RFC 2978, "IANA Charset Registration Procedures."

Media Types

Media types were originally defined in RFC 1590, "Media Type Registration Procedure," which was obsoleted by the MIME RFCs. The MIME RFCs include five parts from RFC 2045 through RFC 2049. MIME part 2, RFC 2046 in particular, deals with MIME media types.

NOTE For the list of the most current media types and subtypes, consult the IANA pages at http://www.iana.org/assignments/media-types/.

A media type is defined as a name and description of the type of content that could be carried in a message. Media types are organized in two main groups, as defined in RFC 2046:

- Discrete
  - Text
  - Image
  - Audio
  - Video
  - Application
- Composite
  - Multipart
  - Message

Text refers to textual information. The text type has a few subtypes:

- **Plain**—Where no formatting characters or commands are used and nonspecial software is required to read it
- **Enriched**—Text that uses special characters and commands that are placed by some special software that is not required to read the text
- **Other subtypes**—Include word-processor formats where special software is required to enhance the text and to read it back

Image refers to data in the form of images. Images typically require special software or hardware to view the information. There are only two subtypes defined in the RFC 2046 specification: JPEG and GIF. Other common image types, some of which are registered and some are not, are BMP (bitmap), PNG (portable network graphic images), PCX (Paintbrush Image), and so on.

Audio refers to data in the form of audio. Audio data typically requires special devices to listen to the data. Audio originally had a single subtype, "basic." Basic audio is a single audio channel using 8 bits at a sample rate of 8000 Hz. Currently, the list of subtypes includes more complex audio format such as G729 and MPEG.

Video refers to data in the form of video, which is considered moving images. MPEG, JPEG, Digital Video (DV), and QuickTime are some of the registered subtypes.

Application refers to some other data type that is understood by an application. The data could be a raw stream of binary information. Two subtypes were defined by the specification: octect-stream and PostScript. Octect-stream deals with arbitrary binary data, and PostScript refers to the PostScript program. Other application types are PDF, visio, ms-powerpoint and msword.

Multipart refers to multiple parts of discrete data types for a single data entity. RFC 2046 defined four multipart subtypes, and a few others have been added:

- **Mixed**—Generic mix of different media types.
- **Alternative**—Same data represented in multiple formats.
- **Parallel**—Multiple parts intended to be viewed simultaneously.
- **Digest**—Multiple parts in which each part has a default type message (subtype RFC 822).

Message refers to an encapsulated message that might contain other objects. The subtypes include the following:

- **RFC 822**—Encapsulated content in an RFC 822 message
- **partial**—A partial RFC 822 message for fragmented transmissions of entities that are too large to transmit as a single unit
- **external-body**—Specifies large entities by reference to an external data source instead of including the actual body of data

HTTP Overview

The HTTP specification and history are rather rich, but before discussing such topics, it is important to describe the impact of HTTP on the Internet and intranets.

TCP is the dominant protocol on the Internet and intranets. HTTP makes up the majority of Internet traffic and is a significant portion of the traffic on private networks. HTTP is also the protocol behind the WWW, and its adoption has extended to private networks, where companies are building their client/server infrastructures based on web technology. You can read a technical description of the use and applications of HTTP in Chapter 2, "Server Architecture Overview," which presents the technical details behind the servers that support HTTP, and Chapter 3, which provides details on application environments that use HTTP.

HTTP was first available in Version 0.9 (HTTP/0.9) as a simple protocol for raw data transfer across the Internet. The first documented version in RFC 1945 for HTTP/1.0, an informational RFC, improved the protocol by allowing messages to be in the format of MIME-like messages, containing meta information about the data transferred and modifiers on the request/response semantics. HTTP/1.0, however, did not address the effects of hierarchical proxies, caching, the need for persistent connections, and virtual hosts. Some incomplete implementations of HTTP/1.0 forced the use of HTTP versions to control the communication capabilities of the hosts attempting to communicate.

The original definition, based on RFC 1945, for HTTP is

> ". . .an application-level protocol with the lightness and speed necessary for distributed, collaborative, hypermedia information systems. It is a generic, stateless, object-oriented protocol which can be used for many tasks, such as name servers and distributed object management systems, through extension of its request methods (commands). A feature of HTTP is the typing of data representation, allowing systems to be built independently of the data being transferred."

A new version of HTTP, HTTP/1.1, was released in RFC 2068, which was further revised by RFC 2616, a standards-track RFC. HTTP/1.1 specifies more stringent requirements than HTTP/1.0 to ensure a consistent implementation of its features. A more pragmatic definition of HTTP, introduced by RFC 2068 and maintained in RFC 2616, describes it as "an application-level protocol for distributed, collaborative, hypermedia information systems."

HTTP has been used in the WWW since 1990 (as part of the WWW global information initiative). HTTP has become the protocol of communication between web browsers and the servers. The use of HTTP has gone beyond the Internet, and it is heavily used on intranets and extranets as well. HTTP is so prevalent as a web communication protocol that most software vendors are developing their applications to utilize web technology, as pointed out in Chapter 1, "Overview of Data Centers."

HTTP Operation

HTTP is a request/response protocol that uses TCP (port 80) as the transport layer.

NOTE TCP port 80 for HTTP is the default port in HTTP server implementations, but it is changeable to fit specific needs.

TIP For the Apache HTTP server, the location where most parameters are controlled on the HTTP daemon is the httpd.conf file in /etc/httpd/conf. The following lines display the two parameters related to the port number associated with HTTP:

```
# Listen: Allows you to bind Apache to specific IP addresses and/or
# ports, in addition to the default. See also the <VirtualHost>
# directive.
#
#Listen 3000
#Listen 12.34.56.78:80
#Listen 80
# Port: The port to which the standalone server listens. For
# ports < 1023, you will need httpd to be run as root initially.
#
Port 80
```

As a request/response protocol, an HTTP client (HTTP browser) sends a request and expects a response. The request uses a method (the purpose of the communication exchange); a version; and a MIME-like message with the specifics of the request, client capabilities information, and potentially other content. The server sends a response back to the client that includes a status line, which shows the protocol version and a return code that indicates success or failure, and a MIME-like message with server information, some entity information, and potentially other entity-body content. Detailed information on the communication exchange between HTTP client/server is presented in the section, "HTTP Connection Overview."

The packet format used by HTTP is unlike other protocols' packet formats. The HTTP header format does not have a fixed size and does not use fixed-size header fields. Typically, a field is terminated by a carriage return and line feed (CRLF), except when the continuation line begins with a space or horizontal tab.

NOTE The entity-body is the exception to the rule that all fields end with CRLF. See RFC 2616, Appendix 19.3, for more details.

An important part of the HTTP transaction is the exchange of HTTP version information between client and server.

HTTP Version

The HTTP version number is specified using a <major>.<minor> numbering scheme to indicate the HTTP version, as described in RFC 2616. The purpose of the version number in an HTTP transaction (the version number is only exchanged once per HTTP transaction between the client and the server) is to indicate the format of the message that HTTP is using and to announce the capability of conducting further HTTP communication. The <major> number is changed (incremented) when the format of a message within the protocol is changed, and the <minor> number is changed to indicate there are new features that do not change the message parsing algorithm but rather indicate the capability of the sender.

The HTTP specification also indicates the conditional compliance of the sending device when utilizing HTTP/1.1. Conditonal compliance indicates that the implementation of the sender is a subset of the full capabilities of a specific HTTP version. The sender, according to the specification, should be able to accept messages and ignore those that are not understood. Furthermore, senders of messages that might not be compatible with HTTP 1.0 should use HTTP/1.1. Consider the HTTP version number as indicating, "This is the maximum version of HTTP that I am capable of understanding," instead of "This is the version of HTTP that I am using," yet keep in mind that conditional compliance is possible.

NOTE RFC 2145 further explains the HTTP version to clarify the details that were ambiguous in previous specifications. RFC 2145 does not attempt to change the intended meaning of the HTTP version numbers in the specifications.

RFC 2145 indicates that the major version can indicate the interpretation of header fields, whereas the minor version does not. The minor version signals the capabilities of the sender.

A clear implication for the rules stated in RFC 2145 is that an HTTP/1.1 message received by an HTTP/1.0 receiver must be interpreted in a way that it remains valid for HTTP/1.0 after all undefined headers are removed. To further clarify this point, and as indicated in RFC 2145, the interpretation of the HTTP message header does not change between minor versions of the same major version, and the receiving end must ignore message headers that are not understood.

The most debated subject around HTTP version is which version of HTTP to send on an HTTP message. RFC 2145 states the following:

- HTTP clients should send a request with a version equal to the highest version supported.
- HTTP clients must not send a version higher than the one supported by the server, if known.
- HTTP servers should respond with a version number not higher than what it supports and less than or equal to the one received in the request.
- HTTP servers may send a lower version than supported if the client is known or suspected to incorrectly implement the HTTP specification.

NOTE The version referenced in the previous bullets is applicable to the <minor> number in an HTTP implementation.

The following section discusses more details on the HTTP message format.

HTTP Message Format

The HTTP message format is defined slightly differently for different versions of HTTP. In general, an HTTP message is either a request or a response, as shown before, and either one has a message header and a message body. The message header has a general header followed by a request of response header, as appropriate, and an entity header (if an entity is present) followed by the message body. The message body contains the entity body.

The following are the format specs for different versions of HTTP.

For HTTP/0.9, the message format is

HTTP-message = Simple-Request | Simple-Response

For HTTP/1.0, the message format is

HTTP-message = Full-Request | Full-Response

For HTTP/1.1, the message format is

HTTP-message = Request | Response

Although there is not much difference between the formats, the version number exchanged during the request and response process determines how to treat the information transferred between client and server.

For HTTP/0.9, the definition for a generic message, which is inclusive of both request or response messages, is the following:

Simple-Request = "GET" SP Request-URI CRLF
Simple-Response = [Entity-Body]

NOTE Simple-Request and Simple-Response prevent the use of any header information and are limited to a single request method (GET).

For HTTP/1.0, the definition for a generic message is

Full-Request = Request-Line * (General-Header | Request-Header | Entity-Header) CRLF [Entity-Body]
Full-Response = Status-Line * (General-Header | Response-Header | Entity-Header) CRLF [Entity-Body]

For HTTP/1.1, the definition for a generic message is

generic-message = start-line * (message-header CRLF) CRLF [message-body]
start-line = Request-Line | Status-Line

NOTE * means repetition, which applied to a request format implies zero or more headers.

An entity, as previously described, is content. This content or object could be the subject of the request for the information included in a response. Note that in a response, the entity or content can be a group of objects, which might include HTML text and images on a single web page. The following examples show the HTTP request and its response from a connection to http://www.apache.org.

Example 8-4 shows the connection request.

Example 8-4 *HTTP Request*

```
GET / HTTP/1.0
Accept: */*
Accept-Language: en-us
User-Agent: Mozilla/4.0 (compatible; MSIE 5.5; Windows NT 5.0)
Host: www.apache.org
Connection: Keep-Alive
Pragma: no-cache
```

The GET, Accept, Accept-Language, and User-Agent lines are Request-header fields, whereas the Connection and Pragma are General-Header fields.

Example 8-5 shows the connection response.

Example 8-5 *HTTP Response*

```
HTTP/1.1 200 OK
Date: Mon, 11 Nov 2002 05:33:54 GMT
Server: Apache/2.0.43 (Unix)
Cache-Control: max-age=86400
Expires: Tue, 12 Nov 2002 05:33:54 GMT
Accept-Ranges: bytes
Content-Length: 7773
Keep-Alive: timeout=5, max=100
Connection: Keep-Alive
Content-Type: text/html
```

The Date, Cache-Control, and Connection lines are general-header fields; the HTTP (status line), Server, and Accept-Ranges lines are response-header fields; and the Expires, Content-Length, and Content-Type lines are entity-header fields describing the content to come.

NOTE Notice that the different fields related to the general, response, and entity headers are not in any particular order. The same is true for the fields in the request message, yet the HTTP method is typically the first field in the request.

The Keep-Alive field is optional and should be used only when the Connection General-Header field is sent.

The message header is the generic referral to four types of headers: the general header, the request header, the response header, and the entity header. All these headers follow the same generic format, defined in RFC 822, in which each header has a field name followed by a colon (:) and the field value. The message body contains the entity body associated with the request or the response.

The following sections present the details of the message header and body.

Message Header

As described earlier, the HTTP header includes a general header, either a request or a response header and an entity header. The generic syntax of an HTTP header (each type of header has its own specific format) is

message-header = field-name : [field-value]

There is no particular order in which these fields should be organized, yet the specification recommends (a good practice) sending general header fields first, followed by request or response header fields, and ending with the entity header fields.

Message Body

The message body, if present, carries the entity body associated with the request or the response. The syntax for the message body is

message-body = entity-body | <entity-body encoded as per Transfer-Encoding>

The message body presence in request and response headers is determined by a different set of rules. The message body on a request could be determined by the presence of the Content-Length or Transfer-Encoding header fields in the message header of the request. The message body on a response depends on the request method and the response status code as follows:

- All HEAD requests must not include a message body.
- All 1xx (informational), 204 (no content), and 304 (not modified) responses must not include a message body.
- All other responses do include a message body, although it can be zero length.

HTTP Connection Overview

After presenting the format of HTTP messages, it is important to analyze a real HTTP transaction. The transaction is based on the same traffic capture presented in Chapter 7, "IP, TCP, and UDP," to illustrate a TCP connection.

As previously mentioned, HTTP uses TCP as the transport layer protocol, which implies that before the HTTP client and an HTTP server can exchange HTTP messages, the TCP connection must be established. Figure 8-6 displays a generic HTTP connection to illustrate the point.

Figure 8-6 *HTTP Connection*

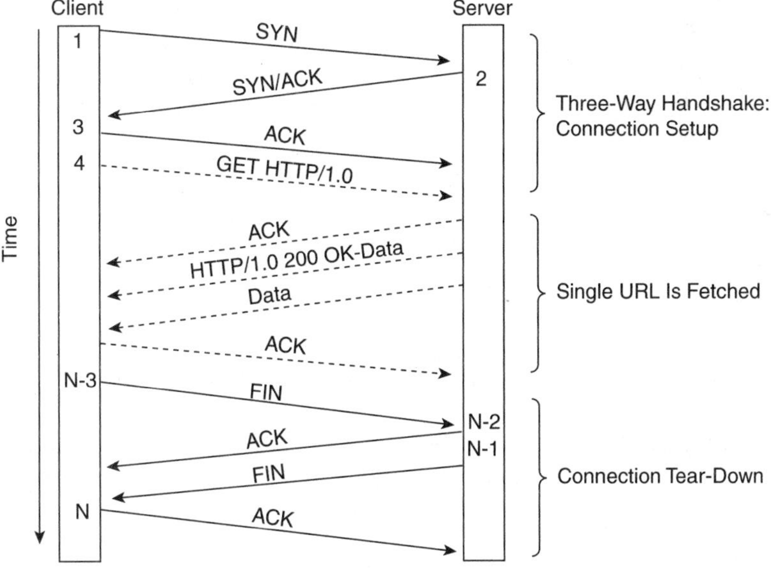

The TCP three-way handshake (SYN, SYN/ACK, and ACK) must occur first before the HTTP transaction can begin. The first HTTP-related message is an HTTP request that establishes the intent of the request through a request method. The server returns an HTTP response indicating to the client the status of the request through the status code followed by the requested data (entity), if any. During the transaction, the flow control and error correction are handled by TCP. Once the HTTP transaction is finished, the TCP connection closes.

Figure 8-7 presents an HTTP connection request (in a TCP packet), which corresponds to frame 14 of the captured transaction used in the previous chapter.

Figure 8-7 *HTTP Connection Request*

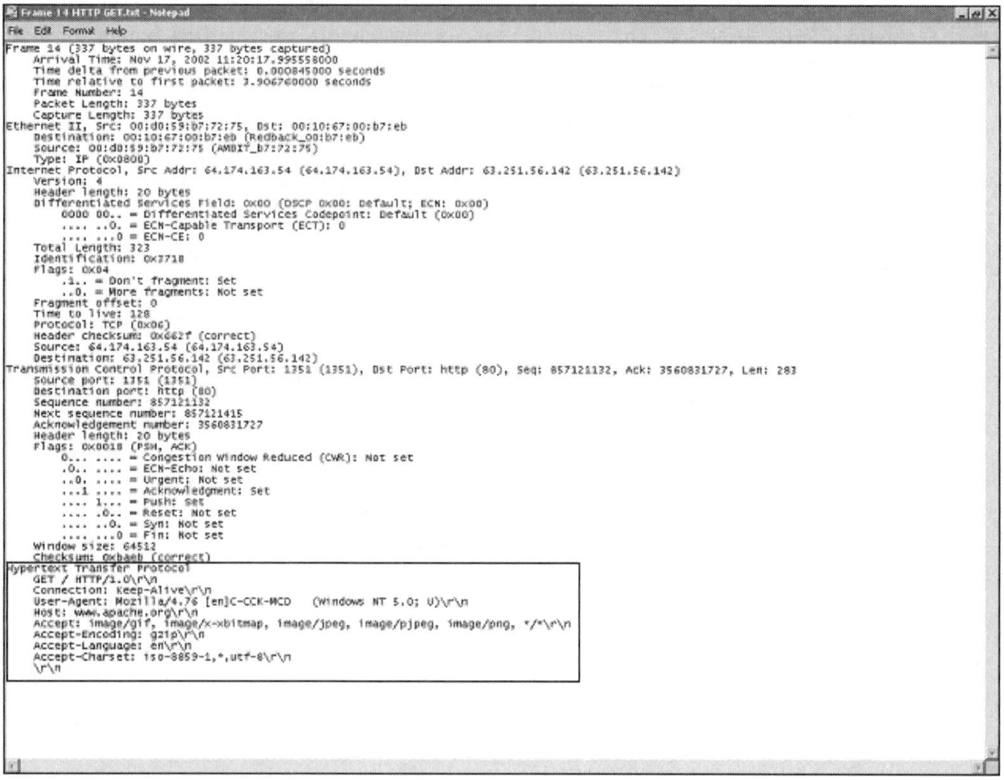

```
Frame 14 HTTP GET.txt - Notepad
File Edit Format Help
Frame 14 (337 bytes on wire, 337 bytes captured)
    Arrival Time: Nov 17, 2002 11:20:17.995558000
    Time delta from previous packet: 0.000845000 seconds
    Time relative to first packet: 3.906760000 seconds
    Frame Number: 14
    Packet Length: 337 bytes
    Capture Length: 337 bytes
Ethernet II, Src: 00:d0:59:b7:72:75, Dst: 00:10:67:00:b7:eb
    Destination: 00:10:67:00:b7:eb (Redback_00:b7:eb)
    Source: 00:d0:59:b7:72:75 (AMBIT_b7:72:75)
    Type: IP (0x0800)
Internet Protocol, Src Addr: 64.174.163.54 (64.174.163.54), Dst Addr: 63.251.56.142 (63.251.56.142)
    Version: 4
    Header length: 20 bytes
    Differentiated Services Field: 0x00 (DSCP 0x00: Default; ECN: 0x00)
        0000 00.. = Differentiated Services Codepoint: Default (0x00)
        .... ..0. = ECN-Capable Transport (ECT): 0
        .... ...0 = ECN-CE: 0
    Total Length: 323
    Identification: 0x3718
    Flags: 0x04
        .1.. = Don't fragment: Set
        ..0. = More fragments: Not set
    Fragment offset: 0
    Time to live: 128
    Protocol: TCP (0x06)
    Header checksum: 0x662f (correct)
    Source: 64.174.163.54 (64.174.163.54)
    Destination: 63.251.56.142 (63.251.56.142)
Transmission Control Protocol, Src Port: 1351 (1351), Dst Port: http (80), Seq: 857121132, Ack: 3560831727, Len: 283
    Source port: 1351 (1351)
    Destination port: http (80)
    Sequence number: 857121132
    Next sequence number: 857121415
    Acknowledgement number: 3560831727
    Header length: 20 bytes
    Flags: 0x0018 (PSH, ACK)
        0... .... = Congestion Window Reduced (CWR): Not set
        .0.. .... = ECN-Echo: Not set
        ..0. .... = Urgent: Not set
        ...1 .... = Acknowledgment: Set
        .... 1... = Push: Set
        .... .0.. = Reset: Not set
        .... ..0. = Syn: Not set
        .... ...0 = Fin: Not set
    Window size: 64512
    Checksum: 0xbaeb (correct)
Hypertext Transfer Protocol
    GET / HTTP/1.0\r\n
    Connection: Keep-Alive\r\n
    User-Agent: Mozilla/4.76 [en]C-CCK-MCD   (Windows NT 5.0; U)\r\n
    Host: www.apache.org\r\n
    Accept: image/gif, image/x-xbitmap, image/jpeg, image/pjpeg, image/png, */*\r\n
    Accept-Encoding: gzip\r\n
    Accept-Language: en\r\n
    Accept-Charset: iso-8859-1,*,utf-8\r\n
    \r\n
```

The HTTP portion of the frame contains the HTTP headers, which include the following information:

```
GET / HTTP/1.0\r\n
Connection: Keep-Alive\r\n
User-Agent: Mozilla/4.76 [en]C-CCK-MCD   (Windows NT 5.0; U)\r\n
Host: www.apache.org\r\n
Accept: image/gif, image/x-xbitmap, image/jpeg, image/pjpeg, image/png,*/*\r\n
Accept-Encoding: gzip\r\n
Accept-Language: en\r\n
Accept-Charset: iso-8859-1,*,utf-8\r\n
\r\n
```

Notice that all the fields, with the exception of the Connection field, are request header fields. Connection is a general header field. The connection request indicates the that client is attempting to retrieve the full contents (GET request) of the / page at the specified URL (http://www.apache.org) and is issuing an HTTP 1.0 request.

Figure 8-8 presents the HTTP response to the HTTP connection request shown in Figure 8-7.

Figure 8-8 *HTTP Response to Connection Request*

```
full http connection to apache.org + FIN.txt - Notepad
File Edit Format Help
Frame 15 (1414 bytes on wire, 1414 bytes captured)
    Arrival Time: Nov 17, 2002 11:20:18.056133000
    Time delta from previous packet: 0.060575000 seconds
    Time relative to first packet: 3.967335000 seconds
    Frame Number: 15
    Packet Length: 1414 bytes
    Capture Length: 1414 bytes
Ethernet II, Src: 00:10:67:00:b7:eb, Dst: 00:d0:59:b7:72:75
    Destination: 00:d0:59:b7:72:75 (AMBIT_b7:72:75)
    Source: 00:10:67:00:b7:eb (Redback_00:b7:eb)
    Type: IP (0x0800)
Internet Protocol, Src Addr: 63.251.56.142 (63.251.56.142), Dst Addr: 64.174.163.54 (64.174.163.54)
    Version: 4
    Header length: 20 bytes
    Differentiated Services Field: 0x00 (DSCP 0x00: Default; ECN: 0x00)
        0000 00.. = Differentiated Services Codepoint: Default (0x00)
        .... ..0. = ECN-Capable Transport (ECT): 0
        .... ...0 = ECN-CE: 0
    Total Length: 1400
    Identification: 0xcace
    Flags: 0x04
        .1.. = Don't fragment: Set
        ..0. = More fragments: Not set
    Fragment offset: 0
    Time to live: 56
    Protocol: TCP (0x06)
    Header checksum: 0x1644 (correct)
    Source: 63.251.56.142 (63.251.56.142)
    Destination: 64.174.163.54 (64.174.163.54)
Transmission Control Protocol, Src Port: http (80), Dst Port: 1351 (1351), Seq: 3560831727, Ack: 857121415, Len: 1360
    Source port: http (80)
    Destination port: 1351 (1351)
    Sequence number: 3560831727
    Next sequence number: 3560833087
    Acknowledgement number: 857121415
    Header length: 20 bytes
    Flags: 0x0010 (ACK)
        0... .... = Congestion Window Reduced (CWR): Not set
        .0.. .... = ECN-Echo: Not set
        ..0. .... = Urgent: Not set
        ...1 .... = Acknowledgment: Set
        .... 0... = Push: Not set
        .... .0.. = Reset: Not set
        .... ..0. = Syn: Not set
        .... ...0 = Fin: Not set
    Window size: 58480
    Checksum: 0x912a (correct)
Hypertext Transfer Protocol
    HTTP/1.1 200 OK\r\n
    Date: Sun, 17 Nov 2002 19:20:13 GMT\r\n
    Server: Apache/2.0.43 (Unix)\r\n
    Cache-Control: max-age=86400\r\n
    Expires: Mon, 18 Nov 2002 19:20:13 GMT\r\n
    Accept-Ranges: bytes\r\n
    Content-Length: 7773\r\n
    Keep-Alive: timeout=5, max=100\r\n
    Connection: Keep-Alive\r\n
    Content-Type: text/html\r\n
    \r\n
    Data (1079 bytes)
```

Frame 15 in Figure 8-8 corresponds to the response to the HTTP connection request presented in Figure 8-6. The HTTP response contains the following information:

```
HTTP/1.1 200 OK\r\n
Date: Sun, 17 Nov 2002 19:20:13 GMT\r\n
Server: Apache/2.0.43 (Unix)\r\n
Cache-Control: max-age=86400\r\n
Expires: Mon, 18 Nov 2002 19:20:13 GMT\r\n
Accept-Ranges: bytes\r\n
Content-Length: 7773\r\n
Keep-Alive: timeout=5, max=100\r\n
Connection: Keep-Alive\r\n
Content-Type: text/html\r\n
\r\n
```

The first line of the response indicates the HTTP version number and the status code that tells the client whether the transaction is successful or, if not, what the nature of the problems is. The server response uses HTTP/1.1 instead of the client's version HTTP/1.0. This difference, however, does not mean that the server and the client are using different HTTP versions. Refer to the section, "HTTP Version" for more information on the HTTP version numbers exchanged by the client and server.

The response message includes the general header fields and the response header fields. The response header fields are "server" and "accept-ranges," which are intermixed with the general header fields.

HTTP/1.0 and HTTP/1.1 might have different behavior during HTTP connections. HTTP/1.1 introduced two concepts: persistent connections and pipelining.

Persistent Connections and Pipelining

Persistent HTTP connections allow a TCP connection to remain open for more than one HTTP request. The behavior prior to persistent connections allowed only a single HTTP request, as depicted in Figure 8-6. In contrast, an HTTP/1.1 persistent connection allows multiple HTTP requests and their responses as part of the same TCP connection. This behavior reduces unnecessary overhead on the network and server because a single TCP connection serves many HTTP requests instead of each TCP connection serving one TCP request. Figure 8-9 presents the contrast between an HTTP/1.0 and an HTTP/1.1 persistent connection.

Figure 8-9 *Persistent Connections*

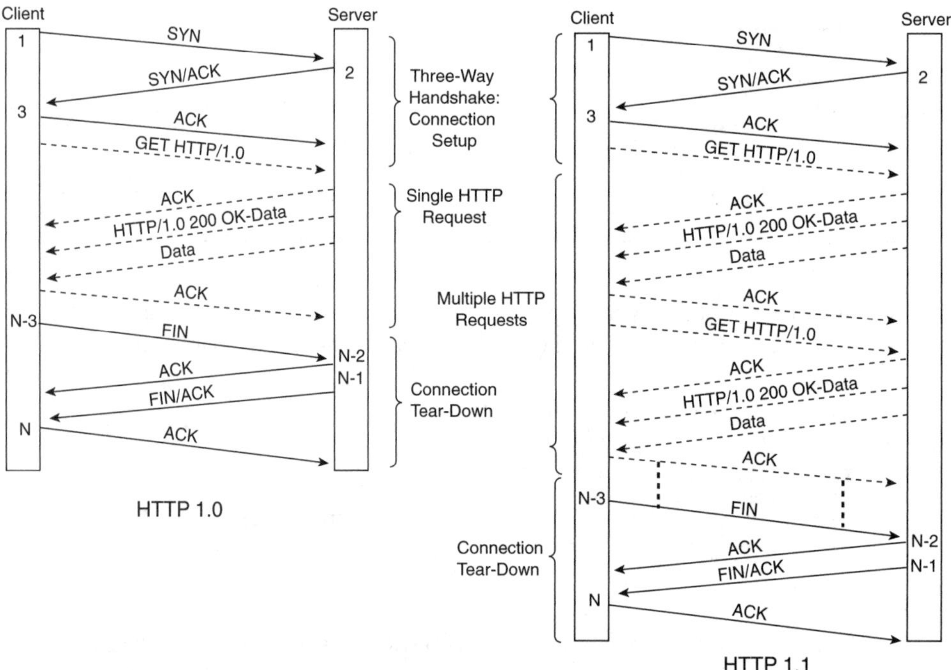

As depicted in Figure 8-9, an HTTP/1.1 connection requires a single TCP connection for multiple HTTP requests, whereas HTTP/1.0 requires a TCP connection per HTTP request. Note that the HTTP requests in the HTTP/1.1 connection are sequential. *Pipelining* allows multiple HTTP requests to be generated without waiting for each response, which implies multiple HTTP requests can be processed concurrently instead of sequentially. Figure 8-10 presents an HTTP/1.1 connection using pipelining.

Figure 8-10 *Connection Pipelining*

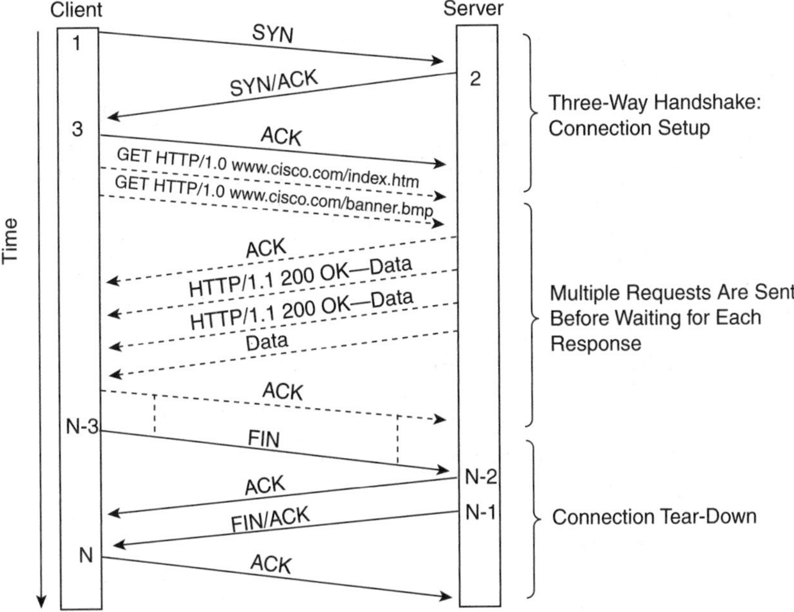

As shown in Figure 8-10, multiple HTTP requests are sent over single TCP connection, and the subsequent requests do not have to wait for the previous ones to complete.

Persistent connections offer a few advantages over nonpersistent connections:

- Less traffic is processed by the network (routers, switches, server load balancers, caches, firewalls, proxies, etc.), the clients, and the servers, which decreases CPU utilization and memory consumption.
- Multiple HTTP requests and responses can be supported on a single TCP connection.
- Clients can make multiple requests without waiting for each response using pipelining.
- Network traffic is reduced by reducing the TCP connection overhead. See the section "HTTP Performance" for more information.

- End-to-end delay on pipelined requests is reduced by avoiding further TCP handshakes, their associated round-trip delays, and the sequential nature of HTTP requests along with their associated round-trip delays.

The persistent-connection behavior is the default in HTTP/1.1. HTTP/1.0 also supports persistent connections, but it is not the default behavior. Persistent connections are controlled by the Connection header, which can have various values: Keepalive, Open, and Close.

Pipelined connections inherit the behavior and characteristics of persistent connections. Additionally, servers are expected to respond to the multiple requests in the same order they were received.

NOTE To date, there are few pipeline implementations, and most load balancers are not currently "pipelining"–aware, which would cause the connection to break. Persistent connections, on the other hand, are fairly common, and load balancers are capable of handling them. Refer to Chapter 16, "Load-Balancing Modes and Predictors," for more information.

HTTP Performance

This section discusses HTTP performance from two viewpoints:

- By presenting the advantages of using HTTP/1.1 over HTTP/1.0
- By using HTTP compression between the client and the server

Performance of HTTP/1.1 Versus HTTP/1.0

The obvious advantages of using HTTP/1.1 over HTTP/1.0 are based on persistent connections and pipelining.

Persistent connections provide a direct savings on the number of packets and bytes that the intermediate devices and the client and server have to process. These savings translate to a lower byte and packet count when downloading the same page with HTTP/1.1 versus HTTP/1.0 and lower CPU utilization on the client and server resulting from a lower number of TCP connections that must be established.

The W3C presented the results of a research project on the effects of persistent connections, pipelining, and link compression on the client and server implementations. The following is a summary of the report:

- The client used was libwww robot.
- The servers used were W3C Jigsaw and Apache.
- Servers supported HTTP/1.0 and HTTP/1.1 with persistent connections, HTTP/1.1 with pipelined requests, and HTTP/1.1 with pipelined requests and deflate data compression.

The results show the following:

- HTTP/1.1 pipelined implementations outperformed HTTP/1.0 in all tests.
- Savings in the packets transmitted were at least a factor of 2 and in certain cases a factor of 10.

The test website was a single page with HTML text totaling 42 KB and 42 GIF images raging from 70 KB to 40 KB totaling 125 KB.

For a test that is equivalent to a browser's first visit to a site, all objects are retrieved because there are none in the cache. This test is equivalent to 43 GET requests, 1 for the page and 42 for the objects (42 objects referenced by the page).

Three network environments were tested:

1. High bandwidth, low latency over 10 Mbps (Ethernet)
2. High bandwidth, high latency over a WAN link
3. Low bandwidth, high latency over a 28.8 Kbps dial-up connection

The round-trip time (RTT) ranges from less than 1 millisecond (ms) on 1, 90 ms on 2, and 150 ms on 3.

Table 8-6 and Table 8-7 present some of the findings. The first table contains the results of the high-bandwidth, low-latency tests using the Apache server, and the second table contains the number for the high-bandwidth, high-latency tests, again on the Apache server.

Table 8-6 *High-Bandwidth, Low-Latency Test Results*

	HTTP/1.0	HTTP/1.1 Persistent	HTTP/1.1 Pipelined	HTTP/1.1 Pipelined with Compression
Packets	489.4	244.2	175.8	139.8
Bytes	215,536	189,023	189,607	156,834
Seconds	.72	.81	.49	.41
% of overhead bytes	8.3	4.9	3.6	3.4

Table 8-7 *High-Bandwidth, High-Latency Test Results*

	HTTP/1.0	HTTP/1.1 Persistent	HTTP/1.1 Pipelined	HTTP/1.1 Pipelined with Compression
Packets	559.6	309.4	221.4	182.0
Bytes	248,655.2	191,436.0	191,180.6	159,170.0
Seconds	4.09	6.14	2.23	2.11
% of overhead bytes	8.3	6.1	4.4	4.4

Table 8-6 shows HTTP/1.1 using persistent connections produces a little less than half the number of packets of HTTP/1.0 and overall produces less bytes and takes less time to transmit the web page. Pipelined requests and pipelined requests with compression also show incremental improvement in all the test results, which indicates that pipelined requests and compression are advantageous.

Table 8-7 shows slightly different numbers resulting from the differences in the transport network used. The numbers also indicate that HTTP/1.1 persistent connections, pipelined requests, and pipelined requests with compression are incrementally advantageous when compared with HTTP/1.0.

NOTE The research project was conducted in 1997 using the browsers available at that time. Although the information is dated and the client behavior has probably changed, these changes are not likely to dramatically alter the experienced behavior that proved HTTP/1.1 is a better-behaved protocol than HTTP/1.0.

For more details, consult the report at http://www.w3.org/Protocols/HTTP/Performance/Pipeline.

HTTP Compression

HTTP compression addresses the performance issues of HTTP transactions by reducing the size or the resources transferred between clients and servers. The initial benefits are realized on both the end-to-end delay perceived by the user, resulting from the lower number of transferred bytes, and the amount of bandwidth and network resources required.

Both HTTP/1.0 and HTTP/1.1 support compression, but the HTTP/1.0 specification did not provide guidance on how the client and the server could negotiate the type of compression to use. The use of compression on HTTP/1.0 was not widespread. The support of compression on HTTP/1.0 is possible through the Content-Encoding and Accept-Encoding fields, which are discussed in the sections, "Entity Header" and "Response Header." Content-Encoding was the mechanism used by the server to signal to the client the transformation applied on the resource so that the client could decode the message to obtain the original resource.

The HTTP/1.1 specification, on the other hand, provides a better definition for the Accept-Coding header and expand the Content-Encoding values. HTTP/1.1 also added Transfer-Coding values that could be used to code the resource. A significant difference between Content-Encoding and Transfer-Encoding is that typically, Content-Encoding is a property of the entity, whereas Transfer-Encoding is a property of the message. The encoded entity already exists at the server when you use Content-Encoding, instead of being coded on the server as the communication between client and server takes places when you use Transfer-Encoding.

The use of Content-Encoding headers implies an end-to-end operation (done at the server and client), and the use of Transfer–Encoding implies a hop-by-hop operation, where the coding could be applied to the message hop-by-hop. Another consideration is whether the content is static or dynamic. If the content is static, a coded version of it could be made before the request arrives, so the server has the option of compressing before or soon after a request is received. However, if the content is dynamically generated, the encoding must take place when the request arrives. The compression that happens when the requests are received is more likely to have an effect on the performance of the server.

A research report on HTTP compression at http://www.cse.lehigh.edu/techreports/2002/LU-CSE-02-002.pdf shows that the average website can achieve 27 percent in byte reductions. Currently, most current browsers and the two dominant web servers support HTTP compression, although in slightly different ways.

Internet Explorer versions 5.01, 5.5, and 6.0 support HTTP compression, and the Internet Information Server (IIS) does too, even though it is not enabled by default.

NOTE For more information on how Internet Explorer and IIS handle HTTP compression and how you can enable it, consult http://www.microsoft.com/technet/prodtechnol/iis/iis5/maintain/featusability/httpcomp.asp.

Netscape 6.2 and 7.0 also supports HTTP compression under HTTP/1.1 by supporting content encoding. You enable under **Preferences > HTTP Networking**.

Apache does not offer native support for HTTP compression, but some third-party modules work with Apache to provide HTTP compression functionality.

The current content encoding values are

gzip (GNU zip compression [the gzip program]): RFC 1952
compress (UNIX file compression [the compress program]): RFC 2616
deflate (deflate compression with zlib format): RFC 1950 and RFC 1951

NOTE The content values currently defined appear at http://www.iana.org/assignments/http-parameters.

HTTP General Header

The general header is used in the communication of general information that is applicable to both requests and return messages but that does not apply to the transferred entity. General header fields apply only to the message being transmitted.

The general header includes the following fields described in more detail in the sections that follow:

- Cache-Control
- Connection
- Date
- Pragma
- Transfer-Encoding

NOTE The following sections do not include all the fields defined in the specification, only the most commonly used. The rest of them are discussed in Appendix B, "HTTP Header Fields."

Cache-Control General Header Field

The Cache-Control field specifies the behavior that caches must follow along the request/response path. The caching behavior, controlled by cache directives under the Cache-Control fields, is changed from the default caching configuration to the intended one.

NOTE HTTP/1.0 caches might not support Cache-Control directives because the HTTP/1.0 specification supported only the Date and Pragma fields.

There a number of directives associated with the requests and responses. Table 8-8 presents the request and response directives specified in RFC 2616. (Note that there is no implied relation between the entries on each column, other than being on the list of directives.)

Following are the request directives:

no-cache
no-store
max-age = delta-seconds
max-stale = delta-seconds
min-fresh = delta-seconds

no-transform
only-if-cached
cache-extension

Following are the response directives:

public
private = "field name"
no-cache = "field name"
no-store
no-transform
must-revalidate
proxy-revalidate
max-age = delta-seconds
s-maxage = delta-seconds
cache-extension

Table 8-8 *RFC 2616 Request/Response Directives*

Request Directives	Response Directives
no-cache	public
no-store	private = "field name"
max-age = delta-seconds	no-cache = "field name"
max-stale = delta-seconds	no-store
min-fresh = delta-seconds	no-transform
no-transform	must-revalidate
only-if-cached	proxy-revalidate
cache-extension	max-age = delta-seconds
	s-maxage = delta-seconds
	cache-extension

For more information on the directives, consult RFC 2616.

Connection General Header Field

The Connection field allows the sender to specify certain option preferences for a particular connection. The specification indicates that these options must not be communicated by proxies over further connections.

The HTTP/1.1 specification defines "close" as a connection option so that the sender can signal that the connection will be closed after completion of the response (using the

Connection: close fields). This specification indicates that the connection is not persistent, which means it is not expected that the TCP connection will remain open after the current HTTP request/response process is complete.

A new field alternative lets you make a connection persistent. It is not part of the HTTP/1.1 specification, but it is widely used by web applications. The field is Connection = Keep-Alive, and it signals that the TCP connection is expected to remain open after the current request/response is complete.

Date General Header Field

The Date field represents the date and time at which the HTTP message was originated. The format of the date, described in RFC 1123, is

Date: HTTP-date

The HTTP-date looks like Mon, 1 Jan 2003 10:37:31 GMT.

Origin servers must include the Date field in all responses, yet there are a few exceptions:

- If the response status code is 100 or 101, the server may include the Date header field in the response.
- If the response status code represents a server error (server status codes are in the 500 range), and it is inconvenient or impossible to generate a valid date, then it is not required.
- If the server does not have a clock that can provide a reasonable approximation of the current time, its responses must not include a Date header field.

If an HTTP message does not have a Date header field, the receiver must assign one.

Clients have the option of sending or not sending the Date header field, yet a client should send a message including the Date header if there is an entity body in the message. If the client, however, does not have a clock, the message must not include the Date header field.

Pragma General Header Field

The Pragma field communicates implementation-specific caching directives to the recipients along the request/response path. Pragma directives, unlike Cache-Control directives, represent an optional behavior, but if it is implemented, it must be consistent with the implementation.

An important Pragma field value is no-cache. The no-cache directive tells the cache to forward the response from the server to the client, even if there is a copy in the cache.

NOTE The no-cache directive is equivalent to the no-cache request-directive of Cache-Control, defined for backward compatibility with HTTP/1.0 implementations.

Clients are supposed to include both the Cache-Control and Pragma no-cache field to servers not known to support HTTP/1.1, and servers must treat Pragma no-cache as Cache-Control no-cache.

Transfer-Encoding General Header Field

The Transfer-Encoding field communicates the type of transformation that has been applied to the message body. The transformation is a security measure for the safe transport of the message through the network between the sender and receiver.

An example of Transfer-Encoding is the chunked type, which modifies the body of the message to transfer it in a series of chunks. Each chunk has its own length, followed by the trailer with the entity-header fields.

When multiple encodings are used, the transfer-encodings must be listed in the order in which they were applied.

NOTE Transfer-Encoding was not part of the HTTP/1.0 specification, so HTTP/1.0 applications do not understand the Transfer-Encoding header.

NOTE The Simple-Request and Simple-Response messages prevent the use of any header information and are limited to a single request method (GET).

Request Header

The *request header* is used by the client to communicate the type of request being made. The request header begins with a method, followed by the request URI and the protocol version, and ends with CRLF. The different portions of the header are separated by spaces. CR and LF are not allowed until the final CRLF.

TIP As part of the HTTP/1.1 specification, the Host header field must be present in all HTTP/1.1 requests. The host specifies the Internet host and port number of the resource being requested, as obtained from the original URL. The URL is specified either by the user or by a referring resource (HTTP URL).

The host allows the origin server or gateway to identify the correct internal URL when multiple host names exist for a single IP address.

Request Header Methods

The HTTP methods define the type of operation that is to take place between client and server. The HTTP/1.0 specification defines only three methods: GET, HEAD, and POST. The HTTP/1.1 specification adds a few more methods to those previously defined by HTTP/1.0 and also adds a few more semantics to the previous definitions of the three methods (GET, HEAD, and POST).

According to RFC 2616, the methods GET and HEAD must be supported by the general-purpose HTTP server, but all other methods are optional. If any of the other methods are implemented, their implementation must be according to the specifications in RFC 2616 Section 9 ("Method Definition").

NOTE The explanations introduced in this section refer to the HTTP/1.1 specification.

The methods defined in the HTTP/1.1 specification are OPTIONS, GET, HEAD, POST, PUT, DELETE, TRACE, and CONNECT.

TIP The methods are case-sensitive, and they are all currently defined in uppercase. This consideration is important even though the end user does not have direct control over whether the methods are specified in lowercase or uppercase.

The following sections introduce the details of each method.

OPTIONS Request Header Method

The OPTIONS method indicates a request for information about the communication options available on the request/response chain identified by the URI in the request. As specified in RFC 2616, this method allows the client to determine the options and requirements associated with a resource, or the capabilities of a server, without implying a resource action or initiating a resource retrieval.

If the URI is an *, the intention is to obtain information about the server, not a resource in the server; otherwise, if the URI is a specific resource, the options apply only to that resource.

GET Request Header Method

The GET method indicates a request to retrieve the information associated with the URI in the request. If the URI refers to a process, the retrieval is the output of the process.

The intend of a GET changes to a "conditional GET" if the request includes an If-Modified-Since, If-Unmodified-Since, If-Match, If-None-Match, or If-Range header field. The conditional GET means it retrieves only if the conditions specified in the additional header fields are met. This conditional behavior is useful for caches to refresh their content without issuing multiple requests and has the added benefit of reducing network traffic.

The GET method could become a "partial GET" if the request message uses the Range header field. The partial GET retrieves only a portion of the requested entity. This GET is particularly useful during file transfer when initial attempts are not successfully completed because it allows the client and server to resume the transfer where they left off.

HEAD Request Header Method

The HEAD method indicates a request to retrieve the meta information contained in the HTTP headers only. This method is exactly like the GET method but without the retrieval of the message body, just the header information.

The intend of a HEAD is to retrieve the information about a URI without having to retrieve the URI resources. This method is useful to test the existence and access of resources and likely changes to them without incurring the overhead of retrieving it.

POST Request Header Method

The POST method indicates to the server that the entity associated with the URI in the request should be accepted. This method allows the client to annotate existing resources, to post messages, to submit information as part of a process, and to extend a database through append operations.

The server has the option of accepting the information transmitted through the post and determines what operation to perform based in the URI.

A good example of the use of POST is when trying to update links on a web page you use as your portal to other areas. Example 8-6 shows a POST request when updating a link on a web page. Typically, a new window opens and the user types the information he or she wants to update. This information is fed to a script, index.cgi in this case, which along with other parameters is sent to the web server. The result is a page with the updated link information. This popular service is offered by portal sites to let their users customize their portal page.

Example 8-6 *POST Request*

```
POST /cgi-bin/cec/ql/index.cgi HTTP/1.0
Accept: image/gif, image/x-xbitmap, image/jpeg, image/pjpeg, application/vnd.ms-
excel, application/vnd.ms-powerpoint, application/msword, */*
Referer: http://www.example.com/cgi-bin/cec/ql/index.cgi
Accept-Language: en-us
Content-Type: application/x-www-form-urlencoded
User-Agent: Mozilla/4.0 (compatible; MSIE 5.5; Windows NT 5.0)
Host: www.example.com
Content-Length: 1577
Connection: Keep-Alive
Pragma: no-cache
Cookie: CP_GUTC=171.69.115.75.18502953227; Trans_ID=2@$2@Q@T.#2T2@$..OLMMZOO$ENI1;
cec_user_id=myid; quicklinks=4746%3CSolutions%
Authorization: Basic bWFycmVnb2M6IXNlY3NteGE=
url=http%3A%2F%2Fwww.example.com%2Fent%2Fese%7C%3D%7Chttp%3A%2F%2F
```

TIP Some of the information in Example 8-6 was purposely changed to hide and protect the information used in the change of the link. Because the POST method could be used to send sensitive information (which might be in cleartext), it is recommended that the communication channel be encrypted.

There are multiple possible responses to a POST request because not all requests result in resource identifiable by a URI. If the resource cannot be identified, the 200 or 204 codes could be used; if a resource is created in the server, a 201 is used. For more information, consult Section 5.9 of RFC 2616.

PUT Request Header Method

The PUT method indicates to the server that the entity associated with the URI in the request should be stored under the URI. If the URI refers to an existing resource, the enclosed entity is considered a new version; however, if it does not refer to an existing resource, the server could create the URI as long as the user agent is capable of defining such resource.

As with POST, PUT allows the user to update some information on a page. With POST, the information is passed on to a site for further analyses to be handled by the URI in the request (like posting a message on a online bulleting board). When using PUT, the information is sent to update the URI in the request. Although the use of PUT gives the user more control and the server less control, it is less commonly utilized than POST for these kinds of transactions.

As with the POST method, the server informs the client about status of the PUT request through a status code. The code could be a 201 for a new resource, 200 or 204 for an existing resource, or a 501 if it is not understood or implemented.

Although the POST and PUT methods appear to be similar, there is a fundamental difference between them. The URI in a POST request identifies the resource that handles the enclosed entity. The URI in a PUT request identifies the entity enclosed with the request as the URI that is the target of the request.

DELETE Request Header Method

The DELETE method indicates to the server that the resource identified by the URI in the request should be deleted. This method allows the client to delete the resource specified by the URI. The client cannot be certain that the request is going to be executed because the server has the option on what to do even if it receives a successful status code in the response.

TRACE Request Header Method

The TRACE method allows the client to determine the intermediate proxies in the request/response path from the client to the origin server. It sends the request with a Max-Forwards value of 0 and receives a response from the first proxy or gateway indicating a successful reception of the message. This method tracks the request chain in conjunction with the Via header.

CONNECT Request Header Method

This method is currently reserved in the HTTP/1.1 specification for use with proxies that can dynamically provide tunneling capabilities.

Request URI

The request URI is a URI that identifies the resource to which the request is to be applied. For more information on URIs, refer to the section "URIs, URLs, and URNs" earlier in this chapter. The syntax for the request URI is

Request-URI = "*" | absoluteURI | abs_path | authority

The intend of the request determines which request URI option to use. The actual options are used as follows:

- *—Indicates the request applies to the server instead of a particular resource. You use it only when the method does not necessarily apply to a resource (such as the OPTIONS method).
- **absoluteURI**—Used (and mandatory) when the request is made to a proxy, which should either forward the request to the origin server or return from its cache.
- **abs_path**—Used to signal the absolute path of the URI.
- **authority**—Only used with the connect method to signal the network location of the URI.

TIP Proxies must not change the absolute path when forwarding the request (except when replacing a NULL path with /).

According to the HTTP/1.1 specification, a client should issue the following request to retrieve a resource from the server:

GET /en/US/netsol/edc.pdf HTTP/1.1Host: www.cisco.com

Notice that the path must not be empty and that the host field is mandatory.

Request Header Fields

The request header includes the following fields, which are described in greater detail in the sections that follow:

- Accept
- Accept-Charset
- Accept-Encoding
- Authorization
- Host
- If-Modified-Since
- Max-Forwards
- Range
- Referer
- User-Agent

NOTE The following sections do not include all the fields defined in the HTTP specification, only the most commonly used. The rest are discussed in Appendix B.

Accept Request Header Field

The Accept field specifies the media types that are acceptable to the client in the response from the server. Each media type can have multiple parameters specified. Figure 8-7 displays frame number 4 of the traffic capture used in Chapter 7. Example 8-7 displays just the HTTP portion of the TCP packet.

Example 8-7 *HTTP Headers*

```
GET / HTTP/1.0\r\n
    Connection: Keep-Alive\r\n
    User-Agent: Mozilla/4.76 [en]C-CCK-MCD   (Windows NT 5.0; U)\r\n
    Host: www.apache.org\r\n
    Accept: image/gif, image/x-xbitmap, image/jpeg, image/pjpeg, image/png, */*\r\n
    Accept-Encoding: gzip\r\n
    Accept-Language: en\r\n
    Accept-Charset: iso-8859-1,*,utf-8\r\n
    \r\n
```

Notice that the Accept field (highlighted) includes multiple image types that include gif, x-xbitmap, jpeg, pjpeg, and png followed by ***/*\r\n**. The character sequence ***/*** implies all media types, followed by **\r\n**, which is how the traffic capture software interprets and displays a CRLF.

Accept-Charset Request Header Field

The Accept-Charset field indicates which character sets are accepted by the client on a response from the server. The character set definition used by HTTP is the same used in the MIME specification. Refer to the section "Character Sets" earlier in this chapter.

In Example 8-7, the client indicates that it is able to accept the following character sets:

iso-8859-1,*,utf-8\r\n

The * character matches every character set, including ISO-8859-1. If * is not present, only the character sets explicitly defined are accepted, except for the ISO-8859-1.

Accept-Encoding Request Header Field

The Accept-Encoding field specifies the content coding that is acceptable in the response to the client in a similar manner to how Accept specifies the media types. The content codings are values that indicate a particular encoding transformation which has been applied to an entity.

Content codings are typically used for document compression. The HTTP/1.1 specification mentions gzip, compress, deflate, and identity as encoding formats.

Example 8-7 displays the following encoding formats in the Accept-Encoding field:

gzip\r\n

The * character in an Accept-Encoding field matches any available content coding that is not explicitly listed in the header field.

Consult RFC 2978 for more details on coded character sets and character encoding schemes.

Authorization Request Header Field

The Authorization field is used by the client, specifically the user agent, to indicate to the server that it wants to authenticate itself. The authentication can occur after a 401 response is received from the server, prompting the client to authenticate. The authentication mechanisms are documented in RFC 2617, "HTTP Authentication: Basic and Digest Access Authentication." See the section, "HTTP Authentication" later in this chapter for more information.

Host Request Header Field

The Host field specifies the name and port number of the host that contains the resource identified by the URI in the request. The host allows the server or proxy to clearly identify the resource being requested when a server uses internally replicated URLs with multiple names and a single IP address.

Figure 8-7 presents the host value of the GET request in the traffic capture.

Host: www.apache.org\r\n

When the port number is not present, the default value is assumed to be port 80.

NOTE Clients are expected to include the host value on all HTTP/1.1 requests. Servers are expected to respond with a 400 (bad request) when an HTTP/1.1 request is received without the host value.

If-Modified-Since Request Header Field

The If-Modified-Since field is used in conjunction with a method to make it conditional, as long as the entity has not been modified since the time specified in the request. If the entity has not been modified, the server does not send the entity, but rather issues a 304 (not modified) status code in the response.

This field is useful for efficiently controlling information that might be cacheable to avoid unnecessary transactions and overhead. Only the resources that have been modified are retrieved. A cache can send a conditional GET request to be fulfilled only if the resource has been modified since the last time a copy of the content was cached.

Max-Forwards Request Header Field

The Max-Forwards field is used in conjunction with the TRACE and OPTIONS methods to limit the number of proxies or gateways that are allowed to forward the request along the request/response path.

The proxy or gateway that received the request is expected to decrement the Max-Forward value by 1 if the value is not 0. If the value is 0, the proxy or gateway does not forward the request any further and responds as the final recipient.

Range Request Header Field

The Range field is used in conjunction with byte-range operations to specify a sequence of bytes of an entity body that the client wants to retrieve. If the byte range requested cannot be fulfilled, the server returns a 416 (requested range not satisfiable) status code in the response; otherwise, the server returns a 206 (partial content), including the bytes of the entity body specified in the request.

NOTE HTTP/1.1 devices are expected to support byte-range operations.

Referer Request Header Field

The client uses the Referer field to specify the address of the resource from which the URI in the request was obtained. It allows the server to know the locations from which the referrals originate. You could use this information for logging, maintenance, and so on. A common practice for online portals is to include the portal URI in the Referer when the client has been redirected or is offered a hyperlink to a different URI. This practice allows the destination site to track the source of the referrals to the site. Example 8-8 shows the referrer field in use in the highlighted line.

Example 8-8 *Referer Field*

```
GET / HTTP/1.0
Accept: image/gif, image/x-xbitmap, image/jpeg, image/pjpeg, application/vnd.ms-
excel, application/vnd.ms-powerpoint, application/msword, */*
Referer: http://search.portal.com/bin/search?cs=nw&p=interesting%20Information
Accept-Language: en-us
User-Agent: Mozilla/4.0 (compatible; MSIE 5.5; Windows NT 5.0)
Connection: Keep-Alive
Host: www.interesting-information.org
```

In the example, the user clicked on a hyperlink on the portal site and was redirected to http://www.interesting-information.org.

NOTE The portal name and destination site were purposely changed.

User-Agent Request Header Field

The User-Agent field indicates the identity of the user agent that originated the request. The user agent is the browser type and version. As shown in Example 8-8, the User-Agent is Mozilla/4.0 (compatible; MSIE 5.5; Windows NT 5.0), which is Microsoft's Internet Explorer Version 5.5.

Response Header

The response header is part of the response message as a result of a client request. The response header begins with the status line followed by the appropriate headers (general, response, or entity) and a CRLF, and ends with the message body (if present). As with the request header, the different portions of the header are separated by spaces.

The status line signals the HTTP version, the status code, and its associated textual explanation (referred to as the *status reason phrase*).

HTTP Status Codes

Each Status-Code is a three-digit result code that signals the status of the request attempt. The reason phrase is intended to give a short textual description of the Status-Code.

TIP Because the Status-Code and phrase are standardized, you could use them to automate actions resulting from the nature of the Status-Code. This process is useful in environments that have server load balancers to take the appropriate action depending on the Status-Code. Chapter 17, "Server Health Management," describes the details behind how load balancers utilize this information to monitor and diagnose the state of the servers in a server farm.

According to RFC 2616, HTTP applications do not need to understand the status code, but they must understand the class of the status code to treat the response as equivalent to the class.

The status codes are organized in five different classes, all starting with a different first digit from 1 through 5. The last two digits are specific to a particular status code. The status code classes are (as defined in RFC 2616)

- 1xx: Informational
- 2xx: Success
- 3xx: Redirection
- 4xx: Client error
- 5xx: Server error

1*xx* Informational Status Codes

The status codes in this class indicate a provision response and signal that the request was received and the process continues. HTTP/1.0 clients do not understand 1xx status codes, so servers are expected not to send a 1*xx* response to an HTTP/1.0 client.

Table 8-9 lists the informational status codes.

Table 8-9 *Informational Status Codes*

Status Code	Status Text	Details
100	Continue	It indicates that the request has been received and the client should continue with the request.
101	Switching protocols	It indicates that the server understands and it is willing to comply with the client's request for a change in the application protocol used in the connection.

2*xx* Success Status Codes

The status codes in this class signal that the action was successfully received, understood, and accepted. Table 8-10 lists the success status codes.

Table 8-10 *Success Status Codes*

Status Code	Status Text	Details
200	OK	It indicates that the request has succeeded. The information returned in the response depends on the method used: GET: Entity referenced in the request HEAD: Entity header referenced in the request POST: Entity containing the result of the action TRACE: Entity containing the request message as received by the server
201	Created	The request was fulfilled and resulted in a new resource being created. The resource is referenced by the URI in the response.
202	Accepted	The request has been accepted for processing, but it has not been completed. There is no guarantee that the processing will be successful and there is no mechanism to notify its completion status.
203	Non-authoritative information	The meta information returned originated not at the origin server but from a local or other party copy.
204	No content	The server has fulfilled the request, and it does not need to return an entity body.
205	Reset content	The server has fulfilled the request, and the user agent should reset the view of document that triggered the request.
206	Partial content	The server has fulfilled the partial GET request for the resource.

3*xx* Redirection Status Codes

The status codes in this class signal that further action must be taken to complete the request. Table 8-11 lists the redirection status codes.

Table 8-11 *Redirection Status Codes*

Status Code	Status Text	Details
300	Multiple choices	The resource referenced in the request corresponds to any one of a set of representations, each with a specific location, and other information so that the user can select the preferred one and redirect the request to that location. Except for HEAD requests, the response should contain the list of resources, their characteristics, and their locations.
301	Moved permanently	The resource referenced in the request has been assigned a new permanent URI, and future references to this resource should use one of the returned URIs.
302	Found	The resource referenced in the request resides temporarily under the URI in the response. Future requests should be made to the URI in the initial request.
303	See other	The resource referenced in the request is found under the URI in the response, and it should be retrieved with a GET method.
304	Not modified	The client's request included a conditional GET in the request and access is allowed, but the document has not been modified.
305	Use proxy	The resource referenced in the request must be accessed through the proxy specified in the location field of the response (proxy URI). The client is expected to generate a new request through the proxy. Only origin servers can negate this type of status code.
307	Temporary redirect	The resource referenced in the request resides temporarily under a different URI. The client should initiate a new request to the URI in the response, but any future attempts should be made to the URI in the original request.

4*xx* Client Error Status Codes

The status codes in this class signal that the request contains bad syntax or cannot be fulfilled. Table 8-12 lists the client error status codes.

Table 8-12 *Client Error Status Codes*

Status Code	Status Text	Details
400	Bad request	The client's request is not understood by the server due to bad syntax.
401	Unauthorized	The client's request requires user authentication. The response includes a WWW-Authenticate field (see "Response Header Fields") with the challenge applicable to the resource.
402	Payment required	Reserved for future use.
403	Forbidden	The server understood the request, and it is refusing to fulfill it. The authentication process will not help, and the request should not be repeated.
404	Not found	The server has not found the resource referenced by the URI in the request.
405	Method not allowed	The method specified in the client's request is not allowed for the resource identified by the URI in the request. The respond includes an Allow header with the list of allowed methods.
406	Not acceptable	The resource identified by the URI in the request generates response entities which have content characteristics that are not acceptable based on the Accept header in the request.
407	Proxy authentication required	The client's request requires user authentication, but they must authenticate first with the proxy. The proxy response includes a WWW-Authenticate field (see "Response Header Fields") with the challenge applicable to the resource.
408	Request time-out	The client did not send a request within the time the server had allocated to wait.
409	Conflict	The request could not complete due to a conflict with the current state of the resource.

Table 8-12 *Client Error Status Codes (Continued)*

Status Code	Status Text	Details
410	Gone	The resource referenced by the URI in the request is no longer available in the server, and no other location is known for it. This condition is considered permanent.
411	Length required	The server refuses to accept the request without a defined content length in Content-Length field.
412	Precondition failed	The precondition given in one or more of the request header fields has resulted in false when tested by the server.
413	Request entity too large	The server is refusing to process the client's request because the entity in the request is larger than the server is willing or able to process. The server might close the connection to prevent the client from continuing the request.
414	Request-URI too long	The server refuses to process the request because the URI in the request is longer than the server is willing to interpret.
415	Unsupported media type	The server refuses to process the request because the entity of the request is in a format not supported by the requested resource in the requested method.
416	Requested range not satisfiable	Servers respond with this code when a request includes the Range field but the range values do not overlap with those of the resource in the request, and the request was not conditional. (The If-Range field was not included.)
417	Expectation failed	The expectation in an Expect field could not be met by the server, or it the recipient is a proxy, it has evidence that the request could not be met by the next-hop server.

5*xx* Server Error Status Codes

The status codes in this class signal that the server is not able to fulfill an apparently valid request. Table 8-13 lists the server error status codes.

Table 8-13 *Server Error Status Codes*

Status Code	Status Text	Details
500	Internal server error	The server detected an unexpected condition that prevented it from fulfilling the request.
501	Not implemented	The server does not support the functionality required to fulfill the request.
502	Ban gateway	The server, while acting as a gateway or proxy, received an invalid response from the upstream server it contacted while attempting to fulfill the request.
503	Service unavailable	The server is currently unable to handle the request because of overload or maintenance. This condition is considered temporary.
504	Gateway time-out	The server, while acting as a gateway or proxy, did not receive a response from the upstream server within the expected time.
505	HTTP version not supported	The server does not support or refuses to support the HTTP version specified in the request.

Response Header Fields

The response header fields allow the server to communicate additional information about the server and access to the resource (identified by the URI in the request) in the response that cannot be placed in the status line. The response header fields are as follows:

- **Accept-Ranges**—The Accept-Ranges field allows the server to indicate its acceptance of the range requests for a resource.
- **Age**—The Age field tells the client about the server's estimation of the amount of time since the response was generated. You can compare the value of the Age field with some "freshness" quantity that would help determine whether the response is still fresh.
- **ETag**—The ETag field indicates the current value of the entity tag (a value associated with a specific version of the content identified by the URL in the request) for the requested representation of the resource. You can use the ETag to determine whether a particular version of the content should be retrieved. For example, the ETag for a particular version could be remembered by the client or cache to be included in a subsequent request for the specific URL associated with the ETag. If the new ETag for

the same URL has changed, the content is downloaded; otherwise, it is not. This check is possible because the server would have changed the ETag value if a new version of the content associated with the URL is available.

NOTE A single resource can have multiple representations (copies) at any one time. The official term for a particular representation of the resource is *variant*.

Etags, or entity tags, identify a particular version of an entity.

- **Location**—The server uses the Location field to redirect the client to a location, other than the one referenced by the URI in the request, to complete the request.
- **Proxy-Authenticate**—The Proxy-Authenticate field is included in a 407 response, and it contains a challenge indicating the authentication scheme and the parameters that are applicable to the proxy for the URI in the request.

  The Proxy-Authenticate field applies only to the current connection and is not passed to downstream clients, unlike the WWW-Authenticate header mentioned later in this section.
- **Retry-After**—The Retry-After field is used with the 503 (service unavailable) status code to indicate how long the service related to the resource referenced by the URI is going to be unavailable. The Retry-After field also is used with the 3xx codes to indicate to the client to retry the redirection after the retry timer has expired.
- **Server**—The Server field carries information about the software running in the origin server that handles the request, typically an HTTP server. Figure 8-5 displays the frame that contains the response to the GET request in the traffic capture to the http://www.apache.org transaction.

  The following line from Figure 8-7 displays the Server field contents:

  Server: Apache/2.0.43 (Unix)\r\n

  The Server field indicates that the HTTP server is Apache Version 2.0.43 running on UNIX.
- **Vary**—The Vary field contains a value that indicates a set of fields which determine whether the cache is allowed to use the response to reply without revalidation. HTTP/1.1 servers are expected to include the Vary field with cacheable responses so that the caches can interpret future requests on the cached resources and negotiate on them.
- **WWW-Authenticate**—The WWW-Authenticate field is included in a 401 (unauthorized) response, and it indicates a challenge (or more than one) that includes the authentication scheme and parameters related to the URI in the request. See the section "HTTP Authentication" for more information.

HTTP Authentication

HTTP authentication is the mechanism used by a user agent to authenticate itself in an HTTP request. The indication of the wish for authentication is the result of the Authorization field in the request header. The actual process of authentication was first documented in RFC 1069, which has been obsoleted by RFC 2617.

NOTE The HTTP/1.0 specification for basic authentication is considered insecure because the username and password traverse the network in cleartext.

RFC 2617 relies on the HTTP/1.1 specification for the basic and digest access authentication schemes.

HTTP uses a simple challenge-response authentication mechanism in which the server challenges a request and asks for user authentication information. To challenge the authorization of a user agent, origin servers use 401 status codes, whereas proxies use 407.

Basic Authentication

The basic authentication mechanism is based on the client authenticating by using a user ID and password for what is called the *realm*. The realm is basically the scope of influence that the user is authenticated to and is typically identified by the absolute URI. The realm is used per authentication scheme to protect other resources that might not be in the scope of what the user is authenticated for.

The server serves the request only after a successful validation of the user ID and password for the context identified by the URI in the request. Once the server, or proxy, receives the request, it responds with a challenge in which the realm for the particular URI is specified. The client then sends the user ID and password separated by a colon (:).

Message Digest Authentication

Message Digest authentication is a more secure alternative to the basic authentication scheme, specified in HTTP/1.0. Message Digest avoids the most serious flaws of the basic authentication scheme, yet it is not intended to be the security mechanism for the WWW. This and other mechanisms are discussed in Chapter 15, "Security Protocols and Technology."

The Message Digest scheme is still based on the challenge/response mechanism. The server or proxy challenges the client request with a nonce value and the client responds with a checksum of the username, password, nonce value, HTTP method, and the requested URI. The checksum by default is based on the MD5 algorithm, which is the only one described in the specification (RFC 2617). This process avoids sending the password in cleartext. For more information on the process of authentication using Message Digest, refer to RFC 2617.

Because the client can use one of multiple authentication schemes, it is recommended that the strongest authentication scheme be used.

Entity Header

The entity header contains the fields used to describe the entity body or the resource referenced in the request. Some of the information in the entity header is optional and some is required. The entity header fields are Allow, Content Encoding, Content Language, Content-Length, Content-Location, Content-MD5, Content-Range, Content-Type, Expires, and Last-Modified and an extension header (identified by "extension-header"), which permits the definition of additional entity header fields without changes to the protocol. Details about the entity header fields follow:

- **Allow**—The Allow field informs the client about the valid methods associated with the resource. The Allow field lists the methods supported by the resource identified by the URI in the request. The field does not prevent the client from trying other methods, yet the client is expected to follow the field values.
- **Content-Encoding**—The Content-Encoding field is used as a modifier of the media type, indicating that additional content codings have been applied to the entity body. This information help the client select the correct decoding mechanisms for the right media type. One of the main applications of Content-Encoding is compression of content without the loss of the media-type identity.
- **Content-Length**—The Content-Length field indicates the size of the entity body in bytes. If the request uses a HEAD instead of a GET method, the valued return corresponds to the entity body that would be sent if the request had been a GET.
- **Content-Location**—The Content-Location field provides the resource location of the enclosed entity when the location was different from the one identified by the URI in the request.
- **Content-MD5**—The Content-MD5 field carries an MD5 digest of the entity body, which serves to provide an end-to-end message integrity check for the entity body.
- **Content-Range**—The Content-Range field carries a partial entity body that indicates the location in the full entity body where the partial entity body fits.
- **Content-Type**—The Content-Type field indicates the media type of the entity body in the message or, when a HEAD is used in the request, the media type of the entity body that would have been sent if the method was a GET.

- **Expires**—The Expires field provides the date and time after which the response is considered stale. The expiration time does not imply that the content has changed but rather that the cached copy of it is stale.
- **Last-Modified**—The Last-Modified field indicates the date and time when the origin server believes the variant (an instant of the resource) was last modified.

Summary

Understanding URIs and URLs, MIME, and the details behind HTTP is important because they are the foundation for the mechanisms to identify, locate, code, and exchange information over the Internet and on intranets.

URIs and URLs make the naming, location, and identification of resources possible and global, which is fundamental to the World Wide Web and the applications that use the web infrastructure.

MIME is also a fundamental framework for the exchange of messages, given the wide variety of applications and either end of the communication exchange. The definition of standard rules for coding and the specification of a global character set allow consistency in the communication exchange.

HTTP and its vast communication structure not only allow but ease the adoption of web technology by providing rules for the actual communication process.

All these protocols make up a substantial portion of the fundamental structure for web communications, and understanding their specifications and the context in which they are likely to appear allows you to better understand the relation between the application world and the network infrastructure.

This chapter covers the following topics:

- Overview of the use of SSL for web-based applications
- SSL operations, with focus on the SSL negotiation phase
- The importance of SSL session resumption to alleviate the performance impact of SSL on the servers
- SSL performance consideration in server farm environments with load balancing
- Public key infrastructure (PKI) aspects of SSL
- The SSL ciphers

CHAPTER 9

SSL and TLS

Secure Sockets Layer (SSL) is a fundamental protocol in today's Data Centers. SSL is used in Internet Data Centers mainly for e-commerce and financial applications. It is used in intranet Data Centers to protect confidential information from being transported unencrypted over the enterprise network.

Besides the traditional applications, SSL today is gaining momentum as a virtual private network (VPN) technology to provide remote access to e-mail and web-based applications. SSL is also used as a server-to-server secure transport protocol.

SSL is a proprietary protocol developed by Netscape. SSLv2 was released in 1995; one year later, SSLv3 was released. Transport Layer Security (TLS) (RFC 2246) is the proposed standard version of SSL and is based on SSL v3.

NOTE Most of today's browsers support SSLv2, SSLv3, and TLS. SSLv3 support was introduced in Netscape 2.*x* and in Microsoft Internet Explorer 3.*x*. TLS support was introduced in Netscape 4.*x* and Microsoft Internet Explorer 4.*x*. SSLv3 and TLS are predominant today.

SSL provides protocols above the transport layer (Layer 4) of the OSI model, with the following services:

- **Authentication**—SSL provides a mechanism for the client to make sure that the server is what it claims to be. As an example, a client connected to an online store can verify that the server to which it is sending a credit card number really belongs to the online store.
- **Data confidentiality**—SSL encrypts the traffic; this protects the data exchanged on SSL from being read by somebody who maliciously captures the traffic.
- **Data integrity**—SSL provides a mechanism to make sure that the data exchanged between client and server is not corrupted.

NOTE Before reading this chapter, you should be familiar with the basic concepts of security, such as authentication and encryption. Refer to Chapter 5, "Data Center Security Overview."

This chapter focuses on the SSL concepts that are necessary to understand HTTPS transactions and their associated design considerations. For detailed information about the cryptographic aspects and the Public Key Infrastructure (PKI) aspects of SSL, see Chapter 15, "Security Protocols and Technologies."

SSL Overview

The SSL protocol runs between the transport layer and application layer. It provides security services to Layer 5 protocols and associated applications. Examples are web-based applications and e-mail applications. Web-based applications can use HTTP on top of SSL (HTTPS). E-mail applications can benefit from the use of the Post Office Protocol (POP3) on SSL (SPOP3), the Simple Mail Transfer Protocol (SMTP) on SSL (SSMTP), and Internet Message Access Protocol (IMAP) on SSL (SSL IMAP).

NOTE SSL requires a connection-oriented transport protocol, which normally is TCP. The Layer 4 port used depends on the Layer 5 protocol. As an example, HTTPS normally uses port 443, SSMTP uses port 465, and SPOP3 uses port 995.

Web-based applications use SSL to encrypt sensitive information and to provide a mechanism for the end user to authenticate the entity (server) to which it is sending or receiving information. Examples of web-based applications using SSL are e-commerce and financial applications.

Usually for e-commerce applications, such as an online store, most of the session is clear text. During the HTTP session, you can select items that you want to buy and fill in the shopping cart. Only when you are ready to pay, you click the check-out button, which forces HTTP to switch to HTTPS (HTTP encrypted with SSL). When you type the credit card number and the billing address, the browser sends this information encrypted. Financial applications such as an online bank tool or a trading tool typically use SSL from the start of the session. SSL is also used to ensure data confidentiality and authentication in server-to-server communication, such as the one that occurs between an application server and a server storing distributed objects.

Figure 9-1 shows an example of use of SSL for a web application that requires the user to sign in. The client application is a browser. The name of the site is www.example.com. This could be a bank, an online store, or an enterprise application. The web site requires the user to sign in before performing financial operations, to buy items, or to change personal information.

At the left of the figure, you can see the username and password fields as they appear in the web page. If you look at the right portion of Figure 9-1, you can see the high-level traffic trace of the packets exchanged between the user and the web server that hosts the application.

When the user clicks the sign-in button, the browser performs an SSL handshake with the web server. The purpose of the handshake is for the browser to authenticate the server and to negotiate the secret key used later to encrypt the HTTP GET request.

The browser then sends the form fields (username and password) encrypted in HTTPS, and the application returns an encrypted page. At this point, you notice that a lock appears on the browser: This means that the page showing on the browser is encrypted.

Figure 9-1 *Use of SSL for a Generic Application*

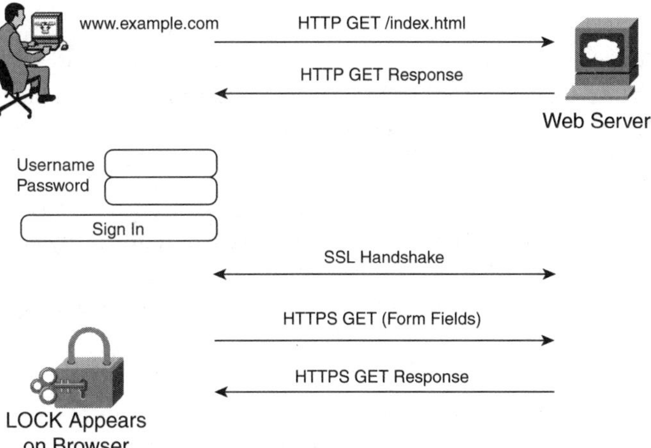

SSL Operations

As previously mentioned, SSL requires a connection-oriented transport protocol such as TCP. A transport connection between a client and a server encrypted with SSL typically is referred to as an *SSL connection*. An SSL connection is characterized by parameters like the encryption keys, MAC keys, cryptographic algorithms. The cryptographic algorithms commonly are referred to as ciphers. The combination of the ciphers typically is referred to as *ciphersuite*. Ciphersuites are negotiated at the beginning of the SSL connection.

Multiple SSL connections can be part of an *SSL session*. All the SSL connections belonging to the same SSL session are characterized by the same security parameters (ciphersuite and master key) and by encryption keys specific to the connection (the encryption keys are generated from the master key of the session).

SSL connections can be described as made of two main phases:

- **SSL session negotiation (or handshake)**—This phase ensures authentication of the server and, optionally, of the client. It is based on public key cryptography, and it allows server and client to agree on a secret master key used for the data encryption. This phase typically uses RSA as the public key algorithm.
- **SSL application data transfer**—In this phase, SSL encrypts the data traffic and ensures data confidentiality and integrity. Confidentiality is achieved by using symmetric algorithms such as DES, 3DES, RC4. Data integrity is achieved by using message digest algorithms such as MD5 and SHA-1.

HTTPS

HTTP is the application layer protocol that is most commonly used in conjunction with SSL. HTTP requests sent over SSL are encrypted and carried on the SSL application data channel; otherwise, they are no different than HTTP requests sent directly over TCP. HTTPS is the acronym that identifies HTTP encrypted with SSL.

URLs for secure connections start with https://. When such a URL is found in an HTML page, the client opens a TCP connection to port 443, followed by an SSL handshake and eventually by a data transfer. The data transfer carries the HTTP traffic. SSL encrypts the HTTP header and payload, which means that the URL and the cookie information in the HTTP GET request are encrypted.

NOTE HTTPS also can use other ports besides the default 443; as an example, a URL such as https://www.example.com:444 would use port 444. This requires that the https daemon is configured to accept SSL on port 444.

Figure 9-2 shows an HTTPS transaction based on HTTP 1.0. Each HTTPS GET request for a new object corresponds to the following operations:

1. A new TCP connection
2. A new SSL handshake
3. HTTP traffic exchange encrypted with SSL
4. TCP connection closure

Figure 9-2 *HTTPS Transaction with HTTP 1.0*

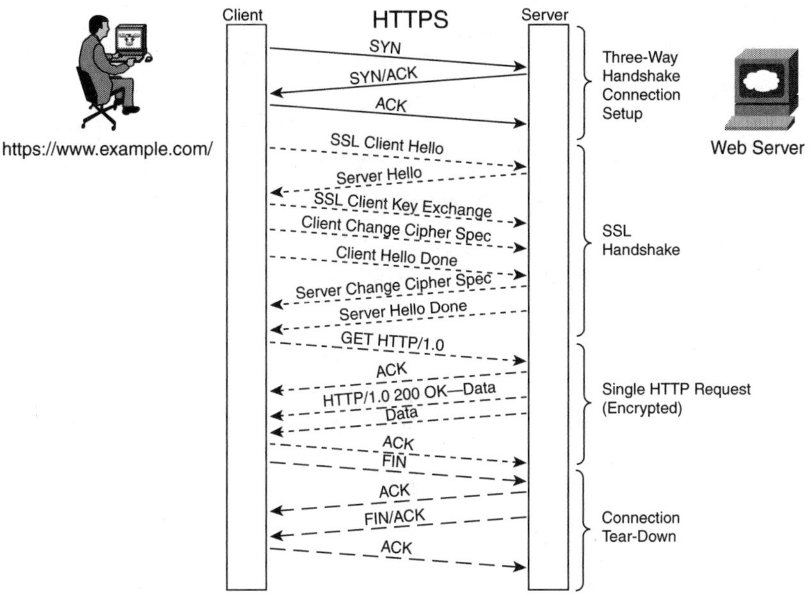

At the right of Figure 9-2, you can see these four steps; at the center, you can see the detailed packet exchange between the client and the server.

As you can see from the figure, with HTTP 1.0 for each HTTPS GET, there is a new connection, and every connection requires an SSL handshake.

Having read Chapter 8, "HTTP and Related Concepts," you should be familiar with the difference between HTTP 1.0 and HTTP 1.1, and with the concept of HTTP persistent connections. With HTTP persistent connections, client and servers exchange multiple HTTP requests and responses on a single TCP connection.

Figure 9-3 shows the effect of HTTP persistent connections on HTTPS. The user requests two objects: https://www.example.com/a.gif and https://www.example.com/b.gif. Because the browser and the server are using HTTP1.1, there is a single SSL connection.

Figure 9-3 *HTTPS Transaction with HTTP 1.1*

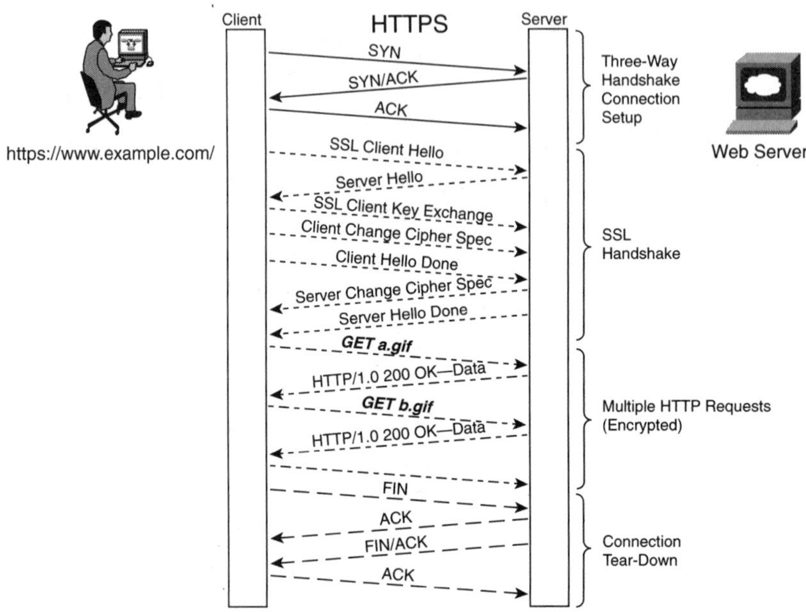

The same HTTP transactions performed with HTTP 1.0 would have created two separate SSL connections.

NOTE HTTP/1.0 also supports persistent connections, but they are not the default behavior. For more information, refer to Chapter 8.

TIP HTTP persistent connections can greatly increase performance for an HTTPS session because they limit the number of connections, which means fewer SSL handshakes. For more information about the SSL performance impact on servers, see the section, "Performance Implications of SSL."

SSL Session Negotiation

This section describes each phase of the SSL handshake. As previously stated, the key purpose of the SSL negotiation is for the client to authenticate the server and, optionally, for the server to authenticate the client; the client and the server must agree on the cryptographic algorithms and keys to use to exchange data securely.

For the purpose of this section, you do not need to have a complete understanding of the ciphers, as long as you realize that the session negotiation relies on public key cryptography (RSA is an example of public key algorithm).

Example 9-1 shows the traffic capture of the SSL negotiation between a browser and an HTTP server. The first number on the left is the record number.

NOTE SSL arranges the messages to be transmitted into blocks called records. These records are processed (encrypted, compressed, and so on) and transmitted. TCP can transmit a single record as multiple TCP segments. As a result, depending on the size, each record of Example 9-1 can be sent on the network as one or multiple packets.

Example 9-1 *SSL Negotiation Trace*

```
1  0.0807 (0.0807)  C>S SSLv2 compatible client hello
   Version 3.0
   cipher suites
   SSL_RSA_WITH_RC4_128_MD5
   SSL_RSA_WITH_RC4_128_SHA
   SSL_RSA_WITH_3DES_EDE_CBC_SHA
   [...]
2  0.0832 (0.0024)  S>CV3.0(980)  Handshake
       ServerHello
         Version 3.0
         random[32]=
           6f 53 23 92 3b ec 53 4e 8d c9 fb 8a 79 31 ed d5
           ba 7e d3 39 bf b2 5b dd 06 7d 7b aa 6d 38 fd 12
         session_id[32]=
           02 00 00 00 2a b7 6f 98 11 a4 13 ad 0a 72 02 d6
           96 80 05 27 e9 00 7e 67 c6 d6 d5 a9 de c3 ba 2d
         cipherSuite         SSL_RSA_WITH_RC4_128_MD5
         compressionMethod                   NULL
       Certificate
         Subject
           C=US
           ST=CA
           O=Cisco
           OU=ESE
           CN=cisco.com
           Email=username@cisco.com
       [...]
       ServerHelloDone
```

continues

Example 9-1 *SSL Negotiation Trace (Continued)*

```
3  0.1019 (0.0187)  C>SV3.0(132)  Handshake
      ClientKeyExchange
        EncryptedPreMasterSecret[128]=
          2e 2c 52 2e 21 f5 a8 b5 af 1e d9 2a 8f e5 40 68
          33 27 16 6c 54 80 c4 76 31 1b 74 70 b1 5b f7 6b
          d2 3f 22 6b 3a 8e a1 03 e3 ba 49 62 47 b6 f2 4f
          37 7c 71 a7 22 0e 1e 9e 1c 9f 9c d1 12 3d 80 20
          79 4b 02 cf e0 c0 4f 6a d7 ab ef d7 e0 90 ff 89
          ec 4b 09 7f 4a d6 9a d5 1d 78 d3 55 b9 08 49 5f
          02 a6 bc 8c 0d dc 44 69 b0 22 3a 47 e6 03 50 62
          31 60 42 34 e6 ca dc 32 30 a1 4d fb fa 64 fc 41
4  0.1019 (0.0000)  C>SV3.0(1)  ChangeCipherSpec
5  0.1019 (0.0000)  C>SV3.0(56)  Handshake
6  0.1126 (0.0107)  S>CV3.0(1)  ChangeCipherSpec
7  0.1126 (0.0000)  S>CV3.0(56)  Handshake
```

The following steps illustrate the SSL session negotiation phases. Not all the steps are always required in the SSL negotiation: Steps 4, 5, and 6 in the following list are optional and are not present in Example 9-1.

Step 1 Client Hello (unencrypted).

The client sends a hello message to the server. This message defines the SSL version that the client understands, a random number used to seed the cryptographic computation, a variable-length session-id, a list of ciphers, and the list of compression algorithms that the client supports. This step corresponds to the first record in Example 9-1; the session-id is not present, which means that the client is generating a new session. The browser on the clients supports the ciphers SSL_RSA_WITH_RC4_128_MD5, SSL_RSA_WITH_RC4_128_SHA, and so on.

Step 2 Server Hello (unencrypted).

The server responds to the client with the protocol version, a random number to seed the cryptographic computation, a session-id number, a cipher, and a compression algorithm. If the session-id is 0, it means that the server does not cache the master key. This corresponds to the second record in Example 9-1.

If there is no need to generate a new master (in case the client already sent the session-id and the server cached it), the negotiation goes directly to the "Client Change Cipher Spec" and Client Finish" (messages 8 through 11).

The Server Hello in record 2 shows a nonzero session-id (a9 de c3 ba 2d), the cipher chosen by the server (SSL_RSA_WITH_RC4_128_MD5), and the fact that there is no compression.

Step 3 Server Certificate (unencrypted).

The server sends its certificate in a standard format (x509). The certificate includes the server's public key. Record 2 in Example 9-1 shows the Server Certificate: The organizational name is Cisco, and the common name is Cisco.com.

The client uses the server certificate to validate the server identity. The browser has a list of Certificate Authorities (CA) that it trusts, and it expects the server certificate to be signed by one of these CAs.

Step 4 Server Key Exchange (unencrypted).

The server key exchange is used to send the server's public key if the server has no certificate or if the certificate is only for signing. This message is signed with the server's private key.

Step 5 Certificate Request (unencrypted).

This message is sent if the server wants to authenticate the client.

Step 6 Client Certificate (unencrypted).

This message is sent by the client to the server when requested.

Step 7 Client Key Exchange (encrypted with server public key).

The client uses this message to communicate the pre-master secret to the server. It is encrypted with the server's public key for confidentiality. The pre-master key is used to generate the shared keys for symmetric encryption. Notice that when the server receives the pre-master secret, this is the most CPU-intensive operation in the session negotiation because of the private key decryption performed by the server.

In record 3 in Example 9-1, you can see the pre-master key encrypted with the server public key.

Step 8 Certificate Verify.

Step 9 Client Change Cipher Spec (unencrypted).

The client sends this message to communicate that it will use the negotiated cipher and secrets. This is record 4 in Example 9-1.

Step 10 Client Finish (encrypted with CLIENT-WRITE-KEY).

This closes the handshake between the client and the server, and contains a hash for all the information previously exchanged. This message is encrypted with the new cipher, key, and secrets. This is record 5 in Example 9-1.

Step 11 Server Change Cipher Spec (unencrypted).

This is like the Client Change Cipher Spec. It is record 6 in Example 9-1.

Step 12 Server Finish (encrypted with SERVER-WRITE-KEY).

This is like the Client Finish message. It is record 7 in Example 9-1.

SSL Data Exchange

The SSL negotiation provides the client and the server with shared secret keys. SSL divides the application data in blocks of 2^{14} bytes or less, called *records*; it compresses them, appends the Message Authentication Code (MAC), and encrypts them with the secret key.

SSL uses two different secret keys, depending on the direction of the traffic:

- Server-to-client traffic is encrypted with the SERVER-WRITE-KEY (which is also the CLIENT-READ-KEY).
- Client-to-server traffic is encrypted with the CLIENT-WRITE-KEY (which is also the SERVER-READ-KEY).

Figure 9-4 illustrates the concept. The client encrypts with the CLIENT-WRITE-KEY, and the server encrypts with the SERVER-WRITE-KEY. Notice that, despite the fact that there are two keys, this encryption is "symmetric," meaning that the CLIENT-READ-KEY is used to decrypt traffic encrypted with the SERVER-WRITE-KEY, and the CLIENT-READ-KEY equals the SERVER-WRITE-KEY.

Figure 9-4 *SSL Data Encryption*

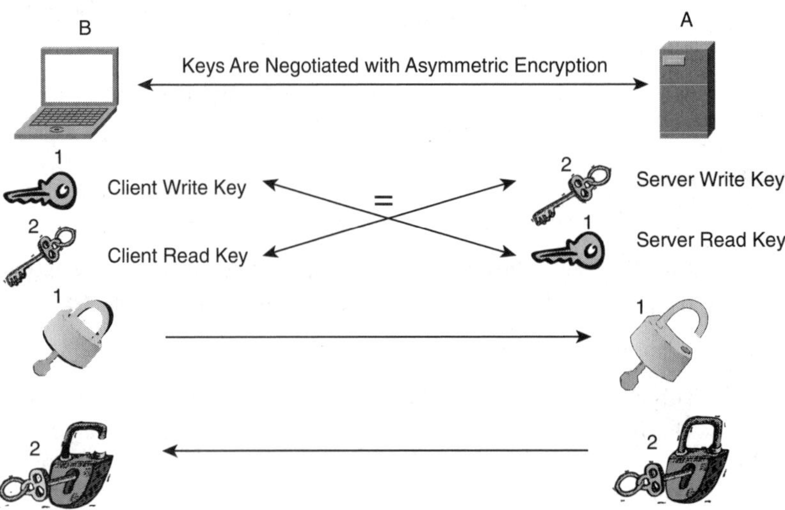

Performance Implications of SSL

SSL has a major performance impact on the web server processing of clients' requests. This is mainly because of the public key encryption rather than the symmetric encryption operated on the application data.

NOTE Public key encryption is used in the session-negotiation phase of SSL. The SSL session negotiation is an important performance factor with HTTPS because of the number of TCP connections generated during a single HTTP session.

The main impact of the symmetric encryption algorithms on the server performance is the achievable throughput, which is a factor in bulk transfers.

The performance of HTTP versus HTTPS on a web server depends on the server's hardware, the operating system, the size of the objects requested by the client, and, of course, the type of cipher used by SSL. The performance impact of SSL on a server can be estimated in terms of CPU utilization, delay in the HTTP response to a given HTTP GET request, buffer utilization on the servers, the maximum number of connections per second that the server can handle, the maximum achievable throughput, and so on.

The following list provides examples of the performance degradation that you can expect from a server handling SSL traffic:

- The CPU utilization of a server processing HTTPS traffic can be ten times the CPU utilization with the same number of clear-text HTTP connections.
- The maximum connection setup rate of a server processing HTTPS traffic can be between 1% and 25% of the maximum connection setup rate of a server processing clear-text HTTP traffic.

For more information about the impact of SSL on the Data Center performance, see Chapter 22, "Performance Metrics of Data Center Devices."

TIP The performance implications of SSL depend on the ciphers, among the other parameters. RSA with a 2048-bit key is, of course, slower than RSA with a 512-bit key. Higher security comes at the price of slower processing speed. See Chapter 15, "Security Protocols and Technology," for more information about the ciphers.

For more detailed information about the SSL impact on servers' performance, you should refer to the whitepaper by Coradiant, "Scaling Security in E-commerce Applications," or the book *SSL and TLS: Designing and Building Secure Systems,* by Eric Rescorla.

Of all the encryption operations that are performed during the SSL handshake, the RSA decryption is the most expensive in terms of CPU utilization. This is the operation that happens on the server when it receives the encrypted pre-master key (Step 7 in the section, "SSL Session Negotiation").

On the client side, the performance implications of SSL are mainly the result of reading the certificate and verifying the CA signature. This operation is at least twice as fast as the RSA private-key decryption. Encrypting the pre-master key with the server's public key is another slow operation.

From the previous description, it appears that a bottleneck is on the server side, but if the server were authenticating the clients with certificates, there would be an additional bottleneck on the client side.

Considering that the slowest SSL operation is the session negotiation, it appears that resuming an SSL session without having to negotiate the master secret would bypass the most expensive operation, thus improving performance. This mechanism is called *session resumption*.

Session Resumption

SSL generates a specific number that uniquely identifies a session. This number is called the *session-id,* and it is 16 bytes in SSLv2 and 32 bytes in SSLv3. The session-id field allows a client to resume a previous session without having to negotiate new ciphers and keys.

Resuming an SSL session has the main advantage of bypassing the most expensive SSL operation in the handshake, which is the exchange of the pre-master–secret between the client and the server. SSLv2 hands out the session-id in an encrypted message; SSLv3 sends the session-id in clear text. Figure 9-5 describes how the session-id is negotiated in SSLv2.

Figure 9-5 shows the SSLv2 handshake. The very first time that the client contacts the server, it does not have any session-id.

The server communicates a *session-id* to the client inside the Server Finish message, which is encrypted with the SERVER-WRITE-KEY. It is impossible for an intermediate device to read the session-id value.

In SSLv3, the session-id is sent in the clear in the Server Hello message. If the client had a valid *session-id,* the handshake would look like Example 9-2.

Example 9-2 shows the SSL handshake when the session-id is reused. You can see the client sending a Client Hello containing a field called resume, followed by the session-id that ends in a9 de c3 ba 2d.

Figure 9-5 *SSLv2 Handshake*

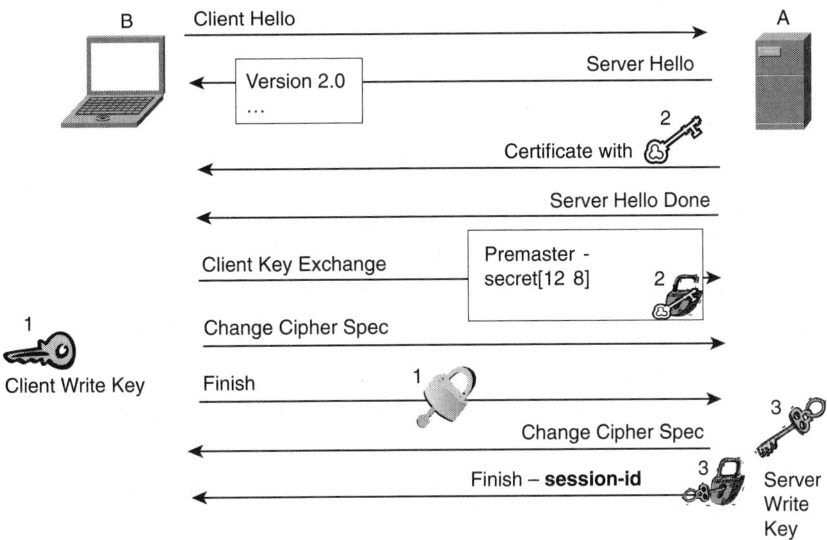

The server accepts to resume the session because it sends a Server Hello containing the same number in the session-id field: a9 de c3 ba 2d.

Example 9-2 *SSLv3 Handshake*

```
1  0.0013 (0.0013)  C>SV3.0(97)  Handshake
      ClientHello
        Version 3.0
        random[32]=
          c4 0b b1 8b c6 1b 48 04 a6 0b 26 b6 67 0d ad a8
          59 b1 4b 8c 75 da e9 7f c7 52 38 de 4c 5c 58 49
        resume [32]=
          02 00 00 00 2a b7 6f 98 11 a4 13 ad 0a 72 02 d6
          96 80 05 27 e9 00 7e 67 c6 d6 d5 a9 de c3 ba 2d
        cipher suites
        SSL_RSA_WITH_RC4_128_MD5
        [...]
2  0.0022 (0.0008)  S>CV3.0(74)  Handshake
      ServerHello
        Version 3.0
        random[32]=
          a0 3b 9a bc ed de b9 73 e6 3d a7 db 81 79 a3 56
          1e 2b a9 40 7d a3 28 1b a3 17 cb b0 8f 52 f2 98
        session_id[32]=
          02 00 00 00 2a b7 6f 98 11 a4 13 ad 0a 72 02 d6
          96 80 05 27 e9 00 7e 67 c6 d6 d5 a9 de c3 ba 2d
```

continues

Example 9-2 *SSLv3 Handshake (Continued)*

```
        cipherSuite          SSL_RSA_WITH_RC4_128_MD5
        compressionMethod                    NULL
3  0.0022 (0.0000)  S>CV3.0(1)  ChangeCipherSpec
4  0.0022 (0.0000)  S>CV3.0(56)  Handshake
5  0.0039 (0.0017)  C>SV3.0(1)  ChangeCipherSpec
6  0.0039 (0.0000)  C>SV3.0(56)  Handshake
7  0.0072 (0.0033)  C>SV3.0(496)  application_data
```

You can also compare Example 9-2 with Example 9-1: Notice that the session negotiation is significantly shorter. The main difference is the fact that there is no need to authenticate the server/client or to exchange the encrypted pre-master. In Example 9-2, you do not see the client sending the *EncryptedPreMasterSecret,* which you see in record 3 of Example 9-1.

It is very important to be able to read the SSL session-id when performing server load balancing for SSL traffic. This is why SSLv3 and TLS are preferable to SSLv2 in a server farm environment.

By using SSLv3 with a load balancer capable of SSL stickiness, you can significantly improve the performance of the server farm (see the next section, "SSL and Load Balancing").

SSL and Load Balancing

When clustering servers configured for SSL traffic, it is possible for multiple connections of the same SSL session to be sent to different servers. Figure 9-6 provides an example. The user connects to https://www.example.com. The web page of www.example.com is made of several objects, and the browser sends one HTTP GET request for each one of those objects.

NOTE A cluster is a group of servers acting as a single virtual server, with the purpose of sharing the load of incoming client requests and providing high availability for the application.

Typically, the browser opens multiple TCP connections to retrieve these objects. It can open one TCP connection per HTTP GET request (as in HTTP 1.0), it can perform one TCP connection every *n* HTTP GET requests (as in HTTP 1.1), or it can open multiple TCP connections simultaneously.

Figure 9-6 *Multiple HTTPS GETs with Load Balancing*

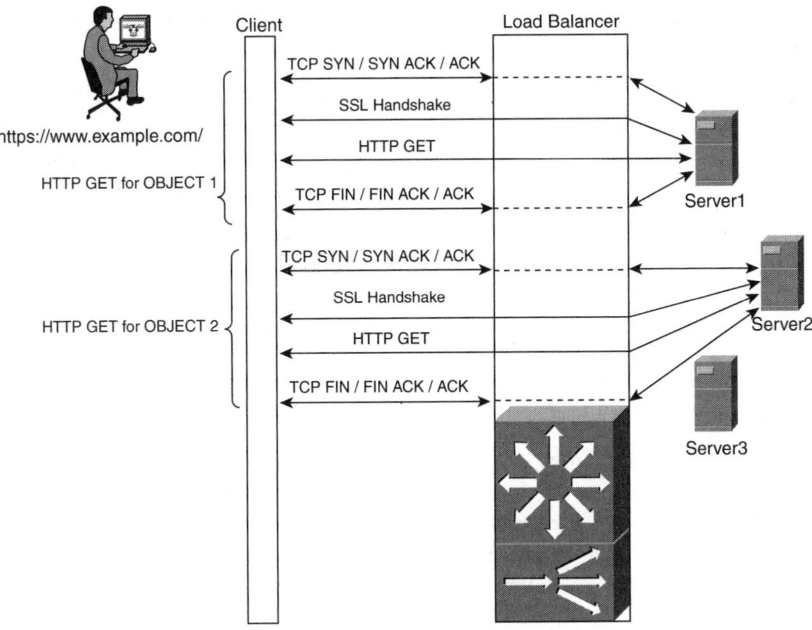

Between the client and the cluster of servers, there is a load balancer. The load balancer can treat each TCP connection independently and send it to a different server. In Figure 9-6, the load balancer sends the HTTPS GET request for object 1 to server 1, and the HTTPS GET request for object 2 to server 2. The reason is that each HTTPS GET in Figure 9-6 opens a separate TCP connection.

During the SSL handshake, server 1 gives out a session number for the client to perform a faster handshake (session resumption). The second HTTPS GET request, for object 2, triggers a new TCP connection (it is HTTP 1.0). The load balancer applies the predictor to the TCP connection and sends it to server 2. The client then sends an SSL handshake with the session-id for the SSL session that exists on server 1. Server 2 does not know anything about this SSL session, so it answers with a new session identifier. The client then understands that there needs to be a new secret key negotiation, which is a full SSL handshake.

As you can see, when a load balancer assigns TCP connections that belong to the same session to different servers, the SSL session-resumption feature cannot be used. This is because the session information is not shared between servers.

Load balancers with Layer 5 capabilities can monitor the SSL session-id inserted by a server. When a client tries to resume a session by sending this session-id in the Client Hello, the load balancer assigns the incoming Hello to the server that is aware of the session, thus allowing the session resumption to work.

SSLv3 displays the session-id field unencrypted in the ServerHello message; SSLv2 does not. This means that SSL persistence with load balancers is possible only with SSLv3 or TLS because the session-id must be in clear text for the load balancer to learn it and match it.

NOTE For more information about SSL session persistence with load-balancing devices, see Chapter 19, "Persistence Mechanisms on Load Balancers."

SSL Performance Optimization

Based on the information provided in the previous section, you can see that the performance impact of SSL session establishment is mitigated by using SSL session resumption. The browser and the servers can cache the SSL master secret so that the negotiation occurs only once in a session, and all the subsequent SSL requests can reuse the previously generated master key. SSL session resumption needs to be preserved in the presence of server clusters.

Improving the performance in SSL transactions can be achieved by doing the following:

- **Make sure that traffic for one SSL session goes consistently to one server**—When operating in a Data Center, SSL connections from the same client to the same virtual IP need to be assigned consistently to one server for the duration of the SSL session. If this does not happen, session-ids cannot be reused, and the new server negotiates a new master key.
- **Use SSLv3 instead of SSLv2**—SSLv3 provides a significant enhancement compared to SSLv2—the session-id is visible in clear text. Load balancers located in the path between a client and a server can read this number and make sure that an SSL session is delivered to the same server, no matter how many different TCP connections are created.
- **Use HTTP 1.1 or HTTP 1.0 with keepalives**—Persistent TCP connections for HTTP greatly improve performance for HTTPS because multiple HTTP requests can be sent over a single TCP connection. Without persistent TCP connections, every HTTPS request requires an SSL connection.
- **Upgrade the client's software**—Historically, some browsers had bugs that caused the SSL session to renegotiate too often. As an example, Microsoft IE 5, 5.01, and 5.5 used to renegotiate the session-id every 2 minutes because of the bug #Q265369.

- **Use acceleration hardware on the server**—Acceleration hardware (SSL NICs) makes it possible to speed up the SSL handshake and the encryption of the application data. SSL acceleration hardware offloads the server CPU from the cryptographic operations; additionally, the dedicated SSL hardware can handle a higher number of RSA requests per second.
- **Use external or built-in accelerators**—External accelerators have several advantages, such as offloading the servers from SSL processing, allowing IDS systems to monitor the decrypted traffic, and allowing HTTP/HTTPS session persistence with load balancers. Like accelerated NIC cards, they offload the servers from cryptographic operations and can handle a high amount of RSA operations per second (higher than a single accelerated NIC card typically can sustain). A network-based intrusion-detection system (IDS) device monitoring the decrypted traffic can identify unwanted activities carried on HTTPS. A load balancer in the path between the accelerator and the servers also can read cookies and rewritten URLs to ensure HTTP session persistence; the impact of renegotiation caused by bugs in the browser would not affect server performance. Acceleration also simplifies virtual hosts design because the server and the load balancer would see the Host TAG in the HTTP request.

Authentication and Digital Certificates

With SSL, authentication ensures that the server the browser is intended to communicate with is the correct server. This is important because keys are negotiated between the two entities for the encrypted data exchange. Optionally, the server can also authenticate the client.

To understand the authentication process, you should be familiar with asymmetric encryption (refer to Chapter 5, "Data Center Security Overview"). The Public Key Infrastructure is analyzed in depth in Chapter 15.

SSL Authentication Overview

SSL achieves authentication by using digital certificates. In the example in Figure 9-7, A is an SSL-enabled server and B is an SSL-enabled client. A digital certificate is basically A's public key and a third-party "signature." CAs are organizations that make sure that A's public key really belongs to A.

Digital certificates are issued and signed by CAs. They contain the public key of a host (it can be a web site as well), together with other information about the host itself. SSL uses the format x.509v3, which is a widely used standard for digital certificates.

Figure 9-7 *Authentication in SSL*

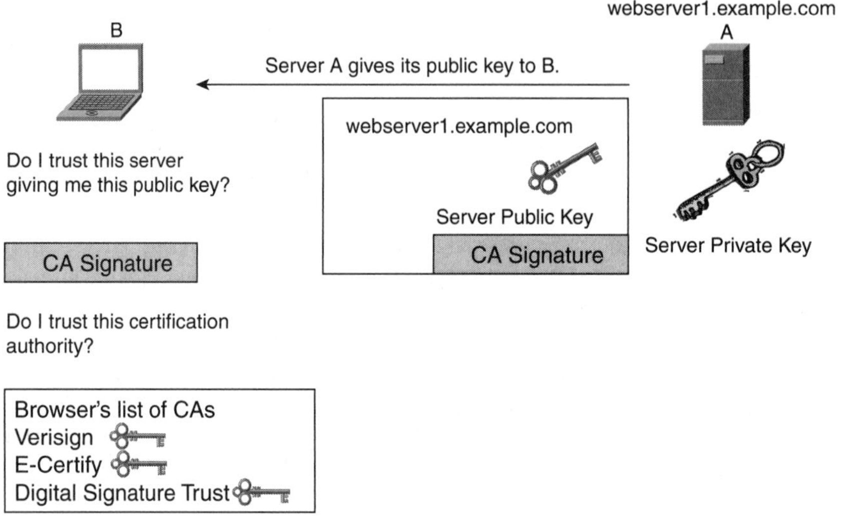

Certificates contain the following fields:

- Version Number
- Serial Number
- Period of Validity
- Issuer
- Subject Public Key
- Subject Common Name
- Signature of the Issuing Authority

The Subject Common Name is the DNS name—for example, www.example.com. This field is visible in IE by looking in Properties, Security, or in Netscape by opening View, Page Info.

Browsers check the common name and compare it to the domain they used in the connection. If they differ, a message is prompted to the user. Figure 9-8 shows the warning message of a browser that receives a certificate in which the common name does not match the domain name of the web site.

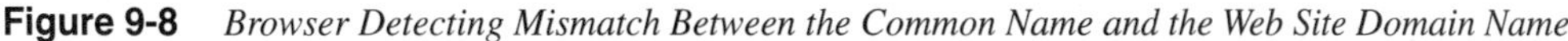

Figure 9-8 *Browser Detecting Mismatch Between the Common Name and the Web Site Domain Name*

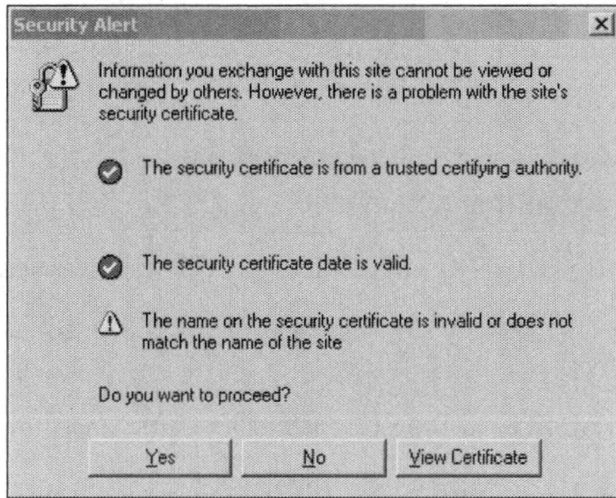

Three main types of digital certificates exist:

- **Server certificate**—This is the certificate that the server sends with the SSL Server Hello. The server certificate delivers the server public key to the client.
- **Client certificate**—This is the certificate sent by the client when the server wants to authenticate the client.
- **CA certificate**—This certificate identifies the CA.

Browsers store a list of trusted CAs (this list can be viewed on Navigator by going to Security View, Certificate, Signers): When a client receives a piece of information signed by a CA, it uses the CA's public key to authenticate the signature. If new certificates need to be installed, the user is warned and decides whether to accept them. Figure 9-9 shows the warning message from a browser that receives a server certificate signed by a CA that the browser does not recognize.

Figure 9-9 *Browser Receiving a Certificate Signed by an Unknown CA*

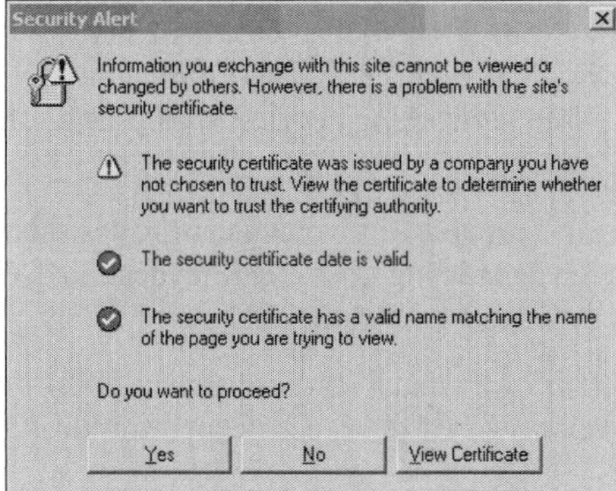

Public Key Infrastructure

The keyword *public* in PKI refers to the fact that a PKI is the infrastructure for the distribution of public keys used by asymmetric encryption (also called public key encryption).

A PKI is a framework of services to support public key technologies such as SSL. A PKI requires the presence of these elements:

- **A CA**—The third-party entity that every device involved in the encryption recognizes.
- **Certificates**—These are documents used to store information about the entity and its public key.
- **A storage structure**—This is used to hold the certificates.
- **A certificate-management structure**—This functionality provides enrollment and revocation of certificates.

The Public Key Cryptography Standards (PKCS) are PKI standards such as these:

- **PKCS#10**—Describes the syntax for certificate-signing requests (see later in this section).
- **PKCS#12**—Defines a format for the storage of certificates. When you exchange certificates between machines or you want to export/import certificates from/to a browser, you can use the PKCS#12 format.

Chapter 5 already introduced the topics of CAs and certificates.

The two key operations in certificate management are enrollment and revocation. The process of having certificates signed by a CA is called enrollment. The enrollment for Internet-facing server farms consists of generating a certification request with a standard format, PKCS#10, and submitting this file to a CA (for example, Verisign).

An enterprise can also have its own PKI, made of an internal CA server and local registration authorities (LRA). LRAs are CA proxies: They protect the CA and offload it from a number of functions—for example, authenticating users who request an enrollment.

The enrollment process of devices of an enterprise network can be automated by using a protocol such as Cisco's Simple Certificate Enrollment Protocol (SCEP). This protocol is normally used by Cisco networking devices, such as SSL offloaders, and is supported by most vendors of CA servers.

A PKI also needs to be capable of revoking certificates. The CA server distributes the list of revoked certificates by creating a certificate revocation list (CRL). The CRL is accessible to the end entities by using LDAP or SCEP.

Clients use the CRL to verify that a server certificate is still valid, while web servers use the CRL to verify the validity of the client certificate. How does a client or a server know where to find the CRL?

X.509v3 certificates have an optional field, called CRL Distribution Point (CDP), where the client can obtain information about the certificates revoked by a CA. Not all certificates include the CDP extension; if they do, and if you enabled the option on the browser (IE 5.*x* has this option), the browser can retrieve the CRL from the CA.

You also can verify manually whether a certificate has been revoked by going to the web site of the CA and providing the serial number of the certificate that you want to verify.

NOTE For more information about PKI, see Chapter 15.

SSL Ciphersuites

The SSL ciphersuites are the cryptography algorithms used for authentication, data confidentiality, and data integrity. Ciphers are negotiated at the session handshake stage. Examples of popular ciphersuites are SSL_RSA_WITH_RC4_128_MD5 and RSA-3DES-EDE-CBC-SHA.

The ciphersuite is made of three fields:

- Key Exchange/Authentication Algorithm (RSA and Diffie Hellman, for example)
- Encryption Algorithm (DES, 3DES, IDEA, RC2, and RC4, for example)
- Message Digest Algorithm (MD2, MD4, MD5, SHA, and SHA-1, for example)

The ciphersuite used by an SSL session is the result of the negotiation between client and server. The Client Hello lists the ciphers supported by the client. Some browsers give you control on the ciphers that you want to use. An example of a browser that supports this option is Netscape 7.0: Edit/Preferences/Privacy and Security/SSL shows the available ciphersuites that you can select.

Servers also enable you to decide which ciphersuites to use. As an example, in Apache, you can configure the ciphersuites with the SSLCipherSuite directive in the httpd.conf file (and, of course, you need to load mod_ssl, the module that provides SSL functionalities to the Apache web server).

Popular ciphersuites include these:

- **SSL_RSA_WITH_RC4_128_MD5**—Uses the RSA algorithm for the key exchange (the RSA key size typically is 1024 bits—or, for even higher security, can be 2048 bits). The data encryption uses RC4 with a key size of 128 bits. The message digest algorithm is MD5, which produces a digest of 128 bits.

- **SSL_RSA_WITH_RC4_128_SHA**—Uses the RSA algorithm for the key exchange (the RSA key size typically is 1024 bits). The data encryption uses RC4 with a key size of 128 bits. The message digest algorithm is SHA, which produces a digest of 160 bits.
- **SSL_RSA_WITH_3DES_EDE_CBC_SHA**—Uses the RSA algorithm for the key exchange. Data encryption uses 3DES, which has a key size of 168 bits; the message digest algorithm is SHA, which produces a digest of 160 bites.
- **SSL_RSA_WITH_DES_CBC_SHA**—Uses the RSA algorithm for the key exchange. Data encryption uses DES, which has a key size of 56 bits; the message digest algorithm is SHA.
- **SSL_RSA_EXPORT1024_WITH_RC4_56_SHA**—Uses the RSA algorithm for the key exchange (1024 bits) and RC4 with a 56-bit key for data encryption. The message digest algorithm is SHA.
- **SSL_RSA_EXPORT1024_WITH_DES_CBC_SHA**—Uses the RSA algorithm for key exchange (1024 bits), and uses DES (56 bits) for data encryption. The digest algorithm is SHA.
- **SSL_RSA_EXPORT_WITH_RC4_40_MD5**—Uses the RSA algorithm for the key exchange with 512 bits of key size, and RC4 with a key size of 40 bits for the data encryption. The digest algorithm is MD5.
- **SSL_RSA_EXPORT_WITH_RC2_CBC_40_MD5**—Uses RSA with a key size of 512 bits for the key exchange, RC2 with a key size of 40 bits for the data encryption, and MD5 as the message digest.
- **SSL_DHE_DSS_WITH_3DES_EDE_CBC_SHA**—Uses Diffie Hellman for the key exchange, together with the Digital Signature Standard (DSS) for key signing. The key size for DH typically is 1024 bits, or 2048 for even higher security. This ciphersuite uses 3DES (168 bits) for data encryption and SHA as the message digest.
- **SSL_DHE_DSS_WITH_DES_CBC_SHA**—Uses Diffie Hellman for the key exchange, together with DES (56 bits) for data encryption. The message digest algorithm is SHA.
- **SSL_DHE_DSS_EXPORT1024_WITH_DES_CBC_SHA**—Uses Diffie Hellman for the key exchange with a key size of 1024 bits, and DES for data encryption. The message digest algorithm is SHA.

NOTE There are more ciphersuites than the ones in the list—for more information, refer to RFC 2246.

For more information about ciphers, see Chapter 15.

Analyzing SSL Traces

In Examples 9-3 and 9-4, you can see the SSL handshake between a client and a server, both running on Pentium III machines. The two machines are on the same LAN segment. The first number of each line of the trace is the SSL record.

The second number is the timestamp from the start of the capture, and in parentheses is the delta time. C>S represents a client-to-server message, and S>C is for server-to-client messages.

Example 9-3 shows the SSL negotiation with Microsoft Internet Explorer browser as the client.

Example 9-3 *SSL Handshake Performed by an IE Browser*

```
1  3.8591 (3.8591)  C>S SSLv2 compatible client hello
  Version 3.0
  cipher suites
  [...]

2  3.8614 (0.0023)  S>CV3.0(980)  Handshake
      ServerHello
        Version 3.0
        random[32]=
          97 80 fc a6 e1 06 ad 81 c9 c2 18 c3 6a dd 7b 03
          ba 4a 59 21 7e f3 6c be 57 6f 93 c0 95 ff 1c 37
        session_id[32]=
          01 00 00 00 c3 e9 3f 61 d7 a6 04 b3 5c de 41 d5
          22 29 9a 71 fd 64 7c 86 5c 77 c8 10 c4 ef 00 b2
        cipherSuite         SSL_RSA_WITH_RC4_128_MD5
        compressionMethod                       NULL
      Certificate
      [...]
      ServerHelloDone

3  3.8912 (0.0297)  C>SV3.0(132)  Handshake
      ClientKeyExchange
        EncryptedPreMasterSecret[128]=
          98 f9 78 fe d5 a7 f7 73 92 f1 d0 31 40 15 be e1
          08 8b 6e e5 db 40 5c 3d 97 f7 39 dc 44 4d 7c d2
          15 c1 54 5d fc 4e f3 3e f2 f8 aa eb 62 da 15 68
          8f 99 f2 16 d8 6a 1d ff f3 d4 26 1b 6a 1e 9b ea
          22 6a 9d e1 6e 15 fc fe 44 8b ad d3 a3 af c3 ec
          50 d5 98 82 b5 d8 a3 ab 93 c1 e6 64 4e 48 2c 93
          0d 9c ff dc a1 a7 8c 5c c7 e5 0b 96 7d 4d f1 a5
          6e 07 02 9b 61 4c 9d 62 99 5a 20 6c 2c e2 b8 6a
4  3.8912 (0.0000)  C>SV3.0(1)  ChangeCipherSpec
5  3.8912 (0.0000)  C>SV3.0(56)  Handshake
6  3.9017 (0.0105)  S>CV3.0(1)  ChangeCipherSpec
7  3.9017 (0.0000)  S>CV3.0(56)  Handshake
```

The delta time of 0.0297 sec between record 2 and record 3 is the result of the client reading the certificate, verifying it, generating the pre-master secret key, and encrypting it with the server public key. The client is buffering multiple records together and transmits them at the same time (this is indicated by the 0.0000 delta time).

The RSA decryption occurs after receiving record 3, which is the client key exchange. Record 6 is sent after the server decrypts the pre-master key. The delta time of 0.0105 sec includes the delay introduced by the RSA decryption, which is typically in the order of tens of milliseconds.

Example 9-4 captures the SSL handshake performed by Netscape with the same server used in Example 9-3. One difference with Example 9-3 is the delay between the Server Hello Done and the Client Key Exchange messages, which is a very high value of 14 sec: Netscape prompts the user with a window asking whether to continue with the encrypted session; only after the user accepts does it send the Client Key Exchange message. This accounts for the 14 sec of waiting between message 2 and message 3—it is the time that it takes for the user to click the Continue button.

Another difference with Example 9-3 is the delta time between the Handshake Finished message from the client and the Change Cipher Spec from the server, which is negligable (0.0008 sec), as if the decryption of the pre-master was extremely fast.

Example 9-4 *SSL Handshake Performed by Netscape*

```
1  0.0279 (0.0279)  C>S SSLv2 compatible client hello
  Version 3.0
  cipher suites
  [...]

2  0.0906 (0.0627)  S>CV3.0(980)  Handshake
      ServerHello
        Version 3.0
        random[32]=
          b7 0d 9b a9 a7 f7 d8 e7 d6 e4 5f 20 c4 78 2f 2a
          95 38 f2 2d 19 bc 84 e2 9b da d8 3e 89 7d 63 eb
        session_id[32]=
          01 00 00 00 95 ec f6 37 36 ef 70 96 28 95 ee 13
          52 82 68 93 73 73 18 d0 11 b8 e1 63 33 2f 8e 92
        cipherSuite         SSL_RSA_WITH_RC4_128_MD5
        compressionMethod                   NULL
      Certificate
      [...]
      ServerHelloDone

3  14.6659 (14.5753)  C>SV3.0(132)  Handshake
      ClientKeyExchange
        EncryptedPreMasterSecret[128]=
          cf 3f 95 33 ea e1 c1 ef 68 1b aa fd dc cc 23 5c
          e1 ed ca e7 f1 b0 ae 3f fe 5f 02 4b de d1 d0 78
          95 06 3b a0 73 96 8e 7a d4 8f 5d 91 39 e7 6e 01
          3b 71 f3 be 6c f4 3c 68 88 dc 4f e8 20 69 d5 71
```

Example 9-4 *SSL Handshake Performed by Netscape (Continued)*

```
          31 6e 34 70 e4 99 d2 6c 11 cb 3a 30 e5 76 d8 a3
          f4 2c ff f6 18 d6 22 fc 6e 23 8d 2b 63 ec 72 13
          5c bf a2 75 b0 3c ac f0 66 7c 8d 44 1f 80 94 7e
          db be 51 dc b8 c7 39 6b f0 96 e1 65 1e 8d 68 a1
4  14.8544 (0.1884)  C>SV3.0(1)  ChangeCipherSpec
5  14.8544 (0.0000)  C>SV3.0(56)  Handshake
6  14.8552 (0.0008)  S>CV3.0(1)  ChangeCipherSpec
7  14.8552 (0.0000)  S>CV3.0(56)  Handshake
8  14.8569 (0.0016)  C>SV3.0(308)  application_data
```

Notice that the Client Change Cipher Spec is sent with 188ms delay after the Client Key Exchange. In this timeframe, the server is already decrypting the pre-master key, and the delay reported in the Server Change Cipher Spec is calculated starting from the Client Change Cipher Spec.

If you now look at Example 9-3, you notice that the Client Change Cipher Spec was sent together with the Client Key Exchange message. This is why the delay for the RSA decryption was accounted for in the Server Change Cipher Spec message.

Also notice that IE is different from Netscape, in that it does not wait for the user to approve the SSL session to complete the handshake. Instead, IE completes the handshake, as shown in Example 9-3; when the user clicks to continue, IE resumes the SSL session by sending the same session-id.

Summary

SSL is a protocol used to provide authentication, encryption, and data integrity. SSL is widely used in conjunction with web-based applications and is increasingly used for SSL-based virtual private networks (VPNs).

The performance implications of using SSL in the Data Center must be considered: Session resumption is a key feature of SSL that helps alleviate the impact on the servers. The load-balancing design needs to preserve the capability of resuming existing SSL sessions by means of SSL persistence. Alternatively, SSL accelerated NIC cards and SSL offloading hardware offload the servers from having to execute the cryptographic algorithms.

A complete SSL design needs to take into consideration how to build the public key infrastructure in the enterprise network, as well as which ciphers are the most appropriate.

For Further Reading

Garfinkel, Simson with Gene Spafford. *Web Security, Privacy, and Commerce.* O'Reilly & Associates.

Rescorla, Eric. *SSL and TLS, Designing and Building Secure Systems*. Addison-Wesley Professional.

This chapter covers the following topics:

- Overview of the DNS architecture—how the DNS namespace is organized, what is a zone, and what resource records (RR) are
- The software and hardware components involved in the DNS resolution process, from the resolver to the DNS servers through DNS proxies and forwarders
- How the resolution process works
- The implications of configuring the DNS servers with multiple NS or A records
- Where to place the DNS servers in the enterprise network
- How to use DNS to distribute the load of application requests to multiple Data Centers

CHAPTER 10

DNS Essentials and Site-Selection Considerations

The domain name system (DNS) is a naming service; this chapter analyzes the use of DNS for the translation of domain names into their associated IP addresses.

NOTE DNS translates a domain name into data, and the data is not necessarily an IP address. This chapter describes DNS with special attention to the translation of domain names to the associated IP address because this is the most relevant aspect of DNS to site selection (also called request routing or global server load balancing).

DNS is the mechanism that, for example, can translate the domain name www.cisco.com to the IP address of the server hosting the Cisco website.

Why do you need this indirection of having a domain name and an IP address, and having to translate? The obvious reason is the fact that a name is easier to memorize than a number. Imagine that you wanted to access the online forums of Communities @ Cisco. You could type http://204.69.199.39/ into your browser, or you could type http://forum.cisco.com/—of course, the name is easier to remember.

NOTE Using an IP address instead of the domain name to request services accessible via HTTP is not recommended. It is used here for pure example purposes.

Another reason exists for using DNS names: It gives flexibility in the use of network addresses. There could be several machines with different IP addresses, all providing the same service and all named www.cisco.com, or there could be a change made to the address of www.cisco.com without having to change the name.

Applications rely on DNS servers for the translation of the names www.cisco.com or forum.cisco.com into the IP addresses. The DNS specifications define how host names are built and which protocol is used for the translation process. A number of RFCs define DNS; RFC 1034 and RFC 1035 are two key specifications.

DNS Architecture

You can think of DNS as a database with the following properties:

- It is hierarchical.
- It is distributed.

DNS names are organized hierarchically. The group of DNS names is referred to as a DNS namespace. The namespace is arranged in domains and subdomains, similar to the directory tree of a filesystem, which is arranged in directories and subdirectories. Figure 10-1 shows the DNS tree structure. A *domain* is the grouping of machines that share a specific subtree of the namespace: example.com or engineering.example.com are domains. A domain within another domain is a *subdomain*: engineering.example.com is a subdomain of example.com.

Figure 10-1 *DNS Tree Structure*

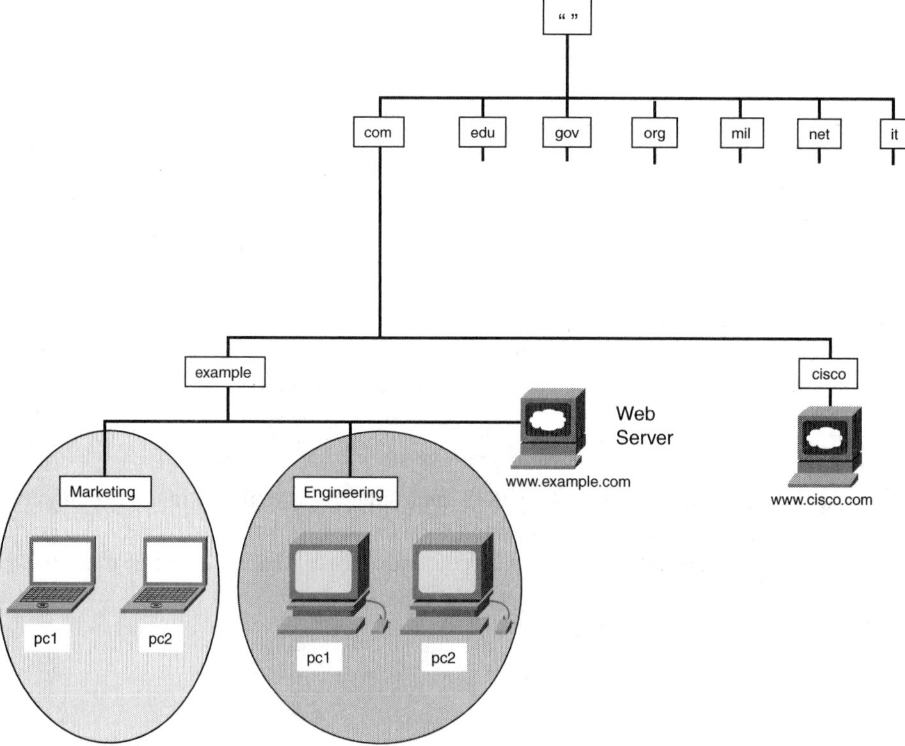

Because of the hierarchical structure, you can assign the same "label" to multiple machines, as long as they belong to different domains. For example, there can be a host called www in the example.com domain (which belongs to a fictitious company), as well as in the cisco.com domain (which belongs to Cisco Systems) because the complete name (called the *fully qualified domain name)* of www in example.com is www.example.com and in cisco.com is www.cisco.com.

At the top of the DNS tree is the root " " (the name of the root zone is the empty string, and the root also is referred to as **.**, where the trailing dot terminates the fully qualified domain name [FQDN]) whose function is provided by special DNS servers, the root DNS servers. If you look down, you recognize some very common trailing strings of Internet sites such as .com, .edu, .org, and .it. These trailing strings correspond to the domains com, edu, org, and ,it and are called top-level domains (TLDs). Among the TLDs, there are generic TLDs (gTLDs) and country code TLDs (ccTLD). gTLDs are the domains that historically were introduced first:

- **com**—For commercial organizations. An example is Cisco Systems (cisco.com).
- **edu**—For educational institutions, such as for Stanford University (stanford.edu).
- **gov**—For U.S. government organizations. An example is the Environmental Protection Agency (epa.gov).
- **mil**—For the military, such as for the Navy (navy.mil).
- **net**—Originally for organizations that provide network infrastructure; today, open also for commercial organizations.
- **org**—For noncommercial organizations. An example is the World Wide Web Consortium (w3c.org).
- **int**—For international organizations, such as the United Nations (un.int).

The Internet Corporation for Assigned Names and Numbers (ICANN), the organization responsible for the root zone, recently introduced additional gTLDs: biz, info, name, pro, aero, museum, and coop.

ccTLDs defines country-specific TLDs, such as us for United States, it for Italy, fr for France, and co for Colombia.

NOTE Root zone information currently is provided by 13 DNS root *servers* (A.ROOT-SERVERS.NET, B.ROOT-SERVERS.NET, and so on). The term *server* in this context means IP address: A DNS proxy machine resolving a name can send queries about the root zone to 13 IP addresses (see the section, "Root Hint").

The current root zone data file indicates that there are 71 gTLD servers and 662 ccTLD servers. As already pointed out, the term *server* here does not indicate a physical server, but rather an IP address used by the DNS proxy during the resolution process.

The information about the number of gTLDs and ccTLDs is based on the root zone data file from ftp://ftp.rs.internic.net/domain/.

You can find information about the existing gTLDs at http://www.iana.org/gtld/gtld.htm.

You can find information about the existing ccTLDs at http://www.iana.org/cctld/cctld-whois.htm.

FQDN

In the DNS namespace, you should refer to a host by using the complete set of labels on the path from the node to the root. Figure 10-1 clarifies this. If you look at the example.com structure, you can see that there are two main branches, marketing and engineering. The two PCs belonging to the marketing are called pc1.marketing.example.com and pc2.marketing.example.com. pc1.marketing.example.com. is a FQDN, or absolute name. Notice the use of *dots* in DNS names to separate labels, and the dot appended to the last label to indicate the end of the FQDN.

Depending on the application, the use of a label sequence without the trailing dot might be interpreted as a *relative* name. As an example, the user of pc2.marketing.example.com connecting to pc1.marketing.example.com might type pc1 in a client application. pc1 would be interpreted as a relative name, and the application might append marketing.example.com. to it. If the user of this application wanted to specify the FQDN, he would have typed pc1.marketing.example.com., with the trailing dot.

NOTE Using relative names is discouraged because it is confusing. For example, in Figure 10-1, if the user of the client application on pc2.marketing.example.com specifies pc1 as the destination host, it is not clear whether he is requesting a connection to pc1.marketing.example.com or to pc1.engineering.example.com.

This book always refers to DNS names as absolute names or FQDNs. The use of the trailing dot to indicate absolute names strictly depends on the application. For the purpose of this book, we typically refer to FQDN names as the fully specified DNS names with or without the trailing dot.

Zones

Figure 10-2 maps the DNS namespace tree to the physical DNS servers that store the information about the domains. These DNS servers are identified by nameserver1.example.com, nameserver.marketing.example.com, and nameserver.engineering.example.com. As you can see, the intelligence is distributed on multiple servers.

A *zone* is the portion of the namespace for which a name server holds complete information (stored in *zone data files*). This server is said to be authoritative for the zone. Figure 10-2 clarifies the concept.

Figure 10-2 *DNS Servers and Namespace*

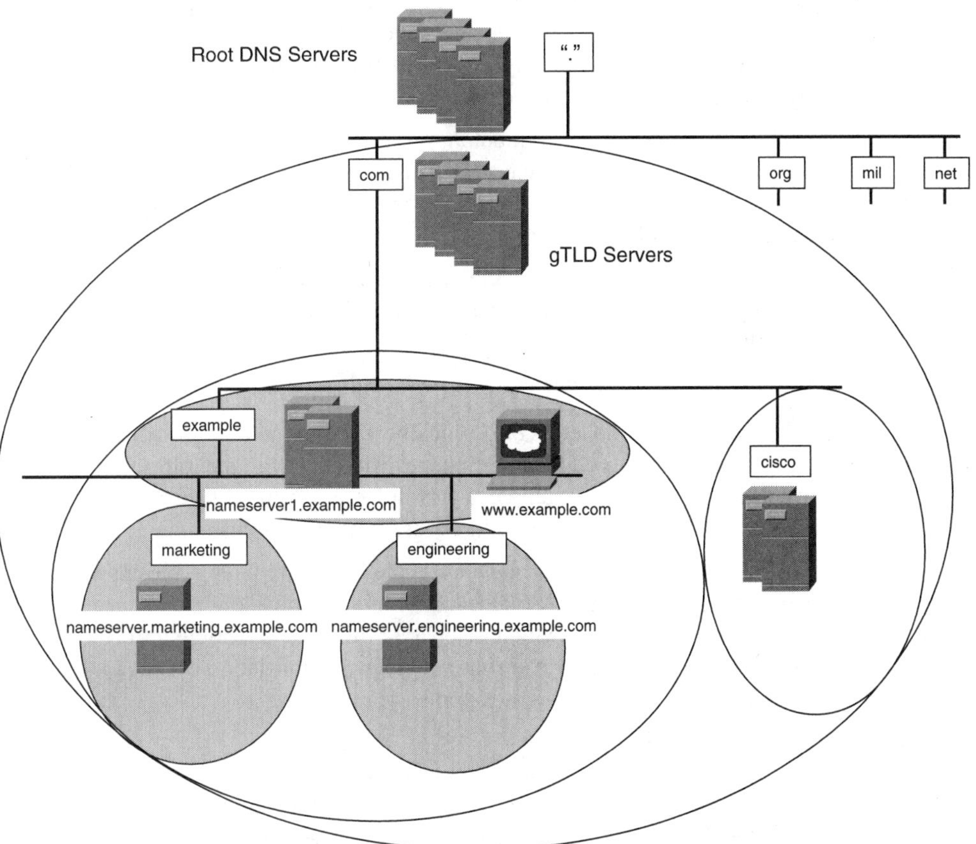

Figure 10-2 shows zones as dark circles and domains as white circles. The big circle represents the com domain. The second big circle defines the example.com domain; its name server is nameserver1.example.com. www.example.com is in the example.com domain and also in the example.com *zone*. This means that nameserver1.example.com can provide an authoritative answer for the translation of www.example.com to its IP address.

Inside the example.com domain are two subdomains: engineering.example.com and marketing.example.com. Their name servers are nameserver.engineering.example.com and nameserver.marketing.example.com, respectively.

The result of the subdivision inside example.com is as follows:

- user1.engineering.example.com belongs to the domain example.com and also to the domain engineering.example.com. The name server that has authority for it is nameserver.engineering.example.com. user1.engineering.example.com is in the engineering.example.com zone.
- user1.marketing.example.com belongs to the domain example.com and also to the domain marketing.example.com. The name server that has authority for it is nameserver.marketing.example.com. user1.marketing.example.com is in the marketing.example.com zone.
- www.example.com is in the example.com domain, and the server that stores the translation information is nameserver1.example.com. www.example.com is in example.com's zone.

Zone data files hold information about *forward* and *reverse* zones:

- **Forward zones**—The term *zone* typically refers to the forward zone, where the *forward* keyword is used to underline the difference with the information used for the inverse mapping. As an example, a forward zone provides the translation between www.example.com and the IP address associated with this name—192.0.2.80.
- **Reverse zones**—A reverse zone defines the inverse mapping, meaning the mapping of IP addresses to their DNS names. The information about the reverse mapping is stored in a zone data file, which is separate from the one holding the forward zone data. As an example, a reverse zone provides the translation between the IP address 192.0.2.80 and its name, www.example.com.

TIP Reverse zones sometimes are used as a simple security check: A server might want to verify the name of the device that it is sending a request to. The information retrieved can be used for logging purposes.

Resource Records

DNS servers are the machines that, among other operations, perform the translation between the names and the IP addresses. Each name server has knowledge of records in DNS that belong to its zone. The zone data files are the databases storing the DNS records, such as name and IP address information. The *resource records* (RRs) are the entries in the zone data file.

Example 10-1 shows the content of the file db.example.com. In the file, you can see a Start of Authority (SOA) record, one Name Server (NS) record, and several Address (A) records. Among the A records, notice the entry that stores the association between www.example.com and the IP address 192.0.2.80.

Example 10-1 *Forward Zone File db.example.com*

```
$TTL 3h
example.com. IN SOA nameserver1.example.com. adminemail.example.com. (
     2003070801     ; Serial
     3h    ; Refresh after 3h
     1h    ; Retry after 1h
     1w    ; Expire after 1 week
     1h )   ; Negative caching TTL of 1 hour
;
; Name servers
;
example.com. IN NS nameserver1.example.com.
example.com. IN NS nameserver2.example.com.
;
;  Addresses
;
localhost.example.com.       IN A 127.0.0.1
nameserver1.example.com.    IN A 192.0.2.150
nameserver2.example.com.    IN A 192.0.2.160
www.example.com.            IN A 192.0.2.80
;
```

The following list explains each type of record:

- **SOA**—The Start of Authority record indicates the zone that the name server is authoritative for. The SOA record starts with the domain name followed by the keywords IN SOA and the name of the master name server for the zone. In Example 10-1, the zone is example.com. The master is nameserver1.example.com. The SOA record has fields used to synchronize the configuration between name servers in case of redundant name servers.
- **NS**—The Name Server records indicate which name servers are authoritative for a zone. In Example 10-1, example.com's authoritative name servers are nameserver1.example.com and nameserver2.example.com. The syntax used to define NS records is the zone name (example.com.) followed by the keywords IN NS and the name servers' names.
- **A**—The Address records provide the mapping between DNS names and IP addresses. Example 10-1 lists the IP addresses for the name servers and for www.example.com. The syntax is the DNS name followed by the keywords IN A and the IP address.

- **CNAME**—The Canonical Name records allow aliases to be defined. As an example, if you want the machine hosting the internal web server to have a different name than www.example.com, you could add the following configuration—www.example.com. IN CNAME server-1.example.com. This means that you can reference the machine as www.example.com and as server-1.example.com.
- **MX**—The Mail Exchange records are used by Simple Mail Transfer Protocol (SMTP) servers to route e-mail messages. If a client (user agent) needs to send an e-mail, it contacts an SMTP server. The SMTP server sends an MX query to a DNS server. The DNS server returns an MX record with the name of the SMTP server to send the message to. RFC 2821 provides details about how mail is routed.
- **PTR**—The Pointer Resource Records are used for reverse lookup; they map the IP address to the DNS name.

NOTE The IN field in the resource records indicates the Internet class. There are other classes, such as the Chaosnet (CH) and Hesiod (HS) records for the Chaosnet and Hesiod networks respectively, but they are seldom used.

DNS Components

This section describes the software components and the hosts involved in the resolution of a DNS name to an IP address. The resolution process originates at the client application (a browser) that needs to send requests to a remote server. The application invokes the DNS resolver (software running on the same host as the application), which, in turn, relies on a DNS proxy for the name resolution.

The resolution of a DNS name is a recursive process in which a DNS proxy typically contacts a number of DNS servers before it finds the IP address it is looking for. A DNS resolver generates a *recursive query* and sends it to the DNS proxy. A recursive query means that the resolver expects either the requested data or an error message.

The DNS proxy sends queries (*nonrecursive* queries) to other name servers until it completes the resolution. Eventually, the DNS proxy returns the IP address to the resolver. The result is that the traffic between a PC and the DNS proxy is just a query and a response. The DNS proxy instead generates queries to several DNS servers.

NOTE Recursive queries carry a bit called the Recursion Desired (RD) bit, which is set to 1. Nonrecursive queries carry the RD bit set to 0.

You can find more information about recursive and iterative (nonrecursive) queries in the section, "Recursive and Iterative Queries." The process of resolving a domain name is described in further detail in the section, "DNS Resolution Process."

DNS Resolver

The DNS resolver is a library of routines used by applications to resolve DNS names. The resolver is software that runs on PCs, workstations, and servers; it is accessible by the local applications via some application programming interface (API) and sends recursive queries to DNS proxies.

NOTE In this book, we use the terminology *DNS resolver* to describe what in RFC terminology is called a *stub resolver*.

A practical example is a browser attempting to connect to www.example.com: It needs the IP address of the www.example.com server before it can connect to it.

Figure 10-3 illustrates the process. user2.cisco.com (10.15.0.4) connects to www.example.com from a web browser. The web browser is the end application; it queries the DNS resolver (that runs on the same computer) via APIs provided by the operating system.

Figure 10-3 *DNS Resolver*

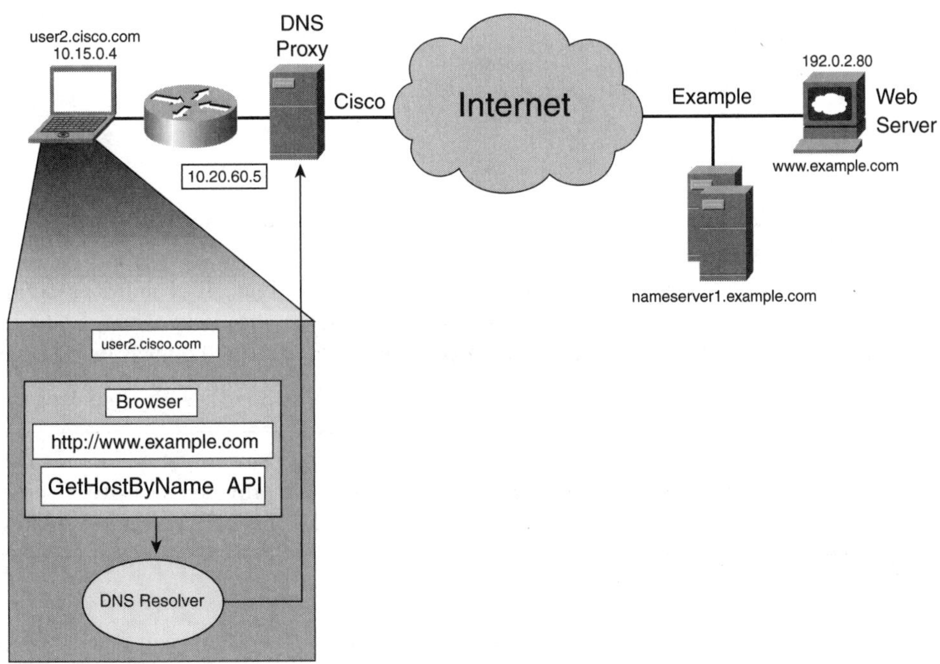

The DNS resolver sends the query to the DNS server 10.20.60.5 (which, in this case, operates as a DNS proxy). The DNS server contacts namserver1.example.com and returns the IP address of www.example.com to the resolver on user2.cisco.com. Example 10-2 shows the response the resolver gets from the DNS proxy.

TIP Windows 2000 and XP come with a built-in DNS cache. You can type ipconfig /displaydns on the client PC to view the information returned by the DNS server to the resolver and cached locally. The DNS resolver uses these records until they expire. On machines running Linux, you can install programs such as dnscache for DNS caching.

The IP address 192.0.2.80 is passed by the DNS resolver to the application (the web browser).

Example 10-2 *Displaying the DNS Cache in a Windows Machine*

```
D:\>ipconfig /displaydns
Windows 2000 IP Configuration
[...]
   www.example.com.
   ------------------------------------------------------
     Record Name . . . . . : www.example.com
     Record Type . . . . . : 1
     Time To Live  . . . . : 10786
     Data Length . . . . . : 4
     Section . . . . . . . : Answer
     A (Host) Record . . . :
                       192.0.2.80
[...]
```

How does the resolver know which DNS server to use? Figure 10-4 shows an example of configuration for a Windows machine. As you can see, the client, whose IP address is 10.15.0.4 (user2.cisco.com), is configured statically to use 10.20.60.5 as its DNS server.

TIP The configuration displayed in Figure 10-4 shows the manual configuration of a DNS server. Normally, the DNS configuration is dynamic and is provided by a DHCP server: The DHCP server can assign both the client's IP address and the DNS server's IP address.

Figure 10-4 *DNS Configuration on a Client PC*

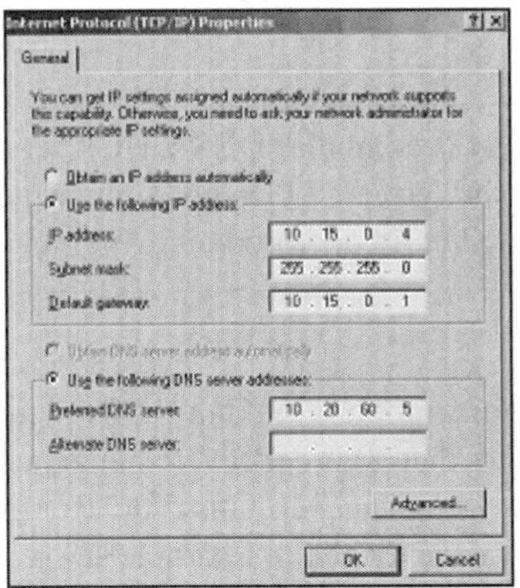

DNS Server

DNS servers are the machines that respond to DNS queries. DNS servers can translate between the names and the IP addresses. A DNS server returns A records for the hosts that belong to its zone, and referrals (basically NS records) to other name servers to which it delegated the authority for the subdomains.

NOTE For more information about referrals, read the section, "Referrals."

An example of the first operation is nameserver1.example.com returning the A record for www.example.com with the IP address 192.0.2.80.

An example of delegation of authority is nameserver1.example.com providing a referral to nameserver.marketing.example.com when resolving user1.marketing.example.com. This is also what happens on the root name servers and the TLD servers during the resolution of Internet names. Referrals are generated when a DNS server receives a nonrecursive query in which the answer, according to the delegation chain, is stored in a subdomain.

The most important DNS servers in the Internet are the root DNS servers. The root DNS servers provide referrals to the TLD servers, such as gTLDs and ccTLDs. In practice, if a DNS proxy on the Internet wants to find out an IP address for the publicly accessible servers of cisco.com, it starts querying the root name servers; they refer the host to the servers that know about the com domain (gTLD servers). These servers, in turn, provide a referral to the name server authoritative for Cisco.com.

The most popular DNS software today is probably the Berkeley Internet Name Domain (BIND), whose UNIX daemon is called *named*.

TIP Cisco Network Registrar is a popular DNS/DHCP server. For more information, refer to http://www.cisco.com/warp/public/cc/pd/nemnsw/nerr/index.shtml and http://www.cisco.com/univercd/cc/td/doc/product/rtrmgmt/ciscoasu/nr/index.htm.

Example 10-3 shows the configuration of a BIND name server. The configuration file (for versions of BIND greater than 8) is called /etc/named.conf. As you can see, the information about the zone example.com is in /var/named/db.example.com. db.example.com is called a zone data file, which was described in Example 10-1.

Example 10-3 *Excerpt from named.conf on a Name Server*

```
options {
        directory "/var/named";
};
zone "example.com" IN {
         type master;
         file "db.example.com";
};
```

Example 10-4 shows the portion of the named.conf configuration that defines where to find the database information for the reverse zone 2.0.192.in-addr.arpa: This is the file db.192.0.2, which you can see in Example 10-5. The records with the reverse mapping information are called PointerRecords (PTR).

Example 10-4 *Reverse Zone Excerpt from named.conf*

```
zone "2.0.192.in-addr.arpa" IN {
         type master;
         file "db.192.0.2";
};
```

Example 10-5 *Reverse Zone File db.192.0.2*

```
$TTL 3h
2.0.192.in-addr.arpa. IN SOA nameserver1.example.com. adminemail.example.com. (
   2003070801       ; Serial
   3h     ; Refresh every 3h
   1h     ; Retry after 1h
   1w     ; Expire after 1w
   1h)    ; Negative caching TTL of 1 hour
```

Example 10-5 *Reverse Zone File db.192.0.2 (Continued)*

```
;
; Name Servers
;
2.0.192.in-addr.arpa.  IN NS nameserver1.example.com.
;
; Addresses point to canonical names
;
150.2.0.192.in-addr.arpa. IN PTR nameserver1.example.com.
```

DNS Proxy

A DNS server can operate like a DNS proxy. This means that the stub resolver on a client in the example.com domain can contact a DNS proxy to resolve www.cisco.com by sending a query with the RD bit set to 1. The client's request is called a *recursive* query: the client wants back an IP address from the proxy, not a referral to other name servers.

The DNS proxy contacts the root name servers, the gTLD name servers, and the authoritative name server for cisco.com sequentially by sending queries with the RD bit set to 0. These queries are called *nonrecursive (iterative)* queries. Using the referrals from each one of these servers, the DNS server eventually finds the IP address for www.cisco.com and returns it to the requesting client.

It should be clear at this point that a DNS server has two different roles:

- **DNS proxy**—When it answers recursive queries (queries with the RD bit set to 1). A DNS proxy typically originates nonrecursive queries (queries with the RD bit set to 0). A DNS proxy can cache resolved DNS names and answer queries from its local cache, thus accelerating the DNS resolution process. A DNS proxy also can generate recursive queries (to a *forwarder,* for example). Query answers from the DNS proxy carry the *Recursion Available (RA)* bit set to 1.
- **DNS server**—When it answers nonrecursive queries. If the name requested is in its zone, the DNS server returns an A record. If the data requested in the query is in a delegated domain of the zones the DNS server is authoritative for, it gives out referrals by returning NS records. You can force a name server to behave purely like a provider of locally stored records by disabling recursive queries. When configured with this option, the DNS server turns off the *RA* flag in its answers.

NOTE In this book, we use the terminology *DNS proxy* for servers answering recursive queries and *DNS server* for servers answering nonrecursive queries. We use the term *resolver* to define the software that runs on client machines and that originates queries but does not understand referrals. The DNS proxy corresponds to a *nonstub resolver*, and the DNS resolver corresponds to a *stub resolver* in RFC terminology.

The boundaries among these three components are blurred because a name server can behave as any of these components.

DNS proxies can be categorized further as DNS forwarders and DNS caching-only servers.

DNS Forwarder

A typical design in enterprise networks consists of having a number of DNS servers resolving DNS queries originated by internal clients for the internal namespace, and only a few name servers used to resolve queries originated by internal clients for external domain names (Internet names). These name servers are called *forwarders*.

Normally, a resolver sends a recursive query to a DNS server, and the DNS server provides the answer. The information returned can be from its local database, if it is authoritative for the domain being requested or is the result of the resolution process (in which case, the DNS server behaves like a DNS proxy).

If a client in the example.com domain requests a resolution of www.cisco.com to a DNS server, this server would have to send queries to the root name servers, com servers, and so on. Another client, which is using another name server in the same company, might send a query for the same name, www.cisco.com. Normally, you do not want all the DNS servers (proxies) in your company to send DNS queries to the Internet for a number of reasons, including the amount of traffic generated and possibly security. The solution consists of electing just a few of the servers as the "forwarders" and pointing the other intranet DNS servers to the selected forwarders.

Aggregating DNS queries for the Internet into the DNS forwarders also allows optimizations such as caching, in which the answer for a domain previously requested would be available for subsequent queries.

Based on the previous definition, a DNS forwarder operates as a DNS proxy: It answers a recursive query on behalf of an internal DNS server, which sends a query with the Recursion Desired (RD) flag on.

Caching-Only Server

A caching-only server is a name server that does not have any zone files, which means that it is not authoritative for any domain. Its function is to send queries to other name servers, following referrals and caching responses.

A caching-only server performs the resolution on behalf of the client, without being authoritative for any specific domain. Or, it can use a forwarder, in which case it sends a recursive query to the forwarder.

DNS Resolution Process

DNS traffic in an intranet or Internet is mainly made of clients sending queries in a single packet to a DNS server and this one sending back a response. If a DNS server is authoritative for the name requested, it responds with the matching IP address; this completes a DNS transaction known as a query type A.

Now consider Figure 10-5. The client represented by the laptop sends HTTP requests to www.example.com. On the left of the figure, you see a rectangle representing the laptop and inside it another rectangle representing the browser with the URL that the client types. The browser needs to find the IP address for www.example.com.

NOTE The IP addresses in the demilitarized zone (DMZ) are public. This chapter uses the RFC 3330 192.0.2.0/24 special range for documentation purposes.

Here is what happens:

1. The browser calls an API the GetHostByName, which invokes a routine from the DNS resolver.
2. The DNS resolver sends a query type A (recursive) to the DNS proxy.
3. The DNS proxy sends a query for name servers for the root zone to one of the servers mentioned in the hint file. The result is cached locally as the current list of root servers.
4. The DNS proxy sends a query type A (nonrecursive) to one of the root name servers. The root name server returns the information about the com name servers (referral).
5. The DNS proxy chooses one of the name servers that knows about the .com domain—for example, c.gtld-servers.net, whose IP address is 192.26.92.30. The DNS proxy sends the query type A to c.gtld-servers.net, and it receives an answer with the referral to nameserver1.example.com.
6. The DNS proxy now contacts the name server authoritative for www.example.com (nameserver1.example.com). The DNS proxy sends a query type A to nameserver1.example.com for www.example.com; in return, it receives the IP address for www.example.com.

Figure 10-5 *The DNS Resolution Process*

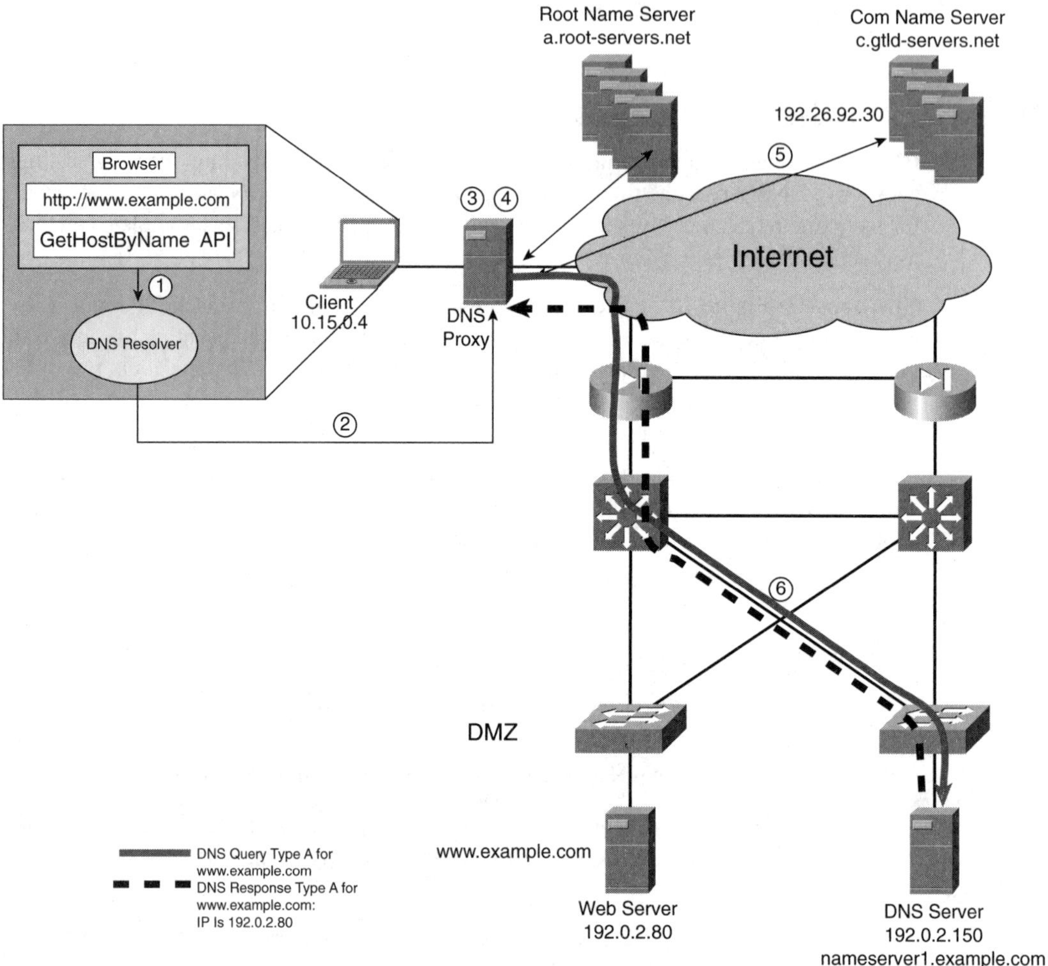

Query Format

The first step in the resolution process is the resolver sending a DNS query type A to the DNS proxy. Example 10-6 shows the content of the query for www.example.com (which is Step 2 in Figure 10-5).

As you can see, the RD bit is turned on. Type A means that the resolver expects to receive A records as a result. The following sections further explain the concept of recursion.

Example 10-6 *Format of a DNS Query Sent by a Resolver*

```
Domain Name System (query)
    Transaction ID: 0x0002
    Flags: 0x0100 (Standard query)
        0... .... .... .... = Response: Message is a query
        .000 0... .... .... = Opcode: Standard query (0)
        .... ..0. .... .... = Truncated: Message is not truncated
        .... ...1 .... .... = Recursion desired: Do query recursively
[…]
    Queries
        www.example.com: type A, class inet
            Name: www.example.com
            Type: Host address
            Class: inet
```

Root Hint

When receiving the query from the *resolver*, the DNS proxy contacts the root name servers (Step 3 in Figure 10-5). The queries sent by the DNS proxy are similar to Example 10-6, with the difference that the RD bit is set to 0.

You might wonder how the DNS knows about the location of the root name servers. The answer is by the root hints. This is information that the system administrator downloads from ftp://ftp.rs.internic.net/domain/named.root and uploads into the name server.

The root hint file looks like Example 10-7, where you can see the NS record for the domain and the IP address for the name server authoritative for the domain. Example 10-8 shows how to configure a BIND DNS server to use the root hint file.

Example 10-7 *An Excerpt from the Root Hint File named.root*

```
.                        3600000  IN  NS    A.ROOT-SERVERS.NET.
A.ROOT-SERVERS.NET.      3600000      A     198.41.0.4
;
; formerly NS1.ISI.EDU
;
.                        3600000      NS    B.ROOT-SERVERS.NET.
B.ROOT-SERVERS.NET.      3600000      A     128.9.0.107
;
; formerly C.PSI.NET
;
.                        3600000      NS    C.ROOT-SERVERS.NET.
C.ROOT-SERVERS.NET.      3600000      A     192.33.4.12
;
; formerly TERP.UMD.EDU
;
```

Example 10-8 *named.conf Configuration for the Root Hint*

```
options {
        directory "/var/named";
};
zone "example.com" IN {
         type master;
         file "db.example.com";
};
zone "." IN {
         type hint;
         file "named.root";
};
```

Referrals

The DNS proxy contacts the root name servers to find out about the www.example.com. The root name servers do not know about www.example.com, but they know about the com DNS servers (gTLD servers). The DNS proxy obtains a referral from the root server to the com servers. Example 10-9 shows how an answer from the root name servers looks: the *ANSWER SECTION* is empty, the *AUTHORITY SECTION* carries NS records for the gTLD servers, and the *ADDITIONAL SECTION* carries the IP addresses for the gTLD servers.

Example 10-9 *Answer from the DNS Root Servers for www.example.com*

```
;; ANSWER SECTION:

;; AUTHORITY SECTION:
com.                    2D IN NS        J.GTLD-SERVERS.NET.
com.                    2D IN NS        K.GTLD-SERVERS.NET.
com.                    2D IN NS        E.GTLD-SERVERS.NET.
com.                    2D IN NS        M.GTLD-SERVERS.NET.
com.                    2D IN NS        A.GTLD-SERVERS.NET.
com.                    2D IN NS        G.GTLD-SERVERS.NET.
com.                    2D IN NS        H.GTLD-SERVERS.NET.
com.                    2D IN NS        C.GTLD-SERVERS.NET.
com.                    2D IN NS        I.GTLD-SERVERS.NET.
com.                    2D IN NS        B.GTLD-SERVERS.NET.
com.                    2D IN NS        D.GTLD-SERVERS.NET.
com.                    2D IN NS        L.GTLD-SERVERS.NET.
com.                    2D IN NS        F.GTLD-SERVERS.NET.

;; ADDITIONAL SECTION:
J.GTLD-SERVERS.NET.     2D IN A         210.132.100.101
K.GTLD-SERVERS.NET.     2D IN A         213.177.194.5
E.GTLD-SERVERS.NET.     2D IN A         192.12.94.30
M.GTLD-SERVERS.NET.     2D IN A         192.55.83.30
A.GTLD-SERVERS.NET.     2D IN A         192.5.6.30
G.GTLD-SERVERS.NET.     2D IN A         192.42.93.30
H.GTLD-SERVERS.NET.     2D IN A         192.54.112.30
```

Example 10-9 *Answer from the DNS Root Servers for www.example.com (Continued)*

```
C.GTLD-SERVERS.NET.     2D IN A          192.26.92.30
I.GTLD-SERVERS.NET.     2D IN A          192.43.172.30
B.GTLD-SERVERS.NET.     2D IN A          192.33.14.30
D.GTLD-SERVERS.NET.     2D IN A          192.31.80.30
L.GTLD-SERVERS.NET.     2D IN A          192.41.162.30
F.GTLD-SERVERS.NET.     2D IN A          192.35.51.30
```

At this point, the DNS proxy queries the com DNS servers about www.example.com (Step 5 in Figure 10-5). The com servers do not know about www.example.com, but they know that nameserver1.example.com might have that information. The com servers provide a referral to nameserver1.example.com, as you can see in Example 10-10. Once more, there is an empty ANSWER SECTION, and the NS records are in the AUTHORITY SECTION.

Example 10-10 *Answer from the DNS com Server for www.example.com*

```
;; ANSWER SECTION:

;; AUTHORITY SECTION:
example.com.               2D IN NS        nameserver1.example.com.

;; ADDITIONAL SECTION:
nameserver1.example.com     2D IN A         192.0.2.150
```

TIP In Example 10-10, the com server gives out the NS record for nameserver1.example.com. You also can see that the server gives the IP address for nameserver1.example.com, even if it does not belong to the com zone. This is because the DNS proxy needs to know how to reach nameserver1.example.com, so the com server provides this section, which is called a *glue* record.

At the end, the DNS proxy contacts nameserver1.example.com and once more sends the query type A for www.example.com, with the RD bit set to 0 (this is Step 5 in Figure 10-5). This time, the DNS proxy receives an answer with the ANSWER SECTION, as you can see in Example 10-11. The ANSWER SECTION has the IP address of www.example.com.

Example 10-11 *Answer from the DNS Server nameserver1example.com for a Query Type A for www.example.com*

```
Domain Name System (response)
Transaction ID: 0x0002
    Flags: 0x8580 (Standard query response, No error)
        1... .... .... .... = Response: Message is a response
```

continues

Example 10-11 *Answer from the DNS Server nameserver1example.com for a Query Type A for www.example.com (Continued)*

```
        .000 0... .... .... = Opcode: Standard query (0)
        .... .1.. .... .... = Authoritative: Server is an authority for domain
        .... ...0 .... .... = Recursion desired: Don't do query recursively
        .... .... 1... .... = Recursion available: Server can do recursive queries
[…]
    Answers
        www.example.com: type A, class inet, addr 192.0.2.80
            Name: www.example.com
            Type: Host address
            Class: inet
            Time to live: 60 minutes
            Data length: 4
            Addr: 192.0.2.80
[…]
```

TIP In Example 10-11, you see that the Authoritative Answer (AA) bit is set. If you look at the DNS records received by the resolver on a workstation, you see that the AA bit is not necessarily set to 1. Why?

The first resolver to request the resolution of www.example.com receives the record with the AA bit set to 1 because the DNS proxy needs to query the authoritative name server for example.com. Other resolvers requesting the same record receive the answer from the DNS proxy cache: As a result, these answers do not have the Authoritative bit set. Another piece of information that you can read in Example 10-11 is the Time-to-Live (TTL), which, in the example, is 60 minutes. The TTL of this same record returned by the DNS proxy cache is less than 60 minutes: The DNS proxy ages the cached entries by decreasing the TTL until they expire.

Now suppose that you want to create a subdomain such as engineering.example.com, and you want nameserver1.example.com to delegate authority for the engineering.example.com zone to another name server. The configuration looks like Example 10-12.

Example 10-12 *Excerpt of db.example.com Modifications to Delegate Authority for engineering.example.com*

```
engineering.example.com. IN NS nameserver.engineering.example.com.
nameserver.engineering.example.com.     IN A 10.30.60.5
```

As you can see in Example 10-12, you create an NS record for the subdomain engineering.example.com, and you declare nameserver.engineering.example.com as the name server. Because nameserver.engineering.example.com belongs to a zone for which nameserver1.example.com has delegated the authority, you also need to give the IP address for this name server (glue record).

As a result, a client sending a query type A for www.engineering.example.com first would contact nameserver1.example.com. It then would receive an NS record for engineering.example.com that tells it to contact nameserver.engineering.example.com. Eventually, nameserver.engineering.example.com translates www.engineering.example.com to its IP address.

The preceding configurations are said to be the *delegation* of authority from nameserver.example.com to nameserver.engineering.example.com for the domain engineering.example.com. During the resolution process, nameserver.example.com answers to the queries for the domain engineering.example.com with referrals to nameserver.engineering.example.com.

Recursive and Iterative Queries

It is evident by now that the resolution of a DNS name is a recursive process in which a DNS proxy must contact a number of DNS servers before it has the IP address it is looking for.

A DNS resolver typically generates a recursive query (RD bit set to 1) and sends it to the DNS proxy. A recursive query means that the resolver expects either the requested data or an error message; it does not want a referral.

For this type of request, the DNS proxy typically sends queries with the RD bit set to 0 to other name servers until it completes the resolution. These queries are called nonrecursive or iterative queries. Alternatively, the DNS proxy can send a recursive query to a forwarder.

Eventually, the DNS proxy returns a query response to the resolver. The query response carries the requested records and the RA bit set to 1. The result is that the traffic between a PC and the DNS proxy is just a query and a response. The DNS proxy instead generates queries to the root name servers, the com servers, and eventually the authoritative name server for the requested FQDN.

In Figure 10-5, Step 2 is a recursive query.

A DNS proxy sending an iterative *(nonrecursive)* query to a DNS server is asking the server to supply the information only if available. If the server does not have the information but the record exists somewhere, it sends back a referral. If a server is authoritative for the name requested in the query and the name does not exist, the server returns an error response code.

In the previous examples, the DNS server resolving www.example.com sends out iterative queries to the root name servers, the com servers and nameserver1.example.com.

In Figures 10-5, Steps 3, 4, and 5 are iterative queries.

Redundant Name Servers

Normally, there are multiple name servers for the same zone:

- **A master**—The server that holds the zone data files (the server that the administrator updates periodically)
- **Multiple slaves**—Servers with the same level of authority on a zone as the master, whose configuration is imported from the master

Master and Slave

The master and slave name servers have the same level of authority in a zone. The master or slave designation indicates which server holds the master zone files.

Use the master to update the name server's zone files. A slave server then pulls the updated configurations from other authoritative name servers. One of these name servers pulls the configuration from the master. The process of retrieving the configurations from another name server is called a zone transfer.

Example 10-13 shows how to configure a name server as the master.

Example 10-13 */etc/named.conf for a Master Name Server (nameserver1.example.com)*

```
zone "example.com" in {
   type master;
   file "db.example.com";
}
```

Example 10-14 shows how to configure a name server as a slave and how to refer the name server to the master for the zone transfers. The named.conf on the slave indicates that the configuration applies to the example.com zone; it contains the IP address for the master name server, and the type slave directive defines the role for the name server.

Example 10-14 */etc/named.conf for a Slave Name Server (nameserver2.example.com)*

```
zone "example.com" in {
   type slave;
   file "bak.example.com";
   masters {192.0.2.150; };
}
```

Zone Transfers

The zone transfer defines the procedure of transferring the zone files from an authoritative name server to another authoritative name server. The slave server sends a query to retrieve what is called the SOA record.

The SOA record (see Example 10-15) has fields containing configuration information for the synchronization process in presence of redundant name servers. The SOA record tells the secondary name server the version number of the zone data files and how often the slave should poll the master. See the refresh time in Example 10-15: After three hours, the client queries for the SOA. If the serial number is higher, the slave downloads the updated zone data file. RFC 1982 has information about SOA versioning.

Example 10-15 *SOA Record in the Zone File db.example.com*

```
example.com. IN SOA nameserver1.example.com. adminemail.example.com. (
     2003070801      ; Serial
     3h     ; Refresh after 3h
     1h     ; Retry after 1h
     1w     ; Expire after 1 week
     1h )    ; Negative caching TTL of 1 hour
;
```

When the secondary name server receives the SOA record, if the serial number is the same as the serial number of the local zone files, there is no need to retrieve the new zone information. If the serial number is higher, the secondary name server retrieves the zone information over TCP.

Figure 10-6 illustrates how zone transfers work. In this figure, the master has the IP address 192.0.2.150, and the slave name server uses 192.0.2.160. The zone transfer is initiated with a query called All of Zone Transfer (AXFR). An AXFR query causes a full transfer of the zone file whose serial number has changed on the master (see Part **a** of Figure 10-6).

Figure 10-6 *DNS Zone Transfers*

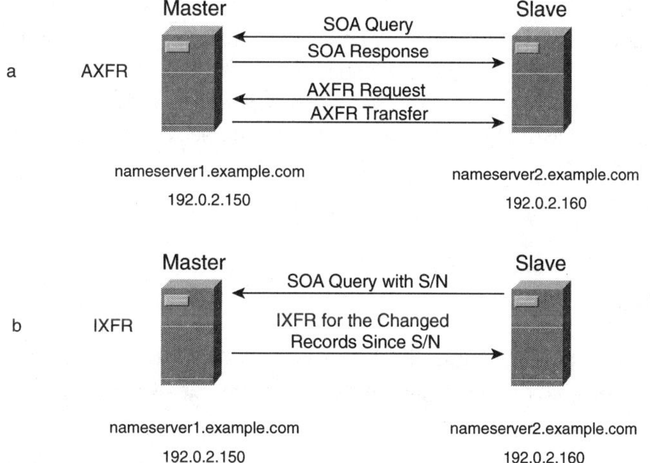

Incremental zone transfer (IXFR) queries allow more granular zone transfers, in which the master just sends the changes in the zone files based on the serial number of the slave name server zone files. To achieve this, the slave name server sends the SOA query with the serial number so that the master can provide the changed information (see Part **b** of Figure 10-6). More information about IXFR queries is available in RFC 1995.

RFC 1996 introduced one additional improvement to zone transfers: the NOTIFY packet. This is sent by a primary name server to all the registered name servers in its zone when the zone files are updated. This is done to accelerate the propagation of the updates; previously, you had to rely on the expiration time in the SOA records.

Transport Protocols

Two main communication flows exist in DNS:

- **From a DNS resolver to a DNS server**—The communication between the resolver and the DNS server is carried on UDP or TCP from a dynamic port on the resolver to port 53 on the server.
- **From a DNS server to another DNS server**—The communication between DNS servers used to have equal source and destination port 53. Newer versions of BIND make this user configurable, with the default behavior being the use of a dynamic source port and port 53 as the destination. The BIND directive **query-source address * port 53** enables you to force the use of the same source and destination port 53. This directive applies only to UDP queries; TCP queries from a DNS server to another DNS server use a random port at the originating node.

The transport for the different query types is as follows:

- **A query**—This typically is carried on UDP, but it also can be done on TCP.
- **SOA query**—A secondary name server that wants to update its zone files first sends an SOA query using UDP to a primary name server. If the secondary server finds that the serial number is higher than its own, it starts a zone transfer. SOA queries use UDP with the destination port of 53. On some name server versions, the source port can be 53 as well.
- **AXFR query**—The zone transfers occur on TCP port 53.

DNS Caching

Caching speeds up the name-resolution process. Caching reduces the amount of processing requested by a DNS server (operating as a proxy) answering recursive queries.

When a DNS proxy receives an A query from a resolver, the following behaviors are possible:

- The DNS proxy checks its local cache for the FQDN requested. If it is present, it sends back the answer to the resolver with the Authoritative Answer (AA) bit not set.
- The DNS proxy does not have any cached A records for the FQDN, but it still has cached NS records for the domain. As an example, the A record for www.example.com might have expired and, as a consequence, might be no longer cached, but the DNS proxy still might have cached NS records for example.com; in that case, it sends a query type A to nameserver1.example.com. It caches the A record for www.example.com and sends the answer to the resolver with the AA bit set. The A record is cached for as long as the TTL in the record indicates.
- The DNS proxy does not have cached A records or cached NS records. In this case, it contacts the root DNS servers and proceeds as described in the "DNS Resolution Process" section. Each record (NS or A) received during the resolution process is stored in the local cache for future use.

NOTE Another aspect to caching is *negative caching*. Negative caching refers to the fact that a resolver can cache an AA about a record that does not exist. The TTL of the negative answer can be configured on the domain name server that is authoritative for a zone so that when this name server returns a negative answer, it also carries the TTL indicating how long this answer can be cached. The time a negative answer is cached is the smallest value between the TTL of the SOA and the TTL value inside the SOA (known as the negative caching TTL). Refer to RFC 2308 for more information.

Caching is good and bad. Caching is beneficial because it reduces delay and the number of DNS packets transmitted. The drawback of caching is stale records, resulting in applications attempting to connect to IP addresses that are no longer available. The TTL settings of resource records provide control over how long a record should be stored in a cache.

TTL

The TTL of a resource record decides how long a cache stores a record that it has received from a DNS server. The TTL is returned by the DNS server together with the answer to the query.

Example 10-16 shows the TTL of the records stored in the cache of a Windows resolver. In this example, you can see an A record for www.example.com and its TTL of 10,793 sec. Originally, the TTL was 10,800 sec; of course, the cache decreases the TTL until it expires.

Example 10-16 *TTL Values in the Cache of a Windows Resolver*

```
www.example.com.
----------------------------------------------------
  Record Name . . . . . : www.example.com
  Record Type . . . . . : 1
  Time To Live  . . . . : 10793
  Data Length . . . . . : 4
  Section . . . . . . . : Answer
  A (Host) Record . . . : 192.0.2.80
```

It is up to the server administrator to configure the zone data files with the appropriate TTL. The configuration of the default TTL setting for a zone is achieved with the statement $TTL, as in Example 10-1.

You can also give explicit TTLs to the records individually. You can see this in Example 10-17. In this case, the TTL is five minutes.

Example 10-17 *Record-Specific TTL Values*

```
www.example.com.     5m     IN A 192.0.2.80
```

Choosing the right TTL is not always easy: A TTL that is too short can cause too many DNS queries to a DNS server, and a TTL that is too long can make the update too slow to work around changes in the records. Typical TTL values range between a few minutes and a few days. You should give a longer TTL (such as 1 to 3 days) to host addresses that do not change often, and a shorter TTL (such as 10 to 15 minutes) to addresses that change frequently.

Client Applications and Caching

Caching of DNS records occurs at many different places: Virtually every device involved with the DNS resolution process caches records. Some of the devices involved with the resolution process are as follows:

- A browser (or, more in general, a client application)
- A resolver
- A DNS proxy

We assume that the DNS proxy and DNS resolver respect the TTL settings for the records, as it should be. Applications do not necessarily honor the TTL.

More generically, an application using the DNS library APIs of a specific machine might not have access to the TTL field—and even if it has access to it, it might not honor it.

Today's browsers keep the A records for an amount of time that differs depending on the browser and the OS. In the case of Internet Explorer 4.*x* and later versions, this amounts to 30 minutes; in previous releases, this time was 24 hours. Other browsers expire the DNS entries with different timings—in the case of Netscape 4.*x*, the default value is 15 minutes.

For more information about how Internet Explorer caches DNS host entries, refer to the Microsoft Knowledge Base article 263558, at http://support.microsoft.com/support/kb/articles/Q263/5/58.ASP.

For more information about how Netscape Communicator caches DNS entries, refer to the Netscape Communicator Preference Index page for the network.dnsCacheExpiration preference, at http://developer.netscape.com/docs/manuals/communicator/preferences/newprefn.html#network_dnsCacheExpiration.

Distribution of Multiple Records

This section discusses how DNS devices use multiple NS records and A records, and how this capability can best be used.

NS Records

Suppose that the company whose domain is example.com has a presence on the Internet at two different geographical locations. In this scenario, it is possible that the company also has one name server for example.com at each location. It is normal in this case for the gTLD servers to give out two NS records for the example.com domain, one for each name server: nameserver1.example.com and nameserver3.example.com in Figure 10-7.

Suppose that the DNS proxy already has a cache with the NS records for the domain example.com. Every time a resolver sends a query for www.example.com, the proxy measures the RTT to get the response from the authoritative name server. For example, the first time it queries nameserver1, it measures an RTT of RTT1 ms. The second time it sends the query to nameserver3, it measures an RTT of RTT2 ms. Further queries for www.example.com are sent to the closest authoritative name server, which, according to Figure 10-7, is nameserver3 (RTT2 < RTT1).

Figure 10-7 *NS Records and RTT*

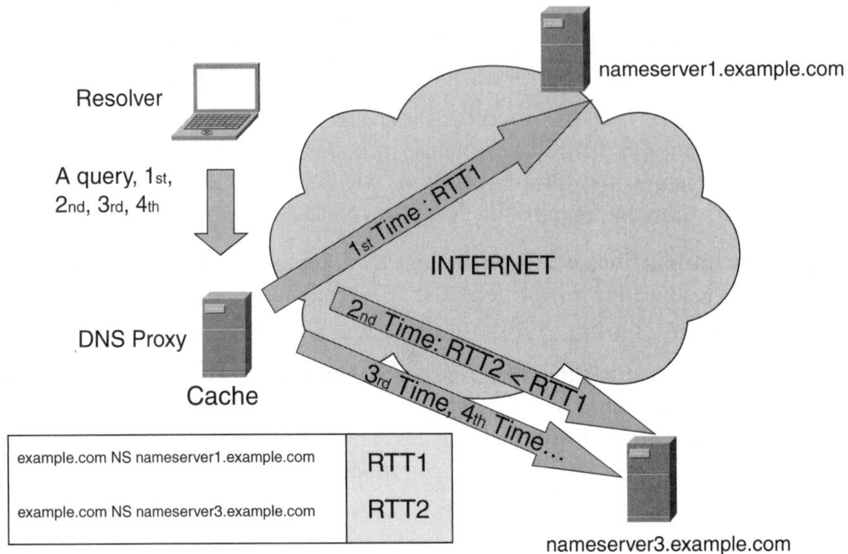

Now suppose that nameserver3 is the closest name server for the DNS proxy. What happens if this name server fails and does not answer the query? Typically, a timeout of a few seconds (three to five sec) allows a retry with another name server. In this example, the DNS proxy would send the query to nameserver1 after waiting for three sec from nameserver3.

TIP The Microsoft Knowledge Base article Q198409 explains how to configure the parameter for the Microsoft DNS server: See http://support.microsoft.com/default.aspx?scid=kb;EN-US;198409.

The RecursionRetry entry in the registry controls the timeout when the Microsoft DNS server is performing a recursive query and a name server does not respond.

So what is the point of giving out multiple NS records? It is redundancy and proximity. By having DNS servers present at different geographical locations, example.com wants to take advantage of both Data Centers and have the DNS proxies direct queries from Internet clients to the closest name server.

In case one name server fails, the DNS proxy sends queries to the remaining DNS server.

A Records

A name server can give out multiple A records for the same domain name. Consider the case in which a DNS proxy queries www.example.com, and nameserver1.example.com has a zone data file that contains the entries displayed in Example 10-18.

The name server gives out both A records for each request and round-robins the order at each request (this behavior can be configurable, depending on the implementation).

A DNS proxy (proxy1) can receive the A record 192.0.2.80 followed by 171.69.0.80 in the same response; another DNS proxy (proxy2) can receive an answer with 171.69.0.80 first. After the TTL expires, proxy1 queries nameserver1.example.com again and obtains, for example, 171.69.0.80 followed by 192.0.2.80.

Example 10-18 *Excerpt of a Zone File with Multiple A Records*

```
www.example.com.        IN A 192.0.2.80
www.example.com.        IN A 171.69.0.80
```

In BIND, you can configure the name server to hand out the A records in a different order or in a fixed order by using the directive **rrset-order** in the /etc/named.conf file, as in Example 10-19.

Example 10-19 *Name Server Configuration to Return A Records with Fixed Order*

```
options {
        directory "/var/named";
        rrset-order {
           class IN type A name "www.example.com" order fixed;
        };
};
```

TIP You can use a DNS server to achieve load distribution of incoming requests (HTTP requests, for example) to a number of servers (web servers, for example).

As an example, www.example.com could be associated with two or three IP addresses and could rely on a DNS server to assign some clients to the first server, some to the second server, and some to the third server.

Using load distribution with DNS for a *local* server farm is not as effective as using load-balancing devices (read Chapter 16, "Load-Balancing Modes and Predictors").

Load distribution among multiple Data Centers effectively can take advantage of DNS. This practice is called request routing, global server load balancing, or site selection, and it is described at the end of this chapter.

Client Applications and Multiple Records

As previously explained, applications running on local machines rely on a resolver to map DNS names to IP addresses. The end user of A records is the application, not the resolver or the DNS proxy.

When an application has received a number of IP addresses for the same domain, it can decide how to use them.

As an example, suppose that a web browser receives two A records in the following order: 192.0.2.80 and 171.69.0.80. The browser opens one or more TCP connections to 192.0.2.80.

In case the TCP connections to 192.0.2.80 fail, the browser can use 171.69.0.80 as a fallback mechanism. The described behavior is the expected one, but it depends on the browser and the operating system.

This behavior, combined with the behavior of DNS proxies with multiple NS records, can be exploited to provide redundancy across geographically dispersed Data Centers.

DNS Server Placement

Placement of DNS servers in the enterprise network must address the following requirements:

- Provide translation services for the internal namespace. This means that name servers that are authoritative for the local domain name must respond to queries from the inside clients.
- Provide the DNS proxy functionalities to resolve Internet names on behalf of the internal clients.
- Provide translation services for the external clients connecting the company's public servers (web servers, for example). This means that DNS servers that are authoritative for the local domain must be accessible by external clients.

The first requirement is addressed by the placement of internal DNS servers in the enterprise data center. These name servers are authoritative for the company's namespace. The DNS proxy functionality is provided by servers in the DMZ. Translation for the company's public servers (such as www.example.com) is provided by servers in the DMZ as well.

Protecting the information about the internal namespace is achieved by splitting internal and external namespaces.

DNS Forwarder Placement

Several DNS proxies exist in an enterprise network; typically, you do not want to grant Internet access to each of them. The solution to this problem is the configuration of DNS forwarders.

See Figure 10-8. When an internal client tries to resolve a domain name such as www.cisco.com, the resolver sends a recursive query to nameinternal.example.com. This DNS server cannot resolve www.cisco.com, and it is configured to forward the query to the forwarders, as in Example 10-20.

Figure 10-8 *Forwarders in the DMZ*

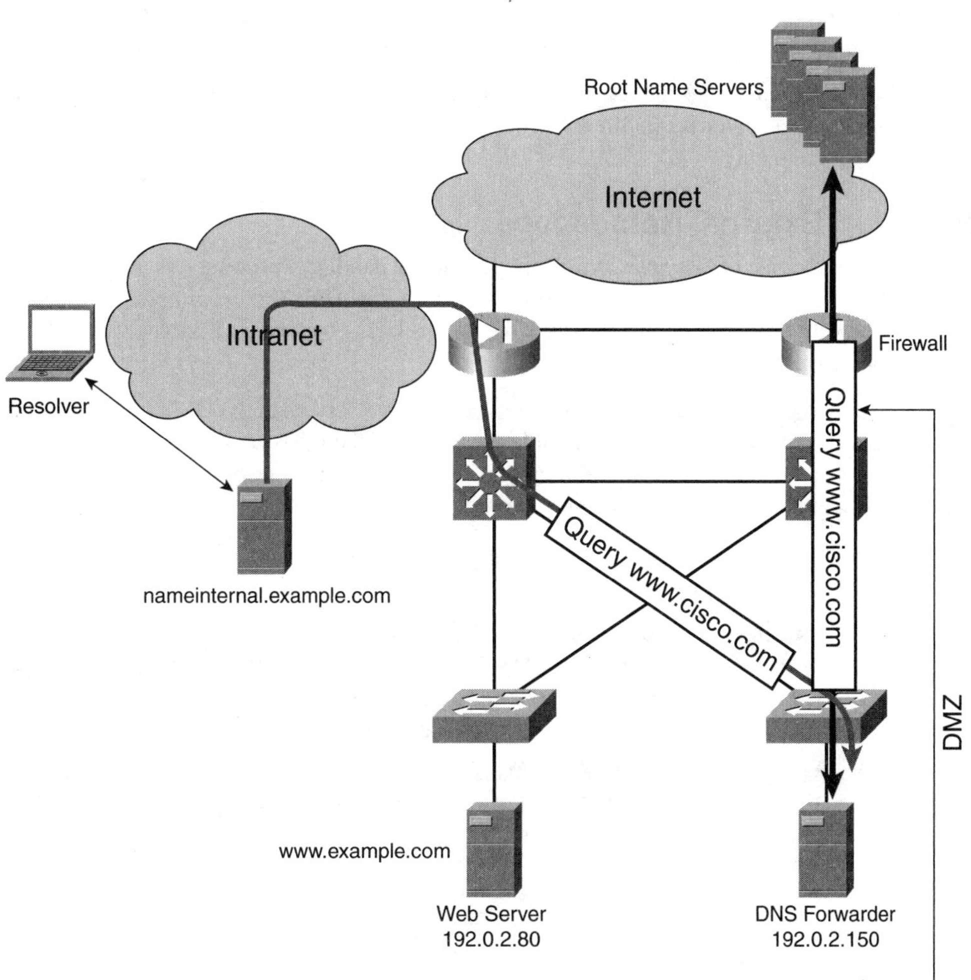

Example 10-20 *Primary DNS Server Configured to Use Forwarders*

```
options {
   directory "/var/named";
   forwarders {192.0.2.150; };
};
zone "example.com" IN {
         type master;
         file "db.example.com";
         forwarders {};
};
```

If nameinternal.example.com has the record in its local cache, it can answer immediately. Otherwise, it forwards the query to 192.0.2.150, which is the forwarder located in the DMZ.

If the forwarder has the record in its cache, it sends an answer immediately; otherwise, it proceeds as described in the section, "DNS Resolution Process."

Internal and External Namespace

The presence of example.com on the Internet is handled by the servers in the DMZ: www servers, SMTP servers, DNS servers, and more. The DNS servers provide the authoritative answer to external clients querying for public-facing servers such as www.example.com and ftp.example.com.

Many organizations typically require that the DNS servers in the DMZ be configured with a zone data file that does not include the names of the internal hosts. The reason is that the information about the internal IP addresses is irrelevant; some organizations also think that hiding the internal domain names provides security.

The design that results from these requirements is called *split namespace.* In this design, there are two DNS servers:

- **An external DNS server**—This one is also called a *delegated* name server, which basically means that the gTLD servers have NS records pointing to this name server. The external name server has a subset of the example.com zone. In Figure 10-9, nameserver1.example.com is such a name server.
- **An internal DNS server**—This is the name server with the information about the internal name space. Different from the external name server, the internal one has the complete zone file information. In Figure 10-9, nameinternal.example.com is such a server.

Figure 10-9 *Configuration of a Split Namespace*

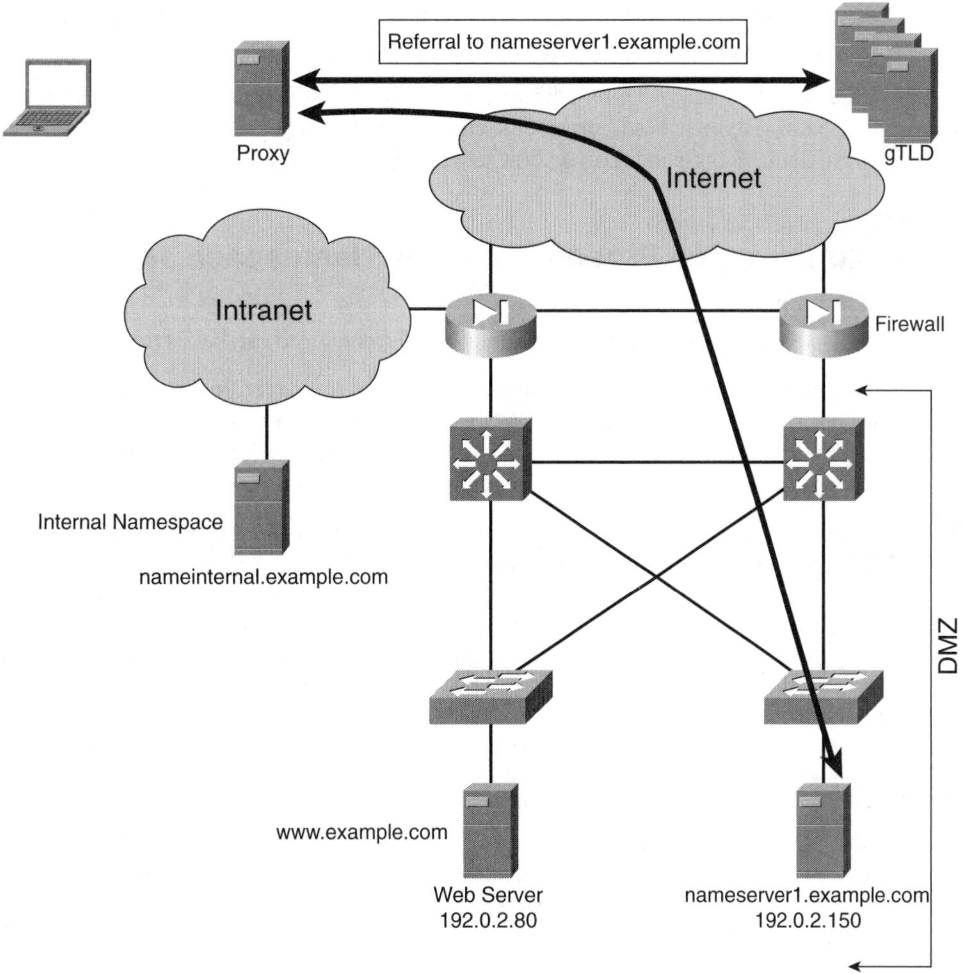

In Figure 10-9, you can see that the client querying for www.example.com receives a referral to nameserver1.example.com. The external name server has information only about the machines available in the DMZ network, which protects the information about the internal name space.

Alternatively, it is possible to host the external name server at the service provider's DNS servers. It is also possible to have one external name server in the DMZ and one at the service provider's, and to configure them as master and slave, respectively: This allows the update the external zone files locally.

Other possible deployment modes for DNS can address security; this section shows one of the common approaches to protect the enterprise internal namespace. This section does not constitute a recommendation on how to deploy DNS servers in the DMZ.

DNS Resolution in the Presence of Split Namespace and Forwarders

In a split namespace design, the external DNS servers also can be used as forwarders.

In Figure 10-9, nameserver1.example.com is also a forwarder. Internal clients connecting to Internet hosts resolve external DNS names by sending a recursive query to the internal DNS server (nameinternal.example.com), which, in turn, forwards this query to the external DNS server. Nameserver1.example.com follows the referrals and resolves the host name.

A special case of an internal client in the example.com is given by the servers in the DMZ. Which name server do the servers in the DMZ use? Normally, the servers in the DMZ need to have access to internal resources, which means that www.example.com's name server in Figure 10-9 would be nameinternal.example.com. If www.example.com asks the resolution of www.cisco.com, this query goes to nameinternal.example.com first and then to the forwarder.

Site-Selection Considerations

DNS often is used to perform site selection, content routing, request routing, or global server load balancing: These terms all mean the same thing. This means that you could have Data Centers in two (or more) different locations and map applications available in both Data Centers to the same DNS name.

As an example, www.example.com could map to 192.0.2.80 and to 171.69.0.80, where 192.0.2.80 is in one geographical location and 171.69.0.80 is in another geographical location.

Site selection makes it possible to resolve www.example.com based on the availability of the Data Center at a certain location. For example, if the servers for 192.0.2.80 are not available, the DNS resolution should hand out 171.69.0.80. This can be achieved with special devices (or features) called site selectors (SS), content routers (CR), request routers (RR), or global load balancers (GLB).

When possible, the site selector should be combined with a routing solution to overcome the limitation of cached DNS entries. DNS should be used for load distribution among Data Centers. Interior Gateway Protocols (IGPs) such as OSPF or EIGRP should be used for rerouting traffic for cached DNS records.

This section describes the main requirements for a solution that provides high availability, load distribution, and proximity.

Site Selection Architecture

Site selectors monitor the availability of servers and application in the Data Centers. Typically, this is achieved by communicating with the local load balancers at each location. Site selectors act as DNS servers that are authoritative for domain names such as www.example.com. Figure 10-10 shows a typical Data Center topology, including the site-selection technology.

Figure 10-10 *DNS and Site Selection*

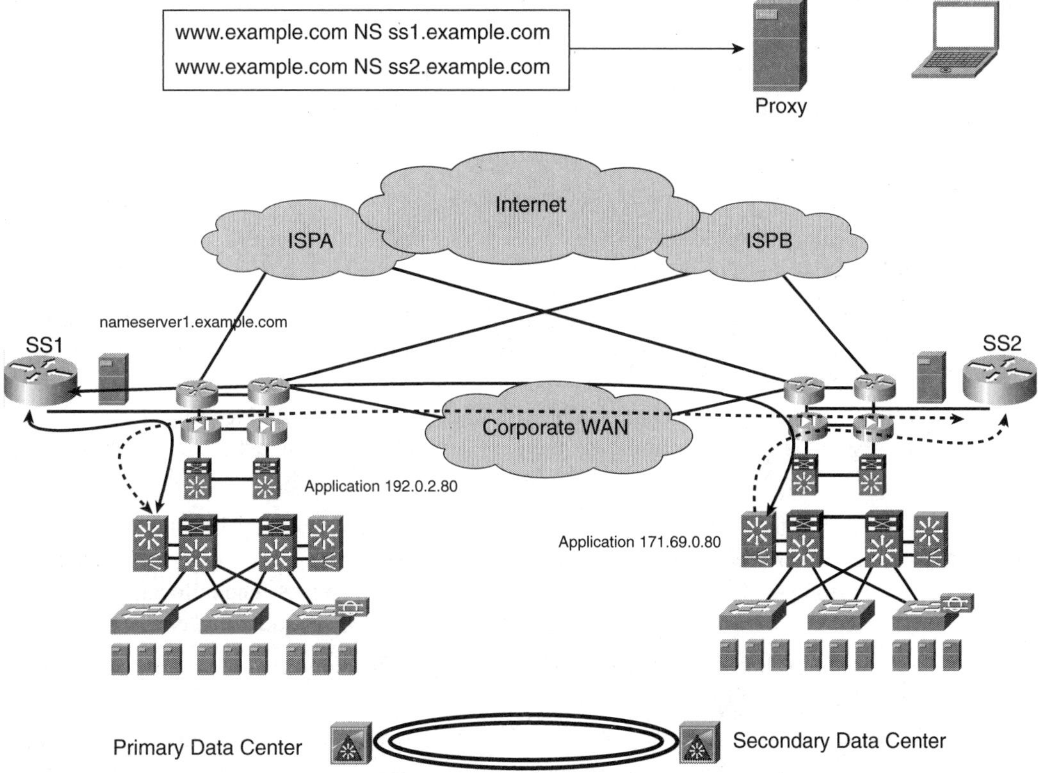

In Figure 10-10, you can see two Data Centers, each dual-homed to different service providers. Each Data Center is designed with redundant network devices, according to the best practices of high availability (see Chapter 20, "Designing the Data Center Infrastructure"). The application data is replicated between the Data Centers over a dense wavelength division multiplexing (DWDM) optical link.

The same application is available at both Data Centers, with two IP addresses: 192.0.2.80 on the West Coast and 171.69.0.80 on the East Coast. Most failure scenarios are recovered by the use of local redundancy: spanning tree, routing protocols, hardware load balancing, and so on.

The two Data Centers are monitored by a site selector (represented as a big router). Monitoring means that the site selector, located in the external network, communicates with the load balancers to find out about the availability of the local servers and applications. The continuous line in Figure 10-10 shows SS1 communicating with the load balancers at each site, and the dashed line shows the communication between SS2 and the load balancers.

The site selector knows when a Data Center application is available. False positives are avoided by knowing the convergence time for local failures that do not bring down the Data Center completely and tuning the site selector accordingly.

In Figure 10-10, the client wants the A record for www.example.com. The example.com name servers return two NS records for www.example.com:

- One points to SS1 (ss1.example.com).
- The other points to SS2 (ss2.example.com).

As a result of the processing of NS records (previously described in this chapter), the DNS proxy sends the A query for www.example.com to the closest SS—in this case, SS1.

SS1 knows whether www.example.com is available locally or remotely; based on the health of the application, it returns either the local IP address 192.0.2.80, the remote address 171.69.0.80, or both (see the previous section, "DNS Caching"). The local address typically is preferred to take advantage of the proximity (if it returns both records, it places the local IP first in the list). To summarize, the main architectural elements of site selection are as follows:

- Each Data Center is designed with a fully redundant topology. Local failures normally are recovered by the use of the Spanning Tree Protocol, routing protocols, hardware load balancing, and active/standby redundant appliances. The failover time is well known and is used to determine when the Data Center should be considered down.
- Data replication makes sure that the same application data is available in both Data Centers.
- A load balancer local to each Data Center monitors applications and bundles information about the status of the applications in a special protocol used to talk to a site selector.

- A site selector external to each Data Center communicates with the local and remote load balancers via dedicated protocols.
- The parent name servers are configured to provide referrals containing the IP address of both site selectors.

Where should the site selectors be placed? If the Data Center hosts applications that are externally accessible, such as an e-commerce website, you should treat the site selectors as external name servers (refer to the section, "Internal and External Namespace").

Referrals to Site Selectors and Subdomains

This section explains how to integrate a site selector into the DNS architecture of an enterprise network. A site selector is a device capable of answering DNS queries for the purpose of distributing clients' traffic to multiple Data Centers. Example.com name servers resolve all queries but the ones for the domain that requires site selection. This is achieved by having example.com name servers delegate authority to the site selector for specific domains.

As an example, assume that the company whose domain name is example.com has a requirement for geographically dispersed Data Centers for an application hosted on www.example.com. The example.com name servers (nameserver1.example.com and nameserver2.example.com) would be configured to provide referrals to the site selectors for www.example.com.

The configuration of the name servers would look like Example 10-21. Notice the delegation of www.example.com to the sites selectors www.example.com. IN NS ss1.example.com. and www.example.com. IN NS ss2.example.com. The DNS configuration lists all the site selectors (in this example, two site selectors), for redundancy purposes.

Example 10-21 *DNS Configuration to Delegate www.example.com to a Site Selector*

```
$TTL 3h
example.com. IN SOA nameserver1.example.com. adminemail.example.com. (
     2003070801      ; Serial
     3h    ; Refresh after 3h
     1h    ; Retry after 1h
     1w    ; Expire after 1 week
     1h )    ; Negative caching TTL of 1 hour
;
; Name servers
;
example.com. IN NS nameserver1.example.com.
www.example.com. IN NS ss1.example.com.
www.example.com. IN NS ss2.example.com.
;
;  Addresses
```

continues

Example 10-21 *DNS Configuration to Delegate www.example.com to a Site Selector (Continued)*

```
;
localhost.example.com.       IN A 127.0.0.1
nameserver1.example.com.     IN A 192.0.2.150
ss1.example.com.             IN A 192.0.2.100
ss2.example.com.             IN A 171.69.0.100
;
```

Figure 10-11 shows the deployment of a site selector in the case of two Data Centers. One site selector is located at each Data Center, and the name server is configured with NS records for both site selectors.

Figure 10-11 *www.example.com or www.gslb.example.com?*

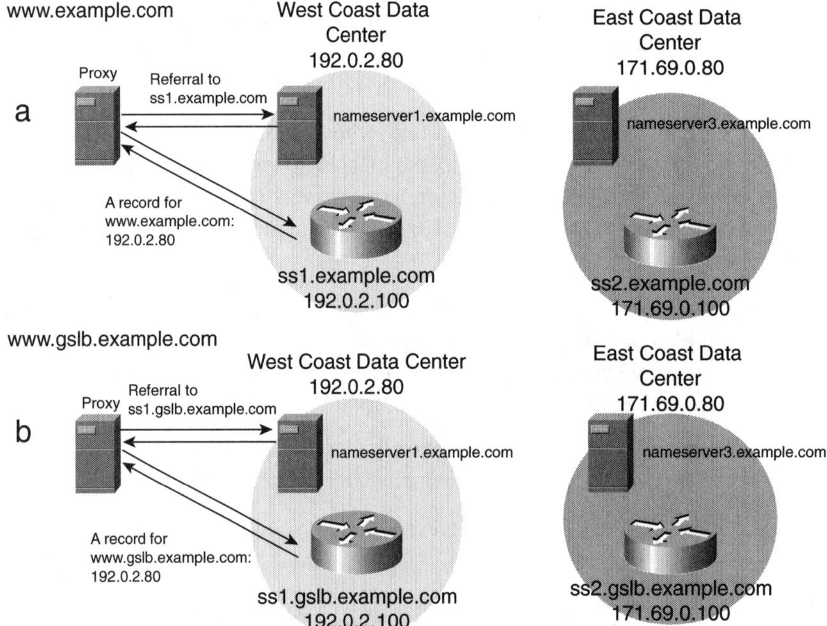

Part **a** of Figure 10-11 illustrates the fact that the client DNS proxy resolving www.example.com would contact nameserver1.example.com or nameserver2.example.com and would be referred to the site selector (ss1.example.com, in the example), which eventually resolves www.example.com to 192.0.2.80.

A different configuration consists of creating a subdomain, such as gslb.example.com, and using www.gslb.example.com as the FQDN. The end user still types www.example.com, and the DNS server "converts" this domain name into www.gslb.example.com by means of a CNAME record. The DNS proxy receives a referral to the site selectors—ss1.gslb.example.com and ss2.gslb.example.com—and eventually it sends a query for www.gslb.example.com to the site selector. You can see these steps in part **b** of Figure 10-11.

Example 10-22 shows the configuration on nameserver1.example.com. The line gslb.example.com. IN NS ss1.glsb.example.com. delegates authority for gslb.example.com to the site selector, and the glue record ss1.gslb.example.com. IN A 192.0.2.100 provides the IP address for the site selector. The line www.example.com. IN CNAME www.gslb.example.com. allows the client to use www.example.com to access www.gslb.example.com.

Example 10-22 *DNS Configuration to Delegate www.gslb.example.com to a Site Selector*

```
$TTL 3h
example.com. IN SOA nameserver1.example.com. adminemail.example.com. (
     2003070801     ; Serial
     3h    ; Refresh after 3h
     1h    ; Retry after 1h
     1w    ; Expire after 1 week
     1h )   ; Negative caching TTL of 1 hour
;
; Name servers
;
example.com. IN NS nameserver1.example.com.
gslb.example.com. IN NS ss1.gslb.example.com.
gslb.example.com. IN NS ss2.gslb.example.com.
;
;  Addresses
;
localhost.example.com.      IN A 127.0.0.1
nameserver1.example.com.    IN A 192.0.2.150
ss1.gslb.example.com.            IN A 192.0.2.100
ss2.gslb.example.com.            IN A 171.69.0.100
;
; Aliases
;
www.example.com.       IN CNAME www.gslb.example.com.
```

Proximity

DNS has a built-in mechanism to lock on to the closest DNS server authoritative for a domain. By simply returning multiple NS records, with each NS record a different site selector (or a regular DNS server at each location), the end client ends up sending A queries to the closest geographical location. This is possible because, as the section "NS Records" explained, the DNS proxies measure the time (RTT) between query and answer from the authoritative name servers for a given domain and, over time, select the "closest" one.

As a result, the site selector of each location should return the local IP address. In Figure 10-10, SS1 should return 192.0.2.80, which is an IP address that belongs to the West Coast Data Center. SS2 should return 171.69.0.80, which is an IP address that belongs to the East Coast Data Center. This ensures that the end client sends the TCP request to the closest Data Center.

As previously stated, you also can return multiple A records. In that case, you would put the local IP address first and the remote IP address second.

TIP If the Data Center hosts stateful applications, be careful with proximity: It takes several DNS resolutions for a DNS proxy to lock on to a location. If the proxy is located the same distance from both locations, it might not be assigned consistently to the same Data Center. See how to achieve stickiness later in the chapter.

Site Selection and Caching

Caching is an important piece of how DNS works. From a client perspective, caching provides the benefit of speeding up the DNS resolution. From the perspective of a Data Center administrator, caching reduces the number of DNS queries to a DNS server.

Caching can have a negative impact on site selection in case of a failure. Suppose that a client is using 192.0.2.80 as the IP address for www.example.com. Suppose now that 192.0.2.80 fails. Until the TTL for the A record for www.example.com expires on the client machine, the application is stuck with the wrong Data Center.

For this reason, it is good practice to lower the TTL to few minutes, such as five minutes, to minimize the effect of caching.

To make this design even more complex, some applications cache the records regardless of the TTL settings. As an example, browsers might not have access to the TTL information of the A records, and they might cache the A records for a certain amount of time. Windows IE caches DNS entries for 30 minutes, and Netscape caches them for 15 minutes, as described in the section, "Client Applications and Caching."

To overcome this problem, instead of returning a single A record, you could configure the site selector to use multiple A records. As an example, if the request for www.example.com is answered by SS1, this selector should return 192.0.2.80 followed by 171.69.0.80.

Listing first the local IP address achieves proximity, while including the remote IP address achieves fault tolerance in case the first location fails and the A records are cached on the browser. The fault-tolerant behavior needs explanation: The browsers have visibility on all the A records returned, and they naturally use the first record in the list. After a number of unsuccessful TCP retransmissions to the first IP, they try the second IP address in the list.

As a result, if a site becomes unavailable and a browser still is using its IP address, after some retries, the browser automatically connects to the backup site.

CAUTION The behavior in the presence of multiple A records is browser dependent. You need to verify this design based on the client applications that get access to the Data Center.

Stickiness

Applications can be stateful or stateless. The requests for a stateless application can be sent to both Data Centers during the same session, with no impact from the user perspective.

Stateful applications require saving the state data locally in the Data Center. If new requests belonging to the same session go to a different Data Center, the user negatively is impacted because he must restart the session.

Previously, we stated that to achieve proximity, the best approach is for the site selector to return the local IP address first in the list of A records. This means that if the DNS proxy of a given client sends DNS queries sometimes to SS1 and other times to SS2, the browser on the client would send HTTP requests to two different sites.

NOTE The assumption in this example is that the site selectors are configured to return the local A records. SS1 returns the A record 192.0.2.80, and SS2 returns the A record 171.69.0.80.

Suppose that a client is browsing the e-commerce area of www.example.com, and the IP address is 192.0.2.80. After 30 minutes, the browser reresolves www.example.com, and the request for some reason is answered by SS2. The result is that new TCP connections go to 171.69.0.80, with disruption of the session.

The easiest solution to this problem is to configure the predictors on SS1 and SS2 appropriately. By changing the algorithms used to return A records from the site selector, you can have SS1 and SS2 act in a consistent way.

There are two algorithms of choice:

- **Active-backup**—This involves electing one Data Center location as the only active site for a specific domain name. The client is routed to the other location only when the first one fails. 192.0.2.80 could be the active location for www.example.com, in which case, both SS1 and SS2 would return 192.0.2.80 as the IP for www.example.com. In case of a failure that makes 192.0.2.80 unavailable, both SS1 and SS2 would return 171.69.0.80 as the IP for www.example.com.

- **Source IP hash**—another solution consists of hashing the IP address of the DNS proxy and returning consistently the same A record to the same proxy querying www.example.com. In this case, a proxy sending a query for www.example.com to SS1 can receive 192.0.2.80 or 171.69.0.80 as the answer. If the same proxy queries SS2 for www.example.com, it would receive the same answer as SS1.

Both solutions can provide load distribution: In the active-backup solution, you achieve load distribution by making some domain names primary for one site and other names primary for the other site. Source IP hash distributes queries for every domain name to both sites, based on the IP address of the DNS proxy.

Summary

DNS is a naming service and provides, among others, a mechanism for translating names to IP addresses. Applications can be invoked by their DNS name, which is easier to remember and also provides more flexibility in IP address assignment. Understanding DNS helps in designing the DMZ of an enterprise network and also providing load distribution to multiple Data Centers.

DNS is structured as a hierarchical tree, in which each DNS server is responsible for a zone and provides referrals for its subdomains.

The resolution of a DNS name involves several components. The application running on the workstation uses the resolver software to obtain the IP address. The resolver sends a recursive query to the local DNS proxy. The DNS proxy sends nonrecursive queries to the DNS servers on the Internet until it receives the A record from the authoritative name server. At the end, the DNS proxy returns this information to the resolver.

One of the key features of DNS is the fact that the DNS proxy can cache previously resolved IP addresses, with the purpose of accelerating the DNS resolution for clients querying the same domain names.

Caching is useful in reducing the number of DNS queries sent by an enterprise network to the Internet, but it has an important drawback when DNS is used for load distribution.

DNS often is used to hand out multiple IP addresses for the same domain name. This allows the client's request to be distributed to multiple Data Centers. The problem with caching is the fact that a client application might use a stale DNS entry, even if the TTL of the DNS entry has expired.

A complete solution to load distribution for multiple Data Centers needs to address the key requirements of local availability before rerouting a request to the remote Data Center (achieved with local redundancy), performing application data replication (provided by technologies such as host-based mirroring), avoiding traffic blackholing due to DNS caching (provided by routing and RHI), assessing service provider availability (provided by multihoming to multiple service providers), and ensuring stickiness (provided by active/standby site selector configurations and by DNS hashing).

By combining DNS, routing, and data replication, it is possible to achieve geographical redundancy for the Data Centers.

For Further Reading

Albitz, Paul, Cricket Liu. *DNS and BIND*, Fourth Edition. O'Reilly & Associates.

Hull, Scot. *Content Delivery Networks: Web Switching for Security, Availability, and Speed.* McGraw-Hill Osborne Media.

Sauter, Dustin R. *Admin 911: Windows 2000 DNS & WINS.* McGraw-Hill Osborne Media.

This chapter covers the following topics:

- HTTP streaming
- UDP versus TCP
- Analog and digital video
- Codecs
- Packetization
- Transport formats
- Trace analysis for streams carried on UDP or TCP
- Control protocols
- Unicast, multicast, and stream splitting
- Streaming products
- Encoding mechanisms

CHAPTER 11

Streaming Protocols Overview

Streaming is a technique used to deliver multimedia objects at the same rate at which they are played. Streaming requires an application on a server to send small chunks of data (video, audio, or both) at a constant rate, and a client application to collect those chunks of data and play them in a continuous fashion. No copy of the streamed media remains on the hard disk of the client.

Understanding streaming requires knowing the formats used to capture, compress, save, and eventually transmit the data. The coder/decoder (codec) defines how the original media is compressed and decompressed. Transport protocols define how the data is delivered to the client; the Real-Time Transport Protocol (RTP) is an example. Control protocols define the establishment of the streaming session; the Real-Time Streaming Protocol (RTSP) is an example.

Streaming is used mainly for two types of applications:

- **Video on demand (VoD)**—Delivering a media stream to a client upon request from the same client
- **Video broadcasts**—Delivering a media stream to a multitude of clients at the same time. A broadcast can be subdivided further into a *live event* and a *rebroadcast*. A live event is broadcasted at the same time it is recorded. A rebroadcast is the broadcast of a previously recorded event scheduled at a particular time. The client has no control over the starting time of the media delivery for a broadcast event.

Delivering unicast video/audio streams to multiple users who share the same network generates a load equal to the sum of each individual traffic stream; this can cause network congestion. Depending on the type of application, you can use three main techniques to minimize the use of bandwidth when delivering streams:

- Multicast
- Stream splitting
- On-demand caching (proxying)

The Layer 4 protocol that typically is used to deliver multimedia streams is the User Datagram Protocol (UDP). UDP is better suited than TCP for delay-sensitive applications, such as multimedia streams, and it can be used with multicast.

Among the vendors that have provided streaming formats for encoding, transport, and file storage are Apple, Real, and Microsoft. Their respective products use a combination of proprietary and standard formats.

NOTE Cisco offers IPTV, a streaming solution based on standard formats: Some of the traces in this book are captured from live broadcasts streamed with IPTV. Cisco also offers proxy services such as splitting and on-demand caching on content engines (caches) with support for the formats of the previously named vendors.

NOTE A useful URL for streaming related technology is http://streamingmedialand.com/.

Download-and-Play, HTTP Streaming, and Real-Time Streaming

HTTP can be used to deliver video and audio objects. A web page can reference a Moving Picture Experts Group (MPEG) file, and the HTTP server serves the file in its entirety to the client requesting it. Notice that just because a file is video or audio, it does not imply that it is going to be streamed. In fact, if the medium is delivered by the HTTP server, the client just downloads and opens it: This technique is called *download-and-play* (the top of Figure 11-1 represents this). A *streaming server* is required instead to do *real-time streaming*.

Video and audio files, by nature, are bigger than the average object size, and their download can take a long time. For example, a movie trailer of 2:20 encoded at a resolution of 480 × 272 using an MPEG4 codec can be as big as 13.3 MB. Downloading this file with a broadband-access Internet connection takes around one minute. Typically, movie trailers are encoded with formats that allow *HTTP streaming*, which means that a player can display the movie before finishing downloading. This is shown in the bottom of Figure 11-1.

HTTP streaming is also called *HTTP fast start* (QuickTime) or *progressive playback* (Windows Media). HTTP streaming is neither a feature of the HTTP protocol nor a feature of the HTTP server, but it is a capability of the browser's plug-ins and a property of the media object itself.

An HTTP server is not a streaming server, which means that serving data (whether text or small graphics) is no different than serving any other object, such as a large video file. Because HTTP uses TCP as the transport protocol, the media is delivered using TCP's windowing and congestion-avoidance algorithms. As a result, delivery of multimedia files on HTTP appears to be bursty.

If the previously mentioned movie trailer was delivered by HTTP on a cable modem network, a traffic analyzer would show an average rate of 1.4 Mbps for the time necessary to download the file (one minute and a few seconds), even if the transport rate for the stream is 761.3 kbps.

Viewing a movie through HTTP (whether this is through download-and-play or HTTP streaming) tends to saturate the network (TCP tries to adjust to the network bandwidth).

Real-time streaming instead means that the server does not deliver the full media at once, but sends small chunks of data at the same rate at which the client plays them. By doing so, streaming does not take all the available bandwidth. Real-time streaming typically uses UDP as the transport protocol to avoid delays introduced by TCP retransmissions (see the section, "UDP vs. TCP").

Figure 11-1 shows that a VoD streamed by an HTTP server takes very little time to download and is delivered on TCP with a big burst that takes almost all the available bandwidth.

Figure 11-1 *Download-and-Play and HTTP Streaming*

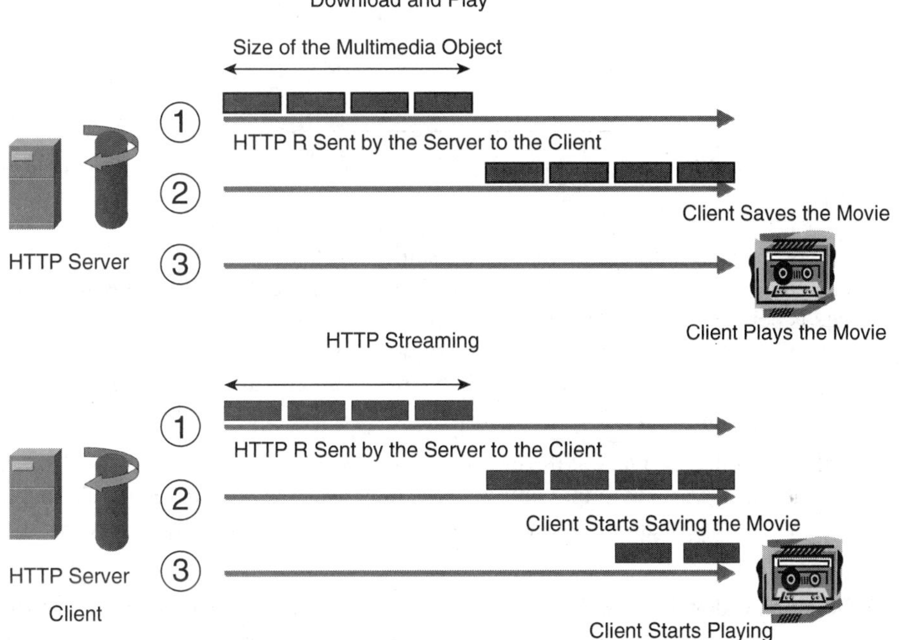

The same VoD streamed by a streaming server takes only the necessary bandwidth and is sent for the entire duration of the VoD (see Figure 11-2).

Figure 11-2 *Real-Time Streaming*

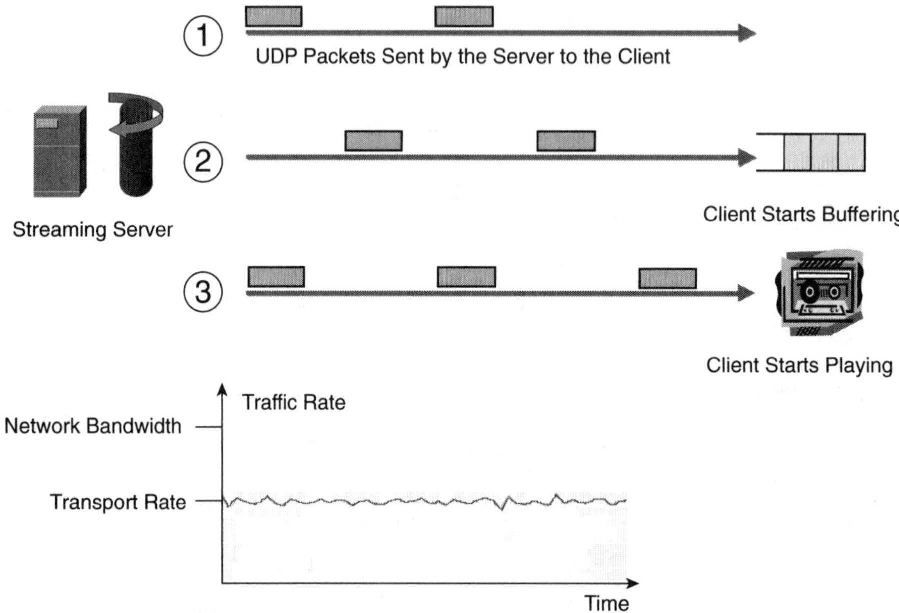

As you can see, real-time streaming consumes less bandwidth for longer periods of time compared with download-and-play. This is an advantage if the streaming media transport rate is below the available network bandwidth. If the transport rate exceeds the network bandwidth, download-and-play is more suitable because the media could be downloaded at a rate that is compatible with the available bandwidth (thanks to TCP) and eventually is played from the hard drive.

Referring to the example of the movie trailer, keeping a 761.3-kbps stream flowing across the Internet is virtually impossible because of congestion and bottlenecks in the transport media: The maximum transport rate that today can be achieved on the Internet is around 500 kbps.

In this case, download-and-play or HTTP streaming works better than real-time streaming. TCP is "greedy" and takes advantage of all the available bandwidth to download the media on the client's hard disk; because it downloads the content at a faster rate than the playing rate, the user can view the trailer without interruptions.

The conclusion is that the choice between download-and-play/HTTP streaming and real-time streaming is dictated by the event type (VoD, live broadcast, scheduled broadcast), the transport rate for the codec being used, and network bandwidth, as follows:

- **Broadcast (live or scheduled)**—You need to use real-time streaming. Be sure to choose a codec whose transport rate is compatible with the network bandwidth.
- **VoD**—If you want to use a very high-quality codec, verify that the transport rate is compatible with the network. If it is, you can use either real-time streaming or download-and-play/HTTP streaming. If not, consider using download-and-play/HTTP streaming.

NOTE The website QuickTime Movie Trailers contains a good collection of clips sent using HTTP streaming; see http://www.apple.com/trailers/index.html.

UDP Versus TCP

Delivery of multimedia streams can be achieved on both TCP and UDP. Generally, UDP is considered to be more suited for delivering real-time traffic than TCP.

This is because real-time traffic is sensitive to delay, yet not so sensitive to packet loss. A missing frame in a video sequence is not necessarily noticeable—or, if it is, it still is preferred to a long pause.

As an example, suppose that you are watching a live event such as the CEO speaking at your company meeting, and the network experiences some congestion. There are two possible outcomes for the network congestion:

- Seeing some glitches in the video, which still continues with no stopping
- Seeing a stop while the client waits for the server to retransmit lost packets

The first behavior is achieved by using UDP as the transport protocol, while the second behavior is typical of using TCP.

Normally, you would prefer the video to continue even with poorer quality rather than watching a black screen, especially considering the fact that some of the distortions in the images probably would go unnoticed by the viewer. Clearly, the delay is more important than losing some packets for this type of applications.

TCP is a reliable, connection-oriented protocol that delivers ordered byte streams. If a segment is lost, TCP ensures its delivery by using the retransmission algorithms. On the receiver side, out-of-order segments are not delivered to the application until the missing segment is retransmitted.

Also, TCP interprets packet loss as a sign of congestion in the network, which requires the sender to slow down transmitting new segments. Two algorithms regulate retransmission and congestion control: *standard retransmission*, when no ACK is received for a segment, and *fast retransmission* when the sender receives three duplicate ACKs. For more details about these algorithms, refer to Chapter 7, "IP, TCP, and UDP."

It should be clear by now that losing a single packet (using TCP), whether it is a data packet or an ACK from the receiver, introduces delay and jitter, which translates into stopping and rebuffering on the client application. With UDP, you would notice degradation only in the quality of the images.

UDP provides unreliable, connectionless, unordered datagram delivery. The main advantage of UDP is that lost packets do not delay the delivery of subsequent datagrams.

UDP is also more suitable for multicast traffic than TCP is. TCP creates bidirectional connections, which involves interaction between the sender and the receiver. Of course, this would overload the multicast server. Instead, UDP is connectionless and unidirectional in nature, which means that a single multicast server virtually can provide streaming for an arbitrary number of clients with no impact on the server performance.

Even if UDP typically is preferred to TCP because of these reasons, TCP has some advantages. Because TCP ensures the delivery of all packets, codecs that do not tolerate loss can be used. Another reason for using TCP is the presence of firewalls that typically block UDP traffic. A dejitter buffer on the client can alleviate the effect of delays introduced by TCP retransmissions. The dejitter buffer requires holding the first received records before playing them, which is also a delay: This delay needs to be compatible with the real-time requirements of the streaming event.

Table 11-1 compares TCP and UDP with regard to the suitability for multimedia delivery.

Table 11-1 *TCP versus UDP for Streaming Delivery*

Feature	TCP	UDP
Smaller delays	No	Yes
Compatibility with multicast	No	Yes
Delivery of ordered packets	Yes	No
Firewall-friendly	Yes	No

The section "Transport Formats" provides more detail on how streaming traffic is transported.

NOTE Good collections of real-time streams can be found at http://wwitv.com/portal.htm and http://www.comfm.com/live/tv/.

Analog and Digital Video

The quality of video streams often is described in terms of broadcast-quality video, Video Home System (VHS)–quality video, and Digital Versatile Disk (DVD) quality video. This section provides a brief description of the characteristics of these different video types for the pure purpose of *classifying* the different compression and decompression techniques.

In the analog world, the resolution of video is measured in scan lines and frequency. The National Television Standards Committee (NTSC) defines a broadcast-quality video as an image made of 525 scan lines and a frequency of 30 frames per second. The Phase Alternation Line (PAL) standard for broadcast defines frames of 625 scan lines and a frequency of 25 fps. In the digital world, the resolution of images is measured in pixels. How exactly the numbers of the analog formats translate into the equivalent number of pixels is beyond the scope of this book. It generally is accepted that the equivalent of a VHS video in the digital world can be estimated to be around 352 × 240 pixels.

Table 11-2 provides a list of video resolutions and frames standards, including the Consultative Committee for International Radio (CCIR) standards for digital video. The Common Intermediate Format (CIF) is a VHS-quality video, while Quarter-CIF and sub-QCIF provide standards with lower resolution.

Table 11-2 lists the video resolution and frame standards.

Table 11-2 *Video Standards for Television*

Standard	Resolution	Frames
NTSC	525 lines interlaced	30 fps
PAL	625 lines interlaced	25 fps
CCIR601 NTSC	720 × 485 pixels	60 fps
CCIR601 PAL	720 × 576 pixels	60 fps
CCIR601 CIF	352 × 288 pixels	30 fps
CCIR601 QCIF	176 × 144 pixels	30 fps
CCIR601 Sub-QCIF	128 × 96 pixels	30 fps

DVDs typically have a resolution of 720 × 480. As a point of reference, typical resolutions for PC video screens are 640 × 480, 720 × 480, 800 × 600, and 1024 × 768.

Standard Definition Television (SDTV) defines a format for digital television that provides quality close to that of a DVD. High-Definition Television (HDTV) defines standards that increase the number of horizontal and vertical pixels. An example of HDTV resolution can be a picture of 1000 vertical lines by 600 pixels.

Codecs

Codec stands for coder/decoder or compressor/decompressor. Encoding refers to how the analog video/audio signal is turned into a digital format and compressed. A codec can be a hardware component as well as a software component. This book focuses on video codecs.

A medium-quality video consists of a sequence of frames of 640 × 480 pixels. Each pixel can be represented (digitized) on a certain number of bits (8 bits, 16 bits, 24 bits). Typically, 24 bits are used to represent the three primary colors, each on 8 bits.

Pure digitization (uncompressed digital video) requires an amount of memory and a transport bandwidth that is unacceptable for current desktops and network bandwidth. In the preceding scenario, sending 24 × 640 × 480 bits per frame, at possibly 30 times per sec, translates to a rate of roughly 221 Mbps. A video of two minutes would take 3.3 GB of disk space. These values are clearly not suitable for the Internet or even for a good number of intranet environments.

Encoding compresses data to a size that is manageable for storage and makes it suitable to be transmitted at a certain *transport* speed. A *transport rate* defines how many bits per second need to be read from a CD-ROM or from a hard drive, or sent on a wire so that the receiving decoder can play the original content without interruption. As an example, a movie trailer might have a transport rate of 761.3 kbps, for a resolution of 480 × 272 pixels.

It is not the purpose of this book to describe in detail how encoding works, but it is important to grasp some of the mechanics of compression, to understand the implications of packetization and data loss.

Basic Encoding Mechanisms

You could think that a compressed video is just a sequence of compressed frames, like, for example, a sequence of Joint Photographic Experts Group (JPEG) frames. Even if this can be true for some encoding techniques, such as Motion JPEG, compression algorithms generally are more sophisticated than this.

In video sequences, there are two main forms of redundancy:

- **Spatial redundancy**—The repetition of patterns within a frame, for example, a pure cyan background, can be thought of as the repetition of the color components of one single pixel for the size of the frame (in Figure 11-3, this is labeled **a**).
- **Temporal redundancy**—The repetition of patterns across frames. A specific object that changes position in different frames is an example (in Figure 11-3, this is labeled **b**).

Figure 11-3 *Basic Encoding Mechanisms*

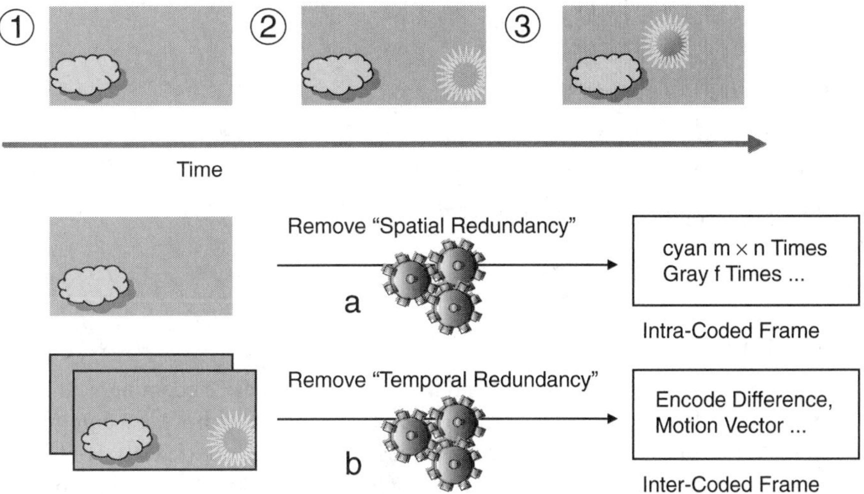

Figure 11-3 shows a sequence of three frames. The repetition of the same background color within a frame is an example of spatial redundancy. The sun changing position across the frames is an example of temporal redundancy.

The processing labeled as **a** in the picture removes the first type of redundancy and produces an "intracoded" frame. This type of frame is described by numbers that define a specific pattern and how to repeat the pattern in the frame.

The processing labeled as **b** removes temporal redundancy and produces an "intercoded" frame. This type of frame has a meaning only if it refers to a previous intracoded frame because it gives information on where objects moved to in the new frame (motion vector).

The compression algorithms also perform a difference between the same object in two different frames. For example, between frames 2 and 3, if the sun changed shape or color, the difference would be encoded. This greatly reduces the amount of information that needs to be carried.

One of the key consequences of encoding is that the encoded frames are not independent of one another. The reason is that some frames are used as a reference, and other frames are derived from the reference by decoding the differences. For more details about how encoding works, see Appendix C, "Video Encoding Mechanisms."

Main Encoding Formats

The following are among some of the most popular encoding formats:

- H.261, H.263
- MPEG1
- MPEG2
- MPEG4
- Sorenson (used by QuickTime)
- Progressive Real Video
- Windows Media Video
- DivX

H.261 and H.263 are formats defined by the International Telecommunications Union (ITU) for videoconferencing. H.261 is a codec designed to provide a compression rate suitable for transport on Integrated Services Digital Network (ISDN). H.263 delivers low-resolution videos—CIF (352 × 288) and QCIF (176 × 144). H.261 and H.263 provide rates in the range of 56 to 768 kbps.

MPEG1 (file extension .mpg) is a standard (ISO 11172) for VHS-quality video (352 × 240 at 30 fps) that was designed mainly for video-CDs. The transport rate is 500 kbps to 1.5 Mbps.

MPEG2 is a standard (ISO 13818) for DVD-quality video (720 × 480 at 30 fps). The transport rate ranges from 2 to 8 Mbps for SDTV, and is 20 Mbps for HDTV (1920 × 1080).

MPEG4 (ISO 14496) streams video at 64 kbps up to 4 Mbps; its optimal transport speed is 385 to 768 kbps.

For more information about how MPEG encodes video, refer to Appendix C.

Other standard formats include Digital Video Compression (DVC), which is a format used by digital cameras that communicate with PCs on Firewire interfaces; Motion JPEG (MJPEG), which is like an MPEG with all I-frames (see the note for more information); and H.324.

NOTE MPEG uses the concept of Group of Pictures (GOP). Several frames (the default is 15) are grouped together to remove temporal redundancies. The first frame is fully coded and is used as a reference for the other frames in the same GOP. The other frames in the GOP are predicted by comparison with the first frame.

The first frame of a group is called an *I-frame*, or *intracoded* frame, because the encoding is meant to reduce spatial redundancy, just like a JPEG picture. The compression ratio for an I-frame is 10:1.

P-frames are forward-prediction frames—they are based on previous I-frames or P-frames. The compression ratio is 20:1.

B-frames are bidirectional frames that reference either past I- and P-frames or future I- and P-frames. The compression ratio for B-frames is 50:1.

Historically, neither MPEG1 nor MPEG2 successfully supported streaming on the Internet, especially at modem speeds. This explains the birth of proprietary format such as Sorenson (used by Quick Time), Microsoft Windows Media, and Progressive Networks' Real. MPEG4, the MPEG version that addresses low bit-rate streaming, came later.

QuickTime, Sorenson, Real Video, and Windows Media are products as well as codecs. These products use their respective proprietary codecs and standard codecs.

QuickTime Apple video produces a high data rate that makes it more suitable for CD-ROM applications. Of the proprietary formats supported by QuickTime, the most notable one is Sorenson, which was introduced in QuickTime 3.

The Sorenson operates very well from low to moderate data rates, such as 160 × 120 low-motion movies. This codec is used by QuickTime as well as Sorenson's products.

Progressive Networks' Real Video is a proprietary codec for a wide range of transport rates, starting from 20 kbps to 450 kbps. Real G2 is a faster codec and, as such, is suited for live broadcast. Real Video 8 is slower, but the quality is much higher. Real Video is used by Real products.

Microsoft developed Windows Media Video, which has a transport rate of 250 kbps for near–VHS-quality videos and 500 kbps for near–DVD-quality videos. Windows Media Screen allows streaming at the very low rate of 15 kbps. Video 8 is based on MPEG4 compression techniques, and its best range of operation is 300 to 900 kbps.

DivX is an MPEG4–based codec that achieves very high compression rates; it is not suitable for real-time live events but is ideal for local playback. It operates with clear images above a 300-kbps transport rate, up to 1.2 Mbps.

Other proprietary codecs include On2, Pixelon, Tranz-Send, Intel Indeo, Cinepak, Motion Vector Quantization Method (MVQM), and LessData.

Table 11-3 lists the various codecs, as well as their resolution, transport rate, and use. Consider this table just a reference; it is far from being exhaustive, and it is also difficult to categorize each format. The key point to remember is the range of transport rates in which each codec operates and the main resolution categories. The QCIF resolution usually is considered the "standard" for the Internet because of the low transport rate required.

Also notice that the VHS format is expressed sometimes as 352 × 240 and sometimes as 320 × 240. This is because the same ratio on a TV screen and on a PC monitor requires a different number of pixels. As an example, MPEG1 was designed to play on TV sets, and the resolution format was set to 352 × 240; you should use a resolution of 320 × 240 to perceive the same ratio on a PC monitor.

Also notice that some of the transport rates are not suited for "transport" on a LAN, let alone the Internet. As an example, an MPEG2 file with a transport rate of 15 Mbps should be used only for local playback or if the size is still manageable for download-and-play. At the time of this writing, it typically is accepted that the maximum transport rate for real-time streaming on the Internet is around 500 kbps. LANs can support higher transport rates in the order of Mbps, for formats such as MPEG1 and MPEG2.

NOTE The maximum transport rate appropriate for streaming on the Internet is subject to change with the adoption of broadband Internet access such as digital subscriber line (DSL) and cable modems by home users. The encoding software typically advises you about the best rate for the type of audience (modem users versus DSL or LAN).

Table 11-3 *Popular Video Codec Information*

Codec	Resolution	Transport Rate	Use
H.261, H.263	CIF(352 × 288) QCIF(176 × 144)	56 to 768 kbps	Videoconferencing, dialup, LAN
MPEG1	VHS (352 × 240)	500 kbps to 1.5 Mbps	CD-ROM, LAN
MPEG2	VHS (352 × 240)	2 to 3 Mbps	LAN
	DVD (720 × 480)	15 Mbps (max)	DVD
	HDTV (1920 × 1080)	80 Mbps (max)	HDTV, film production
	HDTV (1440 × 1152)	60 Mbps (max)	Consumer HDTV
MPEG4	From QCIF to HDTV	5 kbps to 10 Mbps	Dialup, cable, LAN
Sorenson	160 × 120 low motion to 320 × 240	28 to 500 kbps	Dialup, cable, LAN
Real	80 × 60 to 352 × 288	20 to 450 kbps	Dialup, cable, LAN
Windows Media	160 × 120 to 320 × 240	28.8 to 500 kbps	Dialup, cable, LAN
	320 × 240 to 640 × 480	Up to 2 Mbps	Playback or download and play of NTSC broadband quality

Packetization

The purpose of packetization is to bundle portions of the encoded data for delivery in a way that minimizes the effect of packet loss. The *packetizer* is a module in the streaming server software; the corresponding module in the streaming player is the *reassembler*. Both modules must be aware of how the media is encoded, the first to minimize the packet loss, and the second to take appropriate actions when packets are lost.

If the event is a VoD, typically the file being streamed has been preprocessed by appropriate software and saved in a streamable format. This means that the preprocessing already decided how to split the media into packets, and this information is available in the file.

As an example, QuickTime turns encoded media into a streamable format by inserting *hint-tracks*. Hint-tracks are metadata used by the server to decide how to form packets with small portions of the video/audio. Other products achieve the same result by partitioning the media in data units and saving them into a file.

A packetizer must be "media-aware" because packets cannot be formed just by evenly splitting the media. As previously shown, encoding introduces dependencies among frames, and losing some packets (and frames together with those packets) can make other uncorrupted data useless.

NOTE MPEG provides an example for the dependencies among frames. Remember that MPEG uses the concept of GOP. Several frames are grouped together to remove temporal redundancies. The first frame is fully coded and is called an *I-frame*. *P-frames* are forward-prediction frames—they are based on previous I-frames or P-frames.

P-frames have meaning only if referred to the I-frame in the same GOP. Appendix C has more information.

RFC 2250, which is a proposed standard for carrying MPEG on RTP, outlines methods to minimize the effects of packet loss.

NOTE You can find all RFCs online at http://www.isi.edu/in-notes/rfc*xxxx*.txt, where *xxxx* is the number of the RFC. If you do not know the number of the RFC, you can search by topic at http://www.rfc-editor.org/rfcsearch.html.

Transport Formats

The transport format is the format used to deliver multimedia streams on the network. UDP generally is more suited to delivering real-time traffic than TCP, so it is the common denominator for both the standard and proprietary formats. The reason was described in the section, "UDP Versus TCP."

The transport protocol for real-time applications (RTP) is a standard transport format and typically is carried on top of UDP. It is important to understand RTP because it is widely used even by products that have their own proprietary formats, such as Windows and Real.

When UDP cannot be used as the Layer 4 protocol, RTP can be interleaved with RTSP (which is based on TCP port 554), or it can be tunneled in HTTP. This happens because UDP usually is blocked by firewalls. To overcome this problem, streaming servers often have a fallback mechanism to pick another transport protocol if this happens.

RTP is designed to carry real-time traffic. As such, it provides the information necessary to display frames in the correct order independently of their arrival time. RTP is used in conjunction with the RTP Control Protocol (RTCP) so that the server knows how well the streaming session is working. RTCP is carried on UDP as well (despite the name).

Windows and Real developed their own proprietary formats: MSS and RDT.

RTP

RTP, the transport protocol for real-time applications, is the protocol defined by the IETF (RFC 1889) to carry multimedia traffic. RTP is an open-protocol framework in which *profile* and *payload* specifications are defined when new applications need to be carried on top of it. RFC 1890 defines an initial set of payload types.

RTP does not require the use of a specific transport protocol, but it is normally used with UDP. RTP is carried on even port numbers above 5000 (RFC 1890 recommends this number). QuickTime, which makes use of RTP for transport, normally uses ports in the range of 6970 through 6999.

UDP provides RTP with multiplexing and checksum services; on the other hand, UDP is subject to loss of packets and, just like any other Internet protocol, is subject to jitter in the delivery of the packets.

RTP does not prevent out-of-order packets or provide reliable delivery, but it gives the application information on the correct sequence of packets so that these can be decoded independently and presented in the right order. The sequence number also allows the detection of packet loss so that the client then can ask for the retransmission of specific packets.

RTP provides time-stamping. The 32-bit value recorded in the RTP packet is the sampling instant of the first byte in the payload. The time stamp is used so that the application knows when the first frame in the packet should be displayed in relation to the previously received frames, to estimate the network-introduced jitter and adapt to it. The time stamp is provided with a random offset.

RTP provides payload type identification. The payload type identification function describes the media type of the payload as well as the encoding/compression format. RFC 1890 defines the basic payload types. Payload types 96 to 127 are allocated dynamically and negotiated on a per-session basis.

The dynamic payload types make it possible to carry media encoded with proprietary codecs on the top of a standard transport protocol. As an example, Windows and Real use RTP dynamic payload types to carry their respective proprietary formats. This requires the client to know how to interpret the dynamic payload type and decode accordingly.

NOTE Normally, you cannot use a server of one vendor with the player of another vendor just by configuring RTP as the transport protocol. The compatibility between players and servers of different vendors is more likely when using RTP with standard codecs.

Table 11-4 shows a list of payload types. MP2T stands for MPEG2 Transport Stream, MP1S stands for MPEG1 System Stream, and MP2P stands for MPEG2 Program Stream. RFC 2250 describes MPEG encapsulation on RTP; RFC 3016 describes MPEG4 encapsulation on RTP.

Table 11-4 *RTP Payload Types*

Payload Type	Encoding	Audio/Video	RFC
14	MPA	A	RFC 1890
31	H261	V	RFC 2032
32	MPV	V	RFC 2250
33	MP2T	AV	RFC 2250
34	H263	V	
96—127(dyn)	H263-1998	V	
96—127(dyn)	MP1S	V	
96—127(dyn)	MP2P	V	

Example 11-1 shows the trace of an RTP packet from an IPTV session using H.261 as a codec. The Synchronization Source (SSRC) field identifies the source the stream so that even if the IP address changes, the source is recognized. The sequence number is a 16-bit number and increments for every packet in the stream.

Example 11-1 *Example of an RTP Packet*

```
UDP: ----- UDP Header -----
      UDP:
      UDP: Source port      = 54132
      UDP: Destination port = 54132
      UDP: Length           = 267
      UDP: Checksum         = FBD8 (correct)
      UDP: [259 byte(s) of data]
      UDP:
RTP: ----- Real-Time Transport Protocol -----
      RTP:
      RTP: Ver Pad Ext CC: = 80
      RTP:    10.. .... = Version 2 (Current Version)
      RTP:    ..0. .... = Padding 0 (Zero bytes of Padding at the End)
      RTP:    ...0 .... = Header Extension Bit = 0
      RTP:    .... 0000 = Contributor Count = 0
      RTP: Marker  Payload Type: = 9F
      RTP:    1... ....          = Marker 1
      RTP:    .001 1111          = Payload Type 31 (H261 video)
      RTP: Sequence Number       = 46723
      RTP: Time Stamp            = 9942.83280 Seconds
      RTP: Synchronization Src   = 110006392
      RTP:
      RTP: ----- H.261 Header -----
      RTP:
      RTP: Start Bit Position = 7
      RTP: End Bit Position   = 3
      RTP: Intra Frame data   = 1
      RTP: Motion Vector flag = 0
      RTP: GOB Number         = 10
      RTP: Macroblock address = 21
      RTP: Quantizer          = 16
      RTP: Horz Motion Vector = 0
      RTP: Vert Motion Vector = 0
      RTP: Version            = 3
      RTP: Padding            = 0
      RTP: MBZ                = 29
      RTP: PT                 = 21
      RTP: Length             = 47470
      RTP: SSRC               = 1536616473
      RTP: [235 Bytes of H.261 video data ]
```

RTCP

The RTP Control Protocol (RTCP) is used together with the RTP to provide feedback to the streaming server about the quality of the data distribution; this information is mainly the number of lost packets and the jitter.

RTCP normally is carried on UDP, on the first available odd port after the even port used by RTP. RTCP is sent periodically, but its traffic should not take more than five percent of the total traffic.

Fields of interest in the RTCP packet are as follows:

- **SR**—Sender report, for transmission and reception statistics from active RTP senders
- **RR**—Receiver report, for statistics sent by RTP receivers
- **SDES**—Source description items, including CNAME, which identifies the RTP receiver
- **BYE**—The end of participation
- **APP**—Application-specific functions

Example 11-2 shows an RTCP packet and a Reception Report packet, together with the SDES description. Notice the embedded IP of the client in the SDES description. This embedded address can be a problem if the server IP address is subject to NAT. A firewall between the client-side machine and the server might not have the capability to translate embedded IP addresses for this specific protocol.

Example 11-2 *RTCP Packet Format*

```
UDP: ----- UDP Header -----
      UDP:
      UDP: Source port      = 30392
      UDP: Destination port = 30393
      UDP: Length           = 80
      UDP: Checksum         = 588D (correct)
      UDP: [72 byte(s) of data]
      UDP:
RTCP: ----- RTP Control Protocol -----
      RTCP:
      RTCP: Ver Pad RC: = 81
      RTCP:   10.. .... = Version = 2
      RTCP:   ..0. .... = Padding = 0
      RTCP:   ...0 0001 = Reception report count = 1
      RTCP: Packet type          = 201 (Receiver Report)
      RTCP: Length               = 7 (32-bits words)
      RTCP: SSRC of packet sender = 1485723287
      RTCP:
      RTCP: Synchronization source ID     = 3832958433
      RTCP: Fraction lost                 = 0
```

continues

Example 11-2 *RTCP Packet Format (Continued)*

```
RTCP: Cumulative packets lost      = 117
RTCP: Extended highest sequence #   = 80277
RTCP: Interarrival jitter           = 57
RTCP: Last SR timestamp             = 2412820168
RTCP: Delay since last SR           = 5 (Sec)
RTCP:
RTCP: ----- RTP Control Protocol -----
RTCP:
RTCP: Ver Pad RC: = 81
RTCP:  10.. .... = Version = 2
RTCP:  ..0. .... = Padding = 0
RTCP:  ...0 0001 = Source count = 1
RTCP: Packet type           = 202 (Source Description)
RTCP: Length                = 5 (32-bits words)
RTCP:
RTCP: SSRC/CSRC             = 1485723287
RTCP: SDES item       = 1 (SDES_CName)
RTCP:   Length        = 11
RTCP:   User/Domain   = "10.34.13.18"
RTCP: SDES item       = 0 (SDES_End)
RTCP: There are no items
RTCP: SDES item       = 0 (SDES_End)
RTCP: There are no items
RTCP: SDES item       = 0 (SDES_End)
RTCP: There are no items
RTCP: SDES item       = 130 (UNKNOWN)
```

Example of an RTP Session

Example 11-3 shows a portion of the IPTV session from which Examples 11-1 and 11-2 have been captured. Example 11-3 shows that there are two different sources (SSRCs), one for the audio stream and one for the video stream. The RTCP reports are sent to both. Expanding packets 4, 5, 14, and 15 helps you understand which streams they belong to.

Example 11-3 *An RTP Session*

```
1 RTP  Payload=PCMU audio   SEQ=14741 SSRC=3832958433
2 RTP  Payload=H261 video   SEQ=46722 SSRC=110006392
3 RTP  Payload=H261 video   SEQ=46723 SSRC=110006392
4 RTCP Receiver Report PacketLost=7 Jitter=57 Delay=5(sec)
5 RTCP Receiver Report PacketLost=7 Jitter=57 Delay=5(sec)
[. . .]
12 RTP  Payload=H261 video   SEQ=46728 SSRC=110006392
13 RTP  Payload=H261 video   SEQ=46729 SSRC=110006392
14 RTCP Receiver Report PacketLost=20 Jitter=175 Delay=1(sec)
15 RTCP Receiver Report PacketLost=20 Jitter=175 Delay=1(sec)
```

Even without looking at the RTCP packet, just by looking at the UDP ports, it is possible to find out how RTCP and RTP flows are associated.

UDP packet 1 uses the following ports:

- Src Port: 30392
- Dst Port: 30392

UDP packet 2 uses the following ports:

- Src Port: 54132
- Dst Port: 54132

As previously stated, RTCP uses the first available odd port after the even port used by RTP. This implies that RTCP for the audio stream in the example must be using 30393, and RTCP for the video stream must be using 54133.

Looking at packet 4 in Example 11-4, it is clear that packet 4 is an RTCP packet for the audio stream because the Dst Port is 30393, and also because the source identifier matches the SSRC in packet 1 of the traffic trace.

Example 11-4 *Traffic Trace: Packet 4*

```
UDP Src Port: 30392 (30392), Dst Port: 30393 (30393)
Real-time Transport Control Protocol
Packet type: Receiver Report (201)
Sender SSRC: 1485723287
Source 1
  Identifier: 3832958433
    SSRC contents
      Fraction lost: 0 / 256
[. . .]
```

Looking at packet 14 in Example 11-5, it is clear that packet 14 is an RTCP packet for the video stream because the Dst Port is 54133, and because the source identifier matches the SSRC in packet 1 of the traffic trace.

Example 11-5 *Traffic Trace: Packet 14*

```
UDP, Src Port: 54132 (54132), Dst Port: 54133 (54133)
Real-time Transport Control Protocol
Packet type: Receiver Report (201)
Sender SSRC: 3541423131
Source 1
  Identifier: 110006392
    SSRC contents
      Fraction lost: 0 / 256
[. . .]
```

QuickTime, Real, and Windows Media

QuickTime uses RTP for transport on UDP ports 6970 to 6999. In case UDP is not allowed by the firewalls, QuickTime gives the option to encapsulate RTP in HTTP (see the section, "Trace Analysis of UDP, TCP, and HTTP Tunneling"). A streaming session normally consists of a TCP connection for RTSP and two RTP flows, one for the video stream and one for the audio stream. The RTP server in part **a** of Figure 11-4 gives an example of the traffic associated with an RTP streaming session.

Figure 11-4 *Some UDP Transport Formats: RTP, RDT, and MMS*

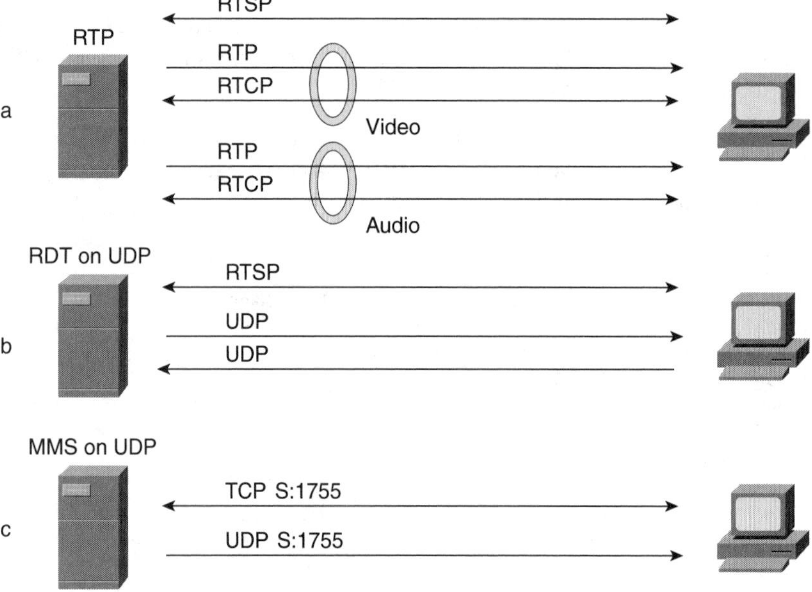

Real can use either RTP or Real Data Transport (RDT) on UDP. If RTP is used, the data traffic flows from the server to the client, and a bidirectional UDP stream is used to carry RTCP and provide information about the client and packet loss.

When using RDT, there is a unidirectional flow from the server to the client, and another unidirectional flow from the client to the server to request retransmission of specific packets. See the second server in part **b** of Figure 11-4 to visualize the transport traffic.

Real tries to use UDP (range between 6970 and 32000 for the server, and between 6970 and 7170 for the client). If UDP does not work, it uses TCP port 554 (which is also the control channel, RTSP). If neither works, Real uses HTTP.

Real can use RTP or RDT also on TCP. In this case, RTP (together with RTCP) or RDT are interleaved with RTSP on TCP port 554. The section, "Control Protocols" provides more detail about RTSP. If RDT is used, one single channel is interleaved; if RTP is used, there are two different channels—one for RTP and one for RTCP.

In addition to standard transport protocols, Windows Media Services use a proprietary transport format, the Microsoft Media Services (MMS) protocol. MMS tries to use UDP, TCP, and eventually HTTP. When MMS is used on UDP (MMSU), Windows Media uses a variety of ports between 1024 and 5000 on the client side and port 1755 on the server. A TCP connection is kept open as well on the server port 1755, as shown in part **c** of Figure 11-4. TCP and HTTP are fallback mechanisms that overcome the problem of passing streaming traffic through firewalls. If the transport protocol is TCP, the port used is 1755. Windows Media also uses DCOM for initial communication between the player and the server. For this purpose, a connection is created from the server TCP port 135.

Figure 11-4 gives an idea of the transport layer traffic associated with the different transport formats.

Trace Analysis of UDP, TCP, and HTTP Tunneling

The section, "UDP Versus TCP" pointed out why UDP is better suited for streaming than TCP.

This section provides an example that should help you understand the implications of using UDP, TCP, or HTTP as a transport protocol. The real-time streaming on HTTP is referred to as HTTP tunneling, to avoid confusion with HTTP streaming, which was described at the beginning of the chapter. The stream that is shown in this example is a live 500-kbps Real stream delivered under congestion conditions.

UDP delivers a better user experience than TCP and HTTP under congestion. TCP and HTTP have similar traffic characteristics because HTTP relies on TCP as the transport protocol. When HTTP tunneling is used by a streaming server, the traffic pattern is different from that when delivering a multimedia file through an HTTP server.

Table 11-5 shows the capture of the 500-kbps stream carried by TCP. The table does not show the IP addresses of the sender and of the receiver. There is a single TCP connection for the entire duration of the streaming session. The sender-to-receiver traffic is from port 554 to port 2343. Table 11-5 identifies this direction of the flow as server-to-client (S->C).

Table 11-5 *500-kbps Live Stream Carried on TCP with Out-of-Order Packets and Retransmission*

	Time	Direction	Flow	Sequence Numbers	Length
1	0	S->C	554 > 2343	Seq=159878630 Ack=4006023452	1360
2	0.00014	C->S	2343 > 554	Seq=4006023452 Ack=159879990	0
3	0.001125	S->C	554 > 2343	Seq=159879990 Ack=4006023452	1360
4	0.139441	C->S	2343 > 554	Seq=4006023452 Ack=159881350	0
5	0.146357	S->C	554 > 2343	Seq=159881350 Ack=4006023452	1360
6	0.147294	S->C	554 > 2343	Seq=159884070 Ack=4006023452	1116
7	0.14738	C->S	2343 > 554	Seq=4006023452 Ack=159882710	0
8	0.148458	S->C	554 > 2343	Seq=159882710 Ack=4006023452	1360
9	0.148643	C->S	2343 > 554	Seq=4006023452 Ack=159885186	0
10	0.244968	S->C	554 > 2343	Seq=159885186 Ack=4006023452	1360
11	0.250875	S->C	554 > 2343	Seq=159886546 Ack=4006023452	1360
12	0.251056	C->S	2343 > 554	Seq=4006023452 Ack=159887906	0
13	0.260396	S->C	554 > 2343	Seq=159887906 Ack=4006023452	1360
14	0.260721	S->C	554 > 2343	Seq=159890626 Ack=4006023452	373
15	0.260854	C->S	2343 > 554	Seq=4006023452 Ack=159889266	0
16	0.261872	S->C	554 > 2343	Seq=159889266 Ack=4006023452	1360
17	0.262008	C->S	2343 > 554	Seq=4006023452 Ack=159890999	0
18	0.340512	S->C	554 > 2343	Seq=159892359 Ack=4006023452	1360
19	0.340633	C->S	2343 > 554	Seq=4006023452 Ack=159890999	0
20	0.340702	S->C	554 > 2343	Seq=159893719 Ack=4006023452	110
21	0.340821	C->S	2343 > 554	Seq=4006023452 Ack=159890999	0
22	0.341825	S->C	554 > 2343	Seq=159890999 Ack=4006023452	1360

The receiver sends ACKs back to the sender. Table 11-5 identifies this direction of the flow as client-to-server (C->S). The SEQ of the receiver of course does not change because the data flow is unidirectional, and the sender is just ACKing the received traffic.

Frame 6 shows a sequence number (159884070) greater than the expected sequence number (159882710) because some frames either have been lost or have taken a different path. As a consequence, the receiver sends an ACK for the missing frame (frame 7), which eventually is received in frame 8.

When the receiver sends the ACK for the same segment three times, it causes the sender to retransmit it. In Table 11-5, the client sends duplicate ACKs in frames 17, 19, and 21 for 159890999. Eventually, the server sends the missing segment in frame 22, SEQ = 159890999. Until frame 22 is received, the client application cannot use segments 159892359 and 159893719.

After doing some calculations (sum of the frame sizes in bytes, times 8 bits/byte, divided by the time), you can see that the rate averages 355 kbps for the portion of the traffic shown:

$$((10 * 1360 + 1116 + 373 + 110) * 8) / 0.342 = 355.532 \text{ kbps}$$

If the object had been encoded for a transport rate of 355 kbps, the application on the server would have placed new data into the TCP send buffer at the same rate as TCP was delivering it to the client. These are the ideal conditions.

By looking at Figure 11-5, you can see the TCP stream statistics from Real Player for a window of 30 sec. The target bandwidth is 500 kbps, but because of retransmission requests, the congestion window on the sender is adapting to the rate that the network seems capable of delivering, which is roughly half of the target bandwidth. This means that the application on the server is playing the stream and delivering the data to the TCP send buffer at 500 kbps. Because the network can sustain only an average rate of 230 kbps, the client experiences continuous interruptions and rebufferings.

Figure 11-5 *TCP 500-kbps Stream in Presence of Congestion*

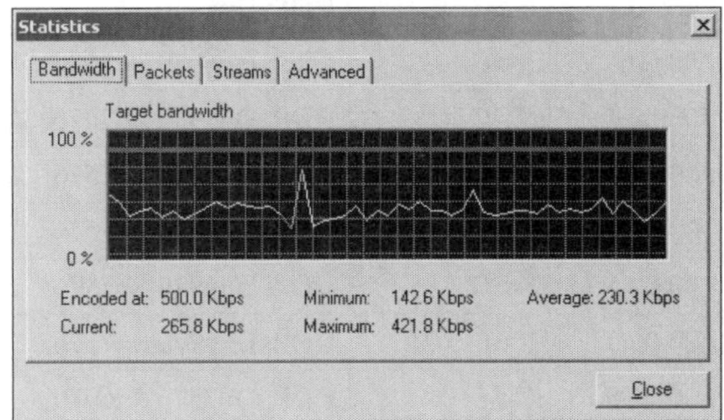

Table 11-6 shows the same stream of Figure 11-5 delivered on UDP. The traffic flows from 6970 to 7576, in the server-to-client (S->C in Table 11-6) direction. Even if a UDP stream is unidirectional, by definition, the client still sends UDP packets back to the server every so often (look at frames 5 and 20—Table 11-6 categorizes these frames as C->S, client-to-server).

The transport rate at frame 9 averages 572.7 kbps, at frame 17 averages 542 kbps, and at frame 26 averages 622.5 kbps.

Table 11-6 *RDT 500-kbps Live Stream Carried on UDP*

Frame Number	Time	Direction	Flow Information	Length (Bytes)
1	00:00.3	S->C	UDP: D=6970 S=7576	1422
2	00:00.3	S->C	UDP: D=6970 S=7576	658
3	00:00.3	S->C	UDP: D=6970 S=7576	620
4	00:00.3	S->C	UDP: D=6970 S=7576	1358
5	00:00.3	C->S	UDP: D=7576 S=6970	37
6	00:00.3	S->C	UDP: D=6970 S=7576	658
7	00:00.3	S->C	UDP: D=6970 S=7576	658
8	00:00.3	S->C	UDP: D=6970 S=7576	377
9	00:00.3	S->C	UDP: D=6970 S=7576	1408
10	00:00.4	S->C	UDP: D=6970 S=7576	461
11	00:00.4	S->C	UDP: D=6970 S=7576	1356
12	00:00.4	S->C	UDP: D=6970 S=7576	658
13	00:00.4	S->C	UDP: D=6970 S=7576	631
14	00:00.4	S->C	UDP: D=6970 S=7576	1415
15	00:00.4	S->C	UDP: D=6970 S=7576	658
16	00:00.4	S->C	UDP: D=6970 S=7576	658
17	00:00.4	S->C	UDP: D=6970 S=7576	938
18	00:00.5	S->C	UDP: D=6970 S=7576	1282
19	00:00.5	S->C	UDP: D=6970 S=7576	475
20	00:00.5	C->S	UDP: D=7576 S=6970	18
21	00:00.5	S->C	UDP: D=6970 S=7576	658
22	00:00.5	S->C	UDP: D=6970 S=7576	1389
23	00:00.5	S->C	UDP: D=6970 S=7576	1330
24	00:00.5	S->C	UDP: D=6970 S=7576	658
25	00:00.5	S->C	UDP: D=6970 S=7576	658
26	00:00.5	S->C	UDP: D=6970 S=7576	1332

Figure 11-6 shows the static window from Real Player for this stream. UDP is sending bursts at a rate of 500 kbps followed by lows, which could be explained either as a consequence of some congestion-control mechanism or because of packets dropped by the network.

Figure 11-6 *RDT/UDP 500-kbps Stream in Presence of Congestion*

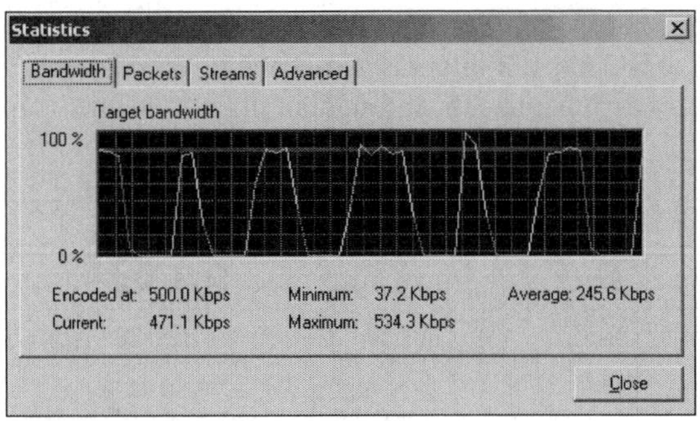

From a user experience point of view, this UDP stream was not subject to pauses. Of course, lost frames are noticeable because of the quality of the video, but overall this is better than the continuous stops when the same stream was delivered on TCP.

The same stream would look much more uniform without congestion, as shown in Figure 11-7.

Figure 11-7 *UDP 500-kbps Stream, No Congestion*

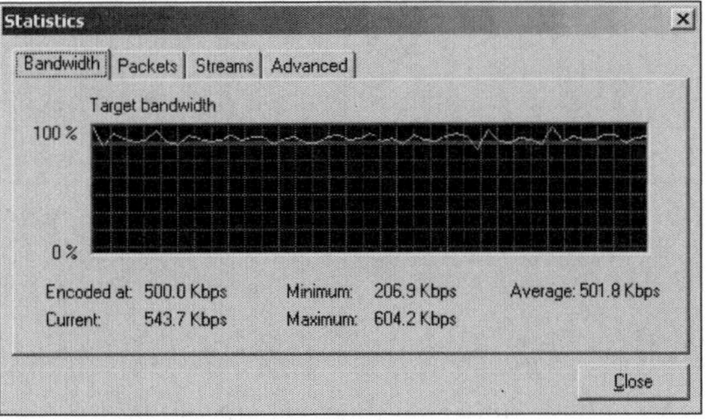

In case neither UDP nor TCP can be used for streaming, the typical fallback mechanism is HTTP tunneling. The meaning of HTTP tunneling is different here than in the earlier discussion of HTTP streaming. The mechanism that was described previously was just the download of a multimedia file by using the HTTP protocol. The server delivering the multimedia was an HTTP server.

When a streaming server (notice, not an HTTP server) uses HTTP, this simply means that the traffic that would be otherwise encapsulated in UDP or TCP is inserted in a TCP packet whose source port is 80. So, the only relation to HTTP is the fact that the connection is established between a client and a server on port 80. The rate at which the traffic is sent is the *streaming* rate, as opposed to the *download* rate.

Table 11-7 shows an example of a 500-kbps stream delivered on HTTP for Real. Notice the transport rate of 643 kbps. If this was a VoD and it was delivered using the HTTP protocol, HTTP would try to maximize the throughput; the traffic rate would be around 1.4 Mbps.

Table 11-7 *A Real RDT Stream Delivered on HTTP*

	Time	Direction	Flow Information	Length
1	00:00.0	S->C	http > 1224 Seq=747659867 Ack=2976954774	1360
2	00:00.0	S->C	http > 1224 Seq=747661227 Ack=2976954774	1360
3	00:00.0	C->S	1224 > http Seq=2976954774 Ack=747662587	0
4	00:00.0	S->C	http > 1224 Seq=747662587 Ack=2976954774	1360
5	00:00.1	S->C	http > 1224 Seq=747663947 Ack=2976954774	1360
6	00:00.1	C->S	1224 > http Seq=2976954774 Ack=747665307	0
7	00:00.1	S->C	http > 1224 Seq=747665307 Ack=2976954774	956
8	00:00.1	S->C	http > 1224 Seq=747666263 Ack=2976954774	851
9	00:00.1	C->S	1224 > http Seq=2976954774 Ack=747667114	0
10	00:00.1	S->C	http > 1224 Seq=747667114 Ack=2976954774	1360
11	00:00.1	S->C	http > 1224 Seq=747668474 Ack=2976954774	801
12	00:00.1	C->S	1224 > http Seq=2976954774 Ack=747669275	0
13	00:00.1	S->C	http > 1224 Seq=747669275 Ack=2976954774	1360
14	00:00.2	S->C	http > 1224 Seq=747670635 Ack=2976954774	1360
15	00:00.2	C->S	1224 > http Seq=2976954774 Ack=747671995	0

Control Protocols

Control protocols provide functionalities that are similar to those of a remote control for a DVD player. Control protocols enable you to start, stop, or rewind a video; they decide the rate of the replication and the method of replication. Examples of control protocols include RSTP (standard), MMS (Windows Media Services), and Progressive Networks Audio (PNA). MMS can be considered both a control protocol and a transport protocol; the details are unknown because the specifications are not available. In this section, the focus is on RTSP.

RTSP

The Real-Time Streaming Protocol (RTSP) is a protocol defined by the IETF (RFC 2326) that allows out-of-band control for streaming protocols. RTSP defines the negotiation process to choose the transport mechanisms for the multimedia stream.

RTSP does not deliver the stream itself, but in certain cases it can be interleaved with data channels. The options that are selected via RTSP are usually these:

- RTP versus other transport protocols
- UDP versus TCP versus HTTP
- Multicast versus unicast
- Bandwidth
- Port number selection for the client

RTSP is a similar protocol to HTTP, in that it is a "text protocol." It uses a similar syntax and similar headers, such as Cookie, Cache-Control, Language, and User-Agent. However, some important differences exist:

- RTSP usually does not deliver data.
- RTSP is bidirectional: Both client and server can send a request.
- RTSP is not stateless.
- Request-URI always contains the absolute URI (as opposed to HTTP, where the Host tag contains the host name).

The main methods used by RTSP are as follows:

- OPTIONS
- DESCRIBE
- SETUP
- PLAY
- TEARDOWN

To understand these methods, refer to the 500-kbps stream described in the section, "Trace Analysis of UDP, TCP, and HTTP Tunneling." In this section, there was no description of the "setup" phase. This phase is described here.

Table 11-8 shows the setup phase for the RDT on a UDP session.

Table 11-8 *RTSP Stream Setup (HTTP -> RTSP -> UDP)*

Frame	Direction	Information
1	C <-> S	HTTP [...]
2	C -> S	HTTP GET /foo/foo_500.raml HTTP/1.0
3	C <-> S	HTTP [...]
4	S -> C	HTTP Cont. -> rtsp://example.com[...]/foo_500.rm
5	C -> S	TCP 1107 > 554 [SYN]
6	S -> C	TCP 554 > 1107 [SYN, ACK]
7	C -> S	TCP 1107 > 554 [ACK]
8	C -> S	OPTIONS rtsp://example.com:554 RTSP/1.0
9	S -> C	RTSP/1.0 200 OK
10	C -> S	DESCRIBE rtsp://example.com[...]/foo_500.rm RTSP/1.0
11	S -> C	SDP RTSP/1.0 200 OK, with session description
12	S -> C	RTSP Continuation
13	C -> S	TCP 1107 > 554 [ACK]
14	S -> C	RTSP Continuation
15	C -> S	TCP 1107 > 554 [ACK]
16	C -> S	SETUP rtsp://example.com[...]/streamid=0 RTSP/1.0
17	S -> C	RTSP/1.0 200 OK
18	C -> S	SETUP rtsp://example.com[...]/streamid=0 RTSP/1.0
19	S -> C	RTSP/1.0 200 OK
20	C -> S	TCP 1107 > 554 [ACK]
21	C -> S	SET_PARAMETER rtsp://example.com[...]/foo_500.rm RTSP/1.0
22	S -> C	RTSP/1.0 200 OK
23	C -> S	PLAY rtsp://example.com[...]/foo_500.rm RTSP/1.0
24	S -> C	RTSP/1.0 200 OK
25	S -> C	UDP Source port: 13264 Destination port: 6970
26	S -> C	UDP Source port: 13264 Destination port: 6970

Table 11-8 shows initially an HTTP GET (frame 2) that returns an RTSP URL as data. At this point, the player opens a separate TCP connection for RTSP (frame 5). At the end of the negotiation phase, the data starts flowing. The RTSP connection stays open. The sequence of RTSP methods is described in the previous bullets.

Each method in the previous sequence now is described. The OPTION Method in frame 8 is used to send a nonstandard request:

```
OPTIONS rtsp://example.com:554 RTSP/1.0
CSeq: 1
[. . .]
```

CSeq identifies a request response pair; the response for the OPTIONS request is this (frame 9):

```
RTSP/1.0 200 OK
CSeq: 1
[. . .]
```

The DESCRIBE method defines the media that the client is looking for (by means of the URL)—the encoding type, the language, cookies, and so on—similarly to what is found in an HTTP GET request. In fact, RTSP can overlap with HTTP for the description of the media. As in this example, it is very likely that the initial contact with the multimedia object will be made through an HTML page. This is captured in frame 10 of the example:

```
DESCRIBE rtsp://example.com/[. . .]/foo_500.rm RTSP/1.0
CSeq: 2
Accept: application/sdp
Session: 19015-1
Cookie:
cbid=ffhgehelmjgkfihheooooopkqkrjrktlufkcgkihldjckilplrnqoluoqmoesltkuefcjdhgi
Bandwidth: 1544000
[. . .]
```

The DESCRIBE response in frame 11 contains the media-initialization information:

```
RTSP/1.0 200 OK
CSeq: 2
Date: Tue, 19 Feb 2002 17:00:02 GMT
[. . .]
Session: 19015-1
Content-type: application/sdp
Content-length: 2652
v=0
o=-   IN IP4 <ip address>
[. . .]
m=audio 0 RTP/AVP 101
[. . .]
m=video 0 RTP/AVP 101
[. . .]
```

The SETUP method specifies the transport protocols that the client is willing to accept if the stream is going to be unicast or multicast. Firewalls should be capable of understanding the SETUP method and opening a channel for the UDP media stream. From frame 18:

```
SETUP rtsp://live.example.com/[. . .]/foo_500.rm/streamid=0 RTSP/1.0
CSeq: 3
[. . .]
```

```
Transport: x-real-rdt/udp;client_port=6970;mode=play,x-pn-tng/
udp;client_port=6970;mode=play,rtp/avp;unicast;client_port=6970-6971;mode=play
If-Match: 19015-1
```

The SETUP response from the server specifies the transport method as well as the ports chosen by the server. It also provides a session identifier. From frame 19:

```
RTSP/1.0 200 OK
CSeq: 3
Date: Tue, 19 Feb 2002 17:00:03 GMT
Session: 19015-1
[. . .]
Transport: x-real-rdt/udp;client_port=6970;server_port=13264
[. . .]
```

The PLAY request is used to start the streaming session. From frame 23:

```
PLAY rtsp://live.example.com/[…]/foo_500.rm RTSP/1.0
CSeq: 6
Session: 19015-1
Range: npt=0-
```

The TEARDOWN method is used to terminate a streaming session.

Interleaving

An interesting feature of RTSP is interleaving, which consists of encapsulating the data channel on top of RTSP, as seen in Table 11-5. Traffic was flowing between port 554 and another port on a TCP connection. This occurs mainly to pass through firewalls.

When data is interleaved with RTSP, the RTP packets are encapsulated in a $ sign followed by the channel identifier and the length of the data.

Usually, RTCP is interleaved on the same connection and is sent on the first channel higher than the RTP channel. For example, RTP uses channel 0 and RTCP uses channel 1.

The following is a capture from the RTSP setup for the 500-kbps TCP stream:

```
RTSP/1.0 200 OK
CSeq: 3
Date: Tue, 19 Feb 2002 16:49:10 GMT
Session: 19044-1
RealChallenge3: 97ace8d8c270ba510bb861eae13d12b04f213d09,sdr=9ecb06e1
RDTFeatureLevel: 2
Transport: x-pn-tng/tcp;interleaved=0
```

Most of the frames seen in Table 11-8 are as follows:

```
RTSP Interleaved Frame, Channel: 0x00, 847 bytes
Magic: 0x24
Channel: 0x00
Length: 847 bytes
Data (847 bytes)
```

According to RFC 2326, this is how the interleaved traffic would look for two channels: channel 0 and channel 1. The $ sign would precede the number of the channel and would be followed by the length of the channel itself:

```
S->C: $\000{2 byte length}{"length" bytes data, w/RTP header}
S->C: $\000{2 byte length}{"length" bytes data, w/RTP header}
S->C: $\001{2 byte length}{"length" bytes  RTCP packet}
```

As for the HTTP stream, if it is decoded like an RTSP stream, you will find that it is implementing the interleaving technique as well. Again, the main difference between HTTP and TCP remains just the port number used for the TCP traffic.

Unicast, Multicast, and Stream Splitting

A streaming server can distribute multimedia traffic using either unicast or multicast packets. Unicast is more resource-intensive for the server but has the advantage that each user can watch the media from the very beginning at any given time. Unicast is more resource-intensive because each user creates a new connection to the server. This also translates into inefficient use of the bandwidth. Unicast is suitable for VoD. Part **a** of Figure 11-8 shows an example of unicast streams: The server generates one flow for each client.

Multicast allows a server to generate a single stream of traffic that gets replicated by routers along the path where viewers are located. Multicast is suitable for scheduled broadcast events, whether live events or prerecorded events, when multiple users watch the same event at the same time and the viewing time is decided by the broadcast channel. A single server suffices for any number of users if multicast is used. Part **b** of Figure 11-8 shows an example of multicast: The server generates a single flow, and the multicast-enabled network replicates this traffic to all the clients subscribed to the multicast group.

Splitting is a technique in which one primary server shares a live media stream with other secondary servers. Clients connect to closer servers that happen to be the secondary ones, thus preserving network bandwidth and allowing the primary server to scale better. The primary server sends unicast streams to downstream secondary servers, which, in turn, deliver the stream to multiple clients. Splitting should be used for scheduled broadcasts to offload the primary server or when portions of the network between the client and servers do not support multicast. In this case, the primary and secondary servers are placed at the edge of the non-multicast–enabled portion of the network. Part **c** of Figure 11-8 shows an example of splitting. The streaming server generates a single flow up to the secondary server. The secondary server "splits" this single flow into multiple streams, one for each client.

Progressive real servers as well as progressive real proxies can be used to achieve stream *splitting*. Sorenson achieves the same with *replication* and *relay* servers, where replication servers deliver unicast streams to the end clients and relay servers deliver a multicast stream to the end client. QuickTime has the concept of relay servers or *reflectors* as well. Microsoft calls these servers *distribution servers*.

On-demand caching is a technique implemented by proxy devices. Upon request from a client, a proxy is capable of contacting, retrieving, and serving the content on behalf of the server to the client. While doing so, the proxy also caches the content so that it can serve it in the future.

Figure 11-8 illustrates unicast, multicast, and splitting.

Figure 11-8 *Unicast, Multicast, and Splitting*

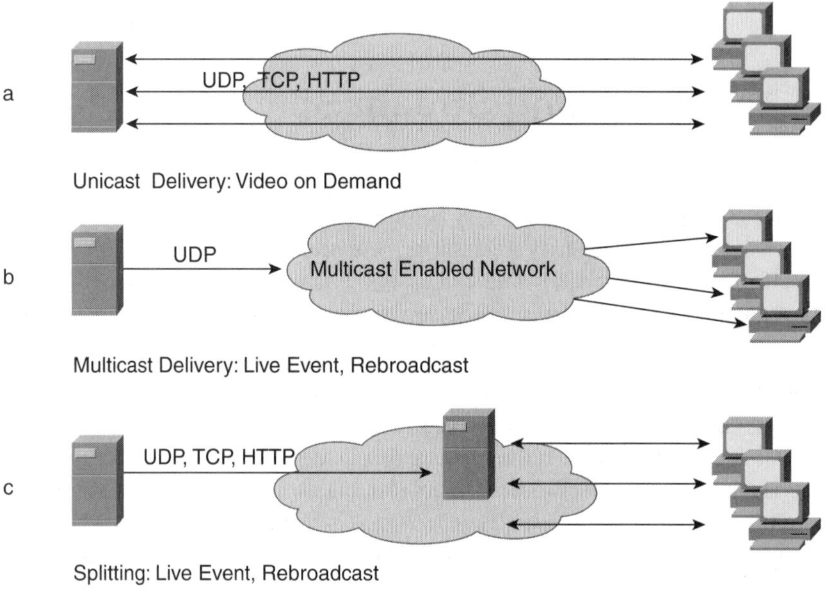

TIP

You can use server load balancing to scale up the performance of servers delivering unicast streams, such as VoD. By using server load balancing, you can cluster several streaming servers together while advertising a single IP address to the client. For more information about load balancing, refer to Chapter 6, "Server Load Balancing Overview."

Load balancers supporting RTP can keep session persistence across RTSP, RTP, and RTCP, and they perform NAT on the IP addresses embedded in these protocols (refer to the section, "RTSP"). If the load balancer does not have explicit support for RTP, you can still achieve load balancing by using dispatch mode and the sticky feature.

If the load balancer does not explicitly support the RTP format, you can provide session persistence across the ports (the RTSP port, RTP, and RTCP) by using sticky groups, also called buddy groups (see Chapter 19, "Persistence Mechanisms on Load Balancers"). You also need to perform load balancing in "dispatch" mode—a load balancer in dispatch mode does not NAT the server IP address, so there is no need to translate embedded IP addresses. For more information about dispatch mode, see Chapter 16, "Load-Balancing Modes and Predictors."

Streaming Products

The market currently offers several streaming products. Some of them are listed here:

- Apple QuickTime
- Progressive Real Systems
- Windows Media Service
- Cisco IPTV

The sections that follow cover how these streaming products interact with codecs and wire formats.

Codecs

Streaming products provide an *encoding*, *storage*, and *playback* system. Streaming can be applied either to a live event or to an existing media object. When encoding a live event, the encoder just compresses the video/audio into a format compatible with the vendor's streaming server.

When an existing media object is used, you first need to process it to make it compatible with the specific vendor streaming server. This is done with the *encoder (packetizer)*. The media already was encoded before going through the *vendor's encoder*, but before this operation, it was not ready to be streamed by the vendor's streaming server.

Streaming products can be categorized based on the codecs supported by the encoder, codecs that the server can stream, codecs that the player can receive, storage format that the encoder can read, the storage format that the encoder uses to save the encoded movie, and wire formats used between server and client.

The list of codecs supported by each vendor changes every year as new and improved codecs are made available. It is important to note the recent adoption of the MPEG4 standard by most vendors. MPEG4 allows high-quality video for a wide range of transport rates, which makes it suitable for streaming on the Internet as well as LANs.

NOTE For more information about codecs and file formats on QuickTime, see http://www.apple.com/quicktime/products/qt/specifications.html.

For more information about production and streaming on Real, see http://service.real.com/help/library/. For more information about Windows Media, consult the Windows Media Series page, at http://www.microsoft.com/windows/windowsmedia/, and look into Technology and Tools, Codecs for the codecs, or Technology and Tools, Server, Previous Version, Deployment Guides for the transport formats (look for "Windows Media Services Deployment Guide").

For more information about Cisco, IPTV go to http://www.cisco.com/univercd/cc/td/doc/product/webscale/iptv/.

Wire Formats

The wire format is the protocol or collection of protocols used to deliver multimedia streams on the network. The wire format of a streaming product mainly is described by the transport protocols, the control protocols, and the associated Layer 4 ports. This section provides information about some of the formats used by QuickTime, Real, and Windows Media.

The wire format used by QuickTime is RTP/RTCP. The control connection uses RTSP. RTP can be tunneled in HTTP if the firewalls cannot open the appropriate UDP ports, in which case RTSP and RTP are encapsulated in TCP traffic port 80.

Real chooses the wire format depending on the presence of a firewall in the path from the server to the client. Real uses RTSP on TCP port 554 for the control connection. If this is not allowed, Real tries using HTTP on port 8080 (a technique called *HTTP cloaking*). The transport format used on UDP, TCP, and HTTP can be either RTP or RDT.

Windows uses standard transport protocols as well as MMS. The range of ports on the client is between 1024 and 5000; port 1755 is used on the server.

Table 11-9 collects the information about the ports used by the different products.

Table 11-9 *Ports Used by the Different Products*

Product	Transport	Layer 4 Protocols
QuickTime	RTP	UDP dynamic port (server), TCP 554 (server), UDP 6970–6999 (client)
QuickTime	HTTP tunneling	TCP 80 (server)
Real	RTP	UDP dynamic port (server), TCP 554 (server), UDP 6970–6999 (client)
Real	RDT	UDP (server), TCP 554 (server), UDP 6970–6999 (client)

Table 11-9 *Ports Used by the Different Products (Continued)*

Product	Transport	Layer 4 Protocols
Real	RTSP interleaving	TCP 554 (server)
Real	HTTP tunneling	TCP 80 or TCP 8080 (server)
WM	MMSU	UDP 1755 (server), TCP 1755 (server), UDP 1024–5000 (client)
WM	MMST	TCP 1755 (server), TCP 1024–5000 (client)
WM	HTTP	TCP 80 (server), TCP 1024–5000 (client)
WM	DCOM	TCP 1024–5000 and 135 on both server and client
Cisco IPTV	RTP	UDP 2n (server), UDP 2n+1 (server), TCP 554 (server), UDP 6970–6999 (client)

Summary

This chapter familiarized you with the streaming protocols for the purpose of designing a Data Center to support VoD or broadcast events, live and scheduled.

Understanding the encoding format of multimedia, especially the transport rate, is required to provision the network and to make sure that there is enough spare bandwidth and that the throughput of the devices being used is sufficient to sustain the expected broadcast quality.

As simple as it can be, it is easy to forget that streaming servers are not HTTP servers. Sometimes, streams are tunneled on HTTP (HTTP tunneling) by the streaming server, which writes to the TCP send buffer with a rate compatible with the transport rate of the media object. Other cases in which traffic is carried over HTTP are HTTP streaming (or fast-start) and download-and-play, which, again, have little to do with streaming.

Choosing between real-time streaming and download-and-play has different effects on the network. Download-and-play is similar to an FTP session, while streaming requirements are those of a very long-lived flow that is delay-sensitive.

Load balancing can help both for download-and-play scenarios and for streaming protocols. For broadcast events with a multicast-enabled network, there is no need for load balancing. However, for live events on unicast networks or VoD applications, load balancing can help scaling the streaming server farm.

Planning a network for real-time applications can be very challenging, especially for people who have to choose among the myriad of (often incompatible) products available. From a networking point of view, the challenge is to understand the underlying transport protocols, the bandwidth requirements, the delay requirements, and the loss tolerance for the specific codecs.

PART III

Infrastructure Protocols

This chapter covers the following topics:

- The fundamentals of the Ethernet technology in switched environments: the frame format (Ethernet v2 and 802.3), the address format, and the frame size
- Characteristics and differences of Fast Ethernet, Gigabit Ethernet, and 10-Gigabit Ethernet
- Ethernet switching: the fundamentals of transparent bridges and the forwarding table
- How to virtualize LAN Ethernet segments with VLANs
- The most commonly used Layer 2 protocols, with special focus on spanning tree (port roles and states, bridge priority, logical ports)
- The most recent spanning-tree improvements—specifically, 802.1w and 802.1s
- How to choose the most appropriate spanning-tree algorithm

CHAPTER 12

Layer 2 Protocol Essentials

The design phase of a Data Center decides the physical medium to be used between network devices and servers, how to connect switches and routers, how many LAN segments will be present, how many servers will be used, where to terminate the Layer 2 domain with a router, which additional services (firewalling, load balancing, Secure Socket Layer [SSL] offloading) will be supported, and so forth.

The choice of the physical medium has to do with considerations of throughput and distances. The focus of this chapter is on Ethernet because most of today's Data Centers use either Fast Ethernet or Gigabit Ethernet as the LAN technology. Multiple Gigabit Ethernet links commonly are used for uplink connectivity, and the server also can be Gigabit Ethernet–attached. The cost of Fast Ethernet and Gigabit Ethernet network interface cards (NICs) is no longer a determining factor in which technology to deploy.

10-Gigabit Ethernet is becoming more available and provides interswitch connectivity as well as interesting possibilities of attachment to metropolitan-area networks (MANs).

The choice of where to terminate the Layer 2 domain is dictated mainly by the interoperability requirements of servers and network devices. In theory, it is possible to use routing protocols at the access layer, but the nature of Data Centers is such that Layer 2 protocols in the access are still preferable. (Refer to Chapter 4, "Data Center Design Overview," for more information.) This chapter provides the basics of Spanning Tree Protocol (STP) and information about its latest improvements. Chapter 20, "Designing the Data Center Infrastructure," provides information about how to use the technologies described in this chapter to design a Data Center.

IEEE 802

The Institute of Electrical and Electronics Engineers (IEEE) 802 is the project that formulates standards for LANs and MANs. The 802.1 working group develops standards for protocols above the MAC layer, and the 802.3 working group is in charge of standards for Ethernet-based LANs. Among the other working groups, it is worth mentioning 802.11 for wireless LANs and 802.17 for Resilient Packet Ring. For a complete list of the current IEEE 802 working groups, refer to http://grouper.ieee.org/groups/802/.

Table 12-1 provides a quick reference to 802 standards that are referenced throughout this chapter.

Table 12-1 *802 Standards Referenced in This Chapter*

Standard	Title	Comments
802.3 CSMA/CD	Access Method and Physical Layer Specifications	
802.3u	Type 100BASE-T MAC Parameters, Physical Layer, MAUs, and Repeater for 100-Mbps Operation	Fast Ethernet.
802.3x	Full-Duplex Operation and Type 100BASE-T2	Defines full-duplex operation and related flow control.
802.3z	Type 100BASE-X MAC Parameters, Physical Layer, Repeater, and Management Parameters for 1000-Mbps Operation	Gigabit Ethernet over fiber.
802.3ab	Physical-Layer Parameters and Specifications for 1000-Mbps Operation over Four Pair of Category 5 Balanced Copper Cabling, Type 1000BASE-T	Gigabit Ethernet over copper.
802.3ae	CSMA/CD Access Method and Physical-Layer Specifications—Media Access Control (MAC) Parameters, Physical-Layer, and Management Parameters for 10-Gbps Operation	10-Gigabit Ethernet.
802.2	Logical Link Control (LLC)	
802.1D	Media Access Control (MAC) Bridges.	Standard that defines the spanning-tree operations. Specifies an architecture and protocol for the interconnection of IEEE 802 LANs below the MAC service boundary.
802.1Q	VLAN Bridge LANs	Standard that describes the bridge operation with VLANs. It references 802.1d as the STP.
802.3ac	Frame Extensions for Virtual Bridged LAN (VLAN) Tagging on 802.3 Networks	802.3ac increases the maximum Ethernet frame size from 1518 to 1522.

Table 12-1 *802 Standards Referenced in This Chapter (Continued)*

Standard	Title	Comments
802.1s	Standard for Local- and Metropolitan-Area Networks Amendment 2 to 802.1q Virtual Bridged Local-Area Networks: Multiple Spanning Tree	802.1s allows multiple instances of spanning tree.
802.1t	Media Access Control (MAC) Bridges Amendment 1	802.1t changes the format of the bridge identifier, also called MAC address reduction.
802.1w	Media Access Control (MAC) Bridges Amendment 2: Rapid Reconfiguration	Fast spanning-tree convergence.
802.3ad	Amendment to Carrier Sense Multiple Access with Collision Detection (CSMA/CD) Access Method and Physical-Layer Specifications. Aggregation of Multiple Link Segments.	802.3ad is a channeling protocol also called the Link Aggregation Control Protocol (LACP).

For detailed information about the IEEE standards, refer to http://www.ieee.org.

Ethernet

Ethernet is the dominant LAN technology. It originally was designed as a protocol for shared media with carrier sense multiple access collision detect (CSMA/CD) being the access method. Today, Ethernet mainly is used on point-to-point links in switched networks between network devices (router and switches), as well as between hosts (workstations and servers) and network devices. The communication links operate in full-duplex mode.

Ethernet supports speeds from 10 Mbps to 10 Gbps, as well as many physical media for each speed (coaxial cable, copper cable, and fiber).

As an example, in the case of copper, Ethernet can run on two pairs of Category 5 unshielded twisted pair (UTP) (most common), four pairs of Category 3 UTP, and so on. In the case of coaxial cable, Ethernet can run on Thicknet or Thinnet cables and, in the case of fiber, can run on multimode fibers and single-mode fibers. Table 12-2 shows the most common Ethernet specifications used for each speed and medium.

Table 12-2 *The Most Commonly Used Ethernet Technologies*

	Coaxial	Copper	Fiber
10 Mbps	10BASE5, 10BASE2	10BASE-T	10BASE-FL
100 Mbps		100BASE-TX	100BASE-FX
1 Gbps		1000BASE-T	1000BASE-LX, 1000BASE-SX
10 Gbps			10GBASE-LR

Many characteristics of Ethernet, such as the speed, duplex, and encapsulation, can be described by explaining the interface settings of a router. Example 12-1 shows some of the information that you can read from the **show interface** command of a Catalyst switch running Supervisor IOS.

After reading this chapter, you should be familiar with most fields displayed in this example.

Example 12-1 *Some of the Fields That Provide Information About Ethernet Interfaces*

```
agg1# show int fa6/9
FastEthernet6/9 is up, line protocol is up (connected)
  Hardware is C6k 100Mb 802.3, address is 0003.6c43.8c0a (bia 00d0.5855.89a8)
  MTU 1500 bytes,
  Encapsulation ARPA
  Keepalive set (10 sec)
  Full-duplex, 100Mb/s
  5 minute input rate 0 bits/sec, 0 packets/sec
  5 minute output rate 0 bits/sec, 0 packets/sec
     Received 2 broadcasts, 0 runts, 0 giants, 0 throttles
     0 input errors, 0 CRC, 0 frame, 0 overrun, 0 ignored
     0 input packets with dribble condition detected
     8488 packets output, 775276 bytes, 0 underruns
     0 output errors, 0 collisions, 3 interface resets
     0 babbles, 0 late collision, 0 deferred
     0 lost carrier, 0 no carrier
     0 output buffer failures, 0 output buffers swapped out
```

Frame Format

The terminology *frame* refers to the data link layer headers and the payload together; the terminology *packet* refers to the Ethernet payload, which typically consists of the IP header and the user data. Ethernet frames range from 64 bytes to 1518 bytes (1522 when you add the VLAN tag).

Figure 12-1 illustrates the format of Ethernet frames. As you can see, Ethernet frames have 6 bytes of destination address and 6 bytes of source address. These are called Media Access

Control (MAC) addresses. In Ethernet v2, the addresses are followed by the Type field, 2 bytes used to indicate the upper-layer protocol. For IP, this value is 0x0800. The data follows the Type field. Table 12-3 shows some common type values.

Figure 12-1 *Ethernet Frame Format*

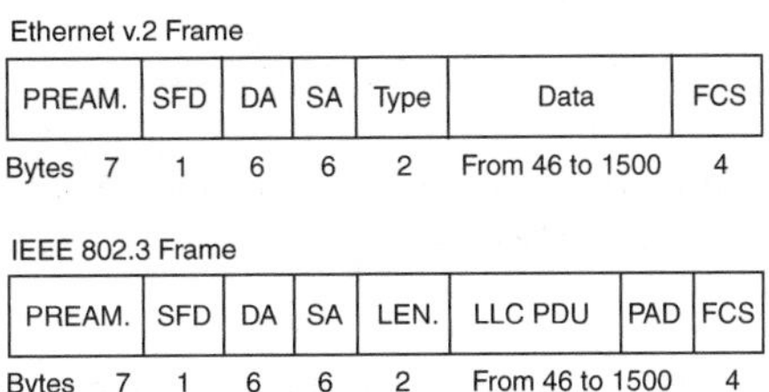

Table 12-3 *Common Protocol Types*

Protocol	Type
IP	0x0800
ARP	0x0806
Novell	0x8137

The bottom portion of Figure 12-1 shows the 802.3 format. The difference with Ethernet v2 is the Length field followed by the logical link control protocol data unit (LLC PDU). LLC (802.2) is a layer between Layer 3 and the MAC layer; it provides services of different types: type 1 is connectionless and type 2 is connection oriented (used, for example, in NetBIOS).

In Figure 12-1, notice the 4-byte frame check sequence, which is a cyclical redundancy check (CRC) calculated on the whole frame.

TIP A device receiving a frame does not know whether it is in 802.3 format or Ethernet v2 until it looks in the Type/Length field. These fields are overloaded, as you can see in Figure 12-1. If the value is more than 1536 (0x600), it is an Ethernet v2 frame. If the value is less than or equal to 1536, it is the length of an 802.3 packet.

Most of today's network traffic uses the v2 format. Example 12-2 highlights the portion of the **show interface** command that shows the encapsulation type. When the encapsulation is Ethernet v2, it is referred to as ARPA.

Example 12-2 *Encapsulation Example*

```
agg1#show int fa6/9
FastEthernet6/9 is up, line protocol is up (connected)
[…]
  Encapsulation ARPA
[…]
```

The Ethernet 802.3 format, in turn, can use one of three other formats. Figure 12-2 presents the possible 802.3 formats. Examples of protocols using the 802.3 encapsulations are listed here:

- **Novell raw format**—Uses 802.3 without the LLC portion; this format is called Novell_Ether in Cisco terminology (see part **a** of Figure 12-2).
- **Novell with LLC encapsulation**—The SAP value is 0xE0; this format is called SAP in Cisco terminology (see part **b** of Figure 12.2).
- **NetBIOS**—Uses the LLC encapsulation with a SAP value of 0xF0.

Cisco Layer 2 protocols typically use the Subnetwork Access Protocol (SNAP) format. (The SNAP format has 0xAA as the SAP field; see part **c** of Figure 12-2.)

Figure 12-2 *802.3 Frame Formats*

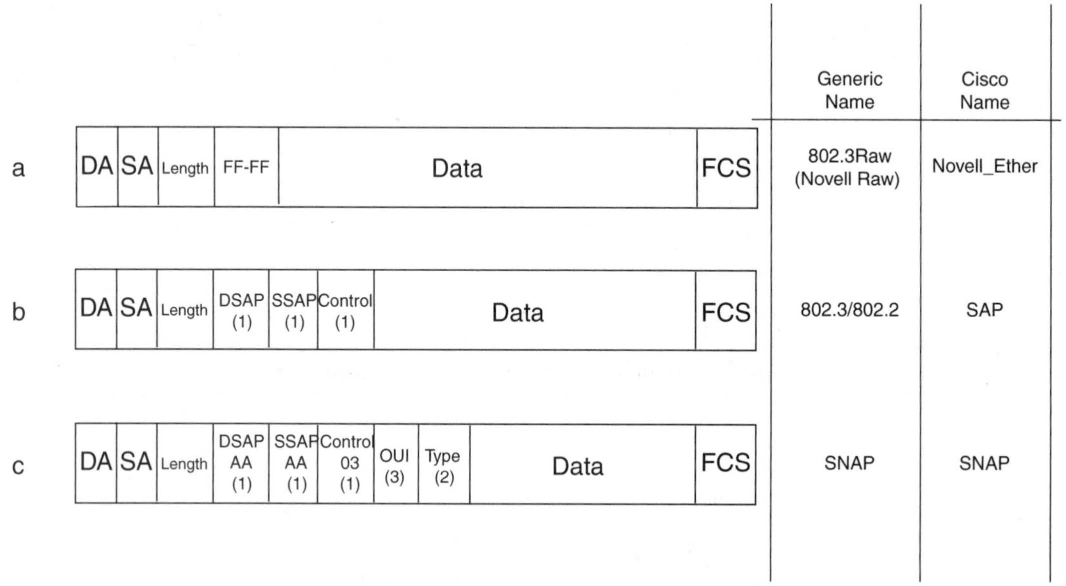

	Frame	Generic Name	Cisco Name
a	DA | SA | Length | FF-FF | Data | FCS	802.3Raw (Novell Raw)	Novell_Ether
b	DA | SA | Length | DSAP (1) | SSAP (1) | Control (1) | Data | FCS	802.3/802.2	SAP
c	DA | SA | Length | DSAP AA (1) | SSAP AA (1) | Control 03 (1) | OUI (3) | Type (2) | Data | FCS	SNAP	SNAP

Address Format

Figure 12-3 shows the format of a MAC address. The first three most significant bytes are called the organizational unique identifier (OUI). They identify the networking vendor; the remaining 3 bytes are decided by the vendor.

Figure 12-3 *MAC Address Format*

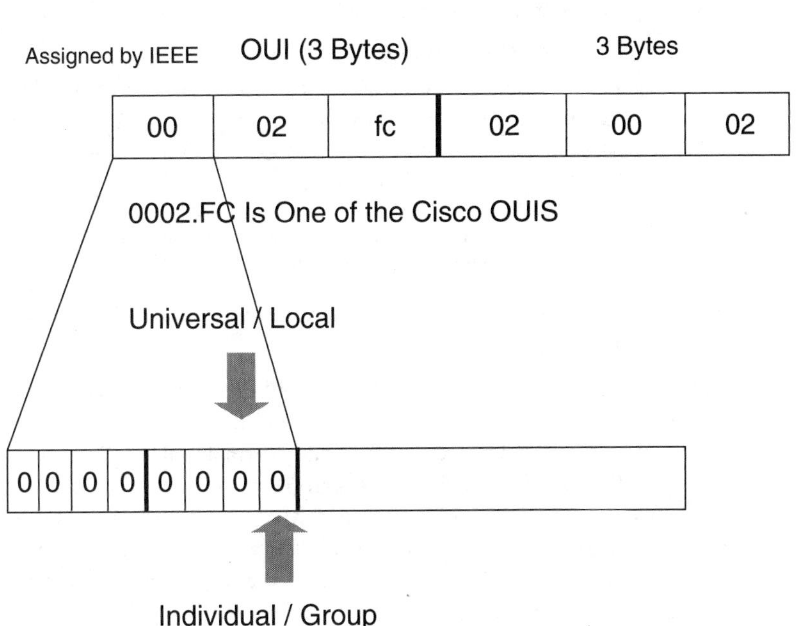

The first bit (the least significant bit) of the most significant byte is called the Individual/Group (I/G) bit. If its value is 0, the address is unicast; if it is 1, it is a multicast address.

The second least significant bit of the first byte is called the Universal/Local (U/L) bit. Burnt-in MAC addresses (BIAs) have the Universal bit set to 0.

In Figure 12-3, you see a unicast address—specifically, a Cisco MAC address (the OUI belongs to Cisco). Notice the values of the I/G and U/L bits.

TIP For more information about the OUI format, refer to http://standards.ieee.org/regauth/oui/tutorials/lanman.html.

To find the OUI associated with a certain manufacturer, you can use the IEEE tool at http://standards.ieee.org/regauth/oui/index.shtml.

In the case of Cisco Systems, the tool returns the following values: 00-00-0C, 00-01-42, 00-01-43, 00-01-63, 00-01-64, 00-01-96, 00-01-97, 00-01-C7, 00-01-C9, 00-02-16, 00-02-17, 00-02-4A, 00-02-4B, 00-02-7D, 00-02-7E, 00-02-B9, 00-02-BA, 00-02-FC, 00-02-FD, 00-03-31, 00-03-32, 00-03-6B, 00-03-6C, 00-D0-58, and so on.

Example 12-1 shows the OUIs 00-03-6C and 00-D0-58. Figure 12-3 uses 00-02-FC. In Chapter 13, "Layer 3 Protocol Essentials," you can see the use of the OUI 00-00-0C for the Hot Standby Redundancy Protocol (HSRP).

MAC addresses can be categorized as unicast, multicast, and broadcasts. Each type of MAC triggers a different behavior on the hosts receiving the frame:

- **Unicast**—A host receiving a unicast frame compares it with its own MAC; If they do not match, it discards the frame.
- **Multicast**—Multicast addresses have the I/G bit set to 1. Multicast addresses have the following format: 0100.5e*xx.xxxx*. They map to the last 23 bits of the multicast IP address. Multicast IP addresses start in binary format with 1110 (Class D): They range from 224.0.0.0 to 239.255.255.255. Figure 12-4 shows the mapping between the multicast used by VRRP 224.0.0.18 and its MAC 0100.5e00.0012. Depending on how the driver programs the NIC, a host receiving multicast traffic either can pass all multicast frames to the CPU or can pass only the frames whose multicast address has been configured on the NIC.
- **Broadcast**—Every host looks at broadcast frames. The format is ffff.ffff.ffff.

Figure 12-4 *Multicast Address Mapping*

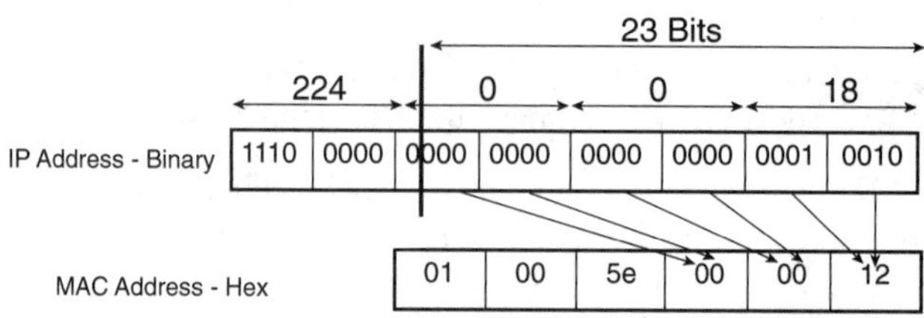

TIP It is a good practice to segregate broadcast domains with Layer 3 devices. Too much broadcast eats CPU cycles from all the devices in the same shared segment.

If a malfunctioning protocol stack generates too much broadcast traffic, you can work around this problem by using a feature called broadcast suppression. A switch configured with *broadcast suppression* measures the amount of broadcast on a port over a certain period of time and drops the traffic exceeding a configured threshold.

Example 12-3 highlights the output of the **show interface** command, where you can see the MAC address associated with the port. Notice that the address (MAC) can be different from the BIA, as it is in this example. The BIA is the MAC that comes with the NIC port of the line card; the other MAC address relates to the configuration that the router pushes to the switch.

Example 12-3 *The MAC Address of Interface FastEthernet6/9*

```
agg1# show int fa6/9
FastEthernet6/9 is up, line protocol is up (connected)
  Hardware is C6k 100Mb 802.3, address is 0003.6c43.8c0a (bia 00d0.5855.89a8)
[...]
```

Frame Size

The minimum frame size for Ethernet is 64 bytes; this number is related to the maximum allowed diameter for CSMA/CD to detect collisions. The maximum frame size including header and the frame check sequence (FCS) is 1518. 802.3ac has increased this number to 1522 bytes to accommodate a VLAN tag.

NOTE The term *diameter* refers to the maximum distance between any two nodes in the collision domain. A collision domain is either a cable or a number of cables connected by repeaters. The minimum frame size and the diameter are correlated because of the CSMA/CD algorithm. A transmitting station needs to be capable of detecting collisions while it is sourcing the frame. If a collision occurs after the frame has been completely transmitted, the frame is lost and no retransmission occurs.

This requires that when a host originates the smallest frame, all the devices on the cable see it before the host finishes transmitting, and the host must be capable of detecting a collision before the transmission is over. In the case of 10-Mbps Ethernet, the maximum theoretical size is about 2500 meters (m) and the smallest frame size is 64 bytes. This means that in

Ethernet, the time that it takes for a host to transmit 64 bytes is enough to detect collisions on a 2500 m cable.

In the case of Fast Ethernet, the minimum frame size is the same as for Ethernet (64 bytes), and the speed is 10 times faster. This speed implies that the diameter is 10 times shorter: about 200 m.

The Maximum Transmission Unit (MTU) specifies the maximum number of bytes in the payload of an Ethernet frame, which is to say that the maximum frame size of 1518 bytes maps to an MTU of 1500 bytes.

One factor that limits the size of an Ethernet frame is the CRC-32 algorithm (the error-detection mechanism), which is not effective above 12,000 bytes. 1518 is well below the limits, which explains why it is possible to use frames bigger than 1518. (See the section, "Giant and Jumbo Frames" for more information.)

You might run into errors related to the frame size when troubleshooting an Ethernet network:

- **Runt**—This is a frame shorter than 64 bytes with an FCS error. This can be the result of duplex mismatch or collisions.
- **Undersize**—This is a frame smaller than 64 bytes with a good FCS. This is typically the result of a problem on the transmitter device.
- **Giant**—This is a frame that is bigger than 1518 bytes with a bad FCS. This can be the effect of misconfigurations such as not setting the MTU of a routed port when the applications actually are using jumbo or baby giant frames. (See the section, "Giant and Jumbo Frames.")

Example 12-4 shows the portions of output from the **show interface** command with an MTU of 1500, which corresponds to a frame size of 1518 bytes. You also can read some counters for the errors previously described.

Example 12-4 *Frame Size and Errors*

```
agg1# show int fa6/9
FastEthernet6/9 is up, line protocol is up (connected)
[...]
  MTU 1500 bytes,
[...]
     Received 2 broadcasts, 0 runts, 0 giants, 0 throttles
     0 input errors, 0 CRC, 0 frame, 0 overrun, 0 ignored
     0 input packets with dribble condition detected
     8488 packets output, 775276 bytes, 0 underruns
     0 output errors, 0 collisions, 3 interface resets
     0 babbles, 0 late collision, 0 deferred
     0 lost carrier, 0 no carrier
     0 output buffer failures, 0 output buffers swapped out
```

Fast Ethernet

One of the most common attachment options for today's servers is Fast Ethernet (100BASE-T), which supports 100 Mbps. The most commonly used Fast Ethernet physical media are as follows:

- **100BASE-TX**—Fast Ethernet on Category 5 UTP with a speed of 100 Mbps. 100BASE-TX allows a maximum distance of about 200m by using repeaters (100m otherwise).
- **100BASE-FX**—Fast Ethernet on either single mode or multimode fiber. 100BASE-FX allows a maximum distance of 400m with half-duplex transmission.

One of the main enhancements introduced by Fast Ethernet is the capability of operating in full-duplex mode. With full-duplex mode, a host can transmit and receive at the same time. A controller operating in this mode does not perform CSMA/CD: Full-duplex Ethernet requires point-to-point links between two devices.

Operating in full-duplex mode has several advantages:

- The transmission on the wire is bidirectional, which allows 100 Mbps of throughput for each direction.
- It eliminates the latency introduced by collisions and the associated CSMA/CD algorithm.
- It eliminates the diameter restrictions of CSMA/CD, which allows for 100BASE-FX to extend up to about 2 kilometers (km) of distance on multimode fiber and about 10 km on single-mode fiber.

TIP If you need to interconnect more than two hosts and you want to use full-duplex Ethernet, you need to use an Ethernet switch. If you use a hub, the hosts operate in half-duplex mode.

Fast Ethernet (defined in IEEE 802.3u) has a negotiation mechanism to choose the speed and duplex of the link and to negotiate flow control. This mechanism is called autonegotiation and is based on fast link pulses (FLP), a link-integrity test. Autonegotiation makes it possible for two connected devices to agree on speed (10 Mbps or 100 Mbps) and duplex (full duplex or half duplex); the preferred choice is to operate at 100 full duplex.

With autonegotiation, it is possible to connect 10BASE-T devices (10 Mbps) with Fast Ethernet devices: Fast Ethernet understands normal link pulses (NLP) emitted by 10BASE-T and adapts accordingly.

Autonegotiation in NICs historically has been problematic because of errors (typically fixed by upgrading NIC drivers) or implementations that do not conform completely to the IEEE 802.3u specifications. As a result of an unsuccessful duplex negotiation, you will have a linkup but performance degradation because of collisions. In case of failure in the speed negotiation, the link stays down.

Table 12-4 shows the possible combinations of autonegotiation between a NIC and a switch, together with the result on the NIC and on the switch port.

Note that hard-coding the speed on one side only causes a duplex mismatch. Even if the interface still sends the FLPs, they do not carry the information about the technology supported, and the peer NIC defaults to half-duplex. This is the case of 2, 3, 5, and 6 in Table 12-4.

TIP Some organizations prefer to hard-code speed and duplex settings for ports that connect network devices. As an example, if a router connects to a switch with Fast Ethernet ports, it often is preferred to force both ports to 100 Mbps and full duplex.

If you statically configure speed and duplex, be sure to do this on both sides of the link; otherwise, you risk having duplex mismatch.

Table 12-4 *Examples of Autonegotiation Combinations*

	NIC	Switch	NIC Result	Switch Port Result
1 (correct)	Auto	Auto	100 full duplex	100 full duplex
2	100 full duplex	Auto	100 full duplex	100 half duplex
3	Auto	100 full duplex	100 half duplex	100 full duplex
4 (correct)	100 full duplex	100 full duplex	100 full duplex	100 full duplex
5	100 half duplex	Auto	100 half duplex	100 half duplex
6	10 half duplex	Auto	10 half duplex	10 half duplex
7	10 half duplex	100 half duplex	Link down	Link down

If you experience problems of duplex negotiation, you can hard-code speed and duplex on both servers and the switches they attach to. Example 12-5 shows how to set the speed on a switch port.

Example 12-5 *Available Speed and Duplex Setting for a Fast Ethernet Switch Port*

```
acc1(config-if)# speed ?
  10    Force 10 Mbps operation
  100   Force 100 Mbps operation
  auto  Enable AUTO speed configuration

acc1(config-if)#duplex ?
  full  Force full duplex operation
  half  Force half-duplex operation
```

Gigabit Ethernet (IEEE 802.3z)

Gigabit Ethernet is Ethernet (same frame size, same frame format) at speeds of 1 Gigabit per second (Gbps). Full-duplex Gigabit Ethernet works similarly to Fast Ethernet. Gigabit Ethernet can operate in half-duplex or full-duplex mode; full duplex is the most common use. Full-duplex Gigabit Ethernet is not subject to the maximum network diameter imposed by the CSMA/CD operation. The distances allowed by full-duplex Gigabit Ethernet are dictated by the physical characteristics of the medium and by the laser transceivers being used.

A gigabit line card can support multiple physical media, by replacing the laser gigabit interface converters (GBICs) on a per-port basis. (For details on how this is possible, read the section, "Ethernet Physical Layers.")

Gigabit Ethernet typically is used with either of the following physical media:

- **1000BASE-SX**—Short-wave laser on multimode fiber, which allows a maximum distance of around 550 m.
- **1000BASE-LX**—Long-wave laser on either multimode or single mode, which allows a maximum distance of 550 m and 5 km, respectively. (Cisco 1000BASE-LX GBICs allow a distance of 10 km on single-mode fiber.)
- **1000BASE-T**—Gigabit Ethernet on UTP, with a maximum distance of 100 m.

TIP Besides 1000BASE-SX and LX, many vendors provide GBICs for longer distances: The Cisco 1000BASE-ZX GBIC allows 70 km on single-mode fiber.

For more information about the length supported by Cisco GBIC, you can consult this URL and look for the data sheets: http://www.cisco.com/en/US/products/hw/modules/ps872/prod_module_series_home.html.

Similarly to Fast Ethernet, Gigabit Ethernet has autonegotiation, but the parameters being negotiated are different. Gigabit Ethernet interfaces do not negotiate speed; instead, they negotiate duplex and flow control. In Example 12-6, you can see the options available when configuring a Gigabit interface of a Catalyst 6500: There is no option to set a different speed; the command **speed nonegotiate** simply disables autonegotiation for flow control and duplex.

Gigabit Ethernet uses PAUSE frames for flow control to protect a host from being overwhelmed by traffic. A NIC supporting PAUSE frame can ask the switch upstream to stop forwarding traffic for a certain amount of time.

The sending and receiving of PAUSE frames is configurable. Example 12-6 shows some of the configuration options of the Gigabit interface of a Catalyst switch. The send configuration of one switch must match the receive configuration of the peer switch.

Example 12-6 *Flow Control Settings on Gigabit Ports*

```
Agg1(config-if)# speed ?
  nonegotiate  Do not negotiate speed

agg1(config-if)# flowcontrol ?
  receive  Configure receiving flow operation
  send     Configure sending flow operation
```

As with Fast Ethernet, negotiation must be verified for interoperability between products from different vendors. Sometimes it is necessary to disable it and hard-code the flow control and duplex settings.

10-Gigabit Ethernet (IEEE 802.3ae)

10-Gigabit Ethernet (10-GigE) is the fastest version of Ethernet available today. 10-Gigabit Ethernet is useful for LAN, MAN, and WAN connections.

10-GigE preserves the following characteristics of the original Ethernet:

- 802.3 Media Access Control protocol
- 802.3 frame size and format

10-GigE differs from previous Ethernet standards for the following characteristics:

- It is full-duplex only.
- It is supported only on fiber.
- The maximum distance is 40 km.
- It is possible to have direct attachment to SONET/SDH.

You can attach 10-GigE to SONET/SDH because of the WAN PHY. (For more information about what a PHY is, read the section "Ethernet Physical Layers.")

10-GigE offers several different transceiver types:

- **10GBASE-SR**—S stands for short wavelength, and R indicates the LAN attachment type with 64B/66B encoding. It is designed for use on multimode fiber (MMF) with a wavelength of 850 nanometers (nm).
- **10GBASE-SW**—S stands for short wavelength, and W indicates the WAN attachment type. It is designed for connection to SONET/SDH equipment.
- **10GBASE-LX4**—L stands for long wavelength (1310 nm), and X indicates the LAN attachment with 8B/10B encoding on single-mode or multimode fiber, for a maximum distance of 10 km (single mode).
- **10GBASE-LR**—L stands for long wavelength (1310 nm), and R stands for the LAN attachment. It is carried on single-mode fiber and allows a distance of 10 km.
- **10GBASE-LW**—This is like 10GBASE-LW but with the WAN attachment option.
- **10GBASE-ER**—E stands for extra long wavelength (1550 nm), and R is for the LAN attachment for single-mode fiber and a total length of 40 km.
- **10GBASE-EW**—This is like 10GBASE-ER but with the WAN attachment option.

TIP Check the details about the supported distances with specific vendors' implementations.

Ethernet Physical Layers

One of the key capabilities of Ethernet is support for several different physical media. IEEE 802.3 defines interfaces (which are not necessarily connectors) between the layers to provide this flexibility.

The physical layer of Ethernet provides encoding and decoding, serialization, and physical connection (mechanical and electrical). Each function belongs to one sublayer of the physical layer.

The MAC function is provided by the *controller*; the physical connectivity is provided by the *transceiver*. A NIC card typically is made up of controller and transceiver together, but it is possible to have a separate transceiver connecting to a controller via a cable.

The connector characteristics are part of the Medium Dependent Interface (MDI) specifications. The MDI defines the mechanical and electrical characteristics for the connection to the physical medium.

Figure 12-5 shows how the Ethernet layers are arranged according to the standards. The next sections describe these layers.

Figure 12-5 *Ethernet Physical Layers*

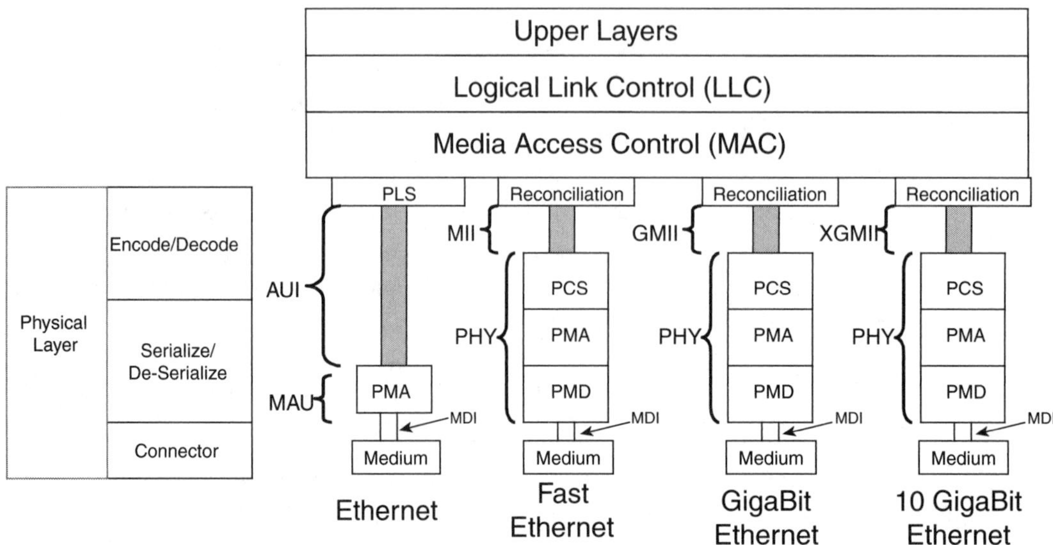

Ethernet Physical Layers

In Ethernet 10 Mbps, the controller provides the MAC layer as well as the encoding and decoding. In Figure 12-5, you can think of the controller as the combination of the MAC layer with the physical layer signaling (PLS) function.

The transceiver in Ethernet is called the media attachment unit (MAU). The MAU consists of the physical medium attachment (PMA), whose job is to serialize and deserialize data, and the physical connector. MAUs for UTP cables use RJ-45 as the connector, MAUs for coaxial cables use British Naval Connectors (BNCs), and MAUs for fiber use straight-tip (ST) connectors.

These two components, PMA and the physical connector, communicate through an attachment unit interface (AUI). This interface can be visible if you use an external MAU; otherwise, the interface is internal to the NIC.

Fast Ethernet Physical Layers

In Fast Ethernet, the controller is independent of the media being used: The encoding/decoding function is implemented in the transceiver.

The transceiver in Fast Ethernet is called PHY. The PHY consists of the following:

- Physical coding sublayer (PCS) for encoding and decoding
- PMA layer for serialization/deserialization (SERDES)
- Physical medium dependent (PMD) layer, which defines the physical layer–dependent functions, such as the MLT-3 encoding for 100 Mbps on UTP

Fast Ethernet connectors include the RJ-45 for copper, the subscriber connector (SC), and the ST connector for fiber.

The equivalent of the AUI in Fast Ethernet is called the media-independent interface (MII): It can function at 10 Mbps or 100 Mbps. The MII typically is not visible; it is built into the NIC card. The possibility exists to attach the controller to the transceiver via a MII connector (SCSI-like).

Gigabit Ethernet Physical Layers

The Gigabit Ethernet layers look similar to the Fast Ethernet layers. The interface between the PHY and the controller is called gigabit media independent interface (GMII), which, unlike the MII, is only an internal interface between chips or boards. The GMII supports 10 Mbps, 100 Mbps, and 1 Gpbs.

1000BASE-SX, 1000BASE-LX, and 1000BASE-CX all share the same PCS and PMA. GBICs typically map to the PMD function in the Gigabit Ethernet stack. This means that on the same switch line cards, you can install GBICs for different Gigabit Ethernet wavelengths.

1000BASE-T uses a separate PCS, PMA, and PMD. 1000BASE-T can run on the existing UTP Category 5 cabling. You can replace 100BASE-T line cards with 1000BASE-T line cards and provide 10/100/1000 Mbps on regular UTP Category 5 cabling.

For fiber connection, you normally would use an SC connector attached to a GBIC or an LC connector attached to a Small Form Factor Pluggable (SFP) converter.

10-Gigabit Ethernet

From a very high level, the 10-Gigabit Ethernet stack can be assimilated to the Gigabit Ethernet stack: You have a MAC layer and a PHY layer, with the PHY layer containing a PCS, PMA, and PMD. The GMII interface is replaced by the XGMII interface (10-gigabit media-independent interface).

Of course, there are differences with Gigabit Ethernet: The MAC layer does not do CSMA/CD anymore, and it supports only full-duplex communication.

The support of the WAN PHY means that you need to have more layers between the PMD and the MAC. This is required for the SONET/SDH framing.

The connector for 10-Gigabit Ethernet line cards is typically the SC connector.

Giant and Jumbo Frames

Ethernet frames have a size that ranges from 64 bytes to 1518 bytes. The minimum frame size is dictated by considerations of supported length of shared media and how the CSMA /CD algorithm works. The maximum frame size is limited by the CRC algorithm. The CRC algorithm loses its effectiveness when the frame size is bigger, around 12,000 bytes.

This means that, with Ethernet, in theory, you could transport bigger frame sizes than 1518 bytes. *Jumbo frames* are Ethernet frames that are bigger than 1518 bytes. The requirement for sending frames bigger than the maximum frame size is dictated mainly by the server CPU load, especially when servers are gigabit-attached to the network. If you have a bulk transfer of data, such as a backup, packaging fewer but bigger frames results in the reduction of the number of CPU interrupts, with a consequent performance improvement.

Normally, a switch categorizes frames greater than 1522 bytes as *giant frames* (refer to section, "Frame Size") and increases an error counter. (For a Catalyst switch, the threshold is typically 1548 bytes.)

Baby giants are legal frames that are slightly larger than 1518 bytes. This is the case of 802.1Q-tagged frames (1522 bytes), multiprotocol label switching (MPLS) frames (1518 + n * 4 bytes, where *n* is the number of stacked labels—2, in the case of MPLS VPNs), and Inter-Switch Link (ISL) frames (1548 bytes). In most cases, baby giants are the result of some protocol-tagging mechanism.

There is no standard definition of the size of a baby giant. A baby giant can be anywhere between 1518 bytes and 8000 bytes, where 8000 bytes could be considered the boundary where jumbo frames start.

If the baby giant is the result of some Layer 2 protocol tagging, you typically do not need to configure anything on the switch. The maximum size is typically 1548 bytes (ISL).

You need to configure a switch to support baby giants bigger than the expected Layer 2 protocols, for example, if you need to support MPLS or if you need to support specific applications.

TIP Read the vendor documentation to find out which baby giant sizes are supported; there is no standard baby giant definition.

No standard definition covers how big a jumbo frame should be, but it commonly is accepted that a jumbo frame should be a frame with an MTU of at least 8192 bytes, to accommodate the size of Network File System blocks. A typical frame size for jumbo frames is 9018 bytes (9000 bytes of MTU).

If you need to use jumbo frames in your network, you need to explicitly configure VLAN interfaces with the MTU size that accommodates the packet size.

TIP Notice that you have control over the maximum frame size that routers can take by configuring the MTU size (the command is **mtu** <size>).

If you need to configure jumbo frames, find out which sizes are supported by the vendor. Some switches support only baby giants with sizes such as 1546 bytes, 1552 bytes, or 2000 bytes. Other switches support jumbo frames with sizes of 8092 bytes, 9216 bytes, and so on.

Keep in mind that there are differences in the frame size supported, depending on these factors:

- The switch model
- The line card that you choose
- The port speed

Example 12-7 shows how to configure a switch interface on the Catalyst 6500 to support jumbo frames. The **mtu** command enables you to define a nonstandard frame size—specifically, 9216 bytes. If you need to support a different size, you can change the default with the command **system jumbomtu**.

Example 12-7 *Configuration of Jumbo Frames on the Catalyst 6500*

```
agg(config-if)# interface GigabitEthernet1/1
agg(config-if)# mtu ?
<9216-9216>  MTU size in bytes
agg(config-if)# mtu 9216
!
mpagg1(config)#system jumbomtu ?
  <1500-9216>  Jumbo mtu size in Bytes, default is 9216
```

When configuring jumbo frames, you also should take into account that routing between an interface configured for jumbo frames and a regular Ethernet interface can cause fragmentation at the IP layer.

TIP Jumbo frames are supported by Ethernet v2. The reason is that Ethernet v2 has no field to indicate the length of the packet. In 802.3 Ethernet, the MTU is limited to 1500 bytes: If the length field has a value greater than 0x600 bytes, the field is considered an EtherType and the packet is categorized as Ethernet v2. (Refer to the section, "Frame Format.")

Ethernet Switching

The key component that provides network connectivity in the Data Center is a switch. Data Centers should be designed with point-to-point full-duplex links connected by switches. Using hubs in a Data Center makes the transmission half duplex, which has at least two drawbacks: It prevents use of the full bandwidth of the network, and it introduces unwanted latencies caused by collisions.

Today's switches, especially the ones that you adopt for the aggregation layer, have Layer 2, Layer 3, and also possibly Layer 4 and Layer 5 processing capabilities. The access switches typically have only Layer 2 capabilities. This chapter focuses on the Layer 2 aspects of a switch.

A Layer 2 Ethernet switch is, first of all, a transparent bridge.

NOTE If a switch supports interfaces of different technologies, such as Ethernet and Token Ring, it also can operate as a translational bridge. This topic is beyond the scope of this book.

Figure 12-6 shows a topology to refresh your memory about the bridging operations.

Figure 12-6 *Ethernet Switching*

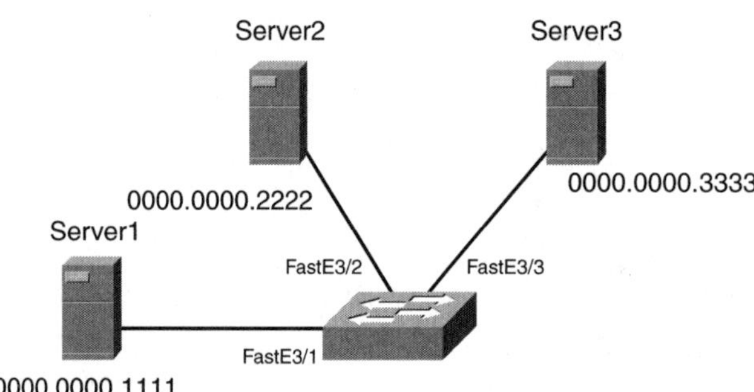

Servers connect to the switch on dedicated links; each link is an Ethernet segment. Even if it is possible to have multiple devices on a single link, it is recommended and most common to have a single device attached to the switch. The second option is required for full-duplex operations.

Because there is a single device on each link, there is no chance for collisions. If multiple devices were attached to the same link, the switch would contain the collision to the specific link.

The servers in Figure 12-6 all belong to the same broadcast domain, which means that if Server1 sends a broadcast, Server2 and Server3 also receive it.

TIP How many collisions domains are there in Figure 12-6? How many broadcast domains? The topology in Figure 12-6 has a single broadcast domain and three different collision domains.

The switch dynamically learns the location of the hosts by looking into the traffic that arrives from Fast Ethernet 3/1, 3/2, and 3/3 and associating the source MAC of the incoming traffic with the port where it appeared.

As an example, when Server1 sends traffic, the switch learns MAC 0000.0000.1111 and associates it with port 3/1. Similarly, when Server3 sends traffic, the switch learns that MAC 0000.0000.3333 belongs to port 3/3.

After the switch builds the table, it knows that traffic whose destination MAC is 0000.0000.1111 needs to be sent out to port 3/1; if the destination MAC is 0000.0000.3333, the destination port is 3/3.

The natural question is what happens if, at this point, Server1 sends traffic to the destination MAC 0000.0000.2222 and the switch has not learned this MAC yet. It is *flooded*, which means that it is sent out to all ports in the broadcast domain, with the exception of the one that the packet entered. This means that the packet goes out to 3/2 and 3/3.

The previous one is an example of *unicast flooding*.

The table that stores MAC addresses and the port where they come from is called the *MAC address table*. When a packet reaches a switch and its destination MAC address appears in the table, it is forwarded to the associated port. If no entry is present, the switch floods the packet on the LAN, except the ingress port.

Example 12-8 shows the content of a MAC address table on a Catalyst switch.

Example 12-8 *MAC Address Table*

```
agg# show mac-address-table
  vlan   mac address     type    ports
------+----------------+--------+-
*    3  0001.64f9.1a01   dynamic  Po261
*   10  0001.64f9.1a01   dynamic  Po261
*   39  0001.64f9.1a01   dynamic  Po261
*   10  00d0.b7a0.84cb   dynamic  Gi4/1
*    5  00d0.b7a0.84cb   dynamic  Po261
*  110  0003.6c43.8c0a    static  Router
```

continues

Example 12-8 *MAC Address Table (Continued)*

```
*   80  0003.6c43.8c0a    static  Router
*  100  0002.fce0.7824   dynamic  Po261
*  802  0003.6c43.8c0a    static  Router
*   50  0030.962a.00f2   dynamic  Gi4/7
*    3  0001.6446.a1c5   dynamic  Gi3/1
```

You can see the MAC address and the type, where dynamic indicates an entry that was dynamically learned as opposed to static entries that are programmed by internal hardware.

In the port field, you see the associated port: Po261 is a channel, Gi4/1 is a Gigabit Ethernet port, and Router is a built-in router.

The MAC address table has an aging timer; after entries in the table are idle long enough, they are cleared. You can manually modify the default timer, which is 300 seconds (s) (5 minutes). The command to use is **mac-address-table aging-time**.

TIP You can also manually configure entries in the MAC address table by using the command **mac-address-table static** <mac address> <vlan> <port>.

A possible use for the static configuration of MAC addresses and associated ports is when a networking device is reachable via multicast MAC addresses (as with some types of firewalls). In such a case, if you do not configure a static MAC address, traffic is always flooded to the LAN.

Layer 2 Protocols

When you connect multiple switches together, you need to have some protocol communication between them, which allows them to build the forwarding topology.

Layer 2 protocols do the following:

- Build loop-free forwarding topologies on top of a "looped" physical topology
- Group ports to form channels
- Encapsulate traffic with tags to carry virtual LAN segments across switches

The protocols are listed here:

- **CDP (Cisco Discovery Protocol)**—This Cisco protocol is extremely useful when troubleshooting the network. It helps understanding how the switch connects to other switches and on which ports. Example 12-9 displays one possible output: it shows that the local switch (agg1) is connected to the other aggregation switch (agg2) and to the access switch (acc1).

- **VTP (VLAN Trunking Protocol)**—This Cisco protocol lets you create VLANs in a centralized location (one switch) and propagate the configuration information to the other switches in the same domain.
- **DTP (Dynamic Trunking Protocol)**—DTP is a Cisco protocol that lets you create trunks between switches by negotiating the creation of the trunk and the encapsulation type.
- **PAgP (Port Aggregation Protocol)**—PAgP is a Cisco protocol that negotiates the creation of channels (bundling of ports) by verifying that the port configurations match at both ends of the links.
- **IEEE 802.3ad (LACP)**—This protocol performs functions similar to that of PAgP.
- **IEEE 802.1D (STP)**—STP is the protocol used to prevent loops in Layer 2 topologies with redundant paths.
- **Per VLAN Spanning-Tree Plus (PVST+)**—This protocol is the Cisco proprietary version of STP, which uses one instance of 802.1D-based spanning tree for each VLAN.
- **ISL**—This protocol is the Cisco encapsulation protocol for trunking.
- **IEEE 802.1Q**—This protocol provides standard encapsulation for VLAN trunking.
- **Unidirectional Link Detection (UDLD)**—This Cisco protocol detects unidirectional links.

Example 12-9 *Output of the* **show cdp** *Command*

```
agg1# show cdp neigh
Capability Codes: R - Router, T - Trans Bridge, B - Source Route Bridge
                  S - Switch, H - Host, I - IGMP, r - Repeater, P - Phone
Device ID     Local Intrfce     Holdtme    Capability  Platform  Port ID
agg2          Gig 1/1            166         R S I     Cat 6000  Gig 1/1
agg2          Gig 4/6            166         R S I     Cat 6000  Gig 4/6
acc1          Gig 4/1            137         R S I     Cat 6000  Gig 1/1
```

Cisco protocols typically use a SNAP format with an OUI 0x00000c (one of the Cisco OUIs). Table 12-5 shows the destination MAC and the LLC information for the listed protocols.

Table 12-5 *Some Layer 2 Protocol MAC Addresses and Types*

Protocol	Destination MAC	LLC
CDP	0100.0ccc.cccc	SNAP, Type 0x2000
VTP	0100.0ccc.cccc	SNAP, Type 0x2003
DTP	0100.0ccc.cccc	SNAP, Type 0x2004

continues

Table 12-5 *Some Layer 2 Protocol MAC Addresses and Types (Continued)*

Protocol	Destination MAC	LLC
PAgP	0100.000c.cccc	SNAP, Type 0x0104
IEEE 802.3ad (LACP)	0180.c200.0002	N/A 0x8809 (Type/Length field)
IEEE 802.1D (STP)	0180.c200.0000	Source service access point (SSAP) 0x42, destination service access point (DSAP) 0x42
PVST+	0100.0ccc.cccd	SNAP, Type 0x010b
ISL	0100.0c00.0000	SNAP followed by proprietary field
IEEE 802.1Q	Original MAC of the traffic	N/A, Type/Length 0x8100
UDLD	0100.0ccc.cccc	0x0111

VLANs and Trunks

Figure 12-6 shows servers attached to a single switch. These servers share the same broadcast domain. If you need to segregate their communication, you can use an additional switch and attach servers to it, or you can also create VLANs and assign the switch ports where the servers are connected to different VLANs. One switch configured with a single VLAN is equivalent to a single LAN segment; one switch with multiple VLANs is equivalent to multiple LAN segments.

A typical requirement in the Data Center is to have servers that are physically located on different switches be able to communicate in the same segment, which you can do by configuring the same VLANs on both switches and connecting them through a trunk that carries the same VLANs.

Figure 12-7 provides an example. You want to attach the servers indistinctly to Switch 1 or Switch 2 and then you want to configure the switches to allow Server 1 to communicate with Server 4 and Server 2 to communicate with Server 3. You can achieve this configuration by using two VLANs, VLAN 2 and VLAN 4: You assign Servers 1 and 4 to VLAN 4 and Servers 2 and 3 to VLAN 2.

The configuration consists in making VLAN 2 the Port VLAN ID (PVID) of the switch ports connecting to Servers 1 and 4 and VLAN 4 the PVID of the switch ports connecting to Servers 2 and 3.

NOTE The PVID is the VLAN that you assign to a switch port. This VLAN is also called native VLAN. If the port becomes a 802.1Q trunk, traffic belonging to this VLAN is treated differently from that of the other VLANs: by default, it is carried on the trunk without a VLAN tag.

Figure 12-7 *Trunking VLANs*

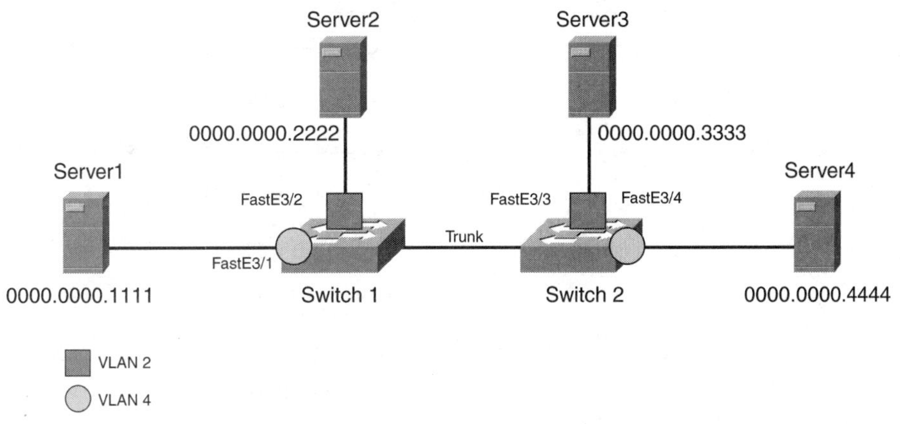

For this design to work, you need to configure the link between Switch 1 and Switch 2 as a *trunk*. A trunk tags the traffic based on the access port it comes from. The receiving switch can read the tag and assign the traffic to the appropriate VLAN.

IEEE 802.1Q is the standard tagging format. Figure 12-8 shows the format of the packets carried on the trunk.

NOTE The Cisco proprietary tagging protocol is called ISL.

Figure 12-8 *802.1Q Trunk*

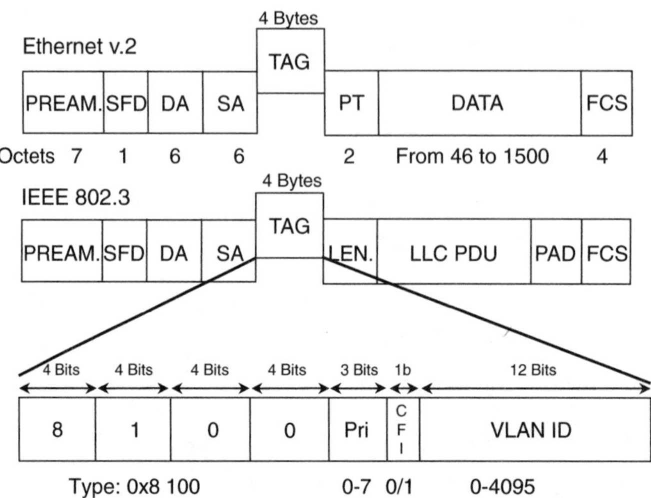

As you can see from Figure 12-8, the 802.1Q tag is placed between the source MAC address and the Type/Length field. A type of 0x8100 indicates that the frame has a VLAN tag. The tag itself is 4 bytes wide, and it contains a field for the priority, used for quality-of-service (QoS) applications; most important is the 12-bit field that indicates the VLAN.

The IEEE standards call for the support of 4096 VLANs, as the presence of a 12-bit field indicates.

Creating VLANs

Creating VLANs on a Cisco switch requires that you first define the VTP domain. If you configure VTP in transparent mode, the switch behaves as if VTP were not present, which means that you need to create VLANs on each switch in the Data Center.

Example 12-10 shows how to create a domain and make it transparent. You should assign the same domain name to all the switches that need to be able to trunk VLANs between each other.

Example 12-10 *VTP Transparent Mode*

```
agg(config)# vtp domain mydomain
agg(config)# vtp mode transparent
```

TIP

If you want to create VLANs on a single switch and have the configuration propagated to the other switches in the Layer 2 domain, you need to use VTP. You make one switch a VTP server (better to have two for redundancy) and the other switches in the domain VTP clients.

When you create a VLAN on the VTP server switch, this VLAN appears on all the other switches in the domain. The only configuration left is the association between VLANs and ports, which you do switch-by-switch.

The configurations in this book assume the use of "VTP transparent," which is equivalent to not using VTP.

Once you create the VTP domain, you need to create the VLANs. Example 12-11 shows how to create VLAN 10 and assign a name to it. If you use VTP transparent, you need to repeat this step on all the switches that need to use VLAN 10.

Example 12-11 *Creating VLANs*

```
acc(config)# vlan 10
acc(config-vlan)# name accessvlan
```

Once you create a VLAN, you can assign ports to it. For example, you can assign Fast Ethernet 3/4 to VLAN 10, as you can see in Example 12-12.

Example 12-12 *Assigning a Port to a VLAN*

```
acc(config)# int fa3/4
acc(config-if)# switchport
acc(config-if)# switchport mode access
acc(config-if)# switchport access vlan 10
```

Port Fast Ethernet 3/4 is an access port; it is the type of port you attach to a server. (For more information, read the section, "Access Ports.")

Creating Trunks

Establishing trunks between Cisco switches is fairly simple because of the DTP. As soon as you configure the ports at the two ends of a link as *switch ports*, a trunk automatically comes up.

TIP If the trunk does not come up, you probably changed the default VLAN for the port (the native VLAN): DTP does not put the port in trunking mode if the PVID does not match at both ends of the link.

Once you have the ports trunking, you might want to choose the encapsulation type and limit the number of VLANs that you carry on the trunk.

Example 12-13 shows how to modify the port configuration to force 802.1Q trunking (Cisco switches by default choose ISL as the encapsulation type) and to limit the number of VLANs to VLAN 10 and 20. If you use the command **switchport trunk encapsulation dot1q**, the peer switch picks up the encapsulation changes. If you use the command **switchport trunk allowed vlan 10,20**, you limit the number of VLANs carried on the trunk.

Example 12-13 *Trunk Configuration*

```
acc1(config)# int giga1/1
acc1(config-if)# switchport
acc1(config-if)# switchport trunk encapsulation dot1q
acc1(config-if)# switchport trunk allowed vlan 10,20
```

If one of the switches is not Cisco, you cannot rely on DTP to bring the trunk up, and you have to explicitly force the port to trunk by using the command **switchport mode trunk**, as in Example 12-14.

Example 12-14 *Trunk Configuration*

```
acc1(config)# int giga1/1
acc1(config-if)# switchport
acc1(config-if)# switchport trunk encapsulation dot1q
acc1(config-if)# switchport mode trunk
acc1(config-if)# switchport trunk allowed vlan 10,20
```

TIP 802.1Q carries untagged traffic that belongs to the same VLAN as the native VLAN of the trunk port. For example, if the PVID or native VLAN of a trunk is 6, the traffic from VLAN 6 is carried on the trunk without any tag. The traffic of all the other VLANs (such as VLANs 5, 7, and 8) carries a 802.1Q tag (for example, 5, 7, and 8).

As a security measure, and to prevent misconfigurations, you should enable **vlan dot1q tag native** to force the tagging of all VLANs on the trunk.

If you do so, the traffic from VLAN 6 on the trunk also carries a 802.1Q tag, specifically the tag for VLAN 6 (which is the native VLAN of the trunk).

EtherChannels

EtherChannels allow you to bundle multiple ports for redundancy and increased bandwidth. Figure 12-9 shows how you connect two switches with a channel. Each switch considers the four ports together as a single port with four times the throughput capacity. (If these were gigabit ports, you'd end up with a 4 Gb port.)

Figure 12-9 *EtherChannel*

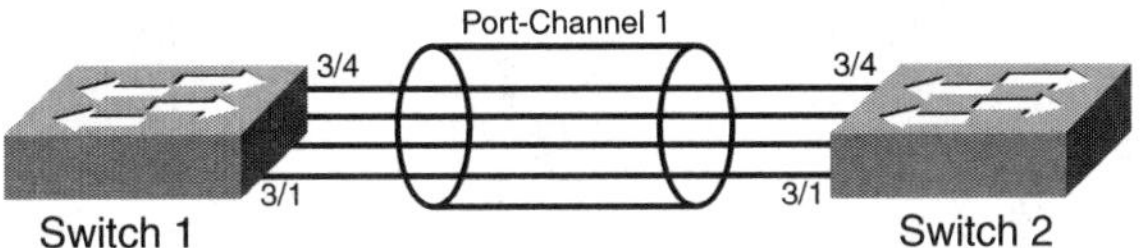

The benefits of channeling are

- **Subsecond convergence for link failures**—If you lose any of the links in the channel, the switch detects the failure and distributes the traffic on the remaining links.
- **Increased bandwidth**—Each port-channel link has as much bandwidth as the sum of the bundled links.

TIP For maximum availability, you should bundle ports that belong to different line cards. In case one line card breaks down, you can still carry the traffic on the remaining links.

Before doing so, make sure that the switch you are using supports channeling across line cards.

It is apparent by now that the key feature which determines the effectiveness of channeling is the load-balancing algorithm that distributes the traffic on the available links. You need to read the specific product documentation to understand the options in distributing the traffic. Typically, they consist of a hashing algorithm that involves the source and destination MAC addresses or a similar algorithm applied on the source and destination IP addresses.

Creating a Channel

This section describes the configuration using LACP as the negotiation protocol, which provides equivalent capabilities to the PAgP protocol. LACP allows the port to successfully form a channel only if the trunking configuration and the port speed match on both sides of the links.

Example 12-15 shows how to configure one of the two switches: You assign the ports that need to form the bundle to the same group (in Example 12-15, group 2). The command **channel-protocol lacp** enables the use of LACP as the protocol for the negotiation.

You configure the ports on the local switch to behave as active; you configure the ports on the remote switch to behave either as *active* or as *passive*.

Example 12-15 *EtherChannel Configuration*

```
interface GigabitEthernet4/1
 switchport
 channel-group 2 mode active
 channel-protocol lacp
end
!
interface GigabitEthernet5/1
 switchport
 channel-group 2 mode active
 channel-protocol lacp
end
```

Once the channel forms, you can configure its switching parameters from the interface Port-channel <group>, which in Example 12-15 is group 2. For example, if you need to configure trunking on top of the channel, you can use the interface Port-channel 2 and the configurations are replicated on the bundled ports.

STP

STP ensures that only one loopless forwarding logical path is present at any given time for a specific VLAN, despite having multiple physical paths for redundancy.

Figure 12-10 shows a topology with two switches connected with redundant links. Suppose that STP is disabled. A host attached to Switch 2 sends a frame with a destination MAC 0000.0000.4444, which has not yet been learned. Switch 2 floods the frame to all the ports, with the exception of the port connecting to the host. As a result, the frame goes to Switch 1 both from port 3/1 and port 3/2.

Switch 1 receives the same frame from port 3/1 and port 3/2. It does not have any entry in its MAC address table for 0000.0000.4444, so it forwards the frame that came in from port 3/2 to port 3/1 and vice versa for the other frame. Figure 12-10 shows only the path taken by one of the two frames. The frame that came in from port 3/2 is sent out to port 3/1. Switch 2 receives the frame with destination MAC 0000.0000.4444 from both ports 3/1 and 3/2; it looks up the MAC address table and does not find the MAC address. As a result, it floods the frame. This process continues indefinitely: Ethernet frames do not have a Time-To-Live field.

Figure 12-10 *Layer 2 Loops*

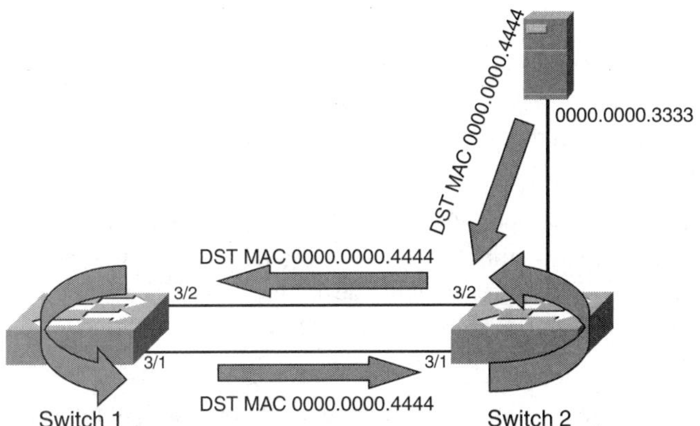

As you can understand from the example, if multiple paths were present and STP disabled, you would have a Layer 2 loop, which means that packets would be replicated and would keep circulating in the network indefinitely.

Layer 2 loops happen, sometimes even with STP enabled, and they have a catastrophic effect. Disabling STP even in loop-free topologies can be disastrous if somebody accidentally introduces a loop by connecting additional network devices.

There are several versions of the STP:

- **IEEE 802.1D**—IEEE 802.1D is the standard spanning tree, also called Single Spanning Tree (SST), which is designed to build a single loopless logical topology.
- **Cisco PVST+**—The Cisco implementation of STP is based on 802.1D but is enhanced to support a separate instance of spanning tree per VLAN, which allows building different logical topologies concurrently, one per VLAN.
- **Cisco Multi-Instance Spanning-Tree (MISTP)**—This Cisco implementation lets you create several instances of a spanning tree and map VLANs to them. Differently from PVST+, MISTP does not execute as many instances as the number of configured VLANs. MISTP executes a user-configured number of instances (topologies) and associates one or more VLANs to each instance.
- **IEEE 802.1s (Multiple Spanning Tree [MST])**—MST lets you define multiple instances of a spanning tree and map VLANs to it (similarly to Cisco MISTP). Referring to MST typically implies the use of 802.1w as well.
- **IEEE 802.1w (Rapid Spanning-Tree Protocol [RSTP])**—This standard improves the convergence time of a spanning tree.

- **Rapid PVST+**—This protocol is a combination of PVST+ and 802.1w; it creates one instance of a spanning tree per VLAN, as does PVST+, and it has the fast convergence behavior of 802.1w.

At the time of this writing, most of the Data Center installations based on Cisco switches implement PVST+. MISTP and MST were introduced mainly to address scalability in presence of a high number of VLANs. PVST+ is still a more flexible protocol and easier to deploy.

Cisco introduced a number of enhancements to PVST+ to improve the convergence time with features such as UplinkFast and BackboneFast. 802.1w supersedes UplinkFast and BackboneFast, which makes it highly desirable to use 802.1w in conjunction with PVST+. This chapter focuses on PVST+ and on 802.1w, which in Cisco terminology has the name *Rapid PVST+*.

For more information about how and why to choose the spanning-tree algorithm, read Chapter 20.

Bridge Identifier

According to 802.1D, each bridge (switch) participating in a spanning tree needs to have a unique bridge identifier. The format of the bridge ID is a number of 8 bytes.

The 8 bytes are used as follows:

- **Priority field**—The two most significant bytes represent the priority of the switch; they are user configurable, and the default value is 32,768. The priority field is used to elect the root bridge. The switch with the lowest priority value wins.
- **MAC Address**—The six least significant bytes ensure the uniqueness of the identifier, and they are derived from the MAC address of the switch.

802.1t modifies the bridge identifier format (which is also called *MAC-address reduction*).

Port Roles and States (802.1w)

Figure 12-11 shows an example of Data Center topology. The aggregation switches operate as Layer 3 switches, which means that they have routing capabilities, but they are still Layer 2 switches.

All the links in the figure belong to the same VLAN, and the aggregation switches bridge traffic between these links, as the access switches do. If all the links forwarded traffic, there would be a loop.

Figure 12-11 *Spanning-Tree Topology in the Data Center*

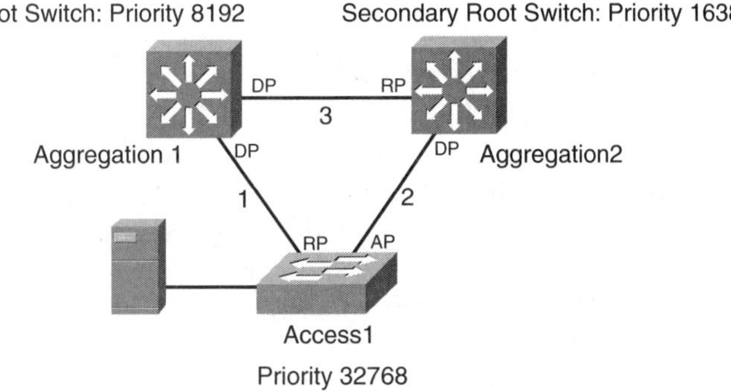

STP solves the looping problem.

When STP is enabled, a port can be in one of these states:

- **Discarding**—In this state, a port does not learn MAC addresses or forward traffic. For the purpose of our discussion, discarding and blocking are equivalent terms.
- **Learning**—A learning port does not forward traffic; it just learns MAC addresses.
- **Forwarding**—In this state, a port learns MAC addresses and forwards traffic.

A port ends up forwarding or blocking (learning is a transient state), based on its role.

Each switch has a priority. (If you have multiple VLANs and you are using PVST+, each VLAN has a priority.) The switch with the lowest priority is called the root switch. The switch with the second lowest priority is called the secondary root. In Figure 12-11, Aggregation1 is the root switch because its priority is 8192: Aggregation2's priority is 16,384, and Access1's priority is 32,768.

TIP It is good practice to set manually the priority of the root and secondary root switches. Such a practice creates a predictable topology. In Figure 12-11, the network administrator defined Aggregation1 as the root switch and Aggregation2 as the secondary root switch. On Catalyst switches, you can use the macro **spanning-tree vlan** *list of VLANs* **root** {**primary** | **secondary**}. The priority for the root switch can be different from 8192 if you use MAC-address reduction.

The port roles of each switch in the topology all depend on the relative distance from each switch to the root switch:

- **Root port (RP)**—The RP is the port on the switch with the best path (best means the lowest cost) to the root. For example, on Access1, the port closest to the root switch is the one attached to link 1. On each switch, there is only one RP.
- **Designated port (DP)**—On a segment, the DP is the switch port with the best path to the root switch. For example, on link 1, the DP is the switch port from Aggregation1. (Aggregation1 is the root switch.) If the cost to the root is the same from both ports on a link, as is the case with link 2, the bridge priority is the tie-breaker. The port from the switch with the lowest bridge priority wins. In Figure 12-11, Aggregation2 has a priority of 16,384, which makes it the designated bridge for link 2. On each segment, there is only one DP.
- **Alternate port (AP)**—An AP is a port that is neither an RP nor a DP. It can provide an alternate path to the root, should the RP become unavailable.

The RP and DP of a switch are forwarding; the AP is blocking. If you look at Figure 12-11, you can see how this system breaks the loop: on link 2, Access1 does not forward any traffic.

STP uses special packets, bridge protocol data units (BPDUs), to build the topology. BPDUs are generated by each switch every 2 sec, and they carry this information:

- **Root ID**—The ID of the root bridge. (The priority of the bridge is embedded in the ID.)
- **Root path cost**—The sum of the cost of the links along the path to the bridge. The higher the bandwidth, the lower the cost of a link.
- **Sender bridge ID**—The bridge identifier of the switch that generates the BPDU.
- **Port ID**—The identifier of the port that forwards the BPDU.

When electing a DP on a segment, the switches that connect to the segment compare the BPDUs to decide which one is "better." Better means a lower root ID, lower root path cost, lower sender bridge ID, or lower port ID. The switch that generates the better BPDU wins, and its port takes the DP role on the segment. Electing the RP on a switch follows a similar procedure.

As a result of the spanning-tree operation, a broadcast or a flood hitting the root switch reaches the leaf nodes as follows:

1. The root switch propagates the broadcast out all its DPs (typically, all the switch ports attached to the root).
2. All the switches attached to the links receive the broadcast from one single port, the RP, and send it out from the DPs.
3. On each segment, the broadcast arrives from one single port, the DP.

Failure Detection (802.1w)

When a switch or a link failure affects a forwarding path, one of the blocking ports in the topology becomes forwarding. For example, if link 1 fails, Access1 detects the link down on link 1 and turns the AP port on link 2 into an RP port, which then becomes forwarding.

In case the switch failure is not accompanied by a link down, the spanning tree detects the problem after losing three consecutive BPDUs. In 802.1w, each switch generates BPDUs every 2 sec and losing three of them is the symptom of a failure in the network.

NOTE In 802.1D, only the root can generate BPDUs and the other switches in the topology relay them on their DPs. In 802.1D, the detection of remote failure is achieved upon expiration of a timer, the Max Age (20 sec), which made convergence extremely slow.

In 802.1w, BPDUs are like heartbeats; each switch generates them every 2 sec, and missing three BPDUs is considered a network failure.

For more information about fast convergence, read Chapter 20.

Multiple VLANs

Rapid PVST+ maintains one spanning-tree topology for each VLAN, whereas 802.1s maintains fewer spanning-tree topologies, called instances of spanning-tree. Suppose that you configured two VLANs in your network: 10 and 20. With PVST+, each switch operates as if there were two different topologies in the network.

Now assume that you want to maintain only one forwarding path, which implies VLAN 10 and 20 would share the same topology. With Rapid PVST+, you adjust the bridge priorities to build a single topology, but each switch still maintains separate information for both VLANs.

By using 802.1s, you instead create one instance, and you assign VLAN 10 and 20 to this one instance.

The difference between Rapid PVST+ and 802.1s is about how they handle Spanning-Tree for multiple VLANs.

4096 VLANs

When using multiple VLANs for each switch, a single switch has multiple bridge identifiers: one per each VLAN or one per each instance.

The allocation of multiple unique bridge identifiers requires each switch to have a pool of MAC addresses, one for each VLAN. (Remember that the 6-byte MAC address field in the bridge identifier ensures the uniqueness of the bridge ID.)

IEEE calls for the support of 4096 VLANs, and this number typically exceeds the available pool of MAC addresses available to a switch.

The solution to this problem is to use *MAC address reduction*, a Cisco feature that implements the 802.1t standard.

In 802.1t, the bridge ID (8 bytes) has the following format:

- **Priority field (4 bits)**—This field is the user-configurable field to assign a priority to a switch.
- **System identifier (12 bits)**—This field is the MST instance identifier or the VLAN identifier. It is not user configurable, but it lets you define a separate instance for every VLAN (with a maximum of 4096 VLANs).
- **MAC address (6 bytes)**—Each switch can use the same MAC address for all the configured instances (or VLANs).

As a result, the range of priorities differs depending on the regular bridge ID format or the extended system identifier:

- **802.1D bridge priorities**—The full range of priorities is given by 16 bits.
- **802.1t bridge priorities**—The minimum priority is 4096, and the other priorities are given in increments of 4096.

TIP When using 802.1s (or MST), Cisco switches default to the extended system ID (or MAC address reduction). As a result, when you use the macro **spanning-tree vlan** *list of VLANs* **root** {**primary** | **secondary**} to set the root and secondary root switches, you see different priorities from the ones that you would see without the extended system ID.

To control the configuration of the extended system ID, you can use the syntax **spanning-tree extend system-id**.

Rapid PVST+

Suppose that you have two VLANs, 10 and 20, and their forwarding topologies are exactly the same. Rapid PVST+ still keeps the information about two separate topologies.

Example 12-16 helps clarify: It is the output from the **show spanning-tree vlan** command on an access switch. You can see that the root ID is 0003.6c43.8c0a and does not match the bridge ID: 0002.1777.780a. The root switch is an aggregation switch, with a priority of 8192, and the local switch has a priority of 32,768.

If you look further down in the example, you see the results of the **show** command for VLAN 20 on the same access switch. The root ID is 0003.6c43.8c14. Is it a different root switch from the one of VLAN 10? No, the switch that is root for VLAN 20 is the same as the one that is root for VLAN 10, but PVST+ keeps a separate topology for each VLAN.

PVST+ achieves this independence between topologies by assigning a separate bridge ID to each VLAN, even if they belong to the same switch.

Example 12-16 *PVST+: One Topology per VLAN*

```
acc1# show spanning-tree vlan 10
VLAN0010
  Spanning tree enabled protocol rstp
  Root ID     Priority    8192
              Address     0003.6c43.8c0a
              Cost        4
              Port        1 (GigabitEthernet1/1)
              Hello Time   2 sec  Max Age 20 sec  Forward Delay 15 sec

  Bridge ID  Priority    32768
              Address     0002.1777.780a
              Hello Time   2 sec  Max Age 20 sec  Forward Delay 15 sec
              Aging Time 300

Interface        Role Sts Cost      Prio.Nbr Type
---------------- ---- --- --------- -------- --------------------------------
Gi1/1            Root FWD 4         128.1    P2p
Gi1/2            Altn BLK 4         128.2    P2p


acc1# show spanning-tree vlan 20

VLAN0020
  Spanning tree enabled protocol rstp
  Root ID     Priority    8192
              Address     0003.6c43.8c14
              Cost        4
              Port        1 (GigabitEthernet1/1)
              Hello Time   2 sec  Max Age 20 sec  Forward Delay 15 sec

  Bridge ID  Priority    32768
              Address     0002.1777.7814
              Hello Time   2 sec  Max Age 20 sec  Forward Delay 15 sec
              Aging Time 300

Interface        Role Sts Cost      Prio.Nbr Type
---------------- ---- --- --------- -------- --------------------------------
Gi1/1            Root FWD 4         128.1    P2p
Gi1/2            Altn BLK 4         128.2    P2p
```

802.1s

With 802.1s, you can create an instance, which means a *number*, to represent the topology, and you can map VLANs to this instance.

Figure 12-12 shows the topology according to 802.1s, or MST (Multiple Spanning-Tree). The instance that represents the topology is MST 1. VLANs 10 and 20 are both mapped to MST 1. On the right of Figure 12-12, you can see the forwarding topology for MST 1.

Figure 12-12 *802.1s Topology*

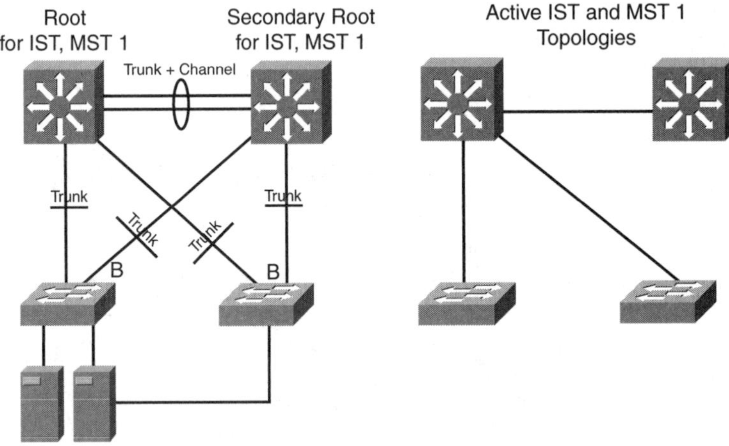

The Internal Spanning Tree (IST) that you see in Figure 12-12 is a default instance (MST 0). You should not map any VLANs to the IST.

If you run the **show spanning-tree vlan 10** command on the access switch, as in Example 12-17, you see that the root bridge is 0003.6c43.8c00. If you type the same command for VLAN 20 on the same switch, you see that the root bridge is the same. VLAN 10 and VLAN 20 on the root switch have the same bridge ID.

802.1s works with instances instead of VLANs: The first line that you see after the **show spanning-tree** command is the MST instance, MST01.

Example 12-17 *MST: One Instance for Multiple VLANs*

```
acc1# show spanning-tree vlan 10

MST01
  Spanning tree enabled protocol mstp
  Root ID    Priority    24577
             Address     0003.6c43.8c00
             Cost        20000
```

Example 12-17 *MST: One Instance for Multiple VLANs (Continued)*

```
             Port        1 (GigabitEthernet1/1)
             Hello Time   2 sec  Max Age 20 sec  Forward Delay 15 sec

  Bridge ID  Priority    32769  (priority 32768 sys-id-ext 1)
             Address     0002.1777.7800
             Hello Time   2 sec  Max Age 20 sec  Forward Delay 15 sec

Interface        Role Sts Cost      Prio.Nbr Type
---------------- ---- --- --------- -------- -------------------------------
Gi1/1            Root FWD 20000     128.1    P2p
Gi1/2            Altn BLK 20000     128.2    P2p

mp_acc1# show spanning-tree vlan 20

MST01
  Spanning tree enabled protocol mstp
  Root ID    Priority    24577
             Address     0003.6c43.8c00
             Cost        20000
             Port        1 (GigabitEthernet1/1)
             Hello Time   2 sec  Max Age 20 sec  Forward Delay 15 sec

  Bridge ID  Priority    32769  (priority 32768 sys-id-ext 1)
             Address     0002.1777.7800
             Hello Time   2 sec  Max Age 20 sec  Forward Delay 15 sec

Interface        Role Sts Cost      Prio.Nbr Type
---------------- ---- --- --------- -------- -------------------------------
Gi1/1            Root FWD 20000     128.1    P2p
Gi1/2            Altn BLK 20000     128.2    P2p
```

TIP Have you noticed the value of the root bridge priority? It is not 8192 but 24,577. The switch is using the extended system ID (MAC address reduction). On Cisco switches, the macro **spanning-tree vlan** *list of VLANs* **root** {**primary** | **secondary**} sets the root switch to a priority of 24,576, which in the preceding examples sums with the system ID (instance 1) and gives 24,577.

Logical Ports

A *logical port* is the sum of the number of forwarding physical ports times the number of VLANs that each port carries. This arrangement is what produces load on the CPU because each port carrying a VLAN has to generate and process BPDUs.

The more VLANs you carry on the trunks, the higher the load on the CPU: It is one of the reasons why you should clear trunks from unnecessary VLANs, as explained in the section, "Creating Trunks."

The upper limit of logical ports that a switch supports depends on the spanning-tree algorithm. With PVST+, each VLAN is a separate instance of the spanning-tree algorithm, which means that PVST+ can support fewer VLANS than MST.

When you have to choose the spanning-tree algorithm, you can follow this approach:

- If you need interoperability between different vendors, you should choose 802.1s (MST).
- If you have only Cisco gear, read the Cisco documentation about the number of logical ports that each algorithm can support, and compare this number with your requirements. 802.1s supports more logical ports than Rapid PVST+. As an example, the Catalyst 6500 with supervisor 2 and 12.1(13)E supports 50,000 logical ports with MST and 10,000 logical ports with Rapid PVST+.
- If you do not need a huge number of logical ports, consider using Rapid PVST+ because it is more flexible when you need to bridge VLANs together.

For more information about how to choose the spanning-tree algorithm, read Chapter 20.

Configuring Rapid PVST+

Use the command **spanning-tree mode rapid-pvst** to enable the spanning-tree algorithm Rapid PVST+.

It is recommended that you make the aggregation switches root and secondary root: This arrangement provides a predictable topology in case the primary root fails because you already know that the secondary root becomes the root.

Example 12-18 shows how to configure the switches to be root and secondary root.

Example 12-18 *Rapid PVST+ Root Switch Configuration*

```
agg1(config)# spanning-tree vlan 10  root primary
agg1(config)# spanning-tree vlan 20  root primary

agg2(config)# spanning-tree vlan 10 root secondary
agg2(config)# spanning-tree vlan 20 root secondary
```

Example 12-18 builds a single topology for both VLAN 10 and VLAN 20. If you need to load balance traffic to the uplinks from the access to the aggregation switches, you then make agg1 the root for VLAN 10 and agg2 the root for VLAN 20.

These macros change the bridge ID priority as follows (remember the default priority is 32,768):

- Root bridge: 8192
- Secondary root: 16,384

Configuring 802.1s

Use the command **spanning-tree mode mst** to enable 802.1s.

The association between VLANs and instances is defined in the **spanning-tree region** configuration. A region for a spanning tree is defined by an alphanumeric identifier, a revision number, and a table that maps the VLANs to their respective instance. The region information in the switches of the Data Center must match; otherwise, they will belong to different regions.

The reason for the region concept is to make sure that you have consistent mapping between VLANs and MST instances. If you notice that you have ports categorized by spanning tree as a boundary port, the problem is likely related to an inconsistent region configuration.

Example 12-19 shows the region configuration.

Example 12-19 *MST Region Configuration*

```
spanning-tree mst configuration
 name data_center_mst
 revision 10
 instance 1 vlan 10,20
```

The name and revision number, as well as the instance mapping, must match on all the switches in the Data Center. You use the name and revision numbers to make sure that all the devices in the MST region are configured consistently in terms of mappings between VLANs and instances.

Notice that you do not map any VLAN to instance 0.

You can decide to have one single spanning-tree topology in the Data Center. If you need to load-balance traffic to the uplinks from the access to the aggregation switches, you configure two instances in addition to the IST. The conclusion is that the total number of instances ranges between two and three, depending on the configuration.

It is a common best practice to assign the root and secondary root roles to the aggregation switches. Example 12-20 shows the configuration with MST.

Example 12-20 *MST Root Switch Configuration*

```
agg1(config)# spanning-tree mst 0 root primary
agg1(config)# spanning-tree mst 1 root primary

agg2(config)# spanning-tree mst 0 root secondary
agg2(config)# spanning-tree mst 1 root secondary
```

These macros change the bridge ID priority as follows (the default is 32,768):

- Root bridge: 24,576
- Secondary root: 28,672

When displaying the spanning-tree information for a VLAN, you see the priority and the system ID together, as in Example 12-14: 24,577 equals 24,576 plus the instance number.

Access Ports

Access ports carry traffic for a single VLAN. You typically connect servers to access ports. Additionally, appliances with Layer 3 interfaces connect to access ports.

In a regular spanning tree when there is a linkup, the port goes through the blocking, learning, and forwarding states. The transition from one state to the other takes 15 sec (called the *forwarding delay*), and the total time to bring up the port is equal to 30 sec.

When a server is attached to an access port and detects a linkup on the NIC, it typically sends out requests for services, such as a Dynamic Host Configuration Protocol (DHCP) request to obtain an IP address. If the switch port takes 30 sec to become forwarding, the server might fail to obtain the IP address. PortFast fixes this problem.

PortFast puts an access port into the forwarding state at linkup, without waiting for the 2 * forwarding delay. If the port is connected to a switch and there is a loop, the port is still participating in a spanning tree and goes into blocking, if necessary.

TIP You should enable PortFast also when a Layer 3 device, such as a router, is attached to an access port.

Example 12-21 shows how to configure an access port.

Example 12-21 *Access Port Configuration*

```
acc(config)# interface fa6/9
acc(config-if)# switchport
acc(config-if)# switchport mode access
acc(config-if)# spanning-tree portfast
```

When using an algorithm based on 802.1w (such as Rapid PVST+ or MST), it is important to assign the PortFast definition to the eligible ports because 802.1w categorizes ports into edge and nonedge. Nonedge ports are regular switch ports susceptible to transition from blocking, to learning, to forwarding.

There are two main advantages in enabling PortFast and making Layer 3 ports explicitly edge ports. If flapping occurs on edge ports, 802.1w does not generate a topology-change notification. Additionally, an edge port does not change its forwarding state when there is a topology recalculation.

For more information about PortFast and its impact during a topology recalculation, read Chapter 20.

Summary

Today's Data Centers use Ethernet as the main LAN technology. Servers attach to the network with Ethernet NICs, whose speed typically ranges from 10 Mbps to 1 Gbps. The network infrastructure consists of Fast Ethernet links (100 Mbps) up to 10-Gbps links.

Ethernet technologies share the same frame size and addressing format, and you can use them on copper and fiber. Designing a Data Center requires choosing the appropriate physical media based on bandwidth and distance requirements.

The Data Center typically consists of a Layer 2 domain segregated by VLANs. Spanning-tree lets you deploy redundant physical links without introducing loops. 802.1Q trunking lets you carry VLANs across switches.

Spanning-tree is available as several different protocols. Rapid PVST+ and 802.1s are likely to replace 802.1D and PVST+, thanks to faster convergence time, reliability, and scalability.

For Further Reading

Clark, Kennedy and Kevin Hamilton. *CCIE Professional Development: Cisco LAN Switching*. Cisco Press, 1999.

This chapter covers the following topics and their relation to the Data Center architecture and design:

- How Address Resolution Protocol (ARP) interacts with routers and servers to translate the IP addresses to the MAC addresses on the local subnet and how ARP interoperates with the MAC address table of the Layer 2 switches
- The operations of Hot Standby Routing Protocol (HSRP), Virtual Router Redundancy Protocol (VRRP), and Gateway Load Balancing Protocol (GLBP) for the purpose of static routing and for the default gateway functionality in the server farm
- The Open Shortest Path First (OSPF) essentials; the link-state advertisement (LSA) types and scope in the areas; the OSPF metrics; OSPF summarization, redistribution, and default route origination; and how to correctly configure and design OSPF routing in the Data Center environment
- The Enhanced Interior Gateway Routing Protocol (EIGRP) essentials; the operation of the Diffusing Update Algorithm (DUAL); the metric calculation; EIGRP summarization, redistribution, and default route origination; and how to correctly configure and design EIGRP routing in the Data Center
- How network address translation (NAT) works, including IOS NAT, NAT on Cisco PIX Firewalls, and NAT on load-balancing devices, and why and where NAT is used in the Data Center

CHAPTER 13

Layer 3 Protocol Essentials

Chapter 4, "Data Center Design Overview," introduces the principles of network design applied to Data Centers. As Chapter 4 covers, Data Center design best practices call for terminating the scope of the Layer 2 domain at the aggregation layer and to route between the Data Center and the core.

Aggregation switches provide the servers' default gateway and route between directly connected subnets on which the servers reside and advertise the Data Center subnets to the core routers. Aggregation switches are Layer 3 switches. Layer 3 switches are Layer 2 switches and full-fledged routers at the same time. They have a high forwarding speed for both Layer 2 and Layer 3 traffic because of application-specific integrated circuits (ASICs).

Figure 13-1 shows where routing occurs in the Data Center. The router icon depicts the routing function of an aggregation switch. In part **a** of Figure 13-1, you can see server farms on three VLAN segments. (Each solid box is a VLAN segment.) The upstream router routes traffic between VLANs and to and from the core routers. The dashed box represents the portion of the Data Center network where routing occurs.

Parts **b** and **c** of Figure 13-1 show the routing design in the presence of firewalls and load balancers. In part **b** of Figure 13-1, the firewall secures and isolates the server farms from one another and the rest of the network and routes between the server farm subnets. The load balancer is in the path between the servers and the firewall and operates in bridge mode. (See Chapter 16, "Load-Balancing Modes and Predictors.")

Part **c** of Figure 13-1 shows the design in the presence of load balancers used in bridge mode and transparent (Layer 2) firewalls. The upstream router routes between server farm subnets and with the core.

Figure 13-1 *Routing at the Data Center*

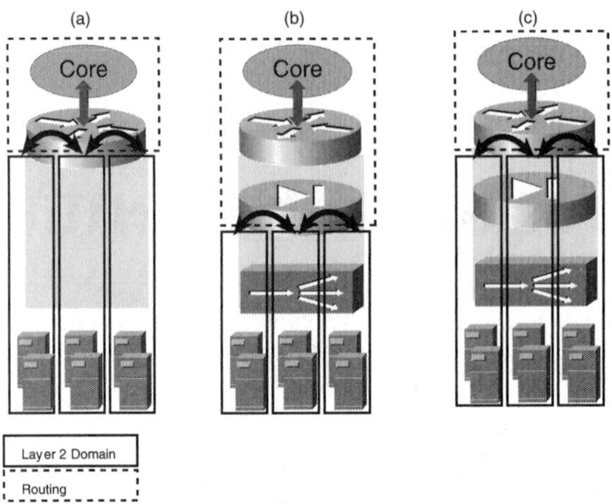

Even if routing is confined between the aggregation switches and the core, sometimes routing also exists between the servers and the aggregation routers. When servers (or mainframes) are multihomed with Layer 3 links, they can use routing protocols to advertise the IP addresses "internal" to the servers or mainframes. Chapter 14, "IBM Data Center Technology," describes in greater detail routing with mainframes.

TIP Configuring routing on the servers requires careful design. Keep in mind that servers might support routing, but they are not designed to be used as a routing device. Servers should not become transit networks, and the CPU utilization for routing should be minimized. For this reason, it is key that you keep to a minimum the number of routing entries present on the servers. Depending on the routing protocol, you can achieve this goal in several ways, which include using summarization, route filtering, and stub areas.

In most cases, multihomed servers do not need routing; you can configure redundancy with Layer 2 features such as network interface card (NIC) teaming. Chapter 2, "Server Architecture Overview," introduced the concept.

This chapter covers the essential information of Layer 3 protocols and functions necessary to design Data Centers. The chapter starts with the topic of ARP, the protocol that "links" routing with Layer 2 forwarding. The chapter then covers the gateway redundancy protocols, the Internal Gateway Protocols (IGP), and NAT. Do not consider this chapter as a tutorial for these technologies but rather as a collection of the essential information that is required to design and build Data Centers.

ARP is used by every Layer 3 device to resolve the MAC address associated with an IP address. Additionally, the ARP table on routers interacts with the MAC address table on switches, and both tables play an important role when the network converges after a change in the topology.

You use HSRP, VRRP, and GLBP mainly to provide the default gateway functionality. Parts **a** and **c** of Figure 13-1 show that the default gateway for the server farms is the upstream router (or routing function within the Layer 3 switch), whereas part **b** of Figure 13-1 shows the server default gateway as the firewall.

IGPs such as OSPF and EIGRP run on the aggregation switches. When using IGPs, you need to consider summarization and redistribution to design scalable, reliable, and stable environments. Summarization and redistribution (combined with route filtering) achieve routing stability because you can limit the impact of topology changes to local routers without forcing route recalculations on all the routers on the network.

NAT is a key feature that provides translation of IP addresses for the purpose of conserving IP address space and security. NAT is available on Layer 3 switches, routers, firewalls, and load balancers. NAT is especially useful in the Internet Data Center because it lets you hide the private address space from outside clients. In addition to the uses already mentioned, stateful devices such as firewalls and load balancers can take advantage of NAT to control the return path of client/server traffic. Stateful devices need to see both directions (client-to-server and server-to-client) of traffic flows.

Chapter 20, "Designing the Data Center Infrastructure," provides more details about the design of the Data Center leveraging the concepts introduced in this chapter.

ARP Protocol and Tables

ARP translates IP addresses into the associated MAC addresses. For example, consider the communication between two hosts (a host can be a server, a PC, a router, a firewall, a load balancer, and so on) on the same Ethernet segment—host 1 with IP address 10.20.5.5 and host 2 with IP address 10.20.5.6. For these hosts to communicate, they need to build frames with source and destination hardware MAC addresses.

A user executing an application on a host specifies the destination of the traffic by means of the IP address. An example is host 1 (10.20.5.5) opening a Telnet connection to host 2 (10.20.5.6). The **telnet** statement specifies the destination IP address (**telnet 10.20.5.6**), and host 1 uses ARP to map the IP address to the MAC address of the destination host:

1 Host 1 sends a broadcast *ARP request* to the LAN segment; the ARP request contains the IP address of the destination host (10.20.5.6).

2 All the hosts on the segment receive the ARP broadcast and look into the IP field of the request.

3. The host that identifies its own IP in the request (host 2) sends an *ARP response* with the information about its MAC address. The ARP response is a unicast to the host that generated the request.
4. Host 2 caches the information from the ARP response into a cache table (the ARP table).

Upon receiving an ARP response, Layer 3 devices keep the IP-to-MAC address association in the ARP table for some time. The aging on a Cisco router is four hours by default, which means that for four hours, a router does not need to send an ARP request for any IP address that it has previously learned. The first row of Table 13-1 provides information about the timers of the ARP table on Cisco routers and on Windows or Linux servers.

Table 13-1 *Timeout Values for the ARP Table Compared with the CAM Table*

	Default Timeout on IOS Routers	Timeout in Presence of Topology Change Notification (TCN)	Default Timeout on Windows and Linux
ARP Table	4 hours	Flushed on the Multilayer Switch Feature Card (MSFC)	Between 5 and 20 minutes
MAC Address Table	300 seconds (sec)	15 sec	N/A

ARP tables are also updated with the mechanism of gratuitous ARPs. A *gratuitous ARP* is an ARP request that a host sends to itself with the purpose of updating the ARP tables of the adjacent devices with MAC address information.

A gratuitous ARP is typically sent when a Layer 3 device initializes the TCP/IP stack of an interface. For example, a router's next-hop MAC address can be a device such as another router, a load balancer, or a firewall. After a change of active/standby status in a pair of such devices, the previously standby and now active peer sends out a gratuitous ARP when it becomes the master. This process updates the router's ARP table.

A positive side effect of the ARP traffic is that it updates the MAC address table. An ARP response triggers an update in the MAC address table of the switch with the source MAC of the host sending the response.

In Table 13-1, you notice that the timeout of idle entries in the ARP table is four hours, but in the MAC address table, it is 300 sec. Because of this difference, it is sometimes possible to have an ARP table up-to-date for a specific MAC without having the corresponding MAC in the MAC address table. The result is flooding because the Layer 3 device (a router, for example) can build a frame with the MAC address of the destination, but this address is not present in the MAC address table. You can fix the flooding problem by configuring a lower timeout for the ARP timer in such a way that periodic ARP traffic updates the MAC address table.

NOTE The MAC address table allows switching traffic at Layer 2 by storing the MAC address, VLAN number, and physical port number association. The absence of the port information causes flooding to all the ports active in a VLAN. Using the MAC address table in Layer 2 switching is described in Chapter 12, "Layer 2 Protocol Essentials."

Another important interaction between the ARP table and the MAC address table relates to effect of a topology change in a spanning tree, which causes the generation of special bridge protocol data units (BPDUs), the Topology Change Notification (TCN) BPDUs.

In presence of TCN BPDUs, the MAC address table ages out entries in 15 sec to avoid blackholing traffic. (Refer to the second column of Table 13-1.) Additionally, if you are using a Catalyst switch with the MSFC, which is the router card in the switch, the TCN makes the MSFC send ARPs for the IP addresses in the table. This process forces the MAC address tables of the switches in the network to be updated with the new location for each MAC address.

HSRP, VRRP, and GLBP

When working with IGP-capable devices, the redundancy is provided by the IGP-specific protocol (OSPF, EIGRP, and so on). The Data Center also has devices configured with static routing, including the following:

- **Servers**—In general, servers are configured with a single static default route pointing to an HSRP, VRRP, or GLBP address. Mainframes, on the other hand, are normally configured for dynamic routing, in which case it is not necessary to configure default gateway redundancy, such as HSRP, on the router interface connected to the mainframe.
- **Load balancers**—Some load balancers are IGP capable and some are not. Because you can use load balancers as a default gateway for server farms, they provide a HSRP or VRRP address for redundancy. Load balancers still need static routes to point to the HSRP or VRRP address of an upstream router or switch.
- **Firewalls**—Just as with load balancers, some firewalls are capable of dynamic routing and some are not. Firewalls use an HSRP or a VRRP address as the next hop in the static routing configuration.

HSRP, VRRP, and GLBP are the key protocols to provide redundancy when working with a static routing environment. HSRP is a Cisco proprietary protocol (RFC 2281, informational), VRRP is an Internet Engineering Task Force (IETF)–proposed standard (RFC 2338), and GLBP is a Cisco proprietary protocol.

Two or more routers with interfaces on a VLAN segment can provide a virtual next hop (default gateway) to a server belonging to the same VLAN by sharing an IP address through HSRP, VRRP, or GLBP.

Table 13-2 shows the protocol characteristics of HSRP, VRRP, and GLBP, and the sections that follow describe these characteristics in more detail.

Table 13-2 *HSRP, VRRP, and GLBP Characteristics*

	HSRP	VRRP	GLBP
Protocol	User Datagram Protocol (UDP) port 1985	IP 112	UDP port 3222
Hello time	3 sec (default)	1 sec (default)	3 sec (default)
Failed Timer	10 sec (default)	3 sec (default)	10 sec (default)
MAC Address	0000.0c07.ac{group}	0000.5e00.01{group}	0007.b4{group}{forwarder}
Hello IP address	224.0.0.2	224.0.0.18	224.0.0.102

HSRP

With HSRP, only one of the two routers (the *active* router) is responsible for routing the servers' traffic; the *standby* router assumes responsibility for the task when the active router fails. The traffic destined to the servers can be forwarded by either router.

Figure 13-2 illustrates HSRP mechanics. Aggregation1 and Aggregation2 both have an interface on VLAN 10: 10.0.0.253 and 10.0.0.254. Together, they provide the default gateway to the servers: 10.0.0.1.

Aggregation1 is the active HSRP router: when the server sends an ARP request for 10.0.0.1, Aggregation1 responds with the MAC address 0000.0c07.ac01, which is a virtual MAC (vMAC) address; the burned-in MAC address (BIA) for Aggregation1 is 0003.6c43.8c0a. Figure 13-2 shows that the servers store the association 10.0.0.1-to-0000.0c07.ac01 in their ARP tables. The servers then send traffic to 0000.0c07.ac01, which is received by Aggregation1. In case the interface of Aggregation1 on VLAN 10 is lost, Aggregation2 takes over 10.0.0.1 and the MAC address 0000.0c07.ac01.

Example 13-1 shows a basic HSRP configuration for Aggregation1. Under the interface VLAN configuration, you specify the IP address for the router interface (10.0.0.253) and the HSRP address: **standby** *group* **ip** *ip address*. In this case, the group number is 1 (see the section, "HSRP Groups" for more information), and the IP address specifies the virtual IP, which is the default gateway used by the servers in Figure 13-2.

Figure 13-2 *HSRP Mechanics*

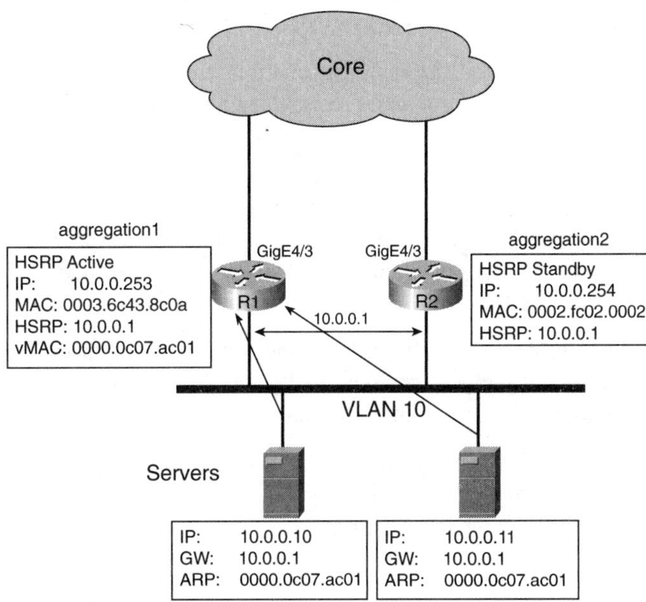

The configuration for Aggregation2 is similar, with the only difference in the priority for the group, 100 (**standby 1 priority 100**). The Priority field is used to arbitrate which router is going to be active on the LAN/VLAN segment.

Example 13-1 *HSRP Configuration*

```
interface Vlan10
 ip address 10.0.0.253 255.255.255.0
 standby 1 ip 10.0.0.1
 standby 1 priority 105
end
```

Active/Standby Election

How does a device become active or standby for a specific group? The priority that you assign to an interface decides. The election happens when both router interfaces are going through the link-up phase. The highest priority determines mastership.

The priority does not count if a new interface comes up on a VLAN where one interface was already active. If the new interface has a priority of 105, it is not going to preempt the one that is already active with a priority of 100.

You can change this default behavior by enabling the **preempt** option, in which case an interface with a higher priority can preempt an existing active interface at any time.

HSRP Groups

One VLAN segment can have multiple groups—that is, multiple virtual IP addresses to be used concurrently by the server farm. One single router interface can belong to multiple groups and be active for one group and standby for another one.

Example 13-2 shows a single VLAN interface on a router with two groups: 1 and 2. Each group has a different priority, which normally would make this router the active for group 1 and the standby for group 2 with both groups on VLAN 10.

The group number decides the value of the vMAC address. Using a vMAC address allows the ARP tables to stay unchanged on the devices that communicate with the routers, even after a change in the active/standby roles.

Example 13-2 *HSRP Groups*

```
interface Vlan10
 ip address 10.0.0.253 255.255.255.0
 standby 1 ip 10.0.0.1
 standby 1 priority 105
 standby 2 ip 10.0.0.2
 standby 2 priority 100
end
```

In HSRP, the virtual interface MAC address is 0000.070c.ac {group number}. The {group number} is derived from the user configuration: **standby** *group* **ip** *IP address*. The MAC address for 10.0.0.1 in Example 13-2 is then 0000.0c07.ac01. HSRP theoretically lets you configure 255 groups; the real limit depends on how many MAC addresses a router recognizes as eligible for routing.

Figure 13-3 illustrates the use of multiple HSRP groups for load distribution. For each VLAN interface, you create as many groups as the number of routers. Figure 13-3 has two groups: group 1 (10.0.0.1) and group 2 (10.0.0.2).

You then assign a higher priority for the first group to Aggregation1 and a higher priority for the second group to Aggregation2. Example 13-2 shows the configuration for Aggregation1. The configuration on Aggregation2 would have the priority reversed: 100 for group 1 and 105 for group 2.

Figure 13-3 *HSRP Groups*

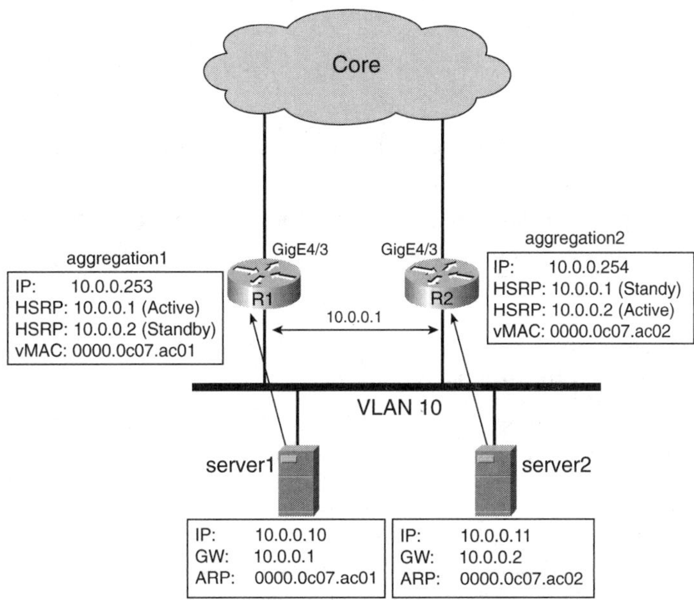

You assign half of the servers to use the HSRP IP address of group 1 (10.0.0.1) as the default gateway and the other half to use the HSRP IP address of group 2 (10.0.0.2).

Figure 13-3 shows the result of these configurations. 10.0.0.1 is active on Aggregation1 and 10.0.0.2 is active on Aggregation2. Server1 is configured with 10.0.0.1 as the default gateway, and server2 is configured with 10.0.0.2 as the default gateway. Should Aggregation1 fail, Aggregation2 takes over the active role for 10.0.0.1 and owns both vMACs: 0000.0c07.ac01 and 0000.0c07.ac02.

Failure Detection

In HSRP, both the active and the standby routers periodically send hello packets to the multicast IP address 224.0.0.2 (all routers) (MAC 0100.5e00.0002). The active router uses the HSRP MAC, 0000.0c07.ac{group}, as the source MAC of the hello packets to keep the MAC address table current.

The periodic hellos make it possible for the routers participating in HSRP on a VLAN to monitor the health of the active router. The routers that are neither active nor standby are in the *listen* state: They listen to the multicast hellos sent by the active and standby router.

HSRP sends hello packets every 3 sec (the default *hellotime*), and when hello packets are not received for a time longer than the *holdtime* (by default, 10 sec, or 3 times the hellotime), the neighbor is declared dead.

Example 13-3 shows how you can modify the HSRP timers by using the following command:

standby *group* **timers** [**msec**] *hellotime* [**msec**] *holdtime*

The timers allow for subsecond convergence: the minimum hellotime is 20 milliseconds (ms). Example 13-3 shows a configuration for convergence in 3 sec: hellos are sent every second, and the holdtime is 3 sec.

Example 13-3 *Timer Configuration in HSRP for Fast Convergence*

```
interface Vlan10
 ip address 10.0.0.253 255.255.255.0
 standby 1 ip 10.0.0.1
 standby 1 timers 1 3
 standby 1 priority 105
end
```

TIP The convergence time in the Data Center depends on the convergence time of all the protocols affected by a failure. Most protocols used in the Data Center today can be configured to converge in few seconds or even to have subsecond convergence times. A spanning tree with the 802.1w optimization converges in less than 1 sec; IGPs can be configured for subsecond convergence.

If you keep the default HSRP settings, you cannot recover from a failure in less than 10 sec. If you configure HSRP to converge in less than 1 sec, you might experience HSRP flapping when the topology changes at Layer 2. In most cases, the settings in Example 13-3 provide fast convergence without flapping.

As usual, before implementing these settings, you need to verify that they are appropriate for the Data Center environment where they are applied.

When a failure occurs, the newly elected peer in the HSRP group starts answering to ARP requests for the virtual IP address on the interface connected to the VLANs where the peers are redundant. The MAC address returned is the vMAC address.

When there is a change in the active/standby roles, the newly active router interface sends out a gratuitous ARP. The gratuitous ARP contains the virtual IP address as well as the vMAC address and the source MAC of the packet is also the vMAC address. The gratuitous ARP makes sure that the ARP tables are up-to-date and refreshes the Layer 2 forwarding tables.

Tracking

You configure tracking to make an active HSRP interface become standby when the router loses an interface used for upstream traffic. For example, suppose that the network in Figure 13-2 uses static routing and that the interface GigabitEthernet 4/3 on Aggregation1 is disconnected because of a failure.

Traffic coming from the core reaches Aggregation2 (Aggregation1 is not connected to the core any more) and then goes to the server, and from the server, it goes to the server default gateway, 10.0.0.1, which is active on Aggregation1. Aggregation1 cannot send the traffic back to the core because the GigabitEthernet 4/3 interface is down.

There are many ways to fix this problem; one of them is to configure HSRP tracking for 10.0.0.1, as demonstrated in Example 13-4.

Example 13-4 *HSRP Tracking*

```
interface Vlan10
 ip address 10.0.0.253 255.255.255.0
 standby 1 ip 10.0.0.1
 standby 1 priority 105
 standby 1 preempt
 standby 1 track GigabitEthernet 4/3
end
```

If the interface GigabitEthernet 4/3 is lost, the router reduces the priority for the HSRP group 1. (By default, it lowers the priority by 10.) Configuring the **preempt** option on both routers ensures that Aggregation2 takes over the active role for 10.0.0.1.

TIP There are several other ways to design the network to work around the failure of GigabitEthernet 4/3 in addition to HSRP tracking. These options include adding an uplink from both Aggregation1 and Aggregation2 to the core routers or connecting Aggregation1 and Aggregation2 with a Layer 3 link.

VRRP

VRRP conceptually is similar to HSRP; the main differences, besides the terminology, concern the use of interface IP addresses, the default preemption, and the fact that only the master sends hello packets.

Master/Backup Election

In the presence of multiple routers on a VLAN segment, VRRP elects a router as *master* and the other routers as *backup* for a given *virtual router* (equivalent to an HSRP group). Figure 13-4 shows a possible configuration: the servers' default gateway is 10.0.0.1 and the MAC address is a VRRP MAC: 0000.5e00.0101.

Figure 13-4 *VRRP*

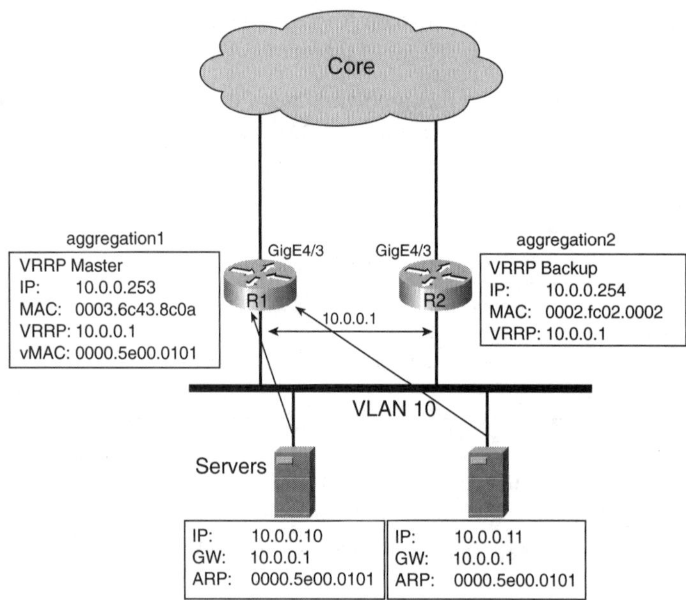

Example 13-5 shows the configuration of router R1 of Figure 13-4. The example uses 10.0.0.1 as the virtual router IP address. The configuration assigns the priority 105 to the virtual router 1 on R1, the default being 100. Unlike HSRP, with VRRP you do not need to allocate an IP address for a virtual router: you can configure VRRP to provide redundancy for the IP address of an interface, and the router that owns that IP address becomes the master automatically. If the configuration specifies **vrrp 1 ip 10.0.0.253** instead of **vrrp 1 ip 10.0.0.1**, the virtual router automatically has a priority of 255. Unlike HSRP, VRRP has preemption enabled by default. You can use the command **no vrrp** *group* **preempt** to disable preemption.

Example 13-5 *VRRP Configuration*

```
interface Vlan10
 ip address 10.0.0.253 255.255.255.0
 vrrp 1 ip 10.0.0.1
 vrrp 1 priority 105
end
```

VRRP Groups

With VRRP, you can create multiple groups of virtual routers on the same segment, similarly to what you can do with HSRP. Example 13-6 shows how. The group identifier (1,2 in the example) is called the virtual router ID (VRID).

Example 13-6 *VRRP Group Configuration*

```
interface Vlan10
 ip address 10.0.0.253 255.255.255.0
 vrrp 1 ip 10.0.0.1
 vrrp 1 priority 105
 vrrp 2 ip 10.0.0.2
 vrrp 2 priority 100
end
```

Failure Detection

The failure detection in VRRP is similar to HSRP. The master router sends hello packets to the multicast IP address 224.0.0.18 (MAC 0100.5e00.0012) every 1 sec, and the backup detects the failure of the master after three hello packets are lost. The source MAC address of the VRRP packets is the virtual router MAC address 0000.5e00.01{VRID}, which is also the MAC address used by the servers to send traffic to the master. This mechanism keeps the MAC address table current.

In VRRP, the equivalent of the hello timer is the *advertisement interval* and the equivalent of the hold down timer is called the *master-down interval*. Example 13-7 shows how you can tune the timers for faster convergence. The following command specifies the advertisement interval; the master down interval is about three times the advertisement interval:

vrrp *group* **timers advertise** [**msec**] *interval*

Example 13-7 *Timer Configuration in VRRP*

```
interface Vlan10
 ip address 10.0.0.253 255.255.255.0
 vrrp 1 ip 10.0.0.1
 vrrp 1 timers advertise msec 300
 vrrp 1 priority 105
end
```

TIP As with HSRP, configuring faster convergence could introduce flapping of VRRP master/backup roles when there is a change in the Layer 2 topology. Before changing the default timers, you need to verify that these settings are appropriate for the environment and the design where they are applied.

VRRP tracking is not specified in RFC 2338, but some vendors implement the tracking feature.

GLBP

GLBP, unlike HSRP and VRRP, makes it possible for the peer routers providing redundancy to the servers to be active concurrently on the VLAN segment. Figure 13-5 shows how.

Figure 13-5 *GLBP*

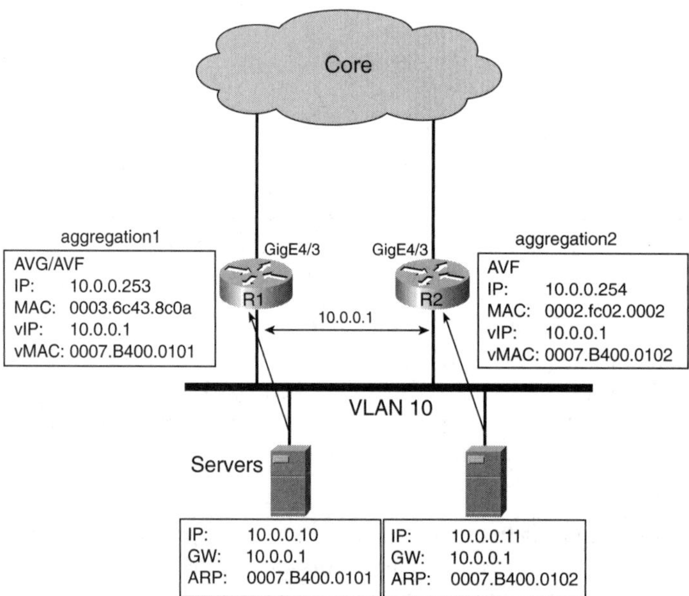

All ARP requests for the default gateway from the servers are directed to the virtual IP address (vIP) 10.0.0.1. Only one of the routers is authorized to respond to the ARP request, the active virtual gateway (AVG). This router answers to the ARP requests by performing a round-robin among a number of vMAC addresses (two MACs used in Figure 13-5). Each vMAC address identifies a router in the GLBP group; for example, 0007.B400.0101 is the vMAC for Aggregation1 and 0007.B400.0102 is the vMAC for Aggregation2.

By answering with different vMACs to different servers, the AVG achieves load distribution: half of the servers in Figure 13-5 use Aggregation1 as their default gateway, and the other half uses Aggregation2. Each router is an active virtual forwarder (AVF) for a given virtual MAC. Aggregation1 is AVF for 0007.B400.0101 and Aggregation2 is the AVF for 0007.B400.0102. Should Aggregation1 fail, Aggregation2 becomes the AVF for both the vMACs.

Example 13-8 shows a basic configuration for GLBP. Under the interface VLAN configuration, you specify the glbp group (1 in the example), followed by the virtual IP address. The command that controls how the AVG answers ARP requests is

glbp *group* **load-balancing** {**host-dependent** | **round-robin** | **weighted**}

Example 13-8 *GLBP Configuration*

```
router(config)#interface Vlan10
router(config-if)#ip address 10.0.0.253 255.255.255.0
router(config-if)#glbp 1 ip 10.0.0.1
router(config-if)#glbp 1 load-balancing round-robin
router(config-if)#glbp 1 priority 105
```

TIP You must assess the use of GLBP as the protocol for default router redundancy based on the server-farm design. GLBP is useful in particular for loop-free designs where both the uplinks from the access switches are forwarding: in this case, GLBP distributes server-to-client traffic on both uplinks. By distributing the server-to-client traffic to both aggregation routers, GLBP also optimizes the utilization of the uplinks from the aggregation routers to the core network.

Using this setup is also possible with HSRP or VRRP by creating multiple groups, as described in the section, "HSRP Groups." Unlike HSRP and VRRP, with GLBP you can configure the same default gateway on all the servers.

Active/Standby Election

When referring to GLBP, the active/standby election refers to the AVG. The routers on a segment elect one device as the AVG based on the priority in a fashion similar to HSRP: one router is the active, one is the standby, and the other routers are in the listen state.

The AVG assigns the MAC addresses to the primary virtual forwarders (VFs) by sending hello messages. Each VF is assigned a MAC address for which it is primary, and it becomes the AVF for that MAC address: the other VFs in the LAN segment are secondary VFs for that same MAC address and in the listen state.

The virtual gateway (VG) by default has preemption disabled. The VF by default has preemption enabled. You can turn on preemption for the VGs with the command **glbp** *group* **preempt**. You can turn off preemption for the VFs with the command **no glbp** *group* **forwarder preempt**.

GLBP Groups

GLBP also has the concept of group. The MAC address in GLBP is 0007.b4{group, AVF}, where the last 24 bits are divided as follows: 6 empty bits, 10 bits for the group number, and 8 bits for the VF number. If one interface is configured with two GLBP groups, 1 and 2, the MAC addresses associated with it look like 0007.b400.01{AVF} and 0007.b400.02{AVF}. With two routers, the AVF takes the values 01 and 02.

TIP With GLBP, you do not need to use multiple groups to achieve load distribution. GLBP is capable of associating the servers to multiple routers while still using one single IP address as the default gateway, and there is no need to explicitly configure different default gateways for a single server farm.

Failure Detection

Failure detection in GLBP works in a similar fashion to HSRP and VRRP, but there are some differences because of the presence of multiple virtual MAC addresses.

Figure 13-6 shows what happens when Aggregation1 fails. Aggregation1 is the primary AVF for 0007.B400.0101 and the secondary AVF for 0007.B400.0102. Aggregation2 is the secondary AVF for 0007.B400.0101 and the primary AVF for 0007.B400.0102. Before the failure, Aggregation1 is the active AVF for 0007.B400.0101 and Aggregation2 is the active AVF for 0007.B400.0102.

When Aggregation1 fails, Aggregation2 takes over the AVG role and becomes the active AVF for 0007.B400.0101. New ARP requests from the servers are answered by Aggregation2, which keeps performing a round-robin of the vMACs. Traffic sent by the servers to 0007.B400.0101 is forwarded to Aggregation2.

Considering that both vMACs are now active on the same router, what is the point in performing a round-robin of the vMAC when answering ARP requests? A timer (called **redirect timer**) controls how long the AVG keeps returning the AVF 0007.B400.0101 to requesting servers. When the timer expires, the AVF still exists for some time, but the AVG does not use it for load balancing any more. A second timer controls when the AVF is completely invalidated.

Example 13-9 shows the GLBP configuration and its timers. The command corresponding to the **standby** command in HSRP is

```
glbp group timers [msec] hellotime [msec] holdtime
```

The command that controls how long the AVG keeps using the AVF for which it became active after the failure is

```
glbp group timers redirect redirect timeout
```

Figure 13-6 *GLBP failover*

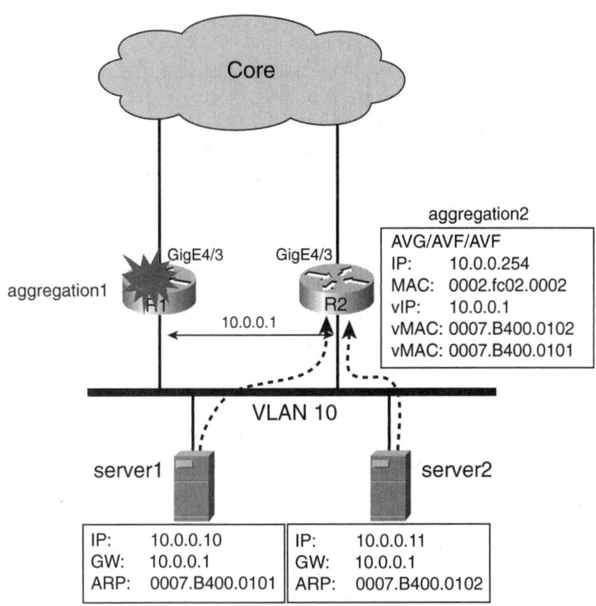

Example 13-9 *GLBP Configuration*

```
router(config)#interface Vlan10
router(config-if)#ip address 10.0.0.253 255.255.255.0
router(config-if)#glbp 1 ip 10.0.0.1
router(config-if)#glbp 1 authentication text datacenter
router(config-if)#glbp 1 load-balancing host-dependent
router(config-if)#glbp 1 priority 105
router(config-if)#glbp 1 timers 1 3
router(config-if)#glbp 1 timers redirect 600 7200
```

Tracking

Tracking in GLBP is a superset of HSRP tracking because it allows tracking of *objects*. An object can be an interface or a routing table entry. Using tracking, it is possible for an AVF to give up mastership for a certain virtual MAC. Example 13-10 shows the configuration. The command **glbp** *group* **weighting** assigns the weight of the AVF to a value of 100. (The weight value is also used for the weighted load balancing.) The AVF weight is decremented by 10 when the interface GigabitEthernet 4/3 goes down with the command **glbp** *group* **weighting track**. The **lower** option in the **glbp** *group* **weighting** configuration states that when the weight goes below 95, the secondary VF takes over as the AVF.

Example 13-10 *GLBP Tracking Configuration*

```
router(config)#track 2 interface GigabitEthernet4/3 line-protocol
router(config)#interface Vlan10
router(config-if)#ip address 10.0.0.253 255.255.255.0
router(config-if)#glbp 1 ip 10.0.0.1
router(config-if)#glbp 1 priority 105
router(config-if)#glbp 1 weighting 100 lower 95
router(config-if)#glbp 1 weighting track 2 decrement 10
```

Load Distribution

You can distribute the server traffic to the routers present on a VLAN segment in two ways: by using multiple groups in HSRP/VRRP, as described in the section, "HSRP Groups," or by using the GLBP protocol.

With GLBP, configuring load distribution does not require you to create multiple HSRP groups or configure a number of the servers with either default gateway's IP address.

With GLBP, the AVG has a pool of as many vMAC addresses as the number of routers present on a subnet. The AVG round-robins return the vMAC as an ARP response to the server. GLBP supports round-robin load balancing, weighted round-robin load balancing, and host-dependent load balancing.

Example 13-11 shows the configuration of GLBP for load balancing with the host-dependent predictor. The host-dependent load-balancing algorithm is such that a given host always receives the same MAC address in the ARP response.

Example 13-11 *GLBP Configuration*

```
router(config)#interface fastethernet 0/0
router(config-if)#ip address 10.0.0.253 255.255.255.0
router(config-if)#glbp 1 authentication text datacenter
router(config-if)#glbp 1 load-balancing host-dependent
router(config-if)#glbp 1 priority 105
router(config-if)#glbp 1 timers 1 3
router(config-if)#glbp 1 timers redirect 600 7200
```

NOTE For more information about GLBP, refer to the document "GLBP—Gateway Load Balancing Protocol" at Cisco.com.

OSPF

You can design the Data Center network to use static routing, dynamic routing, or both. Dynamic routing provides high availability because routes are dynamically injected or withdrawn, thereby adjusting to the changing network conditions. Static routing combined with HSRP or VRRP lets you route around failures as well. Because some firewalls and load balancers support only static routing, you need to design a mixed environment.

This chapter addresses the basics of OSPF routing, starting with the LSA types and the concept of OSPF areas and moving to the toolkit necessary to optimize the routing design in Data Centers, including the following topics:

- Metric tuning
- Redistribution
- Summarization
- Route filtering
- Originating the default route

Chapter 20 provides the design information.

OSPF is a link-state routing protocol where every router knows about every link and every router in the network. An OSPF router is capable of building the shortest-path tree independently of the other routers via the Dijkstra Shortest Path First (SPF) algorithm. For all the routers to have a consistent link-state database, the routers must update each other about changes in link and neighbor state in a reliable way.

They do so through the use of the hello protocol that allows neighboring routers to establish neighbor adjacency. It allows them to periodically exchange information, facilitating the detection of network failures. The section "OSPF Neighbor States" provides information about the most common states between OSPF neighbor routers.

The routers exchange information about the topology with LSAs.

LSAs have the following types (see the section "LSAs" for more information):

- **Type 1,2**—Router LSAs and network LSAs respectively, these LSAs are used for intra-area routing information. (The OSPF routing table displays intra-area routes as "O".)
- **Type 3,4**—Summary LSAs are used for inter-area routing. (The OSPF routing table displays inter-area as "IA".)
- **Type 5**—External LSAs provide information about networks outside the autonomous system (AS).
- **Type 7**—Not-so-stubby area (NSSA) external LSAs inject information about networks outside the AS from a special area, the NSSA.

Read the section "OSPF Areas" to understand the use of the LSAs and the section "LSAs" for more detail about LSA types.

For the purpose of this book, it is important that you fully comprehend how OSPF ensures consistent database information across the routers (a combination of the hello protocol, flooding, and LSA acknowledging) and the purposes of the different LSA types.

Reading the section "OSPF Areas" clarifies the LSA "paths," and the section, "Summarization and Filtering", clarifies how to control the scope of the flooding for building a stable network.

NOTE The document "Open Shortest Path First" at Cisco.com provides additional information about OSPF operations.

OSPF Neighbor States

The hello protocol lets you establish neighbor adjacency between routers and detect network failures. The steady state of a router interface normally is *full*.

On broadcast and nonbroadcast multiaccess (NBMA) networks, OSPF elects a designated router (DR) and a backup designated router (BDR) to reduce the number of adjacencies that each router needs to maintain. On a shared segment, all the routers are in the full state with the DR and with the BDR. The DR allows building a virtual stellar topology as if the DR were the center and the other routers were the spokes. The router with the highest interface priority wins the DR election.

TIP When typing **show ip ospf neighbor** on a router, you typically see the following states: FULL/DR, FULL/BDR, 2-WAY/DROTHER. The router is full only with the DR and with the BDR. The router stays as 2-WAY with the DROTHER routers (the routers others than DR or BDR). This state applies only to broadcast and NBMA networks. The *two-way* state indicates that a router sees its own router ID in its neighbor hello packet.

In a shared segment, you can set the priority of the interfaces of the routers that are not expected to become DRs to zero, and you can increase the priority of the interfaces that you want to be DRs.

You can set the priority using the command **ip ospf priority** *value*, where *value* ranges from 0 to 255, 1 being the default.

For more information about the OSPF neighbor states, refer to the Tech Note "OSPF Neighbor States" (Document ID: 13685) at Cisco.com.

OSPF Areas

OSPF uses the concept of areas to build hierarchical networks. A router running OSPF belongs to one or more areas. Routers belonging to the same area have identical database information.

Routers belonging to multiple areas are called Area Border Routers (ABRs) and perform functions to allow inter-area routing in addition to the intra-area routing functions. Routers at the border of the AS are called Autonomous System Boundary Routers (ASBRs). A router redistributing static routes into OSPF or routes from another routing protocol is an ASBR.

The area types follow:

- **Area 0**—The backbone. Every area needs to interface with area 0 with its own ABRs. Inter-area communication is allowed only through area 0. All LSA types are visible in Area 0.
- **Area n**—Areas adjacent to the area 0. Regular areas flood type 1 and type 2 LSAs internally and exchange type 3/4 LSAs with area 0. (The ABR generates type 3/4 LSAs and injects them into area 0.) Regular areas receive external LSAs (Type 5) as well.
- **Stub Area**—An area that contains a single exit point, which implies that routers inside the area do not have to carry full routing tables. A stub area sees type 1 and type 2 LSAs for intra-area routing and type 3 LSAs for inter-area routing (IA-O routes) but replaces external LSAs with a default route (which is generated by the ABRs as a type 3 LSA). The default route shows as a default IA-O* route. Use the command **area** *area-id* **stub** to create a stub area. Part **a** of Figure 13-7 shows a stub area and which LSAs are allowed in this area.
- **Totally Stubby Area**—A Cisco area type that does not allows external or summary routes into the area. This area sees only type 1 and type 2 LSAs for intra-area routing; it sees no external LSAs and no type 3 LSAs with the exception of the default route generated by the ABR as a IA-O* route (which basically replaces the inter-area and external routes). You do not see any other IA-O route in the routing table. Use the command **area** *area-id* **stub no-summary** to make an area a totally stubby area. Part **b** of Figure 13-7 shows a totally stubby area and which LSAs are allowed in this area.
- **NSSA**—An area that allows external routes to be advertised into the AS but still conserves the characteristics of a stub area to the AS. NSSA is a standard area type (RFC 1587) that defines an area which sees only type 1 and type 2 LSAs for intra-area routing, type 3 LSAs for inter-area routing, and no external type 5 LSAs, but it allows the propagation of type 7 LSAs. The only point of propagating type 7 LSAs is because you want to generate external routes from this area, but you do not want to receive external routes from other areas (one-way propagation). It is why the ABR translates the type 7 LSA into a type 5 LSA before injecting it into area 0. Use the command **area** *area-id* **nssa** to make an area an NSSA. Part **c** of Figure 13-7 shows an NSSA and which LSAs can be used in this area.

Figure 13-7 illustrates the different kinds of stub areas, the types of LSAs exchanged with other areas (stub, totally stubby, and not-so-stubby), and which LSAs are exchanged between these areas and area 0. In a totally stubby area, the routers inside the area just see a default route to the ABRs. In stub areas, the routers see the default route and inter-area routes (routes to specific subnets defined in other areas) because the ABR passes type 3 and type 4 LSAs from other areas.

Figure 13-7 *OSPF Stub Areas, Totally Stubby Areas, and Not-So-Stubby Areas*

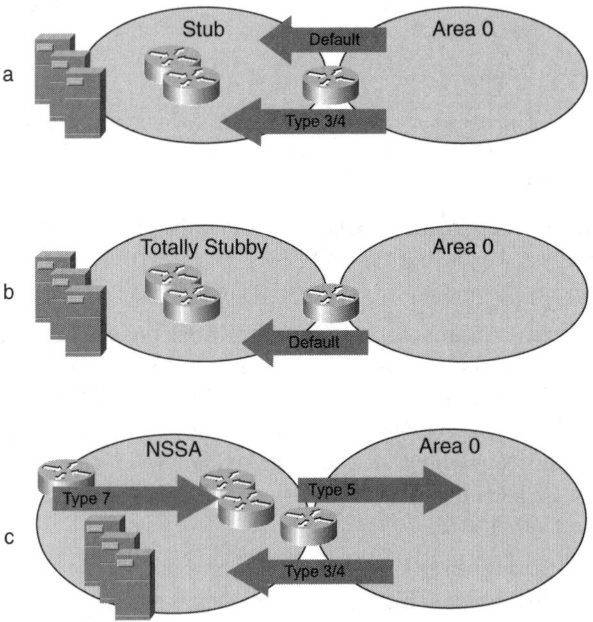

You cannot redistribute static routes in a totally stubby area or in a stub area. They are categorized as external routes and as such, their associated LSAs would not be propagated.

The solution is to use an NSSA (part **c** of Figure 13-7). A router in the Data Center redistributes static routes (type 7 external LSAs), and the ABR turns these LSAs into type 5 LSAs for "unidirectional" flooding into the backbone. The unidirectional nature is because the NSSA does not propagate type 5 areas.

LSAs

All the routers in one area need a consistent database. You keep it consistent by periodically flooding the LSAs to all the OSPF routers (multicast IP 224.0.0.5). LSAs are flooded every 30 minutes or upon occurrence of a change of the topology due, for example, to a router's interface failure. On shared segments, a non-DR router detecting a failure notifies the DR (by using the multicast address 224.0.0.6), and the DR propagates this information to the other routers in an area.

Network design with OSPF is hierarchical because of areas. The scope of the flooding of LSAs is limited by the area boundaries and depends on the LSA type.

There are six different types of LSAs:

- **Type 1**—Type 1 LSAs are also called *router* LSAs. These packets have information about the router links and the neighbor of the router on these links. Type 1 LSAs are limited to the area boundary.
- **Type 2**—Type 2 LSAs are also called *network* LSAs. They are used only for broadcast networks (such as VLAN segments) and include the list of the router on the shared segment. Type 2 LSAs are flooded in the area and generated by the DR of the shared segment.
- **Type 3**—Type 3 LSAs are also called *summary* LSAs. ABRs generate these LSAs to summarize information about a specific area to be advertised in other areas. You can think of the operation of the ABR as combining type 1 LSAs and type 2 LSAs for one area and injecting the result (type 3) into the adjacent area. Notice that summary LSAs are not necessarily summarized routes, just inter-area routes.
- **Type 4**—ASBR summary LSAs provide information about the route to the ASBR. ABRs generate type 4 LSAs.
- **Type 5**—AS external LSAs provide link-state information about networks external to the AS. The metric associated with these networks can be of two types: E1 when it provides the total cost of the route to the external network or E2 when it provides the cost of the external interface. Type 5 LSAs are flooded in all areas with the exception of stub areas.
- **Type 7**—NSSA external LSAs provide link-state information about networks external to the AS. A router in an NSSA generates type 7 LSAs instead of type 5 LSAs. The ABR then translates the type 7 LSA into type 5 LSA when the information is propagated to the backbone (area 0).

Failure Detection in OSPF

The detection of a failure in OSPF is driven by two main mechanisms. The first is, of course, a link down as a result of one of the following:

- A point-to-point link failure (for example, the failure of a Layer 3 link)
- Autostate detecting that no ports are forwarding on a given VLAN

NOTE Chapter 20 explains autostate.

The second mechanism is the hello protocol. By default, a router considers its neighbor down after missing four consecutive hellos. (Each hello is sent every 10 sec.) If a router detects a failure, it sends a link-state update to all the routers in the area. The link-state update is sent through all the point-to-point interfaces and to the DR in a shared segment (224.0.0.5).

Part **a** of Figure 13-8 shows the effect of a failure within the Data Center. The failure of a point-to-point link in an area makes a router flood a type 1 LSA. The ABR translates the type 1 LSA into a type 3 LSA, which is in turn flooded into the backbone (area 0) and into the regular and stub areas. Part **b** of Figure 13-8 shows the effect of a failure in an area other than the Data Center and the backbone. The failure originates a type 1 LSA, and the Data Center receives the type 3 LSA generated by the ABR.

Figure 13-8 *Failure in OSPF and LSAs*

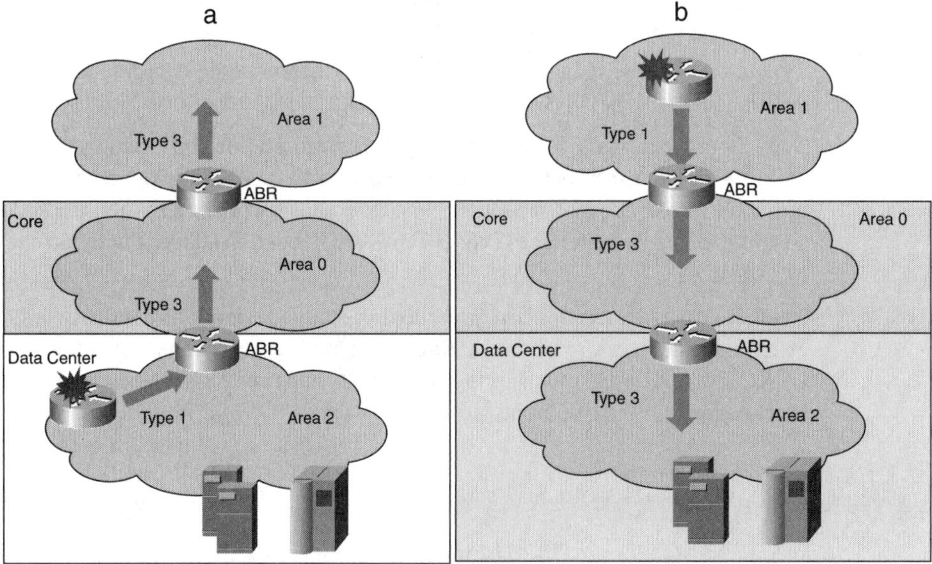

After a router receives the update, it performs the SPF calculation. The total time necessary for recovering after a failure depends on the configured timers, the size of the topology, and whether the SPF calculation is a topological change or a partial route calculation.

A topology change requires a full SPF computation, whereas a route calculation requires a partial SPF computation. Examples of nontopology calculations are the change of a link metric or a link flapping in a different area.

Metric Tuning

When you need to control the path taken by the traffic between the Data Center and the core or between Data Centers or when you redistribute routes, it is important to understand the meaning of the metric that OSPF uses to ensure optimal routing.

OSPF calculates the cost of the links by dividing the reference bandwidth by the bandwidth of the link. By default, the reference bandwidth is 100 Mbps. This means that 10-Mbps Ethernet links have a metric of 10 and Fast Ethernet links have a metric of 1. If the network comprises Gigabit Ethernet links or 10 Gigabit Ethernet links by default, they show a cost of 1, which means that from a routing point of view, a Gigabit link is not necessarily preferred to a 100-Mbps link.

To solve this problem, you can either manually change the cost of Fast Ethernet links by using the command **ip ospf cost**, or you can change the reference bandwidth with the command **auto-cost reference-bandwidth** *ref-value*. The *ref-value* is expressed in terms of Mbps.

The cost of a link given by *ref-value/bandwidth* means that with a ref-value of 10,000 Mbps, a link of 1 Gbps has a cost of 10 and a Fast Ethernet link has a cost of 100.

Redistribution

Redistribution in a Data Center can be useful when you need to run a dynamic routing protocol different from the one that is running in the core, when you need to inject static routes into the routing protocol, or when you use route filtering.

Redistribution consists of importing routing information from one routing protocol or one routing process into another protocol or process. Redistribution is controlled by the receiving protocol; with OSPF, you install the redistribution commands under the **router ospf** *process* configuration.

Example 13-12 shows the configuration of the redistribution of static routes in OSPF. One of the key considerations of configuring redistribution is the metric to assign to redistributed routes. When redistributing static routes in OSPF, you do not need to specify a metric because OSPF automatically derives it from the outgoing interface.

TIP OSPF automatically calculates the metric for redistributed routes if they are imported from another OSPF process, from static routes, or from connected interfaces.

When you redistribute routes into OSPF, the router becomes an ASBR and the routes are considered externals. Example 13-12 shows the use of the **metric-type** keyword to tag the routes as external type 1 (E1). The routes are injected in the area in the form of LSA type 5. The ABR of area 2 passes the type 5 LSA and also generates a summary LSA type 4. Remember that type 4 LSAs provide information about the route to the ASBR.

Example 13-12 *Redistribution Configuration*

```
router ospf 1
 redistribute static metric-type 1 subnets
 network 10.20.40.0 0.0.0.255 area 2
 network 10.50.50.0 0.0.0.255 area 2
```

If you need to redistribute another protocol into OSPF, you use the following syntax:

redistribute *protocol as-number* [**metric** *metric*] [**metric-type** {**1** | **2**}] [*subnets*]

In this case, you need to specify the metric value.

NOTE Read the section "LSAs" for information about the difference between external type 1 and external type 2 routes.

Multiple redistribution points on the network can lead to routing loops and suboptimal routing. Figure 13-9 shows a network with two redistribution points: Aggregation1 and Aggregation2. Both routers redistribute between two OSPF processes.

Figure 13-9 *Multiple Redistribution Points*

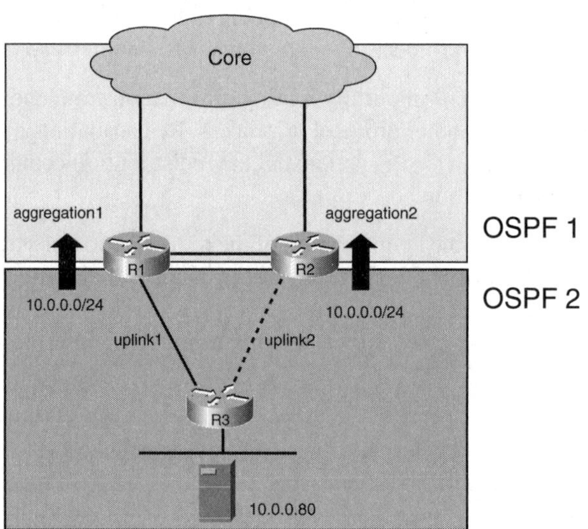

The topology represented in Figure 13-9 uses one-way redistribution: OSPF 1 imports routes from OSPF 2.

TIP Redistribution between two OSPF processes is sometimes used to filter routes. A better design consists in creating an area boundary and using the **area** *areanumber* **range** command. (See the section "Summarization and Filtering.")

Given the topology in Figure 13-9, it is natural that traffic destined to 10.0.0.80 from Aggregation2 be sent to R3 on uplink2. Surprisingly, you might find out that the route installed on Aggregation2 points to Aggregation1 for 10.0.0.0/24.

The reason is that on the Aggregation routers, you have two OSPF processes running; there is no interaction between OSPF processes, and the administrative distance for the routes installed by either process is 110, which is the only parameter used to decide which process should install a route for a given subnet. As a result, on Aggregation2 you might see the external route from Aggregation1 or the route from R3 in the routing table.

To make the route selection deterministic, you need to assign a different administrative distance to the external routes injected into OSPF process 1 by using the command **distance ospf external** *administrative-distance* on the aggregation routers of the example.

Redistribution might introduce loops when there are multiple redistribution points between two routing domains. Having multiple one-way redistribution points does not introduce problems in the following circumstances:

- The protocol you are redistributing into supports different administrative distances for external routes and internal routes. In OSPF, this behavior is not the default, and you can configure a different administrative distance for external routes with the command **distance ospf external** *administrative-distance*. This command has local significance, and you need to configure it on all the routers performing redistribution. Which value should you use for the administrative distance? A value higher than 110 (the OSPF administrative distance).
- The administrative distance of the protocol that you are importing routes from is less than the administrative distance of external routes for the protocol that you redistribute into. For example, if you are redistributing EIGRP into OSPF, this condition is automatically met because the administrative distance of EIGRP is 90. In other cases (such as when you are redistributing Routing Information Protocol [RIP] into OSPF), you might need to tweak the administrative distance of OSPF external routes with the command **distance ospf external**. A special case where the previous recommendation also applies is when you are redistributing one OSPF process into another OSPF process because the administrative distance is the same for both processes.

Summarization and Filtering

Routing designs use summarization for scalability purposes to reduce the number of routing entries that the network has to maintain.

OSPF is a link-state protocol, and it advertises the routing information in the form of database entries that describe the topology of the network. All routers in an area need to have the same database. This rule imposes certain restrictions on where you can perform summarization.

In OSPF, you typically configure summarization at the boundary between two areas. In the specific case of a Data Center, the aggregation routers can be the boundary between the Data Center area and the core area (area 0).

In OSPF, you can configure summarization at the following routers:

- **ABRs**—You can configure summarization of inter-area routes at the ABR with the command **area range**. (See the syntax after this list.) This command controls how the ABR generates type 3 LSAs. You can also configure the ABR to summarize external routes if these are type 7 LSAs that the ABR translates into type 5. In this case, you use the command described in the next bullet.
- **ASBRs**—You can configure the summarization of external routes at the ASBR, which generates type 5 LSAs, with the command **summary-address**. (See the syntax after this list.) This command controls how the ASBR generates type 5 or type 7 LSAs.

The full syntax for the **area range** command and for the **summary-address** command follows:

```
area areanumber range {prefix} {mask}
summary-address {prefix} {mask}.
```

Route filtering is subject to similar requirements as route summarization. You can filter routes at the area boundary or if you have a redistribution point at the ASBR where the redistribution occurs. You can filter routers on either of the following routers:

- **ABRs**—You can configure filtering of inter-area routes at the ABR with the command **area range not-advertise** or with the command **area filter-list**. These commands control how the ABR generates type 3 LSAs. You can also filter type 7 external routes at the ABR by using the command **summary-address not-advertise**. (See the full syntax for these commands after this list.)
- **ASBRs**—You can configure summarization at the ASBR, which generates type 5 LSAs, either by using **distribute-lists** or by controlling the redistribution with **route-maps**.

The full syntax for the **area range not-advertise** command, for the **area filter-list** command, and for the **summary-address not-advertise** command follow:

```
area areanumber range {prefix} {mask} not-advertise
area areanumber filter-list prefix {prefix-list} [in | out]
summary-address {prefix} {mask} not-advertise
```

Default Advertisement

You generate the default route into the Data Center for two main purposes:

- To push nonlocal traffic to the core in case the Intranet Data Center is a stub network
- To inject a default into the core network from the perimeter network (Internet Data Center) to provide Internet access to the internal clients

When configuring stub areas, the ABR automatically generates a default route as an LSA type 3, which is advertised into the local area. The only exception is the use of NSSAs. An NSSA generates the default only if you configure the following command:

```
area area-id nssa default-information originate
```

You can generate the default from a perimeter network in the Internet Edge in two ways:

- The border routers always inject a default with the command **default-information originate always**.
- If you have multiple exit points to the Internet, you can originate the default conditionally with the following command:

  ```
  default-information originate [always] [metric metric-value] [metric-type
  type-value] [route-map map-name]
  ```

The **default-information originate** command injects an external default route into OSPF if a default route is present in the routing table of the border router. (An example is having a static route to an interface.) The **default-information originate route-map** *map-name* makes it possible to advertise a default based on the presence of specific ISP routes (learned through Border Gateway Protocol [BGP], for example).

You can think of the **default-information originate** command as a specialized form of the **redistribute** command: the router becomes an ASBR, the route is considered an external route, and you can specify the metric value as well as whether this route is an external type 1 or external type 2.

EIGRP

EIGRP is a Cisco developed routing protocol. This section provides a quick overview of the protocol mechanisms and provides information about the toolkit necessary to optimize the routing design in Data Centers:

- Metric tuning
- Redistribution
- Summarization
- Route filtering
- Originating the default route

Chapter 20 explains how to deploy EIGRP in the Data Center.

EIGRP is an advanced distance-vector protocol. In EIGRP, as in distance-vector protocols, only neighboring routers exchange routing information, and there is no concept of flooding the topology information across all the routers in the network. Neighboring routers tell each other about the reachable destinations and the distance. Unlike traditional distance-vector protocols, EIGRP does not send periodic routing updates, which is meant to preserve network bandwidth. Routing updates are sent only when there is a change in the topology, and the updates include information only about the routes that have changed. For the preceding mechanisms to work, EIGRP relies on the following:

- **The hello protocol**—EIGRP establishes neighbor adjacency by using a hello protocol as link-state protocols do. Hellos are sent every 5 sec, and a neighbor is considered down after three consecutive hellos are lost.
- **The topology table**—In EIGRP, the topology table stores the information about the routes available through the neighbors. The key purpose is for the router to know about backup routes (the next-hop router providing this path is called the *feasible successor*) that can be used when the primary route fails. Backup routes are calculated according to the DUAL: a backup route needs to satisfy precise metric requirements to avoid creating loops.
- **The routing updates**—The updates have a reliable delivery mechanism with sequence numbers and acknowledgments (ACKs); EIGRP uses the multicast address 224.0.0.10.

NOTE You can find additional information on EIGRP operations at http://www.cisco.com/univercd/cc/td/doc/cisintwk/ito_doc/en_igrp.htm.

Failure Detection

A router detects a failure either because there is a link down or because the hello protocol detects the loss of three consecutive hellos.

If there is a topology change, such as the loss of a link or the failure of a router, the router detecting it checks the topology table for a feasible successor. If the router finds a feasible successor, the route stays in *passive state* (which is the normal state) but changes the next-hop value. The router then sends an update for the route with the changed next hop and distance. The computation that allows the router to switch to the backup route is called a *local DUAL*.

If the router does not have a feasible successor, the route goes *active*, and the router sends a *query* to its neighbors to see whether they still have a route to the destination. If the neighbors send a reply with the routing information, the router updates its topology table, the route goes *passive* again, and the router sends out an update. The mechanism of sending a query to the neighbors and receiving back the replies is called a *diffusing DUAL*.

A neighboring router might receive a query for a route whose next hop was the neighbor itself: it means that the next hop is not valid any more for the route. The router then checks its topology table: if it has a feasible successor, the route goes passive again and the router sends a reply to the query.

If the neighboring routers do not have a feasible successor, they also enter the active state and send queries to their neighbors. At some point, the querying process must stop and replies come back to the router that originated the diffusing DUAL computation.

Each router that entered the diffusing DUAL must wait for all the replies to come back before setting the route back in passive state.

Metric Tuning

It is important to understand the meaning of the metric used by EIGRP so you can control the path taken by the traffic between the Data Center and the core or between Data Centers or when you redistribute routes. EIGRP routes carry a cost, which is the result of a formula applied to the characteristics of the links along the path to the destination. In EIGRP, each link is characterized by the following parameters:

- **Bandwidth**—You can read the bandwidth of an interface by using the command **show interface**, which displays a value in units of kilobits per second (kbps). You can alter the value of the **bandwidth** with the command bandwidth. The bandwidth to a destination is the minimum bandwidth of the path.
- **Delay**—The output of the **show interface** command reports the delay in units of microseconds. You can alter this value on a per-interface basis with the command **delay** followed by the value measured in units of 10 ms. The delay to a destination is the sum of the delays of the path.
- **Load**—The load is a measure of link saturation. The load value represents is a fraction of 255, and a value of 255 means that a link is saturated. The load for a destination is the maximum load along the path.
- **Reliability**—Reliability reflects the link reliability. The reliability value is a fraction of 255, and a value of 255 means 100 percent reliability. The reliability of a route considers the smallest value along the path.
- **MTU**—The maximum transmission unit (MTU) of the path to the destination is the smallest MTU of the links.

You can read the values of the preceding parameters by issuing the **show interface** command, as demonstrated in Example 13-13.

Example 13-13 *Bandwidth, Delay, Load, Reliability, and MTU for a Gigabit Ethernet Interface*

```
GigabitEthernet1/2 is up, line protocol is up (connected)
  Hardware is C6k 1000Mb 802.3, address is 0001.63d1.27ff (bia 0001.63d1.27ff)
  Description: toaggregation2
  MTU 1500 bytes, BW 1000000 Kbit, DLY 10 usec,
     reliability 255/255, txload 1/255, rxload 1/255
```

EIGRP calculates the cost of routes by combining these parameters. Whenever one of the parameters changes, the router needs to run DUAL, and some parameters such as load change continuously. The default is to include only two metrics in the composite cost calculation: the bandwidth and the delay. You can configure it by using the command **metric weights 0 1 0 1 0 0** (which is also the default).

NOTE For more information about the use of the command **metric weights**, refer to the Cisco online documentation for IOS at http://www.cisco.com/univercd/cc/td/doc/product/software/ios123/123cgcr/iprrp_r/ip2_k1g.htm#1040267.

As a result of the default settings, the metric of a route is given by the combination of minimum bandwidth with the total delay according to the following formula:

$$[10^7/(\text{min bandwidth in Kbps}) + \text{Sum (delays in unit of 10 microseconds)}] * 256$$

Redistribution

You can configure redistribution into EIGRP with the following command:

```
redistribute protocol [metric bandwidth delay reliability load mtu][route-map
mapname]
```

Routes redistributed into EIGRP are marked as external and their administrative distance is 170. (The internal EIGRP administrative distance is 90.)

When you configure redistribution, you have to configure the metric for the redistributed routes. If the metrics for redistributed routes are not set, EIGRP sets the metric to infinite and does not propagate the routes. You can set the metric by using the **redistribute** command or by using the following command:

```
default-metric bandwidth delay reliability load mtu
```

TIP You do not need to configure the metric when redistributing from another EIGRP process, from IGRP, from connected networks or static routes.

Even if the default for EIGRP is to use only the bandwidth and the delay, you need to also specify the reliability, the load, and the MTU. You can set the values for the reliability, load, and MTU to 255, 1, and 1500, respectively.

Redistribution sometimes can introduce loops when there are multiple redistribution points between two routing domains. Having multiple one-way redistribution points typically works fine when the following requirements are met:

- **The routing protocols supports different administrative distances for internal versus external routes.**—EIGRP does. EIGRP external routes have an administrative distance of 170, and the internal routes have an administrative distance of 90.
- **The routing protocol from which the redistribution happens has a lower administrative distance than external EIGRP routes.**—An example is the redistribution of OSPF (where the administrative distance is 90) into EIGRP (where external routes have an administrative distance of 170).

Summarization and Filtering

EIGRP lets you summarize and filter routes on a per-interface basis. In EIGRP, you can configure summarization with the following command:

```
ip summary-address eigrp asnumber address mask
```

The metric for the summarized routes is the minimum metric of the specific routes. If you configure summarization, EIGRP automatically installs a summary route pointing to the NULL0 interface to avoid routing loops.

You can do route filtering per routing process, per interface, or per neighbor. The command is **distribute-list** *access-list-number* {**in** | **out**}

If you also specify the interface or the next-hop IP address, you can filter per interface or per neighbor.

You can also use a prefix list as an alternative to access lists by using the following command:

```
distribute-list prefix list-name {in | out}
```

Default Advertisement

In EIGRP, you can generate a default route in two ways:

- You configure a static route **ip route 0.0.0.0 0.0.0.0** *next-hop* and redistribute this route into EIGRP. This configuration has the drawback that the administrative cost of the external EIGRP routes is 170, which means that this route might not be installed on all the routers in the network. For example, in case you configure a summary route 0.0.0.0 0.0.0.0, EIGRP automatically installs a NULL0 route for 0.0.0.0 0.0.0.0 with an administrative cost of 5. The NULL0 route overrides the redistributed default route. The solution consists of configuring summary routes 0.0.0.0 0.0.0.0 with an administrative cost of 200 using the following command:

```
ip summary-address eigrp asnumber 0.0.0.0 0.0.0.0 200
```

- You configure the default network:
  - **ip default-network** *major-network*. EIGRP tags the route with an external flag and the major network becomes a candidate to be the default route. Notice that this command is classful; you need to specify a major network for it to take effect.

NAT

NAT is a key component of the Data Center design, especially for the perimeter network (also called the Internet Edge). NAT was originally described in RFC 1631. Its main function is to provide translation between private and public IP addresses. Private addresses (RFC 1918) belong to the following ranges:

- 10.0.0.0 to 10.255.255.255 (for Class A addresses)
- 172.16.0.0 to 172.31.255.255 (for Class B addresses)
- 192.168.0.0 to 192.168.255.255 (for Class C addresses)

NAT has several uses:

- **Conservation of address space**—You use NAT to dynamically map the private address space to fewer public IP addresses.
- **Security**—You hide the information about the private IP addresses of the server farm and clients and translate them to public IP addresses.
- **Control of return traffic paths**—This use is typical of multihoming, when an enterprise customer is attached to multiple Internet service providers (ISPs). NAT translates the source IP address of traffic leaving the enterprise network. If you have multiple exit points in the network, you can translate traffic from each exit point to a different range of IP addresses. The return traffic enters the enterprise network from the same routers and firewalls it left.
- **Server load balancing**—Load balancers use NAT to hide the real addresses of a cluster of servers behind a single IP address used to access the application (vIP address).

Figure 13-10 illustrates the likely locations for NAT in an enterprise network. Figure 13-10 shows two Internet Data Centers, Data Center 1 and Data Center 2, at two geographical locations. Each location also has a campus network, Campus 1 and Campus 2. You configure NAT either on the border routers (1) or on the firewalls (2) to give Internet access to the campus users. The load balancers (3) provide NAT translation for the publicly accessible servers.

Figure 13-10 *NAT in an Enterprise Network*

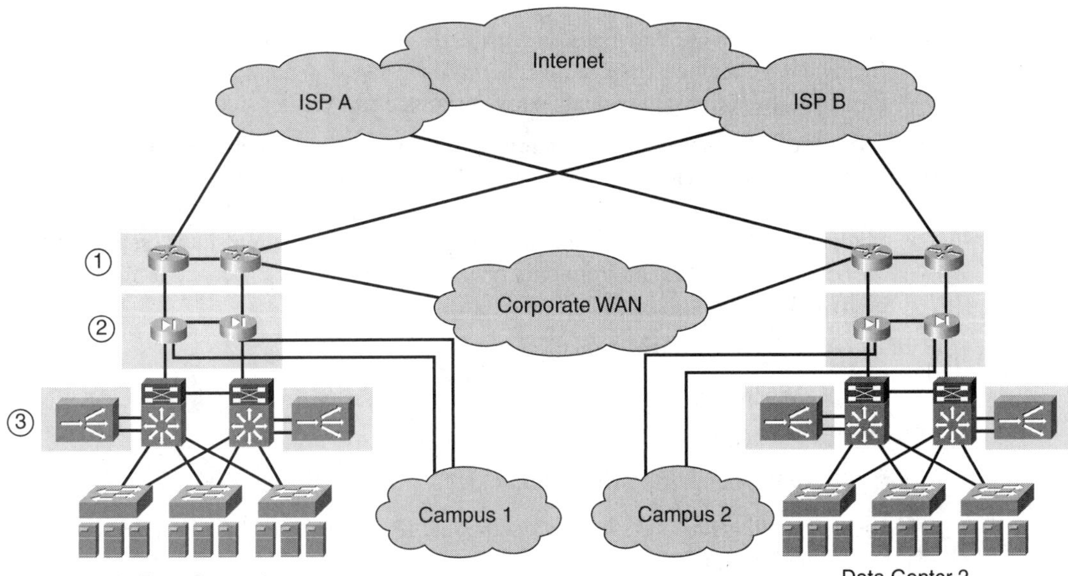

There are at least three devices where you are likely to configure NAT:

- **Routers**—You can configure NAT on routers with different levels of performance that depend on the platform. When working with Layer 3 switches, NAT can happen in hardware or might require software processing. Thanks to the NetFlow-services software, NAT is often performed in the fast-switching path. Figure 13-10 shows the border routers (1) that you are likely to configure for NAT.
- **Firewalls**—Firewalls usually perform NAT with minimal impact on other firewall operations. The range of applications that firewalls understand typically is wider than the applications configurable on a router. Firewalls also provide additional security features together with NAT such as limits on embryonic connections. Figure 13-10 shows the placement of the firewalls (2) performing NAT.
- **Load balancers**—NAT on load balancers provides a single vIP address for applications and translates incoming request to the real IP address of the individual servers in the server farm. Figure 13-10 shows the load balancers (3) performing NAT in the demilitarized zone (DMZ).

The NAT configuration on routers and firewalls typically requires defining an interface as *inside* and another interface as *outside*. The translation can be one of two types:

- **Static**—A statement that maps one inside IP address to an outside IP address. The IP address association (translation slot) is always kept in memory. This setup lets forwarding and translating connections originate from either side of the network.
- **Dynamic**—When using dynamic translations, you configure first an access control list (ACL) to match the traffic requiring NAT and then a pool of IP addresses to draw from. The association between the inside and outside IP addresses (translation slot) is kept in memory for a limited amount of time. The translation slot is created by connections that originate from only one side of the network (outside or inside, not both) and forwards and translates the return traffic.

IP addresses are categorized as either

- **Local**—When they belong to the enterprise address space
- **Global**—When they belong to the public address space

As a result, NAT uses the following terminology:

- **Inside Local**—IP address to indicate the real IP address used by a host that belongs to the enterprise network
- **Inside Global**—IP address that indicates the IP address of an internal host after the translation is performed by NAT
- **Outside Local**—IP address that indicates the IP address of an outside host as seen in the enterprise network after the translation is performed by the NAT
- **Outside Global**—Indicates the IP address of the outside host outside the enterprise network

Figure 13-11 provides an example of NAT. The client, 10.1.1.80 (the inside local IP address), opens a connection to a host on the Internet. The source IP address of this connection is translated by the router to a public IP address: 192.0.2.14 (the inside global IP address).

NOTE This chapter uses the recommendations from RFC 3330 for the use of public addresses for documentation purpose. The "public" IP addresses in this chapter are from the 192.0.2.0/24 subnet.

The inside global address normally comes from a pool of IP addresses available to the enterprise clients. The purpose of NAT in this case is to conserve address space: there are more internal clients (more private IP addresses) than public addresses available in the pool. The assumption is that not every client is continuously connected to the Internet, so statistically there is always a public IP address available for a client requesting a connection.

Figure 13-11 *NAT*

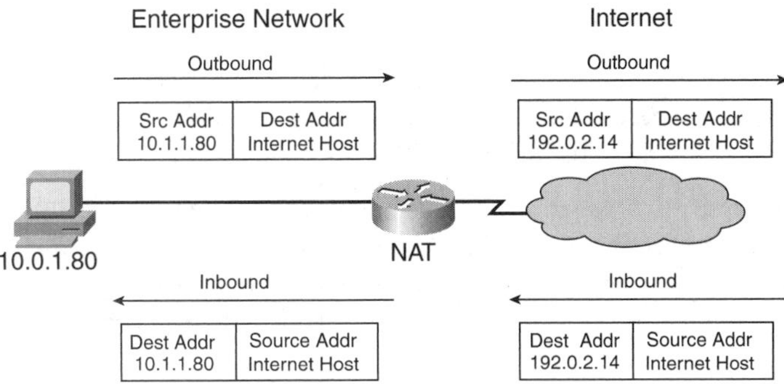

No matter how big the pool is, it is possible that at some point in time, there are more client requests than available public IP addresses. Port address translation (PAT) solves this problem.

PAT associates multiple hosts to a single IP address. PAT uses the Layer 4 ports to provide the many-to-one translation.

In Figure 13-11, if there were a single global IP address, 192.0.2.14, a second client (10.1.1.81) requesting a connection to the Internet would get the same global IP address, but the source Layer 4 port of the connection would be translated by the router to a number that allows the router to uniquely identify the client. For example, 10.1.1.80 could be translated to 192.0.2.14:2031, and 10.1.1.81 could be translated to 192.0.2.14:1506.

NAT Support for Applications

The NAT functionality would be useless for certain applications if routers or firewalls could not understand the applications whose connections are translated by NAT.

Suppose that a host inside the enterprise accesses an outside application. The outside server sees a request with a source IP address equal to the inside global. The application has a control connection that communicates to the server the IP address for the client. This IP address is carried in the payload of the packets.

If the router performing NAT cannot identify the embedded IP address, the outside server sees the inside local IP address embedded in the control connection, and normally the session would fail. If the router understands the application, it can translate the IP address embedded in the control connection from the inside local to the inside global IP.

FTP provides the perfect example. Example 13-14 shows the trace of an FTP control connection for an active FTP transfer. The client IP address is 10.1.1.80, and the server

IP address is 171.69.101.21. Example 13-14 shows the trace at the FTP layer, so you do not see the IP addresses: C->S is traffic from 10.1.1.80 to 171.69.101.21, and S->C is the traffic from 171.69.101.21 to 10.1.1.80.

Now imagine that the client is coming from behind a firewall and the firewall is configured for NAT. You expect the firewall to translate the source IP (10.1.1.80) to a public address (such as 192.0.2.14): this translation alone is not enough.

As you can see in Example 13-14, the client sends the command **PORT 10,1,1,80,6,162**. The server would then see that the source IP of the client is 192.0.2.14 (from the IP headers) and would receive from the client the information that its IP address is 10.1.1.80. An attempt from the server to connect to 10.1.1.80 for the data connection would then fail because it is a private address.

For the FTP transfer to work, the firewall needs to translate the **PORT** command into **PORT 192,0,2,14,6,162**. It requires that the firewall recognize the FTP protocol and translate the PORT command.

Example 13-14 *NAT and the Control Connection of Active FTP*

```
S->C 220 localhost.localdomain FTP server ready.
C->S USER admin
S->C 331 Password required for admin.
C->S PASS mypasswd
S->C 230 User admin logged in.
C->S SYST
S->C 215 UNIX Type: L8
C->S PWD
S->C 257 "/home/admin" is current directory.
C->S TYPE A
S->C 200 Type set to A.
C->S PORT 10,1,1,80,6,162
S->C 200 PORT command successful.
C->S LIST
S->C 150 Opening ASCII mode data connection for /bin/ls.
S->C 226 Transfer complete.
```

Applications like FTP that exchange information about the client/server IP address in the payload require the specific network device to understand where to look for the proper information to perform the translation. Examples of this type of application include FTP, Simple Mail Transfer Protocol (SMTP), Domain Name System (DNS) queries (A and PTR), H.323, Progressive Networks' Real Audio, and Session Initiation Protocol (SIP).

Applications that do not carry any embedded IP address in the application payload are automatically supported. Examples are Telnet, HTTP, and Trivial File Transfer Protocol (TFTP).

TIP A list of the applications currently supported on IOS NAT is available at http://www.cisco.com/warp/public/cc/pd/iosw/ioft/ionetn/prodlit/1195_pp.htm.

New applications are continuously added. For more information, refer to the Cisco IOS Software Release notes.

IOS NAT on Routers

Suppose that the internal network (inside) has addresses in the 10.0.0.0/24 range and that these addresses appear to the external world (outside) as 192.0.2.0/24. Example 13-15 shows a configuration that allows the internal network to communicate with the outside.

The first important configuration step is to assign the inside and outside roles for NAT to the interfaces. This step lets you define inbound and outbound directions and define which NAT operation to perform:

- **ip nat inside source**—Translates the source IP address for outbound traffic and the destination IP address of inbound traffic
- **ip nat outside source**—Translates the source IP address for inbound traffic and the destination IP address for outbound traffic

Example 13-15 *IOS NAT Configuration for Static Translation*

```
interface Ethernet0
 ip address 10.0.0.1 255.255.255.0
 ip nat inside
!
Interface Ethernet1
 ip address 192.0.2.1 255.255.255.0
 ip nat outside
!
ip nat inside source static 10.0.0.4 192.0.2.16
!
```

In Example 13-15, only host 10.0.0.4 can communicate with the outside world: the command **ip nat inside source static** defines a static mapping between 10.0.0.4 and 192.0.2.16. This configuration is suitable for servers accessible from the Internet: external clients can connect to the global IP address, and NAT translates automatically to the local IP.

If you want to give access to the outside network to a number of internal clients, you should use a different configuration based on dynamic translation. Example 13-16 shows how.

Example 13-16 *Dynamic NAT Configuration*

```
interface Ethernet0
 ip address 10.0.0.1 255.255.255.0
 ip nat inside
!
interface Ethernet1
 ip address 192.0.2.1 255.255.255.0
 ip nat outside
!
ip nat pool my_pool 192.0.2.5 192.0.2.14 netmask 255.255.255.0
ip nat inside source list pool 10 my_pool
!
access-list 10 permit 10.1.1.0 0.0.0.255
!
```

The access list must identify the traffic eligible for the translation. Ten internal hosts can get dynamical translation of their source IP address to any of the addresses in the 192.0.2.5 to 192.0.2.14 range, as defined in the NAT pool my pool. This range of addresses is called inside global; the 10.1.1.0/24 range is called inside local.

This configuration effectively allows clients to originate connections to the outside world and creates a translation slot for the return traffic belonging to the connection. Unless the traffic coming from the outside matches a dynamic translation slot, it does not pass through the router. For example, if an external client tries to open a connection to any of the IP addresses in the range 192.0.2.5 to 192.0.2.14, it does not succeed because the router drops the connection attempt.

By operating in this fashion, dynamic NAT provides security for the clients by hiding their IP address and by preventing connections originated by external clients to the internal ones.

In a fully redundant topology (that is, a design with no single point of failure), you typically have the same static and NAT pools configured on a pair of routers. In Example 13-15, which router would answer the ARP request for 192.0.2.16? You need to find a way to arbitrate which device is master for the inside global.

There are two solutions:

- You can bind the NAT configuration to an HSRP group with the **redundancy** command in the static/pool configuration. Example 13-17 shows the use of an HSRP group together with the redundancy option to associate the static translation with the active HSRP router.
- You can disable the NAT routers from answering ARP requests by using the keyword **no-alias** in the static/pool configuration and hard-coding an ARP entry in the neighboring routers with the HSRP MAC. The static NAT configuration would be

  ```
  ip nat inside source static 10.0.0.4 192.0.2.16 no-alias
  ```

Example 13-17 *IOS NAT Configuration with Redundancy*

```
interface Ethernet0
 ip address 10.0.0.253 255.255.255.0
 standby 1 priority 105 preempt
 standby 1 name HSRP1
 standby 1 ip 10.0.0.1
 standby 10 track Ethernet1
 ip nat inside
!
Interface Ethernet1
 ip address 192.0.2.1 255.255.255.0
 ip nat outside
!
ip nat inside source static 10.0.0.4 192.0.2.16 redundancy HSRP1
!
```

In terms of performance, Layer 3 switches might have hardware support for NAT, which allows wire-speed translation; otherwise, NAT is performed in fast switching.

NOTE For more information about the switching paths, refer to Chapter 20.

TIP Cisco IOS Software supports stateful redundancy for NAT, called Stateful NAT (SNAT). It allows the routers to exchange information about the active flows in such a way that upon the failure of one router (router1), the other router (router2) takes over the flows of router1. Because the takeover happens when there is a failure, there is no loss of existing flows. You can find more information at http://www.cisco.com/warp/public/cc/pd/iosw/prodlit/stnat_wp.htm.

NAT on PIX Firewalls

The configurations described in the section on routers are similar to the ones that you can have on Cisco PIX Firewalls. On PIX Firewalls, the concept of inside and outside is extended by security levels. Each interface has a security level, security level 100 being the *inside* interface (the most secure) and security 0 being the *outside* interface (the least secure). Traffic from inside to outside is of course outbound and from outside to inside is inbound.

All the other interfaces have intermediate levels of security, and traffic flowing from a higher security level to a lower security level is *outbound*. Traffic flowing from a lower security level to a higher security level is *inbound*.

The default NAT translation refers to changing the source IP address for the outbound connections and the destination IP address for the inbound connections (same as **ip nat inside source** in IOS NAT).

Example 13-18 shows the configuration that gives an external client access to a server that is in the inside. This configuration is equivalent to the configuration of Example 13-15 in IOS NAT.

Example 13-18 *Static NAT Configuration on the Firewall Services Module*

```
nameif vlan10 inside security100
nameif vlan192 outside security0
ip address inside 10.0.0.1 255.255.255.0
ip address outside 192.0.2.1 255.255.255.0
static(inside, outside) 192.0.2.16 10.0.0.4
```

The **static** command defines the higher security level interface (inside) to lower security level (outside) mapping and is followed by the global IP address and by the local IP address. If there were other interfaces on the firewall with intermediate security levels, the static translation would be defined from the higher security level to the lower security level:

static (*lower, higher*) *globalIP localIP.*

To provide external access to the internal clients, you need to configure dynamic NAT. Example 13-19 shows the configuration that gives internal clients access to the outside. This configuration is equivalent of the IOS NAT configuration in Example 13-16.

Example 13-19 *Client NAT on the Firewall Services Module*

```
nameif vlan10 inside security100
nameif vlan192 outside security0
ip address inside 10.0.0.1 255.255.255.0
ip address outside 192.0.2.1 255.255.255.0
global(outside) 2 192.0.2.5-192.0.2.14 netmask 255.255.255.0
nat(inside) 2 10.1.1.0 255.255.255.0
```

The **nat** command defines which IP addresses are eligible for NATing (local IP addresses). The **global** command defines the range of IP addresses to use as the pool. The number **2** in the example binds the pool with the selected NAT configuration.

TIP An *embryonic* connection is a connection that has been initiated but never completed and has not seen any data. You can append the limit on the embryonic connections to the NAT commands of a firewall to protect the servers from buffer overflow with SYN attacks.

For redundancy on firewalls, see Chapter 22, "Performance Metrics of Data Center Devices."

NAT on Load Balancers

Load balancers largely rely on NAT to forward traffic to the servers, as Example 13-20 demonstrates. The outside clients access 192.0.2.16, and the load balancer translates the destination IP to be either 10.0.0.4 or 10.0.0.5 (**nat server**).

Example 13-20 *Server NAT on the Content Switching Module*

```
vserver HTTP
  virtual 192.0.2.16 tcp www
  serverfarm HTTP-SERVERS
!
serverfarm HTTP-SERVERS
  nat server
  no nat client
  real 10.0.0.4
   inservice
  real 10.0.0.5
   inservice
```

It is also possible for the servers 10.0.0.4 and 10.0.0.5 to initiate connections and be translated to the global IP address, as demonstrated in Example 13-21.

NOTE The load-balancer operations described in this section are commonly referred to as *directed mode* in Cisco terminology. It is also possible to perform load balancing without NAT, in which case the load-balancer operation goes under the name of dispatch mode. For more information, read Chapter 16.

Example 13-21 *NAT on the Content Switching Module for Server-Originated Connections*

```
static nat 192.0.2.16
 real 10.0.0.4
 real 10.0.0.5
!
```

Example 13-21 shows that the internal servers that initiate connections are translated to the global address 192.0.2.16 because they share the same global IP address. The load balancer relies on PAT to differentiate their traffic.

Notice the different meaning of the **static** command in this context compared to the firewall configuration. An external client cannot get access to 10.0.0.4 or 10.0.0.5 if only **static nat** is configured. On a Cisco load balancer, you need to configure a vserver for client-to-server connections.

A third NAT configuration on load balancers consists of using NAT pools to map the incoming clients to an outside local IP address. Example 13-22 clarifies.

Example 13-22 *Client NAT Pools on the Content Switching Module*

```
natpool CLIENT-POOL 10.0.0.6 10.0.0.15 netmask 255.255.255.0
!
vserver HTTP
  virtual 192.0.2.16 tcp www
  policy CLIENT-NAT
  serverfarm HTTP-SERVERS
!
serverfarm HTTP-SERVERS
  nat server
  no nat client
  real 10.0.0.4
   inservice
  real 10.0.0.5
   inservice
!
serverfarm CLIENT-NAT
  nat server
  nat client CLIENT-POOL
  real 10.0.0.4
   inservice
  real 10.0.0.5
   inservice
!
policy CLIENT-NAT
  client-group 10
  serverfarm CLIENT-NAT
!
access-list 10 permit 171.69.102.0 255.255.255.0
!
```

Example 13-22 shows a configuration where clients coming from 171.69.102.0 and accessing the web servers 192.0.2.16 are translated to an IP address in the range 10.0.0.6 to 10.0.0.15 before being sent to 10.0.0.5 or 10.0.0.4.

All the other clients keep their original IP address when dispatched to 10.0.0.5 or 10.0.0.4. The access list defines the clients eligible for Source IP NAT, and the policy maps the access list (client-group) to the server farm where the source NAT is defined (serverfarm CLIENT-NAT).

The only difference between the CLIENT-NAT server farm and the HTTP-SERVERS server farm is the fact that CLIENT-NAT performs both source and destination NAT, whereas HTTP-SERVERS only translates the destination IP to the server IP address.

Summary

Today's Data Centers require careful planning when dealing with dynamic or static routing. Although there are no extensive routing configurations within the Data Center, you do need to connect it to the campus core switches and the Internet Edge.

Some of the key protocols that you need to know to troubleshoot most problems in the Data Centers are ARP, HSRP, VRRP, and GLBP. Whether or not you use dynamic routing between the Data Center and the core of the network, you will be using these protocols in providing the servers' default gateway and for interoperability with firewalls and load balancers.

You typically use dynamic routing between the Data Center and the core of the network. This chapter described the essential operations of OSPF and EIGRP with focus on their main characteristics, which in OSPF relate to the link-state nature of the protocol and in EIGRP relate to the use of DUAL.

For a successful deployment of OSPF, you need to be able to choose the most appropriate area definition for the Data Center and to configure summarization and route filtering. With EIGRP, it is equally important to configure route summarization and route filtering. Sometimes, route filtering requires the configuration of redistribution, which you need to carefully design to avoid routing loops or suboptimal routing.

The injection of the default route also needs attention because this route provides Internet access to the internal clients and also reduces the number of routes in stub networks, such as the Data Center network. A further consideration of the default route is its use in the perimeter network where it is actually generated.

NAT is another key Layer 3 technology that is typically deployed at the perimeter of the network to conserve the enterprise address space, but also to provide protection to clients and servers by hiding their real addresses. NAT can also control the return traffic in multihoming. This chapter explained how to configure NAT on routers and firewalls for all these purposes. Additionally, you use NAT on load balancers to provide a single IP address for a given application hosted on multiple servers.

For Further Reading

Doyle, Jeff. *Routing TCP/IP*, Volume I (*CCIE Professional Development*). Cisco Press, 1998.

Retana, Alvaro, Don Slice, and Russ White. *Advanced IP Network Design (CCIE Professional Development)*. Cisco Press, 1999.

This chapter covers the following topics:

- The essentials of the Systems Network Architecture (SNA), IBM Data Center technology including mainframes, channels, the front-end processor (FEP), and the virtual telecommunications access method (VTAM)
- The mainframe attachment options: enterprise system connections (ESCON), the channel interface processor (CIP), the channel port adapter (CPA), and the Open System Architecture (OSA) card
- The evolution of SNA from subarea SNA to application peer-to-peer networking (APPN)
- How to transport SNA on an IP network via data-link switching plus (DLSW+) and SNA switching (SNAsw)
- The concept of Sysplex for cluster environments
- The design of today's Data Centers for IP-based applications in the presence of IBM mainframes

CHAPTER 14

IBM Data Center Technology

This chapter gives you a basic foundation in IBM networking technology and its evolution from subarea SNA to APPN, and TCP/IP as a basis for understanding today's integration of IBM technology into Data Centers.

If you are interested only in the fundamentals of TCP/IP–based applications running on mainframes, read these sections:

- Mainframe Attachment Options
- Sysplex and Parallel Sysplex

If you are interested in supporting SNA applications on a TCP/IP network, read the following sections:

- Mainframe Attachment Options
- SNA on TCP/IP
- TN3270

Mainframes

This chapter focuses on the use of the IBM mainframe platforms: the S/390 and the zSeries. Mainframes comprise a number of central processors for the execution of program instructions and processors specialized in input/output operations. The I/O subsystem is called a *channel*. Channels allow communication between processors and external devices, such as storage systems or printers.

In this architecture, the central processors delegate the I/O operations to the I/O subsystem, thus allowing several simultaneous I/O operations to run while the central processors execute other tasks. This architecture makes the mainframes extremely powerful for applications in which computing involves frequent data transfers between memory and external devices (this behavior is typical of so-called *data-intensive* applications).

IBM mainframes support several operating systems (OSs):

- **OS/390**—Derived from Multiple Virtual Storage (MVS), this OS runs on the S/390.
- **VM**—VM runs on the S/390.
- **z/OS**—Evolved from OS/390, this OS runs on the zSeries.
- **z/VM**—Evolved from VM, this OS runs on the zSeries.
- **Linux**—The zSeries can be configured to run Linux.

A single mainframe can run many OSs at the same time. This is possible because of logical partitions (LPAR). Logical partitioning consists of dividing the memory, the CPU(s), and the I/O into resources each running their own operating system. Each LPAR can include several CPUs, or a single CPU can be used by multiple LPARs at the same time.

Each LPAR operates as a separate physical server with its own TCP/IP stack.

IBM Data Center Components

IBM Data Center components include mainframes, also called hosts, and potentially front-end processors (FEPs) and terminals. FEPs support physical connectivity from the mainframe to an Ethernet or Token Ring network, and they offload the mainframe from certain network functions, such as routing or bridging.

Figure 14-1 presents the IBM components in a Data Center.

Figure 14-1 shows a simple Data Center with terminals and printers. The easiest way to connect terminals and printers to the mainframe is to use a bus-and-tag connection, as shown for Terminal 1. Remote terminals access the mainframe via serial lines using the Synchronous Data Link Control (SDLC) protocol. The Systems Network Architecture (SNA) defined by IBM makes this communication possible.

A mainframe typically connects to a *FEP*, also called a *communication controller*, which is used to offload the host from performing networking functions such as the routing SNA traffic. The software running on FEPs is called the Network Control Program (NCP).

Between FEPs and terminals, there are *cluster controller* devices, also called establishment controllers, which provide connectivity to terminals and printers. Cluster controllers have no SNA routing capabilities; they basically receive keystrokes from the terminal and send them to the FEP over the serial line.

Figure 14-1 *IBM Data Center Components*

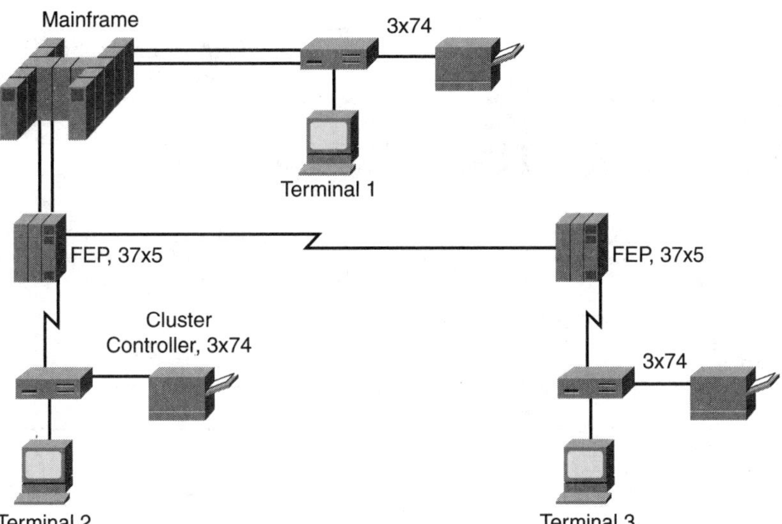

The backbone of the network in this environment consists of mainframes and FEPs. Inside the mainframe, the key component is the virtual telecommunications access method (VTAM).

VTAM is the software that activates and deactivates terminals. It provides directory services by looking up applications, and it establishes sessions between the applications. In the IBM traditional network architecture, SNA, the VTAM in the mainframe holds most of the network intelligence.

All the elements in an SNA network are categorized as physical units (PUs) or logical units (LUs), and are part of the SNA network addressable units (NAU). A PU is the entity that manages a SNA node and is exemplified by a FEP (PU Type 4) or by the cluster controller (PU Type 2). In contrast, a logical unit manages the devices attached to a node, as exemplified by the terminal application TN3270, which is an LU Type 2. The NAUs are the endpoints of SNA sessions.

Table 14-1 maps IBM Data Center components to their name in terms of nodes and NAUs.

Table 14-1 *IBM Data Center Components*

	SNA Nodes	SNA Addressable Units (NAU)	Example of Device
VTAM	Host subarea node	PU Type 5	
FEP	Communication controller subarea node	PU Type 4	37x5
Cluster Controller	Peripheral node	PU Type 2	3276, 3x74, 1174
Terminals		LU Type 2	3270
Character String Printer		LU Type 1	
Data String Printer		LU Type 3	
APPN Nodes		PU Type 2.1	
APPN Programs		LU Type 6.2	

SNA was not designed for client/server applications; it used instead a master/slave architecture in which everything was controlled by the master, which was VTAM. This architecture eventually evolved to allow peer-to-peer communication between the nodes, without requiring VTAM to establish the session between the applications.

IBM introduced the advanced peer-to-peer networking (APPN) architecture to allow client/server communication. With this architecture, every node is a peer and is identified as a PU Type 2.1. Applications that are APPN-capable are also peers and are identified as LU Type 6.2 (see Table 14-1).

APPN introduced a different way to categorize devices:

- **End nodes (ENs)**—The nodes that host the applications and implement a subset of the APPN services.
- **Network nodes (NNs)**—The nodes that provide the complete set of APPN services. NNs are required to provide end-to-end network connectivity between end nodes by maintaining the network topology and helping ENs locate resources on the network.

The elements described to this point represent the foundation of the SNA networks.

IBM Data Centers today support SNA- and TCP/IP–based applications. SNA applications use TCP/IP transport mechanisms such as data-link switching plus (DLSw+) or SNA switching (SNAsw). Often, a Cisco router that provides the previously listed functions is directly attached to the mainframe.

All the mainframe OSs available today (z/OS, z/VM, Linux, and so on) have TCP/IP protocol stacks, the capability to run at least one routing protocol, and access to Gigabit

Ethernet interfaces. As a result, mainframes can be directly attached to a TCP/IP infrastructure via a Gigabit Ethernet card.

How the mainframes attach to a network infrastructure is the topic of the next section.

Mainframe Attachment Options

At the data link layer, mainframes offer at least the following attachment options:

- **Channels**—Allow the connection of mainframes to printers, storage devices, and FEPs, as well as between processors. Enterprise system connections (ESCON) is an example of channel connectivity; it is common to attach mainframes with ESCON to a Cisco 72*xx*/75*xx* router.
- **Synchronous Data Link Control (SDLC)**—Used mainly to connect FEPs to each other and to the cluster controllers over a WAN.
- **LAN protocols**—Include Token Ring and Ethernet, which requires the use of LLC2 for native SNA traffic.

Channel Attachments

Channels are used to connect mainframes to peripheral devices such as storage system and printers, for the attachment of FEPs or routers and for processor-to-processor communication.

The main channel technologies are listed here:

- **Bus and tag**—A parallel bus connection that allows bursting at a maximum of 4.5 MB (notice mega*bytes*) per second and typically is used by the processors at a speed that ranges between 1 MBps and 3 MBps.
- **ESCON**—Uses a serial connection on fiber-optic cables, which can provide a theoretical maximum of 20 MBps. ESCON on multimode fiber allows distances between 2 and 3 km without repeaters; on single-mode fiber with the extended distance facility (XDF), it allows distances of 20 km unrepeated. ESCON allows units to be connected up to 60 km apart. The typical throughput that is achieved on ESCON links on these distances is around 9 MBps. For more information about ESCON, refer to the IBM redbook Enterprise Systems Connection (ESCON) Implementation Guide at http://www.redbooks.ibm.com/.
- **Fiber connectivity (FICON)**—A transport technology based on the physical and transport layers of Fibre Channel. FICON can support up to 2 Gbps. FICON supports distances of 10 km on single-mode fiber without repeaters and can go up to 100 km with repeaters. FICON's effective rate on 1-Gbps links is around 75 MBps. A detailed description of FICON is beyond the scope of this book; for more information, refer to www-1.ibm.com/servers/eserver/zseries/connectivity/ficon_connectivity.html.

The channel terminology refers to the I/O subsystem inside the mainframe whose main task is to offload I/O operations from the main CPUs. The term *channels* on an ESCON card identifies the ports on the card. In Figure 14-2, you can see the mainframe channels attached to several devices: printers, storage devices, and routers.

Figure 14-2 *Mainframe Channel Attachment with ESCON*

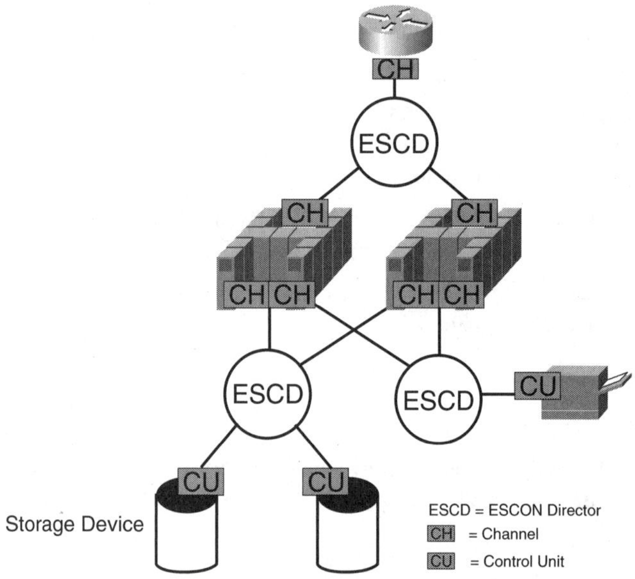

The bus and tag and ESCON technologies support the attachment of the channels to *control units*. The control units operate I/O devices such as terminals, printers, and storage devices. Control units can be separate devices or can be integrated into a single I/O device.

Figure 14-2 shows devices called ESCON directors (ESCD) between the mainframe and the peripheral devices. ESCDs are switches that allow mainframe channels (indicated as CH in the picture) and control units (CU) to be connected. The ESCON director allows multiple hosts (remember that hosts are the mainframes) to share ESCON channels. The back end of Figure 14-2 shows the use of ESCON directors to attach storage devices to mainframes; the front end uses an ESCON director to connect the two mainframes to a router.

Cisco 72*xx*/75xx routers can connect to mainframes with the Channel Interface Processor (CIP) or the Channel Port Adapter (CPA). CIP and CPA are described in the next section.

LAN Attachment Options

The FEP typically provides network connectivity to mainframes (an example is the 3745, shown in Figure 14-3). The 3745 offers SDLC, Token Ring, and Ethernet support, and interfaces with the mainframe with a channel connection. Cluster controllers such as the 3172 can also provide LAN attachment for SNA workstations.

Figure 14-3 *Traditional LAN Attachment Options*

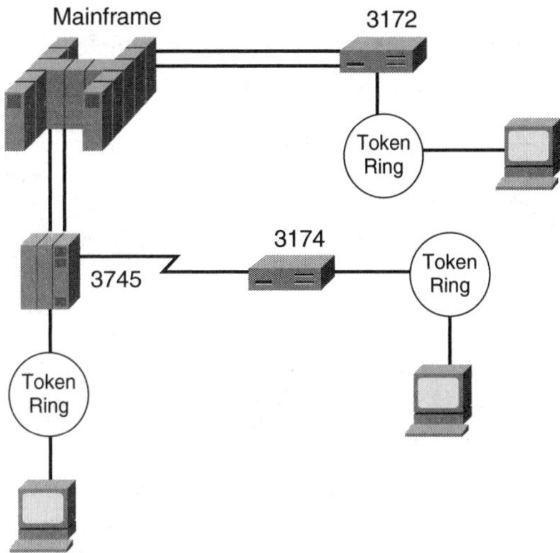

It should be noted that because SNA originally was designed for error-prone networks, the data-link protocols in SNA provide error recovery. This is why SNA on the LAN uses LLC2 (IEEE 802.2).

With the introduction of the external communication adapter (XCA) software in VTAM, it is also possible to have LAN connectivity without a FEP. Previously, the FEP was essential because VTAM would not recognize LAN-attached devices. With the XCA, it is possible to attach 3172s (cluster controllers) directly to the mainframes without FEP (see Figure 14-3).

More recently, it became possible to attach the mainframes to the Cisco 75*xx*/72*xx* routers with the CIP or the CPA. The CIP/CPA connects to the mainframes at the channel level. Like FEPs, CIP/CPAs allow LAN-attached devices to be connected to TCP/IP applications and SNA applications. CIP/CPA can be connected to the mainframe via ESCON.

Communication between the router and the mainframe requires a channel link-layer protocol. Common channel link-layer protocols are Common Link Access for Workstations (CLAW), Link Services Architecture (LSA), and Multipath Channel Plus (MPC+).

In addition to the functions of a FEP, a channel-attached router can perform APPN native routing (see the sections that follow), which allows multiple mainframes to be attached to the same router and for traffic to be routed between them. It can also bridge SNA traffic with DLSw+, and it supports TN3270 servers (read the upcoming section, "TN3270" for more information).

The latest LAN attachment option is open system adapters (OSA). OSAs are basically NICs for mainframes that enable direct attachment from the mainframe to the LAN.

With OSA cards, TCP/IP applications can use IP to connect directly into the mainframe. For example, SNA applications can forward traffic to enterprise extenders, which, in turn, can carry SNA on TCP/IP and connect to the mainframe.

IP Addressing

Typically, inside each mainframe there are several logical partitions that share access to either the channel or the OSA cards. When the mainframe implements a TCP/IP stack, each LPAR has its own IP address, even if all LPARs share the same interface adapters.

Figure 14-4 exemplifies the case in which a mainframe is connected to a channel-attached router and to an Ethernet switch. The LPARs have an IP address for the channel connection and the OSA connection. As an example, LPAR1 has the IP address 10.0.0.1 on the ESCON adapter and 10.0.1.1 on the OSA adapter.

Figure 14-4 *LPARs, Attachment, and Addressing*

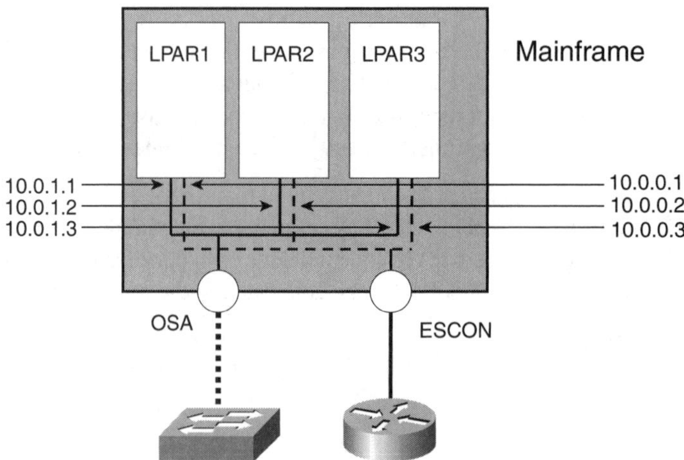

Similar addressing applies to the other LPARs: Each LPAR has two IP addresses, one on the 10.0.0.*x* subnet for the ESCON connection, and one on the 10.0.1.*x* subnet for the OSA connection.

If you want to give an IP address to an LPAR that does not belong to a specific interface, you can configure a static virtual IP address (VIPA). The VIPA then is advertised by the LPAR via routing protocols with a next hop that equals the IP address of the LPAR on the 10.0.0.*x* subnet and the 10.0.1.*x* subnet. If one physical adapter fails, routers can forward traffic destined to the VIPA to the remaining interface. This configuration requires an OSPF server running on the mainframe. For more information about the VIPA, see the section on Sysplex.

IBM Networking

This section provides an overview of the evolution of IBM networking, which helps you understand the need for and use of DLSw+ and SNA switching as the transport mechanism from SNA on a TCP/IP environment.

The networking architecture traditionally used by IBM is SNA. SNA networking can be categorized in two different architectures:

- Subarea SNA
- APPN networking

Subarea SNA

Subarea is the original SNA implementation, in which each operation from each FEP and from each controller is managed by the mainframe. Routing is achieved by configuring static routes called ERs (explicit routes) that map subarea numbers (mainframes and FEPs) to physical links. Failure of a FEP or of a link causes the connections that used that path to be dropped.

Each VTAM controls a specific domain that comprises a number of resources such as terminals and printers. Each SNA network can include multiple domains, in which different mainframes provide support for a separate set of devices. At the same time, however, the VTAM from each mainframe backs up the other VTAMs in case of failure.

SNA addresses are 31 bits long and are divided into a subarea number and an element number. The element number identifies links or devices within a given subarea.

The subarea number is used for routing, whereas the end sessions are established between network addressable units (NAUs). NAUs are categorized as follows:

- Logical units (LUs)
- Physical units (PUs)
- System services control point (SSCP)

The section, "IBM Data Center Components" defined LUs and PUs. However, it did not describe the SSCP. The SSCP is the NAU that controls the resources within a VTAM.

The two main task of the SSCP are as follows:

- To activate and deactivate PUs and LUs
- To initiate and terminate sessions

The following example helps you understand the function of the SSCP and how it interoperates with the other NAUs.

Consider Figure 14-5. When the cluster controllers and terminals are powered on, the mainframe must activate them. The VTAM in the mainframe must activate all the PUs and the LUs. To activate the PU Type 2, VTAM sends a message ACTPU (PU2). This creates an SSCP-PU session. Establishing this session allows the domain software to be loaded and addresses to be assigned. After this session is established, the SSCP can activate the LU that is attached to the PU. For this purpose, it sends a message ACTLU—ACTLU(LU A) in Figure 14-5. The ACTLU message creates an SSCP-LU session.

Figure 14-5 *SSCP Session Establishment*

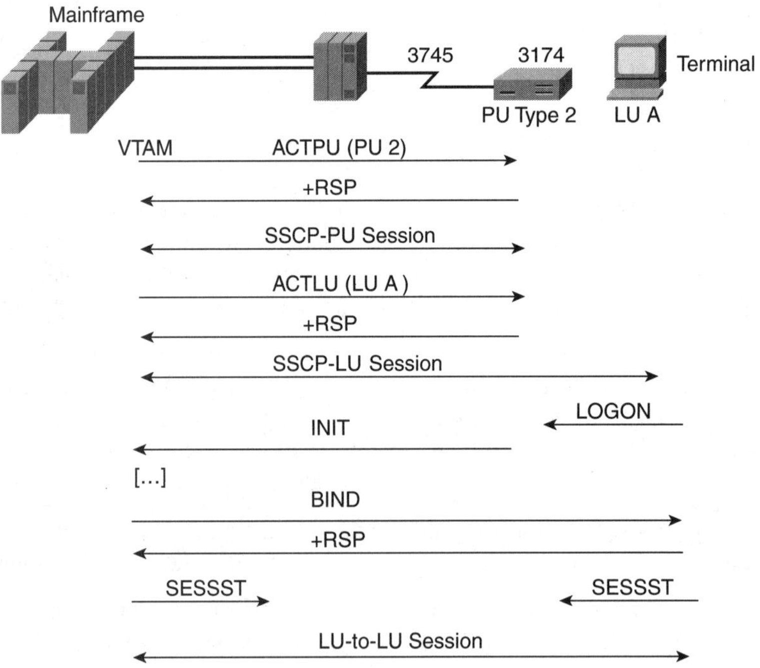

Now imagine that a user from a terminal needs to log onto an application such as the Customer Information Control System (CICS). For the user to work with CICS, an LU-to-LU session must be established. The LOGON request is sent to the controller, which, in turn, originates an INIT request. VTAM locates the application and starts the session (with the BIND): You now have an LU-to-LU session.

SSCP-to-SSCP sessions are established between VTAMs, and they help locate applications that do not belong to the domain owned by the VTAM that received the INIT request.

APPN

The SNA subarea architecture fits a hierarchical network. With the introduction of workstations on LANs, the hierarchical model was insufficient. Workstations needed to communicate without going through a mainframe, which brought the introduction of the Network Basic Input/Output System (NetBIOS) for communication on the LAN. Eventually, requirements for allowing communication across the entire SNA network emerged.

IBM introduced APPN as the SNA solution for peer-to-peer communication. APPN has several benefits over subarea SNA. The main ones are that users can open connections without involving VTAM (peer-to-peer model) and native SNA routing. The migration from subarea SNA to APPN typically is driven by these benefits and by the need to support environments such as the IBM Parallel Sysplex (read the section, "Sysplex and Parallel Sysplex").

In APPN, all the PUs are peers and are called PU Type 2.1. All the LUs are also peers and are categorized as LU Type 6.2. PU Type 2.1 can be either end nodes or network nodes. ENs provide end-user services (you can think of an EN as a workstation); NNs provide the majority of the APPN services (you can think of NNs as routers).

APPN nodes provide *session services:* APPN introduced control points (CP), which are smaller-scale SSCPs (remember that in subarea SNA, the SSCP controls the activations of PUs and LUs, and also establishes the sessions). APPN nodes provide *directory services,* which locate resources in the network. In an APPN network, NNs behave like routers.

The first routing protocol introduced in APPN was Intermediate Session Routing (ISR), which had several limitations, including the fact that an existing session would not recover from the failure of an intermediate node. The next-generation routing protocol was High Performance Routing (HPR). The Rapid Transport Protocol (RTP) is the equivalent of TCP in the HPR architecture. Below the RTP layer is the Automatic Network Routing (ANR) layer, which provides connectionless routing.

The main node types in APPN are the following:

- **Low-entry networking node (LEN) nodes**—LENs were the first PU Type 2.1. They supported some APPN services such as directory services, topology, and routing, but the configurations were mainly static because CP-to-CP capabilities were lacking.

- **ENs**—These are basically workstations. ENs contain LUs and can connect to local ENs or to remote ENs by means of NNs. ENs can locate resources dynamically through the use of CP-to-CP sessions to an NN. ENs cannot route sessions; ENs are the endpoint of sessions. ENs are configured to elect one of the available NNs as the NN server (NNS). CP-to-CP sessions allow the exchange of topology information and registration of LUs.
- **NNs**—NNs implement all the APPN services, such as establishment of LU-LU sessions, routing, and directory search. NNs support CP-to-CP sessions.

SNA over TCP/IP

In today's world, IP is the predominant network protocol, and most enterprises now have an IP backbone. Many companies still have business-critical applications based on SNA. While these applications are being migrated to IP, a scheme needs to be in place to provide access to SNA applications through an IP backbone.

This section is intended to cover only some of these methods and to provide a limited rather than detailed description of these options.

DLSw

Data-link switching is a method of transporting SNA and NetBIOS traffic on top of TCP/IP. DLSw is described in RFC 1795 and RFC 2166. SNA and NetBIOS are non-routable protocols, so when you use them, you must bridge these protocols between remote locations where you have terminals attached to a controller (such as a 3174) and the Data Center where the mainframe resides.

The key challenge that DLSw solves is to provide a service equivalent to LLC2 on top of TCP/IP. For this reason, DLSw is carried on top of TCP. To avoid issues caused by the delay in acknowledging LLC across long distances—possibly over a WAN—DLSw uses local acknowledgments.

Figure 14-6 represents the basic DLSw components on a network. The cluster controller (3174) sends SNA traffic to the communication controller (3745) MAC address. Between the cluster controller and the communication controller, an IP WAN connects the remote offices to the Data Center.

The router at the access receives traffic from the branch cluster controllers destined to the MAC address of the mainframe, encapsulates it into TCP/IP, and sends it to the peer routers. The branch router has several DLSw peers to which it connects over the WAN.

The DLSw router in the distribution layer receives SNA traffic encapsulated in TCP/IP, de-encapsulates it, and forwards it on to the Data Center LAN where the communication controller is located.

Figure 14-6 *Basic DLSw Network*

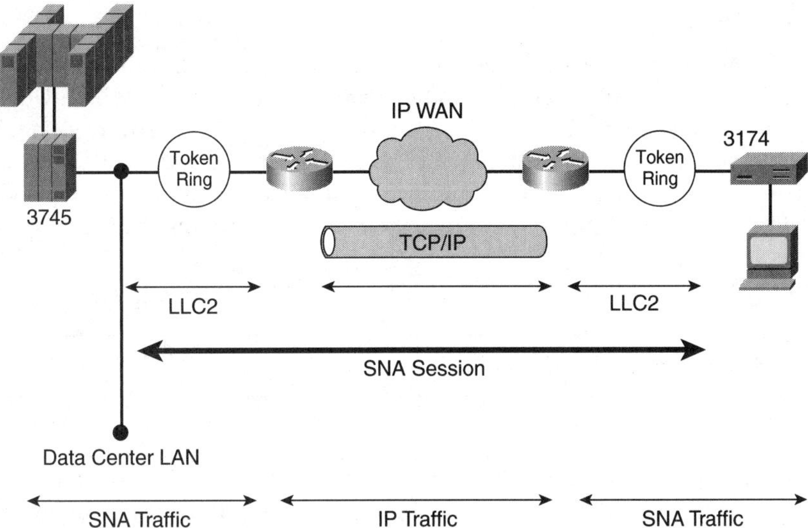

SNAsw

As previously mentioned, customers need to migrate to APPN for reasons that include the need for a routable architecture and support for the parallel Sysplex. Cisco routers operating as a full APPN network node have been widely installed in Data Centers. APPN has proven difficult to scale for a number of reasons, including the need to maintain large topology databases and the amount of control traffic. This is why Cisco introduced SNAsw as the second-generation APPN support, with the main goal of simplicity and scalability.

SNAsw services is a feature set of Cisco routers that supports APPN SNA and is based on the following three APPN technologies:

- Enterprise extenders (EE)
- Branch extenders (called BEX or BXN)
- Dependent LU requester/server (DLUR/DLUS)

SNAsw supports APPN Data Centers by using a combination of these three features: EE, BEX, and DLUR/DLUS. EE allows APPN traffic to be carried on IP, BEX provides for scalability, and DLUR/DLUS makes it possible to support subarea SNA nodes such as the LU Type 2.

Enterprise Extender

IBM implemented the APPN enterprise extender (EE), which is also called HPR over IP, to carry SNA traffic on IP. HRP/IP traffic is carried on top of UDP. With EE, SNA/APPN nodes are mapped to IP addresses. Routing in the network is performed with IP routing protocols such as OSPF. This provides greater integration with the IP infrastructure, compared with DLSw+, which tunnels SNA traffic between two router endpoints. In case of a network failure, the SNAsw EE approach provides nondisruptive rerouting of the SNA session.

NOTE HPR/IP is described in RFC 2353.

Among the main benefits of using EE is that it carries SNA traffic on top of TCP/IP from the remote branch (where you have legacy SNA clients) to the mainframe. Figure 14-7 presents an IP network supporting SNAsw. The terminal in the branch office is connected to a router with SNAsw (as indicated by the support for EE/BXN/DLUR). The mainframes in the Data Center are attached to the IP network with OSA cards.

Figure 14-7 *Enterprise Extender Architecture*

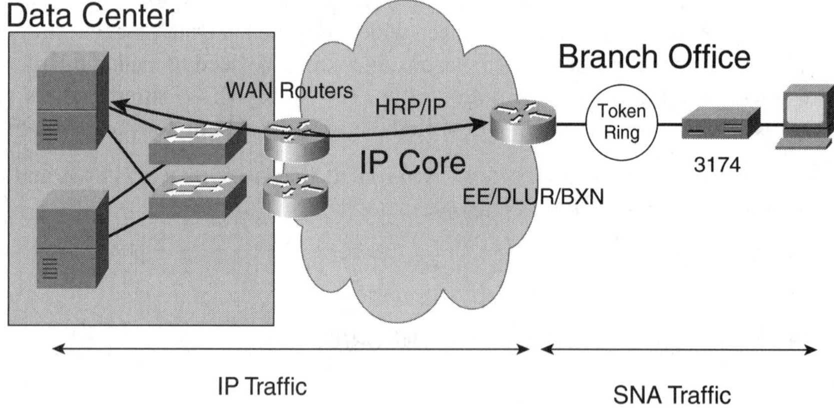

As you can see in Figure 14-7, the endpoints of the RTP session (remember that RTP is the equivalent of TCP in the APPN world) can be an OSA-attached mainframe and a Cisco router supporting EE in the branch office, or a CIP-attached mainframe and a Cisco router supporting EE. EE software runs on both the branch router and the VTAM in the mainframe. Depending on the attachment option, VTAM receives IP traffic either on top of the channel protocol or from the OSA card. If you compare this with DLSw+, there are fewer points of failure because the endpoint of the RTP traffic is the mainframe itself.

Branch Extender

A branch extender node (BEX or BXN) is a node that looks like an end node to the mainframe but looks like an APPN NN to the downstream nodes. The purpose of BXNs is to limit the scope of topology updates and the discovery traffic. The BEX or BXN limits the topology by establishing a boundary, which is an EN, even if nodes are behind this EN. In this architecture, the only real NNs are VTAMs; downstream of the BXN, there are only ENs.

DLUR/DLUS

IBM designed APPN to support independent LUs, such as the LU 6.2. Support for legacy LUs (LU Type 1, LU Type 2, and LU Type 3, which are also called dependent LUs) is achieved through dependent LU requesters and dependent LU servers (DLUR/DLUS). Basically, a DLUR provides SSCP-like services to downstream dependent LUs.

Although the DLUR function is provided by an APPN EN or by an APPN NN, the DLUS function is provided by a VTAM configured as an APPN NN. The request from a dependent LU reaches VTAM through LU 6.2 sessions that have been established between the DLUR and the DLUS.

Figure 14-8 gives an example of how DLUR/DLUS works. A PU with a dependent LU connects to a Cisco router that provides the DLUR function. In Figure 14-8, the PU is Type 2.0, which is a subarea SNA device. The DLUR now knows that it needs to build an SSCP-PU and an SSCP-LU session (Figure 14-8 shows the trace for a subarea SNA session set up). The DLUR sends a REQACTPU (request activate PU) to VTAM; as a result, VTAM sends a response ACTPU (activate PU), which is relayed by the DLUR down to the PU, thus creating the SSCP-PU session. The mainframe then activates the LUs defined under the PU with the ACTLU messages. This, in turn, creates the SSCP-LU session.

Figure 14-8 *DLUR/DLUS*

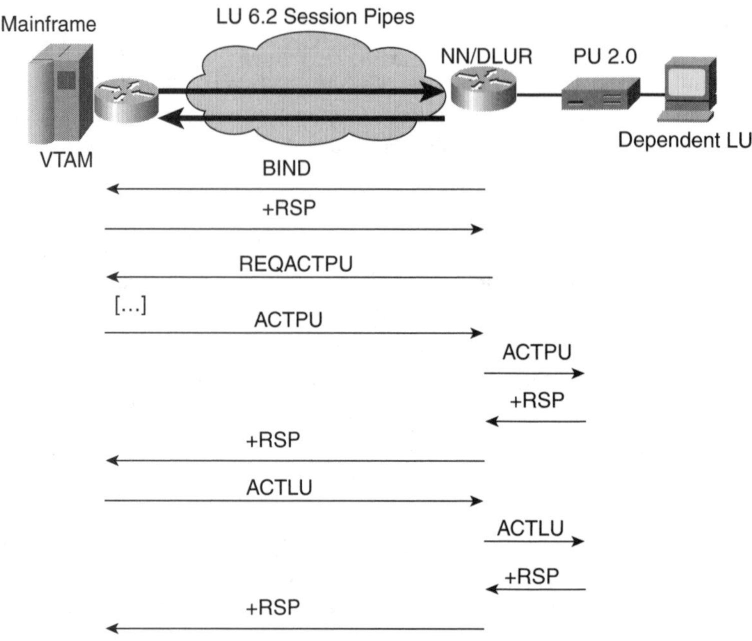

TN3270

In the previous sections, you learned how terminals and SNA workstations can access SNA applications using TCP/IP. This section illustrates some of the methods that allow SNA applications to be accessed from regular PCs.

In a legacy SNA network, terminals provide access to the mainframe applications: The 3270 is a family of SNA display terminals. The section, "IBM Networking" explained how a user logged onto an application running on a host computer. This required two sessions: an SSCP-to-LU session and an LU-to-LU session.

Several mechanisms have been developed to provide mainframe access to IP clients. Most of these mechanisms are based on TN3270 servers. The simplest access method is to Telnet to a computer that implements both a TCP/IP stack and an SNA stack. This computer is a TN3270 server. There is no need for the client computer to implement any specific software; the client must be capable of generating Telnet sessions.

The software running on the TN3270 server translates the characters from the format used on terminals to the ASCII format, and vice versa. It converts clients' characters in SNA data streams. Several standards, such as RFC 1576 and RFC 2355, describe how the TN3270 implementations work.

Typically, a TN3270 server emulates a cluster of PUs and LUs that allow the mainframe to create an SSCP session and an LU-to-LU session. Each LU is assigned to a different Telnet session. The TN3270 implementation assigns LUs randomly to the incoming clients; the TN3270E (defined in RFC 2355) allows LU names to be granted to the sessions so that these sessions are available on multiple connections.

The TN3270 software is categorized in two ways:

- **Inboard**—The TN3270 runs on the mainframe, and the client Telnets to the TCP/IP stack of the mainframe.
- **Outboard**—The TN3270 runs on a separate device that can be directly connected to the mainframe with a channel (as is the case for Cisco routers), or it is connected via SNA, in which case it implements an SNA stack. Clients telnet to the intermediate device connected to the mainframe.

Another way of using the TN3270 emulation software is to integrate it with a web server. End users using a web client access the web server, which, in turn, uses a Telnet session to a TN3270 server to access the mainframe.

A third approach in the integration between mainframes and PCs consists of running a Java applet on the client's computer. The clients would use the browser to connect to a web server, and this browser would download a Java applet onto the client PC. The Java code would communicate directly with a TN3270 server, which provides access to a mainframe.

Sysplex and Parallel Sysplex

IBM introduced Sysplex technology in the 1990s to cluster a number of processors. The Sysplex is a clustering technology to virtualize a number of mainframes or LPARs to simulate a single computer.

If one of the components fails, the system works around the failure and distributes new requests to the remaining ones. In Sysplex, the processors are coupled by using the ESCON channel-to-channel communication.

The *parallel Sysplex* introduced a series of enhancements, especially in terms of data sharing. To make this possible, the parallel Sysplex introduced the coupling facility (CF), which is a processor connected to all the processors in the Sysplex on fiber-optic links called CF channels. Another key component in the architecture (you can see this in Figure 14-9) is the Sysplex timer, which is hardware that synchronizes the processors.

Figure 14-9 gives an example of the Sysplex environment. The LPARs and the mainframes are connected via the ESCON director and exchange traffic with the IP network via the channel-attached router. The shared storage components are attached to ESCON directors and are accessible to the LPARs in the Sysplex (this functionality can be provided via FICON as well).

Figure 14-9 *Sysplex Architecture*

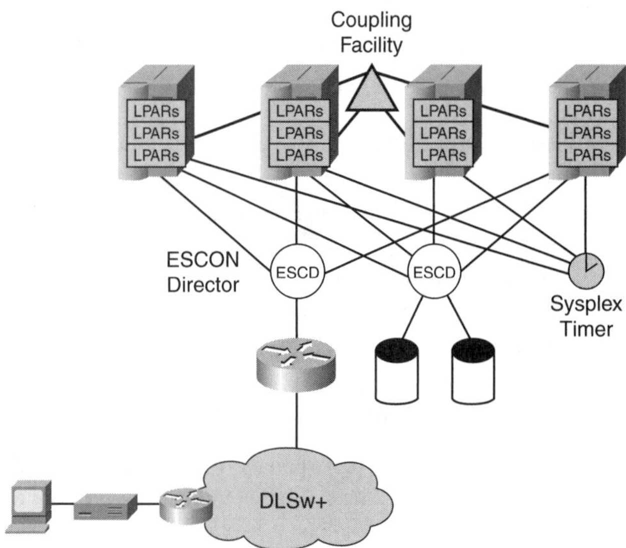

Incoming requests from clients are distributed to the LPARs based on their load. The Workload Manager (WLM) component provides this functionality. In the parallel Sysplex, the WLM runs on the coupling facility.

In terms of IP addressing, you typically configure the Sysplex with static VIPA, dynamic VIPA (DVIPA), and distributed DVIPA. VIPA is categorized as follows:

- **Static VIPA**—An IP address that belongs to the mainframe TCP/IP stack but not to a specific interface adapter. You must run a routing protocol on the mainframe (typically OSPF) to advertise this IP address out of as many interface adapters as needed.
- **DVIPA**—The capability of an LPAR (for example, LPAR2) to take over a VIPA (DVIPA, to be more accurate) from another LPAR (for example, LPAR1) in the event of failure (of LPAR1).

- **Distributed DVIPA** — A "virtual" IP address that identifies one application that is running on multiple machines or multiple LPARs. The Sysplex distributor receives incoming traffic for the distributed DVIPA and sends connections to the available LPARs based on several parameters, including the load information derived from the (WLM).

Figure 14-10 shows a mainframe with three LPARs. Each LPAR runs its own TCP/IP stack and can be accessed through either the ESCON channel or the OSA adapter. Clients can connect to LPAR1 by 10.0.1.1 and to LPAR2 by 10.0.1.2 through the OSA adapter. You can access LPAR1 and LPAR2 also through 10.0.0.1 and 10.0.0.2 through the ESCON channel.

Figure 14-10 *Static VIPA and Dynamic VIPA Concept*

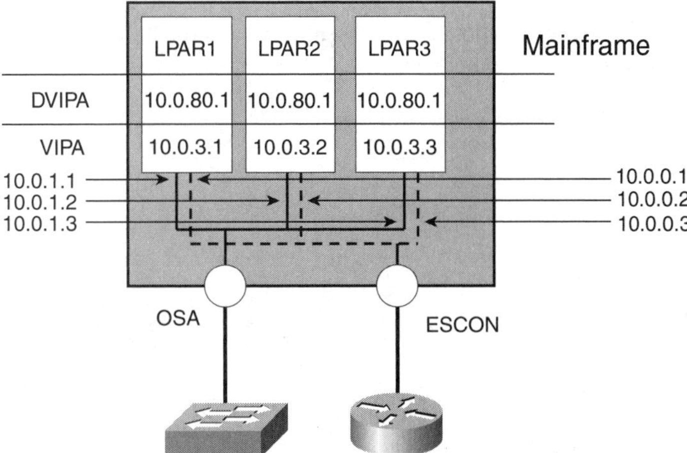

Typically, it is unimportant which interface is used to access the LPAR. For this reason, the concept of static VIPA was introduced. VIPA is equivalent to a loopback address on the LPAR. To access LPAR1, you connect to 10.0.3.1, and the routing devices downstream of the mainframe receive OSPF advertisements for 10.0.3.1 with a next hop equal to 10.0.0.1 and 10.0.1.1. LPAR2 and LPAR3 can be accessed by 10.0.3.2 and 10.0.3.3. The downstream router has two routes for each IP, with each route pointing to either the IP address of the OSA adapter or the IP address of the ESCON channel.

Now imagine that you run the same application on the three LPARs. Although the user mainly connects to LPAR1, in case LPAR1 fails, you want new incoming requests to go to LPAR2. For this to happen, you need to share an IP address called DVIPA between LPAR1 and LPAR2. As you see in Figure 14-10, DVIPA is the same on the three LPARs.

This example can be extended to a number of mainframes coupled with Sysplex. If each system runs a single LPAR, the static VIPA provides high availability for each mainframe in case one interface adapter fails. The DVIPA instead provides high availability for the applications because it is shared across multiple mainframes.

Connections for the same application are distributed to different DVIPAs via the Sysplex Distributor, the equivalent of a load balancer configured for direct server return. The Sysplex Distributor receives incoming requests and, based on the information provided by the WLM, assigns connections to the most suitable LPAR in the Sysplex.

The DVIPAs defined on the master and backup Sysplex Distributors are called distributed DVIPAs. These same IP addresses are defined on the other computers in the Sysplex, but they do not advertise the DVIPA.

Figure 14-11 illustrates the concept by showing that the hidden distributed DVIPA is the loopback address on the target stacks.

Figure 14-11 *Sysplex Distributor in a Sysplex Environment*

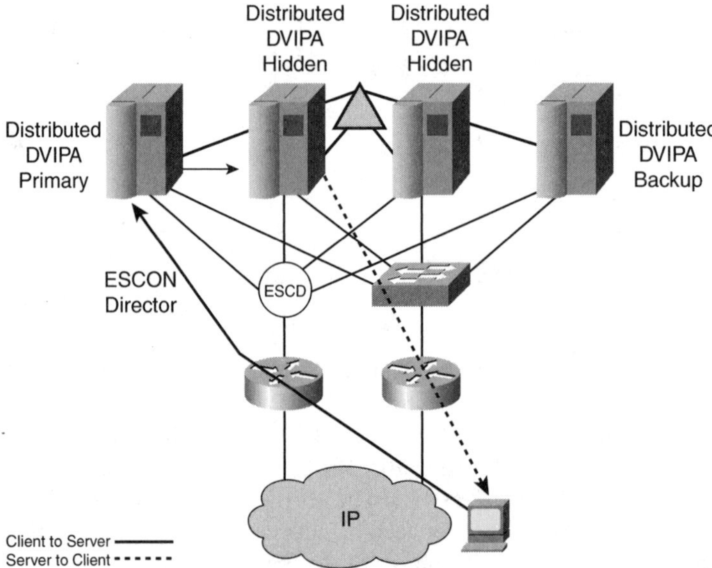

When a client initiates a TCP connection to the DVIPA, the master distributor intercepts it and, based on the information provided by the WLM, forwards it to an LPAR.

Traffic from the target LPAR back to the client takes the shortest path and typically does not go back to the distributor. You can think of this functionality like direct server return.

NOTE For more information about direct server return, see Chapter 16, "Load-Balancing Modes and Predictors."

Alternatively, instead of forwarding packets through multiple mainframe TCP/IP stacks, you can use the Sysplex Distributor to send the load information to a forwarding agent (FA) in 6500 switches or 7*xxx* routers, using multinode load balancing (MNLB).

You can find information about MNLB at wwwin.cisco.com/cmc/cc/so/neso/ibso/ibm/s390/mnibm_wp.htm.

You can also find information about MNLB in the IBM redbook: "Networking with z/OS and Cisco routers: An Interoperability Guide" (see http://www.redbooks.ibm.com).

Geographically Dispersed Parallel Sysplex

Geographically dispersed parallel Sysplex (GDPS) is a solution to provide application availability with mainframes located in different geographical locations (distributed Data Centers). GDPS is used for disaster-recovery and business continuance designs.

GDPS provides the capability to replicate the data stored on ESCON and FICON attached storage at the remote Data Center. Figure 14-12 shows the physical connectivity of the components involved in a Sysplex designed for GDPS. As you can see, the ESCON is extended across Data Centers as well as the channels for the Sysplex timers and the coupling facility. This is possible by connecting the remote sites via dense wavelength division multiplexing (DWDM).

Figure 14-12 *GDPS*

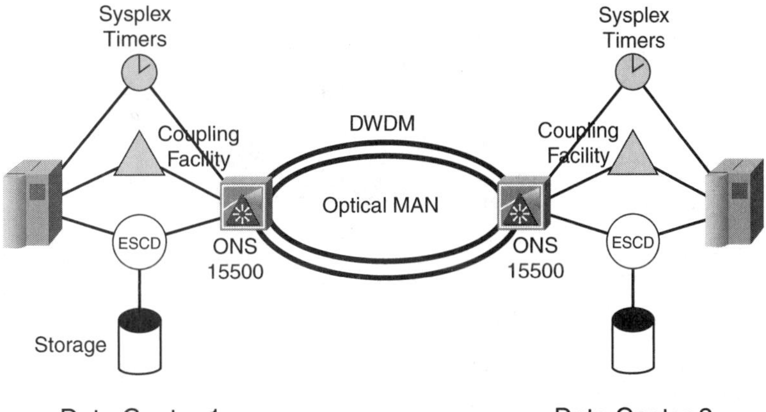

IBM Data Centers Today

This chapter has discussed the evolution of the IBM Data Centers and their networking infrastructure. This section describes a possible topology of an IBM Data Center today.

Figure 14-13 shows an IBM Data Center hosting SNA-based applications as well as IP-based applications. Figure 14-13 shows mainframes clustered together with a parallel Sysplex. These mainframes share a storage system via ESCON or FICON, which, in case a redundant Data Center is present, can be extended geographically for data replication.

The branch routers support SNAsw to allow access to SNA-based applications: These routers operate as EE/BEX/DLUR.

Figure 14-13 *A Possible IBM Data Center of Today*

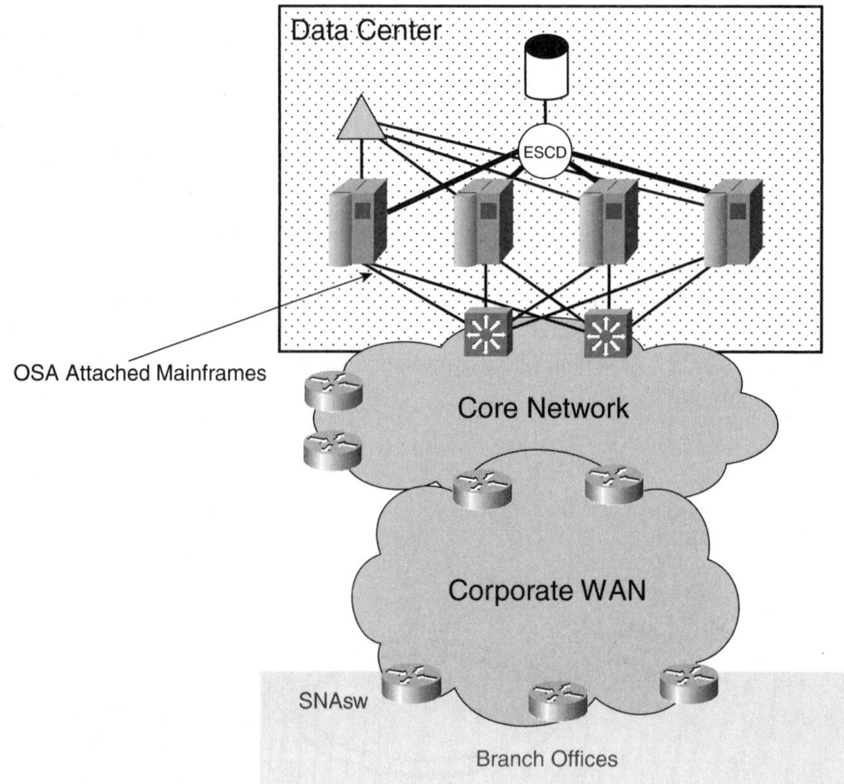

The mainframe front end is attached to the LAN with OSA express cards to a Layer 3 switch (a Catalyst 6500, for example).

Integrating mainframes into the Data Center infrastructure can be different than attaching servers. Servers typically are connected at the access layer. Mainframes typically connect with Layer 3 links to the aggregation layer. Figure 14-14 provides more details.

Figure 14-14 *IBM Attachment to the IP Network*

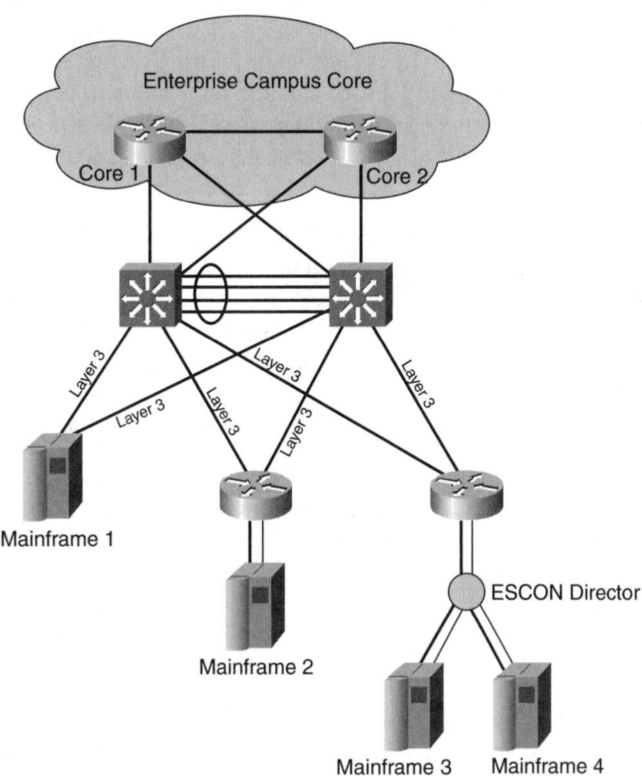

Mainframe 1 is attached to the gigabit port of the aggregation switch (which is a Layer 3 switch) with an OSA card. Each OSA card belongs to a different IP subnet. The links from the mainframe are Layer 3 links. On the Layer 3 switch, you would assign a separate VLAN to each link or assign an IP address to each gigabit port that attaches to the mainframe.

Mainframe 2 has an ESCON connection to a 75*xx*/72*xx* router. The router, in turn, attaches to the aggregation switch with two Layer 3 links. On the switch, you would assign a separate VLAN to each link or assign an IP address to each port that connects to the router. Mainframe 3 and 4 attach to an ESCON director, which, in turn, connects to a 75*xx*/72*xx* router. Connectivity from the router to the aggregation switches is similar to Mainframe 2's router.

Mainframes advertise the VIPAs via OSPF. Mainframes become neighbors with the routers in the aggregation switches. Key considerations in this environment are reducing the number of routes that the mainframe has to maintain and keeping the mainframe from becoming a transit path.

The first concern can be addressed by using OSPF stub areas. Ideally, the mainframe should receive only a default to send traffic to the aggregation routers, which can be achieved by using a totally stubby area. Depending on the existing routing infrastructure, you might need to create a separate OSPF process on the aggregation routers just for the purpose of attaching the mainframes. You also might need to consider the use of redistribution between routing processes. For redistribution best practices, refer to Chapter 13, "Layer 3 Protocol Essentials."

The second important aspect of the design is to make sure that under normal conditions, traffic sent to the mainframe is destined for the mainframe; otherwise, the mainframe performs traffic forwarding like a router. This can be achieved by making sure that the routes provided by the infrastructure always are preferred to the routes advertised by the mainframes. If the design implemented reflects the topology of Figure 14-14, this is achieved by making sure that the aggregation routers always have intra-area routes to the VIPA destinations. In some scenarios, multiple failures might cause the mainframe to become a transit path.

For more information about attaching mainframes to the Cisco 6500 with OSA cards and a recommendation on how to configure OSPF with mainframes, refer to www.ibm.com/servers/eserver/zseries/ networking/pdf/ospf_design.pdf.

Summary

IBM Data Centers are characterized by the use of mainframes. Initially, mainframes ran SNA applications. The SNA architecture defined a master/-slave relationship between mainframes and terminals. This original architecture (called subarea SNA) evolved into APPN, which is a peer-to-peer architecture. Today mainframes support TCP/IP applications as well as SNA applications.

Designing a Data Center with IBM technology typically requires giving access to legacy SNA applications as well as TCP/IP applications. The preferred Cisco solution for transporting SNA on TCP/IP is called SNAsw. With SNAsw, traffic from branch offices is carried on IP and delivered into the mainframe.

Connecting the mainframe to the IP infrastructure can be done with channel-attached routers (CIP/CPA ports on the 72*xx*/75*xx* platforms) or by using OSA Gigabit Ethernet cards installed on the mainframe. The network design must take into consideration the use of the static VIPA, DVIPA, and distributed DVIPA concepts. Typically, the design involves routing protocol considerations, specifically for OSPF.

Mainframes—and, specifically, their LPARs—can be clustered in a parallel Sysplex environment to provide high availability for the applications. In a Sysplex environment, the LPARs share a storage system that is attached to the mainframes via ESCON or FICON directors. For higher availability and disaster recovery, the Sysplex can be extended geographically to a remote Data Center via GDPS.

Part IV

Security and Server Load Balancing

This chapter covers the following topics:

- Symmetric cryptography: Data Encryption Standard (DES), Triple DES (3DES), Advanced Encryption Standard (AES), and Rivest's Ciphers (RC2, RC4, RC5, and RC6)
- Asymmetric cryptography: Rivest, Shamir, and Adleman (RSA); Directory System Agent/Digital Signature Standard (DSA/DSS); and Diffie-Hellman (D-H)
- Hashing algorithms: Message Digest 2 (MD2), MD4, MD5, and Secure Hash Algorithm (SHA)
- Public-key infrastructure (PKI) concepts: standards, key generation, digital certificates, and certificate authorities (CAs)
- PKI deployment, including CA deployment options, chained certificates, enrollment, and revocation
- Transport security, including IP Security (IPSec), Secure Socket Layer (SSL), and Transport Layer Security (TLS)
- Security aspects when designing an SSL solution: which applications can be supported, choice of the ciphersuite, installing 128-bit and 40-bit certificates, and SSL rehandshake
- Security aspects when designing a network that supports IPSec
- Protocols for authentication, including TACACS+, RADIUS, and Kerberos
- Secure management technologies

CHAPTER 15

Security Protocols and Technologies

Chapter 3, "Application Architectures Overview," provided an overview on typical applications that are hosted in enterprise Data Centers. Many of these applications require data transfers over the Internet, which exposes sensitive data to eavesdropping, hijacking, impersonation, or other attacks.

Cryptography is the technology that lets you protect sensitive information from attackers. The information is encoded (encrypted) in a way that can be decoded (decrypted) only by specific individuals or only if some characteristics of the information are preserved (such as its integrity or its origin).

Often, deploying cryptography requires the support of infrastructures to distribute and validate the security parameters used by a given technology. An example of such infrastructure is the authentication, authorization, and accounting (AAA) framework that supports identification of the users of network resources, hosts, or applications. Another example is the PKI that supports the deployment of public-key cryptography.

Before reading this chapter, you should read Chapter 5, "Data Center Security Overview."

Cryptography

Cryptography provides confidentiality, integrity, authentication, antireplay protection, and nonrepudiation. Data Centers use cryptographic services with two primary purposes: maintaining the privacy of the users' data in storage or during transfer over the network and securing the management communications.

As described in Chapter 5, *cryptographic algorithms* (also called ciphers) are categorized based on the key model they use. Algorithms that use the same single key for encryption and decryption are called *symmetric* or *secret-key* algorithms; algorithms that use a private-public-key pair are called *asymmetric* or *public-key* algorithms.

Symmetric algorithms tend to be faster (hundreds of times) than asymmetric algorithms, which is why they are used to provide confidentiality in data transfers. The main challenge with these algorithms is the need to securely exchange the secret key between the entities. You can exchange keys manually or, better, by using asymmetric cryptography.

Asymmetric algorithms are slower than symmetric algorithms, but the key management is easier because one key (the public key) does not need to be protected. Asymmetric algorithms are used for the exchange of symmetric keys previous to the transfer of application data.

Symmetric Cryptography

This section provides basic information about the most popular symmetric algorithms and compares them based on strength and speed. Both parameters change with the evolution of the computer processing power, but the relative strength and speed of the algorithms does not change.

When comparing symmetric algorithms, you can understand the performance if you know whether the cipher is a *block cipher* or *stream cipher*. Stream ciphers tend to be faster than block ciphers.

Block ciphers operate on fixed-length blocks of plaintext; for example, with DES, they are 64-bit chunks.

Stream ciphers operate on smaller plaintext units (typically bit-by-bit). RC4 is a stream cipher. Most of today's e-commerce applications use RC4 for bulk encryption.

DES and its variation 3DES are block ciphers, and they are among the most widely deployed symmetric algorithms. DES is no longer considered secure, which is why financial institutions use 3DES for bulk encryption.

The AES algorithm is a block cipher. It is stronger than 3DES and is being adopted by most secure transport protocols, such as IPSec, SSL, and Secure Shell (SSH).

Digital Encryption Standard (DES)

DES is a symmetric algorithm originally developed by IBM and the National Security Agency (NSA). It was adopted by the U.S. Government as a federal encryption standard in 1977. The DES specifications are available in the Federal Information Processing Standards (FIPS) publication 46-3.

DES uses a fixed key length of 56 bits. The key is actually 64 bits, but 8 bits are used for parity. DES is sometimes used with 40-bit keys (DES with a 40-bit key is used for export grade ciphersuites); this count simply means that 16 bits, out of the 56 bits that form the actual encryption key, are known.

DES is no longer proof against brute-force attacks, which is why the National Institute of Standards and Technology (NIST) has adopted a new algorithm as the U.S. Government encryption standard. This algorithm is referred to as the Advanced Encryption Standard (AES) or Rijndael algorithm.

For illustration purposes, Figure 15-1 shows the high-level operations of DES.

Figure 15-1 *DES Encryption*

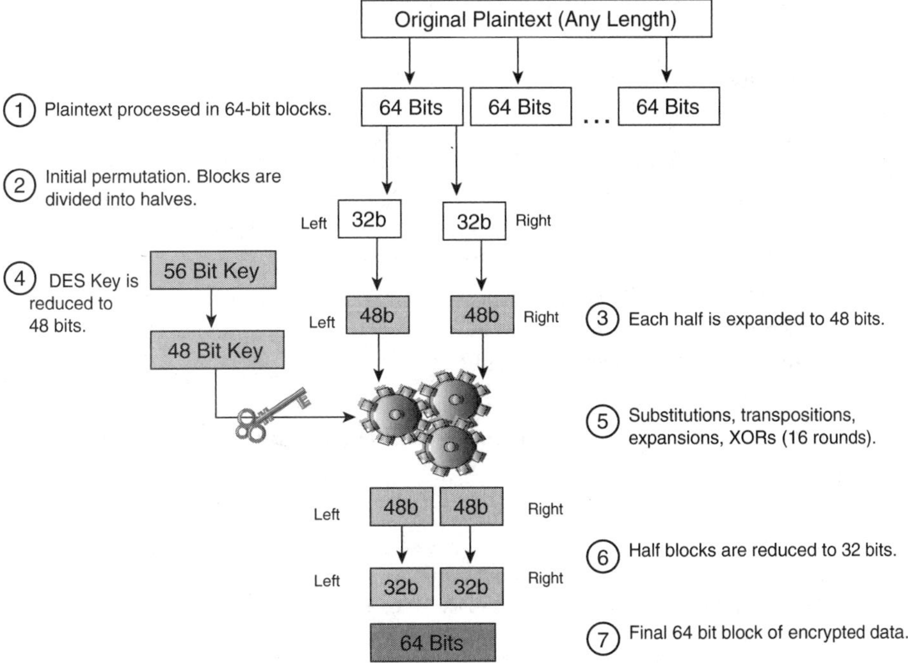

As a block cipher, DES works in fixed-length blocks.

Following are the steps in the operation of DES:

1. The original plaintext is first divided into 64-bit long blocks, which are sequentially processed.
2. Once the plaintext is divided, each resulting block goes throughout an *initial permutation*, which consists of splitting each 64-bit block into two halves, left and right.
3. Each 32-bit half is then expanded to 48 bits using a special expansion algorithm. The resulting data blocks are ready to be handled by the actual encryption process, but before the actual encryption can start, the DES key needs to be formatted.
4. The DES key is 56 bits long and needs to be reduced to the same length as the data blocks (48 bits). A reduction algorithm takes care of that by extracting 48 bits from the original 56 key bits.
5. Next, the 48-bit key material and each data-block half are processed over a series of substitutions, transpositions, and Boolean XOR functions 16 times, until it produces the encrypted version of the half block.

6 A process called *final permutation* reduces each encrypted half block to 32 bits.

7 Finally, each half block is rejoined with its pair to form the resulting 64-bit block of encrypted data.

You use DES in either of the two modes:

- **Electronic code book (ECB)**—ECB encrypts chunks of 64 bits sequentially and independently. There is no dependency between blocks: two identical plaintext blocks encrypted with the same key result in identical cipher blocks. An attacker can identify the repetition of patterns in the plaintext by observing the encrypted data. The cipher block chaining (CBC) mode solves this problem.
- **CBC**—This mode is the most commonly used mode of DES. CBC combines the encryption of each block with the ciphertext from the previous block, which makes it more difficult to decipher than ECB.

DES can also operate in two other modes, which are seldom used: cipher feedback (CFB) and output feedback (OFB). When using these modes, DES operates as a stream cipher.

Triple DES (3DES)

3DES is a variation of DES. Depending on how 3DES is configured, its strength is equivalent to the use of a key of 112 bits (3DES 2-key) or 168 bits (3DES 3-key). Like DES, 3DES is an algorithm approved for use by the U.S. Government.

3DES applies three times the same DES algorithm to the plaintext, using two or three different keys. Figure 15-2 illustrates how 3DES works.

When 3DES uses two keys, the plaintext is initially encrypted with key K1 (Step 1). Then, the resulting ciphertext is decrypted with a different key, K2 (Step 2), which equals to applying another encryption. Finally, the resulting cipher is encrypted again using the same key, K1 (Step 3). In this case, only two keys are used, which provides the strength of a 112-bit key.

When 3DES uses three keys, the encryption process is identical to the one for two keys, but each DES cycle uses a different key, which provides a strength equivalent of a 168-bit key. Because the operations are performed as encryption, decryption and encryption, this version of 3DES is also referred to as 3DES-EDE.

In practice, 3DES is more secure than DES, but because the same DES algorithm is repeated, it is considerably slower.

Figure 15-2 *3DES Encryption*

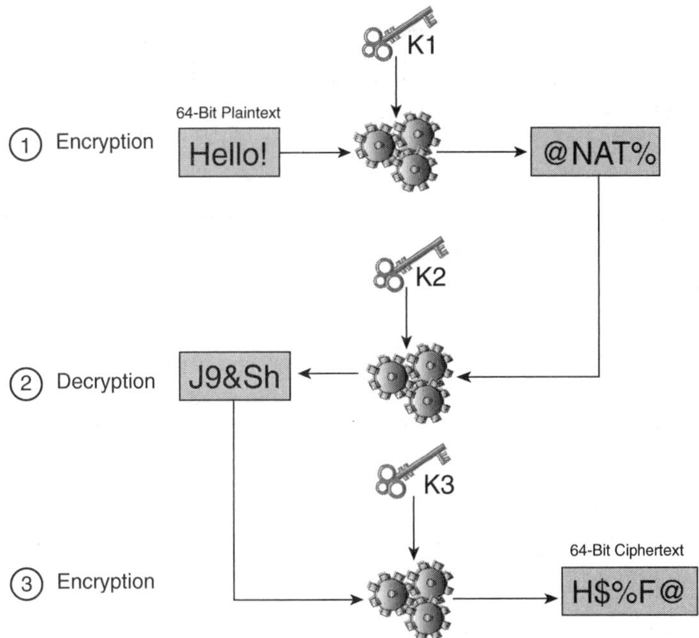

Advanced Encryption Standard (AES)—Rijndael

In 1997, the National Institute of Standards and Technology (NIST) launched the Advanced Encryption Standard (AES) initiative to find an algorithm to replace DES as the standard encryption algorithm used by the U.S. Government to encrypt unclassified information.

In 2000, NIST selected the Rijndael cipher as the AES algorithm. The AES specifications are available in the Federal Information Processing Standards (FIPS) publication 197.

The Rijndael cipher is a block cipher with variable key and block length. The key size can be 128, 192, or 256 bits. To give an idea on the strength of the Rijndael cipher against brute-force attacks, a system capable of recovering a DES key in a second would take approximately 149 thousand-billion years to crack a 128-bit AES key. (Our source is NIST's AES fact sheet at http://csrc.nist.gov/CryptoToolkit/aes/aesfact.html.)

Rivest's Ciphers

Rivest's Ciphers (RC) are a series of cryptographic algorithms designed by Ronald Rivest for RSA Data Security (now RSA Security):

- **RC2**—This block cipher has variable key size, the typical size being 64 bits. RC2 is faster than DES, and it can be more or less secure than DES depending on the key length used. For more information, refer to RFC 2268.
- **RC4**—This stream cipher has byte-oriented operations. RC4 key size can be as big as 2048 bits. RC4 is widely deployed with a key size of 128 bits to secure communications over SSL.
- **RC5**—This block cipher has a variable block length and variable key size (up to 2040 bits).
- **RC6**—This block cipher is based on RC5 and is designed to meet the same requirements as the AES cipher. Like its predecessor, RC6 is a parameterized algorithm where the block length and the key size vary (the upper limit is 2040 bits). The RC6 algorithm is faster than RC5.

For more information on the Rivest's Ciphers, see the RSA Crypto FAQ at http://www.rsasecurity.com/rsalabs.

IDEA

International Data Encryption Algorithm (IDEA) is a block cipher that uses a 128-bit key. IDEA common applications include SSH and Pretty Good Privacy (PGP).

Asymmetric Cryptography

Asymmetric cryptography (also called public-key cryptography) was first introduced by Diffie and Hellman in 1976 and includes a number of encryption schemes that rely on a pair of keys, called the public key and the private key. The public key is published and well known to every entity in the cryptosystem, but the private key is kept secret.

You can use public-key encryption to provide authentication, confidentiality, integrity, antireplay protection, and nonrepudiation.

Public-key encryption is slower than secret-key cryptography, so it is rarely used to provide confidentiality for a large amount of data. The main advantage of public-key cryptography is that the key management is simplified compared to symmetric algorithms.

For the reasons just described, public-key cryptography is used to encrypt small amounts of data, for the exchange of session keys (the secret keys used for bulk encryption), and for digital signatures.

RSA, Diffie-Hellman (DH), and Digital Signature Standard (DSS) are the most used public-key algorithms. You can use RSA for key exchange and for digital signatures. You can use Diffie-Hellman only for key agreement and DSS only for digital signatures.

RSA

RSA is the most popular public-key algorithm. The name RSA carries the first letters of the name of its creators: Ronald Rivest, Adi Shamir, and Leonard Adleman, who designed the algorithm in 1977. RSA is described in the Public Key Cryptography Standards (PKCS) #1 standard.

Typical RSA key lengths are 512 bits, 768 bits, 1024 bits, and 2048 bits. The algorithm used by RSA to generate the public/private key pair does the following:

- Two huge random prime numbers are generated: p and q.
- A number e is chosen that is smaller and prime to (p–1)(q–1). This means that e and (p–1)(q–1) have no common factor except 1.
- The public key is (n,e) with n=pq. The key size in RSA refers to this number, also called the RSA modulus.
- The secret key is (n,d) with d=(1/e)mod[(p–1)(q–1)].

The strength of the algorithm derives from the fact that it is computationally unfeasible to factor large numbers. If somebody could factor n (obtained from the public key) into p and q, it would be possible to calculate d, the secret key. The strength of RSA is that factoring n into p and q is practically unfeasible.

Figure 15-3 provides an example of using RSA between a server and a client; the same concepts apply to the communication between any two hosts (two servers, two clients, two routers, and so forth).

The server needs to send a message to the client in such a way that the client can verify that the message is authentic and coming from the server.

Initially (step 1), an administrator generates the public/private key pair with some tool.

The server sends the pair (n,e) to the client (step 2).

Then, the server converts the plaintext into a number M (which needs to be smaller than n) and encrypts it with the private key . The server calculates S = M^d mod n and sends the resulting encrypted message (step 3).

The client receives the message and decrypts it with the server public key . The client calculates M = S^e mod n to obtain the original message M (step 4). This step authenticates the server because the client would not be able to decrypt the message if it had not been encrypted with the server private key.

Figure 15-3 *Sender Authentication with RSA Encryption*

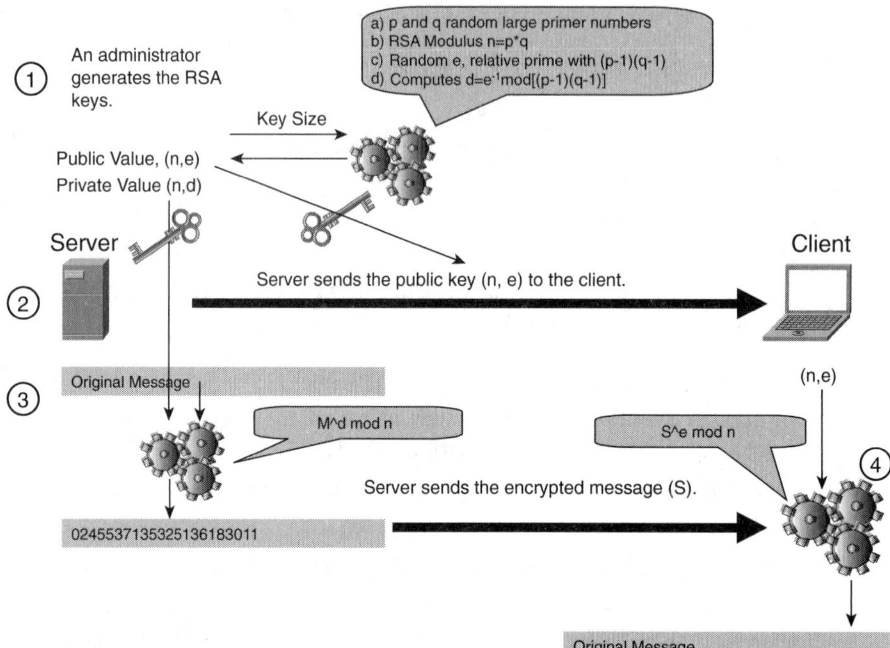

RSA is seldom used to encrypt entire messages. It is instead applied only to a small portion of the data with the purpose of providing authentication. This mode of operation of RSA is typical in digital signatures.

RSA Key Exchange

SSL and TLS have extended the use of RSA to allow the secure exchange of key material, which is referred to as *RSA key exchange*. The key material is a secret key for symmetric encryption, for example.

Suppose that two entities, a client and server (two servers, two clients, two routers. . .), need to negotiate a session key (a shared secret key). If they use the RSA key exchange, the server's public key is sent to the client (Step 1 in Figure 15-4). (This step happens with *digital certificates*.)

The client then sends a session key (for SSL, it would be the premaster-secret key) encrypted with the server's public key (Step 2).

Figure 15-4 *RSA Data Confidentiality Applied to Key Exchange*

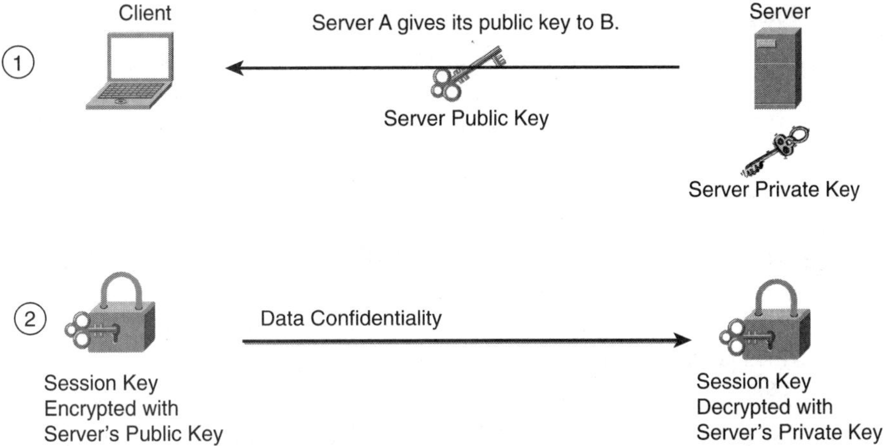

This process provides confidentiality because the session key can be decrypted only by the server that has the private key corresponding to the public used by the client.

It should be apparent by reading the description that the weakness of this mechanism is the delivery of the public key to the client.

In the example in Figure 15-4, a third computer could give its own public key to the client and claim to be the server. This computer would then receive the traffic that was otherwise destined to the server. (This scenario is called a *man-in-the-middle-attack*.)

The client must have a mechanism to verify that the public key really belongs to the server to which it is connecting. The PKI provides the technology to solve this problem.

Digital Signature Standard (DSS)

The DSS, defined in the FIPS publication 186, specifies the algorithms considered appropriate by the U.S. Government for digital signatures. At its publication, DSS specified only the DSA; later, it included the Digital Signature Using Reversible Public Key Cryptography algorithm (an RSA-based algorithm) and the Elliptic Curve Digital Signature Algorithm (ECDSA). Because originally DSS included only the DSA algorithm, it is common to use DSS and DSA as interchangeable terms.

DSA is an algorithm for digital signing only. (It cannot be used for encryption.) Typical DSA key sizes are 512 bits, 768 bits, 1024 bits, and 2048 bits.

The strength of DSA is based on the discrete logarithm problem: it is difficult to calculate the discrete logarithm of large numbers. The Diffie-Hellman algorithm is also based on this problem.

One of the considerations when choosing between DSS/DSA and RSA is that DSA is faster in generating the signature than it is in verifying signatures. For RSA, the opposite is true. RSA is faster in verifying the signature than it is in generating it.

Diffie-Hellman

Diffie-Hellman is a protocol that allows two parties to securely agree on a shared secret key over an insecure medium. Diffie-Hellman is widely deployed as the key exchange method for symmetric encryption algorithms such as DES, 3DES, and IDEA. Diffie-Hellman is described in the standard PKCS #3 and in RFC 2631.

Common Diffie-Hellman key sizes are 768 bits, 1024 bits, and 1536 bits. (They correspond respectively to the Diffie-Hellman groups in IPSec: group 1, group 2, and group 3.)

Figure 15-5 illustrates how the Diffie-Hellman exchange works. In Figure 15-5, a server and a client need to agree on a secret key. The same concepts apply to any two hosts: two servers, two clients, two routers, and so on.

Figure 15-5 *Diffie-Hellman Exchange*

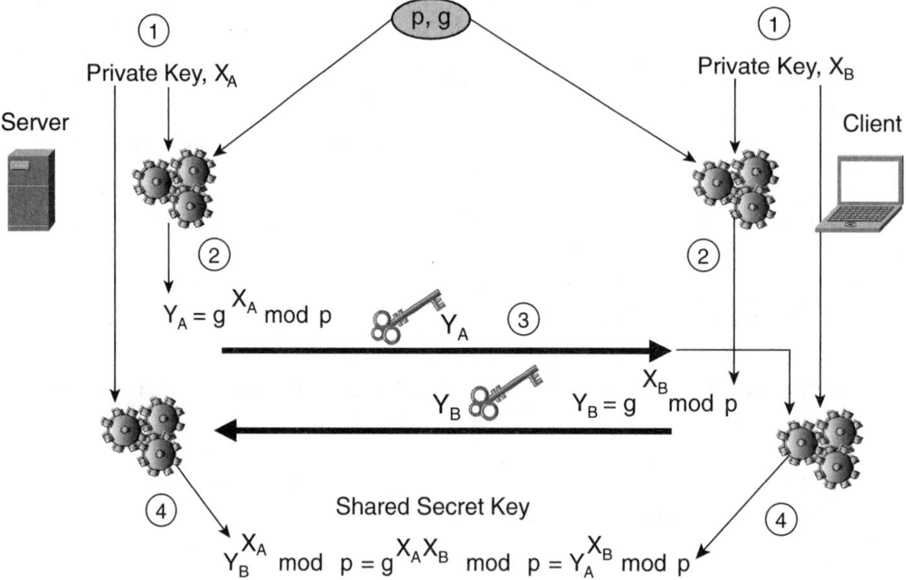

Server and client initially agree on a prime number (p), also called the modulus, and a generator number (g). These numbers are chosen such that p is a large prime number and g is a small number (like 2, 3, 4. . .).

Server and client independently generate a private key (Step 1), the integer X, whose size in bits is less than p. The two hosts generate the corresponding Y public key based on their private keys ($Y=g^X \bmod p$) (Step 2). At this point, both devices have a public and private key pair.

The two hosts exchange their public keys (Step 3). Eventually, each host combines the other host's public key with its own private key to generate the shared secret key (Step 4). For example, host A generates the shared secret key by computing $YB^{XA} \bmod p$, where YB is the other host's public key and XA is host A's private key. The shared key is ($g^{XA}g^{XB} \bmod p$).

The strength of the Diffie-Hellman algorithm is that when g, X, and p satisfy certain mathematical conditions, it is impractical to calculate the shared key ($g^{XA}g^{XB} \bmod p$) by knowing g^{XA} and g^{XB} (This is called the *Diffie-Hellman problem*). It is also unfeasible to calculate the private key X by knowing the public key $Y= g^X \bmod p$ because it is difficult to calculate the logarithm that yields X. (This is known as the *discrete logarithm problem*.)

The strength of the Diffie-Hellman algorithm depends on the size of the large prime numbers used to generate the shared secret key. The key size of Diffie-Hellman refers to the size of the *modulus* p.

Hashing Algorithms

Hashing algorithms provide packet integrity and optionally authentication. Chapter 5 introduced the concepts of cryptographic hash and Hash Message Authentication Code (HMAC). This section provides additional information about the most popular algorithms.

The Message Digests (MD2, MD4, and MD5) and SHA are the most popular hashing algorithms.

MD2, MD4, and MD5

MD2, MD4, and MD5 are hashing algorithms developed by Ronald Rivest to be used in digital-certificate applications. The three algorithms produce a 128-bit digest and their structures are somewhat similar; however, MD2 was optimized for 8-bit machines, whereas MD4 and MD5 were designed for 32-bit machines. MD4 has been proven insecure. MD5 was developed based on MD4 (correcting MD4 design problems), and although it is slightly slower than MD4, it is more secure.

NOTE MD5 is used for many purposes such as routing authentication with Open Shortest Path First (OSPF) or Border Gateway Protocol (BGP). (Two routers are configured with the same secret key and the OSPF/BGP packets carry an MD5 HMAC.) Simple Network Management Protocol (SNMP) and SSL use MD5 for message integrity.

SHA

The Secure Hash Algorithm (SHA) is a message-digest algorithm developed by NIST. You can find information about SHA in FIPS 180-1.

SHA-1 is the second version of the algorithm that fixes an unpublished flaw in SHA. SHA-1 can process messages of less than 2^{64} bits in length and produces a 160-bit message. Because of its larger digest size, SHA-1 is considered to be stronger against brute-force attacks than MD5, but it runs slower.

TIP SHA is also widely used for multiple purposes, including IPSec, SNMP, and SSL/TLS. Generally speaking, you should prefer SHA-1 over MD5 because it is stronger unless performance is critical.

Cipher Summary

Choosing which cipher to enable on a cryptographic module is a tradeoff between performance and security, and obviously, stronger ciphers are typically slower.

Comparing ciphers in terms of strength is difficult because although the key length is an indicator of the strength, different algorithms use the key differently. For example, the strength of RSA 1024 bits can be considered equivalent to the strength of Diffie-Hellman or DSA with a 1024-bit key, but it equates to the strength of a 96-bit key for a symmetric algorithm. (This information is based on the RSA bulletin #13; see the Note.) This strength comparison is an important consideration when choosing ciphersuites in IPSec or SSL because you would want to combine ciphers of similar strength.

NOTE You can find information about the strength comparison between asymmetric algorithms and symmetric algorithms at http://www.rsasecurity.com/rsalabs/bulletins/bulletin13.html.

Table 15-1 lists some of the main cryptographic algorithms in SSL and IPSec for the encryption of the data traffic. The entries in the table are ordered by strength.

A detailed comparison of the strength is out of the scope of this book, so the table just gives some reference points.

Table 15-1 *Cipher Summary*

Cipher	Type	Key Size
DES CBC	Symmetric Block cipher	Fixed key size 56 bits
RC2	Symmetric Block cipher	Up to 1024 bits
RC4	Symmetric Stream cipher	Up to 2048 bits; typically 128 bits
3DES	Symmetric Block cipher	112 bits (2-key) or 168 bits (3-key)
AES (Rijndael)	Symmetric Block cipher	128, 192, or 256 bits

U.S. Government and Cryptography

This section does not intend to be a reference for the legal aspects of cryptography; rather, it is a description of the design aspects of cryptography that can be related to U.S. Government standards or regulations.

NIST and FIPS

NIST is a federal agency that belongs to the U.S. Commerce Department's Technology Administration. The purpose of NIST is to promote standards and technologies to enhance productivity and facilitate trade. You can find more information about NIST mission at http://www.nist.gov/.

NIST operates in various industry sectors, including the computer industry. NIST develops standards for information processing in the form of FIPS: http://www.itl.nist.gov/fipspubs/0-toc.htm.

U.S. Government agencies use cryptography according to the specifications of the FIPS for security.

Examples of FIPS-approved cryptographic algorithms include

- DES (FIPS 46-3)
- DES modes of operations (FIPS 81)
- AES (FIPS 197)
- DSS (FIPS 186-2)
- SHA-1 (FIPS 180-1)

For a reference to the approved algorithms for each cryptographic technology, you can use the cryptographic toolkit at http://csrc.nist.gov/CryptoToolkit/.

When a U.S. Government agency needs to use a cryptographic product, such as an SSL offloader or a virtual private network (VPN) concentrator, it must meet certain requirements in security matters.

FIPS 140-2 specifies the U.S. Government requirements, arranged in different levels of security that cryptographic modules must meet. These requirements include preventing unauthorized operation of a cryptographic module, preventing the disclosure of nonpublic contents of the crypto module such as the plaintext keys, and preventing unauthorized modification of keys and security parameters.

NIST administers a program called Cryptographic Module Validation (CMV), whose purpose is to compare encryption products based on their compliance with FIPS.

FIPS-compliant products must implement specified crypto algorithms:

- DES, 3DES, Skipjack, or AES for symmetric encryption
- DSA, RSA, or ECDSA for digital signatures
- SHA-1, SHA-256, SHA-384, or SHA-512 for hashing

For complete information about the FIPS 140-2 requirements, refer to http://csrc.nist.gov/cryptval/.

NOTE MD5 is not approved by FIPS for hashing. SSL ciphersuites and IPSec transforms that use MD5 are not FIPS compliant. Neither SSLv2 nor SSLv3 are FIPS-accepted protocols, but TLS is. For more information, refer to http://www.corsec.com/copy/pdf/SSL-TLS_whitepaper.pdf.

Export-Grade Ciphers

U.S. regulations dating to the early 1990s mandated that U.S. cryptographic products could be exported only if the key size was "weak":

- The RSA encryption key could not exceed 512 bits.
- The key used for symmetric encryption could not exceed 40 bits.

SSL ciphersuites (or in SSLv2 terminology, cipher kind) that comply with the regulation are SSL_CK_RC4_128_EXPORT40_WITH_MD5 and SSL_CK_RC2_128_CBC_EXPORT40_WITH_MD5, which use RSA 512-bit keys for the key exchange and 40 bits for data traffic.

NOTE Notice that the restriction on RSA keys applied only to encryption, not to authentication (e.g., signing), so you could still use RSA 1024 bits for signing only (http://www.rsasecurity.com/rsalabs/faq/6-4-1.html).

Using RSA 1024-bit keys for signing is what SSL ephemeral RSA does. Read the subsection, "SSL and TLS" under "Transport Security," later in the chapter

---

In December 1998, it became easier to export cryptographic products using 56 bits for data encryption and 1024 bits for the key exchange (Federal Register Citation 63 FR 72156). These changes originated new TLS ciphersuites, specifically the following:

- RSA_EXPORT1024_WITH_DES_CBC_SHA
- RSA_EXPORT1024_WITH_RC4_56_SHA
- DHE_DSS_EXPORT1024_WITH_DES_CBC_SHA
- DHE_DSS_EXPORT1024_WITH_RC4_56_SHA

These ciphersuites are characterized by the use of RSA or DHE 1024-bit keys for the key negotiation and 56 bits for the data transfer.

In January 2000, the U.S. regulation was relaxed (Federal Register Citation 65 FR 2492) and made it possible to export products with any key length to foreign countries after a technical review, as long as the country satisfies certain requirements, such as not being a "terrorist country."

NOTE For more information, refer to the Bureau of Export Administration (BXA): http://www.bxa.doc.gov/.

See also the Federal Register Citations from the Export Administration Regulations (http://w3.access.gpo.gov/bis/): http://w3.access.gpo.gov/bis/fedreg/ear_fedreg98.html#encrypti and http://w3.access.gpo.gov/bis/fedreg/ear_fedreg00.html#65fr2492.

Even if the regulations have changed, the design with cryptographic products must account for the following factors:

- When the regulation prohibited exporting products that used symmetric keys bigger than 40 bits, web browsers were available in two versions: the U.S./Canada version and the export version. The U.S. version would support SSL symmetric encryption with 128-bit key, and the export version would support 40-bit encryption. Even if 128-bit browsers are now available abroad, 40-bit browsers are still in use.
- CAs sell 40-bit SSL certificates and 128-bit SSL certificates.

These factors have implications on the SSL design, which are described in the section "Transport Security."

PKI

The PKI defines services designed to support public-key cryptography. Public-key cryptography is used by protocols such as SSL and IPSec, which are often deployed in Data Centers.

Figure 15-6 illustrates one use of public-key cryptography, digital signatures, and the need for a PKI. The concept of digital signature was introduced in Chapter 5.

In Figure 15-6, host A wants to send a message to B and to attach its digital signature. The purpose of the digital signature is for host B to verify the integrity of the document and the identity of the author of the message:

- The integrity is ensured by the signature, which is the encrypted hash of the document. The receiver performs a hash on the message and compares the result with the attached hash value. If the two values match, the message has not been modified.
- The identity of the author is ensured by decrypting the signature with the sender's public key.

Figure 15-6 shows how the RSA digital signature mechanism works. Host A hashes the message (Step 1); the result is a number (the *fingerprint*). Host A encrypts the number with its private key (Step 2); it is the *signature*. Host A attaches the signature to the message and sends it to host B (Step 3).

Figure 15-6 *RSA Digital Signature*

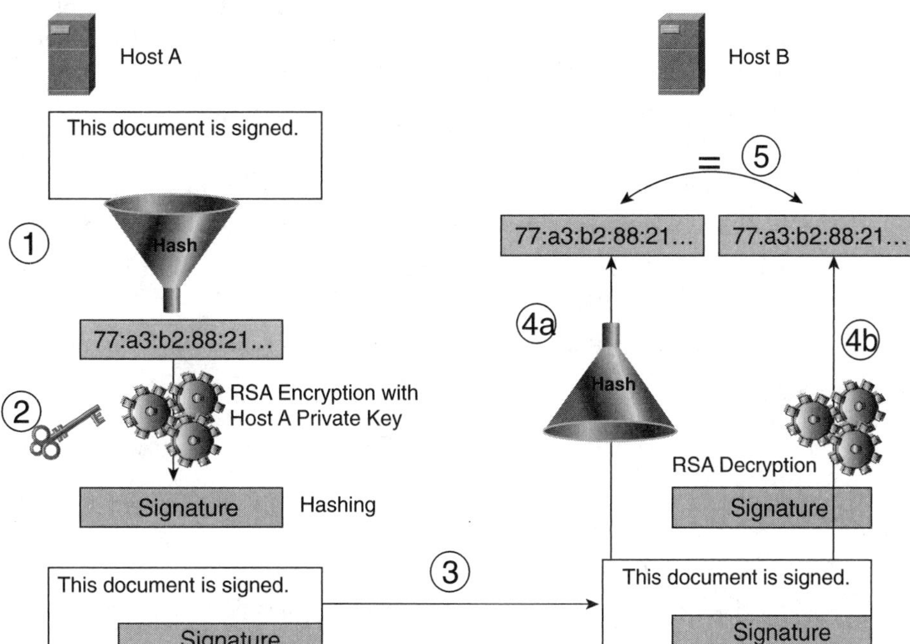

Host B strips the signature from the message, hashes the message (Step 4a), and decrypts the signature with host A's public key (Step 4b). It then compares the results; if they are the same, the message is authentic.

The scheme just described relies on the fact that host B has host A's public key, but nothing prevents an attacker from claiming that he is host A if he manages to provide B with his own public key. The attacker could, at this point, send a message to host B that is considered authentic (a man-in-the-middle attack).

The challenge with public-key cryptography is making sure that the entity delivering the public key is really what it claims to be, which makes key distribution the real issue.

A solution is to entitle a third party, called the CA, to bind public keys with identities by means of digital certificates. Higher-level CAs can in turn bind the identity of a CA to a public key, giving origin to hierarchies of CAs.

The PKI is an infrastructure to solve the problem of public-key distribution; revocation; and, more in general, public-key management.

PKI Standards

PKI standards define algorithms, syntax, formats that relate to the generation of certificates, key exchange, and similar procedures related to public-key cryptography. Among the most widely used formats/standards are

- **International Telecommunication Union Telecommunication Standardization Sector (ITU-T) X.509**—Widely used standard for digital-certificate format and certificate revocation lists (CRLs).
- **Public Key Cryptography Standards**—Standards defined by the RSA laboratories.
- **PKI X.509 (PKIX)**—The Internet Engineering Task Force (IETF) PKIX is a working group that promotes the use of X.509-based PKIs.

X.509v3 describes the format of digital certificates. It is widely used for SSL and IPSec.

PKCS defines standards such as

- **PKCS #1**—"RSA Cryptography Standard"
- **PKCS #3**—"Diffie-Hellman Key Agreement Standard"
- **PKCS #6**—"Extended-Certificate Syntax Standard"
- **PKCS #7**—"Cryptographic Message Syntax Standard"
- **PKCS #8**—"Private-Key Information Syntax Standard"
- **PKCS #10**—"Certification Request Syntax Standard"
- **PKCS #12**—"Personal Information Exchange Syntax Standard"

NOTE For more information about PKCS standards, refer to http://www.rsasecurity.com/rsalabs/pkcs/index.html.

Among the standards issued by PKIX are

- **RFC 3280**—"Internet X.509 Public Key Infrastructure Certificate and CRL Profile"
- **RFC 2587**—"Internet X.509 Public Key Infrastructure LDAPv2 Schema"
- **RFC 2560**—"Internet X.509 Public Key Infrastructure Online Certificate Status Protocol—OCSP"
- **RFC 2585**—"Operational Protocols: FTP and HTTP"

RFC 2587 describes the use of Lightweight Directory Access Protocol Version 2 (LDAPv2) for certificate and Certificate Revocation List (CRL) storage. RFC 2585 defines how to use FTP and HTTP for the transport of PKI operations. The OCSP is a protocol that allows clients to check online whether a particular certificate has been revoked.

TIP Compared to the use of CRLs, OCSP provides a more efficient mechanism for certificate status verification, where clients can query for individual certificates instead of having to download entire revocation lists, which takes longer.

An important PKI protocol for network cryptographic devices is Cisco's Simple Certificate Enrollment Protocol (SCEP). You use SCEP for certificate enrollment and revocation. SCEP uses PKCS #7 as the digital envelop for certificates and certificate requests and PKCS #10 as the certificate request syntax. SCEP is supported by a number of vendors of CA software. SCEP traffic is carried on top of HTTP.

For more information about SCEP, refer to http://www.cisco.com/warp/public/cc/pd/sqsw/tech/scep_wp.htm.

Digital Certificates

A digital certificate could be defined as the electronic counterpart to a driver license that you can use to electronically prove the identity of a subject, such as a server or a router.

To understand the need for digital certificates, keep in mind the problem that PKI addresses: the distribution of public keys. There needs to be a way for a host that receives a public key from another host to verify the identity of the sender. This verification is possible if the sender delivers the public key with a digital certificate.

The digital certificate is a digitally signed data structure that contains the subject's public key along with information about the subject, such as its Domain Name System (DNS) name. For the certificate to be valid, it needs to be signed by a third-party entity called the CA, which is trusted by both communicating devices.

Digital certificates have multiple applications:

- **Server and client authentication in SSL**—An example is in e-commerce applications. When shopping online, before entering the credit-card information, you want to confirm that the server indeed belongs to the online store. This confirmation is possible by verifying the SSL certificate sent by the server.
- **Router authentication in IPSec implementations that use a CA**—Every router is configured with a digital certificate signed by a CA that is trusted by all the routers. When creating an IPSec session, the router sends its certificate (with its public key) to the peer router.
- **IEEE 802.1x used with the Extensible Authentication Protocol-Transport Layer Security protocol (EAP-TLS, RFC 2716)**—IEEE 802.1x is used to assign the enterprise users to certain VLANs based on their identity. The clients are configured

with a digital certificate, which is used by an authentication server such as the CiscoSecure Access Control Server (ACS) to verify the user credentials. The server responds to the switch with the policy to apply for that user.

This section examines the format of a digital certificate through the process of generating the private/public key pair and a certificate signing request (CSR).

Generating Certificates

When building a PKI, you need to generate certificates for servers, routers, and clients. These devices use certificates to deliver their public key to the entity that they need to communicate with.

Notice that when deploying SSL or IPSec solutions, you need to generate private/public key pairs for asymmetric encryption. You can use the key pair for a long time, such as one year.

The generation of *session keys* (that is, secret keys) does not require any configuration. For example, SSL generates the symmetric key at each SSL connection. The lifetime of symmetric keys is short.

This section assumes that you need to generate keys for an SSL device, either for a server or for an SSL offloading device. The first step is to generate the server private key. Example 15-1 shows the use of OpenSSL (http://www.openssl.org/) to generate a 1024-bit RSA private key.

Example 15-1 *Generating the Server Key with OpenSSL*

```
OpenSSL> genrsa -des3 -out server.key 1024
```

NOTE Notice that the **-des3** option just means that the key is encrypted with 3DES before being saved into the **server.key** file.

Once you generate the server key, you need to generate a public key and a certificate to store the public key. You can obtain the certificate by submitting a CSR to a CA. Example 15-2 shows how to generate a Privacy Enhanced Mail (PEM)–encoded PKCS #10 CSR.

Example 15-2 *Generating a Certificate Signing Request with OpenSSL*

```
OpenSSL> req -new -key server.key -out server.csr
Using configuration from D:\openssl\openssl.cnf
Enter PEM pass phrase:
[. . .]
Country Name (2 letter code) [US]:
State or Province Name (full name) [Some-State]:California
Locality Name (eg, city) []:San Jose
```

Example 15-2 *Generating a Certificate Signing Request with OpenSSL (Continued)*

```
Organization Name (eg, company) [Internet Widgits Pty Ltd]:Cisco Systems
Organizational Unit Name (eg, section) []:ESE
Common Name (eg, YOUR name) []:www.cisco.com
Email Address []:admin@cisco.com
```

PEM (RFC 1422) is one of the possible "wrappers" to store keys and certificates on a file. PEM is a base-64 encoding mechanism, and the file extension is .pem. You can use PEM for both CSRs and signed certificates.

The CSR includes additional information besides the public key. This information identifies the entity (the server) with the name of the organization, the common name (DNS name), and so forth. CAs turn this information into a digital certificate. (Read the section, "CAs" for more information.)

Digital Certificate Format

Different standards define the format of digital certificates. X.509v3 is the most widely deployed, and it is adopted by a number of protocols, including SSL, Internet Key Exchange (IKE) for IPSec, and Secure Multipurpose Internet Mail Extensions (S/MIME).

A digital certificate contains the subject's name and public key, a serial number, an expiration date, the identity of the CA that issued the certificate, and the actual encryption algorithm used to sign the certificate.

Example 15-3 shows the content of the digital certificate obtained by signing the CSR from Example 15-2.

Example 15-3 *X.509v3 Certificate*

```
OpenSSL> x509 -noout -text -in server.crt
Certificate:
    Data:
        Version: 3 (0x2)
        Serial Number: 4 (0x4)
        Signature Algorithm: md5WithRSAEncryption
        Issuer: C=US, ST=California, L=San Jose, O=Example , OU=CA Center,
  CN=www.
example.com/Email=admin@example.com
        Validity
           Not Before: May  4 00:51:41 2003 GMT
           Not After : May  3 00:51:41 2004 GMT
       Subject: C=US, ST=California, O=Example , OU=ESE, CN=www.example.com/
  Email=a
dmin@example.com
```

continues

Example 15-3 *X.509v3 Certificate (Continued)*

```
12        Subject Public Key Info:
13             Public Key Algorithm: rsaEncryption
14             RSA Public Key: (1024 bit)
15                 Modulus (1024 bit):
16                     00:d8:d1:cb:64:9d:01:c8:2d:cc:4c:37:b9:d6:2c:
17                     90:b0:56:39:71:75:4e:aa:3c:63:a7:13:1f:97:84:
18                     db:ad:de:3c:1b:61:73:43:31:db:a0:77:15:9d:a9:
19                     4d:1e:3d:5d:98:b1:61:3d:94:90:08:f4:1d:57:8f:
20                     5a:f4:f7:81:58:bf:37:0c:ea:8c:b1:5c:df:3e:c3:
21                     8e:1f:6d:7a:fe:f2:85:dd:9f:4b:72:ba:07:db:33:
22                     ea:20:c6:26:c5:cc:29:57:90:d5:38:5c:d6:47:4b:
23                     45:06:bf:23:4e:f5:14:ae:68:fc:2e:b1:0e:56:a9:
24                     05:e1:63:9b:8e:b4:19:52:a1
25                 Exponent: 65537 (0x10001)
26         X509v3 extensions:
27             X509v3 Basic Constraints:
28                 CA:FALSE
29             Netscape Comment:
30                 OpenSSL Generated Certificate
31             X509v3 Subject Key Identifier:
32                 48:AA:55:BB:DC:F2:8D:0E:EE:BB:E6:25:51:2B:F2:00:DF:6F:41:43
33             X509v3 Authority Key Identifier:
34                 keyid:65:4B:AE:FD:CC:DD:02:DE:61:96:23:DD:C7:88:B6:FF:42:22:51:0
9
35               DirName:/C=US/ST=California/L=San Jose/O=Example /OU=CA Center/CN=
   www.example.com/Email=admin@example.com
36                 serial:00

37     Signature Algorithm: md5WithRSAEncryption
38         56:58:c5:b8:44:e0:08:5d:10:b1:6a:71:dc:a8:07:c2:27:9f:
39         52:54:ff:5e:0d:3c:60:32:1f:78:18:49:d1:b3:4b:1e:f6:dc:
40         2c:fa:69:32:6b:69:4e:65:ad:e5:11:1e:4a:27:85:f4:ae:2b:
41         a0:89:5a:c0:34:87:82:74:ec:9e:73:6d:b2:4d:ec:80:b2:ce:
42         e0:ea:6d:df:ee:cb:0e:d0:03:ed:62:ab:e6:f5:aa:fb:9e:6d:
43         d1:c3:64:f8:2f:7f:f7:72:ab:c3:76:3e:21:e8:f1:a1:e2:c9:
44         09:f8:8c:62:de:a5:b9:b4:c2:35:ff:ba:bc:e5:6c:2b:21:bf:
45         08:37
```

Notice that this certificate is a self-signed certificate, which means that the certificate has been signed by the same organization that owns it: the *issuer name* is Example (line 7) and the *subject* of the certificate is also Example (line 11).

Line 7 shows the information about the issuer of the certificate (the CA).

Line 11 shows the information about the subject (i.e., the entity that requested the certificate), including the domain name of the server that uses the certificate indicated in the field called *common name (CN)*—www.example.com, in this case.

Lines 12-25 includes the subject's public-key information: the key type, which is an RSA public key (indicated in Line 14); the key length (indicated by the modulus value in line 15); and the key itself (lines 16-24).

The validity fields (line 8) specify the period of validity of the certificate and the presence of the RSA public key (line 15).

Line 26 shows the certificate extensions. The CA uses certificate extensions to indicate the use of a certificate. CA:FALSE (on line 28) indicates that this is not a CA certificate but either a server certificate or a client certificate.

NOTE For more information about certificate extensions, refer to http://www.mozilla.org/projects/security/pki/nss/tech-notes/tn3.html.

Line 37 shows the signature of the digital certificate. In this example, the certificate has been signed with an MD5 hash encrypted with RSA. The issuer of the certificate (line 7) is the entity that signed it. This entity is what is called a CA.

Certificate Authorities

A CA is a trusted system that issues and maintains digital certificates. In the driver-license analogy, the CA would be equivalent to the organization that issues and controls the driver licenses, the Department of Motor Vehicles in the United States.

Examples of CAs are organizations such as Verisign, Entrust, Thawte, Equifax, Netscape, and Genuity. A CA can also simply be a server whose signature services can be requested via protocols such as the SCEP.

Public-key encryption calls for the use of CAs together with digital certificates to solve the problem of public-key distribution. The previous sections explained why. The following section explains how two subjects can exchange public keys and verify the identity of the sender in presence of a CA.

Role of CAs During the Key Exchange

Before two hosts can communicate, they need to exchange their public keys, which they send with certificates. Figure 15-7 shows a client and a server willing to communicate with SSL.

Figure 15-7 *Certificate Validation*

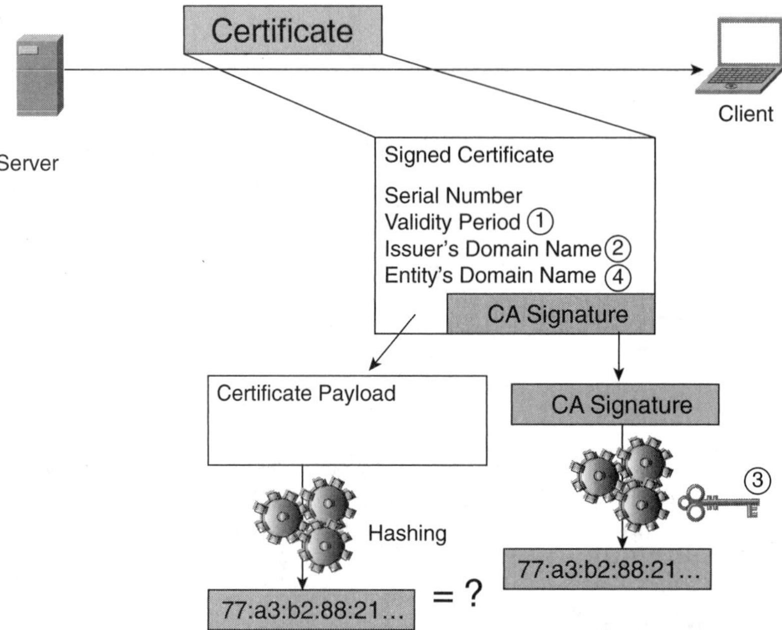

The server sends a certificate signed by a CA to the client's web browser. The web browser comes preinstalled with a list of CAs and their respective public keys; these CAs are the trusted CAs. (See Figure 15-8 in the next section, "CA Certificates.")

The client receives the certificate and decomposes it into the payload and the signature. Following is how the browser verifies the certificate:

1 The validity period is checked against the current date. If the current date is out of the validity period, the authentication fails and the process stops here.

2 The client checks whether the signing CA is a trusted CA. If it does not have a copy of the CA certificate, it requests one. In the example, the browser is pre-installed with the CA certificates of Verisign, E-certify, and Digital Signature Trust.

3 The browser uses the CA public key to validate the entity's certificate. It hashes the payload of the certificate, which in Figure 15-7 produces the string 77:a3:b2:88:21. . ., and compares the resulting fingerprint with the decrypted version of the signature. It calculates the hash by using the CA's public key contained in the CA certificate (from the browser's list of trusted CAs).

4 The browser verifies whether the domain name in the entity's certificate matches the domain name of the entity. It does so by performing a reverse DNS lookup on the IP address of the entity.

A certificate is considered valid after passing all the described steps.

TIP To verify which CA certificates are trusted by default in your browser, with Netscape 7.0 you can look in **Edit > Preferences > Privacy & Security > Certificates** under Manage Certificates on the tab Authorities. With Internet Explorer (IE) 6.0, you can check **Tools > Internet Options** under Certificates on the tab Content.

As the example shows, the validation of a certificate implies the possession of the public key of the signing CA, which is contained in what is called a *CA certificate*. Without the public key of the CA, you cannot validate a signature.

CA Certificates

A CA certificate is a certificate that carries the public key of a CA. The CA certificate can be signed by another CA or by the CA itself (in which case it is a self-signed certificate, similar to the one in Example 15-3 with the difference that line 28 would include CA:TRUE).

Most PCs and web browsers come with a pre-installed list of CA certificates. Browsers also have the capability to request a CA certificate if one is not pre-installed. You typically install a CA certificate to a browser by sending the Distinguished Encoding Rule (DER)–encoded certificate in an HTTP packet with the MIME type set to **"application/x-x509-ca-cert"**. (For more information about MIME types, refer to Chapter 8, "HTTP and Related Concepts.")

Figure 15-8 shows some of the CA certificates pre-installed in Windows 2000. These are some of the CAs that the PC trusts. You can add CAs to the configuration.

Certificates can be chained to create a hierarchy. A *chained CA certificate* is a hierarchy of CA certificates. At the top of the hierarchy is the root CA, a self-signed CA certificate. The subordinate CAs' certificates are signed by the upper-level CAs. Figure 15-9 visualizes the concept. The enterprise CA (2) is a certificate signed by the root CA (1). The enterprise CA in turn signs an SSL certificate (3) to be installed on servers.

A company willing to host an enterprise CA for its SSL clients might consider using certificates chained to a well-known CA. This chain makes its clients trust the enterprise CA itself and its signed certificates.

Figure 15-8 *Default Trusted CAs in Windows 2000*

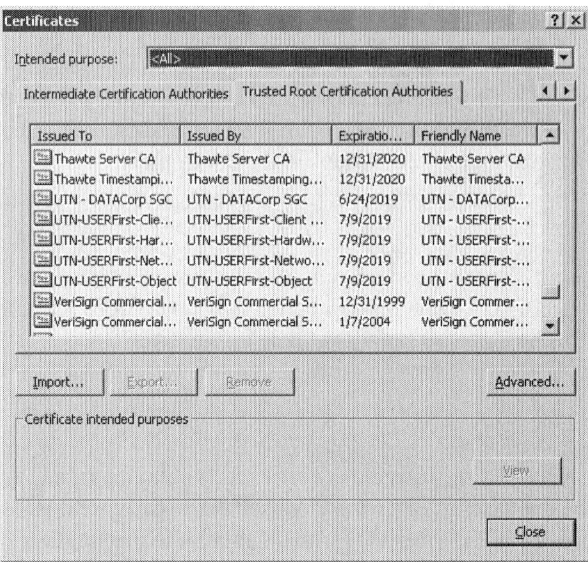

Using chained certificates makes the configuration of Web servers or SSL offloaders slightly more complex, but from the point of view of the browser on the client, the fact that a hierarchy of certificates exists is not noticeable.

Figure 15-9 *Chained Certificates*

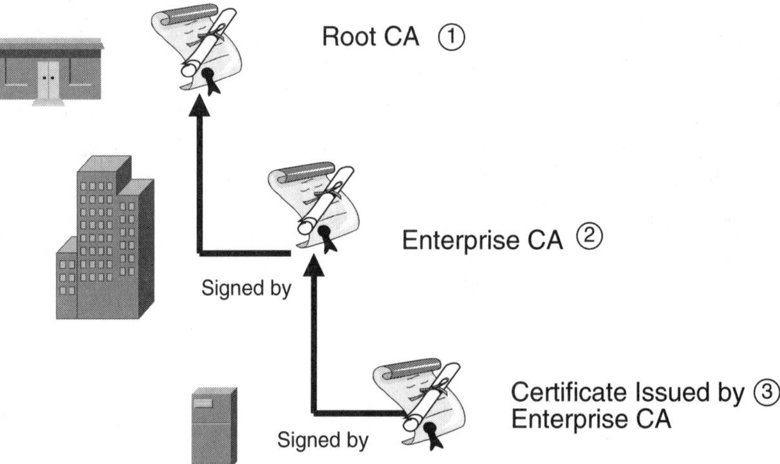

Suppose that a browser receives a certificate signed by an enterprise CA, like certificate 3 in Figure 15-9.

1. The browser verifies the validity period of the server certificate (certificate 3 in Figure 15-9).
2. The browser verifies the issuer's name, which is the enterprise name, and it is not a trusted CA.
3. The browser verifies the certificate signature based on the issuer's public key.
4. The browser then verifies the validity period of the enterprise CA certificate (certificate 2 in Figure 15-9).
5. The browser verifies the issuer's name of the enterprise CA certificate, which in this case is a trusted CA, the root CA (certificate 1 in Figure 15-9).
6. The browser verifies the enterprise CA certificate signature based on the root CA.

If the certificate chain leads to a trusted CA, no warning is displayed to the client. Chained certificates are also used for other purposes, more specifically Server Gated Cryptography (SGC) and step-up certificates. (Read the section "SSL and TLS" in this chapter for more information.)

CA Deployment Options

Several options are available in implementing the CA function in a PKI design:

- **Using a commercial CA**—You can buy certificates from an external CA organization such as Verisign, Entrust, or Thawte.
- **Using an internal CA server**—You can also build an in-house CA by buying CA server software from vendors such as Verisign, Entrust, Microsoft, and Netscape. The network devices that need certificates have access to the CA server by using protocols such as SCEP.
- **Using an outsourced CA server**—You can outsource the PKI by asking CAs to host and manage a CA server for your company. In this case, the network devices get access to the CA server over the Internet, which requires each device in the enterprise network to have access to the external network.

Your choice among these options depends on the purpose of the digital certificate. If the purpose is to build an e-commerce site, you want to use a well-known CA that is trusted by most Internet clients, such as a commercial CA.

If the purpose of the certificate is to build IPSec VPNs or SSL access to internal applications, then you would probably use an enterprise CA server.

Enrollment with an External CA

The process by which an entity obtains its certificate signed by a CA is called *enrollment*. The enrollment consists of these steps:

1. A client generates a private/public key pair.
2. The client composes a Certificate Signing Request (CSR) and sends it to a CA.
3. The CA signs the certificate and sends it back to the client.

The enrollment process is different depending on which entity provides the CA function. To have a certificate signed by an external CA, you need to submit a CSR to one of the commercial CAs—Verisign, Entrust, Microsoft, Netscape, and so on. You can do so through their websites, and then they send you the signed certificate.

You then must install the certificate on the web server, the SSL offloader, or the device that requires this certificate. When performing this operation, it is important to consider the certificate format accepted by the device and the certificate format used by the CA.

CSRs are typically submitted in PEM-encoded PKCS #10 format (with the file extension .pem).

The certificate returned by the CA can use several formats such as Distinguished Encoding Rule (DER) (with the file extension .crt or .cer), which is a binary format based on the Abstract Syntax Notation (ASN.1) or the already mentioned PEM. A commonly used format is PKCS #7 (with the file extension .p7b, but it could also be DER or PEM encoded). PKCS #7 allows CAs to return chained certificates.

Upon receiving the certificate from the CA, you must install it on the web server or SSL offloader. These devices in turn support the import of certificates in various formats, such as DER, PEM, PKCS #7, PKCS #12 (with the file extension .p12 or .pfx), and more.

Enrollment with an Enterprise CA and Use of the SCEP

When you use an in-house CA, a typical configuration would require the administrator of the network device, such as an SSL module, to generate the private and public key pairs on the device and submit the certification request to the CA via SCEP.

Example 15-4 shows how an SSL module requiring a certificate enrolls via SCEP. The trust-point configuration specifies the CA server (http://exampleCA.example.com) as well as the key pair (called MYSITEPAIR in the example) and the information to fill out the X.509v3 fields of the certificate.

Example 15-4 *Enrollment with SCEP on the SSL Module*

```
ssl-off(config)# crypto ca trustpoint CASERVER
ssl-off(ca-trustpoint)# rsakeypair MYSITEPAIR
ssl-off(ca-trustpoint)# enrollment url http://exampleCA.example.com
ssl-off(ca-trustpoint)# subject-name C=US; ST=California; L=San Jose;
  O=Example; OU=Lab; CN=host1.example.com
```

If the CA server does not support SCEP, you would have to copy the certificate with a Trivial File Transfer Protocol (TFTP) transfer, FTP, etc., and the certificate file would be in a format such as PKCS #12 (extension .p12).

A similar configuration procedure applies for client software executing on a PC. Suppose that you are using an IPSec VPN client. The software includes a Certificate Manager, which allows you to generate new certificates and to enroll via the network by using SCEP.

Revocation

CAs revoke certificates if they are compromised before their expiration, if the data contained in the certificate is no longer valid, or when there is a contract termination with an entity.

The CA maintains a CRL, which any party can check before establishing a communication.

Entities can poll the CRL repository by using Lightweight Directory Access Protocol (LDAP) (or SCEP) to receive the current CRL. The CRL list is timestamped and signed by the CA. As an alternative to CRLs, CAs can use PKIX Online Certificate Status Protocol (OCSP).

An example of an application using both protocols is Netscape 7.0. In **Edit > Preferences > Privacy & Security > Validation**, you can configure the options for the CRLs and for OCSP.

The presence of CRLs in the *CRL manager* depends on whether the certificate included a CRL. If a CA specifies a CRL, Netscape shows a CRL rule. You can specify how often Netscape should retrieve the list from each specific CA.

NOTE OCSP is becoming more popular than CRLs because it provides an online mechanism that allows for a faster certificate-status validation.

Transport Security

This section covers the protocols used to secure the transport of data. These protocols provide data confidentiality for specific applications:

- **Secure transactions**—E-commerce, financial, and business-to-business applications require part or all of the transaction to be encrypted with SSL.
- **VPNs**—VPNs were introduced in Chapter 5. They create a secure communication channel from which Internet users can safely access the applications hosted in the Data Center. VPNs can be based on IPSec or on SSL.
- **Management**—The protocols provide for the secure management of network devices and servers.

SSL and TLS

SSL is a protocol developed by Netscape that has been adopted as the de facto mechanism to secure communications on the Internet. SSL security services provide message integrity, data encryption, server authentication, and optional client-side authentication. TLS is an IETF standard (RFC 2246) based on SSL Version 3.

SSL is currently used by online stores to secure transactions and by financial institutions to provide Internet-accessible tools that help you manage accounts, transfer funds, and invest. E-mail clients also use SSL to access enterprise e-mail servers from the Internet.

Deploying SSL in a Data Center requires understanding two main aspects of this technology:

- The use of SSL to secure HTTP transactions and consequently how to optimize a Data Center that supports secure web applications. This topic was addressed in Chapter 9.
- The choice of the ciphers, which certificates to use, and how to build a PKI. This topic is the subject of this section.

As a network designer, you do not need to read this section if the SSL deployment involves load-balancing SSL-enabled web servers; Chapter 9 suffices. If the SSL deployment involves using SSL offloaders, then you need to understand the aspects of SSL described in this section:

- Which applications can be secured
- Choosing the ciphersuites
- Installing certificates

These considerations are necessary when configuring an SSL offloader.

SSLv2, SSLv3, and TLS 1.0

There are three main SSL versions in use today, and they differ in terms of the ciphers supported and how certain SSL mechanisms operate. The list shows the main differences:

- **SSLv2**—The SSL session ID is encrypted (read Chapter 9 for more information), it does not support chained certificates, the hash mechanism is MD5, and it uses RSA for the key exchange.
- **SSLv3**—This version addresses some security flaws in SSLv2 and adds support for SHA as the hash mechanism and Diffie-Hellman and DSS for the key exchange. The session ID in SSLv3 is carried in cleartext.
- **TLS 1.0**—There are few differences between SSLv3 and TLS 1.0. The most important difference is that SSLv2 and SSLV3 use the MD5 algorithm when generating the secret keys, but TLS 1.0 uses a combination of SHA and MD5. MD5 is not a FIPS-approved algorithm, which makes SSLv2 and SSLv3 not FIPS compliant. TLS is compatible with FIPS requirements. For more information, refer to http://www.corsec.com/copy/pdf/SSL-TLS_whitepaper.pdf.

SSL and the TCP/IP Layers

The SSL protocol operates between the transport layer, which needs to be connection oriented, and the application layer of the TCP/IP protocol stack. (For more information about the TCP/IP layers, refer to Chapter 7, "IP, TCP, and UDP.") Virtually any application that uses TCP/IP as the transport protocol can use the services provided by SSL and create SSL connections by using SSL sockets. (For more information about sockets, refer to Chapter 2, "Server Architecture Overview.") Notice that the SSL socket returns the certificate to the application because it is up to the application to verify it. What this means is that applications using SSL need to be SSL-aware.

TIP A popular application toolkit to develop SSL application is OpenSSL. For more information, refer to http://www.openssl.org.

Figure 15-10 shows how SSL relates to the TCP/IP layers.

Figure 15-10 *SSL and TCP/IP Layers*

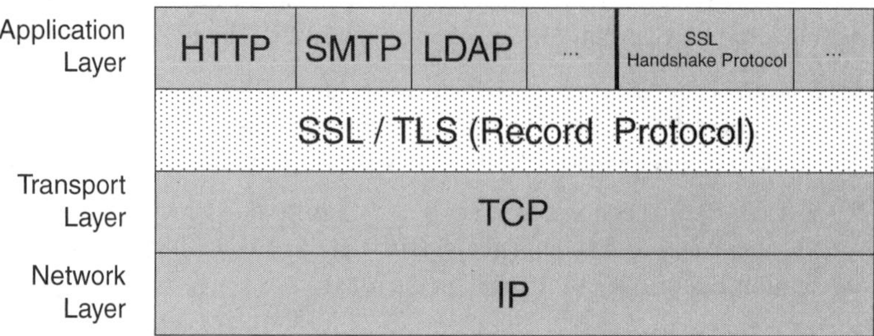

As you can see, SSL provides services between the TCP/IP application layer and the transport layer. The following list provides examples of protocols that use SSL and their associated Layer 4 port when traffic is encrypted and when it is cleartext:

- HTTPS (port 443)—HTTP (port 80)
- SSMTP (port 465)—Simple Mail Transfer Protocol (SMTP) (port 25)
- TELNETS (port 992)—Telnet (port 23)
- SPOP3 (port 995)—Post Office Protocol 3 (POP3) (110)
- SNNTP (port 563)—Network News Transfer Protocol (NNTP) (port 119)
- SIMAP (port 993)—Internet Message Access Protocol (IMAP) (port 143)
- SLDAP (port 636)—LDAP (port 389)
- FTPS (port 990)—FTP (port 21)
- FTPS Data (port 989)—FTP Data (port 20)

TIP When configuring an SSL offloading device, you use the listed ports to intercept SSL-encrypted traffic. For example, if you had to intercept SPOP3 on a Cisco SSL Service Module (SSLSM), you could configure the following:

```
ssl-off(config-ssl-proxy)#virtual ipaddr virtual-ip-address protocol tcp
  port 995
ssl-off(config-ssl-proxy)#server ipaddr server-ip-address protocol tcp
  port 110
```

The virtual configuration defines the IP address used by the client and the port 995, which identifies SPOP3. The server configuration identifies the POP server IP address and the port used by the cleartext traffic. The SSL offloader receives the encrypted traffic, decrypts it, and sends it to the e-mail server in cleartext.

The server response goes through the SSL offloader to be encrypted and sent to the client on SPOP3.

The encryption functionality in SSL is provided by what is called the Record Protocol (see Figure 15-10). Other protocols within SSL, such as the SSL handshake protocol (described in Chapter 9), also use the services provided by the SSL Record Protocol.

The SSL Record Protocol fragments the application data into blocks, compresses them, applies the hashing, encrypts the data, and passes it to the TCP layer.

SSL Certificates

SSL certificates can be one of three types: CA certificates, server certificates, and client certificates. Chapter 9 describes the use of each certificate type in the context of an SSL transaction. This section focuses on SSL server certificates, which are the ones that you normally need to generate or buy for a Data Center deployment.

SSL certificates can be one of two different types: RSA certificates and DSA (also called DSS) certificates. RSA certificates contain an RSA public key and are signed with the RSA algorithm. DSA certificates contain a DSA public key and are signed with the DSA algorithm.

NOTE You can find more information on how to generate DSA certificates with OpenSSL at http://www.openssl.org/docs/apps/CA.pl.html#DSA_CERTIFICATES.

The SSL module on the Cisco CSS11500, which is a load balancer and an SSL offloader, also lets you generate DSA certificates from the command-line interface of the load balancer itself.

SSL ciphersuites are enabled based on the certificate type. Installing an RSA certificate on an SSL device (a server or an SSL offloader) allows the use of the RSA ciphersuites (e.g. RSA_WITH_RC4_128_MD5). Installing a DSA certificate on an SSL device allows the use of the DSS ciphersuites (such as DHE_DSS_WITH_3DES_EDE_CBC_SHA). DSA certificates are seldom used.

CAs sell RSA certificates either as 40-bit certificates or as 128-bit certificates. There are historic reasons behind the existence of these two certificate types. In brief, the two certificate types provide the following:

- **40-bit certificates**—These certificates allow negotiating strong encryption with domestic browsers. If a server uses 40-bit certificates, 40-bit browsers (export browsers developed prior to January 2000) cannot negotiate strong encryption with it. Newer 128-bit browsers sold abroad support strong encryption just like domestic browsers.

- **128-bit certificates**—Also called *global server certificates*, these certificates allow strong encryption with domestic browsers and make it possible to negotiate strong authentication with 40-bit export browsers.

The section, "SGC and Step-Up" provides additional information about the use of the two types of certificates.

SSL certificates follow the X.509v3 format, which was described in the section "Digital Certificate Format," so they include the following information:

- Version number
- Serial number
- Period of validity
- Issuer
- Subject public key
- Subject common name
- Signature of the issuing authority

When web browsers receive a certificate from a server, they verify the information in these fields and they prompt the user if, for example, the certificate has expired or the common name (DNS name) does not match the domain specified in the requested URL.

The common name can carry the fully qualified domain name (FQDN) of a server (for example, www.example.com), or it can have a wildcard (for example, *.example.com). A single wildcard certificate allows securing multiple domains, which is necessary, for example, in name-based virtual hosting. (Read Chapter 2 for more information.)

Even though wildcard certificates are necessary in some cases, it can be argued that their use defeats the principles of Internet trust because a single certificate represents many host machines. In fact, CAs not only recommend that you use a FQDN as the CN, but even when you need to use the same FQDN on multiple servers (for example, load-balanced servers), CAs recommend that you generate separate public/private key pairs and associated certificates for each machine. For more information, refer to the white paper by Verisign, "Building an E-Commerce Trust Infrastructure," available at http://www.verisign.com.au/guide/buildecommerce/.

SGC and Step-Up

As mentioned in the section "SSL Certificates," there are two types of SSL certificates: 40 bits and 128 bits. This section explains the implications on the SSL traffic on the network.

Remember that, prior to December 1998, the U.S. export regulations limited the key size for symmetric encryption to 40 bits for exported products and the key size for RSA encryption to 512 bits. The export version of web browsers (40-bit browsers) would negotiate the SSL session with ciphersuites such as RSA_EXPORT_WITH_RC4_40_MD5 or

RSA_EXPORT_WITH_DES40_CBC_SHA. These ciphersuites were, of course, too weak to address the security requirements of many organizations.

Two mechanisms were built to address the need for stronger cryptography with export-version clients: ephemeral RSA and SGC or Step-Up.

Ephemeral RSA allows a server to install a strong RSA certificate (1024 bits). When the server communicates with domestic clients, it uses the 1024-bit key. When it communicates with an export client, it generates a temporary 512-bit RSA key and signs it with the strong key. The client then uses the temporary 512-bit key to send the premaster secret. This mechanism avoids the risk associated with the use of a permanent RSA 512-bit key, which could be easily broken. The weakness of the 40-bit symmetric key is addressed by the SSL rehandshake mechanism to limit the lifetime of the key. A rehandshake is an SSL handshake transported as encrypted SSL data traffic, so it allows generating a new session key.

NOTE Notice that with ephemeral RSA, the client needs to verify the 1024-bit RSA signature. This signature was allowed by the export regulation because the restriction of 512 bits applied to the RSA algorithm used for encryption, not for signing.

Microsoft SGC and Netscape Step-Up are similar technologies that were made possible by an exception to the U.S. export regulation. The exception allowed eligible institutions to use strong cryptography with an export version client for the purpose of financial transactions.

The idea behind SGC and Step-Up is to add a field in certificates which indicates that the server can perform strong encryption with an export-version client. It requires that the export-version client supports strong encryption but does not use it unless it finds the SGC/Step-Up field in the server certificate. Support for SGC/Step-Up was introduced in Microsoft Internet Explorer 4.0 and Netscape Communicator 4.0, respectively.

In the presence of SGC/Step-Up certificates, the client sends a client hello to the server with an export ciphersuite. The server sends its certificate that the client recognizes as capable of performing SGC/Step-Up. The client then performs a rehandshake to negotiate a strong cipher, or it simply does not complete the SSL connection but restarts the session negotiation by sending a client hello with strong ciphers.

Today, the U.S. regulations have changed, allowing the export of software that implements strong cryptography to most countries. Despite this change, the widespread use of old export-version browsers makes SGC/Step-Up still necessary for companies that want to support strong encryption with non-U.S. clients. SGC/Step-Up certificates are also called 128-bit certificates by CAs.

The implications of the use of SGC and Step-Up are significant for the network design. From a load-balancing design standpoint, the presence of export-grade browsers makes SSL session persistence more difficult to achieve. (Read Chapter 9, "SSL and TLS" and Chapter 19, "Persistence Mechanisms on Load Balancers," for more information.) The reason is that even if these browsers support SSLv3, the rehandshake hides the new session ID. This point is an additional reason for performing SSL offloading on the network because performance optimization by means of SSL persistence would not work.

Choosing SSL Ciphersuites

In SSL, you cannot choose independently the ciphers used for key exchange/authentication and data encryption. Ciphers are combined in predefined ciphersuites. A ciphersuite consists of three fields:

- Key exchange/authentication algorithm (RSA and Diffie-Hellman, for example)
- Encryption algorithm (DES, 3DES, IDEA, RC2, or RC4, for example)
- Message-digest algorithm (MD2, MD4, MD5, SHA, or SHA-1, for example)

Which ciphersuite an SSL session uses is the result of the configuration on the server and the ciphersuites supported by the client. The design of an SSL solution needs to account for the following factors:

- **Security**—Some ciphers are stronger than others, which comes with a performance penalty on the servers. The choice is typically between medium and fast ciphers, strong and slow ciphers.
- **Performance**—SSL has a performance impact on the servers, and there are methods to optimize it, as explained in Chapter 9 as well as Chapter 19.
- **SSL versions**—Not all the clients support the latest version (TLS) or even SSLv3.
- **Export versions of web browsers**—Export-version browsers might support 40-bit encryption and 128-bit encryption if the servers use SGC/Step-Up certificates.
- **FIPS**—Some companies or organizations must comply with FIPS.

According to the RSA security tech note "TWIRL and RSA Key Size," the minimum key size that you should use for symmetric encryption, given today's available processing power, is 80 bits. The minimum key size that you should use for RSA encryption is 1024 bits. You can find the tech note at http://www.rsasecurity.com/rsalabs/technotes/twirl.html.

Based on this report, 1024-bit RSA keys, RC4 (128 bits), and 3DES-EDE (168 bits), as of today, are strong enough ciphers. The design might need to provide enough security for 40-bit browsers, in which case you can deploy two possible solutions: *global certificates* (assuming that the clients support SGC/Step-Up) or a periodical refresh of the session key by means of the rehandshake.

Based on the preceding points and on the description of the cryptographic algorithms, a typical e-commerce design will typically use RSA_RC4_128_MD5 with 1024-bit RSA keys and 128-bit RC4 keys. This ciphersuite provides backward compatibility with SSLv2, and it is a good tradeoff between performance and security.

Financial institutions are more likely to use the ciphersuite RSA_3DES_CBC_SHA because it is stronger. This ciphersuite works with 1024-bit (or even 2048-bit) RSA keys and 3DES keys and uses SHA, which is stronger than MD5. You should disable SSLv2: the RSA_3DES_CBC_SHA ciphersuite is not compatible with SSLv2, and SSLv2 is affected by well-known security flaws.

The main drawback to using 3DES is performance; on most processors, 3DES is 10 or more times slower than RC4. Hardware SSL offloading is often necessary for this deployment.

Companies or institutions installing FIPS 140-2–compliant devices will use TLS only and FIPS approved ciphers such as RSA_3DES_SHA or RSA_DES_SHA.

Internal-only applications protected by SSL can use the same ciphers as e-commerce applications. It is common for a company to create its own CA, which requires generating a company CA certificate, which is typically chained with a well-known CA certificate. If the certificates used by the applications are not signed with the company CA, it is normally acceptable to buy 40-bit certificates (that is, certificates without SGC/Step-Up, which is not needed in this case).

IPSec

IPSec, defined in RFC 2401, is a framework of open standards for ensuring secure communications over public networks such as the Internet. IPSec ensures confidentiality, integrity, authentication, and antireplay protection. IPSec in a Data Center has the following uses:

- In the extranet, it builds tunnels with business partners to share business-to-business applications. (See part **a** of Figure 15-11.)
- It is used for secure management to provide encrypted administrative sessions between the network administrator and the network devices or hosts. (See part **b** of Figure 15-11.)

These two examples summarize the two main deployment types of IPSec—*tunnel mode* and *transport mode*. In transport mode, only the payload of the packet is encrypted, but in tunnel mode, both payload and headers are encrypted.

Part **a** of Figure 15-11 shows an example of IPSec used in tunnel mode. The routers create an encrypted tunnel that carries traffic flowing *through* them. The IPSec datagrams traveling on the Internet carry the source and destination IP addresses of the routers. The IP addresses of the origin and destination hosts are part of the encrypted payload.

Part **b** of Figure 15-11 shows an example of IPSec used in transport mode. IPSec encrypts the IP traffic originating at the PC and decrypts it on the host in the remote Data Center. The source and the destination IP of the IPSec datagram are the same as the origin and destination hosts. The encrypted payload only contains data from the original IP datagram.

Figure 15-11 *IPSec Tunnel Mode and Transport Mode*

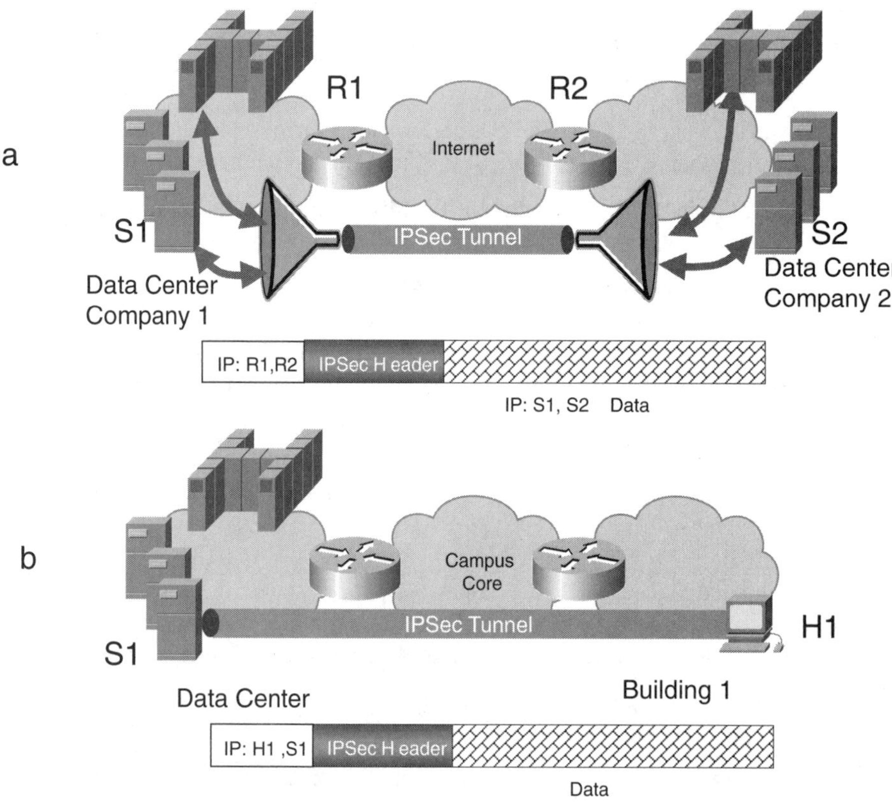

IPSec and TCP/IP Layers

The IPSec protocol operates between the network layer and the transport layer of the TCP/IP protocol stack. (For more information about the TCP/IP layers, refer to Chapter 7.) IPSec is completely transparent to the applications, which, as a consequence, do not need to be IPSec-aware. Figure 15-12 illustrates where IPSec operates with regards to the TCP/IP stack.

Figure 15-12 *IPSec and TCP/IP Stack*

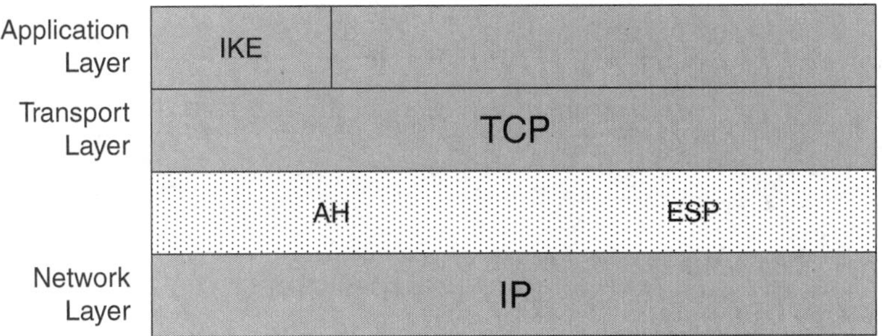

IPSec services are provided by two protocols, IP Authentication Header (AH) and IP Encapsulating Security Payload (ESP):

- **IP AH (RFC 2402)**—AH is a protocol that provides data-origin authentication (the data is really arriving from the IPSec peer), data integrity (the data has not been modified), and antireplay protection. AH uses HMAC algorithms (MD5 and SHA-1) to provide data-origin authentication and data integrity. AH is IP protocol 51.
- **IP ESP (RFC 2406)**—ESP provides data confidentiality, data origin authentication, data integrity, and antireplay protection. ESP authenticates and encrypts only the payload of packets, whereas AH covers most of the header fields as well. ESP uses HMAC algorithms (MD5 and SHA-1) for data integrity and authentication, and it uses DES and 3DES for data confidentiality. ESP is IP protocol 50.

Figure 15-13 illustrates the operations of AH (part **a** of Figure 15-13) and ESP (part **b** of Figure 15-13). AH applies the HMAC to the following fields of an IP datagram: the data and the portions of the IP header that do not change during the transport. The authenticated IP datagram consists of an IP header, followed by the AH header (which includes the HMAC) and by the data portion.

ESP applies the HMAC to the data portion and to the ESP header; it does not include the IP headers in the hashing calculation. The HMAC is appended to the final packet. The data is encrypted with DES or 3DES.

In both AH and ESP, the content of the IP header and the content of the data portion depend on which IPSec mode you use. If you use tunnel mode, the IP header carries the addresses of the routers, and the data portion carries the original IP datagram plus some additional information. If you use transport mode, the IP header carries the IP addresses of the original datagram, and the payload carries the original payload plus some additional information.

Figure 15-13 *AH and ESP*

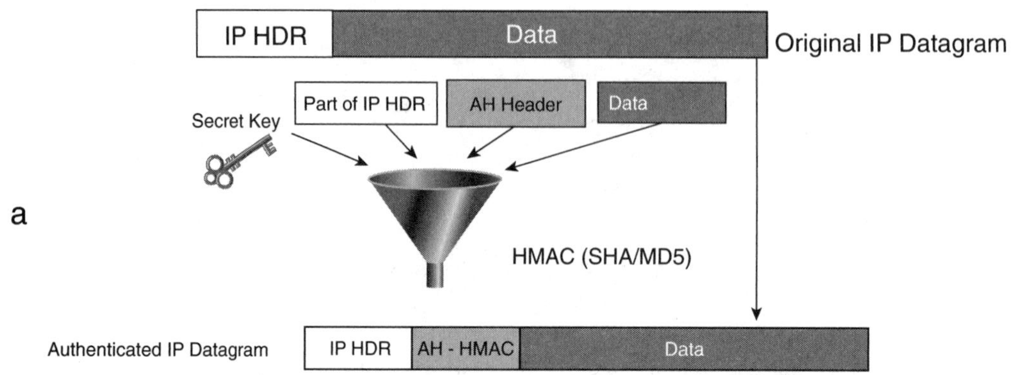

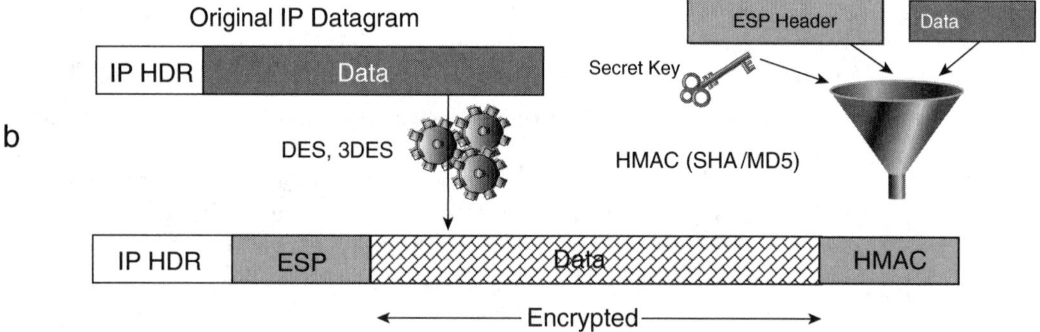

NOTE From the description given so far, you can determine that deploying IPSec requires consideration of the maximum transmission unit (MTU) size. The overhead of the IPSec headers and of the additional IP header (if using tunnel mode) amounts to ~60 bytes (20 bytes of IP headers and 31–38 bytes of ESP headers). If, in addition to IPSec, you tunnel Generic Routing Encapsulation (GRE), you need to consider an additional overhead of 24 bytes. The MTU available to the tunneled IP traffic can be lower than the physical MTU by ~75 bytes.

You must consider MTU size as part of the Layer 3 design; it is also important to ensure that Path MTU discovery packets are not dropped by access control lists (ACLs). For more information about Path MTU discovery, read Chapter 7.

Two IPSec devices negotiate parameters such as whether AH or ESP is used or which encryption algorithm and key sizes are applied. These parameters are known as security associations (SAs).

IKE

When two peers need to communicate, they first open an IKE session. The IKE session provides the transport for the secure negotiation and establishes the IPSec channels used to protect the users' data.

The negotiation of IKE Phase I (which can be one of two types, *main mode* or *aggressive mode*) starts as soon as the origin router receives packets that match the definition of the traffic to be encrypted (a crypto map). Example 15-5 shows the configuration of a crypto map on a Cisco router. The crypto map defines which traffic should be encrypted by specifying an ACL with the **crypto-acl** parameter. The **set peer** command specifies the IPSec peer router.

Example 15-5 *Crypto Map Configuration on a Cisco Router*

```
Router (config)# crypto map name seq ipsec-isakmp
Router (config-crypto-m)# match address crypto-acl
Router (config-crypto-m)# set peer peer
Router (config-crypto-m)# set transform-set transform-set-name
```

The IPSec channels are characterized by what are called Security Associations (SA). SAs define the parameters used to encrypt the traffic. SAs are cryptographic algorithms and encryption keys, for example. In IPSec, there are SAs for the IKE negotiation and SAs for the AH or ESP phase.

During Phase I (main mode), peers agree on hash and encryption algorithms to protect the IKE session, run Diffie-Hellman to agree on a shared secret, and also authenticate each other. After peers agree on those parameters and successfully authenticate, a bidirectional IKE SA is established. The parameters that define how IKE operates in this phase are specified in a policy such as the one in Example 15-6.

Example 15-6 *IKE Configuration on a Cisco Router*

```
Router (config)# crypto isakmp policy priority
Router (config-isakmp)# encryption {des | 3des}
Router (config-isakmp)# hash {sha | md5}
Router (config-isakmp)# authentication {rsa-sig | rsa-encr | pre-share}
Router (config-isakmp)# group {1 | 2}
Router (config-isakmp)# lifetime seconds
```

NOTE Example 15-6 shows the configuration of the policy for the IKE session. Internet Security Association and Key Management (ISAKMP) is one of the protocols that IKE is based on. The configuration is global, and there can be multiple IKE policies. The priority field tells the router which policy to look at first, the highest priority being 1.

IKE Phase II (*quick mode*) starts and routers negotiate the IPSec parameters; SA lifetimes, encryption algorithms, and proxy entities (the source and destination of the tunnel). At the end of this phase, multiple IPSec SAs are established. IPSec SAs are unidirectional, so to protect a single traffic flow, two SAs must be created. The characteristics of the IPSec SAs depend on the configuration present in the *transform set*, such as the one in Example 15-7.

Example 15-7 *Transform Set Configuration on a Cisco Router*

```
Router (config)# crypto ipsec transform-set transform-set-name transform1
[transform2 [transform3]]
Router (cfg-crypto-tran)# mode [tunnel | transport]
```

As the example shows, the transform set lets you choose the IPSec mode, tunnel or transport, and the *transform-set-name* specifies the cipher and whether IPSec will be operating in AH mode or in ESP mode.

As soon as the IPSec SAs are established, routers can start transmitting packets over the IPSec tunnel. In this case, the IPSec tunnel consists of one IKE SA and two IPSec SAs.

Choosing IPSec Security Parameters

The first phase of the IKE negotiation can follow two modes, main mode or aggressive mode. The major difference between the two is that aggressive mode is faster, but the negotiation yields some information about the identity of the peers. Main mode is commonly used when establishing a secure connection between routers or gateways (such as site-to-site VPNs), but aggressive mode is typically used with VPN clients running on systems such as Windows and UNIX and where an extended authentication might be required.

You can configure the IKE negotiation to use different security algorithms, as shown in Example 15-6:

- The choice of the hash and the encryption algorithms is self-explanatory from the sample configuration. SHA-1 is preferable to MD5, and 3DES is obviously preferable to DES. The performance penalty of 3DES on a network device with hardware-accelerated encryption (such as a Cisco 6500 IPSec VPN Acceleration Service Module) is not an important factor, and it is worth the added security.

- The authentication of the peer devices can be based on a shared key (**pre-share**), on RSA encryption (**rsa-encr**), or on an RSA signature (**rsa-sig**). The first option is self-explanatory; the RSA encryption method requires manual distribution of the router public key. The RSA signature method requires building a PKI, and it is the most scalable option.
- The authentication of the IKE peers is fundamental because all the successive VPN security depends on it. For this reason, the authentication should be the strongest possible, that is, at least a 1024-bit RSA key. Considering the small amount of traffic exchanged during the IKE phase, the performance impact of even a 2048-bit key is acceptable.
- You can configure the Diffie-Hellman key exchange to use a 768-bit key (group 1), a 1024-bit key (group 2), or a 1536-bit key (group 5). Based on the previously mentioned RSA report, which calls for 1024-bit keys for asymmetric encryption, as of today group 2 offers a good tradeoff between security and performance. It is good practice to match the Diffie-Hellman key strength to the RSA key strength, so if the RSA key is 2048 bits, you should use group 5.

The data traffic is carried in the VPN tunnel according to the settings of the transform set. The list summarizes the design choices:

- AH is seldom used, and in any case, you should prefer ESP because it provides encryption of the traffic. Moreover, AH is incompatible with network address translation (NAT).
- The ESP options for data encryption are esp-des, esp-3des, esp-aes 192, and esp-aes 256. Use at least 3DES. The ESP options for authentication are esp-md5-hmac and esp-sha-hmac. The best choice is SHA-1.
- You can provide an added layer of protection with Perfect Forward Secrecy (PFS). PFS is a method to generate new keys for encrypting the data traffic in such a way that the new key does not depend on the existing key. PFS is based on Diffie-Hellman. You should configure PFS with the same strength as the Diffie-Hellman group you use for IKE.

SSL VPNs and IPSec VPNs

IPSec VPNs are currently used for remote access (transport mode) and for site-to-site connectivity (tunnel mode). Both modes are present in a Data Center; site-to-site is typically used in the extranet, and remote access VPNs are used to make the enterprise applications available to the remote users.

Remote access IPSec VPNs are characterized by a client application that runs on a PC which encrypts traffic at the network layer. Figure 15-12 (shown previously) illustrated that IPSec operates right above the network layer and below the transport layer of the TCP/IP stack.

SSL VPNs are also becoming more common for remote access. Web browsers and e-mail clients are the SSL VPN clients. No additional software is required on the client's desktop. The only additional configuration required is the installation of client certificates to verify the identity of the remote user from the Data Center, and with e-mail applications, you need to enable SSL on SMTP and POP3. Figure 15-10 (shown previously) illustrated that SSL operates above the transport layer and below the application layer of the TCP/IP stack, which explains why you need to specifically configure the applications to use SSL.

SSL VPNs' main asset is the simplicity of its configuration: SSL VPNs do not require specialized client software. It is true that applications need to be SSL-aware, but because most enterprise applications are web-based or web-enabled, this requirement is not a problem: browsers support SSL.

On the other hand, IPSec supports site-to-site VPNs and is more flexible with the applications because it operates at the network layer.

Authentication Protocols and Technologies

Authentication technologies are deployed in the Data Center for three main purposes:

- To control access to the network devices' configurations (secure management)
- To provide access to Data Center applications only to the allowed users (for example, SSL VPN applications)
- To authenticate client PCs, phones and handheld devices connecting to the campus network (IEEE 802.1x)

Figure 15-14 shows the typical scenarios of authentication. The example shows the authentication of a network administrator that opens a Telnet session to a firewall. You could replace the firewall in the example with a switch, a router, or any other network device, and the example would still apply.

Figure 15-14 *Authenticating Network Administrators*

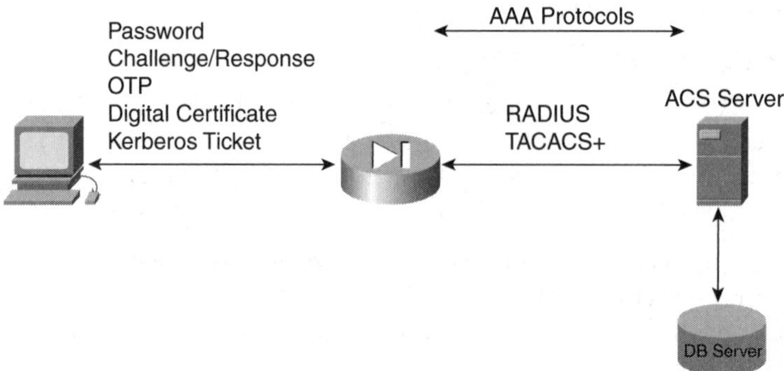

The firewall needs to authenticate the user before giving him access to the configuration. You can achieve this setup by configuring the firewall with the username and passwords of the network administrators. You would save this information on the firewall. (This scenario is called *local authentication*.)

Now imagine that you have to restrict the access to all the network devices in the Data Center: switches, routers, load balancers, and so on. Configuring usernames and passwords on every device is an approach that does not scale well; moreover, if you need to change the user credentials, you would have to reconfigure all the devices in the Data Center.

The solution to this problem consists of using *authentication servers* for the verification of the identity of the user. In this case, the firewall in Figure 15-14 communicates with an authentication server by means of protocols such as TACACS+ or RADIUS.

The firewall sends the user credentials to the server, the server communicates with a secure database that stores the username password associations, and it authenticates the user and returns the authorization information to the firewall.

Authentication Technologies

The username/password is the simplest type of authentication, but it is vulnerable because the password is transmitted in cleartext on the network.

Several authentication mechanisms provide more security:

- One-time passwords (OTPs)
- Challenge/response schemes
- Digital certificates
- Kerberos

OTPs

OTPs are passwords that last for a limited amount of time (a few minutes). OTPs are often used when the username and password needs to be sent in cleartext.

You can implement OTPs with different mechanisms; one of them is called *time-synchronous*. Basically, you configure a *token device* (or software) and the authentication server with the same secret key (seed), and they generate identical new keys that are based on the seed over time.

When the user connects to a device that is configured for OTP, she is prompted for a password. The user then enters her personal identification number (PIN) into the token device, which returns the OTP.

The OTP is sent to the authentication server. The authentication server retrieves the PIN of the user by looking up the username in the database and performs the same exact operation as the token card. If the passwords match, the authentication is successful.

Challenge/Response: IEEE 802.1x EAP-MD5

Challenge/response schemes avoid the problem of sending cleartext passwords by using a secret password combined with a hashing algorithm (such as MD5). IEEE 802.1x provides an example.

IEEE 802.1x is a standard that provides a mechanism for authenticating users on a LAN. With 802.1x, a PC that is attached to a LAN switch is connected to the network only if the authentication is successful. A PC running Windows XP is an example of an IEEE 802.1x–capable client.

The mechanism that allows the authentication of the client is the EAP-MD5 protocol, which is a combination of the Extensible Authentication Protocol (EAP) (RFC 2284) and the Challenge Handshake Authentication Protocol (CHAP) (RFC 1994). The EAP traffic is exchanged between the PC and the switch; the switch communicates with the authentication server with RADIUS and encapsulates EAP into RADIUS. As a result, the authentication really happens between the PC and the RADIUS server. At the end of the authentication, the server sends a *fail* or a *pass* message to the switch.

Figure 15-15 shows a host that is attached to a switch. The switch does not enable the port where the host attaches until it has been authenticated and authorized by the authentication server. The authentication server holds the database of username and passwords for the campus clients.

After the host attaches to the switch, the authentication server generates a random string called a *challenge*. The challenge is sent to the client. The user of the PC inserts his username and password; they are combined with the challenge and hashed with MD5 into a string, which is the *response*. The response is sent back to the server.

The authentication server, after it receives the username and the response, looks up the password in its local data base and performs locally the same operations as the client. If the result of the computation is the same as the response, the authentication is successful.

IEEE 802.1x also supports authentication based on digital certificates by means of EAP-TLS (RFC 2716).

Digital Certificates: Client Authentication in SSL

SSL applications such as web-based applications and e-mail applications can authenticate the users by means of client digital certificates. Chapter 9 described how the SSL negotiation works and the fact that the server can request the client to send a certificate (the message is called a Certificate Request).

Figure 15-15 *Challenge/Response Authentication in IEEE 802.1x*

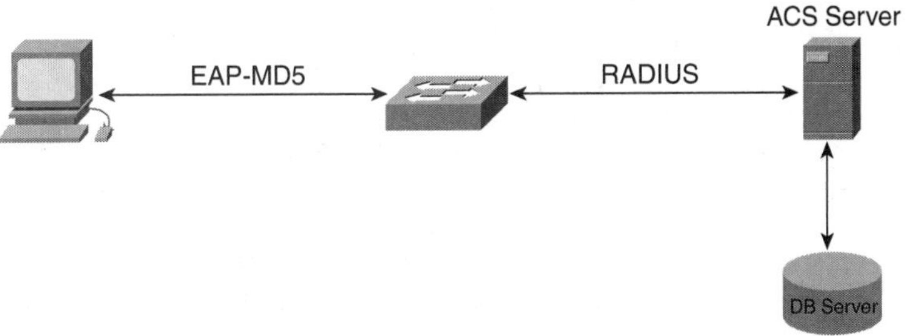

When the client sends a certificate, it is up to the application that uses SSL to verify its content. With SSL offloaders, the certificate is only visible to the SSL offloader itself, so a scheme needs to be in place for this information to be sent to the server where the application resides. You can set up this scheme with *header insertion*.

On the Cisco 11000 Series Secure Content Accelerator, you start this process with the following command:

```
httpheader {client-cert | client-custom fieldname fieldvalue | pre-filter | prefix
prefixstring | server-cert | session}
```

This command lets you insert the client-certificate information into the cleartext HTTP traffic sent to the server so that the receiving application can verify the information about the client.

Verifying the certificate does not authenticate the client. The client needs to send some traffic signed with its private key. The server or the SSL offloader can then verify the signature with the client's public key, which proves that the certificate really belongs to that client.

Example 15-8 shows how the server or the SSL offloader authenticates the client. The server requests that the client send a certificate (Step 5), the client sends the certificate (Step 7), and eventually the client sends the Certificate Verify message (Step 9). The Certificate Verify contains a hash of all previous handshake messages sent or received, signed by the client.

Example 15-8 *Client Authentication in SSL*

```
1  C->S Client Hello  (unencrypted)
2  S->C Server Hello (unencrypted)
3  S->C Server Certificate (unencrypted)
4  S->C Server Key exchange (unencrypted)
5  S->C Certificate Request (unencrypted)
6  S->C Server Hello Done (unencrypted)
7  C->S Client Certificate (unencrypted)
8  C->S Client key exchange (encrypted with server public key)
```

continues

Example 15-8 *Client Authentication in SSL (Continued)*

```
9  C->S Certificate Verify (hash of previous messages signed with clients' private
   key)
10 C->S Client Change Cipher Spec (unencrypted)
11 C->S Client finish (encrypted with CLIENT-WRITE-KEY)
12 C->S Server Change Cipher Spec  (unencrypted)
13 C->S Server finish (encrypted with SERVER-WRITE-KEY)
```

Upon reception of the Certificate Verify message, the server authenticates the client by verifying the signature in the message Certificate Verify.

Kerberos

Kerberos is a network authentication protocol developed by the Massachusetts Institute of Technology (MIT) that provides strong authentication for client/server applications with symmetric cryptography such as DES, 3DES, and IDEA. Kerberos v5 is defined in RFC 1510.

The main use for Kerberos is the authentication of users getting access to network resources. For example, you can use Kerberos to authenticate users requiring Telnet access to a router or switch.

One key component to the Kerberos architecture is the Key Distribution Center (KDC). The KDC is the trusted third party that issues tickets to the client. These tickets guarantee access to the network resource for a certain period of time, after which they expire.

A typical scenario of Kerberos-based authentication is a client PC opening a Telnet session to a router or a switch. The assumption is that the Telnet software is "kerberized," which means that the Telnet software understands the Kerberos authentication mechanism.

NOTE You can use Kerberos authentication without a kerberized Telnet client. In this case, the router or switch becomes the "kerberized" client. The disadvantage is that the client password is unencrypted between the PC and the router.

The following steps describe a kerberized Telnet session to a router:

1. The first time the client PC needs to connect to a network resource such as a router, the PC sends an authentication request to the KDC server. The KDC server has a database with the association of clients and their secret passwords.

2 The KDC responds to the client with the authentication response encrypted with the secret key. The client PC prompts the user for the password (which is also the secret key used by the KDC). If the password decrypts the authentication response, the client is authenticated.

3 The KDC provides the client with a "ticket" encrypted with the router/switch secret key. This key is shared only between the KDC and the router/switch.

4 The client sends the ticket to the router/switch to gain access to it. The client can keep using the ticket to gain direct access to the router/switch until the ticket expires.

Typical kerberized clients include Telnet, FTP, POP, and Remote Procedure Calls (RPC).

Most Kerberos implementations use TCP ports 464 and 749 and User Datagram Protocol (UDP) ports 88, 464, and 4444.

AAA Protocols

Chapter 5 introduced the concepts of Authentication, Authorization, and Accounting. AAA is an architecture that you can use to control the access to sensitive resources, such as servers and network devices, based on users and groups.

As previously described, many authentication mechanisms require consulting a database with the username/password associations. This database can be local on the device that provides authentication or, better, reside on a separate server that a number of devices can consult. This server is called an *authentication server*, and the typical protocols that give access to the authentication server are TACACS+ and RADIUS.

TACACS+

The TACACS+ protocol is the Cisco enhanced version of TACACS. TACACS+ works as a client/server protocol where the client device is called a network access server (NAS) and the server process runs on operating systems such as Windows or UNIX on the authentication server. The NAS can be a router, switch, or firewall requiring AAA services from the server.

NOTE TACACS+ is a TCP-based protocol. It uses port 49.

A fundamental characteristic of TACACS+ is the separation of authentication, authorization, and accounting, which allows users to enable only the services that they need.

In TACACS+, all communications between server and NASs are secured by encryption and authentication. You configure both NAS and server manually with a shared secret key.

TACACS+ communication between server and NAS is characterized by the following traffic patterns:

- **Authentication**—Uses three types of packets: START, CONTINUE, and REPLY. The NAS sends the START packet to the server at the beginning of the authentication process, and it includes information such as the username and the type of authentication to be applied. The server sends REPLY packets to indicate that the authentication has finished or that more information is required. If more information is needed, the clients return it in a CONTINUE packet.
- **Authorization**—Uses two types of messages: REQUEST and RESPONSE. The REQUEST packet includes the user or process name and the services it is requesting. The server replies with a RESPONSE packet, which not only provides a *pass* or *fail* answer but might also include other parameters such as IP addresses.
- **Accounting**—Uses three types of records: START, STOP, and UPDATE. The server sends START when a service is starting and STOP when a service has been terminated. The server periodically sends an UPDATE to indicate that a service continues to be performed.

RADIUS

The RADIUS protocol is a standard access authentication and authorization protocol that was originally developed by Livingston Enterprises, Inc. RFCs 2058 and 2059 define the RADIUS protocol.

RADIUS is also a client/server protocol where the NAS is the client requesting AAA services and the server is a process running in a system such as Windows or UNIX.

RADIUS is carried on top of UDP rather than TCP, which constitutes a disadvantage in respect to TACACS+. UDP is a connectionless protocol that provides a best-effort delivery, and because it cannot guarantee the delivery of packets, RADIUS has to implement all the necessary controls to deal with retransmissions, timeouts, and availability. RADIUS typically uses UDP port 1812 for authentication and UDP port 1813 for accounting. Formerly, UDP ports 1645 and 1646 were used for RADIUS authentication and accounting, respectively.

RADIUS performs encryption and authentication functions to secure the communications but only encrypts passwords, leaving usernames, authorized services, and accounting information in cleartext. TACACS+ encrypts the whole payload.

Another important characteristic of RADIUS is that authentication and authorization are coupled together and cannot be used as independent services. RADIUS cannot provide services such as command authorization, which is supported by TACACS+. Command authorization is useful for the administration of network devices such as routers and switches, and it basically consists of controlling which commands a user or group is allowed to execute in a specific system.

In RADIUS, NAS and server communicate as follows:

- Authentication consists of a query (ACCESS REQUEST) and a response (ACCESS ACCEPT/ACCESS REJECT). The ACCESS REQUEST is sent by the NAS, and it includes the username, encrypted password, NAS IP address, port, and type of service.
- The server can reply with an ACCESS ACCEPT or ACCESS REJECT message. The ACCESS ACCEPT message typically includes a series of attributes used for the session: the service type, protocol type, and IP address to be assigned to the client. The server sends an ACCESS REJECT when authentication fails, and the message is commonly sent with text that indicates the cause for the rejection.

Network Management Security

Network management in the Data Center takes advantage of many security technologies:

- AAA authenticates the administrators of the network devices. This topic is covered in the section, "AAA Protocols."
- SSH is used as a replacement for Telnet to encrypt the management traffic and to authenticate the administrator.
- SNMPv3 is the network management protocol.

SSH

SSH is a protocol that provides secure remote access by using strong authentication and encryption. You should use SSH as an alternative to insecure protocols such as Telnet and rlogin.

For authentication, SSH is deployed with a variety of protocols, including TACACS+ and RADIUS. SSH can use RSA authentication as well. SSH encrypts the traffic with ciphers such as IDEA, 3DES, DES, and RC4-128.

NOTE SSH also provides support for tunneling TCP sessions, which permits you to secure not only login connections, but also e-mail, file transfers such as secure copy (SCP) or secure FTP (SFTP), and X Window commands.

There are two versions of SSH, 1 and 2. Version 2 provides better performance and has addressed a series of security issues in the first version. It is recommended that you use SSH Version 2.

SSH operations can be summarized as follows:

1 The client connects to a server.

2 The server sends its *host public key* and its *server key*. Both keys are RSA or DSA 1024 bits. The host key identifies the server, and the server key changes every hour. The client looks up the server public key in its database; if the key is not found, the client adds it.

3 The client then generates a 256-bit random session number and encodes it with both the host key and the server key.

4 The preceding exchange allows negotiating the session key as well as the symmetric ciphers (DES, 3DES, IDEA, and RC4-128).

5 The client authenticates.

The client authentication can be based on a password or on public-key authentication. The configuration for public-key authentication requires generating an RSA key pair on the client and installing the public key on the server/network device as one of the authorized keys.

From that moment on, the client can log on to the server without a password.

The configuration of SSH in Cisco IOS follows these steps:

Step 1 Configure AAA for authentication.

Step 2 Configure **ip domain-name** *domain-name*, which specifies the default domain name extension that Cisco IOS appends to relative DNS names.

Step 3 Generate the server RSA keys with the command **crypto key generate rsa**.

Step 4 Configure the timeout period for SSH connections and the maximum number of failed attempts with the commands **ip ssh time-out** *seconds* and **ip ssh authentication-retries** *number-of-retries*.

Step 5 Restrict access to the router or switch terminal lines to SSH traffic only with **transport input ssh**.

NOTE You can find more information about SSH at http://www.ietf.org/ids.by.wg/secsh.html.

You can find more information about configuring SSH on Cisco routers at http://www.cisco.com/warp/public/707/ssh.shtml.

SNMPv3

SNMP is a protocol you use to retrieve information from network devices and hosts (*managed devices*) about their configurations, states, and counters for hardware and software components and to set the values of those components for configuration purposes.

Managed devices run an agent. The *SNMP Management Station* remotely controls the agents by periodically sending probes with GET_REQUEST or SET_REQUEST messages, to which the agents reply with "response" messages.

SNMP defines the entities being monitored as *objects*. Objects are identified by their OIDs. The OID is a sequence of numbers separated by a dot, as in .1.3.6.1.2.1.2.2.1.7.

SNMP Versions 1 and 2 do not provide any mechanisms to authenticate the source of a message and do not support encryption, which makes SNMP vulnerable to unauthorized message modification, masquerades (when an attacker gains access to a system by pretending to be an authorized user), and disclosures of sensitive information.

SNMPv3 traffic is encrypted with DES and carries an MD5 HMAC or a SHA HMAC for authentication and integrity purposes.

You can configure SNMPv3 cryptographic options on Cisco IOS routers with the following commands:

```
snmp-server group groupname v3 {auth | noauth | priv}}] [read readview] [write
  writeview] [notify notifyview] [access access-list]

snmp-server user username [groupname remote ip-address {v3 [auth {md5 | sha}

  auth-password ][access access-list]
```

Most of the cryptographic configurations are self-explanatory with the exception of the options **auth**, **noauth**, and **priv**. The **noauth** option specifies no encryption and a cleartext password for authentication. The **auth** option specifies MD5 or SHA authentication but no encryption. The **priv** option specifies MD5 or SHA authentication and DES encryption.

Summary

Cryptographic algorithms (or ciphers) can be categorized as secret-key algorithms, public-key algorithms, or hashing algorithms. Public-key algorithms are typically used for authentication and key exchange, secret-key algorithms for confidentiality, and hashing algorithms for data integrity.

Secure transport protocols such as SSL/TLS and IPSec use a combination of these cryptographic algorithms to maintain the privacy of users' data and to allow the secure management of the Data Center infrastructure. SSL VPNs are becoming increasingly popular as the technology to allow remote access to enterprise web-based applications. IPSec VPNs are used both for remote access and to build site-to-site tunnels, which is often necessary when building extranets.

Both SSL and IPSec combine the use of public-key encryption for authentication and key exchange and symmetric algorithms for the encryption of the data transfer. Symmetric algorithms are significantly faster than asymmetric algorithms, but the distribution of the secret key is more complex with symmetric algorithms.

The use of asymmetric encryption requires a mechanism for distributing public keys in such a way that the receiver of the public key can verify the identity of the entity delivering the key. The PKI is a framework of services that supports key generation, distribution, and revocation.

The design of an IPSec solution or of an SSL solution requires considering the design of the PKI; the considerations of the behavior of the user agents (in SSL, you need to account for the presence of 40-bit browsers and 128-bit browsers); the choice of the ciphers, which is a tradeoff between security and speed; and the need for authentication.

The use of hardware-accelerated cryptographic devices simplifies the design in many ways; one way is that it allows you to choose the ciphers based on the strength of the algorithm without having to worry about the performance impact on a CPU.

Security in the Data Center also calls for the deployment of authentication services, such as AAA, which is based on protocols such as TACACS+ and Kerberos. You can use AAA to authenticate the users of network devices and to provide port-based access control (IEEE 802.1x) on the campus switches.

You can provide secure management in the Data Center by combining strong authentication; SSH, which you can use as an alternative to Telnet; and SNMPv3, which provides authentication and encryption of management traffic.

This chapter covers the following topics:

- The modes of operation of load balancers, including dispatch, directed, client NAT, connection spoofing, and direct server return
- The performance implications of these modes of operation
- Load-balancing algorithms used to load-balance server farms
- Load-balancing algorithms used to load-balance cache farms

CHAPTER 16

Load-Balancing Modes and Predictors

This chapter discusses two key concepts related to load balancing. These concepts are key in understanding the ideas and information introduced in Chapter 19, "Persistence Mechanisms on Load Balancers" and Chapter 22, "Performance Metrics of Data Center Devices." These concepts are listed here:

- Modes of operation
- Load-balancing algorithms (also known as predictors)

The modes of operation and load-balancing algorithms are fundamental to the functions of load balancers and are key to understanding how and why they perform their services in a server farm or cache farm environment.

Modes of Operation

This section discusses the possible mechanisms used by load balancers to perform server selection and packet forwarding. These mechanisms, referred to as modes of operation, are related to how load balancers manipulate packet headers when load balancing traffic.

Modes of operation refer to how load balancers perform the Media Access Control (MAC), IP, and TCP/UDP header rewriting operation on packets being load-balanced. When a packet arrives to a load balancer and is destined for the virtual IP address (VIP), two distinct processes take place:

- Server selection
- Packet forwarding

The server-selection mechanism is triggered when a packet arrives with the destination IP address of the VIP. This server-selection mechanism provides the load balancer with enough information to forward the packet to the selected real server. The information needed to send the packet to the selected real server includes, among other pieces, the real server's MAC address, the real server's IP address, the protocol, and the port number.

NOTE Depending on the underlying hardware architecture of the load balancer, the server-selection mechanism also includes the physical interface, switch port, or VLAN used to reach the selected real server. When the header rewrite takes place in the hardware in which the port is integrated, the specific port becomes very important. The hardware complex uses fast access memory that contains just enough information for the rewrite operation, yet this information is not available for ports that are not part of the same hardware complex.

When all the necessary information to forward the packet is known, the header rewrite takes places, and the packet is sent through the appropriate interface. Typically, the rewrite operation is performed on the destination MAC address, the destination IP address, and possibly the destination port number. If the rewrite operation is performed at Layer 2, the mode is called *dispatch mode*; if the rewrite operation is performed at Layer 3, it is known as *directed mode*.

NOTE In a special case, known as Client Network Address Translation (Client NAT), the source IP address is rewritten. This can be applied to both dispatch and directed modes. Client NAT is explained in the section, "Client NAT," later in this chapter.

Before describing the modes of operation and load-balancing algorithms, it is important to understand the basic operation of bridges and routers. This is because load balancers could operate in bridge and router modes, similar to bridges and routers, in addition to their particular operating modes.

Switching Concepts

The switching operation is described simply as the manner in which the device performs the forwarding decision based on specific header information. Bridges operate at Layer 2 typically by looking at the MAC headers, routers operate at Layer 3 by looking at IP headers, and load balancers have the capability to switch at Layer 4 (TCP/UDP headers) and Layer 5 (HTTP information), in addition to Layers 2 and 3.

Bridging

Bridging and switching, which are analogous terms, refer to forwarding frames based on Layer 2 information. The bridging of frames at Layer 2 occurs by manipulating MAC-layer headers so that frames are forwarded between two or more segments. The two or more segments are on the same Layer 3 network (same IP subnet). Upon receiving a frame, a bridge that connects multiple LAN segments determines the outbound interface or port by searching its Layer 2 forwarding tables for the destination MAC address. Bridges—or, rather, transparent bridges—do not change MAC header information. Bridges simply forward frames to the selected LAN segments, if known, or to all connected LAN segments except the one from which the frame was received.

Routing

Routing, on the other hand, refers to the process of forwarding packets based on Layer 3 information from one LAN segment to another. These two segments are on different Layer 3 networks (different IP subnets). The routing of packets requires the manipulation of Layer 3 headers. Understanding how headers are manipulated by routing processes helps you comprehend how headers are treated by a load-balancing device. Routers follow the process described in Figure 16-1.

Figure 16-1 *Routing Mechanics*

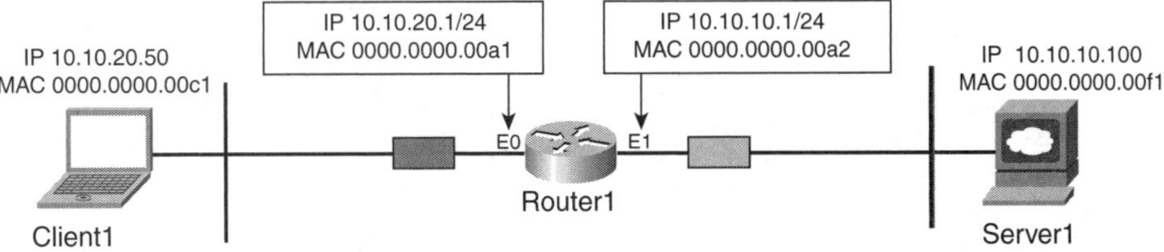

Figure 16-1 presents a simple configuration:

Client1 using MAC address 0000.0000.00c1 and IP address 10.10.20.50, pointing to router1 as the default gateway

Router1 using MAC address 0000.0000.00a1 and IP address 10.10.20.1 on Client1's segment

Router1 using MAC address 0000.0000.00a2 and IP address 10.10.10.1 on Server1's segment

Server1 using MAC address 0000.0000.00f1 and IP address 10.10.10.100, pointing to Router1 as the default gateway

When Client1 is ready to send a packet to Server1, it knows to send an ARP request to the the default gateway, Router1. Router1 responds with its own MAC address. Client1 sends the packet to Server1 using the MAC address of router1 and the IP address of Server1. Router1 rewrites the source and destination MAC address.

Figure 16-2 shows the relevant contents of the packet before and after it is seen by Router1. As the figure describes, the source MAC address, Client1's MAC address (0000.0000.00c1), and the destination MAC address are replaced. The source MAC address is replaced with

Router1's MAC address (0000.0000.00a2), and the destination MAC address is replaced by Server1's MAC address. Notice that the destination MAC address of Router1 corresponds to the MAC address of the interface used to reach Server1.

Figure 16-2 *Client-to-Server Packet Header Rewrite*

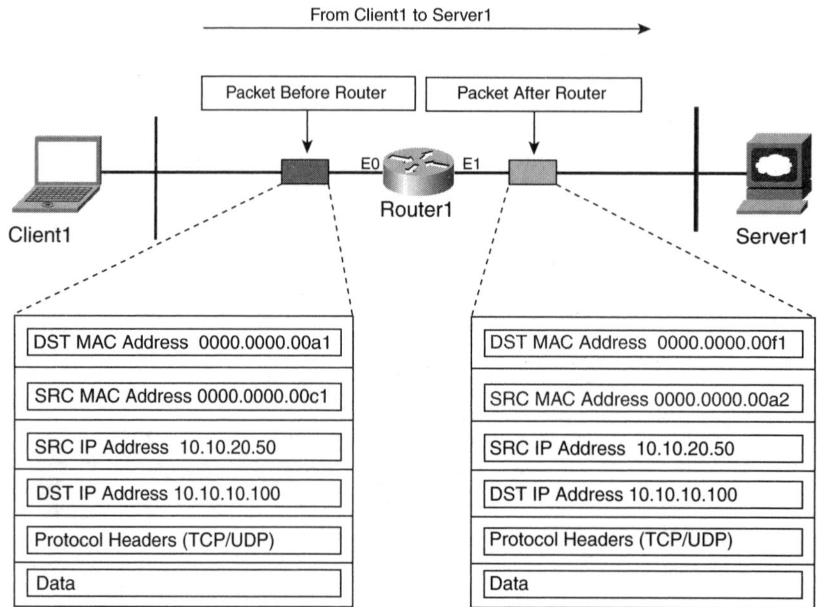

When Server1 sends a packet to Client1, a similar process takes place. Again, both the source and destination MAC addresses are replaced by Router1's MAC address on the interface used to reach Client1 and Client1's MAC address, respectively. Figure 16-3 presents the relevant header information before and after the packets are seen by Router1.

After discussing how routers affect packet headers, it is simpler to understand what the load balancer does as part of the load-balancing function in addition to the routing operation.

Figure 16-3 *Server-to-Client Packet Header Rewrite*

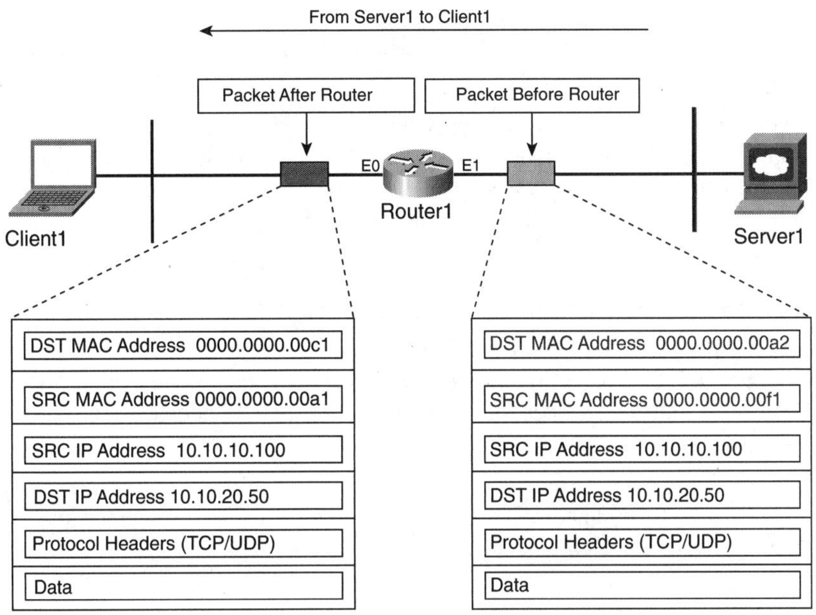

From Server1 to Client1

Packet After Router
DST MAC Address 0000.0000.00c1
SRC MAC Address 0000.0000.00a1
SRC IP Address 10.10.10.100
DST IP Address 10.10.20.50
Protocol Headers (TCP/UDP)
Data

Packet Before Router
DST MAC Address 0000.0000.00a2
SRC MAC Address 0000.0000.00f1
SRC IP Address 10.10.10.100
DST IP Address 10.10.20.50
Protocol Headers (TCP/UDP)
Data

Client1 — E0 Router1 E1 — Server1

Dispatch Mode

Dispatch mode, as previously described, performs its operations at Layer 2. The typical steps followed by a load balancer when operating in dispatch mode are as follows:

1. The packet is received, with the destination address matching a configured VIP.
2. Server selection is triggered based on the VIP configuration.
3. The server-selection process produces information needed to rewrite headers and forward the packet to the selected server through the correct interface.
4. The header is rewritten, replacing the destination MAC with the MAC address of the selected real server. The source MAC and destination IP address are left unchanged.
5. The packet is forwarded to the selected real server.

NOTE In certain cases, the source MAC is changed to use the MAC of the receiving interface. Consult the product pages for specific information.

Because only the MAC-layer information changes in the packet (IP information remains untouched), real servers must be Layer 2–adjacent to the load balancer. Because header rewrite occurs at the MAC layer only, it is necessary for all real servers to also be configured to support the address of the VIP in their IP stack.

NOTE The VIP should be configured as either a secondary or an alias IP address, to avoid potential issues with duplicate IP addresses found in the IP stacks of certain OSs. See Appendix D, "Loopback Interface Configuration Procedures," for more details on how to configure loopback or alias interfaces for secondary or alternate IP addresses.

Figure 16-4 shows changes in the packet headers as they go through the load balancer while configured for dispatch mode.

Figure 16-4 *Dispatch Mode Packet Processing*

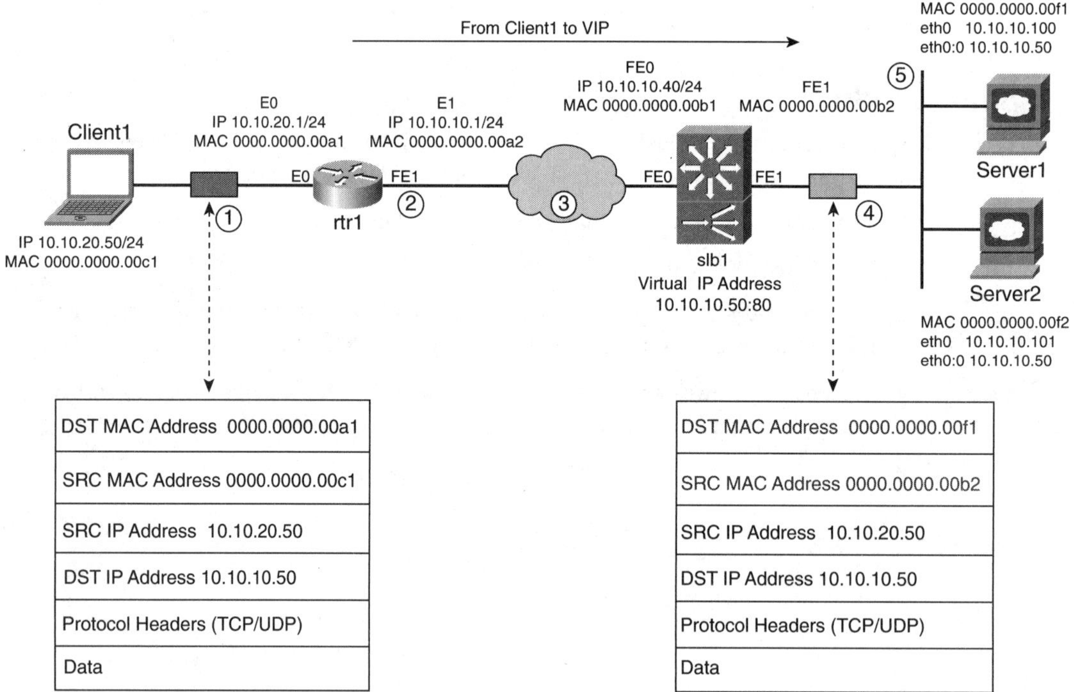

In Figure 16-4, the following transactions occur:

1 Using IP address 10.10.20.50, Client1 attempts to connect to a web server (TCP port 80) identified by the URL www.example.com, which is resolved to the VIP 10.10.10.50. The client sends a TCP connection request using its MAC and IP addresses, its default gateway's MAC address as the destination MAC, and the VIP as the destination IP address.

2 Rtr1 looks up its routing tables performing a longest prefix match to the destination IP address to determine a next-hop device. Rtr1 forwards the connection request to the next-hop device.

3 The packet is routed through the network until it reaches slb1.

4 Slb1 rewrites the destination MAC using the selected server's MAC, and the source MAC using the outbound interface's MAC as it forwards the packet to the server.

5 The selected server receives a packet destined for its MAC and secondary or alias IP.

The server sends a response using its own MAC and IP as the source addresses, the MAC of the default gateway as the destination MAC, and the client source IP of the received packet as the destination IP.

TIP Because real servers must be Layer 2–adjacent to the load balancer when operating in dispatch mode, they can be connected to the load balancer itself or to a Layer 2 switch. Either alternative is workable as long as the Layer 2 adjacency is maintained. Realize that each alternative has its advantages and disadvantages, yet using a Layer 2 switch to connect the real servers gives greater flexibility in the physical deployment of load-balancing services.

The flexibility comes from the fact that load balancers typically do not support the same features found on Layer 2 or Layer 3 switches, do not offer the same port density Layer 2 switches do, and do not deal well with servers changing ports rapidly (in dual-homing scenarios when failing from the primary to the standby NIC port). Load balancers are not Layer 2 or Layer 3 switches, so they do not offer the full range of Layer 2 and Layer 3 capabilities, such as routing protocols, interface tracking, Spanning Tree Protocol, and spanning-tree enhancements. Integrated load balancers inherit all the features available in the switch they are integrated in. For example, the Content Switching Module (CSM) supported in the Catalyst 6500 switch inherits all features available in the Catalyst 6500 IOS. Port density restricts the growth of the server farm, making the process of adding servers burdensome.

In many cases, load balancers have hardware architectures in which ASICs are used to offload the central or load-balancing CPU from performing certain repetitive tasks, such as rewriting Layer 2, Layer 3, or Layer 4 header information, or even NAT functions. This implies that a particular port's ASIC might have an entry for a specific flow and expects to see all packets pertaining to that same flow for processing. Flow information is not exchanged between ports, so during a server failure, the load balancer is forced to rediscover the new interface, leading to the flooding of packets searching for the server's MAC and resulting in potential packet loss.

Directed or Server NAT Mode

Directed mode, unlike dispatch mode, operates on packets at Layer 3, which implies the rewrite of IP header information—specifically, the destination IP addresses. Typically, the rewrite operation implies the translation of destination IP address from the VIP to the selected real server, and vice versa. This translation process allows the placement of real servers on a different subnet than the VIP, thereby permitting more efficient and flexible use of the IP address space and physical deployment configurations.

The typical steps of a load balancer when operating in directed mode are as follows:

1. The packet is received, with the destination address matching a configured VIP.
2. Server selection is triggered based on the VIP configuration.
3. The server-selection process produces information needed to rewrite headers and to forward the packet to selected servers through correct interface.
4. The header is rewritten, replacing the source MAC address with the outbound interface's MAC address, and replacing the destination MAC with the MAC address of the selected server or the next-hop router, if the server is not in the same subnet as the load balancer. The destination IP address is replaced using the selected server's IP address.
5. The packet is forwarded to the selected real server.

TIP Because real servers no longer are required to be Layer 2–adjacent to the load balancer, there could be multiple Layer 3 hops between them and the load balancer. This opens the possibility of having different forward and return paths to and from the server farm. You must remember that the load balancer should process the return traffic, especially when NAT is used in the traffic destined for the server farm.

There is an exception to this mode of operation in which the load balancer can be bypassed by the return traffic. See the "Direct Server Return" section, later in this chapter.

Because the destination IP address is translated to match the selected real server's IP address, there is no longer a need to support the VIP on each real server's IP stack, as is the case in dispatch mode. Because the VIP and real server IP addresses no longer need to share the same IP subnet, real servers might not be connected directly to the load balancer or even a Layer 2–adjacent Layer 2 switch. In fact, the server farm could be several Layer 3 hops away from the load balancer. Figure 16-5 shows the changes in the IP packets as they go through a load balancer in directed mode.

Figure 16-5 *Directed Mode Packet Processing*

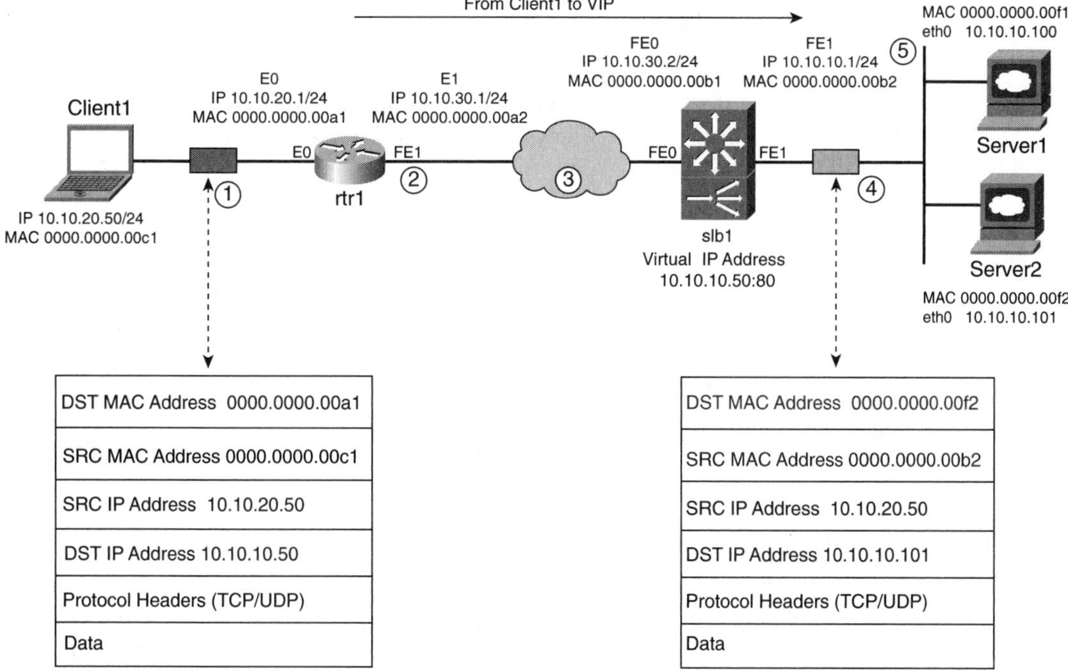

In Figure 16-5, the following transactions occur:

1 Client1 using IP address 10.10.20.50 attempts to connect to a web server (TCP port 80) identified by the URL www.example.com, which is resolved to VIP 10.10.10.50. The client sends a TCP connection request using its MAC and IP addresses, its default gateway's MAC address as the destination MAC, and the VIP as the destination IP address.

2 Rtr1 looks up its routing tables for the longest prefix match to the destination IP address to determine a next-hop device and forwards the connection request to it.

3. The packet is routed through the network until it reaches slb1.
4. Slb1 rewrites the destination MAC and destination IP addresses using the selected server's MAC and IP addresses. Slb1 also rewrites the source MAC using the outbound interface's MAC as it forwards the packet to the server.
5. The selected server receives a packet destined for its MAC and IP addresses.

The server sends a response using the source IP from the connection request packet and the MAC of the default gateway as the destination IP and MAC, and its own MAC and IP as the source addresses.

TIP Server placement can be Layer 2–adjacent to multiple Layer 3 hops away from the slb device. However, utilizing a Layer 2 switch to connect the real servers minimizes the configuration complexity in the deployment of load-balancing devices.

Client NAT

Client NAT refers to the mode in which the source IP address (client IP) in packets destined for the VIP is translated by the load balancer. Client NAT can be applied to both dispatch and directed modes. In the latter case, when both client and server NAT are in effect, the translation mode is referred to as *full NAT* because both the source and destination IP addresses are translated. The load balancer is configured to support a pool of addresses, selecting one to translate the original client IP address. Figure 16-6 presents a full NAT scenario.

In Figure 16-6, the following transactions occur:

1. Client1 using IP address 10.10.20.50 attempts to connect to a web server (TCP port 80) identified by the URL www.example.com, which is resolved to VIP IP address 10.10.10.50. Using its MAC and IP addresses, the client sends a TCP connection request, its default gateway's MAC address as the destination MAC, and the VIP as the destination IP address.
2. Rtr1 looks up its routing tables for the closest match to the destination IP address to determine a next hop. Rtr1 then forwards the connection request to the next hop device.
3. The packet is routed through the network until it reaches slb1.
4. Slb1 rewrites the destination MAC and IP addresses using the selected server's MAC and IP addresses. Slb1 also rewrites the source MAC using the outbound interface's MAC, and the source IP using an available IP address from the NAT pool.
5. The selected server receives a packet destined for its MAC and IP addresses.

Figure 16-6 *Client NAT: Server NAT Scenario*

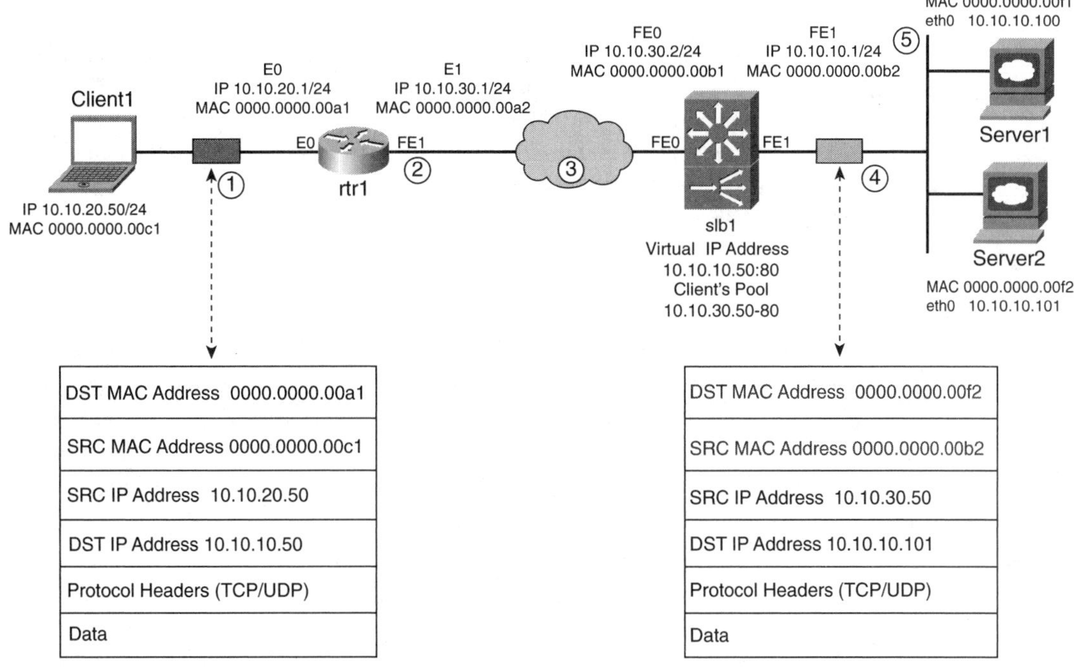

The server sends a response using source IP from the connection request packet as the destination IP (SLB NAT pool address), the default gateway MAC (SLB interface MAC) as the destination MAC, and its own MAC and IP as the source addresses.

TIP Client NAT is used in many cases to ensure that the return traffic is forced back through the load balancer that performed the translation. Keep in mind that after the source IP addresses is translated, demographic information about the clients that use your services is lost. Therefore, make sure the data collection for demographic analysis is done before the NAT process takes place.

Client NAT is the least frequently used NAT method, especially when the NAT is executed close to the server farm. If NAT is executed close enough to the server farm where the load balancer is Layer 2–adjacent to the servers and used as the default gateway, the return path is Layer 2. The servers have a single active load balancer to talk to on the same LAN segment, implying that the primary reason for using client NAT is no longer a requirement.

However, when client NAT is used to force traffic back to the load balancer that performed the initial translation, using the NAT method ensures that the reverse translation process takes place.

While operating in dispatch mode and behaving like a transparent bridge, a load balancer might not have the capability to control return traffic paths if the network is not architected properly. The recommendation is that if a load balancer is used in dispatch mode, there should be no other transparent bridges offering additional Layer 2 paths to the default gateway, to ensure that the load balancer is the only device in the traffic path from the server to the default gateway.

Connection Spoofing

Connection spoofing (also known as TCP termination, delayed binding, or connection splicing) refers to the capability of a load balancer to proxy a connection on behalf of a client. Pretending to be the destination server, the load balancer establishes a connection with a client instead of just NATting the packets between client and server. In addition to the connection from the client to the load balancer, there is a connection from the load balancer to the server.

This is done to take advantage of the capability to perform server selection, which can be based on information found beyond Layer 4 (beyond UDP/TCP). Connection spoofing, however, is applied to TCP because the concept of a connection (in a connection-oriented protocol) to establish a communication channel between two devices lends itself well to the actual spoofing process.

Information beyond Layer 4, which sometimes is referred to as Layer 5 or Layer 7, depending whether the reference is to the TCP/IP suite or the OSI model, respectively, then is leveraged to select specific servers. For instance, HTTP, using TCP as the transport protocol, uses specific *methods* in addition to other fields in the HTTP header to communicate and convey actions between the connected peers. (HTTP methods are explained in Chapter 8, "HTTP and Related Concepts.") The load balancer uses these methods or fields to select specific servers. The HTTP-specific information, however, is available only after the TCP connection has been established—hence the importance of having the capability to support connection spoofing. Server NAT and client NAT both can be implemented while the load balancer is spoofing the connection. Connection spoofing does not change the way in which other modes of operation work. The sections that follow explain the details.

Connection Spoofing Processing

Explaining the operational details that are applied to HTTP traffic best illustrates the basic concept behind connection spoofing. As mentioned in Chapter 8, HTTP uses TCP as the transport protocol. This implies that HTTP-specific information is available only after the

TCP connection has been established—in other words, only after the SYN, SYN/ACK, and ACK exchange has occurred between the client and the load balancer, specifically using the VIP on the load balancer.

After the connection has been established, an HTTP request (in the form of a method) is sent from the client to the VIP. At this point, the load balancer applies the rules or policies to the request and performs the server selection. After a real server is selected, a new connection is initiated with the server. A new SYN, SYN/ACK, ACK exchange takes place between the load balancer and the selected server. The load balancer keeps connections, both to the client and to the server, open for as long as necessary. Typically, after the server selection has taken place, the load balancer controls all communication between client and server. This implies that the load balancer rewrites the IP/TCP header information for both connections. Both client and server are unaware of the load balancer in the middle, rewriting IP addresses and port numbers, and synchronizing SEQ and acknowledgment (ACK) numbers. Figure 16-7 shows the process in more detail.

Figure 16-7 *Delayed Binding: Processing*

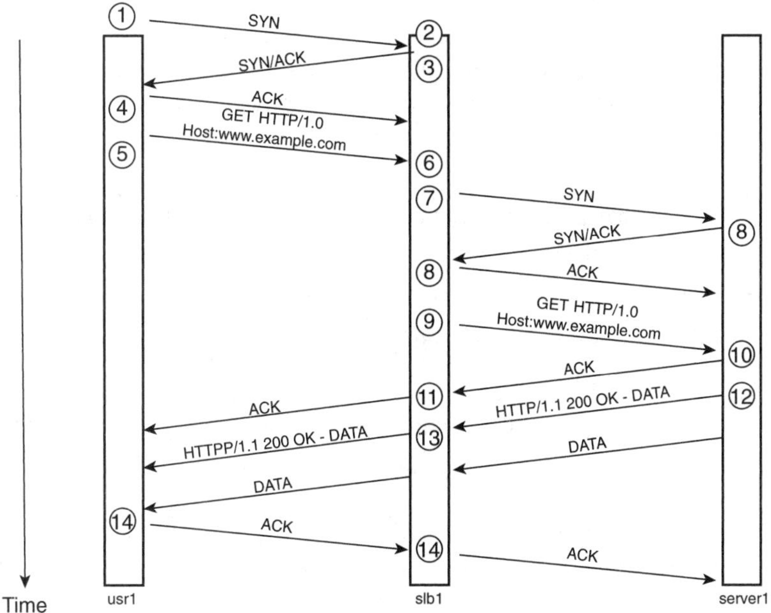

The following sequence of transaction occurs in Figure 16-7:

1 The client, usr1, types www.example.com, which is resolved to a VIP supported by a load balancer—slb1, in this case.

2. Slb1 receives a connection request (SYN) destined for one of its VIPs. The particular destination VIP associated with www.example.com has a content policy applied to the URL that matches index.htm or default.htm. Because a content policy specifies a match to the URL string, the load balancer is forced to spoof the connection until it can parse the URL.
3. Slb1 acknowledges the connection request (ACK) from usr1 and initiates its side of the connection request (SYN) in the same response (SYN/ACK).
4. Usr1 acknowledges the connection request from slb1, and the connection establishment (three-way handshake) is finalized. So far, slb1 has not selected a particular server for the connection because it is still waiting for the URL string.
5. The next packet from usr1 contains the HTTP request, an HTTP GET to /index.htm, in this particular case. The HTTP request has the following format:

```
GET /index.htm HTTP/1.0
Connection: Keep-Alive
User-Agent: Mozilla/4.76 [en]C-CCK-MCD  (Windows NT 5.0; U)
```

NOTE The format HTTP request used in the example is a subset of the actual HTTP request. Only the relevant portions are included, to aid in the explanation.

6. The load balancer parses out the index.htm portion of the HTTP request and uses the information to select a server.
7. Slb1 then sends a connection request to the selected server, server1.
8. Slb1 and server1 go through the TCP handshake (SYN, SYN/ACK, ACK) and establish a connection.
9. Slb1 then sends the HTTP request to the selected server with the original information.
10. Server1 gets the request, acknowledges it, and proceeds to respond.
11. The acknowledgment is received by slb1 and immediately sent to usr1.
12. Server1 responds to the HTTP request from slb1.
13. Slbl adjusts the SEQ and ACK numbers, and sends the response back to usr1.
14. Usr1 acknowledges the previous packet, and slb1 forwards it to server1 after adjusting the SEQ and ACK numbers.

Slb1 rewrites IP header information and adjusts the SEQ and ACK numbers every time a packet is sent to usr1 or server1. This makes it seem as if the client and server are communicating with each other directly.

NOTE In the previous example, there might be a few other packets in the actual exchange of information between client and server. These other packets purposely are omitted to simplify the explanation of connection spoofing.

It is useful to understand what occurs behind the scenes every time a packet associated to the connection between usr1 and server1 is processed by slb1. The processing tasks are as follows:

1. Slb1 rewrites TCP headers, adjusting both the ACK and SEQ number values and the port translation, if required, resulting from the configuration.
2. Slb1 rewrites IP headers based on the currently configured mode of operation.
3. Slb1 performs the TCP checksum calculation on every packet.
4. Slb1 forwards the packet.

These steps and calculations take place on packets destined for either usr1 or server1. This implies that slb1 is required to be in the traffic path to ensure that the rewrite and other associated operations take place.

The concept of connection spoofing mostly is applied to connection-oriented protocols such as TCP. Because TCP is used in many applications, the capability to parse information beyond Layer 4 implies that, for these applications, the load balancer could distribute the load based on application data. This capability opens the door for a number of uses in which the application data determines how and where to ultimately forward traffic. The next section explains an example of such a feature applied to HTTP traffic. This is known as *connection remapping* or *port remappping*.

Connection Remapping

Connection remapping is a concept applied almost entirely to HTTP only. The goal behind connection remapping is to distribute the load of a single TCP connection to multiple distinct servers based on information beyond Layer 4 found on individual HTTP requests. Using a practical example is the best way to understand connection remapping. Figure 16-8 presents the details of a connection remapping example.

Figure 16-8 *Processing of Connection Remapping*

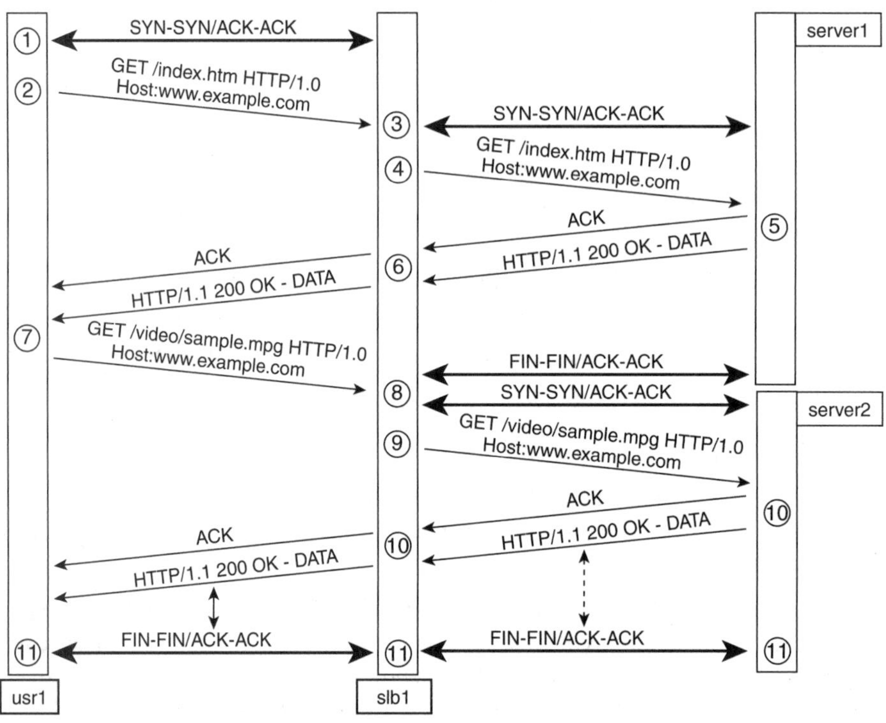

In Figure 16-8, the following sequence of transactions occurs:

1 Usr1 types www.example.com, which is resolved to a VIP supported by slb1. Usr1 establishes a connection with slb1.

2 The particular destination VIP associated with www.example.com has a couple of content policies applied to the URL that match index.htm or default.htm, and *.mpg. Because a content policy specifies a match to the URL string, the load balancer is forced to perform delayed binding on that particular connection.

3 Usr1 sends its first HTTP connection request to slb1 with www.example.com/index.htm as the URL in the request.

4 Slb1 applies the matching content policy, selects the correct server (server1), and establishes a connection with the selected server, server1.

5 Slb1 forwards the HTTP request to server1.

6 Server1 receives the request, acknowledges the requests (ACK), and responds by sending back the web page associated with the URL.

7 Slb1 receives the response from server1, performs the tasks associated with delayed binding, and forwards the response to usr1.

8 Usr1 sends another HTTP connection request destined for /video/sample.mpg, which matches a different content rule.

9 The content rule in Step 7 is associated with a different server farm, so slb1 terminates the connection to server1, selects a new server based on the new URL, and establishes a new TCP connection with the selected server, server2.

10 Slb2 sends the HTTP connection request to server2.

11 Server2 responds to the HTTP request, and slb1 forwards the response to usr1 after performing the delayed binding tasks.

Assuming that there are not more connection requests from usr1, the connection between slb1 and both usr1 and server2 continues until the data exchange triggered by the connection request on Step 7. When completed, the connections are terminated.

Slb1 has the capability to decide, based on HTTP header information, whether to use a different server farm; thus, a different server that might be better suited to handle the request for specific content types would handle the request instead. The existing TCP connection to the current real server is terminated, and a new TCP connection with the newly selected real server is opened, giving much more granular control on how the request load is distributed. As you will see in the "Performance Implications" section, this fancy processing does not come without a price.

Direct Server Return

Direct Server Return (DSR) refers to using the load balancer only to load-balance incoming requests to the server farm, and letting the return traffic from the server bypass the load balancer by being sent directly to the client. The requirements and consequences of this mode are as follows:

- The load balancer is bypassed by the return traffic.
- The load balancer is not required to rewrite header information.
- The load balancer must be Layer 2–adjacent to the server farm and must operate in dispatch mode because any kind of NAT (client or server) would require the load balancer to NAT the return traffic as well.
- The virtual server can be only Layer 4; otherwise, the load balancer would have to process all the return traffic to do the header rewrite operations required by delayed binding.
- Connection spoofing is not possible.
- The load balancer is capable of handling a higher load because it is not required to process the return traffic, so the overall performance is increased.

Figure 16-9 presents the DSR process in more detail.

Figure 16-9 *DSR Processing*

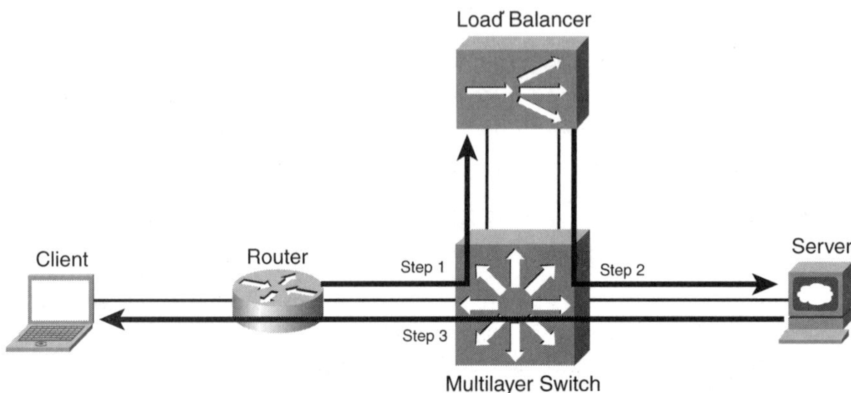

The connection request from the client to the VIP is forwarded by the multilayer switch to the load balancer. The load balancer selects a server and sends the request. The load balancer does not rewrite the L3 header information, which requires the servers in the server farm to be configured with the same IP address used for the VIP. Having all the servers in the server farm use the same IP address is possible by configuring loopback addresses on the servers, yet there are a few caveats. See Appendix D, "Loopback Interface Configuration Procedures," for details on configuring loopback interfaces on different OSs and the possible caveats.

The server receives the request and sends a response using the multilayer as the default gateway, thereby bypassing the load balancer. Because the return traffic is using the same IP address of the VIP as the source IP address, there is no need for the load balancer to be involved.

The load balancer's connection-tracking mechanism requires some modification on a DSR environment. The load balancer typically sees both the inbound and the outbound traffic, yet in a DSR mode, it sees only the inbound traffic. The modification needed by the connection-tracking mechanisms keeps the load balancer from aging entries that might be active because the load balancer sees no return traffic activity.

NOTE The combination of the multilayer switch and the load balancer could be either an L2/L3 switch with an integrated load-balancing module or an external appliance. In either case, the processing is very similar. Yet in a fully redundant environment, it is important to remember the following considerations:

- The default gateway and the load balancer must be adjacent to the servers, thus extending the STP domain from the load balancer through the multilayer switch to the server farm.
- In a fully redundant environment using two load balancers, the need exists for a looped topology in which STP is used to avoid STP loops.
- Load balancers in an active-standby or active-active implementation behave different: Active-standby requires a looped topology, whereas active-active allows a loop-free topology.

Remember that the default gateway and the load balancer must be adjacent to the server farm, thus extending the STP domain from the load balancer through the multilayer switch and up to the server farm, and creating an STP loop in a fully redundant configuration.

DSR typically is used in environments in which the load balancer might be challenged to keep up with the expected load, thus relieving some of its processing capacity to be used for new connections. The restriction is imposed to prevent the use of some of the more useful features of load balancers. For connection-oriented protocols, DSR requires that you figure out the right timeout because the load balancer will not be capable of determining when the connection has been closed. For connectionless protocols, DSR works well because the load balancer is not expecting an explicit connection-termination mechanism.

Performance Implications

This section discusses the performance implications of the different modes of operation and their relation to critical components of load balancers' architectures. Five different modes of operations already have been discussed:

- Dispatch
- Directed or server NAT
- Client NAT
- Connection spoofing
- DSR

Given the choices to configure the load balancers' mode of operation, the selection should be made based on the service requirements and whether the features that support them are available in the particular load-balancing mode. A secondary consideration is performance. The following paragraphs discuss the performance considerations.

The rule of thumb for load balancers is that the more processing tasks are required, the lower the overall performance is. From lowest to highest, the list of modes related to the number of processing tasks follows:

1. DSR
2. Dispatch
3. Directed or server NAT
4. Client NAT
5. Connection spoofing

Table 16-1 points out the main tasks performed under each mode of operation.

Table 16-1 *Performance Considerations of the Modes of Operation*

Mode/Task	Inbound Traffic	Inbound and Outbound Traffic	MAC Header	IP Header	TCP/UDP Header	Connection Spoofing
DSR	√		√			
Dispatch		√	√			
Directed		√	√	√	√	
Client NAT		√	√	√		
Connection spoofing		√	√	√	√	√

DSR sees only the inbound traffic and does not perform L3 or L4 rewrites. Dispatch mode is very similar to DSR, yet the load balancer sees both inbound and outbound traffic. Directed mode is the most common mode, in which the load balancer processes inbound and outbound traffic and rewrites L2, L3, and L4 header information. Client NAT is a special case in which the actual function is not mutually exclusive from other modes that perform L3 rewrites. However, it is analyzed assuming that the rewrite operations are performed on the source and destination IP addresses of inbound and outbound packets, respectively.

NOTE Many load balancers are not optimized for client NAT because the mode operation does not support a key load-balancing function, and its use is not that common. Many other devices on the network could be used as NAT engines for outbound client traffic to hide RFC 1918 addresses.

Finally, connection spoofing is obviously the most expensive mode because it requires the most processing tasks and also performs deep packet inspection on the payload. In this mode, in addition to the L2, L3, and L4 header rewrite, the SEQ and ACK numbers must the kept in sync for the connection from the client to the load balancer and from the load balancer to the server, and for the parsing of content based on content policies.

Expect the performance of a load balancer to lower as the mode or operation changes to require more processing capacity.

Load-Balancing Algorithms

The primary function of load balancers is to distribute the traffic load among the available servers in the server farm or caches in a cache farm. This section discusses the different algorithms used to distribute the traffic load, whether applied to groups of servers or a group of caches (server farms or cache farms, respectively).

Although the purpose of distributing the load is similar, the algorithms for server farm–based and cache farm–based load balancing have subtle differences. Load-balancing algorithms control how traffic distribution occurs and tend to avoid uneven load distribution of traffic to the server farm. This is because all servers in the server farm logically grouped under a single VIP address are expected to have the same application data. Regardless of the server-selection process, every server belonging to the same VIP can serve or provide the requested information.

A load balancer can be placed in front of a cache farm to distribute requests to caches instead of servers. Load-balancing algorithms used for cache farms are applied to solve a different problem than server load balancing. Cache devices are not necessarily expected to have the application data when a request arrives. Caches are expected to retrieve the data as the first request is received and to cache it for potential subsequent requests. This implies that an optimal distribution of requests for content should attempt to select the same cache consecutively to increase the *hit rate*. Hit rate is the average of the number of times that the application data is present in the cache when a request for that specific content has been received.

Because the load balancing for a server farm is done differently than for a cache farm, the load-balancing algorithms are grouped under server farm–based or cache farm–based categories to better describe their details.

Server Farm Load-Balancing Algorithms

A load-balancing algorithm controls the distribution of TCP and UDP connections to the servers in the server farm. Typically, all packets for a single TCP or UDP connection must be sent to the same real server. However, in special situations multiple different TCP or UDP connections should be sent to the same real server (*session persistence*) or a single

TCP connection in which multiple HTTP requests are received and mapped independently to different servers (connection remapping). A load balancer should support all the aforementioned cases for traffic distribution.

NOTE The process of associating multiple TCP/UDP connections from a single client with the same server is called *stickiness*, or more appropriately is defined as *session persistence*. Session persistence is a topic on its own and is discussed in detail in Chapter 18, "Session Tracking and Cookies," and Chapter 19, "Persistence Mechanisms on Load Balancers." HTTP persistence is a different concept that has to do with keeping a single TCP connection open between client and server for all HTTP requests instead of one TCP connection per HTTP request. HTTP connection persistence is explained in Chapter 8, "HTTP and Related Concepts."

The process of load-balancing connections involves two major functions:

1. Server selection criteria
2. Traffic load distribution

The server-selection criteria refer to the type of information used to select the correct server farm and the appropriate server within the server farm. The selection is done by applying Layer 4 or Layer 5 content policies to incoming traffic. The traffic load distribution refers to the actual mechanism of spreading the traffic load across the available real servers.

In case multiple server farms are available for a single VIP, the server-selection mechanism first selects a server farm and then selects a specific server.

For example, assume that you have a VIP 10.10.10.50 that supports services on TCP port 80 for the following URLs:

http://www.example.com/partners/partner-login.htm
http://www.example.com/clients/client-login.htm

When the load balancer processes a new connection that is destined for VIP 10.10.10.50, the server-selection mechanism is triggered. Because there are two distinct server farms, one per URL, the load balancer needs to determine which service and associated server farm supports the specific URL. The load balancer performs a lookup in the HTTP header of the HTTP requests and determines that the server farm associated with client-login.htm should be used. Then, based on the configured load-balancing algorithm, the appropriate server is selected using real-time information such as connection load or response time. Then the traffic is forwarded (traffic distribution). Real-time information on the server is obtained from tables kept in the load balancer that can track connection information, number of connections, response time, and so forth. This connection information is updated as new connections or packets for existing connections are received.

The information needed to perform server farm and server selection includes the following:

- Destination IP address.
- Destination protocol and port number.
- Source IP address.
- Other information might be specific to the application service. For example, on HTTP, the policy could specify URL, host, user agent, and so on.

The information needed to perform traffic load distribution includes the following:

- Current connection load.
- Server response time.
- Other factors, including specific host information that might come through a single compound metric through a protocol such as DFP. The metric might include processor load, available memory, and so on.

NOTE The Dynamic Feedback Protocol (DFP) is used between servers and load balancers to exchange server load information used by the load balancer for load distribution purposes. The server uses a DFP client agent, a process running on the server, to communicate with the DFP server, a process running on the load balancer for the exchange of information in the form of a compound metric that might bias the load balancer's load distribution.

The tuning of traffic distribution across servers in a server farm is typically an ongoing process by which information about the status, load, availability, and respective limits for each server constantly is calculated. This information is used both in the planning stages and during the server-selection process. The actual selection is based on existing and validated information.

Load-balancing algorithms have different characteristics for load distribution and server selection, and some are more complicated than others. The forthcoming sections introduce the following load-balancing algorithms and their detailed characteristics:

- Round-robin
- Weighted round-robin
- Least connections
- Weighted least connections
- Fastest predictor
- Source IP

- Hash address
- URL and hash URL
- Maximum connections

Round-Robin Predictor

Round-robin is the simplest of all predictors. As real servers are configured, a list of servers is assembled. The list is followed in sequential order as the server-selection process is triggered. Under round-robin, the load-distribution information is based strictly on server availability; because of this restriction, it includes only the servers that are currently available and operational. Server load, CPU capacity, and response time are not parameters that factor in the server-selection process. When a request arrives, the next available server in the list is selected, and the connection request is forwarded. Figure 16-10 depicts a round-robin scenario.

Figure 16-10 *Round-Robin Predictor*

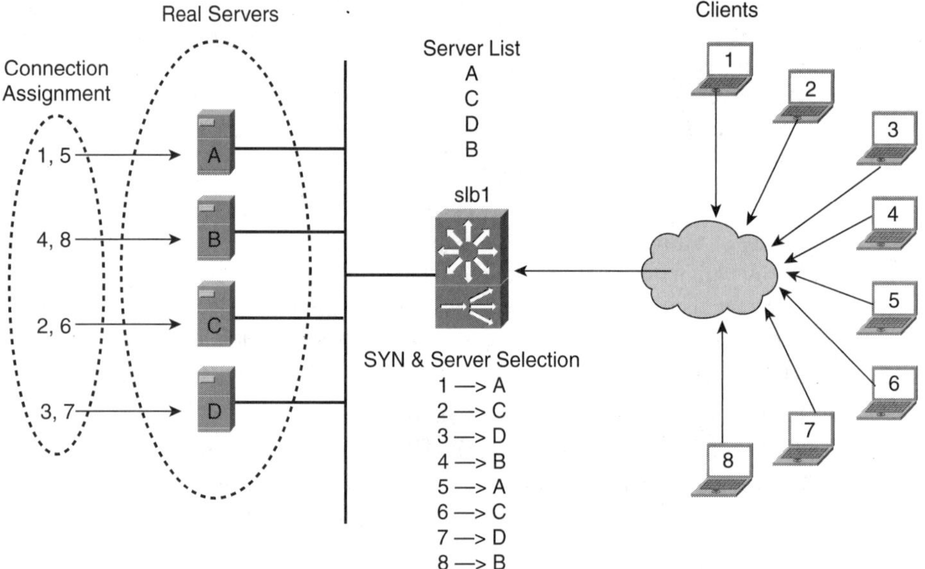

In Figure 16-10, load balancer slb1 is configured to support a VIP associated with four real servers. The servers were configured in the following order: A, C, D, and B. For the purpose of the explanation, assume that clients 1 through 8 have initiated eight connection requests that are received by slb1 in order from 1 to 8. Each request is assigned to the next available server in the server list, which implies an even distribution of requests to servers. Requests are assigned in the following manner:

1 A receives requests 1 and 5.

2 C receives requests 2 and 6.

3 B receives requests 3 and 7.

4 D receives requests 4 and 8.

Round-robin is best suited for homogenous server farms in which both the processing capacity of all servers is alike and the service type or application requirements on each real server are similar. When the server farm is not homogeneous in server capacity or requirements, weighted round-robin may be more convenient. Weighted round-robin is introduced in the next section.

Weighted Round-Robin Predictor

The next load-balancing algorithm to be discussed is the weighted round-robin. The weighted round-robin is an extension of round-robin, in which the load-distribution process can be biased by a weight assigned to each server. The weights assigned to each server should be used as an attempt to even the load distribution on a server farm in which servers have varying processing capacity. Servers with higher weight receive more connections. As in round-robin, the server list is determined by how the real servers were configured. As shown in Figure 16-11, real server A is the first in the list, real server C is the second, B is the third, and D is the last. When the load balancer receives new connection requests, it sends them to the next real server in the list for the number of times indicated by the weight. If weight is *n*, the real server receives n requests before the load balancer moves on to the next real server.

For instance, in Figure 16-11, Server A gets a single request before the load balancer sends the next request to Server C. After Server C gets the next consecutive two requests, the following three subsequent requests are forwarded to Server D. The next two requests are sent to Server B. All other forthcoming requests are handled in the same manner by the load balancer.

Figure 16-11 *Weighted Round-Robin*

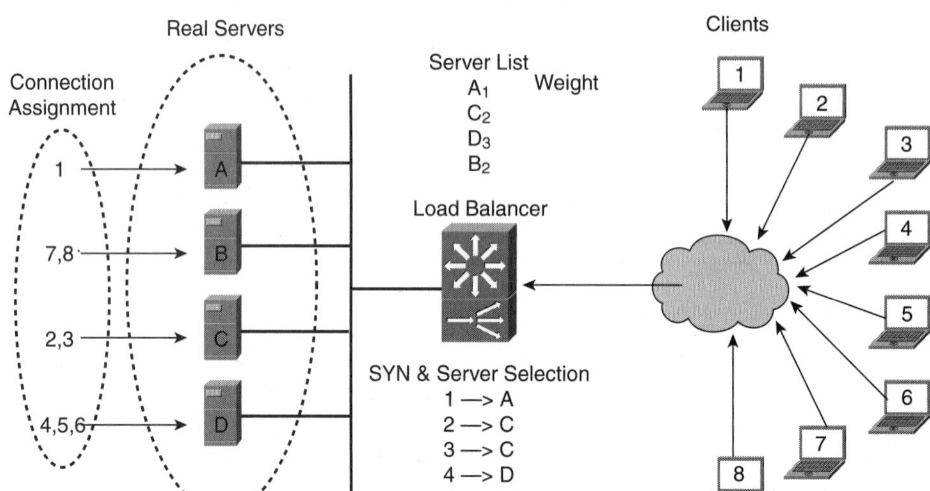

TIP

It is recommended to use the high watermark or an upper-bound value for the number of concurrent connections a server can receive. This prevents the server from reaching its maximum operational limits by exceeding the use of critical system resources such as CPU or memory utilization. Each server could be protected by configuring on the load balancer the maximum number of connections (maxconns) that it can receive. The selection of the maximum number of concurrent connections should be based on either of the following:

- Existing data on the observed maximum number of connections before the response time starts to degrade
- Lab-tested results

See the "Maximum Connections" section toward the end of this chapter for more details.

Least Connections

The next load-balancing algorithm to be discussed is least connections. Least connections uses the lowest number of concurrent connections among the real servers to determine which server receives the next request. When a request arrives, the connection table is searched, and the server with the least number of connections is selected. The request then is forwarded, and after the connection has been established, the connection table is updated. A special case of least connections in which the server-selection process can be biased is available through another predictor referred to as *weighted least connections*.

Weighted Least Connections Predictor

In weighted least connections, each server is assigned a weight, which is used to bias the server-selection process. Each real server in the list is represented by its own weight, *n*, which is defined manually at configuration time. The next real server selected is that with the lowest metric. The metric is defined as the number of active connections divided by the server weight:

$$\text{Metric} = {}^{\text{connections}}/_{\text{weight}}$$

For instance, in Figure 16-12, Server B receives the next request for two reasons: It holds the lowest metric value, and its newly calculated metric, 6/1 = 6, is still the lowest.

Figure 16-12 *Weighted Least Connections*

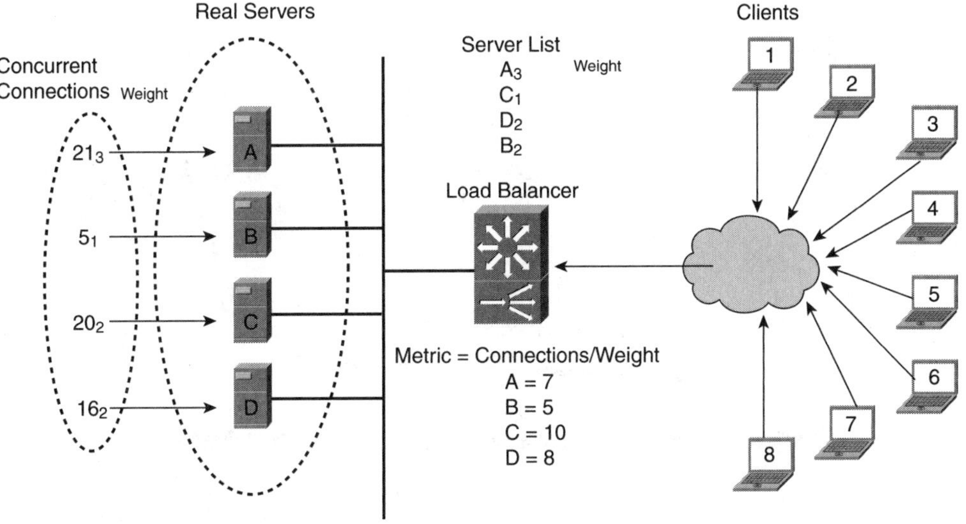

If all servers are assigned the same weight, weighted least connections acts just like least connections. Weighted least connections is utilized when the servers in the server farms have varying capabilities, and the intent is to normalize how the load balancer should treat them. The goal is to distribute higher loads to servers capable of handling more. Furthermore, for less capable servers, a weight can be assigned so that they are not overloaded beyond their capabilities. For more details on how to avoid overloading a real server, see Chapter 17, "Server Health Management."

Fastest Predictor

This load-balancing algorithm selects the next real server based on the fastest response time. The fastest response time is the average delta time between the SYN and SYN/ACK for all successfully established connections.

This load-balancing mechanism should be used with caution because the response time can change drastically and very rapidly, and these changes might not be reflected in the actual response time. With rapid and drastic changes in response time, the server might become overloaded before the load balancer selects a new server. As you have seen, servers do not follow a linear progression between the number of connections and their response times. When the server reaches a certain number of concurrent connections, the response time curve increases sharply. This algorithm, however, could be used in conjunction with the high-watermark connection-control mechanism offered by the specific connection switch, to keep servers out of the danger zone by not sending more connections over the selected limit. Figure 16-13 presents the typical relationship between connections per second and response time.

Figure 16-13 *Concurrent Connections and Response Time*

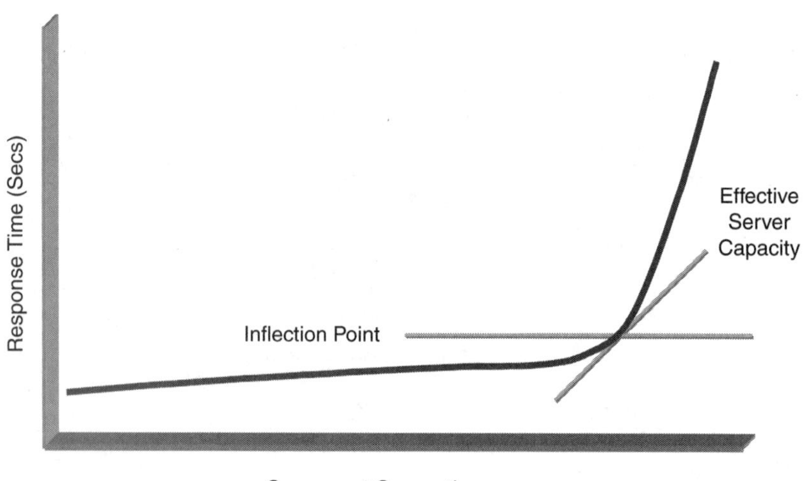

The actual data points are not included because they vary depending on the following factors:

- The server hardware platform
- The software running on the server
- The application used to create the traffic and track the response time

Source IP Predictor

To select the real server, the load balancer uses either the source IP address or a hash value that is based on the source IP address. This predictor could be used for both server and cache farms. Using it for server farms helps to ensure session persistence when no proxy servers used in the client side might change the source IP address for a different connection from the same user. Using the algorithm for cache farms increases the likelihood of a cache hit. A cache hit is important for clients from the same IP address space, typically the same company or organization, to find the requested content already cached in the specific cache in the cache farm.

NOTE A cache hit refers to a request processed by a cache that contains a valid copy of the requested content. Hit rate refers to the number of times a cache hit occurs on an average basis. Conversely, a cache miss is the number of times a request for content does not find the requested content on a cache or cache farm.

Hash Address Predictor

When using hash address as the predictor, the load balancer selects the real server by using a hash value that is calculated by using both the source and destination IP address. This predictor can be used to achieve session persistence when no proxy servers are in front of the clients. The proxy servers issue the requests on behalf of the clients, thus changing the client IP address. The hash value is calculated so that there is statistical distribution based on source and destination IP addresses, which works best when there is a wide range of source or destination IP addresses.

URL and Hash URL Predictors

With the URL and hash URL predictors, the load balancer uses the URL in the HTTP request to determine the real server. This predictor could be used for both server and cache farms. When using it for server farms, the assumption is that distinct groups serve specific types of content. For instance, server farms A and B support services for www.example.com. Server farm A supports *.cgi, and server farm B supports *.jpg, *.mpg, and *.mov.

By using this predictor for cache farms, the likelihood of cache hits is increased by directing requests to the cache farms serving specific content types.

TIP The load-distribution method varies depending on the specific load balancer. Some use the characters at the beginning of the URL defined in the content rule; others use a hash value from a large portion of the URL. Whichever mechanism is in use, the load distribution matches the values to the available number server or caches in the cache farm to even the load they receive.

Hash URL, or URL hash, performs a hash operation on the URL string to come up with a value that matches a server or cache in the farm. Hash URL increases the likelihood of cache hits by sending requests for the same content to the same cache. Depending on the load balancer type, the URL is either partially or fully matched, or pattern matched through a regular expression. For example, the pattern to match could be any of the following expressions:

- www.example.com/default.htm
- www.example.com/*.jpg
- www.example.com/files/movie*

www.example.com is the domain name portion of the URL, often referred to as the FQD. The search for a match does not include the FQD.

Maximum Connections

Maximum connections is not a load-balancing algorithm, but it is important enough to mention in this chapter for the following reasons:

- It prevents each individual server or cache from receiving more than the specified number.
- It prevents the entire server farm from being affected by a single server's load shifting to other servers.

Think of maximum connections as the high watermark that no server should exceed. This watermark requires a basic knowledge of how high the average server load is, which normally comes from observing the behavior of the servers in the server farm. This observation implies some trial-and-error periods in which the wrong values initially are selected and eventually are tuned to the actual server farm.

TIP When fine-tuning the maximum connections number, make sure that the load-distribution algorithm evenly distributes the load among the available servers and that at least 50 percent of the servers in the server farm already are protected with a maximum yet very conservative value. The distribution algorithm could simply be round-robin, and the maximum connection value should be based on observed numbers and controlled with the maxconns mechanism. If you are using an operational environment to determine the correct values, realize that server failure practically is required to discover server limits. Server failure impacts the real client's response time. A better approach for determining the maximum connection limits is to simulate close to real-life traffic conditions in an offline server farm and then use a more conservative number when you go live.

Cache Farm Load-Balancing Algorithms

Unlike server farm predictors, cache farm load-balancing predictors typically control the distribution of a subset of the traffic a server farm would receive. The subset of traffic is composed of connection requests to the objects that a cache can handle, which typically are referred to as *cacheable objects*. Cache farms are deployed to keep copies of the original content close to the user, which implies that the underlying traffic is used to transport such content. When the caches are deployed closer to the server farm, the purpose is to offload the server farm from having to process requests for content that is cacheable. This form of caching is called *reverse proxy caching (RPC)* and is illustrated in Figure 16-14.

As shown in Figure 16-14, the cache farm is connected to the aggregation switches, which is where the load-balancing function for the cache farm is performed. Note that the traffic that the cache farm receives is not processed by the server farm, thus allowing the server farm to scale up the support for other traffic.

For the cache farm to keep copies of this content, the content needs to be cacheable. Because of these considerations, load balancers send only certain connections to cache farms. For example, HTTP is used to transport objects of different kinds. If these objects are marked as cacheable, the HTTP connections (really the underlying TCP connection carrying the HTTP connection) are load-balanced among caches in the cache farm.

Figure 16-14 *Reverse Proxy Caching*

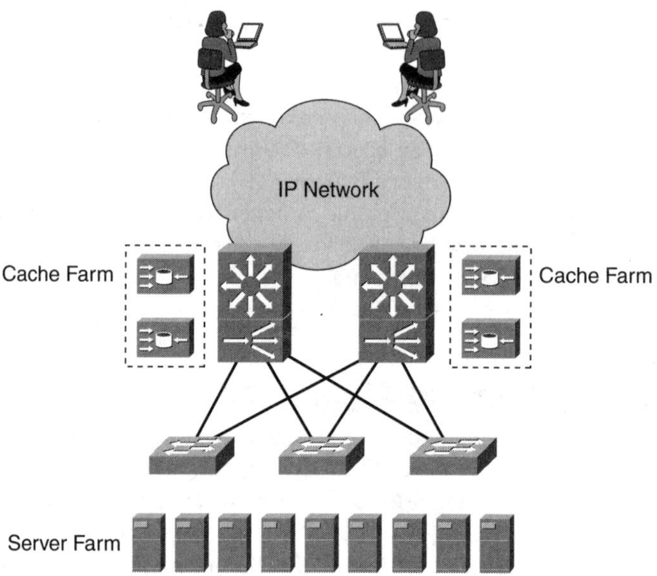

With a caching environment in which the cache farm is close to the user, the requests for content are intercepted long before they reach the origin server, or even the reverse proxy cache farm. This caching type is known as *transparent caching* and is presented in Figure 16-15. The user requests destined for the IP address of the origin servers (or the VIP associated with them) transparently are redirected to the cache farm by multiple mechanisms. These mechanisms can include a load balancer directing traffic to a cache farm, or other mechanisms such as the Web Cache Communication Protocol (WCCP).

In Figure 16-15, the transparent cache is closer to the user and typically behind a link that needs some bandwidth relief. The bandwidth relief comes in part from the request handled locally by the transparent cache farm, but mostly from the content not using the available bandwidth. Other benefits to point out are the likely lower response time to the user by having the content closer and the offloading of processing from the server farm or RPC cache farm. Notice in Figure 16-15 that both the transparent cache farm and the RPC cache farm coexist in a tiered caching environment in which each cache farm type offers a distinct set of benefits.

In the transparent cache farm, just like in RPC mode, the first request for a cacheable object results in the object being cached in the cache farm. As a result, the origin server will not get as many requests, and the propagation delay incurred in bringing the object *n* times (*n* requests) is shortened to one time. This translates to a potentially shorter response time to the user.

Figure 16-15 *Transparent Caching*

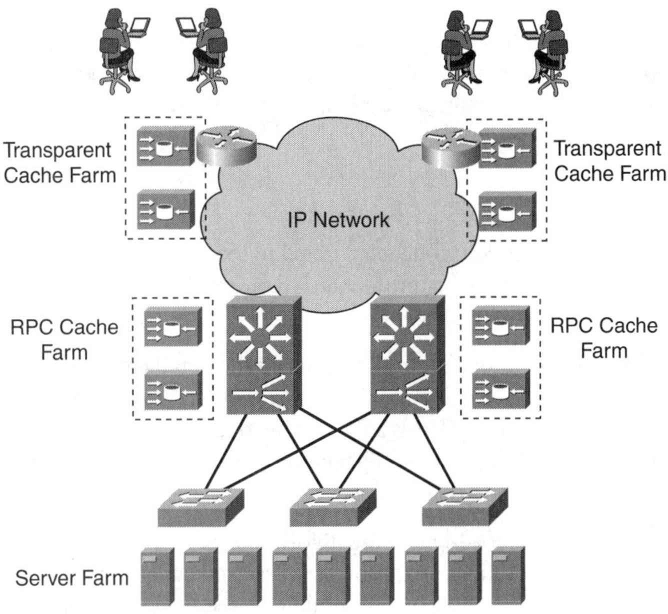

NOTE Two versions of the WCCP exist: V1, which has been submitted as an informational draft, and V2, which has been proposed as an Internet draft. For more information on WCCP, search for WCCP on Cisco's web site (www.cisco.com).

Domain and Domain Hash

The load balancer uses domain name information to perform the cache-selection process. The domain information typically is parsed out the HTTP host tag field and then used to pick a cache. The cache farm is divided by evenly assigning the alphabet letters to each cache in the cache farm so that the cache-selection process is statistically fair.

The host tag is a field in the HTTP header that contains a FQDN, such as www.example.com. In the domain predictor, the load balancer parses a number of characters to then match them to the correct cache. The characters used are determined by the domain name. The domain hash also takes the FQD and produces a value, the hash value, which is used to select the cache or server to send the request. The value is calculated based on an XOR operation on the domain portion of the host tag on the HTTP header. The results of the calculation yield the same value, which ensures that the same cache, or server, is selected on requests for content under the same domain name.

Because the domain hash predictor uses a hash algorithm over the domain name string to come up with a value to select the right cache or server, the selection process increases the cache or server hits. Domain and domain hash both can be used for server and cache farms.

Summary

This chapter described key concepts related to load balancers, load-balancer modes of operation, and load-balancing protocols, which are fundamental to understanding the details behind how load balancers work.

The "Modes of Operation" section introduced the details of how load balancers do their processing work at various depths within the packets, ranging from Layer 2 (MAC) through Layer 3 (IP) and Layer 4 (TCP/UDP), and beyond Layer 4 (HTTP). This illustrated the wide range of capabilities and intelligence supported by load balancers, and the implications of deep packet inspection on performance.

Finally, the numerous load-balancing algorithms, which are the mechanisms used to distribute the traffic load across farms of server and caches, were discussed. The load-balancing algorithms ultimately determine how the load balancers operate, the depth of inspection, and how their intelligent capabilities are used.

This chapter covers the following topics:

- The use of load-balancing devices to gracefully "shut down" servers in a server farm (that is, to gracefully redirect client requests to other servers in the cluster)
- How load balancers can prevent overload on servers by means of slowstart and with maxconnections settings
- How XML and SNMP allow applications to control load-balancing devices
- How load balancers can monitor the health of servers by means of in-band or out-of-band probes, and how to choose the probe to use
- The description of the most commonly used probes
- How to configure load-balancing devices to monitor virtual hosting environments
- How to configure load-balancing devices to monitor web servers receiving clear-text (HTTP) and encrypted traffic (HTTPS)

CHAPTER 17

Server Health Management

Data Center applications execute on servers. A single server can process requests for a certain number of users, and this number depends on the hardware and software capabilities of the server. When the need arises to scale the application to a higher number of users, you need to consider load balancing.

A load-balancing device provides load distribution and application high availability. Load balancers are inserted in the path of the traffic between clients and servers. This makes it possible for the load balancer to redirect requests to the appropriate server (load distribution) and to monitor the status of the application on the servers.

Load balancers provide server health-management capabilities: This means that these devices can detect a malfunctioning server or application, mark it down, and consequently take it out of rotation.

Having redundant servers in conjunction with load balancers achieves two goals:

- **It makes it possible to perform maintenance with minimal disruption**—An operator can configure the load balancer to consider a server as "not in service." As a result, the load balancer does not send any new requests to that server.
- **The failure of one server does not bring down the application**—The load balancer sends new connections to the remaining available server(s).

You can check that a server and an application are available in a multitude of ways. Each monitoring technology has its pros and cons. Technologies with deeper application awareness give more accurate information but are more taxing to the system; technologies that just monitor the TCP stack do not provide as much information about the application, but they have higher scalability.

Using an appropriate health check requires understanding some basic server architecture details and the application protocols; this information is available in Chapter 2, "Server Architecture Overview."

Load-Balancing Terminology

Before reading the rest of the chapter, you should be familiar with some terminology used for the load-balancing technology. This terminology was introduced in Chapter 6, "Server Load Balancing Overview."

In the configurations used in this chapter, you find the following terms:

- **Virtual server** (Shortened to vserver)—A collection of servers that appear to the end client as a single IP address, Layer 4 protocol, and Layer 4 port. The IP address goes under the name of virtual IP (VIP) address.
- **VIP (virtual IP) address**—The IP address that a client uses to access an application.
- **Reals**—The individual servers in the server farm in the cluster of servers that provide an application.
- **Probes or health checks**—The load balancer uses probes to monitor the status of the servers. Probes can be ICMP packets or TCP handshakes whose result provides the load balancer with information about the status of a server.

The status of a server as reported by a load balancer can be either of the following:

- **Operational**—It is defined as "alive."
- **Failed**—When the server fails to respond to a probe, this is also defined as "down."
- **Out-of-service**—The server is administratively down from the perspective of the load balancer. This means that an operator manually took the server out of rotation from the load-balancer configuration. This often is referred to as "suspended."

The configuration commands that allow putting a server into service or taking it out of rotation are named as follows (on Cisco devices):

- **inservice**—Configured under the "real" configuration; equivalent to a **no shut** for a router interface
- **no inservice**—Takes a server out of rotation

As an example, "activating a service" means that a server is going to receive connections because the load balancer puts this device into its pool of servers eligible to receive new connections (that is, in rotation).

Server Management

Server management refers to the fact that by using the load balancer console you can do the following:

- Take a "real" out of rotation
- Put a server back into the cluster of load-balanced servers, and distribute the traffic load to the group of servers

- Protect servers from being overloaded by incoming connections (either by setting a threshold or by distributing load unequally among available servers)

These operations are supported by load balancers and can be executed either manually through the console, through the Extensible Markup Language (XML), or by using the Simple Network Management Protocol (SNMP).

As an example, assume that the load-balancing device is configured as in Example 17-1. Real SERVER1 and real SERVER3 identify two different servers: 10.10.10.11 and 10.10.10.13.

Example 17-1 *Server Farm Configuration on a Load Balancer*

```
real SERVER1
  address  10.10.10.11
  inservice
!
real SERVER3
  address 10.10.10.13
  inservice
!
serverfarm test
  real name SERVER1
   inservice
  real name SERVER3
   inservice
!
 vserver foo1
  virtual 192.168.1.1 any any
  serverfarm test
```

Requests normally are received for the VIP address 192.168.1.1 and are dispatched to the servers 10.10.10.11 and 10.10.10.13. Assume that you need to upgrade the code on the server software running on SERVER3.

Before doing anything on the server machine itself, you can take SERVER3 out of rotation *from the load balancer's console* (see the section, "Graceful Shutdown") so that new incoming connections are sent to SERVER1. When you are done upgrading SERVER3, you want to put it back in service. To do this, you use the load-balancer console and activate the "real" again. At this point, 10.10.10.13 starts receiving connections again. If the predictor was least loaded, the new server receives a huge amount of new connections. A feature called *slowstart* prevents this from happening (see the section, "Slowstart").

Graceful Shutdown

The graceful shutdown feature enables you to take a server out of rotation without terminating existing connections. In Figure 17-1, you can see a server farm made of three servers under the same VIP address: 10.10.10.11, 10.10.10.13, and 10.10.10.15. The value of the

VIP address is 10.10.10.80. Clients request a connection to 10.10.10.80, and the load balancer distributes requests to the VIP among the three servers.

In part **a** of Figure 17-1 (the upper portion of the figure), you can see a client (client A) that has an open connection (connection number 1) with the server 10.10.10.11. An operator needs to perform maintenance on server 10.10.10.11 and decides to take it out of rotation, so he types **no inservice** for SERVER1.

Figure 17-1 *Graceful Shutdown and Connection Assignment*

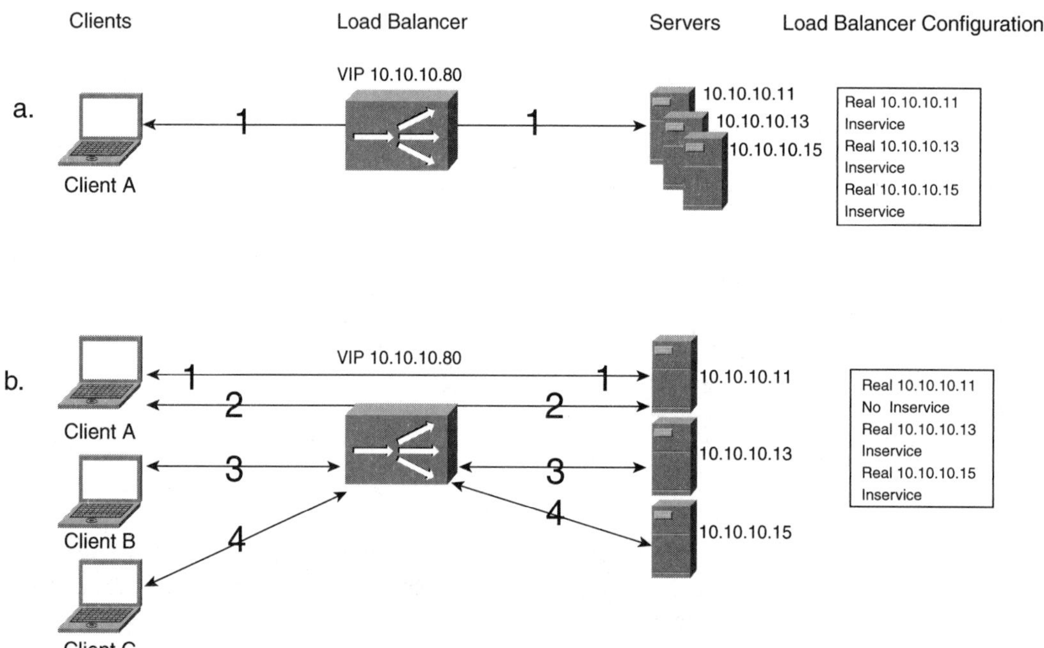

Example 17-2 shows the status of the real server 10.10.10.11 after the operator suspended this service.

Example 17-2 *Connections to a Suspended Server: Graceful Shutdown*

```
10.10.10.11, TELNET, state = OUTOFSERVICE
  conns = 1, maxconns = 4294967295, minconns = 0
  weight = 8, weight(admin) = 8, metric = 0, remainder = 1
  total conns established = 1, total conn failures = 0
```

As you can see from the example, even if the server was suspended, the existing connection (1) is not affected. This is displayed by the total conns established count in the output shown in Example 17-2.

Part **b** of Figure 17-1 shows that the load balancer sends new connection requests (connection number 3 from client B and connection number 4 from client C) to the other servers in the cluster (10.10.10.13 and 10.10.10.15). However, a new connection (number 2 in part **b** of Figure 17-1) coming from client A still is sent to 10.10.10.11 (this is explained in the accompanying note).

NOTE If you are already familiar with the concept of persistence, you probably are asking what happens if you shut down a service and new connections from the same client arrive to the load balancer. Do these connections get load-balanced to another server, or do they go to the same one?

A good implementation of graceful shutdown should not break existing sessions. This implies that a new connection that belongs to existing sessions of the server should not be sent to another server. This is represented in the middle portion of Figure 17-1, when the client that opened connection 1 originates connection 2 after 10.10.10.11 already was taken out of rotation.

The graceful shutdown feature should memorize the IP address of the clients that have opened connections to the server and should "stick" new connections to this same server even if it has been suspended. When the sessions are over (based on some timeout in the sticky table), the server will not accept any new connection.

For more information on session persistence or stickiness, refer to Chapter 6 for the basic concept and to Chapter 19, "Persistence Mechanisms on Load Balancers."

When the specific connections to 10.10.10.11 are closed, the connection count for this server goes to zero.

At this point, an operator can perform maintenance on the server with minimum impact to the clients that are using the application (10.10.10.13 and 10.10.10.15 receive the new connections).

Slowstart

Load balancers typically offer the slowstart feature to avoid overwhelming a server with incoming connections when the server has just been made available for load balancing. The reason for doing this is that when a server has just been started, most likely it is not ready to respond to a large number of connections; at steady state, it will.

Servers do not spawn the maximum number of processes at startup, to avoid overwhelming the CPU, which, in turn, would impair the capability of the server to process incoming requests.

For example, when Apache starts up, it immediately spawns a number of distinct processes—typically, five (StartServers directive). Upon receiving new connections, Apache starts new processes according to the MinSpareServers settings.

The MinSpareServers directive determines how many child processes need to be available that are not processing clients' requests. The creation of new processes is a result of the need to have each connection assigned to a process and the need to have enough "spare" processes. The MaxSpareServer directive, on the other hand, decides the maximum number of idle processes.

When Apache needs to ramp up with the number of processes, it follows this approach: It spawns one process, waits 1 second, it starts two new processes, waits 1 second, spawns four more processes, and so on. When it reaches the rate of 32 children per second, it keeps this forking rate until it matches the required number of servers.

NOTE You can find more information about how Apache handles the process creation at http://httpd.apache.org under the documentation for "Performance Tuning": http://httpd.apache.org/docs-2.0/misc/perf-tuning.html.

Load balancers implementing the slowstart feature give servers placed in rotation time to "catch up" with the connections they receive without being overloaded. The load balancer slowly increments the number of connections sent to the newly activated servers. As a result, the servers are capable of adapting to the connection load until the necessary number of processes is running, as exemplified by the approach used by the Apache servers.

The slowstart feature is most beneficial when used with the "least connections" load-balancing algorithm (see Chapter 16, "Load-Balancing Modes and Predictors").

Max Connections and Min Connections

Max Connections and Min Connections are parameters that you configure under the "real" configuration of a load balancer, to prevent server overload. Example 17-3 shows the lines of a possible configuration.

Example 17-3 *Max and Min Connection Settings in a Server Farm*

```
real SERVER1
  address 10.10.10.11
  inservice
```

Example 17-3 *Max and Min Connection Settings in a Server Farm (Continued)*

```
!
real SERVER3
  address 10.10.10.13
  inservice
!
serverfarm test
real SERVER1
  maxconns 100
  minconns 90
  inservice
real SERVER3
  inservice
!
```

If SERVER1 has 100 active connections, a new incoming connection is sent not to 10.10.10.11, but to another server in the server farm. When the connection count for SERVER1 goes below 90, new connections are sent to 10.10.10.11.

By knowing the architecture of your server software, the operating system, and the amount of RAM, you can estimate the maximum number of connections that a single server can process and protect the server from overload situations (see Chapter 2).

Failure to properly set the max limit of connections on a server can result in a server overload situation. If the server is overloaded, when a new TCP SYN is received, the server will answer with a TCP RST. Load balancers can capture this occurrence with in-band health checks and dispatch new connection requests to servers that are not overloaded.

TIP Setting the maximum number of connections that a load balancer can send to a server requires tuning. It is very possible that the original estimate is simply unattainable, in which case you can change the original settings to a safer number.

Tuning the maxconns and minconns settings is a preventive measure to avoid overload on the servers. Load balancers also provide reactive measures to react to overload (in-band health monitoring).

The conclusion: Use maxconns and minconns as a preventive measure to avoid server overload, and use in-band health monitoring as a reactive mechanism to redirect connections that otherwise would go to an overloaded server.

Server Management Interface

Load-balancing devices enable you to operate on traffic destined to server clusters with command-line interface (CLI) commands such as **inservice** and **no inservice**, as described in the section "Server Management."

Alternatives to using the CLI are the XML interface and SNMP. Both techniques are used either by management applications that provide network administrators with a GUI, or by server-monitoring applications that dynamically can modify load balancers' configurations.

Management software for load-balancing devices typically uses XML for configuration purposes and SNMP for monitoring.

XML

The XML is becoming a popular way to dynamically adjust load balancers configurations, and it simplifies the integration of applications and load-balancer operations. Load balancers run an HTTP server on the main CPU, which listens for HTTP POSTs or PUT and parses the XML content.

XML was invented to describe data. If you are not familiar with XML, think of it as the combination of the description of the fields of a record in a database and their values.

Objects described by XML fields are carried on HTTP. When using XML to configure load balancers, the objects identify specific features, and their value indicates whether the features are enabled or the value assigned to a specific variable used by a feature.

Example 17-4 is an example of an XML object used to configure a load balancer (the Cisco Content Switching Module, specifically).

Example 17-4 *Configuring a Server Farm on a Load Balancer via XML*

```
<?xml version="1.0"?>
<config>
<csm_module slot="5">
<serverfarm name="TELNET">
<real_server ipaddress="10.10.10.11">
<inservice sense="yes"/>
</real_server>
</serverfarm>
</csm_module>
</config>
```

The first lines of configuration specify the configuration mode (<config>) and which load-balancing blade to configure (<csm_module slot="5"> identifies the load balancer in slot 5 of a Catalyst 6500 chassis).

Notice that <serverfarm name="TELNET"> </serverfarm> defines the object whose property is described in the <real_server> </real_server> field.

If the preceding XML lines are sent through an HTTP POST to a load balancer that understands the fields <serverfarm>, <real_server>, and <inservice>, it is possible to activate or suspend a real server.

Applications also can assign weights to servers in the server farm, as shown in Example 17-5.

Example 17-5 *XML Code to Control the Weight of a Real Server on a Load Balancer*

```
<?xml version="1.0" standalone="yes"?>
<config>
<csm_module slot="5">
<serverfarm name="TELNETg>
<real_server ipaddress="10.10.10.11">
<weight value="4"/></real_server>
</serverfarm>
</csm_module>
</config>
```

SNMP

SNMP is used to retrieve information from network devices and hosts (*managed devices*) about their configurations, state, and counters for hardware and software components, and to set the value of those components for configuration purposes. This requires the managed devices to run an agent. The *SNMP Management Station* remotely controls the agents by periodically sending probes with GET_REQUEST or SET_REQUEST messages to which the agents reply with "response" messages.

OID and MIBs

SNMP defines the entities being monitored as objects. Objects are identified by their object identifier (OID). The OID is a sequence of numbers separated by a dot, as in .1.3.6.1.2.1.2.2.1.7.

These numbers are arranged in a hierarchical manner, so .1.3.6.1.2.1.2.2.1.7 and .1.3.6.1.2.1.2.2.1.16 belong to the same category.

Now suppose that the management station wants to retrieve the state of an interface. A way of doing this is to send a GET_REQUEST for .iso.org.dod.internet.mgmt.mib-2.interfaces.ifTable.ifEntry.ifAdminStatus or .1.3.6.1.2.1.2.2.1.7. The agent on the server returns 1 if the interface is up or 2 if the interface is down.

If the management station was interested in the number of output octets sent by the interface, it would have requested the following object: .1.3.6.1.2.1.2.2.1.16 or .iso.org.dod.internet.mgmt.mib-2.interfaces.ifTable.ifEntry.ifOutOctets.

The obvious question at this point is what defines the association between the network, hardware or software properties, and the OID?

Object definitions are described in Management Information Bases (MIBs). Each MIB defines information about different types of software, hardware, or protocols. Some of these MIBs are standard and are defined in RFCs; some of them are proprietary, as with *enterprise MIBs*. The proprietary MIBs start with .1.3.6.1.4.1. Examples are shown here:

.1.3.6.1.4.1.9: The Cisco OIDs
.1.3.6.1.4.1.311: The Microsoft OIDs

NOTE Cisco MIBs can be found at ftp://ftp.cisco.com/pub/mibs/. You can translate between OIDs numeric values and the string format by using the online tool at http://www.cisco.com /pcgi-bin/Support/Mibbrowser/unity.pl.

CISCO-SLB-MIB

In the case of load balancing with Cisco hardware, the management station must use CISCO-SLB-MIB and CISCO-SLB-EXT-MIB.

Example 17-6 shows the result of browsing the virtual server configuration of a Cisco Content Switching Module (IP address 10.20.30.2).

Example 17-6 *SNMPWALK with the Content Switching Module OIDs*

```
[admin@server-4 /]# snmpwalk 10.20.30.2 123 .1.3.6.1.4.1.9.9.161.1.4.1.1
enterprises.9.9.161.1.4.1.1.2.5.9.72.84.84.80.45.86.73.80.49 = 2
enterprises.9.9.161.1.4.1.1.4.5.9.72.84.84.80.45.86.73.80.49 = IpAddress:
  10.20.5.80
enterprises.9.9.161.1.4.1.1.5.5.9.72.84.84.80.45.86.73.80.49 = 80
enterprises.9.9.161.1.4.1.1.6.5.9.72.84.84.80.45.86.73.80.49 = 6
enterprises.9.9.161.1.4.1.1.9.5.9.72.84.84.80.45.86.73.80.49 = "WEB-VIP1"
enterprises.9.9.161.1.4.1.1.18.5.9.72.84.84.80.45.86.73.80.49 = 0
```

The OID being queried shows the table of virtual servers from the Content Switching Module (in this case, there is a single virtual server):

.1.3.6.1.4.1.9.9.161.1.4.1.1 = enterprises . cisco . ciscoMgmt . ciscoSlbMIB . ciscoSlbMIBObjects . slbVirtualServers . slbVirtualServerTable . SlbVirtualServerTableEntry

The first entry in the output from snmpwalk indicates the status of the virtual server, as indicated by the name of the OID. Notice that 5.9.72.84.84.80.45.86.73.80.49 is the identifier of the virtual server:

> enterprises.9.9.161.1.4.1.1.2.5.9.72.84.84.80.45.86.73.80.49 = enterprises . cisco . ciscoMgmt . ciscoSlbMIB . ciscoSlbMIBObjects . slbVirtualServers . slbVirtualServerTable . slbVirtualServerTableEntry . slbVirtualServerState . 5 . 9 . 72 . 84 . 84 . 80 . 45 . 86 . 73 . 80 . 49

The state of this virtual server is 2 (see the second line of Example 17-6), which means "inservice."

Now you should be familiar with the logic of the output in Example 17-6. .1.3.6.1.4.1.9.9.161.1.4.1.1 identifies the table with the virtual server information (slbVirtualServerTable.slbVirtualServerTableEntry).

This table is made of several fields, each providing a piece of information: the status, the IP address, the name of the virtual server, and so forth. Each piece of information is identified by a subfield to the same root:

- enterprises.9.9.161.1.4.1.1.2 = SlbVirtualServState
- enterprises.9.9.161.1.4.1.1.4 = slbVirtualIpAddress
- enterprises.9.9.161.1.4.1.1.5 = slbVirtualPort
- enterprises.9.9.161.1.4.1.1.6 = slbVirtualProtocol
- enterprises.9.9.161.1.4.1.1.9 = SlbServerString
- enterprises.9.9.161.1.4.1.1.18 = slbVirtualTotalConnections

Example 17-7 shows the configuration on the Content Switching Module from which SNMP retrieved the value of the OIDs shown in Example 17-6.

Example 17-7 *Cisco Content Switching Module Configuration Corresponding to Example 17-6*

```
vserver HTTP-VIP1
  virtual 10.20.5.80 tcp www
  serverfarm WEB-VIP1
  inservice
```

RMON

A special category of MIBs are Remote Network Monitoring (RMON) MIBs (.1.3.6.1.2.1.16). RMON MIBs do not provide information about specific elements, but instead provide preprocessed information gathered over time, such as statistics and history. For more information about RMON, refer to RFC 2819.

TRAPs

SNMP allows the managed device to send asynchronous messages (TRAPs), too, when certain events occur. TRAPs typically are originated for events such as these:

- Linkup
- Linkdown

These events obviously are related to the status of the physical interfaces. For more information about SNMP TRAPs, see RFC 1215. A number of other possible TRAPs exist. For example, RMON can compare counters with thresholds and send a TRAP. Alternatively, TRAPs can notify a management station about startup or shutdown of a server.

An example of the use of TRAPs is the SNMP TRAP for the real servers on a Cisco Content Switching Module. Whenever a real changes its state, the load balancer sends a TRAP to the management station with the OID of the real server: 1.3.6.1.4.1.9.9.161.2 (ciscoSlbMIBNotificationPrefix).

Server Failure Detection

Server failure detection is the capability of a load-balancing device to detect that a server is malfunctioning and to mark it down, without the need for an operator to suspend the service manually on the load balancer configuration.

Server monitoring can be done according to two methods:

- **Using probes**—A load balancer originates client traffic (HTTP request, DNS requests, or simply ICMP echo packets) directed to the servers. If the server responds and the response has the expected status code, it is considered alive. Every load balancer implements probes either in the form of in-band monitoring or out-of-band.
- **Using SNMP**—SNMP monitors the status of server hardware and software, and the load-balancing device can adjust the load distribution according to this information. Not all load balancers have the capability to send out SNMP requests.

Server Monitoring Using Probes

Load-balancing devices can perform the following:

- **In-band monitoring**—The load balancer watches the TCP connection setup between a client and a server. This mechanism is driven by clients' requests.
- **Out-of-band probing**—The load balancer itself performs periodic TCP handshakes to the servers (in addition to TCP probes, the load balancer can generate ICMP traffic, HTTP traffic, and so on).

Either of these two mechanisms can detect that a server is malfunctioning and suspend it. As a result, new clients' connections are distributed to the remaining operational servers.

When the load balancer marks a server as "down," it can take two possible approaches:

- Leave the server down until an operator decides to put it back into rotation
- After the expiration of a timer, probe the server again to see if it is healthy, and put it back into rotation (this is called auto-unfail)

NOTE Probes are described in greater detail in the rest of this chapter.

When a probe fails, a syslog or a TRAP message can be generated.

NOTE The informational RFC 3164 describes how syslogs work. Syslogs are carried on UDP port 514. Syslog messages include a time stamp, a host name, and the message itself. Unlike with SNMP TRAPs, the messages are not categorized, so it is not possible to take actions automatically upon reception of a syslog message, unless the receiving application parses the message and identifies previously defined keywords.

Server Monitoring Using SNMP

Memory and *CPU utilizatio*n are the two key parameters to monitor in a server besides checking that the output from the server does not return error codes. Too many processes running concurrently can exhaust the available memory, causing continuous swapping to the disk. This, in turn, can increase the CPU utilization.

SNMP can monitor this information. Administrators typically use SNMP agents on servers to retrieve statistical information on servers' performance and to send a page to support staff if something catastrophic occurs.

Using SNMP for monitoring can be very powerful if coupled with a load balancer in taking preventive measures. The key point is to identify the meaningful object identifiers to monitor.

Some MIBs that are of interest for the management of an HTTP server are the following:

- MIB-II (RFC 1213)
- Host Resources MIBs (RFC 1514)
- WWW-MIB (RFC 2594)

If you use SNMP to monitor the status of physical interfaces, you can use MIB-II. MIB-II defines managed objects for TCP/IP devices and can be used, for example, to monitor the status of interfaces on a server (the reference here is to the specific *Interfaces group* from RFC 1213).

Host Resources MIBs are useful for retrieving information such as CPU, memory, and disk utilization, like the Storage and Device groups. Examples of Host Resources MIB are as follows:

- .iso.org.dod.internet.mgmt.mib-2.host.hrSWRunPerf.hrSWRunPerfTable.hrSWRunPerfEntry.hrSWRunPerfCPU
- host.hrSWRunPerf.hrSWRunPerfTable.hrSWRunPerfEntry.hrSWRunPerfMem

WWW-MIBs or equivalent application MIBs are useful for monitoring the operational status of web servers. In the case of WWW-MIBs, wwwServiceOperStatus provides status information about a web server. WWW-MIBs also define a field for the fully qualified domain name of a virtual host (wwwServiceName), which could be useful with virtual hosting.

NOTE The concept of virtual hosting is described in Chapter 2.

Typically, standard MIBs are available across different operating system platforms: Windows 2000, for example, supports MIB-II and Host MIBs out of the box; otherwise, you must install a specific agent.

In addition to the standard MIBs, there are vendor-specific MIBs to monitor services and operational status. As an example, Microsoft provides MIBs to monitor the following:

- HTTP server (311.1.7.3)
- FTP server (311.1.7.2)
- SQL server (311.1.4.1)

Examples of operational enterprise MIBs are the Windows NT MIBs to monitor CPU utilization (311.1.1.3.1.1.2.1.3.0) and RAM utilization (311.1.1.3.1.1.1.0).

Probe Types

This chapter already introduced the distinction between in-band probes and out-of-band probes. The first ones monitor the connection setup between the client and the server, which has the advantage of being a nonintrusive method to verify the server operations. The disadvantage of in-band probes is that a failed server still can be sent connection attempts, thus introducing a small delay in the client TCP handshake.

Out-of-band probes allow proactive detection of server failures, with the drawback of generating additional traffic on the network and sometimes interoperability with the server process or the Java Virtual Machine.

In terms of which monitoring mechanism provides higher availability, this is a function of the server farm environment and applications. In-band monitoring typically covers more failure scenarios than out-of-band monitoring.

In-Band Health Checks

A load balancer monitors the TCP handshake between the client and the server with in-band health checks or between itself and the servers (if performing delayed binding). Based on how the server handles the TCP handshake, it can take the following actions:

- A connection can be reassigned to a different server.
- A server can be marked as down.

In-band health checks usually are implemented for monitoring TCP connections, but some platforms also support the same functionality on UDP.

NOTE Chapter 2 described the behavior of a server in the presence of process failures. If the process is down on a server that uses UDP as the transport protocol, the TCP/IP stack sends an ICMP port unreachable message when a client sends UDP traffic to the server.

A load-balancing device can capture the ICMP port unreachable and take the server out of service.

Figure 17-2 shows how the in-band health check works. Part **a** of Figure 17-2 shows that the client initiates a TCP handshake, and the load balancer in the middle dispatches the SYN to a server (which, in the first row, happens to be a broken server) and waits for a SYN/ACK. If the SYN/ACK is not received from the server, the load balancer can take it out of service or increase a counter. After a number of unsuccessful attempts to send connection requests to this server, the server is marked as down. The number of attempts normally is user-configurable.

Figure 17-2 *In-Band Server Health Monitoring*

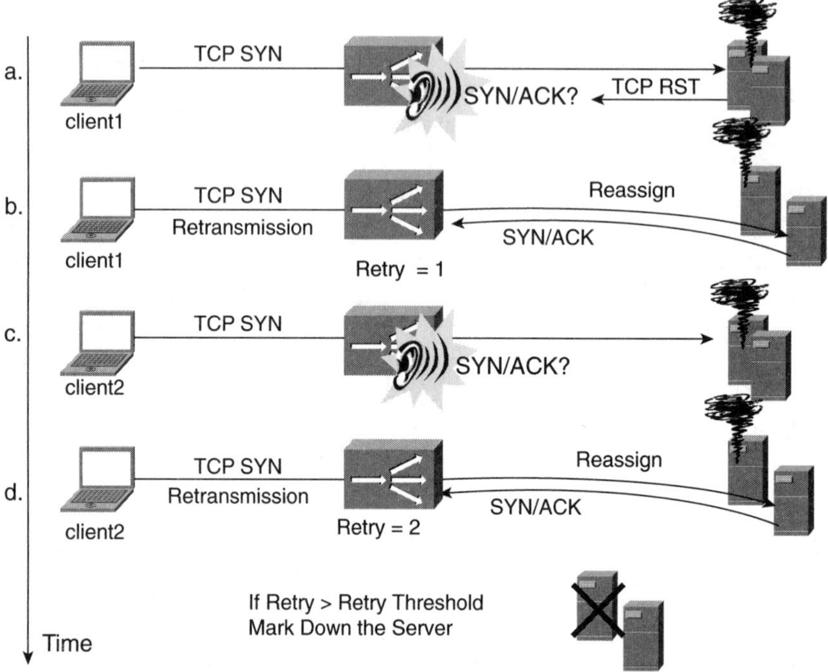

Connection Reassign and Server Markdown

A server failing to respond to a TCP SYN behaves as follows:

- It can send a TCP RST (part **a** of Figure 17-2).
- It simply does not send back any TCP packet (part **c** of Figure 17-2).

If the load balancer notices that the server fails to respond to the TCP handshake, it reassigns the connection to another server. Reassigning a connection means that the load balancer waits for the client to perform a SYN retransmission (parts **b** and **d** of Figure 17-2) and forwards the retransmitted SYN to another server.

NOTE For more information about how the client TCP stack behaves in the presence of server failures, refer to the section, "TCP and UDP Connections to a Failed Server," in Chapter 2.

Servers send a TCP RST if either the server process is down or the server is overloaded because it might be busy with other connections. When a server is overloaded, it might be preferable to try to send the retransmitted SYN to the same server, in the hope that other clients closed existing connections. You can achieve this by configuring a threshold (the reassign threshold) on the load balancer so that connections are reassigned to a different server only after the client has sent SYNs for a "threshold" number of times.

As an example, if the value of the reassign threshold is 2 and the server does not respond to two consecutive SYNs, the load balancer reassigns the third SYN to a different server.

When the load balancer reassigns a connection, it does not necessarily take the faulty server out of rotation. As an example, in part **b** of Figure 17-2, client1 has just been reassigned; client2 (part **c** of Figure 17-2) sends a SYN, and the load balancer sends this SYN to the faulty server again. The server does not send any ACK, client2 retransmits the SYN, and the load balancer assigns the SYN to another server (part **d** of Figure 17-2).

After each SYN "failure," the load balancer increases a counter (the failed counter or retry counter). When the counter goes above a threshold (the retry threshold), the server is taken out of service. In part **d** of Figure 17-2, the retry counter goes above the threshold of 2; as a result, the faulty server is marked as down.

NOTE Notice that in Figure 17-2, the same server responds first with a TCP RST and then just does not respond: This is for explanation purposes. In a real scenario, most likely a server consistently will respond with a TCP RST (if the server Layer 4 port is not listening) or simply does not respond (if the server is disconnected, for example).

TIP When deciding on the threshold to reassign connections to a different server, you have to know how the TCP stack of the client operates. In Windows 2000, for example, the TCP stack attempts the same connection three times (one transmission and two retransmissions).

If the reassign threshold on the load balancer is 3, the Windows 2000 client connection going to a malfunctioning server does not get reassigned and eventually times out. If the client has a browser, for instance, the Reload button would have to be clicked to generate a new connection request.

Server Recovery (auto-unfail)

Load balancers typically wait for a certain amount of time (this is user-configurable) before sending new traffic to servers that previously failed.

When the timer has expired, the load balancer sends a new TCP SYN (upon a connection request from a client) to the previously failed server. The server is considered in "testing" mode. If the SYN fails, the server still is considered down and the TCP SYN retransmission from the client is sent to another server. If the server answers the SYN, the connection is established with this one and its status is changed to up or alive.

HTTP Return Code Checks

In-band monitoring typically provides the monitoring device with information about the status of Layer 4 of the server hosting the application. An HTTP server could be returning error status codes, but the server still would accept a TCP handshake on port 80.

HTTP return code checks allow monitoring of the HTTP responses from the server to the client. The load-balancing device can identify status codes that are not expected and increment a counter; if these unexpected status codes happen too frequently (the counter reaches a user-configured threshold), it can suspend the server.

Figure 17-3 provides an example of HTTP return code checks. Client1 sends HTTP requests to an HTTP server. The load-balancing device forwards the HTTP requests and monitors the status code in the responses. In the example, the GET request for the object 123.gif returns a 500 server error, as well as the request for page.html. The load balancer increases a counter each time it detects the status code 500 until a threshold is reached, at which point the server is marked as down.

Client2 sends HTTP requests for the same application; the load balancer sends these requests to another server and monitors the status code. This time, the server responds with a 200 Ok status: The server is healthy.

Notice that an HTTP server that can respond correctly to some HTTP requests (such as index.html) and returns error codes for other HTTP requests (such as 123.gif) is taken out of service over time because of the counters increasing.

TIP This mechanism is more powerful than HTTP application probes because it gives the load-balancing device the capability of monitoring all the available web pages or scripts on a server, as opposed to just one URL specified in the probe configuration.

Application probes typically monitor only one web page by periodically sending an HTTP GET to a user-configured URL, such as index.html. HTTP return code checks monitor all the client requests to a web server, which means that the load balancer verifies the status code for each and every object retrieved by the client: index.html, 123.gif, and so on.

Figure 17-3 *HTTP Return Code Checks*

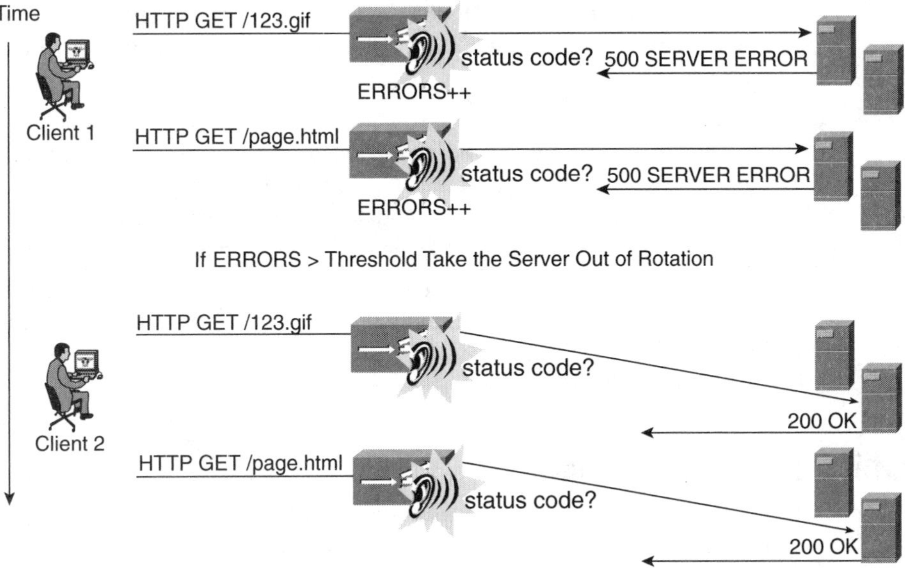

Out-of-Band Probes

Out-of-band probes are packets generated by the load-balancers CPU. These packets are real protocol requests, such as ARP or ICMP ECHO or HTTP GET requests.

The load-balancers CPU implements an IP stack and can generate probes of all types, from very simple ARP requests to specific application requests; the most typical is an HTTP GET.

Probes can be categorized based on the protocol layer that is being used:

- **Layer 2 probes**—An example is ARP probes. The CPU sends an ARP request periodically to resolve the MAC address for the IP of each server in its server farm.
- **Layer 3 probes**—An example is ICMP probes, which are just like pings. The CPU of the load balancer pings the servers. If no response is received, the server is marked as down.
- **Layer 4 probes**—These are normally TCP handshakes, such as SYN, SYN ACK, and RST. TCP probes can be used to monitor many servers whose applications are TCP based. They cannot provide information about the application itself.

- **Layer 5 probes**—These probes are used to monitor servers at the application layer or Layer 5. An example is the use of HTTP probes to monitor a web server. The load balancer sends an HTTP GET for a specific URI or an HTTP HEAD and monitors the response status. If this is not 200 Ok, the load balancer marks the server as down.

NOTE Out-of-band probes sometimes do not interoperate well with servers. This can be caused by how the probe closes the TCP connection. On most load balancers, this is done with a TCP RST directed to the server. Servers often log the RST as an error. You must modify the configuration of the load balancer to use the FIN handshake as the closing mechanism.

On the other hand, closing probe connections with a FIN might keep open sockets on the load balancer, eating resources and limiting the number of probes that can be open at the same time.

Dynamic Feedback Protocol

Cisco invented the Dynamic Feedback Protocol (DFP) to have the server communicate status information to load-balancing devices in the form of a compound metric called weight.

DFP includes agents and a Load Balancing Manager. The DFP Agent is software that runs on servers and collects information about the following:

- CPU
- Memory
- Disk space
- Concurrent connections
- Application response times
- Queue lengths
- Threshold levels

DFP does not define which elements to monitor; it just provides a communication infrastructure between load balancers and servers. The DFP software interface provides the freedom to customize DFP agents to monitor specific applications and specific server parameters.

A DFP agent can monitor any information that it deems necessary. The only restriction for DFP to work with the Load Balancing Manager is to report a meaningful value for the load balancer.

The information is made of BindIDs and weights. A BindID defines an IP address, a protocol, and a port. Each physical server machine running an agent can have multiple

BindIDs. Weights are used to change the way that the predictor assigns new connections, especially the weighted round-robin and weighted least-connections predictors.

DFP agents can run on servers as well as other devices. For example, a load balancer in one location could be part of a group of load balancers that are geographically distributed and load-balanced as well. Load balancers communicate site load information among themselves or between them and a global load balancer. Metrics to determine the site selection could be communicated through DFP.

Probes Comparison: Determining What to Use

Choosing the right type of probe for your network is a trade-off between performance and intelligence.

Regular in-band health checks are almost equivalent to TCP out-of-band probes, with the difference being that in-band checks usually provide for much greater scalability than out-of-band health checks.

Although out-of-band probes are a very powerful tool for monitoring servers, the main problem that they pose can be scalability. The more probes you use, the smaller the rate is at which the load balancer can generate them. Additionally, application layer probes are more resource-intensive than Layer 2 probes because they involve more computation.

HTTP return code checks are in-band check mechanisms, but they can have a more significant impact on performance because their operation is not limited to the TCP handshake phase; they need to look into HTTP responses. HTTP return code checks are probably the most complete mechanism for monitoring the availability of an HTTP-based application.

NOTE Make sure you understand the difference between HTTP return code checks and HTTP probes. HTTP return code checks involve the load balancer monitoring HTTP requests generated by a client and the associated response from the server. HTTP probes involve the load balancer generating HTTP requests for the server and reading the response from the server.

Even if HTTP return code checks are an in-band mechanism, they require the load balancer to inspect the Layer 5 information throughout the duration of the TCP connection, which has a performance impact.

Regular in-band health monitoring (Layer 4) applies only at connection setup, which does not introduce performance penalties.

External applications can use SNMP to monitor servers and can use XML to configure load balancers. SNMP usually comes in the form of lightweight software to run on servers and can monitor applications by using both standard and enterprise MIBs. There are MIBs for all sort of applications.

When using SNMP, you can implement preventive measures by triggering configuration changes when the memory utilization exceeds a certain value or when the CPU utilization rises to high values. The drawback is that for each server, you must send several SNMP GET_REQUESTs to retrieve all the information that you need; a DFP agent, on the other hand, consolidates and processes the information on the server itself and just sends a single metric number.

Out-of-Band Probes

This section describes how the main out-of-band probes work. Understanding the application layer probe mechanisms requires familiarity with the specific application being checked. Figure 17-4 represents the three main categories of probes:

- Layer 3 probes (part **a** in Figure 17-4)
- Layer 4 probes (part **b** in Figure 17-4)
- Layer 5 probes (part **c** in Figure 17-4)

Figure 17-4 *Out-of-Band Probes and Their Pseudotraces*

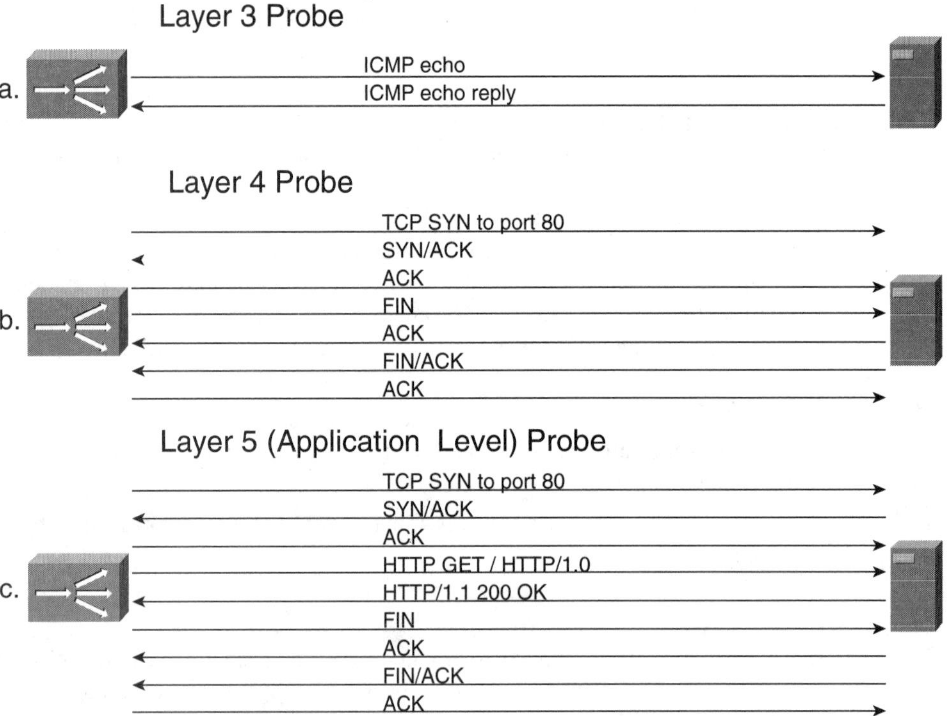

Layer 2 Probes: ARP

ARP is *the* Layer 2 probe. Typically, a load balancer is the default gateway for the servers that it load-balances; as a result, it ARPs the IP addresses of the configured servers to populate the ARP table.

If a server becomes unreachable and the load balancer receives no response to its periodic ARP requests, it suspends the server.

NOTE The ARP probe works only if the load balancer is the default gateway for the servers. If the design is such that there is a router in the path between the load balancer and the servers, obviously ARP cannot be used to check whether a server is available.

Layer 3 Probes: ICMP

The ICMP probe is nothing more than a ping that is sent by a load balancer to a server. The load-balancing device sends an ICMP ECHO request and receives an ICMP ECHO REPLY, as can be seen in part **a** of Figure 17-4.

An ICMP probe is not really giving information about the status of the server running on the physical machine. It simply reports that the IP stack is working fine; the proof is that it is capable of answering an ICMP ECHO request.

Layer 4 Probes

Layer 4 probes are more effective in detecting server availability because they send a request that is received by a Layer 4 port. These probes verify that the TCP or UDP stack is listening on the port where the application expects requests, but they do not give information about the status of the application itself.

TCP Probe

A TCP probe performs a TCP three-way handshake (TCP SYN, SYN/ACK, ACK) (see part **b** of Figure 17-4) with a server on a given port and closes the TCP connection right away with a TCP RST or, alternately, the four-way handshake (TCP FIN, ACK, FIN/ACK, ACK).

Example 17-8 is an example of configuration for a TCP probe.

Example 17-8 *TCP Probe Configuration*

```
probe TCPPORT80 tcp
  port 80
  interval 3
  failed 5
serverfarm HTTP-FARM
 nat server
 no nat client
 real 10.10.10.11
  inservice
 real 10.10.10.13
  inservice
  probe TCPPORT80
```

The probe specifies the Layer 4 port to open the TCP connection to and is associated with the *serverfarm* HTTP-FARM. The probe configuration also specifies the interval between keepalives when the server is operational and when the server is not operational (failed).

UDP Probe

To verify that a specific application is listening to a UDP port, the load balancer sends a UDP probe with a Layer 4 port corresponding to the application being monitored. If the server responds with an ICMP port unreachable message, the server is taken out of rotation; otherwise, traffic is sent to it. Example 17-9 shows an example of a UDP probe. The first packet is the probe sent by a load balancer, and the ICMP port unreachable message is the response from the server.

Example 17-9 *Trace of a UDP Probe and the Server Response*

```
Ethernet II
    Destination: 00:d0:b7:a0:84:fc (INTEL_a0:84:fc) (server MAC)
    Source: 00:02:17:76:50:0a (Cisco_76:50:0a) (Load balancer MAC)
Internet Protocol, Src Addr: 10.10.10.2, Dst Addr: 10.10.10.11
User Datagram Protocol, Src Port: 1563 (1563), Dst Port: domain (53)
    Source port: 1563 (1563)
    Destination port: domain (53)

Ethernet II
    Destination: 00:30:b6:36:9b:d4 (CISCO_36:9b:d4) (Load balancer MAC)
    Source: 00:d0:b7:a0:84:fc (INTEL_a0:84:fc) (server MAC)
Internet Protocol, Src Addr: 10.10.10.11, Dst Addr: 10.10.10.2
Internet Control Message Protocol
    Type: 3 (Destination unreachable)
    Code: 3 (Port unreachable)
    Checksum: 0x12c4 (correct)
```

Application Layer Probes

Application layer probes (also called Layer 5–7 probes) are built on top of either TCP or UDP, and send requests to the server from which a specific answer is expected.

The type of answer that a load balancer expects from a server can belong to one of the following types:

- Status code
- A successful login sequence
- A specific "content"

A simple example of the first type of probe is an HTTP HEAD request for a specific URI. If the server is in good health, it responds with a status code of 200 Ok. The same principle can be applied to other applications for which a status code is returned in the response, such as FTP, SMTP, POP, and IMAP.

An example for the second type of probe can be an FTP, POP, or IMAP probe in which a username and a password are sent to verify the health of the authentication mechanism.

An example of the third type of probe is an HTTP GET probe in which a hash of a web page is compared with a previously cached result; if there is a change, this is considered an error. Another example is a DNS probe that requests the resolution of a specific domain name; the result is compared with a predefined IP address.

Example 17-10 shows the configuration of a DNS probe for DNS load balancing. Assuming that the DNS servers are authoritative for foo.com, the load balancer can verify the health of these servers by sending periodically (every 3 sec) an "A query" for www.example.com and comparing the result with the IP address specified in "expect address." If the DNS server returns a different IP address or an error message, the server is taken out of service.

Example 17-10 *DNS Probe Configuration*

```
probe DNS dns
  name www.example.com
  expect address 172.26.193.16
  interval 3
  failed 5
```

Application probes are CPU intensive (for both the load balancer and the servers). They require the load balancer to generate protocol traffic and perform parsing on the results returned by servers. The remainder of this section provides more details on the operation of the mentioned application probes.

HTTP Probe

When an HTTP probe is associated with a real server, the load balancer sends an HTTP request to a server just like a client browser would do. The load-balancer CPU acts as the client.

The HTTP probe can be any of the following types:

- HTTP HEAD (checking for the status code)
- HTTP GET (checking for the status code) (see part **c** in Figure 17-4)
- HTTP GET (checking the content in the returned page)

The health of the server can be assessed according to two different mechanisms—the status code or the content of the page itself. When the status code is used, the load balancer typically matches 200; if the status code is different, the server is marked as down.

A different approach is to compare the page content with the web page that was retrieved the very first time that the real was enabled. This typically is done by hashing the page returned by the server and comparing the value of the hash with the very first hash performed on the same page.

The **probe** command typically allows you to define the URI that the switch retrieves from the servers.

The HTTP probe can use HTTP/1.1 so that the TCP connection is kept open for a number of HTTP requests, which depends on the configuration of the HTTP server. Example 17-11 shows the HEAD request followed by the server response. The server IP address is 10.10.10.11. Notice that the Keepalive Max field decreases in the server response: When it is 0, the TCP connection is closed.

Example 17-11 *HTTP HEAD Probe*

```
HEAD / HTTP/1.0
Connection: Keep-Alive
User-Agent: Mozilla/4.06 [en] (WinNT; I)
Accept: image/gif, image/x-bitmap, image/jpeg, image/pjpeg, image/png, */*
Accept-Language: en
Accept-Charset: iso-8859-1,*,utf-8
Host: 10.10.10.11

HTTP/1.1 200 OK
Date: Wed, 17 Apr 2002 23:17:45 GMT
Server: Apache/1.3.12 (Unix)  (Red Hat/Linux)
Last-Modified: Thu, 23 Aug 2001 20:12:51 GMT
ETag: "43ba5-2ae-3b8563c3"
Accept-Ranges: bytes
Content-Length: 686
Keep-Alive: timeout=15, max=71
Connection: Keep-Alive
Content-Type: text/html
```

Example 17-11 *HTTP HEAD Probe (Continued)*

```
HEAD / HTTP/1.0
Connection: Keep-Alive
User-Agent: Mozilla/4.06 [en] (WinNT; I)
Accept: image/gif, image/x-bitmap, image/jpeg, image/pjpeg, image/png, */*
Accept-Language: en
Accept-Charset: iso-8859-1,*,utf-8
Host: 10.10.10.11

HTTP/1.1 200 OK
Date: Wed, 17 Apr 2002 23:17:48 GMT
Server: Apache/1.3.12 (Unix)  (Red Hat/Linux)
Last-Modified: Thu, 23 Aug 2001 20:12:51 GMT
ETag: "43ba5-2ae-3b8563c3"
Accept-Ranges: bytes
Content-Length: 686
Keep-Alive: timeout=15, max=70
Connection: Keep-Alive
Content-Type: text/html
```

When servers are configured for name-based virtual hosting, the HTTP probe needs to specify the Host tag for the domain being hosted. In this case, the HTTP request would contain the fully qualified domain name in the Host tag, as shown in Example 17-12.

Example 17-12 *HTTP Probe for Virtual Hosting*

```
GET / HTTP/1.0
Connection: Keep-Alive
User-Agent: Mozilla/4.06 [en] (WinNT; I)
Accept: image/gif, image/x-bitmap, image/jpeg, image/pjpeg, image/png, */*
Accept-Language: en
Accept-Charset: iso-8859-1,*,utf-8
Host: www.example.com
```

The HTTP probes can check additional HTTP header fields, such as the Cookie header. A probe can be set to match the cookies set by a server to be a specific NAME = VALUE set. The probe just sends a GET / HTTP/1.0 and expects a response with set-cookie: NAME = VALUE. If this differs from the setting on the load balancer, the server is marked as down.

SSL Probe

When an HTTP server is enabled to serve HTTPS, it listens on port 443. In theory, the health of this service could be checked by monitoring the TCP handshake between the client and the server on port 443 (in-band health check). It also is possible for the load balancer to generate a TCP connection request to port 443 that does not include the SSL handshake (out-of-band probe). Either method does not really prove that SSL is working; even if SSL is working, the server could complain with log messages because the handshake on port 443 was not followed by the SSL handshake.

A better approach to verify the server health status for SSL is to have the load balancer perform an SSL handshake with the server. This handshake does not require the load balancer to install certificates or to encrypt data with the server's public key. A subset of the SSL handshake is performed, as seen in Example 17-13. The server IP address is 10.10.10.11, and the load-balancer IP address is 10.10.10.2.

Example 17-13 *An SSL Probe*

```
New TCP connection #1: 10.10.10.2(1148) <-> 10.10.10.11(443)
1 1  0.0990 (0.0990)  S>C  Handshake
      ServerHello
        Version 3.0
        session_id[0]=
        cipherSuite         SSL_RSA_WITH_RC4_128_MD5
        compressionMethod                   NULL
1 2  0.0991 (0.0000)  S>C  Handshake
      Certificate
1 3  0.0991 (0.0000)  S>C  Handshake
      ServerHelloDone
1    0.1088 (0.0097)  C>S  TCP RST

New TCP connection #2: 10.10.10.2(1149) <-> 10.10.10.11(443)
2 1  0.0978 (0.0978)  S>C  Handshake
      ServerHello
        Version 3.0
        session_id[0]=
        cipherSuite         SSL_RSA_WITH_RC4_128_MD5
        compressionMethod                   NULL
2 2  0.0979 (0.0000)  S>C  Handshake
      Certificate
2 3  0.0979 (0.0000)  S>C  Handshake
      ServerHelloDone
2    0.1074 (0.0095)  C>S  TCP RST
```

Example 17-13 shows two consecutive probes. Each creates a new TCP connection. The load balancer expects the server to send a valid version number, a server Hello, and the ServerHelloDone. If these messages are not received, the load balancer declares the server to be down. Notice that the TCP connection is closed by the load balancer with a TCP RST. As previously mentioned, this sometimes causes error logs on servers; if this is the case, make sure that you change the closing sequence with a TCP FIN handshake.

For more information about the SSL handshake, refer to Chapter 9, "SSL and TLS."

DNS Probe

DNS probes can be implemented in several different ways. Some load-balancing products can send only a query type A and consider valid every response from the server: Receiving a response is a sign that the process is up.

A better approach is to send a DNS query with a user-configurable domain name, and possibly a user-configurable IP address to match. The assumption is that a DNS server capable of responding to an A query for a specific domain is capable of responding to any other query for the other configured domains.

For more information about DNS, refer to Chapter 10, "DNS Essentials and Site-Selection Considerations."

FTP Probe

The FTP probe opens a control connection to port 21 on the server and can be configured to expect a specific status code. Example 17-14 shows the trace of an FTP probe: The load balancer (10.10.10.2) opens a connection to the server (10.10.10.11), and the server responds with "220 Service ready for new user." The load balancer eventually sends a **QUIT** command to close the FTP control connection.

Example 17-14 *An FTP Probe*

```
10.10.10.2        10.10.10.11    TCP     4129 > ftp [SYN]
10.10.10.11       10.10.10.2     TCP     ftp > 4129 [SYN, ACK]
10.10.10.2        10.10.10.11    TCP     4129 > ftp [ACK]
10.10.10.11       10.10.10.2     FTP     Response: 220 localhost.localdomain FTP
  server ready.
10.10.10.2        10.10.10.11    FTP     Request: QUIT
10.10.10.11       10.10.10.2     TCP     ftp > 4129 [ACK]
10.10.10.11       10.10.10.2     FTP     Response: 221 Goodbye.
10.10.10.11       10.10.10.2     TCP     ftp > 4129 [FIN, ACK]
10.10.10.2        10.10.10.11    TCP     4129 > ftp [ACK]
10.10.10.2        10.10.10.11    TCP     4129 > ftp [FIN, ACK]
10.10.10.11       10.10.10.2     TCP     ftp > 4129 [ACK]
```

As can be seen from the trace, the load balancer sends a **QUIT** command right after Response 220. A regular FTP transaction instead sends a USER request, and the server would ask for a password.

More sophisticated FTP probes enable you to specify a USER and a password to send for a more complete health check.

SMTP Probe

The Simple Mail Transfer Protocol (SMTP) is the protocol used to deliver electronic mail (e-mail).

The SMTP probe opens a TCP connection to port 25 and expects a message from the server: "220 foo.com Simple Mail Transfer Service Ready."

The probe can stop here or can go further—for example, sending, a HELLO message and waiting for a 250 OK status code.

POP3 Probe

The Post Office Protocol (POP) is used to access mailboxes from various user agents. The POP3 probe opens a TCP connection to port 110 and waits for a "+OK POP3 server ready" message.

Additionally, the probe can test the authorization mechanism by sending a **USER** command, checking that the server sends a +OK, and eventually sending a **PASS** command and again waiting for a +OK from the server.

Depending on the probe implementation, you can have a TCP RST from the client (the load balancer) or a cleaner closure via the **QUIT** command followed by the server's +OK.

IMAP4 Probe

The Internet Mail Access Protocol is a protocol similar to POP; it is used to access a mailbox from a user agent running on a client machine.

A probe opens a TCP connection to port 143 and waits for an * OK message from the server. The probe can stop at this point and send an a1 LOGOUT message to close the session, or it can go further to test the authentication mechanism health. In this case, the load balancer sends A001 LOGIN <username> <password> and waits for a1 OK. The load balancer eventually closes the connection with A002 LOGOUT and waits for A002 OK.

The A001 and A002 flags are used in IMAP to identify each command sent by the client.

Case Study: Server Health for Virtual Hosting

This section applies the concepts of health management to the specific virtual hosting environment. If you are not familiar with the concept of virtual hosting, refer to Chapter 2 for more information.

Virtual hosting consists of partitioning a physical server into several web servers, according to one of these methods:

- Using multiple IP addresses on the same physical machine (IP-based virtual hosting)

- Using multiple Layer 4 ports (port-based)
- Using the HTTP Host tags (name-based)

The challenge of monitoring servers in which each hosts several websites is being able to virtualize operations and health checks as if each website was a separate physical server.

You could argue that a single physical server hosting several customers can be monitored by just making sure that one of the websites is up and assuming that all the others are also. As an example, a server hosting www.foo1.com and www.foo2.com could be monitored by sending an HTTP probe to www.foo1.com and looking at the status code. If it is 200 Ok, the load balancer can assume that www.foo2.com is also in good health.

The argument to support this choice is that even if there are two websites, in the end the same set of processes is handling requests for both of them.

The reality is that the directories where the content comes from are different (for example, /home/httd/html/foo1 and /home/httpd/html/foo2), and in some scenarios human operation might adversely affect one website without affecting the one that the probe is monitoring.

The recommendation is to have a separate "real" for each hosted site, even if the IP address used is the same, for two reasons:

- Ease of management
- Granularity of server health checks

As an example, if you have two servers—10.10.10.11 and 10.10.10.13, each shared between www.foo1.com and www.foo2.com—and you configured port-based virtual hosting (www.foo1.com maps to port 8081, and www.foo2.com maps to port 8082), you can create four reals, as in Example 17-15, that are grouped in two different server farms.

Example 17-15 *Server Farm Configuration for Virtual Web Hosting*

```
serverfarm HTTP-FOO1
  nat server
  no nat client
  real 10.10.10.11 8081
   inservice
  real 10.10.10.13 8081
   inservice
!
 serverfarm HTTP-FOO2
  nat server
  no nat client
  real 10.10.10.11 8082
   inservice
  real 10.10.10.13 8082
   inservice
```

Server farm HTTP-FOO1 is assigned to www.foo1.com, and server farm HTTP-FOO2 is assigned to www.foo2.com in Example 17-15. The map states that the HTTP request is matched against the Host header value of www.foo1.com or www.foo2.com. The policy assigns each host header to a different serverfarm. The vserver configuration pulls it all together under a single IP address: 192.168.1.1.

Example 17-16 *Virtual Web Hosting: Host-Based on the Load Balancer, Port-Based on the Server*

```
map FOO1 header
  match protocol http header Host header-value www.foo1.com
!
policy FOO1
  header-map FOO1
  serverfarm HTTP-FOO2
!
map FOO2 header
  match protocol http header Host header-value www.foo2.com
!
 policy FOO2
  header-map FOO2
  serverfarm HTTP-FOO2
!
vserver VIRT-WEB-HOSTING
  virtual 192.168.1.1 tcp www
  persistent rebalance
  slb-policy FOO1
  slb-policy FOO2
  inservice
!
```

This enables you to take one real server out of service at a time. For example, you might want to change the content in /home/httpd/html/foo1 on 10.10.10.11. To prevent users from getting load-balanced to 10.10.10.11 for www.foo1.com, you can just suspend the real 10.10.10.11 under server farm HTTP-FOO1.

Depending on the virtual hosting environment, you need to use different types of probes to verify the availability of your servers.

For server farms implementing IP-based virtual hosting, you can configure a TCP probe to port 80 and assign this probe to each server farm. The load balancer performs a TCP handshake to each of the IP addresses, verifying that the server is capable of serving requests for all the websites. Remember that each physical server is configured with multiple IP addresses; each IP identifies a separate website. From the load balancer standpoint, it is irrelevant whether the IPs are different machines or are just loopbacks on the same machine.

For server farms implementing port-based virtual hosting, you can configure a TCP probe to the specific ports; the configuration looks like Example 17-17. Remember that different Layer 4 ports on the same real identify a different web server.

Example 17-17 *Port-Based Virtual Web Hosting and Probes*

```
probe TCP_PORT tcp
  port 8081
  interval 3
  failed 5
!
serverfarm HTTP-FOO1
  nat server
  no nat client
  real 10.10.10.11 8081
   inservice
  real 10.10.10.13 8081
   inservice
  probe TCP_PORT
```

For server farms implementing name-based virtual hosting, you need to use Layer 5 probes—specifically, HTTP probes carrying the Host tag of each specific website, as in Example 17-18. Remember that in host-based virtual hosting, different Host tags in the HTTP header identify different web servers on a physical machine. As an example, an HTTP request to 10.10.10.11 with the Host tag www.foo1.com invokes the web server www.foo1.com. An HTTP request to 10.10.10.11 with the Host tag www.foo2.com invokes the web server www.foo2.com.

Example 17-18 *Probe for Servers Configured for Host-Based Virtual Hosting*

```
probe HTTP-FOO1 http
  header Connection Keepalive
  header Host www.foo1.com
  request method head
  interval 3
  failed 5
!
serverfarm HTTP-FOO1
  nat server
  no nat client
  real 10.10.10.11
   inservice
  real 10.10.10.13
   inservice
  probe HTTP-FOO1
```

A different way to monitor servers running virtual hosting is to use SNMP. If the web server supports WWW-MIBS (RFC 2594), it is possible to retrieve information for each virtual host (wwwServiceName) and, specifically, to know whether the service is up or down (wwwServiceOperStatus).

Case Study: HTTP and HTTPS

Server availability for HTTP and SSL requires special attention because, in many scenarios, a server that is in good health for HTTP but not for SSL should be taken out of rotation.

Typically, an HTTPS connection is not the first connection from a client to a server. Most of the time, a client starts a browsing connection, normally on port 80; at some point during the session, a new connection to port 443 (HTTPS) is started when sensitive information needs to be transmitted.

The need for session persistence would imply that the HTTPS connection is directed to the server that the original HTTP connection was directed at. If you have a multitier network that stores the session information in a centralized database, this is not a problem, but if the session information is stored on the specific server, you need to ensure persistence, as described in Chapter 18, "Session Tracking and Cookies."

Imagine that you designed the server health management in such a way that the server can be independently taken out of rotation for port 443 and for port 80. A server might appear to be down for the virtual server that dispatches traffic for port 443, but it might appear to be up for the virtual server that dispatches traffic for port 80.

As a consequence, it could be possible that an HTTP connection is directed to this server. When the session shifts to HTTPS, the virtual server rule does not send the HTTPS connection to the same server because SSL does not work on this server. As a result, the session information is lost.

The key problem is that the same physical server can appear down for one protocol and up for another one. The solution is to be sure to take down the server for both HTTP and HTTPS if either the HTTP probe or the HTTPS probe has failed.

Example 17-19 provides a server load balancer's configuration that fixes this problem. As you can see, both virtual servers load-balance connections to the same set of real servers (they both use the same server farm). If 10.10.10.11 does not respond to the keepalive on port 443, it is marked as down for both the virtual server HTTP and HTTPS. This ensures that new incoming connections for port 80 (HTTP) do not go to this server, where the transition to port 443 eventually would fail.

Example 17-19 *Probe Configuration for Web Servers with HTTPS Enabled*

```
probe TCP_PORT tcp
  interval 3
!
serverfarm HTTP-FARM
  nat server
  no nat client
  real 10.10.10.11
   inservice
  real 10.10.10.13
   inservice
  probe TCP_PORT
!
vserver HTTP
  virtual 192.168.1.1 tcp www
  serverfarm HTTP-FARM
  persistent rebalance
  inservice
!
 vserver HTTPS
  virtual 192.168.1.1 tcp https
  serverfarm HTTP-FARM
  persistent rebalance
  inservice
!
```

In the configuration, a probe called TCP_PORT is assigned to the server farm without specifying which port to open. The port to which the probe is sent depends on the vserver that the probe is assigned to; in this case, a probe is sent for both ports 80 and 443 without needing you to configure this.

To reinforce the concept, look at the output from some **show** commands in Example 17-20. As you can see, the load balancer is sending a probe to both port 443 and port 80 for each server in the server farm: 10.10.10.11 is marked as failed. This does not mean that 10.10.10.11 is taken out of rotation yet because this **show** command just shows the status of the probes.

Example 17-20 *Output of* **show module csm** *module* **probe detail**

```
real               vserver         serverfarm      policy          status
------------------------------------------------------------------------------
10.10.10.11:443    HTTPS           HTTP-FARM       (default)       FAILED
10.10.10.13:443    HTTPS           HTTP-FARM       (default)       OPERABLE
10.10.10.11:80     HTTP            HTTP-FARM       (default)       OPERABLE
10.10.10.13:80     HTTP            HTTP-FARM       (default)       OPERABLE
```

Another **show** command, represented in Example 17-21, indicates that the real 10.10.10.11 is taken out of rotation for ports 80 and 443.

Example 17-21 *Output of* **show module csm** *module* **reals**

```
real              server farm       weight  state         conns
----------------------------------------------------------------
10.10.10.11       HTTP-FARM         8       PROBE_FAILED  0
10.10.10.12       HTTP-FARM         8       OPERATIONAL   0
```

Summary

Hardware load balancing provides several benefits in addition to just load distribution. Load balancers help in case you need to perform maintenance on one server of the pool: Taking one real out of service allows existing connections to still go to this real server until the user closes them; new connections are sent to the other servers in the pool.

Load balancers also provide features to avoid overloading servers by limiting the number of connections sent to a particular server, either because the server has just been added to the pool or because the number of incoming connections exceeds a threshold that you configured.

Deploying load balancers in the path between the client and the servers allows these devices to monitor the TCP connection setup and take actions based on the success or failure of TCP handshakes.

Deeper inspection capabilities even allow the load balancer to monitor the HTTP responses from a server and identify failure conditions by reading into the HTTP status codes returned to clients' requests.

In addition to these mechanisms, load balancers can generate protocol traffic of their own to periodically monitor the capability of servers to respond correctly to client requests. By means of Layer 4 probes, you can monitor almost every application, as long as you know which ports the application uses. In addition to Layer 4 probes, load balancers support several applications level probes.

You can integrate load-balancing devices with management applications by using XML or SNMP. XML enables you to build custom applications that can modify the configuration of the load balancer dynamically. SNMP enables you to monitor the load balancer from a management station.

SNMP also can be used to monitor the health of servers in terms of CPU utilization, memory, number of connections, and more. By knowing the MIBs supported by a given server, you can build applications to monitor servers and modify the load distribution on the load balancer accordingly.

This chapter covers the following topics:

- Overview of how today's server applications track user sessions and how the tracking mechanism relates to the network protocols
- What *cookies* are and why they are used for session tracking
- How browsers handle the cookie attributes, and how they behave in presence of multiple cookies
- How servers perform session tracking by means of hidden fields, rewritten URLs, and cookies
- How Apache mod_session provides session tracking with cookies and rewritten URLs
- How Java servlets allow tracking sessions with cookies and rewritten URLs

CHAPTER 18

Session Tracking and Cookies

If you are a network designer, you might have been asked how to integrate BEA Weblogic, Siebel, IBM Websphere, or Oracle application server in the network, or how to help migrate the Data Center to Java-based applications. By reading this chapter and Chapter 19, "Persistence Mechanisms on Load Balancers," you will learn how.

It is important to understand how applications work for you to be able to integrate correctly *hardware load balancing* and *SSL offloading* with application servers. Chapter 6, "Server Load Balancing Overview," introduced the concepts of *session persistence*, which relates to load-balancing multiple web and application servers. Chapter 3, "Application Architectures Overview," explained the predominant application servers architecture of today and how Java applications are built.

This chapter explains how and why a stateful application on a single server tracks a *session*, from both application and networking points of view. Application developers use the tools described in this chapter and those provided by web and application servers for the purpose of session tracking.

Chapter 19 explains how network devices—specifically, load balancers—can provide application services for stateful applications for the purpose of session persistence.

What a Session Is and Why It Matters

As Chapter 3 explained, one of the key trends in application environments is the fact that enterprise applications have become web-enabled. E-commerce, business-to-business, supply-chain management, messaging, resource-planning, and customer relationship applications are web-based—or, in case of legacy applications, web-enabled. The "web" keyword indicates that the access method to these applications is mainly based on the HTTP protocol: the client is typically a browser, and the server is an application server (whose routines can be invoked through HTTP) or a web server.

E-commerce applications provide a perfect example of web-based application. Imagine that you need to buy a book online. You would normally open a browser; provide the URL of an online store, such as http://www.example.com; look up the categories of your choice; select books; and eventually check out.

The e-commerce application running on the server needs to track the progress of your selections for the duration of the session: The session is the entire transaction with the e-commerce site.

Another example of a session is the use of an online e-mail application via a browser. The session identifies the fact that, through the browser, you sign in, check e-mails, and compose and send messages.

From the point of view of web-based applications, a session starts when the user makes contact with a web site, and ends when the user finishes the transaction, whether closing the browser, timing out, or checking out.

Session tracking refers to the fact that a server tracks the client that is using the application: For the duration of the session, the e-commerce application running on the server needs to keep in memory the "shopping cart" information until the transaction is over; the e-mail application needs to memorize the messages being composed and eventually send them. How can the applications identify a session and keep state information?

Server applications can correlate HTTP requests belonging to the same client and differentiate them from requests from other clients by using *cookies* or *rewritten URLs*.

Cookies

HTTP is a stateless protocol, in that it does not provide mechanisms for a server to relate a specific HTTP request to previous HTTP requests from the same client. Netscape introduced *cookies* to overcome this limitation of the HTTP protocol; the specifications are available at http://wp.netscape.com/newsref/std/cookie_spec.html.

RFC 2109 and RFC 2965 introduced an HTTP state-management mechanism based on cookies.

Cookies are small strings that servers send to clients in HTTP response packets (refer to Chapter 8, "HTTP and Related Concepts," to see the format of HTTP response packets). Servers store information about a visiting client or identify a user through the use of cookies.

Session Cookies and Persistent Cookies

Cookies are categorized based on their use as *session cookies* and *persistent cookies*; this section explains the differences.

Servers use the information contained in the cookie for the purpose of keeping the state information of the application: The state information is the result of the specific sequence of the client's HTTP requests.

In the case of e-commerce applications, cookies are used to associate a client with its shopping cart. This is done by assigning a number (called session-id) as the value of the cookie that is sent by the server to the client. The client must send the cookie in every single subsequent request to the same site. The server associates the shopping cart with the session-id. Cookies used for this purpose have a short life: When the browsing session is over, they are not saved on the client's PC. These cookies are called *session* cookies or *temporary* cookies.

Checking e-mails online is another example of using a session cookie. Imagine that you have an e-mail account on a web portal of your choice, and you use a browser to check e-mails. The advantage of these e-mail accounts is that you can open e-mail from any PC that has a browser and Internet connectivity.

When you open the e-mail web page, you are asked to sign in with your username and password. As a result, the server sends you a session cookie, which is basically a random number. For the time you spend checking e-mails, you keep sending this random number to the server. The server uses this number as your identifier. You might have deleted e-mails and composed new ones: The server displays the inbox without the deleted e-mails and with the information about the e-mails that you have sent. This is possible because the server identifies you by means of the random number.

When you sign out, the number in the session cookie has no value for the application. This is why when you close the browser, this cookie is lost.

Another typical use of cookies is for applications in which a server needs to know the identity or preferences of its clients. Instead of explicitly asking the client to provide its identity every time it visits the site, the browser provides the identification information automatically through cookies. The server reads the cookies provided by the browser; it looks up a database and finds the client's information. The browser saves these cookies in a file on the hard disk. These cookies are called *persistent* cookies.

An example of this use is when you visit an online store and are welcomed with your name and prompted with advertisement of books or CDs that match your personal taste. This behavior is possible because the online store previously sent this kind of cookie to your PC.

Cookie Format

Cookie strings are in the format NAME=VALUE and are inserted after the Set-Cookie: header in the HTTP response packet. The attributes of the cookie are also stored in the Set-Cookie field, separated by semicolons.

Cookies have the following attributes:

- **Domain**—The HTTP Response header specifies the domain name with the Set-Cookie field domain=DOMAIN. An example is domain=.example.com.
- **Path**—The HTTP Response header specifies the path with the Set-Cookie field path=PATH. An example is path=/.

- **Expire**—The HTTP Response header specifies the expiration date with the Set-Cookie filed expire=DATE. An example is expire= Sun, 1-Feb-2003, 00:00:00 GMT.
- **Secure**—The server specifies this option to indicate that the client should send the cookie in the HTTP request only if the browser is using HTTPS (secure HTTP).

The client uses the Cookie: field in the HTTP Request header to send cookie information back to the server. Unlike the Set-Cookie Response header, it does not contain information about the expiration date, path, and domain.

NOTE For information about the HTTP Request and Response headers, refer to Chapter 8.

This is because the client is not setting cookies on the server; the client is just providing the server with the values that the server already has set on the client's browsers.

Figure 18-1 illustrates what happens when a client sends an HTTP GET to www.example.com. Initially, the cookie table in the browser is empty (Step 1). The client sends an HTTP GET for index.html (Step 1) without any cookie information, and the server sends an HTTP response with a Set-Cookie field. The cookie name is user, and the cookie value is 123.

Figure 18-1 *How Cookies Work*

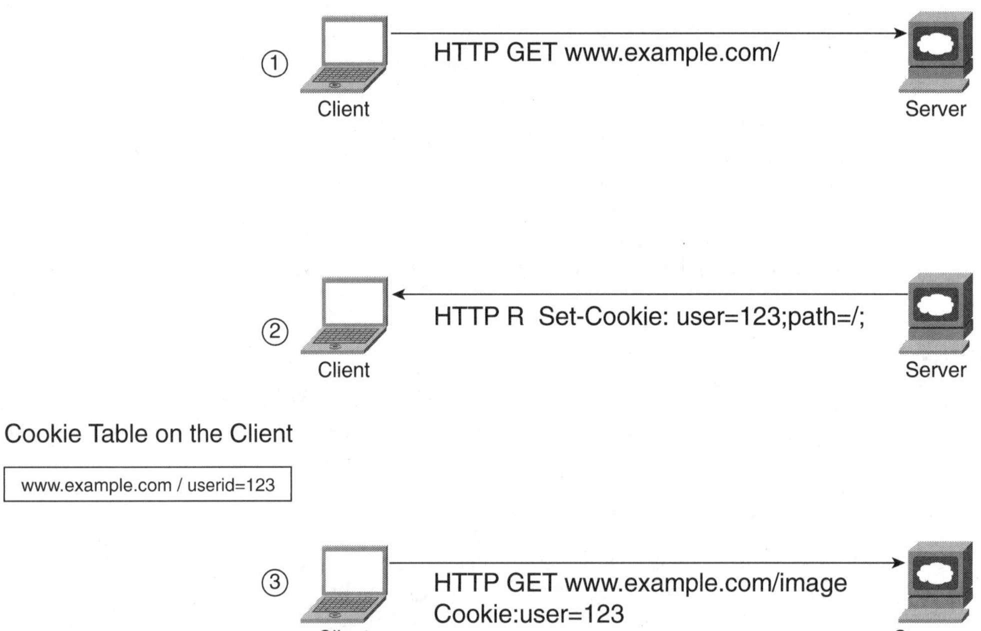

When sending a new HTTP GET request (Step 3 in Figure 18-1) to the previously visited server, the browser sends the cookie information that it previously received from the server. The cookie attributes control whether the browser should send the cookie to the server.

A more realistic example is given by a server providing a generic application written with Java servlets: Such a server might send an HTTP response with a field of Set-Cookie: JSESSIONID=ECB59CFA334DA26A6F875535F7FB98DF.

When the browser on the client receives an HTTP response with a Set-Cookie header, it saves the information either in memory or on the disk itself (see the upcoming section, "Where Cookies Are Stored"). Session cookies typically are saved in memory. The cookie information is made of NAME=VALUE associations (such as JSESSIONID= ECB59CFA334DA26A6F875535F7FB98DF), plus the other fields previously described.

How Browsers Handle Cookies

This section describes how cookies are handled by clients—more specifically, browsers. The upcoming section "How Servers Track User Sessions" provides information on how servers handle cookies. Clients can return one or multiple cookies per HTTP request, depending on how the attributes of the cookies are set.

It is important to understand the role of path, domain names, and expiration date because they decide the order in which cookies are sent in the GET request and for how long they are stored in the browser's memory or in the PC hard disk.

This, in turn, helps when troubleshooting session persistence issues in the presence of hardware load balancing because the load balancer needs to read the relevant information from the cookies for it to operate correctly.

How Browsers Handle Cookie Attributes

The following list explains how the client saves the cookie attributes received from the server:

- **Domain**—If the Set-Cookie specified by the HTTP Response header does not carry a domain attribute, the cookie in the client table inherits the domain name of the server. If the Set-Cookie specifies a domain name, the client stores this attribute together with the cookie value. A server cannot specify a Set-Cookie with a domain name different from its own, for security reasons.
- **Path**—The path attribute is subject to similar rules as the domain attribute. If the server does not set the path attribute in the HTTP Response header, the client saves the cookie using the path of the URL. If the server sets a path that is not a prefix of the URL, the browser discards the cookie.

- **Expire**—A cookie that has no explicit expiration time set by the server is deleted when the browser is closed. It is also possible for the server explicitly to force a client to delete a cookie by sending a Set-Cookie response header with an expiration date in the past.

Figure 18-2 helps in understanding the logic that regulates how a client sends cookies back to the server in HTTP Request headers. The server www.example.com has several directories, including /images, /books, and /dvd.

Figure 18-2 *Cookies, Domain Name, and Path*

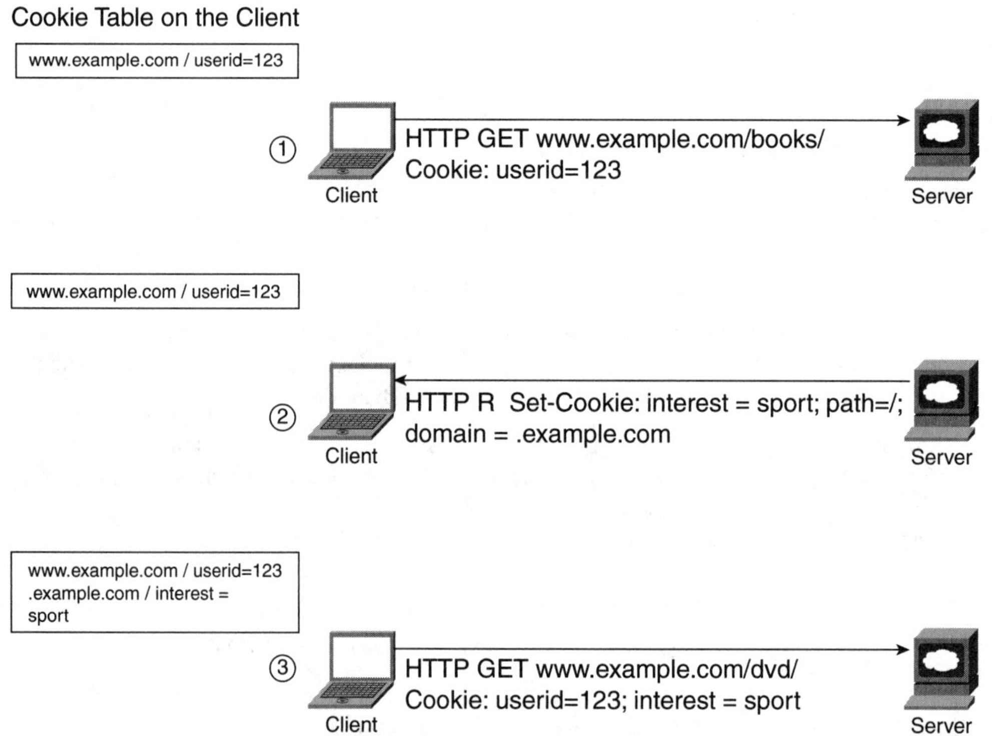

At Step 1 of Figure 18-2, the client sends an HTTP GET Request to the URL http://www.example.com/books. The cookie table on the client has a cookie userid=123 for the domain www.example.com. As a result, the HTTP GET Request carries the Cookie header field userid=123.

A cookie is sent back to a server if the domain name specified in the URL matches the domain attribute and if the path specified in the URL matches the path specified in the path attribute of the cookie. When the secure option is specified, the cookie is sent only on HTTPS.

In Step 1 of Figure 18-2, the client sends the cookie user=123 to www.example.com because www.example.com matches the domain www.example.com, and because the path requested /books is more specific than the / path specified in the cookie attributes.

NOTE A domain matches the domain attribute of the cookie if it is equal or more specific. For example, an HTTP GET for http://www.example.com matches the domain attribute www.example.com, but it would also match .example.com because www.example.com is more specific than .example.com. Similarly, the path in a URL matches the path attribute if the path attribute of the cookie is equal or more specific. As an example, an HTTP GET for http://www.example.com/books matches the path / because /books is more specific than /.

At Step 2 of Figure 18-2, the HTTP response from the server carries a cookie interest=sport with the following attributes:

- Domain = .example.com
- Path = /

At Step 3 of Figure 18-2, the client HTTP request for www.example.com/dvd/ carries the cookie userid and interest. The example shows that the field interest is inserted as a response to http://www.example.com/books, and the client sends it back even when requesting http://www.example.com/dvd. This is a result of the servers sending cookie attributes that are less specific than the domain or path requested (as in Step 2 of Figure 18-2).

How Browsers Handle Multiple Cookies

If a server needs to place multiple cookies on a client, it uses multiple Set-Cookie fields in a single HTTP response. Similarly, if a client sends an HTTP GET request with a URL that matches multiple cookies' paths and domains, the HTTP request header contains a line such as this:

```
Cookie: NAME1=VALUE1; NAME2=VALUE2; NAME3=VALUE3…
```

NAME1, NAME2, and NAME3 represent the cookie names, and VALUE# represents the cookie value.

Rules govern the order that the client uses to place cookies in an HTTP request. If multiple cookies match the URL, all of them are inserted in the header, giving precedence to the most specific paths. Two cookies with equal names but different paths are considered different cookies.

RFC 2065 recommends that user agents (browsers) support NAME=VALUE associations of 4096 bytes, 20 cookies per domain (where www.example.com and .example.com count as multiple domains), and 300 total cookies.

Figure 18-3 shows how a browser behaves if a URL matches multiple cookies in its memory. The browser sends all the cookies that match the domain and the path. The browser orders the list of cookies with the most specific match first in the list. Figure 18-3 clarifies this.

Figure 18-3 *Multiple Cookies*

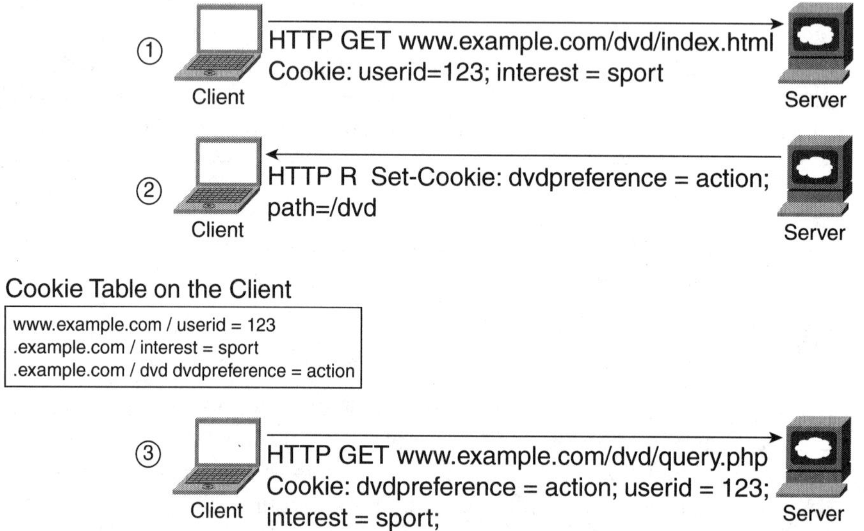

In Figure 18-3, a client sends an HTTP request to www.example.com/dvd/index.html (Step 1). The HTTP response (Step 2) includes a Set-Cookie header of dvdpreference = action with an attribute of path=/dvd.

An additional HTTP request (Step 3) to www.example.com/dvd/query.php includes the Cookie header with dvdpreference first in the list. This is because www.example.com/dvd/ produces a match in the cookie table with the following cookies: userid, interest, and dvdpreference. The difference between dvdpreference and the other cookies is the path attribute: dvdpreference specifies /dvd as the path, while the other cookies specify /. For this reason, dvdpreference is the most specific "match."

Where Cookies Are Stored

When a browser receives cookies from a server, it stores them in the memory. If no expiration time is set, or if it was set in the past, cookies are lost when the browser is closed.

If cookies have a valid expiration time, they are saved in text format either in a file or as multiple files in a specific directory.

Netscape 7.02 saves the cookies in the file cookie.txt, which on Windows machines is located in the directory D:\Documents and Settings\username\Application Data\Mozilla\Profiles\default\. The format of the cookie is as follows:

```
.example.com      TRUE /     FALSE          1016602330      userid     123
```

The first field is the domain, followed by a flag that indicates whether all machines in a domain can use the same cookie. The path follows, then the security attribute, and finally the expiration date in seconds counted from January 1, 1970, 00:00:00 GMT. The last field in the cookie.txt file is the name of the cookie, followed by its value.

Internet Explorer 6.0 saves the cookies in the directory D:\Documents and Settings\username\Cookies. Each cookie is a different file with the following format:

username@domain_name.txt

An example follows:

username@example[1].txt USERID 123 example.com/ [...]

You can manage cookies on Internet Explorer 6.0 from Tools/Internet Options/General Tab/Temporary Internet Files—Settings/View Files.

Netscape, RFC 2109, and RFC 2965

Cookies originally were introduced by Netscape. The specification is found at http://wp.netscape.com/newsref/std/cookie_spec.html. RFC 2109 is a proposed standard that supersedes Netscape format; RFC 2965 is the current proposed standard that obsoletes RFC 2109.

The proposed standard uses quotes for the values of cookie names and attributes, and additional attributes in the Cookie: field of an HTTP request besides the cookie name. Netscape specifications do not use quotes for the cookie value. For example, an HTTP request compatible with RFC 2965 would contain the following:

```
Cookie2: $Version="1"; userid="123".
```

Web applications use the version number to identify the user agent (browser). The absence of the version number in the Cookie: request header indicates the Netscape implementation; $Version= 1 together with the Cookie2 field indicates that the client supports RFC 2965.

The $ sign identifies attributes in HTTP requests. In the Netscape specification of cookies, attributes are sent only from server to client, not vice versa.

RFC 2109 replaces Expires with Max-Age. RFC 2109 includes more attributes than the ones defined by Netscape—the Comment and Version attributes. The Comment attribute is used by the server to provide explanations on how the cookie will be used.

RFC 2965 also has the Version attribute, but it uses new state-management headers—Set-Cookie2 and Cookie2. The Version number used by both RFC 2109 and RFC 2965 is 1.

RFC 2965 also introduces new attributes: CommentURL, Discard, and Port. These attributes are used to increase the security of transactions that rely on cookies.

As an example, the Port field specifies which TCP port was used by the server to send the HTTP response with the cookie so that the user agent can compare this value with the port it is using for the HTTP request.

How Servers Track User Sessions

This section explains how server applications track user sessions by means of cookies, rewritten URLs, and form hidden fields. It also explores how these methods are combined for interoperability with clients that have no cookies or with clients that have disabled cookies.

The mod_session and Java servlet examples provide a case study that helps you understand the application programming side of session tracking and how this interacts with the network.

Session Tracking Overview

Servers need to track user sessions for the reasons explained previously. Session tracking implies that the server needs to do the following:

1. Track a session by generating a session identifier (session-id) to uniquely recognize a session.
2. Hand out the session identifier at the client's first HTTP request with either of the mechanisms described later in this chapter (cookies, typically).
3. Associate the client's further HTTP requests to the same session (by reading the session-id in the cookie or in the rewritten URL).
4. Expire the session after a configurable timeout.
5. Clean up the temporary data associated with the client's session.

The main techniques that can be used to keep state information during an HTTP session to avoid the shopping cart problem are listed here:

- Form hidden fields
- URL rewrite (URL encoding)
- Cookies

These techniques are described in the following sections.

Session Tracking with Form Hidden Fields

Hidden fields can be used in the HTML code so that when the user fills in a form and submits it, the hidden value is carried with the HTTP request from the client. A field can be inserted in the HTML code that is of TYPE="hidden", and it is preset by the server to a value that provides session information. When the client sends an HTTP request (a POST or a GET method) to the server, this field is sent together with the request. The main problem of this technique is that it allows session tracking only when the user is filling in forms.

Figure 18-4 shows how session tracking works when using forms with hidden fields. The server sends an HTTP response with the HTML code for the web page (Step 1). The client sees a web page with a field called Username, followed by a space to type the username. When the user clicks the button that shows the text "Click to submit," the browser sends an HTTP POST with the username, together with the hidden field userid = 123 (Step 2). The HTTP POST invokes the ACTION http://www.example.com/cgi-bin/selection.pl.

Figure 18-4 *Session Tracking with Form Hidden Fields*

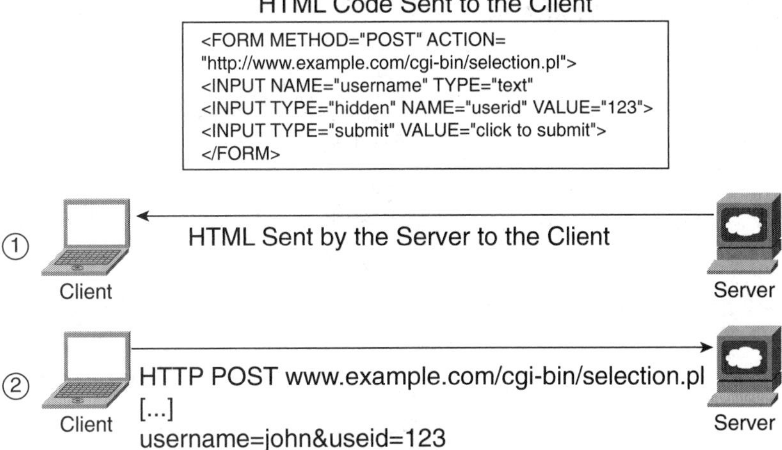

NOTE In a real application, the hidden field is more likely to be called SESSIONID, and the value is typically a random number that identifies the HTTP session.

Session Tracking with URL Rewrite

URL rewriting is another technique for session tracking. With URL rewriting, the server changes the URLs in the HTML code to include the session-id information. When the client requests a page referenced by the initial page, it sends the session information together with the rewritten URL in the HTTP GET request. A specific software on the server processes the HTML code and appends the session information.

NOTE The URLs are rewritten by the server, not by the client. As a result, the client requesting a certain URL originates a GET request that contains fields appended originally by the server.

Figure 18-5 shows how session tracking works when using URL rewrite. The upper portion of the figure shows the original HTML code. The session module processes the code: The server appends the jsessionid number to the <href>s in the HTML code.

Figure 18-5 *Session Tracking with URL Rewrite*

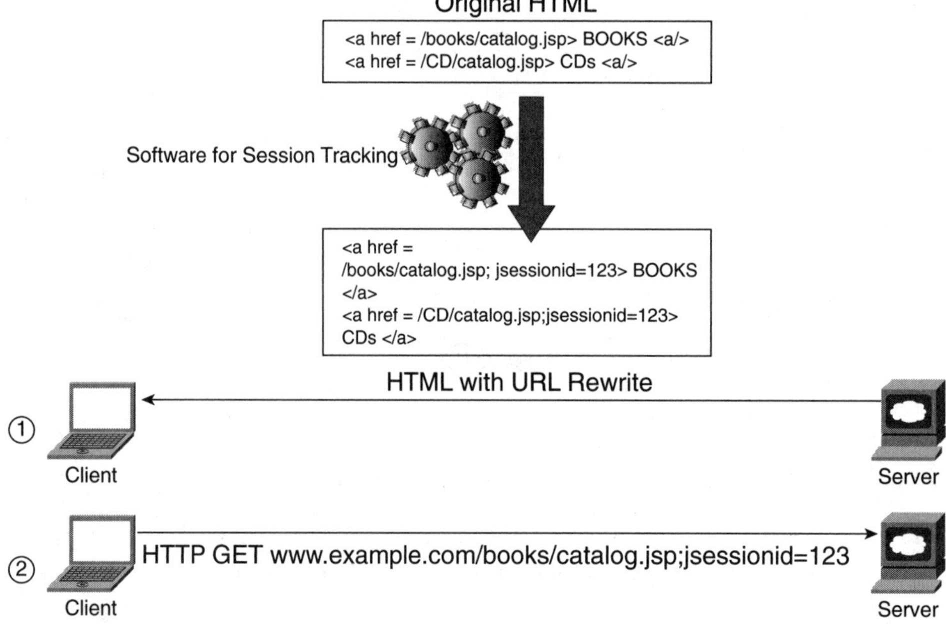

As a result, when the user clicks a hyperlink, the browser sends an HTTP request for the URL indicated in the <href>. The number jsessionid=123 that was appended to http://www.exmaple.com/CD/catalog.jsp provides the server with the session information.

NOTE The HTML create hyperlinks with the anchor (<a>) element. The HREF attribute of an anchor element defines where to locate a resource. In Figure 18-5, the resource is http://www.example.com/CD/catalog.jsp.

Session Tracking with Cookies

Cookies were invented to maintain state during an HTTP session. This can be achieved in at least two different ways using cookies:

- By inserting information about the client into the cookie
- By associating each visiting client to a cookie (the most common method)

The first method makes it possible to have "stateless servers." A stateless server does not know anything about the visiting client, except from the information provided in each HTTP GET. Such a server relies completely on the client to provide it with information about previous actions of the browser. An example is to have the cookie to store the books, CDs, and so on selected by a user during an e-commerce session.

This approach is discouraged because the size and the number of cookies to hold all the information could grow to a point that it could become a burden for the browser. The other reason that this approach is not recommended is that it is easy for someone capturing the traffic to read the client's information in the cookie field as HTTP information traverses the network in clear text.

Instead of using stateless servers, it is preferred to save information about the client on the server and insert cookies just for identification purposes. A returning client would provide a specific session-id stored in the cookie that the server associates with the session state it is maintaining on behalf of the client.

Applications usually generate cookies with session-ids that are used to keep state for the duration of an HTTP session. These numbers are randomly generated to reduce the risk of a user counterfeiting cookies.

Session Tracking Methods Combined

Cookies are the most commonly used method to track users' sessions. Despite this, some clients do not support cookies because this requires memory and possibly disk space. Users might even disable cookies on browsers for security and privacy reasons.

Therefore, it is important to design applications that address the requirements of the clients, regardless of whether they support cookies. The most typical approach consists of combining cookies and rewritten URLs.

The following list describes the sequence of events of a client/server interaction for an application designed to work with all clients:

1. Initially, the client sends an HTTP request to the server.
2. The HTTP response from the server includes HTML code with the session-id appended at the end of the URLs.
3. The HTTP response also includes a cookie with the session-id of session_id = 1023419940.

If the client supports cookies, the session information is sent back to the server in the **Cookie:** field of the HTTP request header. If the client disabled cookies, this information is included in the URLs requested by the client.

Several available software mechanisms track user sessions. mod_session in Apache and specific libraries on application servers, such as the HttpSession APIs for Java servlets, are used to provide the session-tracking functionality.

Case Study: Apache mod_session

Like other HTTP session-tracking mechanisms, mod_session makes the tracking process transparent to the application developer. The session module uses cookies, rewritten URLs, and hidden fields in forms without requiring any modification of the HTML code from the developer; all you need to do is configure the mod_session in the web server.

Example 18-1 shows the configuration for session cookies and rewritten URLs on mod_session for Apache.

Example 18-1 *Apache Configuration for Session Persistence*

```
<Location />
 SessionCookieName session_cookie
 SessionCookiePath /
 SessionUrlSidName session_id
 SessionFilter /perl/filter
</Location>
```

As you can see, the configuration allows you to assign a name to the cookie (session_cookie in the example) as well as the path. It is recommended that you use the / path so that this information is always sent to the server, no matter which URL the client requests (refer to the section, "How Browsers Handle Cookies" for more information about the rules of cookie attributes).

SessionUrlSidName decides the name of the variable used when encoding the session in the URLs. SessionFilter tells the web server which script to use to parse the HTML code and rewrite the URLs with the session number.

In Figure 18-6, you can see the web server 172.26.200.137 inserting session_cookie (consistently with the configuration in Example 18-1) with the random value of 1023419940_10. This number is the session identifier; it has no expiration time, so it disappears when the browser is closed.

Figure 18-6 *Session Cookies Inserted by Apache mod_session*

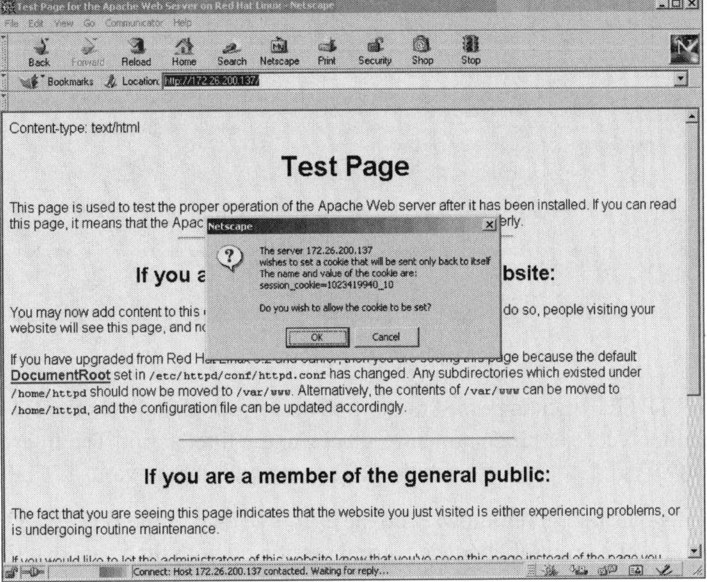

As previously explained, a complete session-tracking mechanism works regardless of whether the clients support cookies. This is achieved by using cookies combined with rewritten URLs, as described in the following paragraphs.

Figure 18-7 illustrates how Apache operates with mod_session when cookies are disabled on the browser. As you can see, the browser loads the same web page as in Figure 18-6: The only difference with the page that shows in Figure 18-7 is that the URL for the hypertext DocumentRoot has the additional characters ?session_id=1023419940_10:

http://172.26.200.137/manual/mod/core.html#documentroot?session_id=1023419940_10

If you click on DocumentRoot, the web server receiving the request calls the filter script that identifies the string session_id, reads its value (1023419940_10), and updates the environment variable SESSION_KEY.

Figure 18-7 *Session Persistence with URL Rewrite in Apache mod_session*

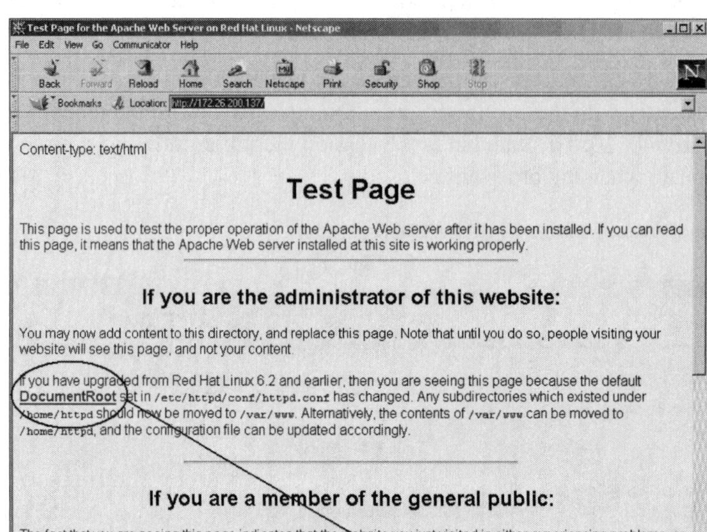

The HTTP GET then is passed to the web server, which delivers the HTML code for manual/mod/core.html#documentroot back to the filter script. The filter appends the SESSION_KEY to the URLs in the HREFs, as with the previous HTTP responses.

By doing this, the server knows who the user is as long as the HTTP GET requests are sent from the user's browser appended string session_id with the value that the server assigned to it.

URL rewrite also rewrites the ACTION field of forms. For example, this form

```
<FORM METHOD = "post" ACTION = "/cgi-bin/action">
```

would be changed by the URL rewrite by appending the session-id to the ACTION field, like this:

```
<FORM METHOD = "post" ACTION =
"/cgi-bin/action?session_id=1023419940_10">.
```

Similarly, mod_session rewrites URLs for image maps. For image maps, you see this type of URL:

```
http://172.26.200.137/map/imagemap1.map/session_id=1023822792_10?62,7
```

If you look at the HTML rewritten code, it looks like this:

```
<a href="/map/imagemap1.map/session_id=1023822792_10">
<img ismap src="/icons/apache_pb.gif" width = "200" heigh="40">
</a>
```

In brief, the session modules from web servers make it easier for the developer to track sessions because there is no need to deal with the details of where to embed the session information.

As previously pointed out, the filter script /perl/filter/ updates the environment variable SESSION_KEY with the session-id. The application then can use this variable to store temporary data about the user.

Case Study: HTTP Sessions with Servlets

Java servlets were described in Chapter 3. This section illustrates how servlet APIs provide tracking of a user session. The key purpose of this section is to show the interaction among the mechanisms of cookies, URL rewriting, and forms.

This section requires a minimum knowledge of object-oriented programming as it shows object creation and applying methods to objects. Remember that *method* in object-oriented programming is a concept similar to a function and is applied to an object. Even if you are not familiar with object-oriented programming, you can follow the flow of the code displayed as this section explains what happens on the network at each step of the application.

The key idea behind this section is to show that the servlet code creates a *session object* (with the method getSession) to store the information about the user selection (which is saved with the method setAttribute). The session object is referenced by the session-id exchanged between the servlet and the client by means of cookies or rewritten URLs. A specific method provides the functionality of detecting whether a client supports cookies; based on this information, it rewrites URLs (this is the method encodeUrl).

The following list shows the key Java methods used and is provided for reference:

- **Public HttpSession getSession(boolean create)**—Enables you to retrieve the session information from an HTTP request (both GET and POST apply here). The session information is retrieved from the cookie or the URL sent by the client. If no session information is available and the create field value is TRUE, this method creates a new session identifier.
- **public void setAttribute(java.lang.String name, java.lang.Object value)**—Enables you to associate objects to the session.
- **public java.lang.String encodeUrl(java.lang.String url)**—Rewrites the URL string with the session-id. If this method detects that the client is using cookies, it stops appending the session-id to the URLs.

Figure 18-8 shows the result of invoking the example application SessionTracking. This application enables you to select from two musical genres, either classical or rock, or to type the preferred one in the form field.

Figure 18-8 *Tracking Sessions with the Example Servlet SessionTracking*

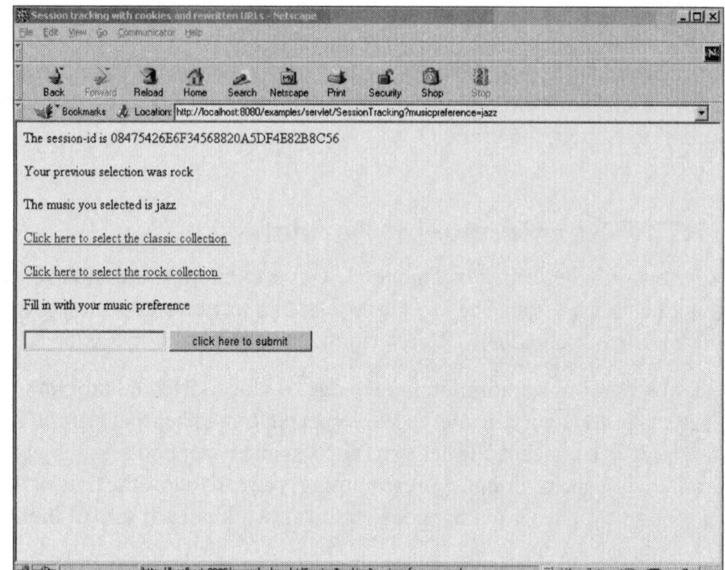

The first line shows the session-id, which is generated at the first HTTP request sent to the server. This number should not change for the duration of the session.

Below the session-id, you see two hyperlinks. Clicking the first one selects the classic collection; clicking the second one selects the rock collection. Below this is the form field to fill in.

The application saves the last selection with the session information to demonstrate that the server is tracking the session.

After you click the first hyperlink, you see the same screen with the line "The music you selected is classical." When you click the second hyperlink, you see the lines "The music you selected is rock" and "The previous selection was classical." If you type in the form field and click the Submit button, you see the line "The music you selected is" followed by the string that you typed, and the string "The previous selection was" followed by the last selection.

Figure 18-8 shows the output result of the following sequence of events:

1 Clicking the hyperlink Click Here to Select the Rock Collection:

```
http://localhost:8080/examples/servlet/
SessionTracking?musicpreference=rock
```

2 Typing jazz in the form field and submitting it—notice that the URL requested is this:

```
http://localhost:8080/examples/servlet/
SessionTracking?musicpreference=jazz
```

Example 18-2 shows the HTML code generated by the servlet corresponding to the screen capture in Figure 18-8.

Example 18-2 *Example of HTML Code Generated by the Servlet SessionTracking*

```
<html>
<head><title> Session tracking with cookies and rewritten URLs </title></
head><body>
<p> The session-id is 08475426E6F34568820A5DF4E82B8C56</p>
<p><a href="SessionTracking?musicpreference=classical" > Click here to select the
classic collection </a></p>
<p><a href="SessionTracking?musicpreference=rock" > Click here to select the rock
collection </a></p>

<form action="SessionTracking" method = GET>
<p> Fill in with your music preference </p>
<input type=text name=musicpreference>
<input type=submit value="click here to submit">
</form>

</body>
</html>
```

In Example 18-2, you see that the URLs in the HREFs have no session information, like this:

```
<a href="SessionTracking?musicpreference=classical" >
```

You can also see that the form does not have any session information:

```
<form action="SessionTracking" method = GET>
```

This is because the client browser has cookies enabled, and, at the very first HTTP request, the application sent the cookie JSESSIONID = 08475426E6F34568820A5DF4E82B8C56. The servlet understood that the client supports cookies and did not rewrite any URL.

If you disable cookies on the browser and request the same application http://localhost:8080/examples/servlet/SessionTracking, you see a similar output to Figure 18-8, but when you click on the hyperlink for classical music, you see that the browser sends a request for this URL:

```
http://localhost:8080/examples/servlet/
SessionTracking;jsessionid=2FA9BA8083B77523A091469A3ECDF1CD?musicpreference=classical
```

The URL contains the session information jsessionid=2FA9BA8083B77523A091469A3ECDF1CD, followed by the selection musicpreference=classical. To see why, compare Example 18-3 with Example 18-2.

Example 18-3 *Example of HTML Code Generated by the Servlet SessionTracking with Rewritten URLs*

```
<html>
<head><title> Session tracking with cookies and rewritten URLs </title></
  head><body>
<p> The session-id is 2FA9BA8083B77523A091469A3ECDF1CD</p>
<p><a
href="SessionTracking;jsessionid=2FA9BA8083B77523A091469A3ECDF1CD?musicpreference
  =classical" >
Click here to select the classic collection </a></p>
<p><a
href="SessionTracking;jsessionid=2FA9BA8083B77523A091469A3ECDF1CD?musicpreference
  =rock" >
Click here to select the rock collection </a></p>

<form action="SessionTracking;jsessionid=2FA9BA8083B77523A091469A3ECDF1CD" method
  = GET>
<p> Fill in with your music preference </p><input type=text name=musicpreference>
<input type=submit value="click here to submit">
</form>

</body>
</html>
```

Example 18-3 shows the source HTML code generated by the SessionTracking servlet when the browser disables cookies. The HREFs in Example 18-3 have the field jsessionid followed by the session identifier. The form action carries the jsessionid as well.

By looking at the source code for SessionTracking.java, you can understand the following:

- How the servlet sends cookies and rewrites URLs
- How the servlet stores the client's last selection

NOTE This sample code is simply meant to illustrate some of the functions provided by some servlet APIs from the point of view of the generation of cookies and rewriting of URLs.

We recommend using the existing literature for recommendations on how to write servlet applications. If you use servlets to track user sessions, you will find this chapter useful in understanding the effect of these APIs on the network traffic.

Example 18-4 shows the source code for the example servlet SessionTracking.java.

Example 18-4 *SessionTracking.java Source Code*

```
import javax.servlet.*;
import javax.servlet.http.*;
import java.io.*;
import java.util.*;


public class SessionTracking extends HttpServlet {

    public void doGet(HttpServletRequest request,
                      HttpServletResponse response)
        throws IOException, ServletException
    {
        response.setContentType("text/html");
        PrintWriter out = response.getWriter();

       // Get the session-id from the HTTP request or generate a new one if none is present
        HttpSession session = request.getSession(true);

        out.println("<html>");
        out.print("<head>");
        out.print("<title> Session tracking with cookies and rewritten URLs </title>");
        out.print("</head>");
        out.println("<body>");
        out.println( "<p> The session-id is " + session.getId() + "</p>" );



        // Retrieve the client's previous music selection from the session information
        if (session.getAttribute( "musicpreference" ) != null) {
          String previous = session.getAttribute( "musicpreference" ).toString();
           out.println( "<p> Your previous selection was " + previous + "</p>");
        }

        String music = request.getParameter("musicpreference");

          // Save the client's current music selection in the session information
        if (music != null) {
            session.setAttribute("musicpreference", music);
            out.println( "<p> The music you selected is " + music + "</p>");
        }
```

continues

Example 18-4 *SessionTracking.java Source Code (Continued)*

```
31         // HREFs with encoded session-id
32         out.print("<p><a href=\"" +
response.encodeURL("SessionTracking?musicpreference=classical"));
33         out.println("\" > Click here to select the classic collection </a></p>");
34         out.print("<p><a href=\"" +
response.encodeURL("SessionTracking?musicpreference=rock"));
35         out.println("\" > Click here to select the rock collection </a></p>");

36         // form GET with the encoded session-id
37         out.print("<form action=\"" + response.encodeURL("SessionTracking") + "\"
method = GET>");
38         out.print("<p> Fill in with your music preference </p>");
39         out.println("<input type=text name=musicpreference>");
40         out.println("<input type=submit value=\"click here to submit\">");
41         out.println("</form>");
42         out.println("</body>");
43         out.println("</html>");
44     }
45 }
```

This is what the code does:

- request.getSession(true) looks for the session information in the HTTP request. If this is not found, it creates a new session object (Line 13).
- The code displays the session-id by invoking session.getId() (Line 19).
- If this is not the first HTTP request and there are already values associated with the session, the servlet retrieves the locally stored value of the musicpreference parameter: session.getAttribute("musicpreference") (Lines 21 and 22). Notice that session.getAttribute is the client's previous music selection.
- Request.getParameter("musicpreference") (Line 25) looks for a parameter named musicpreference= <value> in the HTTP request.
- If found, the servlet associates the <value> (the variable music) with the session-id: session.setAttribute("musicpreference", music) (Line 28). The servlet displays this value at the next HTTP request as the client's previous music selection.
- The servlet generates the HTML code: It passes the HREFs and the FORM ACTION through response.encodeURL() (Lines 32, 34, and 37). If the client accepts cookies, response.encodeURL() does not really do anything; if the client disabled cookies, encodeURL appends the jsessionid to the URLs in the HREFs or in the form ACTION field.

Session Persistence for Server Clusters

So far, you've seen how to track a user session on a single server. In a Data Center, you have multiple servers that provide the same type of information, and they all implement individually the mechanisms to ensure persistence that we have described so far.

When you use multiple servers and you load-balance traffic (with or without a load balancer), it is possible that HTTP requests belonging to one session are sent to two different servers: Each TCP connection could be sent to a different server based on the predictor algorithm.

Server farms can be made of the following:

- **Servers that do not share state information**—They store the session information locally in memory. Scattering TCP connections for the same HTTP session to different servers is an issue.
- **Servers that share state information**—Distribution of TCP connections to any server in the farm does not cause any problem.

For the first type of server, a hardware load balancer provides several mechanisms that achieve session persistence. One of them, which is also the most flexible, consists of dynamically learning the *session cookie* that the application (mod_session or servlets, for example) is using and associating the session cookie consistently with the server that generated it.

The second type of server stores session information in a shared location in two ways:

- Writing to a shared folder
- Writing to a database

These two approaches are self-explanatory, and the assumption is that there is either a shared folder or a shared database that all the web servers in the cluster can access.

Notice that the servers need to share the session-id generated by the first server, plus the attributes that the application assigned to that identifier.

Chapter 19 provides more information on session persistence and analyzes the design options based on the features available on load balancers.

Summary

Stateful applications need to track clients that are using the application to keep state information. The classic example of an application is an e-commerce website where users buy items such as books or CDs online. A single user keeps selecting items and filling a shopping cart. The application needs to show consistent information about the shopping cart to each user connected to the server.

Web-based applications use several mechanisms to track user sessions. The most popular mechanism is based on cookies. Cookies are strings carried in the HTTP request and response headers with sequences of NAME=VALUE, plus additional attributes. Cookies are inserted by the server in the HTTP response and are stored in the client's memory or disk drive. For session tracking based on cookies to work, the client needs to send them back at each request.

The most common type of cookie is a *session cookie*, which is made of a name followed by a random number. This random number has local meaning on the server: It is used to reference the shopping cart of a specific user.

Some clients do not support cookies, for several reasons: The simplest one is that cookies are disabled on the browser. Some mechanisms allow applications to work even if cookies are disabled: These mechanisms are cookies, rewritten URLs, and form hidden fields.

This chapter showed the example of session tracking with mod_session, the software for the Apache web server, and the Java servlet methods.

When you know that a web-based application is stateful, you typically can expect that this application exchanges cookies with the client, as demonstrated by the mod_session and Java servlet examples. In this case, a hardware load balancer can provide session persistence transparently by dynamically learning the session information from the cookies. Chapter 19 provides information about session persistence with hardware load balancers.

For Further Reading

Deitel, Harvey M., Paul J. Deitel, T.R. Nieto. *Internet & World Wide Web How to Program*, Second Edition. Prentice Hall.

http://java.sun.com/products/servlet/

This chapter covers the following topics:

- The concept of session persistence as it relates to the HTTP, the Secure Socket Layer (SSL) protocol, and application protocols that open multiple Layer 4 ports
- The use of proxy servers for Internet access, what a mega-proxy is, and how it affects the design of server load balancing
- Load balancing in the presence of servers that share information about user sessions
- Persistence mechanisms provided by server load balancers: predictors and sticky methods such as source IP sticky, cookie sticky, URL cookie sticky, HTTP redirection sticky, and SSL sticky
- How to implement session persistence for web-based applications by using the sticky methods on load balancers and SSL offloading devices

CHAPTER 19

Persistence Mechanisms on Load Balancers

Before reading this chapter, be sure you have read Chapter 3, "Application Architectures Overview"; Chapter 6, "Server Load-Balancing Overview"; Chapter 8, "HTTP and Related Concepts"; Chapter 9, "SSL and TLS"; and Chapter 18, "Session Tracking and Cookies."

Distributing a client's connections to multiple servers in a farm introduces the need for ensuring persistence. In fact, it is often a requirement that connections from a given client be associated with a certain server until the transaction is completed, but with load distribution, multiple TCP connections from the same client could be dispatched to different servers. This distribution can break user transactions—a problem that is referred to as the "lost shopping cart" issue. (Refer to Chapter 6 for more information.)

You might think that a client's source IP address could be used as an identity mechanism to maintain the client/server association. Unfortunately, this assumption is not valid because Internet clients often use proxy servers; as a result, clients change source IP address during a transaction.

Among the advantages of using load balancers instead of Domain Name System (DNS)–based load distribution is that load-balancing devices provide tools to ensure session persistence.

This chapter describes the concept of session persistence as it relates to HTTP and SSL and to applications that open multiple ports concurrently (such as FTP, e-commerce applications, streaming protocols, or RADIUS, for example).

NOTE Most applications open multiple connections sometimes to the same L4 port as part of the same transaction. These applications also require persistence.

This chapter then analyzes the solutions to provide successful user transactions. One solution consists of performing load distribution to servers that share session information; another solution consists of configuring load balancers with predictors that inherently ensure session persistence; the last and most common solution consists of configuring load balancers with persistence mechanisms (also called *sticky methods*), such as source IP sticky, cookie sticky, URL sticky, and SSL sticky.

TIP Persistence mechanisms offered by load balancers rely either on the client IP address or on Layer 5 information. The Layer 5 persistence mechanisms are typically used for HTTP and SSL.

A load balancer with Layer 5 capabilities must perform connection spoofing to read the Layer 5 information. By terminating the TCP connection and waiting either for the HTTP request or for the SSL hello, the load balancer can find the information necessary to ensure session persistence. For more information on connection spoofing, refer to Chapter 16, "Load-Balancing Modes and Predictors."

The configuration examples in this chapter are based on the Cisco Content Switching Module (CSM), which is a module available in the Catalyst 6500 family that offers Layer 4 and Layer 5 load-balancing capabilities.

The Concept of Session Persistence

Chapter 6 introduced the concept of *session persistence*, which refers to the capability of the load balancer to logically group multiple connections that belong to the same client transaction to the same virtual server (vserver).

This section provides an overview of the concept of persistence as it relates to HTTP and SSL and to protocols that open multiple ports on a single transaction.

HTTP Session Persistence

Chapter 18 introduced the concept of an *HTTP session*.

HTTP session persistence consists of assigning HTTP connections that belong to a certain HTTP session consistently to one server. Failure to do so results in a broken user session. With load balancing for e-commerce applications, this problem is often described as the "lost shopping cart" issue.

Suppose that a client is using a web-based application, and assume that the initial HTTP request is assigned to a certain server. This server starts tracking the user session and locally memorizing data about the client, as described in Chapter 18. Later, a new HTTP request from the same client goes to a different server. The second server is not aware of the session information present on the first server, so it starts a new session, which from the user point of view is equivalent to restarting the web-based application. You can fix this issue by using load balancers that support HTTP persistence by means of cookies or URL mechanisms. If the clients do not use nonpersistent proxies (see the section, "Persistence Considerations for Clients Using Proxy Servers"), it is also possible to ensure HTTP session persistence with source IP–based mechanisms.

SSL Persistence

Chapter 9 introduced the concept of an *SSL session*, which consists of assigning SSL connections that belong to an SSL session consistently to one server. Failure to do so significantly decreases the server performance. If multiple SSL connections that belong to the same user session go to different servers, it is impossible to resume existing SSL sessions, thus forcing a full SSL handshake for each new connection. The full SSL handshake is computationally more intensive than just resuming an existing SSL session, as described in Chapter 9. You can solve this problem by using the *SSL sticky* method or, if the clients do not use nonpersistent proxies (see the section, "Persistence Considerations for Clients Using Proxy Servers"), by using source IP mechanisms.

Persistence with Protocols Using Multiple Ports

The concept of persistence also applies to generic applications that use multiple ports concurrently: several TCP connections from the same client to different but related ports must be assigned to the same server. It is also possible that an application uses different Layer 4 protocols, such as User Datagram Protocol (UDP) and TCP, in which case the load balancer needs to maintain the association between client and server for the protocol/port pairs.

The FTP protocol provides a good example of an application that uses multiple ports. The FTP protocol is characterized by two separate *channels*:

- The *control channel*, which is the TCP connection that is used to send commands to the servers
- The *data channel*, which carries the actual data

The control channel uses port 21 on the server side. With FTP active, the server uses port 20 for the data channel; with FTP passive, both client and server use a dynamic port for the data channel.

In Example 19-1, you can see the control connection established between the client 10.21.99.246 and the FTP server 192.168.10.101. The client asks for the list of files as indicated by the Request LIST.

Example 19-1 *The FTP Control Connection*

```
10.21.99.246      192.168.10.101  TCP      1778 > ftp [SYN]
[...] handshake continues
192.168.10.101    10.21.99.246    FTP      Response: 220 FTP server ready
10.21.99.246      192.168.10.101  FTP      Request: USER admin
[...]
10.21.99.246      192.168.10.101  FTP      Request: PASV
192.168.10.101    10.21.99.246    FTP      Response: 227 Entering Passive Mode
(192,168,10,101,147,113)
10.21.99.246      192.168.10.101  FTP      Request: LIST
192.168.10.101    10.21.99.246    TCP      ftp > 1778 [ACK]
192.168.10.101    10.21.99.246    FTP      Response: 150 Opening ASCII mode data
connection for /bin/ls.
10.21.99.246      192.168.10.101  TCP      1778 > ftp [ACK]
192.168.10.101    10.21.99.246    FTP      Response: 226 Transfer complete.
[...]
```

Because the client is using the passive FTP mode (**Request: PASV**), it is up to the client to open the data channel. You can see this step in the Example 19-2.

Example 19-2 *The FTP Data Connection*

```
10.21.99.246     192.168.10.101 TCP      1779 > 37745 [SYN]
[...] handshake continues
192.168.10.101   10.21.99.246   FTP-DATA FTP Data: 418 bytes
192.168.10.101   10.21.99.246   TCP      37745 > 1779 [FIN, ACK]
[...] the connection is closed
```

If there is a load balancer between the client and the FTP servers and the client connects to a VIP address, there is the risk of load balancing the two TCP connections to two different servers.

If you look at Example 19-1, the server sent **Response: 227 Entering Passive Mode (192,168,10,101,147,113)** on the control channel. As you can see in Example 19-2, the server communicated to the client the IP address and the Layer 4 port (37745) to use on the data channel.

If the client's TCP SYN for port 37745 goes to a different server from the one that sent the **Response 227**, the FTP fails because the newly selected server does not know about the control channel negotiation.

You can fix this issue by using sticky groups on server load balancers (see the section, "Sticky Groups") configured for source IP stickiness.

Even if this example is specific to FTP, the same concept applies to a multitude of protocols that rely on different port numbers for the communication between the client and the server.

Additional examples of applications that use multiple protocol/ports include

- **E-commerce applications**—These applications are characterized by an HTTP session composed of cleartext HTTP and HTTP encrypted with SSL (HTTPS). Such a session uses port 80 and 443 and these ports are related: assigning HTTP to one server and HTTPS to a different server would break the HTTP session. A solution that provides persistence for HTTP/HTTPS is typically based on the use of cookie sticky groups in conjunction with SSL offloaders. Alternatively, you could use source IP sticky groups, assuming that the clients do not use nonpersistent proxies.
- **Streaming applications**—Chapter 18 described how streaming applications work and their traffic profiles. One of the key characteristics of streaming applications is that they support a UDP transport mechanism (typically RTP), a TCP transport mechanism (typically Real Time Streaming Protocol [RTSP] interleaving), and an HTTP transport mechanism. If the firewall in between client and server blocks UDP traffic, the application tries the TCP transport; if it is also blocked, it tries HTTP. Session persistence for streaming applications needs to maintain the client/server association for all the available protocol/port pairs.

  A solution that provides persistence for streaming protocols consists of configuring one vserver (virtual server) per each protocol port association (the vserver for the RTP traffic would just be a UDP with a wildcard port) and grouping them together with the use of sticky groups based on the source IP address.

NOTE The QuickTime server protocol/port associations are as follows: TCP port 554 (RTSP), TCP port 80 (for HTTP tunneling), and UDP with a range of ports (for RTP and RTP Control Protocol [RTCP]).

Real uses the following protocol/port associations: TCP port 554 (RTSP), TCP port 80 (for HTTP tunneling), and UDP with a range of ports (for RTP, RDT, and RTCP).

Windows Media uses UDP port 1755 and TCP port 1755 (for MMSU and MMST) and TCP port 80 (for HTTP tunneling).

- **RADIUS**—As described in Chapter 15, "Security Protocols and Technologies," RADIUS servers provide authentication and accounting. Load balancing RADIUS servers requires maintaining the association between UDP port 1812 (for the authentication) and UDP port 1813 (for the accounting). You can maintain this association by using sticky groups based on the source IP address.

Persistence Considerations for Clients Using Proxy Servers

As previously explained, load distribution of client TCP connections to a server farm might result in requests that belong to a given session being sent to different servers.

The choice of the persistence mechanism must account for the possibility that requests being sent to the load balancer might be sent from a client using proxies. This possibility applies mainly to Internet clients whose Internet service provider (ISP) uses large clusters of proxy servers. The problem that this configuration poses to a load balancer is often referred to as the *mega-proxy* issue.

Proxy Server Overview

Proxies are devices that send requests for a given protocol on behalf of a client. An example of proxy-server use is ISPs that use web-proxy devices to provide Internet access to dial-up users. When a client requests objects from the Internet, the HTTP requests go to a proxy device that has a public IP address; it retrieves these objects and returns them to the client.

Figure 19-1 shows how a proxy server works. Imagine that the user buys books on the site called http://www.example.com. The PC has a private address (10.0.0.20). The browser is set up to use the proxy server.

TIP The proxy settings for Internet Explorer 6.0 appear under **Tools > Internet Options > Connections > LAN Settings > Proxy Server**.

The proxy settings for Netscape 7.0 appear under **Edit > Preferences > Advanced > Proxies**.

As a result, the server sees 192.0.2.20 as the source IP address of the HTTP requests. This IP address is not the IP address of the PC; it belongs to the proxy server.

Figure 19-1 *How a Proxy Server Works*

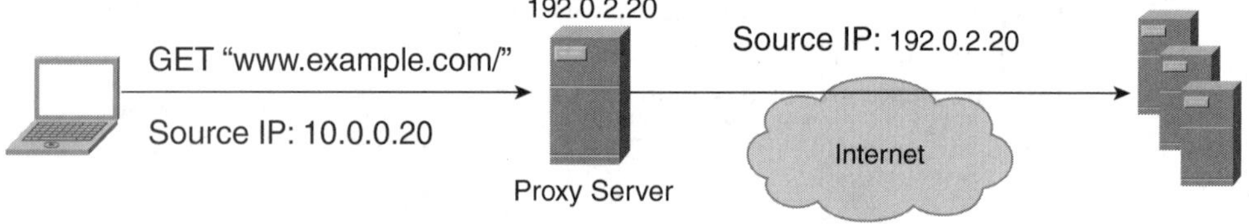

Service-provider clients and enterprise clients use proxies for the following purposes:

- **Providing Internet access**—Internal clients do not need to have a public IP address, nor do they need to be able to send DNS queries for the resolution of external domain names. Proxies take care of both operations.
- **Speeding up the delivery of content retrieved from the Internet**—Proxies cache previously requested content and give it back to the client if the same object is requested. If the content was not requested before or has expired, the cache performs an HTTP request using its own IP address.
- **Filtering**—Proxies let you define which websites (by URL) are accessible to the clients and which ones are not and can also control which object types the users can retrieve.

Clustered Proxy Servers

Usually, proxies are grouped together, forming a cluster for scaling and redundancy purposes. Multiple clients use these clustered proxies to get access to the Internet.

Clusters of proxy servers are categorized as

- **Persistent proxies**—When the user is assigned to one proxy server for the duration of a session
- **Nonpersistent proxies**—When the user is assigned to different proxy servers for different TCP connections of the same session

When clients access the Internet with persistent proxies, sessions can be identified by the source IP address (which is the IP address of the proxy server).

When clients use nonpersistent proxies (and this case is the so-called *mega-proxy farm*), requests coming from the same client might be proxied by different proxy servers, so a single session might show different source IP addresses. In this case, the source IP address of the clients' requests cannot be used to identify a session.

Implications of Proxy Servers on Load Balancing

Consider the example of Figure 19-2, which shows the default behavior of a load balancer when a client uses nonpersistent proxies for Internet access. The servers in this example do not share session information.

Figure 19-2 *Proxies, Load Balancers, and the Shopping Cart*

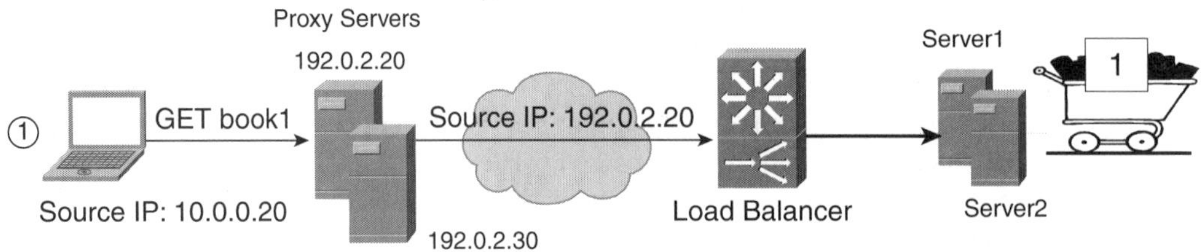

Initially (Step 1 in the figure), the client 10.10.10.20 sends an HTTP request (**GET "book1"**) to the online store http://www.example.com, and the load balancer assigns this request to server1. Server1 builds the shopping cart with item number 1. Notice that the IP address of the client, as seen by the load balancer, is 192.0.2.20. This address really is the IP of the proxy server that the client is using.

Later (step 2 in the figure), the client sends an HTTP request (**GET "book2"**) to the same online store. The source IP that the client uses for accessing the Internet has changed to 192.0.2.30, so the load balancer believes that this request is from a different client and assigns it to server2. Notice that at the moment of the client request for book2, the shopping cart for this client on server2 is empty.

The result of this behavior is a broken session (the "lost shopping cart" problem): server1 was holding the state information for the client's shopping cart, and suddenly the client's requests are assigned to server2, which does not have the shopping-cart information. This problem was also described in Chapter 6.

This example points out that session persistence in the presence of proxy devices should take into account that the source IP address of the clients is not a reliable mechanism of identification. The section, "Source IP Sticky" provides more details about the design options.

Persistence Using Session Sharing Servers

It is sometimes possible to design load balancing without session persistence. For example, you could design web-based applications in such a way that servers share session information as it is described in this section.

Session persistence is always required for protocols that open multiple ports, such as FTP or streaming protocols, or for performance optimization of SSL traffic.

When servers share the session information, typically there is no need to configure session persistence on the load-balancing device. This setup has the following advantages:

- **Better load distribution**—The load balancer can assign connections that belong to the same session more equally to the servers.
- **Automatic failure detection**—Taking one server out of rotation is not a problem because any other server can take connections belonging to any session.
- **Easier server management**—You can set the weight to 0 on a real so that no new TCP connections are sent to it and existing connections are not disrupted. When the server has no connections, it could be removed.

The drawback of this approach is the performance penalty on the achievable performance of the server farm because of the higher amount of operations that need to be performed for each client request.

In fact, servers share the session information by writing to a shared folder or to a database. Reading the session information with either mechanism is slower than reading it from the local memory as happens when the load balancer ensures session persistence.

Session Persistence Mechanisms

This section compares the use of predictors that ensure session persistence with the persistence or sticky methods available on load balancers.

Predictors

Predictors indicate how load balancers distribute incoming connections to the servers. Examples of predictors are round-robin, weighted round-robin, and source IP hash.

A *hashing* predictor is a mathematic function that operates on a field in the incoming request and generates a number that identifies a server. Hashing predictors inherently achieve persistence as long as the following conditions are met:

- The field to which the hash is applied does not change during the session. For example, source IP hash always produces the same server selection for the same client IP address. This condition requires that the source IP not change during a session.

- The information used by the load balancer to identify the session and to elect the server needs to be present in the very first request. An example of using hashing that does not provide persistence is the hash predictor applied to cookies: the first request from the client does not carry a cookie, and as a result, the hash predictor applied to the second request would elect a different server.

Figure 19-3 clarifies how the hashing predictor works.

Figure 19-3 *Hashing Predictor*

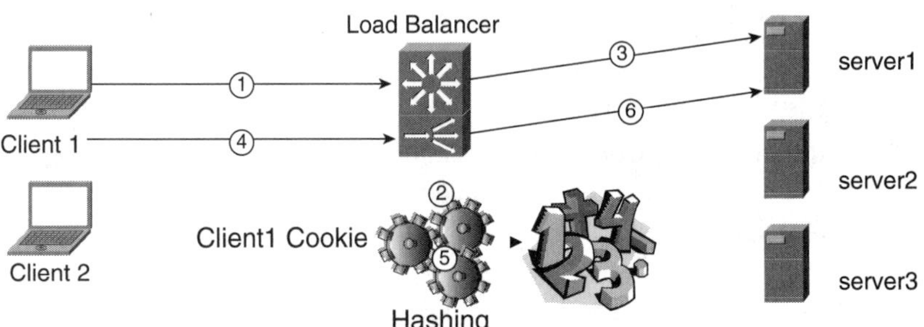

Client1 opens a TCP connection with the website (Step 1). The load balancer performs a hash on the client's information (Step 2). The operation returns a number that identifies server1 and the load balancer assigns the connection to this server (Step 3). Each connection from the client goes through the path indicated by Steps 4, 5, and 6, and each time the client's information is hashed to return a number that matches a server.

NOTE For more information about load-balancing predictors, refer to Chapter 16.

There is a difference between using a predictor that achieves persistence and a persistence mechanism.

Sticky Methods

Sticky methods let a load balancer send clients' requests to the server where a session started.

Based on the predictor, the first request of a new session is sent to the most suitable server; subsequent requests belonging to the same session are assigned to servers based on the sticky information.

Sticky methods can be further categorized as

- **Learning methods**—These sticky methods memorize information that uniquely identifies the client during the first phase of a session. This information can be, for example, the source IP of the client, the cookie sent by the server, or the SSL session ID. The load balancer matches specific fields in client requests to the information previously stored to identify the server. The *sticky table* saves the information that is dynamically learned with the sticky method.
- **Matching methods**—These sticky methods require manual configuration of strings that identify the servers, whose value typically appears in HTTP requests or cookies.

Figure 19-4 shows persistence based on learning sticky methods.

Figure 19-4 shows a client that opens a new connection (Step 1) to the website. Based on a round-robin predictor, the load balancer assigns this connection to server2 (Step 2a) and populates a table (Step 2b) (the sticky table).

The next connection from this client (Step 3) has the load balancer to look up the sticky table (Step 4). The switch finds that it previously chose server2, so it forwards the new connection (Step 5) to server2.

Figure 19-4 *Sticky Methods on Load Balancers*

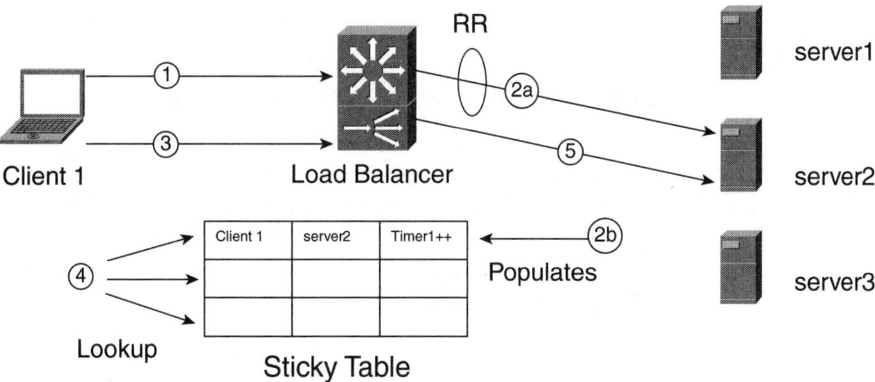

Table 19-1 shows that the sticky table allows choosing the predictor, with the drawback that the sticky table takes memory and thereby limits the number of sessions. (Typical limits are between tens of thousands to over a million of entries.)

Table 19-1 *Pros and Cons of the Main Sticky Methods*

	Allows Choice of Predictor	Limits on Number of Sessions
Sticky Table	Yes	Yes
Hashing Predictor	No	No
Cookie or URL Matching	Yes	No

The hashing predictor has the drawback that it spreads traffic in a way that is not necessarily equal for the servers. A key advantage, however, is that the load balancer does not have to hold any information in memory.

Cookie or URL matching (described in more detail later) neither impose the choice of a predictor nor do they take memory.

Sticky Groups

Session persistence for protocols that use multiple ports can be achieved with sticky groups. Example 19-3 shows how to configure sticky groups using the Cisco CSM. The required configuration is as follows:

- One vserver for each VIP address, Layer 4 protocol, and Layer 4 port (for example, one vserver for TCP port 80 and one vserver for TCP port 443).
- Assignment of the same server farm to all the vservers that need to be bundled together (in this example, the server farm HTTP-FARM).
- One sticky group that defines the sticky method (the sticky method could be source IP or cookie, for example), the group identifier, and the timeout. (You can configure this timeout globally or in vserver submode, and it needs to be consistent across the vservers.) Example 19-3 does not show the sticky method because it could be the source IP, cookie, cookie-url, and so on. The syntax of the command on the Cisco CSM is

  ```
  sticky sticky-group-id {netmask netmask | cookie cookie-name | ssl} [timeout
    timeout] [address {source | destination | both}]
  ```

- Assignment of the same group identifier (group 5 in Example 19-3) to the vservers that need to be logically bundled. The syntax of the sticky group command in vserver submode is

  ```
  sticky timeout group sticky-group-id
  ```

  In Example 19-3, the timeout is 30 minutes (min).

The initial HTTP request to port 80 populates the sticky table with the source IP address of the client. When a request comes in for port 443, the switch looks up the client IP (or the cookie, depending on the sticky method) in the same sticky table, and it assigns the request to the server found in this table.

Example 19-3 *Using Sticky Groups for Session Persistence Between HTTP and HTTPS*

```
sticky 5 ...
!
serverfarm HTTP-FARM
 nat server
 no nat client
 real 10.10.10.11
  inservice
 real 10.10.10.13
  inservice

vserver HTTP
  serverfarm HTTP-FARM
  sticky 30 group 5
  virtual 171.69.0.137 tcp 80
  inservice
!
vserver HTTPS
  serverfarm HTTP-FARM
  sticky 30 group 5
  virtual 171.69.0.137 tcp 443
  inservice
```

Source IP Sticky

The simplest and easiest way to identify a client is by its IP address. The approach has at least two drawbacks, however:

- If clients are coming from nonpersistent proxies where their IP addresses might change several times, this mechanism does not work.
- If many clients come from the same proxy devices, the distribution in the server farm is unbalanced.

This section explains how to configure a load balancer for source IP stickiness with the source IP sticky methods and with the source IP hash predictor.

Source IP Sticky Configuration

Example 19-4 shows how to configure source IP stickiness on a Cisco CSM. The global command to enable the feature is

`sticky` *`sticky-group-id`* **`netmask`** *`netmask`* **`address source`**

The *sticky-group-id* is then applied to the vserver with the command

`sticky` *`timeout`* **`group`** *`sticky-group-id`*

Example 19-4 shows a vserver (171.69.0.137) that load-balances connections to two different reals: 10.10.10.11 and 10.10.10.13.

Example 19-4 *Using Source IP Stickiness*

```
sticky 5 netmask 255.255.255.255 address source

serverfarm HTTP-FARM
 nat server
 no nat client
 real 10.10.10.11
  inservice
 real 10.10.10.13
  inservice

vserver HTTP
  serverfarm HTTP-FARM
  sticky 30 group 5
  virtual 171.69.0.137 tcp 80
  inservice
```

With this configuration, the sticky table stores the source IP of the client for 30 min and retains information on which server was elected by the load balancer the first time the request was received.

As an example, client 192.0.2.20 issues a GET request, and is assigned to 10.10.10.11. If after 20 min, it sends another GET request, the switch reselects server 10.10.10.11.

Notice that in the configuration, the **sticky** command specifies a mask, 255.255.255.255. The sticky table creates an entry for 192.0.2.20 (the 32-bit address).

Configuration for Mega Proxies

As explained in the section, "Persistence Considerations for Clients Using Proxy Servers," the load-balancer configuration needs to take into account that the source IP of the clients might change during a session.

The configuration described in Example 19-4 would not work if applied to the scenario of Figure 19-2. The reason is that the client source IP can change from 192.0.2.20 to 192.0.2.30. The predictor, which originally elected 10.10.10.11 as the server for 192.0.2.20, is allowed to send the new request to 10.10.10.13.

Example 19-5 shows how you can fix this problem. If you know which range of IP addresses the service provider assigns to the clients visiting your site, you can change the mask in the sticky table to aggregate multiple IP addresses in one single sticky entry.

Example 19-5 *Source IP Sticky Configuration for Clients Using Mega-Proxy Servers*

```
sticky 5 netmask 255.255.240.0 address source

serverfarm HTTP-FARM
 nat server
 no nat client
 real 10.10.10.11
  inservice
 real 10.10.10.13
  inservice

vserver HTTP
  serverfarm HTTP-FARM
  sticky 30 group 5
  virtual 171.69.0.137 tcp 80
  inservice
```

In Example 19-5, the assumption is that even if a client changes IP address during a session, the main subnet (/20) does not change.

The drawback of this approach is that you might assign many other clients to the same server as long as they match the same subnet. As a result, the load distribution can be unequal.

If you know that the clients use nonpersistent proxies, and that the masking of the source IP address does not solve the issue of session persistence, you should consider providing stickiness by means of URL or cookie persistence.

NOTE When dealing with client requests that are proxied, it is important to know the following information about their service providers:

- What range of IP addresses are used by the proxy servers?
- Do they use persistent or nonpersistent proxies?
- If the ISP uses a nonpersistent proxy, does it assign addresses from a specific range? If, for example, clients are assigned addresses from one subnet and the first three octets do not change during the session, you can define a sticky mask of 255.255.255.0.

ISPs usually make this information available. For example, AOL provides a useful page for webmasters at http://webmaster.info.aol.com/.

This information helps decide which sticky method is the most appropriate.

Source IP Hash

When you configure a load balancer to distribute traffic based on a hash for the source IP, connections are consistently assigned to one server as long as the source IP does not change.

The hash predictor lets you specify the masking on the source IP address. If you can use the client IP address to identify the session, you can set the mask to 255.255.255.255. If the source IP changes because of the mega-proxy problem, you can change the masking for the hashing, as shown in Example 19-6.

Example 19-6 *Using Source IP Hash and the Netmask*

```
serverfarm HTTP-FARM
  nat server
  no nat client
  predictor hash address source 255.255.240.0
  real 10.10.10.11
   inservice
  real 10.10.10.13
   inservice
```

Cookie Sticky

HTTP servers configured to track the user session send cookies with random numbers to the client's browser. Load balancers with Layer 5 capabilities are able to match cookies inside HTTP GET requests and assign those to the servers that originated them.

There are two substantial categories of persistence mechanisms based on cookies:

- **Cookie passive**—When the cookie is sent by the server to the client and the load balancer spoofs the value of the cookie
- **Cookie active**—When the load balancer inserts an additional cookie into the client/server communication and uses this cookie to identify which server a client should be assigned to

A load balancer that ensures persistence based on cookies inserted by a server provides the following choices:

- Caching session cookies (cookie passive)
- Matching the value field in the cookie with a preconfigured string (cookie match)
- Hashing the value field of a cookie (cookie hash)

Cookie Passive

The best approach to achieving persistence with session cookies is to have a load balancer retain the association "session cookie"—server.

Figure 19-5 shows the example of a browser receiving a session cookie called JSESSIONID with the value of A479F3AD060C7BF5CE1F917347F862C3 from a servlet engine. This example is based on the use of the servlets. Remember that the application, called SessionTracking, was described in Chapter 18.

Figure 19-5 *Browser Accepting a Session Cookie*

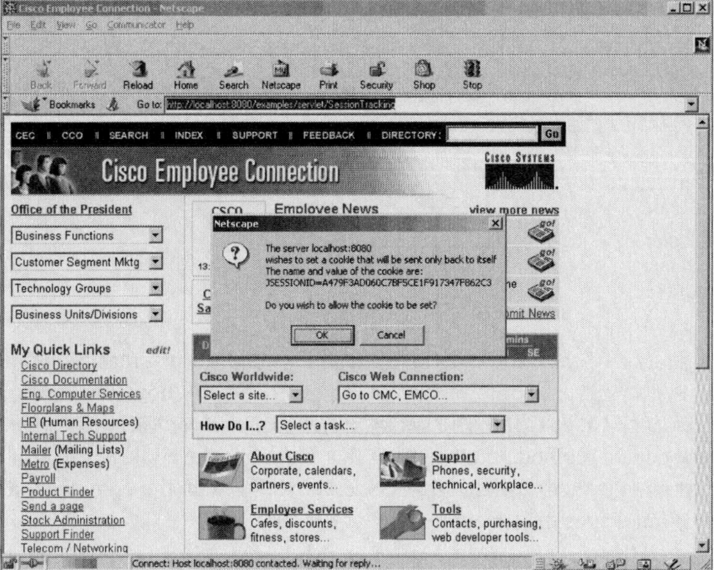

Load balancers can retain information about these cookies and associate a returning client with the server that originated the cookie.

Figure 19-6 shows how cookie passive works.

In Figure 19-6, the client initially sends a GET request to http://www.example.com (Step 1).

The load balancer uses the round-robin predictor to select the server (Step 2). The server responds and inserts a cookie: JSESSIONID = A479F3AD060C7BF5CE1F917347F862C3 (Step 3a).

The load balancer reads the Set-Cookie: field of the HTTP response and saves the value in its sticky table (Step 3b). Subsequent requests from the client carry the Cookie: field (Step 4a). The switch looks up the cookie name and value in the sticky table (Step 4b) and assigns the request to the server where the session started (Step 5).

Figure 19-6 *Cookie Passive*

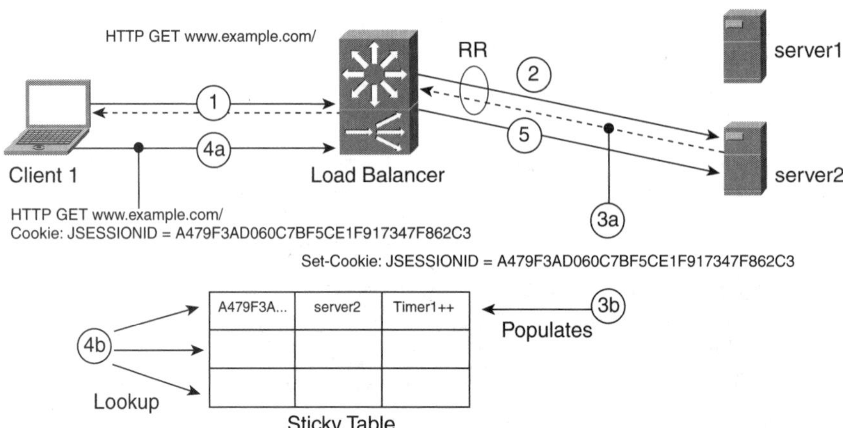

Configuration of the cookie-passive capability requires just turning on the feature in the context of a vserver configuration. Example 19-7 shows how you can configure cookie passive on the Cisco CSM. The **sticky** *sticky-group-id* **cookie** *cookie-name* command specifies the cookie method and the string that identifies the cookie, JSESSIONID. The sticky configuration is then assigned to the vserver HTTP with the command **sticky 30 group 3**, where 30 indicates the timeout.

Example 19-7 *Cookie Passive Configuration*

```
serverfarm HTTP-FARM
  nat server
  no nat client
  real 10.10.10.11
   inservice
  real 10.10.10.13
   inservice
!
sticky 3 cookie JSESSIONID
!
 vserver HTTP
  virtual  171.69.0.137 tcp www
  serverfarm HTTP-FARM
  sticky  30 group 3
  parse-length 4000
  inservice
!
```

Cookie Match

Another solution to HTTP persistence is to match the actual value of the cookie with some predefined string. With this mechanism, you have to keep consistent configurations between servers and load balancers. Appendix E, "Configuring Servers to Insert Cookies," explains how to insert cookies that the load balancer can match.

There are two different implementations:

- Matching a specific cookie introduced by the server
- Matching a fixed portion of a session cookie

Figure 19-7 shows a client sending a request to http://www.example.com (Step 1). The load balancer sends the request to a server according to the configured predictor.

Figure 19-7 *Cookie Match*

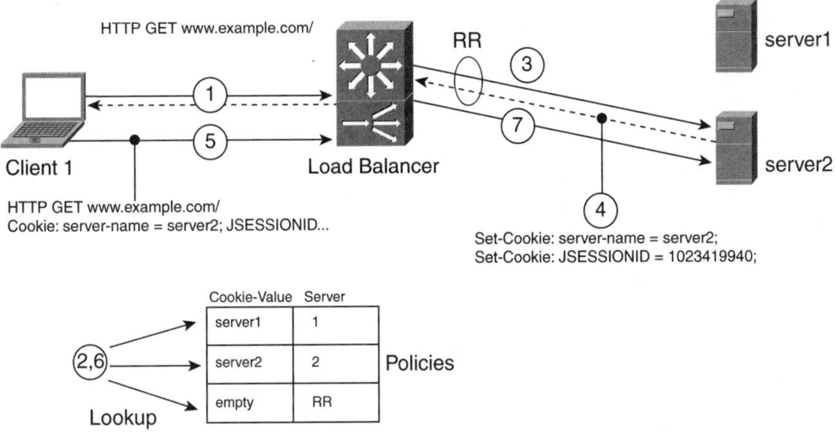

This time, the server inserts two cookies—JSESSIONID and an additional cookie that identifies the server ("server-name = server2").

NOTE The insertion of the JSESSIONID is immaterial to the example, but it shows that the server might be inserting cookies in addition to the server-name cookie.

Further requests from the client to http://www.example.com carry the cookie server-name. The load balancer can match this value and assign the HTTP request to the appropriate server.

As you can see from Example 19-8, each real server has an associated cookie value. When an incoming request carries the server-name cookie (configured in the policies POLICYSERVER1 and POLICYSERVER2), the value is compared against the string under each "map" and forwarded accordingly.

Example 19-8 *Cookie Match Configuration*

```
!
map COOKIESERVER1 cookie
  match protocol http cookie server-name cookie-value server1
!
map COOKIESERVER2 cookie
  match protocol http cookie server-name cookie-value server2
!
serverfarm HTTP-FARM
  nat server
  no nat client
  real 10.10.10.11
   inservice
  real 10.10.10.13
   inservice
!
serverfarm SERVER1
  nat server
  no nat client
  real 10.10.10.11
   inservice
!
 serverfarm SERVER2
  nat server
  no nat client
  real 10.10.10.13
   inservice
!
policy POLICYSERVER1
  cookie-map COOKIESERVER1
  serverfarm SERVER1
!
 policy POLICYSERVER2
  cookie-map COOKIESERVER2
  serverfarm SERVER2
!
vserver HTTP
  virtual 171.69.0.137 tcp www
  serverfarm HTTP-FARM
  slb-policy POLICYSERVER1
  slb-policy POLICYSERVER2
  inservice
!
```

The following list explains how to read the configuration in Example 19-8:

1 A client sends an HTTP GET request for 171.69.0.137. This initial GET request does not carry a cookie.

2 The load-balancing device (a Cisco CSM in this example) looks up the vserver configuration. It first looks up the slb-policy POLICYSERVER1 and then the slb-policy POLICYSERVER2. (slb-policy contains Layer 5 information about the cookie matching.) The GET request does not contain a cookie, so it does not match any policy.

3 The load balancer selects a server from the default server farm (serverfarm HTTP-FARM) and sends traffic to it. Suppose the server is server2 (10.10.10.13).

4 Server2 sends the response to the HTTP GET request to the client together with cookies. One response includes the cookie name value server-name=server2.

5 The client sends a new HTTP GET request for 171.69.0.137, and this time, the GET request contains a cookie (server-name=server2).

6 The load balancer looks up the slb-policies, and server-name=server2 matches the policy POLICYSERVER2 because this policy is associated with the map COOKIESERVER2. The map COOKIESERVER2 matches the cookie with the server2 value.

7 As a result, the load balancer chooses the server farm SERVER2 that contains the server 10.10.10.13.

A special case of cookie matching is the one where an application server sends a cookie with a random portion (which could be defined as the HTTP session identifier), followed by a string that uniquely identifies a server, such as SERV1 for server1 and SERV2 for server2. The cookie would be as follows:

JSESSIONID= A479F3AD060C7BF5CE1F917347F862C3-SERV1

Example 19-9 shows the configuration of a Cisco CSM for session persistence with cookie match. The configuration is very similar to Example 19-8 with the exception of the cookie maps, where the value is replaced with a string that matches any cookie ending in -SERV1 for the map COOKIESERVER1 and in -SERV2 for the map COOKIESERVER2.

Example 19-9 *Matching a Predictable String of the Session Cookie*

```
!
map COOKIESERVER1 cookie
  match protocol http cookie JSESSIONID cookie-value
????????????????????????????????-SERV1
!
map COOKIESERVER2 cookie
  match protocol http cookie JSESSIONID cookie-value
????????????????????????????????-SERV2
```

continues

Example 19-9 *Matching a Predictable String of the Session Cookie (Continued)*

```
!
serverfarm HTTP-FARM
  nat server
  no nat client
  real 10.10.10.11
   inservice
  real 10.10.10.13
   inservice
!
serverfarm SERVER1
  nat server
  no nat client
  real 10.10.10.11
   inservice
!
 serverfarm SERVER2
  nat server
  no nat client
  real 10.10.10.13
   inservice
!
policy POLICYSERVER1
  cookie-map COOKIESERVER1
  serverfarm SERVER1
!
 policy POLICYSERVER2
  cookie-map COOKIESERVER2
  serverfarm SERVER2
!
vserver HTTP
  virtual 171.69.0.137 tcp www
  serverfarm HTTP-FARM
  slb-policy POLICYSERVER1
  slb-policy POLICYSERVER2
inservice
!
```

TIP Session persistence with cookie passive where the cookie is learned dynamically is preferable to the cookie-match methods because it requires fewer configurations on both the load balancer and the server.

Cookie Active

Cookie active or *cookie insert* is the mechanism of sending cookies from a load balancer. Figure 19-8 illustrates how cookie active works.

Figure 19-8 *Cookie Active or Cookie Insert*

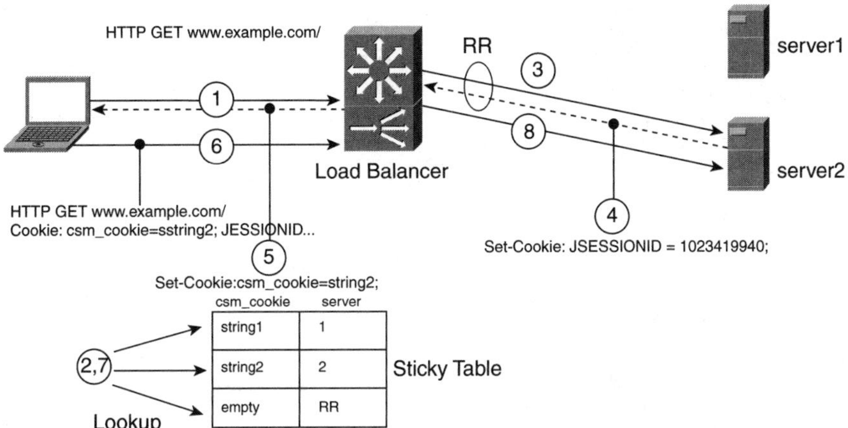

The following sequence explains the different transactions, as numbered in Figure 19-8:

1. A client sends an HTTP request.
2. When the load balancer receives the request, it looks up the sticky table.
3. The load balancer selects a server with a certain predictor.
4. The load balancer intercepts the reply.
5. The load balancer inserts a cookie in it that uniquely identifies the server (for example, the IP address of the real server) and forwards the modified HTTP response to the client.
6. Further HTTP requests from the client include the cookie set by the load balancer. This cookie contains the information necessary for the load balancer to ensure session persistence.
7. The load balancer looks up the sticky table.
8. The load balancer selects the appropriate server.

Example 19-10 gives a sample of the configuration of cookie active. The global configuration for the cookie mechanism specifies the name of the cookie inserted by the load balancer. The value is determined by the load balancer based on the server selected by the predictor algorithm.

Example 19-10 *Cookie Active Configuration*

```
serverfarm HTTP-FARM
  nat server
  no nat client
  real 10.10.10.11
   inservice
  real 10.10.10.13
   inservice
!
sticky 3 cookie csm_cookie insert
!
 vserver HTTP
  virtual 171.69.0.137 tcp www
  serverfarm HTTP-FARM
  sticky  30 group 3
  parse-length 4000
  inservice
!
```

URL Sticky

As described in Chapter 18, when the client disables cookies, servers typically embed the session information into the URLs.

An additional field carrying the session ID is attached to URLs so that a client clicking on hyperlinks carries the ID number in its HTTP requests.

Figure 19-9 shows a web page with rewritten URLs.

If you click the hyperlink "Click here to select the classic collection," the browser sends an HTTP GET to /examples/servlet/SessionTracking;jsessionid=A479F3AD060C7BF5CE1F917347F862C3?musicpreference=classical.

A load balancer capable of reading URLs can assign the HTTP request to the server that originated the session, whose identifier is A479F3AD060C7BF5CE1F917347F862C3. But how would the load balancer know which server originated this session ID? The following section answers the question.

URL Cookie

When servers perform URL rewrite, the information about the session ID is embedded in the HTML page, and the load balancer cannot read this information, but it can still find it and store it as described in the next paragraph.

A web server with session tracking enabled does not know whether the clients disabled cookies, so the server sends a page with rewritten URLs as well as a cookie. Both the cookie and the rewritten URLs carry the same session number. You can see how it works in Figure 19-10 and Example 19-11.

Figure 19-9 *Page with Rewritten URLs*

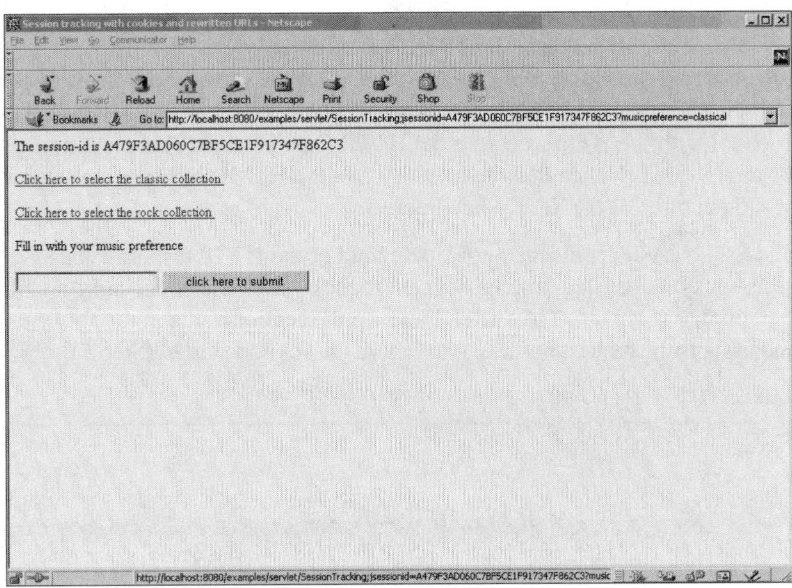

Figure 19-10 *URL Cookie Persistence*

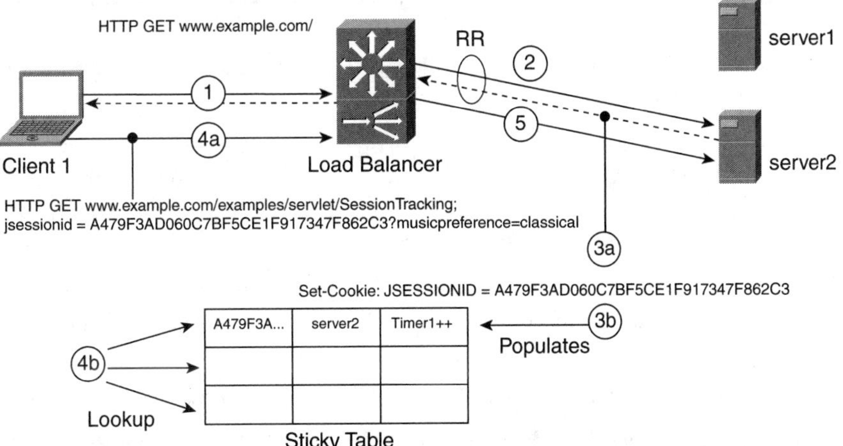

The load balancer in Figure 19-10 is configured for URL cookie persistence, and the client in the picture disabled cookies.

The client initially sends an HTTP request to http://www.example.com (Step 1). The load balancer uses the round-robin predictor to select the server (Step 2). The server responds and sends a cookie, JSESSIONID= A479F3AD060C7BF5CE1F917347F862C3 (Step 3a), together with the HTML code in the HTTP Data portion. This response is visible in Example 19-11. Notice that the **href** fields in the HTML code are rewritten with the same session number as the Set-Cookie field.

The load balancer reads the Set-Cookie field of the HTTP response and saves the value in its sticky table (Step 3b). Subsequent requests from the client carry rewritten URLs ;jsessionid= (Step 4a). The switch looks up the session value in the sticky table (Step 4b) and assigns the request to the server where the session started (Step 5).

Example 19-11 *Traffic from an HTTP Server with Session-Tracking Enabled*

```
<HTML>
 [...]
<p><a
href="SessionTracking;jsessionid=A479F3AD060C7BF5CE1F917347F862C3?musicpreference
=classical" > Click here to select the classic collection </a></p>
<p><a
href="SessionTracking;jsessionid=A479F3AD060C7BF5CE1F917347F862C3?musicpreference
=rock" > Click here to select the rock collection </a></p>
[...]
HTTP/1.1 200 OK
Date: Fri, 07 Jun 2002 18:32:50 GMT
Set-Cookie: jsessionid=A479F3AD060C7BF5CE1F917347F862C3; path=/
```

The *URL cookie* mechanism (also called *URL learn*) on a load balancer captures the information in the cookie and uses it to match the URL.

The URL cookie technology solves problems that relate to users who disable cookies on their browsers and problems that relate to user agents (this differs from regular browsers) that do not support cookies. Typical user agents that do not support cookies are wireless application protocol (WAP) applications.

Example 19-12 shows how to configure a URL cookie on the Cisco CSM to achieve session persistence with the servers of Example 19-11. The following **sticky** command specifies the cookie name and enters the sticky cookie submode:

```
Router(config-module-csm)# sticky sticky-group-id cookie cookie-name
```

The following command issued from the sticky cookie submode specifies the string used in the URL:

```
Router(config-slb-sticky-cookie)#secondary url-string
```

The *cookie-name* is the name of the session cookie and the url-string is the string used in the URL to pass the session information to the server.

Example 19-12 *URL Cookie Configuration on the Cisco CSM*

```
serverfarm HTTP-FARM
  nat server
  no nat client
  real 10.10.10.11
   inservice
  real 10.10.10.13
   inservice
!
sticky 3 cookie jsessionid
  secondary jsessionid
!
 vserver HTTP
  virtual 171.69.0.137 tcp www
  serverfarm HTTP-FARM
  sticky  30 group 3
  parse-length 4000
  inservice
!
```

URL Match

URL match is similar to cookie match. Web or application servers can set the session ID in such a way that a portion of it never changes so that it uniquely identifies the server. An example could be a session ID such as the following: JSESSIONID=*XXXXXXXXXXXXXXXXXXXXXXXXXXXXXXXX*-SERV1 to identify server1, JSESSIONID=*XXXXXXXXXXXXXXXXXXXXXXXXXXXXXXXX*-SERV2, and so forth. A special character, the hyphen in this example, typically precedes the server identifier. Changes in the format of the identifier depend on the application server that you use.

This session ID can be carried inside cookies or it can be embedded in URLs. If this session ID is carried inside URLs, you can configure a load balancer to match it, as you can see in Example 19-13.

Example 19-13 *How to Match the Server ID in the Session ID of a URL*

```
!
map URLSERVER1 url
  match protocol http url  *JSESSIONID=????????????????????????????????-SERV1*
!
 map URLSERVER2 URL
  match protocol http url  *JSESSIONID=????????????????????????????????-SERV2*
```

continues

Example 19-13 *How to Match the Server ID in the Session ID of a URL (Continued)*

```
!
serverfarm HTTP-FARM
  nat server
  no nat client
  real 10.10.10.11
   inservice
  real 10.10.10.13
   inservice
!
serverfarm SERVER1
  nat server
  no nat client
  real 10.10.10.11
   inservice
!
 serverfarm SERVER2
  nat server
  no nat client
  real 10.10.10.13
   inservice
!
policy POLICYSERVER1
  URL-map URLSERVER1
  serverfarm SERVER1
!
 policy POLICYSERVER2
  URL-map URLSERVER2
  serverfarm SERVER2
!
vserver HTTP
  virtual 171.69.0.137 tcp www
  serverfarm HTTP-FARM
  slb-policy POLICYSERVER1
  slb-policy POLICYSERVER2
  inservice
!
```

The key portion of the configuration is the URL MAP. URLSERVER1 matches any URL containing the JSESSIONID string followed by 32 characters (the random portion of the session ID) and by the –SERV1 string. This format is defined by the regular expression ***JSESSIONID=????????????????????????????????-SERV1***.

URL Hash

The URL hash is a predictor. Figure 19-11 shows how the hash works.

Figure 19-11 *URL Hash*

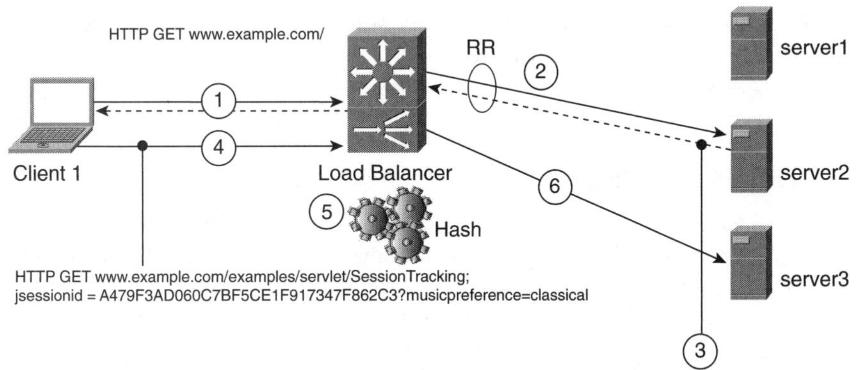

The first request (Step 1) does not have any session information, so it can be sent to any server (Step 2). Server2 inserts a session ID in the <hrefs> of the web page (Step 3). The second request (Step 4) carries the session information and is hashed to server3 (Step 5).

The hashing predictor causes some shuffling in the server selection because you cannot really assign a client to a server on the first request: one server inserts the session ID and then all other client requests are assigned to another server based on the result of the hashing.

Example 19-14 shows how a URL hash could be configured on a load balancer to provide stickiness with the rewritten URLs shown in Figure 19-11.

Example 19-14 *How to Hash a Session ID in the URL*

```
vserver HTTP
  serverfarm HTTP-FARM
  virtual 171.69.0.137 tcp 80
  url-hash begin-pattern ;jsessionid=
  url-hash end-pattern ?
  inservice
!
serverfarm HTTP-FARM
  nat server
  no nat client
  predictor hash url
  real 10.10.10.11
   inservice
  real 10.10.10.13
   inservice
!
```

NOTE URL hash is not really a perfect mechanism to ensure session persistence.

The URL hash used for persistence can work as long as the servers can accept a session ID that was generated on another server.

HTTP Redirection Sticky

HTTP redirection is a feature of HTTP that allows pointing a client to a different URI. A server could send a message "302 found" with the "location" information of a URI different from that originally selected by the client. For more information about HTTP redirection, refer to Chapter 8. Example 19-15 clarifies how HTTP redirection works.

A load balancer can use HTTP redirection to assign a client to a server for the duration of a user session. Figure 19-12 illustrates how an HTTP redirection sticky works. Initially, the load balancer receives an HTTP request from a client directed to the VIP address (Step 1); the load balancer applies the predictor algorithm, elects a server, and sends an HTTP redirect to the client with a URI that identifies the elected server (Step 2) (server-1.example.com in the example). Example 19-15 shows the traffic trace of these two steps: the client requesting index.html from the destination host http://www.example.com and the load-balancer reply indicating the location http://server-1.example.com.

Figure 19-12 *HTTP Redirection Stickiness*

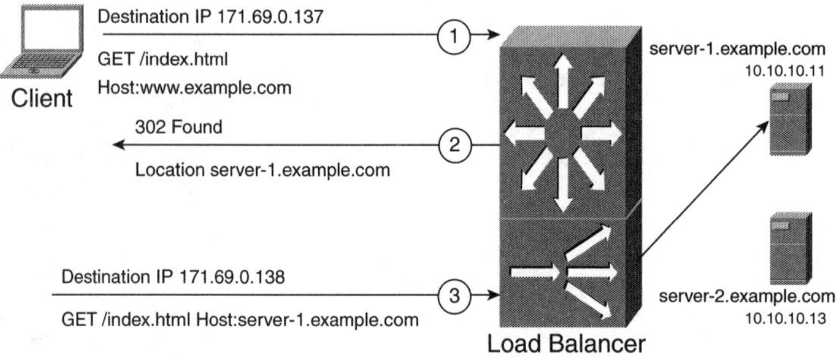

The client receiving the redirection information sends a new HTTP request to server-1.example.com (Step 3 in Figure 19-12). The traffic trace of this request appears in Example 19-15.

Example 19-15 *How HTTP Redirect Works*

```
! Client request (step 1):
GET / HTTP/1.0
Connection: Keep-Alive
User-Agent: Mozilla/4.7 [en] (WinNT; U)
Accept: image/gif, image/x-xbitmap, image/jpeg, image/pjpeg, image/png, */*
Accept-Language: en,pdf
Accept-Charset: iso-8859-1,*,utf-8
Host: www.example.com

! Reply (step 2):
HTTP/1.1 302 Found
Location: http://server-1.example.com
Connection: close
Content-Type: text/html

! Client request (step 3):
GET / HTTP/1.0
Connection: Keep-Alive
User-Agent: Mozilla/4.7 [en] (WinNT; U)
Accept: image/gif, image/x-xbitmap, image/jpeg, image/pjpeg, image/png, */*
Accept-Language: en,pdf
Accept-Charset: iso-8859-1,*,utf-8
Host: server-1.example.com
```

Notice in Figure 19-12 the IP addresses associated with the requests. The IP address for http://www.example.com is 171.69.0.137, which is the VIP address. The IP address for server-1.example.com is 171.69.0.138.

Notice that this IP address identifies server1, but it does not need to be the real IP address of the server. The load balancer provides network address translation (NAT) between the public IP address space and the real IP address of the server. you configure the CSM with a one-to-one mapping between the VIP addresses used for the redirection and the servers.

Example 19-16 shows the configuration corresponding to Figure 19-12. In Example 19-17, there are *redirect* vservers, and they are assigned to reals. The purpose of these vservers is just NATing the public IP address to the server private IP address, just as 171.69.0.138 maps to 10.10.10.11. The **webhost** statement is the string sent into the Location field of the HTTP redirect message.

Example 19-16 *Example of Configuration for HTTP Redirection Stickiness*

```
serverfarm HTTP-FARM
  nat server
  no nat client
  redirect-vserver http-server1
   webhost relocation server-1.example.com 302
```

continues

Example 19-16 *Example of Configuration for HTTP Redirection Stickiness (Continued)*

```
    virtual 171.69.0.138 tcp www
    inservice
   redirect-vserver http-server2
    webhost relocation server-2.example.com 302
    virtual 171.69.0.139 tcp www
    inservice
   real 10.10.10.11
    redirect-vserver http-server1
    inservice
   real 10.10.10.13
    redirect-vserver http-server2
    inservice
 !
 vserver HTTP
   serverfarm HTTP-FARM
   virtual 171.69.0.137 tcp 80
   inservice
 !
```

One of the drawbacks of using HTTP redirect for persistence is that a client could potentially bookmark the server name instead of the main site, and a future connection might be dropped because the server is out of service.

Load balancers offer a fix for the problem of connections being dropped. The fix consists of configuring a backup server farm, as described in Example 19-17.

Example 19-17 *Backup Server Farm Example*

```
serverfarm HTTP-FARM
  nat server
  no nat client
  redirect-vserver http-server1
   webhost relocation server-1.example.com 302
   webhost backup server-2.example.com 302
   virtual 171.69.0.138 tcp www
   inservice
  redirect-vserver http-server2
   webhost backup server-1.example.com com 302
   webhost backup server-1.example.com 302
   virtual 171.69.0.139 tcp www
   inservice
  real 10.10.10.11
   redirect-vserver http-server1
   inservice
  real 10.10.10.13
   redirect-vserver http-server2
   inservice
```

Example 19-17 *Backup Server Farm Example (Continued)*

```
!
vserver HTTP
  serverfarm HTTP-FARM
  virtual 171.69.0.137 tcp 80
  inservice
!
```

As you can see from the example, server-1.example.com and server-2.example.com are backing up each other. For example, if the user bookmarks server-1.example.com, an HTTP request comes to the load balancer for 171.69.0.138. If 10.10.10.11 is down, the load balancer sends an HTTP redirect to server-2.example.com.

If you configure more servers, such as server-1, server-2, server-3, you can configure the backup in such a way that server-2 backs up server-1, server-3 backs up server-2, and server-1 backs up server-3.

SSL Sticky

The key reason to implement SSL stickiness is for performance, as described in Chapter 9.

When clustering servers configured for SSL traffic, it is possible that multiple connections of the same SSL session are sent to different servers. Consider the example of a client using HTTPS (HTTP on SSL) to connect to a web server.

The browser opens multiple TCP connections to retrieve web objects. It can open one TCP connection per HTTP request (like HTTP 1.0), it can perform one TCP connection every n HTTP requests (like HTTP 1.1), or it can open multiple TCP connections simultaneously.

Because the traffic is carried on top of SSL, for each separate TCP connection there is an SSL session negotiation. For example, the HTTPS request for object 1 requires a TCP handshake, followed by an SSL session negotiation, followed by the HTTP GET.

As described in Chapter 9, the SSL session negotiation has an important performance impact on the server. SSL offers a shortened negotiation scheme, called *session resumption*, to accelerate the initial phase of the SSL connection between client/server pairs that have already gone through the full SSL negotiation. For this reason, it is important that the load balancing preserves the client/server association for the duration of a session. Assigning each SSL connection to a different server would impair the session resumption capability, thus affecting server performance.

SSL Sticky Configuration

Load balancers with Layer 5 capabilities can monitor the SSL session ID inserted by a server. When a client tries to resume a session by sending this session ID in the SSL client hello, the load balancer assigns the incoming hello to the appropriate server based on the session ID, thus allowing the session resumption to work. This technology is called *SSL persistence* or *SSL sticky*. Figure 19-13 illustrates how SSL sticky works.

Figure 19-13 *SSL Sticky*

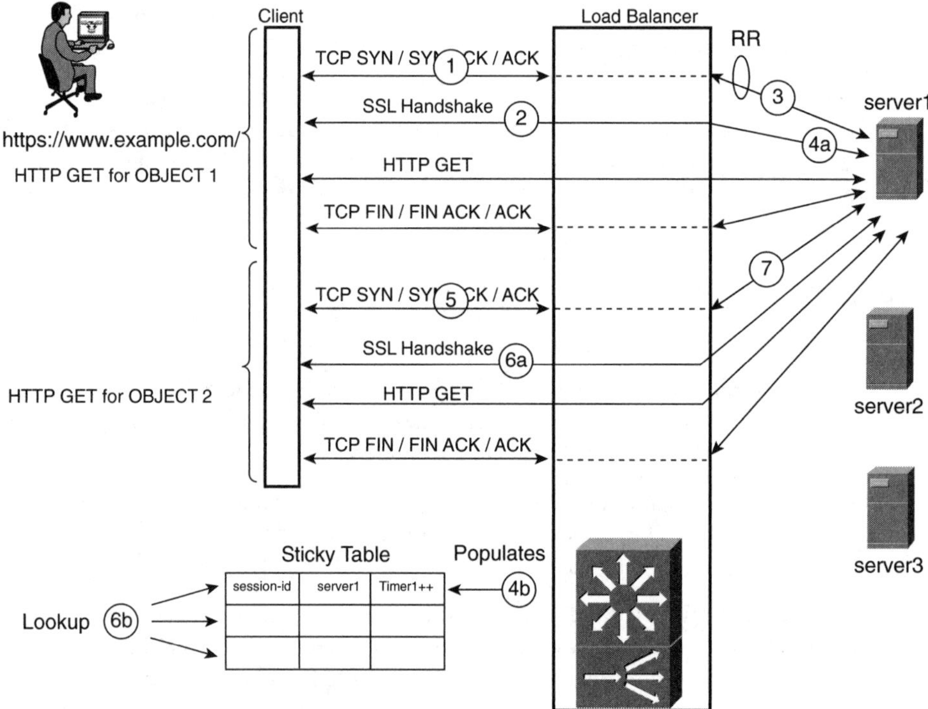

In Figure 19-13, a client sends HTTPS requests to a virtual IP address. The client opens a TCP connection to the VIP address (Step 1). The TCP connection is terminated at the load balancer. The client sends an SSL client hello (Step 2). Because the SSL session ID is not present, the load balancer applies the round-robin predictor and elects server1. The load balancer opens a connection to server1 (Step 3), sends the SSL client hello, and monitors the SSL server hello (Step 4a). The load balancer reads the SSL session ID in the server hello and populates the sticky table with the association session ID–server1 (Step 4b).

A new HTTPS request from the client causes the browser to open a TCP connection to the VIP address (Step 5). The client sends an SSL client hello (Step 6a) carrying an SSL session ID. The load balancer looks up the SSL session ID in the sticky table (Step 6b), which identifies server1. The load balancer then opens a TCP connection to server1 (Step 7) and forwards the client hello to this server.

Example 19-18 shows the configuration of a Cisco CSM for SSL persistence. The vserver intercepts traffic on port 443 (HTTPS) and is assigned the sticky group 3. This sticky group uses the SSL method. The timeout for this sticky group is 60 min (1 hour), consistent with the SSL timeout on the Apache servers, which is 3600 seconds (1 h).

NOTE For more information on Apache's timeout details, consult http://www.apache-ssl.org/docs.html#SSLSessionCacheTimeout.

Example 19-18 *SSL Sticky Configuration on the Cisco CSM*

```
serverfarm HTTPS-FARM
  nat server
  no nat client
  real 10.10.10.11
   inservice
  real 10.10.10.13
   inservice
!
sticky 3 ssl
!
 vserver HTTPS
  virtual 171.69.0.137 tcp https
  serverfarm HTTPS-FARM
  sticky 60 group 3
  inservice
!
```

SSL Persistence Caveats

Implementing a solution that guarantees SSL persistence is often difficult because it requires that several conditions are met. The clients should use SSLv3 or Transport Layer Security (TLS), and if a rehandshake happens, the load balancer cannot ensure persistence. Additionally, some clients expire the session very often, minimizing the advantages of SSL session resumption.

The main consequence of broken SSL sessions is performance degradation. If the network designer planned to use SSL persistence to also ensure HTTPS persistence, the limitation can cause the "lost shopping cart" problem. The case-study section "E-Commerce Applications" shows how to design web-based applications for HTTP, HTTPS, and SSL persistence. This section describes the limitations of SSL persistence in greater detail.

The SSL sticky method relies on the SSL session ID, the field present in client and server hellos that uniquely identifies SSL sessions.

As explained in Chapter 9, SSL persistence works with SSLv3 and TLS, but it does not work with SSLv2 because in SSLv2, the session ID is encrypted. In fact, the SSL session ID needs to be visible to the load balancer for this device to populate the sticky table and to associate the client hello with the appropriate server. If the clients use old versions of browsers, it is very possible that they use SSLv2 for HTTPS traffic, breaking SSL persistence.

SSL sessions can be resumed until the session cache times out either on the server or on the client. When this happens, clients and servers need to perform a full SSL handshake at the start of a new TCP connection. Old versions of Netscape Communicator used to renegotiate the session every 30 sec, and Internet Explorer would renegotiate every 2 min. If the clients use these older browser versions, SSL session persistence does not provide significant performance improvements. Upgrading the clients' software typically solves the problem. For example, IE running on Windows 2000 SP2 or Windows XP caches the session ID for 10 h.

NOTE You can find more information about the IE browsers renegotiating every two min (Microsoft Knowledge Base article 265369) at http://support.microsoft.com/default.aspx?scid=kb;EN-US;265369.

Find more information about the settings for the SSL cache time in Microsoft Windows (Microsoft Knowledge Base article 247658) at http://support.microsoft.com/default.aspx?scid=kb;EN-US;q247658.

It is also possible for the server and the client to go through a full handshake in the middle of a TCP connection; this occurrence is called *rehandshake*. The result of the rehandshake is the creation of a new SSL session ID and possibly new ciphers. These elements might be created to negotiate stronger ciphers when the client needs to get access to more sensitive information during a session.

The server could send a hello-request message during the regular application data exchange, and the client receiving the hello request might or might not proceed to send the client hello encrypted with the shared secret and perform an "encrypted" handshake. The client can also initiate this autonomously.

When the TCP connection is closed and a new one is opened, the client tries to resume the session that was negotiated in the encrypted data. It is impossible for a load balancer to spoof the value, thus breaking persistence based on the SSL session ID.

When the SSL rehandshake occurs, HTTPS persistence might be lost, unless, of course, SSL is terminated on an SSL offloading device. In this case, if it supports this capability, the SSL offloader needs to enforce the SSL rehandshake with the client on behalf of the server.

The conclusion from this section is that, considering the SSL caveats, you should use SSL persistence mainly for performance optimization because in this case, the consequence of a *broken* SSL session would only be performance degradation.

The only solution to all the caveats described in this section is to use an SSL offloader device. SSL offloaders perform encryption and decryption instead of the server CPU.

Case Study

The previous sections in this chapter illustrated the mechanisms available on load balancers to provide session persistence. Each mechanism addresses different requirements that depend on the application type (e-commerce applications, streaming applications, etc.), the client characteristics (whether the clients use nonpersistent proxies), and the server characteristics (whether servers share the session information).

Table 19-2 shows the main persistence mechanisms and their use. The rest of this section applies these persistence mechanisms to some common application scenarios.

Table 19-2 *Main Persistence Mechanisms and Their Characteristics*

Persistence Mechanism	Applications	Persistence Type	Compatible with Mega-Proxy	Compatible with Cookieless Clients	Works with SSL Encrypted Traffic	Vserver Type
Source IP	All	Multi-port protocols, HTTP, SSL	Requires changing the mask	Yes	Yes	L4
Cookie passive	Web-based	HTTP	Yes	No	Requires SSL offloader	L5
URL cookie	Web-based	HTTP	Yes	Yes	Requires SSL offloader	L5
SSL sticky	Applications using SSLv3	SSL, HTTPS	Yes	Yes	Yes	L5
HTTP redirection	Web-based	HTTP, SSL	Yes	Yes	Yes	L4

As Table 19-2 indicates, the most generic persistence mechanism is the source IP sticky method. It is applicable to all the applications: e-commerce, streaming, and FTP. The only drawback of source IP persistence is the fact that when clients use mega-proxies, this method might not work.

The other sticky methods are mainly designed for web-based applications. For pure HTTP traffic, URL cookie is the most flexible mechanism because it works regardless of whether the clients support cookies. If traffic is encrypted in SSL, you need to consider the use of SSL offloading devices (see the section, "E-Commerce Applications") for the load balancer to be able to read decrypted HTTP traffic and ensure persistence.

HTTP redirection works for both cleartext HTTP and encrypted HTTP traffic (HTTPS). The main drawback of this mechanism is the need to allocate one public IP address for each server in the server farm.

SSL sticky addresses mainly a performance problem. It also provides session persistence for HTTPS traffic, but it cannot provide persistence in the transition from cleartext in HTTP to encrypted text in HTTPS.

The sticky methods based on cookies, URLs, and SSL session ID work with the load balancer performing connection spoofing (see Chapter 16), as indicated by the vserver type Layer 5 (L5).

E-Commerce Applications

The design of session persistence for e-commerce applications can easily be extended to other web-based applications. E-commerce applications are characterized by an HTTP session composed of cleartext HTTP and encrypted text using SSL (HTTPS).

Cleartext traffic is used to select items to buy and to fill in the shopping cart. Once you are ready to pay, you click the checkout button, which forces HTTP to switch to HTTPS. When you type the credit-card number and the billing address, the browser sends this information encrypted.

Session persistence for e-commerce applications requires consideration of

- Cleartext HTTP persistence
- HTTPS persistence (persistence for encrypted HTTP)
- SSL persistence (for performance)
- Persistence in the transition from HTTP to HTTPS

The possible solutions that address these requirements are the following:

- Using servers that share session information (no need for HTTP persistence) and using the load balancer for SSL persistence.

- Ensuring HTTP, HTTPS, and SSL persistence by using source IP stickiness on a load balancer. (This solution requires careful configuration for clients using mega-proxy.)
- Ensuring HTTP, HTTPS, and SSL persistence by using the HTTP redirect sticky method on a load balancer.
- Ensuring HTTP persistence with cookie/URL sticky methods on a load balancer; ensuring HTTPS persistence by decrypting SSL with an SSL offloader and by applying the load balancer cookies/URL sticky methods to the decrypted traffic.

SSL Persistence and Servers Sharing Session Information

One possible e-commerce design consists of using servers that replicate the HTTP session information in the cluster. This design requires no configuration on the load balancer for HTTP persistence. (You do not need to configure the sticky cookie method.)

When the session switches to HTTPS, the load balancer provides SSL session persistence to optimize the server performance.

Example 19-19 shows the configuration of a load balancer for this design. The vserver HTTP provides load distribution with no persistence. The vserver HTTPS is configured for SSL persistence.

Example 19-19 *Configuration of an E-Commerce Server Farm for HTTP/HTTPS with Servers Sharing Session Information*

```
serverfarm HTTP-FARM
 nat server
 no nat client
 real 10.10.10.11
  inservice
 real 10.10.10.13
inservice

sticky 5 ssl

vserver HTTP
  serverfarm HTTP-FARM
  virtual 171.69.0.137 tcp 80
  inservice

vserver HTTPS
  serverfarm HTTP-FARM
  sticky 60 group 5
  virtual 171.69.0.137 tcp https
  inservice
```

Source IP Persistence

If the session information is local to the server, you need to ensure session persistence with the load-balancing device. The source IP sticky method ensures persistence for HTTP, HTTPS, and SSL and for the transition of HTTP to HTTPS, as long as you can use the source IP address to identify the user session.

Example 19-20 shows the configuration. The same sticky group is assigned to the vserver that intercepts cleartext HTTP traffic and HTTPS traffic. The mask 255.255.240.0 is used to provide persistence for mega-proxy clients, assuming that during a session the client takes IP addresses that belong to the same /20 subnet.

Example 19-20 *Using the Source IP Sticky Method for E-Commerce Applications*

```
serverfarm HTTP-FARM
 nat server
 no nat client
 real 10.10.10.11
  inservice
 real 10.10.10.13
  inservice

sticky 5 netmask 255.255.240.0 address source

vserver HTTP
  serverfarm HTTP-FARM
  sticky 30 group 5
  virtual 171.69.0.137 tcp 80
  inservice

vserver HTTPS
  serverfarm HTTP-FARM
  sticky 30 group 5
  virtual 171.69.0.137 tcp https
  inservice
```

HTTP Redirection Persistence

If the web and application servers do not share session information and the masking used with source IP persistence does not work for mega-proxy clients, you might consider the use of HTTP redirection stickiness.

As described previously, with HTTP redirection you can configure a VIP address that is used for the main domain name, such as http://www.example.com. Upon receiving an HTTP request for http://www.example.com, the load balancer selects a server and sends an HTTP redirect to the client with the name of the real server.

After receiving the HTTP redirect, the client sends all new HTTP requests (including HTTPS requests) to an IP address associated with the real server. This IP address typically is a public IP address that maps to a single server in the server farm. The load balancer provides the NAT function. The configuration would look like Example 19-21.

The section "HTTP Redirection Sticky" already explained the server farm HTTP-FARM and the redirection configuration. The only addition to the configuration is the presence of the vservers HTTPS-1 and HTTPS-2 for the HTTPS traffic directed to server-1.example.com and server-2.example.com, respectively.

Example 19-21 *HTTP Redirection Sticky Method for E-Commerce Applications*

```
serverfarm HTTP-FARM
  nat server
  no nat client
  redirect-vserver http-server1
   webhost relocation server-1.example.com 302
   webhost backup server-2.example.com 302
   virtual 171.69.0.138 tcp www
   inservice
  redirect-vserver http-server2
   webhost relocation server-2.example.com 302
   webhost backup server-1.example.com 302
   virtual 171.69.0.139 tcp www
   inservice
  real 10.10.10.11
   redirect-vserver http-server1
   inservice
  real 10.10.10.13
   redirect-vserver http-server2
   inservice
!
serverfarm SERVER-1
  nat server
  no nat client
  real 10.10.10.11
   inservice
!
serverfarm SERVER-2
  nat server
  no nat client
  real 10.10.10.13
   inservice
!
vserver HTTP
  serverfarm HTTP-FARM
  virtual 171.69.0.137 tcp 80
  inservice
!
vserver HTTPS-1
  serverfarm SERVER-1
  virtual 171.69.0.138 tcp https
  inservice
```

continues

Example 19-21 *HTTP Redirection Sticky Method for E-Commerce Applications (Continued)*

```
!
vserver HTTPS-2
  serverfarm SERVER-2
  virtual 171.69.0.139 tcp https
  inservice
!
```

SSL Offloading and URL Cookie Persistence

HTTP redirection provides a complete solution to HTTP persistence, SSL persistence, and HTTPS persistence. The drawback of HTTP redirection is the fact that clients can bookmark the new location, which in turn requires configuring the load balancer with backup servers.

A cleaner solution that is increasingly popular consists of decrypting SSL traffic on a network device, an SSL offloader. An SSL offloader is a device that terminates SSL sessions originated by a client and forwards the cleartext HTTP to any device, which is most likely a load balancer. The load balancer can read HTTP fields such as Cookie, URI, and Host TAG.

The use of SSL offloaders combined with URL cookie persistence on load balancers offers a complete solution for HTTP/HTTPS persistence.

NOTE SSL offloaders are used for reasons that go beyond the need for HTTP/HTTPS persistence. These devices alleviate the load of SSL decryption from the servers, and they allow you to centralize SSL decryption operations and configurations on a single device that provides services for multiple operating systems.

Figure 19-14 shows the use of an SSL offloader in conjunction with a load-balancing device.

Cleartext traffic, such as regular HTTP requests, goes to the load balancer, which distributes the requests to the servers listening on port 80. The load balancer is also used to intercept encrypted HTTP traffic (HTTPS) and forwards this traffic to the SSL offloader (identified as the Cisco SSL Service Module [SSLSM] in Figure 19-14).

The SSL offloader returns the decrypted traffic to the load-balancing device, which can see the cookie field and the URI field. As a result, it is possible to ensure HTTP/HTTPS persistence. The SSL offloader returns the decrypted traffic to the load balancer on a port different from 443; in this example, it is 445.

Figure 19-14 *Traffic Path Using an SSL Offloader and a Load Balancer*

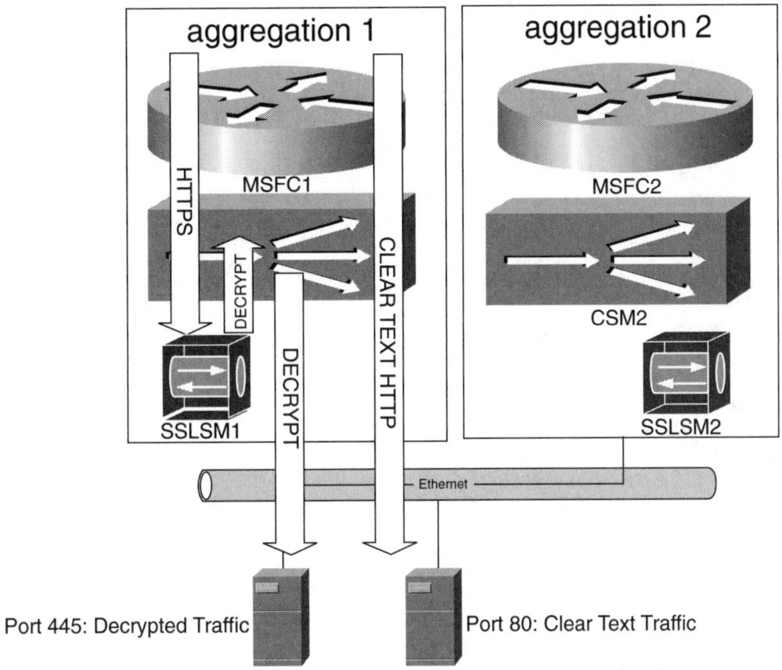

TIP Most SSL devices give the option to re-encrypt the traffic before sending it to the servers. In this case, the decrypted arrow in Figure 19-14 would go to the load-balancing device and back to the SSL device. The SSL offloader would then encrypt the traffic and send it directly to the server elected by the load balancer.

This configuration is called *back-end encryption*.

Example 19-22 shows the configuration of a load balancer for session persistence with the use of an SSL offloader device. The server farm consists of Java-based application servers configured for session tracking, as described in Chapter 18.

Example 19-22 *HTTP/HTTPS Persistence Configuration on a Cisco CSM in Presence of SSL Offloading*

```
serverfarm SSLOFFLOADER
  nat server
  no nat client
  real 10.20.3.80 445
   inservice
  real 10.20.3.90 445
   inservice
!
 serverfarm HTTP-FARM
  nat server
  no nat client
  real 10.10.10.11
   inservice
  real 10.10.10.13
   inservice
!
 sticky 3 ssl
 sticky 5 cookie JSESSIONID
  secondary JSESSIONID
!
 vserver HTTP
  virtual 171.69.0.137 tcp www
  serverfarm HTTP-FARM
  sticky 30 group 5
  parse-length 4000
  inservice
!
 vserver HTTPS
  virtual 171.69.0.137 tcp https
  serverfarm SSLOFFLOADER
  sticky 60 group 3
  inservice
!
vserver WEB-DECRYPT
  virtual 10.20.3.81 tcp 445
  serverfarm HTTP-FARM
  sticky 30 group 5
  parse-length 4000
  inservice
```

In Example 19-22, cleartext HTTP traffic matches the vserver HTTP and follows the known rules of load distribution and session persistence based on the sticky group 5 (URL cookie sticky).

HTTPS traffic matches the vserver HTTPS and the load balancer distributes incoming requests to two SSL offloading devices: 10.20.3.80 and 10.20.3.90 (server farm SSLOFFLOADER). SSL persistence is used (sticky group 3) for even higher performance on the SSL offloader.

The decrypted traffic from the SSL offloader uses TCP port 445 (which has been configured on the SSL device) and matches the vserver WEB-DECRYPT. The load balancer reads into the cookie and URL fields to apply persistence based on the sticky group 5. The same server that was used by the HTTP traffic for a given session is used for the decrypted HTTP traffic that belongs to the same session.

Summary

Load distribution inherently introduces the need to ensure session persistence, which means the need to group together multiple connections that belong to the same session. HTTP session persistence refers to assigning multiple HTTP requests that belong to the same HTTP session consistently to one server. SSL session persistence refers to assigning multiple SSL connections that belong to the same SSL session consistently to one server. Session persistence for applications that open connections on multiple ports refers to preserving the same client/server association for all these connections.

A load balancer provides mechanisms to ensure HTTP session persistence when the servers in a cluster do not share session information. The best mechanisms provided by load balancers today rely on cookies and URLs. This process makes hardware load balancing well integrated with the session-tracking mechanisms of today's application servers because the load balancers can learn dynamically the session cookies and preserve the client/server association for a given session.

Load balancers provide SSL session persistence to optimize the performance of servers by making it possible to resume SSL sessions. SSL session persistence is made difficult by the use of old browsers that renegotiate the SSL session, or implement SSLv2, or by the need to perform an encrypted rehandshake.

A complete solution to the need to optimize servers' performance and ensure HTTPS persistence consists of using an SSL offloading device combined with a hardware load balancer capable of URL cookie persistence.

You can use source IP sticky methods for the application protocols that open connections on multiple ports, such as streaming protocols, FTP, and RADIUS. Source IP sticky methods might not work for clients using mega-proxy servers. Knowing the mega-proxy design of the service provider makes it possible to fix the problem by changing the masking of the source IP method.

PART V

Data Center Design

This chapter covers the following topics:

- The processing of packets through Cisco devices using router processor (RP) switching paths or application-specific integrated circuits (ASICs)—process switching, fast switching, Cisco Express Forwarding (CEF) switching, flow-based Multilayer Switching (MLS), and CEF-based MLS.
- Basic design concepts applied to the Data Center, which include Layer 3 links, VLANs, switched virtual interfaces (SVIs), and autostate.
- Load distribution on Layer 2 and Layer 3 links with VLAN load balancing, the Gateway Load Balancing Protocol (GLBP), and equal-cost path load balancing.
- Use of internal redundancy features such as Router Processor Redundancy (RPR), Stateful Switchover (SSO), Nonstop Forwarding (NSF), and CatOS high availability.
- Using spanning tree in the Data Center, why to use Rapid Per VLAN Spanning Tree Plus (PVST+) or Multiple Spanning Tree (MST), how to maximize Data Center availability by correctly configuring spanning tree and by using Unidirectional Link Detection (UDLD) and Loopguard.
- Layer 2 Data Center design, including best practices in configuring VLANs, access ports, trunks, and Spanning-Tree. How to limit the number of Layer 2 topology recalculations.
- Layer 3 Data Center design, including default gateway redundancy best practices with Hot Standby Router Protocol (HSRP), Open Shortest Path First (OSPF) design, Enhanced Interior Gateway Routing Protocol (EIGRP) design best practices in the Data Center, and how to limit the number of Layer 3 topology recalculations.

CHAPTER **20**

Designing the Data Center Infrastructure

The purpose of the Data Center *infrastructure* is to provide scalable port density, high availability, and security for the servers and for the mainframes and attachment for the appliances (firewalls, load balancers, Secure Socket Layer [SSL] offloaders, caches, and intrusion detection system [IDS] sensors).

Chapter 4, "Data Center Design Overview" outlined Data Center design principles. This chapter illustrates the following:

- The key physical components of the Data Center infrastructure—switches and Ethernet links
- The forwarding characteristics of switches and routers
- How to optimize the use of multiple physical links and paths in the Data Center
- How to use VLANs to virtualize the links and switches in the Data Center
- How to enhance the Layer 2 stability and convergence time
- The design best practices for the Layer 2 and Layer 3 features in the Data Center, which were described in Chapter 12, "Layer 2 Protocol Essentials," and Chapter 13, "Layer 3 Protocol Essentials"

Topology Overview

Figure 20-1 illustrates the reference architecture of the Data Center described in this chapter. You can identify the access layer, which provides ports for the servers and connects with the uplinks to the aggregation layer.

Aggregation switches connect to the access switches and to core routers or core switches.

The aggregation layer provides aggregation from the access switches; routing functions between the Layer 2 segments in the access switch; and connectivity for firewalls, load balancers, SSL offloaders, IDS sensors, and reverse proxy caches. The aggregation switches also provide connectivity to the mainframes. (Read Chapter 14, "IBM Data Center Technology," for more information.)

Figure 20-1 *Data Center Infrastructure*

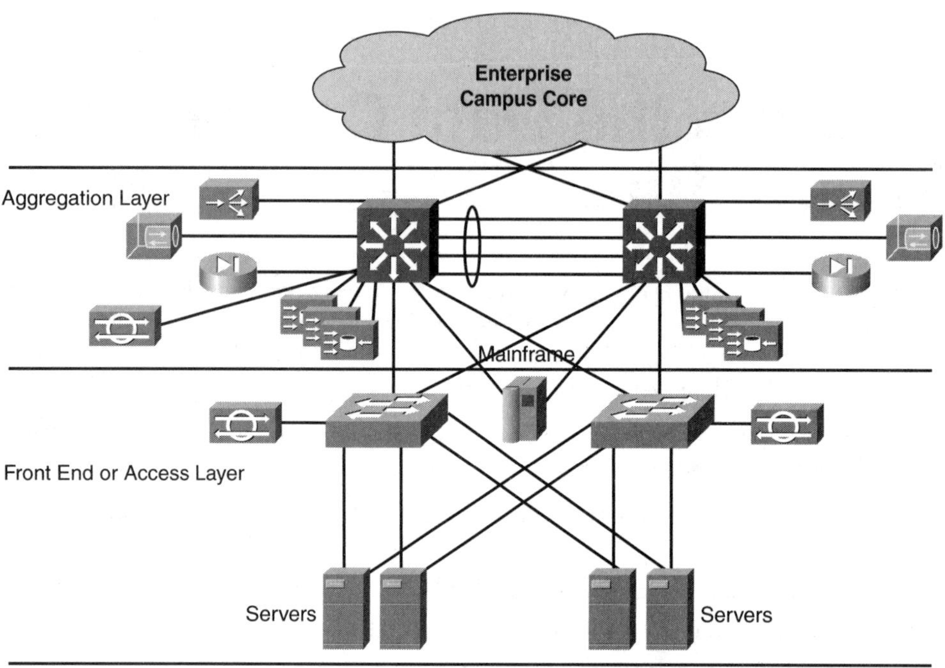

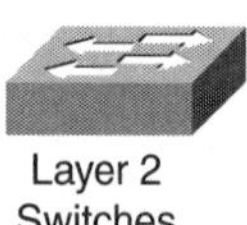

The design described in this chapter uses a Layer 2 access. The need for Layer 2 access was described in Chapter 4. The reasons for a Layer 2 access include the following:

- The flexibility of being able to virtualize the physical infrastructure by using VLANs
- The need for stateful devices (such as firewalls and routers) to see client-to-server and server-to-client traffic, which is easier when these devices are Layer 2–adjacent to the servers

VLANs make it possible to attach servers to any access switch in the topology and to logically place the server in the Layer 2 segment that it belongs to. For example, an application server of a certain vendor might need to be on the same Layer 2 segment as the other application servers of the same vendor. You can attach the application server to any access switch in the Data Center and assign it to the "vendor's application server" VLAN.

Stateful devices, such as load balancers and firewalls, keep state information about sessions between clients and servers. This process implies that these devices need to be in the path of the traffic. Such a path is easier to achieve with a Layer 2 access because these devices can bridge traffic between the server VLANs and the upstream router that provides the default gateway. If the servers were several hops away from the firewalls and the load balancers, there could be a direct Layer 3 path from the server to the client bypassing the stateful devices.

Figure 20-2 pictures the scope of the Layer 2 domain, which spans from the access switches to the aggregation switches. The scope of broadcasts and unicast flooded packets on Layer 2 segments terminates at the aggregation switches. The aggregation switches route traffic between the Layer 2 segments and traffic going to and coming from the campus core to the Data Center.

Figure 20-2 *Layer 2 and Layer 3 in the Data Center Infrastructure*

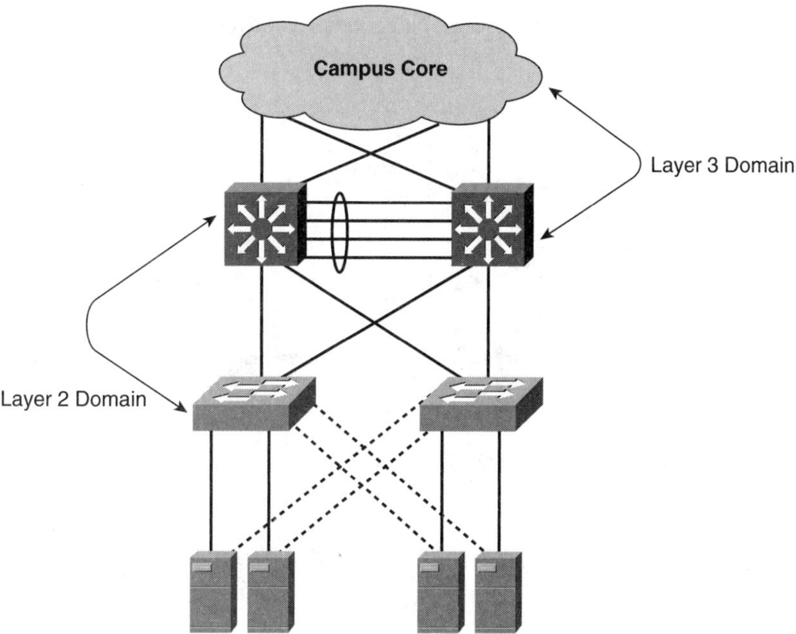

The network devices used for the infrastructure are Layer 3 switches in the aggregation layer and Layer 2 switches (or Layer 3 switches performing mainly Layer 2 functions) in the access/front-end layer.

NOTE The section "Switching Paths" provides architectural information about the forwarding paths of Layer 3 switches and routers.

Figure 20-3 shows the physical connections between the switches in a Data Center. The links between switches are typically Gigabit Ethernet. The links from the servers are either Fast Ethernet or Gigabit Ethernet.

NOTE The section "Link Redundancy and Load Distribution" describes the use of redundant links for the purpose of scaling bandwidth and high availability.

You should design the Data Center with a fully switched topology: there should be no hubs. All the links should be full-duplex point-to-point. If you follow these guidelines, there are no collisions, and no latency is introduced by the carrier sense multiple access/collision detect (CSMA/CD) algorithm. (Read Chapter 12 for more information.)

Some of the links in Figure 20-3 are categorized as Layer 3 links, and some are categorized as Layer 2 links.

Figure 20-3 *Switches in the Data Center Connected with Layer 2 and Layer 3 Links*

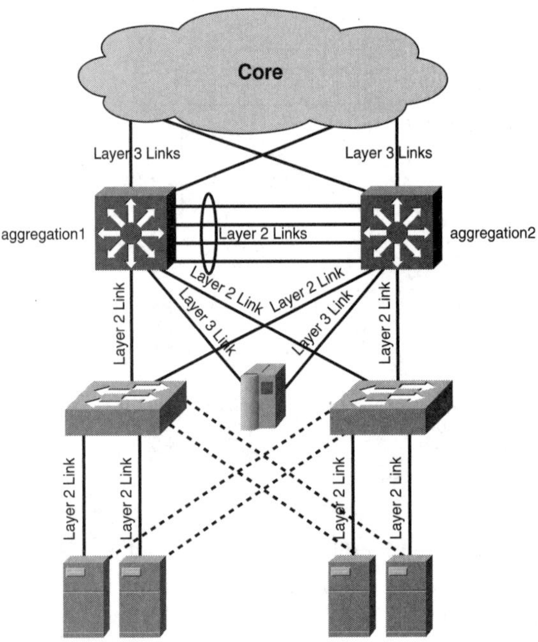

By partitioning the topology of Figure 20-3 with VLANs, you can virtualize the Data Center Layer 2 domain. Figure 20-5 illustrates the concept.

In the Data Center architecture, the Layer 3 links are the links connecting Layer 3 interfaces. A Layer 3 interface is a physical interface with an IP address. Routers forward traffic between Layer 3 links. Example 20-1 shows the configuration of a Gigabit Ethernet interface attached to a Layer 3 link.

Example 20-1 *Configuration of a Layer 3 Link*

```
interface GigabitEthernet4/1
 description a_L3_interface
 ip address 10.0.2.2 255.255.255.0
end
```

The links between the aggregation switches and the core in Figure 20-3 are Layer 3 links; the links between the mainframe and the aggregation switches are Layer 3 links.

In the Data Center architecture, the Layer 2 links are the links that attach to a Layer 2 interface. A Layer 2 interface does not have an IP address. Switches forward traffic between Layer 2 interfaces.

Example 20-2 shows the most basic configuration of a port connecting to a Layer 2 link on a Catalyst switch. Figure 20-2 shows that Layer 2 links connect the switches together and connect servers to the access switches.

Example 20-2 *Configuration of a Layer 2 Link*

```
interface GigabitEthernet4/1
 description a_L2_interface interface
 switchport
end
```

From a network-design perspective, all the Layer 2 links in the Data Center can potentially belong to the same broadcast domain. VLANs allow segregating and isolating the scope of broadcast domains. A Layer 2 interface can carry either a single VLAN (access port) or multiple VLANs (trunk).

NOTE The section "Using VLANs to Virtualize the Physical Data Center Infrastructure" illustrates the use of VLANs in the Data Center.

Depending on the placement of VLANs on the links and the switches, a topology can be "looped" or "loop free," as described in Chapter 4.

NOTE Remember that spanning tree breaks the loop of looped topologies by putting some ports into a blocking state; should a forwarding port fail, one blocking port goes forwarding.

In loop-free topologies, no port is blocking; all ports are forwarding.

Each topology is mandated by different requirements:

- In the presence of dual attached servers, VLANs need to span at least two access switches, which typically requires a looped topology. (See the section, "Dual Attached Servers.")
- In presence of redundant load balancers or redundant firewalls that support active/standby redundancy, looped topologies are preferred.
- Loop-free topologies are possible with Direct Server Return designs. (Read Chapter 16 "Load-Balancing Modes and Predictors.")
- Loop-free topologies are possible in the absence of server load balancing or firewalls.

The Layer 2 design described in this chapter applies equally to both looped and loop-free designs.

If the reason for designing a loop-free topology is mandated by concerns about spanning-tree failures, you should first consider the use of Rapid PVST+ or MST in conjunction with Loopguard and UDLD.

802.1w (used by Rapid PVST+ and MST) overcomes the limitation of the 30 to 50 second (sec) convergence time of 802.1D by providing subsecond convergence. UDLD and Loopguard provide protection from failures that Spanning-Tree alone cannot recover from.

Switching Paths

A Cisco router can forward traffic using different processing paths: they are normally categorized as process switching, fast switching, or CEF. The path taken by the traffic depends on the router platform, on the release of code running on the router, and on the features that are applied to an interface. CEF is the preferred and recommended forwarding mechanism.

The Data Center architecture described in this book uses routing at the aggregation layer and Layer 2 switching at the access layer. The routing function can be provided by routers as well as Layer 3 switches. The architecture presented in this book uses Layer 3 switches in the aggregation.

A Layer 3 switch is a device capable of performing Layer 3 forwarding at the same speed as Layer 2 switching. A Layer 3 switch comprises a router processor (RP) and a switch processor (SP) as well as the ASICs for traffic forwarding. The SP handles Layer 2 protocol processing. The RP handles routing protocol processing. The RP can be on a daughter card attached to the supervisor. (A supervisor is a linecard in a switch, which manages the other linecards, handles the protocol traffic, and has the intelligence about how to forward traffic.) The ASICs handle forwarding for both Layer 2 and Layer 3 traffic.

Layer 3 switches, such as the Catalyst 6500, feature a number of ASICs that perform several features in hardware. As a result, traffic arriving to a Layer 3 switch can be processed in hardware by the ASICs, or it can be processed by the RP; this choice depends on the features enabled on the interface.

Traffic switched by the RP can take the same switching paths as a standalone router (process switching, fast switching, and CEF).

Cisco IOS Switching Paths

Cisco routers and the RP of a Layer 3 switch offer three levels of traffic forwarding:

- **Process switching**—This method involves the CPU for routing and rewriting each individual packet that the router receives. This method is the slowest because the packet is processed in the "IP input" process, and the time that it takes for this process to run depends on how many outstanding processes are waiting. Once the IP input process is scheduled, the packet is subject to a lookup of the entire routing table. Equal-cost routes load balancing is performed on a per-packet basis.
- **Fast switching**—Fast switching increases the forwarding performance of a router by caching the result of the routing lookup for the first packet (process switched) destined to a certain IP address. Further packets destined for an IP address that was previously looked up are processed at the *interrupt level*, which means by functions invoked as the result of the receive interrupt without having to wait for the IP input process to be scheduled. If the user configured additional features besides pure routing, there might be the need to copy the packet to the system memory for process switching. Fast switching performs load balancing per-destination.
- **CEF**—CEF is the fastest of the three switching paths and normally is the default on Cisco routers (and RPs in a Layer 3 switch). CEF calculates a table, called the forwarding information base (FIB), with all the destinations derived from the routing table. The FIB table is a copy of the routing table stored in a cache for fast lookup. CEF uses the FIB table in conjunction with a table that has the next-hop link layer information (the *adjacency* table). CEF occurs at the interrupt level for every packet, which is different from fast switching where the first packet for a given destination would be process switched. Load balancing in CEF can be per-packet or per-destination. CEF can also run distributed (which is called dCEF); each line card in a router has a copy of the FIB table and performs CEF locally.

TIP

An interesting feature introduced with CEF is unicast reverse path forwarding (described in Chapter 21, "Integrating Security into the Infrastructure").

CEF is the preferred switching path and is the default on the IOS releases that support this feature. Features such as network address translation (NAT) and access control lists (ACLs) are supported in the CEF path.

TIP

This tip provides some terminology that can be useful when troubleshooting routing configurations.

The adjacency table stores the association of the next-hop IP address together with the VLAN, the MAC address of the next hop, and the encapsulation type.

With Layer 3 links, the adjacency table has information about the interface (for example, interface GigabitEthernet 3/1) in place of the VLAN information.

Adjacency types include the following:

- **Punt adjacencies** pass the incoming packet to the next switching path.
- **Glean adjacencies** are used when a router has an interface on a LAN segment. Instead of populating the adjacency table with the MAC addresses for all the hosts available on the segment, the router just programs the subnet information with a glean adjacency. When traffic comes in destined to a host on the directly connected subnet, the router ARPs for the host and caches the resolved MAC address. (For more information about Address Resolution Protocol [ARP], refer to Chapter 13.)
- **Host-route adjacencies** are used for a directly connected IP address. Typically, it is the next-hop address of a router on a point-to-point link.
- **Load-share adjacencies** achieve load balancing for equal-cost routes.
- **Incomplete adjacencies** mean that the ARP table does not have yet the rewrite information for the next hop.

NOTE

For more information about IOS switching paths, refer to http://www.cisco.com/warp/public/105/20.html and http://www.cisco.com/univercd/cc/td/doc/product/software/ios122/122cgcr/fswtch_c/index.htm.

Multilayer Switching (MLS)

As previously mentioned, Layer 3 switches are the key platform for the Data Center infrastructure. MLS products, such as the Catalyst 6500, the Catalyst 4000, or the Catalyst 5000, are capable of performing Layer 3 forwarding in hardware (Layer 3 switching).

At a very high level, a Layer 3 switch is primarily a Layer 2 switch (transparent bridge) integrated with a router. An RP (which could be on a separate line card, on a daughter card on the supervisor, or simply a processor on the supervisor) provides the routing intelligence: running the routing protocols. ASICs capable of performing cache lookup on the Layer 3 headers of a packet provide the Layer 3 forwarding capabilities.

The two key architectures for MLS are as follows:

- **Flow-based**—With flow-based forwarding, the first packet to a certain destination is processed by the RP, and the forwarding decision is cached in a hardware cache. Further packets destined to the same IP address are forwarded according to the cache table.
- **CEF-based**—With CEF-based forwarding, the router installs the FIB table and the adjacency table in the hardware ASICs. As a result, no packet goes through the router daughter card; all the traffic is switched in hardware. Of course, exceptions with specific features enabled on either the input or output interface might require processing on the RP.

With Layer 3 switches, the forwarding is performed in hardware with the exception of traffic requiring special handling because of feature processing. For example, the Catalyst 6500 Supervisor Engine I and Supervisor Engine II perform some NAT processing by the RP. (Notice that the newest Catalyst 6500 supervisor, Supervisor Engine 720, performs NAT with ASICs.)

NOTE In CEF-based Layer 3 switching, the amount of traffic that goes to the RP is very small because the FIB and the adjacency tables are programmed in hardware. An example of an exception is the traffic that requires the resolution of glean adjacencies. This traffic goes to the RP and is rate-limited by the hardware.

The design discussion in this chapter assumes that the aggregation switches are Layer 3 switches based on either MLS architecture.

Using VLANs to Virtualize the Physical Data Center Infrastructure

This section illustrates the concept of virtualizing the Data Center network by using VLANs and the associated concepts of SVI and autostate.

VLANs virtualize Layer 2 segments, making them independent of the physical topology: two servers can be on different access switches in the topology of Figure 20-3 and be logically connected via a VLAN. Another pair of servers can be connected to the same access switches as the previous servers yet on a different logical segment, which is a different VLAN.

The router that forwards traffic between VLANs is built into the Layer 3 switches, and its Layer 3 interfaces are called SVIs. An SVI is a "virtual interface" on a VLAN. An SVI is virtual because it is not a physical interface, but like a physical interface, it can go up and down by sensing whether there are physical ports connected on a VLAN. This feature is called autostate.

Figure 20-4 summarizes the steps in virtualizing the physical infrastructure by using VLANs, SVIs, and Layer 3 switching.

Part **a** of Figure 20-4 shows a Layer 2 switch not capable of supporting VLANs. The servers that connect to it belong to the same broadcast domain, and it is not possible to create two separate Layer 2 domains without introducing an additional switch connected through a router.

Part **b** of Figure 20-4 shows a Layer 2 switch capable of supporting VLANs. The two servers are assigned to two different VLANs, preventing communication between them unless you introduce an external router, as in Part **c** of Figure 20-4. The external router connects two physical interfaces to two different VLANs. The interfaces on the router are identified by FastEthernet0/1 and FastEthernet0/2.

The next step is to integrate the router and the switch. In this case, there is no external interface connection to the Layer 2 switch. The router references the interfaces by means of the VLAN number itself: interface VLAN1 and interface VLAN2, as shown in part **d** of Figure 20-4, are called SVIs.

VLAN Topologies

On top of the physical architecture of Figure 20-3, you can build a logical LAN architecture made of VLANs. Each VLAN is a broadcast domain, as described in Chapter 12.

Figure 20-4 *From Layer 2 Switching to Layer 3 Switching*

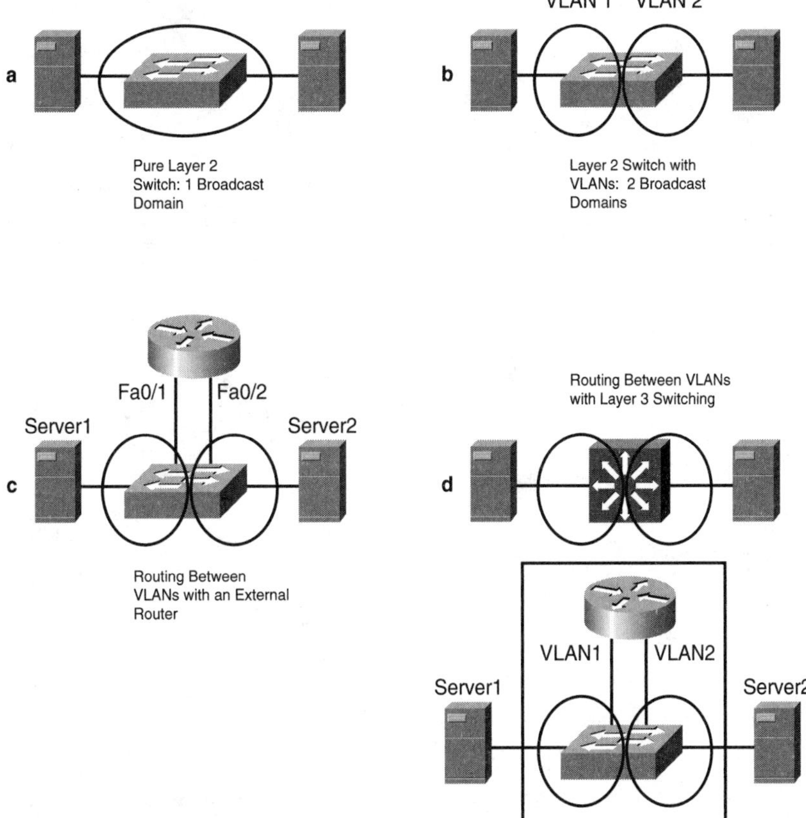

Part **a** of Figure 20-5 shows the topology of a Data Center where multiple pairs of Layer 2 switches provide separate LAN segments for each type of server. Right below the routers is a LAN segment for web servers. The web servers in turn have an interface connecting to the application servers on a separate pair of Layer 2 switches.

Part **b** of Figure 20-5 shows the recommended architecture for a Data Center with multiple server tiers. Web servers are connected to Layer 2 ports on a VLAN called "web," and application servers are connected to Layer 2 ports on a VLAN called "app." VLAN web and VLAN app are configured on all the switches in Figure 20-5. As a result, you can attach web and application servers to any access switch, as long as the Layer 2 port is assigned to the appropriate VLAN.

Figure 20-5 *Server Tier Segregation with VLANs*

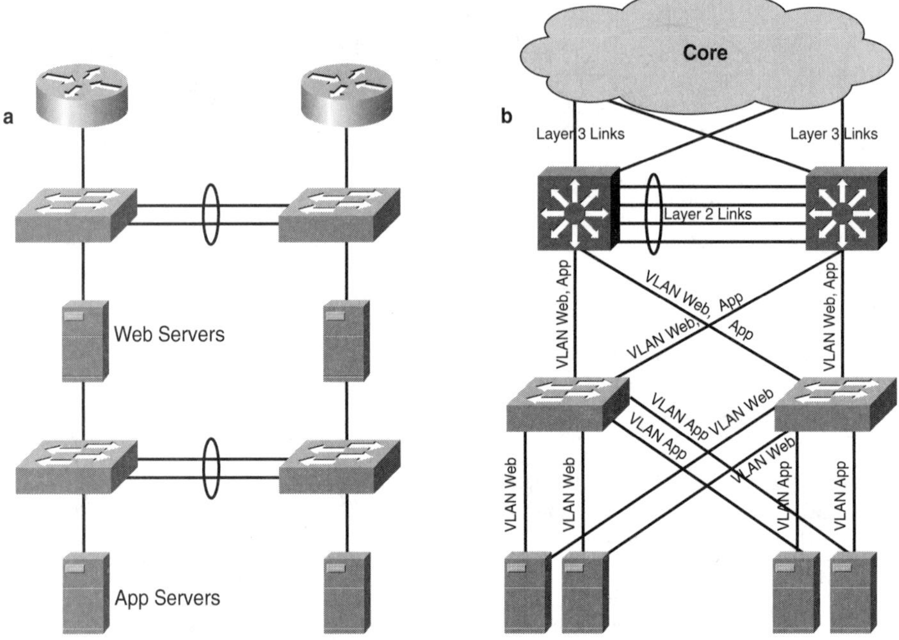

The result is that part **b** of Figure 20-5 is logically equivalent to the design in part **a** of Figure 20-5 with more scalability, flexibility, and high availability.

Routing between the VLANs requires the configuration of switched VLAN interfaces, which is the topic of the next section.

TIP We use VLANs as a mechanism to segregate server farms. VLANs are secure as long as the Layer 2 configurations are correct. For example, you can avoid VLAN hopping, which is often considered a concern for architectures based on VLANs, by tagging the native VLAN on 802.1Q trunks. Chapter 15, "Security Protocols and Technologies," provides detailed information about Layer 2 security.

SVIs

Data Centers use VLANs to assign servers to separate Layer 2 virtual segments on a single physical infrastructure. Layer 3 switches route between the virtual segments (VLANs).

You can configure Layer 3 switches with VLAN interfaces called SVIs, which are the equivalent of a Layer 3 interface of a router attached to a physical segment.

Example 20-3 shows an SVI with IP address 10.0.2.2. As you can see, the interface is neither a Gigabit Ethernet port nor a Fast Ethernet port; it is just a VLAN interface on VLAN 2.

Example 20-3 *Switched VLAN Interface Configuration*

```
interface Vlan2
 description default_gateway_cluster1
 ip address 10.0.2.2 255.255.255.0
end
```

VLAN 2 is associated with specific physical ports. You achieve this association by assigning ports to VLAN 2, as in Example 20-4. You can verify which ports are assigned to a certain VLAN, as in Example 20-5: the Gigabit Ethernet port 4/9 belongs to VLAN 2, as well as the port-channel (EtherChannel) 2.

Example 20-4 *Assignment of a Port to VLAN 2*

```
interface GigabitEthernet4/9
 switchport
 switchport access vlan 2
 switchport mode access
end
```

Notice that the router interface is not mentioned among the ports. The router is built into the switch, but it has an interface on this VLAN; otherwise, it would not be able to pick up any Layer 3 traffic.

NOTE The "connection" between the VLAN and the SVI is the backplane of the Layer 3 switch. Remember that VLANs and SVIs are the virtualization of a physical Layer 2 segment and of a physical Layer 3 interface, respectively.

Example 20-5 *VLANs and Physical Ports*

```
agg1#show vlan id 2

VLAN Name                             Status    Ports
---- -------------------------------- --------- ----------------
2    default_gateway_cluster1         active    Gi4/9, Po2
```

Autostate

One of the advantages of the integration between Layer 2 switching and routing is that when no devices are active on a VLAN, the SVI goes down, preventing the route associated with the VLAN subnet from being advertised, thus avoiding traffic black-holing.

For example, consider Figure 20-4. Think of the scenario where server2 is disconnected from the switch: it was the only device on the subnet VLAN2. In part **c** of Figure 20-4, the router still routes traffic to VLAN2 and advertises this subnet as reachable.

In part **d** of Figure 20-4, the SVI of VLAN2 goes down when there is no active port on it. (The router "port" does not count.) As a consequence, the router stops advertising reachability for VLAN2, preventing traffic from black-holing.

This feature is called autostate, and it is possible only when routers and switches are tightly integrated. When you design networks with redundant Layer 3 paths, autostate makes it possible for the network to reroute traffic to the servers from another Layer 3 path.

Consider Figure 20-6. Figure 20-6 represents a loop-free topology. As you can see, VLAN 10 is specific to access1, and VLAN 20 is specific to access2; VLANs 10 and 20 are not trunked between aggregation1 and aggregation2.

Figure 20-6 *Autostate and Layer 3 Redundant Paths*

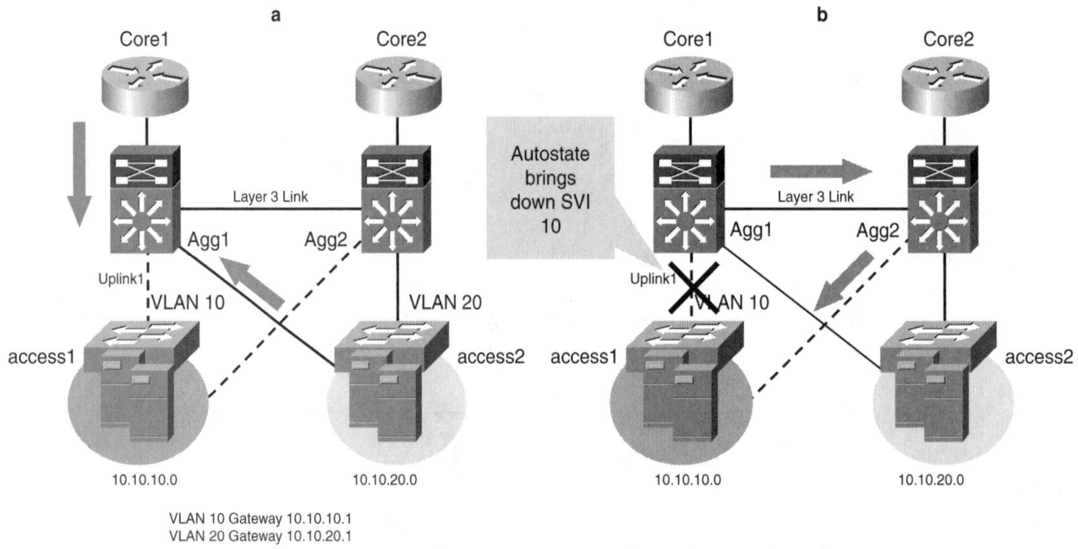

At steady state (no failures on the network), the traffic destined to 10.10.10.x can take either aggregation1 or aggregation2. Part **a** of Figure 20-6 shows that the traffic reaching aggregation1 destined to 10.10.10.x can be either client-to-server traffic (from the core) or server-to-server traffic (from access2). If uplink1 fails (part **b** of Figure 20-6), the traffic to 10.10.10.x should be routed to aggregation2.

The autostate feature brings down the SVI for VLAN 10 from aggregation1 when uplink1 fails so that aggregation1 routes traffic to aggregation2 on the Layer 3 link. If you use autostate, neither client-to-server traffic nor server-to-server traffic is affected by the link failure.

Link Redundancy and Load Distribution

This section focuses on the use of redundant links in the Data Center. You can use redundant links as backups in case the active link fails, or you can use them at the same time as the active link for the purpose of load distribution.

Having backup links has the advantage that when the active link fails, you get the same bandwidth as you would under normal operations. The drawback is that the backup link is not used until a failure occurs.

Distributing traffic on multiple links provides for more bandwidth under normal operations, but when a failure occurs, the remaining link might not have enough capacity to carry the extra traffic. Careful bandwidth provisioning can obviate the problem by adding bandwidth in excess of what you normally need.

This section focuses on the configuration of load distribution on multiple active links in the Data Center:

- Load distribution on Layer 2 links via EtherChannels
- Load distribution on multiple Layer 2 paths with a choice of VLAN load balancing, multigroup HSRP, or GLBP
- Load distribution on multiple Layer 3 links by using equal-cost route load balancing

The servers can also attach to the infrastructure with redundant links. This section examines the use of the fault-tolerant configuration, whose purpose is high availability.

Scaling the Bandwidth with EtherChannels

Chapter 12 introduced the use and configuration of EtherChannels. EtherChannels are used as a high-availability mechanism and to scale bandwidth.

You can use EtherChannels to scale bandwidth at Layer 2: The bundled links appear to the higher-layer protocols as a single link. Spanning-Tree treat EtherChannels as a single physical link (with greater bandwidth, which means lower cost). All the ports in the channel are forwarding or blocking for a certain VLAN.

Every link in a Data Center can be an EtherChannel depending on the bandwidth requirements: servers can be attached to the access switches with EtherChannels, the uplinks from the access switches can be EtherChannels, and the links to the core can also be EtherChannels. (A channel can also be a Layer 3 link.)

The link between the aggregation switches should be an EtherChannel both for bandwidth and for reliability. Connectivity between the aggregation switches should always be guaranteed so that appliances, such as load balancers and firewalls, have a direct communication path and the routers inside the Layer 3 switches also have direct connectivity for neighbor establishment.

The channels can be formed with up to 8 ports. The load distribution of frames on a channel can be based on the IP addresses or on the MAC addresses. On the Catalyst 6500 switch, this option is configurable with the command in Example 20-6.

Example 20-6 *EtherChannel Load Balancing*

```
agg1(config)#port-channel load-balance ?
  dst-ip         Dst IP Addr
  dst-mac        Dst Mac Addr
  dst-port       Dst TCP/UDP Port
  src-dst-ip     Src XOR Dst IP Addr
  src-dst-mac    Src XOR Dst Mac Addr
  src-dst-port   Src-Dst TCP/UDP Port
  src-ip         Src IP Addr
  src-mac        Src Mac Addr
  src-port       Src TCP/UDP Port
```

It is recommended that you create an EtherChannel with ports from different line cards in each switch. This setup prevents the failure of a single line card from affecting the entire channel. Examples 20-7 and 20-8 show a possible configuration that creates a channel between two switches, switch 1 and switch 2. Switch 1 GigabitEthernet4/6 connects to switch 2 GigabitEthernet2/4. Switch 1 GigabitEthernet5/6 connects to switch 2 GigabitEthernet3/4.

Example 20-7 *Channel Configuration on Switch 1*

```
interface GigabitEthernet4/6
 description to_aggregation2
 switchport
 switchport trunk encapsulation dot1q
 switchport trunk allowed vlan  5,10,20
 switchport mode trunk
 channel-group 2 mode active
 channel-protocol lacp
!
interface GigabitEthernet5/6
 description to_aggregation2
```

Example 20-7 *Channel Configuration on Switch 1 (Continued)*

```
 switchport
 switchport trunk encapsulation dot1q
 switchport trunk allowed vlan 5,10,20
 switchport mode trunk
 channel-group 2 mode active
 channel-protocol lacp
```

Example 20-8 *Channel Configuration on Switch 2*

```
interface GigabitEthernet2/4
 description to_aggregation1
 switchport
 switchport trunk encapsulation dot1q
 switchport trunk allowed vlan  5,10,20
 switchport mode trunk
 channel-group 4 mode passive
 channel-protocol lacp
!
interface GigabitEthernet3/4
 description to_aggregation1
 switchport
 switchport trunk encapsulation dot1q
 switchport trunk allowed vlan 5,10,20
 switchport mode trunk
 channel-group 4 mode passive
 channel-protocol lacp
```

It is also recommended that you use the aggregation protocols to help hold bundling ports together. Port Aggregation Protocol (PAgP) is a Cisco-proprietary protocol, and Link Aggregation Control Protocol (LACP) or 802.3ad is the equivalent IEEE standard.

Each switch uses the same channel group on the two ports that are part of the bundle. The channel group has local significance: on switch 1 it is group 2, and on switch 2 it is group 4.

The protocol that Examples 20-7 and 20-8 use for bundling is LACP, which requires the switch to be either in active or passive mode. *Active mode* means that the switch is actively negotiating the port channel, whereas *passive* means that the port does not initiate a LACP negotiation. Switch 1 is configured in active mode and switch 2 in passive mode. Switch 2 could have been configured for active mode as well. You can form channels between active and passive ports or active and active ports only; you can form no channels between passive ports.

Traffic Distribution on Layer 2 Links

Figure 20-7 shows that the links between the access switches and the aggregation switches are Layer 2 links. Based on the VLAN assignment on these links, the Layer 2 topology can be

- **Loop free**—You can see this topology in part **a** of Figure 20-7. VLAN 10 is present on access1; VLAN 20 is present on access2. VLAN 10 and VLAN 20 are defined on aggregation1 and aggregation2 but are not allowed on the trunk between them. As a result, there is no loop.
- **Looped**—You can see this topology in part **b** of Figure 20-7. VLAN 10 and VLAN 20 are present on both access1 and access2, which makes the topology looped. VLAN 10 and VLAN 20 are defined on aggregation1 and aggregation2, and for design reasons, it should be allowed on the trunk between them.

Figure 20-7 *Traffic Distribution with Loop-Free and Looped Topologies*

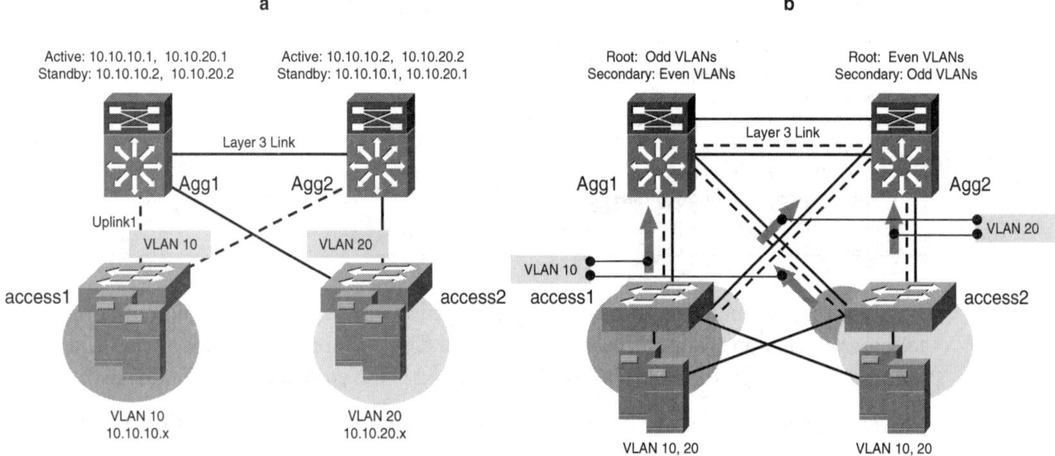

Part **a** of Figure 20-7 shows how in loop-free topologies, you can achieve load distribution with the following:

- **MHSRP**—On VLAN 10, aggregation1 is made active for one HSRP group that corresponds to the IP address 10.10.10.1 and standby for the HSRP group that corresponds to the IP address 10.10.10.2. Aggregation2 is made active for the HSRP group that corresponds to 10.10.10.2 and standby for the HSRP group 10.10.10.1. Half of the servers on VLAN 10 are assigned to 10.10.10.1 as their default gateway, and the remaining half is assigned to 10.10.10.2. The design for VLAN 20 is identical with the difference that the default gateways are 10.10.20.1 and 10.10.20.2.

- **GLBP**—On VLAN 10, aggregation1 is the active virtual gateway, which answers ARP requests for 10.10.10.1, and it returns the MAC address of aggregation1 and aggregation2 with a configurable load-distribution mechanism. The servers on VLAN 10 are assigned to 10.10.10.1 as their default gateway. The configuration for VLAN 20 is identical with the difference that the default gateway is 10.10.20.1

Chapter 13 provides further configuration and protocol details about load distribution with HSRP, Virtual Router Redundancy Protocol (VRRP), and GLBP.

In a looped physical topology, Spanning-Tree keep a loop-free forwarding topology by blocking one uplink from the access switches. To perform load distribution on both uplinks, you need to make sure that each uplink is blocking only for half of the configured VLANs and forwarding for the remaining half.

Consider part **b** of Figure 20-7. Traffic for VLAN 10 from access1 goes to aggregation1, and traffic for VLAN 20 from access1 goes to aggregation2. This setup is possible if you do the following:

- Make aggregation1 the root switch for VLAN 10 and secondary root for VLAN 20. (A more generic approach consists of making aggregation1 root for odd VLANs and secondary root for even VLANs.)
- Make aggregation2 the root switch for VLAN 20 and secondary root for VLAN 10. (A more generic approach consists of making aggregation2 root for even VLANs and secondary root for odd VLANs.)

Before deploying uplink load balancing, it is important to consider that these designs offer a more efficient bandwidth utilization at the expense of a more complex configuration. For more information about the spanning-tree configuration of root and secondary root switches, refer to Chapter 12.

Traffic Distribution on Layer 3 Links

As displayed in Figure 20-7, the links between the aggregation switches and the core are typically Layer 3 links, and it is desirable to take advantage of the bandwidth provided by all these links. Equal-cost route load balancing is the feature that you use to distribute the traffic on Layer 3 links.

When a router has multiple routes with the same cost for the same destination, it can load-balance traffic for those destinations. OSPF allows four equal-cost routes by default, which you can extend to eight routes with the command **maximum-path** under the **router ospf** configuration. In the design of Figure 20-7, there are typically two equal-cost routes from each aggregation switch to every destination.

Similarly to OSPF, EIGRP allows load balancing for four equal-cost routes by default. You can modify this parameter with the **maximum-path** command. Differently from OSPF, EIGRP can also load-balance unequal-cost routes if you use the **variance** command.

Load-balancing routes can follow any of the following approaches:

- **Per-packet**—Each packet is treated independently, and the router round-robins the packets on all the available routes (equal-cost routes). The main problem of per-packet load balancing is that packets belonging to a flow (source IP, destination IP, Layer 4 protocol, source Layer 4 port, and destination Layer 4 port) might arrive to the final destination out-of-order. This lack of order could lead to performance degradation for TCP-based applications and real-time UDP applications.
- **Per-destination**—Traffic destined to a specific host always takes the same next hop; packets from different clients for the same destination take the same next hop. Per-destination load balancing solves the problem of misordered packets. The drawback is that traffic from several different clients can take the same next hop, which implies the load distribution is not optimal.
- **Per-source-and-destination**—With per-destination load balancing, there might be many clients sending traffic to the same host with no load balancing of the next hop because the destination IP address is the same. Load balancing on both the source IP address and the destination IP address allows better load distribution without breaking the packet sequence for a specific flow (unless the client is behind a proxy and changes its source IP address during a session).

Typically, the load-balancing algorithm depends on the switching path as follows:

- Process switching uses per-packet load balancing.
- Fast switching uses per-destination load balancing.
- CEF uses either per-packet or per-source-and-destination load balancing.
- Flow-based MLS typically uses no load balancing by default. You can configure it to per-source-and-destination load balancing by changing the flowmask to source-destination.
- CEF-based MLS typically uses per-source-and-destination load balancing (source and destination IP address) by default.

NOTE The load-balancing behavior of flow-based MLS and CEF-based MLS is really platform-dependent. You should verify the information in the section with the product documentation.

If you use hardware-based forwarding (MLS), available on products such as the Catalyst switches, the forwarding is performed at wire speed by the ASICs.

With flow-based MLS, only the first packet of a flow is processed by the router daughter card. All subsequent packets to the same destination are forwarded by the hardware to the same next hop. You can change the behavior to achieve per-source-and-destination load balancing by modifying the flowmask to be source-destination in such a way that packets with different source IP addresses and the same destination IP are sent to different next hops. The drawback of this approach is that the cache fills up more quickly because it has to store as many entries as the client—destination IP pairs as opposed to the destination IP only.

CEF-based MLS has a built-in capability to provide per-flow load balancing by using hashing functions built in the hardware.

Based on the information provided in this section, you should be able to configure load distribution on the Layer 3 links that connect the Data Center to the core. The most likely options that you are going to use for equal-cost path load balancing are the per-source-and-destination load balancing with two equal-cost routes for every destination. If you need more bandwidth on the links to the core, you can bundle additional links to form EtherChannels. These EtherChannels should still be configured as Layer 3 links.

Dual-Attached Servers

For maximum servers' availability, it is recommended that you have dual network interface cards (NICs). Chapter 2, "Server Architecture Overview," illustrated the options available for server connectivity in the Data Center. This section focuses on the fault-tolerance option. Figure 20-7 illustrates the fact that servers are dual-attached with Layer 2 links to the access switches.

The reason for this design is apparent if you look at Figure 20-8. A server attached as in part **a** of Figure 20-8 is subject to the failure of the access switch. A failure of access1 brings down this server together with all the other servers attached to the same switch. Of course, there are still servers attached to access2, and a load balancer could dispatch new requests to these servers, but you are still giving up a number of functional machines because of the failure of one single component in the network.

A better approach is depicted in part **b** of Figure 20-8; the server is attached both to access1 and access2. This requires two NICs: one is active, the other one is standby. (The link is up, but it does not send out any traffic.) In case of the failure of access1, the server activates the NIC that connects to access2.

The newly active NIC inherits the same MAC address as the other one. The IP address stays the same as well, and as a consequence, there is no need to update ARP tables. It takes less than 1 sec for the transition to happen, which normally is unnoticeable to the clients.

Having dual-attached servers has an important consequence for the network design: the VLAN on access1 needs to be present on access2 as well. The presence of the same VLAN on multiple access switches imposes a looped topology in the network. You can see the blocking ports in the topology in part **b** of Figure 20-8.

Part **c** of Figure 20-8 shows a third option to attach dual NIC servers to a Layer 2 infrastructure for a loop-free design.

Figure 20-8 *Server Attachment Options*

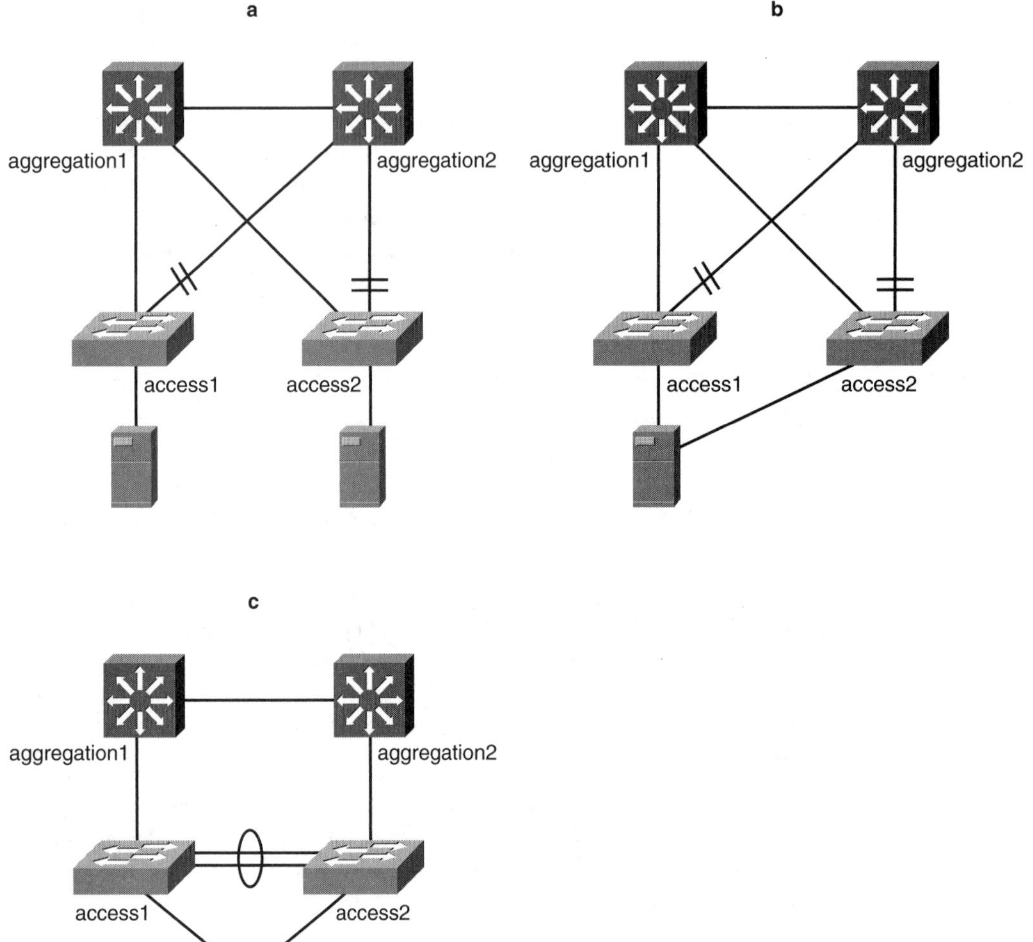

Spanning-Tree Considerations

Spanning-tree is required in a Data Center infrastructure to ensure a loop-free forwarding topology in presence of redundant Layer 2 paths. You should never disable spanning-tree even in topologies that by design are loop free.

Additionally, Cisco features such as UDLD and Loopguard make Layer 2 loop failures very unlikely.

The most generic and flexible architecture needs to accommodate looped topologies to address the need of active/standby service appliances (load balancers, firewalls) for redundant Layer 2 paths.

Spanning-tree has gone through significant improvements with the introduction of 802.1w, the protocol that provides fast convergence. You can use Rapid PVST+ or MST to achieve subsecond convergence for any failure. Chapter 12 describes both protocols.

The choice between Rapid PVST+ and MST is a tradeoff between flexibility and scalability. Rapid PVST+ provides more flexibility and an easier migration from PVST+. The use of MST should be driven by the need for a high number of logical ports.

If you take advantage of 802.1w with Rapid PVST+ or MST and if you combine them with Loopguard and UDLD, the Layer 2 portion of the Data Center is capable of subsecond convergence and unlikely to fail with a Layer 2 loop.

This section assumes that you are familiar with the basics of Spanning-Tree, such as bridge protocol data units (BPDUs); VLAN instances; blocking, learning, and forwarding states; topology change notification (TCN); and so on.

Choosing the Spanning-Tree Algorithm

On Cisco products, you can choose between PVST+ and 802.1s. Either algorithm can be combined with 802.1w for fast convergence.

In Cisco terminology, using PVST+ in combination with 802.1w is called Rapid PVST+ (**spanning tree mode rapid-pvst**), and using 802.1s in combination with 802.1w is called MST (**spanning tree mode mst**).

NOTE Chapter 12 explains how to configure Rapid PVST+ and MST.

MST achieves higher scalability because it limits the number of spanning-tree instances, but it is less flexible than Rapid PVST+ with bridging devices that do not support spanning-tree (that we define as *transparent* because they "merge" or, more correctly, bridge traffic of two different VLANs, including BPDUs, just like a wire).

TIP If you have a topology that includes transparent devices such as load balancers used in bridge mode (such as a Cisco Local Director) and Layer 2 firewalls, you should consider the use of Rapid PVST+. Rapid PVST+ is also recommended as a migration from PVST+ to take advantage of the fast-convergence features of 802.1w. If the main concern is scalability, you should consider MST.

The rest of this section assumes that you are familiar with the concept of spanning-tree instances, as described in Chapter 12.

NOTE You can also find information about how MST and 802.1w work at http://www.cisco.com/warp/public/473/147.pdf and http://www.cisco.com/warp/public/473/146.pdf.

The *scalability* of a spanning-tree algorithm is measured by how many logical ports it can support. Logical ports are counted as the sum of access ports plus trunks, where the trunk weight is given by the number of VLANs that it carries.

For example, assuming that the Layer 2 links connected to aggregation1 in Figure 20-7 carry one VLAN, the number of logical ports on aggregation1 is three. Three is the number of Layer 2 links: the uplinks from access switches and the channel between aggregation1 and aggregation2.

If the Layer 2 links in Figure 20-7 are trunks, each carrying two VLANs, the count of logical ports is 3 * 2 = 6 logical ports.

On Cisco Catalyst switches, you can verify the number of logical ports by using the command **show spanning tree summary totals**.

The online documentation for Cisco switches tells you how many logical ports Rapid PVST+ and MST support on a given platform. MST supports more logical ports than Rapid PVST+. If the Data Center requires thousands of VLANs, you should use MST.

MST has some limitations compared to Rapid PVST+ when you need to bridge VLANs together.

With Rapid PVST+, bridging VLANs is not a problem; in MST, there could be a single logical topology for multiple VLANs that presents some challenges with devices that bridge VLANs. Figure 20-9 presents the main challenges.

Figure 20-9 *Transparent Devices and MST*

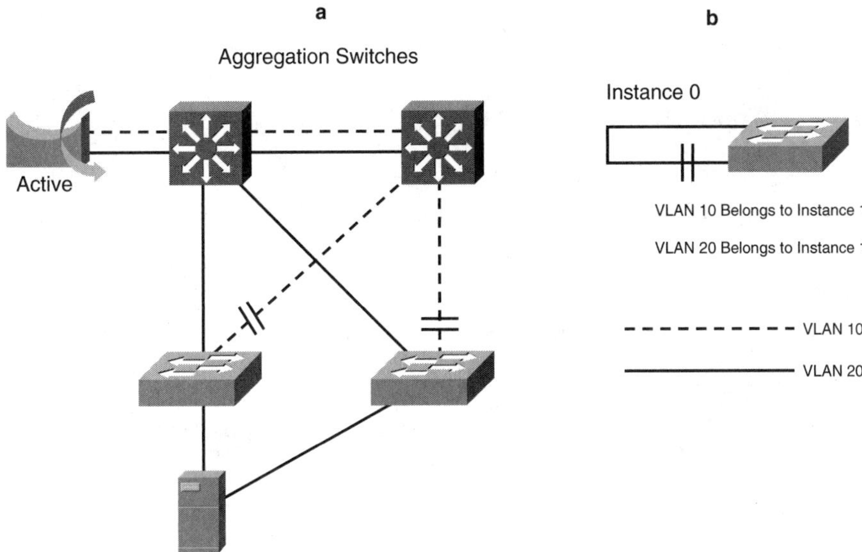

Suppose that both VLAN 10 and VLAN 20 are mapped to the MST instance 1. Even if there is no loop, MST blocks one of the two ports (either on the side of VLAN 10 or on the side of VLAN 20) because the "instance" has a loop. If you look at Part **b** of Figure 20-9, you see that the link that bridges VLAN 10 with VLAN 20 is actually creating a loop on instance 1. This loop is not causing any real problem; as a matter of fact, it is not really a forwarding loop, but MST works on instances not on VLANs.

Rapid PVST+ creates a forwarding topology for each VLAN independent of the other VLANs. Figure 20-10 explains the concept. The aggregation switch in part **a** of Figure 20-10 holds the information about VLAN 10 and VLAN 20 as two separate instances, as in part **b** of Figure 20-10. The result of merging VLAN 10 and VLAN 20 is that, depending on the priorities and other parameters, aggregation1—VLAN 10 could be the root bridge for aggregation1—VLAN 20, as in part **c** of Figure 20-10.

Figure 20-10 *Transparent Devices with PVST+*

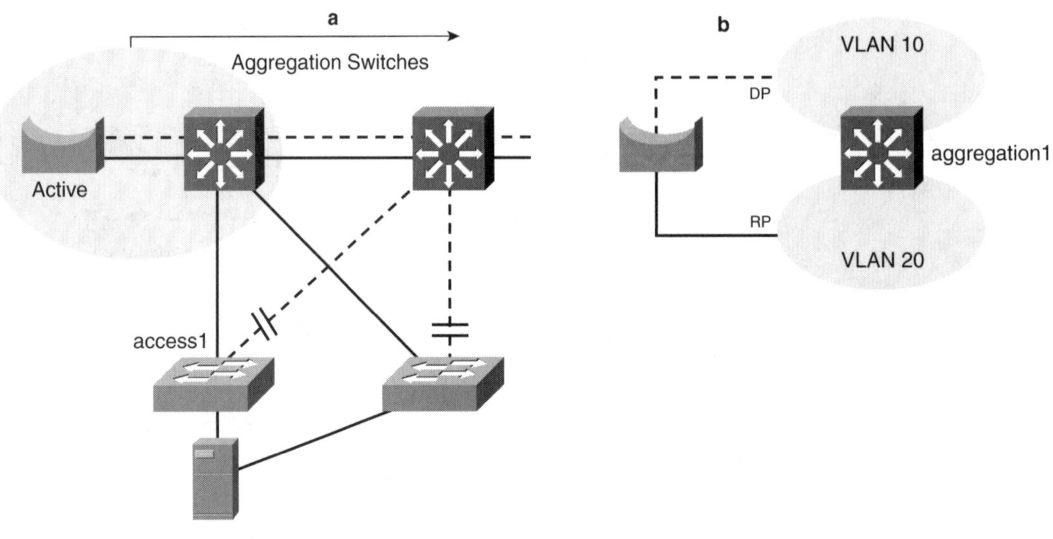

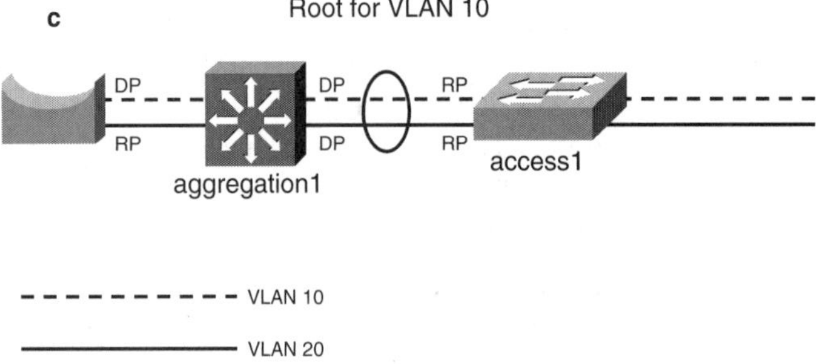

Looking at Example 20-9 from the **show** commands on the switch helps clarify the concept.

Example 20-9 *Spanning-Tree for the Client-Side VLAN*

```
agg1#show spanning tree vlan 10
  Root ID     Priority    4096
              Address     0003.6c43.8c0a
              This bridge is the root
  Bridge ID   Priority    4096
              Address     0003.6c43.8c0a
```

Example 20-9 *Spanning-Tree for the Client-Side VLAN (Continued)*

```
agg1#show spanning tree vlan 20
  Root ID     Priority    4096
              Address     0003.6c43.8c0a
  Bridge ID  Priority    4096
              Address     0003.6c43.7414
```

VLAN 10 becomes the root bridge for VLAN 20. The bridge ID for VLAN 10 is 0003.6c43.8ca0; the bridge ID for VLAN 20 is 0003.6c43.7414.

The conclusion is that with Rapid PVST+, merging VLANs is easier: as long as there is no loop, the access ports connected to the bridging device are forwarding.

With MST, to be able to merge VLANs together, you need to filter BPDUs on the access ports connected to the bridging device. Otherwise, an access port would be blocking.

Rapid Convergence

High availability means not only having a redundant physical topology and recovering from failures, but also having fast convergence so that service degradation or interruption is avoided.

This section deals with fast convergence of Layer 2 environments by using the recent standard enhancements to the Spanning Tree Protocol (STP).

The convergence time of STP (802.1D) is between 30 sec (two times the forward delay) and 50 sec (max age + two times the forward delay). This convergence time is not acceptable for current Data Centers, considering that most routing protocols can converge in less than 1 sec.

Cisco introduced features such as BackboneFast and UplinkFast to accelerate the convergence of STP. You can use these features with PVST+. With BackboneFast, you can expect a convergence time of 30 sec for indirect failures (instead of 50 sec), and with UplinkFast, you can expect a convergence time of a couple of seconds for uplink failures. Cisco UplinkFast and BackboneFast features addressed specific failure types and required understanding of the topology in order to know on which switch each feature should be enabled.

The introduction of IEEE 802.1w has significantly improved the convergence time of STP from the 30 to 50 sec of 802.1D to few hundred milliseconds. If you use Rapid PVST+ or MST, which both use 802.1w, fast convergence does not require additional configurations, and the convergence time is independent of the location in the topology where the failure occurs.

PortFast is a spanning-tree fast-convergence feature that is equally important in PVST+, Rapid PVST+, and MST. You must correctly apply PortFast and TrunkFast (which is the equivalent of PortFast for trunks) to minimize the downtime in case of topology changes.

Fast Convergence in PVST+

Cisco introduced proprietary mechanisms to bring down the convergence time of 802.1D spanning tree. PVST+ is the Cisco version of spanning tree that supports one spanning-tree instance for each VLAN. The following features reduce the convergence time on switches running PVST+:

- **BackboneFast**—Removes 20 sec, that is, max age, from the convergence time so that the total convergence time for indirect failures goes down to 30 sec. Enable BackboneFast on aggregation switches and access switches. The command is **spanning tree backbonefast**.
- **UplinkFast**—Makes STP converge in 3 to 5 sec for failure of uplinks from the access switches; compare this number with at least 30 sec without this optimization. Enable UplinkFast only on access switches. The command is **spanning tree uplinkfast**.
- **PortFast**—Allows forwarding traffic immediately after the linkup. In PVST+ by default, once a port comes up it goes through the following states—blocking, listening, learning, and forwarding—which takes 30 sec before traffic can really be sent out of that port. Ports with PortFast enabled when changing state do not send TCN BPDUs, thus reducing the amount of flooding in the network. Enable PortFast on ports used by servers. The command in interface mode is **spanning tree portfast**.

TIP UplinkFast raises the priority of the switch to prevent it from becoming a root switch. Do not enable UplinkFast on aggregation switches: you would prevent them from being root and secondary root switches!

Routed ports can also benefit from PortFast: these ports do not need to go through the blocking, listening, learning, and forwarding states.

TrunkFast is a slight variation of PortFast: this feature puts all the VLANs of a trunk into forwarding right after the linkup. See Example 20-10 for how to configure TrunkFast.

Example 20-10 *Enabling TrunkFast in Supervisor IOS*

```
Router# configure terminal
Router(config)# interface GigabitEthernet 4/1
Router(config-if)# spanning tree PortFast trunk
%Warning:PortFast should only be enabled on ports connected to a single
 host. Connecting hubs, concentrators, switches, bridges, etc... to this
 interface  when PortFast is enabled, can cause temporary bridging loops.
 Use with CAUTION
```

Fast Convergence in Rapid PVST+

Cisco calls Rapid PVST+ the combination of PVST+ and 802.1w. IEEE 802.1w (Rapid STP) is the standard that improves the convergence time of the spanning tree.

If you use 802.1w, you do not need BackboneFast or UplinkFast any more; in a well-designed network, 802.1w spanning tree converges in less than 1 sec for any failure, mainly thanks to a mechanism that allows neighboring switches to agree on the transition of a designated port to a forwarding state.

This section explains how Rapid PVST+ works, and it is important to introduce some 802.1w terminology.

In 802.1w ports are categorized based on their roles:

- **Root port (RP)**—The port of the switch that is closest to the root switch. The state of a root port in a converged topology is forwarding.
- **Designated port (DP)**—The port on a segment that sends the BPDUs with the lowest-cost path to the root switch. The state of a designated port in a converged topology is forwarding.
- **Alternate port**—A port that has an alternate path to the root switch. An alternate port is blocking.
- **Backup port**—The blocking port when two links are connected to the same shared LAN segment.

NOTE Notice that we call blocking the state of a port that in 802.1w is defined as *discarding*.

Besides the port role, 802.1w has the concept of link *type*. 802.1w links can be *point-to-point* or *shared*: a link is categorized as point-to-point based on the duplex settings of the ports. If it is full duplex, it is considered a point-to-point link; if it is half duplex, it is considered shared.

In 802.1w, there are *edge* or *nonedge* ports. An edge port is connected to an end device, such as a server. A nonedge port is connected to another switch. In the Cisco implementation of 802.1w, you need to turn on PortFast to classify a port as edge.

Example 20-11 shows how you can verify how 802.1w has categorized a port: in the sample interface FastEthernet 6/9 is an access port assigned to VLAN 65. PortFast is enabled on this interface.

Example 20-11 *Showing the 802.1w Port Type with Supervisor IOS Syntax*

```
Router#show spanning tree int fa6/9

Vlan             Role Sts Cost      Prio.Nbr Type
---------------- ---- --- --------- -------- --------------------------------
VLAN0065         Desg FWD 19        128.329  Edge P2p
```

The fast convergence in 802.1w is based on mechanisms to quickly transition ports into the forwarding state. These mechanisms include a proposal and agreement scheme and a mechanism similar to Cisco UplinkFast.

The proposal/agreement sequence happens between switches to quickly place in forwarding state a port that moved into the designated role on a point-to-point link. Traditionally (with 802.1D) before a port could be forwarding, you would have to wait around 30 sec (twice the forwarding delay). With 802.1w, the switch where the port is located sends a proposal and waits for the neighboring switch to reply with an agreement before moving the port into forwarding. The proposal/agreement mechanism takes less than 1 sec to converge.

802.1w can converge in very few seconds for uplink failures: the transition from an alternate port to a root port role and forwarding state is triggered when a switch loses its root port using a mechanism similar to UplinkFast.

Edge ports provide benefits equivalent to those of PortFast plus some key functionalities: an edge port keeps its forwarding state during topology changes, whereas a nonedge port connecting to a non-802.1w–capable device would take 30 sec to become forwarding after a topology change.

TIP It is important to configure the switch ports as edge if they attach to a Layer 3 interface such as a router interface, load-balancer interface, firewall interface, or cache interface.

These devices typically do not understand 802.1w, and if the port is categorized as nonedge, it goes through the blocking, learning, forwarding sequence when a topology change occurs. This process accounts for 30 sec before the port is forwarding.

Also, notice that a flapping port of type edge does not cause topology changes, differently from what a PortFast port would do with PVST+. You can find more about topology changes later in this chapter.

NOTE For more information about 802.1w, see http://www.cisco.com/warp/public/473/146.html.

Fast Convergence in MST

IEEE 802.1s (MST) lets you define multiple instances of spanning tree and map VLANs to it, as described in Chapter 12. When enabling MST on a Cisco switch, enable 802.1s and 802.1w, which means that fast convergence does not require any additional configuration.

Fast convergence in MST relies on 802.1w, as described in the section, "Fast Convergence in Rapid PVST+."

Minimizing Topology Changes

Having a lot of flooding in the Data Center is a sign that something is malfunctioning. One possible cause is malfunctioning server NICs.

Server NICs sometimes have interoperability issues with the networking equipment for many reasons; one possibility is that either the NIC vendors or the switch vendors do not completely conform to the IEEE specifications. Other times, the interoperability problems result from software bugs or proprietary hardware features not described in the IEEE specifications.

One single malfunctioning NIC causing continuous linkup/linkdown is extremely detrimental to the network: continuous TCN BPDUs can generate large amounts of flooding in the network. Here is why.

Topology changes in STP interoperate with the *MAC address table* and rely on flooding to make sure that traffic reaches its destination until the table is completely up-to-date.

Under normal conditions, when entries in the MAC table reach an aging time of 300 sec (5 minutes), they are cleared. When there are topology changes in PVST+, the TCN packets traversing a switch bring down the aging timer to 15 sec (forwarding delay).

In MST or in Rapid PVST+ (as a consequence of 802.1w), the TCN mechanism is slightly different, but the principle is the same: a TCN causes flushing of entries in the MAC table to update this table with the new logic topology. When a topology change occurs, there is some amount of flooding as a consequence of the flushing of the MAC table.

You can fix the problem in several ways: using NIC vendor patches to avoid the continuous linkup/linkdown that is causing the TCN, enabling PortFast on the server ports, or using the *debounce* feature on Cisco switches.

Enabling PortFast on access ports limits the generation of TCNs for all the spanning-tree algorithms supported by Cisco switches. For example, PortFast-enabled ports in Rapid PVST+ are categorized as 802.1w edge ports, and edge ports do not generate TCNs when changing status.

The debounce option lets you increase the tolerance of a switch for a jittery NIC card. When the jitter exceeds the specifications, the switch can wait for a longer amount of time before bringing down the port.

TIP Although too many and unnecessary TCNs are a problem, TCNs accelerate the update process of the MAC address table in Layer 2 convergence after a failure.

A nice feature available on the RP of the Catalyst switches allows even quicker updates of the MAC table when a topology change occurs. The RP, upon receiving a TCN on a VLAN, sends ARPs for the IP addresses that belong to the VLAN. This process forces the MAC address tables of the switches in the network to be updated with the new location for each MAC address.

Loop Prevention: UDLD and Loopguard

Despite the fact that STP is designed to prevent loops, certain types of failures can still create loops. There are two main categories of loops:

- Loops caused by misconfigurations (incorrect cabling, STP disabled on certain VLANs, misconfigured pairs of bridging devices)
- Loops caused by failures in the network that STP is unable to recover from

Incorrect wiring, especially with fiber links, can cause a link to be up while BPDUs are not either received or transmitted. The consequence is a loop; the feature that fixes this type of problem is UDLD.

Part **a** of Figure 20-11 shows an example of incorrect wiring between access1 and aggregation2. Two strands of fiber from access1 (port1) go to two different ports on aggregation2 (port2 and port3), causing a linkup on port1 and port3 even if aggregation2 cannot send traffic to access1.

The consequence is the active topology depicted in part **a** of Figure 20-11, where all the ports are forwarding.

Another typical cause of loops is a port that becomes unidirectional (either the receive or the transmit direction of the transceiver breaks down), as shown in part **b** of Figure 20-11.

With this scenario, the port state is up, but it stops sending BPDUs, causing the uplink2 on access1 to change state to forwarding. The faulty port can still receive traffic; this event just created a loop. The feature that fixes this problem is Loopguard.

You can only use Loopguard on switched networks, that is, when there are no hubs. Because all the links are point-to-point, Loopguard categorizes the absence of BPDUs as the symptom of a unidirectional link preventing the spanning tree from opening a blocked port.

Figure 20-11 *Loop Failures in the Data Center*

a

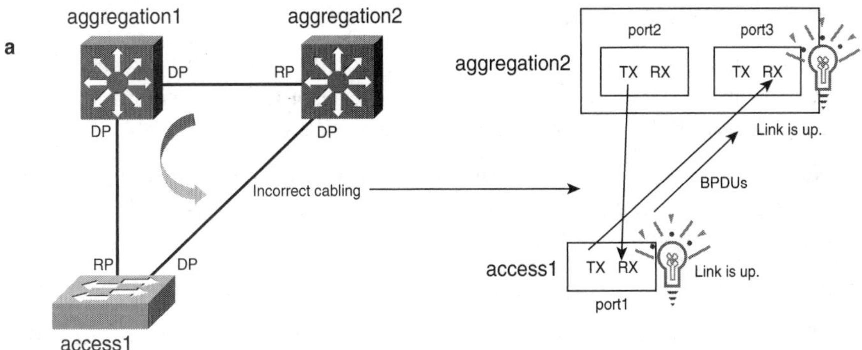

b

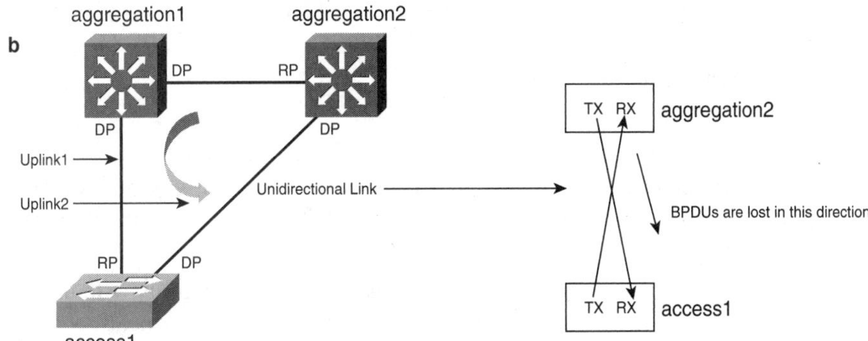

Both Loopguard and UDLD fix the problem of unidirectional failures by putting the ports where the problem is detected in a state where traffic forwarding is prevented. (For UDLD, the state is **errordisable**, and for Loopguard, it is **port inconsistent**.)

Enable Loopguard and UDLD globally with the commands **spanning tree loopguard default** and **udld enable**.

Internal Redundancy Considerations

The designs presented in this book always describe a fully redundant topology, which is a topology with no single point of failure. A Data Center infrastructure has two aggregation switches, multiple access switches, and dual-attached servers. The approach of using redundant devices provides *external* redundancy: if one device fails, the redundant peer takes over the traffic for the failed one.

Depending on the hardware platform and the operating system, some switches offer a feature called supervisor redundancy, high availability, or RP redundancy. These features provide redundancy internally to the switch itself.

You can configure a switch supporting internal redundancy with two supervisors (that is, two SPs and two RPs) so that if the active supervisor fails, the redundant supervisor takes over without the need for the external device to take over.

You should design a Data Center with external redundancy, which does not prevent it from taking advantage of internal redundancy if the failover is as fast as or faster than external redundancy and if it is stateful.

Internal redundancy has the following main uses in the Data Center:

- It can increase the availability of the Data Center if the failover time is so short that external redundancy does not detect the failure.
- You can use it on switches connected to single attached servers to avoid losing these servers when the supervisor fails.
- You can use it to perform maintenance on the active supervisor without disrupting the network traffic.

TIP A good example of internal redundancy is the case of a server with mission-critical applications that is attached to a single access switch. In this case, you cannot afford to lose the access switch.

If the access switch is a Catalyst 6500, you can use high availability with the CatOS operating system. If the supervisor fails, the redundant supervisor takes over in a few seconds, keeping the state of the switch ports.

You need to explicitly enable high availability by using the command **Console(enable)> set system highavailability enable**.

Because internal redundancy has failover time and state-synchronization characteristics that differ between switch platforms and operating systems, it is up to you to assess whether a specific implementation of this feature meets your Data Center requirements. This section provides an overview of the main redundancy implementations.

Supervisor Redundancy

Supervisor redundancy refers to the use of two supervisors in a single switch. When you use two supervisors in the chassis, one becomes the active and the other standby.

The active supervisor switches traffic at both Layer 2 and Layer 3. The SP handles spanning-tree calculations as well as the other Layer 2 protocols; the RP handles the routing protocols.

The standby supervisor is fully initialized and configured but is not operational: it does not forward traffic or participate in protocol handling.

The state synchronization between the active and standby supervisors and the switchover time depend on the redundancy scheme available. In IOS, internal redundancy is categorized as:

- **Route Processor Redundancy (RPR)**—Active and standby supervisors synchronize their configurations. The MAC address table, and STP state are not synchronized.
- **Route Processor Redundancy Plus (RPR+)**—It is like RPR with improvements for a faster switchover (30 to 60 sec).
- **Stateful SwitchOver (SSO)**—It supports the synchronization of the Layer 2 state, the MAC address table, the spanning-tree state, the trunk state, and the EtherChannel state. It is similar to the CatOS high-availability feature. The switchover time is a few seconds (between 3 and 7 seconds).

NOTE For more information about CatOS high availability on the Catalyst 6500, see http://www.cisco.com/warp/public/cc/pd/si/casi/ca6000/tech/hafc6_wp.htm.

The standby supervisor takes over when either the SP or the RP on the active supervisor fail or when the administrator configures a switchover to perform maintenance. When supervisor redundancy is stateful, the failure of the active supervisor goes unnoticed from the point of view of traffic forwarding because forwarding ports do not change state and the forwarding tables are unchanged.

After the switchover, the newly active RP has to re-establish adjacencies with the neighboring routers and rebuild the routing table, which is eventually installed on the supervisor. With stateful redundancy, the hardware FIB table is synchronized between active and standby supervisors, so while the newly active RP calculates the routing table, traffic can still be Layer 3–switched.

Non-Stop Forwarding (NSF) is a feature that allows a router to forward traffic when the primary RP failed and the standby is taking over the active role. NSF requires SSO.

NSF

Consider part **a** of Figure 20-12. This design uses external redundancy: aggregation1 and aggregation2 are concurrently active and create adjacencies with core1, core2, and between them. Should aggregation1 fail, core1, core2, and aggregation2 take notice of the failure and adjust their routing tables.

Figure 20-12 *External Redundancy and Internal Redundancy*

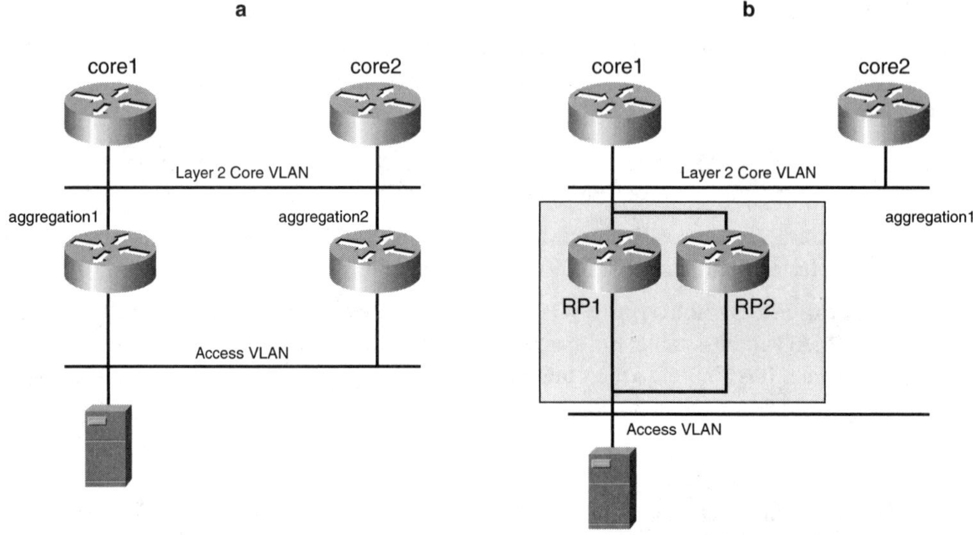

Consider now part **b** of Figure 20-12. This design uses internal redundancy. The two RPs inside the box belong to aggregation1; RP1 is active and establishes neighbor adjacencies with core1 and core2. Routing protocols run only on RP1.

If RP1 fails, RP2 takes over, but it has to re-establish adjacencies with core1 and core2 and start as if a new router was inserted in the network. Core1 and core2 find out about the failure of RP1, which causes route flapping in the network.

NSF is a feature available on some routing platforms where the switchover between RPs goes undetected by the neighboring routers. NSF achieves this goal by doing the following:

- Synchronizing the FIB information and the adjacency data base between the active and standby RPs
- Rebuilding the routing tables on the standby RP (once it becomes active) with the cooperation of the neighboring routers

As a consequence, if RP1 fails, it takes some time for RP2 to become active, and traffic forwarding continues because RP2 received the forwarding information from RP1. In the meanwhile, RP2 rebuilds the routing-table information and updates the FIB and adjacency table.

For NSF to work in the topology shown in Figure 20-11**b**, you need the following:

- **Aggregation1 to be NSF-capable**—Aggregation1 can probe its neighbors to find out whether they are NSF-aware and can rebuild the routing-information base using a procedure called the Link State Database (LSDB) out-of-band resynchronization.
- **Core1 and core2 to be NSF-aware**—Core1 and core2 understand the special hello packets sent by RP2 and must be capable of performing an LSDB out-of-band resynchronization with RP2.
- **An RP switchover that is faster than the dead interval (40 sec).**

NOTE For more information about NSF, refer to http://www.cisco.com/univercd/cc/td/doc/product/software/ios120/120newft/120limit/120s/120s22/nsf120s.htm and http://www.cisco.com/univercd/cc/td/doc/product/software/ios122/122newft/122t/122t15/.

Layer 2 Data Center Design

The configuration of the Data Center in terms of Layer 2 features follows the Cisco multilayer architecture described in Chapter 4.

Chapter 12 described the key steps in configuring VLANs and trunks. The Data Center design from a Layer 2 perspective entails choosing the VLAN allocation scheme, which forwarding spanning-tree topology you want to create for each VLAN, which spanning-tree algorithm to use, where to enable features such as PortFast and TrunkFast, and how to optimize the convergence time.

VLAN Configuration

The first step in configuring the Data Center infrastructure consists of creating VLANs to host the server farms.

You can follow the steps in this list and find additional information about each feature in Chapter 12:

Step 1 Configure Virtual Terminal Protocol (VTP) mode transparent, with **vtp domain** <*name*> followed by **vtp mode transparent**, on aggregation and access switches.

Step 2 Enable MAC address reduction, with **spanning tree extend system-id**, on aggregation and access switches.

Step 3 Create VLANs, with **(config)vlan** <*number*> and assign a name with **(config-vlan) name** <*name*> on aggregation switches and on the access switches where the VLAN is required.

Step 4 Configure trunks to carry the VLAN traffic between switches and limit the scope of each VLAN by defining the VLANs allowed on trunks.

Figure 20-13 provides an example of VLAN allocation with dual-attached servers, four server farms, and a pair of load-balancing devices. Each server farm is assigned to a VLAN: 10, 20, 30, and 40.

Figure 20-13 *VLAN Allocation in the Data Center*

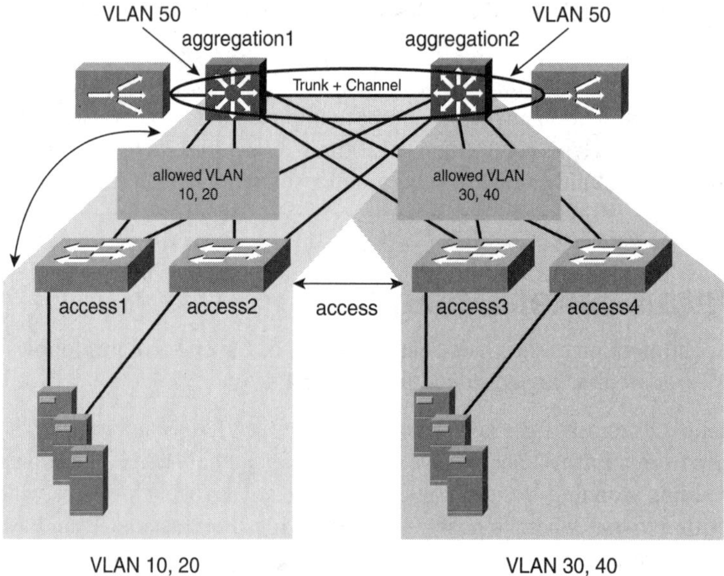

The servers assigned to VLAN 10 and VLAN 20 are connected to access1 and access2; the servers assigned to VLAN 30 and VLAN 40 are attached to access3 and access4.

Figure 20-13 shows the scope of VLANs 10, 20, 30, and 40. Notice that the trunks between aggregation1 and aggregation2 and access1 and access2 do not carry VLAN 30 nor VLAN 40, and the trunks between aggregation1 and aggregation2 and access3 and access4 do not carry VLAN 10 nor VLAN 20.

This choice is a design choice: by limiting the scope of the VLANs and aggregating servers on switch pairs, you spare bandwidth on the uplinks that would otherwise be used by unicast flooding or broadcasts.

This design does not prevent you from attaching a new server on access4 on VLAN 10 in case there are no more ports available on access1 and access2. You would then change the configuration of the trunks to access4.

You use VLAN 50 for the communication between the load balancers. The redundant pair of load balancers uses VLAN 50 for their redundancy protocol. VLAN 50 should only be configured between the aggregation switches.

Also, notice that the presence of dual-attached servers and active/standby load balancers requires the use of a looped topology: VLANs 10, 20, 30, and 40 are trunked between the aggregation switches.

Based on the design of Figure 20-13, you need to create VLANs as follows:

- VLANs 10 and 20—On access1, access2, aggregation1, and aggregation2
- VLANs 30 and 40—On access3, access4, aggregation1, and aggregation2
- VLAN 50—On aggregation1 and aggregation2

The section "Spanning-Tree Topology" explains which ports are blocking and which ports are forwarding with this design.

TIP Some network administrators use VTP server/client to propagate the VLAN configuration; other administrators prefer the manual configuration. Considering that most Data Centers use a limited number of VLANs, VTP in Data Centers is seldom necessary, which means that VTP transparent mode is typically sufficient.

With VTPv1 and VTPv2, it is possible to delete VLANs accidentally as a result of a misconfiguration. VTP version 3 addresses this problem and introduces the support for 4,000 VLANs and private VLANs.

Access Ports

Access ports carry traffic for a single VLAN. Servers are typically connected to access ports.

Additionally, external appliances such as load balancers, firewalls, SSL offloaders, and caches are typically connected to access ports.

When a server is attached to an access port, or when a device (that does not operate as a bridge) is attached to an access port, it is recommended that you enable PortFast with the command **spanning tree portfast** in interface configuration mode.

PortFast puts an access port into the forwarding state at linkup, without waiting for two times the forwarding delay (a total of 30 sec), thus allowing the device to start transmitting right away. Should the port become blocking because the access port is incorrectly connected to a switch and there is a Layer 2 loop, PortFast does not prevent the port from transitioning into blocking.

With a spanning-tree algorithm based on 802.1w (such as Rapid PVST+ or MST), it is important to assign the PortFast and TrunkFast definitions to the eligible ports to make sure 802.1w categorizes these ports as edge. Edge ports do not change state during a topology change.

Nonedge ports should be connected to devices that understand the 802.1w protocol. If they are not, when a topology change occurs, these ports go through the blocking, learning, forwarding sequence.

TIP When connecting a Layer 3 device or an end host to a switch, it is usually better to configure PortFast or TrunkFast and to hard-code the settings for channeling and trunking.

You should configure channeling by either setting the channel mode to on if necessary or explicitly disabling the protocol if channeling is not used.

You should either set the trunk mode to on if necessary or explicitly disable the protocol (the Dynamic Trunking Protocol [DTP] on the Catalyst switches) if trunking is not used.

These configurations cut down the time it takes for an interface to come up and prevent unexpected effects on protocols that negotiate master/backup roles, such as HSRP and VRRP.

Trunk Configuration

After creating the VLANs on the switches in the Data Center topology and assigning these VLANs to the server ports, you need to make sure that the VLAN traffic is carried across switches. You do so by creating trunks on the links between the switches.

You should configure trunks between the following network devices:

- Aggregation switches (carrying basically all the VLANs)
- Access switches and aggregation switches (carrying only the server VLANs)
- Aggregation switches and the service appliances

By default, a trunk carries all the VLANs configured on a switch. You should restrict the VLANs carried on trunks to the ones that are actually present on both switches you have connected. You can do so by using the command **switchport trunk allowed**.

You can define the VLANs allowed on a trunk with the command **switchport trunk allowed vlan 10,20** in interface configuration mode.

You can modify the list of the VLANs allowed on a trunk with the following commands:

```
(config-if)#switchport trunk allowed vlan add vlan number
(config-if)#switchport trunk allowed vlan remove vlan number
```

After deciding the VLANs that you want to carry on the trunk, you need to decide the encapsulation type to use on the trunks. The traffic can be encapsulated with the VLAN tag according to two different encapsulation types:

- **802.1Q**—The standard encapsulation in which the VLAN tag is inserted between the source MAC address and the type/length field of the Ethernet frame. The traffic belonging to the native VLAN of a trunk port is carried untagged.
- **ISL (Inter Switch Link)**—Cisco-proprietary encapsulation type that is really a "tunneling" protocol. The traffic is encapsulated in frames with a destination MAC of 0100.0c00.0000.

The recommended trunk encapsulation is 802.1Q mainly because it is the standard. The configuration command in interface configuration mode is **switchport trunk encapsulation dot1q**.

In 802.1Q, the *native VLAN* of a port is carried untagged, which could lead to the problem of VLAN hopping, as described in Chapter 15. When you use the 802.1Q encapsulation, it is recommended that you configure the switches to tag the native VLAN with the global command **vlan dot1q tag native**.

Use the command **switchport mode trunk** to put the port into a permanent trunk. In this mode, the port also sends DTP frames to turn the neighboring port into a trunk as well. If the trunk does not form, verify the VTP domain configuration. VTP domain names must match between the neighboring switches.

Trunks are often configured between the aggregation switches and service devices (load balancers, firewalls). A service device routes between VLANs and provides Layer 3 interfaces on the VLAN, which are equivalent to SVIs. If the trunk is configured between the switch and such a device, you should enable TrunkFast, for the reasons mentioned in the section, "Rapid Convergence." The command is **spanning tree portfast trunk**.

Spanning-Tree Topology

This section explains the configuration of Spanning-Tree in the Data Center network. The key steps can be summarized as follows:

Step 1 Enable spanning tree, (For Rapid PVST+, the command is **spanning tree mode rapid-pvst**.)

Step 2 Assign the root and secondary root roles to the aggregation switches on a per-VLAN basis. (The commands are **spanning tree vlan** *vlan number* **root primary** and **spanning tree vlan** *vlan number* **root secondary**.)

Part **a** of Figure 20-14 shows a typical Data Center topology. In part **a** of Figure 20-14, aggregation1 is configured to be the root for all the VLANs, and aggregation2 is configured to be the secondary root for all the VLANs.

Figure 20-14 *Redundant Topologies and Failure Recovery with Spanning-Tree*

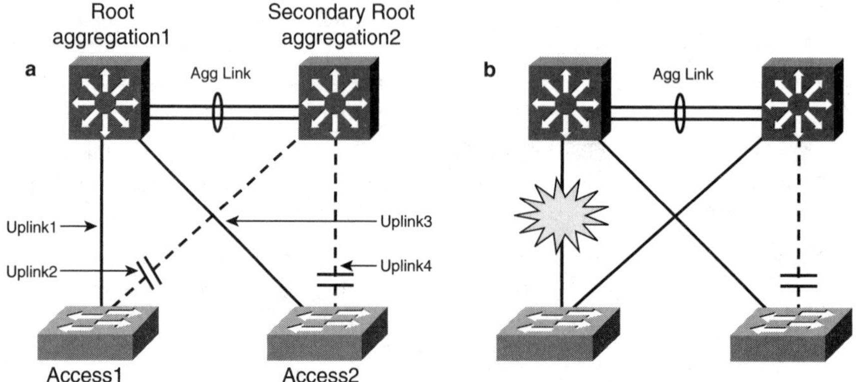

TIP If you want to forward traffic to both uplinks from each access switch, you can assign root and secondary root priorities to the aggregation switches in such a way that each uplink is forwarding for one VLAN and blocking for another VLAN. This approach was described in the section, "Traffic Distribution on Layer 2 Links."

Uplink1 connects access1 with aggregation1, and uplink2 connects access1 with aggregation2. In Figure 20-13a, uplink2 does not forward any traffic (the dashed line) because the port on access1 to aggregation2 is in the blocking state.

The continuous links and the dashed links belong to the same VLAN. The continuous line shows the active topology, whereas the dashed line is a link where no traffic is flowing because one of the switch ports on the link is blocking. The blocking port is represented with the double line.

Make sure that the VLANs configured on the access switches are trunked between the aggregation switches (called "Agg Link" in the figure). This link has the following properties:

- It is typically made redundant through the use of EtherChannel, which means it is highly available.

- The link is also a trunk that carries traffic for all the VLANs present in the Data Center topology.
- It is always forwarding because it is attached to the root switch and secondary root switch.
- Control protocol communication between the aggregation switches takes this link. (For example, the HSRP hellos are exchanged through this link instead of through the access switches.)

NOTE Trunking the server VLANs on this link is not required if the topology is loop free.

The topology described in this section is the most generic possible in that it accommodates the requirement for dual-attached servers as well as active/standby load balancers and firewalls.

This section describes a looped topology. In a looped topology, you should use the link between the aggregation switches to carry server VLANs.

In case of failure of a forwarding link, one blocking port becomes forwarding. You can see this change in Figure 20-13b, where uplink2 from blocking becomes forwarding.

Notice that the upper-layer protocols like HSRP or VRRP are unaffected by the failure of uplink1 because the control traffic is exchanged on the link between the aggregation switches.

If the direct link between aggregation1 and aggregation2 were not present, the failure of uplink1 would interrupt the HSRP communication for the time that it takes the spanning tree to converge, which could potentially change the active/standby roles of the SVIs on the routers.

Having a direct "channel" of communication between devices at the aggregation layer, and having this channel continuously forwarding, keeps the topology deterministic.

The convergence time for the failure depends on the spanning-tree algorithm, as described in the section, "Rapid Convergence."

Layer 2 Configuration Summary

This section summarizes the key Layer 2 design recommendations explained in this chapter.

Figure 20-15 displays the topology.

Figure 20-15 *Data Center Design: Layer 2*

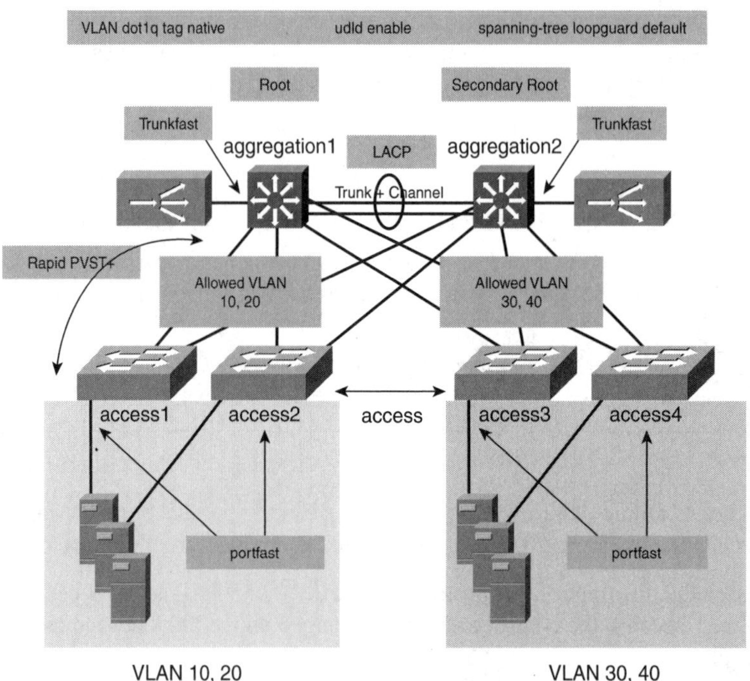

This Data Center design uses Rapid PVST+ for reasons of design flexibility and to take advantage of 802.1w rapid convergence (a choice of Rapid PVST+ versus PVST+). The root switch is aggregation1, and the secondary root switch is aggregation2. The two aggregation switches are connected through a channel. The aggregation protocol is LACP (802.3ad). The channel is built bundling ports across line cards to maximize its availability. This channel is also a trunk carrying VLANs 10, 20, 30, and 40.

The access1 and access2 switches use only VLANs 10 and 20, which is why you clear VLANs 30 and 40 from their uplinks. The access3 and access4 switches carry only VLANs 30 and 40, so VLANs 10 and 20 are removed from their uplinks.

The access ports on access1, access2, access3, and access4 are configured with PortFast. Configure PortFast on the switch ports from aggregation1 and aggregation2 that attach to an external device, which is a load balancer in this case, but it could be an SSL offloader or a firewall. If the load balancers or the firewall are attached with a trunk, configure TrunkFast on the link.

Loopguard and UDLD are enabled globally on all the switches in the figure to prevent Layer 2 loops in case of unidirectional links with malfunctioning switches. **vlan dot1q tag native** is enabled globally on all the switches for security reasons.

NOTE For more information about the best practices in designing networks with the Catalyst switches, refer to http://www.cisco.com/warp/public/473/103.pdf and http://www.cisco.com /warp/customer/473/185.html.

Layer 3 Data Center Design

This section covers different design options for redundant Layer 3 topologies using dynamic routing. Chapter 13 described the Layer 3 features that you are likely to use in the Data Center. This section explains how and where to apply these features.

Figure 20-16 shows from a very high level possible Data Center designs. The router icon in Figure 20-16 is the RP in a Layer 3 switch. The server load balancer in these designs operates as a bridge. The firewall provides packet filtering and stateful inspection, and it can be the default gateway for the servers.

Figure 20-16 *Layer 2, Layer 3, Firewalls, and Load Balancing in the Data Center*

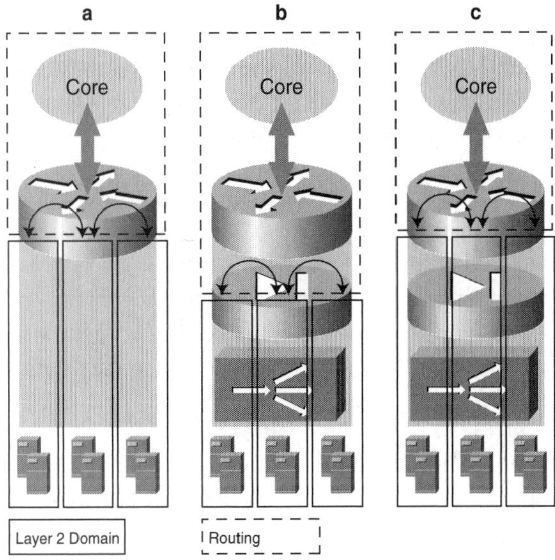

Part **a** of Figure 20-16 shows the design without firewalls or load balancers. The default gateway is the RP in the Layer 3 switch.

Part **b** of Figure 20-16 shows the design with firewall and server load balancing. The firewall is the default gateway.

Part **c** of Figure 20-16 shows the design with a transparent firewall. The default gateway is the RP in the Layer 3 switch.

As you can see in Figure 20-16, in a typical Data Center routing is performed between the aggregation switches (these are Layer 3 switches) and the core switches (Layer 3 switches or routers). In parts **a** and **c** of Figure 20-16, the Layer 3 switch also routes between directly connected subnets (VLANs), and it provides the function of default gateway with protocols such as HSRP, VRRP, and GLBP.

This chapter, which focuses on the infrastructure design, mostly reflects the topology of part **a** of Figure 20-16, where the default gateway for the servers is the RP (also referred to as the aggregation router) in the Layer 3 switch. The presence of firewalls and load balancers as in parts **b** and **c** of Figure 20-16 requires additional considerations.

Routing Between Core and Aggregation Routers

The Data Center network attaches to the core as a stub network, as you can see in Figure 20-17. The core routers only need to advertise a default route, and the aggregation routers in the Data Center advertise the local subnets in summarized routes.

Sometimes, it is necessary to advertise host routes. Figure 20-17 shows a load balancer that uses Route Health Injection (RHI) to advertise a VIP address based on the availability of the servers. RHI installs a host route on the aggregation switches, and this route is redistributed into the Interior Gateway Protocol (IGP).

NOTE For more information about RHI, refer to http://www.cisco.com/univercd/cc/td/doc/product/lan/cat6000/cfgnotes/csm_3_1/helthmon.pdf.

The connectivity between the Data Center aggregation and campus core switches can be

- Pure Layer 3 links (each link is a different subnet)
- A shared-core VLAN

Figure 20-18 illustrates the design with Layer 3 links between the core routers and the aggregation switches. Part **a** of Figure 20-18 shows a sub-optimal design: if core1 fails, server-to-client traffic cannot leave the Data Center. Part **b** of Figure 20-18 shows a Layer 3 link between the aggregation switches; this link provides a redundant path in case the Layer 3 link with core1 is lost. The same problem can also be fixed by configuring HSRP tracking on all the SVIs facing the serverfarms.

Figure 20-17 *Routing Between Core and Aggregation Routers*

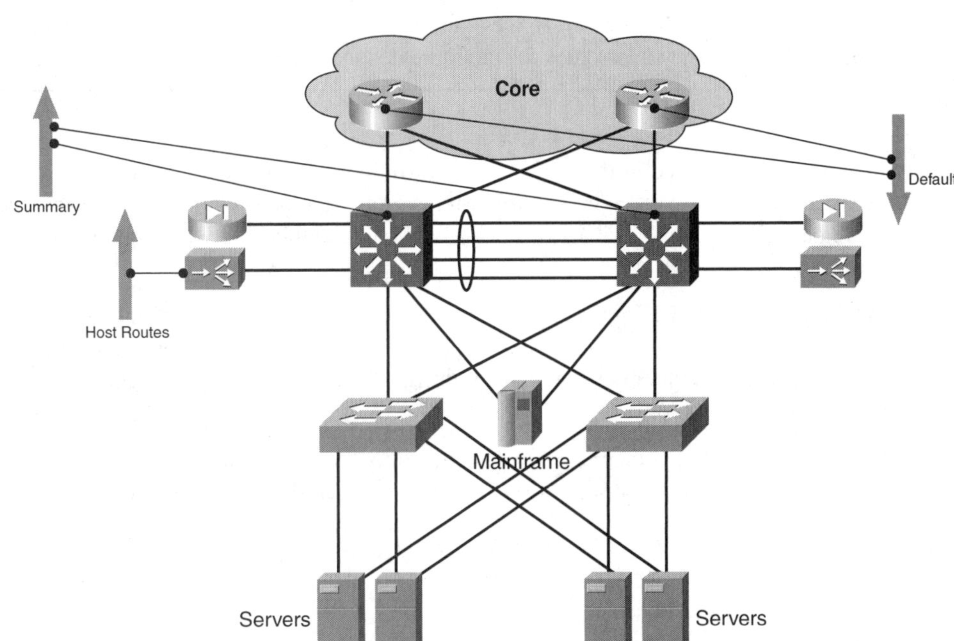

Figure 20-18 *Layer 3 Links Between Core and Data Center*

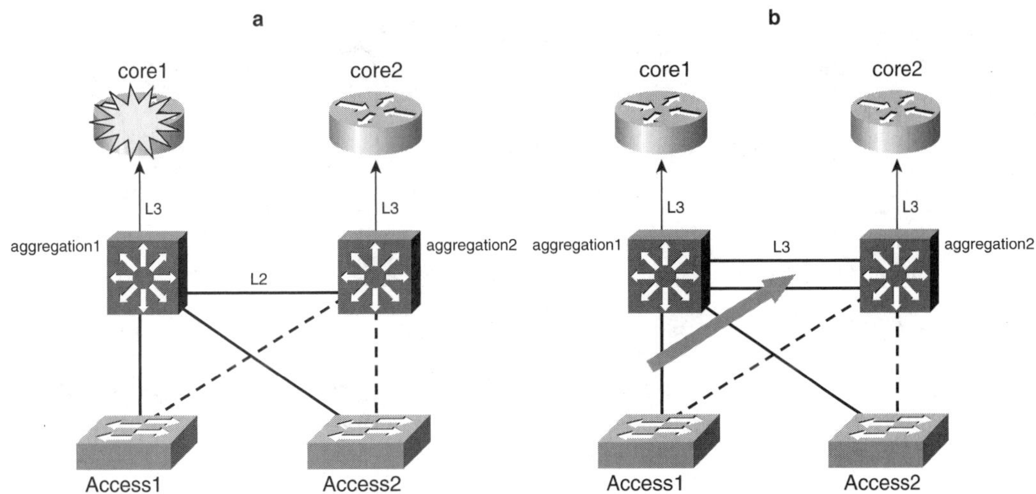

TIP In addition to having the Layer 3 link between the aggregation switches, you could have a full mesh of Layer 3 links between the aggregation switches and the core, which provides additional redundancy and routes for the same destination IP.

In the design displayed in Figure 20-18, you would typically run a dynamic protocol between the core and the aggregation switches. Aggregation1 would be neighboring with aggregation2 and core1, and aggregation2 would be neighboring with aggregation1 and core2.

In this topology, the RP on the aggregation switch detects the failure of one of the Layer 3 links instantaneously. This failure brings down the Layer 3 interface on the aggregation switch, which immediately triggers the routing protocol to notify the neighbors and recalculates the topology.

Figure 20-19 shows another possible design. In this case, the connectivity between the core Layer 3 switches and the aggregation switches is a shared segment, a core VLAN.

Figure 20-19 *Layer 2 Core VLAN Between Core and Data Center*

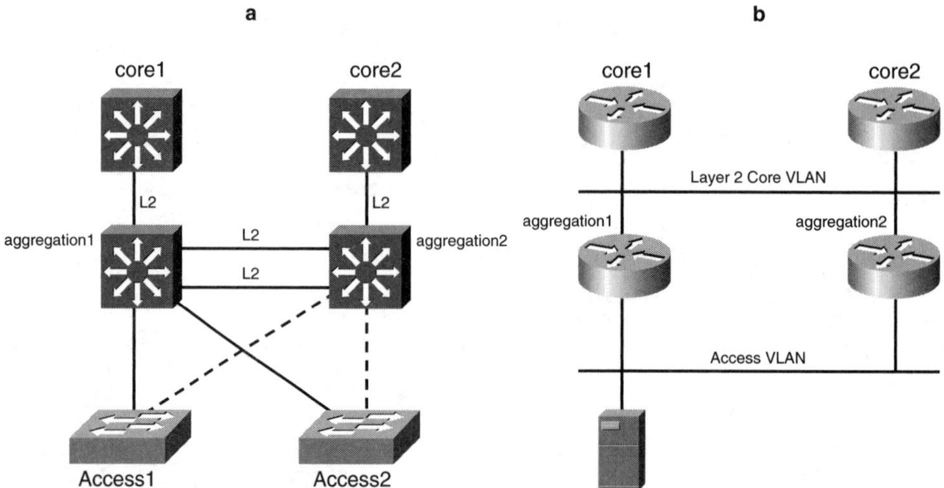

Part **a** of Figure 20-19 represents the physical topology, whereas part **b** of Figure 20-19 gives the logical representation of the connectivity between the RP in the Layer 3 switches and the core routers.

NOTE Notice that there is no Layer 2 loop in the core: the aggregation switches are providing the bridging for the core VLAN, but the core switches do not trunk the core VLAN between them.

One of the main differences with the design of Figure 20-18 is the convergence time. The failure of a link with the core routers does not bring down the SVI on the aggregation switch. As a result, the failure is detected by the expiration of the dead interval, which with OSPF by default is 40 sec and with EIGRP is 15 sec.

TIP If you use the design where the core and the aggregation switches share a VLAN, you can make the failure detection faster by modifying the default hello-interval and hold-time per-interface. You should be careful to configure these values to match on the adjacent router interfaces; otherwise, the routers will not become neighbors. The commands to use with OSPF are **ip ospf hello-interval** *seconds* and **ip ospf dead-interval** *seconds*. A possible configuration for a Data Center environment is **ip ospf hello-interval 1** and **ip ospf dead-interval 4**.

The commands to use with EIGRP are **ip hello-interval eigrp** *autonomous-system seconds* and **ip hold-time eigrp** *autonomous-system seconds*. A possible configuration for a Data Center environment is **ip hello-interval eigrp 1 1** and **ip hold-time eigrp 1 3**. Notice that the first number is the autonomous system (AS) number.

You must test the preceding values in your specific environment to make sure that they are appropriate.

Using Layer 3 links between the aggregation routers is preferable because of the faster convergence time.

Default Gateway Redundancy: HSRP, VRRP, and GLBP

HSRP, VRRP, and GLBP were discussed in Chapter 13. These protocols provide the default gateway to the servers.

The design choices of using the gateway redundancy protocols include the following:

- Which aggregation router should be active for each HSRP group
- The use of multiple groups for load distribution on the uplinks
- Whether to use preemption
- Tuning the timers

This section explains the design with HSRP, but the same concepts apply to VRRP and GLBP.

Matching Layer 3 and Layer 2 Topologies

The choice of which aggregation switch should be HSRP primary router or secondary router on a given VLAN should follow the same policy as the assignment of the root and secondary root roles for the VLAN. Under normal conditions, the root switch for a VLAN should also be HSRP active on the SVI.

A topology that performs uplink load distribution is the perfect example to explain this concept.

Figure 20-20 shows a looped topology: the uplinks on each access switch are forwarding for one VLAN and blocking for another VLAN, according to the design described in the section, "Traffic Distribution on Layer 2 Links." Access1 sends traffic for VLAN 10 to aggregation1 and traffic for VLAN 20 to aggregation2. You achieve this design by making aggregation1 the root switch for the odd VLANs and aggregation2 the root switch for the even VLANs.

Figure 20-20 *Matching the HSRP Topology to the Spanning-Tree Topology*

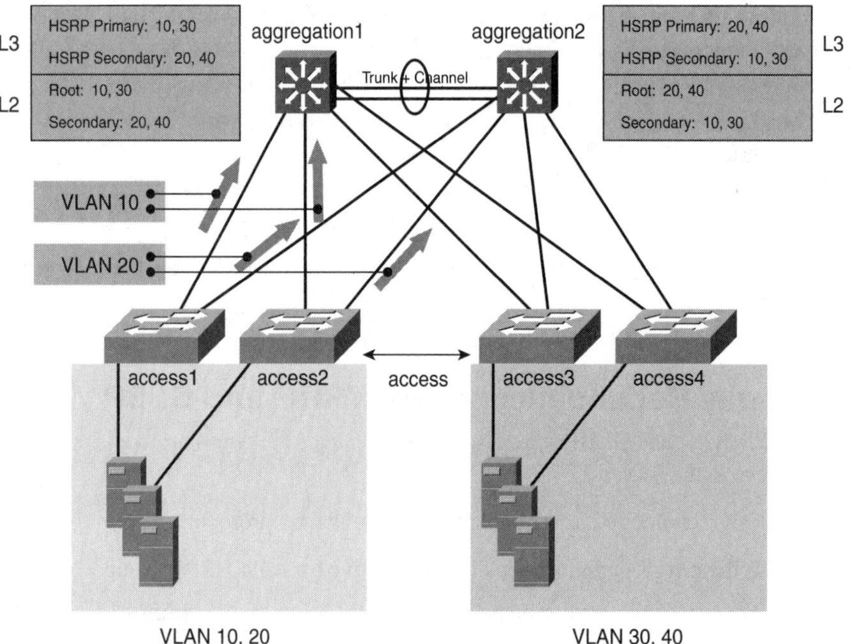

If you consider the Layer 2 forwarding topology, it is clear that the default gateway for the servers on VLAN 10 should be aggregation1 and the default gateway for the servers on VLAN 20 should be aggregation2. You can achieve this design by assigning the priorities to HSRP as described in Chapter 13: aggregation1 could have a priority of 105 for the HSRP on VLANs 10 and 30 (and more generically, the odd VLANs) and 100 for the HSRP on VLANs 20 and 40 (and more generically, the even VLANs).

With loop-free topologies, you should use multiple HSRP groups or GLBP.

To Preempt or Not to Preempt?

Preempt or not preempt? If you do not configure preemption, the active/standby role of the HSRP router interface depends on which router is brought up first on a VLAN and on the sequence of RP failures. With the **preempt** option, the order in which the routers are brought up is irrelevant; the interface with the higher priority always wins.

Considering that in a spanning tree the root switch always "preempts" the other switches, and considering that the Layer 2 and Layer 3 topologies should match for optimal traffic forwarding, the conclusion is that it is preferable to enable the preempt option.

Preemption also has its drawbacks: after reloading, the HSRP primary router could preempt before rebuilding the routing table and installing the FIB entries in the hardware. As a result, servers could send traffic to the HSRP primary, but this router might be incapable of forwarding traffic for some time.

The solution to this problem is to configure preemption delay. By configuring the preemption delay option, you make sure that a router waits for a configurable delay before preempting the neighbor. This configuration provides enough time for the router to rebuild the routing table and to populate the forwarding table. A possible configuration in interface configuration mode is **standby 1 priority 105 preempt delay 60** on the HSRP primary router and **standby 1 priority 100 preempt delay 60** on the HSRP secondary router. With this configuration, preemption is delayed by 60 sec.

Timer Tuning

Failure detection with the default HSRP timers takes 10 sec. As explained in Chapter 13, HSRP can be tuned for subsecond convergence. Although the configuration for subsecond convergence is good from a recovery-time standpoint, it could also cause the flapping of the HSRP active/standby roles when the Layer 2 protocols are converging.

A safer setting is to send hellos every second and configure a hold time of 3 sec: **standby 1 timers 1 3**. This configuration assumes that the convergence of the Layer 2 protocols takes less than 3 sec, which is possible with Rapid PVST+ and MST, as described in the section, "Rapid Convergence."

Using OSPF in Data Center Design

Before configuring OSPF in the Data Center, you should be familiar with the concepts and features described in Chapter 13.

The goal of the OSPF design is to maximize the stability of the routers in the Data Center, contain the scope of route flapping in the Data Center, and minimize the convergence time.

OSPF Topology

Figure 20-21 shows a possible design with OSPF. In this figure, the core routers are the area border routers (ABRs). It is also possible to place the ABR at the aggregation routers as well.

By making the core routers the ABRs, you minimize the amount of routing processing on the aggregation switches in the Data Center. On the other hand, the core routers have topology information for the Data Center area, which means that route flapping in the Data Center is perceived in the core. Making the aggregation routers the ABRs prevents this problem.

Figure 20-21 *OSPF Routing in the Data Center*

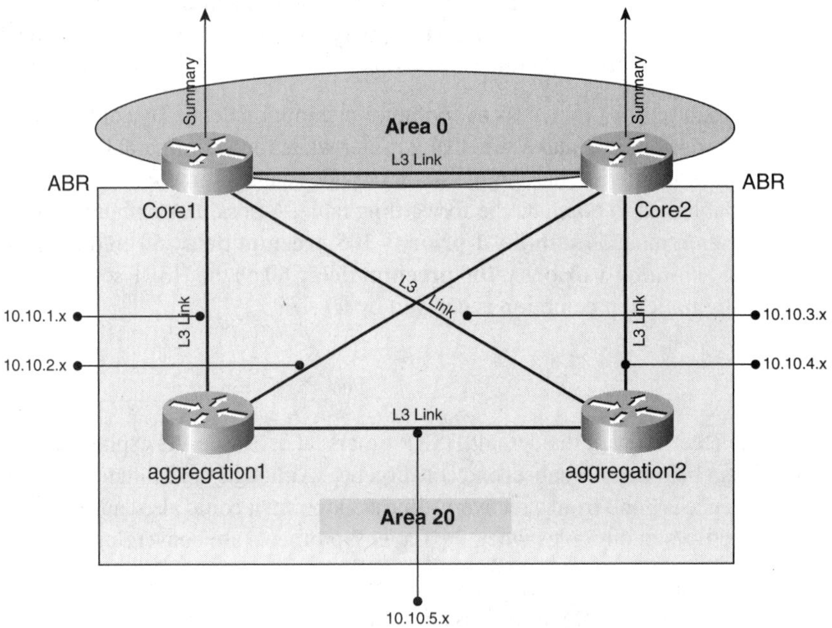

The following list describes the design:

- The core routers belong to area 0, and they are also the ABRs for the area 20, the Data Center area.
- The Data Center belongs to a separate area (area 20); this area can be a totally stubby area, a stub area, or a not-so-stubby area (NSSA).
- Connections to the core are Layer 3 links.
- If possible, the routing devices in the Data Center receive a default route pointing to the core—which is the result of configuring a totally stubby area, a stub area, or an NSSA. When configuring an NSSA, you also need to use the command **area** *area-id* **nssa default-information originate** to generate the default.
- Summarization occurs from the Data Center to the core, which you achieve using the **area** *area-id* **range** *network mask* command.
- Inside the Data Center, the **network** statements in the **router ospf** configuration match all the necessary subnets, and the **passive-interface** command reduces the number of neighbors that each aggregation router needs to maintain. It is recommended to keep Layer 3 connectivity between the aggregation routers either with one SVI (which should not be passive) or with a Layer 3 link.

The next sections explain these design choices.

Area Assignment and Summarization

Two key features allow OSPF to scale well, and you should use them when designing the Data Center:

- Stub areas
- Summarization

Flooding link-state advertisements (LSAs) in the AS can generate a significant amount of traffic for the routers to handle. Additionally, failures in one area can generate LSA flooding in many other areas, which in turn triggers new shortest path first algorithm (SPF) calculations.

If you have a flapping link in the Data Center, you must avoid flooding LSAs into all the other areas. Similarly, you do not want the routers in the Data Center to be affected by a flapping link from another area.

The solution to the first problem is to configure summarization. *Summarization* prevents the propagation of unnecessary LSAs. The placement of an OSPF area needs to take into account where you want to summarize routes because summarization in OSPF can only happen at the area boundaries.

OSPF can perform summarization at two levels:

- **Interarea routes**—By using the command **area** *area-id* **range** *network mask* on the ABR
- **External routes**—By using the command s**ummary-address** *network mask* on the AS boundary router (ASBR) or **summary address** *network mask* **not-advertise** on the ABR

The result of summarization is that when a failure occurs which affects only one of the subnets that the ABR summarizes, the ABR does not generate a Type-3 LSA for such a failure.

The solution to the second problem is to assign the Data Center to an area as stub as it is allowed by the routing requirements: a failure in an area other than the Data Center would not cause an SPF calculation if the Data Center was a totally stubby area because a totally stubby area does not receive LSA Type 3.

Stub Areas

The configuration of the Data Center as a stub area limits the impact of failures in the campus network on the Data Center routers.

An NSSA limits the scope of LSA flooding and gives you the possibility of redistributing static routes (which is often useful when dealing with load balancers and firewalls and of course at the Internet edge for routing to the Internet).

By default, NSSA ABRs do not generate a summary default as do stub and totally stubby areas. You can configure the ABRs to inject a default route into the Data Center area by using the command **area** *area-id* **nssa** *network mask*.

If the aggregation routers need to redistribute static routes (**redistribute static subnets**), these routers become ASBRs, and they generate Type-7 LSAs. The ABRs then turn the LSAs into Type-5 LSAs before injecting them into area 0.

Advertising the Local Subnets

You have two choices in including the local subnets in OSPF:

- Using the **network** command in router configuration mode
- Using the **redistribute connected** command in router configuration mode

The **network** command is preferred because the **redistribute connected** command introduces external routes.

When you use the **network** command, the aggregation routers become neighbors on every subnet defined in the configuration. If there are few VLANs, this occurrence is not a problem, but as the number of VLAN grows, it can consume RP CPU time without providing any benefit. Figure 20-22 shows why.

Figure 20-22 *Router Neighbors on Too Many VLANs*

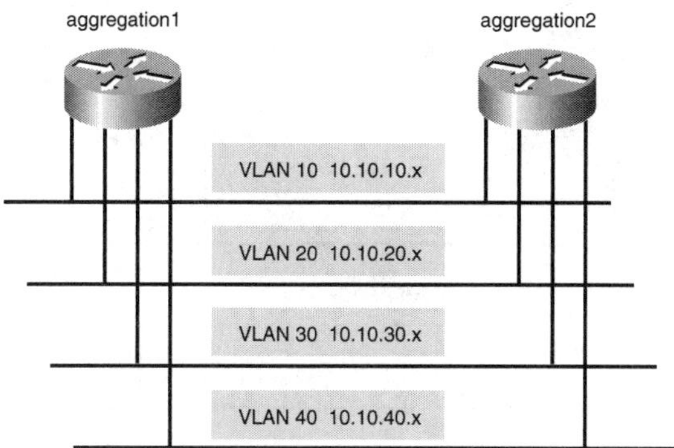

In Figure 20-22, you see the logical representation of the RP of a Layer 3 switch connected to VLANs 10, 20, 30, and 40 via SVIs. Configuring the aggregation routers with **network 10.10.10.x**, **network 10.10.20.x**, **network 10.10.30.x**, and **network 10.10.40.x** means that aggregation1 and aggregation2 see each other as four neighbors: it is too much redundancy.

You can prevent the routers from becoming neighbors on a VLAN by using the command **passive-interface**. In router mode configuration, you can configure **passive-interface vlan10**, **passive-interface vlan20**, **passive-interface vlan30**, and **passive-interface vlan40**.

When you make SVIs passive, you need to be make sure to preserve at least one SVI, or you have a Layer 3 interface on which the aggregation routers are neighbors. Figure 20-23 clarifies the concept.

Assume for the purpose of the example that aggregation1 and aggregation2 are the ABRs. As such, they summarize the Data Center subnets into 10.10.x.x.

All the SVIs in the topology are passive. Imagine that aggregation1 loses connectivity on VLAN 10 (10.10.10.x). Still, aggregation1 and aggregation2 advertise the summarized subnet 10.10.x.x. Aggregation2 can still receive traffic from the core destined to 10.10.10.x. Aggregation1 needs to route this traffic to aggregation2.

This setup is not possible because aggregation1 and aggregation2 are not neighbors any more because all the SVIs are passive. For this topology to work, you need to "unpassive" one SVI, such as interface VLAN 20. Another possibility consists of adding a Layer 3 link between the aggregation switches, which would be included in the **network** configuration.

Figure 20-23 *ABR Router Neighbors on No VLANs*

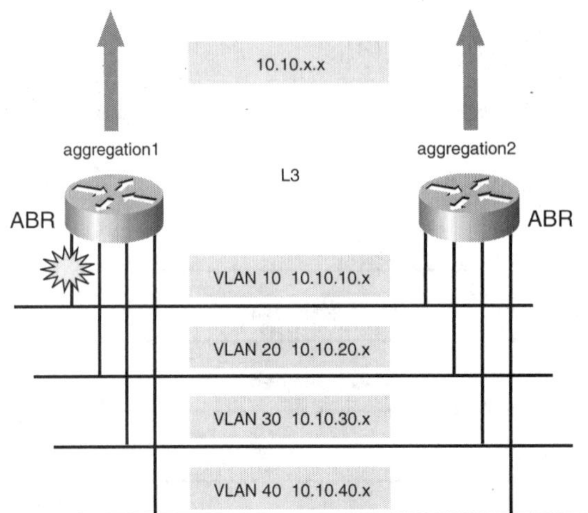

OSPF Metric Tuning

As described in Chapter 13, OSPF calculates the cost of the links by dividing a reference bandwidth by the bandwidth of the link. By default, the reference bandwidth is 100 Mbps.

In Data Center environments, there are typically Gigabit Ethernet links and even 10 Gigabit Ethernet links. To address this problem, you can change the reference bandwidth to 10 Gbps with the **auto-cost reference-bandwidth 10000** command. You should use this change consistently in the OSPF network.

Convergence Time

When you use OSPF, the convergence time for link or router failures is given by the time required to do the following:

- Detect the failure. The detection of a Layer 3 link failure is very quick; the detection of a failure on a VLAN can take longer (40 sec).
- Propagate the LSA.
- Wait before the SPF calculation. Having received the LSAs, a router calculates the SPF after a delay of 5 sec (a timer that you can configure with **timers spf** *spf-delay spf-holdtime*).

- Run the SPF algorithm. This time is the time it takes for the CPU to run the algorithm, which depends on the size of the area, typically a few hundred milliseconds.
- Update the routing table.

A number of other factors influence the convergence time in OSPF, as you can see in Example 20-12. Here you can read the default value for the SPF schedule delay (5 sec), the hold time between two SPF calculations (10 sec), and the rate at which LSAs can be sent (5 sec) and received (1 sec).

Example 20-12 *OSPF Timers*

```
Router#show ip ospf
 Routing Process "ospf 20" with ID 4.4.4.4
 Supports only single TOS(TOS0) routes
 Supports opaque LSA
 It is an area border and autonomous system boundary router
 Redistributing External Routes from,
 SPF schedule delay 5 secs, Hold time between two SPFs 10 secs
 Minimum LSA interval 5 secs. Minimum LSA arrival 1 secs
 Number of external LSA 0. Checksum Sum 0x000000
 Number of opaque AS LSA 0. Checksum Sum 0x000000
 Number of DCbitless external and opaque AS LSA 0
 Number of DoNotAge external and opaque AS LSA 0
 Number of areas in this router is 2. 1 normal 0 stub 1 nssa
```

With the default timers, the convergence time for failures in the Data Center network for a Layer 3 link failure can be around a few seconds (5 or 6 sec).

TIP You can bring down the convergence time to a couple of seconds by using the command **timers spf 1 5**. As always, when changing the default settings, take care to assess whether they are appropriate for your specific Data Center environment.

OSPF Configuration Summary

Examples 20-13 and 20-14 provide a summary of the configurations described in this section, assuming that the core routers provide the ABR function:

- Both aggregation and core routers use the reference-bandwidth 10000.
- Area 20 is defined as NSSA.
- The core routers inject the default into area 20.
- The aggregation routers use the SPF timers of 1 sec for the delay and 5 sec for the holddown.

- The aggregation routers are configured with VLAN 10, VLAN 20, VLAN 30, and VLAN 40 as passive SVIs.
- The core routers summarize the Data Center subnets into 10.10.x.x.

Example 20-13 *Aggregation Switch Configurations*

```
router ospf 20
 log-adjacency-changes
 auto-cost reference-bandwidth 10000
 area 20 nssa
 timers spf 1 5
 passive-interface Vlan10
 passive-interface Vlan20
 passive-interface Vlan30
 passive-interface Vlan40
 network 10.10.0.0 0.0.255.255 area 20
```

Example 20-14 shows the configuration of the core routers.

Example 20-14 *Core Router Configuration*

```
router ospf 20
 log-adjacency-changes
 auto-cost reference-bandwidth 10000
 area 20 nssa default-information originate
 area 20 range 10.10.0.0 255.255.0.0
 network 172.16.0.0 0.0.255.255 area 0
 network 10.10.0.0 0.0.255.255 area 20
```

Using EIGRP in Data Center Design

Before configuring EIGRP in the Data Center, you should be familiar with the concepts and features described in Chapter 13.

EIGRP converges faster than other distance-vector protocols, thanks to Diffusing Update Algorithm (DUAL). DUAL uses a query-reply mechanism between routers to find alternate routes to a destination.

The goal of the EIGRP design is to maximize the stability of the routers in the Data Center and contain the scope of the EIGRP queries.

EIGRP Topology

Figure 20-24 shows an example of an EIGRP configuration in the Data Center.

Figure 20-24 *EIGRP Routing in the Data Center*

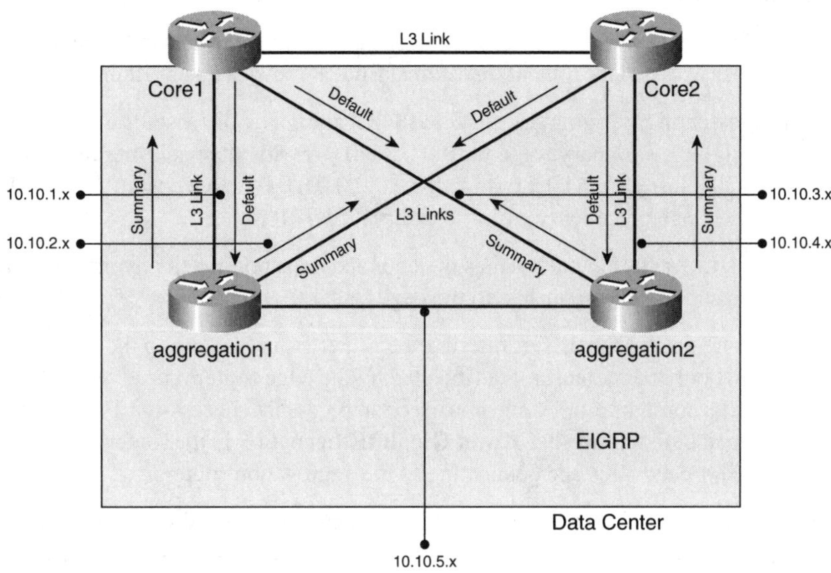

The following list describes the design:

- Connections between the aggregation routers and the core are Layer 3 links.
- The core routers advertise default routes to the Data Center by using distribute lists.
- Summarization is configured per-interface from the Data Center to the core and uses the **ip summary-address eigrp** command.
- Inside the Data Center, the **network** statements in the **router eigrp** configuration match all the necessary subnets, and the **passive-interface** command reduces the number of neighbors that each aggregation router needs to maintain. It is recommended to keep Layer 3 connectivity between the aggregation routers either with one SVI (which should not be passive) or with a Layer 3 link. Read the section, "Advertising the Local Subnets" under "Using OSPF in Data Center Design" for more information. The same concepts apply to EIGRP.

Default Routes

The core routers can advertise default routes to the Data Center in two ways:

- By using the **ip summary-address eigrp** *asnumber address mask* per-interface
- By using the command **distribute-list** *access-list-number* **in/out** *interface*

If you use the first option, it is important to configure an administrative cost of 200 for the default route that the core advertises to the Data Center.

The reason derives from the need to honor the default route advertised by the edge routers for Internet access. This route is an external EIGRP route (with an administrative cost of 170).

When you configure summary routes, EIGRP automatically installs a NULL0 route. So if you configure a summary route for 0.0.0.0 0.0.0.0 without specifying the administrative cost, EIGRP installs a NULL0 route for 0.0.0.0 0.0.0.0 with a cost of 5. The NULL0 route would then take precedence over the external EIGRP route.

As a result, any traffic that reaches the core and does not match any route would be black-holed instead of getting pushed to the edge routers.

The second option consists of filtering the routes from the core to the Data Center in such a way that only the default route (injected by the edge routers) is advertised to the Data Center. The configuration would consist of an access list, **access-list 10 permit 0.0.0.0**, and the command **distribute-list 10 out GigabitEthernet4/7** in the router configuration mode, repeated for each interface connecting to the aggregation routers.

Both options are valid, with the second one being preferred. With the first configuration, a router that has just been powered up would immediately advertise the default even without having a complete routing table.

With the second configuration, the router needs the routing information to reach the edge routers before advertising the default.

Summarization

Summarization is fundamental to EIGRP scalability because it limits the scope of EIGRP queries. When you summarization, if a topology change occurs in the Data Center, the query reaches the core routers. The core routers do not know anything about subnets more specific than the summarized route, which causes the query to stop. The core routers would then report an infinite metric in the reply, thus accelerating the diffused DUAL computation.

You configure summarization from the aggregation routers to the core routers per-interface with the command **ip summary-address eigrp** *asnumber address mask*.

EIGRP Configuration Summary

Examples 20-15 and 20-16 provide a summary of the configurations described in this section. You can see the use of the **network** command and the **passive-interface** command in the aggregation router configuration. You can also see the configuration of summarization under the interface GigabitEthernet4/7. The configuration of the core router shows the use of distribute lists to advertise the default to the Data Center.

Example 20-15 *Aggregation Router EIGRP Configuration*

```
router eigrp 20
 network 10.10.0.0 0.0.255.255
 passive-interface Vlan10
 passive-interface Vlan20
 passive-interface Vlan30
 passive-interface Vlan40
 no auto-summary
 no eigrp log-neighbor-changes
!
interface GigabitEthernet4/7
 description to_core1_
 ip address 10.10.1.1 255.255.255.252
 ip summary-address eigrp 20 10.10.0.0 255.255.0.0 5
end
```

Example 20-16 *EIGRP Core Router Configuration*

```
router eigrp 20
 network 10.10.0.0 0.0.0.255
 network 172.16.0.0 0.0.255.255
 distribute-list 10 out GigabitEthernet4/7
 no auto-summary
 no eigrp log-neighbor-changes
!
interface GigabitEthernet4/7
 description to_aggregation1
 ip address 10.10.1.2 255.255.255.252
end
!
access-list 10 permit 0.0.0.0
```

NOTE For more information about the use of EIGRP in a Gigabit campus design, refer to http://www.cisco.com/warp/public/cc/so/neso/lnso/cpso/camp_wp.pdf.

Layer 3 Configuration Summary

This section summarizes the key Layer 3 design recommendations explained in this chapter.

Figure 20-25 displays the topology.

Figure 20-25 *Data Center Design: Layer 3*

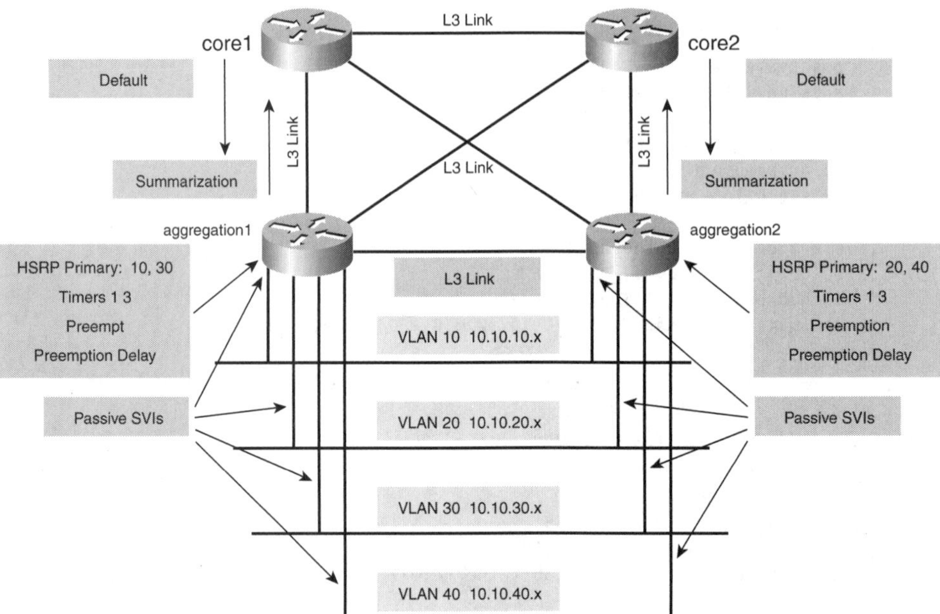

The core routers are connected with the aggregation routers (where aggregation routers are the RPs in the aggregation switches) with Layer 3 links. The key design goal with the routing protocols is to advertise a default from the core routers to the aggregation routers and summarized routes from the Data Center to the core network.

The default gateway function is provided by HSRP, VRRP, or GLBP. You assign the priorities to match the Layer 2 topology for optimized traffic forwarding. Use preemption and the preemption delay feature. You configure the HSRP timers to detect a failure in few seconds.

You configure dynamic routing according to the sections "Using OSPF in Data Center Design" and "Using EIGRP in Data Center Design." The router configuration has passive SVIs on VLANs 10, 20, 30, and 40. Layer 3 links between the aggregation routers ensure that the aggregation routers are neighbors.

Summary

This chapter provides information on how to design the Data Center from a Layer 2 and Layer 3 perspective. The building blocks of the Data Center are Layer 3 switches. Layer 3 switches provide high-performance Layer 3 forwarding and allow virtualizing the physical infrastructure with the use of VLANs and SVIs.

You can design today's Data Centers to converge in few seconds. Layer 2 features such as IEEE 802.1w, tuning the gateway redundancy protocols, and IGP provide fast convergence in the Data Center.

IEEE 802.1w combined with PVST+ (called Rapid PVST+) provides flexibility for integration with transparent firewalls or load balancers, whereas IEEE 802.1w combined with IEEE 802.1s provides scalability for Data Centers with thousands of VLANs.

Proper Layer 2 configuration with features such as PortFast and TrunkFast limits the number of topology recalculations at Layer 2. Similarly, Layer 3 configurations with summarization and default routes limit the number of topology recalculations at Layer 3.

You can add internal redundancy with features such as IOS SSO/NSF and CatOS high availability to external redundancy for additional router and switch availability.

This chapter covers the following topics:

- The definition of the different security zones around the topology of the Data Center
- Security designs pertaining to the Internet Edge, including antispoofing filtering, Unicast Reverse Path Forwarding (uRPF), traffic rate limiting, routing protocol security, stateful firewalling, and intrusion detection
- Core security, including device hardening and routing protocol security
- Aggregation layer security using stateful firewalls, packet filters, and network-based intrusion detection systems (IDSs)
- Server farm security deploying host-based and network-based intrusion detection, private VLANs, port security, VLAN access control lists (ACLs), and stateful firewalls
- Implementation of a secure management infrastructure based on isolating the management infrastructure, using strong encryption and authentication, and deploying host-based and network-based intrusion detection

CHAPTER 21

Integrating Security into the Infrastructure

This chapter assumes the existence of a security policy, and it primarily focuses on the design phase of the security cycle. The design focuses on explaining how you can systematically deploy the security technologies described in Chapter 5, "Data Center Security Overview," and Chapter 15, "Security Protocols and Technologies," to reduce risk to acceptable levels for your organization.

The design approach proposed in this chapter follows the security-zone strategy, in which distinct portions of a Data Center are divided by their functions. You analyze each zone individually and secure it according to its unique requirements.

For information about the deployment of a public-key infrastructure (PKI) and security design considerations when deploying Secure Socket Layer (SSL) offloading, refer to Chapter 15.

Defining Security Zones

Selecting the security technologies and products to use in a design cannot start without the prior identification of the critical assets they are supposed to protect. Following is the recommended procedure:

1. Identify the critical elements, such as mission-critical applications, servers, and network resources.
2. Group these elements in security zones based on functional areas that might have specific security requirements.
3. Secure each security zone individually, yet approach the design considering the interaction between different security zones.
4. Analyze how the complete security design would work as a whole.

A *security zone* is a group of computing resources under a common administration and similar security needs. All the entities under a security zone have similar security requirements; therefore, you can apply some of the security controls to the group as a whole rather than to individual systems. This modular approach helps keep the design simple and consistent, which directly translates into a more effective architecture.

The number and nature of the security zones vary depending on the uniqueness of each design; however, some typical network areas that appear in almost every Data Center could be selected as security zones. For example, web servers can be grouped in one zone given their functional similarities, and the routers connecting to the Internet can be part of another different security zone.

NOTE The concept of security zones is intended to provide a structured approach to security designs. In practice, you can use other valid zone definitions for design purposes that are different from the ones proposed in this chapter. You might define these other zones around applications instead of network areas. In this case, you can define multiple zone instances to map specific applications that are supported by servers at different tiers (web, application, and database).

Figure 21-1 shows a typical Data Center and the security zones based on network functions. This design and its zones serve as the reference model throughout the chapter.

Figure 21-1 *A Typical Data Center Design*

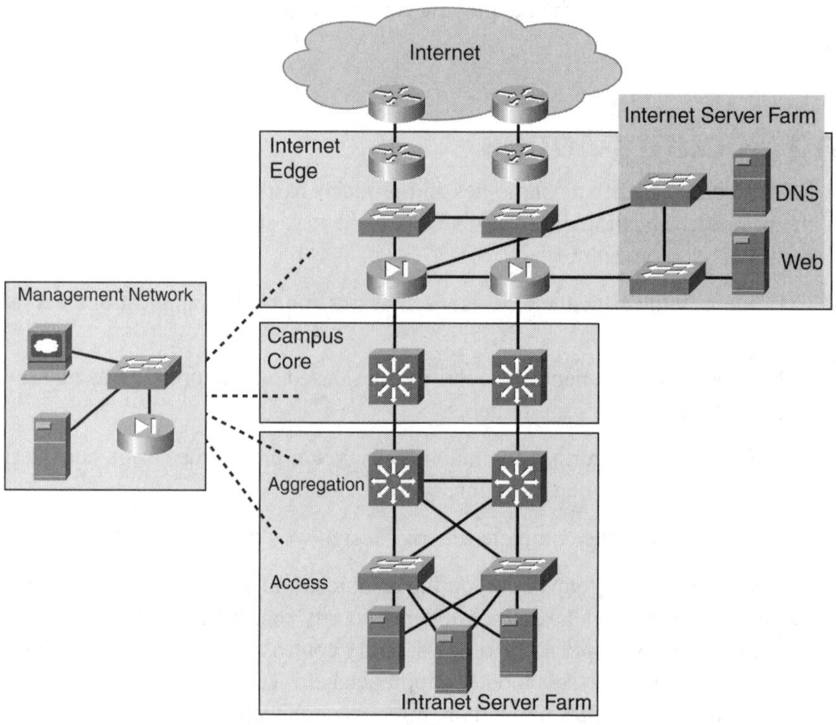

The security zones are as follows:

- **Internet Edge**—Provides connectivity to the Internet, which includes the routing and security functions at the edge of the enterprise. The Internet Edge includes the Internet server farm, which provides connectivity to servers that support Internet-based services (i.e. external website), and infrastructure services such as Domain Name System (DNS).
- **Campus core**—Provides connectivity between the enterprise's major network areas, such as the Data Center, the campus network, and the WAN. Its functions include both high-speed switching between network areas and the core routing functions to maintain a map of the overall network.
- **Intranet server farm**—Provides connectivity to internal servers (web servers and application servers) and the traditional Layer 2 or access layer functions, and it houses the servers that support the enterprise's internal applications. The intranet server farm infrastructure includes the aggregation switches that provide the aggregation point for Data Center services, such as load balancing, SSL offloaders, firewalls, and IDSs, in addition to the traditional distribution layer functions. The aggregation switches connect to the campus core.
- **Management network**—Provides management and monitoring for the resources in the Data Center.

Having selected the different security zones that compartmentalize the Data Center, you can start a systematic process to secure them individually while making sure the overall design integrates well. This approach lets you focus on each zone in detail, determine the critical elements and the possible internal and external threats that pose a risk to them, and identify the technologies and security mechanisms that you can put into place to achieve an adequate level of security. Once you properly secure each individual zone, you must analyze the complete design as a whole to identify any areas that could still be open to exploits.

One fundamental concept in security designs is the use of the same or similar security technologies at different network locations. In other areas of network design, this coverage can be seen as undesirable overlapping, but in security, it is a common practice for building multiple lines of defense. For example, you can use a router with ACLs and a stateful firewall, providing two distinct security barriers. If the first line of defense is compromised, an intruder would still have another line of defense to penetrate.

Figure 21-2 shows a two-layer firewall design that combines a packet-filtering firewall (a router with ACLs) with a stateful firewall.

Figure 21-2 *Complementary Use of Security Technologies*

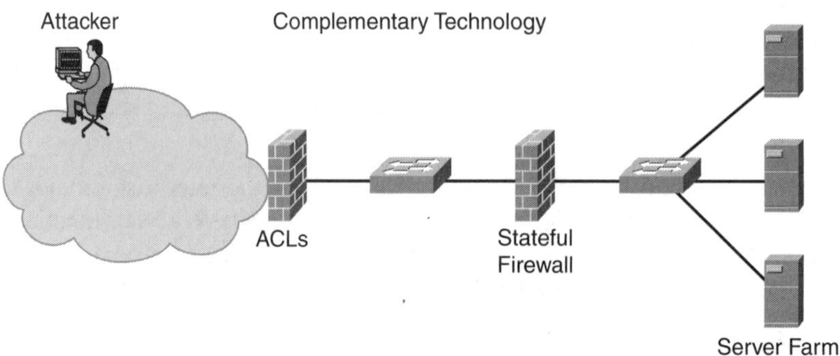

Another security design best practice is the tiered approach to the use of ACLs. Under this approach, you use ACLs as a packet-filtering mechanism at different levels:

- Internet Edge routers
- Campus core switches
- Aggregation layer firewalls

These ACLs get more granular as they are closer to the critical systems they are designed to protect.

The first tier of ACLs protects from spoofing attacks; you typically apply this tier at the Internet Edge. A second tier of ACLs limits the access to the network only for valid application types, such as port 80 for web services or port 53 for DNS services, without specifying the exact IP address of the servers for the Internet Edge firewalls. Finally, a third tier of ACLs provides the most granular control based on the definition of the exact systems and protocols that are configured at the aggregation layer firewalls.

NOTE In Chapter 7, "IP, TCP, and UDP," a discussion on firewall configuration preventing Path Discovery maximum transmission unit (PDMTU) indicated that the best practice should include a number of filters (ACLs) specifically allowing Internet Control Message Protocol (ICMP) traffic to go through the firewalls. The following ACLs are common in the configuration in this chapter and are designed to address reachability issues:

```
firewall(config)# access-list 100 permit icmp any any echo
firewall(config)# access-list 100 permit icmp any any echo-reply
firewall(config)# access-list 100 permit icmp any any time-exceeded
firewall(config)# access-list 100 permit icmp any any unreachable
```

How explicit the ACLs are depends on the requirements and restrictions of your network. Typically, you only need reachability to the publicly advertised addresses, not the internal network numbers, so allowing traffic related to these ICMP ACLs should not pose a security threat. Also, remember that PMTUD is initiated by the host, which means that you should apply the ACLs consistently on all the firewalls in the path to the likely destination.

The following sections discuss the integration of security based on the previously defined security zones.

Internet Edge

The Internet Edge is the portion of the network infrastructure that connects the enterprise to the Internet. As such, the Internet Edge is the gate used by external users to access the public services offered by the enterprise and by internal users to reach the Internet services. As a primary entry point to the enterprise, the Internet Edge must be the first line of defense against external attacks and malicious activity such as distributed denial-of-service (DDoS) attacks and scanning activity.

The Internet Edge is where you should implement filtering to allow only legitimate traffic to go through and to keep all undesirable traffic out.

This section recommends the use of different types of filters at the Internet edge. These filters are designed to allow only the traffic destined to the public services provided by the Internet server farm in the Data Center and to also control the rate of traffic to mitigate the effect of DDoS attacks.

Network-based intrusion detection can monitor any attack attempts and general scanning activity. This detection helps you identify malicious activities so that you can take the proper measures before an actual intrusion takes place. For example, if the IDS detects some recognizance activity on web servers, an action response is triggered. The action response is to block the port associated with the recognizance activity, to ensure that the latest patches are applied to the servers, and to determine that no additional processes are unnecessarily running on the servers.

The Internet Edge security design should also include the necessary mechanisms to protect the exchange of routing information between the enterprise and the Internet service provider (ISP) by using route authentication.

You can provide security at the Internet Edge using the following methods:

- Deploying antispoofing filtering to prevent DoS attacks by limiting IP spoofing
- Using uRPF, also to prevent DoS attacks by limiting IP spoofing
- Implementing traffic rate limiting to reduce the effect of DoS and DDoS attacks
- Securing routing protocols to avoid trust exploitation and routing disruptions
- Deploying stateful firewalls to prevent unauthorized access
- Implementing intrusion detection to detect network reconnaissance activities and to identify threats and intruders

Deploying Antispoofing Filtering

Antispoofing filtering consists of defining ACLs that help mitigate source-address spoofing attacks from outside the enterprise or from inside the enterprise against external networks. This definition implies that antispoofing filtering has two key purposes:

- The enterprise should never receive packets whose source IP addresses correspond to the enterprise's public address space or the private address space (RFC 1918). They are invalid packets that could make the attacker look like an internal or trusted system.
- Packets originating from the enterprise should always carry source IP addresses from the enterprise's public address space. Other packets should be blocked because they are invalid and are likely the result of a spoofing attack either initiated or perceived to be coming from inside the enterprise network.

You can successfully implement antispoofing by combining filtering techniques such as filtering RFC 1918 addresses and the filtering techniques discussed in RFC 2827.

NOTE In this book, RFC 1918 filtering refers to the filtering of RFC 1918 addresses, and RFC 2827 filtering refers to the filtering techniques described in RFC 2827.

These filtering techniques are explained as follows:

- **RFC 1918 filtering**—RFC 1918 defines a private space of Internet nonroutable IP addresses to be used internally by organizations. RFC 1918 filtering makes sure that no packets using source IP addresses from the private address space are sent to or received from the Internet. This type of filtering is typically implemented at the ingress point on the Internet Edge router on ISP edge routers.

- **RFC 2827 filtering**—This filtering is typically deployed at the Internet Edge routers and ISP routers and prevents spoofing from being conducted against the enterprise public address space as well as from being initiated from inside the enterprise network. RFC 2827 filtering prevents the spoofing of the enterprise address space by blocking incoming packets with source IP addresses belonging to the public address space reserved for the enterprise's public services. On the other hand, RFC 2827 filtering prevents source-address spoofing from being initiated from inside the network by ensuring that only packets with legitimate source IP addresses leave the enterprise. Legitimate addresses under this context refer to the IP address blocks publicly assigned to the server-farm services.

Figure 21-3 illustrates the use of RFC 1918 and RFC 2827 filtering at the Internet Edge. In this figure, 192.0.2.0/24 is the IP address block publicly assigned to the enterprise public services. The ISP router is configured for ingress RFC 2827 filtering. This practice is common among service providers to ensure that their customers forward only packets with the source IP addresses assigned to them. The ISP router configuration is presented in Example 21-1. It applies the access-list 101 as an ingress filter, allowing only traffic coming from 192.0.2.0/24.

Figure 21-3 *RFC 1918 and RFC 2827 Filtering*

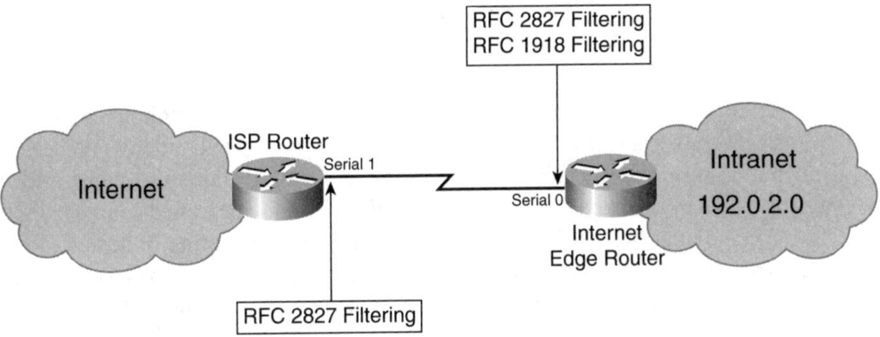

Example 21-1 *RFC 2827 Filtering at an ISP Router*

```
interface Serial 1
  ip access-group 101 in
!
access-list 101 permit ip 192.0.2.0  0.0.0.255 any
access-list 101 deny ip any any
```

The Internet Edge router in Figure 21-3 is configured according to the configuration in Example 21-2. The Internet-facing interface is configured with both ingress and egress filters. Access-list 130 is an egress RFC 2827 filter that allows only outgoing traffic with legitimate IP addresses (in this case, within 192.0.2.0/24). Access-list 120 is an ingress filter that combines RFC 1918 and RFC 2827 filtering to deny incoming packets with a source IP belonging to the enterprise network or the private address space. No legitimate external client would be using either IP address space.

Example 21-2 *Combined RFC 2827 and RFC 1918 Filtering at the Internet Edge Router*

```
interface Serial 0
  ip access-group 120 in
  ip access-group 130 out
!
access-list 120 deny ip 192.0.2.0  0.0.0.255 any
access-list 120 deny ip 10.0.0.0 0.255.255.255 any
access-list 120 deny ip 192.168.0.0 0.0.255.255 any
access-list 120 deny ip 172.16.0.0 0.15.255.255 any
access-list 120 permit ip any any
!
access-list 130 permit 192.0.2.0  0.0.255.255 any
access-list 130 deny ip any any
```

Using uRPF

Routers forward packets based on the destination IP addresses without checking other information, such as the source IP address of the packet or the IP address of the device from which the packet was received. This process facilitates IP address spoofing. uRPF is a feature designed to check packets to ensure that they are coming from the intended sources and the expected interfaces, helping mitigate source-address spoofing. When uRPF is enabled, each packet is checked not only for its destination IP address but also for the routing table of the source IP addresses. The check consists of verifying that there is a routing-table entry with the destination to the source IP address of the packet and that the route is associated with the interface the packet came from. You can deploy this feature instead of the traditional RFC 2827 filters at the ISP and the Internet Edge routers for antispoofing. Using uRPF simplifies the configuration because you do not have to define ACLs.

NOTE uRPF is based on Cisco Express Forwarding (CEF), and it was originally introduced in Cisco IOS software Release 11.1(17)CC. For current platform and IOS version support, use the Cisco navigator tool available at http://www.cisco.com/go/fn.

Figure 21-4 shows the same scenario as Figure 21-3 but using uRPF for antispoofing filtering.

Figure 21-4 *Antispoofing Filtering with uRPF*

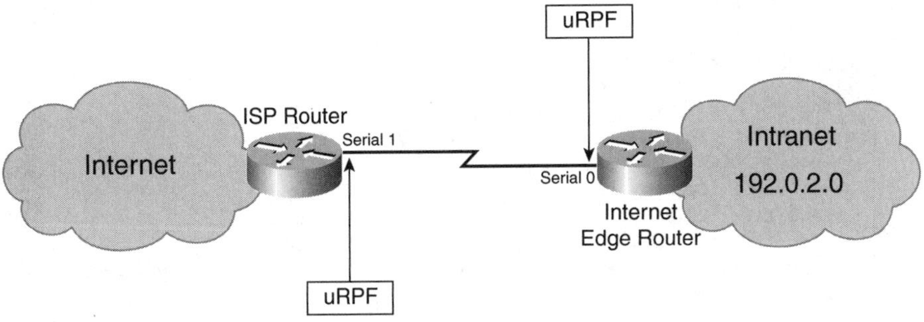

Example 21-3 shows uRPF enabled on the customer ingress interface of the ISP router.

Example 21-3 *uRPF on the ISP Router*

```
interface Serial 1
 description HDLC Link to DataCenter Customer XYZ
 ip verify unicast reverse-path
!
```

Example 21-4 shows uRPF enabled on the Internet-facing interface of the edge router.

Example 21-4 *uRPF on the Internet Edge Router*

```
interface Serial 0
 description HDLC Upstream Link to Internet
 ip verify unicast reverse-path
!
```

Using ACLs

You can configure the Internet Edge routers with ACLs to allow only access to and from the public services provided by the enterprise. You do this configuration only at the TCP or UDP level, without defining the IP addresses of the servers providing the services. You use more granular filters downstream. Example 21-5 shows the filters deployed on the Internet edge routers. This example applies filters to the Internet-facing interface, and in addition to implementing antispoofing, these filters permit the typical services used in a Data Center, such as DNS, HTTP, Simple Mail Transfer Protocol (SMTP), ICMP, and Network Time Protocol (NTP).

Example 21-5 *Internet Edge Filters*

```
interface Serial 0
  ip access-group 120 in
  ip access-group 130 out
!
! Ingress ACL - RFC 2827 Filtering
access-list 120 deny ip 192.0.2.0  0.0.0.255 any
! Ingress ACL - RFC 1918 Filtering
access-list 120 deny ip 10.0.0.0 0.255.255.255 any
access-list 120 deny ip 192.168.0.0 0.0.255.255 any
access-list 120 deny ip 172.16.0.0 0.15.255.255 any
! Ingress ACL - Allowed Basic Services
access-list 120 permit icmp any any
access-list 120 permit tcp any any established
access-list 120 permit tcp any any eq www
access-list 120 permit tcp any any eq smtp
access-list 120 permit udp any any eq domain
access-list 120 permit tcp any any eq domain
access-list 120 permit udp any any eq ntp
access-list 120 permit udp any any gt 1023
!
! Egress ACL - RFC 2827 Filtering
access-list 130 permit 192.0.2.0  0.0.255.255 any
access-list 130 deny ip any any
```

Implementing Traffic Rate Limiting

Traffic rate limiting consists of implementing queuing mechanisms that control the volume of traffic forwarded through a router. The traffic is usually classified based on protocol, source and destination IP address, and port numbers. Each defined traffic type is assigned a threshold, after which packets are processed at a lower priority or are simply discarded.

You can use traffic rate limiting to reduce the effects of DoS attacks and their large volumes of data by making sure that a single traffic type does not take all the bandwidth and resources available. During this type of DoS attack, the target system typically experiences an unusual volume of packets that follow a particular pattern. For example, during a SYN flood, the system under attack experiences an abnormal volume of SYN requests. Rate limiting allows you to define beforehand the thresholds after which traffic is considered abnormal, and once those thresholds are reached, packets of that type are dropped or processed at a lower priority, depending on the configuration. This process ensures that even in a DoS attack, the victim system continues working while maintaining bandwidth for other applications based on different packet types.

One drawback of implementing traffic limiting is that the mechanism is based on fixed thresholds, and many times, traffic patterns vary because of normal use and not because of a DoS attack. Another limitation of rate limiting is that legitimate packets often cannot be distinguished from DoS packets, so when the rate limiting starts, some DoS packets are likely to be forwarded while other valid packets are dropped.

Committed Access Rate (CAR) limiting and traffic shaping are IOS features on routers that provide these capabilities.

Example 21-6 shows a rate-limiting configuration that helps control the effects of DoS attacks such as TCP SYN floods against subnet 192.0.2.0. In this example, new connections are only rate-limited, but already established connections are allowed to flow normally. The **rate–limit** command tells the router to drop TCP SYNs exceeding the rate of 64 Kbps.

The value of the maximum rate depends on the amount of traffic received by the network under normal conditions and on the bandwidth of the connections to the service provider.

Example 21-6 *CAR Limiting*

```
! Limit inbound TCP SYN packets to 64 Kbps
interface serial0/0
      rate-limit input access-group 103 64000  8000 8000
      conform-action transmit exceed-action drop
!
access-list 103 deny tcp any 192.0.2.0 0.0.255.255 established
access-list 103 permit tcp any host 192.0.2.0 0.0.255.255
```

Securing Routing Protocols

As previously explained, the Internet Edge supports routing between the enterprise and the Internet, which you do through dynamic routing protocols or static routing. When you use dynamic routing, you implement Border Gateway Protocol (BGP) between the ISP and the Internet Edge routers, and you deploy an Interior Gateway Protocol (IGP) such as Open Shortest Path First (OSPF) or Enhanced Interior Gateway Routing Protocol (EIGRP) to propagate routing information to the interior of the enterprise network. The routers supporting these routing protocols can be the subject of attacks that compromise the overall stability of the routed network, consequently affecting the Data Center applications.

Some routing protocols do not provide any security mechanisms and are subject to disruption by the injection of illegitimate routing updates. Protocols such as BGP, OSPF, Intermediate System-to-Intermediate System (IS-IS), EIGRP, and Routing Information Protocol Version 2 (RIPv2) provide mechanisms to ensure that routing updates are valid and are received from legitimate routing peers. They achieve this goal by using route filters and neighbor router authentication.

Route Filters

Route filters are typically deployed at the ISP router to ensure that only the public networks assigned to the enterprise are externally advertised. This setup represents several benefits: the route filters protect the stability of the ISP network by blocking the injection of bogus routing information while also preventing the enterprise from being used as a transit area between different networks coming from multiple ISP connections.

The Internet Edge routers can also use route filters to allow only specific routes, including the default route. You might use them to control which outbound connection to the Internet is used when there are multiple connections to the Internet.

Neighbor Router Authentication

Internet Edge routers should use *neighbor router authentication* to ensure that routing updates are valid and are received only from legitimate peers. Neighbor router authentication, sometimes called route authentication, certifies the neighbors' authenticity and the integrity of routing updates. In some cases, you can also statically configure the neighbors to ensure that only peers with known IP addresses are able to exchange routing updates.

When you use route authentication, you initially configure the routers with a common secret key to validate each routing update. A sending router signs each update using the secret key. The update is verified by the receiver to probe its authenticity and integrity.

There are two ways that secret keys are used:

- Some implementations send the secret key in clear inside each update, which does not provide much security because keys can be intercepted while in transit.
- Other implementations use a keyed-hash function (i.e. Hashed Message Authentication Codes with Message Digest 5 [HMAC-MD5]) to generate a digest, which is sent along with the routing update. This method is more secure because the actual secret key is never sent over the network.

Most routing protocols are configurable in either manner.

Figure 21-5 shows how route authentication works using a hashing algorithm to provide route authenticity.

Figure 21-5 *Route Authentication with Hashing*

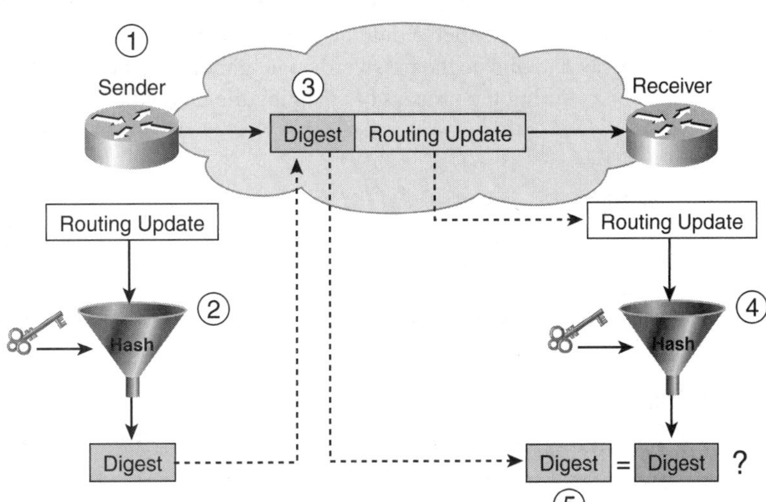

The transactions depicted in Figure 21-5 are as follows:

1 The routers are configured with a shared secret key that is used to sign and validate each routing update.

2 Every time a router has to send a routing update, the routing update is processed with a hash function that uses the secret key to produce a digest.

3 The resulting digest is appended to the routing update. In this way, the routing update message contains the actual routing update plus its corresponding digest. The routing update message contains the actual routing update plus its corresponding digest.

4 Once the message is sent, the receiving router processes the routing update with the same hash function and secret key.

5 The receiving router compares the result with the digest in the routing update message. A match means that the sender has signed the update using the same secret key and hashing algorithm and that the message has not changed while in transit.

Example 21-7 shows the configuration of OSPF MD5 authentication. Notice that the key configuration is per-interface and that you need to enter the same key on both routers.

TIP Also notice that the **ip ospf message-digest-key** command is followed by a key number. You use this number because there could be multiple keys per interface. This feature is useful when you need to update the password on neighboring routers, and you want to keep neighbor adjacency during the process of changing the passwords.

Example 21-7 *OSPF Authentication*

```
! OSPF MD5 authentication
interface Ethernet0
  ip address 192.0.2.1 255.255.255.0
  ip ospf message-digest-key 10 md5 mypassword
!
router ospf 10
  network 192.0.2.0 0.0.0.255 area 0
  area 0 authentication message-digest
```

Deploying Stateful Firewalls

In the recommended design, the Internet edge incorporates a layer of stateful firewalls as another line of defense against external attacks. The concept of stateful firewalls is introduced in Chapter 5. The use of stateful firewalls has two main goals, protecting the Internet server farm and controlling the traffic between the Internet and the rest of the enterprise network. Each goal requires a particular firewall configuration, presented as follows:

- The filters defined to protect the Internet server farm need to be precise, defining the exact protocols, ports, and IP addresses of the expected communication flows. Typically, this layer is the only line of firewalls protecting the Internet-facing servers, which explains why filters need to be as granular as possible. It is also important to note that you should apply filters for ingress traffic and egress traffic because you need to control egress traffic as well. Applying filters in both directions makes attacks more unlikely to succeed and helps prevent attackers from using a compromised server as the launch platform to compromise other systems. If they are available, you should also enable any DoS mitigation mechanisms in the firewall to protect servers.
- The firewall configuration used to protect the rest of the network is significantly different; filters at this level do not need to be very granular because other lines of protection are likely to be implemented downstream. These filters typically define the protocols and UDP/TCP ports expected, with rules based on networks rather than individual IP addresses.

Example 21-8 shows the configuration of a PIX Firewall deployed at the Internet edge. The demilitarized zone (DMZ) interface is the segment that corresponds to the Internet server farm, and the inside interface connects to the campus core. Note the difference on the filters.

The first portion of ACL 100 defines the exact protocols, ports, and IP address to protect the web server at the DMZ. The remaining portion of the ACL controls the traffic returning to the enterprise network, with more generic rules applied to the 192.0.2.0/24 network rather than individual systems. Also, note that this portion of the ACL only specifies ICMP. Traffic is expected only to be initiated from the inside out and not the other way around. As a stateful firewall, the PIX tracks the status of the TCP and UDP sessions, automatically letting the returning traffic flow in.

NOTE For more information on configuring **static** and **global** commands on the PIX Firewall, refer to Chapter 13, "Layer 3 Protocol Essentials."

Example 21-8 *Firewall Filters at the Internet Edge*

```
! Address Translation for Web Server at DMZ
firewall(config)# static (dmz,outside) 192.0.2.7 192.0.2.7
! Address Translation for internal clients going to the Internet
firewall(config)# global(outside) 1 192.0.2.10-192.0.2.200 netmask 255.255.255.0
firewall(config)# nat (inside) 1 172.16.1.0 255.255.255.0
! Ingress filter portion to Internet Server Farm
firewall(config)# access-list 100 permit tcp any host 192.0.2.7 eq www
firewall(config)# access-list 100 permit icmp any host 192.0.2.7 echo
firewall(config)# access-list 100 permit icmp any host 192.0.2.7 echo-reply
firewall(config)# access-list 100 permit icmp any host 192.0.2.7 time-exceeded
firewall(config)# access-list 100 permit icmp any host 192.0.2.7 unreachable
! Ingress filter portion to Enterprise network
firewall(config)# access-list 100 permit icmp any 192.0.2.0 255.255.255.0 echo
firewall(config)# access-list 100 permit icmp any 192.0.2.0 255.255.255.0 echo-
  reply
firewall(config)# access-list 100 permit icmp any 192.0.2.0 255.255.255.0 time-
  exceeded
firewall(config)# access-list 100 permit icmp any 192.0.2.0 255.255.255.0
  unreachable
firewall(config)# access-group 100 in interface outside
! Egress filter from Internet Server Farm
firewall(config)# access-list 101 permit udp host 192.0.2.7 any eq domain
firewall(config)# access-list 101 permit icmp host 192.0.2.7 any echo
firewall(config)# access-list 101 permit icmp host 192.0.2.7 any echo-reply
firewall(config)# access-list 101 permit icmp host 192.0.2.7 any time-exceeded
firewall(config)# access-list 101 permit icmp host 192.0.2.7 any unreachable
firewall(config)# access-group 101 in interface dmz
```

Implementing Intrusion Detection

Chapter 5 introduced IDSs. You should deploy both network-based and host-based IDSs in the Internet Edge. You use a network-based IDS to monitor the segment that connects the

ISP edge routers and the firewalls and in inside segments such as the DMZ to monitor activities on the intranet server farm. The outside segment works as a funnel that concentrates all traffic coming from the Internet, so a single IDS sensor connected here can sound the alarm on any attack attempts or recognizance from the Internet, even before an actual intrusion takes place. Another advantage of connecting a network sensor on that segment is that a single sensor can monitor all traffic even when there are multiple connections to the Internet.

You use a host-based IDS to prevent known vulnerabilities on hosts from being used for attacks. Host-based IDSs are obviously related to hosts that you can place in an Internet server farm for specific purposes, such as DNS, FTP, and SMTP servers, or for Internet application, such as e-commerce, which relies on web-based servers (HTTP).

When you deploy the network-based sensor in a switched infrastructure, you must use features such as switch port analyzer (SPAN) or capture to forward traffic to the monitoring interface of the IDS sensor. Example 21-9 shows how to use the SPAN feature on a Catalyst 6500 to forward traffic from VLAN 5 (the monitored VLAN) to the IDS sensor plugged into the port FastEthernet 2/1.

Example 21-9 *Using SPAN on a Catalyst 6500 with Intrusion Detection*

```
Router(config)# monitor session 1 source vlan 5
Router(config)# monitor session 1 destination interface Fa2/1
!
Router(config)# interface FastEthernet2/1
Router(config-if)#switchport
Router(config-if)#switchport mode access
```

Example 21-10 shows how you can use a VLAN ACL (VACL) on a Catalyst 6500 to capture traffic on VLAN 5 and how to send it to an IDS sensor on the port FastEthernet 2/1. Differently from the SPAN configuration, the VACL configuration lets you define which traffic type you want to monitor. In Example 21-9, **access-list 110** specifies that only traffic 80 should be matched, and in the **vlan access-map**, line 10 applies the capture only to this traffic.

The remaining traffic types (matched in access-list 120) are subject to regular forwarding (vlan access-map 120).

The switch forwards the HTTP traffic based on the destination IP address, but it also sends the traffic to the port FastEthernet 2/1 (because this port is configured as "switchport capture").

You can control the monitoring scope of the IDS sensor by using the VACL capture feature.

Example 21-10 *Using Catalyst 6500 VACL Capture with Intrusion Detection*

```
Router(config)# access-list 110 permit tcp any any eq 80
Router(config)# access-list 120 permit ip any any
!
Router(config)# vlan access-map idsfilter 10
```

Example 21-10 *Using Catalyst 6500 VACL Capture with Intrusion Detection (Continued)*

```
Router(config)# match ip address 110
Router(config)# action forward capture
Router(config)# vlan access-map idsfilter 20
Router(config)# match ip address 120
Router(config)# action forward
!
Router(config)# interface FastEthernet2/1
Router(config-if)#switchport capture
```

The signatures you use in the Internet Edge are those that protect the servers and applications likely found in the Internet Edge server farm. A list of common signatures to use includes the following:

- **DNS signatures**—Examples are 6050 - DNS HINFO Request, 6051 - DNS Zone Transfer, 6052 - DNS Zone Transfer from High Port, 6053 - DNS Request for All Records, 6054 - DNS Version Request, 6055 - DNS Inverse Query Buffer Overflow, and 6056 - DNS NXT Buffer Overflow.
- **HTTP signatures**—Examples are 5188 - HTTP Tunneling, 5055 - HTTP Basic Authentication Overflow, 3200 - WWW Phf Attack, 3202 - WWW .url File Requested, 3203 - WWW .lnk File Requested, 3204 - WWW .bat File Requested, 3212 - WWW NPH-TEST-CGI Attack, and 3213 - WWW TEST-CGI Attack.
- **FTP signatures**—Examples are 3150 - FTP Remote Command Execution, 3151 - FTP SYST Command Attempt, 3152 - FTP CWD ~root, 3153 - FTP Improper Address Specified, 3154 - FTP Improper Port Specified, 3155 - FTP RETR Pipe Filename Command Execution, 3156 - FTP STOR Pipe Filename Command Execution, 3157 - FTP PASV Port Spoof, 3158 - FTP SITE EXEC Format String, 3159 - FTP PASS Suspicious Length, and 3160 - Cesar FTP Buffer Overflow.
- **E-mail signatures**—Examples are 3100 - Smail Attack, 3101 - Sendmail Invalid Recipient, 3102 - Sendmail Invalid Sender, 3103 - Sendmail Reconnaissance, 3104 - Archaic Sendmail Attacks, 3105 - Sendmail Decode Alias, 3106 - Mail Spam, and 3107 - Majordomo Execute Attack.

TIP The Cisco Secure Encyclopedia lets you browse the information about the signatures available for Cisco IDS devices and provides updates about the latest security vulnerabilities and associated signatures. The URL is http://www.cisco.com/cgi-bin/front.x/csec/search.pl.

A list with all the signatures supported by the Cisco IDS is available at http://www.cisco.com/cgi-bin/front.x/csec/idsAllList.pl.

A list with the signatures grouped per service is available at http://www.cisco.com/cgi-bin/front.x/csec/idsServiceList.pl.

Host-based IDSs specifically target host vulnerabilities, including the following:

- Protection against e-mail worm attacks such as GONER or NIMDA
- Protection against application hijacking using a dynamic link libraries (DLLs) control hook
- Protection against downloading files using instant-messenger applications
- Protection against known buffer-overflow attacks
- Control of application execution in the system

Host-based IDSs also provide prevention in addition to detection. Prevention is possible by enforcing the appropriate system behavior defined using behavior policies. This approach does not require signatures; therefore, it can prevent attacks before they occur.

Internet Edge Design

This section is a summary of the various security considerations previously discussed. Figure 21-6 depicts a complete security design of the Internet Edge.

Figure 21-6 *Internet Edge Design*

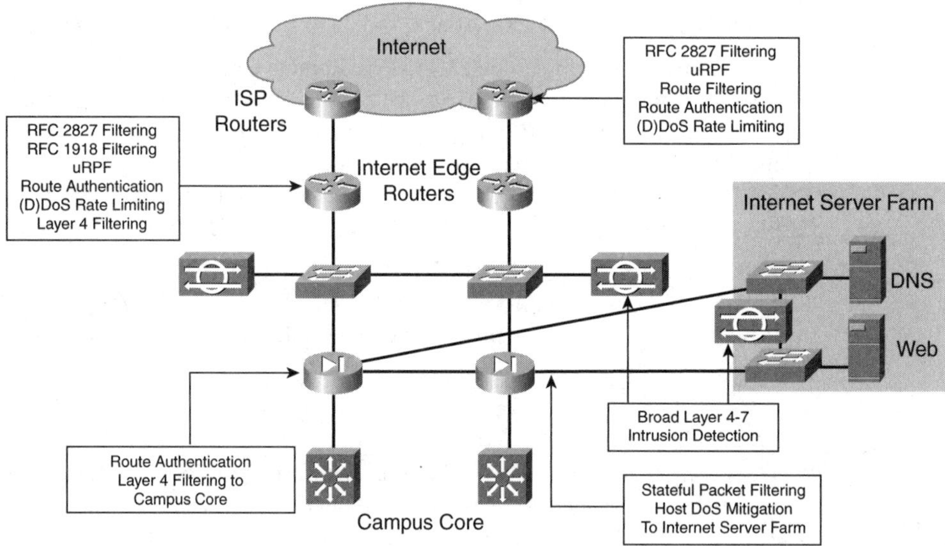

This design provides antispoofing by combining RFC 1918 filtering and RFC 2827 filtering on the edge routers.

You can also use uRPF at both the ISP routers and Internet Edge routers to mitigate source-address spoofing attacks by making sure packets are coming only from the proper links.

You apply rate limiting to both ISP and Internet Edge routers to make sure DoS attacks do not consume all available bandwidth.

You configure the ISP routers with route filters to make sure only the public networks assigned to the enterprise are propagated to the Internet. This configuration also prevents the enterprise from being a transit network for Internet traffic.

Neighbor route authentication is configured on the links connecting to the ISP routers as well as the campus core routers to ensure the peer's authenticity and route integrity.

In this design, the Internet Edge also implements a line of stateful firewalls to protect the servers at the DMZ with very precise filters and DoS controls and the rest of the enterprise with less granular filters based on networks rather than specific hosts.

Another important element of this design is the use of a network-based IDS. The network-based IDS should be deployed on the segment between the Internet Edge routers and the stateful firewalls and in the internal segments such as the DMZ to monitor server-farm activities.

Finally, you should disable all unnecessary services on all routers. Disable the following list of services:

- IP redirects
- Proxy Address Resolution Protocol (ARP)
- Cisco Discovery Protocol (CDP)
- Directed broadcasts on a per-interface basis

Example 21-11 shows how to disable these services on VLANs 1 through 10.

Example 21-11 *Unnecessary Services That Should Be Disabled on Routers*

```
router(config)# no ip domain-lookup
router(config)# no cdp run
router(config)# no ip http server
router(config)# no ip source-route
router(config)# no service finger
router(config)# no ip bootp server
router(config)# no service udp-small-servers
router(config)# no service tcp-small-servers
!
! interface level commands
router(config)#int range GigabitEthernet 6/1 - 16
router(config-if-range)#no ip redirects
router(config-if-range)#no ip directed-broadcast
router(config-if-range)#no ip proxy-arp
router(config-if-range)#no cdp enable
```

The next security zone to deal with is the campus core.

Campus Core

The *campus core* provides connectivity to multiple distinct modules of an enterprise network, and it is expected to provide high-speed switching services. The security measures applied to the campus core switches simply address the following issues:

- Disable any unnecessary services and harden the configuration of the switches and routers that build the campus core. Example 21-11 describes the list of services that should be disabled in the Layer 3 switches. You should also manage the switches as securely as possible.
- The second recommendation is to secure the exchange of routing updates with routing-update authentication, route filters, and neighbor definitions. These configuration commands appear in Chapter 5.

The following are additional best practices to secure the core switches:

- Use secure protocols such as Secure Shell (SSH) and Simple Network Management Protocol Version 3 (SNMPv3), and avoid insecure protocols that do not protect usernames and passwords.
- Turn off any unnecessary services; for example, do not run CDP unless necessary.

Figure 21-7 illustrates where these concepts are implemented at the campus core.

Figure 21-7 *Campus Core Design*

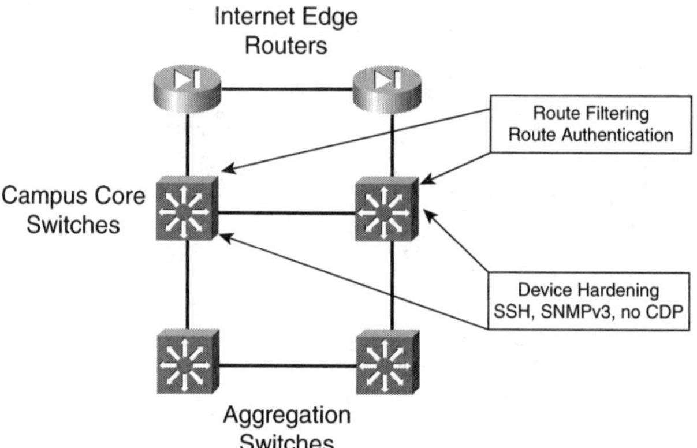

The design in Figure 21-7 mitigates issues with route authentication and trusted routing peers. Additionally, the use of SNMPv3 and SSH for secure management is important to ensure privacy and authenticity when performing management functions.

Intranet Server Farms

The intranet server farm contains the aggregation and access switches, any device-supporting services such as load balancers and SSL offloaders, the servers supporting the internal application environments, and monitoring tools for network analysis that monitor application traffic paths and latencies and allow remote troubleshooting.

The intranet server farm requires more granular controls than those at the Internet Edge, and it constitutes an additional line of defense against external attacks, while providing an intranet's first line of protection against internal threats.

Security requirements are distinctly applied to both the aggregation and access switches.

The aggregation layer should achieve the following goals:

- Protect the server farm and the network infrastructure against external and internal attacks. You typically achieve this goal by using stateful firewalls and a network-based IDS.
- Control the communication between server farms. Typically, different server farms have distinct security requirements; therefore, you must put into place the proper controls to protect one farm from each other. You do so by either using ACLs at the switches or segregating the server farms using firewalls. When you use ACLs, in addition to blocking traffic flowing between server farms, they can also mitigate spoofing by using uRPF.

The access layer should achieve the following goals:

- Protect the server farm and the network infrastructure against internal attacks at the server-farm level and help control the communication between server farms. You typically use stateful Layer 2 features, ACLs, and network-based IDSs.
- Protect servers against known and unknown host vulnerabilities. Target the types of servers in the server farm through the use of host-based IDSs.

Figure 21-8 illustrates the security measures applied to the aggregation switches.

In this design, the server farms and the supporting network infrastructure are protected by a layer of stateful firewalls. These firewalls are configured with granular ACLs based on protocols, ports, and destination/source IP addresses, which control ingress and egress traffic to and between the server farms. Additionally, you set up the available DoS controls per-server.

The principle goal of the access layer is to support the server farm. The server farm maintains the accessibility and availability of the application services for internal users, hence the name intranet server farm. The access layer switches should use features such as port security, ARP inspection, PVLANs, and VLAN tagging to avoid the typical server-farm level attacks, and switches at the host level should use the host-based IDS to prevent and detect attacks to the various servers.

Figure 21-8 *Security Measures at the Aggregation Switches*

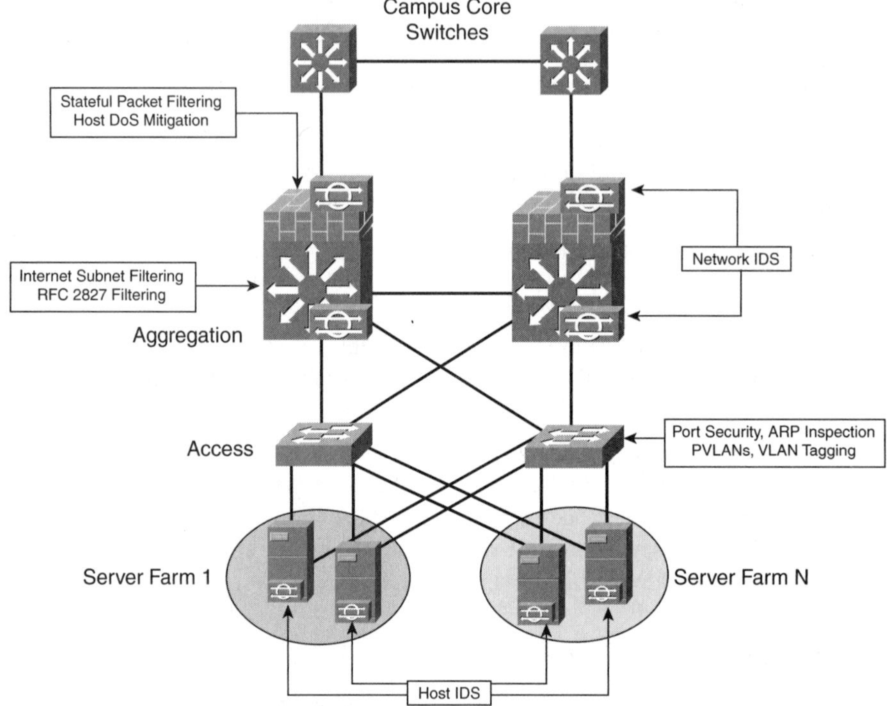

You must take additional security measures when dealing with a multitier server farm. As explained in Chapter 4, "Data Center Design Overview," a typical server farm supports applications that fall in to the classic client/server or n-tier models. The n-tier model translates into a multitier design, which includes the following types of servers:

- **Web servers**—Provide the front-end or presentation services to the users
- **Application servers**—support the business logic and perform the computing aspect of a transaction
- **Database servers**—Contain the data used by the applications

Figure 21-9 illustrates the communication between the server tiers and the client.

Notice in Figure 21-9 that the communication flows in the multitier environment as follows:

- Client to web server
- Web to application server
- Application to database server
- No other communication flows allowed

Figure 21-9 *Communication Flows in a Server Farm*

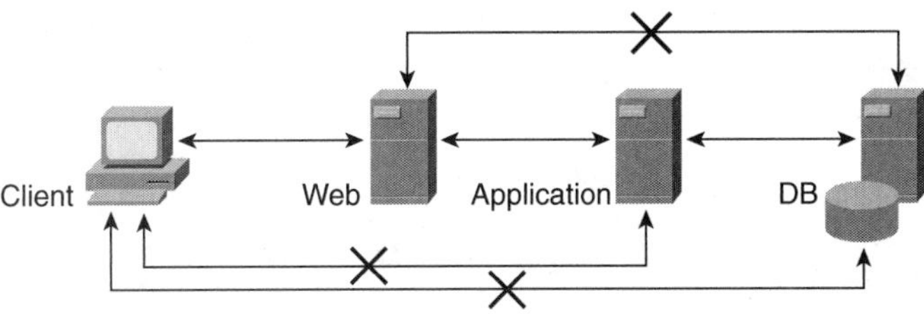

The design of a multitier server farm can use either physical or logical separation between tiers, yet the implementation of the security rules does not change. The firewalls and additional features must support the outlined communication flows.

In practice, server farms supporting specific applications are likely to have different tiers, and the communication flows between the tiers might be different. If the goal is to establish a security zone around a specific application environment, the security controls must be granular enough to differentiate the security applied to the distinct zones (application environments). The server-farm design section later in the chapter discusses the different alternatives.

Assigning the server farms to separate VLANs and using firewalls, ACLs, and static translations lets you enforce the described traffic paths between web, application, and database.

Besides these measures, other security measures are applicable to the access layer:

- Deploying stateful firewalls and ACLs
- Deploying intrusion detection
- Enabling other security features

The following sections discuss the security measures applied to both the aggregation and access layers.

Deploying Stateful Firewalls

At the aggregation level, the primary role of the stateful firewalls is to control the traffic destined to the intranet server farms. The access control rules defined at this level need to be more granular than those used at the Internet Edge. The access rules should enforce not only protocols but also the devices and the ports numbers used to communicate. You must apply filters in both directions to control inbound and outbound traffic.

Example 21-12 illustrates a granular filter configured on a Firewall Service Module (FWSM) at the aggregation layer. In this example, the egress and ingress filters permit web traffic from and to a web server. These filters also allow basic services such as DNS and ICMP.

NOTE For more information on configuring **static** and **global** commands on the PIX Firewall, refer to Chapter 13.

Example 21-12 *Granular Filters on an Aggregation Firewall*

```
firewall(config)# static (inside,outside) 172.16.1.2 172.16.1.2
! Ingress filter
firewall(config)# access-list 111 permit tcp any host 172.16.1.2 eq www
firewall(config)# access-list 111 permit icmp any host 172.16.1.2 echo
firewall(config)# access-list 111 permit icmp any host 172.16.1.2 echo-reply
firewall(config)# access-list 111 permit icmp any host 172.16.1.2 time-exceeded
firewall(config)# access-list 111 permit icmp any host 172.16.1.2 unreachable
firewall(config)# access-group 111 in interface outside
! Egress filter
firewall(config)# access-list 112 permit udp host 172.16.1.2 any eq domain
firewall(config)# access-list 112 permit icmp host 172.16.1.2 any echo
firewall(config)# access-list 112 permit icmp host 172.16.1.2 any echo-reply
firewall(config)# access-list 112 permit icmp host 172.16.1.2 any time-exceeded
firewall(config)# access-list 112 permit icmp host 172.16.1.2 any unreachable
firewall(config)# access-group 112 in interface inside
```

Most stateful firewalls also provide some mechanisms to control the effects of DoS attacks, such as TCP SYN rate limiting and SYN_COOKIES. It is highly recommended that you use such DoS controls and, whenever possible, apply the control parameters to individual systems rather than networks. Configuring these DoS controls per-system helps you better deal when not all servers receive the same type and volume of traffic. Example 21-13 shows that you can use the FWSM **static** command to limit the maximum number of concurrent and embryonic connections for a particular server. The **static** command sets the limit to 2000 concurrent connections and 200 embryonic connections.

Example 21-13 *Firewall Configuration*

```
firewall(config)# static (inside,outside) 172.16.0.2 172.16.0.2 2000 200
```

The next major role of firewalls at the aggregation layer is to segregate server farms in different security zones that have different security requirements. The FWSM configuration in Example 21-14 illustrates that concept. This configuration segregates two server farms: one supports the company portal, portal-net, and another one supports a payroll application, payroll-net. Note that ACL 111 restricts access to the payroll-net server to be only initiated from 171.69.2.0/16, the portal-net, while allowing any external access to the payroll-net web server (172.16.1.5). Example 21-14 presents the configuration of the firewall segregating the two server farms.

Example 21-14 *Granular Filters on an Aggregation Firewall*

```
firewall(config)# nameif vlan402 portal-net-webdmz security50
firewall(config)# nameif vlan403 payroll-net-webdmz security60
firewall(config)# nameif vlan400 outside security0
firewall(config)#ip address portal-net-webdmz 172.16.1.1 255.255.255.0
firewall(config)#ip address payroll-net-webdmz 172.17.2.1 255.255.255.0
firewall(config)#ip address outside 192.0.2.1 255.255.255.0
firewall(config)# static (portal-net-webdmz,outside) 172.16.1.5 172.16.1.5
firewall(config)# static (payroll-net-webdmz,portal-net-webdmz) 172.17.2.3
  172.17.2.3
! Ingress filter
firewall(config)# access-list 111 permit tcp any host 172.16.1.5 eq www
firewall(config)# access-list 111 permit icmp any host 172.16.1.5 echo
firewall(config)# access-list 111 permit icmp any host 172.16.1.5 echo-reply
firewall(config)# access-list 111 permit icmp any host 172.16.1.5 time-exceeded
firewall(config)# access-list 111 permit icmp any host 172.16.1.5 unreachable
firewall(config)# access-list 111 permit icmp any host 172.17.2.3 echo
firewall(config)# access-list 111 permit icmp any host 172.17.2.3 echo-reply
firewall(config)# access-list 111 permit icmp any host 172.17.2.3 time-exceeded
firewall(config)# access-list 111 permit icmp any host 172.17.2.3 unreachable
firewall(config)# access-group 111 in interface outside
! Egress filter portal-net-webdmz
firewall(config)# access-list 112 permit tcp host 172.16.1.5 host 172.17.2.3
firewall(config)# access-list 112 permit udp host 172.16.1.5 any eq domain
firewall(config)# access-list 112 permit icmp host 172.16.1.5 any echo
firewall(config)# access-list 112 permit icmp host 172.16.1.5 any echo-reply
firewall(config)# access-list 112 permit icmp host 172.16.1.5 any time-exceeded
firewall(config)# access-list 112 permit icmp host 172.16.1.5 any unreachable
firewall(config)# access-group 112 in interface portal-net-webdmz
! Egress filter payroll-net-webdmz
firewall(config)# access-list 113 permit udp host 172.17.2.3 any eq domain
firewall(config)# access-list 113 permit icmp host 172.17.2.3 any echo
firewall(config)# access-list 113 permit icmp host 172.17.2.3 any echo-reply
firewall(config)# access-list 113 permit icmp host 172.17.2.3 any time-exceeded
firewall(config)# access-list 113 permit icmp host 172.17.2.3 any unreachable
firewall(config)# access-group 113 in interface payroll-net-webdmz
```

You use stateful firewalls at the access layer only in multitier environments where the requirements call for physical separation between the different tiers of servers. The same design principles and configuration used at the aggregation layer are applied to the firewalls at the access layer if it is in use.

Applying Packet Filters

You perform packet filtering by applying ACLs. ACLS are discussed in Chapter 15. At the aggregation switches, ACLs are implemented to control high-speed traffic such as backup traffic flowing between different server farms. You commonly do this task using VACLs or router ACLs (RACLs). VACLs are processed in hardware in many switching platforms, such as the Catalyst 6500, which makes them ideal for server-to-server communication when high throughput is required because there is no performance degradation.

The RACLs used in this module can help control access to the aggregation switches strictly from the management subnet or the list of management hosts.

Example 21-15 shows the use of a VACL to allow only traffic going to and coming from a web server. This VACL also allows primary services such as DNS and ICMP.

Notice that the lines of configuration 1 and 7 and 2 and 8 are symmetric. VACLs do not have a concept of direction; consequently, they apply to all the traffic traversing a VLAN. So if you configure only the entry **access-list** 101 **permit tcp any host** 172.16.1.2 **eq** www, the client-to-server traffic would flow, but not the return traffic from the server. This reason is why you need to specify access-list entries for both directions of the traffic.

The configuration line 13 allows server-to-server communication on the VLAN, which happens in hardware.

Example 21-15 *VLAN Access Lists*

```
1  access-list 101 permit udp any eq domain host 172.16.1.2
2  access-list 101 permit tcp any host 172.16.1.2 eq www
3  access-list 101 permit icmp any host 172.16.1.2 echo
4  access-list 101 permit icmp any host 172.16.1.2 echo-reply
5  access-list 101 permit icmp any host 172.16.1.2 time-exceeded
6  access-list 101 permit icmp any host 172.16.1.2 unreachable
7  access-list 101 permit udp host 172.16.1.2 any eq domain
8  access-list 101 permit tcp host 172.16.1.2 eq www any
9  access-list 101 permit icmp host 172.16.1.2 any echo
10 access-list 101 permit icmp host 172.16.1.2 any echo-reply
11 access-list 101 permit icmp host 172.16.1.2 any time-exceeded
12 access-list 101 permit icmp host 172.16.1.2 any unreachable
13 access-list 101 permit ip 172.16.1.0 0.0.0.255 172.16.1.0 0.0.0.255
14 Aggregation(config)#vlan access-map vaclwebserver
15 Aggregation(config-access-map)#match ip address 101
16 Aggregation(config-access-map)#action forward
17 Aggregation(config)#vlan filter vaclwebserver vlan-list 10
```

NOTE VACLs do not have a concept of direction; consequently, the filter applies to all traffic entering the VLAN. This condition limits the use of VACLs for RFC 2827 filtering. You should use RACLs when the purpose is to prevent the source-spoofing of the local networks without blocking intra-VLAN traffic.

VACLs at the access layer control the traffic between servers. As with any other filters deployed in the Data Center, VACLs are deployed to control ingress as well as egress traffic; however, VACLs could make a significant difference.

Deploying Intrusion Detection

You can implement intrusion detection, as previously described, by monitoring the network (with a network-based IDS) or monitoring hosts (with a host-based IDS). The following sections discuss the details of each type of intrusion detection in the intranet server farm.

Network-Based Intrusion Detection

You use network-based intrusion detection at the aggregation layer with two major purposes:

- Identify any attacks attempts and detect intruders on the outside or the inside of the layer of firewalls. The outside is recommended when the intent is to monitor all traffic before it reaches the server farms. The inside is recommended when the goal is to perform more specific monitoring on a subset of the server farms. In either case, you should select a specific set of signatures in the IDS that closely match the intent of traffic monitoring.
- Identify the action steps to take when a suspicious activity is detected. The identification process requires tuning the signatures by monitoring the alarms and determining what is normal and abnormal. You can deploy a single sensor to inspect the multiple server farms, and you should configure it to specifically alert on those protocols allowed by the firewalls. It is a way to aggregate IDS services in a single chassis instead of using a dedicated sensor at each server farm.

You can deploy network-based IDSs either at the aggregation layer or directly at the Layer 2 infrastructure of each server farm, the access layer. Another consideration for IDS at the access layer is performance; if the IDS at the aggregation layer is not capable of monitoring the aggregate server farm traffic, the alternative is to deploy more than one and distribute the load between them or to deploy it at the access layer where the traffic load could be reduced to a subset of the server farms, which VLANs could identify.

You can connect network-based sensors to each one of the LAN segments where servers connect. In this way, each sensor can analyze all the traffic flowing from and to every server connected to the same segment. IDSs at the access layer deal with traffic that has already made it through the firewalls; therefore, it needs to be configured accordingly. Another good practice is to set the sensors to alert only on the traffic that is allowed by the firewalls because any other traffic should be blocked. This recommendation especially helps in cases where you need to improve the sensor's performance.

Signatures are templates used by IDSs to determine unusual behaviors on the network that could be considered security violations. Note that you can apply any of these signatures to the location where the IDSs are placed. It is recommended that you be liberal in your selection of the initial set of signatures to monitor but relate them to the security policy. Given the hundreds of available signatures, the selection process should focus on those signatures that match the policies and that are applicable to the specific environment.

The following is a sample of signatures used in the detection of attacks destined to various server types in the server farm:

- **HTTP signatures**—3455 - Java Web Server Cmd Exec, 5087 - WWW Sun Java Server Access, 5312 - *.jsp/*.jhtml Java Execution, 5375 - Apache mod_dav Overflow, 5103 - WWW SuSE Apache CGI Source Access, and 5160 - Apache ? indexing file disclosure bug.
- **RPC-based application signatures**—6101 - RPC Port Unregistration, 6102 - RPC Dump, 6103 - Proxied RPC Request, 6104 - RPC Set Spoof, 6105 - RPC Unset Spoof, 6110 - RPC RSTATD Sweep, 6111 - RPC RUSERSD Sweep, 6112 - RPC NFS Sweep, 6113 - RPC MOUNTD Sweep, and 6114 - RPC YPPASSWDD Sweep.
- **Windows/NetBIOS signatures**—3300 - NetBIOS OOB Data, 3301 - NETBIOS Stat, 3302 - NETBIOS Session Setup Failure, 3303 - Windows Guest Login, 3304 - Windows Null Account Name, 3305 - Windows Password File Access, 3306 - Windows Registry Access, and 3327 - Windows RPC DCOM Overflow.

The signatures used in the server farm belong to *signature groups* such as the HTTP group, because HTTP is used to gain access to most applications; the RPC group, because RPC is widely used for server-to-server communication; and groups specific to certain operating systems such as Windows/NetBIOS, if applicable.

NOTE For a better understanding of the application types and their associated architectures, refer to Chapter 3, "Application Architectures Overview."

You can fine-tune the HTTP signatures to the specific server platform used in the Data Center. For example, if the servers are BEA Weblogic or IBM WebSphere, you can make the HTTP signatures specific to attacks directed to Java code such as servlets, and you might disable Common Gateway Interface (CGI) signatures.

With databases, you might enable the signatures that belong to the SQL group, and if the Data Center also hosts collaborative applications, you might need to turn on the signatures that belong to the Post Office Protocol (POP) and Internet Message Access Protocol (IMAP) groups.

NOTE When dealing with tuning signatures and alarms on a Cisco Network-based IDS, consult the network security database (NSDB) to determine what alarms are relevant to the particular environment and at what level they should be logged. NSDB is an HTML-based encyclopedia of network vulnerability information that includes specific information about the attacks, hot links, potential countermeasures, and related vulnerabilities. The NSBD is integrated with the CiscoWorks Monitoring Center for Security.

You can also browse the latest signatures on the online Cisco Secure Encyclopedia at http://www.cisco.com/cgi-bin/front.x/csec/search.pl.

Host-Based Intrusion Detection

Host-based IDSs, also referred to as host-based intrusion protection systems (HIPS), are implemented on each critical server and depend on the security policies on each server or server tier in the server farm. As explained in Chapter 5, a host-based IDS consists of software agents that directly run on the end systems to be protected. Because they are agents that reside in the end systems, they have visibility of all the system parameters, which is different from network-based systems. This visibility allows host-based IDSs to identify some attacks and vulnerabilities that complement those detected by network-based IDSs.

Host-based IDSs monitor system calls to the host operating system and determine whether the requested action is permitted. As with network-based IDSs, host-based IDSs require tuning so that alarms related to normal activity are not generated.

The vulnerabilities that a host-based IDS should target relate to the functions performed by the server. The generic set of vulnerabilities tied to the operating system include buffer overflow, control of application execution, protection against dynamic link library (DLL) hijacking, and so on, which should be considered the baseline. The other set relates more to the applications. This set includes signatures for Windows and Solaris systems.

The following are subsets of the available signatures for both Windows and Solaris. For more information, consult the product documentation.

Windows signatures are

1127 IIS %u (UTF) encoding
941 IIS .htw cross-site scripting
942 IIS .shtml cross-site scripting
876 IIS +.htr file fragment reading
431 IIS 4.0 FTP buffer overflow
873 IIS ASP sample site advsearch.asp DoS
875 IIS ASP sample site query.asp DoS
1129 IIS authentication method disclosure
869 IIS catalog_type ASP sample page
1132 IIS chunked encoding heap overflow
854 IIS CodeBrws.asp file access
1121 IIS CodeRed / index server idq.dll buffer overflow
1133 IIS COM extension request
1114 IIS cpshost.dll file upload

940 IIS cross-site scripting
1106 IIS details.idc remote command execution
1207 IIS envelope - file execution by IIS process
1224 IIS envelope - file execution by IIS web user
1210 IIS envelope - registry mod. by IIS process
1229 IIS envelope - registry mod. by IIS web user

Solaris signatures are

1331 /bin/login buffer overflow
1308 admintool buffer overflow
1502 Apache artificially long slash path
1504 Apache chunked-encoding memory corruption
1419 Apache envelope - file access by CGI
1420 Apache envelope - file modification by CGI
1503 Apache test-cgi directory listing
1313 ARP buffer overflow
26 aspppd insecure file link
1318 at buffer overflow
1336 cachefsd mount file and remote buffer overflow
391 Cancel buffer overflow
1300 CDE dtmail buffer overflow
1324 mailx buffer overflow -F argument
1303 netpr -p buffer overflow
1555 Netscape Enterprise Server JHTML view source
59 ping hname buffer overflow
325 rpc.cmsd buffer overflow
1326 sendmail tTdvect GOT buffer overflow
1332 snmpdx buffer overflow

The following section discusses the signatures used by IDSs to determine security anomalies on the network.

Enabling Other Security Features

Layer 3 and Layer 2 switches offer features that increase the security by preventing certain vulnerabilities from being exploited. Following is the list of features used to prevent very specific attacks or to increase security in the server farm. For more information about how to configure the following features, consult Chapter 5.

Port Security

You apply *port security* to ports where the servers are connected to help mitigate some data-link level attacks such as MAC flooding. You use port security to configure the switch ports to accept only packets with trusted source MAC addresses.

The intranet server farm supporting the enterprise applications could be designed and implemented in many ways. All the previous security measures are included into the designs. The following section discusses design alternatives that include both the aggregation and access layers.

ARP Inspection

ARP inspection prevents ARP spoofing and man-in-the-middle attacks by ensuring an attacker cannot hijack the default gateway address and therefore intercept all the server traffic.

Chapter 5 introduced three different commands:

- **set security acl arp-inspection match-mac enable**
- **set security acl arp-inspection address-validation enable**
- **set port arp-inspection** *mod/port* **drop-threshold** *rate* **shutdown-threshold** *rate*

From a design perspective, it is recommended that you implement the three commands to achieve a consistent state when dealing with something as delicate as ARP inspection. The consequence of someone hijacking the identity of the default gateway is that a device could monitor all the server traffic.

For the **set security acl ip arp-inspection** command, it is important to "log" the information for later analysis. The ARP rate-limiting feature requires some tuning until you find the right value, yet you should consistently apply it to all ports where devices are connected. You should also disable unused ports.

Private VLANs

Private VLANs at the server farm help enforce the isolation of servers to prevent them from communicating with other servers in the same VLAN, reducing the chances of trust-exploitation attacks. When using private VLANs, you should configure the port's connection firewalls and routers as promiscuous, and set the server ports as isolated or community, in case a group of servers need to communicate with each other. Additionally, private VLANs also help mitigate Layer 2 attacks such as ARP spoofing.

Private VLANs are a great alternative to separating application environments that still share the same services infrastructure and the same IP subnet yet need to be isolated from one another. For instance, a payroll application and a web-based directory could coexist in the same IP subnet yet they must be isolated. While they are isolated, they could use the content switching or an SSL module to achieve higher scalability.

VLAN Tagging

You use *VLAN tagging* to prevent untagged traffic from reaching any VLAN. The **vlan dot1q tag native** command forces the switch to drop untagged traffic and to admit only 802.1Q-tagged frames on trunks.

VLAN tagging, referred to as "802.1 tag all" in Chapter 5, should be implemented on the aggregation and access switches on every VLAN used by servers. Unused VLANs should not have enabled ports so that they are not used as the source of attacks.

NOTE For more information about the Layer 2 design in the Data Center and how this command relates to the other Layer 2 configurations, refer to Chapter 12, "Layer 2 Protocol Essentials," and Chapter 20, "Designing the Data Center Infrastructure."

Server-Farm Design Alternatives

This section discusses server-farm design alternatives and the application of security in the design.

The following designs are the two recommended alternatives for implementing multitier server farms, as shown in Figure 21-10:

- The *collapsed design* locates all server tiers in the same layer of switches, separating the different tiers and application with VLANs. All the switches in the access layer are connected to the aggregation switches, which implies that firewalls and other service devices logically support each server group within each tier from the aggregation layer, as shown in part **a** of Figure 21-10.
- The *expanded design* locates each server tier in a different set of switches, which are connected to each other instead of to the aggregation switch. You can separate the server groups per tier or separate applications with VLANs and separate the access switches with firewalls. As depicted in part **b** of Figure 21-10, the services in the expanded design are at the aggregation layer for the first tier of servers and at the access layer for the second tier of servers.

Whether the design is collapsed or expanded, the filters defined at the server farm need to be restrictive yet flexible enough to allow the normal application and management traffic flows. You should precisely configure the filters in the server farm, indicating not only protocol and ports but also source and destination IP addresses. The filters should be designed to control both ingress and egress traffic. When implementing stateful firewalls, the recommended practice is to turn on the available DoS controls and apply them to the individual servers.

Figure 21-10 *Collapsed and Expanded Server-Farm Design*

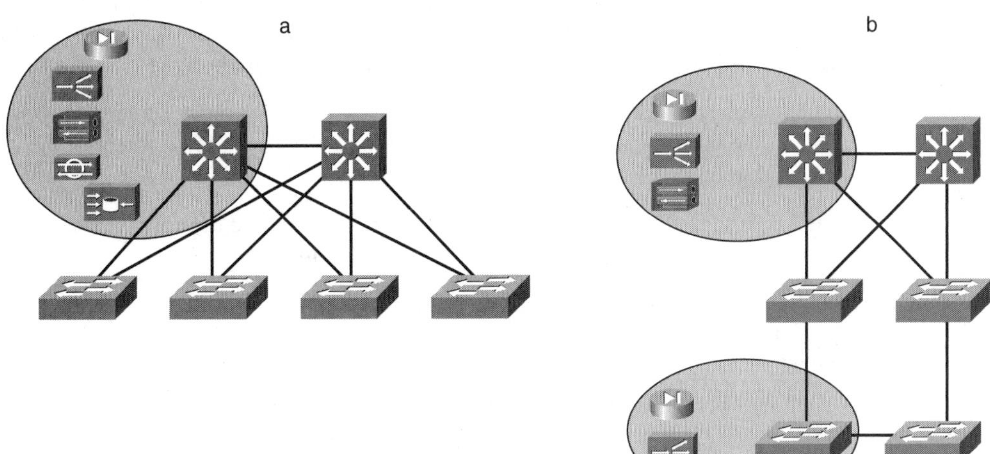

The following sections explore the details of each design.

Collapsed Server-Farm Design

The collapsed design, presented in Figure 21-11, has a single access layer in which all access switches are connected to the aggregation switches.

Figure 21-11 *Collapsed Server-Farm Design*

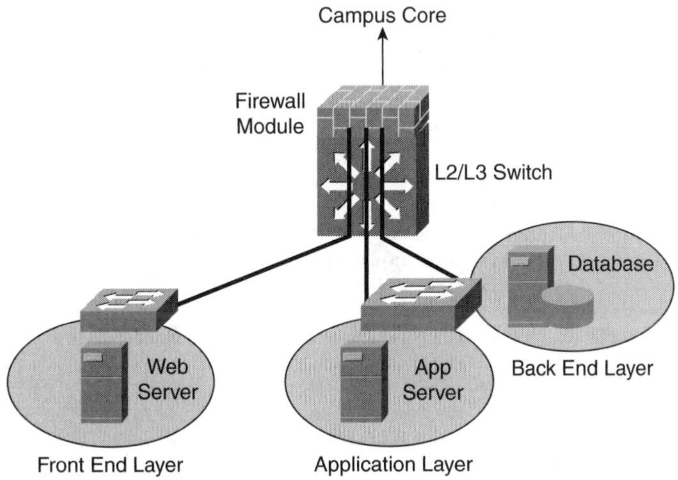

In the collapsed design, the server farms are on the same or on different access switches grouped by VLANs. As shown in Figure 21-11, you can use a single switch to house servers belonging to a single VLAN, or you can use it to house more than one VLAN. Whether you use one or more switches is strictly a port-density or server dual-homing requirement.

Collapsed designs require that the firewall concurrently support many server VLANs. For each VLAN, the firewall can provide default gateway services while it protects the VLAN from inbound or other VLAN traffic.

Example 21-16 shows how to configure the FWSM to implement the collapsed design and allow only traffic that follows the flow illustrated in Figure 21-9.

As you can see in Example 21-16, the core of the network is considered untrusted (security level 0), and the segment hosting the application servers is considered more trusted (security level 20) than the segment hosting the web servers (security level 10). The static translations in the example allow the communication between the outside (core) and the web server (10.20.5.10) and between the web server and the application server (10.20.6.11). The web server is expected to be accessed by outside clients using HTTP. Access-list 111 opens HTTP access to the web server while allowing basic services such as DNS and ICMP. At the same time, DCOM connections are expected to be initiated from the web server to the application server using TCP port 135 and a negotiated port in the range 3000–4000. Access-list 112 allows that access. Access-list 113 restricts traffic coming from the application server farm, allowing basic DNS and ICMP services. Note that the traffic corresponding to Distributed Component Object Model (DCOM) connections is automatically allowed by the stateful engine for the firewall. There is no need to add extra lines to ACL 113 for DCOM traffic returning to the web server. Finally, the static commands also set the maximum number of concurrent connections and embryonic connections, helping mitigate DoS attacks.

Example 21-16 *Partial Configuration of a FWSM for Multitier Server Farms*

```
nameif vlan30 outside security0
nameif vlan5 web security10
nameif vlan6 app security20
ip address outside 10.20.30.5 255.255.255.0
ip address web 10.20.5.1 255.255.255.0
ip address app 10.20.6.1 255.255.255.0
static (web,outside) 10.20.5.10 10.20.5.10 10000 500
static (app,web) 10.20.6.11 10.20.6.11 200 20
! Outside Ingress filter
access-list 111 permit tcp any host 10.20.5.10 eq www
access-list 111 permit icmp any host 10.20.5.10 echo
access-list 111 permit icmp any host 10.20.5.10 echo-reply
access-list 111 permit icmp any host 10.20.5.10 time-exceeded
access-list 111 permit icmp any host 10.20.5.10 unreachable
access-group 111 in interface outside
! Web Server Farm Ingress filter
access-list 112 permit tcp host 10.20.5.10 host 10.20.6.11 eq 135
access-list 112 permit tcp host 10.20.5.10 host 10.20.6.11 range 3000 4000
access-list 112 permit icmp host 10.20.5.10 any echo
```

Example 21-16 *Partial Configuration of a FWSM for Multitier Server Farms (Continued)*

```
access-list 112 permit icmp host 10.20.5.10 any echo-reply
access-list 112 permit icmp host 10.20.5.10 any time-exceeded
access-list 112 permit icmp host 10.20.5.10 any unreachable
access-group 112 in interface web
! Application Server Farm Ingress filter
access-list 113 permit icmp host 10.20.6.11  any echo
access-list 113 permit icmp host 10.20.6.11  any echo-reply
access-list 113 permit icmp host 10.20.6.11  any time-exceeded
access-list 113 permit icmp host 10.20.6.11  any unreachable
access-group 113 in interface app
```

NOTE It is possible to restrict the dynamic ports used with DCOM. In the example here, the dynamic ports have been restricted to the 3000–4000 range. Check Microsoft documentation to see how you can configure servers with port restrictions (http://www.microsoft.com/com/wpaper/dcomfw.asp).

Figure 21-12 shows how you can deploy the different security technologies in a collapsed design.

Figure 21-12 *Security in a Collapsed Server-Farm Design*

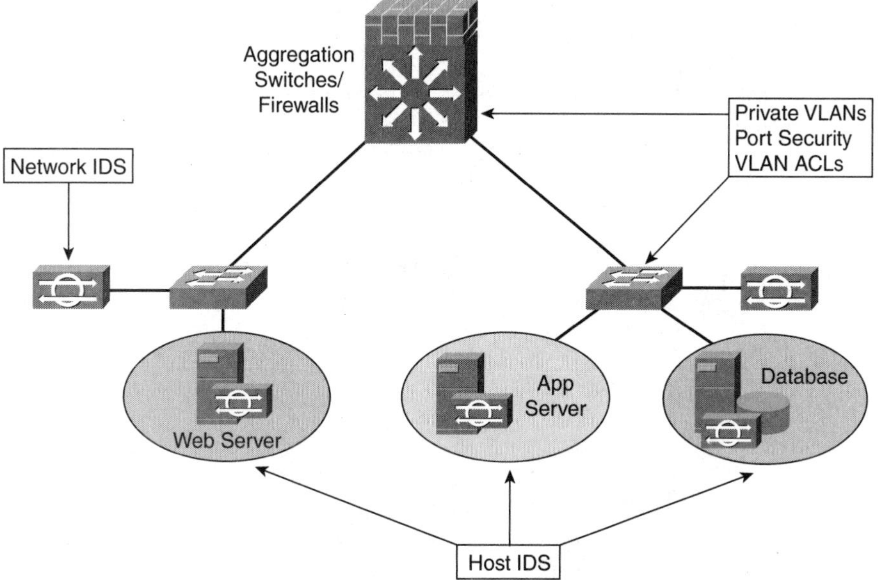

The proposed security design for a collapsed server farm incorporates private VLANs to enforce the isolation of those servers that do not need to communicate. The ports connecting the firewalls are configured as promiscuous, so they talk to all the other devices in the same segment. Web servers, application servers, and database servers are connected to the same Layer 2 infrastructure, but their traffic is separated in different VLANs.

Port security is also implemented on both server and firewall ports to mitigate some data link layer attacks.

Intrusion detection is implemented in the form of network-based and host-based IDSs. A network sensor is connected to the Layer 2 infrastructure to inspect all traffic flowing through the server farm. At the same time, a host-based IDS is implemented on the critical servers to help with host-driven attacks.

Expanded Server-Farm Design

You use the expanded design to achieve physical separation between the different server tiers or groups of servers. The physical separation is possible through the use of different access layer switches to house the server groups, but unlike in the collapsed design, the access switches are connected to each other directly. Figure 21-13 shows the expanded design.

Figure 21-13 *Expanded Server-Farm Design*

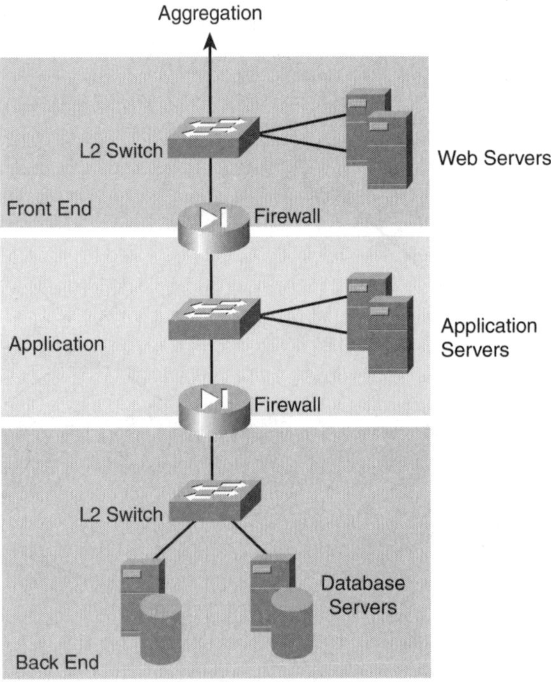

As shown in Figure 21-13, each Layer 2 switch supports a different tier of servers, and the connectivity between tiers is through firewalls. This design lets you specifically configure each tier's firewall to communicate between tiers, which simplifies each firewall's configuration yet requires more firewalls. Notice that this design can use both appliances and modules. An appliance, a PIX Firewall, is connected to both switches, forcing all traffic to go through it. You can also use a FWSM on the Layer 2 switches. In this scenario, the switches are connected to each other, and the firewalls are configured on each access layer switch so that all traffic between server tiers is force to traverse the FWSM. For illustration purposes, Figure 21-14 presents an expanded design supporting a multitier server farm that contains a web server and a database server. In this example, clients are expected to open HTTP sessions to the web server while the web server communicates with the database server over SQLNet. Two layers of firewalls are implemented to protect this scenario.

The first layer, called the front end, protects the web server by controlling the traffic flowing to and from the IP network. The second layer, the back end, protects the database server, making sure it can only receive SQLNet connections initiated by the web server.

Figure 21-14 *Expanded Multitier Server Farm*

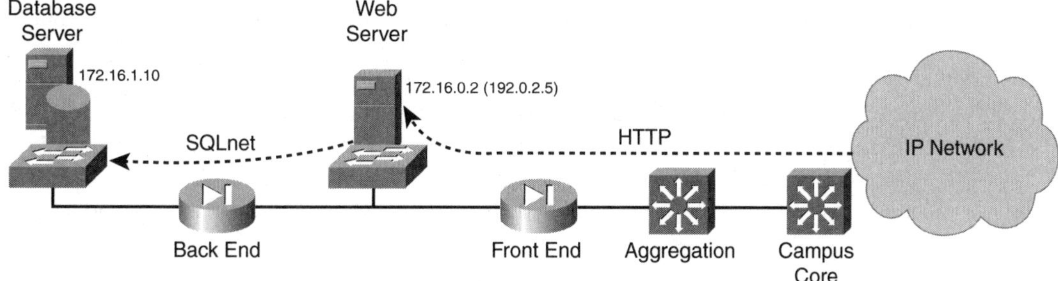

Example 21-17 shows the configuration of the front-end firewall using a Cisco PIX. As you can see, the front-end firewall performs address translation between the web server's public and private IP addresses. In this scenario, the web server is the only system accessible from the IP network; hence, it is the only one with a public IP address. The **static** command used for the address translation also sets the DoS control to a maximum of 10,000 concurrent connections and 500 embryonic connections. The front-end firewall is also configured with precise ingress and egress filters. The ingress filter permits incoming HTTP connections to the web server and allows some basic ICMP services. On the other hand, the egress filter allows DNS queries and ICMP services for the web server. Note that the egress filter does not include any entry permitting HTTP packets corresponding to client sessions. Those packets are automatically permitted by the stateful firewall, thanks to its ability to inspect and track the connections. In the PIX Firewall configuration, the inspection of HTTP traffic is enabled with the **fixup protocol http 80** command.

Example 21-17 *Front-End Firewall Filters at a Multitier Server Farm*

```
! Front-End-Firewall Configuration
fixup protocol http 80
static (inside,outside) 192.0.2.5 172.16.0.2 10000 500
! Ingress filter
access-list 111 permit tcp any host 192.0.2.5 eq www
access-list 111 permit icmp any host 192.0.2.5 echo
access-list 111 permit icmp any host 192.0.2.5 echo-reply
access-list 111 permit icmp any host 192.0.2.5 time-exceeded
access-list 111 permit icmp any host 192.0.2.5 unreachable
access-group 111 in interface outside
! Egress filter
access-list 112 permit udp host 172.16.0.2 any eq domain
access-list 112 permit icmp host 172.16.0.2 any echo
access-list 112 permit icmp host 172.16.0.2 any echo-reply
access-list 112 permit icmp host 172.16.0.2 any time-exceeded
access-list 112 permit icmp host 172.16.0.2 any unreachable
access-group 112 in interface inside
```

Example 21-18 presents the configuration of the back-end firewall. The **static** command indicates that the database server does not need address translation and sets the DoS control to a maximum of 200 concurrent connections and 20 embryonic connections. The ingress filter permits SQLNet sessions initiated by the web server. Both ingress and egress filters allow basic ICMP services. **fixup protocol sqlnet 1521** enables the inspection of SQLNet traffic. A typical SQLNet session consists of two connections, one of them dynamically negotiated. If you did not turn on the inspection of SQLNet, the firewall would not be able to recognize the dynamically negotiated connection and the SQLNet traffic would be dropped.

Example 21-18 *Back-End Firewall Filters at a Multitier Server Farm*

```
! Back-End-Firewall Configuration
fixup protocol sqlnet 1521
static (inside,outside) 172.16.1.10 172.16.1.10 200 20
! Ingress filter
access-list 111 permit tcp host 172.16.0.2 host 172.16.1.10  eq sqlnet
access-list 111 permit icmp any host 172.16.1.10  echo
access-list 111 permit icmp any host 172.16.1.10  echo-reply
access-list 111 permit icmp any host 172.16.1.10  time-exceeded
access-list 111 permit icmp any host 172.16.1.10  unreachable
access-group 111 in interface outside
! Egress filter
access-list 112 permit icmp host 172.16.1.10  any echo
access-list 112 permit icmp host 172.16.1.10  any echo-reply
access-list 112 permit icmp host 172.16.1.10  any time-exceeded
access-list 112 permit icmp host 172.16.1.10  any unreachable
access-group 112 in interface inside
```

The recommended security design for an expanded server farm uses most of the principles described in the collapsed design. The most important difference is the incorporation of multiple layers of stateful firewalls physically separating the tiers. Figure 21-15 presents the expanded design, including security.

Figure 21-15 *Expanded Server-Farm Design, Including Security*

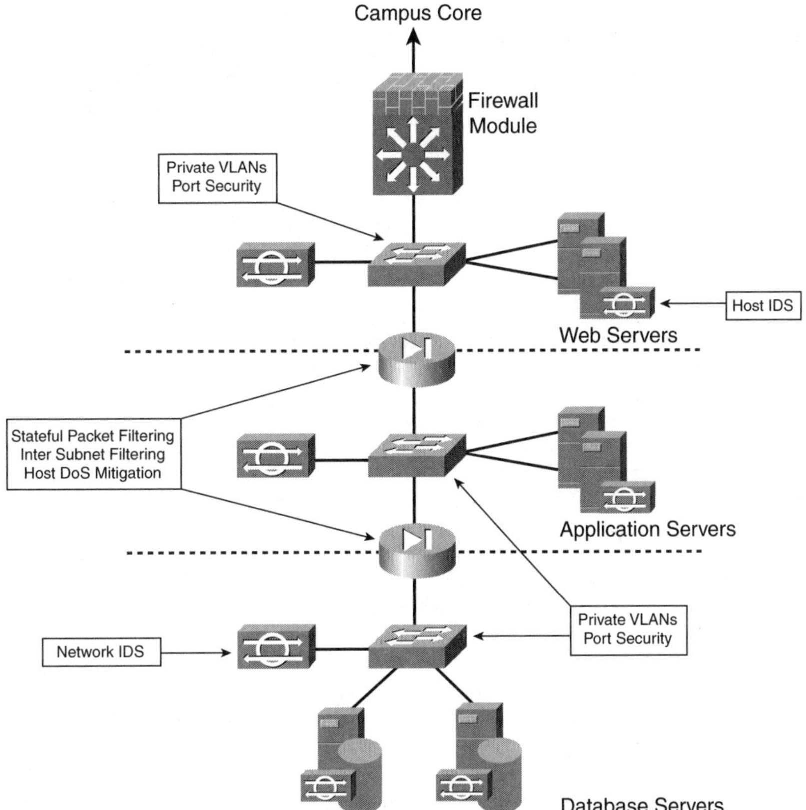

Private VLANs, port security, and intrusion detection are implemented as described for the collapsed design.

The major difference in the expanded design is the additional layer of switches and stateful firewalls. You must configure these firewalls with very precise rules indicating the exact systems that can communicate using what protocols. These rules should consider traffic flowing in all directions and from all interfaces.

Finally, the firewalls should implement any available DoS controls on a system basis.

Redundant Firewall Designs

Deploying redundant firewalls presents challenges that are very similar to those in deploying redundant load balancers. This section describes active-standby and active-active firewalls, using the PIX and FWSM as examples for the active-standby mode.

Active-Standby Firewall Environments

When you deploy firewalls in active-standby mode, only one device forwards traffic at any given time. The standby device is ready to take over should the primary fail. Example 21-19 shows the failover configuration from a firewall module. The rest of this section explains each portion of the configuration.

Example 21-19 *FWSM Failover Configuration*

```
nameif vlan200 foverif security99
[...]
ip address outside 10.20.30.5 255.255.255.0
ip address inside 10.20.10.1 255.255.255.0
ip address failover 10.20.200.1 255.255.255.0
failover
[....]
ip address foverif 10.20.200.1 255.255.255.0
failover lan unit primary
failover lan interface foverif
failover timeout 0:00:00
failover poll 15
failover ip address outside 10.20.30.6
failover ip address inside 10.20.20.2
failover ip address foverif 10.20.200.2
failover link foverif
```

The communication exchange between a redundant pair of firewalls follows one of the following two schemes:

- **Failover cable**—A dedicated serial cable connecting the pair of firewalls (applicable only to the PIX line of firewalls). This approach typically allows the configuration of one single device and the synchronization of the configurations between the active and standby devices. The dedicated serial line is not subject to congestion, and it offers a fast failover. There are, however, length restrictions on how far apart you can place the redundant firewalls from each other. Convergence time is faster with the failover cable because the detection of a failure on the active device is more immediate (as in a reload or a power failure, for example).
- **Failover VLAN**—Just a VLAN used to transport firewall status between the pair of firewalls. The VLAN is trunked between the aggregation switches housing the redundant firewall pair. This approach requires at least some basic configuration on both

the master and standby device for the election process to take place properly. You synchronize the configurations with external software tools. A failover VLAN might be subject to link congestion (for which there are workarounds), and there are no length restrictions.

Example 21-19 shows the creation of VLAN200 as the carrier for the failover communication with the commands **nameif vlan200 foverif security99** and **failover lan interface foverif**.

MAC Address

The MAC address association to the IP address of a firewall can follow the same schemes as the ones described for the load balancers.

With the PIX Firewall and the FWSM, when a device becomes active, it inherits both the MAC address and the IP address of the previously active unit. There is no need to update the ARP tables of the adjacent routers.

Example 21-20 shows the configuration: each device is configured with the IP address to use as primary and the IP address to use as standby. The following command indicates the IP address that a firewall uses if it is primary:

```
ip address interface IP address
```

The following command indicates the IP address that the firewall uses if it is secondary:

```
failover ip address interface IP address
```

The following configuration command means that this firewall should be standby. Its outside IP address would be 10.20.30.6; otherwise, its outside IP address is 10.20.30.5:

```
failover ip address outside 10.20.30.56
```

Election Process

With the PIX Firewall or on the FWSM, a command explicitly assigns the role for each device. **failover lan unit primary** makes the firewall the primary device; similarly, **failover lan unit secondary** makes the firewall the standby device.

When you use the failover cable on a redundant set of PIX firewalls, the cable determines which is primary and which is secondary by the connector on the cable. The end of the cable labeled primary (if you're using the failover cable for redundancy) should be connected to the firewall that you configured first.

Failure Detection

In the PIX and the FWSM, the detection of a failure on the active unit is a combination of these mechanisms:

- The active device sends a hello packet every 15 seconds (sec). (This timer is configurable with the command **failover poll** and can be brought down to 3 sec.) Hello packets are sent to all the interfaces.
- The standby unit monitors both the hello packets and the failover communication.
- Two consecutive missing hello packets trigger the failover tests.
- The failover tests consist of sending hello messages both on the interfaces and the failover connection. The units then monitor their interfaces to see whether they have received traffic.

The firewall performs additional tests to determine which unit is faulty. The tests include a linkup/linkdown test of the network interface cards (NICs), a network activity test, an ARP test, and a broadcast ping test.

The conclusion is that the convergence time by default is around 30 sec (twice the poll timer) and can be brought down to around 6 sec.

Stateful Failover

The state information on a firewall consists primarily of the following elements:

- Connection information (the 5-tuple information per connection)
- Translation information (network address translation [NAT] and port address translation [PAT])

The routing table information typically is not synchronized.

The command **failover link** in Example 21-19 enables stateful failover on the PIX and FWSM.

Active-Active (Clusters)

Certain models of firewalls can be clustered for redundancy in an active-active configuration. What this configuration means is that both firewalls accept traffic, and by a messaging mechanism, they decide which one forwards the incoming packets. This mechanism ensures both load distribution and redundancy.

Figure 21-16 shows how this process works. Part **a** is the physical topology, and part **b** represents the logical topology.

Figure 21-16 *Firewall Redundancy with Multicast MAC*

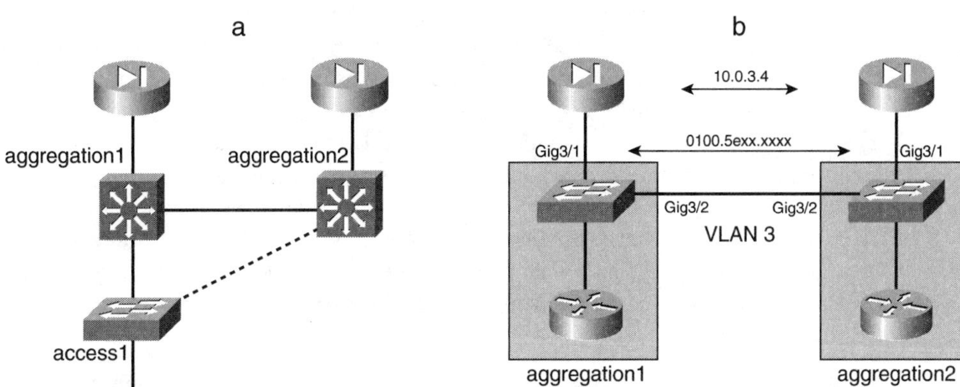

These firewalls share a common IP address, 10.0.3.4. Because both devices are active, it is a requirement to forward traffic to both firewalls at Layer 2.

The solution consists of associating their "virtual" IP address, 10.0.3.4, to a multicast MAC address, 0100.5exx.xxxx. If you do so, traffic at Layer 2 is flooded and reaches both firewalls.

This design has two main limitations: the first is that you are asking a router to ARP a unicast IP and to learn a multicast MAC address, and the second is that every time traffic is sent to the firewalls by the router, there is flooding on the VLAN (VLAN 3 in the example).

You can fix the problems by doing the following:

- Create a static ARP entry on the router in the Layer 3 switch: **arp** 10.0.3.4 0100.5exx.xxxx.
- Create a static entry in the cam table pointing to the firewall and to the trunk: **set cam permanent** 0100.5exx.xxxx 3/1,3/2 in CatOS or **mac-address-table static** 0100.5exx.xxxx in GigE3/1 GigE3/2 in native IOS.

The following section discusses Data Center management aspects.

NOTE For more information about the MAC address table on a Layer 2 switch, refer to Chapter 12.

Management Network

The *management network* refers to the part of the Data Center infrastructure that provides a secured environment for the configuration, monitoring and maintaining the different elements and devices that form the Data Center, such as routers, switches, and firewalls. The services typically provided by the management infrastructure include configuration management, monitoring, user authentication, and software updates. You usually implement configuration management and monitoring by using network management systems and servers running protocols such SNMP, remote monitoring (RMON), and syslog. You frequently use RADIUS and TACACS+ servers for user authentication, authorization, and accounting (AAA). FTP and Trivial File Transfer Protocol (TFTP) are protocols commonly used for software upgrades. You can group all these systems and services in a single security zone.

The following sections discuss these principles applied to the management infrastructure.

Management Isolation

The isolation of the management infrastructure consists of creating a management segment separated from the production network by physical or logical means. This isolation prevents the data plane from being used as a path to the management systems, reducing the effects of a possible compromise on the production network.

In an ideal case, you should achieve the isolation by using separate switches and dedicated ports on the managed devices, which is known as out-of-band (OOB) management. Figure 21-17 illustrates the use of physical segregation, where a terminal server connects to the console ports of a router and a switch and where a firewall connects to an OOB switch using a dedicated interface. In this example, the dotted lines represent the management interfaces and VLANs, and the solid lines are the links carrying normal user traffic.

Physical isolation is the most secure method, but in some situations, it might not be possible to implement a truly OOB management in a Data Center. The alternative, in-band management, also allows segregation but logically through the use of virtual private networks (VPNs) and VLANs. Figure 21-18 shows an example that uses multiple VLANs to securely manage a firewall.

This example creates two VLANs: the solid lines represent the VLAN carrying the normal user traffic, and the dotted lines are the VLAN for the management traffic.

NOTE VPN is a technology that Data Centers can use to segregate traffic in multiple isolated communication channels. VPNs typically provide services such as encryption and strong authentication, which are discussed in the following sections. The Data Center can use VPNs to securely manage those devices that you cannot directly connect to the management segment.

Figure 21-17 *OOB Management with Physical Segregation*

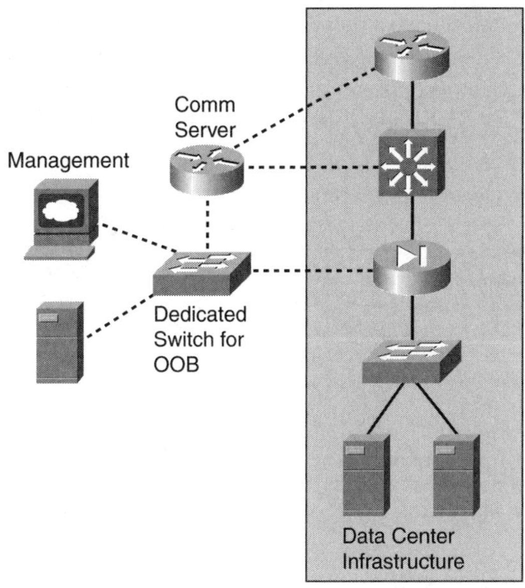

Figure 21-18 *Logical Segregation*

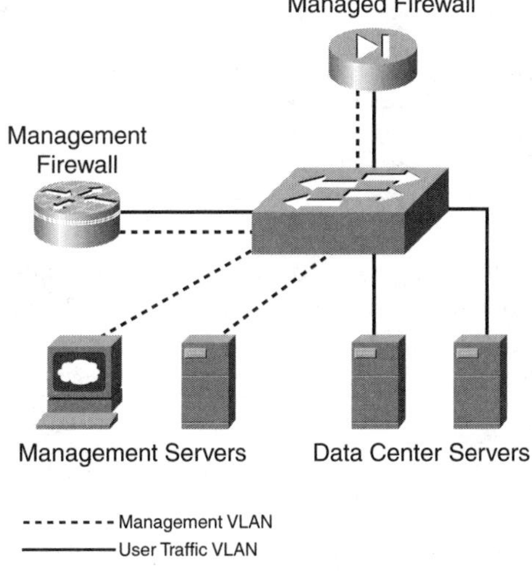

You can also use firewalls to enforce the separation between the management segment and the production network. Example 21-20 shows the configuration of an IOS firewall for in-band management. This example applies ingress inspection to the interface connecting the management segment. An ingress filter is applied to the interface connecting to the data plane. This ACL allows primary management services such as SNMP, TFTP, syslog, and POP. It also allows IP Security (IPSec) traffic destined to the same router for secure remote management.

Example 21-20 *IOS Firewall Used for In-Band Management*

```
ip inspect name myfw ftp timeout 3600
ip inspect name myfw http timeout 3600
ip inspect name myfw rcmd timeout 3600
ip inspect name myfw tftp timeout 30
ip inspect name myfw udp timeout 15
ip inspect name myfw tcp timeout 3600
!
interface Ethernet0
  description Management Plane
  ip address 10.1.1.5 255.255.255.0
  ip inspect myfw in
!
interface Ethernet1
  description Data Plane
  ip address 172.16.2.1 255.255.255.0
  ip access-group 117 in
!
access-list 117 permit esp any host 172.16.2.1
access-list 117 permit udp any host 172.16.2.1 eq isakmp
access-list 117 permit udp 172.16.1.0 0.0.0.255 host 10.1.1.47 eq syslog
access-list 117 permit udp 172.16.1.0 0.0.0.255 host 10.1.1.45 eq 45000
access-list 117 permit udp 172.16.1.0 0.0.0.255 host 10.1.1.44 eq tftp
access-list 117 permit udp 172.16.1.0 0.0.0.255 host 10.1.1.48 eq snmp
access-list 117 permit tcp 172.16.1.0 0.0.0.255 host 10.1.1.43 eq tacacs
access-list 117 deny   ip any any log
```

In real life, it is very unlikely that you can implement an entire management infrastructure under a purely OOB model, so most cases implement the management segment as a combination of OOB and in-band mechanisms.

Encryption

The use of encryption is a recommended practice to protect the transport of all administrative data corresponding to the switches, routers, firewalls, and other infrastructure elements that build the Data Center. This practice becomes mandatory in in-band and remote management.

Many of the protocols used in network administration and monitoring send all data in cleartext. If intercepted, sensitive information such as usernames and passwords can end up in the wrong hands. Telnet and SNMPv1 are examples of protocols that do not provide any confidentiality. Whenever it is possible, you should replace these protocols with those that work in a secure manner. For example, instead of Telnet, you can use SSH or SSL, which provide strong encryption and authentication. Instead of using SNMPv1, use SNMPv3, which supports encryption, integrity, and authentication.

In some situations, you might need to still use insecure protocols. A typical example is TFTP, which is still the only mechanism some products use for file transfer and software upgrade. You can secure this type of protocol by using IPSec, which works at the IP level. Example 21-21 illustrates the configuration of an IPSec VPN for secure management using an IOS router and Cisco VPN Client 3.x. Under this configuration, users are authenticated against a RADIUS server using XAuth (extended authentication).

Example 21-21 *IOS Configuration for Secure Management Access*

```
aaa new-model
aaa authentication login clientauth group radius
aaa authorization network groupauth group radius
!
crypto isakmp policy 10
 encr 3des
 authentication pre-share
 group 2
!
crypto ipsec transform-set mgmset esp-3des esp-sha-hmac
!
crypto dynamic-map dynmap 10
 set transform-set mgmset
!
crypto map mgmmap client authentication list clientauth
crypto map mgmmap isakmp authorization list groupauth
crypto map mgmmap client configuration address respond
crypto map mgmmap 10 ipsec-isakmp dynamic dynmap
!
interface Ethernet1
description Data Plane
ip address 172.16.2.1 255.255.255.0
crypto map mgmmap
!
ip local pool mgmpool 10.1.1.100 10.1.1.105
radius-server host 10.1.1.43 auth-port 1645 acct-port 1646 key mysecretkey
```

Strong Authentication

The use of strong authentication is another recommended practice that becomes mandatory with in-band and remote management. Strong authentication becomes essential for effective control of the access to management systems and managed devices that form the Data Center infrastructure.

You can implement multiple technologies for user identification and authentication, from simple mechanisms such as static passwords up to more sophisticated technologies such as biometrics. One of the most convenient and secure methods uses One-Time Passwords (OTPs).

NOTE Biometrics systems are automated mechanisms that identify and authenticate a person by looking at physiological or behavioral characteristics, such as fingerprint patterns, hand geometry, and keyboard typing style. Biometric systems are effective, but the technology is still significantly expensive.

As the name indicates, OTPs are passwords that can be used only once. OTP uses a password-generator device called a token. When a user needs to authenticate, he uses the token device to generate a valid password, and once he uses the password, it is no longer valid. You can use this type of mechanism in conjunction with AAA protocols such as TACACS+ and RADIUS. Figure 21-19 shows the RSA SecurID 520 PINpad, a token device.

Figure 21-19 *Photo Token Device*

Once a user is authenticated, she must be authorized. This process provides access to specific devices and commands that are preselected to be adequate to her role or responsibility. Using authorization, you can divide the administration and monitoring responsibilities based on users, groups, or functional roles. In this way, you can create different groups, each with different privileges. In most organizations, security and network operations are handled by different teams. In this scenario, you could create two groups, netops and secops. You can configure netops with privileged access to all network devices and with restricted access to security devices such firewalls. At the same time, secops can be assigned unrestricted privileges over all the security devices and limited access to the security elements of the network devices.

Example 21-22 shows the TACACS+ profiles corresponding to two groups and two users in those groups: groups netops and secops and users netops1 and secops1. Under this configuration, the secops group has full privilege access to the managed devices in the 10.1.1.0/24 subnet, and netops has a restricted access that allows users in that group only to execute the commands **show ver**, **ping**, and **logout**.

Example 21-22 *TACACS+ Profiles for the Netops and Secops Groups*

```
group = netops {
password = clear "ag&^hg"
allow mynas.cisco.com ".*" "10\.1\.1\.*"
refuse ".*" ".*" ".*"
     privilege = clear "cisco" 15
         service = shell {
                  cmd = show {
                  permit "ver"
                  }
                  cmd = ping {
                  permit "."
                  }
                  cmd = logout {
                  permit ".g
                  }
         }
}
user = netop1 {
         member = netops
         default service = permit
         }
group = secops {
         password = clear "G3^%C"
   allow mynas.cisco.com ".*" "10\.1\.1\.*"
refuse ".*" ".*" ".*"
         privilege = clear "cisco" 15
         service = shell {
                  default cmd = permit
                  default attribute = permit
         }
}
user = secop1 {
         member = secops
         default service = permit
         }
```

Example 21-23 shows the commands on IOS to enable AAA using TACACS+. This configuration separates the authentication of the console port from the VTYs. Console access is authenticated with the line password, but VTY access is controlled with TACACS+.

Example 21-23 *AAA Configuration on an IOS Router*

```
aaa new-model
aaa authentication login use_tacacs group tacacs+
aaa authentication login use_line line
aaa authorization exec default group tacacs+
aaa authorization network default group tacacs+
aaa accounting exec default start-stop group tacacs+
aaa accounting network default start-stop group tacacs
!
tacacs-server host 10.1.1.43 single-connection
tacacs-server key mysecretkey
!
line con 0
 exec-timeout 2 0
 login authentication use_line
line vty 0 4
 login authentication use_tacacs
!
```

NOTE You can configure authorization up to the command and attribute level, but this process is supported only by TACACS+. RADIUS does not provide any command authorization.

Secure Management Design

The design of the management infrastructure requires that all the management systems be in the same security zone and that there is a consistent mechanism that gathers logs, makes configuration changes, and accesses and monitors devices. Figure 21-20 illustrates a design of the management infrastructure based on the principles previously explained.

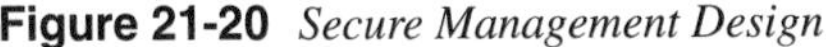

Figure 21-20 *Secure Management Design*

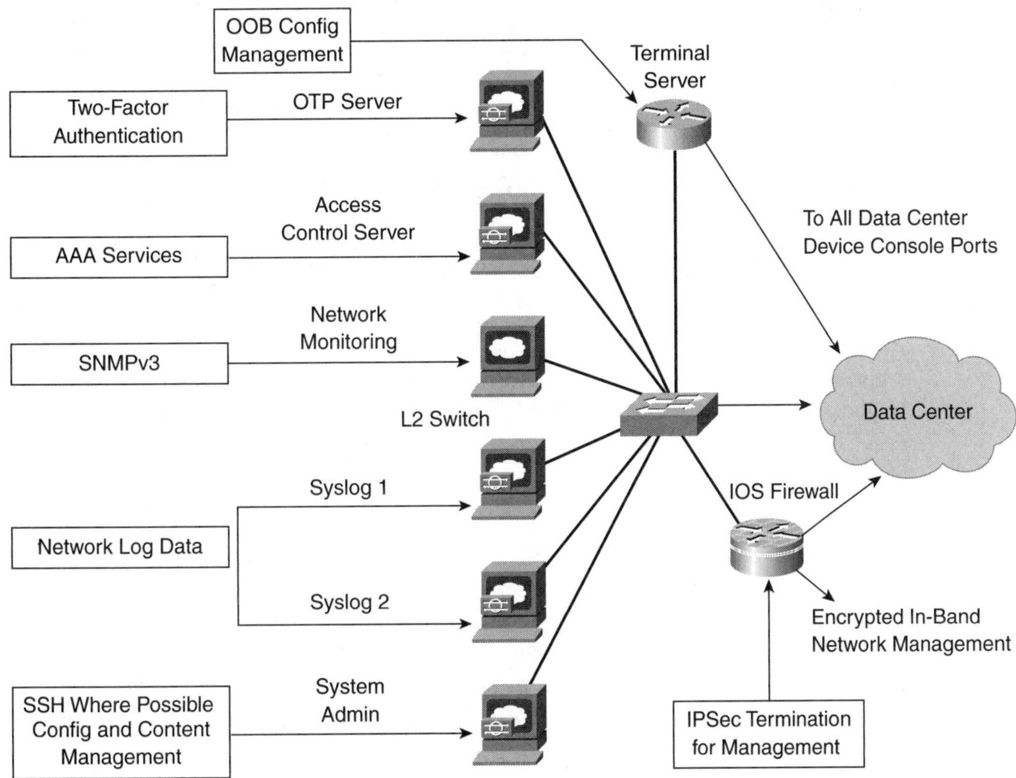

In this design, the OOB management is implemented with a separate Layer 2 infrastructure and with a terminal server that connects to the console ports of the devices managed OOB. This design also incorporates a router that acts as the termination point of the IPSec tunnels used for secure in-band management. The same router is configured as a stateful firewall to maintain the segregation of the management segment from the production network. Host-based agents are installed on the critical servers. For strong access control, an access control server (AAA) is deployed in conjunction with the OTP server, which provides strong authentication, and SNMPv3 is used to manage the network devices.

Summary

Designing the security of the Data Center network requires that you consider multiple factors that include defining the security zones, selecting the security tools and the features to use, understanding where and how these tools and features should be applied, and deciding how the entire Data Center security should be monitored and managed.

The security zone definition involves understanding the likely attacks, threats, and vulnerabilities; the criticality of the systems within the zone; and ultimately the specific requirements that the design should support.

The design of ACLs, the placement of firewalls, and the signatures enabled on IDS sensors are based on the requirements of each security zone.

At the Internet Edge, it is typical to use RFC 1918 and RFC 2827 filtering and uRPF. In this security zone, the firewalls filter the traffic directed to the servers hosted in the DMZ and limit external access to the enterprise campus to the connections originated by the internal users. Typical intrusion-detection signatures belong to the HTTP, DNS, FTP, and SMTP protocol families.

At the intranet server farm, the firewalls enforce traffic paths between the enterprise users and the servers and among servers. In addition to providing these functions, the firewalls protect the servers from DoS attacks of TCP SYN cookies by limiting the number of allowed embryonic connections. IDS signatures at the intranet server farm are tailored to the application environment; as a result, they typically belong to the HTTP family. Within the HTTP family, you can fine-tune the signatures to the specific application server platforms, such as Java signatures or Active Server Pages (ASP) signatures. The IDS sensor can also monitor server-to-server communication protocols, such as RPC.

At the intranet server farm, it is important to deploy Layer 2 security features such as port security, ARP inspection, and private VLANs to limit the chance that a compromised server could attack other servers or that somebody could divert the traffic path of sensitive traffic by performing ARP spoofing.

The security design of the Data Center can follow two different approaches:

- Providing physical segregation between the security zones and deploying multiple firewall devices to segregate the server farms
- Segregating the server farms with VLANs

The second design provides the security services mainly at the aggregation layer of the Data Center. In either design, it is important that security does not compromise high availability, which is why you must deploy the devices in the path of the traffic, specifically the firewalls, in redundant pairs.

The design is not complete until you consider the network management. You must secure the network management in the Data Center with encryption and strong authentication for device access.

This chapter covers the following topics:

- Traffic patterns overview
- Performance metrics concepts
- Overview of performance metrics used on routers, switches, and firewalls
- In-depth analysis of performance metrics for load balancers and Secure Socket Layer (SSL) offloaders
- Performance benchmark-testing efforts

CHAPTER 22

Performance Metrics of Data Center Devices

This chapter introduces multiple topics related to benchmarking the performance of devices typically found in Data Centers, such as switches, routers, server load balancers, and firewalls. The discussion includes a short analysis of data traffic patterns, testing tools, testing tips, and server performance metrics. The chapter also discusses the metrics you use to measure the performance of these devices.

Firewalls, load balancers, and SSL offloading devices perform different functions than Layer 2 or Layer 3 switches and they are therefore benchmarked differently. For instance, to accurately measure the performance capabilities of load balancers, you must measure connections and session related metrics. These metrics collectively describe different aspects of their capabilities in dealing with specific traffic types and overall indicate their behavior under extreme load conditions.

Routers and Layer 3 and Layer 2 switches do not need to track connection or session state.

Understanding the performance characteristics of the Data Center devices allows you to design a network that is capable of withstanding the expected load and helps you do capacity planning for bottlenecks as the traffic load increases over time.

Before you learn the metrics used to benchmark the performance of Data Center devices, it is important to understand the traffic patterns that you are likely to see in the Data Center.

Traffic Patterns Overview

This section discusses traffic patterns observed on the Internet and intranets and their relation to Data Center environments. The discussion includes an analysis of how to look at traffic patterns from the perspective of the network devices that have to process the packets associated with such traffic.

By observing the traffic patterns present on the Internet or intranets, it is possible to infer the likely traffic that the server farms have to process. This inference is useful when it is not possible to observe the actual traffic processed by the server farm, or you have no preexisting traffic patterns to use for capacity planning or testing purposes.

The simulation of real-world traffic conditions implies the use of a data-traffic mix that resembles traffic patterns in operating networks. Because every network experiences different traffic patterns, it is impossible to determine through a single set of tests the behavior of the devices for a specific network. You must approximate by using existing statistical data on traffic patterns to select the most descriptive set of tests. This approximation process includes gathering real-world data, based on the observation of real traffic statistics on various Internet backbone points or intranet locations, and averaging the multiple data points to produce a single set of protocols and their percentages, the *traffic mix*.

You should determine this traffic mix for both Internet and intranet traffic patterns because they are different. Internet traffic patterns are based entirely on Internet-centric information, which would not necessarily reflect enterprise backbone traffic conditions. Each enterprise has its own traffic patterns, and because the data is more accessible, it becomes easier to observe an equivalent set of patterns, or a data mix, for testing purposes. For instance, a firewall located in the Internet Edge of an enterprise network deals with traffic and traffic volumes that are different from those for a firewall at the edge of a server farm in the intranet. The Internet Edge firewall might perform network address translation (NAT) functions that the intranet firewall does not.

Internet Traffic Patterns

Internet traffic patterns are based on measurements taken multiple times at a number of points on the Internet. These measurements reflect the status and traffic conditions at the time of the measurements, which typically happen over long periods of time to produce a more accurate average. Multiple measurements produce Internet traffic statistics that describe the traffic patterns.

There are ongoing efforts to both measure and characterize various aspects of Internet traffic. As a result, many research organizations and projects focus on providing valuable information used in and produced by such analysis. A few of these organizations include the following:

- **San Diego Supercomputer Center (SDSC)**—An organized entity within the University of California, San Diego, that deals with how to resolve "demanding computational science problems" through the use of computing technologies. This work ultimately fosters scientific research. There are two groups under SDSC, CAIDA and NLANR. For more information on SDSC, consult http://www.sdsc.edu/.
- **The Cooperative Association for Internet Data Analysis (CAIDA)**—Provides tools and analyses promoting the engineering and maintenance of a robust, scalable, global Internet infrastructure. For more information on CAIDA, consult http://www.caida.org/.

- **The National Laboratory for Applied Network Research, Measurement Network Analysis Group (NLANR)**—Focuses on characterizing the behavior of high-performance connection networks. The research provides a great deal of scientific data and practical measurements of Internet traffic. In the Data Center, you should apply Internet traffic patterns to the Internet Edge, which includes the edge routers, edge firewall, an Internet server farm, and devices such as load balancers and SSL off-loaders. For more information on NLANR, consult http://www.nlanr.net/.

NOTE If you place load balancers and firewalls in front of devices other than servers and caches such as virtual private network (VPN) terminators and wireless gateways, load balancers are exposed to the same traffic conditions that the devices they front-end.

When devices such as load balancers or firewalls front end other devices such as VPN terminators or wireles gateways, you might need to include some of this traffic in the mix to benchmark the load balancers and firewalls in conditions similar to those found on your network.

Use the traffic statistics available through these and other organizations as guidelines for the traffic types on the Internet Edge of an enterprise. A key consideration when using the statistics to produce a traffic mix for testing purposes is that although most traffic types might apply to your own environment, some might not be appropriate.

You must analyze your current traffic statistics at the Internet Edge of the enterprise network. You use NetFlow statistics from the edge routers to create a realistic traffic mix. This approach, however, requires that NetFlow information be readily available for a fair length of time so that you can calculate a representative average.

NOTE For more information on NetFlow, consult http://www.cisco.com/univercd/cc/td/doc/cisintwk/intsolns/netflsol/nfwhite.htm.

The research project "Wide-Area Internet Traffic Patterns and Characteristics," conducted by Thompson, Miller, and Wilder and published in 1997, gathered data from two different locations of the public MCI backbone. The project found the following:

- TCP averages 95 percent of bytes, 90 percent of packets, and at least 75 percent of flows on the link.
- User Datagram Protocol (UDP) averages 5 percent of bytes, 10 percent of packets, and 20 percent of flows.

- Web traffic makes 75 percent of bytes, 70 percent of packets, and 75 percent of flows in the TCP category.
- In addition to Web traffic, Domain Name System (DNS), Simple Mail Transfer Protocol (SMTP), FTP data, Network News Transfer Protocol (NNTP), and Telnet are identified as contributing a visible percentage.
- DNS represents 18 percent of flows but only 3 percent of total packets and 1 percent of total bytes.
- SMTP makes 5 percent of bytes, 5 percent of packets, and 2 percent of flows.
- FTP data produces 5 percent of bytes, 3 percent of packets, and less than 1 percent of flows.
- NNTP contributes 2 percent of bytes and less than 1 percent of packets and flows.

Table 22-1 presents the top-six TCP and UDP protocols that are part of the results of a protocol mix for data traffic collected as part of a research project, "Trends in Wide Area IP Traffic Patterns," done by McCreary and Claffy during May 1999 and March 2000.

Table 22-1 *Top 10 Protocols*

Protocols	Packets	Bytes	Average Size
TCP	374,801,201	176,706,563,104	471
UDP	62,456,731	9,842,511,709	157
Generic Routing Encapsulation (GRE)	7,566,415	5,272,240,819	696
Internet Control Message Protocol (ICMP)	5,938,044	1,350,011,401	227
Encapsulating Security Payload (ESP)	517,353	197,216,792	381
IP in IP	265,103	179,257,606	676
Authentication Header (AH)	74,423	43,454,671	583
IPIP	143,502	41,707,350	290
SKIP	117,050	41,633,952	355
Internet Group Management Protocol (IGMP)	68,404	7,729,038	112

The TCP and UDP traffic make more than 96 percent of both the packets and bytes of the data mix. Note that TCP alone is roughly 82 percent of the packets and slightly 91 percent of the byte count.

The top TCP protocols include HTTP, FTP, SMTP, and NNTP, and the top UDP protocols include RealAudio and DNS.

More recent analysis still shows WWW traffic dominating the traffic mix yet not as high as previously seen. WWW traffic includes web-related applications such as HTTP, Secure HTTP (HTTPS), and SQUID (web caching). Other application traffic that belongs to peer-to-peer applications such as the file-sharing applications Gnutella, Napster, and eDonkey is on the rise. The CAIDA organization has obtained more recent traffic traces, which show the changes in the protocols mix. Check them at http://www.caida.org/analysis/workload/. Some of the peer-to-peer applications are likely to appear in university environments. The University of Wisconsin, Madison, performed an example of such research, "Internet Traffic Flow Size Analysis."

Keep in mind that although some of these protocols are increasing in the mix, their applicability to selecting a proper data mix should be based first on whether these protocols are present on your network and second on whether the devices in the Data Center have to process them.

Intranet Traffic Patterns

Intranet statistics are in many ways easier to obtain than Internet-based statistics. In the enterprise, you can easily monitor the traffic on enterprise backbones and even the enterprise connections to the Internet. Some important considerations related to an enterprise backbone are the protocols other than IP and the location to monitor the traffic.

Protocols different from IP are difficult to test partly because not many testing tools support protocols other than TCP/IP. The majority of enterprise networks, however, have or are migrating to an IP-only infrastructure, which makes the need to test those other protocols irrelevant.

Traffic patterns on internal networks include both client-to-server and server-to-server communications. You can easily monitor client-to-server traffic in the aggregation switches using NetFlow. Monitoring server-to-server traffic depends on the type of servers and the location where that traffic is present. Web-to-application-server traffic has different characteristics from application-to-database traffic, and in both cases, the location to monitor is typically a VLAN related to a specific application.

NOTE A good source of information for measuring performance of IP networks is the paper "Measuring IP Network Performance" by Geoff Houston on the Internet Protocol Journal at http://www.cisco.com/warp/customer/759/ipj_6-1/ipj_6-1_measuring_ip_networks.html.

The traffic mix to use in the enterprise should reflect what is found in the backbone, trimmed down to traffic patterns that devices such as the load balancer or firewall are likely to handle. In many cases, choosing the mix might be as easy as taking the list in Table 22-1, including the breakdown of TCP and UDP protocols, adding a few other protocols that might be relevant, and changing the percentages to reflect those of your own environment.

Traffic Patterns in the Data Center

Data Center devices are exposed to various traffic characteristics depending on the location of the device. In general, when considering which metrics to use to benchmark the performance of various devices, it is important to first classify the likely traffic types and to then identify how the classified types of traffic are handled by the relevant Data Center devices.

This second point of correlating classified traffic types to specific devices is relevant in determining how you should measure performance on the different Data Center devices. For instance, routers, Layer 2 switches, and Layer 3 switches process packets and are not aware of whether those packets belong to connections or sessions. This fact implies that routers, Layer 2 switches, and Layer 3 switches do not keep state information that could be used to recover the connections or sessions in case of a failure of the primary processing device. Routers, Layer 2 switches, and Layer 3 switches process packets and, for the most part, are not concerned with information in the payload of the packet or whether the packet is a control packet (such as a connection request or response) that is part of a connection that needs to be tracked. In a few exceptions, some features on routers or switches do recognize connection requests such as TCP intercept or SYN rate limiting used for denial-of-service (DoS) protection. These features, however, do not necessarily force the devices to track connections or sessions.

Other devices such as load balancers, firewalls, and SSL offloaders are aware of connection and in some cases sessions. These devices do keep state information for connections or sessions. Tracking connections and sessions implies these devices can recognize packets that belong to connections and sessions and can also understand the meaning of some of these packets. For example, a load balancer knows of connection requests (SYN), HTTP requests (GET or PUT), and URLs.

Routers, Layer 2 switches, and Layer 3 switches are measured on how they process packets, whereas firewalls, load balancers, and SSL offloaders can be measured on how they process connections. For example, if a load balancer is configured to load-balance connections, its performance might be better measured on how well it processes connections.

Classifying traffic in this case refers to how the devices consider the traffic patterns instead of the protocol mix. For devices that are aware of connections and sessions, the classification is based on the types of connections or sessions. Devices that process packets do not need such classification because one packet might not require specific processing requirements and does not belong to a logical traffic entity the device is aware of.

Connections in the context of these discussions refer to both TCP connections and single UDP transactions, which include packets with a common 5-tuple of protocol, source and destination IP addresses, and port numbers. The following sections discuss the more generic classifications of connections: short-lived and long-lived.

Short-Lived Connections

Short-lived traffic is best described as traffic that belongs to connections between client and servers which only lasts or "lives" a few seconds. Because the connections are only a few seconds in length, a relatively small number of packets are exchanged between client and server.

Figure 22-1 provides an example of the events of a short-lived connection using HTTP.

Figure 22-1 *Short-Lived Connection Example*

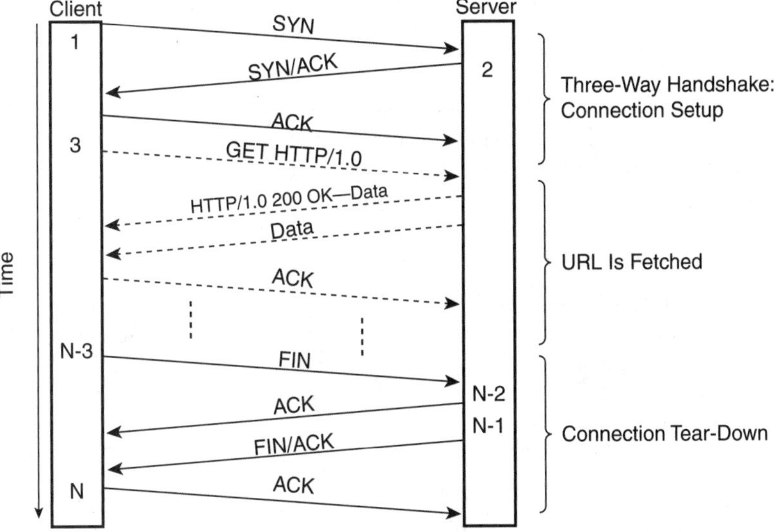

After the user types the URL, a connection request is sent (SYN) and the connection is established. The web page associated with the URL in the request is loaded, and the TCP connection is torn down. This connection generates just a few packets, as follows:

- Connection setup packets (SYN, SYN/ACK, and ACK)
- The HTTP connection request and the HTTP response
- Download of the web page, including ACKs
- Connection teardown packets (FIN, FIN/ACK, and ACK)

According to Brownlee and Claffy, in some Internet links roughly 45 percent of the connections last less than 2 seconds (sec). Short-lived connections are also present on intranets. The following list gives examples of typical short-lived connections in both Internet and intranet environments:

- **A search for a specific document**—A search engine that finds a specific document generates a short-lived connection. The result of the search engine is a list of the likely locations of the document, if any.
- **An HTTP session used to browse the Web looking for information**—Browsing for information generates a number of short-lived connections in which the contents of each page are downloaded, after which the connection is terminated. In certain cases, a new connection is initiated before the previous connection is terminated, and in some cases, the connections are terminated when the client browser is closed down.
- **A DNS request**—This example is self-explanatory because DNS primarily uses UDP as the protocol for finding the IP address of a particular host name. Referring to the previous example (the document search), it is important to remember that for every HTTP request generated, a DNS request was also generated (assuming the client's browser did not have the IP address for the specific site in its cache).

Figure 22-2 shows an actual example of a short-lived connection, along with its summary. The connection is the first connection of a session to http://www.amazon.com, and it required 10 packets, lasted less than 0.5 sec, and transferred 1692 bytes. Note that Figure 22-2 displays both the packets and the connection summary.

Figure 22-2 *Summary of a Short-Lived Connection*

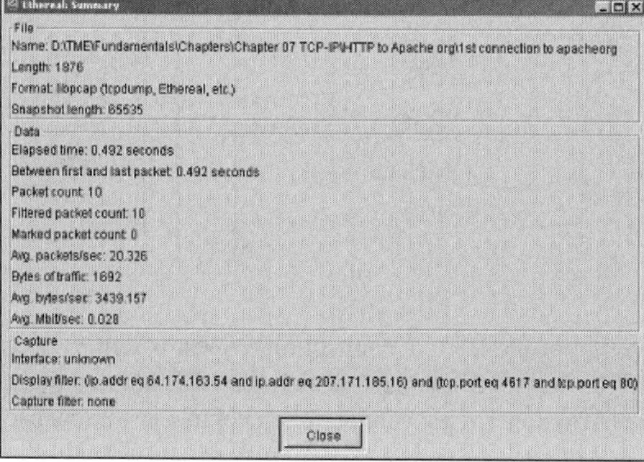

Other short-lived connections last longer than 1 or 2 sec and are in the 10 to 15 sec range. Notice that the reference is to individual connections instead of sessions. Sessions are in fact made by a number of connections. The session length is measured from the beginning of the first connection to the end of the last connection.

Sessions are also important, particularly when the Data Center device is supposed to recognize and track specific sessions, as load balancers and SSL offloaders do. Figure 22-3 shows an example of a session.

NOTE In many of the connections that are part of the session example with http://www.amazon.com, the TCP connection remained open. TCP connections are not necessarily closed after other connections for the same session are subsequently opened. Because many of these connections can remain open, the load balancer is forced to also keep state information for each open connection until they are closed or aged out because of a lack of activity. In either case, tuning the load balancer to better match the likely behavior would relieve it from the unnecessary burden of keeping the connections active in its connection table.

A descriptive example of a short-lived connection in the 10 to 15 sec range is the connection shown in Figure 22-3 to http://www.apache.org. Notice that in this example, the connection lasted roughly 12.8 sec. A Data Center device keeping track of the connection would only need to keep connection-state information for approximately the same time if it is not part of a session.

Another example of short-lived connections, this time associated with a session, is a number of the TCP connections of a session to http://www.amazon.com, introduced in Figure 22-4. The first connection, which corresponds to the connection in Figure 22-2, lasted less than 0.5 sec, and the successive connections were not that much longer. There were a total of seven TCP connections to port 80 for browsing and selecting items to buy, and one connection to port 443 (HTTP) to finish the transaction and pay for the items, including exchanging sensitive information such as credit cards and personal information.

It is worth noting that the duration of the session, almost two minutes (min), is not all attributed to the sum of the individual connections. The user "thinking" time is also included in the actual browsing, selecting, and marking the items of interest. Regardless of the reasons why the sessions last as long, Data Center devices keeping track of such sessions and the related connections still need to track all of them for as long as they are active.

Figure 22-3 *Short-Lived Connection to http://www.apache.org*

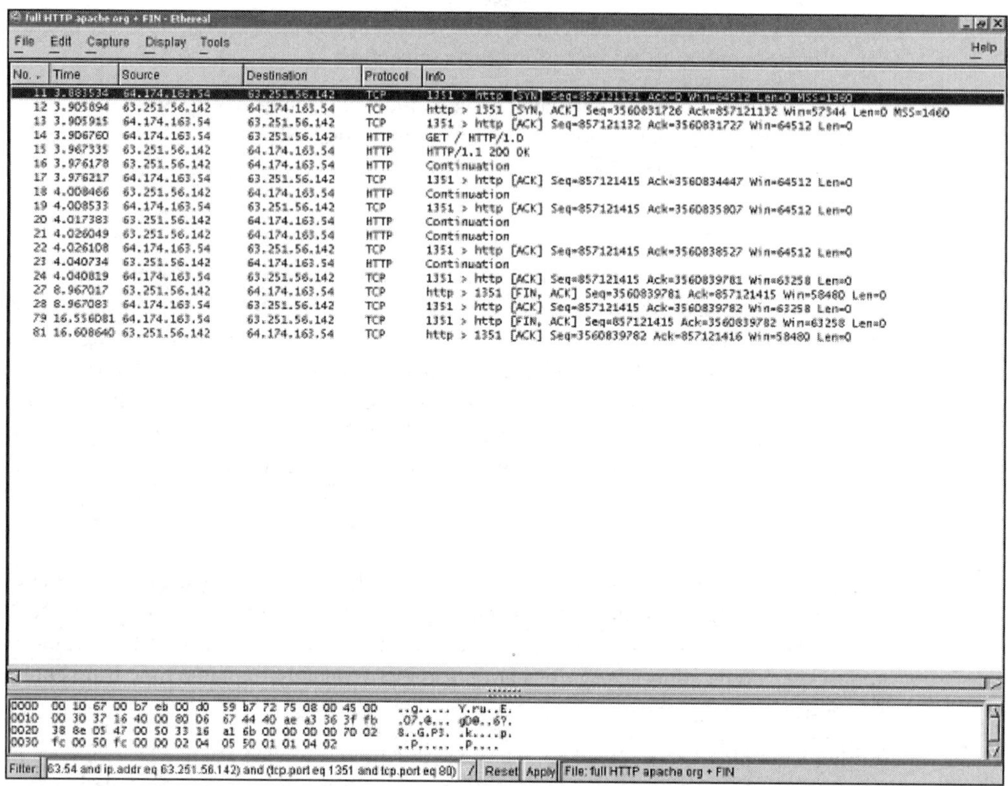

A high number of short-lived connections over a short period of time demands a high rate of processing. For Data Center devices such as routers or switches, the processing demand is based on how many packets are processed per unit of time. However, for Data Center devices that are connection- and session-aware, the demand is based on how many connections are processed per unit of time. The rate of packets per unit of time leads to a packets-per-second (PPS) metric, whereas the rate of connection per unit of time leads to a connection-per-second (CPS) metric.

Figure 22-4 *Short-Lived Connection Associated to a Session*

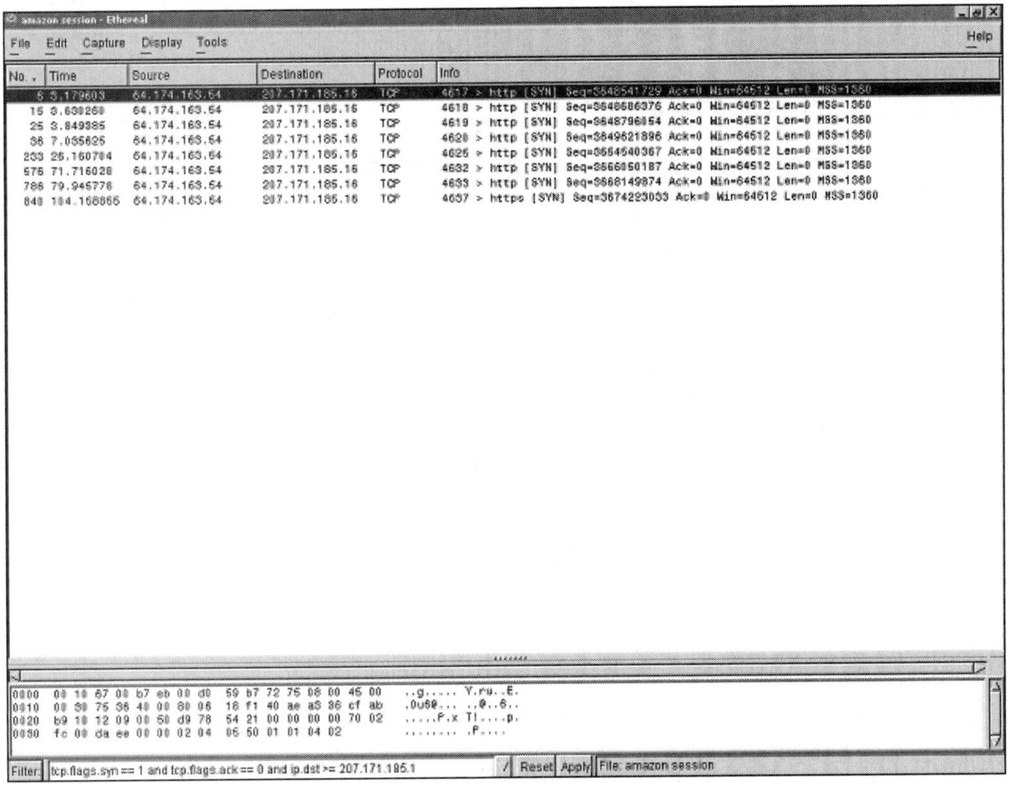

Long-Lived Connections

Long-lived traffic is best described as traffic that belongs to connections between clients and servers that last or "live" more than 15 sec—and might last more than a few minutes, hours, and even days. The duration of the connection ranges from a few seconds to a few days and might involve the exchange of good number of packets before the connection is terminated. The number of packets and the duration of the connection vary depending on the type of connection, the protocol in use, and other variables. According to Brownlee and Claffy, these long-lived connections can carry a high load, 50 to 60 percent, of the total number of bytes on a given link.

You can see an example of a long-lived connection in a Citrix session. The Citrix session includes a few connections that get started with a client browser applet. (For more information on applets, refer to Chapter 3, "Application Architectures Overview.") Figure 22-5 shows the summary of the long-lived connection between a Citrix client and a Citrix server.

Figure 22-5 *Example of a Citrix Long-Lived Connection*

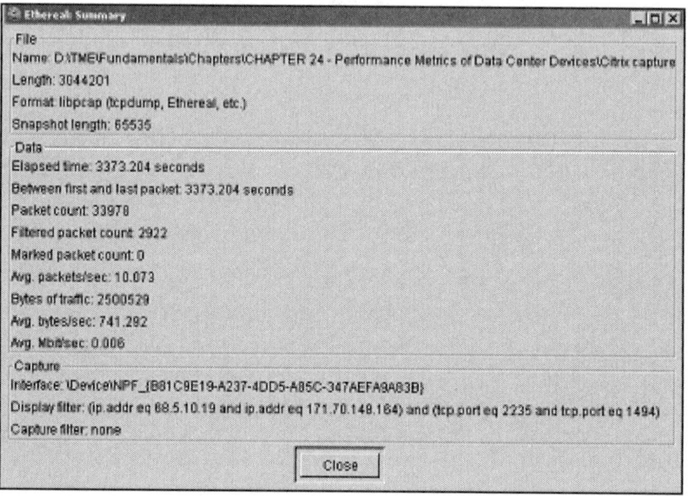

Figure 22-5 presents the headers of the initial packets and a summary of the entire connection. Similar to a Telnet connection, the connection is strictly controlled by the user, so the duration and information exchange is strictly driven by the user's actions. The connection lasted 56 min and 2,500,529 bytes were exchanged, for an average of 741 bytes per second. This connection was idle most of the time, yet each packet sent from client to server had the PSH flag on. Refer to Chapter 7, "IP, TCP, and UDP," for more information on how interactive applications use the TCP flags.

Other long-lived connections using Telnet, FTP, video streaming, or audio streaming could last hours. A Data Center device tracking connection information for long-lived connections is forced to keep the connection information in the connection table as long as the connections are active. An example of another long-lived session is an audio-streaming session. In this case, a connection is made to http://www.npr.org (National Public Radio) to hear a live broadcast of a radio show. The session consists of two different connections: a TCP connection to http://www.npr.org in selecting the program and a second TCP connection to the actual streaming server. The entire session lasted approximately 22 minutes. Figure 22-6 shows a summary of the TCP/ Real Time Streaming Protocol (RTSP) connection.

Notice the bytes transferred, 4,379,606, are a lot less than the ones transferred during the file download; the connection lasted longer. This statistic shows that the duration and size are independent, yet on a specific link, a greater amount of the bytes of traffic is related to long-lived connections.

Figure 22-6 *Long-Lived Audio Streaming Connection*

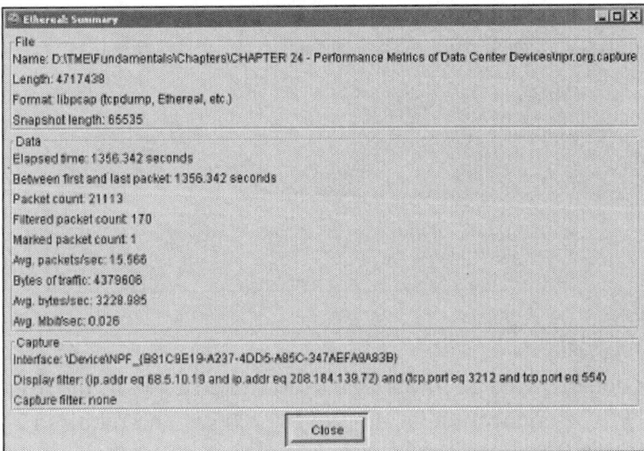

A few descriptive examples of long-lived connections follow:

- **A Telnet connection left open minutes or hours at a time**—This connection is not intensive in the amount of data transferred from the server to the client.
- **The transfer of a large file using FTP or HTTP**—Depending on the file size, the number of packets, size of packets, and the duration, the time it takes to transfer large files using FTP or HTTP tends to exceed the average duration of a connection.
- **An audio- or video-streaming session, which again varies in the number of packets, average packet size, and connection duration**—A particular video-streaming session uses a different set of protocols, which typically include both a control connection used for synchronization and a transport connection used for the actual delivery. Consult Chapter 11, "Streaming Protocols Overview," for more information.

Figure 22-7 displays another interesting example of a connection whose duration is dependent on the available bandwidth of the traffic path. Figure 22-7 presents an example of a connection in the time range between a short-lived connection and a long-lived connection, in this case to http://www.apache.org.

Figure 22-7 *Example of a Long-Lived Connection*

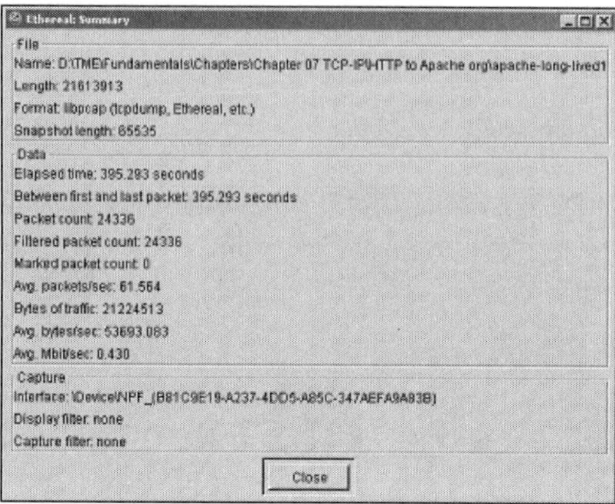

The connection in Figure 22-7 was used to download a 19 MB file from http://www.apache.org using HTTP. The connection lasted roughly 6.6 sec and required 24,336 packets. This example is included in the long-lived connection section because the download happened over a fast connection to the Internet. If the download had happened over a 800 Kbps link, the connection would have lasted approximately 26 sec, and if it had happened over a 50 Kbps link, the connection would have lasted roughly 7 min.

A high number of long-lived connections poses different demands on Data Center devices than short-lived connections. The demands depend on how many of these long-lived connections are being tracked and how many packets need to be processed. If the Data Center device tracks connections, it should measure how many of them it can track, and if the device does not track connections, it simply should measure how many packets it can process per unit of time. The connections being tracked lead to the concurrent connections (CC) metric, and the packets processed per unit of time to PPS.

Because some Data Center devices are aware of connections and sessions, it is important to understand the metrics used to benchmark their performance. The following section deals with the metrics introduced so far.

CPS, CC, and PPS

You can classify most traffic in the Data Center as either short-lived or long-lived by selecting an arbitrary time distinction between the two types of connections, one that represents your particular environment. As discussed earlier, you should benchmark the devices just processing packets using the PPS metric and the devices that process connections and sessions using CPS and CC. We also discussed that short-lived connections are closely related to CPS and long-lived connections are closely related to CC.

CPS, CC, and PPS are by no means the only metrics to benchmark the performance of the different Data Center devices, yet they are key to measuring the fundamental performance properties of such devices. The section "Performance Metrics Overview" discusses other appropriate performance metrics.

An important consideration when measuring performance is the likely bottleneck for a particular metric. The *likely bottleneck* is the component that first limits the overall capacity of the device when it is placed under a heavy load. For the PPS metric, which measures throughput, the likely bottleneck is based on the hardware and software architecture of the device. The bottleneck component could be the router processor (rp) if switching at Layer 3, the switch processor (sp) if switching at Layer 2, a line card, the connection from a line card to the switch fabric, or the switch fabric. For the CPS metric, the likely bottleneck is the processor that deals with connection establishment or deep packet inspection, the port ASIC that performs intensive processing tasks, and so forth. Notice that a line card or switch fabric is also a potential bottleneck yet they are less likely because they are designed to deal with a higher magnitude of processing capacity. For the CC metric, the likely bottleneck is the memory used to keep connection and session state, whether in main memory or at the port or interface level.

Other factors such as the buffer capacity, the interface ASICs, and the number of processors also influence the overall performance behavior of a device. These factors are particularly important when the performance-testing efforts focus on devices that understand and keep track of connections besides just packets.

Another important consideration influencing performance is the switching path of a device. The *switching path* refers to the processing capabilities of a device that leverages hardware rather than software for the processing itself. The most common descriptions refer to the fast path, which typically relies on hardware-based processing, and the *slow path*, which is supported by software. These concepts are analogous to process switching and fast switching, which are software-based (slow path) or hardware-based (fast path). These concepts are explained in Chapter 20, "Designing the Data Center Infrastructure."

NOTE Lookups on hardware are faster than software lookups. When you perform the lookups using a hash value, the original table being searched is divided into smaller portions related to the likely hash values, so the search yields the location of the table or a location close to it. Other search mechanisms, such as the ones based on MAC or IP address, tend to be slower than a hash search if done sequentially, yet if you organize the tables in a predetermined fashion and use hardware, the searches are also fast.

Ternary Content Addressable Memory (TCAM) is an example of hardware used for fast lookups and increased processing capacity. You can use TCAMs to store a Forward Information Base (FIB) table. A FIB table is an example of an IP address prefix table, which speeds up the lookup function. You can also perform FIB lookups on hardware.

You can find more information on these performance metrics in the section, "Testing Performance Metrics," later in the chapter.

Performance Metrics Overview

Before delving into the details of performance metrics, it is important to define a few concepts. First is the concept of a metric. Paraphrasing RFC 2330, "Framework for IP Performance Metrics," a metric is a carefully specified quantity related to the performance and reliability of the operational Internet. A more practical explanation is that a metric describes the performance or reliability of a system—in the context of this book, the Data Center infrastructure. Although metrics can measure reliability, the more practical approach centers on performance as it directly relates to whether the device is able to perform as expected. Therefore, the main concern in this chapter is to describe performance metrics and no other metrics that might be applicable to reliability. Measuring methodologies for reliability are typically specific to the equipment under test and therefore not generic enough on how you can apply them.

Performance metrics and their associated measurement methodologies are well documented for several network devices, such as LAN switches in RFC 2889, "Benchmark Methodology for LAN Switching Devices," and firewalls in RFC 3511, "Benchmarking Methodology for Firewall Performance." Other RFCs, such as RFC 2544, "Methodology for Network Interconnect Devices," offer in-depth discussion on benchmarking methodologies that you could apply to several types of devices, such as routers and switches. There are, however, a number of devices for which measurement methodologies do not exist, such as load balancers, and SSL offloaders. This chapter discusses the key metrics and measurement mechanisms for some of these devices for which official methodologies do not exist or are not well documented. Before discussing metric and measurement information on these devices, specifically load balancers and SSL offloaders, we discuss some key concepts applied to LAN switches and firewalls.

Performance Metrics

Performance metrics indicate the capability of a device to perform under load. This performance level determines how much traffic the device could process and at which traffic level the device experiences a loss of packets while sustaining a steady load. The maximum performance levels without traffic loss indicate the maximum capabilities of the device, which are important for capacity planning, design practices, and troubleshooting efforts.

The following are the most commonly used metrics to benchmark the performance of networking devices:

- Throughput
- Frame loss

- Latency
- Connection processing rate
- CC

These terms and metrics must be defined to avoid confusion when applying the metrics to specific devices later in the chapter.

The definitions for throughput, frame loss, and latency were obtained from RFC 1242 exactly as written. Connection processing rate and CC capacity are not terms officially defined, but RFC 2647 provides some basic definitions that we expanded for the explanations in the book:

- **Throughput**—The maximum rate at which none of the offered frames are dropped by the device.
- **Frame loss**—Percentage of frames that should have been forwarded by a network device under steady state (constant) load that were not forwarded due to lack of resources.
- **Latency for store and forward devices**—The time interval starting when the last bit of the input frame reaches the input port and ending when the first bit of the output frame is seen on the output port.
- **Latency for bit-forwarding devices**—The time interval starting when the end of the first bit of the input frame reaches the input port and ending when the start of the first bit of the output frame is seen on the output port.
- **Connection processing rate**—The maximum rate of new connections the device is able to process.
- **CC**—The number of simultaneous connections the device is able to track and process.

The context of a connection is the same that is used in Chapter 7, which is also applicable to UDP and implies an exchange of information between two hosts where the 5-tuple (source and destination IP addresses, source and destination port numbers, and protocol) remains constant. This definition includes UDP transactions, which, although UDP is a connectionless protocol, are treated as connections when measuring connection rates. Whether traffic is TCP or UDP, a device keeping track of connections or sessions needs to treat packets that belong to the 5-tuple as related, even in UDP transactions.

NOTE The expanded definitions for connection processing rate and CC are the result of including devices that do not have official performance-benchmark metrics defined, such as load balancers and SSL offloaders.

The next two sections discuss at a high level the different metrics traditionally used on multilayer switches and firewalls because performance-benchmarking methodologies are readily available. The metrics associated with load balancers and SSL offloaders are discussed in depth in their own separate sections.

Multilayer Switch Metrics

Multilayer switches are switches that offer integrated Layer 2 and Layer 3 functionality. Testing the performance of these devices requires testing both Layer 2 and Layer 3 characteristics. Typically, you measure performance in LAN switches by testing the following metrics (which were initially defined in RFC 1944 and RFC 2544):

- Throughput
- Frame loss
- Latency

RFC 2889 extended the test definition to include address learning, congestion control, and meshed traffic topologies.

All these metrics describe the operational capabilities of LAN switches applied to Layer 2 and extendable to Layer 3 processing. In Layer 2 and Layer 3 processing, there is no concern for the identification of connections for processing purposes.

Most tests associated with the different metrics test, in isolation, a single metric at a time. Single metric results do not indicate how a device behaves in the network as part of a system and under realistic traffic conditions. They describe the maximum performance of a device when dealing with a specific test scenario, which is a good indication for it limits, questionable value for real-life behavior.

Throughput

Multilayer switches process frames or packets, and as a result, metrics such as throughput, obtained with varying frame and packet sizes, describe the processing behavior of the device under test (DUT). Note that throughput is analogous to forwarding rate.

RFC 2455, "Benchmarking Methodology for Network Interconnect Devices," suggests that you use the following frame sizes to test Ethernet: 64, 128, 256, 512, 1024, 1280, and 1518.

The average frame size on an intranet ranges from 200 to 500 bytes, which suggests testing the device with a frame size between 256 and 512. These results would more accurately represent the device behavior under load. If you use jumbo frames, you should add to the list of tests a particular test with the expected jumbo frame size.

Throughput is measured in bits per second (BPS) or PPS. BPS gives the absolute throughput number, but PPS multiplied by the packet size (or frame size) also gives the absolute throughout number. As the packet size increases, the overall throughput of the device also increases. You obtain the maximum throughput values using the maximum transmission unit (MTU) size.

On Ethernet, the maximum PPS number is predetermined by how many bits can fit in the wire, in addition to the interpacket gap delay, as documented in Table 22-2.

Table 22-2 *Wire Speed Packet Size Distribution on Ethernet Media*

Media	64 Byte Packets	1518 Byte Packets
Ethernet	14,881	812
Fast Ethernet	148,810	8128
Gigabit Ethernet	1,488,100	81,280

The maximum PPS numbers for either packet size are considered wire speed.

NOTE Note that some testing tools let the user select the actual packet size or frame size to use during testing. If the tool you are using does not let you specify the exact size, simply calculate the actual frame or packet size by adding the appropriate header bytes and padding bytes.

Frame and Packet Loss

Other metrics such as frame or packet loss describe a somewhat undesirable behavior that helps to discover the actual processing limits of the DUT under a constant load, which is often limited by the maximum capacity of the media supported (wire speed). This metric measures whether the device is able to process at wire speed, and the test could show limitations on either the interface and/or the switch fabric.

Latency

Latency-related benchmark results provide a view of the time delays that might be experienced by traffic through the DUT, typically measured in microseconds. When you deal with devices that are connection-aware, an important latency consideration is that latency generally increases as the depth of packet inspection increases.

Inspecting Layer 4 information is more resource intensive than performing Layer 3 lookups. When you deal with the maximum PPS capacity of the DUT, more lookups imply higher overall latency. Layer 4 and Layer 5 inspection is also different, especially when processing TCP connections. Layer 5 information is not available until after the TCP handshake has occurred, which means that to take appropriate action, the DUT must wait until the handshake is finished. A good example is described in Chapter 16, “Load-Balancing Modes and Predictors.”

Firewall Metrics

Some firewalls, unlike routers and switches, do keep connection-state information. These types of firewalls are often referred to as *stateful firewalls* and perform operations beyond mere packet filtering. Benchmarking performance on a firewall requires running the tests not only for the basic metrics throughput, frame or packet loss, and latency but also for more meaningful metrics such as the connection processing rate and CC. The same definitions presented earlier for throughput, frame or packet loss, and latency are applicable to firewalls, and the new connection processing rates and concurrent connection are also defined as CPS and CC, respectively.

Another major difference when testing firewalls instead of routers or switches is the need for real traffic instead of simulated traffic. Firewalls perform basic security checks on such things as TCP initial sequence numbers (ISNs), which, if not valid, deny the packet.

A number of additional tests, as defined in RFC 3511, focus on specific yet common features, including the following:

- DoS handling
- HTTP transfer rate
- HTTP transaction rate
- Illegal traffic handling
- IP fragmentation handling

The DoS handling tests determine how the firewall deals with a high rate of TCP connection requests (SYN packets). This maximum rate indicates how well the firewall would fare under such an attack (a SYN flood attack).

HTTP transfer rate refers to how the firewall handles entire HTTP transactions that include the TCP connection request, the transfer of the objects associated with the URL in the request, and the final connection teardown. An option of the HTTP transfer rate test excludes the HTTP headers, connection requests, and teardowns to measure only the protocol payload; this option is called *goodput*.

HTTP transaction rate refers to the transaction rate per unit of time that the firewall is able to support.

Illegal traffic handling refers to the capability of the firewall to handle both legal and illegal traffic concurrently. *Illegal traffic* is traffic that has been explicitly identified in a rule which intends to drop or deny it.

IP fragmentation handling refers to the capability of the firewall to process fragments that might require re-assembly before a rule could be applied.

A more realistic test to conduct is a combination of many of these tests, where the firewall configuration is meant to address multiple issues at the same time, as on real networks. The expectation is that metrics such as CPS are affected by the increased processing demand resulting from more features being enabled. For more information on measuring firewall performance, consult RFC 3511.

Load Balancer and SSL Offloader Metrics

In several ways, you benchmark load balancers and SSL offloaders using the same metrics, yet the metrics are applied slightly differently to each device. For example, measuring CPS on a load balancer requires a count of the full connections processed per unit of time, whereas in an SSL offloader, it means a count of full connections, including the encryption key negotiation. The next section discusses performance benchmarking metrics used on load balancers and SSL offloaders.

Load Balancer Performance Metrics

Currently, there are no standard metrics, performance benchmarks, or even methodologies to test and measure the performance of load balancers.

The following information might help you decide on which metrics to test and how to conduct the tests in a way that the results are beneficial to understanding their true capabilities.

Because load balancers track connections, and because the traffic is classified as short-lived or long-lived connections, it is expected that the metrics you use are the ones that describe their operation when processing the different traffic types.

The following section discusses the short-lived and long-lived concepts applied to load balancers.

Traffic Patterns and Load Balancers

Whether dealing with short-lived or long-lived traffic, an important consideration is the location of the likely bottleneck of the load balancer.

Presuming that the rate at which short-lived connections is steady, you would see the CPU utilization increase until the load balancer experiences packet loss or other potential symptoms, such as retransmissions. At this connection rate, the performance limit would have been determined. Our experience in measuring load-balancer performance indicates that when dealing with short-lived connections, the limits are typically related to the CPU capacity of the load balancer.

Figure 22-8 depicts the observed behavior of a load balancer from the perspective of receiving and establishing an increasing number of connections per unit of time.

Figure 22-8 *Load-Balancer Connection Rate Curve*

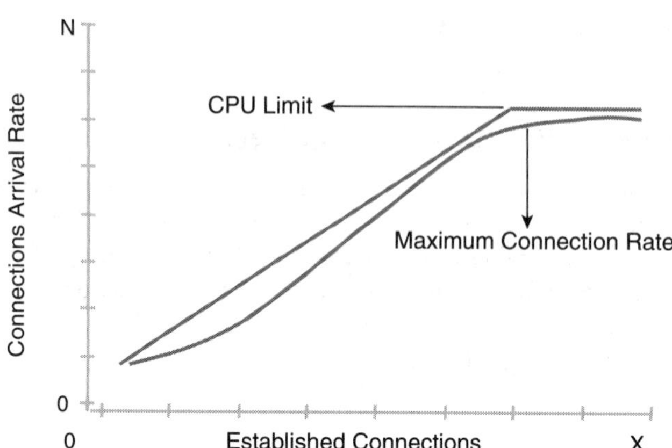

Note in Figure 22-8 that as the number of new connections increases, the number of connections the load balancer can establish and process also increases. As these two parameters increase, so does the load balancer's CPU utilization, which might refer to more than one processor performing the load-balancing functions. At some point, the load balancer reaches its capacity and the curve flattens, which indicates that regardless of the new connection arrival rate, the load balancer has reached its maximum connection rate.

The load balancer also reaches its maximum CPU utilization and maintains it as the maximum connection rate remains steady. Clearly, a metric worth benchmarking is the connection rate that the load balancer supports. This metric is CPS.

In Figure 22-8, the traffic is assumed to be from short-lived connections because they do not live long enough to tax other components of the load balancers or increase the CPU utilization. The traffic load from short-lived connections is related to the CPS metric; therefore, it is CPU bound.

If the connections last long enough on an average basis, the load balancer might experience a different behavior. "Long enough" means that the rate at which new connections are received is higher than the rate at which connections are torn down. This behavior leads to an increasing number of active connections that the load balancer must keep in memory.

NOTE Load balancers use various memory types to hold the following pieces of information: connection, connection state, session state, and shortcut tables for fast lookups. Memory can be DRAM, TCAM, or space in certain ASICs. For the time being, the term memory refers to the general definition or concept of space that stores connection information, regardless of the specific type.

The conclusion is that the number of active connections in the load balancer is limited by memory space instead of CPU capacity.

Long-lived connections are related to the CC metric and are memory-bound. A real traffic mix includes both short-lived and long-lived connections and any combination in between. The combined demands therefore affect different aspects of load balancers.

Furthermore, different traffic types can also affect the maximum limits that you find using individual metrics. For instance, the CC affects the rate of CPS and vice versa. Figure 22-9 illustrates this relation.

Figure 22-9 *Relation between CC and CPS*

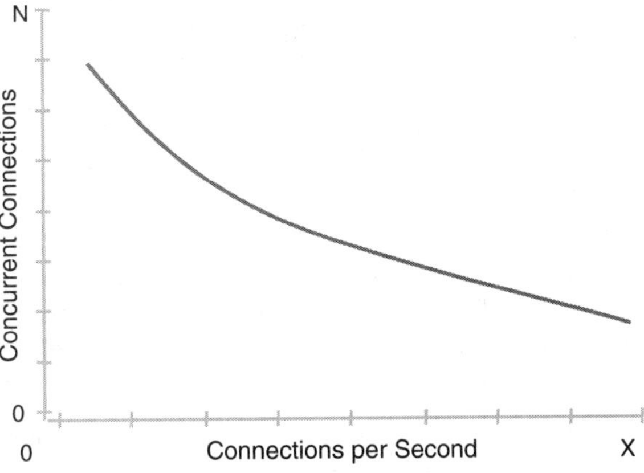

Figure 22-9 shows that as the number of CC increases, the CPS rate decreases. This behavior is normal, and it has been recorded on actual networks. As the long-lived connections increase, the number of new connections that the load balancer can process decreases. The actual impact on one versus the other depends on the traffic types, the bytes associated with each connection, and the distribution of short-lived and long-lived connections.

To summarize, Chapter 6, "Server Load-Balancing Overview," introduced the generic architecture of load balancers, and this chapter has discussed the kind of traffic a load balancer is likely to process. With that foundation established, it is possible to discuss the performance metrics of load balancers. The following sections discuss the relevant metrics.

Thus far, we have explored the following topics:

- Relationships between short-lived sessions and CPU processing and between long-lived sessions and memory
- The effects of traffic on performance and the relationship between different metrics
- The capability of the load balancer to track connections and sessions

In addition to CPS and CC, another important metric relevant to the actual switching capacity of a load balancer is throughput or PPS measured in bytes. Although in real conditions the throughput is really determined by the packets belonging to real connections, it is important to know the packet-switching limits of the load balancer.

Adding a metrics column to Table 6-1 of Chapter 6, the metrics in Table 22-3 correspond to the components and their critical areas.

Table 22-3 *Relationship Between Components and Metrics*

Performance Impact Areas	Critical Components	Performance Metrics
Processing capacity	Main or central CPU, port ASICs, dedicated processors	CPS
Memory	DRAM, port memory, content-addressable memory (CAM)	CC
Switching capacity	Shared BUS, switch fabric, port capacity	PPS

Two other metrics are not necessarily related to a single architectural component, yet they are important to measure, particularly as they relate to server farms. These metrics relate to timing issues that can affect the server farm and consequently the client connections to the servers, which are perceived by users as how well the application behaves. These two metrics are response time and latency.

Latency as a metric applied to load balancers has the same meaning and describes the same capabilities as it does when applied to store and forward devices, because load balancers are in fact store and forward devices. Although response time is more applicable to server farms, it is measured from the user perspective. The response time is influenced by latency, but there are many other contributing factors, such as the bandwidth capacity of the client-to-server path, propagation delay, and the server load.

The following sections introduce the details of the performance metrics used to benchmark load balancers.

CPS

CPS describes how many new connection requests per second a load balancer can process. The term *processing* implies the successful completion of the connection handshake and connection teardown. A test that is aimed at measuring CPS should include a complete connection setup and teardown cycle. The traffic used for testing should closely match the kind of traffic that represents a common connection on an intranet or on the Internet. This requirement implies that the connection transports valid application traffic. For example, in a Web transaction, you should include one or more HTTP requests and their responses, along with the connection-teardown portion.

Often, the processing of the connection setup, SYN-SYN/ACK-ACK, describes the capabilities of a load balancer. Taken as a metric, it does not provide enough valid information that could lead to understanding the true capabilities of a load balancer. The results of these tests are used to advertise artificially high values for load-balancing performance that cannot be achieved in an operating network because real traffic conditions do include the processing of the payload.

Simply measuring connection setup and teardown omits the load imposed by processing the payload. This additional processing could be merely additional packets that need load balancing, but it could also imply deeper packet inspection in case of Layer 5 processing (connection spoofing).

Connection setup and teardown tests describe the best performance capabilities of a load balancer. You must expect, however, that once the load balancer is placed in front of a server farm, the performance of the load balancer will be lower than that indicated by the results of connection setup and teardown tests.

NOTE In the early days of load balancing, the tools that were used to measure performance did not offer more than connection setup and teardown. Even today, the tools we use to obtain an accurate performance view of a load balancer rely on actual clients and servers controlled by a number of scripts that facilitate management of the testbed. Commercial benchmark testing tools are improving but often use TCP/IP stacks tuned for performance. These TCP/IP stacks prove to be challenging when dealing with a actual network that uses firewalls, load balancers, and real clients or servers because they do not necessarily follow standard TCP/IP implementations.

CC

As described previously, CC refers to the number of simultaneous connections a load balancer can support. When engineering the testbed to benchmark CC, the key is to control the duration of connections that force the load balancer to keep the connection information active. Just as for CPS, you should use actual connections including valid application data to best measure the load balancer's behavior. Long-lived connections might also differ from one another. A Telnet connection that lasts one hour would affect a load balancer very differently than an HTTP download that lasts one hour. Because the goal is to measure maximum CC capacity, it is simpler to use the Telnet connection because it is less taxing than the HTTP download and therefore represents the best CC watermark of the load balancer.

Throughput (PPS)

PPS describes how many packets per second a load balancer can process. Because these packets belong to the connections being processed, they are used as the means to measure switch fabric or port capability similarly to how it is done for Layer 2 and Layer 3 switches.

Although throughput measures switch fabric or interface capacity, it becomes a metric of lesser importance for load balancers. An average connection uses inbound or outbound packets of unequal sizes. In addition, packets are not isolated entities but are part of an active connection for which state is being kept. Because there is a practical limit to the number of CPS and CC a load balancer supports, the upper limits of PPS are bound to the sum of packets of all active connections. In other words, the sum of connection packets is unlikely to tax the throughput capabilities of a load balancer, but if it does, the connections are likely long-lived and the packet size is much larger than the average. The characteristics of these types of connections are representative of FTP or HTTP downloads, streaming video feeds, and bulk data transfer in general. However, knowing the performance limits in terms of throughput for a load balancer is useful as a means of understanding its upper operational limits.

NOTE This limit might be imposed by the maximum processing capacity of the main CPU, and that capacity is typically related not to packet size but to the number of packets. If the number of processed packets remains constant and the packet size increases, the overall throughput increases as well. A sound recommendation is to find the packet processing limit using tools with controllable packet sizes, and if the number of PPS remain constant at different packet sizes (big and small), you can easily find the throughput by multiplying the number of packets by the packet size.

Latency

The description of latency in this chapter is based on the definition in RFC 1242 when applied to store and forward devices. As mentioned previously, like all network devices, a load balancer adds latency. In many ways, a load balancer has the potential to add more latency than other devices because it can execute tasks deeper in the payload of packets. Furthermore, the latency at Layer 5 is expected to be higher than that at Layer 4 because of connection spoofing and deeper packet inspection. To better understand the likely additional latency, it is important to know the tasks at both Layer 4 and Layer 5.

At Layer 4, the load balancer must perform the following tasks:

- 5-tuple lookup
- Lookup of content policy information on TCP/IP headers
- Rewrite of MAC header information

- Rewrite of IP header information
- Checksum calculations for TCP
- Calculation and rewrite of other TCP/UDP header information

At Layer 5, the load balancer performs all Layer 4 tasks in addition to the following:

- Spoofing TCP connections toward the client side
- Lookup of content policy information on packet payload
- Initiating new TCP connections with the server
- Maintaining both client and server connection synchronization, which requires SEQ and checksum calculation, in addition to other header rewrite operations for both connections

Although the additional operations required for processing at Layer 4 or Layer 5 are likely to increase the latency when compared to just the Layer 2 and Layer 3 operations, the architecture of the load balancer (software or hardware) actually determines the kind of impact.

Measuring latency on a server farm is, however, extremely difficult. Isolating the latency of a single device in the presence of other devices, including clients and servers, is difficult. Given the random nature of connection loads, server behavior is somewhat unpredictable, and testing tools are not designed to provide this kind of information based on real clients and servers.

Response Time

Response time is loosely defined as the elapsed time between the end of an application layer request (the user presses the Enter key) and the end of the response (the data is displayed in the user's screen). Response time is typically measured in milliseconds, and it is assumed that the path is loss-free and that the latency is equal for all packets between client and server. The importance of response time is that it determines in a measurable way whether the content is readily available to the client and, most importantly, whether the client perceives that the content is readily available. The perception of speediness is subjective and differs from user to user, yet the response time indicates exactly how much time a user has to wait for the requested information. Although response time is not a metric to calculate on load balancers, it is one metric to measure server behavior. This server behavior could be normalized by the load balancer, thus indirectly improving response-time issues. For instance, the response time of a web server on the Internet, as shown in Figure 22-10, is relatively predictable and linear over time as the number of connection requests increases. Then, it reaches its maximum connection point and the response time becomes exponentially higher.

Figure 22-10 *Server Response Time*

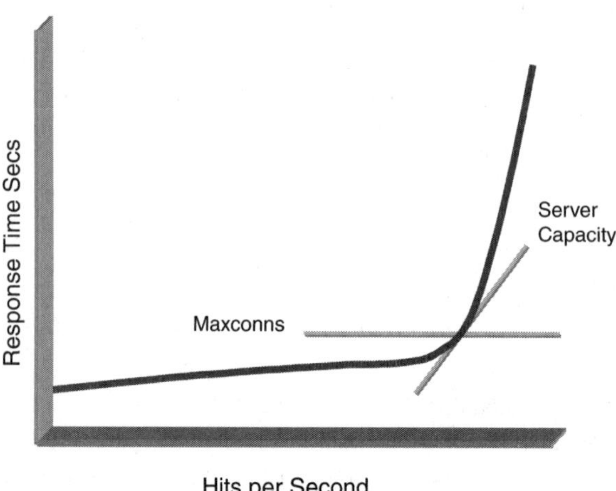

The performance curve of each server and the overall server farm has its own inflection point where the response time increases rapidly. This infection point is determined by the effective server capacity and the connection rate. In many cases, you must observe rather than calculate the infection point because each server's capacity is influenced by a number of factors, including other processes running, the number of service threads or processes configured, and number of connections. A good source of information to understand server behavior and tuning is *Web Performance Tuning* by Patrick Killelea (O'Reilly & Associates, 1998).

SSL Offloaders Performance Metrics

SSL offloaders, unlike load balancers, are not placed in front of server farms to load balancer traffic. Load balancers distribute the multiple types of traffic, and SSL offloaders deal only with SSL traffic. The key functions SSL offloaders execute on behalf of the server farm are key negotiation and encryption. These two operations could shift a significant portion of the CPU load from the server to the SSL offloaders when the server farm supports SSL.

Some of the same metrics discussed for load balancers are applicable to SSL offloaders, and some are less relevant because the SSL offloaders are only subject to a subset of the traffic the load balancers process. The previously discussed classification of traffic patterns of short-lived and long-lived connections is also applicable to SSL offloaders, yet they are specifically applied to SSL traffic, which can be used for HTTPS, SMTP, and other application protocols using SSL.

Short-lived SSL connections are likely to be related to sessions, where SSL is used mostly for the secure part of the transaction when you need to exchange sensitive information. This arrangement is typical of an e-commerce transaction when the user browses the site using port 80 and pays for the items online using port 443. Contrast it with long-lived connections that are more likely related to sessions which use SSL from the beginning of the transaction. These sessions are typical of banking applications on the Internet (online banking) or intranet applications that deal with sensitive information which cannot be transmitted in cleartext, such as human-resource benefits or salary information. Note that some SSL-only transactions could also consist of a number of short-lived connections, particularly when using HTTPS.

Like load balancers, SSL offloaders track connections and SSL sessions. For scalability reasons, an SSL offloader might remember an existing SSL session to be reused at a later time. This reuse of the SSL session avoids the most intensive of the tasks of an SSL or HTTPS transaction: the SSL handshake. Chapter 9, "SSL and TLS," explains this concept in detail.

The *SSL handshake* includes the negotiation of cryptographic algorithms, the verification of the identity of the client, and a new session key. The computationally expensive task is when the server uses its RSA private key to decrypt the premaster secret that was encrypted by the client using the server's public key. The performance improvement on SSL transations, from a user perspective, results from the use of SSL hardware offloading, the performance improvement on servers comes from offloading this task from the servers and performing the key encryption/decryption (in hardware), and the performance improvement in the number of SSL transactions on SSL off loaders comes from reusing previous session keys. The data encryption/decryption process is less computationally intensive; however, the CPU savings on the server farm could be significant on long-lived transactions. The cryptographic algorithm used for encryption is generally RC4, which is less intensive compared to other encryption algorithms.

The key metrics used to benchmark the performance of SSL offloaders are

- CPS
- CC
- PPS
- Latency

Because SSL offloaders could relieve one or more servers from having to process SSL transactions, it is important to know the SSL transaction capacity of the server farm to compare it to the capacity of the load balancer. The following sections discuss the details of these metrics applied to SSL offloaders.

CPS

The CPS rate that you should measure for SSL offloaders is related to the number of SSL handshakes it can complete. This metric is often called transactions per second (TPS) or sessions per second, but they all refer to the same concept: new SSL sessions the device is able to support. The CPS number is different depending on the length of the key of the cryptographic algorithm in use. 2048-bit keys are more intensive than 64-bit keys; therefore, an SSL offloader is expected to perform better when using a smaller key, although the environment is less secure. Figure 22-11 presents the results of different key sizes and measuring the CPS rate.

Figure 22-11 *SSL Handshake Rates Using Different Key Sizes*

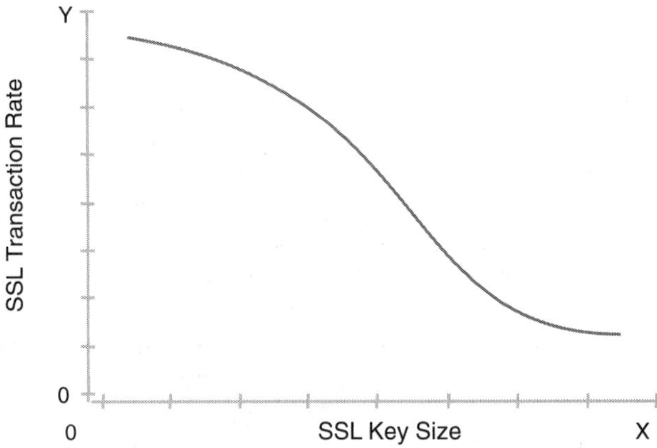

Note that the ciphersuite in use is also relevant on SSL performance. RSA with RC4 and Message Digest 5 (MD5) is less intensive than RSA with Triple Data Encryption Standard (3DES) and Secure Hash Algorithm (SHA), with the latter being more secure than the former.

One additional factor to consider in CPS-related tests is whether the SSL offloader is expected to reuse SSL sessions. If so, the overall performance is expected to be higher, but the difference is only significant if SSL reuse will apply in the real network environment.

CC

Concurrent connections or rather concurrent SSL sessions are mostly related to long-lived sessions and therefore indicate the memory capacity to hold them.

PPS

The PPS metric measures throughput, which, with an SSL offloader, is throughput the server farm would have to process. As with load balancers, measuring PPS requires real traffic or at least real SSL connections. Because the packet size cannot necessarily be the same for all packets in the same real SSL session, you can engineer the web page to test certain limits by forcing the SSL transaction to transfer a predetermined number of bytes.

Algorithms used for bulk encryption have an effect on the throughput of the SSL offloader. For example, an interesting consideration is that for the same transaction (a download of the same page), the CPS rate of an SSL offloader is roughly 9 percent higher when using DES than with 3DES. When comparing the results of just the RC4 algorithms, MD5 performs roughly 5 percent higher than SHA.

Latency

Latency on an SSL offloader indicates the time it would take the device to process the data, which in this case is the SSL handshake and subsequent encryption/decryption of packets. Because SSL offloaders are not necessarily used in the primary path to the server farm and might not be configured for back-end encryption, the latency can vary through SSL offloaders. The variation comes from the SSL being used only in the encrypted part of a session (non-SSL traffic does not need to go through the SSL offloader) and that the SSL offloader may or may not support an encrypted tunnel back to the server which would add more processing latency. The recommendation when measuring latency is to compare the processing of a page using plain HTTP with the same page using HTTPS. Downloading the page should not be interactive (no user should be involved in the process), so the timing is strictly based on the actual process of processing traffic through the SSL offloader withour the user/client factor. Latency and the following metric, response time, are related. The higher the latency induced by the SSL offloader, the higher the response time. Latency measures the device processing time instead of response time, which would measure the network and application processing time.

Response Time

Response time, as it was suggested for load balancers, is not necessarily an SSL offloader metric, yet it provides an accurate view of how users perceive the application behavior. This metric is particularly interesting because the SSL offloader is deployed to reduce, among other factors, the response time by processing SSL-related packets. For response time having an existing value to compare the effects of using an SSL offloader is important. The baseline consists of performance results of the server and application environment running SSL natively on the server and processing SSL transactions. You compare these results to the same environment using an SSL offloader, which increases the processing rate and reduces the overall response time. The response-time reduction is the result of the processing speeds (latency) of the SSL offloader being lower than that of a server running SSL in software for the same transactions.

Testing Performance Metrics

The more realistic you want the test results to be, the more complex your testing environment needs to be.

Ultimately, the goal driving the tests is to determine the performance behavior of the network devices so that your network design is sound, flexible, scalable, and highly available. In thinking through the methodology, you must remember the following principles:

- Two test environments are never the same.
- You cannot exactly duplicate a real network environment with a test setup.
- Two different network environments experience different traffic patterns.

Following are some recommendations when performing tests or analyzing their results:

- Use traffic patterns that closely resemble actual traffic patterns from your network. Select the most significant protocols of your traffic distribution for your test data mix.
- Test methodology, test scenarios, and test results should be available and verifiable. Without them, the validity of the test is unknown and the usability questionable.
- Performance-test results that include packet loss are not representative of the device's real behavior because they appear higher than test results in which packet loss is not experienced. The effects of packet loss are unpredictable and hard to quantify. For instance, TCP can back off; retransmissions can occur; and, depending on which packet types get lost, congestion can occur.
- Testing should also include other network components connected as they would be in the real network. This setup factors interoperability and design issues that could change the test results. First, test the device to determine its capabilities (baseline); then, test it in the actual design that mirrors the real network environment.

The testing methodology also includes the application layer pieces that you use to test application environments with load balancers, SSL offloaders, or firewalls. These pieces recreate a working application environment.

The major areas covered under testing methodology are

- Testing tools
- Staging the testbed

These are practical guidelines used to aid in understanding the effort of benchmarking devices. An important consideration is the need for baseline testing and results.

You use baseline testing results for comparison between a baseline environment without the DUT and the same environment including the DUT. In the baseline environment, you conduct tests on servers first to determine their own capabilities (CPS, CC, and response time). This task is simplified in environments with homogenous servers because you can test one and presume all the others behave similarly. Once you place the servers behind the device, such as a load balancer, the load balancer must at least support the sum of all server metrics. It is recommended, however, to have room to spare for bursts and growth. The following section focuses on the tools you use to benchmark the server application environments that include application-aware devices instead of just the Layer 2, Layer 3, and firewall devices. The technology is newer, and there is plenty of information on testing Layer 2, Layer 3, and firewall devices. Some of the testing tools traditionally used for Layer 2, Layer 3, and firewall tests, however, do support testing of load balancers and SSL offloaders.

Testing Tools

Currently, no single tool supports the measurement of all previously proposed metrics. And the absence of testing tools providing capabilities to test all metrics speaks to the fact that much of the Data Center network equipment is fairly new technology. It includes load balancers, SSL offloaders, and integrated services when they are used in a chassis that support the traditional Layer 2 and Layer 3 services. Furthermore, when a particular metric is supported, there is not enough flexibility to simulate a real traffic environment, partly because in a server environment, it is difficult to simulate real application traffic. With respect to load balancers and SSL offloaders, the state of tools is more a reflection of the newness of the technology than the quality of the tools and the fact that no standardized metrics, testing methodology, or standard testing traffic patterns exist. As a result, testing load balancers requires more time and is more complex, more involved, and more expensive than testing Layer 2 or Layer 3 devices.

The ability to conduct simulated real-world tests implies that you actually need multiple tools.

Before moving on, it is important to remember that load balancers deal primarily with web-based traffic (HTTP) and SSL offloaders with secure web traffic (HTTPS), which explains why most test tools focus on HTTP and HTTPS functionality. Our expectations are that tools will get smarter as load balancers and other technology in application environments grow smarter. The following sections present testing tools organized in two categories:

- Strictly software based
- Combination of hardware and software

These sections provide pointers about the general capabilities of tools. The discussion, however, is not meant to be a detailed explanation of what testing tools do, how their internals work, and how well they function.

Software Testing Tools

Software-based testing tools are written to run on existing operational systems such as UNIX, Linux, or Windows. This feature implies that the tools must be able to run on existing hardware platforms with little or no change to either the operating system or the tools' own code. Some tools have their own customized IP stacks, and others use the existing IP stack. The customized IP stack is optimized to increase the connection rate; this optimization has its advantages and disadvantages. The advantages lie mainly in the reduction of the number of servers you need to support the desired connection rates, and the disadvantages lie in the fact that the stack is modified or rewritten and it might not offer all enhancements or new additions in the stacks that come with the operating system.

Most software testing tools are shareware, and their support is what you can expect for free software: you get what you pay for. In some cases, the source code is available, so you could tweak, fix, and enhance it. Software tools in general are more flexible than hardware/software tools in that they can be easily enhanced to provide more functionality. On the other hand, software tools do not perform as fast as hardware-based tools and are highly dependent on the operating system and the hardware they run on.

Following are lists of shareware tools and their URLs. First are the web load tools:

- http://www.testingfaqs.org/t-load.html lists a number of tools.
- http://www.softwareqatest.com/qatweb1.html lists a number of tools under the category of load and performance tools.
- http://www.aptest.com/resources.html lists a number of testing tools under the category of web test tools.

The next list outlines specific testing tools:

- HTTPLOAD from ACME offers a variety of tools for HTTP-related tests at http://www.acme.com/software/http_load/.
- The Web Application Stress Tool from Microsoft is at http://msdn.microsoft.com/library/default.asp?url=/library/en-us/dnw2kmag00/html/StressTool.asp.
- WebStone from Mindcraft for benchmarking Web servers is at http://www.mindcraft.com/webstone/.
- WebBench from Ziff Davis is at http://www.etestinglabs.com/benchmarks/webbench/webbench.asp.
- SPECweb99 from Standard Performance Evaluation Corporation is at http://www.spec.org/osg/web99/.

Instead of Web resources, many people prefer homegrown tools. Some of these tools are based on scripting languages such as Perl, and others are readily available programs such as wget. Tuning these tools lets you measure specific values such as server response time.

Hardware Testing Tools

Hardware-based testing tools are hardware devices built for special purposes and designed to benchmark the performance of networking devices. The hardware tools come with software that lets you configure the tool, specify the tests to run, control the execution of the test, and gather the results. Most tools have been developed for Layer 2 and Layer 3 devices and, in certain cases, for other networking gear such as firewalls. Some of these tools have been and are being enhanced to test load balancers and SSL offloaders. The software of hardware-based testing tools typically runs on any PC as a controller, which also acts as the storage location for test scripts and results. Hardware tools are typically more expensive than software tools.

Hardware-based tools have better performance capabilities than software tools, yet they are less flexible in their ability to develop new features quickly and advanced features without hardware replacements. Hardware tools come with a predetermined set of tests that might be sufficient for your needs. Software tools typically allow you to add or change tests fairly rapidly. Hardware tools are much more accurate than software tools and much easier to control. Accuracy and control are both key features, particularly when you measure latency or packet loss. In addition, hardware tools come with technical support.

Our experience using the hardware and software tools has been less than ideal. The available tools are not suited for real-world testing conditions, which is not a surprise because the complexity is a problem even when using a single software tool. Even more important, these tools are not traditionally set up to simulate real application environments that include meaningful information in the payload. It is highly unlikely that the tools can perform the following tasks: stuff various valid HTTP header information (specific HTTP fields) on HTTP requests; generate DNS requests; establish SSL connections; and allow FTP, Telnet, or even UDP traffic, particularly through a single tool. On the other hand, a number of software tools do allow you to generate these types of connections and use real application data. Obviously, simulating real-life conditions is advantageous, but it is also more time-consuming.

The following is a list of vendors of hardware and software and their respective URLs:

- SmartTCP from Spirent Communications is at http://smartbits.spirentcom.com/solutions/products/applications/pdf/SmartTCP/index.htm.
- Ixweb from Ixia is at http://www.ixiacom.com/products/paa/webstressing/.
- WebAvalanche from CAW Networks is at http://www.cawnetworks.com/product/wa_technical_specs.shtml.

Staging the Testbed

You should read this section of the chapter if you have little or no experience in staging a testbed and running systems tests. If you are experienced, you are likely to find this information rather obvious, mostly likely of little relevance to your operational best practices.

This section introduces simple, practical tips on how to set up the testbed, run the tests, and validate the results. In staging the testbed, the main prerequisite to a successful completion is a solid target goal. The goals should be focused on acceptable convergence times, deterministic traffic paths, predictable failover and fallback mechanisms, and scalability on terms of performance, services and servers. Whether they are device limits or system limits, make sure that your testing tools are capable of reaching the limits (CPS, CC, PPS, IP addresses or servers). In addition, make sure your testing tools can generate the type of traffic, such as DNS, HTTP, FTP, SMTP or other relevant protocols, you need to measure.

In reaching the limits, use the vendor-advertised numbers as the top end of your testbed capacity. Once you introduce a realistic data mix, the performance is likely to be lower than the advertised performance.

Testing Environment

The test environment includes the clients, servers, and network infrastructure.

A client—typically the software used by the user sitting behind the keyboard—originates the requests for information or content from the server farm. For web-based applications, the client is the browser, but for FTP, SMTP, or Telnet, the client is a specific piece of software that provides the user interface to the application requesting information on behalf of the user.

A good recommendation for the client side is to use a real client running on top of an unmodified TCP/IP stack so that the interaction between the client and the server is as real as possible. When you use software-based testing tools, the hardware platform running the client software limits the number of requests that can be made per unit of time. This number is crucial for the typical server so that you can determine whether your test client is capable of taxing the server side at your target goal. Considering the target goal for the maximum value of each relevant metric, it is more than likely that you need a good number of client machines to generate the proper load if you are using software-based tools.

Even if you are using hardware-based tools, you need a fair amount of equipment when dealing with high-end devices such as service modules that have multiple processors dedicated to specific processing functions.

Another recommendation concerns the software used to control the testbed. This software controls the clients and potentially servers, triggers the start of the tests, and might control the output and how it is displayed. Whether you use software or hardware, ensure that you have a mechanism in place to control the testbed, and to save and retrieve the results from each test cycle.

Servers are the destination of the client requests, and as such, they either contain the information themselves or retrieve it and serve it to the clients. As with the client software, using an unmodified TCP/IP stack and generally available server software ensures that your traffic patterns are real. Again, if using software-based tools and generally available software, it is important to gather the performance numbers for a single server to establish a baseline that can be shared by all other servers in the testbed.

Our experience simulating real application environments is that the testbed is much simpler if you are dealing only with the front-end tier (web, Telnet, FTP, and SMTP servers). It is complicated to build or simulate a multitier environment, particularly the actual intertier traffic patterns, yet there are tools in the market that use scripting to simulate user traffic conditions. In these cases, your goal would be to determine the performance of a device that could scale this tier, but also to determine the capacity of the system, possibly measured in transactions per second, which includes many server tiers.

If you use standard server platforms and generic server software, one challenge on the server side is to keep the content on all servers equal (particularly when testing scalability with load balancers or SSL offloaders).

TIP To make this process easy when testing HTTP, we copied the contents of the Cisco documentation CD to all the servers and rooted the HTTP server on the directory with the content of the CD. The content included text and other objects all of which helped save time in setting up the test environment.

The network infrastructure includes the routers, Layer 2 and Layer 3 switches, firewalls, load balancers, and SSL offloaders. Typically, you are interested in benchmarking only one type of device, yet you need some portion of the infrastructure for the test.

NOTE A number of special cases occur when service modules inserted into a Layer 2 or Layer 3 switch offer load-balancing or SSL-offloading capabilities. This setup makes the overall switch Layer-3-through-Layer-5-capable, yet the metrics for each service provided by the service module are specific to the function it performs. In these instances, both the metrics used for multilayer switches and the metrics used for load balancer and SSL offloaders are applicable. You must apply each set of metrics and their associated tests to the appropriate switch role, whether as Layer 2, Layer 3, Layer 4, or Layer 5.

The recommendations are simple: if you are benchmarking a single device, the topology is not too important, so focus on using the right levels of software and building a simple topology. If you are benchmarking more than one identical device (for example, a pair for redundancy), or if you are testing more than one type of device (firewalls and load balancers), use the code you would use in production and build the infrastructure to resemble the real infrastructure as closely as possible. If you expect to enable security and management features that have potential impact on your results, consider whether they relevant to your goals.

Selecting Your Data Mix

A realistic traffic mix is complex to engineer, maintain, and run, so you should simplify as much as possible without sacrificing the main goals. Table 22-4 provides a potential protocol mix to use at the Internet edge for Internet-facing server farms.

Table 22-4 *Sample Data Mix*

Protocol	Connections %	Packets %	Bytes %
TCP-WWW	60		
TCP-SMTP	5		
TCP-FTP Data	10		
TCP-NNTP	5		
UDP-Domain	10		
UDP-RealPlayer	10		

Table 22-4 describes a good traffic mix that you could use as the starting point to tailor a specific mix for your own environment. Notice that the percentages for packets and bytes are not completed because they are defined by how you actually set up the connections. Because the web traffic is so significant, it is important to include some guidelines on the specific traffic conditions. The following information comes from the "Wide-Area Internet Traffic Patterns Characteristics" study conducted by Thompson, Miller, and Wilder:

- **Client per flow statistics**—1 KB, 14 to 16 packets, and an average of 67 bytes per packet
- **Server per flow statistics**—9 to 12 KB, 14 to 18 packets, and an average of 620 bytes per packet

For SSL-related tests, which are more specific to the SSL offloader from a processing perspective, you could make some of the web pages used for regular HTTP available for HTTPS. The short-lived and long-lived traffic classifications suggest that two types of transactions are engineered: one type to last just a few seconds and the other one to last longer, beyond 15 sec and perhaps in the minutes range.

Running the Tests

Before running the tests, you should perform the following steps:

1. Identify the tests to run.
2. Develop the scripts for each test.
3. Determine the duration test.
4. Determine the number of test runs for each test type.
5. Identify expected results for verification purposes.

Many of these points are driven by the actual test, yet it is recommended that you run tests at least twice and ideally three times. It will be evident if the results are consistent and repeatable.

Before the actual run, verify that basic connectivity works as expected. Basically, make sure that

1. Clients can reach the servers and applications ping the server from the default gateway and from a client behind the default gateway, access the application under test. This ensures the server is reachable, and the application is available.
2. Servers can reach the clients. Ping the clients from the server which ensures reachability through the default gateway.
3. Clients and servers can ping other devices in the path. Ping clients and servers from the firewalls or load balancers after they are added to the primary path, then attempt 1 and 2 to make sure the additions of the new devices did not break reachability.

TIP Building testbeds, we found that most problems discovered during testing were related to items 1, 2, or 3 in the previous list.

It is recommended that you first obtain a baseline set of tests as a starting point for comparing other test results. This baseline enables you to measure the impact as you turn on features or change the configuration of the testbed or the DUT.

Summary

This chapter discussed various topics related to performance testing for Data Center networking devices. Various Data Center devices such as routers, switches, firewalls, load balancer, and SSL offloaders might be exposed to different traffic types, determined by their location on the network and the function they perform.

We discussed both Internet and intranet traffic patterns, leading to how you can classify the patterns from a Data Center perspective. The traffic classifications of short-lived and long-lived connections leads to concrete metrics (CPS, CC, and PPS) that are useful to benchmark devices that track connections and sessions.

We discussed performance metrics in reference to all the devices in the Data Center and also specifically to multilayer switches and firewalls. This discussion is an informative overview of the current metrics and documents testing methodologies for LAN interconnected devices and firewalls.

We also include a more in-depth discussion on the metrics you use to benchmark load balancers and SSL offloaders. This discussion concluded that you need to benchmark Data Center devices which track connections using CPS and CC primarily and PPS, latency, and response time secondarily.

A final section on testing performance metrics included the types of available testing tools and how to stage a testbed.

PART VI

Appendixes

APPENDIX **A**

Character Sets

This appendix presents the ASCII and International Organization for Standardization (ISO)-8859-1 character sets.

ASCII Character Set

ASCII is a standard seven-bit code to represent characters that was proposed by the American National Standards Institute (ANSI) (http://www.ansi.org) in 1963 and finalized in 1968. Other sources also credit much of the work on ASCII to Robert W. Bemer. ASCII was established to achieve compatibility between various types of data-processing equipment. Standards that document ASCII include ISO-14962-1997 and ANSI-X3.4-1986(R1997).

The standard ASCII character set consists of 128 decimal numbers (7 bits), ranging from 0 through 127, assigned to letters, numbers, punctuation marks, and the most common special characters. The extended ASCII character set also consists of 128 decimal numbers and ranges from 128 through 255 (using the full 8 bits of the byte), representing additional special, mathematical, graphic, and foreign characters.

Standard Set Nonprintable Characters

Table A-1 lists the standard set of nonprintable ASCII characters.

Table A-1 *Standard ASCII Characters: Nonprintable*

Dec	Hex	Character (Code)	Dec	Hex	Character (Code)
0	0	Null	16	10	Data link escape (DLE)
1	1	Start of heading (SOH)	17	11	Device control 1 (DC1)
2	2	Start of text (STX)	18	12	Device control 2 (DC2)
3	3	End of text (ETX)	19	13	Device control 3 (DC3)

continues

Table A-1 *Standard ASCII Characters: Nonprintable (Continued)*

Dec	Hex	Character (Code)	Dec	Hex	Character (Code)
4	4	End of transmission (EOT)	20	14	Device control 4 (DC4)
5	5	End of query (ENQ)	21	15	Negative acknowledgement (NAK)
6	6	Acknowledge (ACK)	22	16	Synchronize (SYN)
7	7	Beep (BEL)	23	17	End of transmission block (ETB)
8	8	Backspace (BS)	24	18	Cancel (CAN)
9	9	Horizontal tab (HT)	25	19	End of medium (EM)
10	A	Line feed (LF)	26	1A	Substitute (SUB)
11	B	Vertical tab (VT)	27	1B	Escape (ESC)
12	C	Form feed (FF)	28	1C	File separator (FS) right arrow
13	D	Carriage return (CR)	29	1D	Group separator (GS) left arrow
14	E	Shift out (SO)	30	1E	Record separator (RS) up arrow
15	F	Shift in (SI)	31	1F	Unit separator (US) down arrow

Standard Set Printable Characters

Table A-2 lists the standard set of printable ASCII characters.

Table A-2 *Standard ASCII Characters: Printable*

Dec	Hex	Character	Dec	Hex	Character	Dec	Hex	Character
32	0x20	<space>	64	0x40	@	96	0x60	`
33	0x21	!	65	0x41	A	97	0x61	a
34	0x22	"	66	0x42	B	98	0x62	b
35	0x23	#	67	0x43	C	99	0x63	c
36	0x24	$	68	0x44	D	100	0x64	d
37	0x25	%	69	0x45	E	101	0x65	e
38	0x26	&	70	0x46	F	102	0x66	f
39	0x27	'	71	0x47	G	103	0x67	g
40	0x28	(	72	0x48	H	104	0x68	h
41	0x29	)	73	0x49	I	105	0x69	i

Table A-2 *Standard ASCII Characters: Printable (Continued)*

Dec	Hex	Character	Dec	Hex	Character	Dec	Hex	Character
42	0x2A	*	74	0x4A	J	106	0x6A	j
43	0x2B	+	75	0x4B	K	107	0x6B	k
44	0x2C	,	76	0x4C	L	108	0x6C	l
45	0x2D	-	77	0x4D	M	109	0x6D	m
46	0x2E	.	78	0x4E	N	110	0x6E	n
47	0x2F	/	79	0x4F	O	111	0x6F	o
48	0x30	0	80	0x50	P	112	0x70	p
49	0x31	1	81	0x51	Q	113	0x71	q
50	0x32	2	82	0x52	R	114	0x72	r
51	0x33	3	83	0x53	S	115	0x73	s
52	0x34	4	84	0x54	T	116	0x74	t
53	0x35	5	85	0x55	U	117	0x75	u
54	0x36	6	86	0x56	V	118	0x76	v
55	0x37	7	87	0x57	W	119	0x77	w
56	0x38	8	88	0x58	X	120	0x78	x
57	0x39	9	89	0x59	Y	121	0x79	y
58	0x3A	:	90	0x5A	Z	122	0x7A	z
59	0x3B	;	91	0x5B	[	123	0x7B	{
60	0x3C	<	92	0x5C	\	124	0x7C	|
61	0x3D	=	93	0x5D	]	125	0x7D	}
62	0x3E	>	94	0x5E	^	126	0x7E	~
63	0x3F	?	95	0x5F	_	127	0x7F	<del>

Extended Set

Because the extended set was undefined, vendors created a few different versions to use the extended values (greater than 127). Table A-3 lists a common set of these extended values.

Table A-3 *ASCII Characters: Extended Set*

Character	Dec	Hex	Character	Dec	Hex	Character	Dec	Hex	Character	Dec	Hex
€	128	80		160	A0	À	192	C0	à	224	E0
	129	81	¡	161	A1	Á	193	C1	á	225	E1
‚	130	82	¢	162	A2	Â	194	C2	â	226	E2
ƒ	131	83	£	163	A3	Ã	195	C3	ã	227	E3
„	132	84	¤	164	A4	Ä	196	C4	ä	228	E4
…	133	85	¥	165	A5	Å	197	C5	å	229	E5
†	134	86	¦	166	A6	Æ	198	C6	æ	230	E6
‡	135	87	§	167	A7	Ç	199	C7	ç	231	E7
ˆ	136	88	¨	168	A8	È	200	C8	è	232	E8
‰	137	89	©	169	A9	É	201	C9	é	233	E9
Š	138	8A	ª	170	AA	Ê	202	CA	ê	234	EA
‹	139	8B	«	171	AB	Ë	203	CB	ë	235	EB
Œ	140	8C	¬	172	AC	Ì	204	CC	ì	236	EC
	141	8D	-	173	AD	Í	205	CD	í	237	ED
Ž	142	8E	®	174	AE	Î	206	CE	î	238	EE
	143	8F	¯	175	AF	Ï	207	CF	ï	239	EF
	144	90	°	176	B0	Ð	208	D0	ð	240	F0
‘	145	91	±	177	B1	Ñ	209	D1	ñ	241	F1
’	146	92	²	178	B2	Ò	210	D2	ò	242	F2
“	147	93	³	179	B3	Ó	211	D3	ó	243	F3
”	148	94	´	180	B4	Ô	212	D4	ô	244	F4
•	149	95	µ	181	B5	Õ	213	D5	õ	245	F5
–	150	96	¶	182	B6	Ö	214	D6	ö	246	F6
—	151	97	·	183	B7	×	215	D7	÷	247	F7
˜	152	98	¸	184	B8	Ø	216	D8	ø	248	F8
™	153	99	¹	185	B9	Ù	217	D9	ù	249	F9
š	154	9A	º	186	BA	Ú	218	DA	ú	250	FA
›	155	9B	»	187	BB	Û	219	DB	û	251	FB
œ	156	9C	¼	188	BC	Ü	220	DC	ü	252	FC
	157	9D	½	189	BD	Ý	221	DD	ý	253	FD
ž	158	9E	¾	190	BE	Þ	222	DE	þ	254	FE
Ÿ	159	9F	¿	191	BF	ß	223	DF	ÿ	255	FF

Table A-4 represents the Microsoft extended ASCII set, which you can find at http://msdn.microsoft.com/library/default.asp?url=/library/en-us/vsintro7/html/_pluslang_ascii_character_codes.asp.

Table A-5 and Table A-6 provide two other common ASCII extended character sets. Credits given to http://cplusplus.com for the charts.

Table A-4 *ASCII Characters: Microsoft Extended Set*

Dec	Hex	Char	Dec	Hex	Char	Dec	Hex	Char	Dec	Hex	Char
128	80	Ç	160	A0	á	192	C0	└	224	E0	α
129	81	ü	161	A1	í	193	C1	┴	225	E1	ß
130	82	é	162	A2	ó	194	C2	┬	226	E2	Γ
131	83	â	163	A3	ú	195	C3	├	227	E3	π
132	84	ä	164	A4	ñ	196	C4	─	228	E4	Σ
133	85	à	165	A5	Ñ	197	C5	┼	229	E5	σ
134	86	å	166	A6	ª	198	C6	╞	230	E6	µ
135	87	ç	167	A7	º	199	C7	╟	231	E7	τ
136	88	ê	168	A8	¿	200	C8	╚	232	E8	Φ
137	89	ë	169	A9	⌐	201	C9	╔	233	E9	Θ
138	8A	è	170	AA	¬	202	CA	╩	234	EA	Ω
139	8B	ï	171	AB	½	203	CB	╦	235	EB	δ
140	8C	î	172	AC	¼	204	CC	╠	236	EC	∞
141	8D	ì	173	AD	¡	205	CD	═	237	ED	φ
142	8E	Ä	174	AE	«	206	CE	╬	238	EE	ε
143	8F	Å	175	AF	»	207	CF	╧	239	EF	∩
144	90	É	176	B0	░	208	D0	╨	240	F0	≡
145	91	æ	177	B1	▒	209	D1	╤	241	F1	±
146	92	Æ	178	B2	▓	210	D2	╥	242	F2	≥
147	93	ô	179	B3	│	211	D3	╙	243	F3	≤
148	94	ö	180	B4	┤	212	D4	╘	244	F4	⌠
149	95	ò	181	B5	╡	213	D5	╒	245	F5	⌡
150	96	û	182	B6	╢	214	D6	╓	246	F6	÷
151	97	ù	183	B7	╖	215	D7	╫	247	F7	≈
152	98	ÿ	184	B8	╕	216	D8	╪	248	F8	°
153	99	Ö	185	B9	╣	217	D9	┘	249	F9	∙
154	9A	Ü	186	BA	║	218	DA	┌	250	FA	·
155	9B	¢	187	BB	╗	219	DB	█	251	FB	√
156	9C	£	188	BC	╝	220	DC	▄	252	FC	ⁿ
157	9D	¥	189	BD	╜	221	DD	▌	253	FD	²
158	9E	₧	190	BE	╛	222	DE	▐	254	FE	■
159	9F	ƒ	191	BF	┐	223	DF	▀	255	FF	

Table A-5 *ASCII Characters: ANSI Extended Set (Windows)*

	0	1	2	3	4	5	6	7	8	9	A	B	C	D	E	F
8	□	□	‚	ƒ	„	…	†	‡	ˆ	‰	Š	‹	Œ	□	□	□
9	□	‘	’	“	”	•	–	—	˜	™	š	›	œ	□	□	Ÿ
A		¡	¢	£	¤	¥	¦	§	¨	©	ª	«	¬	-	®	¯
B	°	±	²	³	´	µ	¶	·	¸	¹	º	»	¼	½	¾	¿
C	À	Á	Â	Ã	Ä	Å	Æ	Ç	È	É	Ê	Ë	Ì	Í	Î	Ï
D	Ð	Ñ	Ò	Ó	Ô	Õ	Ö	×	Ø	Ù	Ú	Û	Ü	Ý	Þ	ß
E	à	á	â	ã	ä	å	æ	ç	è	é	ê	ë	ì	í	î	ï
F	ð	ñ	ò	ó	ô	õ	ö	÷	ø	ù	ú	û	ü	ý	þ	ÿ

Table A-6 *ASCII Characters: OEM Extended Set*

	0	1	2	3	4	5	6	7	8	9	A	B	C	D	E	F
8	Ç	ü	é	â	ä	à	å	ç	ê	ë	è	ï	î	ì	Ä	Å
9	É	æ	Æ	ô	ö	ò	û	ù	ÿ	Ö	Ü	¢	£	¥	₧	ƒ
A	á	í	ó	ú	ñ	Ñ	ª	º	¿	⌐	¬	½	¼	¡	«	»
B	░	▒	▓	│	┤	╡	╢	╖	╕	╣	║	╗	╝	╜	╛	┐
C	└	┴	┬	├	─	┼	╞	╟	╚	╔	╩	╦	╠	═	╬	╧
D	╨	╤	╥	╙	╘	╒	╓	╫	╪	┘	┌	█	▄	▌	▐	▀
E	α	ß	Γ	π	Σ	σ	µ	τ	Φ	Θ	Ω	δ	∞	φ	ε	∩
F	≡	±	≥	≤	⌠	⌡	÷	≈	°	∙	·	√	ⁿ	²	■	

ISO-8859-1 Character Set

The ISO defined the ISO-8859-1 as a single-byte, coded, graphic character set.

ISO-8859-1 explicitly does *not* define displayable characters for positions 0–31 and 127–159, and the HTML standard does not allow them to be used for displayable characters. The only characters used in this range are 9, 10, and 13, which are tab, newline, and carriage return, respectively. Table A-7 lists the ISO character set.

Table A-7 *ISO-8859-1 Character Set*

Char	Code	Name	Description	Char	Code	Name	Description
	32	-	Normal space	0	48	-	Digit 0
!	33	-	Exclamation	1	49	-	Digit 1
"	34	quot	Double quote	2	50	-	Digit 2
#	35	-	Hash	3	51	-	Digit 3
$	36	-	Dollar	4	52	-	Digit 4
%	37	-	Percent	5	53	-	Digit 5
&	38	amp	Ampersand	6	54	-	Digit 6
'	39	-	Apostrophe	7	55	-	Digit 7
(	40	-	Open bracket	8	56	-	Digit 8
)	41	-	Close bracket	9	57	-	Digit 9
*	42	-	Asterisk	:	58	-	Colon
+	43	-	Plus sign	;	59	-	Semicolon
,	44	-	Comma	<	60	lt	Less than
−	45	-	Minus sign	=	61	-	Equals
.	46	-	Period	>	62	gt	Greater than
/	47	-	Forward slash	?	63	-	Question mark

continues

Table A-7 *ISO-8859-1 Character Set (Continued)*

Char	Code	Name	Description	Char	Code	Name	Description
@	64	-	At sign	P	80	-	P
A	65	-	A	Q	81	-	Q
B	66	-	B	R	82	-	R
C	67	-	C	S	83	-	S
D	68	-	D	T	84	-	T
E	69	-	E	U	85	-	U
F	70	-	F	V	86	-	V
G	71	-	G	W	87	-	W
H	72	-	H	X	88	-	X
I	73	-	I	Y	89	-	Y
J	74	-	J	Z	90	-	Z
K	75	-	K	[	91	-	Open square bracket
L	76	-	L	\	92	-	Backslash
M	77	-	M	]	93	-	Close square bracket
N	78	-	N	^	94	-	Caret
O	79	-	O	_	95	-	Underscore

Table A-7 *ISO-8859-1 Character Set (Continued)*

Char	Code	Name	Description	Char	Code	Name	Description
`	96	-	Grave accent	p	112	-	p
a	97	-	a	q	113	-	q
b	98	-	b	r	114	-	r
c	99	-	c	s	115	-	s
d	100	-	d	t	116	-	t
e	101	-	e	u	117	-	u
f	102	-	f	v	118	-	v
g	103	-	g	w	119	-	w
h	104	-	h	x	120	-	x
i	105	-	i	y	121	-	y
j	106	-	j	z	122	-	z
k	107	-	k	{	123	-	Left brace
l	108	-	l	|	124	-	Vertical bar
m	109	-	m	}	125	-	Right brace
n	110	-	n	~	126	-	Tilde
o	111	-	o	X	127	-	(Unused)

continues

Table A-7 *ISO-8859-1 Character Set (Continued)*

Char	Code	Name	Description	Char	Code	Name	Description
	160	nbsp	Non-breaking space	°	176	deg	Degree sign
¡	161	iexcl	Inverted exclamation	±	177	plusmn	Plus-minus sign
¢	162	cent	Cent sign	²	178	sup2	Superscript 2
£	163	pound	Pound sign	³	179	sup3	Superscript 3
¤	164	curren	Currency sign	´	180	acute	Spacing acute
¥	165	yen	Yen sign	µ	181	micro	Micro sign
¦	166	brvbar	Broken bar	¶	182	para	Paragraph sign
§	167	sect	Section sign	·	183	middot	Middle dot
¨	168	uml	Umlaut or diaeresis	¸	184	cedil	Spacing cedilla
©	169	copy	Copyright sign	¹	185	sup1	Superscript 1
ª	170	ordf	Feminine ordinal	º	186	ordm	Masculine ordinal
«	171	laquo	Left angle quotes	»	187	raquo	Right angle quotes
¬	172	not	Logical not sign	¼	188	frac14	One quarter
-	173	shy	Soft hyphen	½	189	frac12	One half
®	174	reg	Registered trademark	¾	190	frac34	Three quarters
¯	175	macr	Spacing macron	¿	191	iquest	Inverted question mark

Table A-7 *ISO-8859-1 Character Set (Continued)*

Char	Code	Name	Description	Char	Code	Name	Description
À	192	Agrave	A grave	Ð	208	ETH	ETH
Á	193	Aacute	A acute	Ñ	209	Ntilde	N tilde
Â	194	Acirc	A circumflex	Ò	210	Ograve	O grave
Ã	195	Atilde	A tilde	Ó	211	Oacute	O acute
Ä	196	Auml	A umlaut	Ô	212	Ocirc	O circumflex
Å	197	Aring	A ring	Õ	213	Otilde	O tilde
Æ	198	AElig	AE ligature	Ö	214	Ouml	O umlaut
Ç	199	Ccedil	C cedilla	×	215	times	Multiplication sign
È	200	Egrave	E grave	Ø	216	Oslash	O slash
É	201	Eacute	E acute	Ù	217	Ugrave	U grave
Ê	202	Ecirc	E circumflex	Ú	218	Uacute	U acute
Ë	203	Euml	E umlaut	Û	219	Ucirc	U circumflex
Ì	204	Igrave	I grave	Ü	220	Uuml	U umlaut
Í	205	Iacute	I acute	Ý	221	Yacute	Y acute
Î	206	Icirc	I circumflex	Þ	222	THORN	THORN
Ï	207	Iuml	I umlaut	ß	223	szlig	sharp s

continues

Table A-7 *ISO-8859-1 Character Set (Continued)*

Char	Code	Name	Description	Char	Code	Name	Description
à	224	agrave	a grave	ð	240	eth	eth
á	225	aacute	a acute	ñ	241	ntilde	n tilde
â	226	acirc	a circumflex	ò	242	ograve	o grave
ã	227	atilde	a tilde	ó	243	oacute	o acute
ä	228	auml	a umlaut	ô	244	ocirc	o circumflex
å	229	aring	a ring	õ	245	otilde	o tilde
æ	230	aelig	ae ligature	ö	246	ouml	o umlaut
ç	231	ccedil	c cedilla	÷	247	divide	division sign
è	232	egrave	e grave	ø	248	oslash	o slash
é	233	eacute	e acute	ù	249	ugrave	u grave
ê	234	ecirc	e circumflex	ú	250	uacute	u acute
ë	235	euml	e umlaut	û	251	ucirc	u circumflex
ì	236	igrave	i grave	ü	252	uuml	u umlaut
í	237	iacute	i acute	ý	253	yacute	y acute
î	238	icirc	i circumflex	þ	254	thorn	thorn
ï	239	iuml	i umlaut	ÿ	255	yuml	y umlaut

Table A-7 information was extracted from the Web Design Group pages at http://www.htmlhelp.com/.

APPENDIX B

HTTP Header Fields

This appendix discusses the following HTTP header fields not included in Chapter 8, "HTTP and Related Concepts."

General Header Fields

- Trailer
- Upgrade
- Via
- Warning
- Cache-Control
- Connection
- Date
- Pragma
- Transfer-Encoding

Trailer General Header Field

The Trailer field indicates that a number of header fields are present in the trailer of a chunked transfer-coding encoded message. This is partly because HTTP/1.1 messages must include a Trailer field when using chunked transfer coding. This tells the recipient which fields to find in the trailer.

If there is no Trailer field in the header, the trailer should not include any header fields other than the Transfer-Encoding, Content-Length, and Trailer fields.

Upgrade General Header Field

The Upgrade field signals to the server which protocols the client wants to include in the list of supported communication protocols. If the server is switching protocols, it must use the Upgrade field with the 101 status response code.

The Upgrade header does not give the client an option to indicate which protocol to use. The server has the option to use the preferred protocol.

Via General Header Field

The Via field indicates the intermediate protocols and recipients between the user-agent and the server for requests, and between the origin server and client for responses. This header must be used by gateways and proxies.

Warning General Header Field

The Warning field carries additional information about the status or transformation of a message that might not be reflected in the message. This information warns about a possible lack of semantic transparency from caching operations or transformations applied to the entire body of the message. The response can carry more than one warning. Table B-1 presents the warning codes in the HTTP/1.1 specification.

Table B-1 *HTTP/1.1 Specification Warning Codes*

Warning Code	Description
110	Response is Stale
111	Revalidation Failed
112	Disconnected Operation
113	Heuristic Expiration
199	Miscellaneous Warning
214	Transformation Applied
299	Miscellaneous Persistent Warning

NOTE Simple-Request and Simple-Response prevent the use of any header information and are limited to a single request method (GET). For more information on request methods, see Chapter 8.

Request Header Fields

This appendix discusses the highlighted HTTP header fields not included in Chapter 8:

- Accept-Language
- Expect
- From
- If-Match
- If-None-Match
- If-Range
- If-Unmodified-Since
- Proxy-Authorization
- TE
- Accept
- Accept-Charset
- Accept-Encoding
- Authorization
- Host
- If-Modified-Since
- Max-Forwards
- Range
- Referer
- User-Agent

Accept-Language

The Accept-Language field specifies the set of natural languages that is preferred in a response to the client. The languages (spoken, written, or used by humans—not computers—to communicate) are identified by a language tag. Current language tags include en, en-US, en-cockney, i-cherokee, and x-pig-latin. Example B-1 displays the language tag that a client is capable of accepting.

Example B-1 *Accept-Language Field*

```
GET / HTTP/1.0\r\n
Connection: Keep-Alive\r\n
User-Agent: Mozilla/4.76 [en]C-CCK-MCD   (Windows NT 5.0; U)\r\n
Host: www.apache.org\r\n
Accept: image/gif, image/x-xbitmap, image/jpeg, image/pjpeg, image/png, */*\r\n
Accept-Encoding: gzip\r\n
Accept-Language: en\r\n
Accept-Charset: iso-8859-1,*,utf-8\r\n
\r\n
```

NOTE The IANA administers the language tag namespace. The latest language tags can be found at http://iana.org/assignments/language-tags.

Expect

The Expect field indicates that the client requires particular server behaviors. The server responds with an error status if it cannot understand the expectation of the request, if the server cannot fulfill the expectation, or if the expectation is not supported.

From

The From field indicates the e-mail address of the user behind the client that has sent the request. This information can identify the person behind the request for multiple purposes, including these two:

- Logging, to correlate unwanted requests with a person
- Contact information, in case the request is done by some kind of automatic process and a problem occurs

The client is not expected to send the user e-mail address without approval, so the specification recommends that the user be able to disable, enable, and change the value of the field before the request is sent.

If-Match

The If-Match field is used in conjunction with a method to make it conditional. Entity tags perform the matching operation. If no match occurs, the server is expected to respond with a 412 (Precondition Failed) status code. When the If-Match field is used with the asterisk

(*), as in If-Match:*, the server is expected to respond if the representation for the entity exists; the resource then is sent back to the client. For example, when sending a conditional GET request, the resource is sent back in the response only if the condition has been met.

This field provides more control over the operation of cacheable resource and to avoid unnecessary transactions and their associated overhead.

If-None-Match

The If-None-Match field is used in conjunction with a method to make it conditional; this is similar to how the If-Match field is used with the exception of comparing a *none-match* instead of a match. The server responds with a 304 (Not Modified) status code in the response if there is a match of the entity tags. If none of the entities matches, the server can perform the requested method (as if the If-None-Match field did not exist—under these conditions, any If-Modified-Since fields are ignored).

When If-None-Match is used with the asterisk (*), as in If-None-Match:*, the server does not perform the method if the representation for the entity exists, but it does perform the method when the representation for the entity does not exist.

This field provides more control over the operation of cacheable resources and avoids unnecessary transactions and their associated overhead.

If-Range

If a client has a partial copy of an entity in its cache and is attempting to retrieve the remaining portion, it uses a Range request with a conditional GET. The condition might fail if the entity has been modified and the client is forced to issue a second request to retrieve the entire entity.

The If-Range field is used to avoid the second request when the entity has been modified by the server interpreting the If-Range request as follows: Send the missing portion if the entity has not changed; otherwise, send the entire entity.

The server responds with a 206 (Partial Content) status code and the subrange if a match occurs on the entity tag. If the entity tag does not match, the server responds with a 200 (OK) status code and returns the entire entity.

If-Unmodified-Since

The If-Unmodified-Since field makes the method in the request conditional. If the resource has not been modified, the server is expected to respond to the request and perform the operation indicated by the method in the request. If the resource has been modified, the server does not perform the operation and responds with a 412 (Precondition Failed) status code in the response.

Proxy-Authorization

The Proxy-Authorization field allows the client to identify itself to the proxy requiring the authentication. The field contains the user-agent information needed by the proxy for the resource or realm indicated in the request.

TE

The TE field indicates which extension transfer codings the client is willing to accept, in addition to trailer fields in a chunked transfer coding. The TE field applies only to the immediate connection.

Response Header Fields

Before listing the response header fields, it is important to discuss the status line that signals the HTTP version, the status code, and its associated textual explanation.

HTTP Status Codes

Each status code is a three-digit result code that signals the status of the request attempt:

- 1*xx*: Informational
- 2*xx*: Success
- 3*xx*: Redirection
- 4*xx*: Client error
- 5*xx*: Server error

The following sections present a subset of the information presented in Chapter 8 as a quick-reference list.

1*xx* Informational Status Codes

The status codes in this class indicate a provision response and signal that the request was received; the process continues. HTTP/1.0 clients do not understand 1*xx* status codes, so servers are expected not to send a 1*xx* response to an HTTP/1.0 client.

Table B-2 lists the informational status codes.

Table B-2 *Informational Status Codes*

Status Code	Status Text
100	Continue
101	Switching Protocols

2*xx* Success Status Codes

The status codes in this class signal that the action was successfully received, understood, and accepted. Table B-3 lists the success status codes.

Table B-3 *Success Status Codes*

Status Code	Status Text
200	OK
201	Created
202	Accepted
203	Nonauthoritative Information
204	No Content
205	Reset Content
206	Partial Content

3*xx* Redirection Status Codes

The status codes in this class signal that further action must be taken to complete the request. Table B-4 lists the redirection status codes.

Table B-4 *Redirection Status Codes*

Status Code	Status Text
300	Multiple Choices
301	Moved Permanently
302	Found
303	See Other
304	Not Modified
305	Use Proxy
307	Temporary Redirect

4*xx* Client Error Status Codes

The status codes in this class signal that the request contains bad syntax or cannot be fulfilled. Table B-5 lists the client error status codes.

Table B-5 *Client Error Status Codes*

Status Code	Status Text
400	Bad Request
401	Unauthorized
402	Payment Required
403	Forbidden
404	Not Found
405	Method Not Allowed
406	Not Acceptable
407	Proxy Authentication Required
408	Request Timeout
409	Conflict
410	Gone
411	Length Required
412	Precondition Failed
413	Request Entity Too Large
414	Request-URI Too Long
415	Unsupported Media Type
416	Requested Range Not Satisfiable
417	Expectation Failed

5*xx* Server Error Status Codes

The status codes in this class signal that the server cannot fulfill an apparently valid request. Table B-6 lists the server error status codes.

Table B-6 *Server Error Status Codes*

Status Code	Status Text
500	Internal Server Error
501	Not Implemented
502	Ban Gateway

Table B-6 *Server Error Status Codes (Continued)*

Status Code	Status Text
503	Service Unavailable
504	Gateway Timeout
505	HTTP Version Not Supported

The list of response header fields is as follows (the details of each field are explained in Chapter 8):

- Accept-Ranges
- Age
- ETag
- Location
- Proxy-Authenticate
- Retry-After
  Server
- Vary
- WWW-Authenticate

Entity Header Fields

The following is the list of Entity header fields. The details of each field are explained in Chapter 8:

- Allow
- Content-Encoding
- Content-Length
- Content-Location
- Content-MD5
- Content-Range
- Content-Type
- Expires
- Last-Modified

APPENDIX C

Video Encoding Mechanisms

The coder/decoder (codec) defines how the original media is encoded. Encoding is required to reduce the amount of data necessary to represent the video/audio. This, in turn, reduces the amount of bandwidth necessary to stream video/audio on the network.

The secret to encoding involves removing the redundant information present in a single frame or across multiple frames. As an example, a single frame representing a blue sky is made of the repetition of the same pattern, a blue pixel. A good encoding mechanism can represent this frame as the color code followed by the number of times that it needs to be repeated. This reduces the number of bytes necessary to store the encoded information. This is an example of removal of spatial redundancy.

Another example of redundancy is the still background of a scene in which one object is moving. Instead of saving the background in each frame, a good encoding algorithm should save the background information in a single frame and provide the information about the moving object in the following frames. This is an example of removal of temporal redundancy.

The section, "Basic Encoding Mechanisms," in Chapter 11, "Streaming Protocols Overview," introduced the concept of the removal of spatial and temporal redundancy. This section provides more details on how redundancy is removed.

Removal of Spatial and Temporal Redundancy

Removal of spatial redundancy is achieved typically by applying the following techniques in sequence:

1. Chroma subsampling
2. Discrete cosine transform
3. Quantization

Each pixel is, by definition, represented in terms of a luminance component (gradation of black and white) and two chrominance components (colors). Because the human eye is more sensitive to luminance, typically this component is not subsampled. The chrominance component is spatially subsampled instead. With a block of 8 × 8 pixels to represent in terms of luminance and chrominance, by subsampling, it is possible to use one 8 × 8 block of luminance values and two blocks of 4 × 4 chrominance values. This ratio is called 4:1:1 because, for every 4 pixels, only 1 pixel is sampled for the chrominance.

A *discrete cosine transform* (DCT) is applied to blocks of pixel values to obtain the coefficients for spatial frequencies. By doing this, it is possible to reconstruct the original image with few coefficients.

Quantization is applied to the coefficients to scale them based on their degree of importance. Typically, neighboring pixels have very slow variation of their luminance and chrominance; this allows the removal of higher frequencies without any noticeable effects. Quantization preserves the most important frequencies (the lowest ones).

Figure C-1 shows the use of these steps to remove spatial redundancy. Each of these steps is applied to a small block (8 × 8) of the original frame. The frame represents a blue sky with a cloud.

Figure C-1 *Removing Spatial Redundancy*

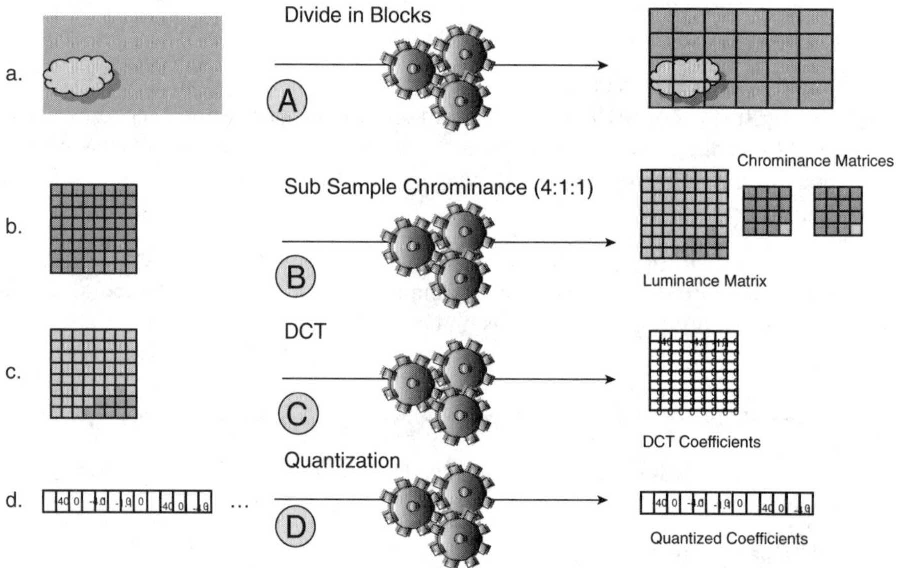

Part **a** of Figure C-1 shows the frame being divided in small blocks.

Part **b** of Figure C-1 shows the chrominance subsampling—the original block is turned into a 8 × 8 block of luminance (grayscale matrix) and two 4 × 4 blocks of chrominance (color components). If the original block had not been subsampled, it would have required 8 × 8 pixels of 24 bits to represent it: 192 bytes. After the subsampling, only (8 * 8 * 1 bytes) + (4 * 4 * 1 bytes) + (4 * 4 * 1 bytes) = 96 bytes are required, with almost no noticeable effect to the human eye.

Part **c** of Figure C-1 shows the next compression phase—the DCT. The transform is applied to each matrix to obtain its spatial frequency components. These are represented as a matrix of coefficients: The value in the (0,0) high corner on the left of the matrix is the continuous component—basically, the background. Most of the other coefficients are very small. Given the size of the block, there will not be high frequency variations, and most of the information is in the (0,0) component.

Part **d** of Figure C-1 shows the quantization of the DCT coefficients, which further removes irrelevant information about the block. Quantization is performed on each coefficient by reading the matrix in a zigzag fashion and saving the result into another string (quantized coefficients).

Temporal redundancy is removed typically by applying the following techniques:

- Encoding the differences between frames
- Using motion vectors

One method of reducing the size of a movie stream is to subtract the previously transmitted frame from the current one and encode only the difference. Areas in which no movement occurred are not encoded because the difference would be a blank space. Another method of reducing temporal redundancy is to track where areas of the previous frame moved in the current frame (*motion estimation*). These two techniques are combined so that first the new location of a previous object is found and then the difference is performed between the two. Only the difference (*residual macroblock)* is encoded.

Figure C-2 gives an example of removing temporal redundancy. Part **a** of Figure C-2 shows a sky with a sun that changes position from Frame 2 to Frame 3. In part **b** of Figure C-2, frames 2 and 3 are compared to produce the "motion vector"— the sun moved from the low right corner to the center of Frame 3, so the motion vector is the arrow in the picture.

The second operation (part **c** of Figure C-2) is the difference between the sun as it appears in frames 2 and 3. The result of the difference is encoded with the "intracoding" techniques previously described.

Figure C-2 *Removing Temporal Redundancy*

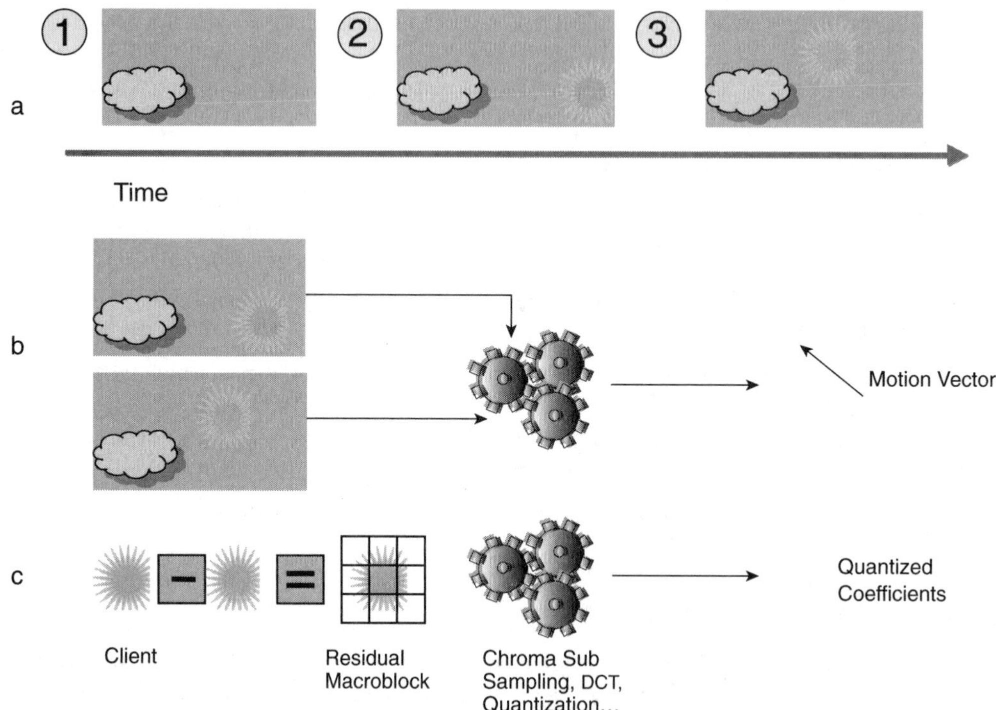

MPEG Encoding

The Motion Picture Experts Group (MPEG) is a codec. This section provides a brief description of the techniques used by MPEG, to help you better understand how MPEG is packetized. Similar concepts can be applied to other codecs.

MPEG uses the concept of Group of Pictures (GOP). Several frames (the default is 15) are grouped to remove temporal redundancies. The first frame is fully coded and is used as a reference for the other frames in the same GOP. The other frames in the GOP are predicted by comparison with the first frame.

The first frame of a group is called an *I-frame,* or *intra-coded* frame, because the encoding is meant to reduce spatial redundancy, just like a JPEG picture. The compression ratio for an I-frame is 10:1.

P-frames are forward-prediction frames—they are based on previous I-frames or P-frames. The compression ratio is 20:1.

B-frames are bidirectional frames that reference either past I- and P-frames or future I- and P-frames. The compression ratio for B frames is 50:1.

The process of compression starts splitting the picture into *slices*. A *slice* is the unit of recovery in case of data loss. The reason is that each slice can be decoded independently of the other slices—when a slice is lost, a media player should just skip to the next slice. This becomes very important when an MPEG medium is packetized for delivery on the network (see the section, "Packetization" in Chapter 11).

Each slice has a certain number of *macroblocks*. A macroblock is an element of 8 × 8 pixels. A discrete cosine transformation is applied on each macroblock, producing an array of 64 coefficients.

For each macroblock, MPEG allows performing a chroma subsampling. The typical ratio is 4:1:1 (four samples of luminance and one for each chrominance component). This means that for every macroblock of 8 × 8 pixels, the matrix of luminance is still 8 × 8, and the two chrominance components are represented on a matrix of 4 × 4. Notice that these are spatial frequencies, not time frequencies.

This process is applied both to the I-frame and to the *residual macroblock* for the P-frames. As a result, the MPEG-encoded stream is a sequence of I-pictures followed by P-pictures. Each P-picture is a sequence of macroblocks. Each macroblock is made of a motion vector followed by quantized DCT coefficients for luminance, followed by the chrominance coefficients.

Figure C-3 shows how a sequence of frames is encoded in MPEG. Frames are grouped to remove temporal redundancy: They form the GOP (part **a** of Figure C-3). The result is a sequence of an I-picture followed by two P-pictures (part **b** of Figure C-3, on two lines). The first P-picture is expanded to show the components; the dashed line indicates what forms the P-picture.

P-pictures are made of several macroblocks; two are represented in part **b** of Figure C-3, and they are expanded in their components: the motion vector, followed by the information about the luminance matrix and the two chrominance matrices.

Figure C-3 *MPEG Encoding*

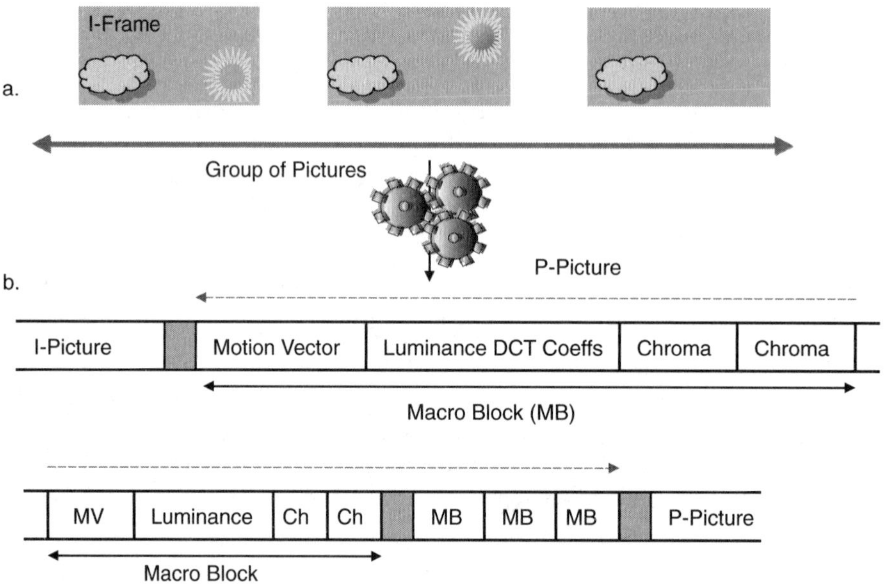

NOTE More information on MPEG can be found at http://mpeg.telecomitalialab.com/.

APPENDIX D

Loopback Interface Configuration Procedures

This appendix presents the steps you follow to configure a loopback interface on multiple operating systems to support the dispatch and DSR load-balancing modes. Under these modes of operation, the servers in the server farm must be configured with the IP address of the VIP to ensure the packets sent by the load balancer are processed by the servers. If the servers are not configured with the IP address of the VIP, the packets are dropped because the destination IP address does not match the server's IP address. An important note to remember is that the load balancer does not rewrite Layer 3 header information in dispatch or DSR modes. The operating systems include Windows 2000, Windows NT, and Linux.

Windows 2000

The following are the steps to configure the loopback interface on Windows 2000:

Step 1 Click the Start tab and go to Settings and Control Panel. Double-click the Add/Remove Hardware icon (see Figure D-1).

Figure D-1 *Control Panel*

Step 2 A window displaying the Add/Remove Hardware Wizard opens. Click Next. In the next window (see Figure D-2), select the Add/Troubleshooting a Device task and click Next.

Figure D-2 *Add/Remove Hardware Wizard*

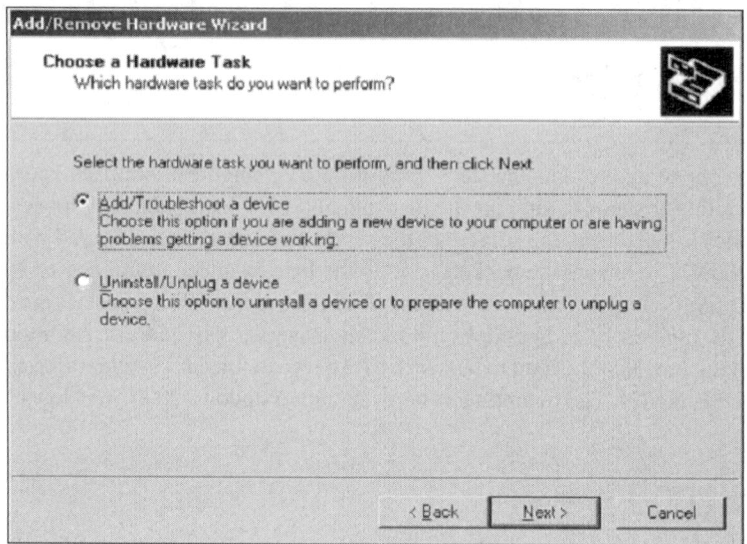

Step 3 You see a message indicating, "Windows is searching for hardware." Wait until you see a new window. Select Add a New Device and click Next (see Figure D-3).

Step 4 In the next window, select "No, I Want to Select the Hardware from a List and click Next. You see a window displaying the type of hardware to install. Scroll down to Network Adapters, select it, and click Next (see Figure D-4).

Figure D-3 *Choose a Hardware Device*

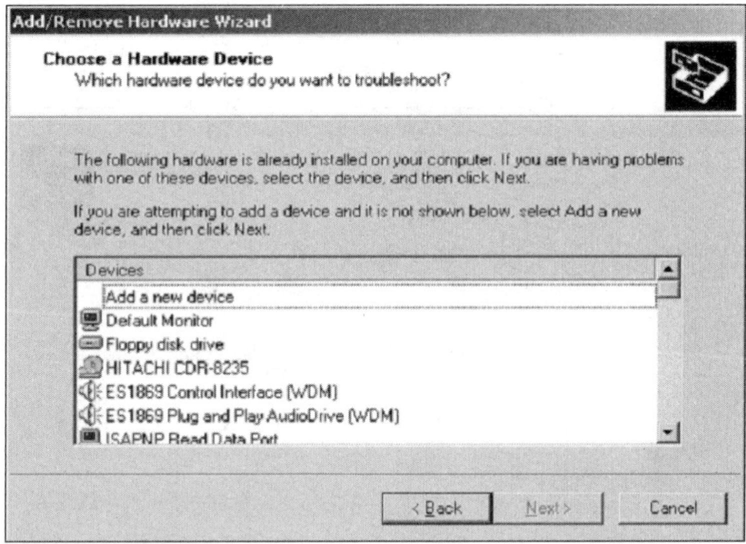

Figure D-4 *Hardware Type*

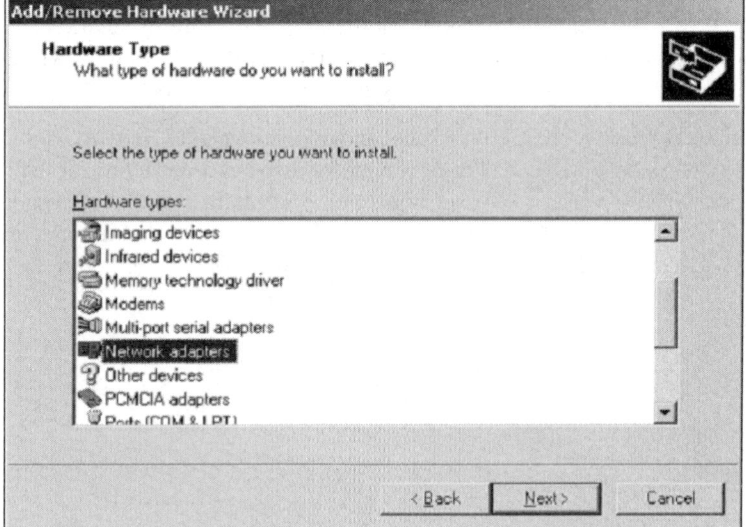

Step 5 In the new window under the Manufacturers column, scroll down and select Microsoft. Under the Network Adapter column, select Microsoft Loopback Adapter. Click Next (see Figure D-5).

Figure D-5 *Select Network Adapter*

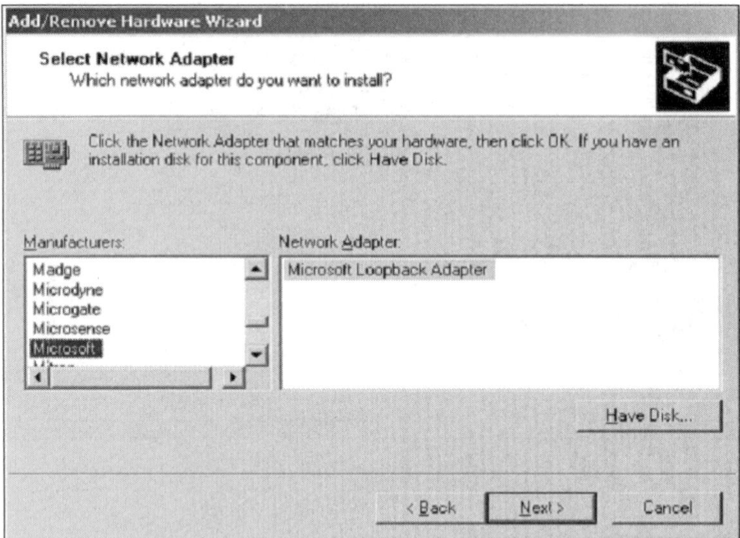

Step 6 On the following window, choose Start Hardware Installation and click Next. You see a final window, Completing the Add/Remove Hardware Wizard. Click Finish (see Figure D-6).

Step 7 Go back to the Control Panel and double-click the Network and Dial-up Connections icon. The next window displays a few icons for the current Dial-Up or Local Area Connections. Select the one that corresponds to the loopback adapter. If you leave the cursor on the icon long enough, you can see which adapter the icon is for, as shown in Figure D-7.

Figure D-6 *Completing the Hardware Add/Remove Wizard*

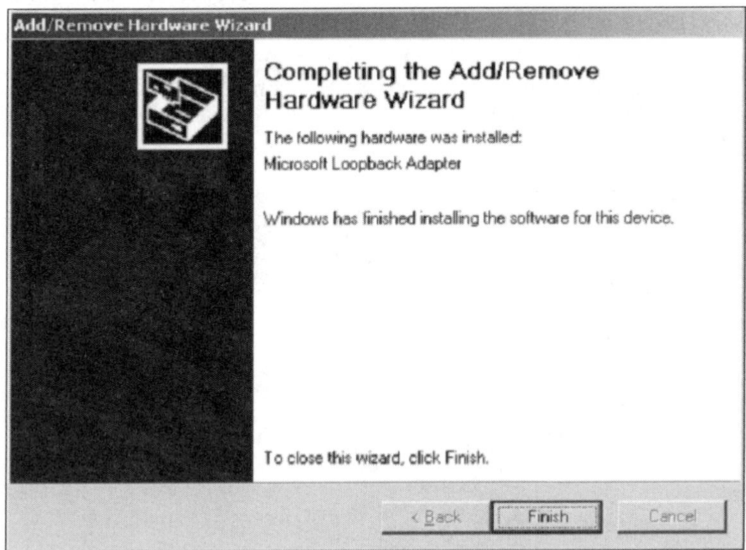

Figure D-7 *Selecting the Microsoft Loopback Adapter*

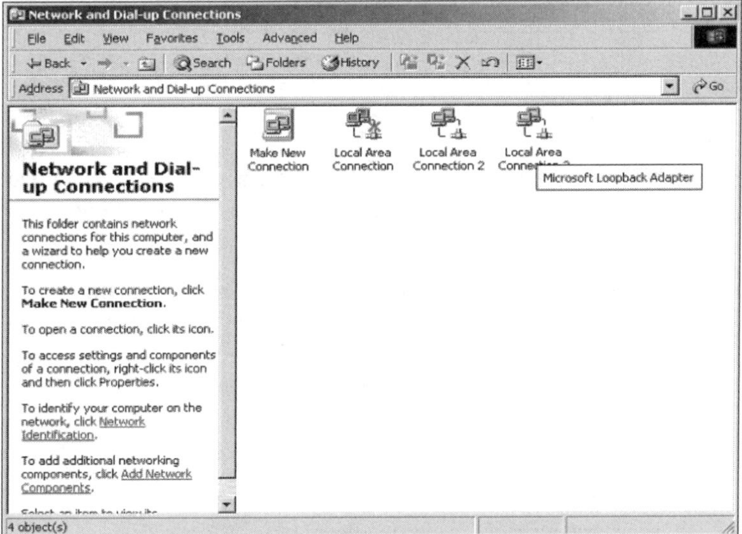

Step 8 Right-click the proper icon and go to Properties. Select Internet Protocol (TCP/IP) and click Properties. Type the VIP address and the correct subnet mask (See Figure D-8). Do not define the default gateway. Presumably, because you have an adapter already defined, you do not need to include the primary and alternate Domain Name System (DNS) servers.

Figure D-8 *TCP/IP Properties*

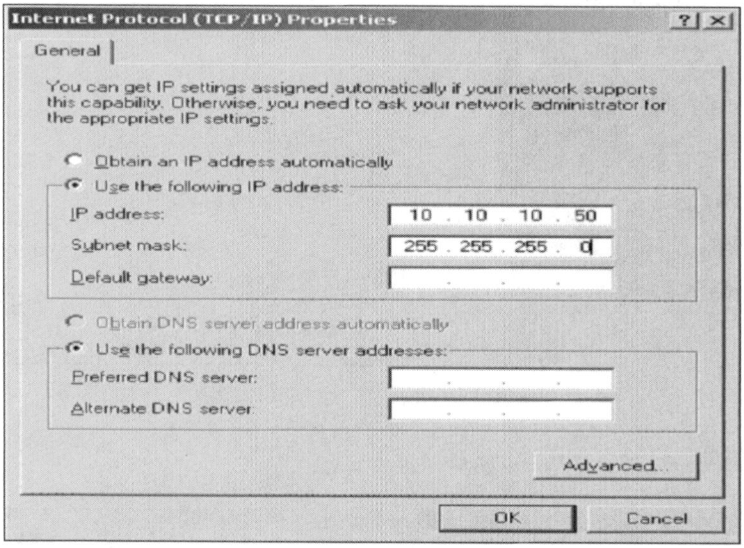

Click OK and OK again to exit.

Step 9 Make sure the adapter and its address are active. Go to a command-prompt window and run **ipconfig** (see Figure D-9) and **netstat** to verify (see Figure D-10).

Step 10 The last step is to make sure you can reach both the main IP addresses and the loopback IP address from the default gateway.

Figure D-9 *ifconfig Output*

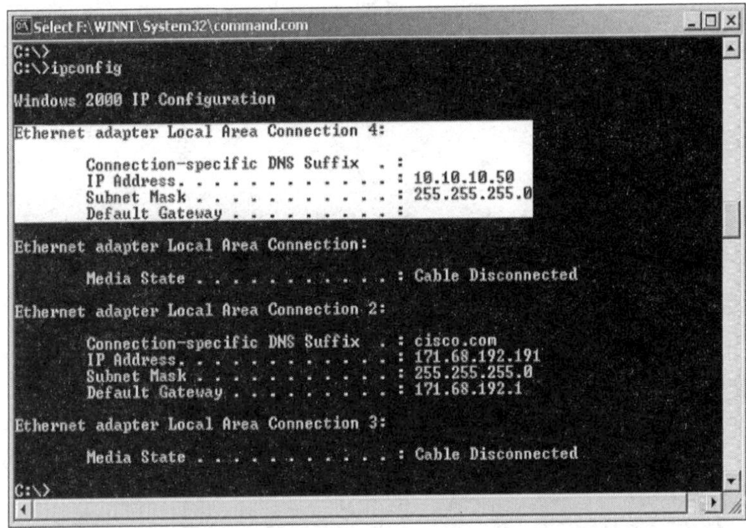

Figure D-10 *netstat Output*

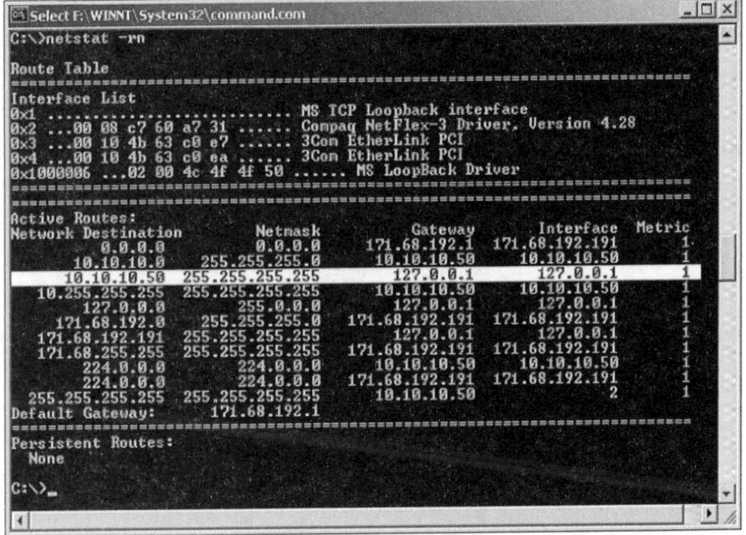

Windows NT

Following are the steps to configure the loopback interface on Windows NT:

Step 1 Right-click the Network Neighborhood icon and click Properties (see Figure D-11).

Figure D-11 *Network Neighborhood*

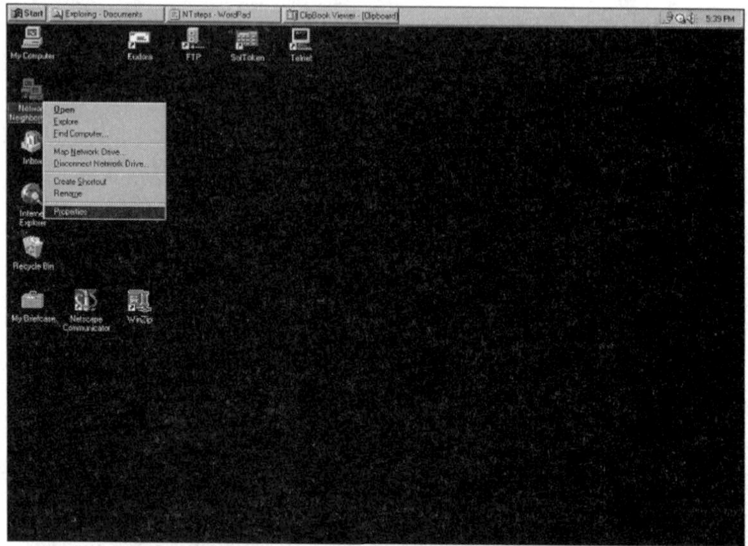

Step 2 Click the Adapters tab and then on the Add button (see Figure D-12).

Figure D-12 *Network Window*

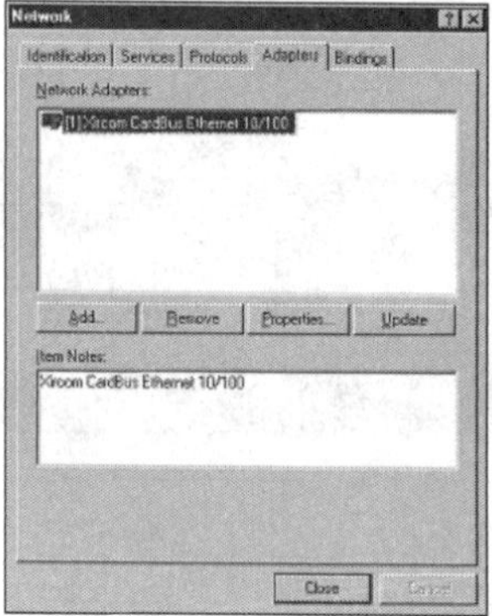

Step 3 Scroll down to Microsoft Loopback Adapter. Click OK (see Figure D-13).

Figure D-13 *Selecting Network Adapter*

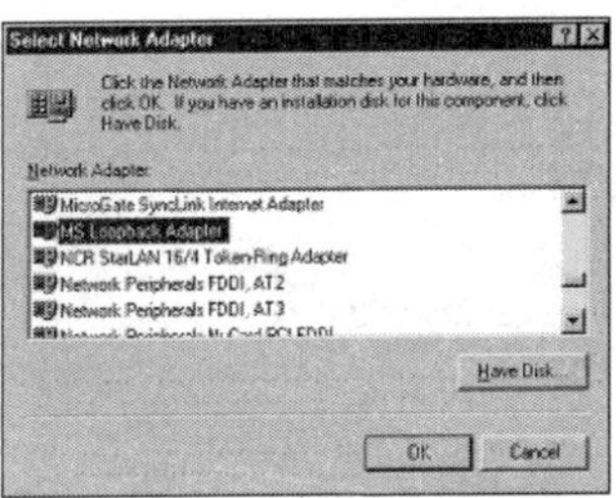

Step 4 The Microsoft Loopback Adapter Setup window opens so you can select the frame type. Leave the default frame type, 802., and click OK (see Figure D-14).

Figure D-14 *Selecting the Frame Type*

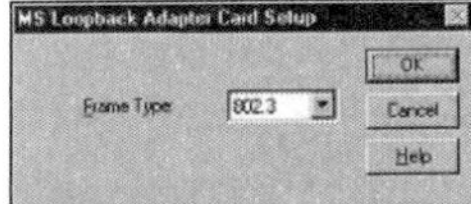

Step 5 Have the installation disks or CDs available to finish the Windows setup (see Figure D-15).

Figure D-15 *Copying Windows Files*

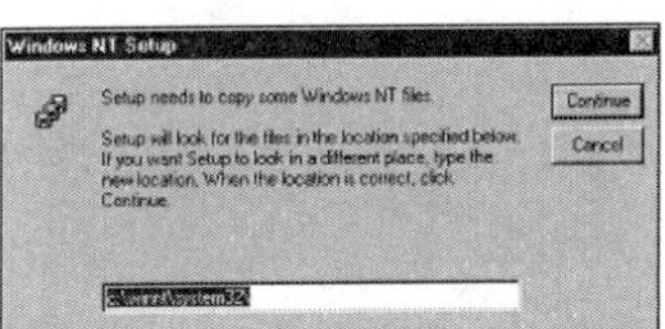

Step 6 You are back to the network windows. Click Close to accept the Microsoft Loopback Adapter (see Figure D-16).

Figure D-16 *Selecting the Loopback Interface*

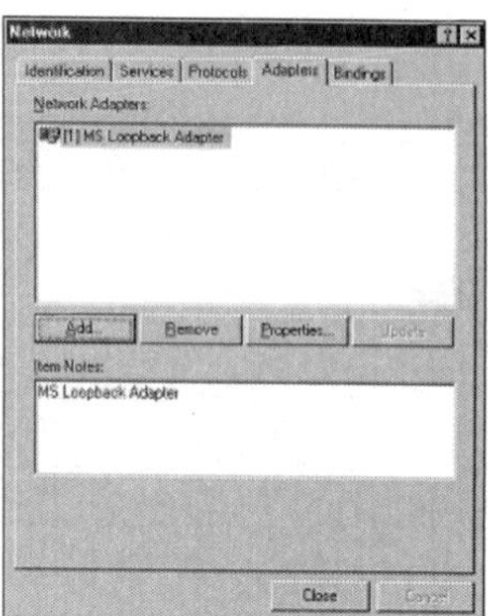

Step 7 The next page is the Microsoft TCP/IP Properties, which Windows opens to let you configure the IP information for the loopback adapter. Use the VIP address and a network mask that matches the real server's IP address (see Figure D-17).

Figure D-17 *Configuring TCP/IP Properties*

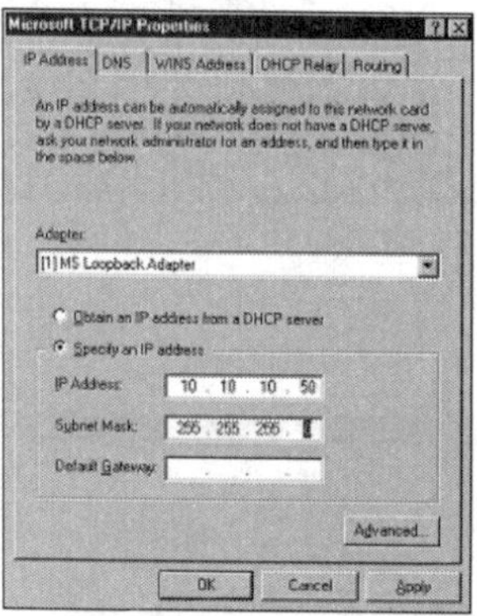

Step 8 Reboot the system. When the system comes up, ensure that both addresses are active by typing **netstat -rn** and **ipconfig /all** in a command-prompt window.

Linux

In UNIX, setting up a second IP address on an interface is called *aliasing*. Following are the steps to configure an alias address that matches the VIP needed for dispatch and DSR mode. The following example is specific to Linux:

Step 1 Configure the alias addresses. Server R3, in the testbed diagram, has a real address of 10.10.10.103, and you should configure it with an alias address of 10.10.10.50, which is the virtual address for both HTTP and FTP server farms. Log in to R3 and **su** to root. Change directory to /etc/rc.d/rc3.d/ and display its contents (see Figure D-18).

Figure D-18 *Content of rc3.d*

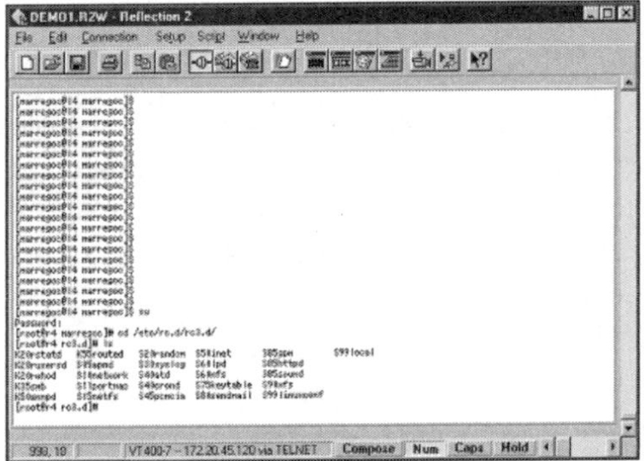

Step 2 You need to create a file that will get executed at boot time to create the alias IP address. We selected **S12ipalias** as the name of the file, and following are the lines you should include in that file. Make sure to copy the file in the cwd. Notice that the line makes reference to eth0:0, which is the first alias address for that adapter. If you need more addresses, use the next consecutive available number. For instance, if you already have eth0:0 in use, configure eth0:1. Notice that a host route into the routing table is added for the address, so packets for the aliased addresses are forwarded to the correct virtual adapter. The MAC address used for eth0 and eth0:x instances is the same (see Figure D-19).

Figure D-19 *Copying S12ipalias File*

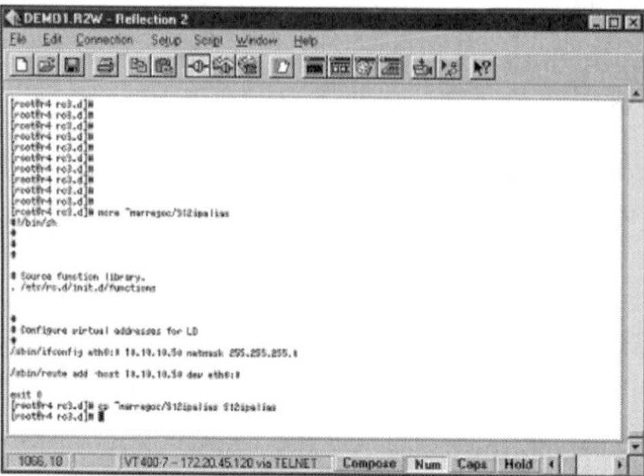

Step 3 After you copy the file, check that it has the right content (see Figure D-20) and then reboot the server. Other ways of restarting the TCP/IP stack do not require rebooting the server, yet it is recommended that you reboot the server to make sure the changes you made are active after the system comes up normally.

Figure D-20 *Verifying Contents of S12ipalias File*

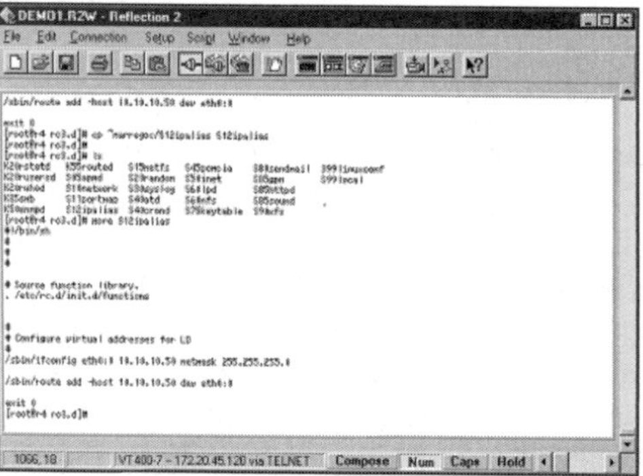

Step 4 After the server is back up, use **ifconfig –a** and **netstat –rn** to make sure both IP addresses are active (see Figure D-21).

Figure D-21 *Verifying Alias IP Address*

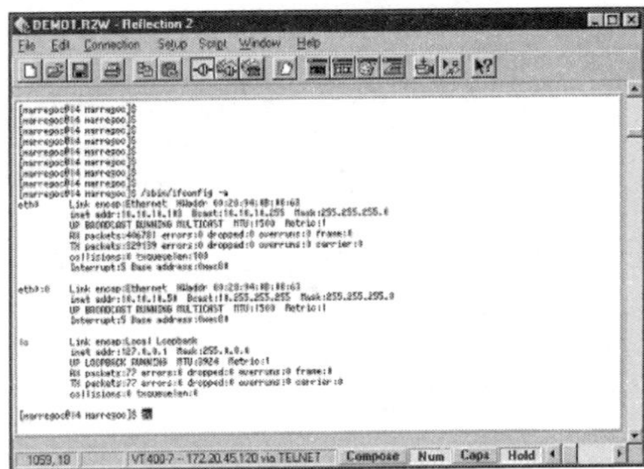

Step 5 Make sure that you can ping your default gateway and that your default gateway can ping both the primary address and the alias address.

APPENDIX **E**

Configuring Servers to Insert Cookies

Using hardware load balancers in conjunction with web servers and application servers lets you provide session persistence by using cookie or URL stickiness on the hardware load balancer.

If you use a J2EE-based application server (refer to Chapter 3, "Application Architectures Overview") and you have an application that tracks sessions (which the mechanisms offered by Java servlets do, as described in Chapter 18, "Session Tracking and Cookies"), there is no additional configuration required on the server.

You can configure the load balancer for cookie-passive or URL-cookie methods so that it automatically learns the session cookie and uses it for HTTP session persistence.

If you want the servers to introduce a separate cookie for pure identification purposes to use in conjunction with cookie-match mechanisms, web servers offer several mechanisms.

One possibility is to use the META tags in the HTML code of the entry page of a website. You can use the following HTML configuration:

```
<META HTTP-EQUIV="Set-Cookie" CONTENT="cookie_server=server4; path=/">
```

The META tag works well for cookie-match sticky methods; it does not work well for cookie-passive sticky methods. The reason is that **Set-Cookie** does not show in the HTTP response as an HTTP header field. **Set-Cookie** is sent as part of the HTTP data, and the browser interprets it.

As a result, the browser sends the cookie **cookie_server**, but the load balancer never sees a server sending a **Set-Cookie: cookie_server=server4**.

META tags are an option, and they require changes in the HTML code of the web page.

Web servers, on the other hand, offer options that do not require changes in the HTML code. The Internet Information Services (IIS) server offers an example. Figure E-1 shows how to modify the IIS server in such a way that it introduces the cookie **server-name=server1**.

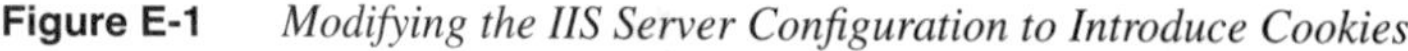

Figure E-1 *Modifying the IIS Server Configuration to Introduce Cookies*

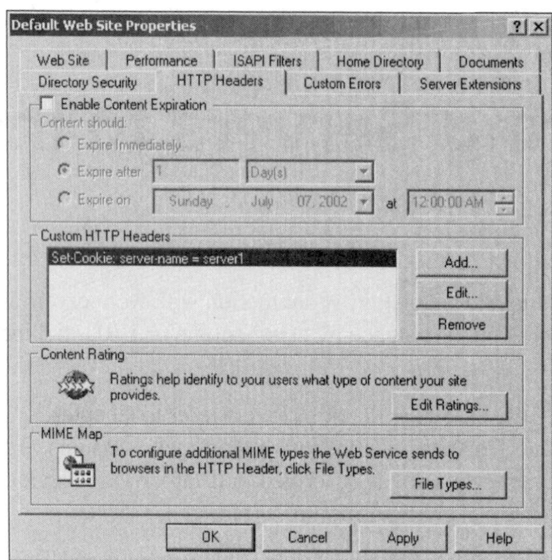

Another way of inserting cookies consists of using scripts (Perl or PHP scripts, for example). Each scripting language has libraries that provide this functionality.

APPENDIX **F**

Client-Side and Server-Side Programming

This appendix provides information about the technologies for client-side programming, such as JavaScripts, Java applets, and ActiveX controls, with code examples that help you understand how these technologies work. The server-side programming part explains the architectural differences between Common Gateway Interface (CGI), Java servlets, and Active Server Pages (ASP), which helps you understand the wide adoption of servlets and ASPs and the implications that it has on server availability.

Understanding the role that these technologies play in the Data Center helps when integrating application servers with hardware load balancers and when deploying firewalls and intrusion detection systems (IDSs). Without knowing these technologies, it is difficult to make a meaningful choice about which signatures to enable and where to enable them or how to protect internal clients and servers from attacks carried on HTTP.

Client-Side Programming

This section provides details about the client-side programming technologies described in Chapter 3, "Application Architectures Overview."

JavaScript

JavaScript is a client-side scripting language that is interpreted by the browser.

NOTE JavaScript originated from Netscape. The Microsoft version of JavaScript is called Jscript. The information provided in this section refers to the technology rather than the specific implementation.

You can find more information about JavaScript at http://devedge.netscape.com/central/javascript/. You can find more information about Jscript at http://msdn.microsoft.com/scripting/jscript/.

JavaScript provides the HTML code with several functionalities that can be implemented on the client side (in the browser). They include control of the browser windows, graphic capabilities, and mathematical computations. Example F-1 shows a JavaScript sample embeded in HTML.

Example F-1 *JavaScript Example*

```
<html> <head> <title>
    Simple JavaScript Example
  </title>
  <script type ="text/javascript">
    <!--
    for (var count = 1; count <= 5; ++count) {
      document.writeln ("Hello:" + count + "<br />");
    }
    // -->
  </script>
</head> <body> </body> </html>
```

As you can see in Example F-1, the HTML code references scripts with the tag <script> followed by the tag <type>. The type indicates the language for the script. (You will also see the tag <language>.) type="text/javascript" indicates the presence of a JavaScript, which is probably one of the most popular client-side scripting languages, along with VBScript.

Applets

Applets are Java applications compiled in *bytecode* format that can be executed in a Java Virtual Machine (JVM) on any operating system. A JVM is an abstraction of a processor with its own registers and instruction set. The JVM is what makes the compiled Java code portable across operating systems and hardware platforms because it provides virtualization of the underlying hardware.

A JVM runs as a separate process on the client machine or can be embedded in the browser as a plug-in.

NOTE You can find detailed information about JVM specifications at http://java.sun.com/docs/books/vmspec/.

Example F-2 shows a simple segment of Java code, which you can compile into HelloWorld.class, the bytecode format.

Example F-2 *Simple Java Program*

```
/*
 * HelloWorld
 */
public class HelloWorld {
  public static void main(String args[]) {
  System.out.println("Hello World!");
 }
}
```

You can execute this code separately by typing **java HelloWorld**; to make this an applet, you change the code as shown in Example F-3, where the HelloWorld class extends the Applet class.

Example F-3 *Java Applet*

```
import java.awt.Graphics;
import java.applet.Applet;
public class HelloWorld extends Applet {
 public void paint(Graphics g) {
  g.drawString("Hello World!", 100, 50);
 }
}
```

If you include the applet reference in the HTML code as shown in Example F-4, you can run the applet from within the browser. The statement <applet code="HelloWorld.class"> indicates the name of the bytecode to execute. The bytecode is typically downloaded from the web server where the HTML code comes from.

Example F-4 *HTML Code with a Java Applet*

```
<html>
<body>
<h1>HelloWorld Applet</h1>
<applet code="HelloWorld.class">
Your browser doesn't support applets
</applet>
</body>
</html>
```

NOTE Java applets and JavaScript are two different technologies, but they both use Java syntax. A Java applet is a compiled bytecode; a JavaScript is source code that must be interpreted by the browser. Applets are independent of the HTML code, which merely references them for the browser download; a JavaScript is part of the HTML code.

Example F-5 shows the pseudo-code for the HelloWorld applet in a client/server application. The codebase option specifies the location of the class, whereas the code option specifies the name of the class. The archive specifies the zip or jar archive (jar is another archiving format, just like zip), which contains multiple files that form the application. Param specifies parameters used by the applet.

Example F-5 *Remote Java Applet*

```
<html>
<body>
<h1>HelloWorld Applet</h1>
<applet codebase="http://www.example.com/myapp" archive=hello.zip
  code="HelloWorld.class" >
<param name="helloname" value="world">
</applet>
</body>
</html>
```

When the web browser downloads the HTML page from http://www.example.com, it downloads also the applet and the archive along with it. The browser then runs HelloWorld.class in the JVM.

Figure F-1 shows a browser downloading the applet myapp.class from the server. This Java application then opens connections back to the same server by using a TCP socket. In the example, the parameters (param name = "serverport") specify the TCP port 8500.

The communication between the applet running on the client and the server can use these schemes:

- **Sockets**—The client and server open a number of sockets for the duration of the communication.
- **Java Database Connectivity (JDBC)**—The applet connects directly to a database, or as it typically happens, the applet connects to a middle-tier server to get access to the database.
- **Remote Method Invocation (RMI)**—The applet invokes a remote method from a server using the RMI abstraction.
- **Internet Inter Object Request Broker [ORB] Protocol (IIOP)**—Common Object Request Broker Architecture (CORBA) technology allows calls to a remote method on a server.

Figure F-1 *Applet Opening Connections to the Server*

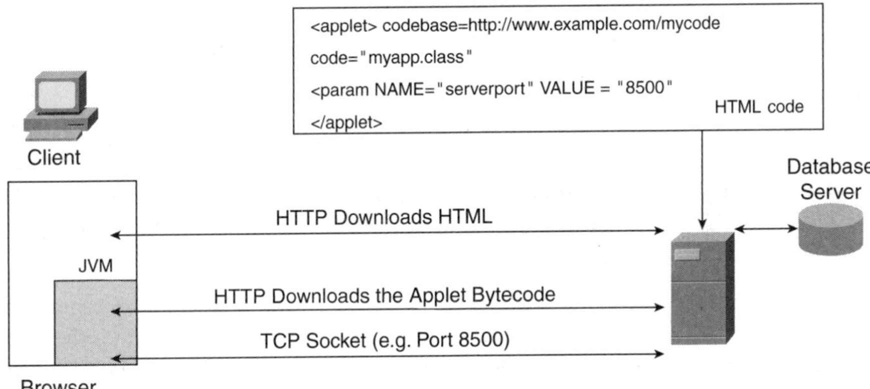

ActiveX Controls

ActiveX means many things, but for the purpose of our discussion, we are interested in ActiveX controls, which are a technology developed by Microsoft that is similar to applets.

NOTE For more information about ActiveX controls, refer to http://www.microsoft.com/windows/ie/press/whitepaper/iwhite/white003.htm.

ActiveX controls are binary code downloaded to the client machine by a browser. They execute on the client machine just as applets do. Example F-6 shows the HTML pseudocode that you could potentially see in a web page containing ActiveX controls.

Example F-6 *ActiveX Control in HTML*

```
<OBJECT CLASSID="clsid:02304043-bde8-120a-132f-005030042a00"
  CODEBASE="http://www.example.com/myapp.dll">
</OBJECT>
```

The CLASSID uniquely identifies the component that is to be downloaded. If the component is already registered in the Microsoft Windows Registry, the browser is not required to download it again. The tag CODEBASE indicates the location from which the component is downloaded. The code itself can be developed in C, C++, Java, and Visual Basic.

NOTE Unlike applets, ActiveX controls have full access to the operating system, which makes ActiveX more powerful than applets and at the same time more dangerous. To overcome the security issues, the ActiveX code is "signed" with a technology called Authenticode.

An ActiveX control can in turn open connections to a remote server, just as an applet does. The protocol that is used to invoke remote methods is the Distributed Component Object Model (DCOM). Alternatively, the ActiveX control can access databases directly by using Open Database Connectivity (ODBC).

Figure F-2 shows a client downloading an ActiveX control from a web page. The ActiveX control is registered in the client computer, and when the client executes the code, it uses the parameters passed by the PARAM statement in the HTML code. In this example, the ActiveX code opens a socket on the specified port.

Figure F-2 *ActiveX Control Opening Connections to the Server*

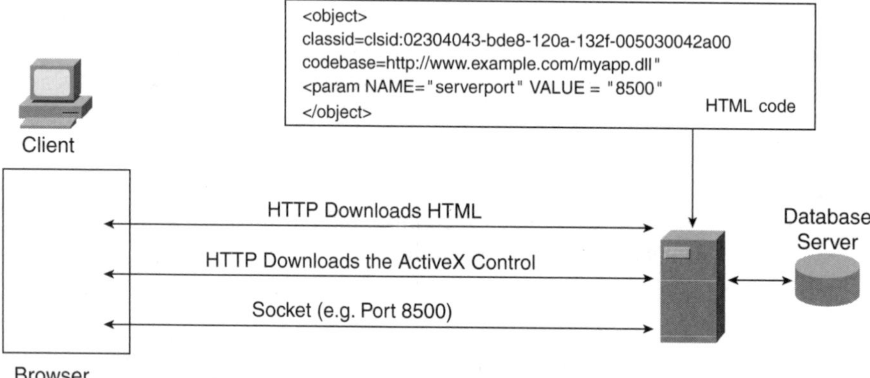

Server-Side Programming

This section provides details about the server-side programming technologies described in Chapter 3.

CGI

CGI is a technology for exchanging information between a web server and a program that complies with the CGI specifications. Like PHP: Hypertext Processor (PHP) and other techniques, CGI was developed to provide dynamic web pages. CGI is particularly useful in processing forms and providing access to databases. You can develop CGI programs in several languages, such as Perl and C.

Unlike other scripting techniques, CGI programs run in a separate process. This fact makes CGI application more robust: in case the CGI script should crash the process, the web server is unaffected. Although it provides higher web server availability, processing is slower because each client request results in the server spawning a new process. FastCGI addresses the performance problems.

CGI scripts communicate with the web server via environment variables. The web server knows where to find CGI scripts based on the configuration of a directive such as ScriptAlias /cgi-bin/, as shown in Example F-7.

Example F-7 *Apache Configuration for CGI Scripts*

```
ScriptAlias /cgi-bin/ "/var/www/cgi-bin/"

<Directory "/var/www/cgi-bin">
    AllowOverride None
    Options ExecCGI
    Order allow,deny
    Allow from all
</Directory>
```

Figure F-3 exemplifies CGI processing. In Part **a** of Figure F-3, one client (client1) fills in the field name of a form with the string abc and clicks the Submit button. The web server receives a GET for the URL http://www.example.com/cgi-bin/form.pl?name=abc.

Continuing with Figure F-3, the Web server matches the /cgi-bin/ string against the ScriptAlias configuration (see Example F-7) and looks up the Perl script form.pl in the /var/www/cgi-bin/ directory. A new CGI process is spawned (process 123) to interpret form.pl, and the web server passes name=abc information to form.pl by means of global variables or via the STDIN.

In Part **b** of Figure F-3, a new client (client2) requests the execution of a cgi-bin (again form.pl), and a new process is spawned that executes the script and processes the input field name=def.

When the first client (client1) again requests the execution of the cgi-bin form.pl with the input field lastname=ghi (see Part **c** of Figure F-3), a new process is spawned (process 789). Notice that this process is not the same process that handled the request name=abc for the same client.

The fact that CGI spawns separate processes for requests from the same client makes it difficult to keep data persistence for the duration of a client session because each request goes to different processes, which means that the memory space is not shared. To overcome this limitation, CGI typically saves data into temporary files.

Figure F-3 *CGI Processing*

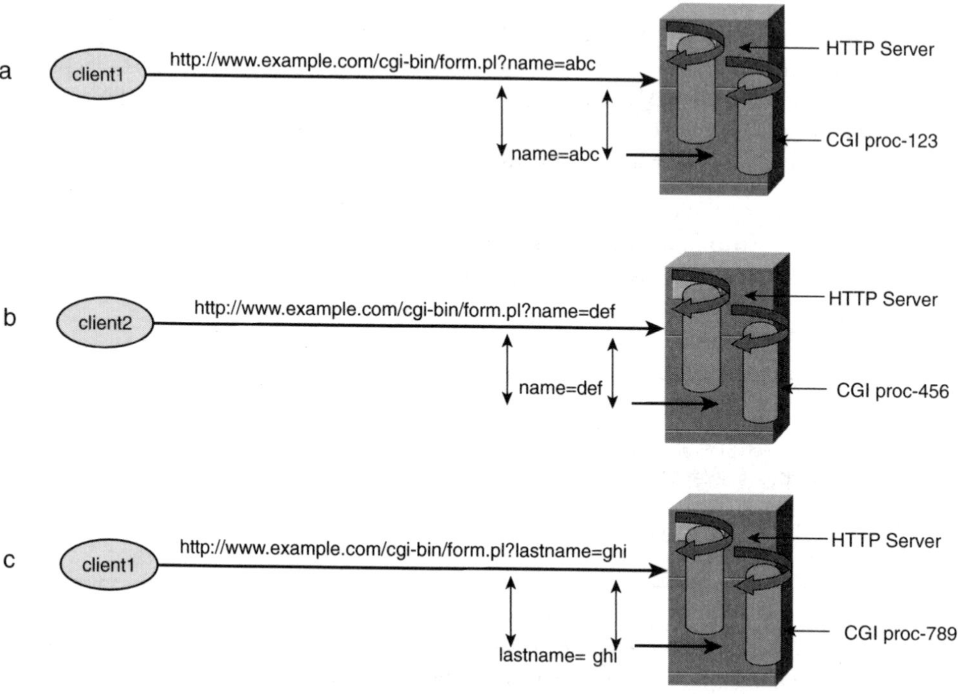

To summarize, the main limitations of CGI processing are the following:

- **Performance**—Processes for each request are created and deleted even if the client remains the same.
- **Complex data persistence**—Creating separate processes for requests that belong to the same client session requires CGI to continuously save on the disk temporary data that must be shared.
- **Complex handling of database server connectivity**—When multiple requests from the same client require access to the database, new database connections close and open because processes are created and killed for each connection.

TIP FastCGI provides easier session affinity (or data persistence) than CGI because a single client can be assigned to the same application process for the duration of a session, making it possible to cache previous selections in the process memory.

Servlets and JSP

Servlet technology is similar to applet technology, with the difference that servlets run on servers instead of clients. A servlet is a Java class (which is bytecode) that executes on a server.

Servlets run in a special environment called a container or a servlet engine. A container handles the creation of servlet instances, the initialization, and the distribution of incoming requests; in brief, the servlet engine manages the life cycle of the servlet. Like applets, servlets are loaded and executed in a JVM.

Unlike CGI, servlets use multiple threads instead of processes to handle multiple clients requesting the same servlet. Because of the threaded architecture, data persistence for a returning client is typically easier to manage than in CGI.

Figure F-4 shows the differences between servlets and CGI. Part **a** of Figure F-4 shows that new requests for a servlet are executed in threads within the same process (thread1, thread2, and thread3), whereas the servlet instance is kept in memory across all the requests.

Figure Part **b** of F-4 shows that in CGI, new requests, even from the same client, cause CGI to spawn the child processes 123, 456, and 789. (Refer to Figure F-3.)

Figure F-4 *CGI and Servlets*

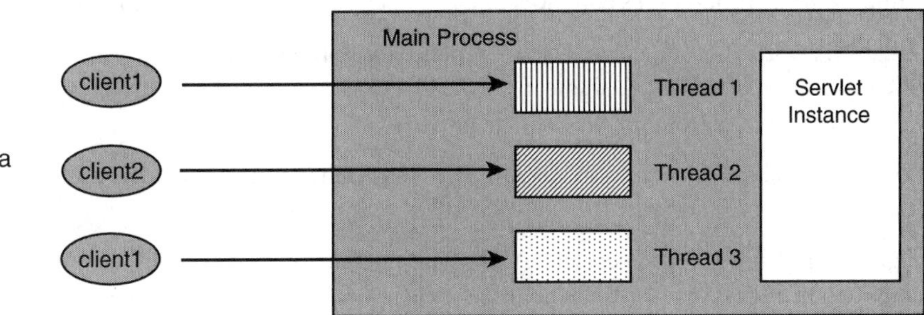

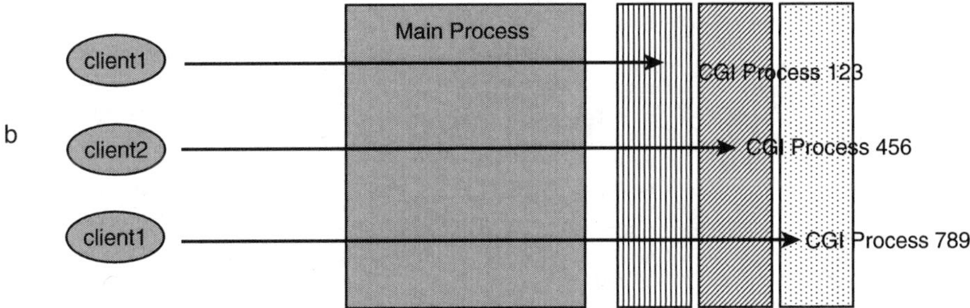

Servlet engines can run inside application servers or inside web servers. Examples of web and application servers that support servlets include Apache, BEA Weblogic, and IBM WebSphere. Typically, the servlet engine and the web server run on the same physical machine, in which case the web server uses interprocess communication to pass HTTP requests to the servlet engine. In case the servlet engine runs on a separate machine from the one used by the web server, HTTP requests that require application processing are exchanged on the network with a format that depends on the application server vendor. An example is the Apache JServ Protocol (AJP).

Java Server Pages (JSP) embed programs based on servlet application programming interfaces (APIs) in the HTML code. JSP code embedded in the HTML code is translated into a servlet, which is compiled at the first request.

The main difference between JSP and pure servlets is that JSP is easier to write, especially because you can code the static content directly in HTML instead of using Java functions to generate HTML code.

ASP

Microsoft ASP is a server-side scripting technology. ASP scripting provides similar functionalities as JSP scripting. The main differences concern the operating systems that support these technologies and the languages that you can use to develop the applications.

Like JSP, ASP is not subject to the performance limitations that originally affected CGI, and the robustness of ASP is guaranteed by the fact that it is possible to run the applications in a separate process from the web server process.

You can develop ASP scripts in VBScript or Jscript (the Microsoft equivalent of JavaScript) and run them on Microsoft Internet Information Server (IIS).

Differently from JSP and servlets, ASP scripts are interpreted at runtime. When the IIS receives an HTTP request with the .asp extension, the server invokes the scripting engine asp.dll, which interprets the ASP script.

INDEX

Numerics

A

B

C

D

E

F

G

H

I

J

K–L

M

N

O

P

Q

R

S

T

U

V

W

X–Z